Architectural

SECOND EDITION

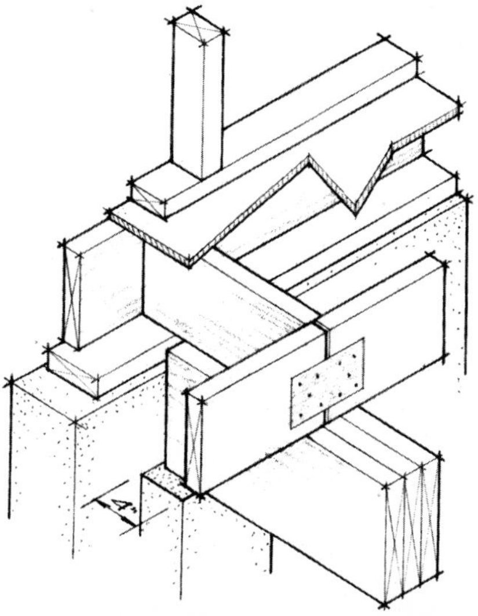

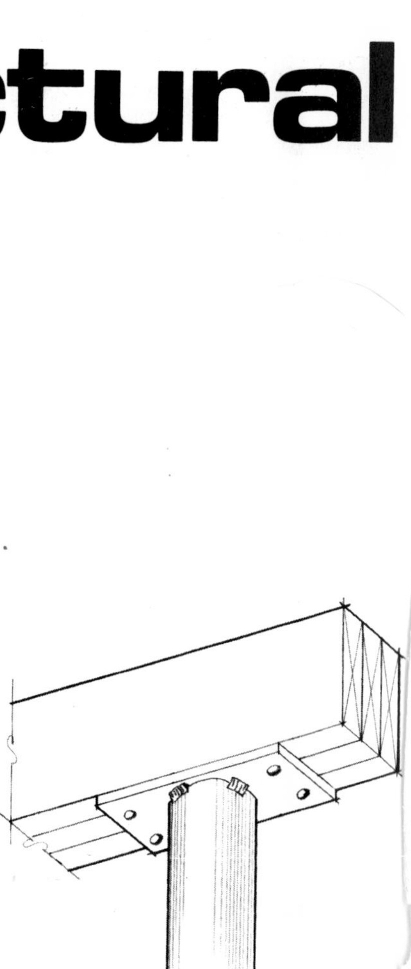

Architectural Drawing

and Light Construction

Drawing
and Light Construction

EDWARD J. MULLER

Architectural Engineering Technology Department
Southern Technical Institute

Prentice-Hall, Inc., Englewood Cliffs, New Jersey

Library of Congress Cataloging in Publication Data

MULLER, EDWARD JOHN
Architectural drawing and light construction.

Bibliography: p.
Includes index.
1. Architectural drawing. 2. Building—Tools and implements—Drawings. I. Title
NA2700.M8 1976 720'.28 75-23212
ISBN 0-13-044578-9

10 9 8 7

Printed in the United States of America

PRENTICE-HALL INTERNATIONAL, INC., *London*
PRENTICE-HALL OF AUSTRALIA, PTY. LIMITED, *Sydney*
PRENTICE-HALL OF CANADA, LTD., *Toronto*
PRENTICE-HALL OF INDIA PRIVATE LIMITED, *New Delhi*
PRENTICE-HALL OF JAPAN, INC., *Tokyo*
PRENTICE-HALL OF SOUTHEAST ASIA (PTE.) LTD., *Singapore*

Contents

2 LETTERING 22

3 BASIC TECHNICAL DRAWING 40

4 ISOMETRIC AND OBLIQUE PICTORIAL DRAWINGS 62

8 DRAFTING EXPRESSION 205

9 TYPICAL ARCHITECTURAL DETAILS 232

10 WORKING DRAWINGS OF SMALL HOMES 265

13 PRESENTATION DRAWINGS AND RENDERING

14 DRAWING A SMALL COMMERCIAL BUILDING

15 BUILDING MODELS

16 WRITING SPECIFICATIONS

17 CAREERS IN CONSTRUCTION 444

APPENDICES 451

INDEX 491

Prefaces

FIRST EDITION

This book is intended for the student who likes to draw and who is interested in achitectural construction. Although not exhaustive in the many categories of architecture, this work is meant to introduce the important, fundamental areas dealing with the drawing of small buildings. It assumes that the starting point is at the drawing board, and that the first requirement is learning the "graphic language."

The first five chapters are devoted to the mechanics of representing graphic ideas on paper—to be learned in their proper order. Architectural lettering, drafting, geometry, conventional projection principles, and methods of showing sections must be understood before original construction representations are attempted. Some technical schools require a prerequisite of elementary technical drawing before architectural drawing courses are taken. The basic material is included in the book mainly for those students who have not been exposed to technical drawing, for those who may need it for review, or for those who may use the book for home study. The material selected for the introductory work and exercises is architectural in nature, however, rather than mechanical, keeping it within the realm of the title.

Each step is progressive, and simplified procedures are used to develop the principal building representations. The wide variety of detail drawings will provide excellent exercises, not only for developing drafting skill, but for learning construction background information.

Considerable work on freehand sketching is included. Ability to sketch must be given emphasis in drawing courses. Most architectural ideas start with a sketch, and technical discussions are limited unless sketches are used to supplement verbal descriptions. Freehand lettering rather than mechanical lettering is used throughout the material to maintain a consistent architectural appearance. Skill in lettering can be acquired by duplicating plates directly from the text.

The author has tried to bring together written information needed by the student to understand construction problems and examples of good drafting techniques to show him how they are drawn. Where practical, application is made to new products and materials available to the dynamic construction industry. To add variation to the student's work and to make the book more adaptable to classroom use, supplementary exercises are given at the end of appropriate chapters. Additional architectural data are to be found in the Appendices.

Principles of perspective drawing, shades and shadows, rendering, as well as model building, also are included for the purpose of completing the necessary background experience now required in architectural drawing.

In acknowledging the assistance afforded in the preparation of this book, the author wishes to express his sincere gratitude to the following people and organizations: to H. Alan Dale, Jr., A.I.A., of Dale & Smith, Architects for his invaluable council and the generous contribution of Figs. 12-32, 13-29, 13-30, 14-5, 14-6, 14-7, 14-8, 14-9, 14-10, 14-11; to my colleagues—Dean George L. Carroll for his relentless help with the manuscript; to Robert W. Hays and Ted R. McClure for their help; to Chester R. Orvold, L.A., Wilton W. Vaugn, P.E., Robert L. Myatt, P.E., Charles T. Holladay, P.E., Turner M. Sullivan, P.E., also colleagues, for their assistance; to Seiss Wagner and Charles Stormes for their work on many of the drawings; to Julia Parker for her dedicated library research; to Bob Carter for photos (Figs. 1-1, 1-2, 1-3); to Prentice-Hall, Inc., for permission to adapt Fig. 2-8 from Warren J. Luzadder, *Fundamentals of Engineering Drawing,* 5th Ed.; to Keuffel & Esser Co., for Fig. 2-21; to Master Plan Service, Inc. for Figs. 4-18, 12-29, 12-51, 12-54, 13-4, 13-5, 13-6; to Summer-White & Associates for Figs. 6-6, 6-7, 6-8, 10-15, 12-31; to Aeck Associates Inc., Architects for Fig. 5-29; to General Electric Company for Fig. 6-36; to Lumber Dealers Research Council, Inc. for the material for Figs. 6-45, 6-46, 6-47; to Brown & Wright Associates, Registered Architects for Figs. 8-30, 8-31; to Andersen Corporation for Fig. 9-11; to Curtis Companies, Incorporated for Fig. 9-15; to Glide Corporation, division of Aluminum Extrusion Co., for Fig. 9-16; to The Donley Brothers Company for Fig. 9-20; to General Aniline & Film Corporation for Fig. 8-35; to American Radiator & Standard Sanitary Corporation for Figs. 11-21, 11-29; to Rolscreen Company for Figs. 12-5, 13-17; to Bob Allen for material on professional perspective; to Hugh Stubbins, F.A.I.A., for Fig. 13-2; to Paul Lyons for Fig. 13-3; to Ed Moulthrop of Robert & Co. Associates, Architects & Engineers for Figs. 13-1, 13-12, 13-14, 13-15; to Stevens & Wilkinson, Architects for Fig. 15-1; to Larry Cuba for photos (Figs. 15-2, 15-3, 15-5, 15-6, 15-11, 15-12); to Sholtz Homes, Inc. for many of the chapter-opening drawings; to National Warm Air Heating and Air Conditioning Association for permission to reproduce Worksheet Form J-1 (Appendix G); to Sara Howard for the final typing of the manuscript; to the others who may have been overlooked; and especially to my wife, Colette, for her indulgence and help in so many ways.

SECOND EDITION

Since the original edition was published in 1967, hundreds of schools throughout the country and abroad have found the book effectual in their drawing, architectural, and construction courses. Almost all levels of instruction in a wide variety of applications have shown favorable responses to the material and its presentation. Home study programs as well have found it readily adaptable, which, needless to say, has been gratifying to the author.

Therefore, much of the first edition has been retained, and suggestions by the many users have been added wherever possible to make the second edition even more applicable.

New lumber sizes have required some updating, many illustrations have been added, new material on basic drawing, lettering, sketching, residential site planning, roofs, insulation, metric conversion, perspective drawing, reflections, and others have been included. An entirely new chapter on careers in construction, an expanded glossary, and a set of residential working drawings also have been added. You will notice other refinements throughout the book that will make the new edition a most valuable tool for classroom or homestudy instruction as well as a handy reference for the many areas of architectural drawing and building construction.

Acknowledgment is gratefully made to the following, and others who may have been overlooked, for their generous help in furnishing photos or material for this edition: to Keuffel &

Esser Company for Fig. 2-21; to Cheshire-Baldwin, Architects for Figs. 5-42, 5-43; to Pella Windows and Doors for Fig. 6-58; to Brown Brothers for Figs. 6-60, 6-62; to Hedrich-Blessing, Architectural Photographers, for Figs. 6-51, 6-52, 6-53, 6-54, 6-55, 6-56, 6-57, 6-59; to John Jobson, student, for Fig. 6-63; to Bob Carter Photos for Figs. 6-64, 6-65, 17-1, 17-3, 17-5, 17-6; to Western Wood Products Association for Fig. 7-54; to California Redwood Association for Fig. 7-59; to American Plywood Association and Southern Forest Products Association for the material in Fig. 8-32; to Mr. Klok and U.S. Gypsum Company for Fig. 12-27; to Grayson Evans, student, for Fig. 13-7; to Ed Moulthrop, architect, for Figs. 13-15, 13-21; to Robert Sussenback, student, for Fig. 13-28; to W. Roy Reese, Jr. & Associates for Fig. 14-4; to Ken Sargent, student, for Chapter 15 opening drawing; to Frank Vella for Fig. 17-2; to National Forest Products Association for Appendix E, Plank-and-Beam Design Data; to Charles H. Stormes for Appendix I, Residential Working Drawings; and finally to Rosalie Herion and her co-workers in the Prentice-Hall College Editorial-Production Department for their diligent care in putting it all together.

EDWARD J. MULLER
Marietta, Georgia

1

"Handle your tools without mittens."—Ben Franklin

Drafting Equipment and Its Uses

The first consideration in the mastery of the mechanics of drafting is, naturally, the selection of the proper equipment. Many instruments are available at drafting supply stores, so many in fact, that it would be bewildering for a beginning student to select appropriate and proper equipment without getting a few words of preliminary advice. Comparatively few pieces of equipment are necessary if carefully chosen. In selecting any of the instruments, the first advice is—buy the best quality you can afford. Second, purchase only equipment produced by reputable manufacturers; you will then be assured of accuracy and good design. Many instruments and pieces of equipment are continually being improved and redesigned to aid the draftsman. Third, good equipment deserves proper care and treatment; do not abuse it nor use it for any purpose other than the purpose for which it was designed.

To get the most from his equipment, the aspiring architectural draftsman must develop enough skill to have complete control of his instruments. This comes with *practice*, deliberate and well-directed practice, which develops good work habits and eventually leads to the attainment of speed. Early training in drawing places particular emphasis on accuracy and skill until correct work habits are formed; speed will develop gradually with experience.

1.1 A LIST OF NECESSARY EQUIPMENT

The following list is the recommended minimum equipment for student use. Refer to Fig. 1-1 of basic equipment which illustrates each piece listed below. Although some of the equipment is identical to that used in engineering drawing, it is nevertheless specifically appropriate for architectural drawing:

1. Drawing board (24″ × 36″) (32″ × 48″);
2. T square or parallel bar (36″–48″);
3. 30°– 60° plastic triangle (14″);
4. 45° plastic triangle (10″);
5. 12″ architect's scale, triangular;
6. 2 semiautomatic pencils, several 3H, 2H, H, F leads;
7. Pencil pointer, either sandpaper or mechanical pointer;
8. Erasers, 1 Pink Pearl, 1 Artgum;
9. Roll of drafting tape;
10. Erasing shield;
11. Irregular curve;
12. Adjustable triangle;
13. Small set of case instruments;
14. Lettering guide;
15. Architectural template (1/4″ = 1′- 0″); and
16. Dusting brush.

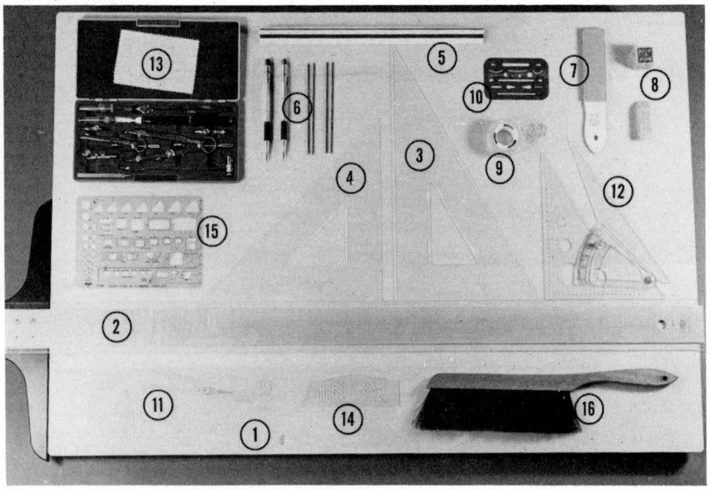

Fig. 1-1 Basic drafting equipment.

The following list of supplemental equipment (Fig. 1-2) would be found useful for advanced students or draftsmen working in architectural offices:

1. Large drawing table (38″ × 72″), drafting stool (30″);
2. Parallel bar (60″);
3. Flat architect's scale, 4-bevel;
4. Drafting fountain pen, India ink;
5. Beam compass;
6. Mechanical pencil pointer;
7. Electric eraser;
8. Protractor, semicircular;
9. Civil engineer's scale;
10. Additional achitectural templates;
11. Linoleum or vinyl plastic pad for drawing surface; and
12. Large 45° plastic triangle (14″).

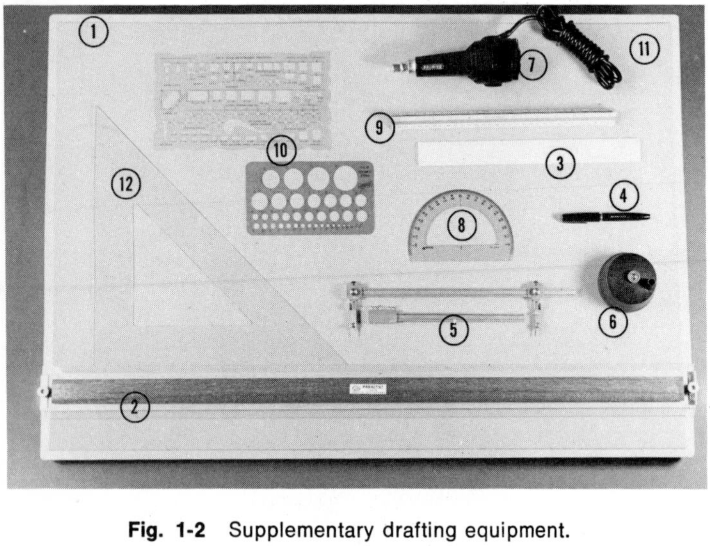

Fig. 1-2 Supplementary drafting equipment.

1.2 DRAWING BOARDS AND TABLES

The drawing board or table should be large enough to accommodate anticipated paper sizes. In architectural offices, drawings may be 3′ or 4′ long by 2′ or 3′ wide, requiring rather large boards; beginning work need be no larger than 22″ × 34″, requiring a minimum board size of 24″ × 36″. Larger boards are recommended, however, as larger drawings are occasionally required. See Fig. 1-3. The board should have a perfectly smooth surface and should be rigid enough to prevent warping and bending, which would impair the quality of the work. The working edge, usually the left edge, guides the head of the T square; therefore, this edge must be straight and true. Since students must often rely on portable drawing boards for beginning work, a board must be selected that is light as well as rigid. Boards are made of seasoned basswood or clear white pine, laminated or constructed to prevent warping and splitting. Soft basswood surfaces allow some flexibility under the paper, which is desirable, yet the depressions resulting from continual use of the board will eventually require the use of a pad or paper under the drawing. If the portable drawing board is used, some method must be utilized to incline it at the correct angle. A slope of 10° or 15° from the horizontal is satisfactory. If the slope exceeds this angle, instruments have a tendency to roll off; if it is less than 10°, the draftsman has difficulty working on the upper part of the drawing, and he does not get the proper view of his work. A direct, frontal view of the work is always necessary. Portable boards with collapsible supports under the upper corners are available for working on small desks or regular tables.

Many experienced draftsmen economically use a flush door as a board, supported by cabinets or adjustable wooden horses. The door should be 1¾″ thick, 2′–6″ or 3′–0″ wide, 6′–8″ or 7′–0″ long, solid core; with a 60″ parallel bar and a good board cover, this is a very satisfactory arrangement. It is possible to purchase "rejected" doors from some manufacturers, but care should be taken to select a door which is not warped and which has at least one good surface. The parallel bar placed near the center of the door would allow leg room near the center and offer sufficient board space on either side of the drawing for reference material and instruments (see Fig. 1-4).

Drawing board heights should be convenient for work while standing, usually 36″ high at the lower side. The body has more freedom and flexibility in the standing position, however, it alleviates fatigue to change occasionally from a standing to a sitting position when drawing for long periods of time. Many tables on the market are too light and unstable; they should not be purchased by anyone who intends to do a great deal of drafting. More elaborate tables are available with adjustable, sturdy basswood tops and storage drawers below. Metal edges on some of the various drawing boards not only prevent warping but provide an easy sliding edge for the T square. The ideal drafting arrangement would be a sturdy, 4-post, wood table and 42″ × 84″ basswood board with a 60″ parallel bar. A smaller, level reference table, slightly lower than the drawing board, can be placed conveniently to the left, if used by a right-handed draftsman (see Fig. 1-5).

Fig. 1-3 Using the drafting equipment on the drawing table.

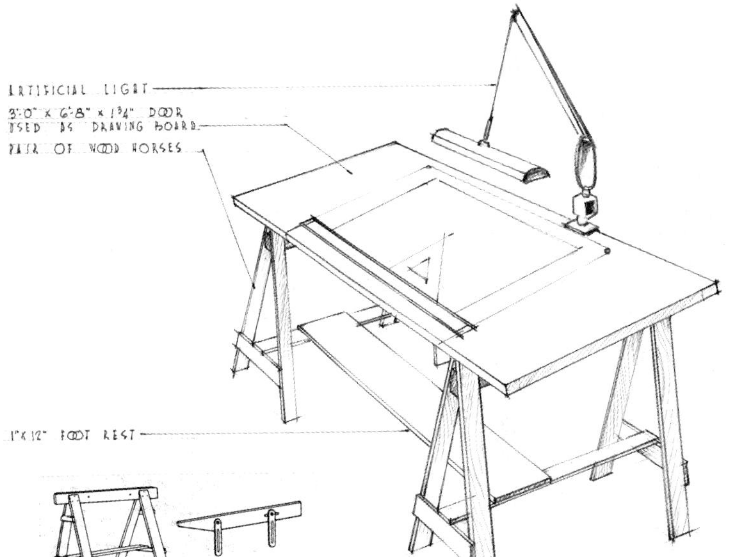

Fig. 1-4 An economical table can be made from a flush door.

The sizes of equipment shown here are the author's personal preferences; dimensions and equipment may have to be modified to meet individual requirements and budgets.

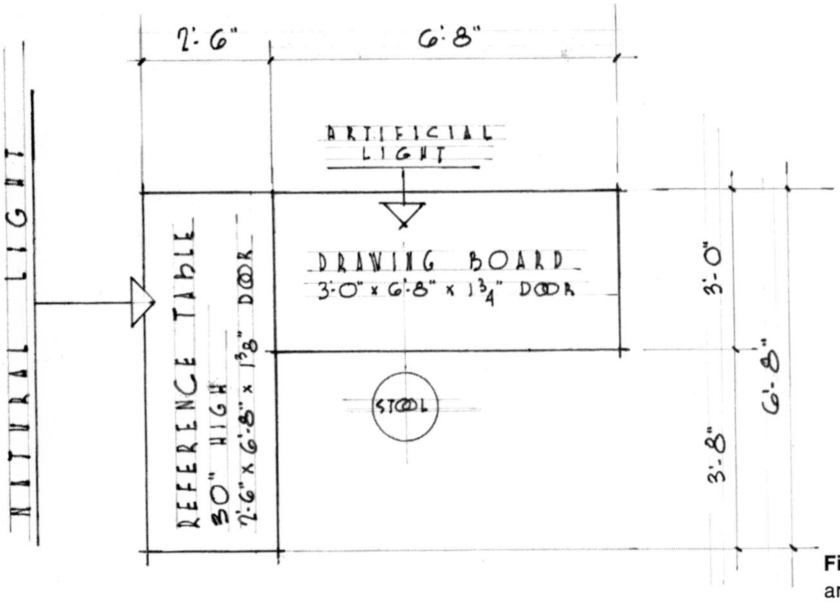

Fig. 1-5 A convenient layout of a drafting board and a reference table.

1.3 BOARD COVERS AND DRAFTING SURFACES

The surface of the board is very important if good drafting technique is to be attained. When drawing on heavy drawing paper, the mere thickness of the paper will take up depressions from pencil lines, but when working on thin tracing paper or vellum some type of flexible pad should be used underneath. Paper underlays are satisfactory if they have a slight spongy effect; however, paper usually will retain the grooves from line work, occasionally necessitating replacing of paper pads. Green paper underlays can be obtained with $\frac{1}{8}''$ vertical and horizontal coordinates. They have a smooth, plastic-coated surface and "give" sufficiently when placed over a wooden drawing board. These pads are especially desirable when sketching on thin tracing paper; the pale green lines show through the tracing paper enough to provide guide lines for quick, accurate sketches.

Linoleum pads, also available at drafting supply stores, are more permanent and are used by many professional draftsmen. Under tracing paper these pads will give the proper resiliency and sensitivity, resulting in desirable line contrasts from different pressures in linework. A newer, sheet-vinyl pad, available in several light colors, is more flexible than linoleum and is preferred by some draftsmen. Off-shades of white and light green colors on the drawing surface help to prevent glare and reduce eye strain. The heavier pads can be adhered permanently to the board surface with linoleum mastic or merely tacked temporarily at the top corners. Vinyl pads tend to expand slightly after they have been on the board for a while.

1.4 T SQUARES

The standard, fixed-head T square is still preferred by many architectural draftsmen. Select one that is rigidly secured at the head; long T squares especially have a tendency to become loose where the head joins the blade. Both the edge of the head and the edges of the blade should be perfectly straight and true. The straightness of the blade can be checked by, first, drawing a line the full length of the top edge of the blade; then, after turning the T square upside down, comparing the line with the same, overturned edge of the blade. A warped blade can be quickly revealed by this method. The most satisfactory T squares have wooden heads and hardwood blades with clear plastic edges (see Fig. 1-1). The plastic edges on the blade should not only be tough and smooth, but they should be transparent so that the draftsman can see work on the drawing that may be slightly below the edge of the blade. Avoid using a T square longer than the board length. Blade lengths should vary according to board sizes; however, a T square over 42″ long becomes unwieldy and is seldom required unless it is for some special purpose. The T square is needed for drawing horizontal lines and as a rest for triangles when drawing vertical or inclined lines. Only the top edge of the blade is used, and it is referred to as the working edge.

A right-handed draftsman should hold the head of the T square firmly against the left edge of the board with the left hand (see Fig. 1-6). A left-handed draftsman should reverse the T square and hold it firmly on the right side of the board with the right hand. To draw a horizontal line, the right-handed draftsman should position the T square with the left hand on the T-square head, then slide the left hand over on the top surface of the blade and hold with a slight pressure so the T square will not move until the line is drawn. Keep the pencil point against the top edge of the blade and lean it slightly in the direction the line is advancing. The pencil should maintain the same slope and pressure in relation to the T square throughout the entire length of the line, otherwise a variable line will result. Experienced draftsmen can draw several close, parallel lines without moving the T square, and the pencil should be revolved slowly when the line is drawn so that the point will wear evenly and last longer. The line can be positioned more accurately on the paper if the side of the pencil point is first brought in contact with the edge of the T square before touching the paper. The habit of putting pressure on the beginning and the end of each line should be developed early by the student. Avoid going back and forth over a line.

1.5 PARALLEL BARS

Time can be saved by using a parallel bar on larger boards. The bar is always kept parallel by the use of cords or wires attached to the board at the corners and running on pulleys through the bar (see Fig. 1-2). Standard lengths are 42″, 48″, 54″, 60″, 72″, 84″, and 96″. Hardwood or hard plastic parallel bars with edges of clear plastic are considered best. Some are adapted with small ball-bearing rollers underneath to minimize direct contact with the paper and facilitate sliding the bar up

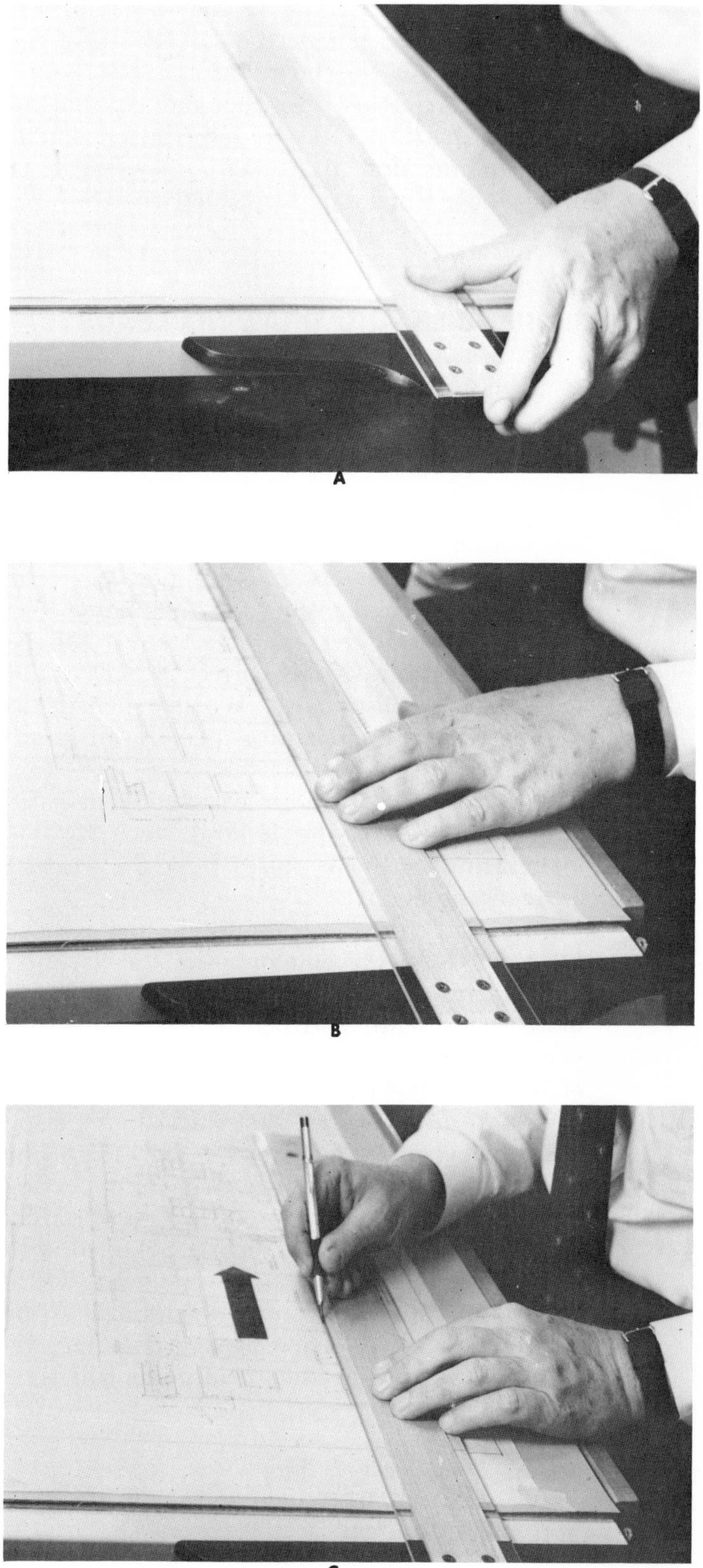

A

B

C

Fig. 1-6 Drawing horizontal lines with the T square. (A) Placing T square in position on board; (B) holding T square with slight pressure; (C) drawing horizontal line. (Left-handed draftsman would use opposite side of board.)

and down the board. On long tabletops the parallel bar need not be the full length of the board; some of the board's space can be reserved for reference material and equipment. Drafting machines are not especially popular with architectural draftsmen; they seem to prefer the use of a long blade and triangles.

1.6 PENCILS AND DRAWING LEADS

The selection and care of pencils should be the student's as well as the professional draftman's primary consideration. Wooden drawing pencils are hexagonal so they can be easily manipulated between the fingers, and they will not roll off the drawing board. Their hardness is indicated by letters and numbers near the end of the pencil. When sharpening a new pencil, this hardness symbol should not be cut away, otherwise the correct pencil would be difficult to distinguish. Wooden pencils, as well as leads for mechanical pencils, are available in 18 degrees of hardness (see Fig. 1-7). Different brands of leads vary slightly in hardness. For example, the H lead made by one manufacturer may be softer than the H lead made by another.

To sharpen the wooden pencil, first, remove the wood from the end opposite the hardness symbol; it can be cut with a pen knife or, more conveniently, sharpened in a draftsman's pencil sharpener. About three-eighths of an inch of lead should be exposed. Then, the exposed lead is formed into a long, conical point using a sandpaper pad or file (see Fig. 1-8). The point should be carefully formed by revolving the lead over the abrasive surface. More accurate and uniform points can be obtained with one of the mechanical pencil pointers. Occasionally, if many long, straight lines have to be drawn, the "chisel" point as shown in Fig. 1-9 can be utilized. The wide lead point will wear longer than the conventional "cone" point. However, since it is time-consuming to frequently have to remove the wood from wooden pencils, and since they have to be discarded or attached to extensions once they have become short, it is advisable to obtain several mechanical pencils. These pencils (sometimes called draftsmen's lead holders) usually have a finger area which is knurled or covered with a grooved rubber surface for easy manipulation. In mechanical pencils the lead is held by a spring chuck and can be quickly released for sharpening or removal by pressing the cap. A different lead in each of several mechanical pencils makes any required weight of lead quickly available.

One of the secrets of good line technique is the continual resharpening of the lead point; many draftsmen draw only several lines with a point, then resharpen it again. The leads can be sharpened on sandpaper pads, but the most professional point will be obtained, as mentioned previously, by using one of the mechanical lead pointers. See Fig. 1-10. They are now available in many different models; students would be wise in investing in any suitable one.

The majority of achitectural drawings can be done with 3H, 2H, H, F leads or pencils. The main considerations, of course, are the sharpness of the lines and their opaqueness for reproduction. Softer leads wear faster and require constant resharpening, whereas harder leads may groove or even cut the paper if too much pressure is applied. Different students also seem to produce various line weights with the same leads. Only after experience with several lead or pencil grades will the draftsman find the correct lead to use for the desired lines. The following factors should be considered in the selection of the proper pencil leads:

1. Pressure used by the individual draftsman;
2. Type of paper—texture, tooth (surface ability to retain the graphite);

Fig. 1-7 Pencil hardness chart.

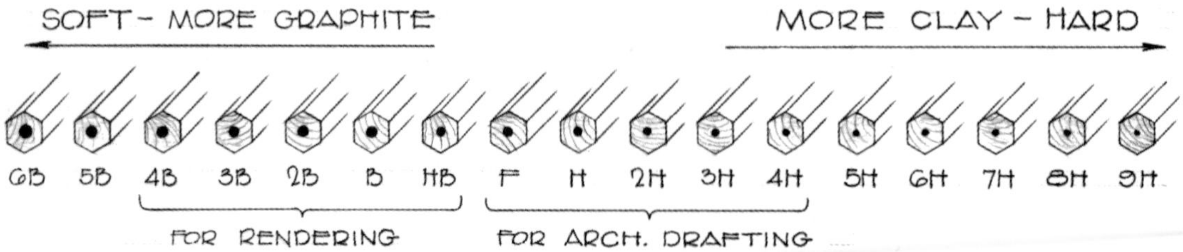

Fig. 1-8 Pointing the wood pencil with a sandpaper pad. (Do not sharpen over drawings.)

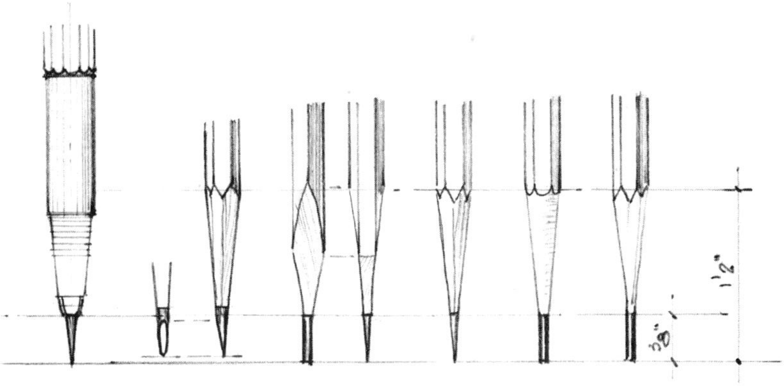

Fig. 1-9 Sharpening drafting pencils.

3. Atmospheric conditions, humidity;
4. Accuracy required on the drawing; and
5. Opaqueness necessary for reproduction.

1.7 TRIANGLES

Larger triangles are needed for architectural drawing than for most engineering drawing work; a 10″ 45° triangle and a 14″ 30°–60° triangle are satisfactory for the work covered in this book. Both the 45° and 30°–60° triangles should be made of heavy, transparent acrylic plastic about 0.06″ thick. The thinner, inexpensive triangles are difficult to pick up, and they often warp and become useless. Triangles should have true, accurate edges, with their inside edges beveled to facilitate picking up with the fingernails; care should be taken not to damage the outside ruling edges.

Lucite plastic triangles are available in several tinted fluorescent colors. They seem to transmit the overhead light out through their edges, thus reducing confusing shadows near the edges of the triangles.

Lettering triangles are discussed in Chapter 2.

To draw vertical lines, use either the 45° or the 30°–60° triangle. First, move the head of the T square into position and hold it firmly against the edge of the board. Lay the triangle on the drawing with one of its legs against the upper edge of the T square; then slide the left hand to the lower part of the triangle and blade of the T square. Maintain a slight pressure on the instruments until the line is drawn *upward* along the vertical edge of the triangle,

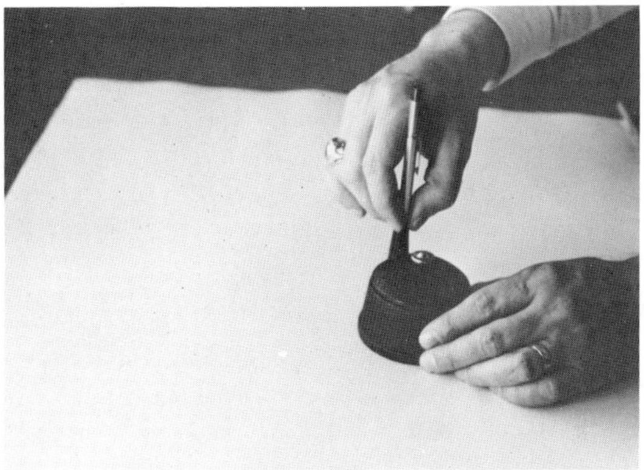

Fig. 1-10 Pointing the lead with a mechanical lead pointer.

as shown in Fig. 1-11. The left-handed draftsman should hold the T-square blade and the triangle with his right hand and draw vertical lines *upward,* away from the body. Whether right- or left-handed, remember that the vertical, ruling edge of the triangle should be placed so the vertical line will be drawn along the edge closest to the head of the T square. Beginning students often make the mistake of pulling the pencil down along the vertical side of the triangle, which necessitates looking over the hand and thus obscures the work on the board. The correct use of triangles must be developed at the very outset to overcome this tendency; otherwise an undesirable habit will result.

If long, vertical lines are required, the line is drawn slightly short of the end of the vertical side of the triangle; then both the triangle and the T square must be moved up so that the line can be continued. The pencil should be leaned

Fig. 1-11 Drawing vertical lines with triangle. (Reverse for left-handed draftsman.)

Fig. 1-12 Drawing lines with the adjustable triangle.

slightly in the direction in which the line is being drawn and kept in a plane perpendicular to the paper. The arrow in Fig. 1-12 indicates the direction in which inclined lines at standard angles should be drawn.

1.8 THE ADJUSTABLE TRIANGLE

The adjustable triangle is used often and is very convenient for lines other than 45°, 30°, and 60° angles. It has a protractor scale adjustment which permits the drawing of any angle from 0° to 90° from the horizontal or base line. The outer protractor scale indicates angles from 0° to 45° from the longer base, while the inner scale indicates angles from 45° to 90° from the shorter base. The set screw also serves as a convenient lifting handle. Rather than use the two regular triangles in combination for drawing angles in increments of 15°, it is much simpler to set the adjustable triangle for the correct angle, eliminating the manipulation of two triangles for the correct position as shown in Fig. 1-13.

1.9 ERASERS

Erasing can be considered by the draftsman as a necessary evil. Even the most advanced draftsman must erase occasionally, but excessive erasing indicates poor planning, inadequate organization, or lack of concentration and should be avoided. (Refer to Chapter 8 on drafting techniques.) To erase a line properly should be as important as drawing a line properly. Care should be taken in selecting an eraser—those that damage or discolor the paper should be discarded. Several types of erasers are needed: one for rubbing out darkened lines, and one for taking out light lines and for general paper cleaning. The most popular is the Pink Pearl, available in various shapes and sizes. One paper-wrapped, pencil-shaped pearl eraser can be resharpened by peeling the paper from the pointed end; other pencil-type eraser holders are available in which the eraser core can be let out from the holder as needed. Many draftsmen prefer a soft, white vinylite eraser for use on vellum, tracing paper, or film. Artgum is the standard eraser for cleaning a drawing, and it should always be available on the drawing board. Be sure the Artgum is clean; before applying it to the drawing, the dark areas should first be rubbed off on scrap paper. Avoid rubbing over finished pencil lines with Artgum; doing so will take the life out of the lines. The 1″ × 1″ × 2″ size is most convenient.

To erase, place several fingers near the area to be erased and hold the paper down firmly to prevent the paper from wrinkling or pulling out of position on the board. Use only as much pressure with the eraser as is needed to eradicate the line. See Fig. 1-14. Rubbing in several directions will speed up the removal. Stubborn lines can be removed more easily by placing a plastic triangle or other smooth, hard surface under the area to be erased. Avoid scraping tracing paper with a knife or other sharp instruments. The roughened surface may make repenciled lines appear darker, and the spot will appear as a ghost on the reproduction.

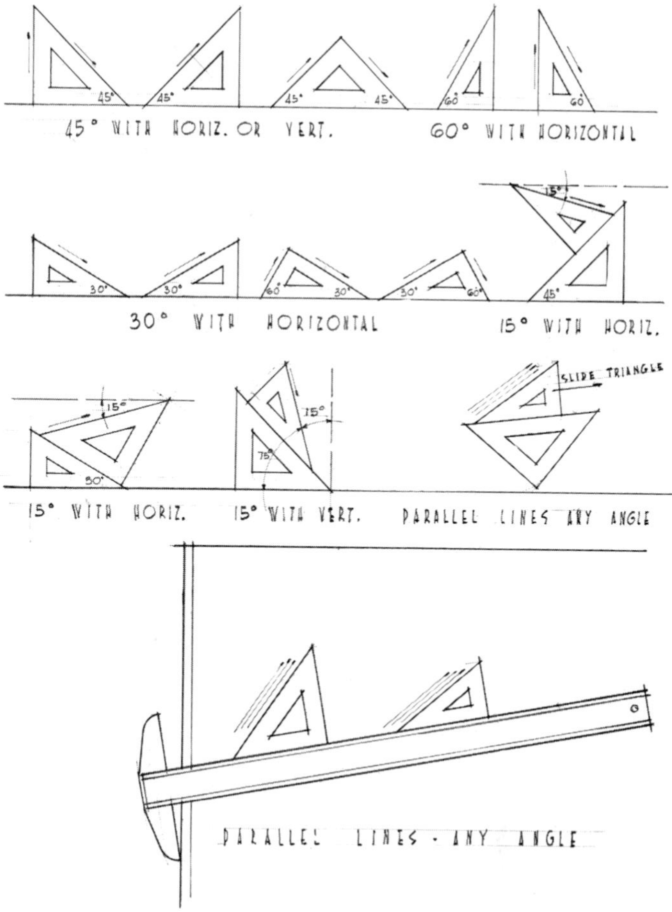

Fig. 1-13 Drawing various lines with the use of the triangles.

1.10 ELECTRIC ERASING MACHINES

Many drafting rooms use an electric erasing machine because this device saves time when considerable erasing must be done. Nevertheless some draftsmen consider it a luxury item. Several successful models are on the market; a satisfactory model is shown in Fig. 1-2. The erasing machine selected should be light in weight and well-balanced. It should be designed so the rubber tip is easily visible when the machine is in operation, and it should have some provision for stalling if too much pressure is exerted on the paper; otherwise the machine may rub a hole through the paper and ruin the drawing. A variety of eraser plugs are available for each machine; they are held securely on the shaft end with a screw-type collet.

1.11 ERASING SHIELD

The erasing shield is a thin, metal instrument with holes of various shapes. It is a comparatively inexpensive tool that is frequently used by the professional draftsman. Not only is it required when eradicating small lines in confined areas without disturbing surrounding lines, but it can also save time in many other situations. For example, thin columns in front of an elevation view can be quickly erased from the wall symbol linework much faster than starting and stopping the linework around the columns. Section views with finished crosshatch lines can be easily corrected with the aid of the shield. In addition, the shield can be used as a template if a particular hole is of suitable shape. Railings also can be put in elevation views after the wall symbols have been completed. Contrasting corners or edges on buildings can be easily executed on renderings, and many other situations will make the erasing shield a handy instrument to have on the drawing board.

To erase with the shield, select the opening that best fits the line or area to be eradicated, and hold the erasing shield down firmly on the drawing. Then rub the line within the opening carefully with the Pink Pearl eraser. See Fig. 1-15. A worn shield with thin edges around the different openings becomes more useful; it allows the eraser to make contact over its entire opening, and it can be set more accurately. Before

Fig. 1-14 Erasing with a holder-type eraser.

Fig. 1-15 Using the erasing shield.

using the eraser, its dirty surface can be removed by rubbing it directly on the shield. Like other instruments, the shield should be clean when it is placed on the drawing.

1.12 IRREGULAR CURVES

Regular curves, namely true circles and arcs, are drawn with a compass or circle templates. But often it is necessary to draw irregular curves—those with nonuniform curvature. Many clear plastic curves are manufactured. Architectural draftsmen will find numerous applications for their use, especially when drawing floor plans. The nonmonotonous nature of irregular curved lines on a working drawing sets them apart from the horizontal and vertical lines, as well as from circles, which gives them emphasis and provides more interest to an otherwise mechanical looking drawing. Experience has shown that the most useful plastic irregular curve is one that has a number of small curvatures as well as a few long, slightly curved edges.

Accurate, plotted curves, such as those often found on molding profiles, can be neatly drawn with an irregular curve if care is used in selecting the proper curved edge, and in placing this edge carefully along the path of the intended curved line.

To draw an irregular curved line, first plot the points accurately through which the curve should pass, then select the edge on the irregular curve that will coincide with the most points on the paper—the entire group of points if possible. If only a few points will match the curvature, more difficulty is encountered in producing a smooth curved line, and more care must be used in advancing along the curvature. Intersecting lines on the curve should be continuous, and the general nature of the curved line should not be bumpy. If considerable curved work is involved, an *adjustable curve* will not only save time, but will produce neater lines if no small curvatures are required. This instrument is made of a flexible metal core covered with a rubber or metal ruling edge; it can be bent to the desired curvature before the line is drawn. Long, accurate curves often require the use of a *flexible spline curve.* This curve is held in place on the drawing with metal weights or "ducks." The entire curve can be drawn with one smooth, uninterrupted line. *Ship curves,* originally used in hull design, or *highway curves* are occasionally useful for driveway layouts and roadways on plot plans, as well as for other uses.

1.13 PROTRACTOR

Odd angles, other than those drawn with a 45° triangle, a 30°–60° triangle, or a combination of both, can be laid out with the protractor. It is a semicircular plastic instrument with degree calibrations marked off along its curved edge and a center or apex identified in the center of its straight side. The two reversed scales along the curvature of the protractor allow angles to be laid out in either direction from the horizontal. More expensive protractors have ruling bars attached to the pivot point or apex for easier angle layout. Many draftsmen use the calibrated adjustable triangle instead of a protractor when odd angle layout is required.

1.14 THE ARCHITECT'S SCALE

Most of the measurement and scaling on drawings can be done with the architect's scale, an instrument with which every student should

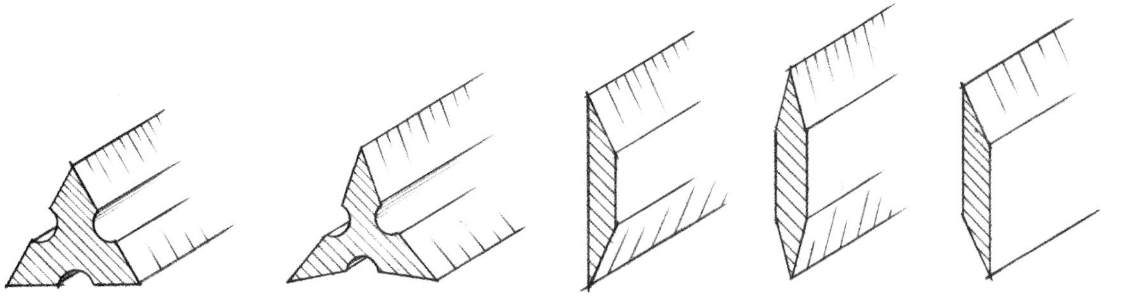

Fig. 1-16 Sectional shapes of drafting scales.

become proficient. Scales are made of boxwood or plastic; the more expensive ones are made of boxwood with laminated, white plastic faces. While the all-wood scales will not break when accidentally dropped on the floor, their edges cannot be made as sharp as edges on the plastic scales. Sharp edges and distinct, machine-divided markings on the scale are necessary for accurate measurements. Figure 1-16 shows the cross sections of the various shapes available.

Most experienced draftsmen prefer the *flat* scales because the triangular types require one continually to look over the upright portion of the scale, thus losing considerable time in hunting the correct markings. Flat scales are available in 6″, 12″, and 18″ lengths; the 6″ length is a convenient size for the pocket. The *4-bevel* and *opposite bevel* types can be easily picked up by merely bearing down on their edges. For student use the triangular type is more economical. It combines eleven different scales and can be satisfactorily picked up and handled on the drawing board. *Fully divided* scales have each main unit throughout the entire scale fully subdivided. *Open divided* scales have the main units undivided, and a fully subdivided extra unit placed at the zero end of the scale; the architect's scale is open divided. Listed below are the eleven scales found on the triangular architect's scale:

Two scales are combined on each face except the full-size scale, which is fully divided into sixteenths. The combined scales are compatible; one is twice as large as the other, and their zero points and extra subdivided units are on opposite ends of the scale. In architectural drawing the major units of measurement are feet and inches. In addition, the architect's scale is calibrated into these units in conventionally reduced scales so that large buildings and details can be conveniently drawn on manageable sizes of paper. The fraction or number near the zero end of each scale indicates the unit length in inches that can be used on the drawing to represent one foot on the actual structure. The extra unit near the zero end of the scale is subdivided into twelfths of a foot or inches, as well as fractions of inches on the larger scales.

Inaccuracy in measuring with the scale weakens a drawing and often results in a worthless piece of work. *To measure correctly with the scale,* select the proper scaling edge and place it on the drawing so that the edge is away from the body and the numbers can be easily read. See Fig. 1-17. The edge of the scale must be *parallel* with the line to be measured. First, count from zero the full feet in the dimension and make a short dash at right angles to the scale, then count the inches (if the dimension

Full scale—1/16″ graduations

1/8″ = 1′–0″	1/4″ = 1′–0″ (one-forty-eighth size)
3/8″ = 1′–0″	3/4″ = 1′–0″
1/2″ = 1′–0″ (one-twenty-fourth size) .	1″ = 1′–0″ (one-twelfth size)
1 1/2″ = 1′–0″ (one-eighth size)........	3″ = 1′–0″ (one-quarter size)
3/32″ = 1′–0″	3/16″ = 1′–0″

Fig. 1-17 Using the triangular architect's scale.

has both feet and inches) from the same zero in the opposite direction on the scale and mark the other limit of the dimension. (Refer to Fig. 1-18.) Laying out fractional parts of an inch in the smaller scales will require interpolation or estimation between inch calibrations for accurate measurement. When transferring smaller scales to the paper, the pencil must be kept sharp. To avoid accumulative errors, a series of dimensions or spaces should be marked off, if possible, without moving the scale. Each successive measurement should be added to the preceding one. Never move the scale to a new position for each dimension in a consecutive series; slight errors in each may accumulate into a significant error of the total. Unequal dimensions should be added by arithmetic and marked off consecutively from the original reference or starting point on the scale. If a series of dimensions is stepped off with the dividers, the total length should be rechecked to ensure that no accumulative error has resulted.

1.15 CIVIL ENGINEER'S SCALE

Occasionally a civil engineer's scale is needed by architectural draftsmen for drawing plot plans, land measurement, and stress diagrams.

Fig. 1-18 Measurements with various architectural scales.

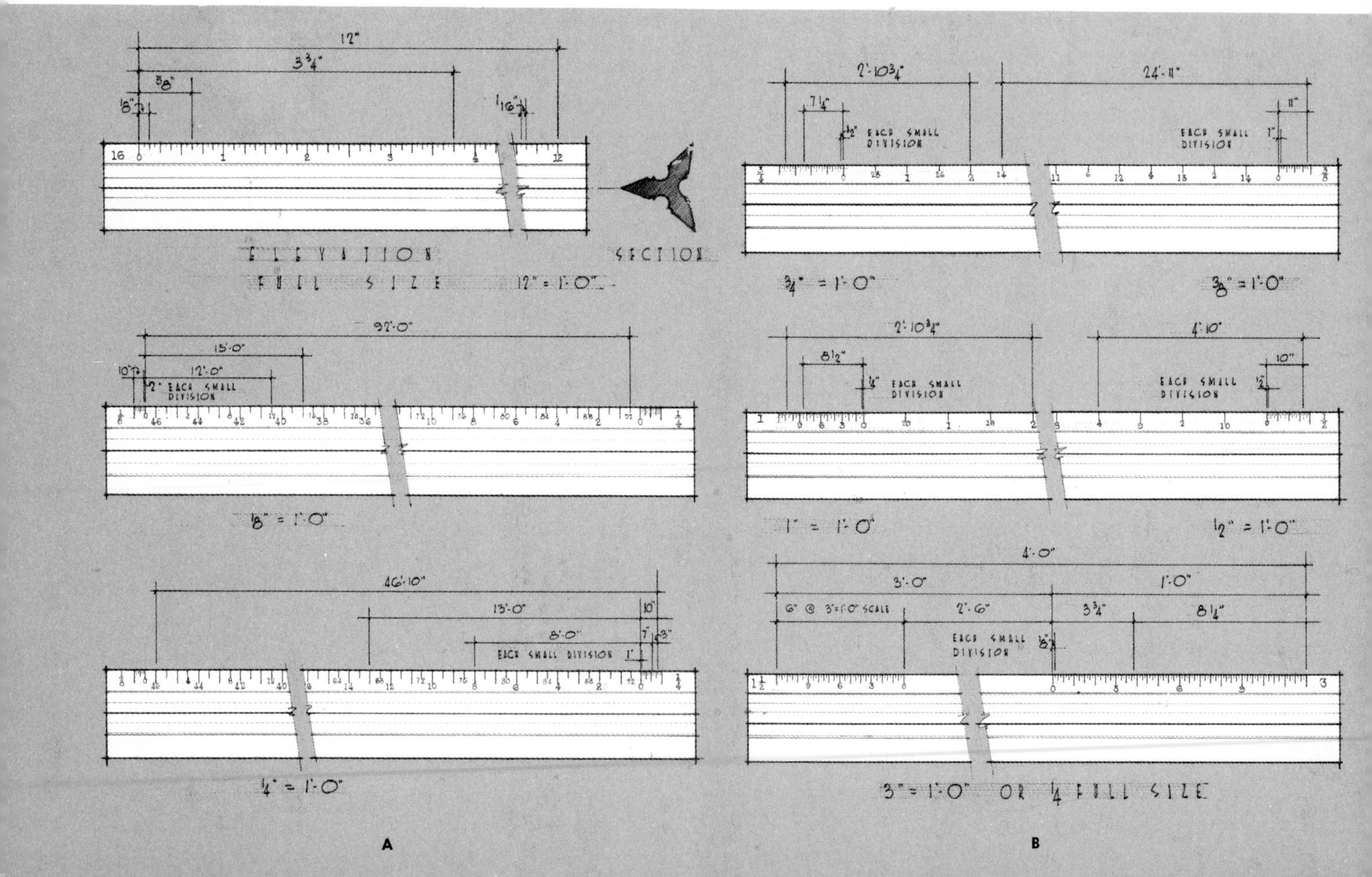

Civil engineer's scales are always fully divided and can be obtained in any of the flat or triangular types (see Fig. 1-16). Scales found on the triangular type are: 1″ = 10′, 1″ = 20′, 1″ = 30′, 1″ = 40′, 1″ = 50′, 1″ = 60′. Land measurement is always recorded in feet and decimal parts of a foot, rather than in inches. Therefore, the inch unit on the 1″ = 10′ scale would have 10 divisions, and the inch unit on the 1″ = 20′ scale would have 20 divisions, each representing feet throughout the other scales. If a scale of 1″ = 100′ were needed, the 1″ = 10′ scale could be used by merely letting each inch represent 100′ instead of 10′. This method applies to other scales as well.

1.16 DRAFTING TEMPLATES

Many good drafting templates are available for architectural draftsmen, and they should be used if speed is important. Templates are made of thin plastic with machine-cut, accurate openings; the thicker templates have tapered openings edges so that the pencil point will follow the lower part of the edge. Circles, for example, can be drawn more quickly with a template than with a compass.

To be effective, templates must be used properly. *To draw a circle* with the template, lay out center lines on the drawing where the circle is to be drawn. Then superimpose the correct circle opening over the center lines. When the quadrant lines on the template coincide with the center lines on the paper, draw the circle, using a sharp, conical point on the pencil. *To draw an arc,* lay out the tangent lines on the drawing first; then place the correct size circle on the paper so that the quadrant lines coincide with the tangent lines, and draw the arc. In using the template, the figure or circle must be drawn with the correct line weight on the first setting as it is difficult to replace the template in the exact position. Architectural templates are made in scales of: 1/8″ = 1′, 1/4″ = 1′, 1/2″ = 1′. Many of the symbols used in architectural drawing can be found on one or the other of these sizes. Openings for blocks of different shapes, so often needed on working drawings, can be executed quickly. North-point arrows, plumbing fixtures, steel sections, furniture outlines, even stair profiles are found on different templates. Care should be taken to avoid using inaccurate, poorly made templates. When using the template, it must be held down firmly to keep it from slipping out of position. Allowance must be made for the width of the pencil line in placing the opening in the right position on the drawing.

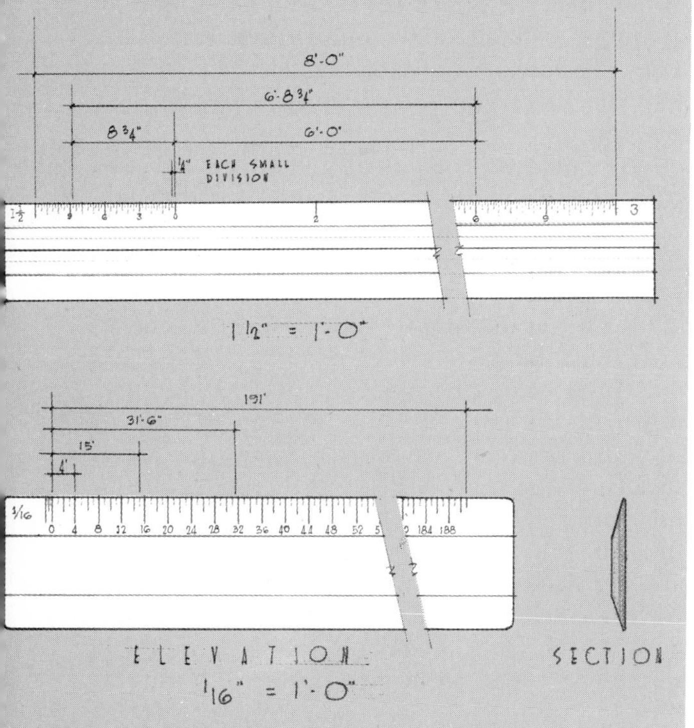

c

1.17 CASE INSTRUMENTS

If the student purchases a sturdy, well-made set of instruments, it will give excellent service and last a lifetime. Good instruments can be recognized by their carefully finished and well-fitted parts. If there is any play or too much tolerance in their joints or threaded parts, accuracy cannot be attained, and they should not be purchased or used.

An elaborate set of instruments is not necessary for architectural drawing. Figure 1-1 shows a set of professional quality that will fill all the necessary requirements. The main instrument is a sturdy 6″ or 6 1/2″ *big bow compass.* It can be accurately set with the center thumb wheel,

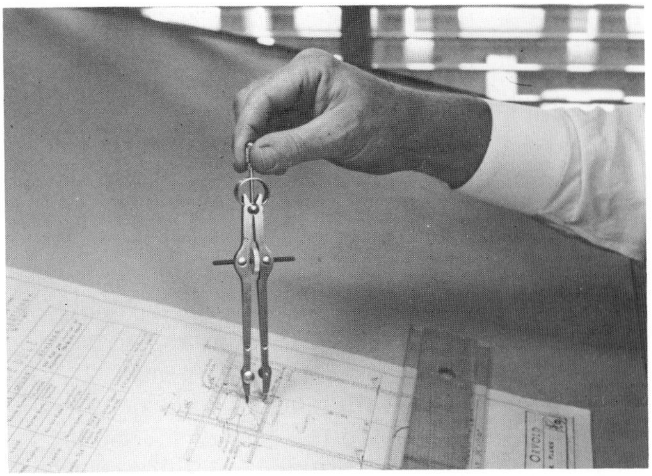

Fig. 1-19 Drawing an arc with the compass.

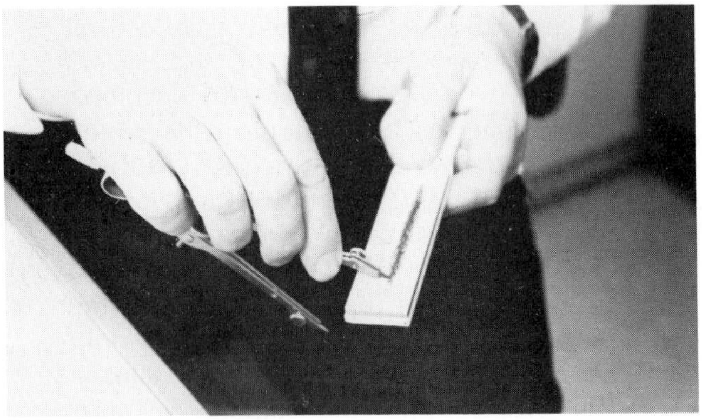

Fig. 1-20 Sharpening compass lead point with sandpaper pad.

Fig. 1-21 Ruling pen, Swedish border pen, lettering fountain pen, and black drawing ink.

and the setting cannot be accidentally altered. When drawing a circle with the big bow compass, hold it with the thumb and forefinger, and lean it slightly in the direction of travel as it is twirled between the fingers (see Fig. 1-19). Diameters can be drawn $\frac{3}{16}''$ to 13″. A divider point can be attached in place of the pencil lead if the compass is needed to step off equal distances or to transfer measurements. The points should be equal in length if the compass is to be used as a divider. If used as a compass for drawing circles, the needle point should be kept slightly longer than the pencil lead point.

To sharpen the compass pencil point, refer to Fig. 1-20, which shows the simplest and easiest method. Hold the compass with a slight angle in reference to the surface of the sandpaper pad, and form a single outside bevel on the lead. Care should be taken to make the surface of the bevel perpendicular to a line running to the center of the pivot point of the compass. Do not let the metal of the compass touch the sandpaper.

A ruling pen attachment can be inserted in place of the pencil attachment if ink circles or arcs are to be drawn. Some of the large bow compass sets are equipped with beam lengthening bars which can be attached if circles up to 26″ diameter are needed. For still larger circles the standard *beam compass,* with a rigid metal beam, adjustable needle point, and pencil and ink attachments, will be found to be more reliable and useful (see Fig. 1-2). They are very accurate for diameters up to 36″, and the better ones have micrometer adjustment heads.

A *ruling pen* is usually included in the large bow compass set and is used for drawing various width ink lines. See Fig. 1-21. For more extensive work, a *border pen,* also known as a Swedish pen, will be found most useful since it holds a larger ink supply. When using these pens, care must be taken when loading them with ink. Insert only about $\frac{1}{4}''$ of ink between the nibs with the use of the dropper cap or squeeze tip; wipe off any excess ink from the outer surface of the nibs. Never dip the pen into the ink bottle. If the nibs of the pen are too sharp, ink will not be held close to the ends; if they are too flat or uneven, ink will flow out from them too rapidly and blot or run over at the ends of the lines. Pens and inking equipment should be wiped clean after using with an ammonia soaked cloth. Black drawing ink can be purchased in bottles or in the newer plastic tubes, which are squeezed to supply the ink. These tubes are practical in that they prevent the ink from spilling and evaporating, as well as eliminate the danger of breaking if accidentally dropped on the floor.

1.18 DRAFTING BRUSH

A drafting brush (shown in Fig. 1-14) should be a part of every draftsman's equipment. It will quickly remove eraser, dust, and graphite particles from the drawing without smudging the linework. Students can use an inexpensixe 3″ paint brush on small drawings as a substitute, but the regular drafting brush will save time on larger drawings. A clean cloth in the drafting kit is indispensable for wiping instruments and minor cleaning jobs.

1.19 DRAFTING TAPE

Drafting tape, either 5/8″ or 3/4″ wide, provides the most convenient method for securing drawing or tracing paper to the board. Tape can be purchased in rolls of 10 or 60 yd; some rolls come in packages with handy "tear-off" cutting edges. Small pieces are used at the corners of a drawing; they can be removed without leaving marks or gum residue on the paper.

1.20 DRAWING PAPERS AND FILM

The majority of commercial architectural drawing work is done on tracing papers or vellums; however, for beginning student work a good grade of opaque white or buff heavy drawing paper is recommended. For student use, *cut sheets* 12″ × 18″ or 18″ × 24″ are the most popular and convenient sizes. White paper will show the linework best, yet off-white or buff is easier on the eyes and will not show smudges and dirt as readily. A good drawing paper should have a medium grain or "tooth" to take the pencil, should erase well, and should be sturdy enough not to groove when pressure is exerted in linework or tear when handled. Usually the rougher side of the paper is the better drawing surface, and the student should check the surface before securing the paper to the board.

Thin, transparent *tracing paper* should be used for sketching, and the better grades of tracing paper are recommended for more advanced architectural drawing. For sketching work, the economical tracing papers are adequate. A 24″ roll that has been sawed in half to make two 12″ rolls is a convenient width and is used by many draftsmen; the 12″ width can be torn off at any length needed. Others use a 12″ × 18″ sketching pad. Because of the temporary nature of sketches and the frequent need for numerous preliminary sketches, sketching paper should be inexpensive so that draftsmen will not be concerned about wasting it. When executing more permanent drawings that will be reproduced in blueprint or other types of duplicating machines, a high grade of tracing paper or vellum should be used, available in many types and grades. The better quality tracing papers are made from 100 per cent rag stock; the better vellums are rag stock that have been transparentized with a synthetic resin. Either paper can be obtained in sheets or rolls of various sizes. The most transparent papers are not necessarily the best papers for reproduction; only testing can reveal their true reproductive qualities.

Listed below are the characteristics to look for in choosing a tracing paper:

1. Good transparency for reproduction;
2. Suitable "tooth" for pencil work;
3. Good erasing qualities;
4. Nonyellowing qualities;
5. Strength and resistance to tearing; and
6. Resistance to brittleness and shrinkage.

Cut sheets 22″ × 34″ are large enough for working drawings of residences and small buildings of light construction. Many drafting offices use standard-sized cut sheets of tracing paper with the borders and title blocks custom printed for this type of work. Preprinted borders and title blocks are not only time-saving, but also give the drawings a uniform, commercial appearance.

Development of polyester films in recent years has resulted in a *tracing film* that has many advantages over paper. Film takes pencil lines with less pressure than paper; films are exceptionally strong and durable, they can be filed indefinitely without deterioration, and they have good reproductive qualities. Films, however, are more expensive than papers and should be used mainly for tracings that are expected to be kept on file for long periods of time, especially if drafting modifications are anticipated. Ordinary graphite pencil lines tend to dissipate on film after repeated use—manufacturers recommend the use of a plastic-type lead for more permanence of linework. Films are available in several thicknesses and in rolls 36″, 42″, and 48″ wide. One side of the film is matte coated; however, some films have this coat on both surfaces, making it possible to draw on either side.

1.21 OPTIONAL EQUIPMENT

Occasionally it becomes necessary to change the scale of a drawing. An aid for reducing or enlarging a drawing is the *proportional dividers* (Fig. 1-22). This instrument can be used to divide straight lines or circles into equal parts, or it can be used to change meters into feet. *To use the dividers,* move the legs together and set the sliding pivot to the desired ratio mark or setting on the leg. When the legs are spread, the relative distance between the two needle points at one end and the two needle points at the other end will always be in the same indicated ratio. For example, when the sliding pivot on the dividers is set to the ratio of 3:1, the distance between the two long needle points will always be three times greater than the distance between the two short points. Measurements are taken from one drawing with one end of the dividers and laid out on another drawing with the other end; thus saving the draftsman considerable time in calculating the different scale.

Fig. 1-22 Using the proportional dividers.

A *drafting fountain pen* is convenient for uniform inked lines and ink lettering. Some draftsmen do all the lettering on working drawings in ink; it seems to read easier on reproductions. The continuous ink supply is fed to a hollow point, available in seven different sizes, which makes the fountain pen adaptable and versatile for many drafting uses.

Drawings or tracings should never be folded, but they can be neatly rolled up. For this reason, students especially, will find sturdy *pasteboard tubes* handy for carrying and storing their work. A convenient size would be 3″ diam by 36″ long. Such tubes can be purchased with either screw-on caps or slip-on pasteboard caps.

A 12″ or 14″ large *paper shears* has many uses, among them trimming drawings and cutting paper from rolls. If a shears is not available, a razor-blade cutting tool can be substituted. However, cutting directly on a drawing board with a razor blade will soon ruin the board.

Use *transparent mending tape* for mending or reinforcing torn drawings or tracings. It is sold in rolls ¾″ wide by 5 or 36 yd long. The tape can be drawn over with ink or pencil, is hardly visible, and will not reproduce when the tracing is printed. *Mending kits* are available with transparent patches and heating tools that weld the invisible patch securely to the paper.

1.22 LIGHTING AND LIGHT FIXTURES

Proper lighting on the drafting board is often overlooked. Because of the exacting nature of drafting, the importance of correct lighting must be emphasized and always be kept in mind. Natural north light of the proper intensity is the easiest on the eyes, yet most drafting rooms must be supplemented with some type of artificial light because natural light is not dependable and is not always available in the most desirable intensity or direction. Direct sunlight should never fall on the drawing board; it is usually too intense and produces blind spots or highlights on either the paper or the instruments. Soft, natural light from the upper left is the most effective for right-handed draftsmen, vice versa for left-handed.

Most drafting rooms are equipped with overhead fluorescent lighting that is well-diffused when it falls on the drawing board, and very few shadows will develop if the fixtures are properly installed. Light intensity should be from 60 to 100 footcandles on the drawing surface; this can be easily checked with a small light meter placed on different parts of the board. If adequate overhead or natural light is not available, an adjustable, drafting lamp fixture should be used. One type fixture with an adjustable "floating arm" has two 15-watt straight fluorescent tubes in the reflector head and a base that can be clamped to the edge of the drawing board. The head is balanced so it can be moved to any position with a touch of the hand. Other similar fixtures are made with incandescent instead of fluorescent bulbs; others are made with a combination 60-watt incandescent bulb in the center of the reflector and a circular fluorescent tube surrounding it. Some models have illuminated magnifiers attached for small detail work. Two different color bulbs should be used in the straight, fluorescent fixtures; for example, one daylight and one white bulb.

Fluorescent lighting produces a stroboscopic effect when instruments are moved under the light. This can be annoying as it renders the moving instrument more visible at certain points along its path. This disadvantage can be minimized by purchasing a fixture with a high power factor, or by using the combination fluorescent and incandescent type lamp fixture. Most of the standard fixtures are satisfactory as long as confusing shadows are eliminated and the light intensity is sufficient.

EXERCISES IN THE USE OF INSTRUMENTS

The following problems should be drawn accurately in pencil. They should be drawn lightly with a 3H pencil, then carefully retraced with an H pencil. Construction lines need not be erased if they are light and hardly visible. Keep the pencil *sharp* and bear down slightly at the beginning and end of each line.

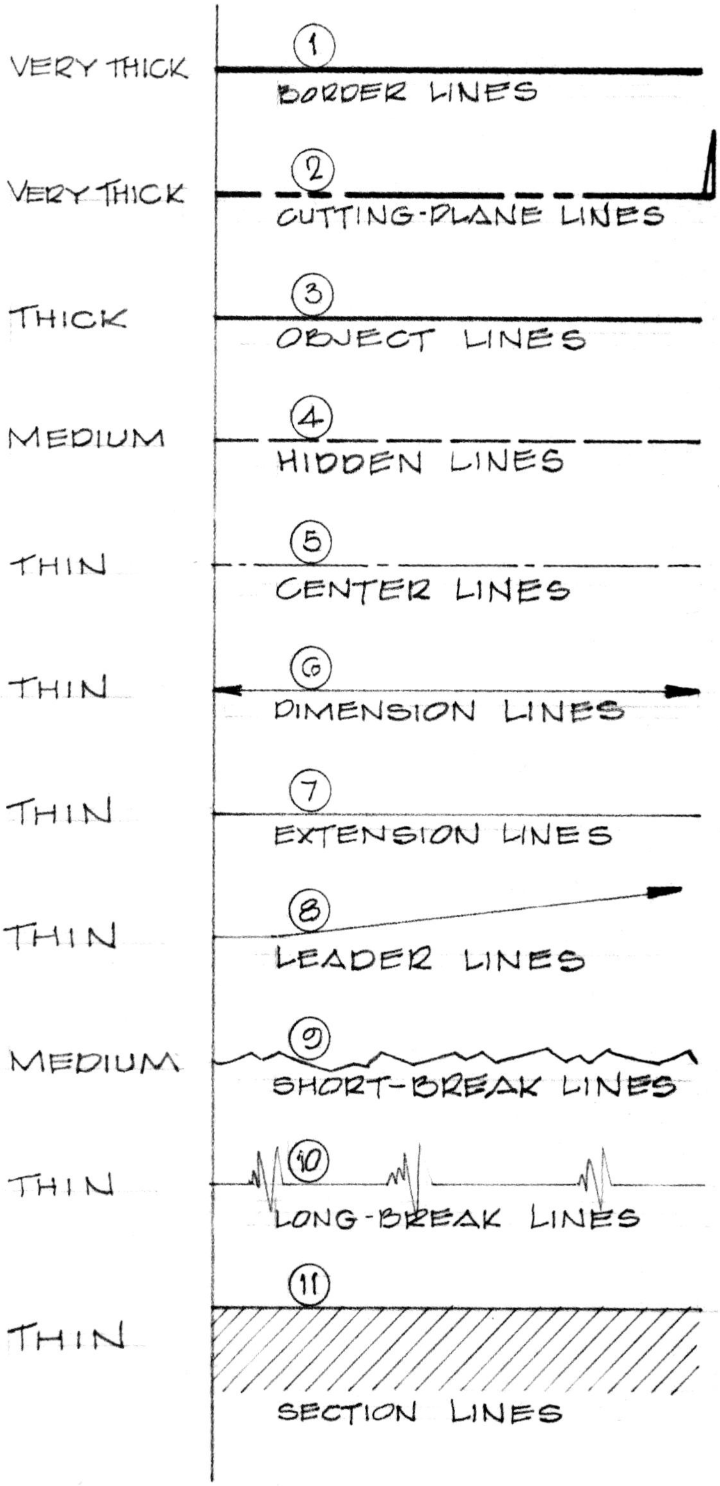

Fig. 1-22a Types of lines on architectural drawings.

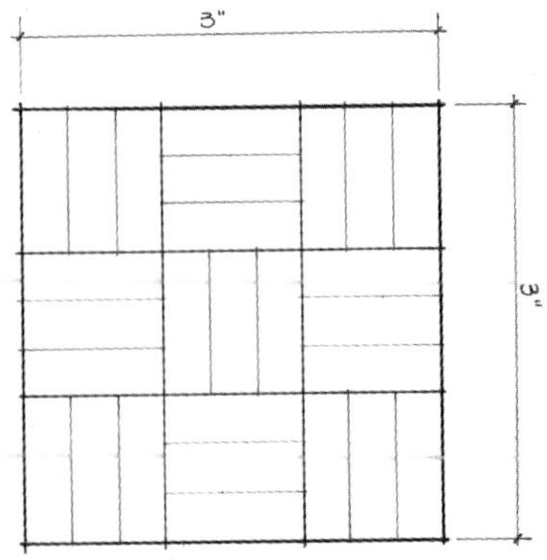

Fig. 1-23

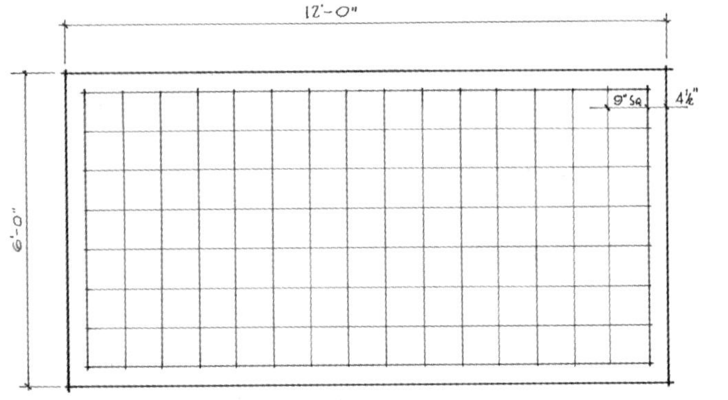

Fig. 1-24

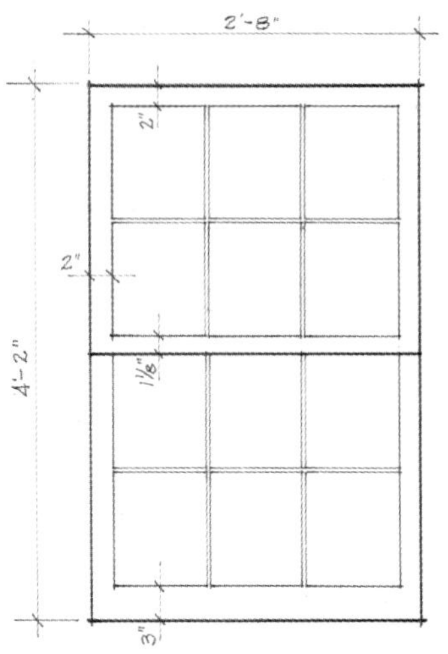

Fig. 1-25

1. Parquet flooring (Fig. 1-23). Draw a 3″ square. Divide the top and side into 3 equal parts and draw in the nine squares. Complete the figure by drawing the horizontal and vertical lines as indicated.

2. Asphalt tile floor layout (Fig. 1-24). Using the scale: ½″ = 1′–0″, draw the rectangle 12′–0″ × 6′–0″. Draw a 4½″ border within the rectangle, then fill the space with 9″ square tile as indicated in the figure.

3. Wood double-hung window (Fig. 1-25). Using the scale: 1″ = 1′–0″, draw the rectangle 2′–8″ × 4′–2″. Divide the height in two and draw the 1⅛″ sash rail in the center of the height. Draw the inside of both sash according to the dimensions shown. Complete the drawing by dividing the inside of the sash in half vertically and in thirds horizontally. Show the muntins with close, sharp lines.

4. Six-panel colonial wood door (Fig. 1-26). Using the scale: 1″ = 1′–0″, draw the rectangle 3′–0″ × 6′–8″. Draw the outside lines of the panels as shown by the dimensions, show the panel bevels 1½″ wide.

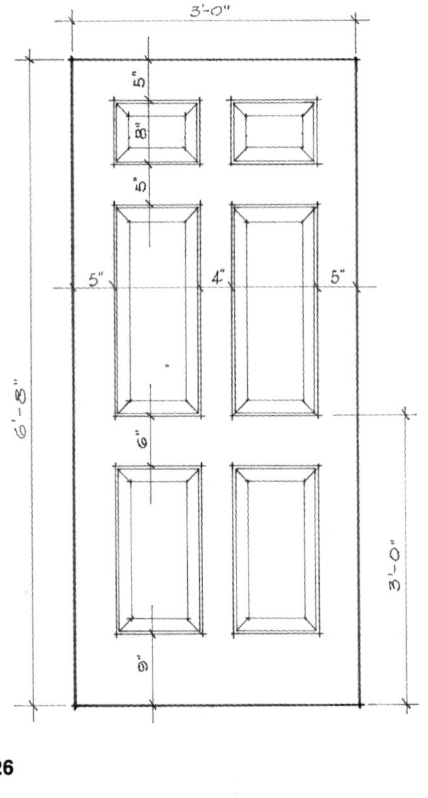

Fig. 1-26

5. Concrete block—top view (Fig. 1-27). Using the scale: 3″ = 1′–0″, draw the 8″ × 16″ rectangular shape. Divide the 16″ length into four equal parts and draw vertical center lines for the cavities. Make the webs 1½″ thick at their thinnest points.

6. Casement window in block wall (Fig. 1-28). Using the scale: ½″ = 1′–0″, draw the outside rectangle 8′–0″ × 12′–0″ and lay out 8″ course-height lines. Lay out 8″ lengths horizontally and draw vertical joints of 16″ block in alternate pattern. Allow two block lengths for the width of the casement window and six course heights for its height and stone sill. Make the sill 4″ thick.

7. Kitchen cabinet detail (Fig. 1-29). Using the scale: 1″ = 1′–0″, draw the basic rectangle 3′–0″ × 6′–0″, lay out and draw the 6″ splash board, the 4″ toe recess, the 2″ space around the 15″ × 20″ doors and drawer fronts as indicated. Draw all lines very lightly, erase lines between features, then darken lines where required and indicate pulls. Dotted lines indicate door swing.

8. Marble floor pattern (Fig. 1-30). Using the scale: 1″ = 1′–0″, draw the 18″ squares and 8″ border as indicated. Draw horizontal and vertical center lines in the squares that will locate the 12″ circles and the small squares. Erase the center lines within the circles and small squares and darken the center lines between the same figures as indicated.

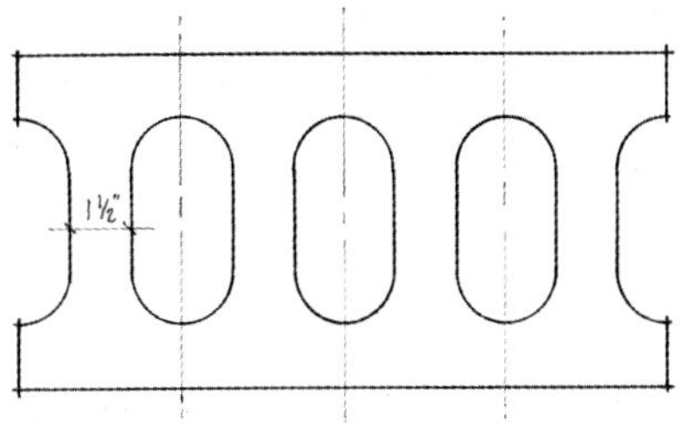

Fig. 1-27

Fig. 1-28

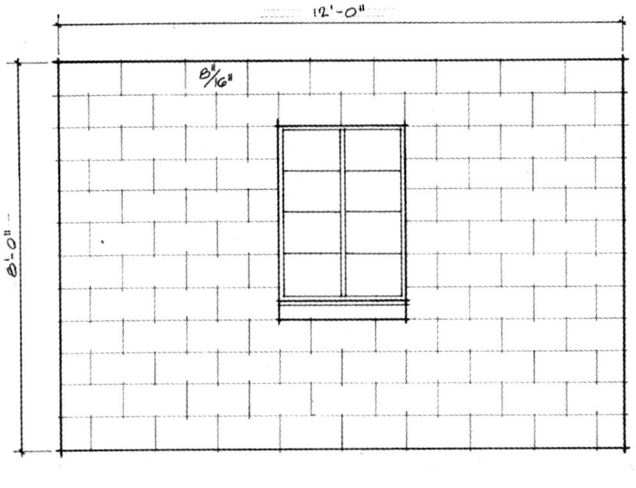

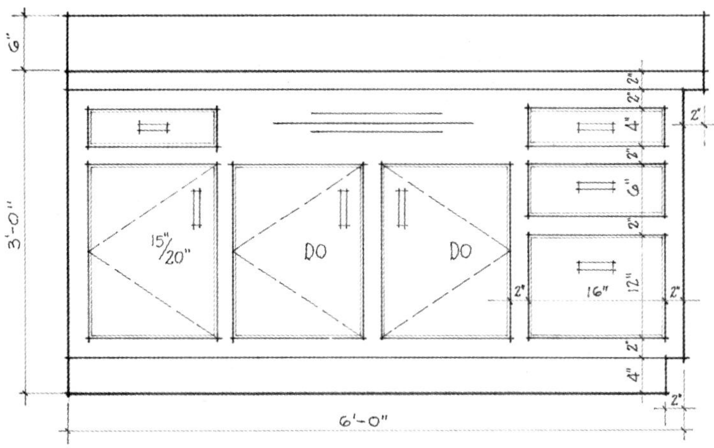

Fig. 1-29

Fig. 1-30

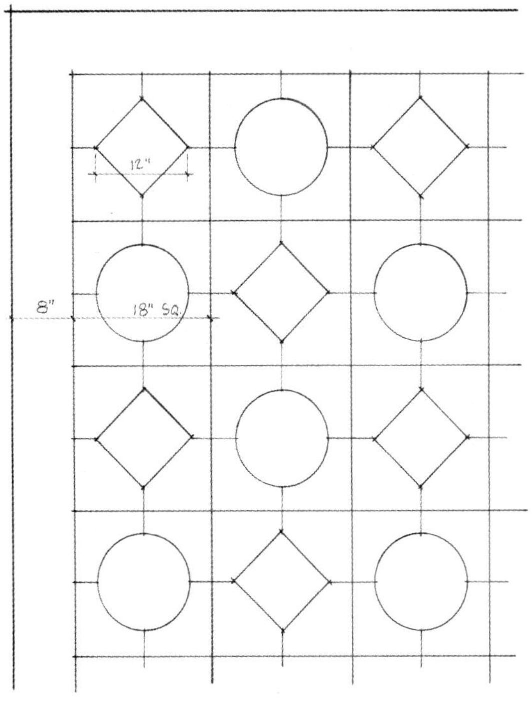

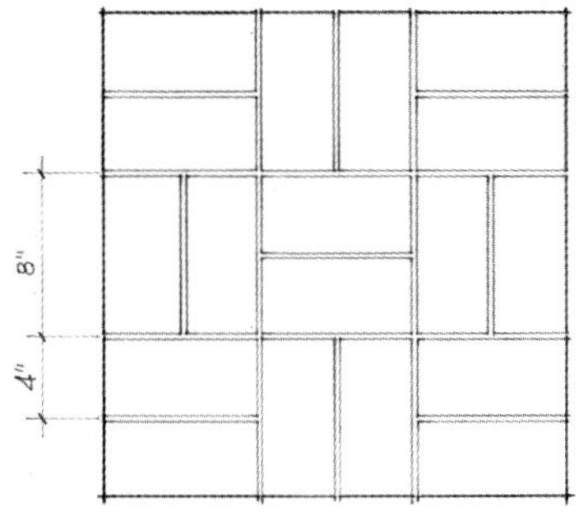

Fig. 1-31

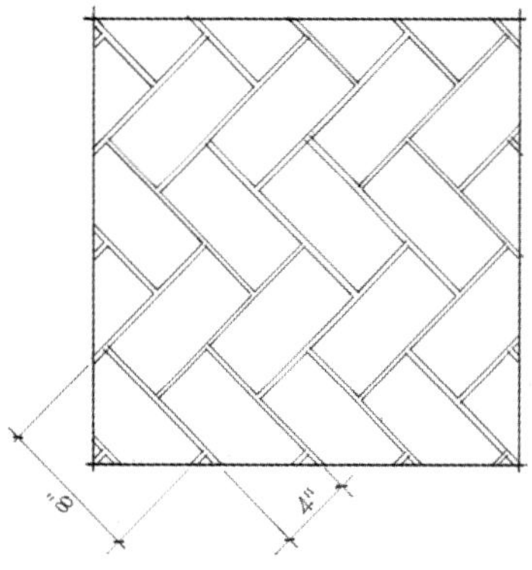

Fig. 1-32

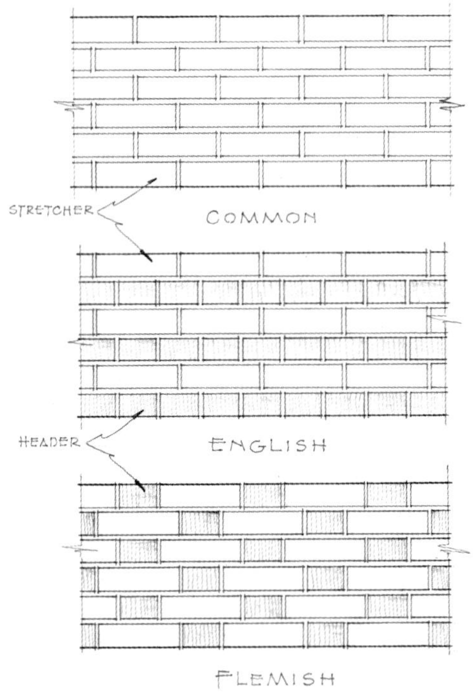

Fig. 1-33

Fig. 1-34

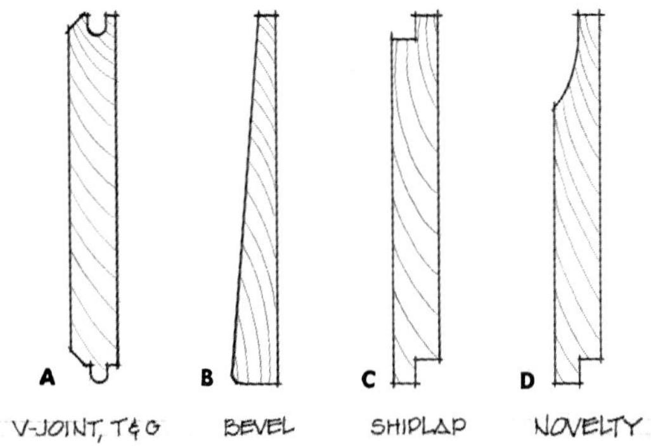

9. Basket weave brick pattern (Fig. 1-31). Using the scale: $1\frac{1}{2}'' = 1'\text{–}0''$, lay out a $2'\text{–}0'' \times 2'\text{–}0''$ square with light lines. Divide the height and width into thirds and lightly draw the nine squares. Allow $\frac{1}{2}''$ mortar joints between the brick, and lay out the alternate brick as indicated. Erase the original lay-out lines and darken the lines around each brick.

10. Herringbone brick pattern (Fig. 1-32). Using the scale: $1\frac{1}{2}'' = 1'\text{–}0''$, lay out a $2'\text{–}0'' \times 2'\text{–}0''$ square with light lines. With the 45° triangle, draw the diagonals. From the diagonals lay out 4″ squares and fill the entire space. Then lay out the $\frac{1}{2}''$ mortar joint lines $\frac{1}{4}''$ on each side of the 4″ square lines. Erase the proper construction lines and darken the lines surrounding each brick as indicated.

11. Brick bonds (Fig. 1-33). Using the scale: $1\frac{1}{2}'' = 1'\text{–}0''$, draw the vertical break lines $2'\text{–}11''$ apart. Draw six vertical courses of brick by allowing three heights of brick and three mortar joints to equal 8″. All mortar joints are $\frac{1}{2}''$ wide. Allowing one brick and one vertical mortar joint 8″ long, lay out the horizontal stretches so alternating vertical joints are midway on the common bond layout. The English bond pattern will have one course of stretchers and one course of headers as shown on the figure. Use the same dimensions for the brick and mortar joints on all three layouts. The Flemish bond will have alternate stretchers and headers in each course, with the headers centered both above and below the stretchers. Darken in outlines of each brick after construction lines have been erased. Headers can be shaded by light, vertical, freehand lines.

12. Wood siding (Fig. 1-34). Using the scale: $6'' = 1'\text{–}0''$, draw four, equal-spaced rectangles $\frac{3}{4}''$ × 6″ long. Part A of Fig. 1-34: draw the tongue $\frac{1}{2}''$ × $\frac{1}{4}''$, the groove $\frac{5}{16}''$ × $\frac{5}{16}''$, the bevel 45° × $\frac{1}{4}''$. Part B: the tongue $\frac{5}{16}''$ wide, the butt $\frac{3}{4}''$ wide with a $\frac{1}{4}''$ round. Part C: the rabbet joints on each end $\frac{3}{8}''$ × $\frac{3}{8}''$. Part D: the rabbet joint $\frac{3}{8}''$ × $\frac{3}{8}''$, the tongue $\frac{3}{8}''$ wide, the curved cut $1\frac{1}{2}''$ from top. Fill each with freehand, end-grain wood symbol. Darken outside object lines.

13. Wood trim profiles (Fig. 1-35). Using the scale: $12'' = 1'\text{–}0''$, draw the figures as shown full size. Keep the pencil sharp and let the intersection of lines run over at the corners. Draw the end-grain symbol of the wood freehand.

14. Garage plan (Fig. 1-36). Using the scale: $\frac{1}{4}'' = 1'\text{–}0''$, draw the $4'\text{–}0'' \times 4'\text{–}0''$ grid lines lightly. Lay out the 6″ wide walls on the inside of the $12'\text{–}0''$ and $24'\text{–}0''$ grid lines. Center the doors and make the small door and windows $2'\text{–}0''$ wide. Fill the walls with a gray tone.

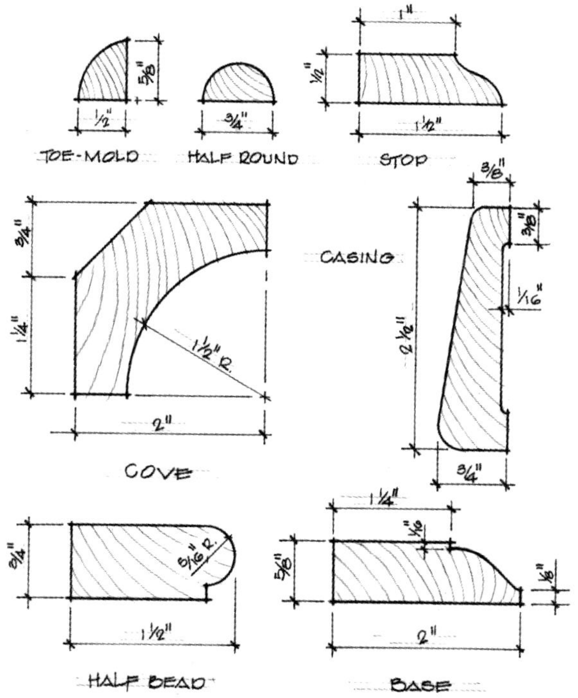

Fig. 1-35

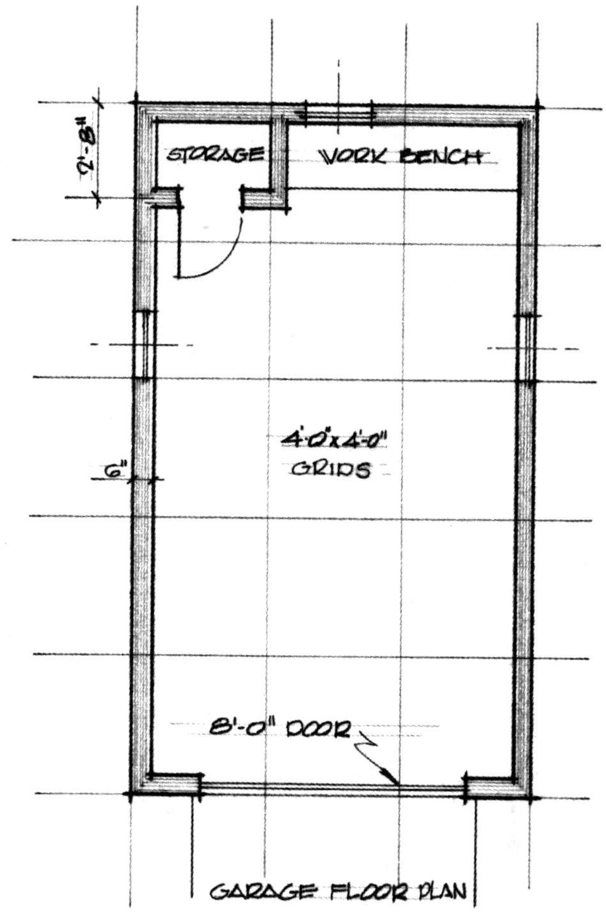

Fig. 1-36

REVIEW QUESTIONS

1. Why are quality drafting instruments important for good work?

2. Why is the drawing board slightly inclined?

3. For what purpose is a pad used under tracing paper?

4. Do left-handed draftsmen place the triangles on the T square in the same manner as right-handed draftsmen? If so, why?

5. What is the advantage of transparent equipment such as triangles?

6. Why are drawing pencils often hexagonal in shape?

7. Is the 2H lead harder than the 2B?

8. For what purpose is the pencil turned between the fingers when drawing a line?

9. Why is the adjustable triangle timesaving?

10. What is the difference between the architect's scale and the civil engineer's scale?

11. List the necessary qualities of suitable tracing paper.

12. What are the most ideal lighting conditions for drafting?

"Practice is the best of all instructors."—Publitius Syrus

2

Lettering

Legible lettering on a drawing fulfills an important requirement. Information that cannot be revealed by graphic shapes and lines alone must be included in the form of notes, titles, dimensions, and identifications, to make the drawing informative and complete. The lettering can either enhance the drawing by making it simple to interpret and pleasant to look at, or ruin an otherwise good drawing by making it difficult to read and unsightly in appearance.

2.1 LETTERING SKILL

Skill in freehand lettering adds style and individuality to a draftsman's work. Even though the various mechanical devices available aid in producing the uniform technical lettering required in some offices, freehand lettering is generally preferred on architectural drawings and should be an important phase of draftsmanship training. In fact, many employers evaluate drafting skill in direct relation to lettering skill. If the student learns the basic letter forms (Fig. 2-2) and gives deliberate application to their mastery during early practice, he will soon be able to do a creditable job of lettering. Anyone who can write can learn to letter. After considerable experience, every draftsman's freehand lettering acquires an individuality—much the same as his handwriting—which is soon identifiable and which contributes favorably to "good technique" in architectural drawing.

Lettering is also occasionally incorporated into the design of structures. Inscriptions, plaques, signs, and other applications comprising well-designed letter forms in the architectural aspects of the building often fall upon the draftsman for their execution. Therefore, the basic styles of alphabets and their characteristics should be of particular interest to him.

2.2 ALPHABET CLASSIFICATIONS

By closely observing the alphabets and typefaces in use by the modern commercial world, you will notice that each fits one of the following basic letter classifications (see Fig. 2-1).

Roman Perfected by the Greeks and Romans, and modernized during the eighteenth century by typefounders, this alphabet imparts a feeling of grace and dignity, and is considered our most beautiful typeface. The classic example can be found on the column of Trajan in Rome. Thick- and thin-width strokes and "serifs" are the distinguishing features. Serifs are the spurs or "boots" forming the ends of the strokes, which can be used on gothic letters as well as roman. Although the lettering found on old Roman stonework is lightface, modern roman lettering has a bolder characteristic. Extensive modifications of this beautiful alphabet are in wide use today.

Gothic This basic alphabet has been in use for many years as a "commercial" block-type letter, which is comparatively simple to execute and easy to read. Its distinguishing characteristic is the uniformity in width of all strokes. Its modifications include—inclined, addition of serifs, rounded, squared, boldface, and lightface. The gothic alphabet is the base from which our "single-stroke" technical lettering has evolved. It was standardized by C. W. Reinhard, a chief draftsman for *Engineering News,* during the latter part of the nineteenth century.

Script This completely different basic alphabet is cursive in character and resembles handwriting. Interconnected lowercase letters are used within words; capital letters, of course, are used only at word or sentence beginnings, a practice not required of roman or gothic letters. The free-flowing, continuous strokes produce a delicate and personal temperament, making this alphabet popular for many commercial trademarks. Modifications of either vertical or inclined scripts range from very thin lines to bold or thick-and-thin varieties of many modern interpretations.

Fig. 2-1 Basic alphabet types. All lettering can be classified under one of these types.

Text Sometimes referred to as "Old English," this alphabet was first used by central European monks for recording religious manuscripts before the advent of the printing press. The strokes of different width are due to the fact that a flat quill pen was employed. Because of its connection with religious writings, this alphabet is usually identified with formal religious work and the Scriptures. Testimonials and fraternal certificates are often hand-engrossed with variations of the alphabet. It is similar to script in that lowercase letters must be used throughout the words, with the use of capitals restricted to word beginnings only. Text is difficult to read and draw, yet simplified versions of it are still widely used in Germany today.

The term "italics" is generally given to typefaces having inclined, lightface, and curved characteristics. It is not given a separate grouping because all of the above-mentioned letter types can be made in the italic form.

2.3 UPPERCASE AND LOWERCASE LETTERS

Nearly all alphabets have both uppercase (capitals) and smaller, more rounded lowercase letters. The height of the lowercase body is usually two-thirds the height of its capitals, with ascenders extending to the capital line and descenders dropping the same amount below (see Fig. 2-29). If a great deal of copy or an unusually large note is necessary on a drawing, lowercase letters will be found to require less space, and they are usually more readable. Yet capitals are used for the majority of the lettering done on architectural drawings. Because of the universal acceptance and popularity of capitals, the material in this chapter will mainly consider their characteristics.

2.4 BASIC LETTERING PRACTICE

The vertical, single-stroke gothic alphabet shown in Fig. 2-2 is the basic style used by draftsmen for most of the small lettering found on technical drawings. Because of its legibility and simplicity of execution, it has been universally accepted as a standardized alphabet. Lettering on architectural drawings is known for its freedom of style and individuality, yet no style can be developed that is easily read unless the student thoroughly learns the basic alphabet. The architectural variations should not be attempted until the rudiments of letter construction are accomplished. (For a beginning lettering exercise, it is suggested that a sheet of tracing paper is fastened over Fig. 2-2, and a direct duplication of the basic characters is made.)

Select an H or 2H drawing pencil for lettering and keep the point medium sharp at all times. Figure 2-3 shows the proper method of holding the pencil. A comfortable, natural posture is the most desirable. Be sure the entire forearm rests on the flat table surface; this position allows for more stability than trying to letter over instruments or equipment on the drawing table. Rotate the pencil continually between strokes to maintain a uniform pencil point. A point that is too sharp is difficult to control—it will either break or create grooves in the paper if a desirable, firm pressure is applied. A pencil that becomes too dull, on the other hand, pro-

Fig. 2-2 The vertical, single-stroke technical alphabet, showing proportion and sequence of strokes. Master this basic alphabet before trying the architectural variations.

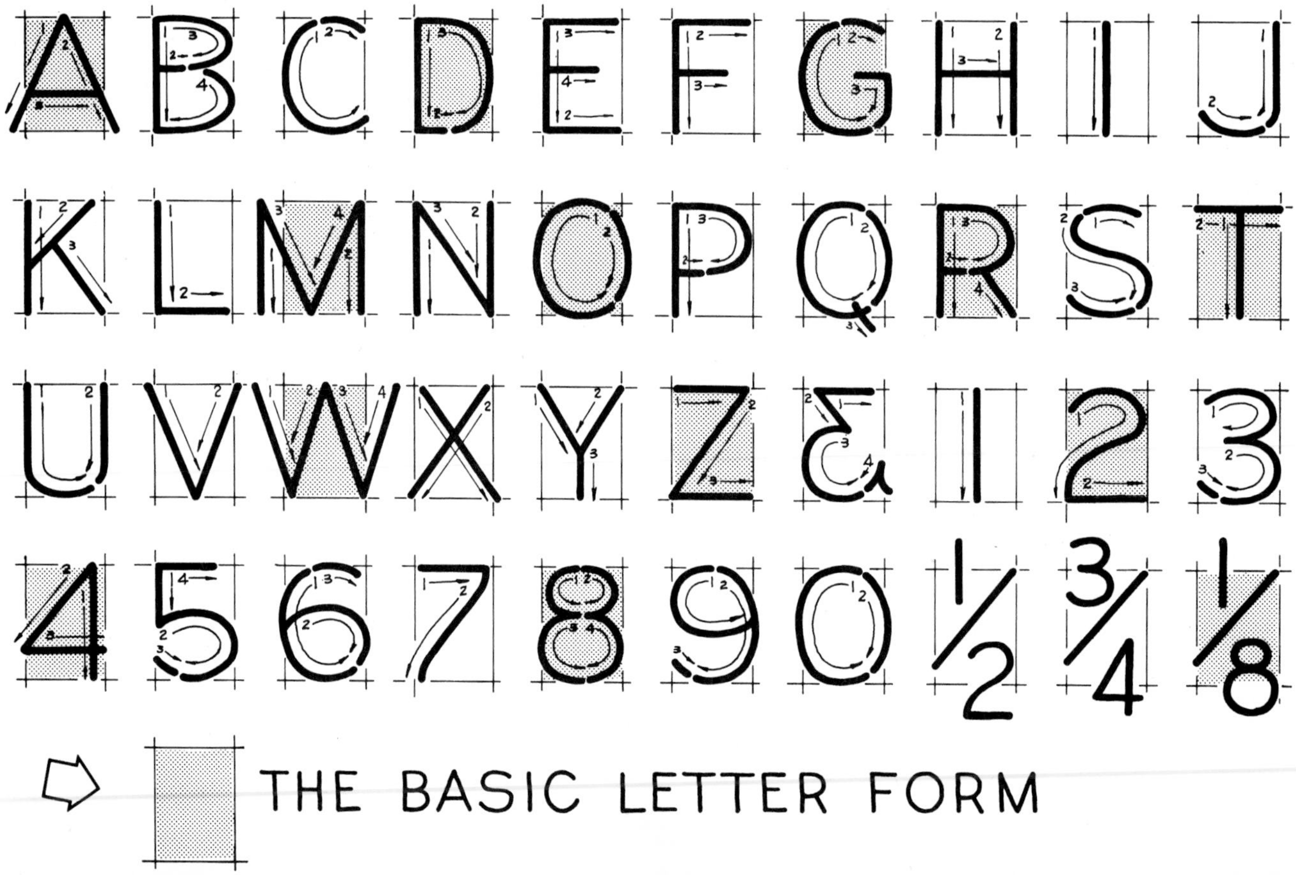

duces ragged and awkward strokes (see Fig. 2-4). Other unsatisfactory results are shown in Figs. 2-5 and 2-6. As a preliminary exercise, try a few of the practice strokes shown in Fig. 2-7 before starting the actual letter forms.

2.5 GUIDE LINES

All lettering is done with the aid of penciled guide lines. Even experienced draftsmen carefully draw horizontal guide lines for their lettering. It is nearly impossible to maintain straight lettering without guide lines—use them like the experts do. See Fig. 2-8 for the method of drawing uniform guide lines with one type of plastic lettering guide. Until you have developed skill in *vertical* lettering strokes, use vertical guide lines also; after you have attained confidence, dispense with the vertical guide lines—but never with the horizontal ones. In pencil lettering, the guide lines are always left on the drawing; therefore, care should be taken in placing the lines neatly on the paper with a sharp pencil. Architectural draftsmen give more prominence to their horizontal guide lines, and make no effort to minimize them; in fact, they usually draw guide lines well beyond the intended extremities of the actual letters. The lines then contribute a "brushy" appearance to the lettering. Only on inked lettering are the lines erased. To give a title more emphasis, a series of close, horizontal lines can be drawn throughout the height of the letters (see Fig. 2-9). Such practice should be consistent with similar titles on the drawing, however.

One of the available lettering guides or triangles (Braddock, Ames) will aid in maintain-

Fig. 2-3 Holding the pencil for lettering.

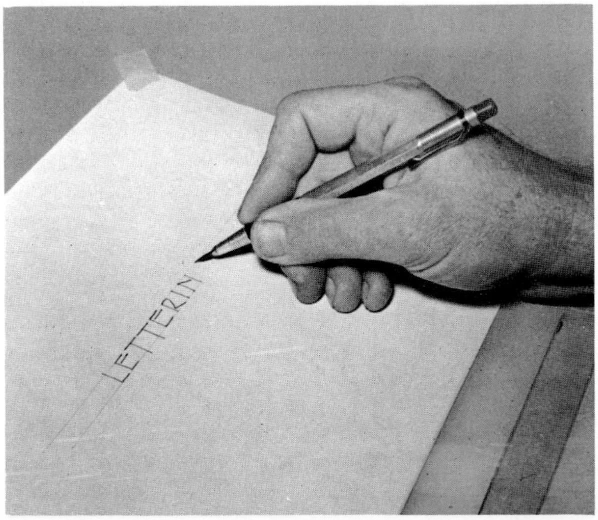

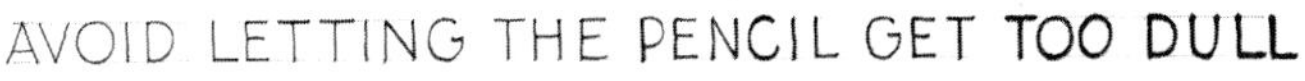

Fig. 2-4 Maintain a medium-sharp point to avoid variations in stroke width.

Fig. 2-5 Nonintersecting strokes create this careless appearance.

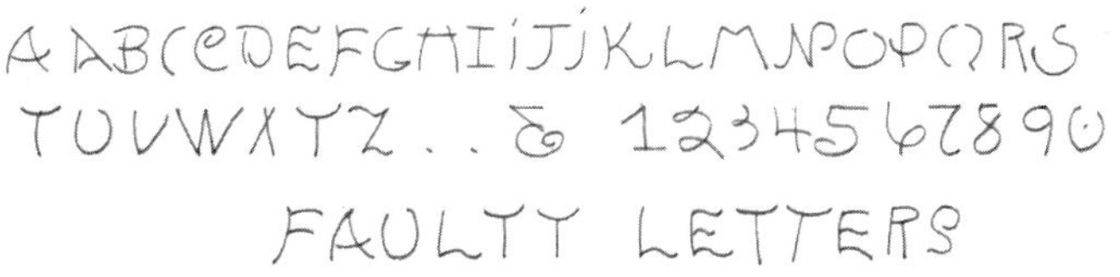

Fig. 2-6 Examples of faulty letter forms.

Fig. 2-7 Preliminary practice strokes.

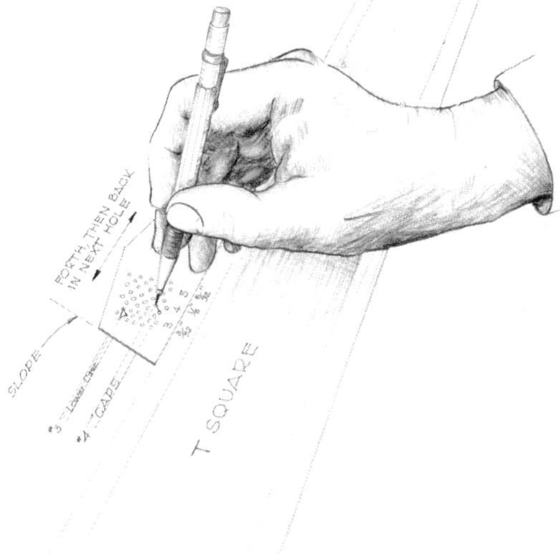

Fig. 2-8 Using the lettering guide.

Fig. 2-9 Use of guide lines for emphasizing titles.

ing uniform letter heights. *To draw lines with the guide,* a sharp pencil is inserted into the proper countersunk hole and the guide is pulled along the top edge of the T square, then the pencil is inserted into a lower hole to form the height of the letters and returned along the T-square blade. A series of uniform guide lines can be easily drawn in this manner. Holes in the guide are grouped for capitals and lowercase; the numbers below each group indicate the height of the caps in thirty-seconds of an inch. For example, holes in the No. 4 row would lay out lines for capitals $\frac{4}{32}''$ or $\frac{1}{8}''$ high.

2.6 HEIGHT OF LETTERS ON WORKING DRAWINGS

Generally, small lettering carefully fitted into open spaces on a drawing is more legible than larger letters crowded into insufficient spaces. For the sake of readability, never allow lettering to touch any of the drawing linework. On work drawn to the $\frac{1}{4}'' = 1'\text{–}0''$ scale, $\frac{1}{8}''$ high lettering can be used for minor titles such as room names on floor plans, and $\frac{3}{32}''$ lettering can be used for small notes. On smaller drawings, the minor titles can be made $\frac{3}{32}''$ high and the small notes $\frac{1}{16}''$ high. Slight variations are permissible, depending upon the layout and the preference of the draftsman, but if lettering is kept small and neat, a more professional appearance will result. Beginning lettering exercises should be done with letter heights of $\frac{1}{4}''$ or $\frac{3}{8}''$ until correct letter forms have been mastered. The distance between sets of guide lines for long notes should be spaced the same as the height of the letters, that is, if the letters are $\frac{3}{32}''$ high, the vertical space between each line should be $\frac{3}{32}''$, which will prevent a crowded appearance. A short note having only several lines of lettering can be made with the rows of letters slightly closer together and still be satisfactory.

2.7 LETTER PROPORTION

After studying the basic letter forms in Fig. 2-1 with the suggested sequence and direction of strokes, you will notice evidence of different letter widths relative to the basic rectangular shape. These definite letter widths are identified with each character and should be maintained if the lettering is to be legible and harmonious. Not only do widths vary from the single line of the letter I to the widest character, the W, but all alphabets as a whole can be distorted, if necessary, in general width (see Fig. 2-10). The narrower distortion is called "compressed" lettering, the wider is called "extended." In either method the letters vary in width, yet retain the relative basic characteristics. Condensed lettering occasionally becomes necessary in confined areas on drawings, yet it is more difficult to read than standard or extended letters. Extended lettering is appropriate when a word or title must identify a large area or a group of drawings. Remember that visual unity is attained when condensing or extending has been consistent and the recognizable silhouette or design of the individual letter has not been altered.

CONDENSED

STANDARD

EXTENDED

Fig. 2-10 Condensed and extended lettering.

The effect of "visual gravity" is evident in correct letter construction. If the horizontal center bar of the letters B, E, F, and H is placed at midheight, it will appear to be below center. This effect is called visual gravity, and all lines, especially horizontal, are influenced by it when observing a graphic figure. Lines on a page have optical weight. To counteract visual gravity, notice that the central horizontal stroke of the above-mentioned letters is placed slightly above center. Even the upper portions of the B, S, 3, and 8 are reduced in size to gain stability. Each character is a well-designed form in itself, and you should not attempt to improve or alter an accepted letterform. Put more grace in the letter M by extending the center "V" portion to the bottom guide line, rather than terminating it above the line. Keep the W vertical by making the third stroke parallel with the first, and the fourth stroke parallel with the second. Both "V's" in the W are narrower than the regular letter A or V. Make circular letters full height, even slightly larger than the space between the guide lines, with smooth, curving strokes. If vertical lettering is used, make the vertical strokes perfectly vertical. Check your work occasionally with a triangle—strokes that may appear to be perfectly vertical may nevertheless be slightly inclined.

Fig. 2-11 Spacing of letters.

2.8 LETTERING TECHNIQUE

The beginning and ending of each stroke are important—emphasize them with a slight pressure of the pencil, to bring the strokes to sharp and clean-cut terminations. Eliminate careless gaps in lettering by carefully intersecting the strokes. A few consistent gaps in architectural lettering can be used if they are planned and do not detract from its legibility (see Fig. 2-25). Make each stroke definite and firm; going over a stroke twice ruins the appearance of the letter. To gain positive pencil control, pull strokes toward yourself when lettering rather than away from yourself. Develop perfection of the letters before attempting speed. *There is no substitute for diligent practice.* Concentrate on letter forms before you concern yourself with spacing.

2.9 SPACING OF LETTERS AND WORDS

Because each letter has a different profile and width, the spacing of characters within each word becomes a visual problem rather than one of mechanical measurement between letters. The spaces between letters should be nearly identical in *area* if the word is to appear uniform in "tone." This can be done only by "eye" or by optical judgment (see Fig. 2-11). Notice that the letters of the lower line are incorrectly spaced when they are equidistant from each other. Letters with vertical adjacent sides or edges must be kept well apart to allow a similar amount of space between very irregular adjacent characters. The relatively wide space between the I and N can be seen in the top row of Fig. 2-11. On the other hand, an LT, AT, or other similar offset combination may require the letters actually to overlap, if a uniform background area is to be attained throughout. Adjacent circular shapes, such as OO or DC, usually must be kept comparatively close together. The exact area between each letter cannot always be made identical, yet the general area should appear somewhat uniform. Good spacing can be evaluated by squinting the eye and observing the gray tone throughout the lettering; if the tone appears spotty or varies too much, it is poorly spaced. Beginning students tend to compress individual letters and space them too far apart. Poor spacing often results in awkward appearance or difficult legibility.

Spaces between words should be adequate to make word divisions obvious. A good rule of thumb would be to make the space between words about twice the area between letters within the words, since spacing is a variable problem. If letters are tightly spaced, words can be put rather close together. If a group of words must be spread over a wide space, the space between each word must be sufficient to give the words identity and make the note readable. Too much space between words, however, produces a disconnected, spastic effect.

2.10 INCLINED LETTERING

Occasionally, to produce contrast or variety on drawings inclined lettering can be used. Although vertical lettering is used primarily, inclined letters, if used appropriately for minor notes, will often add more expression to the lettering. Figure 2-28 shows an architectural, inclined alphabet; the sequence and direction of strokes are similar to the vertical alphabet. To keep the incline uniform, random guide lines can be lightly drawn, using the $67\frac{1}{2}°$ inclined edge of the lettering guide. This is the American Standard slope of 2 to 5 for inclined letters.

Fig. 2-12 Making larger, vertical lettering with the use of a triangle.

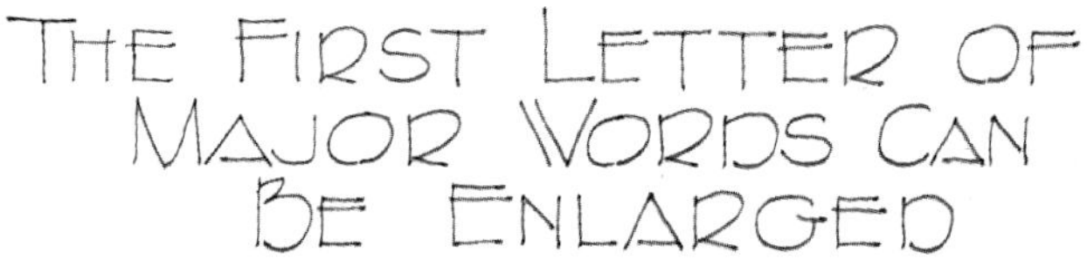

Fig. 2-13 Enlarging the first letter of each word improves legibility.

2.11 LETTERING WITH A TRIANGLE

Some experienced draftsmen, who have developed unusual speed in lettering, use their triangle for drawing all vertical strokes (see Fig. 2-12). They simply slide the triangle along the T square with their left hand as they letter; when a vertical stroke is needed, they quickly set the triangle into place and draw perfectly vertical strokes with the edge. All the other strokes are made freehand, and a personalized lettering style results. The system is used mainly for lettering titles 3/8″ or 1/2″ in height and with the alphabet shown in Fig. 2-33.

2.12 LETTERING TITLES

More skill in composition and spacing is demanded in designing titles with larger lettering. Defects that may go unnoticed in small notes of a drawing, frequently become obvious in larger titles. The size of a title should be consistent with the importance it carries—titles of similar magnitude should be similar in size. Select the guide line heights after establishing title magnitudes so the titles will have the correct importance throughout the drawing. Often titles can be given more importance by the use of extended lettering, or by using a thicker stroke with the pencil. Underlining also provides a means of emphasis. See Fig. 2-14.

Another important consideration is the finished silhouette formed by the title; if a number of words are used, care should be given to the general shape of the completed title, especially if the words must be put on two or three lines (see Fig. 2-15). Allow sufficient surrounding space to avoid a crowded appearance. Be sure it is close enough to the view or detail it identifies to ensure positive association. Titles can easily be misinterpreted if they are placed

Fig. 2-14 Title variations for architectural drawings.

Fig. 2-15 Arrangements of lettering blocks.

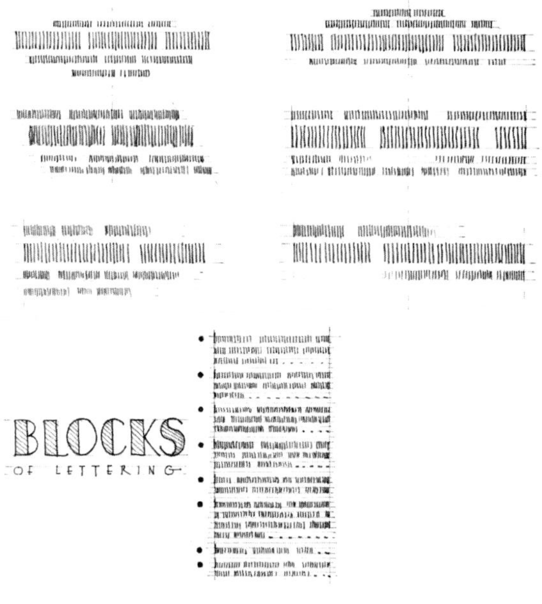

midway between two views. If a title must identify two views, position it to indicate an obvious relationship to both views. Extended lettering with spread spacing must be used if a title is to ramble over a wide area. If possible, place a title directly below the view or detail, rather than above or at the side of the view or detail. A reader will search below a drawing for its title when reading blueprints, and consistent relationships between title sizes and their placement will make drawings easier to interpret.

2.13 SYMMETRICAL TITLES

Occasionally a title must be "justified" or centered within a given space. This presents the problem of spacing and layout to make the end of a line fall at a predetermined point. For example, lettering that must be put into title blocks appears more pleasing if it is centrally located (see Fig. 2-24). Several methods can be used to determine the title's length and control its symmetry. One method is to count the number of letters (include the space between words as one letter width) to find its exact center. Then, after the guide lines and a vertical center line have been drawn in the desired space, the title can be put in by starting with the middle letter, or space, on the center line. Complete the last half of the line, then, working from the center letter toward the beginning, complete the first half of the title (see Fig. 2-16). Differences in letter widths are usually compensated for by similar-size letters on both sides of the center. If more wide letters, especially W or M, happen to fall on one side, adjustments can be made to allow for them. Another method which may be preferred by some draftsmen is first to lay out the required title on a separate slip of paper. The length is measured, and its center is indicated with a mark. This mark establishes symmetry and is centered directly above the space to be titled. The final title can be duplicated below with the spacing taken from the preliminary layout. These methods are only suggestions for fitting titles into given spaces; each individual may find various methods for arriving at the desired result.

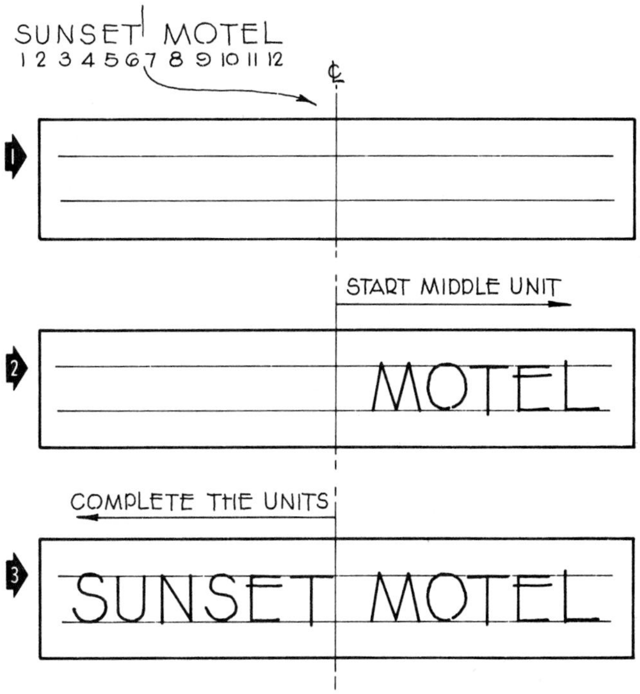

Fig. 2-16 Steps in laying out a symmetrical title within a title block.

2.14 LAYING OUT LARGE TITLES

To be graceful in appearance, large letters usually require the use of instruments for making both straight and curved strokes. Unless one is very accomplished in lettering art, freehand letters over an inch or so in height are difficult to make. After guide lines of the proper height are laid out, begin by constructing the letter forms lightly in pencil first, working over the construction until spacing and proportion have been perfected (from an established alphabet). Then, using a triangle and T square for straight lines and a compass and irregular curve for curved lines, carefully finish each letter in a mechanical technique. The freehand construction can be erased as soon as the settings for the instruments have been established. Width of lines should be uniform, and tangencies between curves and straight lines should be neat and unbroken. When straight lines are tangent to an arc (as in the U, B, etc.) the arc should be drawn first and the tangent lines attached to it. This method is much simpler than joining an arc to existing straight lines. If roman lettering is used, be sure the correct inclined strokes are thick, and the established thickness is uniform on both straight and curved strokes.

Avoid mixing freehand and mechanical lines on the same lettering. If instruments are used, make all the lines with instruments.

If a freehand technique is desired on a large title (often on display drawings), construct all letters lightly with instruments after they have been spaced and proportioned by sketching. Then go over the mechanical lines freehand, using neat, deliberate pencil lines. The mechanical guides will maintain straightness and form, and the freehand finish will soften the appearance.

Fig. 2-17 Use a thick point to give important titles a boldface characteristic.

2.15 LETTERING WITH INK

The student should devote some practice to ink lettering, since ink is often the medium used for presentation drawings. Also, if the lettering on working drawings is expected to

Fig. 2-18 Curved-stroke alphabet made with "B" Speedball pen.

Fig. 2-19 Single-stroke alphabet with serifs made with "B" Speedball pen.

reproduce very clearly, draftsmen may do the lettering in ink. Small, freehand lettering and titles can be effectively done with the use of a technical fountain pen, such as shown in Fig. 1-2. Many point sizes are available, and regardless of the pressure applied, the width of the line will always remain uniform. Usually, lightface freehand ink lettering is more readable than boldface. Observe the comparison in Fig. 2-17. Care should be taken in selecting the proper size point according to the height of the letters. Large, bolder letters can be made with the type "B" or "D" Speedball pens, if the student is willing to devote a little practice to their mastery. The alphabet in Fig. 2-18 is designed for the use of type "B" Speedball pens; the curved nature of each stroke is simpler to master than rigid straight strokes. See also Fig. 2-19.

When inking large, precise titles, the ruling pen and ink compass should be used. The accurate layout of each letter should first be done in pencil, centers for circles and arcs should be perfectly plotted, and all ink lines should be done with ruling edges. Handling inking instruments requires more skill and experience than pencil work. If single-stroke lettering is used, care must be taken in adjusting the instruments to ensure identical widths from ruling pens and compasses. Letters with strokes wider than the settings of ruling pens can be made by outlining each letter and filling in the spaces with a Speedball pen or a small brush dipped in the same ink. Waterproof, black India ink should be used for all inkwork.

An example of one of the many pressure-sensitive alphabets suitable for major titles is shown in Fig. 2-20. Many sizes and styles are available at drafting and art supply stores. If a title is to be put on tracing paper, a grid sheet placed below the tracing will facilitate their layout.

ABCDEFG
HIJKLMN
OPQRSTU
VWXYZ &
123456789
abcdefg
hijklmn
opqrstu
vwxyz.!

Fig. 2-20 Boldface alphabet suitable for major titles. Various sizes and styles on pressure-sensitive paper are available for draftsmen, and the lettering is easily applied to drawings.

Fig. 2-21 Leroy lettering device, used for uniform mechanical lettering.

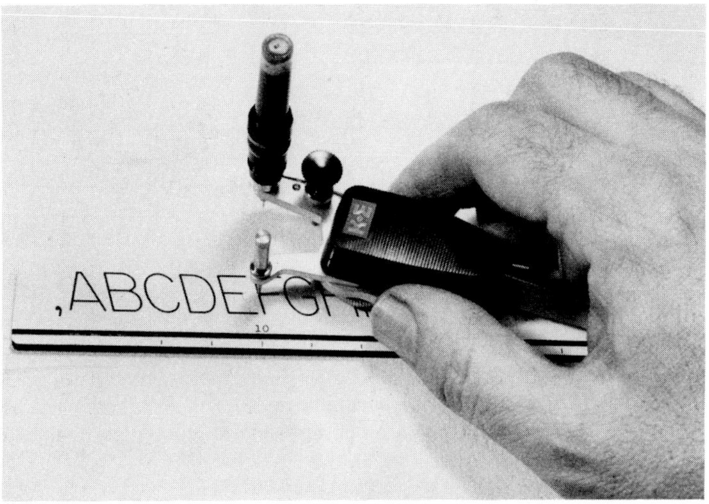

2.16 LETTERING DEVICES

Several types of lettering sets are available for making uniform technical letters in ink or pencil. Although they produce lettering stiff in appearance, they are sometimes used in offices when uniformity is essential. The most widely accepted type is the *Leroy* device shown in Fig. 2-21. It consists of a scriber with changeable points and different size template guides.

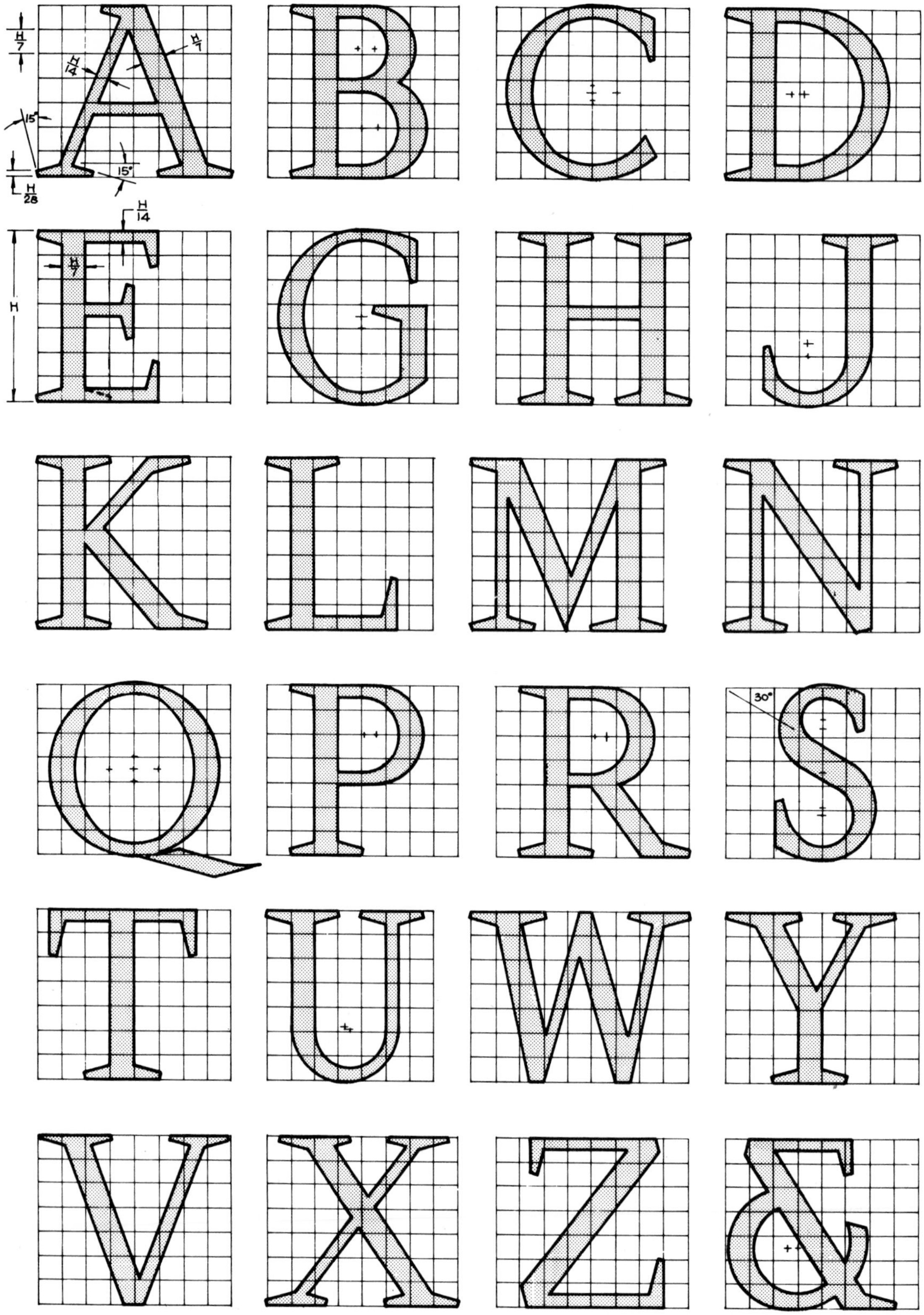

Fig. 2-22 A modified Roman alphabet suitable for major titles on drawings. Notice that this alphabet can be quickly drawn with a compass and an adjustable triangle set at 15 degrees. Heights of the letters (H) may vary according to the need, but the proportions shown should be maintained.

Either vertical or inclined lettering can be made with each template by adjusting the scriber. The template controls the shape of each letter form, but the draftsman must space the characters by sliding the template back and forth along the edge of the T square. Many special Leroy templates are available for other than standard lettering. Another device is the *Wrico* set, consisting of various size plastic templates and a stylographic fountain pen with variable size points.

Other templates are made for both small and large letters. A very inexpensive paper template of 1″ "stencil"-type letters is handy for quickly tracing large numerals or letters frequently needed on working drawings.

2.17 TITLE BLOCKS

Each sheet of a set of drawings requires identification, usually in the form of a title block placed in the lower right-hand corner of the sheet. Various types and sizes of blocks can be used. School projects need to have only simple title blocks; architectural offices often require more complex ones. Several examples are shown ing Figs. 2-23 and 2-24. Many offices have sheets with borders and title blocks preprinted ready for drafting use; others have title block stamps, called hand stamps, made up that can be quickly imprinted on each sheet before the drafting is started; others use *appliqué* preprinted title blocks of transparent plastic that will adhere to tracing paper and reproduce effectively. The use of either type conserves drafting time.

Information in title blocks varies, but a completed title block usually contains the following data:

1. Name and location of the structure;
2. Name and location of the owner or client;
3. Name and address of the architect;
4. Date drawing is made;
5. Date of revisions of drawing, if any;
6. Initials of the draftsman;
7. Initials or signature of the checker;
8. Architect's or engineer's seal; and
9. Identification number of sheet.

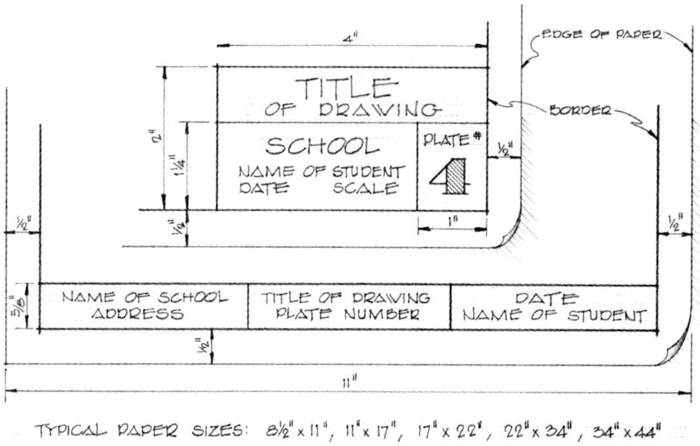

Fig. 2-23 Title blocks satisfactory for school drawings of small size.

Fig. 2-24 (A) Title block for a set of architectural working drawings. (B) Folding a print to file size so the title block is exposed.

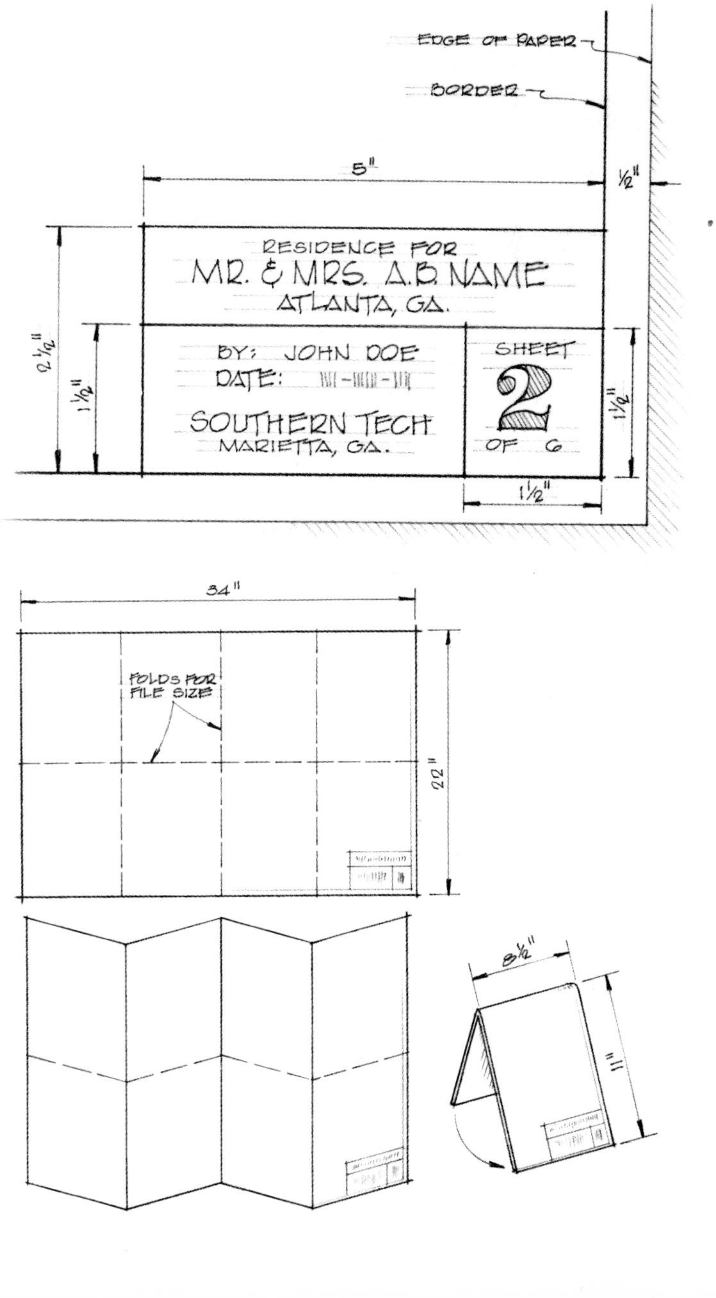

2.18 LAYING OUT SIMILAR TITLE BLOCKS ON CONTINUOUS SHEETS

A very convenient method for laying out similar title blocks on a number of sheets in a set is as follows: First, carefully lay out the required block on a small piece of paper or Bristol board. Then simply slip the layout under each sheet of tracing paper as it is needed, and duplicate the block. Most of the lettering can be accurately spaced on the original layout, and considerable time will be saved in duplicating the linework. Keep the lettering symmetrical within the block for the most pleasing appearance. To aid in quick observation, sheet numbers are usually made very bold and placed in the lower right of the block.

2.19 DEVELOPING AN ARCHITECTURAL STYLE

The architectural alphabets (Figs. 2-25 to 2-32) are included as suggested letter styles for the student. Each sample has been taken from competent draftsmen's work and represents accepted lettering currently being used on working drawings. It is recommended that the most appropriate styles be duplicated carefully and tried experimentally on several drawings. A few trials will indicate whether they satisfy the personal taste of the student, and whether they can be drawn easily and rapidly. The one style that seems to be the most satisfactory should be studied in detail and practiced until every character can be done automatically. Uniformity in appearance should be attained, even in different sizes. Refinement should be a continual process until a polished style develops that can proudly be put on drawings. If the need arises, one or two of the other alphabets can be used as alternates, for emphasis or deemphasis. Regardless of the alphabet selected, avoid extreme modifications—flairs with no meaning, or awkward curves which only result in faulty letter structure. Straightforward and uncomplicated lettering will be found to be the most acceptable.

Condensed No. 1 (Fig. 2-25) is extremely condensed and gains its distinction from the spread spacing between the letters. Each character is made as condensed as possible without destroying its recognizable features. Spacing must be uniform, and word divisions must be obvious for readability. The letter S is made with one reverse-curve stroke. Other letters are also made with fewer strokes than are required for similar basic letters. Ends of strokes are made with prominent points, thus giving the appearance of slight serifs.

Extended No. 2 (Fig. 2-26) is an extended style with very little space between each letter—the opposite of Alphabet No. 1. It is widely used and represents the practice of extending each letter. Each word should appear as a tight unit; otherwise use of the alphabet would require an extensive amount of space on the drawing. It is very readable, even in small sizes. If the low middle bar is used on the E and F,

Fig. 2-25

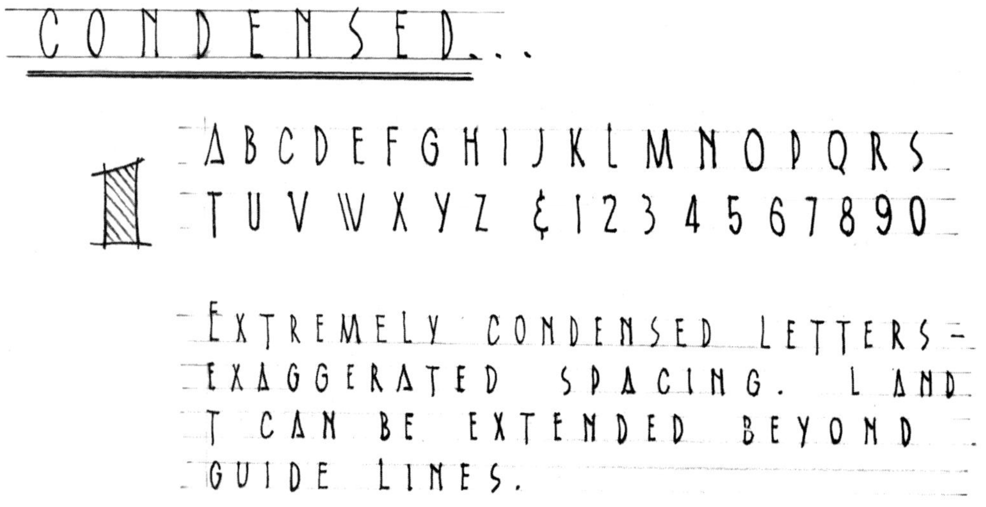

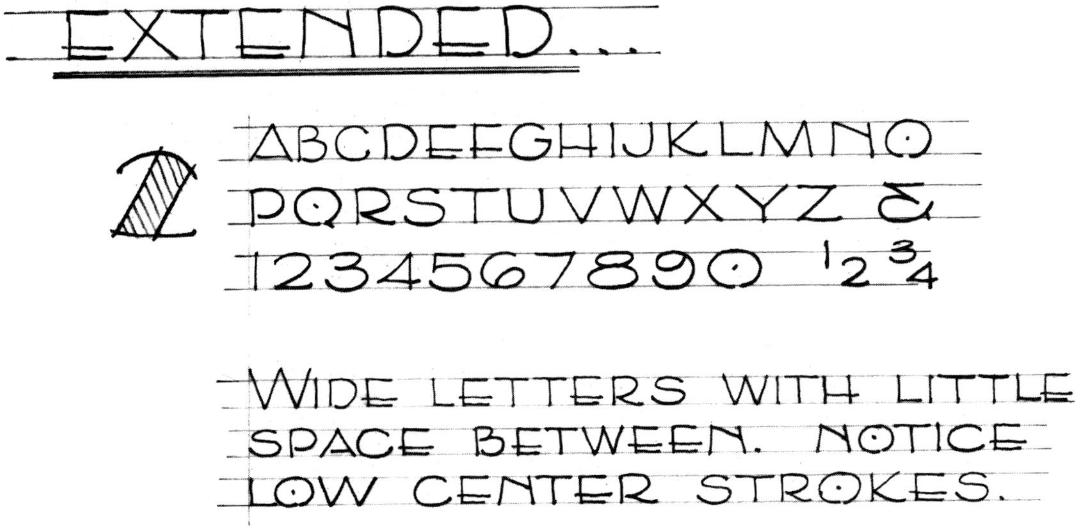

Fig. 2-26

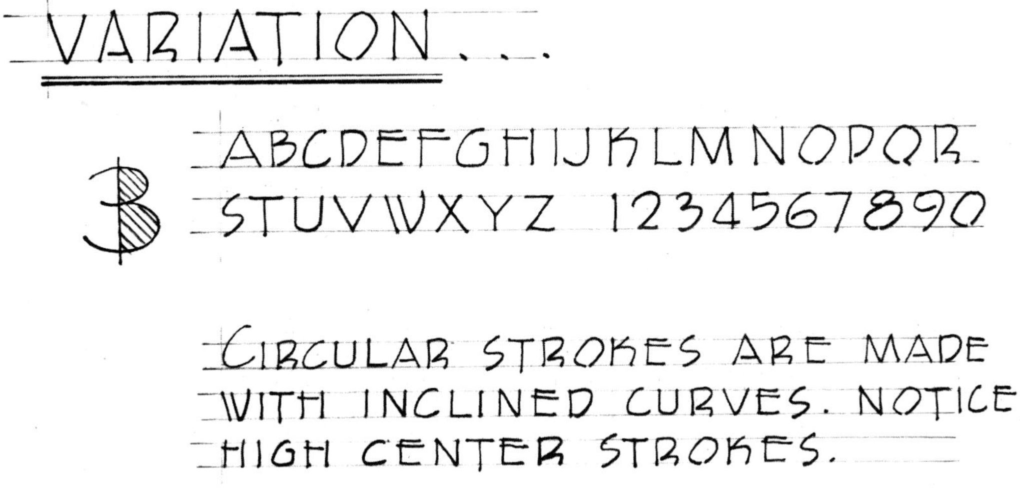

Fig. 2-27

similar low strokes should be used on the H, K, R, etc.

Variation No. 3 (Fig. 2-27) obtains its character from the inclined nature of all curved strokes. The O and Q appear to be tipping over, and possess a rectangular rather than full-round nature to their form. Small openings or gaps may be left in a number of the curved letters. Center bars are placed high for stability, and care should be taken not to condense the letters.

Kabel Modern No. 4 (Fig. 2-28) is similar to a typeface originated by a type designer who gave it his name. Contrast is provided between the full-round circular letters and the remaining condensed characters, thus giving it interest and variety. Spacing can be either spread or tight. Some draftsmen place a dot in the center of the circles; often the O, C, G, and Q are exaggerated.

Inclined No. 5 (Fig. 2-29) is the standard, inclined technical alphabet with a few minor architectural variations. Many draftsmen find inclined letters easier to execute. Every student should be able to do a lowercase alphabet well for occasional minor notes. To attain proficiency in the lowercase letters, practice making a graceful, inclined ellipse, which forms the basic shape for many of the characters; very little space should be used between the letters in each word. Use inclined guide lines if necessary.

KABEL MODERN...

4 ABCDEFGHIJKLMNOPQRST
UVWXYZ & 1234567890

FOR CONTRAST, THE CIRCULAR
LETTERS ARE MADE TRUE CIRCLES,
THE OTHERS ARE CONDENSED.

Fig. 2-28

INCLINED...

5 *ABCDEFGHIJKLMOPQR*
STUVWXYZ 123456789

abcdefghijklmnopqrstuvwxyz

Large blocks of minor notes can
be quickly made with Inclined
Lower Case lettering.

Fig. 2-29

Fig. 2-30

THICK & THIN...

6 ABCDEFGHIJKLMNOPQ
RSTUVWXYZ 123456789

SATISFACTORY FOR EMPHASIS.
AVOID A HEAVY APPEARANCE.
SIMILAR TO THE ROMAN
ALPHABET.

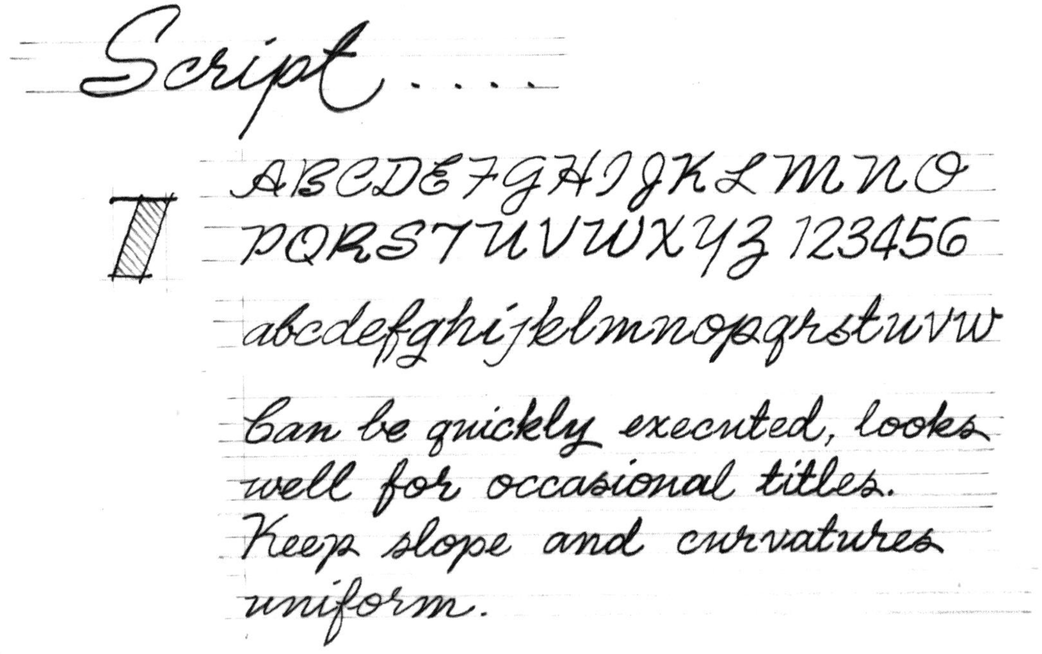

Fig. 2-31

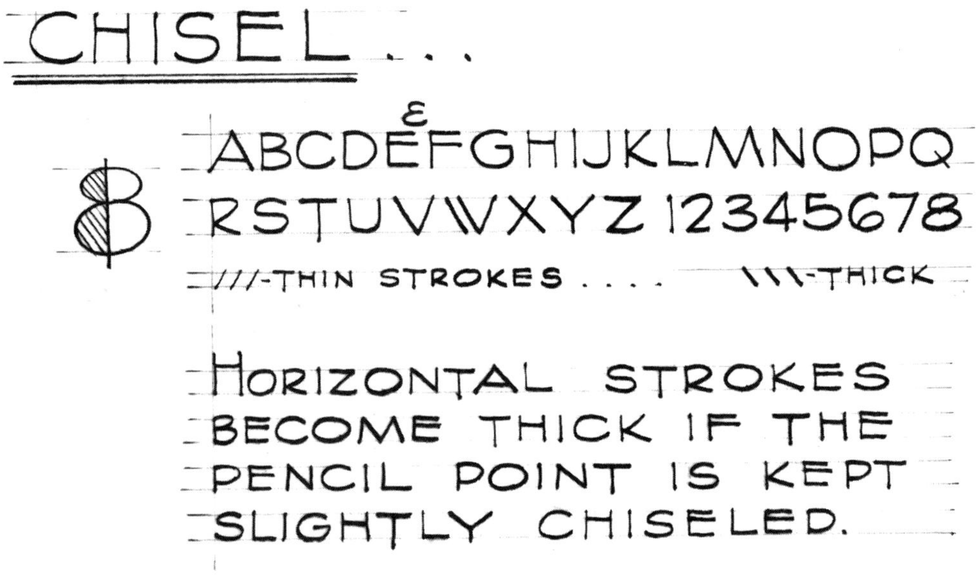

Fig. 2-32

Thick and Thin No. 6 (Fig. 2-30) can be used for important titles, but because of the extra strokes required, it would be too time-consuming for general lettering. To appear pleasing, it should resemble lightface roman lettering; the closer the resemblance, the more pleasing it will become. Avoid making the serifs too prominent.

Script No. 7 (Fig. 2-31) is suggested as an occasional style on display drawings, for titles of a special nature on working drawings, or for other incidental uses. Script is seldom used as the main lettering on drawings, unless the draftsman has developed a good, legible hand and desires to give more individuality to his work. Execution should be rapid, using smoothly curved strokes. Few straight lines are used, and it can be either vertical or inclined, depending on preference and adaptability. Usually each letter in a word is connected; however, an occasional break gives additional interest.

Chisel No. 8 (Fig. 2-32) is an adaptation of the extended style. The wide horizontal and narrow vertical strokes are a natural development of the pencil wearing to a flat, chiseled point. However, care must be taken to keep the point trimmed to a uniform chisel or the strokes will not maintain their contrast in width. The inclined strokes that slope in the same direction as the center stroke of the N should always be thick, the others thin. For example, the first stroke of the letter A should be thin, the second inclined stroke thick, thus resembling the roman thick and thin letters. The only exception is the letter Z, which usually has a thick center stroke.

Triangle No. 9 (Fig. 2-33) is an alphabet used by many architectural draftsmen. Use a small triangle for all the vertical strokes. Place the T-square above the lettering area and use the lower horizontal edge for guiding the triangle so the instruments will not interfere with your hand. The other strokes are quickly made freehand. Keep the letters in each word close together.

Alphabets for Large Titles (Figs. 2-18 through 2-20 & 2-22) are used for major titles on drawings; for numerals in title blocks; or for identification letters, which find incidental use on working drawings. Several styles are included to allow latitude in choice and appropriateness. The large letters can be traced directly from the book onto tracing paper, if they are suitable in size and style. Incidentally, boldface lettering when placed adjacent to very small, lightface lettering creates interesting contrast in the composition of titles for display drawings.

LETTERING EXERCISES

1. On $8'' \times 11''$ drawing paper, lay out a $\frac{1}{2}''$ border and the title block shown in Fig. 2-23B. Using guide lines $\frac{3}{8}''$ high and $\frac{1}{2}''$ between each set, draw four each of the basic lettering strokes shown in Fig. 2-4 in the first set. On the next two rows letter the complete basic single-stroke alphabet twice, centering each row. On the fourth row letter two sets of the numerals. In the space below the numerals lay out $\frac{1}{4}''$ guide lines $\frac{1}{4}''$ apart, and centered both vertically and horizontally, letter the following:

GOOD LETTERING MUST BE
MADE EASY TO READ BEFORE
ANY ATTEMPT IS MADE TO
DO IT RAPIDLY.

2. On similar drawing paper, with border and title block as in Exercise 1, lay out similar guide lines and letter the same copy in inclined capitals (see Fig. 2-29). Use inclined guide lines lightly drawn.

3. On similar paper, also prepared with the border and title block as in Exercise 1, duplicate the architectural lettering and layout of Fig. 2-26.

Fig. 2-33

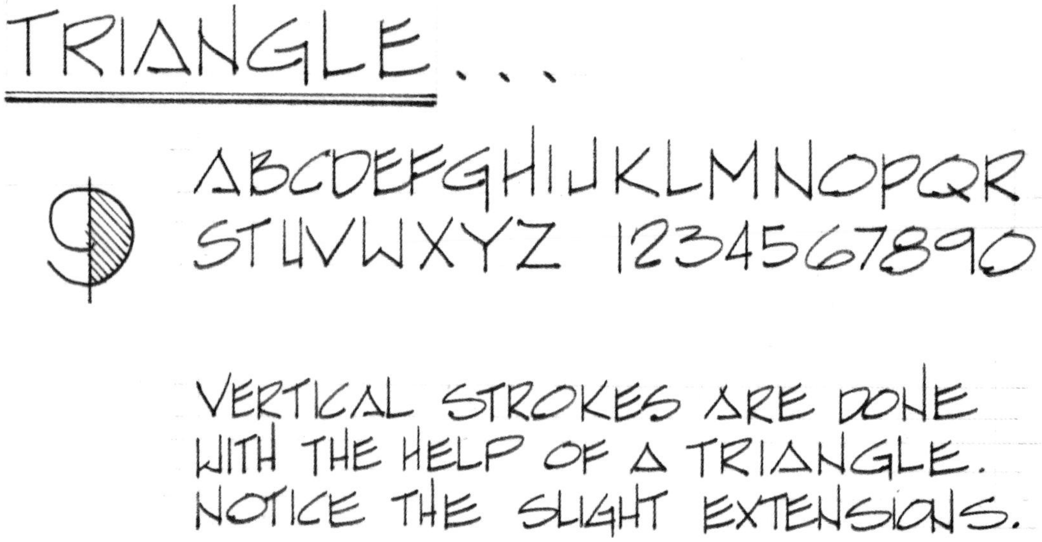

4. On similar paper, again with border and title block as in the previous exercises, lay out and center the title: ROMAN, in large roman letters 1¼″ high. Allow a 1½″ space from the top border. One inch below the title lay out ½″ guide lines, ⅜″ between each set. Letter the thick and thin architectural alphabet in Fig. 2-30, with all rows of lettering symmetrical. Keep the numerals on a separate line. Use instruments for the title only.

5. Repeat Exercise 4 using the word GOTHIC for the title and the lettering from Fig. 2-28.

6. On similar paper, with border and title block of Exercise 1, make your own layout, using large, instrument-drawn roman letters for the title and an architectural alphabet of your own choice.

7. Draw guide lines for 3/32″ high lettering and letter the following exercises using one of the architectural alphabets:

WELD VERTICAL LEG TO SIDE OF COLUMN

UNDERCUT ALL DOORS WHERE AIR PASSAGE IS REQUIRED

SEE DETAIL SHEET S-4

THIS PORTION OF WALL TO BE PIERCED BRICK (SEE FRONT ELEV.)

SHADED AREA IN PLAN INDICATES FURRED CEILINGS

PROVIDE WEEP HOLES EVERY 4′–0″

TURN DOWN REINF. 3″ FROM EDGE

SET THRESHOLD IN ELASTIC BEDDING MASTIC

REVIEW QUESTIONS

1. What are the distinguishing characteristics of the roman alphabet?

2. Why has the gothic alphabet been the most adaptable to technical lettering?

3. What are serifs?

4. Describe in your own words the meaning of "lowercase" lettering.

5. Which letter is the widest in the alphabet?

6. Why are guide lines needed for lettering on working drawings?

7. What is meant by a "boldface" alphabet?

8. List several methods of giving titles emphasis.

9. What is meant by "architectural style" in lettering?

10. Where is the title block usually placed on a working drawing?

"Geometry . . . is the only science that it hath pleased God to bestow upon mankind."—Thomas Hobbs

3

Basic Technical Drawing

Applied geometric construction, orthographic projection, sectioning, and auxiliary projection are the basic training areas needed for a solid foundation in drawing architecture as well as other fields of drawing. Each of these basics is of equal importance; they are discussed here for the benefit of those students who may not possess the necessary background, and for those who may need an accelerated review. Further study of architectural drawing assumes that these essential concepts have been mastered. Applied geometric construction provides the methods for arriving at general graphic shapes and intersections of various lines. The knowledge of orthographic projection serves as the conventional and universally accepted method for representing 3-dimensional objects on working drawings. Sections are necessary to show information about construction that is ordinarily hidden on exterior views. Auxiliary projection shows how views that lie on other than orthographic planes are drawn.

3.1 GEOMETRIC CONSTRUCTION

The T square, triangles, compass, and irregular curve are the tools required for beginning geometric construction exercises. To gain accuracy in draftsmanship, use a well-sharpened 3H or 4H pencil. Often the locations of center points from which arcs or circles are drawn become the important steps in the construction. Place these carefully.

3.1.1 To Draw a Line Through Two Points (Fig. 3-1)

After the two points have been established, hold the pencil firmly on either point and pivot the triangle or T square edge against the anchored pencil until the other point is aligned. (The eye need concentrate only on the second point.)

3.1.2 To Divide a Line Into Equal Divisions

First Method (Fig. 3-2A). Given line AB to be divided into, for example, five equal parts, draw line BC at any convenient angle and along it, measure or step off five equal divisions. Any suitable increment can be measured with the scale or stepped off with the dividers. Connect point A with the fifth point on line AC and transfer the remaining points to line AB with parallel connectors.

Alternate Method (Fig. 3-2B). Draw a perpendicular from line AB as shown and place the scale between point B and the perpendicular. If five divisions are required, select five divisions on the scale and pivot it from point B and the perpendicular until the end of the five divisions coincides with point B and the other with the perpendicular. (Slightly larger divisions on the scale must be used than the intended divisions on line AB.) Indicate the remaining divisions along the scale, and transfer them with perpendiculars to line AB. Any number of divisions can be made, and considerable latitude in choice of increment size on the scale can be employed. However, the smaller the angle between the line to be divided and the edge of the scale, the more accurate the divisions will be.

Division by Trial and Error Many draftsmen merely step off the divisions with the use of the dividers, if the number of divisions is not excessive. Several trials usually result in an accurate division.

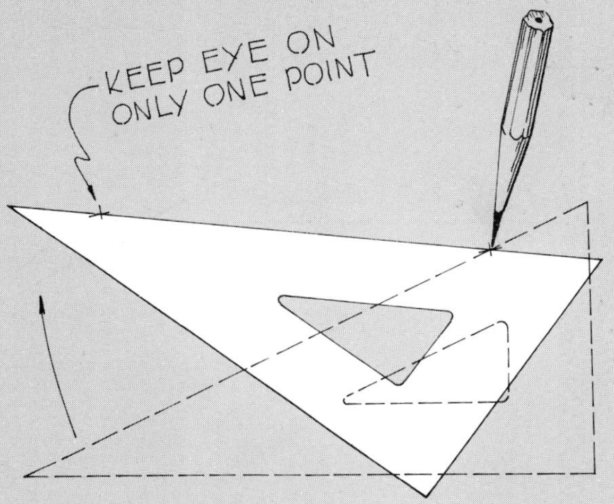

Fig. 3-1 Convenient method of drawing a line through two points.

Fig. 3-2 (A) Dividing a line into equal divisions (first method); (B) dividing a line into equal divisions (alternate method).

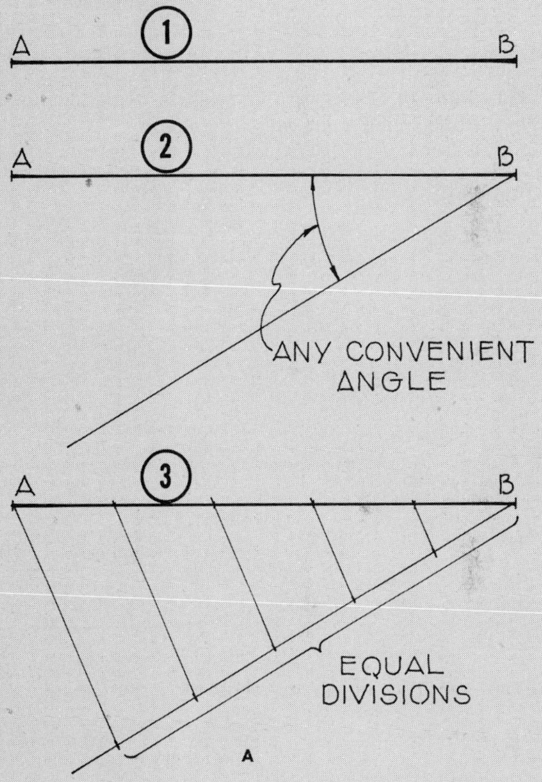

A

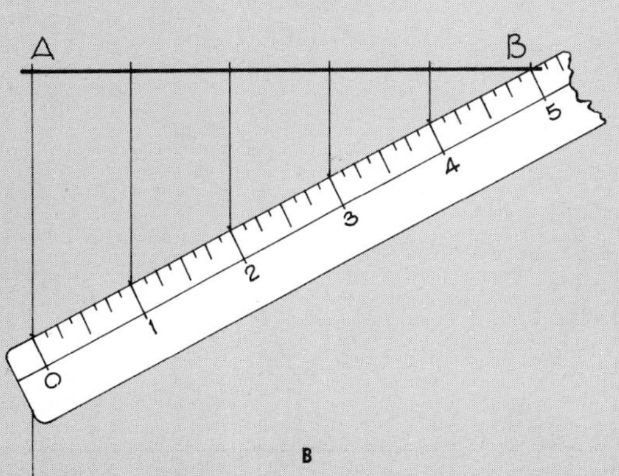

B

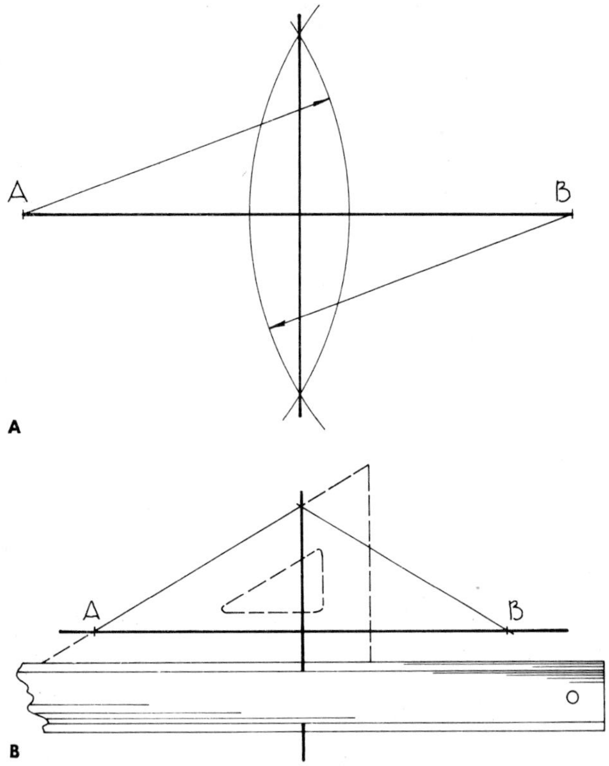

Fig. 3-3 (A) Bisecting a line with a perpendicular bisector; (B) bisecting a line with a triangle.

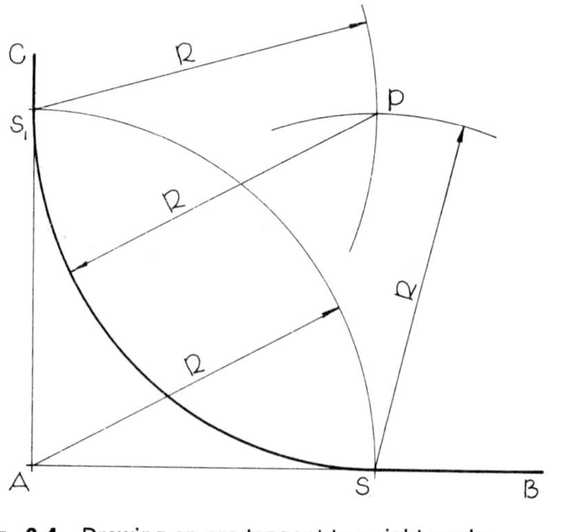

Fig. 3-4 Drawing an arc tangent to a right angle.

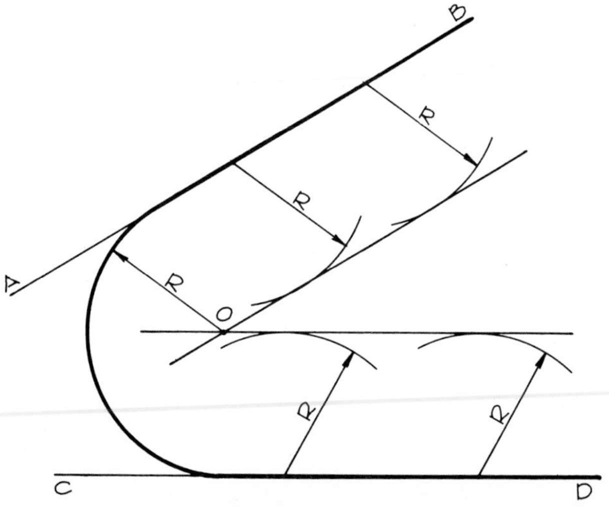

Fig. 3-5 An arc tangent to two straight lines (the arc center must be equidistant from both lines).

3.1.3 To Bisect a Line With a Perpendicular Bisector

With the Compass (Fig. 3-3A). Given line AB, with the compass set larger than half the length of the line, draw the same arc from both ends. A line passing through both intersections of the arcs will divide line AB with a perpendicular bisector.

With the T square and Triangle (Fig. 3-3B). Given line AB, from both ends draw equal angles, as shown, with the triangle. A perpendicular from line AB passing through the intersection of the angular lines will bisect line AB with a perpendicular bisector.

3.1.4 To Draw an Arc Tangent to the Lines of a Right Angle (Fig. 3-4)

Given right angle CAB, with its center at corner A, draw the arc with given radius R, intersecting AB at S, and AC at S_1. Then, using points S and S_1 as centers, construct arcs of the same radius. Their intersection at P forms the center for the given radius arc R, which will be tangent to the lines of the right angle.

3.1.5 To Draw an Arc Tangent to Two Straight Lines Which are Not Perpendicular (Fig. 3-5)

Given lines AB and CD forming an acute angle as shown (use the same procedure for lines forming an obtuse angle). Set the compass for the given radius and draw arcs R at random points on each line. The intersection O is located by drawing light lines through the extremities of the arcs. The lines will be parallel to the given lines AB and CD and be equidistant.

3.1.6 To Draw an Arc of Any Radius R Tangent to a Given Circle and a Straight Line (Fig. 3-6)

Let R_1 be the radius of the given circle or arc, and XY the given line. Draw line ST parallel to XY at R distance away as shown. Using P as the center and the Sum $R_1 + R$ as the radius, construct an arc intersecting line

ST at point O. The arc of R radius drawn from point O will be tangent to the given circle and line XY.

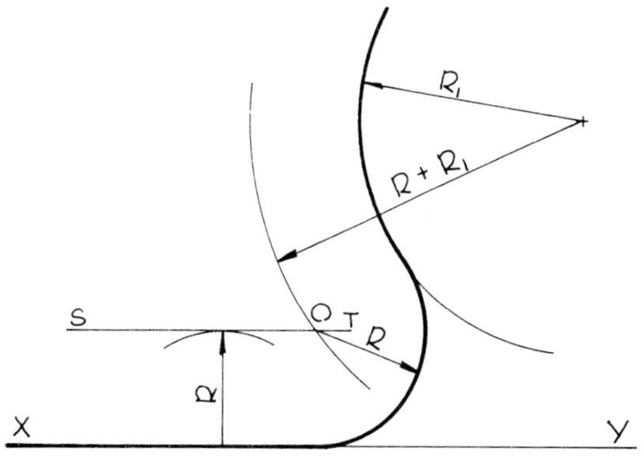

Fig. 3-6 Drawing an arc tangent to a circle and straight line.

3.1.7 To Draw an Ogee or Reverse Curve (Fig. 3-7)

Given two parallel lines BC and ED, connect B and D with a line and upon it indicate the reversal point A. (The placement of point A is arbitrary, depending upon the desired nature of the ogee curve.) Erect perpendiculars from line BC at B and line ED at D. Construct perpendicular bisectors of BA and AD. The intersections of the bisectors and the previous perpendiculars are the centers for the required arcs. Set the compass at the required radii, established graphically by the perpendiculars. A line intersecting both centers of the arcs will pass through point A, revealing the accuracy of the construction and the tangent point of the two arcs.

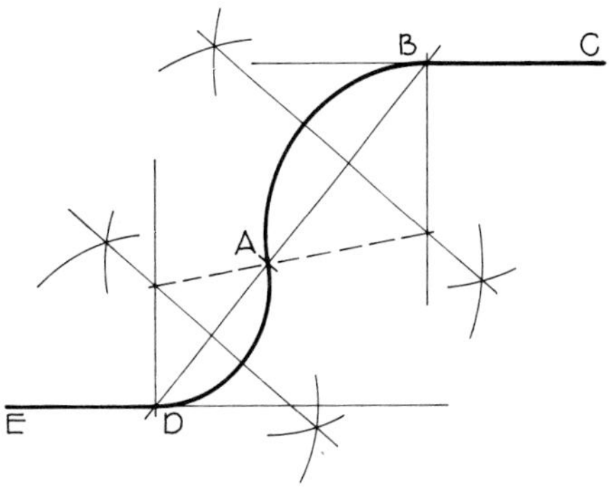

Fig. 3-7 Drawing an ogee curve.

3.1.8 To Draw a Regular Pentagon (Fig. 3-8)

Given the size of the circle within which the pentagon is to be inscribed, draw the circle and divide its circumference into five equal parts by trials with the dividers, and connect the points. The points on the circle can also be located with the protractor—step off five 72° angles (360° ÷ 5).

Fig. 3-8 Drawing a regular pentagon.

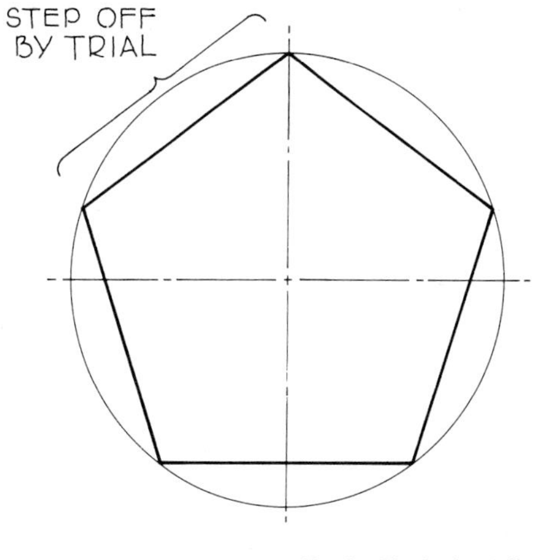

3.1.9 To Draw a Regular Hexagon

When the Distance Across Flats Is Given (Fig. 3-9A). The flats are the parallel sides. A hexagon can be dimensioned either across its parallel sides or across its corners. Construct a circle with a diameter of the given distance across flats. Circumscribe a hexagon around the circle which is tangent to the center of each side using the 30°–60° triangle and T square.

When the Distance Across Corners Is Given (Fig. 3-9B). Construct center lines and draw a circle of the diameter required across corners of the hexagon. Using the 30°–60° triangle and T square, inscribe the hexagon within the circle starting at an intersection of one center line and the circle. The radius of the given circle will be the length of each side.

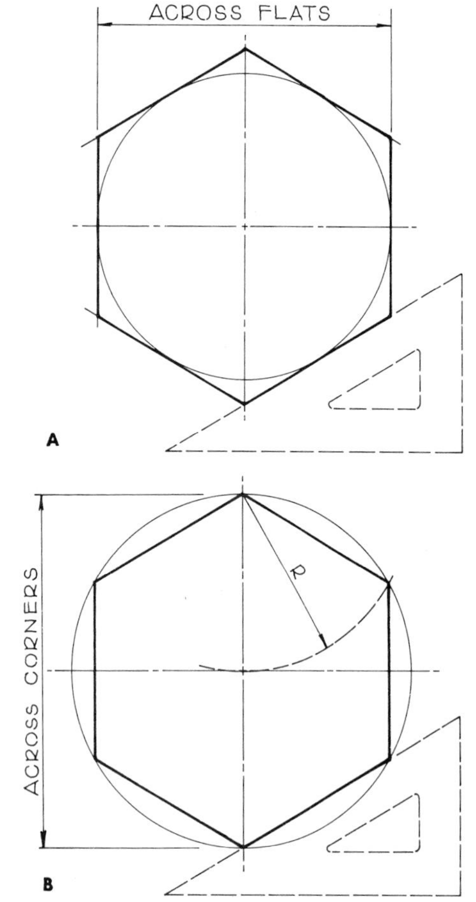

Fig. 3-9 (A) Drawing a hexagon with distance across flats given; (B) drawing a hexagon with distance across corners given.

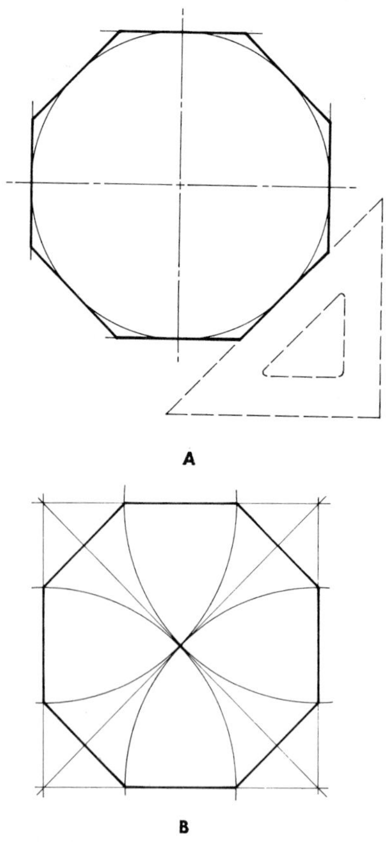

Fig. 3-10 (A) Drawing an octagon with a circle; (B) drawing an octagon with a square.

3.1.10 To Draw a Regular Octagon

Construction Around a Circle (Fig. 3-10A). Given distance across flats (between parallel sides), draw center lines and construct a circle of the given diameter. Using a 45° triangle and a T square, draw the sides of the octagon tangent to the circle as indicated.

Construction Within a Square (Fig. 3-10B). Draw a square with sides equal to the required distance across flats. Draw diagonals and, using half the length of the diagonal as a radius and the corners of the square as centers, draw the arcs as shown. Connect the intersections of the arcs and sides to form the octagon.

3.1.11 To Construct a Regular Polygon With Any Number of Sides (Fig. 3-11)

Given the length of one side and, for example, let seven sides be required. From any point A, draw the semicircle CDB using AB as the radius. By trial with the dividers, divide the semicircle into seven equal parts. AD will become the second side. Bisect side AB and AD with perpendicular bisectors to locate point O, which will be the center of the polygon. Draw the circle through points A, B, and D. The remaining vertices can be located by stepping off chord AB along the remainder of the circle, or by extending lines A3, A4, etc. to the circle.

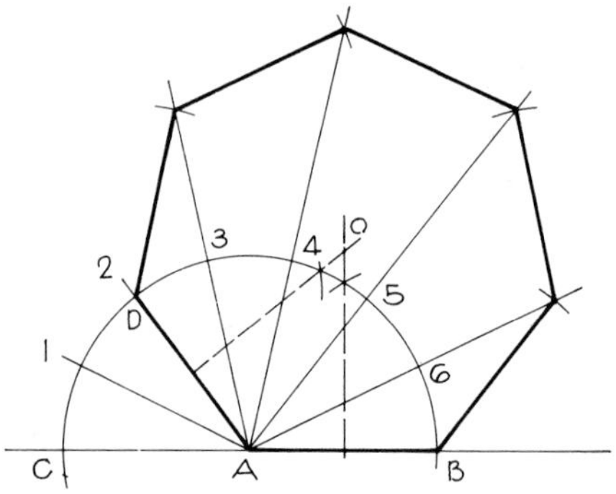

Fig. 3-11 Drawing a polygon.

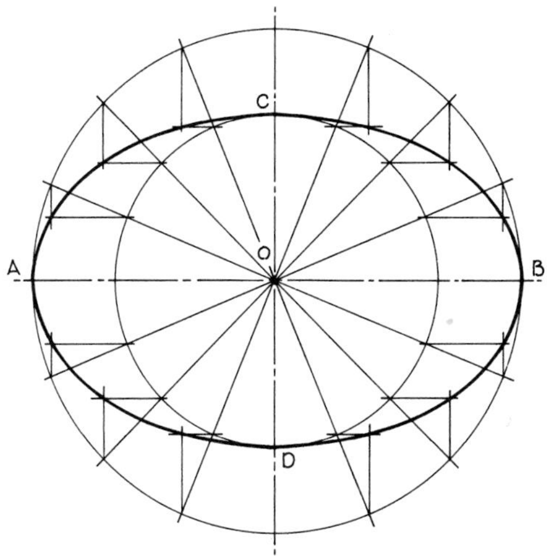

Fig. 3-12 Drawing an ellipse (concentric-circle method).

3.1.12 To Draw an Ellipse by the Concentric-Circle Method (Fig. 3-12)

Given the major axis AB, and the perpendicular minor axis CD, draw concentric circles of both diameters from point O. Divide each quadrant into an arbitrary number of angular dimensions; the example shows four divisions in each quadrant which have been conveniently laid out with the triangles—more accuracy can be obtained by more divisions. From the intersections of the division lines and the outer circumference, draw vertical lines parallel to CD. From the intersections of the angular division lines and the inner circle, draw horizontal lines parallel to AB as indicated. The intersections of these perpendicular construction lines produce points from which the ellipse can be constructed. Completion is achieved by smoothly connecting the points with the use of the irregular curve. If all the points in one quadrant of the ellipse can be aligned with one setting of the irregular curve, the other quadrants can be completed by merely marking the curve and tipping it over for the remaining curved lines. Elliptical arches can be quickly drawn with the foregoing construction.

3.1.13 To Draw an Ellipse by the Parallelogram Method (Fig. 3-13)

Given the major axis AB and minor axis DF. From the axes draw a rectangle or parallelogram with sides equal to the axes. Divide AO and AC into equal number of parts. Draw light lines from point E through the AO divisions and from point D through the AC divisions. Intersections of similar numbered lines will create points along the ellipse. Complete the remaining three quadrants by the same procedure and draw the ellipse with an irregular curve.

3.1.14 To Draw an Approximate Ellipse by the Four-Center Method (Fig. 3-14)

Given the axes AB and CD. Connect points A and D with a diagonal line. With AO as the radius, draw the arc AA_1 using O as the center. With DA_1 as the radius draw the arc FA_1 using

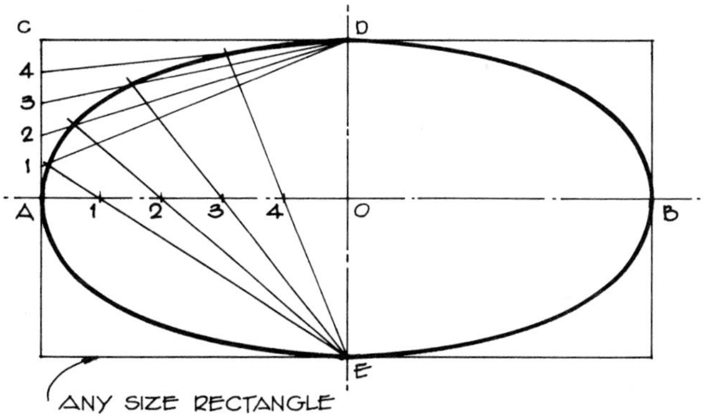

Fig. 3-13 Parallelogram ellipse.

Fig. 3-14 Four-center approximate ellipse.

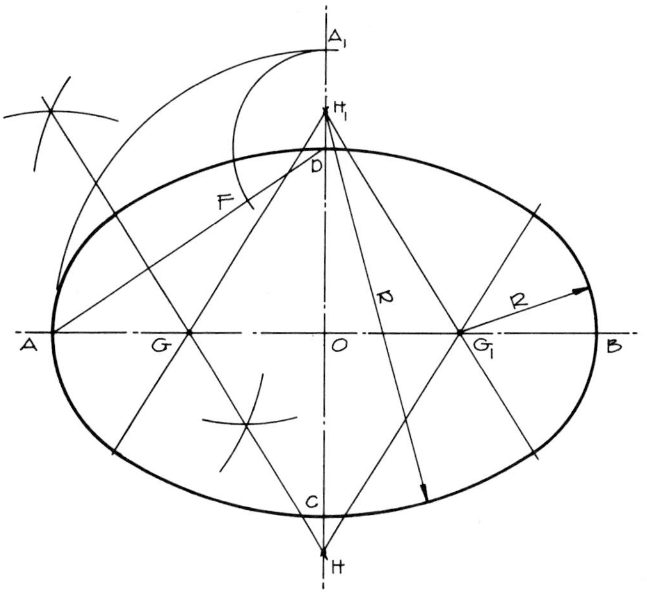

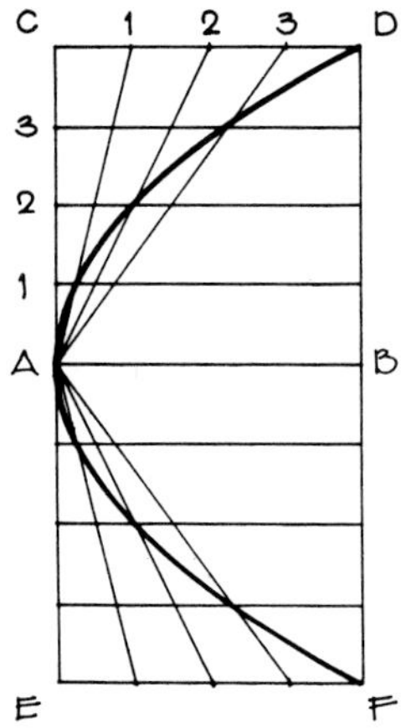

Fig. 3-15 Drawing a parabola within a rectangle (use equal increments).

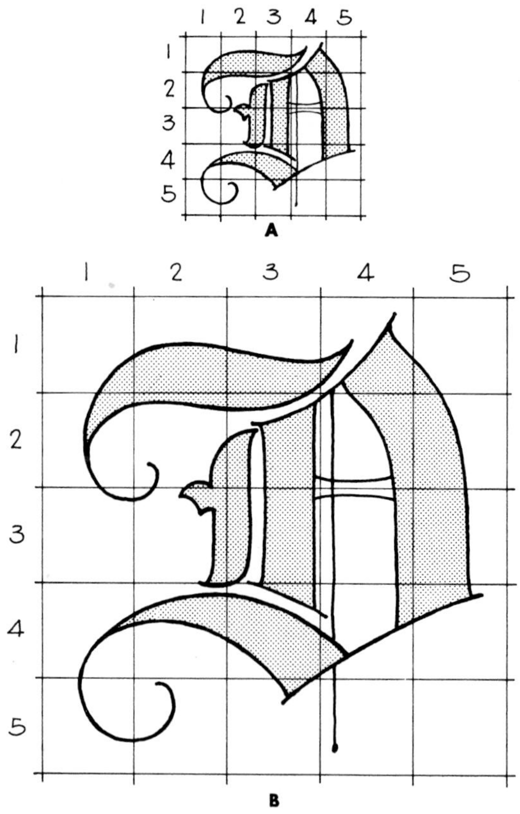

Fig. 3-16 Enlarging or reducing a figure.

D as the center. Bisect line AF with a perpendicular bisector as shown; this locates points G and H which become the centers for the required arcs. Points G_1 and H_1 are located equidistance from O as points G and H respectively. The distance GO equals OG_1 and HO equals OH_1. Draw the radius AG arc from points G and G_1 and the radius HD arc from points H and H_1 to complete the ellipse.

3.1.15 To Draw a Parabola Within a Rectangle (Fig. 3-15)

Given a rectangle CDEF. Usually these are the given dimensions, indicating the width and depth (or span and rise) of the needed parabola. Divide AC and CD into the same number of parts as shown. The intersections of like-numbered lines become points on the parabola. Notice that one set of lines is parallel and the other radiating. Connect the points with the use of an irregular curve.

3.1.16 To Enlarge or Reduce an Irregular Drawing (Fig. 3-16)

If a drawing is to be enlarged, first lay out a uniform grid field over the figure as shown. Use a grid size convenient for enlargement. For example, if a drawing is to be enlarged, say, five times or 500 per cent then it would be appropriate to select a spacing for the grid lines of the smaller field which could be conveniently increased five times for the larger grid. Next, lay out a larger, compatible grid field, using the same number of grid lines as the smaller field. For convenience, number the corresponding grid spaces in both fields as shown. The detail within each small grid space can then be enlarged within the corresponding larger grid block. Complete one block at a time until the entire figure is enlarged. *To reduce the size of a drawing,* the opposite procedure is used; the detail is taken from the larger grid field and reduced to the corresponding smaller one.

3.1.17 Esthetic Proportions Through Geometry

There are a number of interesting geometric proportioning methods which have appeared from time to time in the history of architecture and art. Some have withstood the test of time and should be accepted for their esthetic worth, even by modern standards. Not only do they provide the student of drawing with valuable construction exercise, but they indicate an application of geometry to the esthetics of structures.

The "Golden Section" –originally a Greek method of dividing lines and form into pleasing proportions (Fig. 3-17A). Mathematically, its ratio may be expressed as follows: $(\sqrt{5}+1)/2 = 1.618$. The ratio of one division to the other, then, can be stated: 1/1.618. Given line AE, to be divided according to the Golden Section, first bisect the line at point C. Erect a perpendicular to line AE at point E, equal in length to CE. On the hypotenuse (AD) of the triangle, locate point B so BD equals DE. On the original line AE, locate point F so that AF equals AB. F divides AE according to the proportions of the Golden Section.

The "Golden Rectangle" (Fig. 3-17B). The Golden Section provides the stable proportions for the Golden Rectangle. The long side of the rectangle is in proportion to the short side as AF is to FE in Fig. 3-17A. For convenience in drawing a predetermined size of the rectangle, the numerical proportion 76–47 units will provide a satisfactory method of scaling. As a matter of interest, the short side of the rectangle can be laid out within it to form a square, and the remaining space will always be another Golden Rectangle (see dotted line).

Construction of the Basic Triangle for a Classic Pediment (Vignola) (Fig. 3-17C). Given width of the base AB, bisect line AB with a center line intersecting it at C. With AC (one half of AB) as the radius, construct the semicircle AEB. With the radius EB, construct the arc AGB from point E. Connect points AG and GB.

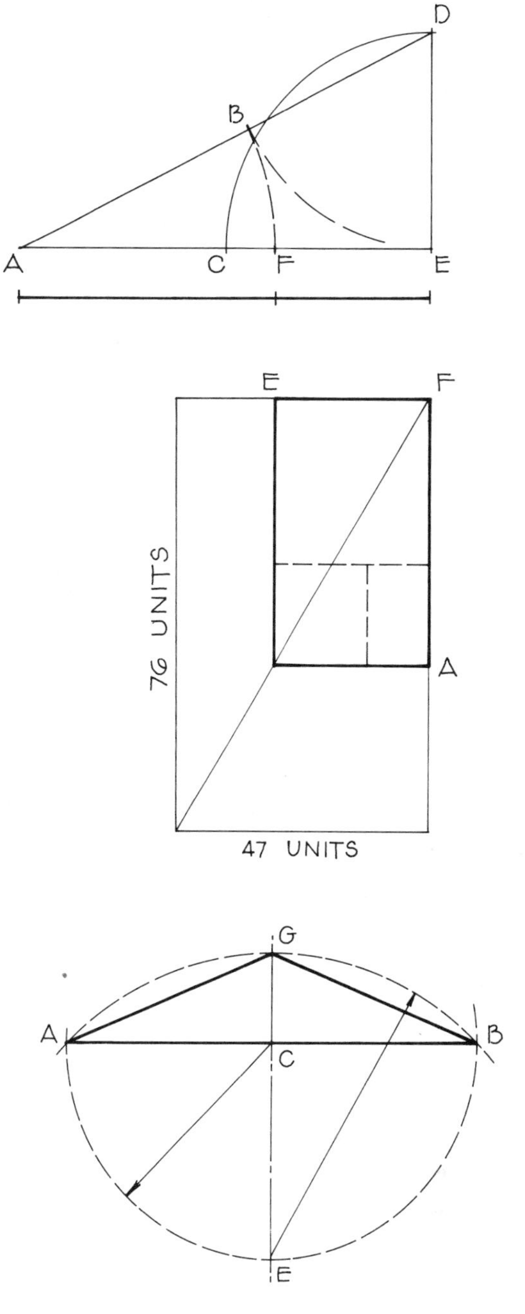

Fig. 3-17 (A) The "Golden Section"; (B) the "Golden Rectangle," made from the "Section" proportions; (C) the classic pediment triangle (Vignola).

3.2 ORTHOGRAPHIC PROJECTION

The representation of a 3-dimensional object, such as a structural member or a building, on the flat plane of a piece of drawing paper is a fundamental and important consideration of the draftsman. A pictorial representation, of course, would be the most realistic in appearance, and this in itself has certain advantages; yet from the standpoint of accurate graphic description for technical use, an "orthographic projection" has been found through the years to be the clearest method for showing true shapes, relationship of features, and necessary dimensions. ("Ortho" means "perpendicular" or "at right angles.") It has proven to be the most reliable way of presenting technical description graphically and, therefore, has literally become a *graphic language*.

Sometimes referred to as a "multiview" drawing, an orthographic drawing requires as many related views as necessary to reveal all necessary

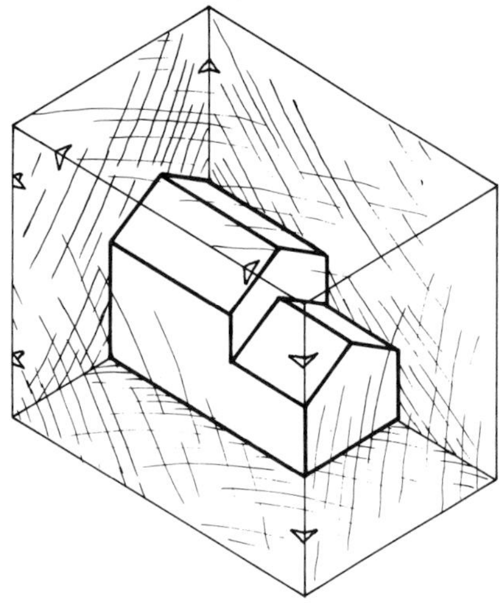

Fig. 3-18 The glass box.

information about an object. Some objects, such as simple gaskets for example, require only one view, since the slight thickness can better be shown by a note rather than by graphic methods. On the other hand, if a more complex object, such as a building is drawn, often four or five views might be needed. Graphic experience, together with knowledge of construction, provides the architectural draftsman with the means to determine the number and type of views necessary to accurately represent a structure on paper.

3.2.1 Principles of Projection— "The Glass Box"

For the simplest method of understanding this graphic language, let us think of an object, such as the basic house shown in Fig. 3-18, as being enclosed by transparent picture planes, or actually a glass box. Notice that the sides of the house are parallel to the glass planes, and if we viewed each side through each transparent plane, a true-shape image of the side would result.

The inclined surfaces of the roof are not parallel to the upper horizontal glass plane, therefore, they do not appear in their true shape. The ridges of the roof, on the other hand, appear as full length lines on the top view because they are parallel to the top picture plane. The profile of the gable roof, which is not evident on the top view, appears in true shape on the end views. Theoretically, the surfaces of the house that are perpendicular to

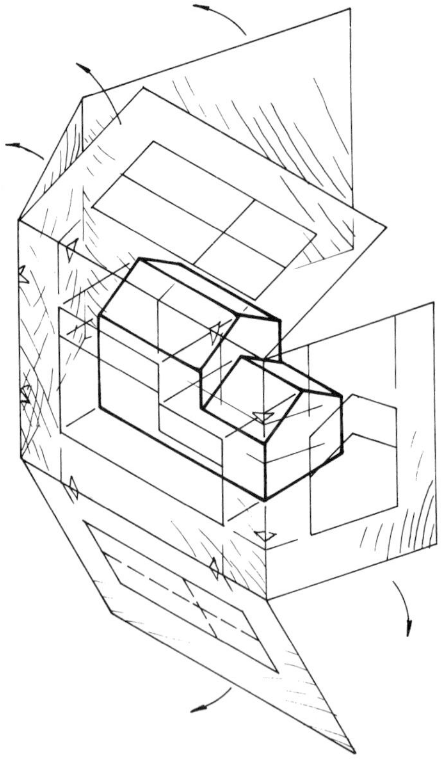

Fig. 3-19 Opening the box to form a flat plane.

the transparent planes, and lines formed by the intersections of inclined surfaces, are brought to the projection planes with parallel "projectors." And the images created by these projectors on the planes are known as "an orthographic projection."

3.2.2 The Relationship of Views

If the glass box is then opened, using theoretical hinges as shown in Fig. 3-19 an orthographic multiview drawing is formed on a flat plane. If required, six views of the house could be extended to the planes of the box; however, six views would seldom be necessary. After opening the box, you will notice that the top view is directly over the front view, the right-side view is directly to the right of the front, the left-side view is directly to the left of the front, etc. This alignment of views allows features of the house to be clarified by cross-observation of more than one view. Only two dimensions (height and width) can be shown on each orthographic view; thus, by aligning the views an accurate, 3-dimensional description can be obtained from the combined views.

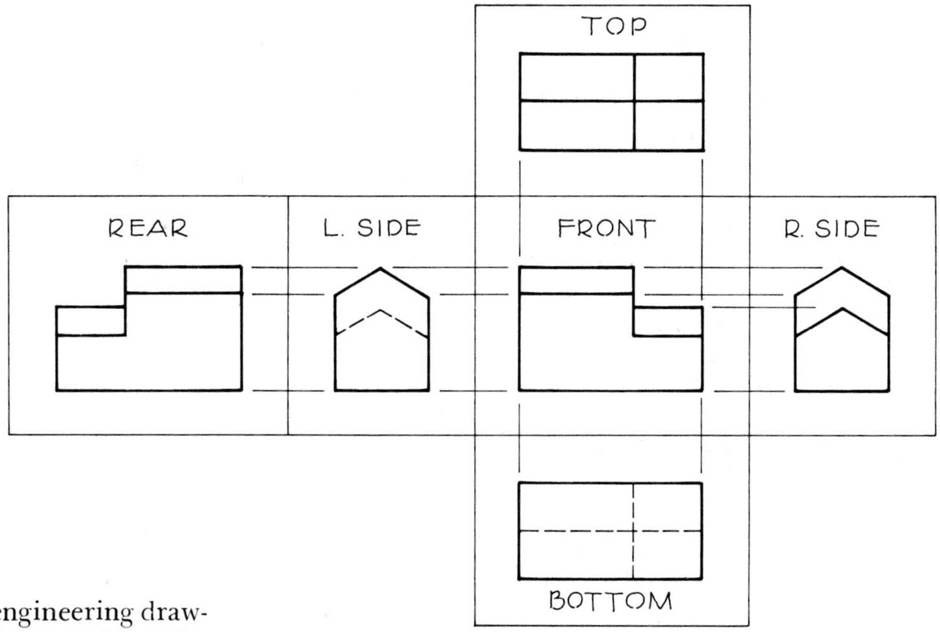

Fig. 3-20 The relationship of orthographic views.

3.2.3 Third-Angle Projection

It is conventional, for most engineering drawings in this country, to use the front view (the principal view), the top view, and the right-side view. Usually, these three views will give a complete graphic description of the object. (If important information is located on the left side, this view is substituted for the right-side view.) Ordinarily, the left-end view of the house would only duplicate the information shown on the right end, and the left-end view also has the disadvantage of showing part of the roof as hidden surfaces. The same is generally true of the rear or bottom views—they only duplicate information and are therefore unnecessary. As long as all information is shown, a minimum number of views is used. The three conventional views (front, top, and right side) are produced by placing the object within the third octant of the transparent plane assembly shown in Fig. 3-21. The top view is projected to the horizontal plane, the front view is projected to the frontal plane, and the right-side view is projected to the profile plane. This method of projection and relationship of views is called *third-angle projection* and is universally used for technical drawings throughout the United States and Canada.

Fig. 3-21 Third-angle projection planes.

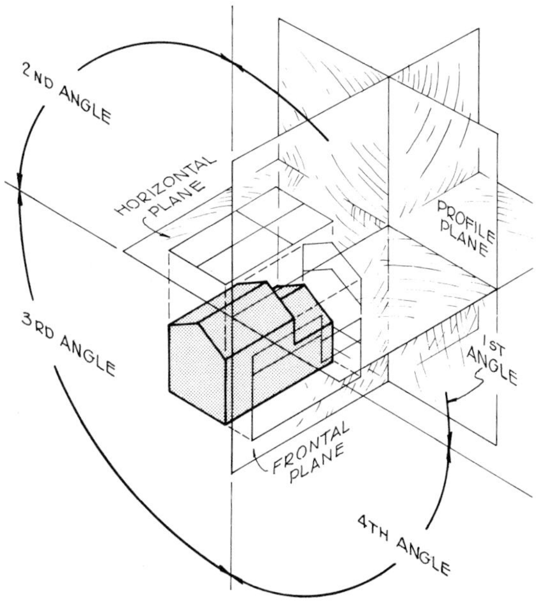

3.2.4 Hidden Surfaces

Often surfaces and features on orthographic views are hidden from the observer. If these features contribute necessary information, they are represented by dashed (hidden) lines. In Fig. 3-20 the hidden roof surfaces are shown as dashed lines on the left-side view since they are behind the higher portion of the object. Dashed lines should be carefully made by the draftsman. Uniform dashes should be used, very little space is left between each dash, and the ends of each dash should be made prominent (see Fig. 8-6).

3.2.5 Architectual Views

In architectural drawing, orthographic views that are projected to vertical planes, such as the front, side, and rear views, are called "elevations." Views that are projected to horizontal planes and observed from the top (or bottom) are called "plans." Hereafter, this terminology will be used when referring to the different architectural views.

Another variation in architectural work is the placement of the different elevations and plans on paper. As previously mentioned, when drawing the orthographic views of a small object, the views must be related for proper cross-reference. Because the elevations and plans of a building are often comparatively large, it becomes difficult to place them all on the paper in definite orthographic relationship. For convenience, the plan and the elevations are frequently put on separate sheets. Such an arrangement allows the draftsman to draw each view large enough to facilitate reading and interpretation. However, each plan and elevation must be properly identified so that all views can be related in the reader's mind. Elevations should be shown horizontally and, if space permits, the right elevation should be to the right of the front, and the left elevation to the left of the front. Avoid an elevation "on end" on the paper —it would not appear in a natural position. Otherwise, the elevations are true orthographic projections with few, if any, hidden surfaces or features shown.

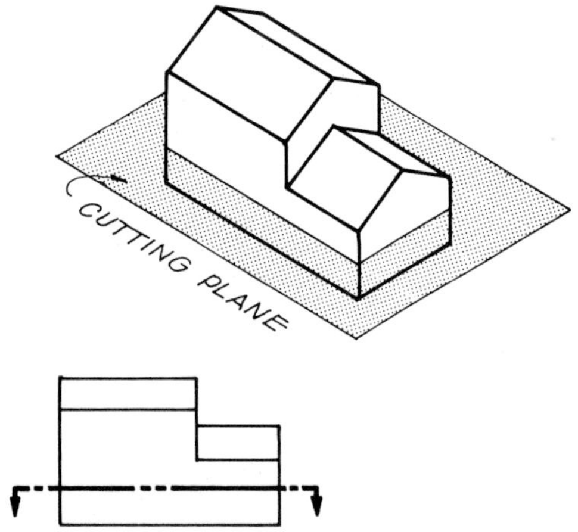

Fig. 3-22 The imaginary cutting plane of a first-floor plan.

Fig. 3-23 The first-floor plan is shown as though the upper part of the house is cut away to reveal the layout of rooms.

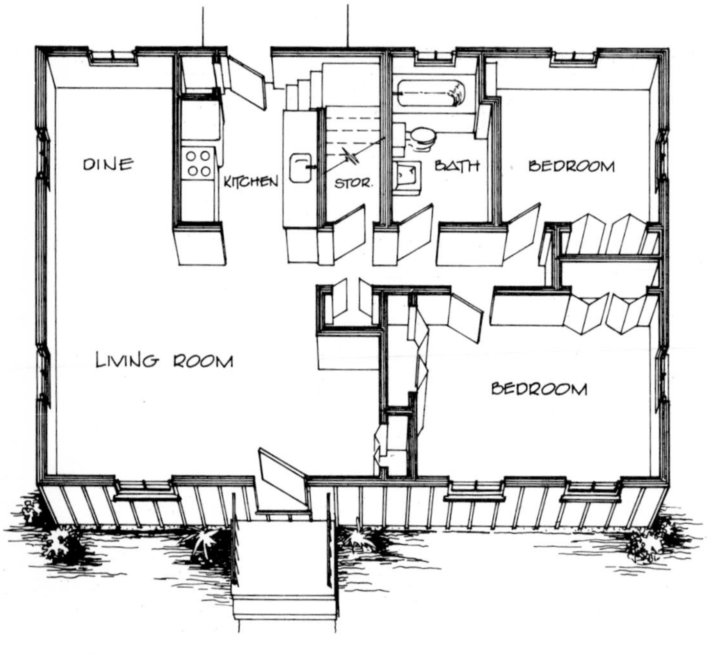

Top views of buildings are limited mainly to "roof framing plans" showing the layout of complex roof structural members. Occasionally a roof plan is necessary to show skylight, drains, and other important information on commercial buildings. Top views of houses would be largely for the purpose of developing different roof intersections and overhang treatments during planning stages. It is seldom necessary to draw a top view of a house showing only the roof surface.

The main drawing of a set of working drawings—the *floor plan,* is actually a horizontal section view of the building as seen from above. The cutting plane (see Fig. 3-22) is theoretical and passes through important vertical features such as doors, windows, walls, stairs, fireplaces, etc., to show their location and size within the building. To do this, the cut must often have offsets to pass through features that might be located high or low on the walls. Yet, the offsets are not shown on the plan. This conventional method of floor plan representation will be seen after studying a number of the floor plans shown throughout the book. Floor plans will be considered further under Working Drawings in Chapter 10.

Other architectural views of only portions of a building, such as structural members, small sections, etc., come under the broad, general heading of *details,* and will be discussed throughout later chapters.

3.3 SECTIONING

A section is defined as an imaginary cut made through an object, or a combination of objects, with the material in front of the cut removed.

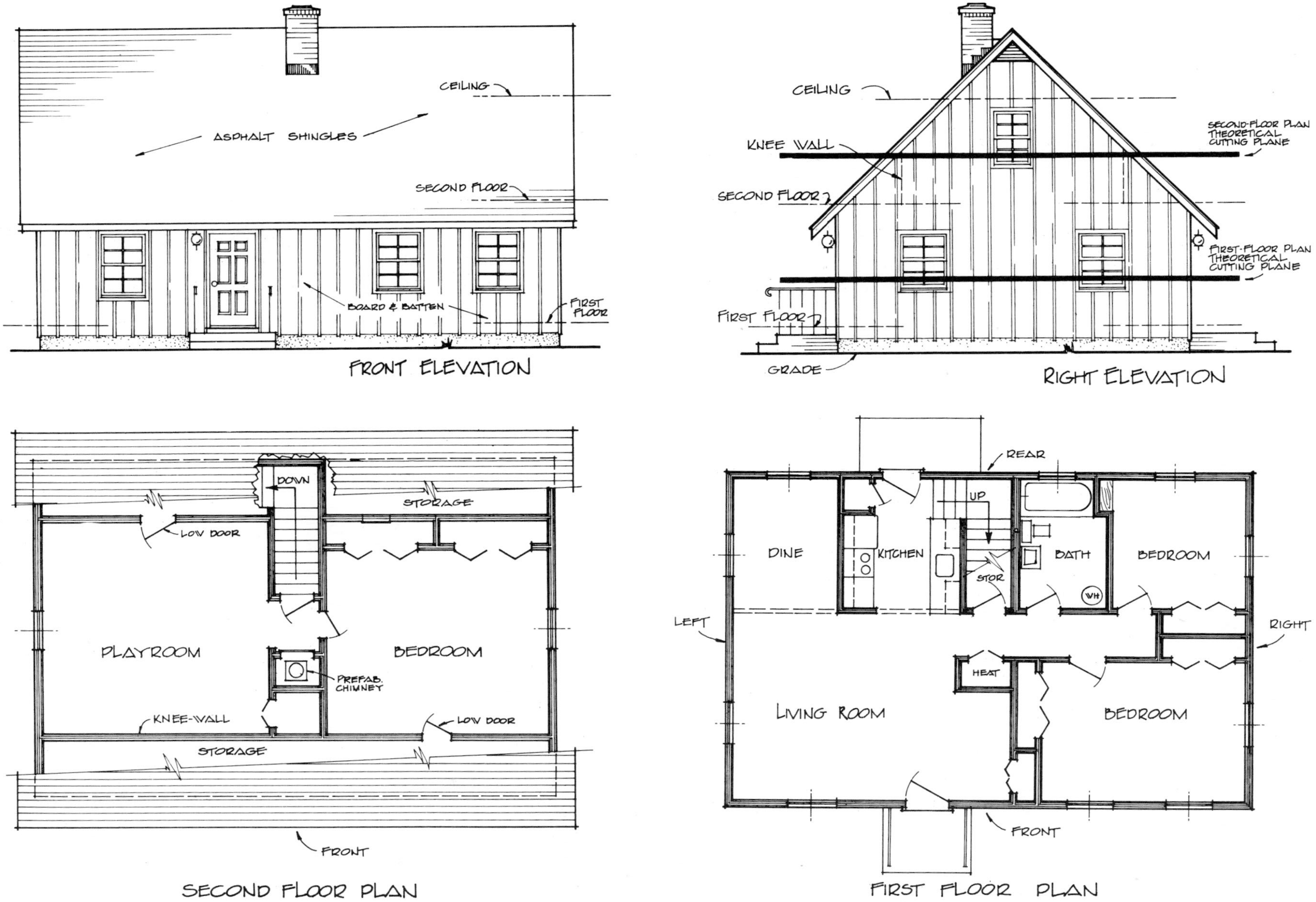

Fig. 3-24 Architectural views of a small 1½-story house.

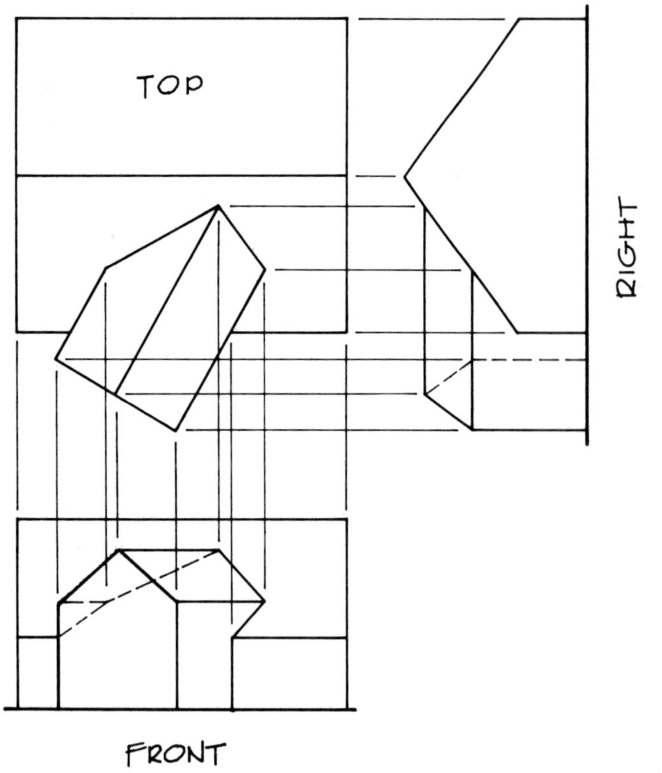

Fig. 3-25 Projecting roof intersections on architectural views.

A view of this cut or plane, then, becomes a direct method of revealing important internal information about the object. Usually, sections are drawn through walls, floors, windows, doors, structural members, cornices, fireplaces, stairs, footings, trim moldings, cabinet work, special construction, etc.

3.3.1 Importance of Architectural Sections

When looking at the elevation of a building, only the exterior materials and features are visible. If dashed lines were used to indicate the many hidden materials, their shapes, and their interrelationships, the resulting hodgepodge of lines would make the drawing impossible to read. A simple method must be used, therefore, to show clearly each important feature of interior construction on working drawings for the benefit of builders and workmen. Sections are drawn mainly for this structural purpose, although occasionally a simplified section is used on design drawings. On typical architectural working drawings draftsmen seldom employ the use of "hidden" lines to the extent that they are employed on many engineering drawings. Rather, the architectural draftsman uses a series of sections taken through strategic points of the construction throughout the building and arranges them for easy reference to the other views. Different types of sections are used—each has an appropriate application, determined by the draftsman, to show necessary information simply and comprehensibly. Often, for clarity in dimensioning, sections are drawn at a larger scale than the view from which they are taken.

3.3.2 Indicating the Cutting Plane

Unless the plane of the section is obvious, a "cutting-plane line" should be used to identify the imaginary cut on the related drawing (see Fig. 3-22). Cutting planes are usually represented by a heavy dash and double-dot line; usually arrows are placed at the ends of the line to indicate the direction of observation revealed by the section view. If the section is identical when looking in either direction, the arrows would be unnecessary.

As previously mentioned, floor plans are actually horizontal sections, and no cutting plane is conventionally needed to identify them. This is understandable if we think of the floor plan as a means for showing information about only one floor level—as long as the theoretical cut is somewhere through that floor level, there is no reason for showing a cutting-plane line on an elevation view. Even if the cut is offset in some parts of the building to encompass features found at different heights in the walls, no cutting plane is needed since the elevation views show the correct heights of such features.

Also, typical wall sections, showing uniform construction throughout major exterior walls, require no cutting planes for identification.

On drawings having two or more cutting planes and section views, each section must be related to the proper cutting plane; usually letters, such as A–A, B–B, etc., are used for this identification. Complex drawings having section views on several sheets must have letter identifications as well as sheet identification to relate the view correctly. Figure 9-6 shows a satisfactory method for relating numerous sections to their cutting planes when views must be arranged on different sheets. The small circles can be quickly drawn with a circle template.

3.3.3 Sectioning Conventions

The section must distinctly show the outline of all solid materials that have been cut and also the voids or spaces that may fall between the materials. Occasionally, features lying beyond the cutting plane must also be shown for clarity (see Fig. 3-26). These features are brought to the plane of the section by perpendicular projectors, very much like the features of an object are brought to the projection plane of an orthographic projection drawing. Usually, hidden features are not shown on section views; dashed lines only confuse sectioned details. On some views, however, it is necessary to violate true projection for added clarity; features such as holes, ribs, spokes, etc., which do not fall on the cutting plane of a symmetrical object, are revolved to the cutting plane and then projected to the section view (Fig. 3-27). It is also conventional practice not to section bolts, screws, rivets, shafts, rods, etc., which may fall in the plane of the section. They are more clearly shown unsectioned (see Fig. 3-28).

3.3.4 Crosshatching Sections

Other than the above-mentioned conventions, the materials that are cut must be crosshatched (symbol line tone) with the proper material symbol. (See Fig. 8-11 for the various standard sectioning symbols used on construction drawings.) Adjacent materials are crosshatched in different directions for easier identification; the 45° triangle can be used for the majority of the linework; and to conserve time, the spacing of crosshatch lines should be done by eye—experience will develop uniformity of tone. Small, sectioned pieces should have darker tones; larger surfaces can be lighter. Wood structural members are merely indicated with diagonals—drawn with instruments; others such as "finish lumber" and concrete are executed freehand. Thin members, such as sheet metal, building paper, or gaskets are filled-in solid black—usually only a heavy line. If the same member is revealed in several places in a sec-

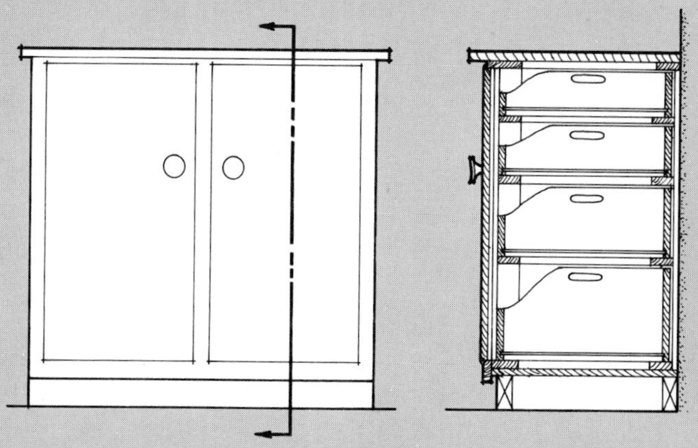

Fig. 3-26 Section showing features beyond cutting plane.

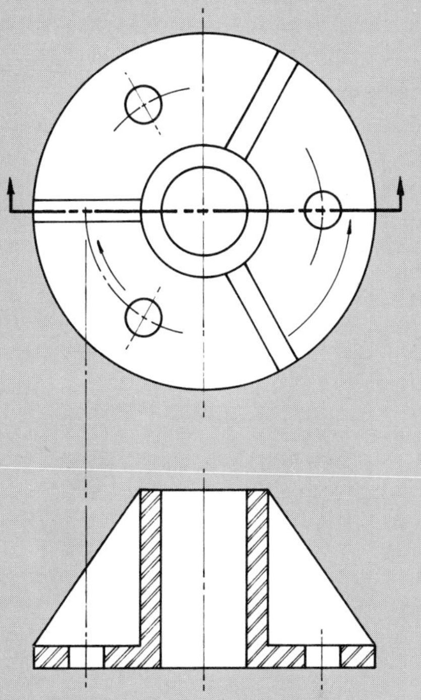

Fig. 3-27 Conventional symmetry in sections.

Fig. 3-28 Fasteners on the cutting plane are not cut.

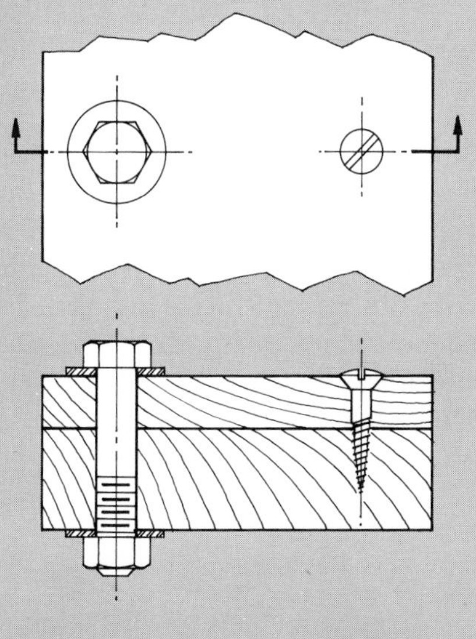

tion view, or in different sections, the crosshatch technique should always be identical. Important profile lines of a section should be made prominent.

3.3.5 Full Sections

A full section shows an object or a building *cut entirely across* so the resulting view is completely "in section." The cutting plane can be a straight plane, or it can be offset, to pass through features it may have missed if it were a straight, nonoffset plane. An offset does not show on the section view, as the change in plane is purely imaginary, and is meant to gather as many features as necessary to make the section inclusive and complete. Sections can be either horizontal or vertical. Although drawings showing horizontal section views through a building are in reality one of the types of sections, it is customary to call these "plans"; whereas drawings showing vertical section views are commonly referred to as "section details." This is the usual method of showing cuts through walls and is the most predominant way of showing sections in architectural drawings. A vertical section, if completely taken through the narrower width of a building, is called a *transverse section;* taken through the long dimension of a building, it is called a *longitudinal section* (Fig. 14-8). Either type is usually informative and often reveals construction detail that is difficult to show with other drawing procedures.

3.3.6 Half-Sections

Instead of the cutting plane passing entirely through the object, as in the full section, the cutting plane in a half-section goes only to the center and gives the appearance of having the front quadrant removed (see Fig. 3-29). On symmetrically shaped objects, half-sections conveniently show both the interior and the exterior in only one view. Because of symmetry, some objects do not warrant a full section. When drawing a half-section, the hidden features on the uncut half of a symmetrical object need not be shown with dashed lines, since they would merely duplicate the features of the section. Notice that a center line separates the interior and exterior portions of the half-section view.

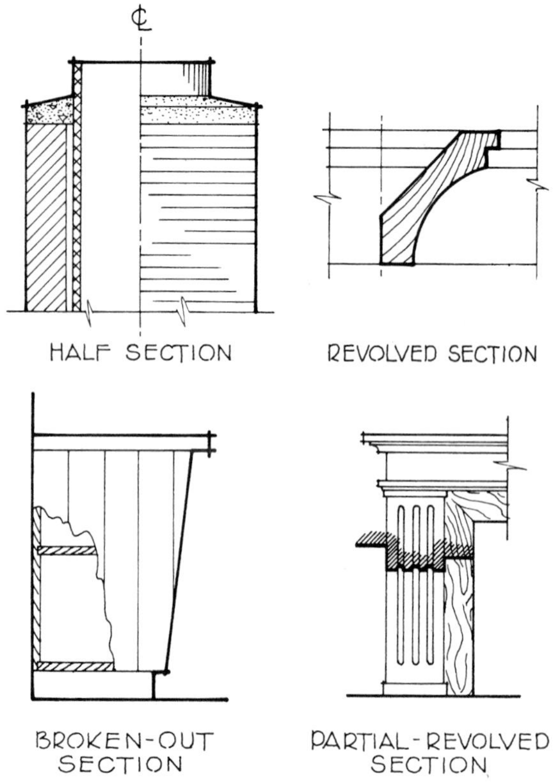

Fig. 3-29 Various types of minor sections used on drawings.

3.3.7 Broken-Out Sections

A broken-out section is a convenient method of showing important interior features which can be given sufficient description in a small area of an exterior view. Usually, the removal of only a small portion of exterior material will not affect the appearance of a view, and the flexibility of a broken-out section allows it to be placed where important exterior features need not be removed (see Fig. 3-29). Irregular break lines indicative of the material removed are used to show the limits of the sectioned area.

3.3.8 Revolved Sections

The cross-sectional shapes of I beams, wood moldings, irregular shaped structural members, etc., can be effectively shown by the use of revolved sections. Each is drawn by assuming a cutting plane perpendicular to the axis of the member, as shown in Fig. 3-29, which has been revolved through a 90° arc to the frontal plane and superimposed directly upon the elevation view of the member. Lines of the elevation view that may underlay the section should be removed before the crosshatch lines are applied.

3.3.9 Revolved Partial Sections

Occasionally, elevations of traditional fireplaces, exterior door trim, molded woodwork, etc., requiring only information about their exterior profiles, can conveniently employ a revolved partial section (see Fig. 3-29). Using a bold line, only the profile is drawn directly over the elevation. (Notice that the offsets in the profile coincide with the lines on the elevation which represent the offsets.) Short crosshatch lines may be drawn along the "material" side of the heavy profile line for more emphasis. This method of sectioning clearly shows the projection and contour of the elevation surface without the need for a separate view.

Fig. 3-30 Plotting the profile of a rake molding (partial revolved section).

1. Layout profile of horizontal molding and slope of roof with side view.
2. Draw reference plane—X vertically and RP-Y perpendicularly to roof slope.
3. Establish arbitrary points A, B, C, D. Transfer distances A-a, B-b, etc., to RP-Y on the projection lines.
4. Connect points A′, B′, C′, etc., with an irregular curve to form the profile of the rake mold.

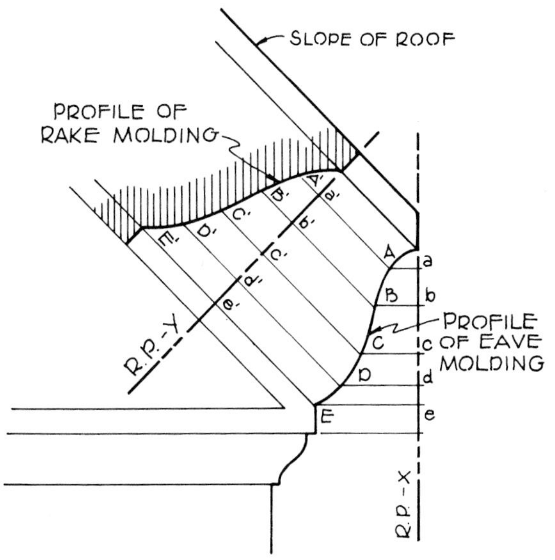

3.3.10 Removed Sections

Removed sections are similar to revolved sections; instead of being superimposed on the exterior view, they are removed to a convenient position near the view from which they are taken, and a cutting plane line is used to show their origin. Identification letters (Section 3.3.2) relate the cutting planes to their sections; several methods can be used (refer to Fig. 9-6). The advantage of the removed section over the revolved section is the possibility of enlargement, if necessary. Small details can be shown and dimensioned more easily at larger scales. If a series of sections relating to a main view is drawn, each section should be arranged in a logical manner and located, if possible, near its cutting plane. Whenever workable, a removed section should be drawn in its natural projected position. Sections difficult to orient will create complications in interpreting a drawing.

3.3.11 Pictorial Sections

Sometimes a pictorial section becomes the most effective method of showing structural assemblies or other construction features which become awkward to explain with orthographic views alone (see Fig. 4-13). Pictorial sections are discussed in Chapter 4.

3.4 AUXILIARY VIEWS

As previously mentioned under Orthographic Projection, the principal surfaces of a rectangular object, such as our miniature building, are shown in true shape when their features are observed from the surface in a perpendicular manner. That is, the surfaces, or elevations, appear in true shape if their projection planes are parallel to each surface. However, when the sloping roof appears on the front and rear elevations, the view of the roof is not a true shape because the surfaces are inclined to the front and rear projection planes (see Fig. 3-20). The top view also shows the roof surfaces distorted because of their inclination to the horizontal projection plane. Usually, inclined roof surfaces do not require true-shape representa-

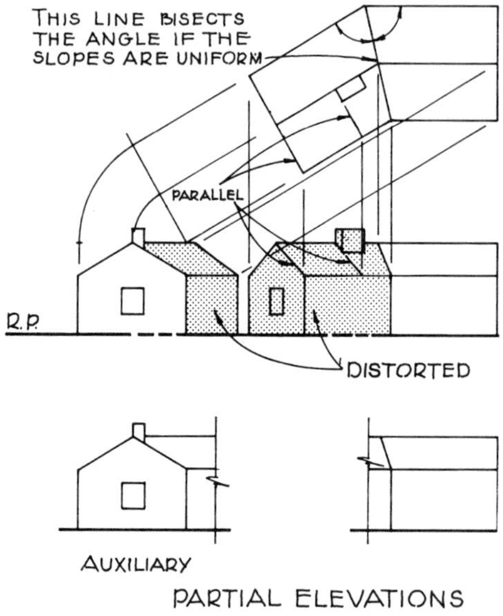

Fig. 3-31 Auxiliary elevation views.

tion, therefore, principal elevations are adequate. But suppose we have a building with a wing, or part of an elevation, extending in a nonparallel direction from the other elevations. In contemporary architecture, many buildings have oblique wings or nonparallel sides, cabinets are designed at angles other than right angles, and structural members have elevations and surfaces that are sometimes inclined to the principal planes. These inclined surfaces would appear distorted on the principal views or elevations. Occasionally several important surfaces are inclined and often must be shown in true shape on working drawings (see Fig. 3-31). To reveal the true shape of an inclined surface, an *auxiliary view* is necessary.

This is done by assuming an auxiliary plane *parallel* to the inclined surface; the features of the surface are then projected to the auxiliary plane with parallel projectors that are perpendicular to the surface. The direction of observation, also, becomes perpendicular to the inclined surface and the auxiliary plane. In most respects, an auxiliary view is similar to an orthographic view, except that the plane to which it is projected is *inclined* from the principal orthographic planes of projection. It is also convenient to think of the auxiliary plane as being "hinged" to the (profile) plane from which it is developed. *Reference planes,* one of which appears as a line on a principal view and the other as a line parallel to the auxiliary projection plane, are assumed to facilitate the construction of the auxiliary view. An auxiliary view then, is a view projected to any plane *other than* one of the six orthographic planes, and has been projected from a surface that is parallel to the auxiliary plane.

3.4.1 To Draw an Auxiliary View of an Irregular Object

The step-by-step construction shown in Fig. 3-32 is meant to simplify the procedure for developing a typical auxiliary view.

STEP NO. 1. Draw two views of the object, one showing the profile of the auxiliary surface,

Fig. 3-32 Steps in drawing an auxiliary view.

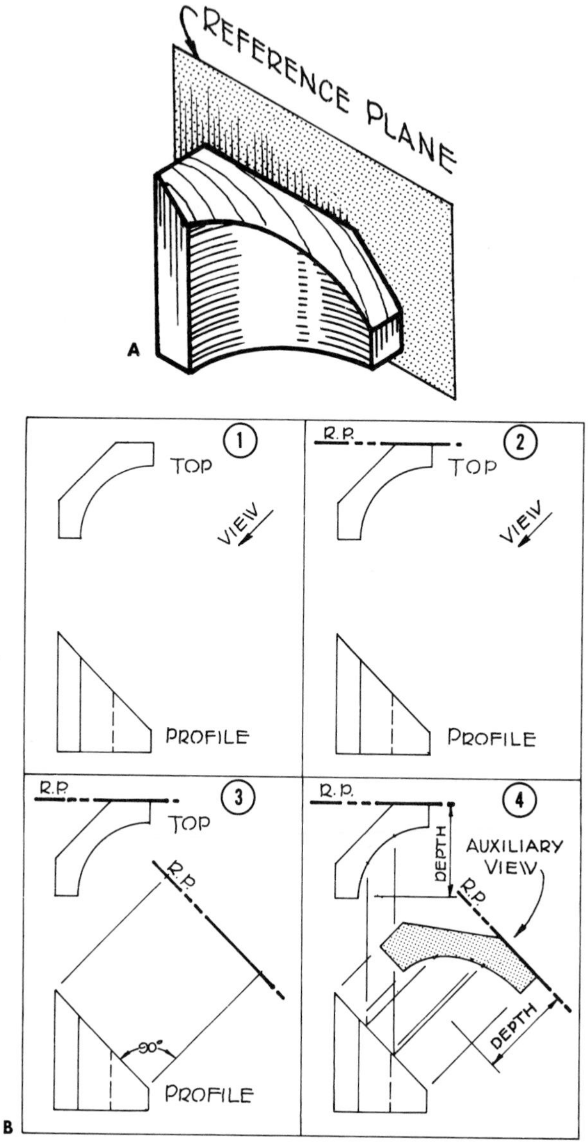

and one showing the top and depth characteristics. Indicate the direction from which the auxiliary is to be taken.

STEP NO. 2. Assume a "reference line" on the top view, from which depths of the auxiliary are taken. A reference plane is established in back of this object for convenience, and it will show as a line on both the top view and the auxiliary view. (On symmetrical objects, the reference plane is best established on the center line.) Draw the reference line (a heavy dash and double-dot line) on the top view.

STEP NO. 3. Draw the auxiliary reference line parallel to the inclined surface of the front view. Be sure it is located far enough away from the front view to allow enough space for the auxiliary view.

STEP NO. 4. Draw projection lines from the front view perpendicular to the reference line, as shown. Transfer the measurements of the various necessary points of the top view to the corresponding features of the auxiliary view, with the dividers or by measurement. Notice that the auxiliary view will form between the auxiliary reference plane and the front view, because the reference plane has been assumed to be in back of the object on the top view. Irregular or curved surfaces can be plotted accurately by projecting as many points as needed along the curved surface of the top view to the inclined surface of the profile view, then to the auxiliary reference line as shown. Depth measurements are transferred in the same way that other features are transferred. Use an irregular plastic curve to connect the plotted points with a smooth line.

STEP NO. 5. Connect all the proper points on the auxiliary surface with lines, noting the visibility of each. Strengthen the lines. Usually, only a partial auxiliary is necessary, but the complete object as viewed from the auxiliary plane can be drawn for graphic experience.

3.4.2 Partial Auxiliary Views

The draftsman will encounter auxiliary views, mainly, in drawing elevations of buildings whose exterior walls are nonparallel to the principal planes (see Fig. 3-31). If these elevations have important information and need to be shown in true shape, a "partial auxiliary" elevation is drawn. If the complete elevation is drawn on the auxiliary plane, a portion of the elevation will appear distorted and therefore have little pictorial value. Generally this distorted portion

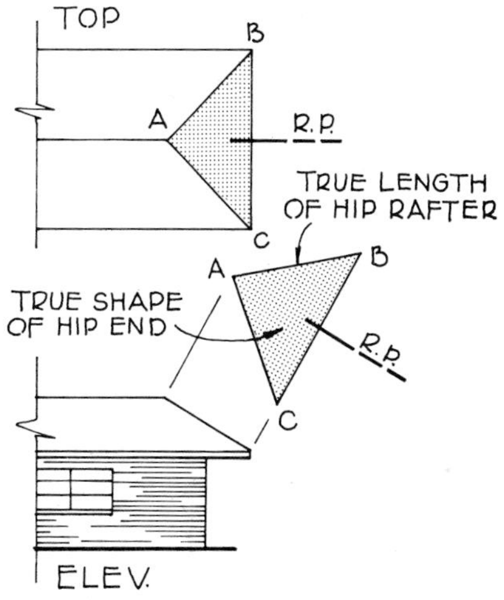

Fig. 3-33 Drawing the true length of a hip rafter.

is not drawn; the same holds true for the inclined surface in the principal elevation. The termination between the true shape and the distorted shape in either elevation is shown with a conventional break line.

To draw a *partial auxiliary elevation,* assume an observation direction perpendicular to the auxiliary surface. (The projection plane then becomes parallel to the auxiliary surface, as previously mentioned.) It is preferable to draw the auxiliary view in a natural, horizontal position, rather than in its projection position. Show all features, such as windows and doors, in true shape and size, and all horizontal dimensions in true length. These features can be projected from the plan view which has been fastened above the drawing and inverted in a position to make the auxiliary wall horizontal. Take the heights from the other main elevations, or assume a horizontal reference plane at the ground line of the other elevations, and transfer the heights with the dividers or by measurement.

3.4.3 Inclined Oblique Auxiliary Views (Secondary Auxiliary Views)

If an inclined surface cannot be seen as a line in any of the six principal views, and is not perpendicular to any of the six principal planes, its true shape must be constructed by the use of a "secondary auxiliary" rather than a direct projection method. Such views are rarely required, yet the draftsman should be able to

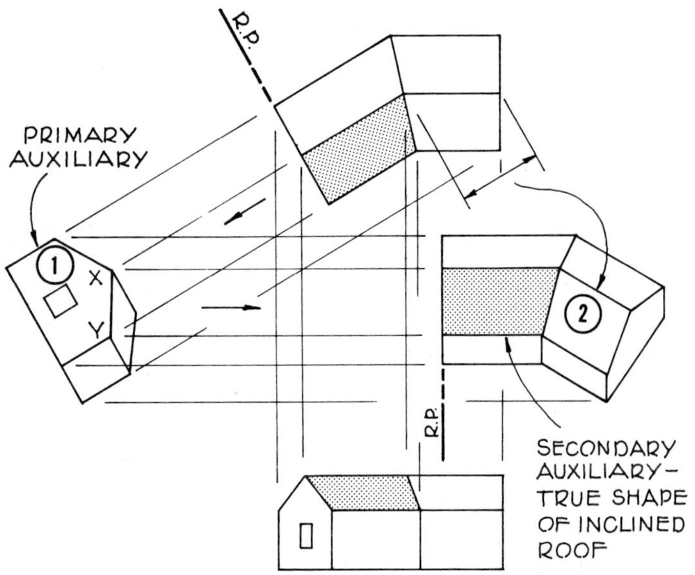

Fig. 3-34 Drawing the true shape of an inclined oblique plane (secondary auxiliary).

develop inclined oblique surfaces, principally to determine the true length of structural members that may have to be placed in an inclined oblique position within a building.

A convenient method is shown in Fig. 3-34. *To construct the true shape* of the shaded portion of the roof, first, draw a primary auxiliary (1) projected from the top view. This auxiliary view is needed first because it shows the *edge view* of the shaded roof; the required surface is represented as a line (X–Y). It must be remembered that auxiliary views of inclined surfaces are projected from views that show the inclined surface as a line. From the primary auxiliary view, construct parallel projectors that are perpendicular to the edge view line X–Y; these projectors form the true width of the shaded surface. For convenience, place the reference plane on the end of the oblique wing of the top view, and on the secondary auxiliary view draw it parallel to line X–Y of the primary auxiliary. Transfer the true lengths of the shaded surface on the top view to the second auxiliary view (2). Connect all visible points of intersection. The entire house can be drawn by projecting all points from the primary auxiliary view and by transferring lengths of all points from the reference line of the top view to the corresponding projection lines of the second auxiliary.

EXERCISES

Geometric construction. On 8½″ × 11″ paper lay out a ½″ border and divide into nine equal spaces similar to Fig. 3-35. With the following information, complete the exercises as shown.

1. Construct a 1″ arc tangent to the given right angle.

2. Find the center of the given circle using chord perpendicular bisectors.

3. Construct a ¾″ arc tangent to the given arc and straight line.

4. Divide line AB into five equal divisions.

5. Construct a ⅞″ arc tangent to the given circle arcs.

6. With the compass bisect the given angle.

7. Construct a hexagon 1½″ across corners.

8. Construct a 1⅜″ octagon.

9. Construct an ogee curve from point A to point B, passing through point E. (EB = 2AE) The line passing through A is parallel to the line passing through B.

Orthographic projection. Study the pictorial drawings in Fig. 3-36 (pp. 59–60) and develop the orthographic views of each problem. The exercises are meant to provide you with experience in understanding projection principles, and upon completion should be examined by your instructor to ensure proper interpretation.

Sectioning. On 8½″ × 11″ paper draw the following exercises:

1. Draw a full section of Fig. 4-11 (double size). With the use of dividers, take the dimensions directly from the figure in the book.

2. Draw a half-section of Fig. 4-12 (double size).

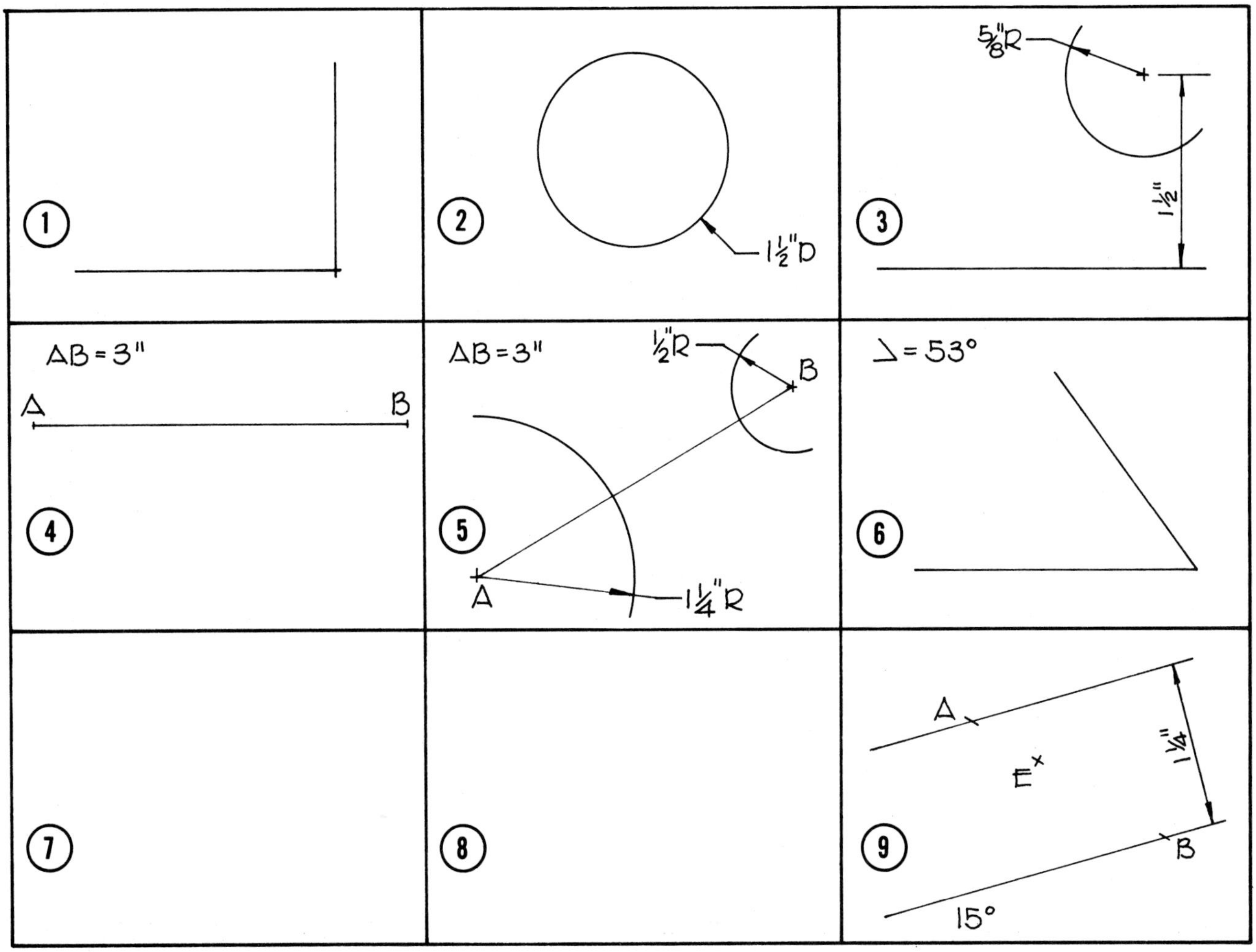

Fig. 3-35 Exercises in geometric construction.

Fig. 3-36 Exercises in orthographic projection drawing. With the use of dividers, double or triple each exercise.

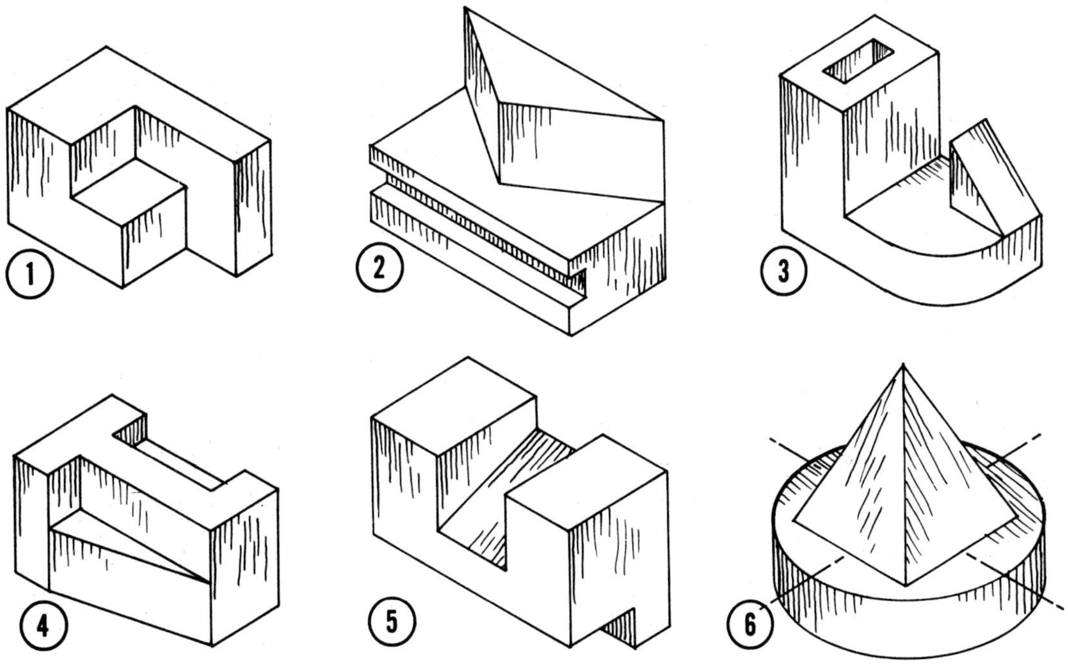

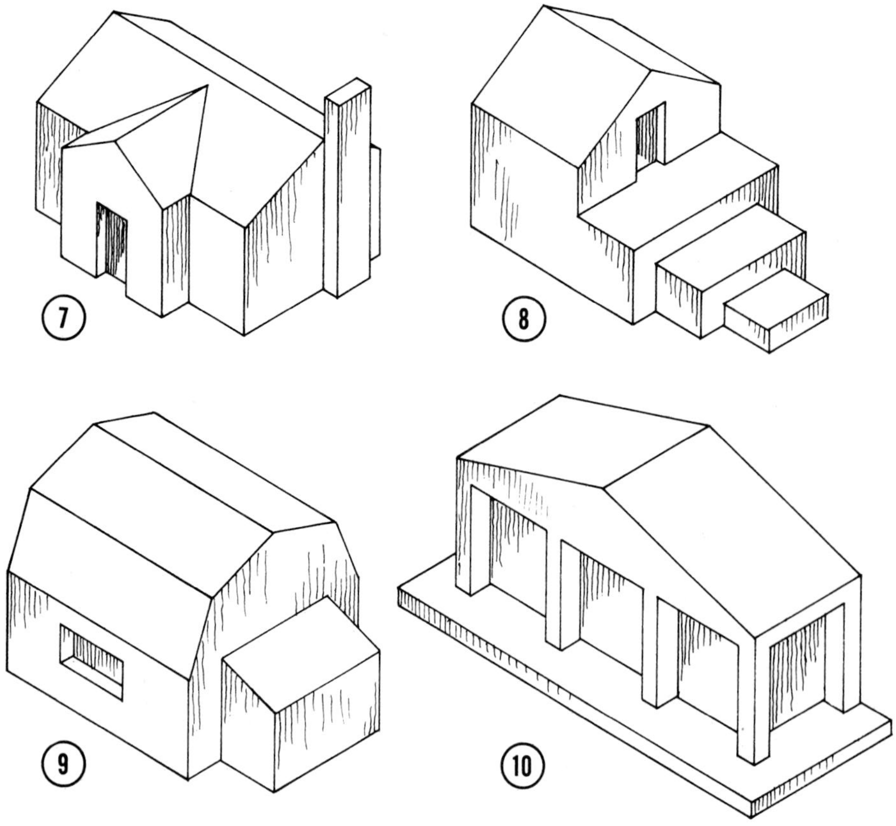

Fig. 3-36 *continued.*

Fig. 3-37 Exercises in auxiliary projection.

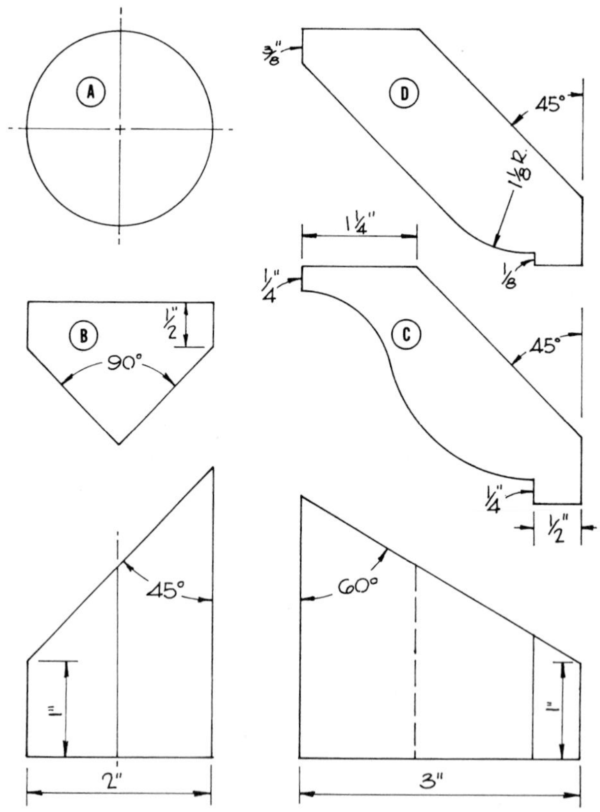

3. Draw a longitudinal and transverse section of Fig. 4-21. Scale: 6″ = 1′–0″. Hatch sections with the steel symbol.

4. Draw the orthographic section of Fig. 4-13. Take dimensions directly from the figure.

5. Draw a footing and box sill section detail of a wood frame building; see Chapter 9. Scale: ¾″ = 1′–0″.

AUXILIARY VIEWS

1. Construct the true shape of the end of the hip roof shown in Fig. 3-33 (surface ABC). Select a convenient scale to fit your paper.

2. Construct the true shape of a 45° miter cut from wood profiles (Fig. 3-37):
a. 1¼″ dowel
b. 2″ × 2″ molding
c. 3″ × 3″ ogee molding

REVIEW QUESTIONS

1. Describe the term "orthographic projection."

2. What is a "frontal" plane?

3. Why do drawings of many objects require more than one orthographic view?

4. Which orthographic view is considered the major view?

5. How are hidden surfaces shown on an orthographic view?

6. Why are orthographic views of a building often drawn in an unrelated position on working drawings?

7. What is the "cutting plane" of a section?

8. Why are cutting planes sometimes offset rather than straight planes?

9. Why are hidden lines seldom used in section views?

10. What is the advantage of a partial section?

11. Why are auxiliary surfaces projected to planes, parallel to the surfaces?

12. How are numerous sections identified as to their position on the major view?

"Step after step the ladder is ascended."—George Herbert

4

Isometric and Oblique Pictorial Drawings

Isometric and oblique drawings are pictorial in nature, yet they are compatible with orthographic drawings in that three sides are shown and the principal lines of each side or plane are measured directly. As we mentioned previously, orthographic views have certain advantages, but they also have limitations: two or three isolated views are required to present the information clearly. This information must be shown only on the orthographic planes; visualizing their features makes training in technical graphics a prerequisite. Even trained persons find that orthographic views are not always entirely adequate for representing construction in the best way. A pictorial drawing, on the other hand, is easy to interpret by the average person because three surfaces are combined into one realistic view. To represent an object pictorially so the height, width, and depth can be observed in one composite representation, the object is turned to make three sides visible (isometric); or the top and side are shown by projecting oblique lines from a frontal orthographic view (oblique). An example of each is shown in Fig. 4-1. The sides of an object on either type of drawing are represented with parallel lines, conveniently executed with T square and triangles, and are sometimes collectively termed "paraline" drawings.

Because these pictorial views are easy to

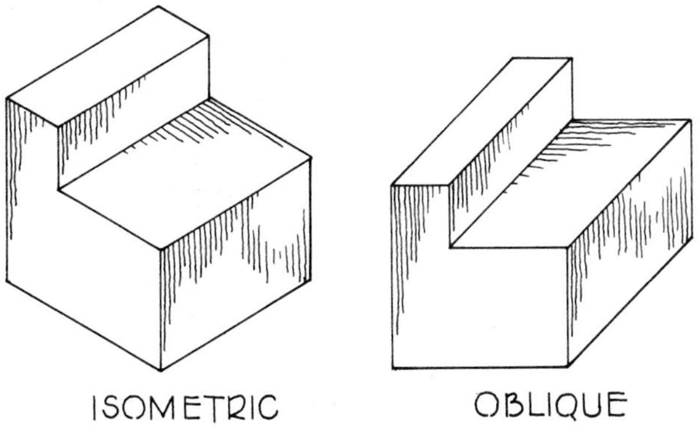

Fig. 4-1 Comparison of isometric and oblique pictorial drawings.

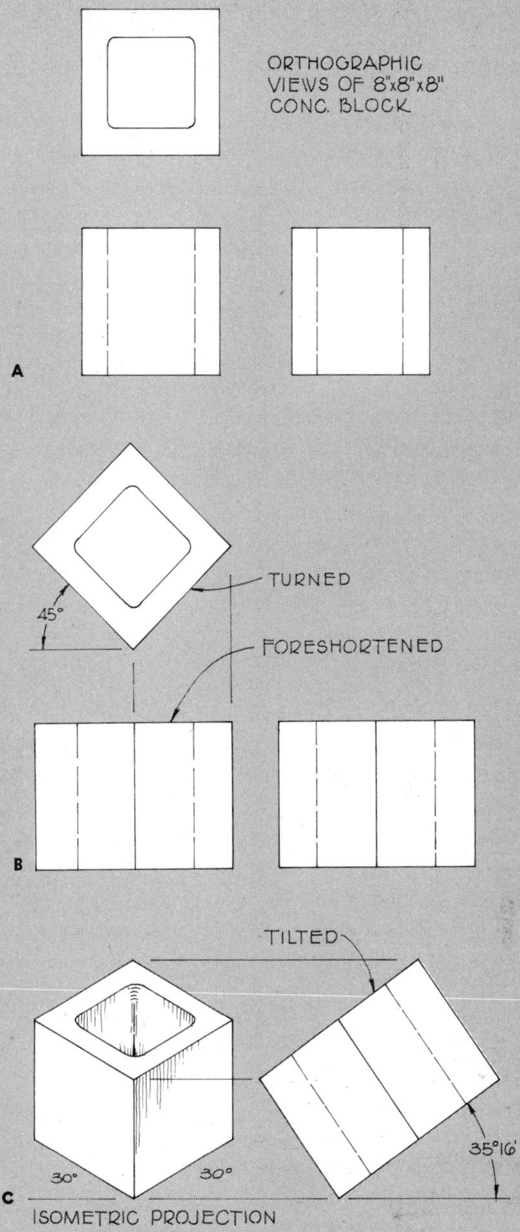

Fig. 4-2 Method of developing a true isometric projection, which is time-consuming for the draftsman.

Fig. 4-3 The three isometric axes.

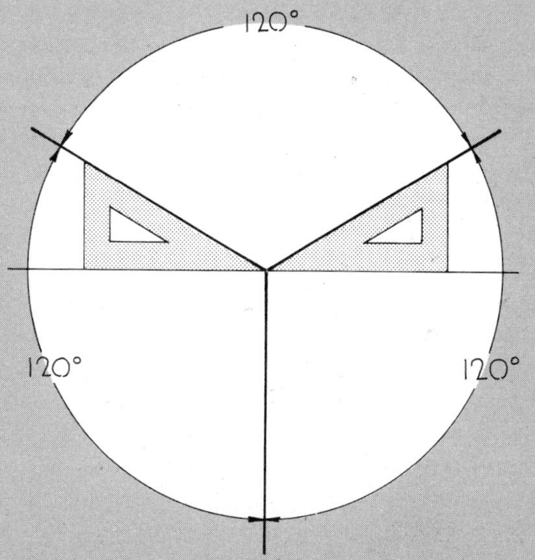

draw with instruments, they become suitable for use on working drawings and are satisfactory for occasional design drawings. They are also handy for quick freehand sketches (see Chapter 5)—for analyzing construction details or for graphic communication between coworkers. Draftsmen should, therefore, be able to draw and interpret the conventional pictorial drawings covered in this chapter. Other types of technical–pictorial drawings have been devised; however, they are more time-consuming and they do not find application in architectural work. Isometric and oblique drawings, used intelligently, will be found entirely adequate for presenting supplementary construction information whenever needed.

4.1 ISOMETRIC DRAWINGS

A drawing is called isometric when it depicts an object that has been rotated and inclined from a regular, parallel position to give it a pictorial appearance. The rotation and inclination are such as to result in a drawing with three equally divided axes about a center point. (Hence, the prefix "iso," from the Greek word *isos,* meaning equal.) In Fig. 4-2 we have used a hollow concrete block with equal exterior dimensions to show the uniformity of the angles and sides. The axes may be turned in several positions, but the most pleasing and generally the most convenient position shows one axis vertical and the other two 30° above the horizontal. Regardless of the position of the axes, the three faces of the block are equally foreshortened; intersecting edges of the mutually perpendicular surfaces produce equal 120° angles (Fig. 4-3), and similar intersections of the surfaces produce parallel lines. Because the lines which recede from the viewer must be foreshortened in a true projection, which makes them difficult to measure, the draftsman merely uses scaled lengths for convenience and speed. For example, if the actual size of the concrete block in Fig. 4-4 is 8″ × 8″ × 8″, then the lines representing the surfaces are scaled to the same measurement. No allowance is made for foreshortening, but all measurements must be made on the axis lines. The front, top, and side view of the block are given equal importance, and they can be easily drawn with the 30°–60° triangle. If it becomes necessary to show the underside of an object (so it appears to be observed from below), the draftsman employs a "reverse axis" (see Fig. 4-5). This axis position is more appropriate when drawing a high cornice view, or an overhead structural feature, etc. The object appears to have been tilted backward instead of forward, as in the conventional position. Care must be taken to keep the major planes of the reverse axis clearly in mind.

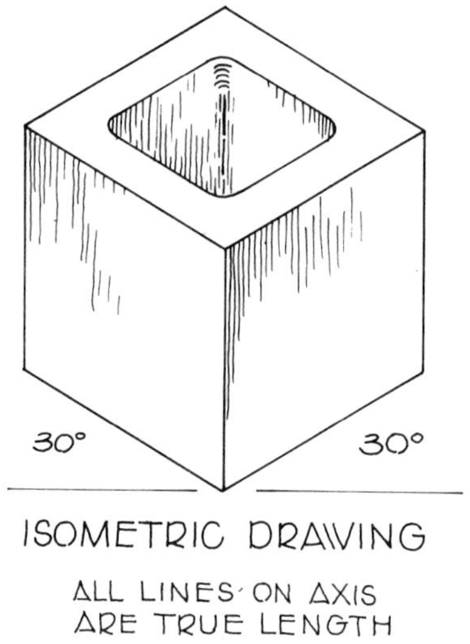

Fig. 4-4 The same block drawn with lines on the axis the same length as the orthographic views. An isometric drawing is about 22½ percent larger than an isometric projection, yet it has equal pictorial value and is simpler to draw.

Fig. 4-5 An isometric drawing exposing the underside.

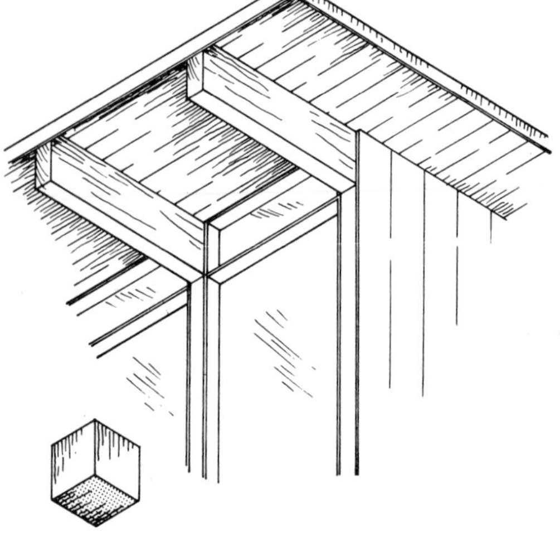

4.2 CONSTRUCTING AN ISOMETRIC DRAWING

First, consider the most advantageous angle from which to view the object. Adopt the view that will show the important information on the three isometric planes, even if it requires turning the object around. Avoid the need for hidden lines; they are usually omitted on paraline drawings. Then look for the major geometric forms. These forms are "boxed in," first by drawing the correct axis lines, measuring the lines, and completing the boxed-in effect by drawing the surrounding parallel lines (see Fig. 4-6B). This becomes a framework (very much like a cage) from which minor shapes or features can be taken away or added. The preliminary box construction aids in placement of the drawing; if the view seems to be developing off to one side, the construction lines can be changed quickly and little time is lost. The basic enclosure also acts as reference surfaces, from which offset features can be measured during the development of the drawing.

If an object similar to Fig. 4-7 is to be drawn, a "block-on-block" method of construction may be simpler. Each basic shape is added to one another, much like blocks are piled together, rather than by drawing a complete cage around the entire area of the object. After the base block is drawn, using this method, care should be taken to locate correctly the position of the succeeding block. Notice that the position of each new block is first laid out on the surface of the previous block. If the adjacency of the blocks falls on a hidden surface, often the features of the hidden surface must be constructed, even though they will not show and must be erased later. The block-on-block

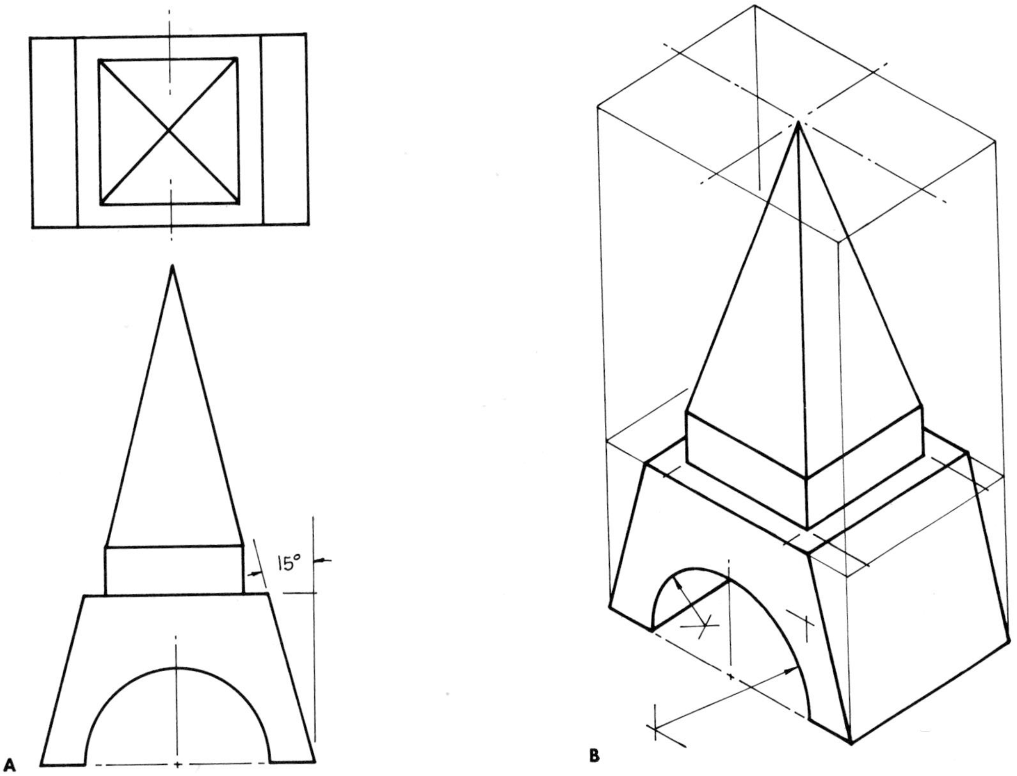

Fig. 4-6 Constructing an isometric drawing within a box framework with axis distances taken from the orthographic views.

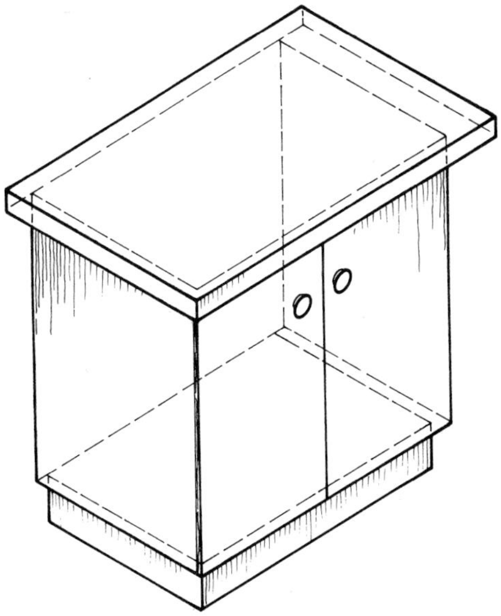

Fig. 4-7 Some objects are better drawn by placing one block on the other.

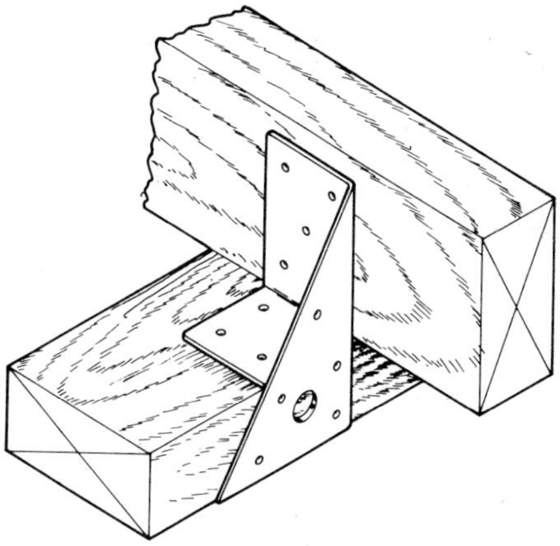

Fig. 4-8 Isometric drawing of a metal framing anchor connection.

method usually requires less construction linework than the boxed-in method.

Isometric Angular Shapes Angles specified in degrees do not appear in their shape on an isometric drawing. The construction of an angular shape generally requires the use of coordinates from an orthographic view to determine the angular extremities (see Fig. 4-6A and B). The coordinate lengths are then transferred to the corresponding isometric planes.

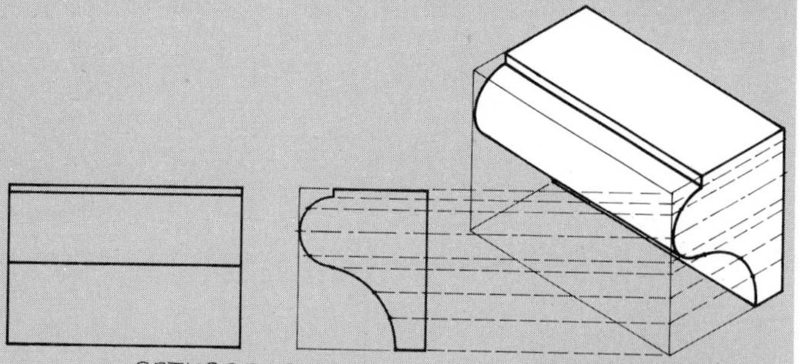

Fig. 4-9 Constructing irregular curved shapes from orthographic views.

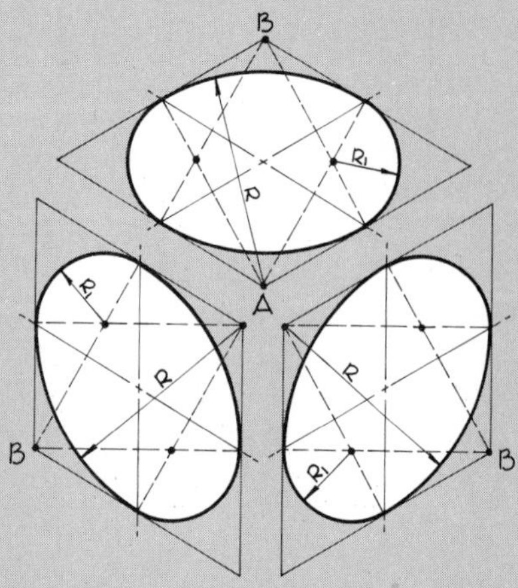

Fig. 4-10 The "4-center" method of drawing isometric circles on the three axes.

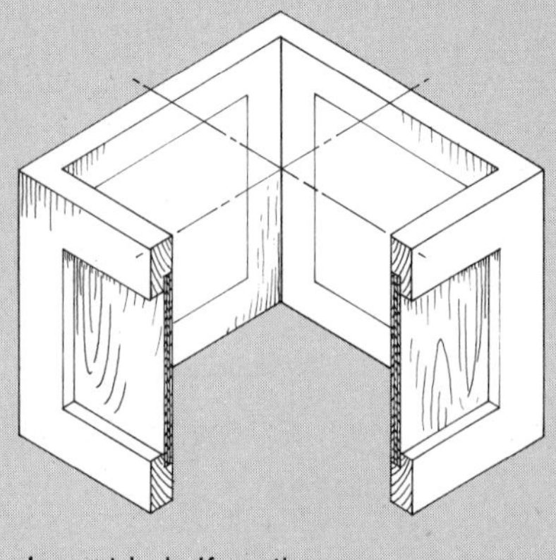

Fig. 4-11 Isometric half-section.

Fig. 4-12 Isometric section, partially broken.

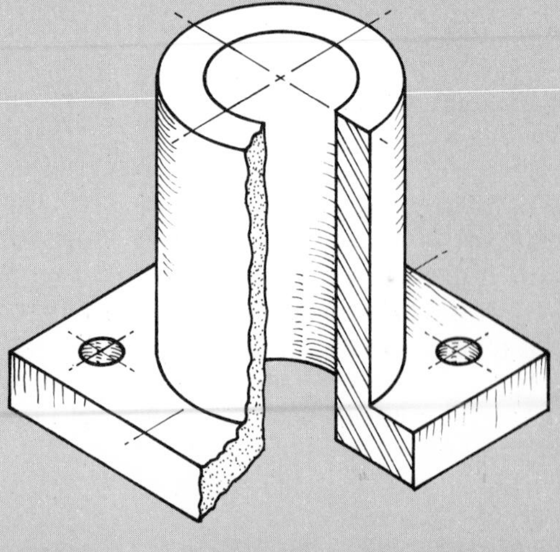

Irregular Curved Shapes In isometric drawings, irregular curved shapes are executed with the use of offsets (see Fig. 4-9). The draftsman takes points from an orthographic view and transfers these to the framework of the isometric projection. Profile sections can be used, or after the points are located on the drawing, they can be connected with curved lines to produce the pictorial feature. Coordinate distances must be obtained from orthographic views of the same scale, and they are projected on the isometric planes.

Isometric Circles Circles also appear distorted on isometric drawings. A true circle becomes an ellipse. Other than construction with an ellipse template, satisfactory circles are generally constructed by the "4-center" method (see Fig. 4-10). The following procedure is used for drawing an isometric circle:

1. Construct center lines to locate it;
2. Construct an isometric square (rhombus) the size of the required diameter;
3. From corners A and B construct lines to the midpoint of the opposite sides of the square, which become perpendiculars of the sides;
4. The intersections of these construction lines become the centers of the small arcs; draw the arcs using radius R_1;
5. Points A and B become centers of the large arcs; draw both arcs of R radius, taking the size of R from the construction.

All the construction is done with the use of the T square, 30°–60° triangle, and the compass. If an isometric template is available, the center lines are first drawn, then the template is lined up accurately on the center lines. Circles and arcs on the three isometric planes can be drawn by either method. If the circles fall on non-isometric planes, they can be plotted by the coordinate method from an orthographic view (see Fig. 4-9).

4.3 ISOMETRIC SECTION VIEWS

Because hidden lines are seldom used in pictorial drawings, sectioned surfaces showing interior assembly or construction often become necessary. The object is cut on either of the isometric planes. If it is symmetrical, it is cut on center-line planes (Fig. 4-11), and principles similar to orthographic sectioning are followed. On small, symmetrical objects, generally a *half-section* is used (see Fig. 4-11). First, the major shapes are drawn lightly; then the profiles of the sectioned surfaces are established, and the remaining lines are completed. The front quadrant of the object is removed to best reveal the interior. Usually more of the exterior of a symmetrical object can be shown if a *broken-out* pictorial section is used (see Fig. 4-12). The axis cut is made on only one center-line plane, and only enough of the frontal material is removed to reveal the profile of the sectioned surface. The other broken edge of the opening is drawn with a freehand line. Crosshatch lines indicating the material are made less prominent, and their angle should not run parallel to the outline of the section. Diagonals are sufficient to indicate wood structural members (see Fig. 4-13 and Fig. 8-11, p. 216 for building material symbols).

When strengthening the finish lines of isometric drawings, start with the nearest features and continue toward the back of the object. This procedure is timesaving because it minimizes erasing; the result will be a neater piece of work.

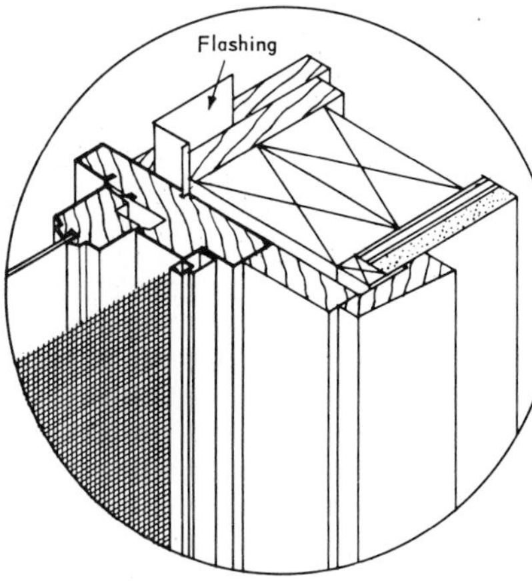

Fig. 4-13 Isometric section of a window detail.

4.4 OBLIQUE DRAWINGS

An oblique drawing shows an object with one set of planes in true orthographic projection on the frontal surface. The receding perpendicular sides are represented with parallel lines at various angles, which are projected from the frontal, true shape (see Fig. 4-14). It resembles an isometric drawing in that three sides are shown, and the three sides are represented with parallel lines upon which a draftsman can make true measurements. The concrete block shown in the illustration has a true square, similar to an orthographic view, as its front surface. The receding top and right sides appear nearly isometric.

Various Pictorial Effects One of the advantages of oblique drawings is their versatility in creating pictorial effects. By varying the angles of the receding axes, either one of the receding sides can be emphasized (see Fig. 4-14A, B, and C). Because drafting triangles conveniently provide angles of 30°, 45°, and 60°, these angles are most commonly used for the oblique axes. A 30° axis from the horizontal

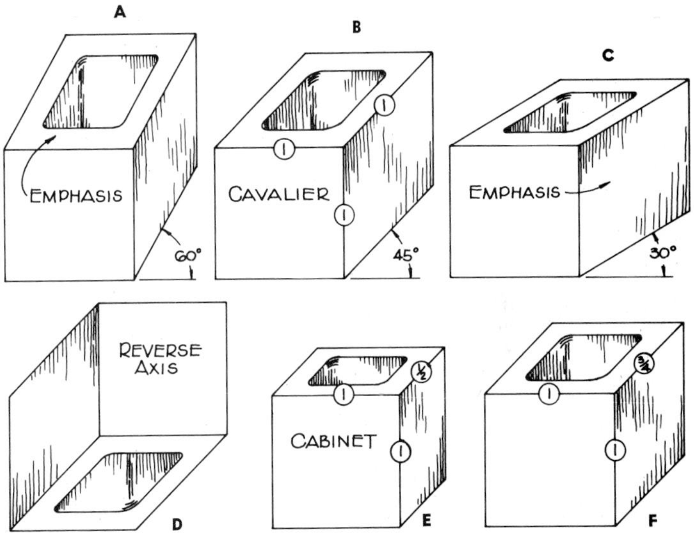

Fig. 4-14 Pictorial appearance of various types of oblique drawings.

adds side-view emphasis; a 45° axis gives equal emphasis to both of the receding surfaces (commonly called a Cavalier drawing); and a 60° axis results in emphasis on the top view. If important information falls on one of the receding planes, the angle should be given careful consideration.

The axis can be projected to either right or left, dependent on which side better describes the object. Also, the axis can be projected below the horizontal if the bottom surface yields more information than the top (see Fig. 4-14D).

On conventional oblique drawings, as we mentioned, the receding lines are measured true-length, producing a distorted effect. This applies especially to objects of considerable depth. The heavy appearance on receding sur-

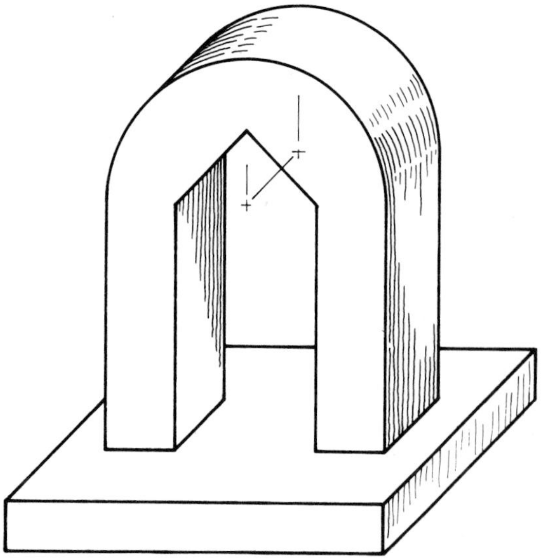

Fig. 4-15 Circles and irregular shapes should be placed on the frontal plane of oblique drawings.

faces often makes an oblique rendition objectionable. However, more pleasing proportions and a more realistic appearance can usually be achieved by reducing the depth by 1/4, 1/3, or 1/2. The lines on the frontal planes remain full scale, giving the oblique lines proportional ratios of 1 to 3/4, 1 to 2/3, or 1 to 1/2, (see Fig. 4-14E and F). The ratio of 1 to 1/2 is referred to as a Cabinet drawing and generally has a too-thin appearance for most objects, other than shallow cabinets.

One of the other expediencies of oblique drawings is their convenience for showing circles or irregular shapes on the frontal planes. Circles can be drawn easily with a compass, and the other shapes do not have to be distorted (see Fig. 4-15). This is a definite advantage in giving technical information. Therefore, when selecting the layout of an oblique drawing, if possible, place the circular and irregular features on the frontal plane. Also, if a long object is drawn, place the long dimension on the frontal plane; the drawing will appear shallower in depth. Actually, objects of little depth are better suited to oblique drawing because the distortion on their receding surfaces will hardly be noticeable.

If *circular shapes* fall on one of the oblique planes, they are made elliptical, similar to isometric circles. Because of the construction involved, circles on oblique axes should be avoided; but if they become necessary, a rhombus similar to isometric drawing is constructed around the intended circle, and the approximate, 4-center method of ellipse construction is used. Different angular axes, necessarily, require differently shaped rhombus construction; the appropriate method can be taken from Fig. 4-10. Notice that the large arcs are drawn from the intersection of the two perpendicular bisectors of the two sides that form the larger rhombus angle; the smaller arcs are drawn from the intersection of the perpendicular bisectors of the two sides that form the smaller angle. The circle arcs must be tangent to the midpoints of the oblique-square sides. On the oblique axes, arcs representing rounded corners, etc., are drawn by the same method, even though they may require only part of the construction.

4.5 OBLIQUE SECTION VIEWS

Oblique drawings, like isometric ones, are often more informative if sectioned to show interior construction. On small objects the cutting surfaces are usually made on the oblique centerline planes. Half-sections have the advantage of showing both interior and exterior features. The characteristics of oblique sections are similar to isometric sections and are drawn in a similar manner. Center lines are placed on all circular shapes to show symmetry.

Fig. 4-16 Sectioned orthographic details can be given a pictorial appearance by the addition of oblique receding surfaces.

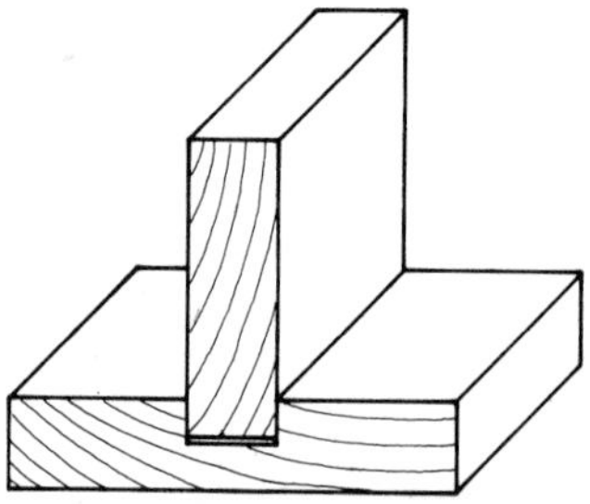

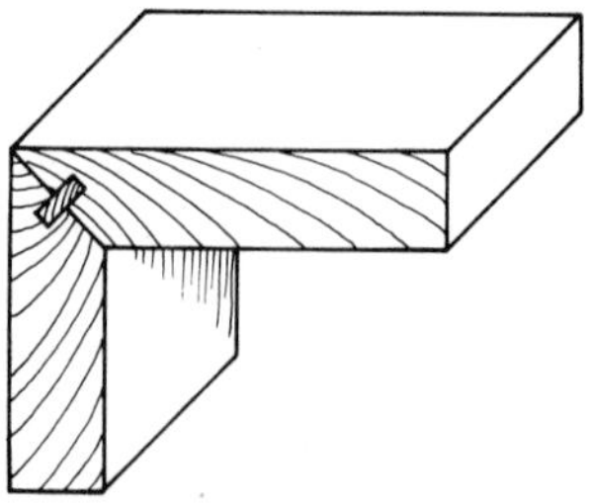

On orthographic sections of walls, structural members, moldings, etc., oblique object lines can be projected from the section to give a pictorial quality to the drawing (see Fig. 4-16). Although infrequently used, such a drawing will often explain construction information that is not entirely evident on the section.

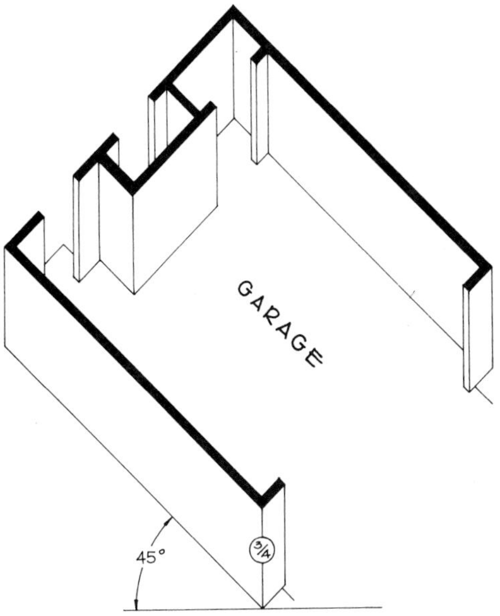

Fig. 4-17 The addition of vertical lines to a turned floor plan to produce a pictorial appearance.

4.5.1 Oblique Section Variation—Using an Inverted Plan View

A useful variation of the conventional oblique pictorial drawing can be introduced by turning true-shape plan view at a 45° angle. Then project its depth with vertical lines drawn three-fourths full size (see Fig. 4-17). This method is versatile in its application and is appropriate when a slightly distorted appearance is not objectionable. Pictorial drawings of uncovered rooms or 3-dimensional plan layouts can be quickly executed from a previously completed plan view. The plan can be slipped under tracing paper and inverted to the 45° position; after it has been traced, the three-fourths full length depth lines are added with a triangle, to produce a pictorial drawing with a fair degree of realism. See Fig. 4-18.

4.6 PICTORIAL DIMENSIONING

Although many of the rules for dimensioning orthographic drawings are also valid for pictorial drawings, the rules have slight variations due to the pictorial nature of the drawings. The following rules should be observed:

Fig. 4-18 A residential floor plan given a pictorial nature with the addition of oblique lines. Cabinetwork and furniture may also be represented.

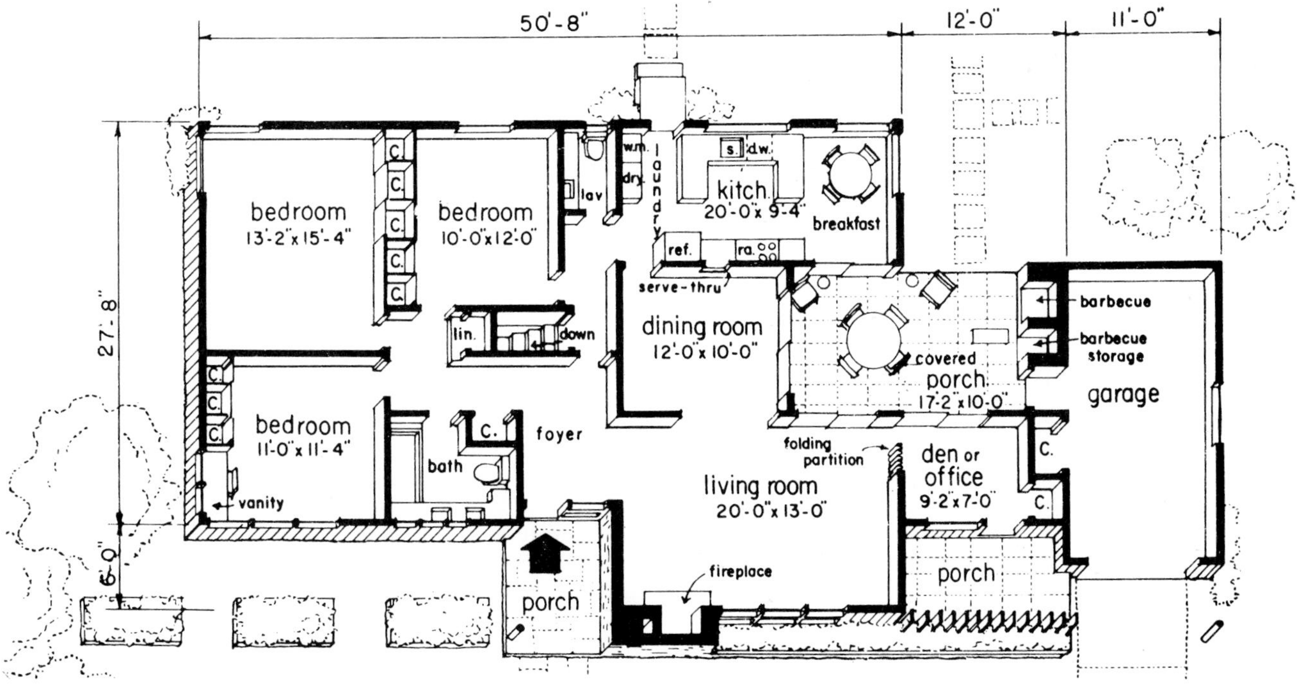

1. If possible, dimension *visible* surfaces and features only.
2. Dimension lines must not connect extension lines that lie on different planes. Each plane has two axes—stay on these axes. Keep extension lines and dimension lines on the surface in question.
3. Occasionally, dimensions can be placed directly on the object, provided clarity is maintained and there is sufficient space. This method will usually eliminate unnecessary extension lines running through the object. Otherwise, place dimensions out beyond the extremities of the view, so that they do not seem to crowd the exterior profile of the drawing.
4. Leaders should not be made parallel with the axes of the drawing. Leaders that dimension circular shapes should just touch the arc, and the arrowhead should point toward the center point. The other end of the leader should extend out to an uncrowded space and have a ¼″ line attached, which should lie on the same axis as the circle center lines (see Fig. 4-19). Arc leaders dimensioning radii should originate at the center point of the arc, and the arrowhead should touch the *inner side* of the arc line.
5. Notes may be lettered on either of the pictorial planes, or in a horizontal position. Whichever method is adopted should be maintained throughout the drawing.
6. On construction drawings, dimension lines should be made continuous, and the dimension number placed just above the line (see Fig. 4-19). Letter the number so that it appears to lie on the same plane as the surface being dimensioned. This is accomplished by using vertical lettering, yet the vertical axis of the lettering is kept parallel with the extension lines of the dimension. To make the lettering appear pictorial, each figure is distorted very much like a square is distorted into a rhombus when it is placed on a pictorial plane. Keep the dimension number midway between the arrowheads, and use a logical system to place the smallest dimension closest to the view and the successively larger farther out.

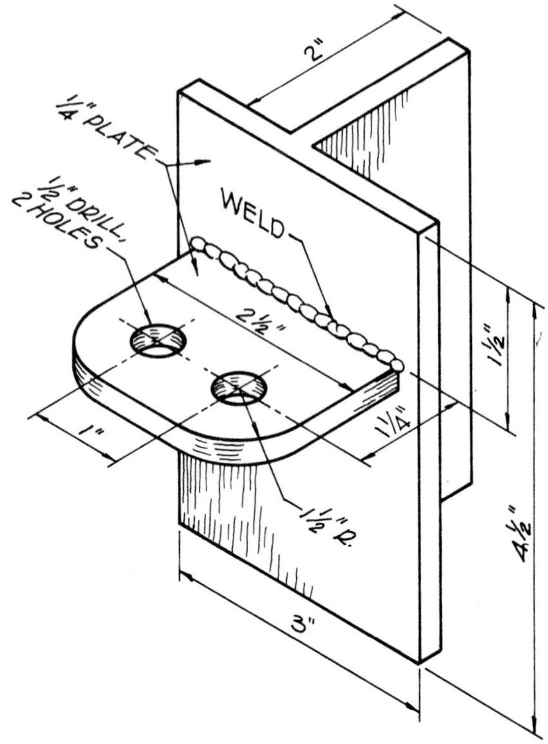

Fig. 4-19 Dimensioning pictorial drawings.

PICTORIAL DRAWING EXERCISES

The pictorial drawings in Figs. 4-20 through 4-23 should be made with instruments on small-sized (8½″ × 11″) sheets of drawing paper. All problems are shown in orthographic projection for the purpose of converting them into both isometric and oblique drawings. Double the size of each problem shown in Fig. 4-20; dimensions can be transferred with dividers. When drawing Figs. 4-22 and 4-23, merely let the grids equal any convenient size to fit your paper.

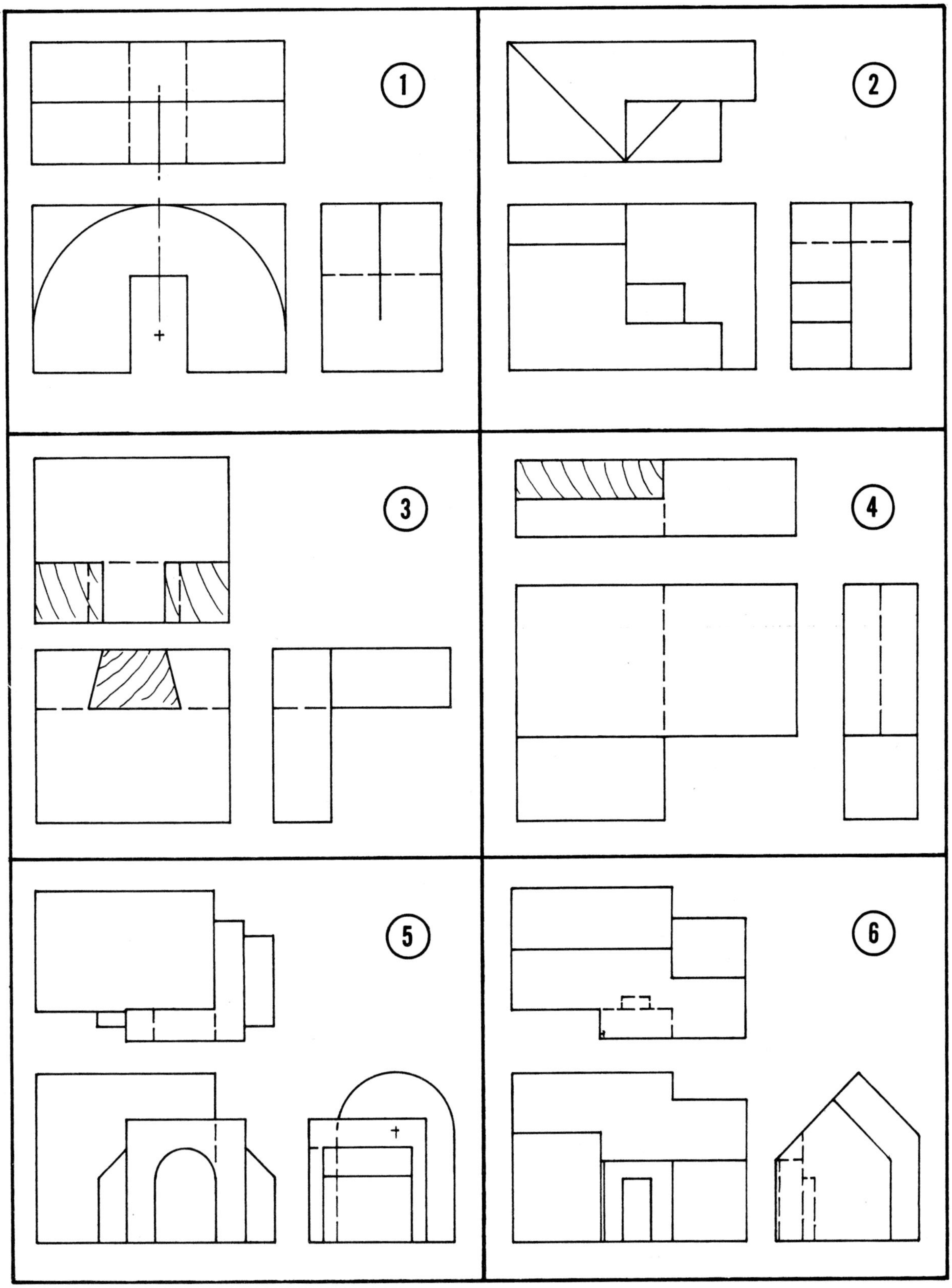

Fig. 4-20 Exercises in isometric and oblique drawing. The exercises should be enlarged to suitable scale.

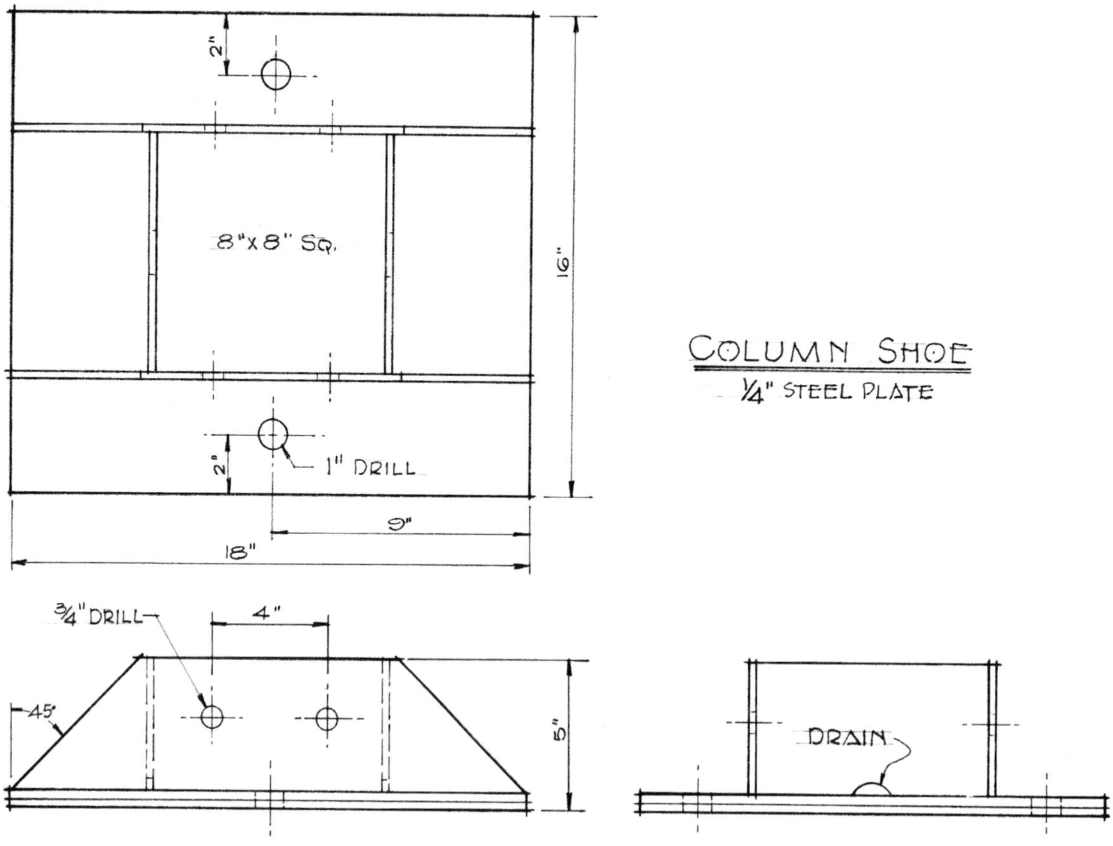

Fig. 4-21 Exercise in isometric or oblique drawing.

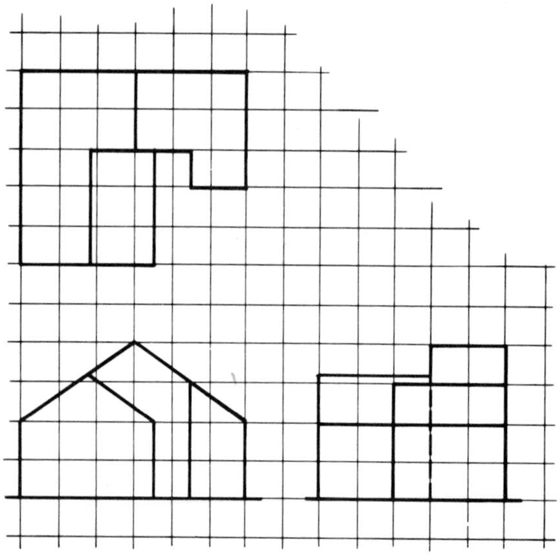

Fig. 4-22 Exercise in isometric or oblique drawing. Enlarge the grids to a convenient size.

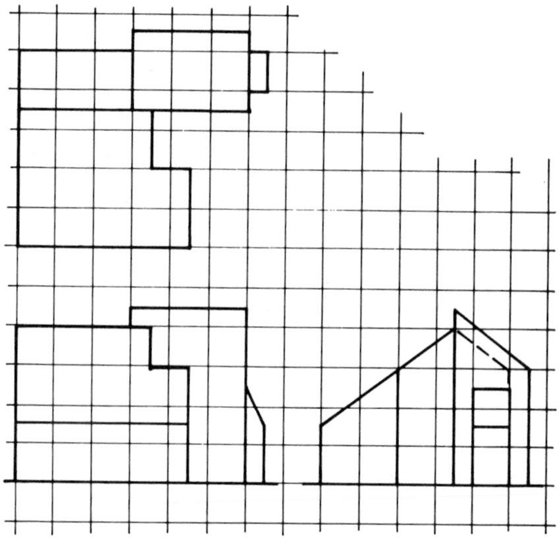

Fig. 4-23 Exercise in isometric or oblique drawing. Enlarge the grids to a convenient size.

REVIEW QUESTIONS

1. What is the advantage of a mechanical pictorial drawing over an orthographic drawing?

2. What are the applications of isometric and oblique drawings on working drawings?

3. Why does the oblique type of drawing have more versatility than the isometric?

4. What angle from the horizontal gives emphasis to the top view in an oblique drawing?

5. Describe a "Cabinet drawing."

6. Why is it advantageous to place irregular shapes of an object on the frontal plane when making an oblique drawing?

7. How may a plan view of a building be quickly made into a pictorial drawing?

8. In dimensioning pictorial drawings, why are leaders drawn at angles other than those of the principal axes?

9. How are dimension numbers made to appear as though they lie on the planes of the drawing?

10. Are the longest dimensions placed closest to the view or farthest from the view, as compared to the shorter dimensions?

"For the ordinary business of life, an ounce of habit is worth a pound of intellect."—Thomas B. Reed

5

Freehand Sketching

The often overlooked freehand sketch is a vital means of technical expression, not only for the "idea man," but also for the person concerned with making concepts workable realities. The draftsman frequently finds himself in this position. Without sketching ability, he is handicapped in many of his day-to-day drafting situations. Generally, every structure, no matter of what size, and each graphic problem that confronts the draftsman or designer originates with a pencil sketch. Whether crudely or meticulously done, the sketch becomes an important thinking instrument, as well as a means of conversing effectively between technically trained people. Whether one is concerned with the esthetic aspects of a building or with its structural properties, the ability to make spontaneous sketches is a considerable asset for the architectural draftsman, and therefore sketching should be an important part of his training.

To gain proficiency in this mode of expression, the student must invite situations entailing sketches at every opportunity. Graphic problems requiring solutions should be analyzed by preliminary sketches—not one, but as many as need be to develop the problem before it is put in final form on the drawing. Therein lies one of the many advantages of sketching—graphic ideas can be quickly developed on scratch paper before being drafted to scale on the board.

In addition, the sketch is necessary in planning and organizing intelligently the sheet layout of a complete set of drawings, which often include many views and details. Numerous layout sketches are necessary to arrange drawings in their right sequence and to utilize the paper efficiently.

However, students are occasionally reluctant to resort to sketches when experimenting with their initial concepts. They seem to feel, evidently, that their early attempts will look unprofessional; but this is inconsequential at the outset. Rather, the desire to develop the concepts graphically should be their incentive for using sketches—appearance will improve with experience. Even the most proficient have had to start with crude beginnings.

The secret of learning to sketch, especially for those who are doubtful of their aptitude, is to begin by drawing simple things, such as lines and rectangular views, circles and circular shapes, and complete orthographic sketches. Then advance to isometric and oblique pictorial sketches, and finally to realistic perspective drawings. This sequence, which leads the student to more difficult work progressively, also provides experience in all the necessary types of drawings encountered by the draftsman.

So that the beginner will not be burdened with rules and restrictions, the following material is suggested as a series of guides for making freehand sketching as simple and easy as possible, and as a means for eventually making it an enjoyable and rewarding accomplishment.

5.1 SKETCHING MATERIALS

Few materials are needed—pencils, paper, sandpaper pad, and an eraser. The majority of linework can be done with an H or B pencil, occasionally a 2B will be handy for darker accents, and a 2H pencil, if one is available, can be used for preliminary construction layout. Points on the pencils can be conical, or if both wide and thin lines are required (on floor plan sketches), a chisel-type point (see Fig. 5-1) can be dressed on a sandpaper pad to allow variation with the same point. Dressing the pencil point becomes very important in later shading exercises to represent various architectural textures, but for beginning work the medium-sharp point is satisfactory.

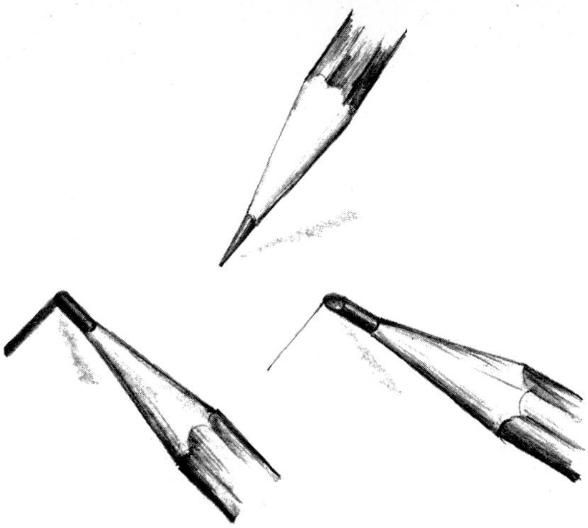

Fig. 5-1 Pencil points used for sketching.

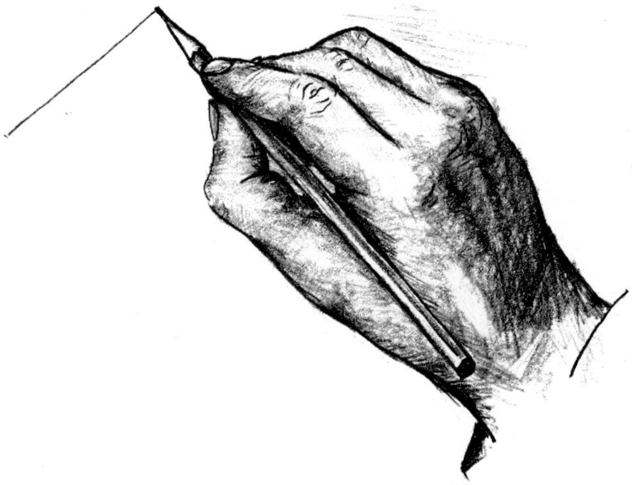

Fig. 5-2 Hold the pencil in a natural, comfortable position.

Fig. 5-3 An alternate position for holding the sketching pencil during preliminary layouts.

The pencil should be held in a natural way; avoid clutching it too close to the point. Some draftsmen prefer to hold the pencil in a horizontal position, shown in Fig. 5-3, when laying-in preliminary construction lines.

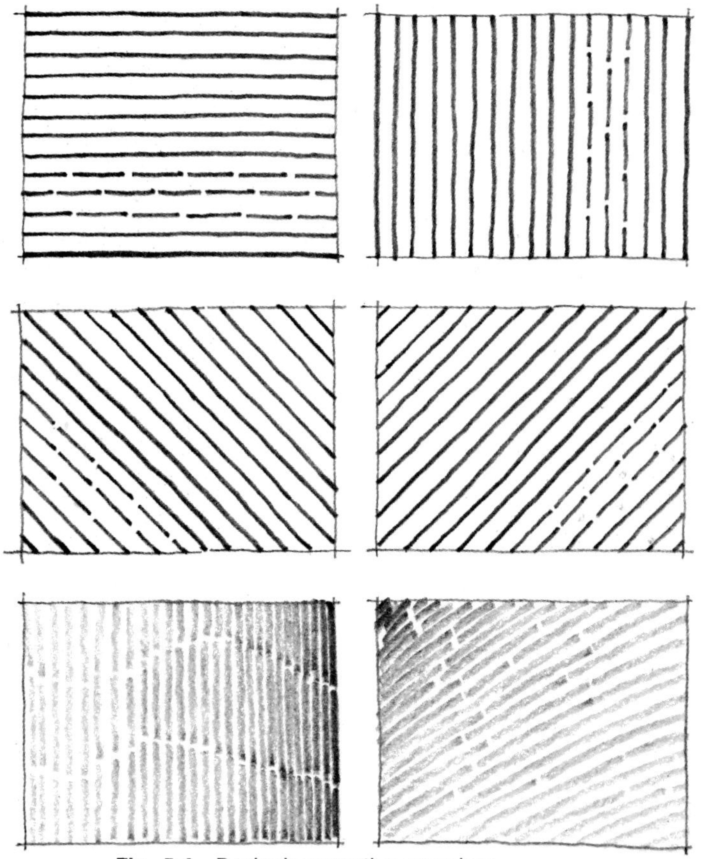

Fig. 5-4 Beginning practice exercises.

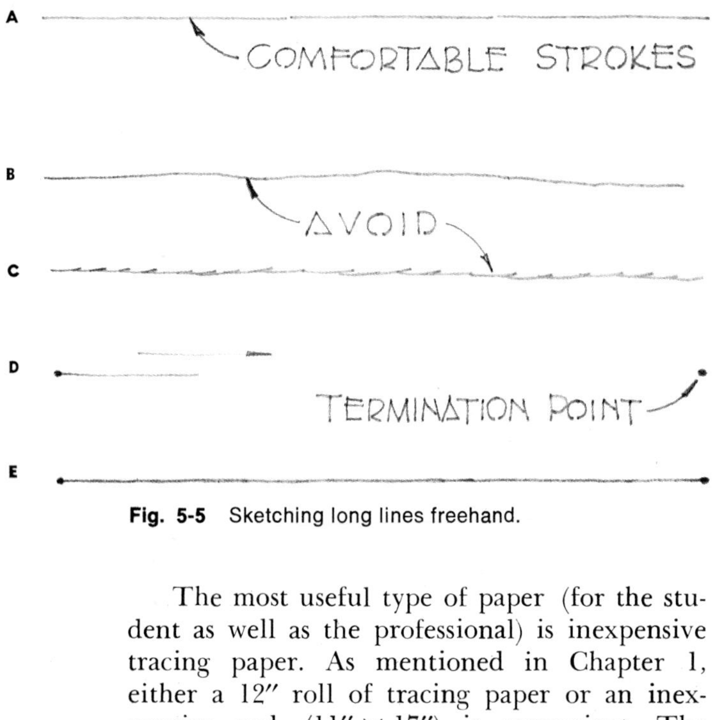

Fig. 5-5 Sketching long lines freehand.

The most useful type of paper (for the student as well as the professional) is inexpensive tracing paper. As mentioned in Chapter 1, either a 12″ roll of tracing paper or an inexpensive pad (11″ × 17″) is convenient. The advantage of sketching on tracing paper is the ease with which sketches can be modified or redeveloped simply by placing the transparent paper over previously done sketches to minimize repetitious construction. Also, flaws that might possibly go unnoticed can be found by turning the paper over and observing the sketch in reverse. An eraser on the end of the pencil will be handy, but generally most erasing will be unnecessary when sketches can be redrawn quicker than mistakes can be erased.

5.2 BEGINNING LINE EXERCISES

Start your sketching practice with simple line exercises, drawn horizontally, vertically, and inclined in several directions (see Fig. 5-4). Make the short lines with finger and wrist movements, and longer lines by attaching a series of shorter, more comfortable-length lines to each other (see Fig. 5-5). After each stroke, move the ball of the hand to a new position along the path of the long line. Usually, a very light trial line will help to establish the general direction of a long line. Or, before the long line is started, a termination point can be indicated; concentrate on the point as the line progresses, and almost without exception the line will end at the point. Establish *parallel lines* by placing a few points along the original line, equidistant from it, and sketch the parallel line through the points, as in Fig. 5-6.

The right-handed person should sketch horizontal lines from left to right (the reverse if left-handed), and vertical lines should be drawn toward oneself. If a small sheet of paper is being used, the paper can be turned in a favorable position when sketching lines; usually it becomes easier to sketch a line in a horizontal direction. For practice exercise, sketch straight lines in all directions without turning the paper however, mainly to gain coordination of the hand and eye.

If a board or pad is used when sketching, a semifreehand method of drawing long lines, shown in Fig. 5-7, can be employed. The edge of the board or pad is used as a guide, and the free hand holds the paper in a position parallel to the edge of the board. This method is especially helpful in establishing important center lines or major horizontal roof lines on an elevation, from which other lines on the sketch can be made parallel. Borders are also easily made with this method.

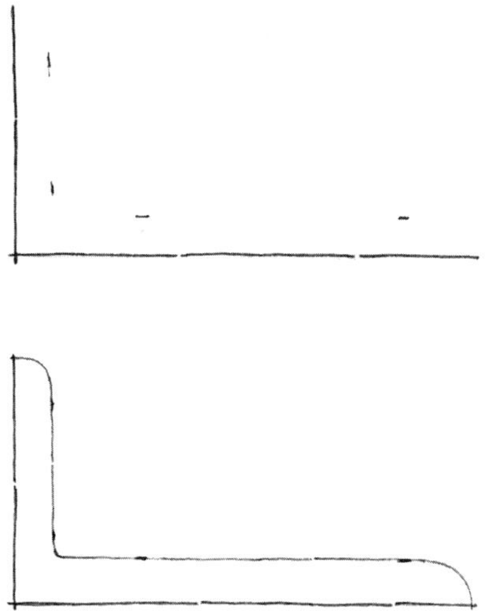

Fig. 5-6 Laying out parallel lines.

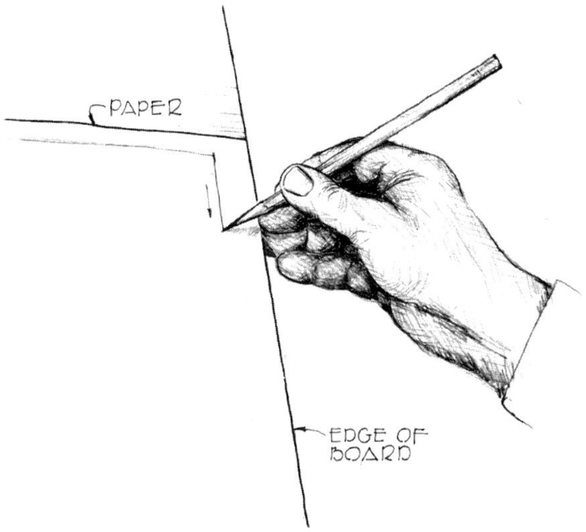

Fig. 5-7 Drawing semifreehand lines with a convenient edge.

5.3 DIVIDING LINES AND AREAS EQUALLY

Ability to divide lines and areas into equal spaces is frequently necessary in arriving at many of the common geometric forms found in sketches. A line can be quickly divided if the pencil itself is used as a measuring stick. With the aid of the pencil, lay off approximate half-lengths of the line from each end; if the approximation is not exact, the remaining small space is easily bisected by eye to produce an accurate division of the entire line.

Another method of bisecting lines is by *visual comparison*. An entire line is observed and "weighed optically" in determining its fulcrum, or point of balance. Each half is compared visually before placing the bisecting point. This procedure can be repeated any number of times to divide a line into any number of equal divisions, merely by dividing and redividing its line segments (see Fig. 5-8). It is especially effective in maintaining symmetry of sketches when lines as well as spaces must be kept uniform.

Centers of rectangular figures are also found by drawing their diagonals. If necessary, the halves can be divided with diagonals for smaller divisions, etc. (see Fig. 5-9).

5.4 SKETCHING ANGLES

The 90° angle is a predominant feature in the majority of construction sketches. Thus, it becomes important to be able to sketch right angles rather accurately, even if it entails checking them with the triangle occasionally. Frequently the perpendicular edges of the drawing paper can serve as a guide for comparison. It is also helpful to turn the sketch upside down; nonperpendicular tendencies of horizontal and vertical lines will become evident. Correct shape

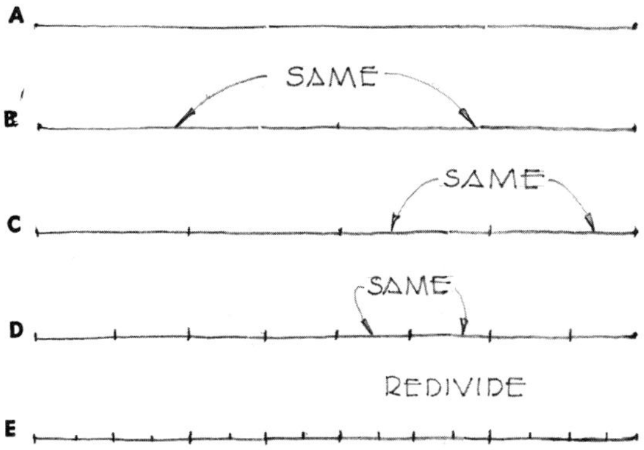

Fig. 5-8 Bisecting lines by visual comparison.

Fig. 5-9 Finding centers by sketching diagonals.

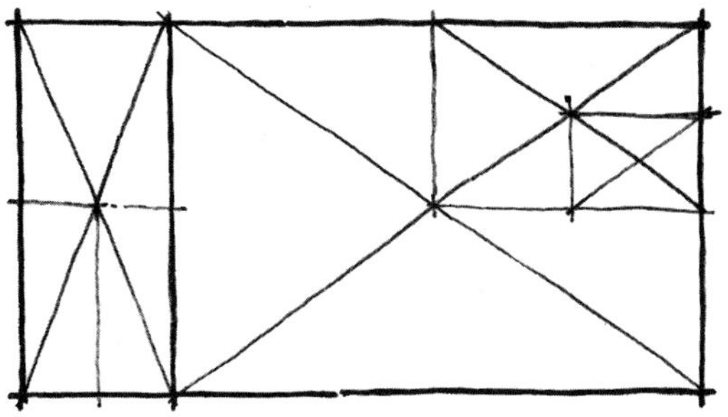

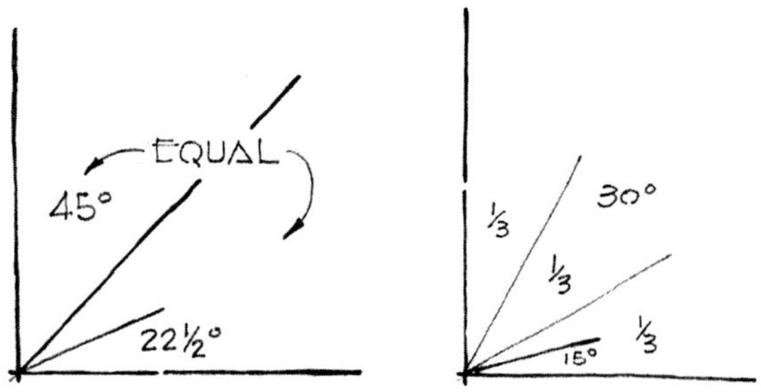

Fig. 5-10 Sketching angles by convenient divisions.

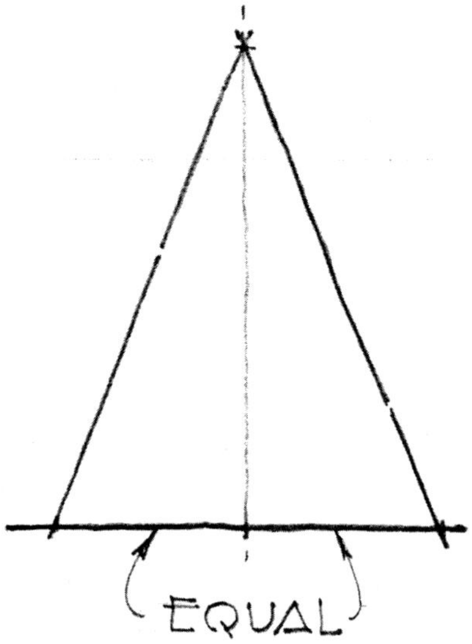

Fig. 5-11 Using a center line for symmetry.

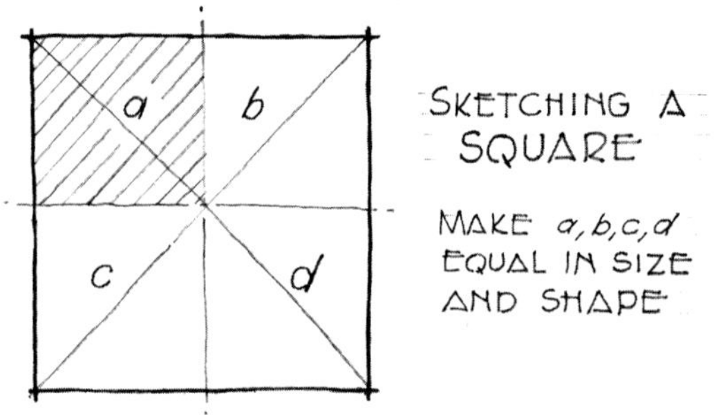

Fig. 5-12 Sketch an accurate square by starting with center lines.

Fig. 5-13 Sketching a circle.

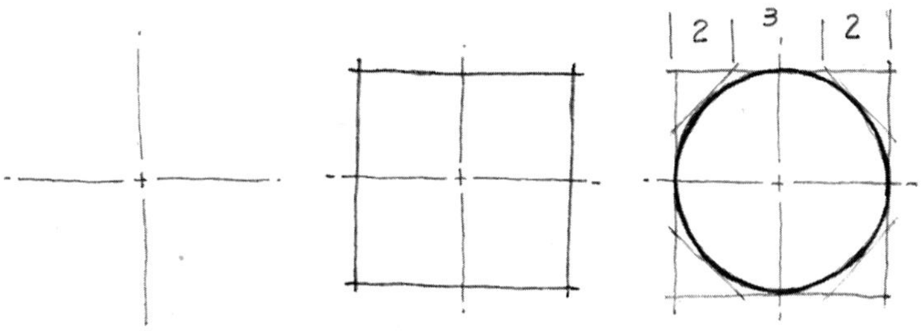

of the right angles gives the sketch stability, without which effectiveness is lost.

A 45° angle is made by dividing a right angle equally by visual comparison; a 30° or 60° angle by dividing the right angle into three equal parts, which is slightly more difficult. Always start with the right angle for the most accurate estimation of angle shape (Figs. 5-10 and 5-11).

5.5 SKETCHING CIRCLES AND ARCS

Small circles are usually sketched without construction other than center lines, but larger circles require some preliminary construction to help maintain their symmetry, and also to locate them properly on the sketch. Start larger circles (over ½″) with perpendicular center lines, around which lay out a square and carefully check each quadrant of the square as it develops for unity of size and shape (see Figs. 5-12 and 5-13). If the square is not true, the finished circle will not come out round. Then, starting at the intersection of the top of the square and the center line, sketch each half of the circle with full, curved strokes that touch each center-line intersection within the square. Practice sketching circles of different sizes until they become balanced and well rounded. Be careful to maintain a "blown-up," full character on all circles rather than a flattened or elliptical appearance.

Fig. 5-14 Sketching a circle with the use of two pencils.

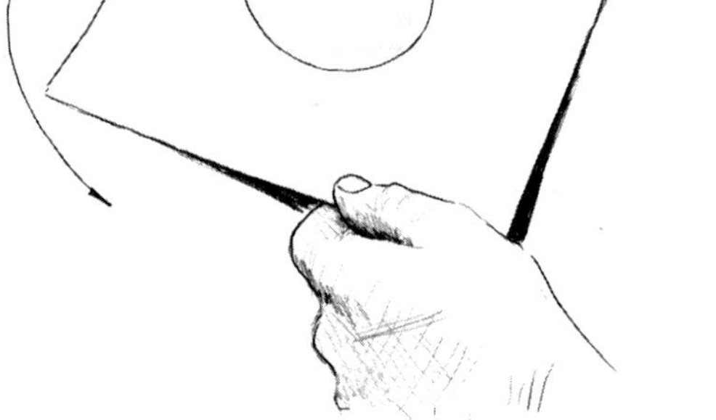

If several circles are required on a sketch, a *semimechanical* technique shown in Fig. 5-14 will produce them accurately and save considerable time. Try a few of different sizes for exercise. Hold two equally long pencils rigidly in the hand so that they act very much as a compass. One pencil becomes the pivot; the other scribes the circle when the paper is revolved under the pencils with the other hand.

Freehand arcs are drawn with similar construction, as mentioned for circles (see Figs. 5-15 and 5-16). Often it is advisable to construct an entire square and circle in order to maintain the character of a regular curve on arcs. The construction linework can be quickly erased.

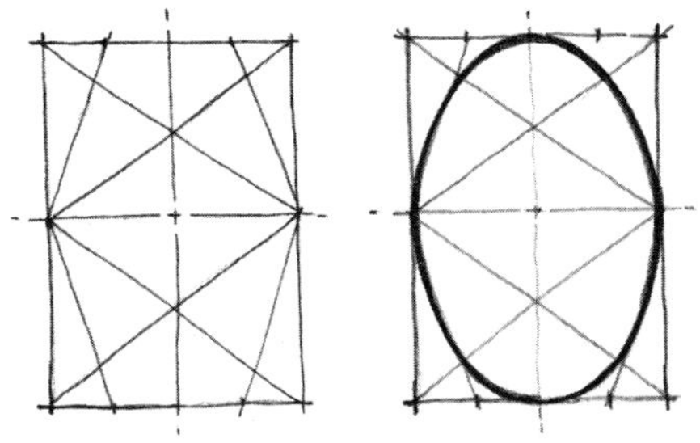

Fig. 5-17 Construction for sketching an ellipse.

5.6 DEVELOPING GOOD PROPORTION

Proportion is an illusive characteristic of sketching—it is mastered only after training the eye to see correctly. Without a feeling of proper proportion the sketch can be misleading and therefore of little value. Continually strive for correct proportion by astute observation and analysis of your sketching subject. Drawing in proportion is largely a matter of discerning how one thing relates to another—for instance, how length relates to width, height to length, the size of one feature to another, one space to another, etc. The trained draftsman automatically sees these relationships and checks for accuracy at frequent intervals while sketching.

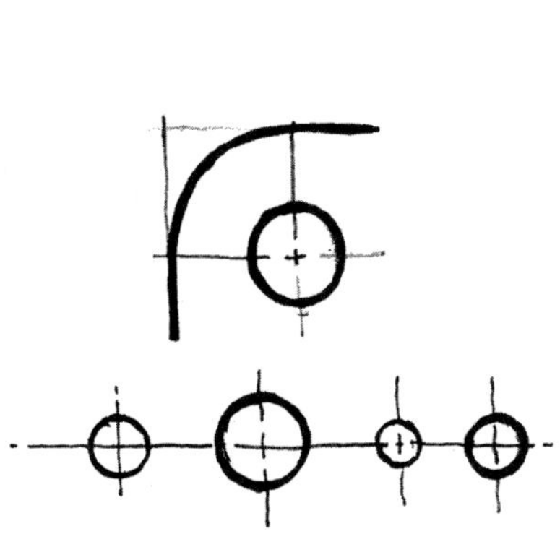

Fig. 5-15 Sketching small circles.

Fig. 5-16 Sketching arcs with construction.

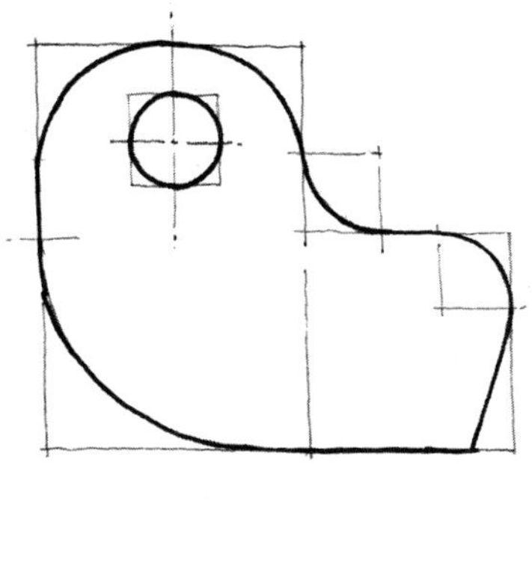

One of the simplest methods of arriving at correct proportion is seeing through incidental details of the subject and recognizing the *basic geometric forms* inherent in it, whether the subject is orthographic or pictorial. If these basic forms can be recognized, an important step in proportion has been accomplished. At this point we are mainly concerned with plane figures; pictorial sketches are discussed later.

When sketching from a dimensioned drawing, the dimensions themselves provide a definite basis for proportion—if they are carefully observed. To set the general size of a sketch, establish a major line or feature first; the remaining lines are then made proportional to that original line according to the given dimensions. For example, if a 20′ × 40′ floor plan is to be sketched, the 20′ is represented with a line of any convenient length, depending on the size of the paper (preliminary sketches should be small), the line for the 40′ should then be drawn twice this length. Similarly, if a partition within the plan is, say 10′ long, the line representing it should be only one-half as long as the 20′ line, etc. This procedure introduces an adequate proportion throughout the sketch.

But suppose we are sketching an object or view that has no given dimensions for measurement or tangible means for proportion. This presents more of a problem to the easily discouraged beginner, and some system must be developed to help create this necessary sense of

Fig. 5-18 A page from the sketchbook of a thirteenth-century French architect, Villard D'Honnecourt, showing the use of geometric forms in sketching.

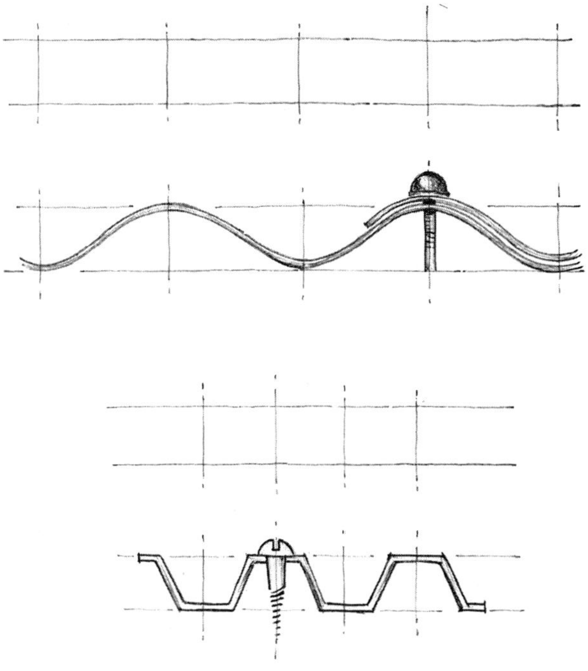

Fig. 5-19 Sketching construction for simple shapes.

Fig. 5-20 Adaptation of basic shapes to detail sketches.

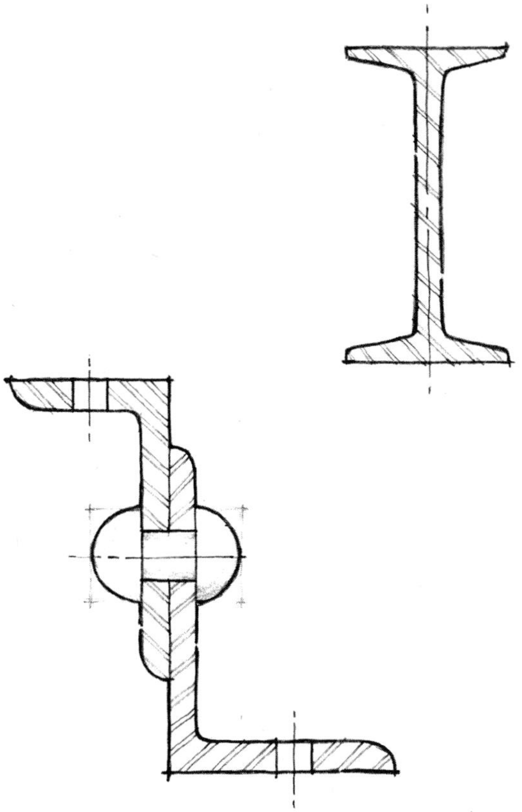

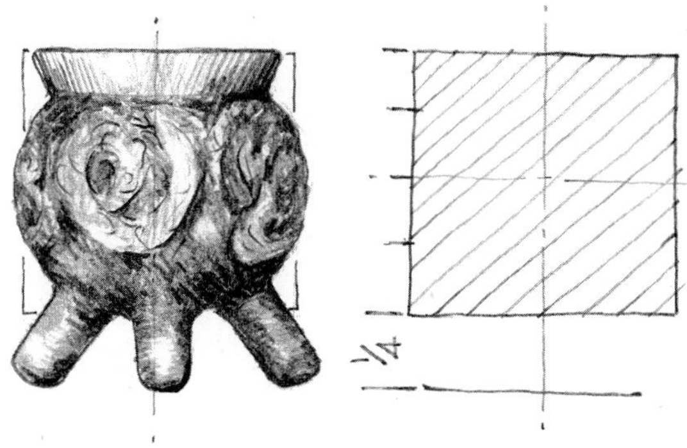

Fig. 5-21 Using a simple square for arriving at proportion.

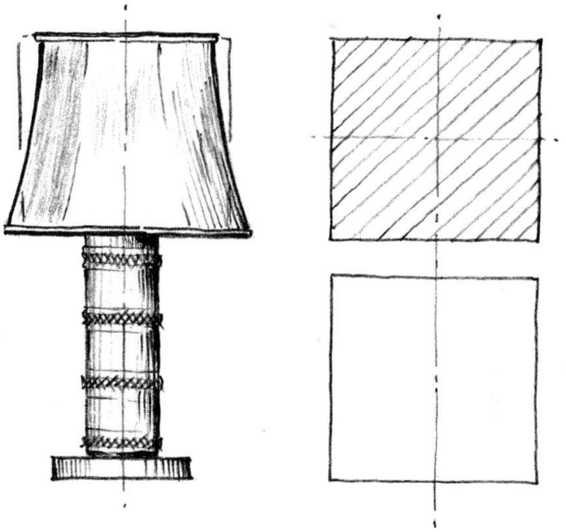

Fig. 5-22 Arriving at proportion in sketches.

relationship. The simple *square*, as a shape for comparing basic proportion, is the most effective and appropriate method. Although not particularly attractive in itself, the square is the ideal geometric form to look for when arriving at proportion of height and width. It has uniform sides, regardless of its size, and can be accurately sketched by comparing these sides. If you were analyzing the proportion of the Mexican vase (Fig. 5-21), you would observe that the body of the vase will fit neatly into a square, and the legs raise the body about one-fourth of the height of the square. In sketching the lamp (Fig. 5-22), its shade has the general shape of a square, and its height is a little more than twice the height of the square. The width of the stem is one-third of the width of the square. Two squares quickly give you the basic proportion of the piece of furniture

Fig. 5-23 Many sketching subjects can be fitted into squares.

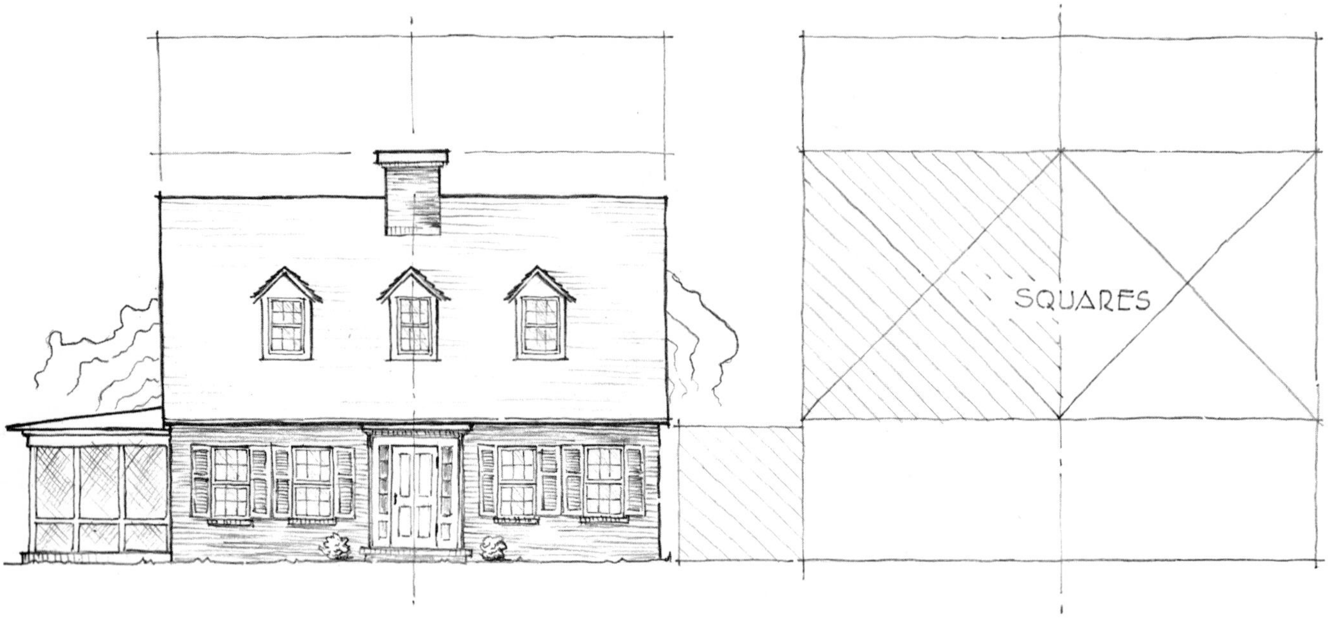

Fig. 5-24 The use of the square in sketching elevations.

(Fig. 5-23). If you were sketching the exterior elevation of the colonial house (Fig. 5-24), a square would organize its general shape and smaller squares would give you the proportions of minor details.

The square, therefore, makes a suitable unit for simplifying a subject under observation and for quickly duplicating the units in the sketch. When you become "square conscious," you will automatically see squares of different sizes in your subjects; when these same squares are used as guides in your sketch, you will have arrived at a handy method of proportioning plans, elevations, and section sketches of buildings as well as other subjects.

It is also imporant to be familiar with the general proportions of commonly used building materials, such as lumber, brick, concrete block, stock moldings, stock doors, etc. (see Figs. 5-25 and 5-26). Once the proportions of these materials are committed to memory, other aspects of the sketch will assume relative proportions.

5.7 ACQUIRING GOOD LINE TECHNIQUE

At the start of a sketch, make the lines light and indefinite while the forms are still in a plastic state of development. These exploration and trial lines should be retained until satisfactory shapes emerge and the general nature of the sketch takes on a realistic proportion. Next, perfect and strengthen important lines, so that

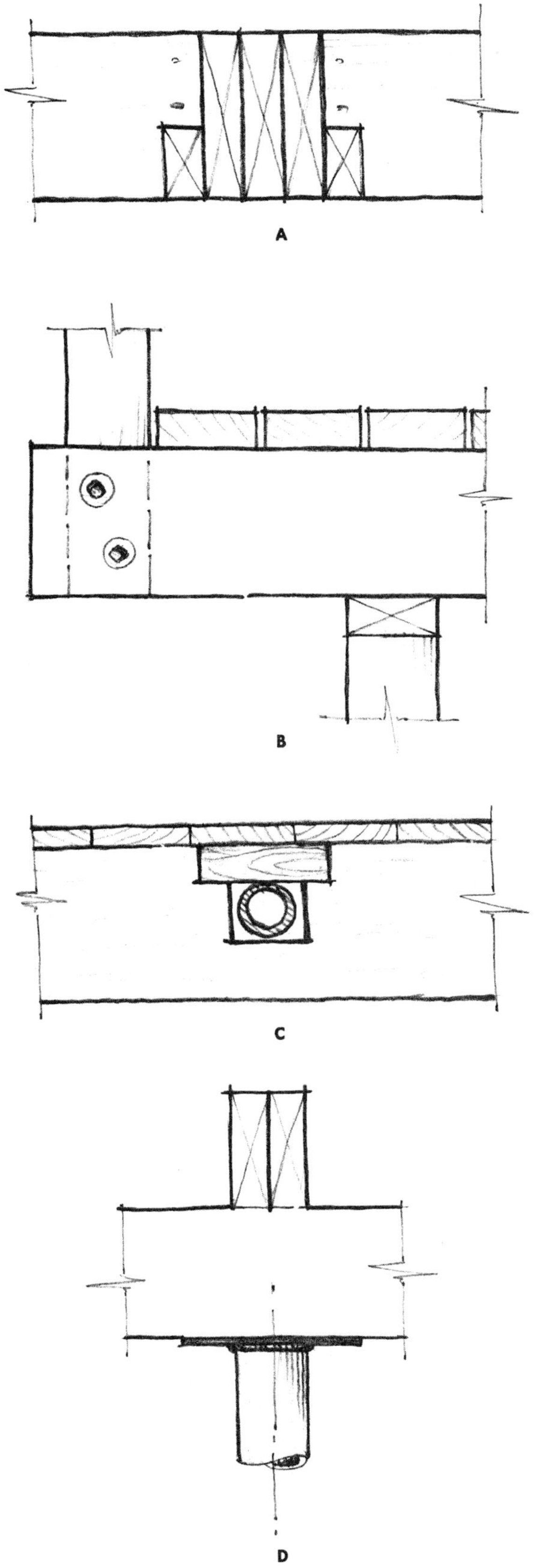

Fig. 5-25 The use of parallel lines in detail sketches.

the corrected shapes predominate the trial lines; work on minor details after major shapes seem right; in this way, the entire sketch will mature simultaneously. Light trial lines can be erased as the sketch progresses, although if they are left in, the light lines throughout the drawing seem to soften it and give it a "sketchy" quality.

The finished lines should have weight variations according to their importance. Object lines and key profile lines are made bold, whereas less important lines are made accordingly less prominent. Line variations provide the sparkle and depth so important in a successful sketch. Occasionally a freehand line is broken at uneven intervals rather than made continuous, and the beginning and end of each stroke are made definite instead of appearing feathered out. One of the interesting qualities of a freehand line is its slight waviness as compared to the sharp straightness of a mechanical line. This quality adds personality to the finished sketch, and there is no reason for trying to avoid it. On the other hand, a choppy, hesitating line technique, shown in Fig. 5-5C, is neither forthright nor pleasing in appearance. Progress in sketching is made only with *practice;* each successive exercise should be a deliberate effort to improve.

5.8 SKETCHING PLANS AND ELEVATIONS

The floor plan sketch is the logical start for depicting the architectural idea. After preliminary planning has produced a few general concepts of the structure, but definite limitations are not yet established, a "schematic sketch" showing possible room locations is drawn. Use only circular shapes for these trial layouts (see Fig. 5-27). Make similar sketches if necessary for second-floor plans as well. From these schematics a more developed plan is made.

The best procedure for working out preliminary studies of tentative floor plans and elevations is the use of $\frac{1}{8}''$ coordinate paper. Either work directly on $8\frac{1}{2}'' \times 11''$ sheets, or tape your sketching tracing paper over a coordinate underlay pad, which has been fastened to the drawing board, as mentioned in Chapter 1. The coordinate paper facilitates sketching horizontal and vertical lines and provides a

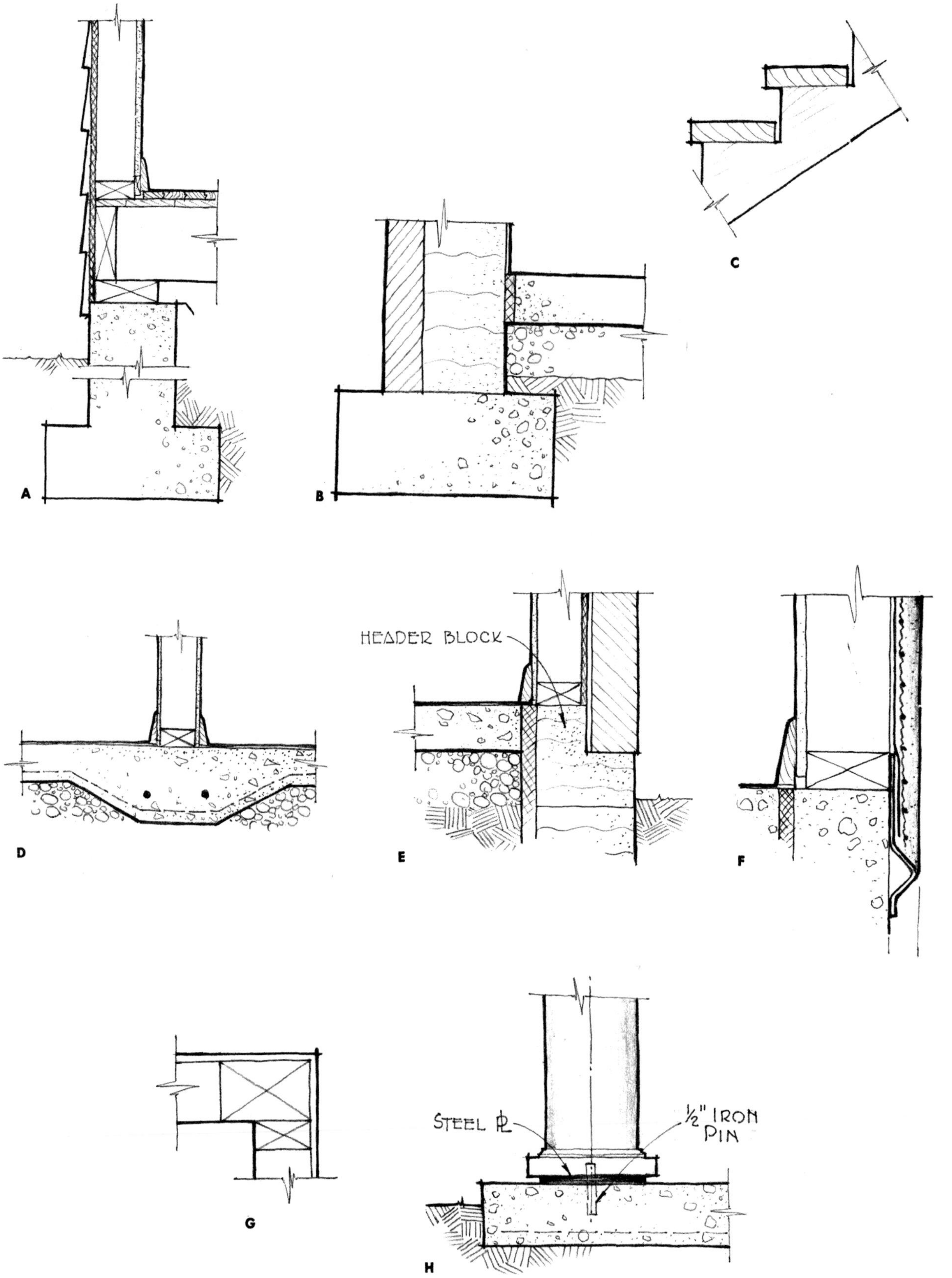

Fig. 5-26 Quick construction sketches.

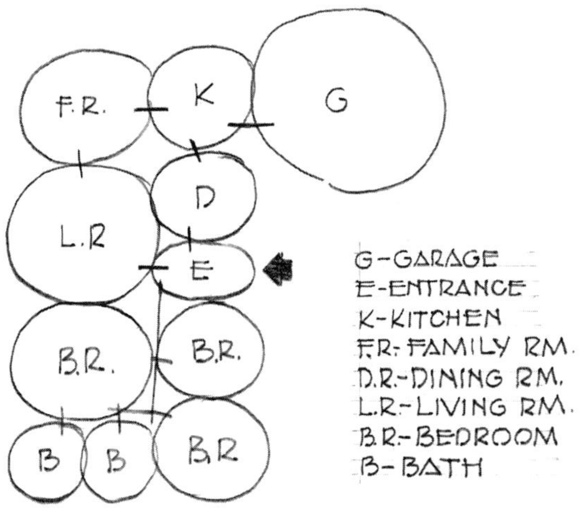

Fig. 5-27 A schematic sketch for starting a floor plan.

preliminary sense of scale. Each coordinate space represents 1 sq ft, and the sketch will have a convenient scale of $\frac{1}{8}'' = 1'\text{-}0''$. This scale is satisfactory for early studies. Frame walls on coordinate paper can be made a half-space wide (6″), large buildings can be put on a small sheet, and more important, the small scale allows more command of the development. Even the scale of $\frac{1}{16}'' = 1'\text{-}0''$ will be found adaptable to beginning sketches on coordinate paper. Large sketches are clumsy to handle during the planning stage.

To sketch a plan, lightly draw the exterior walls with a single, continuous line; do not show windows and doors yet. Lay out all the partitions with a fine line; let the lines continue through doors and other openings. Establish all clothes closets with a minimum of 2′ in depth and fill in with close lines parallel to the 2′ dimension. Indicate the placement and width of all windows and doors on the wall lines. With the pencil dressed to a chisel point, widen the exterior walls and partitions with a broad line; stop at the window and door openings. Next, complete the window and door symbols (see Fig. 5-28) with a sharp point. On design sketches, door indications can merely be left as openings. Sketch the approximate locations of stairs; indicate risers with parallel lines (actual size about 10″ apart), and indicate the direction of travel with an arrow and the note UP or DOWN, as the case may be. Draw in fireplaces, entrance platforms, terraces, walks, and other minor features. Kitchen cabinets and bathroom fixtures are blocked-in freehand. Label the rooms and add as many dimensions as needed; usually only interior room sizes are indicated at this stage. Show the plan with the front side *down* on the paper.

If a second-floor plan is necessary for a 2-story house, develop the second-floor plan on tracing paper placed over the completed first-floor plan. Place bearing walls and major partitions above first-floor walls, if possible, for sounder construction. Stairwells and chimneys must coincide, and plumbing wet-walls are best aligned above each other. The vent stack of a first-floor bath must pass through a second-floor partition. Draw an end elevation of $1\frac{1}{2}$-story houses before attempting the second-floor plan. Locations of half-walls and dormer windows become simpler on elevation views showing the roof profile.

Before the elevations can be sketched, a preliminary roof layout must be made on the plan view. The character of the roof plays an important role in the total design of a house, not only for the sake of appearance, but also from a standpoint of accommodating the outline of the plan. Consequently, several sketches may be necessary to find the most desirable type of roof. For economy keep the roof simple; on the other hand, if an unassuming single gable or hip roof is used, its austere silhouette usually appears monotonous and contributes little architectural character to the structure. (Refer to p.183 for description of roof types.) Uniform roof overhangs are easier to frame than various extensions. But protection from the weather over entrances, walks, and terraces makes the roof more serviceable. Show the roof overhang with dashed lines and indicate ridges, valleys, hips, and roof offsets. If the roof slopes are uniform, the intersections of gables and hips are always shown with 45° lines.

To sketch an elevation, place the floor plan sketch under a fresh sheet of tracing paper, take the longitudinal features from the plan, and merely transfer features from each exterior wall (see Fig. 5-28). The ridge and eave lines of sloping roofs can be established by first sketching the end elevations if necessary. Then they are transferred to the other elevations after satisfactory roof slopes have been developed. Stock door heights are shown about 6′–8″ above the estimated finished floor level, and the tops of windows are usually aligned with door tops in residential construction. Impor-

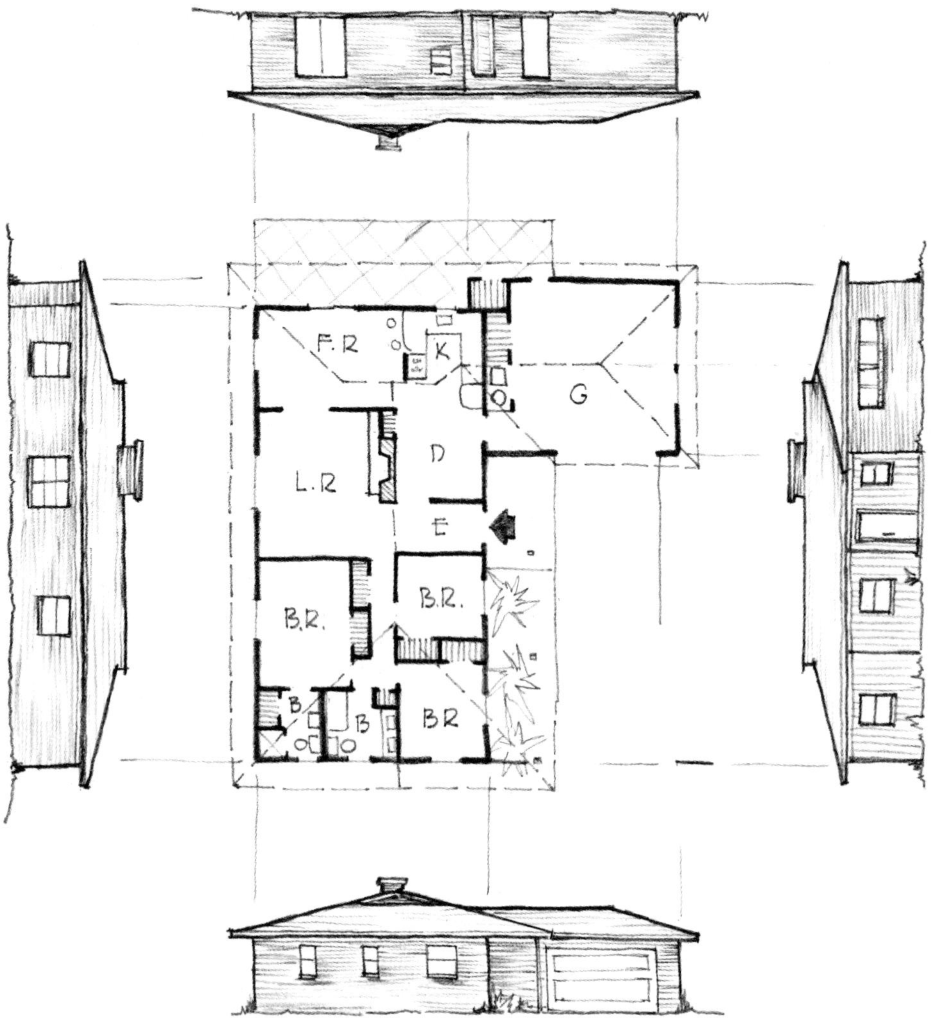

Fig. 5-28 Plan development sketch and relating elevations.

tant details showing the character of the windows and doors should be added, as well as other significant features such as chimneys, columns, exterior steps, symbols of exterior materials, etc. Sketching some foliage near the ends of the elevation will project an impression of unity with the landscape (see Fig. 5-29).

Sketching section details requires definite information about the construction of the tentative structure; nevertheless, exploratory section sketches must be made in conjunction with plan and elevation development.

Start details by blocking in important structural members, around which subordinate materials are added. If masonry is involved in the section, establish its shape before applying wood framing or other details. Add exterior and interior wall coverings, moldings, finish flooring, etc., after major structural pieces are oriented correctly. Care must be taken to relate each member according to its structural position; proportion is important to reveal workability of the detail. Because section details are composed mainly of parallel and perpendicular lines, the right-angle nature of the lines deserves attention. Strengthen the outlines of important elements and make the symbols of the different sectioned materials lighter. In large areas of sectioned surface, except for the periphery of the surface, much of the symbol linework can be omitted (see Fig. 5-26).

Coordinate paper with 12×12 divisions within each 1″ square can be used to sketch accurate details in the following conventional scales: $\frac{1}{4}'' = 1'\text{-}0''$, $\frac{1}{2}'' = 1'\text{-}0''$, $1'' = 1'\text{-}0''$, and $3'' = 1'\text{-}0''$ (see Fig. 5-30). Especially

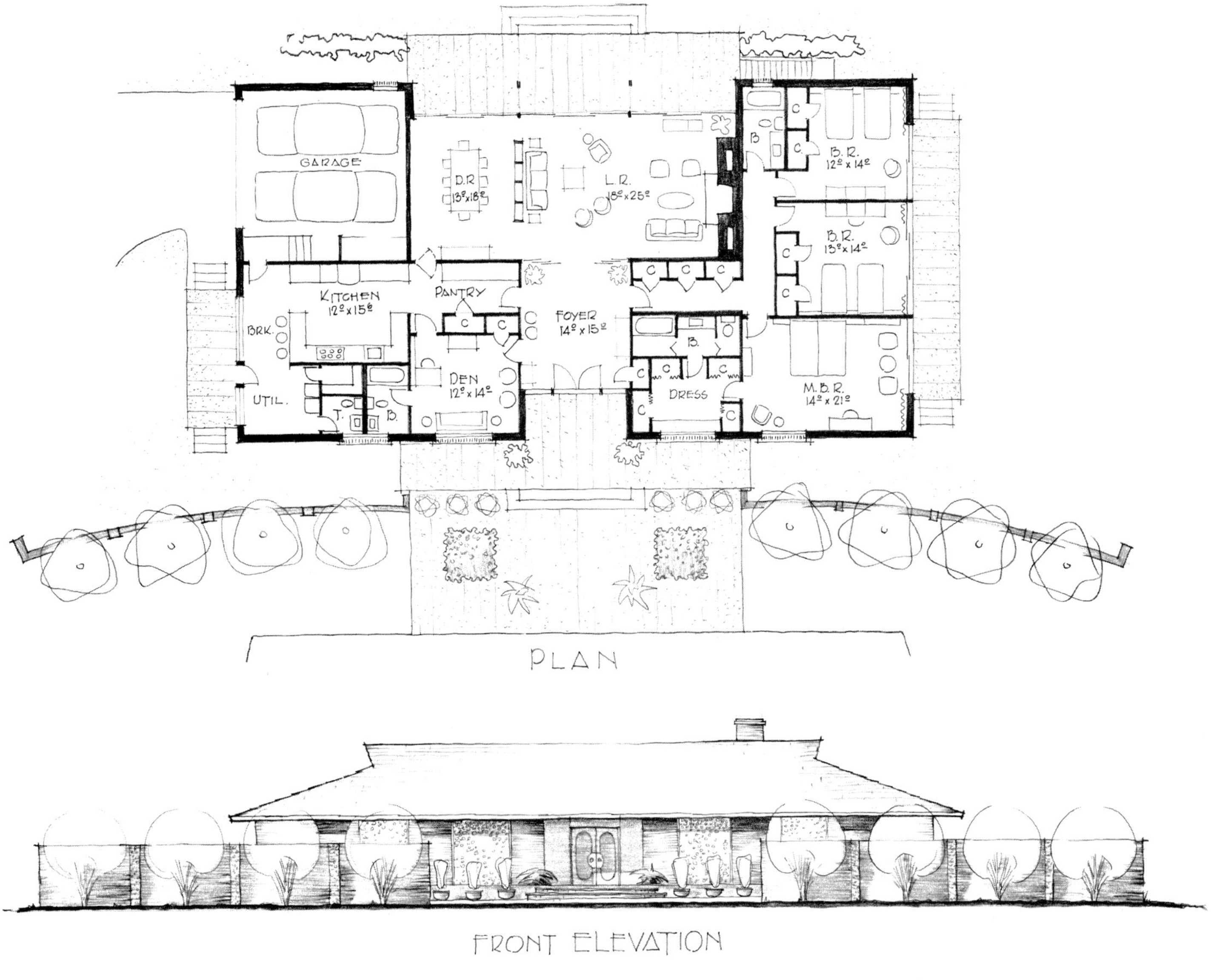

Fig. 5-29 A professional preliminary sketch of a residence.

when using the 1″ = 1′–0″ scale, you will find that section details can be quickly sketched over this paper, if scaled sketches are needed. In fact, many draftsmen find that details sketched over 12 × 12 per inch coordinate paper are perfectly satisfactory for working drawings. Using the different scales with the paper, each small square is equal to the following number of inches:

¼″ = 1′–0″	4″
½″ = 1′–0″	2″
1″ = 1′–0″	1″
3″ = 1′–0″	(3 small squares = 1″)

5.9 ISOMETRIC AND OBLIQUE SKETCHING

Not only are isometric and oblique sketches the next step in the logical development toward perspective sketching, but they also provide a quick method of examining tentative construction details pictorially if the need arises.

The principles of pictorial and orthographic sketching are similar, except that now we will deal with volumes rather than flat planes. Instead of the square being a convenient unit of proportion as in orthographic views, the *cube* becomes the ideal unit of pictorial proportion.

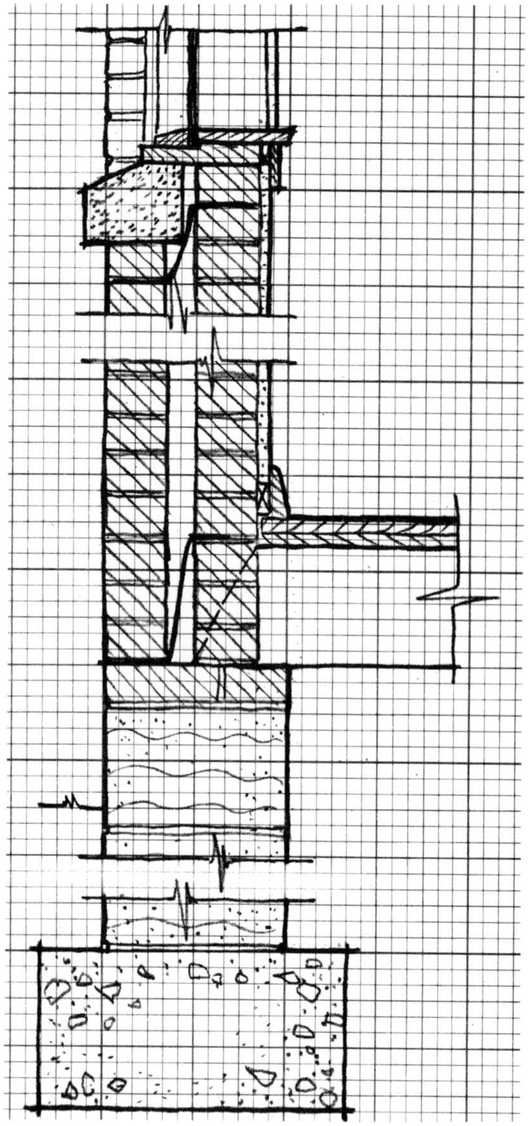

Fig. 5-30 A scaled detail sketch on 12″ × 12″ coordinate paper.

In addition, all objects are simplified to their basic volumetric forms, and these forms are the first consideration in the pictorial sketch (see Fig. 5-38). *Block out the basic forms of the object before attempting the minor details.* Since this simple procedure is effective for experienced technical illustrators, it should serve the student equally well. Study the forms shown in Fig. 5-31—careful analysis of any object being sketched, reveals that these basic shapes are inherent forms, although sometimes only parts of these shapes or several of them in combination are perceived.

First, practice sketching the basic geometric shapes, using the construction principles indicated in Chapter 4, Isometric and Oblique Pictorial Drawings. Then, look for these shapes in the object you are about to sketch and concentrate on the basic form representation. The object can be enclosed in a cube or box (Fig. 4-6), or it can be "built up" by a series of differently shaped blocks, one on top of the other (Fig. 4-7), depending on the nature of the object. Details are added or "carved" from these main blocks after shape and proportion are established.

If you are sketching from orthographic plans or elevations, the lines of each view can often be laid out on their respective pictorial planes for easier construction. Occasionally it becomes advisable to combine a pictorial sketch with an orthographic section sketch. Partial pictorial sections are also revealing sketches. Appropriate exercises should be devoted to sketching from actual models, drawing equipment, even books, or anything at hand.

5.10 SKETCHING A QUICK THUMBNAIL PERSPECTIVE

The realistic appearance of a perspective sketch is often helpful, not only in analyzing many of the esthetic aspects of the structure before the working drawings are completed, but in presenting preliminary ideas to a client. Exterior features that appear quite satisfactory on elevation views may not always be pleasing when observed from an oblique angle. Isometric and oblique drawings usually are not entirely reliable for scrutinizing these design aspects, whereas perspective sketches are especially adaptable to critical examination of architectural ideas during their planning stages.

Briefly, a perspective drawing or sketch is based on the fact that all horizontal lines that recede from the observer appear to converge at a distant point (that is, if one side of the building is parallel to the picture plane). The receding lines will appear to vanish at two distant points if the building is observed from an angular position (see Fig. 5-32). Also, these points of convergence, called vanishing points, fall on a horizontal line or plane which is theoretically at the same level as the observer's eye, and which appears on the drawing very similarly as the actual horizon appears on a landscape. Depending on the placement of the

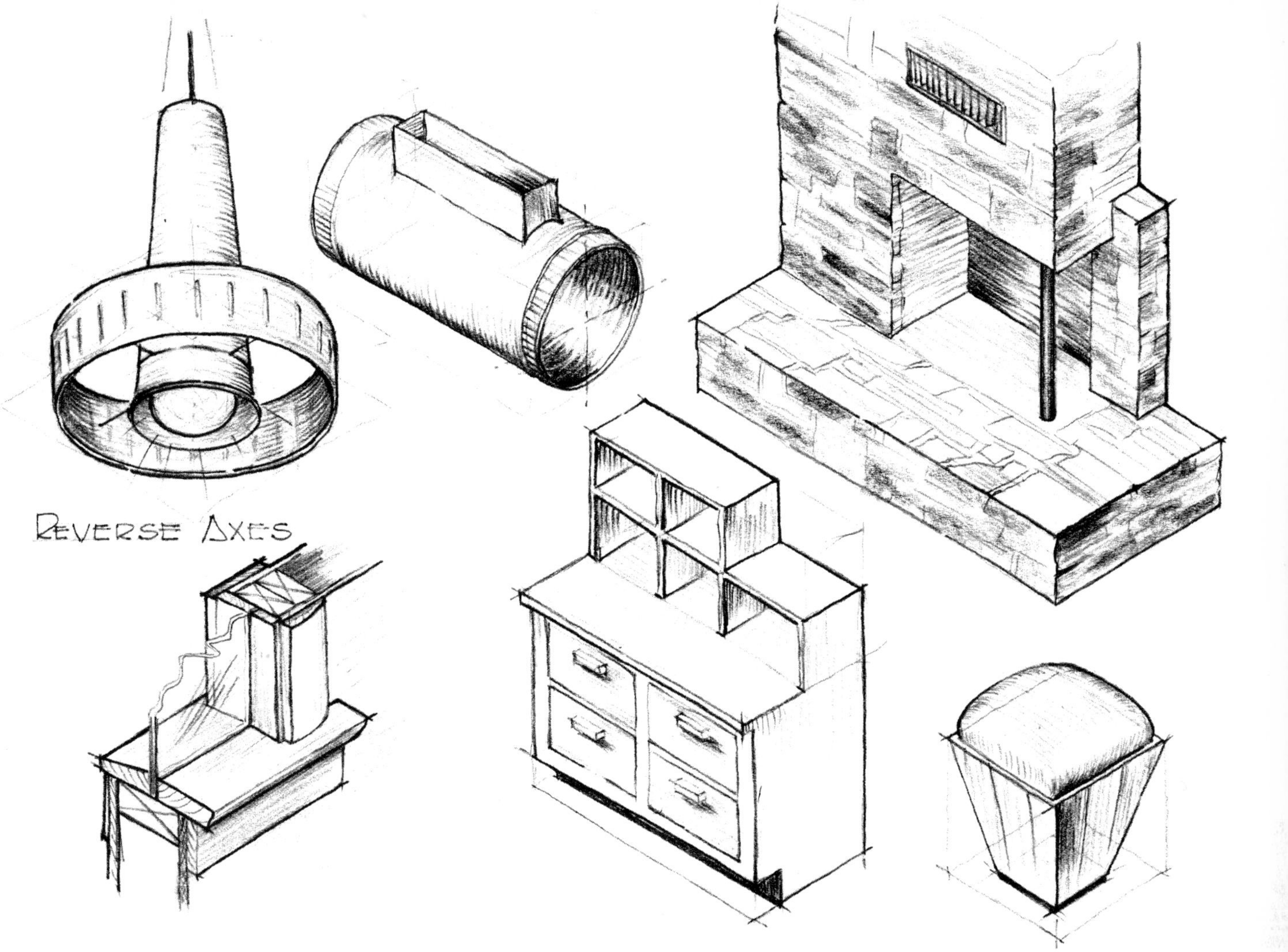

Fig. 5-31 Isometric sketches.

Fig. 5-32 A perspective layout using a plan and elevation view.

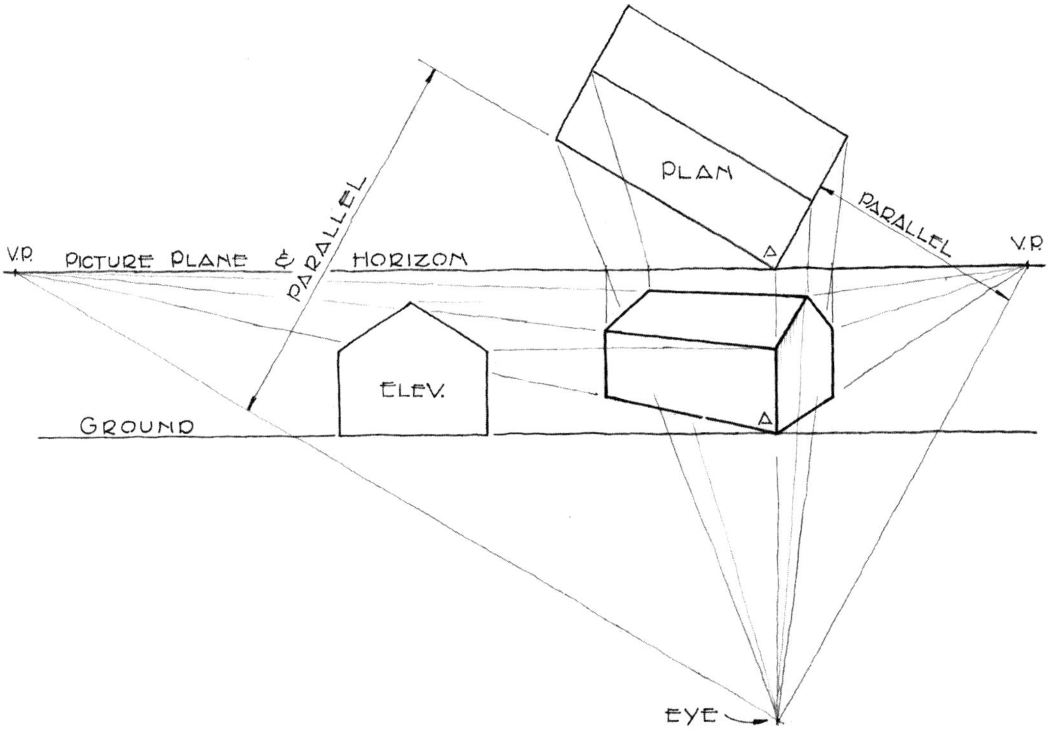

horizon line on the drawing, a structure will appear to have been viewed from either a raised or lowered position. Usually the sketch is made with the natural height of observation in mind: about 6′ high, the height of a person's eye above the ground.

In sketching a thumbnail perspective, vanishing points and proportion are usually arrived at by eye; in fact, the points are commonly omitted except in early exercise sketches because the eye soon becomes trained to establish their correct position and horizon level mentally. Often the points do not fall within the confines of the paper.

Early exercises should consist of simple block studies as shown in Figs. 5-33 and 5-34. Basic building forms and shapes with a minimum of detail should be sketched in various positions until they look realistic; then more complex shapes can be attempted.

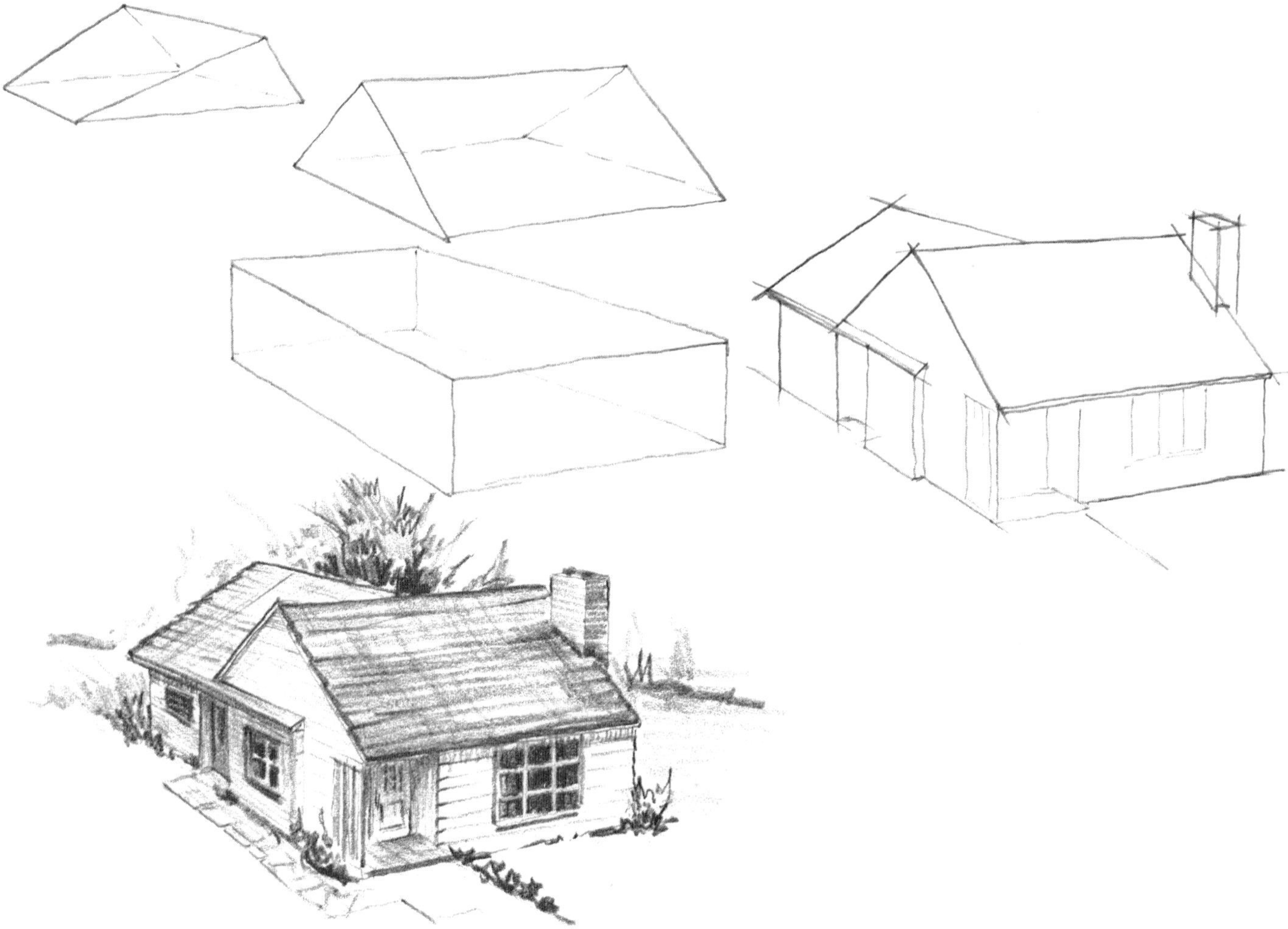

Fig. 5-33 The basic geometric forms in a perspective sketch.

Fig. 5-34 Blocking-in forms to get proportion.

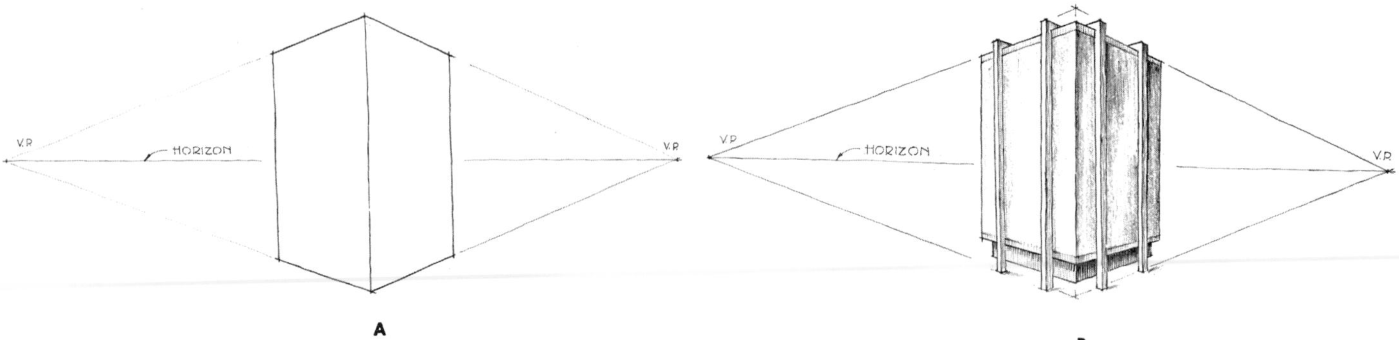

A

B

It will be beneficial at this point to turn to Chapter 12 and study the principles of perspective drawing. A background in the theory of perspective projection will definitely be helpful in learning to sketch freehand perspectives. Generally the angular-type perspective, as shown in Fig. 5-35, is appropriate for small, planning-stage sketches.

For sketches of interiors, the 1-point parallel perspective, shown in Fig. 5-37, is adequate for most situations.

In general, follow these simple steps in sketching thumbnail perspectives of architectural subjects:

STEP NO. 1. Draw a vertical line to represent the closest vertical corner of the building. On this line, assume a sense of vertical scale by stepping off equal divisions of, say 5′, to any height needed for the building. The divisions can be actually about ½″, 1″, or any similar length, depending upon the desired size of the finished sketch.

STEP NO. 2. At a point near 6′ high (height of the average man) on the vertical line, sketch a horizontal line across the paper to represent the horizon (see Fig. 5-35). Occasionally, the appearance of the building will be improved by raising the horizon line to more than 6′; however, avoid placing it at a level coinciding with major roof lines or other important horizontal features of the building.

STEP NO. 3. Establish vanishing points on the horizon line by trial (see Fig. 5-36). Place the points on the horizon line well out beyond the area for the intended building, so that the receding lines from the vertical forecorner will result in realistic forms.

STEP NO. 4. From the vertical line, sketch a

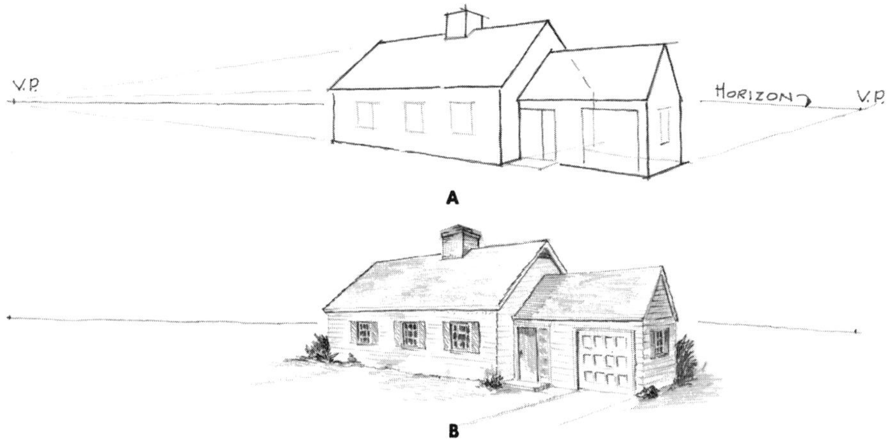

Fig. 5-35 Blocking-in residential forms.

Fig. 5-36 Vanishing points too close together produce a distorted appearance.

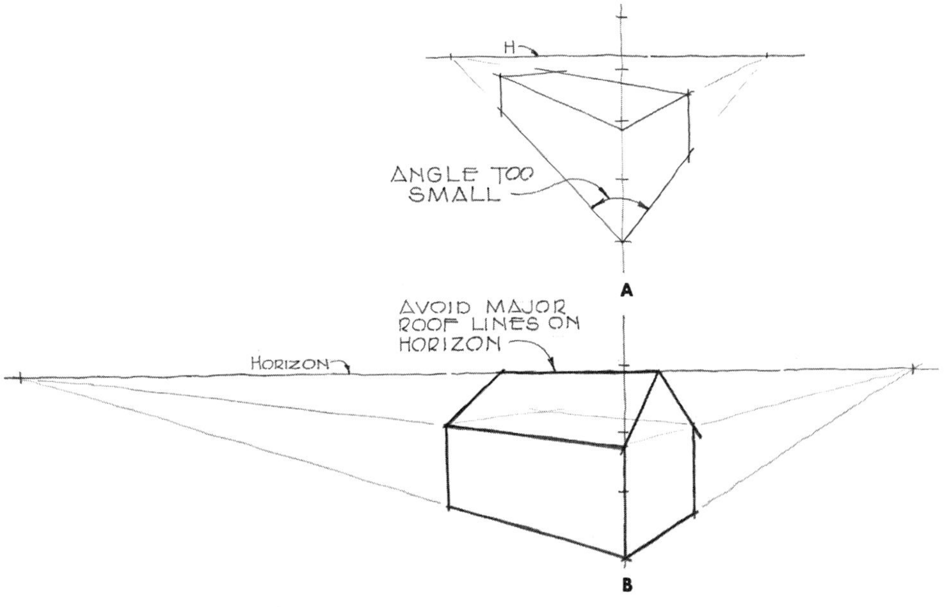

trial block of the general size and proportion of the building. The scale of the plan can be taken from the vertical line, but depth proportions become smaller as they recede from the viewer. If the basic block does not appear to have the desired shape, move the vanishing points to new locations on the horizon line. Even the horizon can be moved to create more desirable appearances. A few trials will produce the correct construction for the building. Wall lines of the block must converge at their respective vanishing points; and care should be taken to avoid a sharp angle formed by the receding walls at the bottom of the forecorner (see Fig. 5-36). If the building is a house with a gable or hip roof, block in the entire height of the roof at the ridge height; use the ground line as the bottom of the block.

STEP NO. 5. Develop the irregularities and offsets of the building, using the basic block as a cage or framework. Symmetry can be maintained with the proper use of center lines. Remember that similar features will appear wider near the observer than they will farther away. Depth proportions are established by eye so that the entire sketch maintains a satisfactory appearance.

To simplify beginning perspective sketches, grid sheets are available that can be placed under tracing paper when sketching. These sheets or charts are laid out for various angles of view, and the grids eliminate the need for establishing vanishing points. A suitable scale is adopted to establish the basic block of the sketch; after this appears to be correct, the details are added with grid lines serving as a guide for receding lines.

Interior sketches are started with an orthographic rectangular view of the facing wall (see Fig. 5-37), inasmuch as we will be looking directly into the wall if we sketch a parallel perspective sketch. The height of the rectangle on the vertical plane can be considered to be the standard 8′ ceiling height, for convenience, and the length is made accordingly. For example, if the wall is 16′ long, it is drawn twice as long as whatever height we have made the 8′ ceiling. Place a vanishing point about 6′ high near the center of the rectangle. Sidewall lines are drawn from the corners of the rectangle outward. Notice that the sidewall lines, if extended into the rectangle, converge at the vanishing point. All lines that are perpendicular to the picture plane converge at this point. Heights of relative features are horizontal on the facing wall and can be carried along the sidewalls as long as they vanish toward the vanishing point. This construction forms the basis for the sketch; all features such as, doors, windows, beams, furniture, etc., are added in proportion after completion of the basic room interior.

Fig. 5-37 Interior sketch using 1-point perspective.

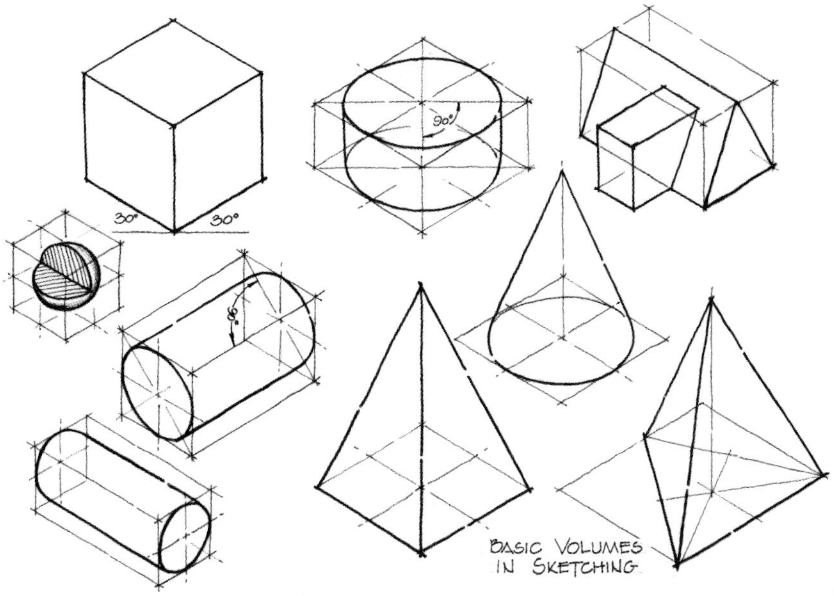

Fig. 5-38 Basic isometric forms.

Fig. 5-39 Shading of basic forms and masses found on sketches.

5.11 SHADING PICTORIAL SKETCHES

A limited amount of shading on pictorial sketches adds to the effect of realism, although only lines may define the limits of a 3-dimentional object. Shading also makes interpretation much simpler for the untrained person, and therefore its use is justified. A few major points seem appropriate here for the purpose of improving sketching technique, but, it would be best to first refer to Chapter 12, under shades and shadows, for projection principles.

The observation of light as it affects the images of objects is especially helpful to students when learning to add shading to their sketches. Without light we would see nothing; light, therefore, must be considered if we are to represent a 3-dimensional object realistically.

The light source is generally regarded as coming from an upper-left position, slightly in front of the object. We can think of the source as coming over our left shoulder as we work on the sketch. The top of our object, then, would be the lightest in value or tone, since it receives the most intense light; the front side would have a lesser value, and the right side would appear darkest (see Fig. 5-39). Also, reflected light plays on the sides of an object and must be shown. For that reason, surfaces are not usually shaded with a monotone over their entire area; generally, a graduating shade is more effective.

Highlights, which appear entirely white, are the result of direct reflection of the light source from a surface into our eyes. These white areas play an important part in representing the character of each surface and, therefore, should be handled carefully (see Fig. 5-39, which

Fig. 5-40 A quick thumbnail perspective sketch.

shows the nature of highlights on basic forms). Usually it is advisable to omit the highlight in small areas until the shading is complete; then the exact shape of the highlight is rubbed out with an eraser. Overhangs and undercuts, as well as holes and recesses, require the use of shadows to reveal their relief and give them emphasis. Cylindrical surfaces must be made to appear round by applying a parallel highlight slightly to the side of the light source, and darker tones near their receding edges.

Light patterns created by strong sunlight on outdoor subjects require more contrast at the shadows than interior subjects.

Contrast can be a useful tool for emphasizing important features on a sketch. When a white area and an extremely dark tone are placed adjacent to each other, the contrast provides a definite emphasis at their junction and gives the impression of bringing the white area forward. This quality is helpful in obtaining 3-dimensional effects, especially when adjoining surfaces form abrupt intersections. Remember that shading indications merely supplement the outlines of the sketch and should not be overdone, nor should they produce conflicting geometric shapes which interfere with the important features of the drawing.

An example of good shading technique, made with careful pencil strokes, is shown in Fig. 5-39. Darker tones of the shade are made with wide strokes spaced closely together and with considerable pressure on the pencil. Lighter tones are produced with fine lines spaced farther apart, and the lines are usually feathered out at their ends. Shade lines should reveal the basic form of the surface they represent—straight lines on flat planes and curved lines on curved surfaces. Other shading techniques, such as a series of dots, or smudging, can be employed to depict definite surface textures; smudge tones give the impression of a smooth, satiny surface, whereas dots appear to represent a rough texture. See Chapter 13, Section 13.4, for further information on pencil rendering.

5.12 SKETCHING WITH THE FELT-TIP PEN

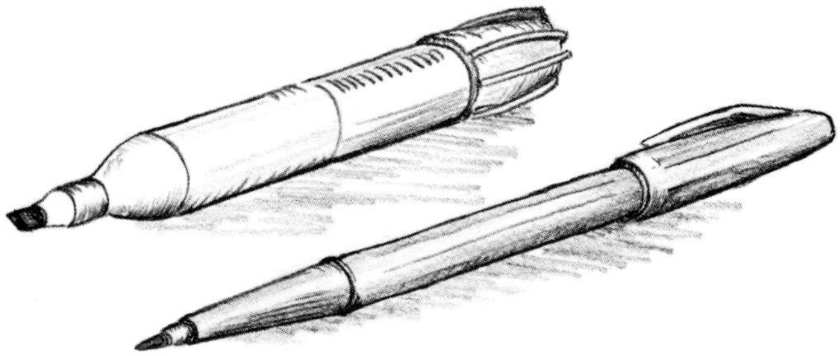

Fig. 5-41 Many types of felt-tip pens with chisel or pointed tips are available for sketching.

Many architects now use the felt-tip pen on tracing paper for quick sketches that can be reproduced if necessary like working drawings. The pens are convenient and responsive, lending themselves to many architectural subjects. They are economical and easily available in most stationery and drafting supply stores. Many stores carry a full line of colors as well as black. Their only drawback for the student is that the lines are positive and cannot be erased like pencil lines. For that reason, use the felt tip only after you have gained confidence with the pencil, or lay out the principle lines of the sketch with pencil first before completing the drawing with the pen.

Several types of tips are available, but the most popular are the *cone* and *chisel* points (see Fig. 5-41). The cone point is best for outlines and finer detail requiring uniform width lines, whereas the chisel is more versatile and allows different width lines with the use of the corner, edge, or the broadside for flat sweeps when larger areas need to be covered. Various pressures also produce different widths with either point. Experiment with the chisel point by holding it in different ways to see the many free-flowing lines that are possible.

Avoid using the felt-tip pen on porous paper since the ink will blot and spread throughout the paper. On some thin papers the ink may soak completely through and even stain paper below. A sized paper should be used; as previously mentioned, tracing paper is very satisfactory.

Keep the pens tightly capped when not in use or they will soon dry out. Rather than trying to revive a dried out point, you will find that it is usually better to discard it. Points, however, can be redressed with a razor blade should they become worn and blunt from repeated use.

After you have tried a few felt-tip sketches, it will be evident that they take on their own definite character, different from other mediums. Black linework combined with bold areas of soft gray or very light tan produces interesting architectural combinations. Bright colors should be avoided. Often masses of foliage can be stroked with bold sweeps and the edges of the masses given repeating, character lines with the fine point to quickly represent landscaping. The pen is also well-adapted to masses of light and shadow on buildings (see Figs. 5-42 and 5-43).

Fig. 5-42 Sketch done with the felt-tip pen.

Fig. 5-43 Interior sketch with the felt-tip pen.

Fig. 5-44 Making a mat and mounting a small drawing.

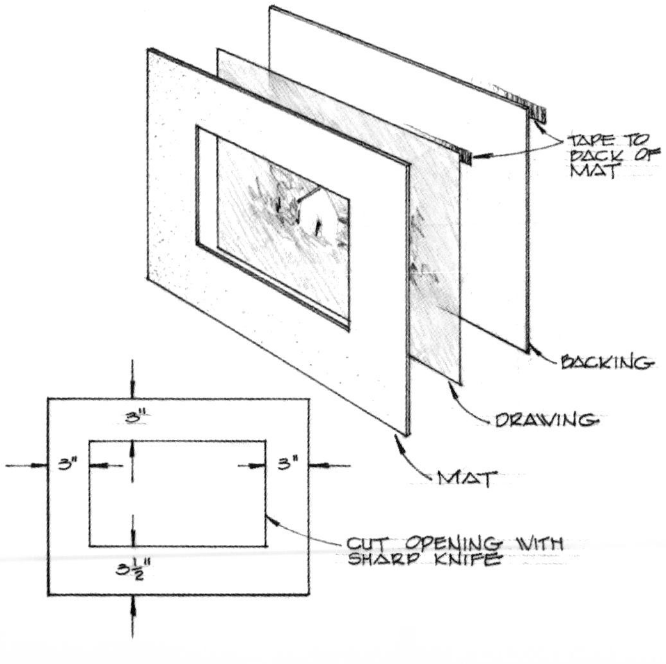

Black line sketches on tracing paper can be easily mounted over colored board so the tint shows through, and then framed with a white mat to dramatize or display the sketch if necessary (see Fig. 5-44).

SKETCHING EXERCISES

1. On 8½" × 11" drawing paper lay out a border and divide the paper into twelve equal rectangles freehand, as shown in Fig. 5-45. With an HB pencil carefully fill the rectangles with horizontal, vertical, and inclined lines as shown.

2. Sketch a 3" square and bisect each side by eye. Connect the points to form an inverted square

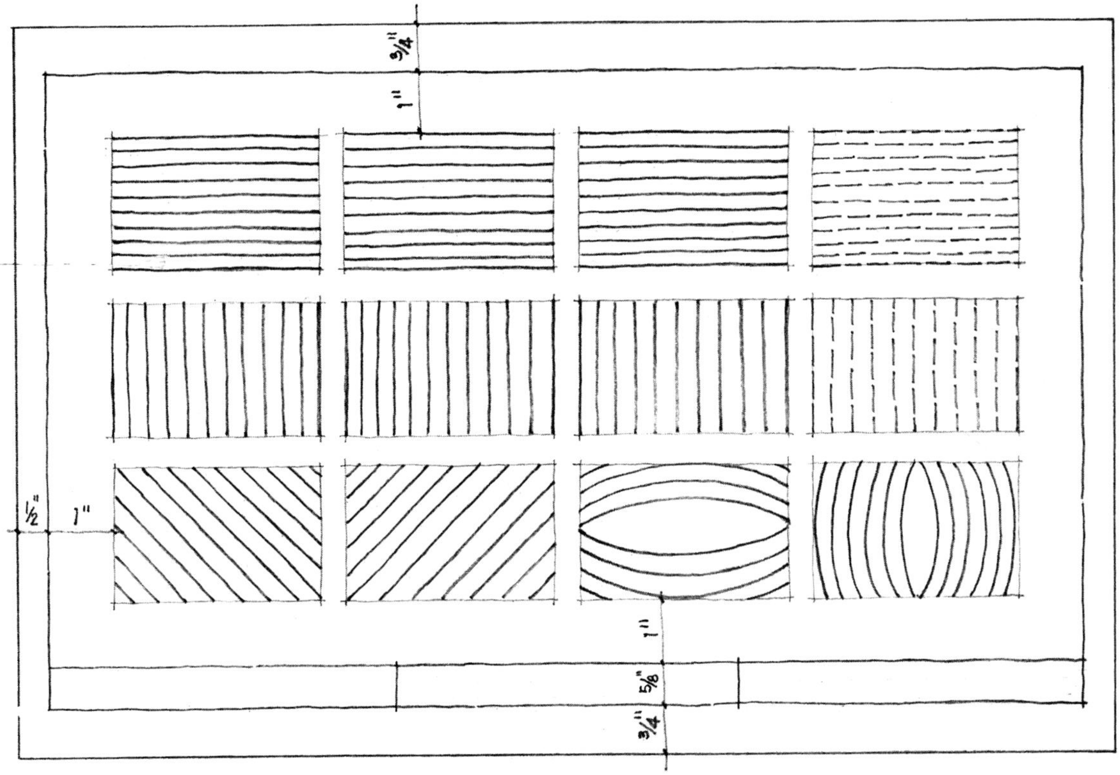

Fig. 5-45 Layout of sketching exercises.

within the original, as shown in Fig. 5-46; continue drawing squares within squares until the space is filled.

3. Sketch Fig. 5-20, showing the angle-iron assembly.

4. Sketch a section view of an I beam as shown in Fig. 5-20.

5. Sketch four $1\frac{1}{4}''$ squares and draw circles within each (Fig. 5-13).

6. Sketch an ellipse as shown in Fig. 5-17, major axis 3″, minor 2″.

7. Sketch the corrugated metal sections, Fig. 5-19.

8. Sketch the lamp, Fig. 5-22.

9. Sketch three orthographic views of the sheet-metal boot in Fig. 5-31.

10. Sketch the box sill section, Fig. 5-26A.

11. On coordinate paper sketch the floor plan shown in Fig. 5-50.

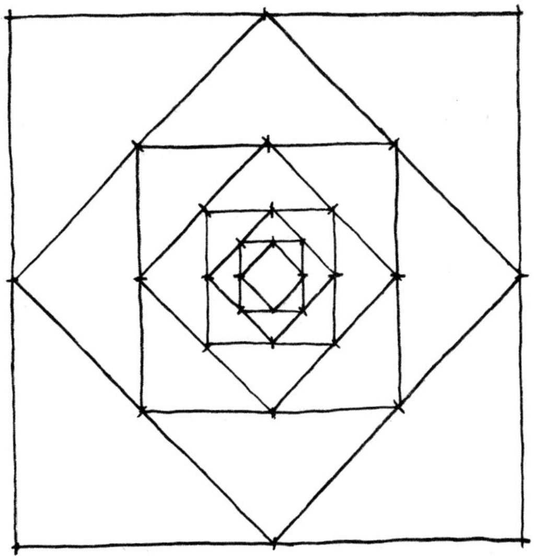

Fig. 5-46 Sketching exercise.

12. On coordinate paper sketch the front elevation shown in Fig. 5-50.

13. On $8\frac{1}{2}'' \times 11''$ drawing paper sketch the basic isometric shapes, Fig. 5-38.

14. Sketch the fireplace in an isometric view, Fig. 5-31C.

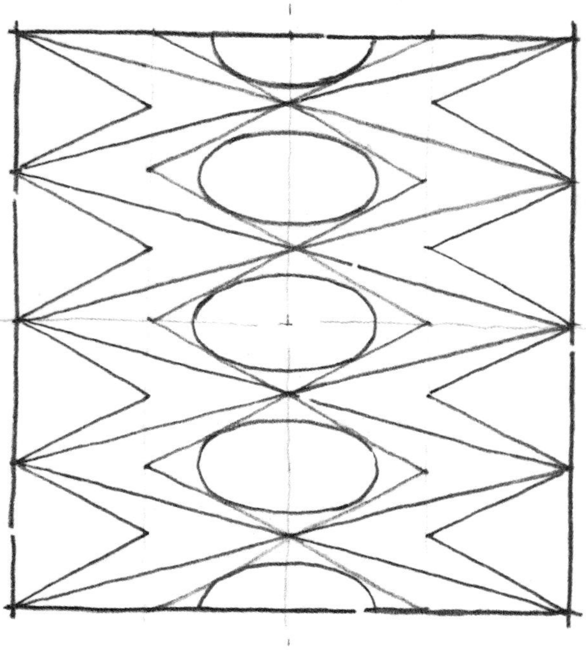

Fig. 5-47 Sketching exercise.

Fig. 5-48 Sketching exercise.

Fig. 5-49 Sketching exercise.

15. Make an isometric sketch of the lamp, Fig. 5-22.

16. Sketch an isometric section view of Fig. 5-25A.

17. Sketch a small object of your choice in an isometric rendition.

18. Make a perspective sketch of the piece of furniture, Fig. 5-23.

19. Make a perspective sketch of the small house, Fig. 5-50.

20. Make a perspective sketch of a small home from a magazine.

REVIEW QUESTIONS

1. Why does ability in sketching require a strong sense of observation?

2. Explain the "structural" or "skeleton" method of developing a sketch.

3. Why is a sketching subject reduced to its simplest geometric forms in organizing the sketch and the details drawn later?

4. What type of practice sketches should precede pictorial sketches?

5. Which simple geometric form aids in establishing proportion?

6. Why do architectural draftsmen prefer to do their sketching on inexpensive tracing paper?

7. For what reason is sketching a necessary part of draftsmanship training?

8. What is meant by a "schematic" sketch of a floor plan?

9. Why is the use of coordinate paper underlays especially helpful in sketching floor plans?

10. In perspective sketching, why may it be necessary to try several basic-block forms before arriving at suitable vanishing points when drawing a building?

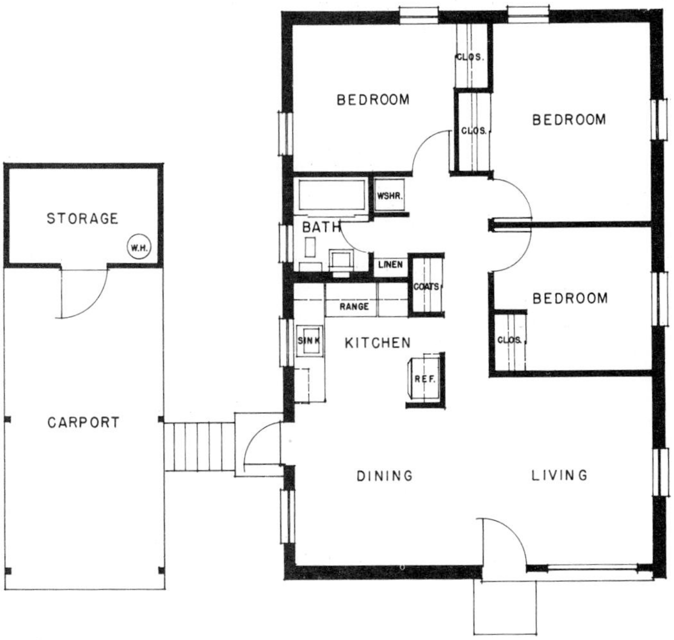

Fig. 5-50 Sketching exercise.

FLOOR PLAN

"The beautiful is as useful as the useful. More so perhaps."—Hugo

6

Basic Residential Planning

Because of the universal interest and the various aspects involved in home planning, the house is the most appropriate starting problem for students. It is appropriate, not only because nearly everyone has been subjected to either the good or the bad qualities of residential planning at one time or another and has formed various opinions of his own, but because the principles of good residential planning can be adapted to many of the other types of structures.

The successful design of buildings requires a deep insight about abstract design, the many construction methods, factors of cost, and even human psychology—all are important; and few individuals are generously gifted with such varied qualifications. However, the draftsman who can grasp the basic planning principles as he works on the drawing board has a definite advantage, whether he contributes creatively or not. Minor decisions must continually be made during the development of working drawings. Prudent decisions reflect the draftsmen's background and will certainly contribute to his advancement. Planning also provides an insight into the real meaning of "architecture" and challenges the ultimate thinking ability of the student. Good planning should start with correctly sized and oriented living spaces.

6.1 USE A PLANNING CHECKLIST

One of the inevitable aspects of residential planning is the unlimited variety of tastes and needs of different individuals. Almost every planning job brings together dissimilar combinations of these aspects. Realistic planning often becomes a matter of compromise—choosing between features which will genuinely contribute to the livability of the plan and those which the client feels he would like to have. Occasionally, choices are difficult to resolve. Within the limits of the budget, the custom-designed home should be a representation of the tastes and needs of the occupants, and it should please them. The role of the designer often becomes that of an arbitrator with a practical-minded attitude, yet one with a flair for individuality, if he is to be successful. He must be able to reconcile the special requests of individuals with their actual needs and come up with satisfying solutions. As a rule this is not easy. His first step, then, must be a definite understanding of the tastes and needs of the client. To be certain that no important details have been overlooked or forgotten, a procedure must be followed which helps to organize these requirements before planning is started. One of the simplest methods for this purpose is a *checklist* similar to the following:

PLANNING CHECKLIST

1. SITE:
   - _______ Size of lot
   - _______ Shape of lot
   - _______ Type of contours (level, slope to rear, slope to front, slope to side)
   - _______ Utilities available (water, electricity, gas, sewage)
   - _______ Drainage (good, poor)
   - _______ Type of trees, if any
   - _______ Direction of most desirable view
   - _______ North direction
   - _______ Convenience to schools, shopping, churches, etc.
   - _______ Satisfactory top soil

2. OCCUPANTS:
   - _______ Number and age of adults
   - _______ Number and age of boys
   - _______ Number and age of girls
   - _______ Profession of owner
   - _______ Provision for guests
   - _______ Provision for maid, if any
   - _______ Others (in-laws, etc.)
   - _______ Pets

3. INDIVIDUAL REQUIREMENTS:
   - _______ Formal entertaining
   - _______ Separate formal dining area
   - _______ Informal living areas
   - _______ Outdoor living and eating areas
   - _______ Supervised outdoor play area
   - _______ Nursery
   - _______ Recreation areas
   - _______ Hobby areas (music, sewing, woodworking, gardening, etc.)
   - _______ Study or reading areas
   - _______ Laundry area
   - _______ Screened porch or breezeway

4. GENERAL DESIGN:
   - _______ One-story ranch
   - _______ Two-story (_______ elaborate stairway)
   - _______ Split-level
   - _______ Crawl space
   - _______ Concrete slab
   - _______ Basement (_______ exterior entrance)
   - _______ Traditional exterior
   - _______ Contemporary exterior
   - _______ Type of roof
   - _______ Exterior materials (brick, clapboard, stone, board-and-batten, plywood)
   - _______ Finish floor materials
   - _______ Garage (number of cars)
   - _______ Carport (number of cars)
   - _______ Provision for eventual expansion
   - _______ Open planning

5. BUDGET RESTRICTIONS:
   - _______ Size of house in sq ft (1000 and under, 1500, 2000, 2500 and over)
   - _______ How the house is to be financed
   - _______ Number of bathrooms (tub or shower) (wall and floor material)
   - _______ Fireplaces
   - _______ Type of entrance
   - _______ Quality of interior trim

6. MECHANICAL EQUIPMENT REQUIRED:
   - _______ Central heating (warm air, hot water, radiant, heat pump, etc.)
   - _______ Air conditioning
   - _______ Washer-dryer
   - _______ Dishwasher
   - _______ Ironer
   - _______ Food freezer
   - _______ Garbage disposal
   - _______ Exhaust fans
   - _______ Water softener
   - _______ Size of hot water heater

7. STORAGE AREAS REQUIRED:
   - _______ Entrance closet
   - _______ Bedroom closets

_______ Linen closets
_______ Toy storage
_______ Kitchen equipment storage
_______ Cleaning equipment storage
_______ Tool storage
_______ China storage
_______ Gardening equipment storage
_______ Hobby equipment storage
_______ Others

6.2 DETERMINE THE COST LIMIT OF THE HOUSE BY THE BUDGET

The cost of a house should be based primarily upon the yearly income of the owner. Unless the client has a considerable amount of money for a down payment, monthly loan payments can become very difficult on a house which is overambitious. According to lending institutions, the maximum cost of a home should be based upon two, or at the very most—two and one-half, times the yearly income. For example, if a man's income is $16,000 per yr, he should build a home costing up to approximately $32,000 to $40,000. If the local cost for general residential construction is, say, $22.00 per sq ft, he then would be prudent to build a home no larger than 1500 to 1800 sq ft in size. Because the cost per square foot varies so widely in different areas of the country, home building costs must be based on local conditions. Local contractors or architects should be consulted for local construction costs.

For the average family the cost of a new home represents the most important investment they will make. About 20 percent of the annual budget can be spent for shelter. Usually only one or two homes are purchased during an entire lifetime, and each purchase should be made wisely. Life in the most pleasantly designed home can soon lose its luster if the occupants are overburdened with financial worries.

6.3 REVIEW THE RESTRICTIONS AND LEGAL ASPECTS OF THE LOT

First, make a thorough investigation of the property upon which the house is to be built. If possible, check for any restrictions created by easements; acquaint yourself with the zoning regulations of the property. All legal restrictions must be carefully followed. *Easements* are the legal means by which a party other than the owner has been given access or certain rights to the property for various reasons. Utility companies have easements on property in many areas. For example, if electric power lines run across a piece of property, the power company no doubt has an easement on the property for the explicit purpose of running and maintaining the lines. The right is irrevocable and must be honored by the owner and future owners. Occasionally easements are granted to individuals for trespass privileges on property and must be honored as well.

Zoning regulations or ordinances, usually binding to residential property, restrict the minimum size of a dwelling which can be put on a lot in a given area. These restrictions protect property owners from encroachment of undesirable structures, which might devaluate surrounding property values. From the standpoint of future resale of a house, it is wise to neither overbuild nor underbuild in a restricted area; it is advisable to maintain a consistent quality in keeping with neighboring homes. Overbuilding simply means the construction of a much larger or more expensive house than those in the immediate area, whereas underbuilding is the reverse—building a house much smaller or one in a lower price bracket than surrounding homes. Ordinances usually restrict the placement of a house on a lot (setback from the street as well as the side lot lines).

Of course, it is taken for granted that all conditions of lot selection, such as availability of utilities, convenience to shopping centers, schools, churches, transportation, and suitable zoning regulations have been considered by the prospective home builder. The selection of the lot and an investigation of the clear-title legality of the deed (usually done by title guarantee companies) are the responsibility of the owner.

If possible, make a personal inspection of the lot. No written description is as valuable as first-hand observation of the property.

A "plat," which is a graphic description of a subdivision or tract of land, is on file in county or city land registering offices. The plat and a written description constitute the legal documents of the property. Photostats of registered plats may be obtained by the landowner for a small fee. The usual registered-plat drawing (Fig. 6-1) contains the following information: name of subdivision, district or section, county or city, state, north-point arrow, scale,

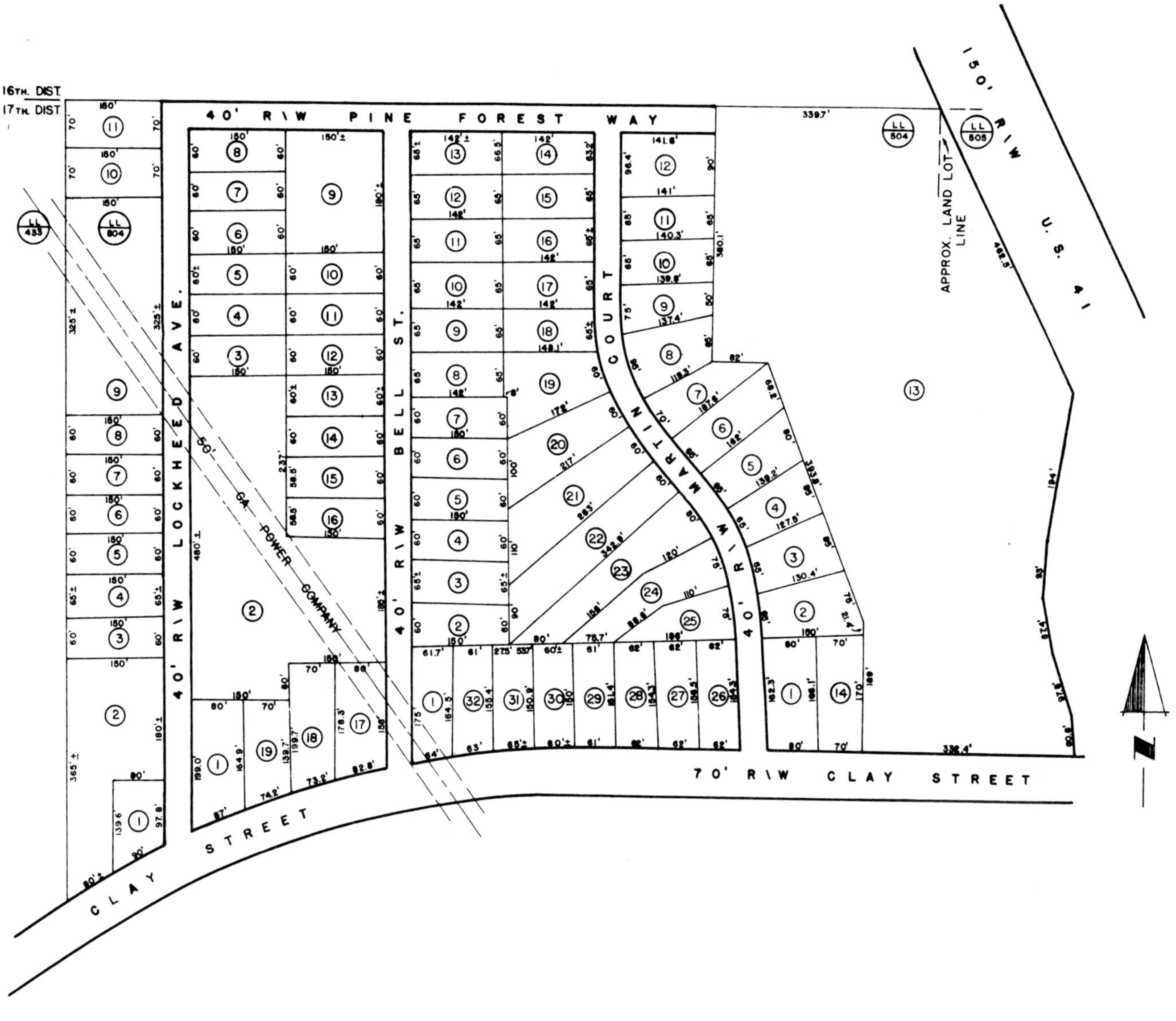

Fig. 6-1 A plat map of a residential subdivision.

name and width of all streets, bearing of street lines, lot lines, lot dimensions and numbers, description of any easements, setback lines, utility mains, protective covenants, references to adjoining property, and certification as to the correctness of the plat by a registered land surveyor. Although the name is similar, a plat should not be confused with a "plot plan," which will be described later with working drawings. The plot plan is drawn by the draftsman to show the exact placement of the structure on the property, but it does not become part of the property's legal description.

Linear measurements describing the boundaries of land are usually given in feet and decimals of a foot carried to two places, such as 87.41′, 264.92′, etc. Bearing angles are indicated in degrees and minutes from either north or south, whichever results in the smaller angle, such as N31° 17′E, S24° 45′W, etc. Land surface heights shown on plats or survey maps can be either distances in feet above sea level, or they can be distances above or below local permanent datum points, called "bench marks." Either method is satisfactory for indicating various land surface heights.

Prior to construction planning, owners often have survey maps made of their property by a registered land surveyor. A survey map (Fig. 6-2) containing *contour lines* as well as other pertinent physical descriptions of the property will help the designer orient the structure properly. Contour lines indicate the elevation variations of the property. Each contour is plotted

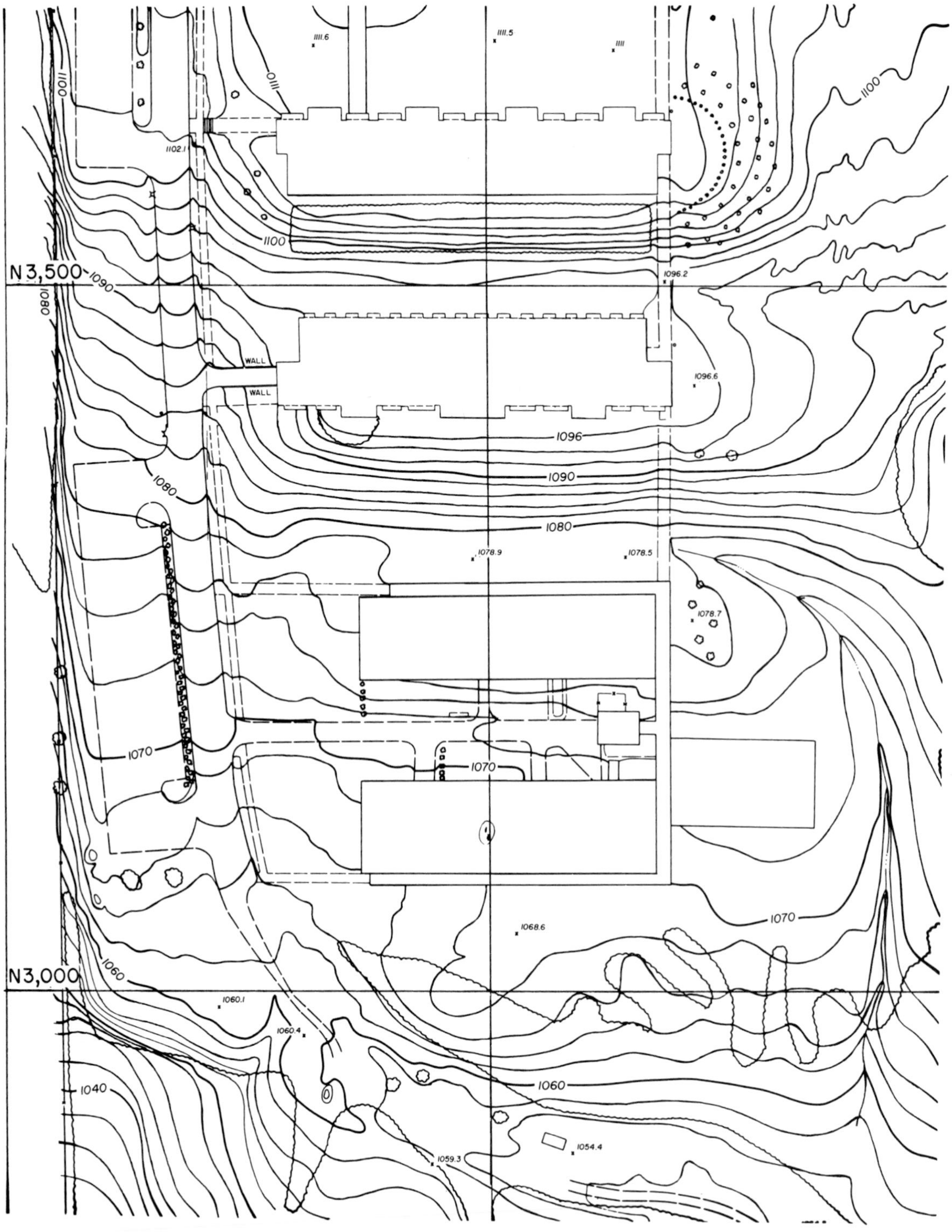

Fig. 6-2 A survey map showing the use of contour lines to indicate surface variations.

to represent similar elevations along the entire line. If one were to actually walk along a contour line, he would continually walk on the same level. The shoreline of a lake is a good example of a natural contour line. As the water's edge continues around the lake, it varies in shape and curvature depending on the nature of the terrain along the shore. If a small stream empties into the lake, the water's edge turns and follows the bed of the stream for a distance, then crosses the stream and returns toward the mouth and continues around the edge of the lake. Each contour on the ground closes on itself, such as the complete shoreline of the lake, and eventually returns to itself. This fact is not always apparent on most contour maps as the closures usually fall off the map.

Adjacent contour lines normally have similar characteristics because of natural surface formations (see Fig. 6-3). Lines close together indicate a steep rise in elevation, whereas lines farther apart indicate a more level area. Lines will not cross each other except when indicating unusual conditions such as caves or overhanging cliffs; nor will they touch each other except when a vertical wall or cliff is represented. On riverbeds, the contour lines point upstream. Figure 6-4 shows typical contour indications.

The vertical distance between contour levels is known as the "contour interval." These contour intervals are usually 2′, 5′, or 10′, depending on the scale of the map. Heights above sea level or heights above or below local datum points are usually shown along every fifth line, which is often drawn darker to facilitate identification. Because of the uneven nature of land surfaces, contour lines are generally drawn freehand on topographic maps; on plane surfaces they would appear more mechanical, and therefore are occasionally drawn with instruments.

Slopes of land surfaces or roadbeds are generally expressed in percent of grade. A slope of 5 percent, for instance, rises vertically 5′ over a horizontal distance of 100′.

$$\frac{\text{Rise}}{\text{Run}} = \text{Slope (expressed in percent)}$$

$$\frac{5}{100} = .05 = 5\%$$

Figure 6-5 shows the contour lines of a typical building lot. The contour profile of line A–A is constructed by projecting the intersections of line A–A and the contour lines that pass through it to the contour levels laid out horizontally below. If the lot is to be leveled for a more desirable construction area, finish contours would appear similar to those shown in the lower drawing. The finish profile of line B–B could be found by projecting the new contour intersections as shown. Fills and cuts are accurately defined by superimposing original and finish contour profiles. Notice that on contour maps showing required surface changes, the finish contour lines are usually made solid and the original lines where the changes occur are shown as broken lines.

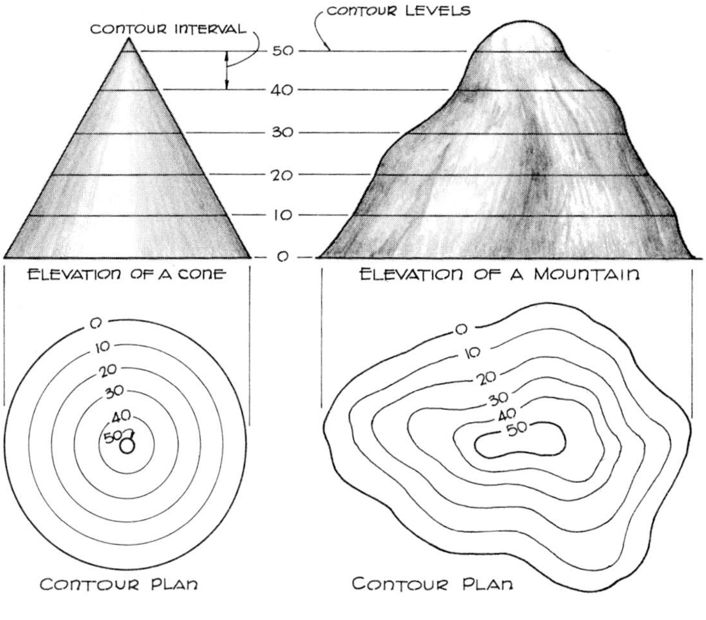

Fig. 6-3 Contour lines showing the shape of a cone and a mountain.

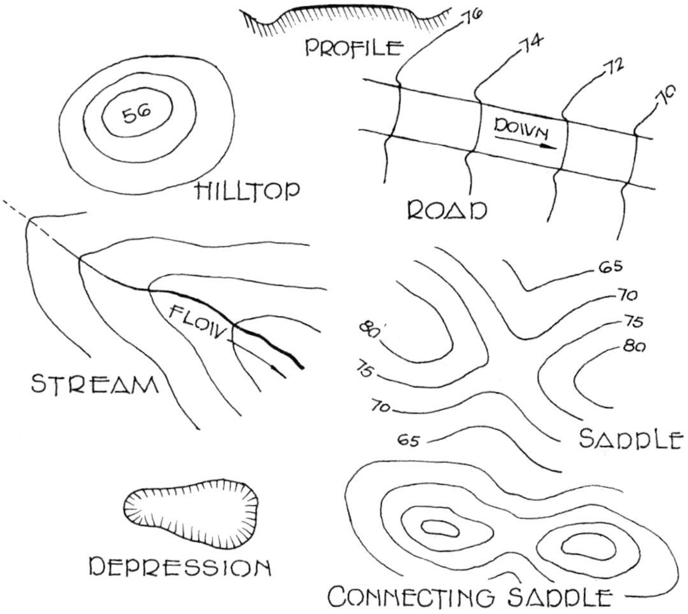

Fig. 6-4 Contour representations of various land surfaces.

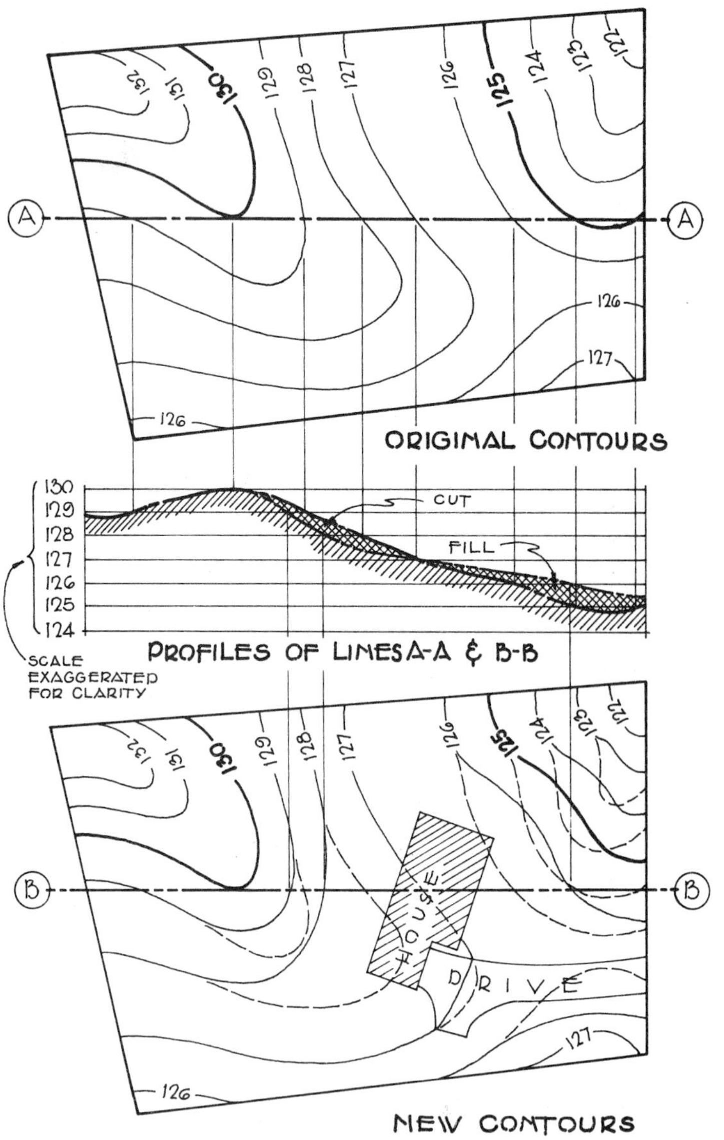

Fig. 6-5 The method of plotting a "contour profile" and of indicating new contours on plot plans.

Fig. 6-6 Layout of "row houses."

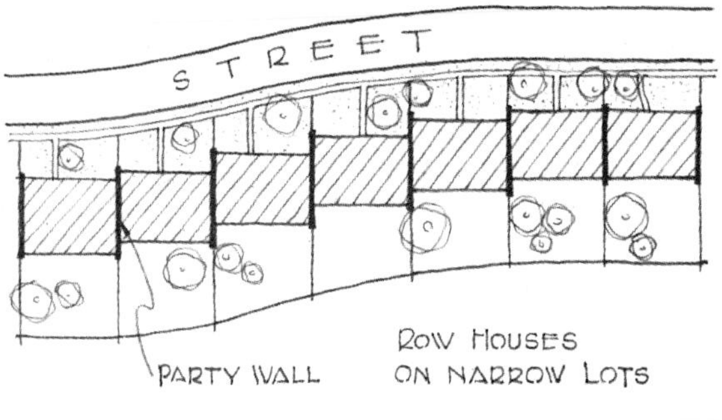

6.4 PLAN THE HOUSE TO FIT THE SITE

After reviewing the legal restrictions of the lot, analyze the natural advantages of the area so that the house will become an integral and compatible part of its environment. Study the following points for their individual adaptability:

Plan a 1-story house if you have enough space to spread out Houses on one level are easiest to build and maintain; there are no stairways that use up valuable floor space and constitute possible hazards for children and elderly people. Rambling 1-story houses are often referred to as "ranch-type" (Fig. 6-6). If the contours of the lot will accommodate offset floor levels, plan a "split-level" house (Fig. 6-7). If the space is limited, plan a 2-story house (Fig. 6-8); build up instead of out. Less roof and less foundation will make the 2-story house more economical than a 1-story of comparative size. In areas where expensive land must be divided into very narrow lots, the best solution is "row houses" (Fig. 6-9). Their party walls afford more privacy than do facing windows 10′ or so apart on adjacent conventional houses. However, row houses can be considered only in tract or subdivision planning.

Make the house part of the land By utilizing the entire lot for livability (see Fig. 6-10) even a modest size home can seem spacious if the inside is made to communicate with the exterior. Level areas adjacent to the house are the most inexpensive living space your planning can provide. If possible, open the back to private outdoor areas by the use of glass and a view—easily created with landscaping if necessary. On noisy streets, "turn your back" to the public by using few, if any, windows on the front.

Avoid excessive excavation Usually selection of the proper house type will minimize expensive excavation work. You will find that the less you disturb the natural contours of the land, the kinder Nature will be to the future inhabitants of the home (see Fig. 6-11).

Orient the house to the sun Living areas are more pleasant with southern exposures. However, not all lots can easily accommodate this favorable exposure and still provide the most desirable view. On lots with the street side facing south, a walled patio near the front of the house may be the only method of obtaining a southern exposure and privacy as well (Fig. 6-12). To gain southern exposure on other lots

Fig. 6-7 Split-level house.

Fig. 6-8 Two-story house.

Fig. 6-9 Ranch-type house.

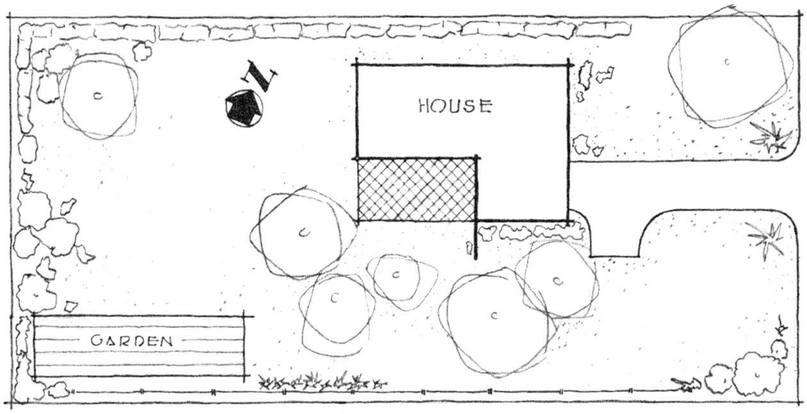

Fig. 6-10 Landscaping sketch showing good site utilization.

Fig. 6-11 Planning for minimum excavation.

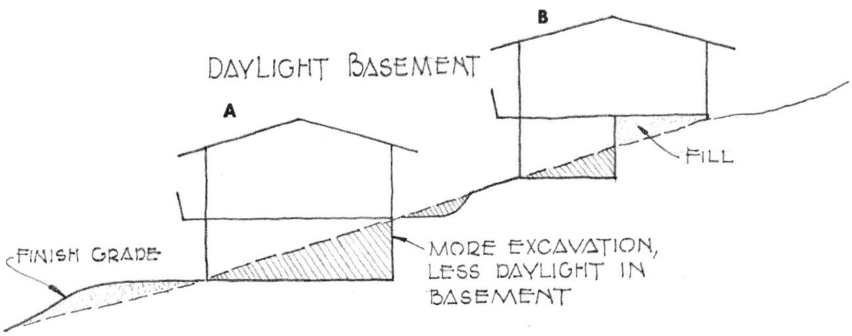

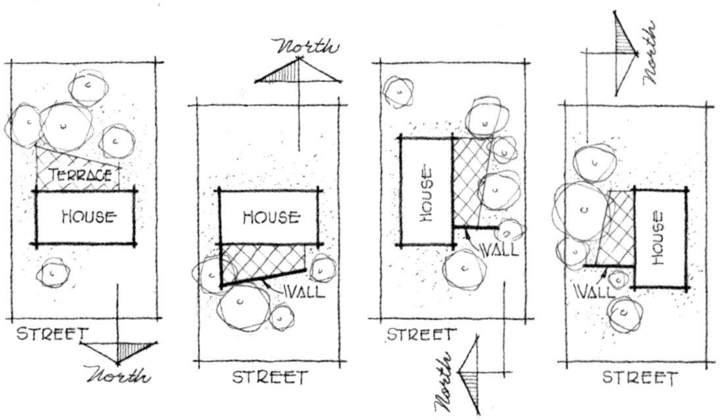

Fig. 6-12 Orienting the house to the sun.

it may become necessary to turn the plan, or place living areas on various sides of the building. With correctly designed overhangs and sunshades, window walls can harness the sun in summer and provide warmth and comfort within the house during the winter (see Fig. 6-13). Sun charts, showing exact angles of the sun throughout various times of the day and year, should be consulted for accurate solar orientation of large glass walls, especially in warm climates. Plan the roof overhangs accordingly. Sunlight in moderation can be pleasant, but in excess it can be severe and damaging.

Make maximum use of the existing trees as noise barriers and as shade producers during months of intense summer sun. Shade on a house reduces inside temperatures considerably (as much as 10°) during the summer, and reduces the maintenance of painted surfaces. Deciduous trees are especially effective; by dropping their leaves in winter, they allow desirable winter sunshine to penetrate a house when it is needed; and in summer they block the sun when it becomes destructive. For maximum utility, trees should be on the south side of the house. Evergreen trees, on the other hand, are more effective as windbreaks; they often make it possible to prolong the use of outdoor living areas well into the colder months of the year.

Consider prevailing winds By proper planning, breezes can be funneled through a house for additional comfort in warmer climates, and bitter winds can be diverted in colder climates (see Fig. 6-15).

Keep bedrooms and quiet zones isolated from noise-producing conditions. Cars, trains, play areas, etc., must be considered in house orientation.

Provide a sense of privacy from possible observers on public streets or from surrounding buildings or property. The house should be a sanctuary where the occupants can relax and feel protected.

Fig. 6-13 Harnessing the sun with overhangs for year-round comfort.

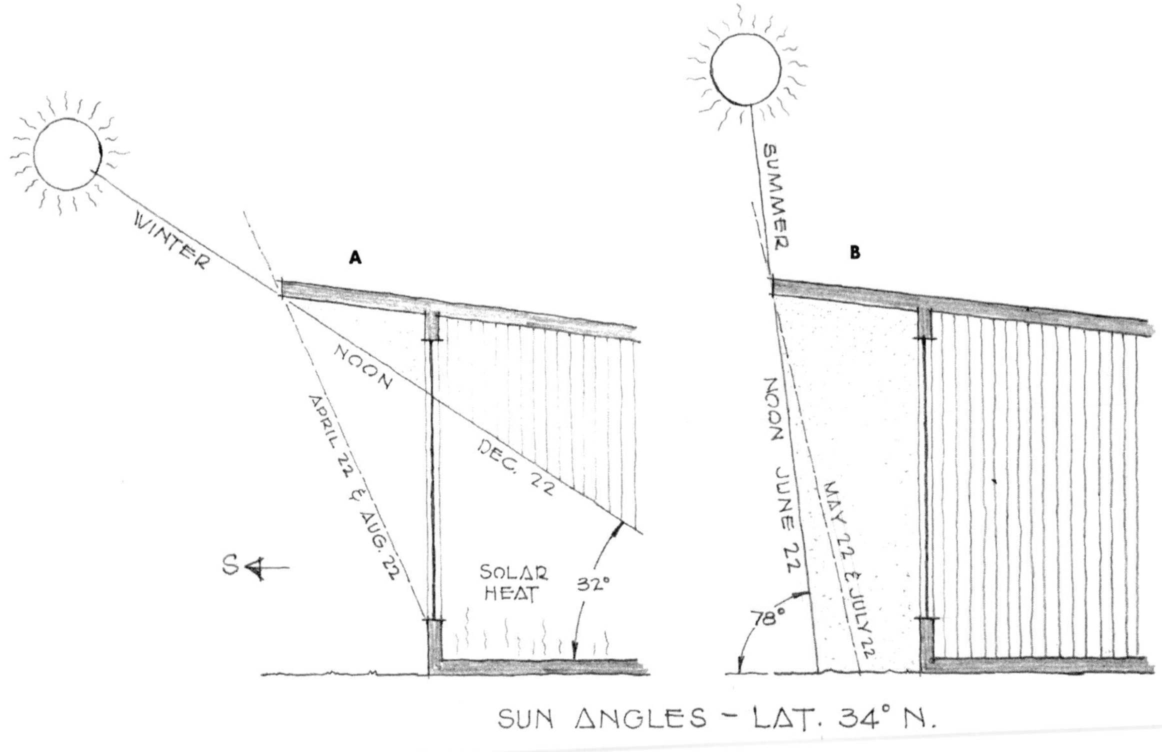

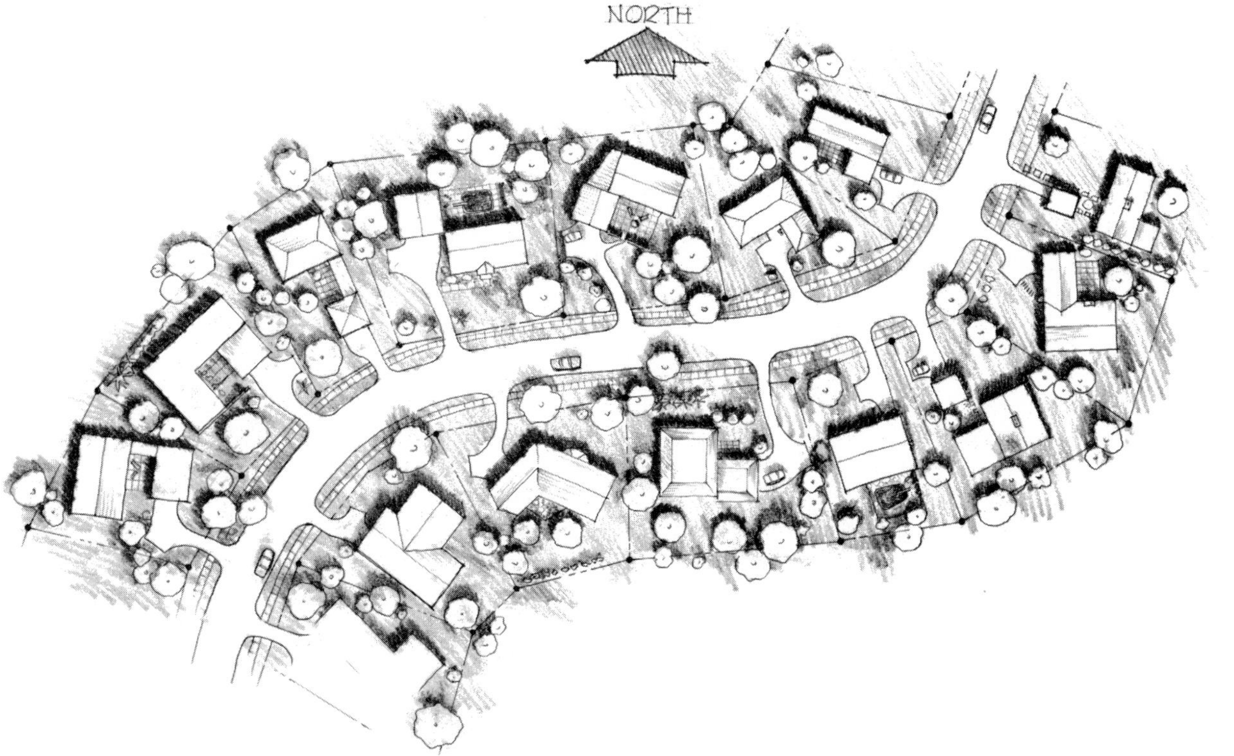

Fig. 6-14 Plan the site for interest and privacy.
1. Avoid the "lined up" look; vary the position and placement of the house on each lot.
2. Use curved streets; they prevent speeding.
3. Cut lots into a variety of shapes and sizes.
4. Curved driveways are more pleasing than straight drives.
5. Control the view from windows by planting or walls to gain privacy.
6. Place living areas on the south side if possible; avoid a western exposure.
7. Combine a variety of housing styles, some one-story, others two-story, to prevent the uniform roofline look.
8. Use deciduous trees on the south side for summer shade; use conifers for windbreaks.
9. A rolling terrain improves interest and ground-line variety.
10. Planting should be done in clusters to retain the "natural" look.
11. If possible, provide a turn-around drive so cars will not have to back out into a busy street.
12. Split-level houses should be placed on a sloping lot, a flat-roof house on a flat site.
13. Preserve natural contours to prevent harsh drainage problems.
14. Avoid high planting near intersection of driveway and street which will obstruct the view.
15. Provide greenery backgrounds for flowering shrubs.
16. Do not hide the front entrance; have planting lead the eye to the door.

6.5 CHOOSE THE MOST APPROPRIATE BASIC STRUCTURE

There are many basic structures to consider and analyze before the most suitable is decided upon. Each of the following have both advantages and disadvantages, but after considering the needs carefully, one type will prove to be the most appropriate.

One-story with a pitched roof and flat ceilings (see Fig. 6-16). This popular house type is built with conventional rafter and ceiling-joist framing methods, or the roof framing can be quickly erected with prefabricated roof trusses. It lends itself easily to prefabrication, which is gaining in acceptance throughout the United States. It also has the advantage of having its

Fig. 6-15 Using shape and orientation for natural ventilation in warmer climates.

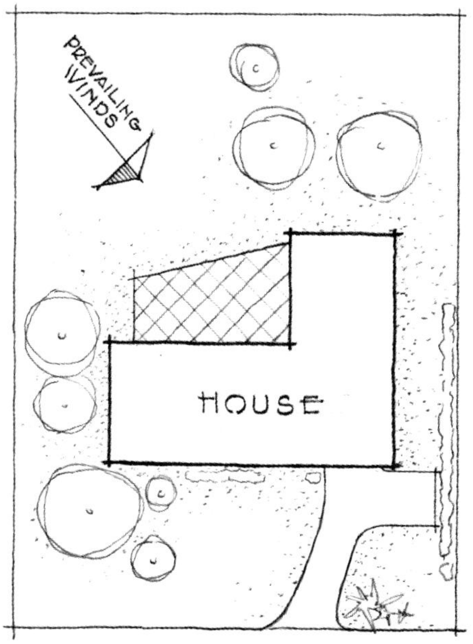

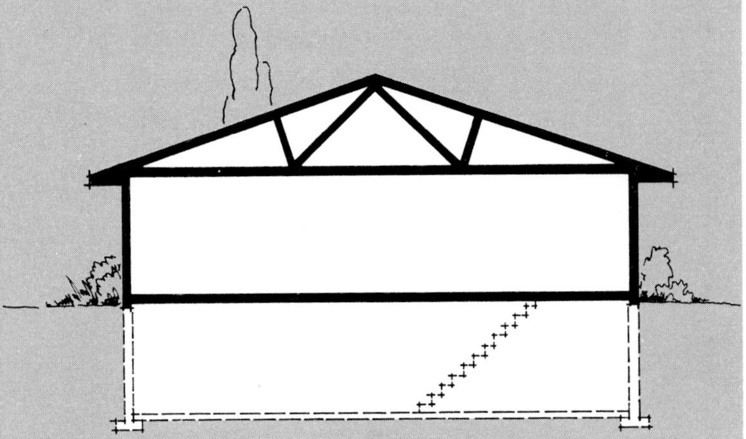

Fig. 6-16 One-story house with pitched roof and flat ceilings.

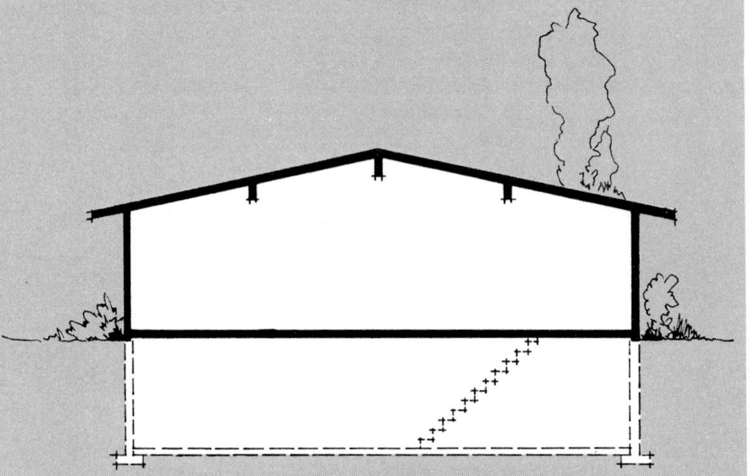

Fig. 6-17 One-story house with pitched roof and sloping ceilings.

Fig. 6-18 One-story house with a flat or shed-type roof and ceilings.

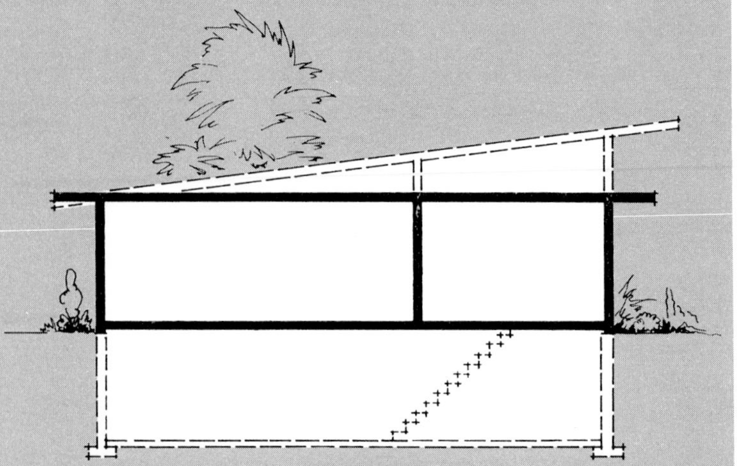

living areas on one level. This type of house can be built with or without a basement, with a crawl space, on a concrete slab, or it can be used in conjunction with multilevel designs to produce many of our traditional home styles.

One-story with a pitched roof and sloping ceilings (see Fig. 6-17). This type has evolved from the plank-and-beam type framing and its popularity is due mainly to the massive exposed beams and sloping ceiling interiors, as well as the interesting architectural effects produced by the extensions of the beams on the cornice exteriors. The type looks well with large overhangs, which produce expansive, unbroken roof lines. Many exciting examples of this structural type can be found in contemporary designs.

One-story with a flat roof and ceilings (see Fig. 6-18). With built-up roofing materials comparing favorably with conventional roofing, this type has become definitely contemporary in nature and is a very economical type of construction (the same structural members are used for both the ceiling and the roof). It requires skillful design of its elevation views to overcome a boxy appearance, and its strong horizontal roof lines often appear monotonous unless broken with offsets or various roof levels. The flat roof can be combined effectively with the shed-type roof (see dotted lines in Fig. 6-18), or it can be used with gable roofs as carports, garages, or other attached wings for variety of roof lines.

One-and-one-half-story with two living levels–less living space on the top level (see Fig. 6-19). This structural type is associated with the New England "Cape Cod" house. The basic simplicity of the true Cape Cod design should be retained, in proportion and in detail, if an approach to historical authenticity is desired. Even though the shape is traditional, many contemporary type houses have resulted from the use of the steep roof and various adaptations of the story-and-one-half principle.

Two-story with two living levels–pitched roof and flat ceilings (see Fig. 6-20). Numerous 2-story houses are rich in traditional charm. Their heritage can be captured only by the correct proportion and detail usually associated with many of the New England houses. Either gable or hip roofs of various slopes can be used with the 2-story design; often lower roofed additions to the main box seem to enhance the overall silhouette. Upper-story projections (see Fig. 10-14) not only increase the second-story living space, but tend to reduce the strong vertical appearance.

Split-level with three living levels—pitched roofs and flat ceilings (see Fig. 6-21). The majority of the comparatively new split-level type houses have three living levels and an optional basement level. All levels are connected with stair segments that combine in pairs to make one full-story height. Multilevels provide excellent zoning for different activities, and their exteriors can be given interesting variety. On sloping lots the split-level can be oriented to the site and still have full-story height exposure to outdoor living areas. Stair arrangements can become complicated, requiring considerable study to develop a successful design.

Split-level with three living levels—continuous sloping roofs and various ceilings (see Fig. 6-22). This second type of split-level is identified by low-pitched roofs (usually 2:12 or 3:12 slopes) which continue over several levels to create sloping ceilings in various upper and middle rooms. The continuous ceilings produce several ceiling heights, thereby adding interest to the interior living spaces. Roof slopes and floor levels must be carefully controlled to result in satisfactory wall heights and proper proportions. Both types of split-levels are similar in livability and popularity.

6.6 SPEND THE MOST TIME IN PERFECTING THE PLAN

Probably no other aspect of home planning plays as important a role in the character of the structure as the living patterns of the family. Design the home from the inside by starting with a good plan carefully conceived in terms of the activities of the occupants. Think of the rooms and spaces as 3-dimensional volumes as you travel from one room to another on the graphic plan. Keep the following points in mind while developing the plan with numerous preliminary sketches:

Keep the general shape of the plan simple if you are looking for economy But if vitality and appearance are more important, other shapes can add interest with some sacrifice of economy. A *square* plan offers the most economy from a standpoint of mere enclosure of a

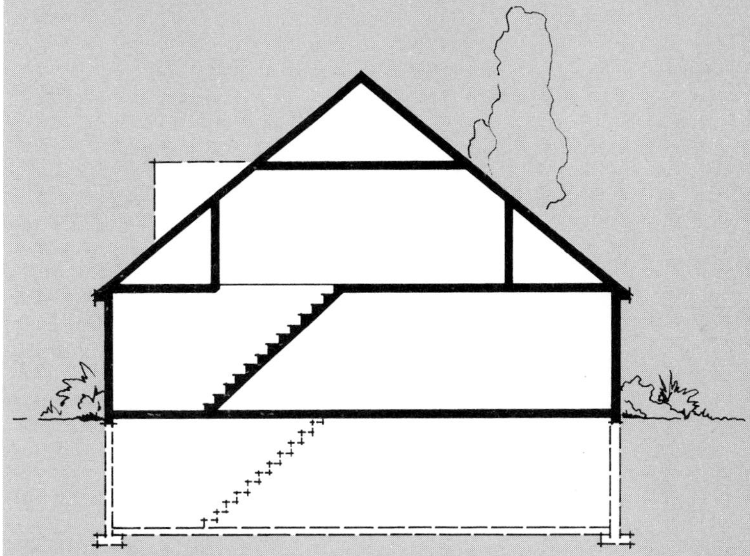

Fig. 6-19 One-and-one-half-story house with the steep roof allowing partial living space on the second level.

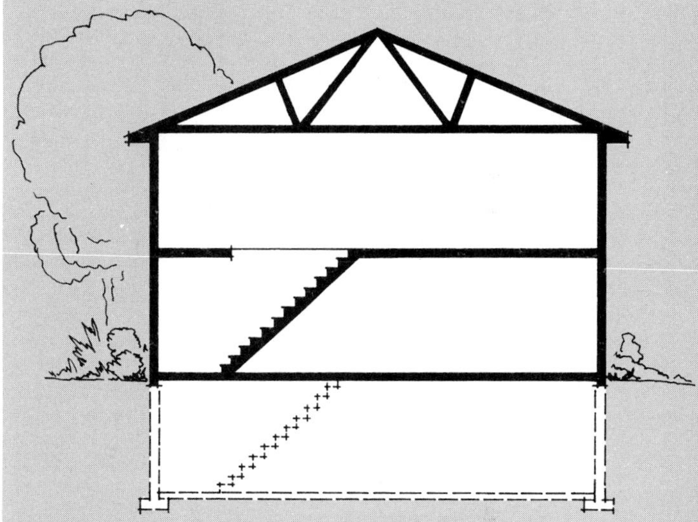

Fig. 6-20 Two-story house with a pitched roof and flat ceilings.

Fig. 6-21 Split-level house with three living levels—pitched roof and flat ceilings.

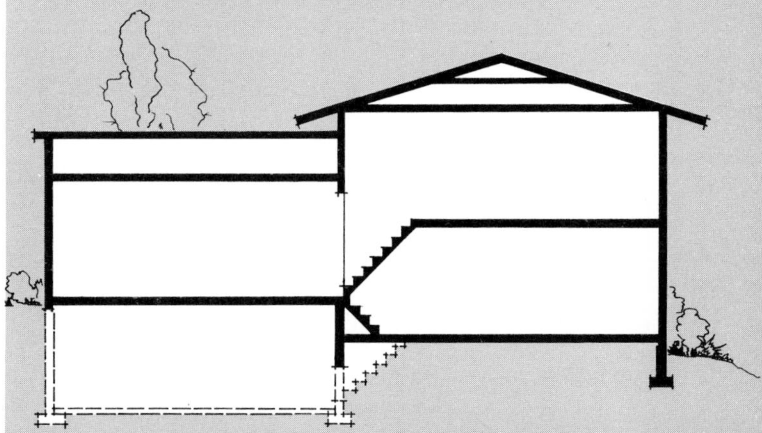

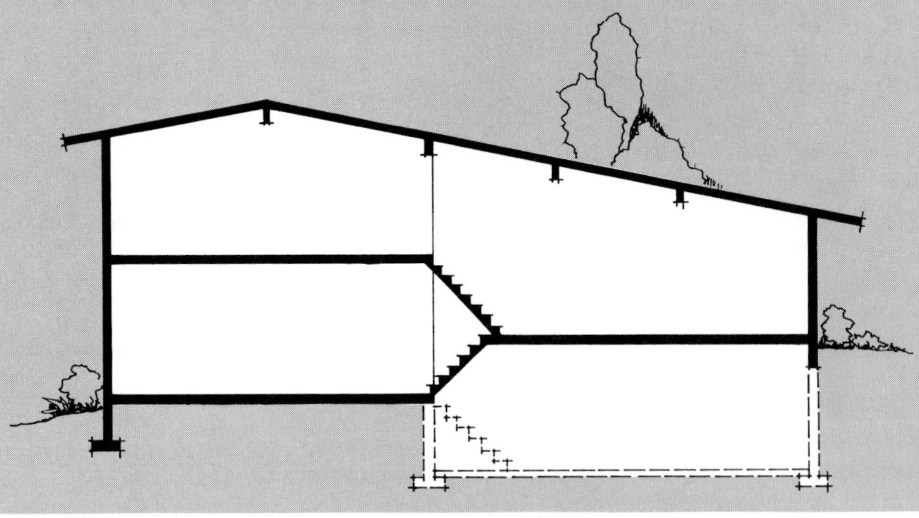

Fig. 6-22 Split-level house with three living levels—pitched roof and various ceilings.

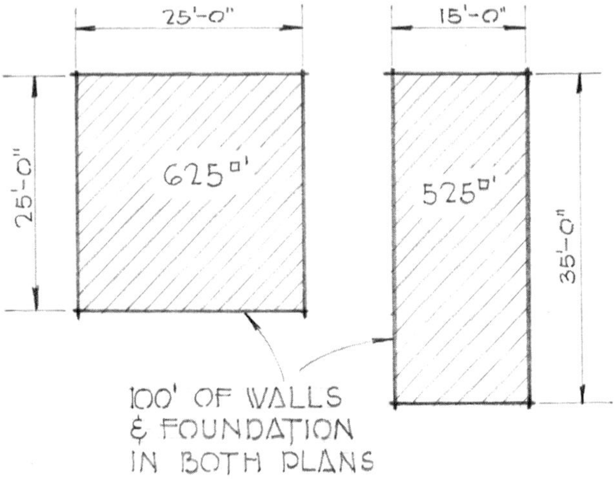

Fig. 6-23 A square plan offers the most economy.

given space (see Fig. 6-23). Notice that the square shape provides 100 additional sq ft of floor space in comparison to the rectangle having the same lineal feet of exterior walls and the same number of corners. Corners, whether inside or outside, increase the basic cost of a house. However, with the square it is difficult to provide light and ventilation to interior areas, unless the plan is small, or unless skylights have been introduced to the roof. The square is a static shape which requires skillful handling to give it interest.

The *rectangle* compromises economy with more visual interest and has become the most popular floor plan shape. Various combinations of the rectangle can be used to produce unlimited relationships of rooms and zones as well as nonmonotonous spaces and interior forms (see Fig. 6-24).

Even though it has more corners, the *L shape* (Fig. 6-25) creates interest because of the offset. This shape provides a simple means of isolating quiet zones, and hallway space can be reduced without sacrificing efficient traffic patterns. A *T-shaped* plan (Fig. 6-26) results in still more corners, but roof shapes can be combined over it for comparatively simple roof framing. Often, bedroom wings can be given isolation and cross-ventilation with this shape and yet be favorably oriented to the living spaces.

Dramatic effects can be obtained with the *U-shaped* plan (Fig. 6-27). This shape integrates itself easily with the surroundings to gain isolated outdoor living space with a minimum of fences or screens. Abundant natural light and ventilation can be provided to each room. Conversely, heating and cooling are more difficult in extreme climates, which usually makes the shape more expensive than those previously mentioned. The *H shape* (Fig. 6-28) possesses similar advantages and disadvantages to those of the U shape; often more space must be devoted to hallways and passages. This shape does not lend itself to modest homes; yet it is ideal for expandable plans. Either the H plan or the U plan requires generous lots, and, if correctly oriented, effects strong house-land relationships.

Departing from boxy shapes, the *hexagonal* or diagonal shape (Fig. 6-29) offers unusual and often distinctive patterns. These shapes were brilliantly used by the late Frank Lloyd Wright

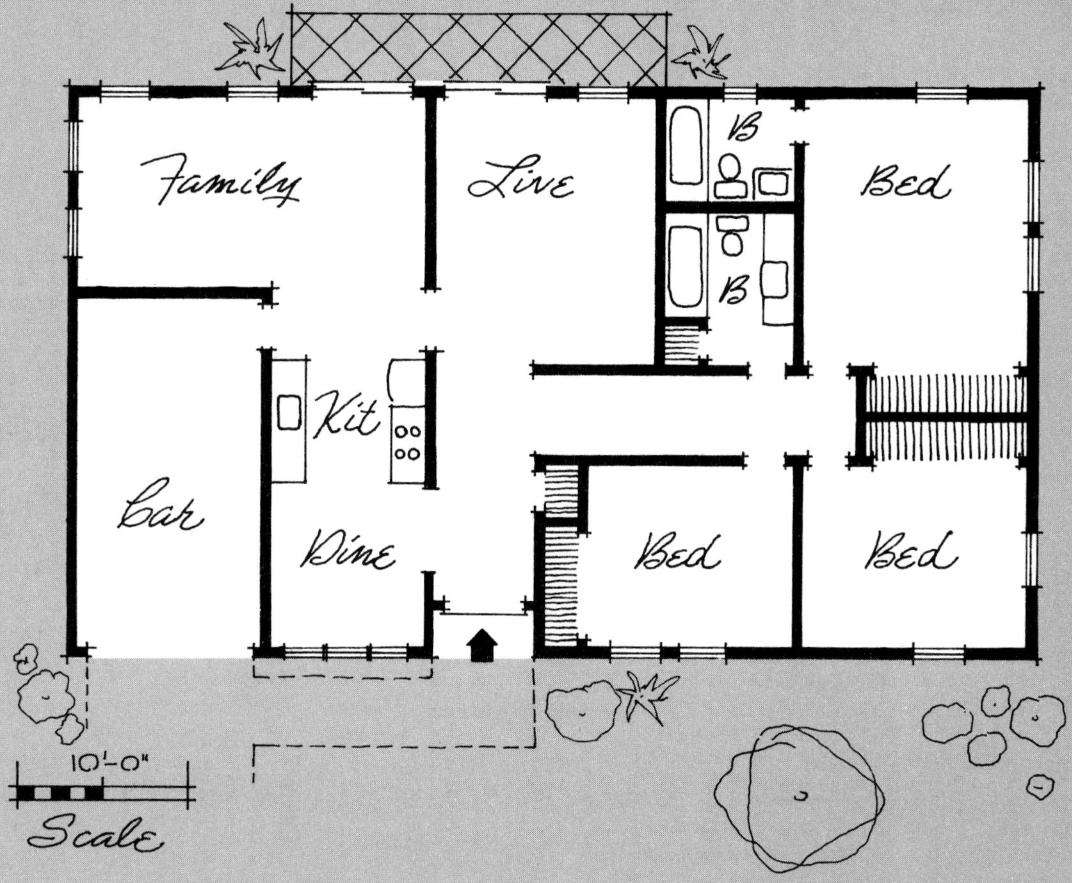

Fig. 6-24 A rectangular floor plan.

Fig. 6-25 An L-shaped floor plan.

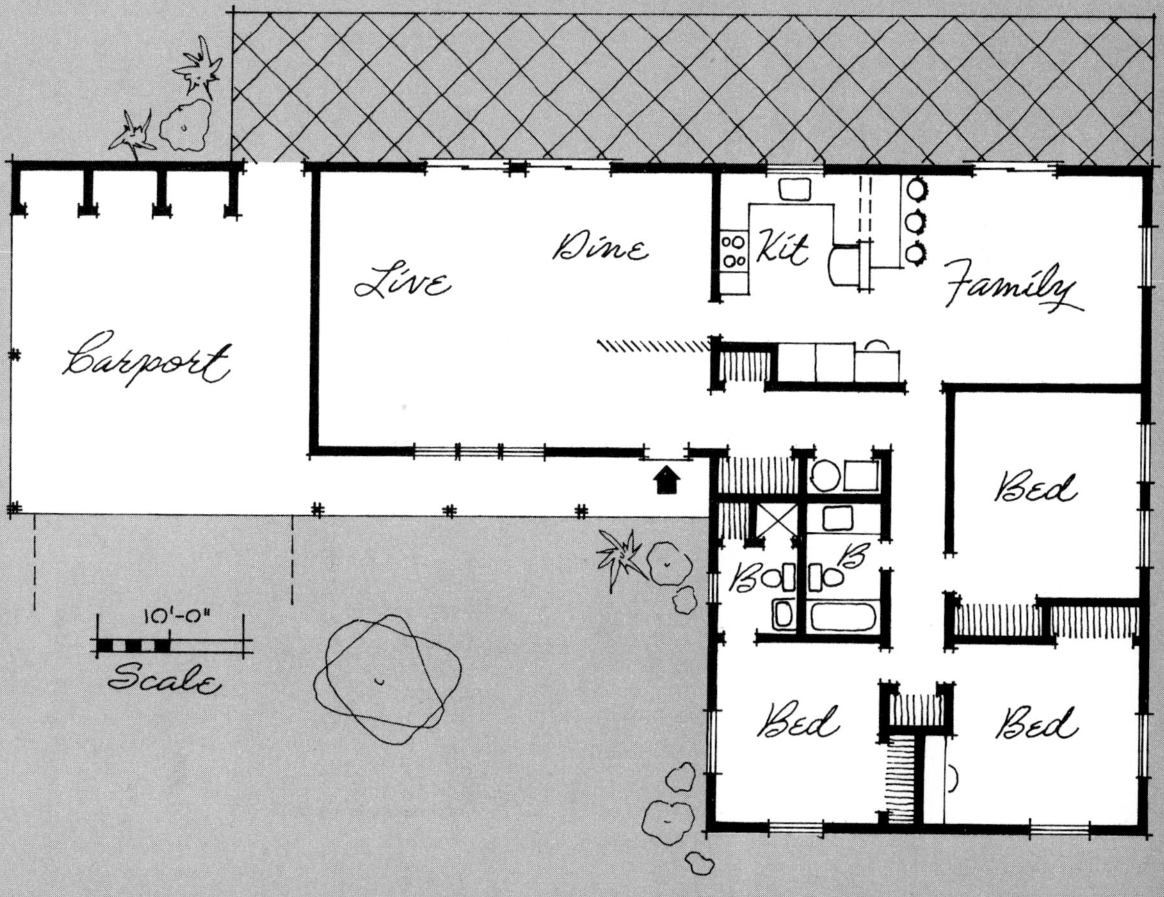

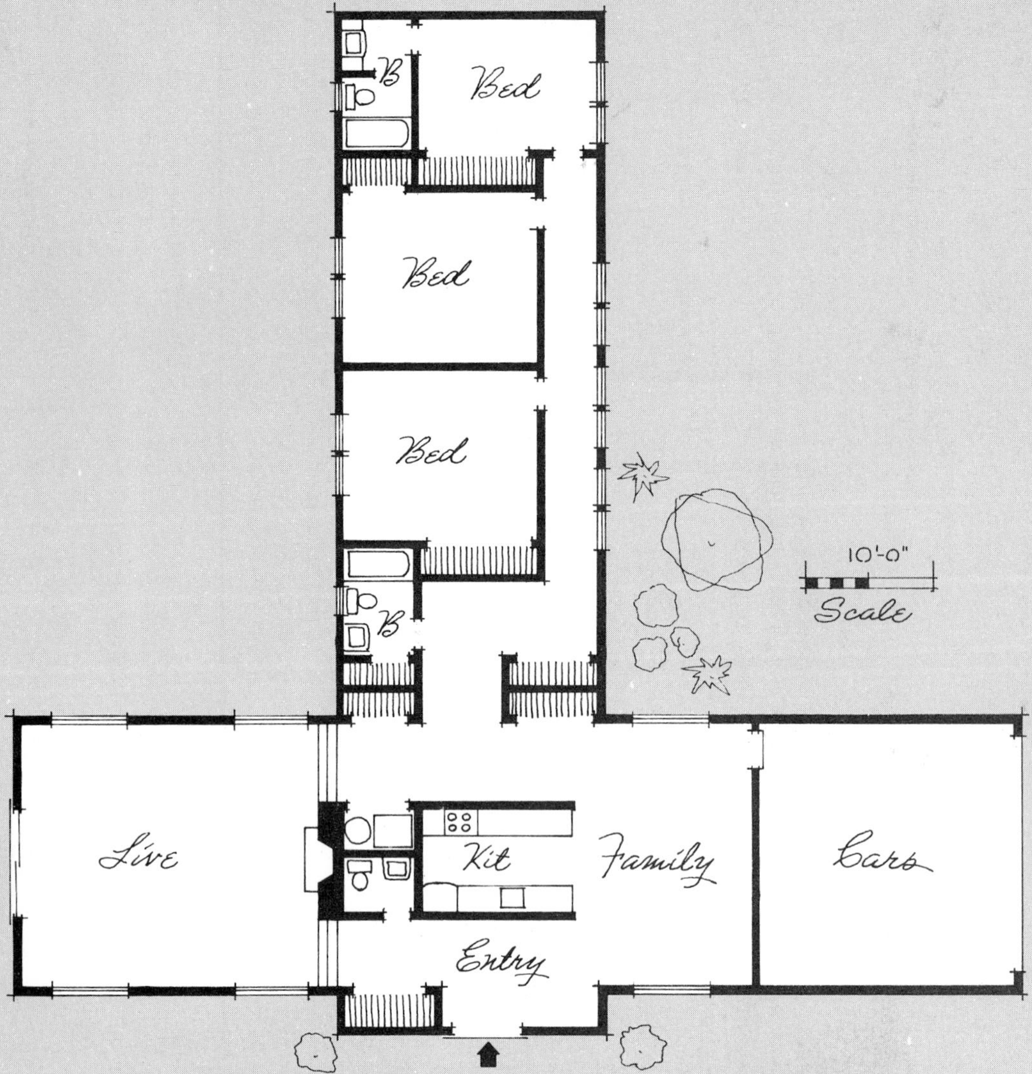

Fig. 6-26 A T-shaped floor plan.

Fig. 6-27 A U-shaped floor plan.

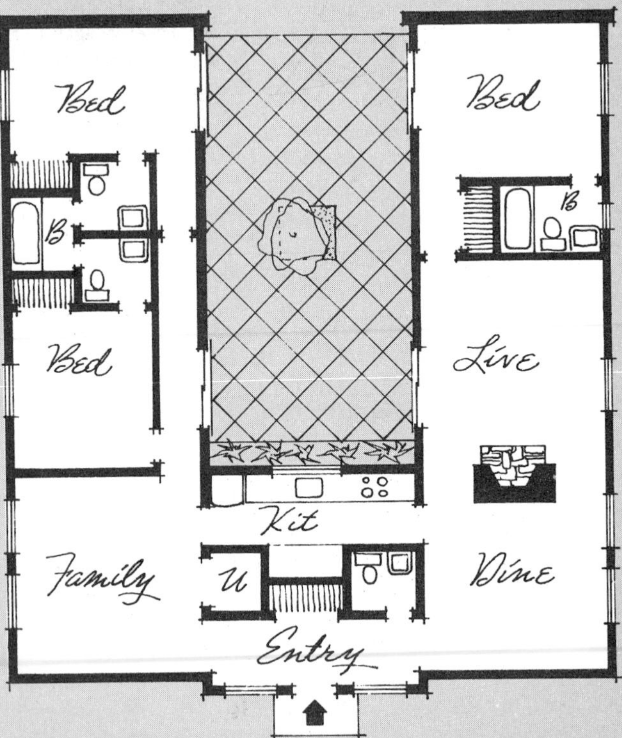

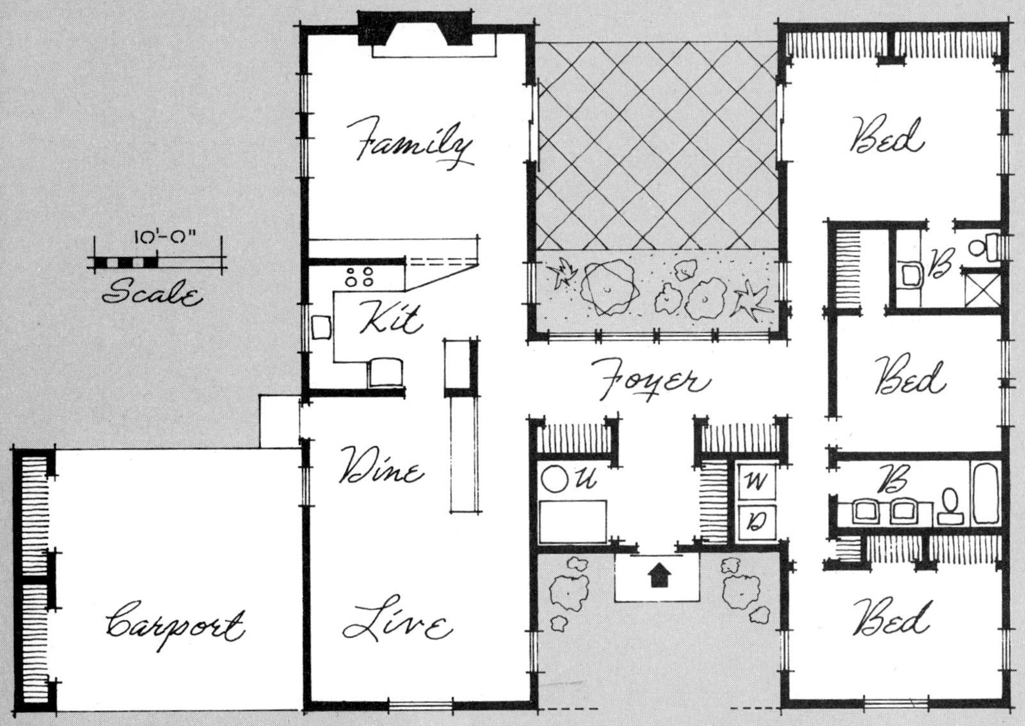

Fig. 6-28 An H-shaped floor plan.

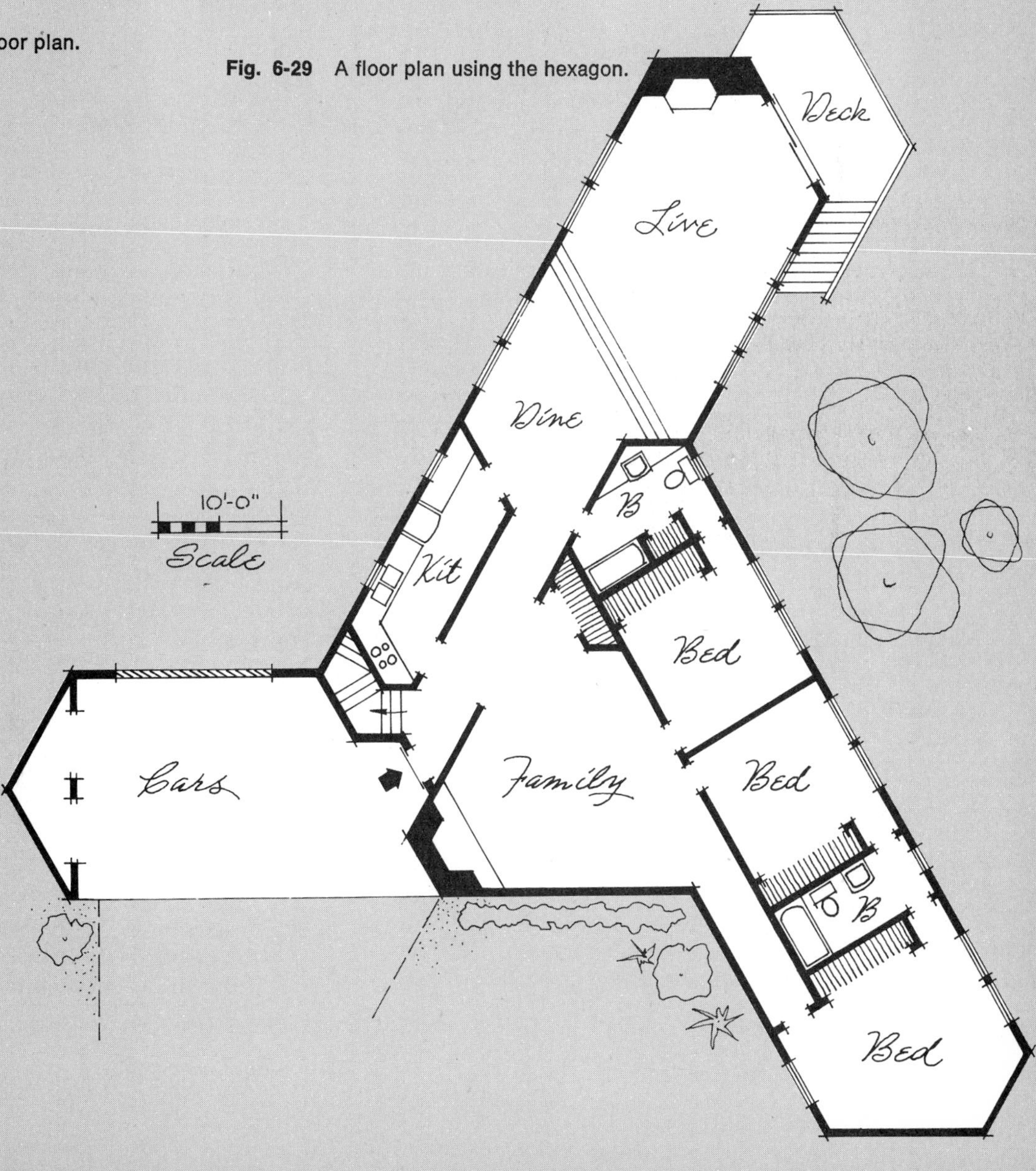

Fig. 6-29 A floor plan using the hexagon.

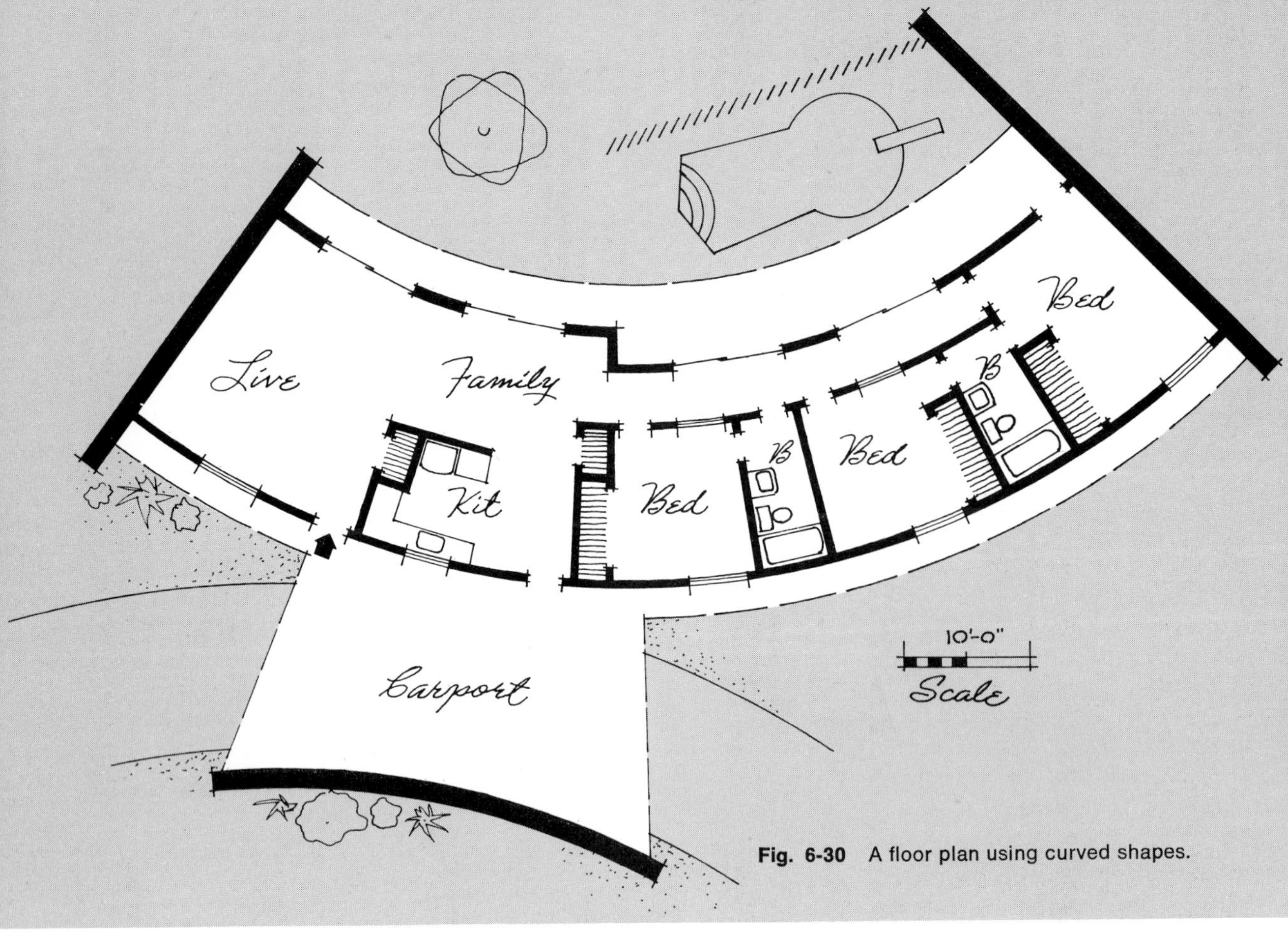

Fig. 6-30 A floor plan using curved shapes.

in many of his famous structures. Construction costs mount tremendously when other than right angles are used on plans; acute corners become difficult to utilize efficiently. *Curved shapes* (Fig. 6-30) offer free-flowing spaces and novel, unconventional interiors. Wood construction does not lend itself to curved walls nor do conventional fixtures and furniture. But the curved shape definitely deviates from the cubical forms we have been accustomed to, and occasionally a curved plan is devised which offers a break from the traditional living patterns of the past.

The *atrium* or court plan, taken from ancient Roman architecture, (Fig. 6-31) offers an entirely private outdoor living area and literally "turns the outside in." An interesting interior atmosphere is created when unexpected openings to the sky greet the vistor as he enters the house. Vistas of openness as well as closely integrated interiors characterize a plan with good circulation around an atrium. Where well-located lots offer little opportunity for outdoor privacy, the atrium plan (if carefully devised) might well be the logical solution for gaining exterior living space. This plan can be adapted to almost any climate; but in extreme tropical areas the enclosed atrium may become a heat pocket, unless sunlight is controlled by blinds or other shading devices.

Allow the correct amount of space for each major activity From a general standpoint you can think of the basic activities in a home as being *eating, sleeping,* and *living.* Give each activity its proper allotment of space, according to the living habits of the inhabitants and the size of the plan. Use precious space generously where it counts most—in living and entertainment areas. And restrict floor space in individual-activity areas, such as kitchens and baths, where careful planning can make them adequately efficient. Living rooms set the interior atmosphere of the home and should not convey the impression of confinement. Isolate quiet zones—bedrooms, studies, etc.—from noisy family and recreation rooms. If possible, use closets for sound-barrier walls; a closet full of clothes makes the simplest method of preventing sound transmission between rooms.

Make areas serve dual, nonconflicting purposes if you want maximum space utilization

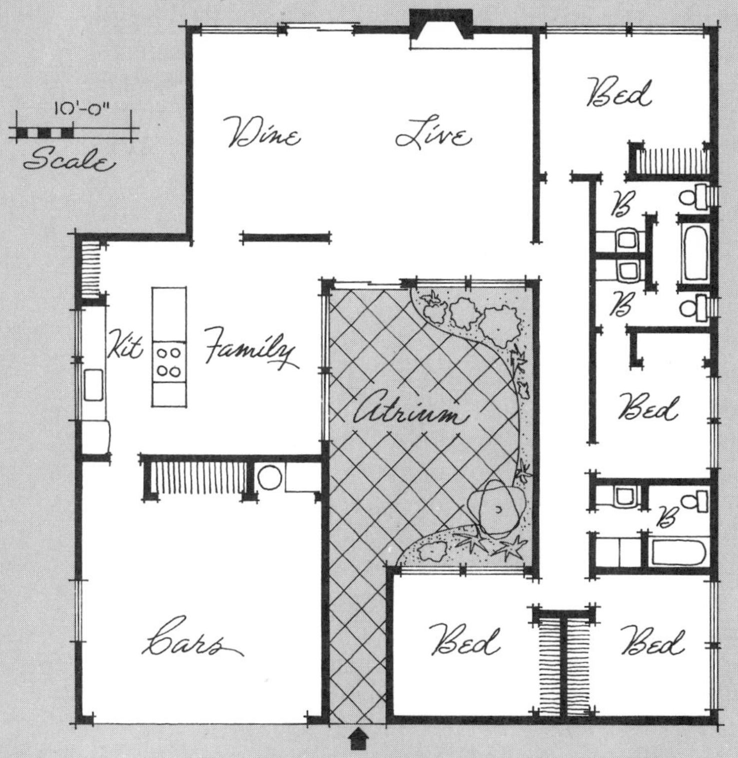

Fig. 6-31 A floor plan with an atrium.

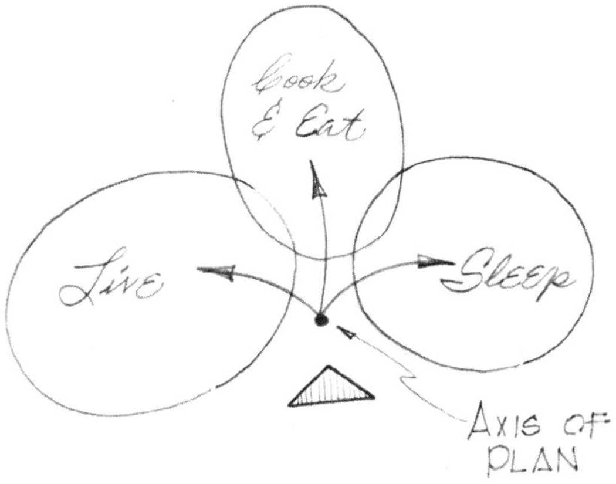

Fig. 6-32 Using major activities in preliminary planning.

Table 6-1 Typical Room Sizes (inside dimensions)

Living	14′ x 20′
Dining	12′ x 14′
Kitchen	8′ x 16′
Bath	5′ x 9′
Bedroom, Master	12′ x 15′
Bedroom	11′ x 13′
Entrance Hall	7′ x 8′
Powder Room	4′ x 5′
Utility	8′ x 12′
Hall Width	3′–6″ to 4′
Stairs Width	3′
Garage (Single)	12′ x 20′
Garage (Double)	20′ x 20′
Workshop	12′ x 14′

and a flexible plan. See if any of the following typical combinations might gain additional living space in the plan:

1. Living-dining
2. Living-family
3. Kitchen-laundry
4. Bath-laundry
5. Garage-laundry
6. Hall-laundry
7. Garage-workshop
8. Large bedroom with room divider
9. Carport adjacent to terrace

Plan the size of each room to fit the furniture to be used in it, especially the dining room and bedrooms. Minimize partitions, if possible, by eliminating offsets and by keeping partition walls in line with each other—unnecessary corners (as we have mentioned before) are expensive and they make furniture arrangement difficult.

Refer to Table 6-1 to help you size the various home areas.

Keep major traffic routes short Consider day-to-day activities so that the traffic patterns are minimized and hallways do not deprive the plan of important living space. Time, space, as well as maintenance of floors can be saved by efficient circulation. Traffic through rooms (especially through the center) is a characteristic of many older houses, which were designed around formal exteriors; little concern was given to the routes between different activity areas. If the main entrance of a plan is placed near the center (see Fig. 6-32), major traffic patterns can "fan out" in each direction and thus increase usable space within rooms and reduce hall lengths. The route from the carport or garage to the kitchen should definitely be short. If traffic must pass through a room, arrange the doors so that the traffic affects only a corner or an end. Often the correct placement of doors will reduce the length of routes. Avoid major traffic through an activity area, such as a kitchen work center. The activities of some families require many rooms, even if they are small; other families prefer fewer and larger rooms—commonly known as "open planning." To sum up, provide convenient relationships between rooms, minimize traffic through rooms, and provide access to outdoor living areas if you want good traffic flow in your plan.

Plan for adequate storage space not only for clothes storage, but for the many items required in a modern home. Design the space to fit the items, provide it where it is needed, and make the storage easily accessible. Many types of modern closet-door units are available for built-in storage spaces. Sliding doors eliminate swinging space needed within a room, and full, 8′ high closet doors provide maximum storage space above clothes rods. Walk-in closets are satisfactory if clothes rods can be installed along two long walls, otherwise they are inefficient (see Fig. 6-33). Avoid a narrow closet with a door in the narrow end; the storage space has poor accessibility. Lining part of a carport or garage with 1/4″ pegboard provides inexpensive storage for garden tools. Even built-in cabinets installed above the hoods of stored cars make efficient use of otherwise wasted space. Diagonal areas below stairways can be devoted to storage. Often the attic can be utilized for dead storage by introducing a "scuttle" or disappearing stair unit in a convenient hall ceiling. If a basement is planned, a considerable amount of its space can be reserved for storage. However, according to experts, in most cases basement storage space is more expensive than above-ground storage space. The average home must provide storage for the following items (excluding kitchen equipment): clothes, linens, cleaning equipment, toys, hobby and sports equipment, sewing needs, guests' coats, tools, and lawn and garden equipment. Well-designed storage units make for a better organized home and thereby help to simplify housekeeping.

Plan a functional kitchen The housewife spends much of her time in the kitchen, planning meals, storing food, cooking and serving, and cleaning after meals. The kitchen should, first of all, be easy to work in, conveniently located, and pleasant in appearance, to make these tasks no more difficult than necessary. Unlike furniture, kitchen cabinets and appliances are permanently installed and cannot be rearranged by merely pushing them about to rectify planning errors. Kitchens can be placed at the front of the house—to be close to the garage and front door; or they can be placed in the back—to be accessible to outdoor eating and play areas. Kitchens serve various purposes besides food preparation; many are designed to furnish room for snacking and informal meals. Others incorporate informal living and play

Fig. 6-33 Closet layouts.

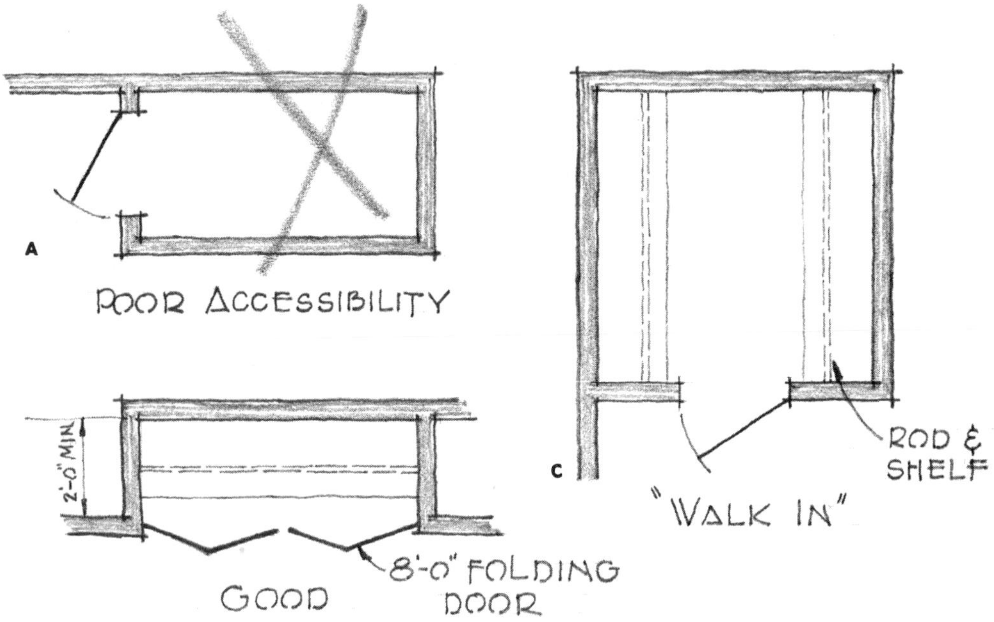

areas for children. Some are even combined with entertainment centers. Many housewives, on the other hand, prefer a completely independent kitchen that can be closed off from other areas when cooking and eating are completed.

The layout of the actual work center of the kitchen deserves careful attention. The basic activity of this area is largely controlled by the placement of the sink, the cooking unit, and the refrigerator. If we were to connect these three major appliances with a triangle on the plan, it would represent the bulk of the travel within the kitchen and is known as the "work triangle" (see Fig. 6-34). Keep the perimeter of this triangle from 12′ to 20′ in length if you want an efficient kitchen; if it becomes longer, a rearrangement of the basic appliances should be made. Check manufacturers' literature for the actual size of the appliances to be included in your kitchen (to be sure they fit) before progressing too far with the planning of the cabinets and other features. According to the arrangement of the cabinets and appliances, kitchens can be made in these basic shapes: U shape, L shape, two-wall or corridor type, and the modest one-wall type (see Fig. 6-35). Tests have shown the U shape to be the most efficient. Occasionally a peninsula or "island" cabinet is incorporated into the L shape or U shape to isolate the work center or to utilize excessive space within large kitchen areas. The ideal arrangement is to have the major appliances efficiently placed with continuous cabinets between and sufficient countertop space on each side of the appliances for satisfactory work surfaces (see Fig. 6-36). Whether or not the kitchen is used for eating, countertop sur-

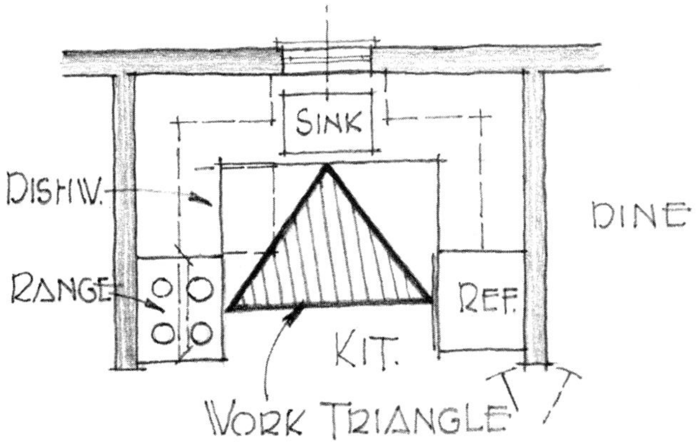

Fig. 6-34 The efficiency of a kitchen depends upon the size of the work triangle.

Fig. 6-35 Basic kitchen layouts.

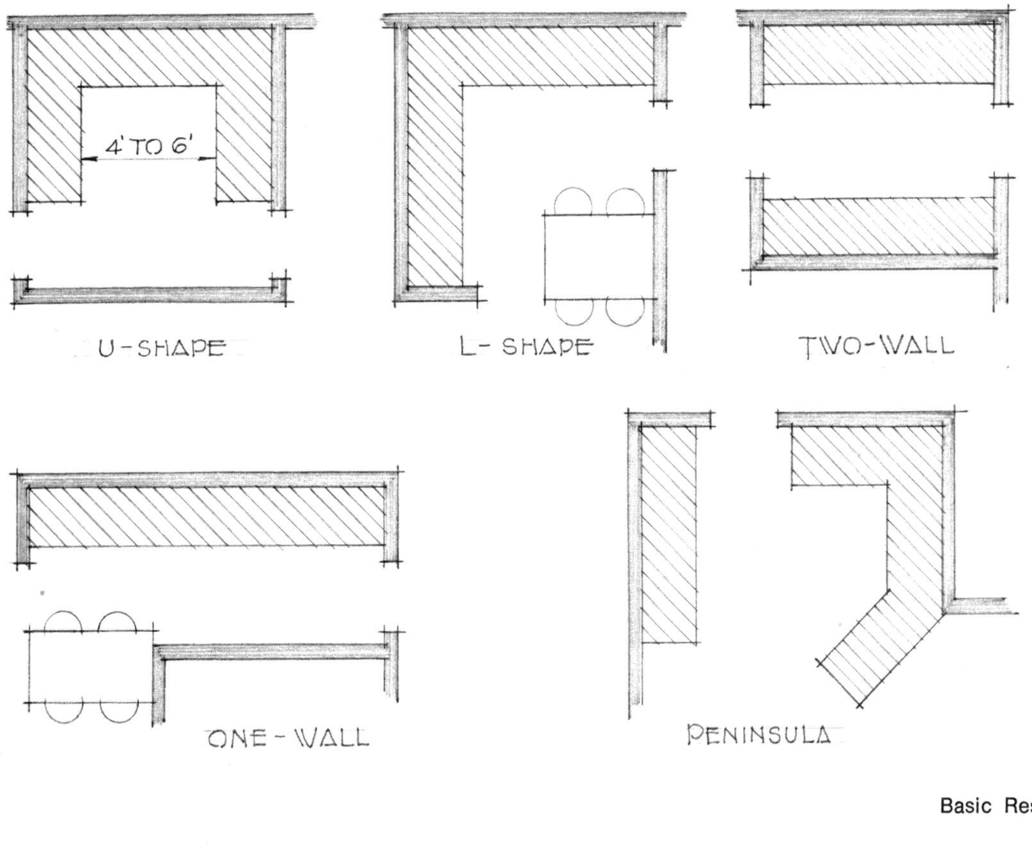

Fig. 6-36 Several examples of functional kitchens.

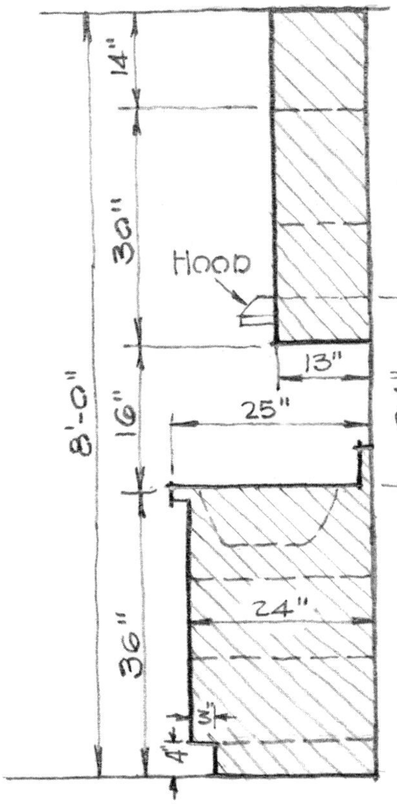

Fig. 6-37 Standard kitchen cabinet heights and widths.

face must be provided for many activities: menu planning, actual food preparation (mixing, chopping, etc.), cooking, serving, as well as for cleaning up. These countertops should be surfaced with heatproof, easy-to-clean material. Through traffic should bypass the kitchen work center to avoid interference with the preparation of meals. Provide maximum kitchen storage with both base cabinets and wall cabinets where possible. Run wall cabinets to the top of the standard 8′ high wall, and use the top 14″ for dead storage (see Fig. 6-37). Allow at least 40 sq ft of shelf space for general kitchen storage, with an additional 6 sq ft for each person living in the home. In U-shaped and two-wall type kitchens, allow between 4′ and 6′ of floor space between faces of opposite cabinets. Various modifications of the basic arrangements can be made to create interest and to utilize the kitchen space effectively without destroying the function of the work center.

Water vapor, cooking odors, and heat should be controlled in a modern kitchen with the use of an exhaust fan. Such fans are especially important in open-plan kitchens. Range hoods usually incorporate quiet-running fans for the rapid disposal of the undesirable side effects of food preparation.

Plan efficient, well-placed bathrooms The bathrooms in American homes are world-famous for their conveniences. We have become insistent upon comfortable facilities because the bathroom is the place where each member of the family can attend his health and grooming in complete, much desired privacy. Most homes now require at least 1½ or 2 baths. A half bath comprises a lavatory and a water closet and is commonly called a powder room if it is accessible from a hall. Two-story homes should have a bath on each floor. For the most economy without crowding, use the 8′–0″ × 5′–0″ size for a full bath (Fig. 6-38). Put the standard 5′ tub across the end so that the other fixtures will fit along one plumbing wall. A 4″ vent stack is necessary in the wall near the water closet, which is usually placed between the other fixtures. To accommodate the vent stack an 8″ wet-wall is generally indicated. To shorten the plumbing runs put baths back to back, and plan, if possible, a compact arrangement for the baths, sink, washer-dryer, and water heater (see Fig. 6-38). However, do not sacrifice a good plan for the extra cost of separating the baths or other plumbing.

Locate the doors in bathrooms to give maximum privacy and isolation. Often the bathroom door is left open, and direct views from living areas are undesirable. Minor rearrangements of bathroom positions in relation to halls usually eliminate this situation. Doors

Fig. 6-38 Compact plumbing arrangement.

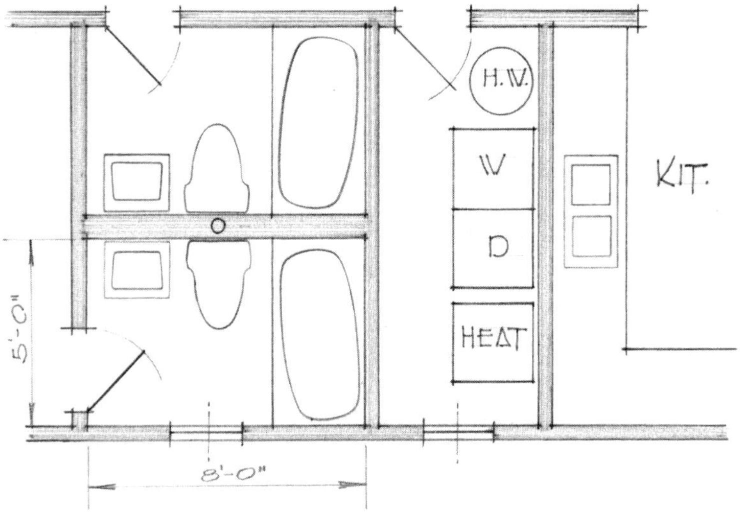

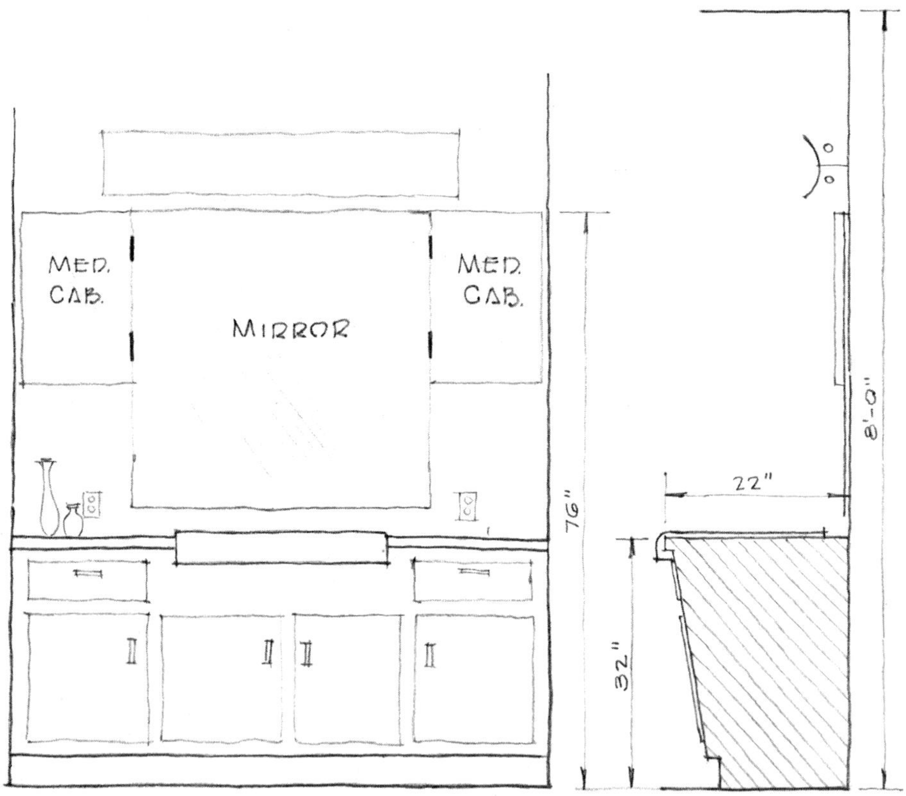

Fig. 6-39 Standard heights and widths of bathroom vanities.

Fig. 6-40 A combination dressing and bath area.

should swing into the bathroom (never into halls) without hitting bathroom fixtures. Use narrow doors; usually 2′–2″ or 2′–4″ widths are sufficient. By isolating the water closet or tub into compartments, the bathroom can be made useful to more than one person simultaneously. With children in a home, twin lavatories will reduce peak demands on the bathroom. Built-in lavatory cabinets (Fig. 6-39) will result in more storage space and allow countertop areas for grooming use. Large mirrors attached to the wall directly above the cabinets will further facilitate grooming and will also give the room a more spacious appearance. Do not center medicine cabinets directly over the lavatory; use a mirror or a window above. Many master bedrooms have accessible private baths with adjacent dressing facilities (generous closets) resulting in complete master suites (see Fig. 6-40). Shower stalls are preferred by some people and require less floor space than tubs. A minimum shower should be 2′–6″ × 2′–6″. Forced-air exhaust fans allow windowless inside bathrooms to be satisfactory; but bathrooms with windows should also have an exhaust fan for more positive ventilation to the outside. Floors and wainscoting in bathrooms should be finished with durable, easily maintained materials that produce sanitary and pleasant interiors. Lighting should be soft and adequate, especially in front of mirrors.

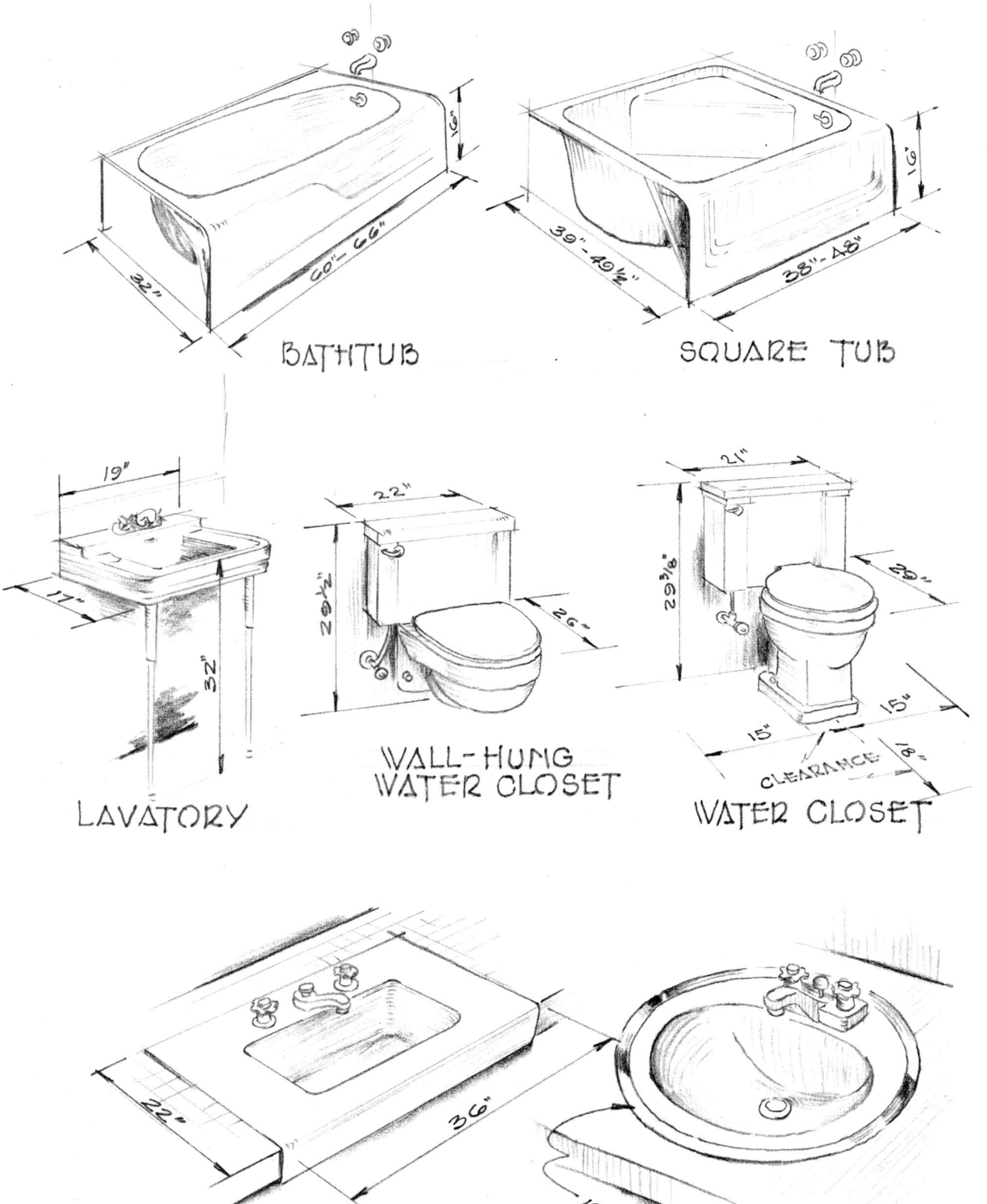

Fig. 6-41 Standard bath fixture sizes.

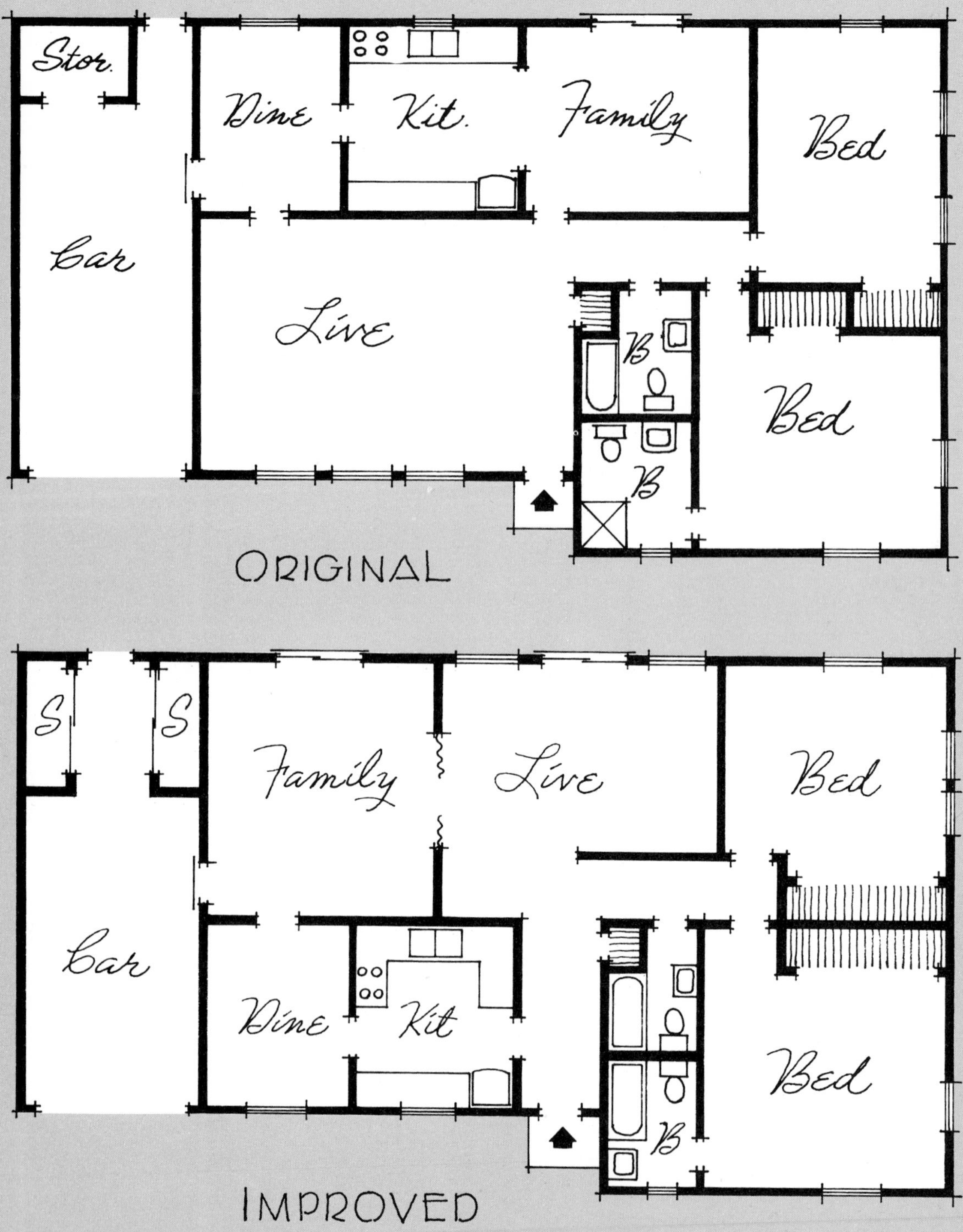

Fig. 6-42 Improving preliminary plan layouts.

IMPROVEMENTS

1. Family room is isolated from quiet bedroom zone.
2. Traffic is eliminated through living room as well as kitchen work area.
3. An isolated front entrance is provided.
4. Living room and family room may be opened to rear outdoor living areas.
5. More closet space is provided in bedrooms.
6. Plumbing is more compact.
7. Communication is provided between family room and living room for large gatherings.

6.7 MAKE THE ELEVATIONS EXPRESS THE SPIRIT OF THE INTERIOR

The exterior of a house should evolve from the requirements of the inside; if a formal interior is planned, the exterior should reflect it; if the interior is informal, the exterior should create an impression of freedom and casual living. Traditional exteriors are usually based upon the use of symmetry: identical features on both sides of a vertical center line, resulting in positive balance (see Fig. 6-43A). Informality is gained by combining areas and features of dissimilar size and placement, unrestricted by identical balance, to produce a different type of visual balance (see Fig. 6-43B). Either type should create a sense of tranquility. Both can be in good taste if they provide interest without too much busy "make-up" and if they reflect simplicity without being austere.

Consider the basic structural masses Give them good proportions and pleasing visual shapes (Fig. 6-44). Unless its general form and silhouette are good, no amount of texture or ornament can improve upon a structure. Avoid extreme deviations from accepted building forms unless you are creative enough to start a new trend in architecture. Traditional shapes of the past have lived because their general proportions have been pleasing. Avoid the "too-high" look.

Keep important roof lines simple Complex roofs not only look uncomfortable, but they are unnecessarily expensive to build. Steep roof pitches produce houses that are dominated by the roof texture and shape. If you use an L-shape or T-shape plan, make the wings the same width, if possible, so that the roof will be unified. If one wing must be narrower, be sure the narrower span roof is received against the larger span (Fig. 6-45). Avoid artificial gables (Fig. 6-46). Complex roofs are the result of complicated plans; therefore roof planning must be started when the plan is developed.

Select window sizes according to the inside room requirements In living areas where the view is important, windows can be large—to the floor if necessary. Incidentally, do not make the mistake of putting a picture window in a wall where there is no view. In dining rooms, windowsills are kept about 3′–0″ from the floor; in kitchens, the cabinets require sills to

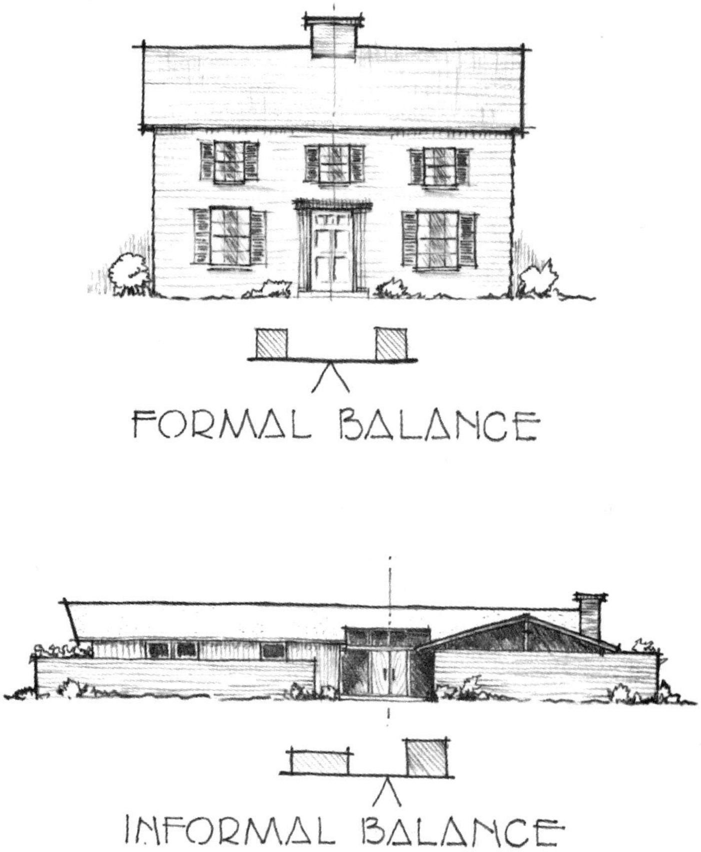

Fig. 6-43 Formal and informal elevations.

Fig. 6-44 Providing a silhouette with pleasing proportions.

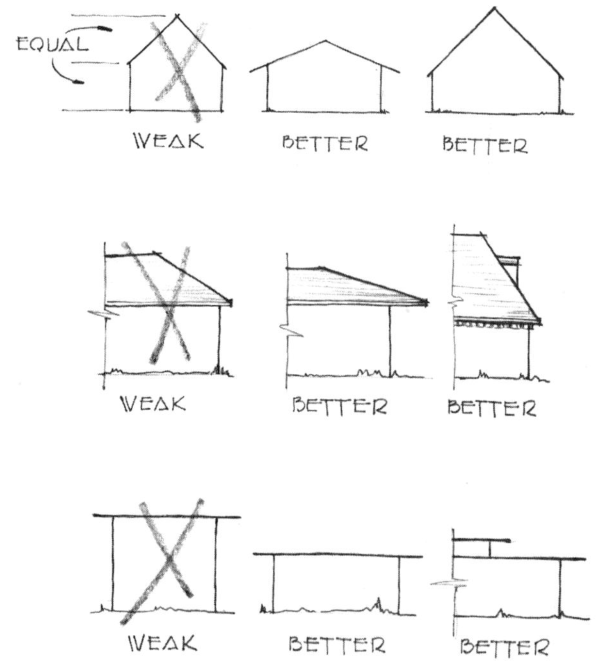

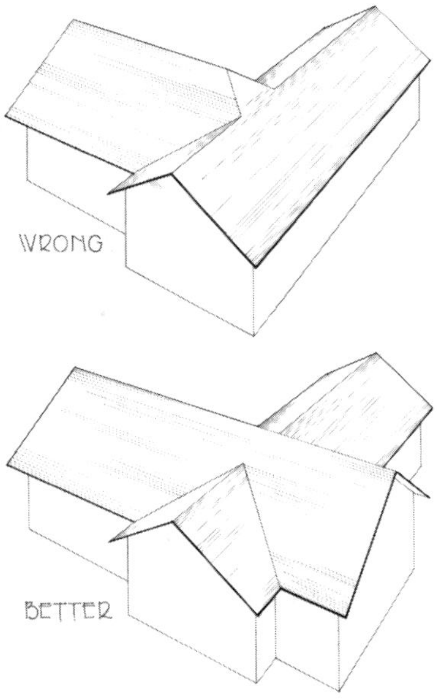

Fig. 6-45 Arranging smaller gable roofs against larger ones.

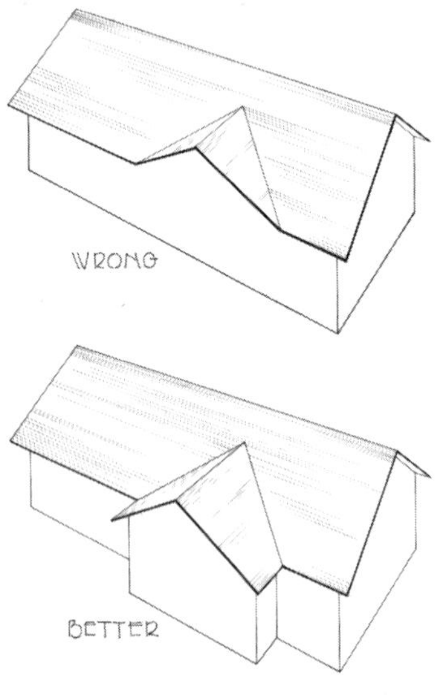

Fig. 6-46 Avoiding artificial gables.

be at least 3′–8″ from the floor; in bedrooms and baths, where privacy is important, windowsills should be at least 4′–0″ from the finished floor.

Coordinate the window sizes and types Almost every house requires windows of different sizes, yet good fenestration (placement and sizing of window openings) will unify the exterior if you select window sizes of similar proportions. Use the graphic method of drawing a diagonal through one of the selected window shapes to find the correct proportions of the other windows (see Fig. 6-47). Today's wide range of window sizes and styles permits almost unlimited freedom in correct window coordination. Double-hung windows with small lights are typical of traditional exteriors; large window-walls are typical of contemporary exteriors. Line up the heads of windows and doors on the elevations. When making preliminary sketches, consider the appearance of the wall areas around window openings as well as the windows themselves. If these shapes are

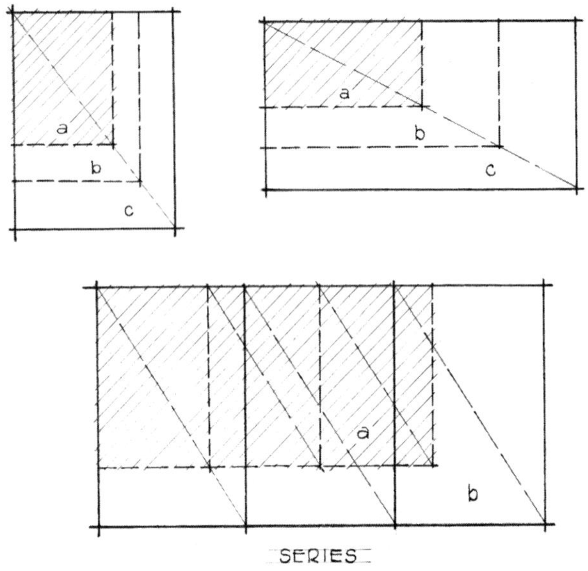

Fig. 6-47 Graphic method of arriving at similar window proportions.

Fig. 6-48 Placement of windows.

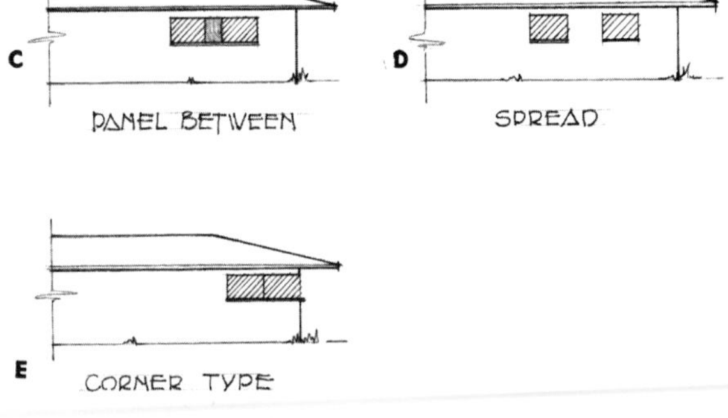

not pleasing, or if the wall areas fail to produce the desired character, consider moving the windows one way or another without restricting their effectiveness from the interior. Avoid windows so close together or so near to exterior corners as to create extremely narrow interjacent wall areas (Fig. 6-48A). These areas appear unstable, especially if the wall is masonry. Bring the windows together by joining them with a narrow mullion, or place a unifying panel between the windows, or spread the windows farther apart (see Fig. 6-48C and D).

Select an appropriate front door style (as well as the other exterior doors) in keeping with the style of the house, and give this door the prominence it deserves. The treatment of the front entrance in traditional styles of the past has been highly ornamental. In present versions of these styles various adaptations of the *panel door,* with or without lights are appropriate. Otherwise, the *flush door,* painted or with natural wood finish, is the best selection for most contemporary entrances. If the front hall needs natural light, sash doors should be used, or side lights can be installed along the door frame (see Fig. 10-13). As a safety measure, it is advisable to place some type of small window in or near the front entrance so that the housewife can identify callers before admitting them. Many types of *sliding glass doors,* framed in wood or metal, are available for easy access to outdoor living areas. To prevent serious accidents, sliding glass doors should be installed with tempered glass, or protection bars across the doors should be used. Refer to manufacturers' catalogues for details and availability of the various doors before you indicate the selection in your planning.

Relate the four elevations by carrying out a repeating, interesting theme. Let some of the structural members be exposed, if appropriate, to contribute rhythmic enrichment. One exterior material should dominate, both in texture and color; use few additional materials. Especially avoid the pretentious use of too many contrasting materials on the front and only plain materials on the sides and rear. Design all four sides. Above all, select materials for the exterior that require minimum maintenance throughout the years.

Fig. 6-49 Cornice treatments should be consistent with the character of the elevations.

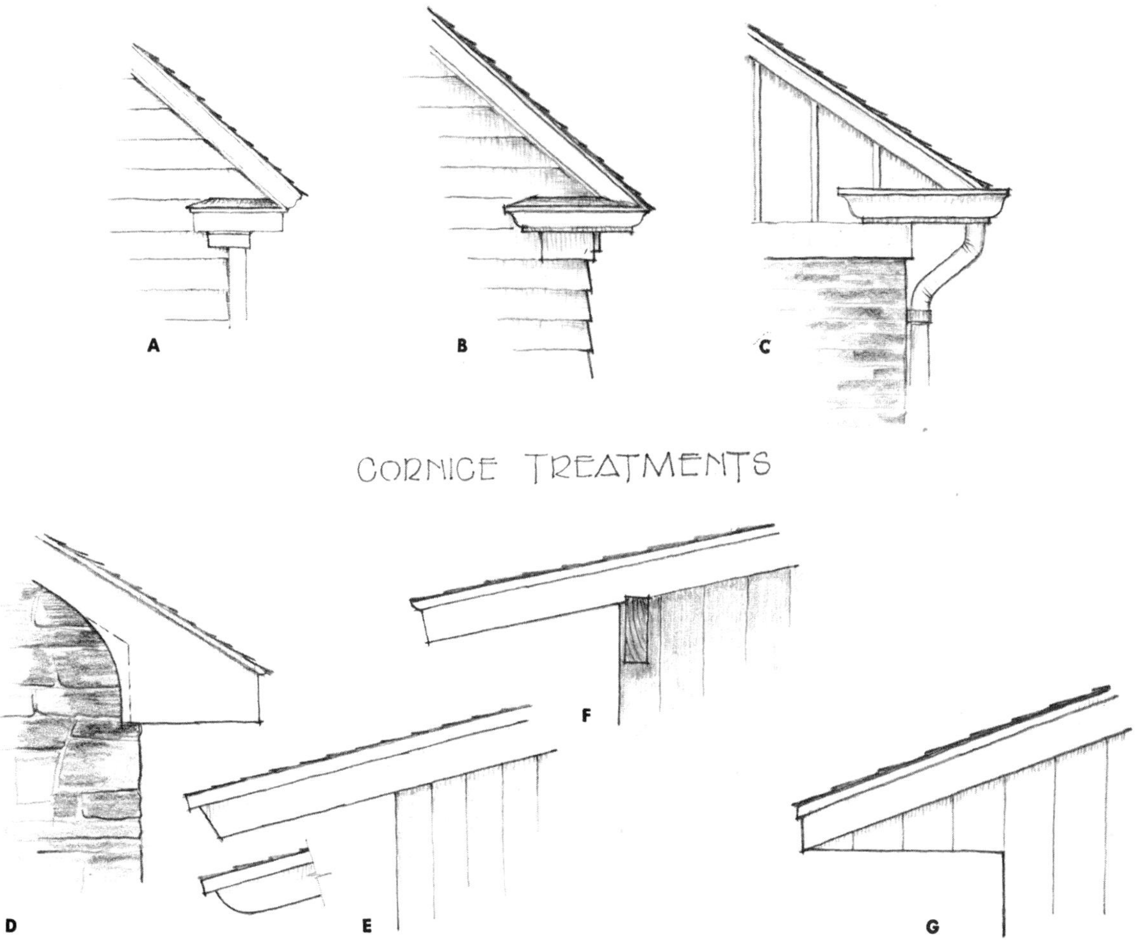

Accent horizontal lines if you want the house to appear lower and longer. A "lofty" appearance is usually not pleasing. Wide overhangs of the roof and wall extensions from the house produce protected areas and help integrate the house to the land.

Make the chimney massive if you want this important design element to contribute character to the structure.

Keep details in scale Many of the details found on large traditional homes will not be successful on a small home. Suitable cornice detail is especially important.

Remember that much of the value of a house is created by the design If the design is simple and in good taste, the house will continue to be desirable for many years.

Study the prizewinning residential designs in leading architectural journals and home magazines. See if you can determine why prominent architects and home specialists have chosen these over other designs, and what makes a house, whether large or small, exceptional and appealing. This understanding should provide you with one of the important requirements of successful planning—good taste.

6.8 COMBINE EXTERIOR DESIGN ELEMENTS THAT ARE IN KEEPING WITH ACCEPTED HOME STYLES

Study the following home photographs for their identification with a definite style. Like our culture, home styles have their roots in many other countries. Each style, however, because of local climate, materials, topography, and the needs of individuals is strictly American in development.

Colonial styles have survived because they are honest houses, usually unpretentious and simple, yet having pleasing architectural features. Many were passed on to descendants after having given each generation a lifetime of enjoyment. Houses erected in early colonial days in New England were built by carpenters and masons skilled in traditions of England, the Netherlands, and Germany. The styles in Louisiana were influenced by the French, in Florida, California, and Texas by the Spaniards, and some areas give evidence of oriental influences.

It can be said that many of the most admirable American homes were built 150-200 years ago; some are still in use. The value of these early houses lies in the degree to which they were copied as the population spread.

Today, very few houses exist that are "pure" examples of any one architectural style. All vary in proportion, window fenestration, or decorative treatment. These variations, however, give each house individuality and tend to show the stamp of a particular architect. But many retain enough features to allow us to make positive identification of their basic style. This is important—a well designed home should give evidence of a definite styling, and you should be able to recognize those characteristics that identify it with a particular style. Today's home designer would be wise to keep an eye on tradition while focusing on the new materials and innovations available in contemporary building.

Fig. 6-50 An example of poor exterior design. Notice that too many materials have been used, details have no unity, and the house has not been oriented to the site.

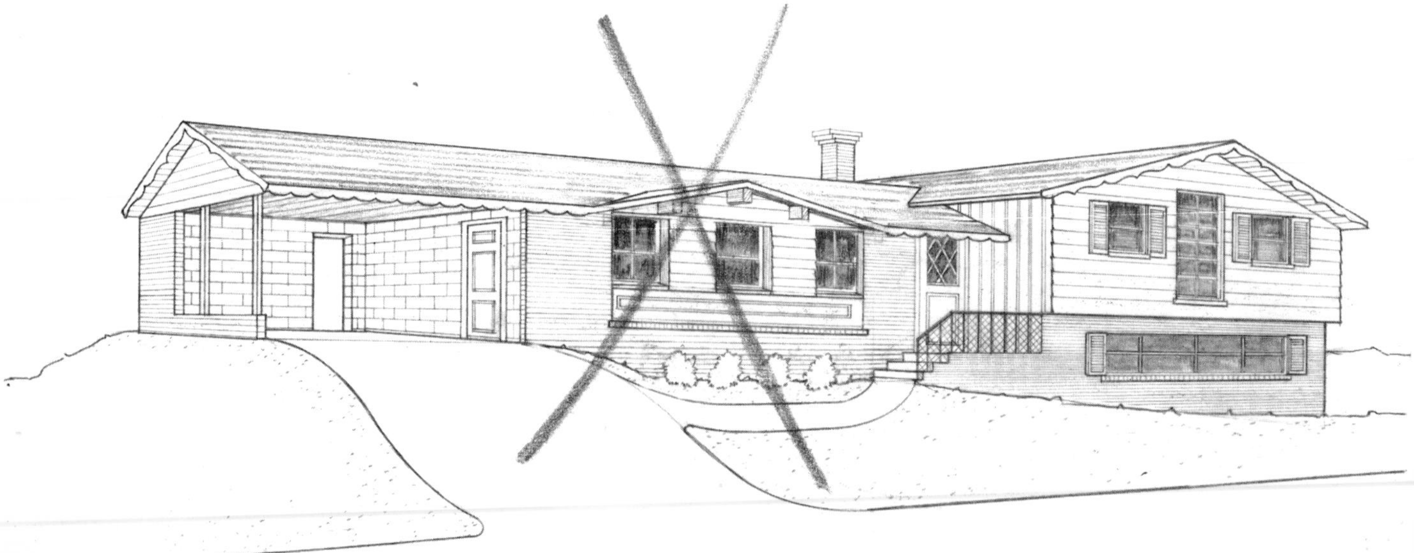

Fig. 6-51 Colonial "saltbox" styling. *(Hedrich-Blessing Photos.)*

Fig. 6-52 New England Colonial styling. *(Hedrich-Blessing Photos.)*

Fig. 6-53 Cape Cod styling. *(Hedrich-Blessing Photos.)*

Fig. 6-54 Regency styling. *(Hedrich-Blessing Photos.)*

Fig. 6-55 Dutch Colonial styling. *(Hedrich-Blessing Photos.)*

Fig. 6-56 Southern Colonial styling. *(Hedrich-Blessing Photos.)*

Fig. 6-57 Ranch house styling. *(Hedrich-Blessing Photos.)*

Fig. 6-58 French Provincial styling.

Fig. 6-59 Garrison styling. *(Hedrich-Blessing Photos.)*

Fig. 6-60 English Half-timber styling.

Fig. 6-61 Contemporary styling.

Fig. 6-62 Early Adobe houses in the southwest.

Fig. 6-63 Student ink sketch of Spanish styling.

Fig. 6-64 Williamsburg styling.

Fig. 6-65 Contemporary styling.

RESIDENTIAL PLANNING EXERCISES

The following planning exercises should first be done freehand on tracing paper or 1/8″ coordinate paper. After you have gathered various residential ideas from books, magazines, newspapers, and other sources, develop the problems as indicated in Chapter 5, under sketching plans and elevations. The plan sketch cannot be developed entirely before trials of elevation views, and possibly floor levels, have been established. Develop the plan and elevations together; do not be discouraged if numerous sketches are needed, or if completely different approaches to the problem are necessary before a workable layout is finally attained.

1. Plan a *small beach house* for a young couple with a small daughter. The beach house should have minimum accommodations yet a festive spirit for vacation and weekend living. Provide for the following:
   a. Lot size: 65′ ocean front, 200′ deep
   b. 700 sq ft floor space, contemporary design
   c. Large living, dining, kitchen combination area with small kitchen utility unit behind folding doors
   d. Set house on preserved wooden piers to prevent damage from high water
   e. One easily accessible bath with shower
   f. Two sleeping rooms
   g. Fireplace, redwood exterior

2. Plan a bachelor's *retreat house*. The occupant to be is a young professor who requires space for books and study, and space for occasional entertaining of large groups. Provide for the following:
   a. Lot size: 100′ × 185′, level and wooded
   b. 1500 sq ft floor space, plank-and-beam construction
   c. Master bedroom and guest bedroom
   d. Large living-dining room, modest kitchen
   e. One full bath
   f. Carport for one car, outdoor terrace area

3. Plan a *home for a young family* with one child. They are interested in a 1-story, colonial-type house with the following specifications:
   a. Lot size: 100′ × 200′, the lot slopes downward 10′ from the left to the right side
   b. 1800 sq ft maximum floor space
   c. Kitchen near family room with guest accommodations
   d. Two bedrooms, 1½ baths
   e. Full basement to be partially used as garage for one car
   f. Provision for outdoor play area with supervision possible from kitchen
   g. Brick-veneer construction with gable roof

4. Plan a *medium-priced home* for a family with two children, boy and girl. The clients indicate a preference for a ranch house on one level, with the following requirements:
   a. Lot size: 150′ × 225′, with wooded view in rear
   b. 2000 sq ft maximum floor space, exclusive of double carport
   c. Two full baths, one to be private for master bedroom
   d. Three bedrooms, separate dining room, family room, living room, kitchen, and utility area
   e. Outdoor living area, rear entrance "mud room"
   f. Adequate storage space

5. Plan a *traditional 2-story home* for a family of five (two boys and one girl), with the following specifications:
   a. Lot size: 100′ × 175′
   b. 2200 sq ft floor space plus double garage
   c. Kitchen, dining room, entrance hall, powder room, and large living room on first floor—concrete slab-on-grade
   d. Three bedrooms and double bath on second floor
   e. Outdoor terrace off living room with brick fireplace
   f. Stone and/or wood exterior
   g. Traditional-styled front entrance

6. Plan a *split-level home* for a family of four (two teen-age daughters). Provide the following:
   a. Lot size: 125′ × 185′, rolling and wooded
   b. 2000 sq ft floor space plus double carport
   c. Separate dining and living room, three bedrooms, two full baths
   d. Utility and laundry area
   e. Large recreation room with fireplace and access to outdoor living area
   f. Brick-veneer and board-and-batten exterior

7. Plan a modest *duplex for elderly people*. Two retired couples are interested in homes that will be easy to maintain and convenient to live in. They specify the following:
   a. Lot size: 90′ × 200′, provision for gardening
   b. 1000 sq ft in each unit
   c. Frame construction, masonry party wall between units
   d. Adequate storage, guest space, carport for one car for each unit

REVIEW QUESTIONS

1. In arriving at a general size for a family's home, what price range should be selected if they have a $13,000 annual income?

2. What is meant by an easement?

3. Do contour lines crossing a small stream point upstream or downstream?

4. Why is a southern exposure generally the most satisfactory direction in solar orienting a window-wall?

5. Which part of a home should have the most isolation and quiet?

6. What geometric shape is the most economical for a basic plan?

7. Evaluate the "traffic flow" in your own home from the standpoint of convenience.

8. What is the maximum length of a satisfactory kitchen "work triangle"?

9. Define the word "fenestration"

10. Why are simple, uncomplicated exteriors usually the most pleasing?

"*Ah, to build, to build. That is the noblest art of all the arts.*"—Longfellow

7

Light Construction Principles

This chapter introduces and explains many of the accepted principles and methods of light construction found in residences and small commercial buildings. The written material is supplemented with typical sections taken through walls, floors, roofs, and structural members. Pictorial drawings are also used when necessary to present this information as simply as possible. Some of the methods shown are adaptable to one area of the country; others are common construction practice in other areas, depending on building codes and local conditions. Some methods are conventional practice, having been in use for years, others are comparatively new. Together, they form details widely used and generally found satisfactory. More exhaustive treatments of construction details can be found in specialized texts to supplement this material. The actual drawing of details is treated later, but design drawing should not be attempted until a thorough study of construction methods has been made.

7.1 DEVELOPING A BACKGROUND IN LIGHT CONSTRUCTION METHODS

At this point in their training, students should acquire as much information and background relative to construction as they can find from various sources. Architecture, whether it is pursued by people who create and design the most elaborate structures or by others called upon to draw the various working drawings of the simplest buildings, requires a searching interest and enthusiasm about the methods of building. To be successful in this field not only requires skill in knowing *how to draw,* but equally important, requires the acquisition of background information in knowing *what to draw.* Unless a draftsman continually strives to increase his knowledge of construction details, he can expect to become no more than a junior draftsman or merely a tracer.

Technical courses in architectural blueprint reading, building materials, and construction methods, which in technical schools often precede or are prerequisites to architectural drawing, provide this needed background. For supplemental information, refer to the Selected Bibliography; it lists suitable books on construction, many of which are available in libraries. Monthly periodicals and trade magazines containing current and up-to-date information should be continually read by students and draftsmen. Literature from the many building construction trade organizations will be found valuable. Various governmental agencies concerned with housing and standardized construction practice, as well as the United States Government Printing Office, offer inexpensive manuals that should not be overlooked. Draftsmen must become familiar with *Sweet's Architectural Catalog File* (F. W. Dodge Corp., N.Y.) for convenient reference on many of the construction materials available.

Part-time employment with builders or contractors, as an adjunct to drafting training, is desirable for learning construction methods. In fact, actual on-the-job observation of a building in the process of construction is time well spent by the draftsman. Not only is it a thrilling experience, but it offers the opportunity of seeing many of the building materials in use and how they are put together within the building—mainly the structural members that are often concealed once the building is completed. The student who has familiarized himself with the methods and techniques of construction will certainly be better equipped to draw more intelligently, progress more rapidly, and grow in stature as an architectural draftsman.

No attempt has been made to treat special situations requiring structural engineering design to solve the problems. Such information, which is beyond the scope of this book, is left to specialized texts.

7.2 CONSTRUCTION TERMINOLOGY

Figure 7-1 is a guide to the terms found in light construction. A student should memorize these terms and know where they apply within a typical building. Definitions of other terms, which may be unfamiliar to him, can be found in the Glossary of Construction Terms, found in the Appendix. Students will occasionally encounter several designations for similar features in construction terminology because workmen frequently use terms that are indigenous to their particular region; elsewhere the terms might have quite different applications. Despite widespread national distribution of building construction products, terminology has not been entirely standardized; but as a student continues to improve his vocabulary and construction background, the ambiguities will become less confusing.

Some of the present terms used in residential construction, especially in wood framing, have been handed down from New England colonial history. For example: "collar beam," "soleplate," "ridge pole," etc. Some terms have come from the ancient Greek civilization, especially terms relative to classic building exteriors, such as: "frieze," "plinth," "dentils," etc. Other parts derive their names from their physical shapes. For instance, the box sill, which has a boxed-in characteristic, the K brace, which has the shape of the letter K, the T post, which resembles the letter T when shown in cross section, the I beam as well, are just a few of the terms that are so labeled because of their shape. Most of the terms, however, have been derived from the logical use or placement of the part in relation to the building, i.e., "footing," "foundation," "baseboard," "toemold," "doorstop," etc.

"Girders," "beams," and "joists" are terms given to horizontal structural members used in buildings. Often the heavy, structural support for the floor framing in light construction is referred to as either a "girder" or a "beam." In more complex construction, however, the heaviest members are referred to as "girders." They

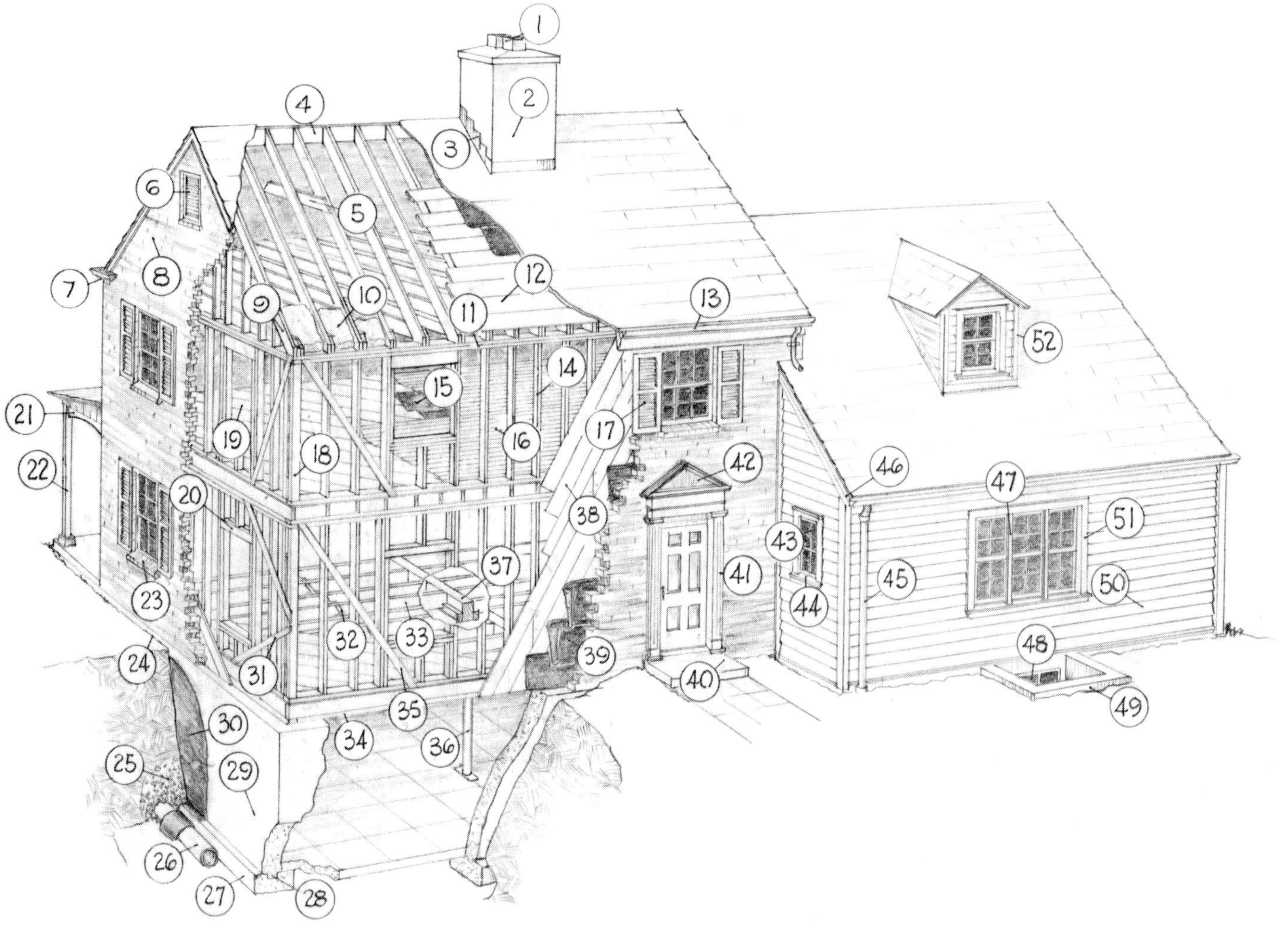

Fig. 7-1 Typical residential terms.

1. Chimney flues or pots
2. Chimney
3. Flashing
4. Ridgeboard
5. Collar beam
6. Vent; louver
7. Cornice return
8. Brick veneer
9. End rafter
10. Insulation
11. Top double plate
12. Roof decking
13. Gutter
14. Stud
15. Flooring paper
16. Finish flooring
17. Shutter
18. Corner post
19. Subfloor
20. Lintel; header
21. Porch frieze board
22. Porch post
23. Brick sill
24. Grade line
25. Cinder or gravel fill
26. Drain tile
27. Footing
28. Keyway
29. Foundation wall
30. Waterproofing
31. Knee brace
32. Bridging
33. Floor joists
34. Sill plate
35. Corner brace
36. Steel column
37. Beam; girder
38. Wall sheathing
39. Building paper
40. Stoop
41. Trim pilaster
42. Pediment door trim
43. Double-hung window
44. Windowsill
45. Downspout
46. Rake mold
47. Mullion
48. Basement window
49. Areaway wall
50. Bevel siding
51. Wood window trim
52. Dormer

support the "beams," which are of intermediate weight, and which support the "joists," the lightest members of the floor or roof structure.

7.3 FOOTINGS AND FOUNDATIONS

Every properly constructed building must be supported by an appropriate foundation, which will support the weight of the building and sustain the structure throughout all weather conditions to which it may be subjected. The footing, the enlarged base of the foundation wall, must be massive enough, depending on local soil conditions, to distribute the weight of the building to the ground below; and it must be deep enough to prevent frost action below. Poured concrete is usually the best and most widely used material. Footings can be formed and poured or, in warmer climates where soils are stable enough to hold their shape, trenches

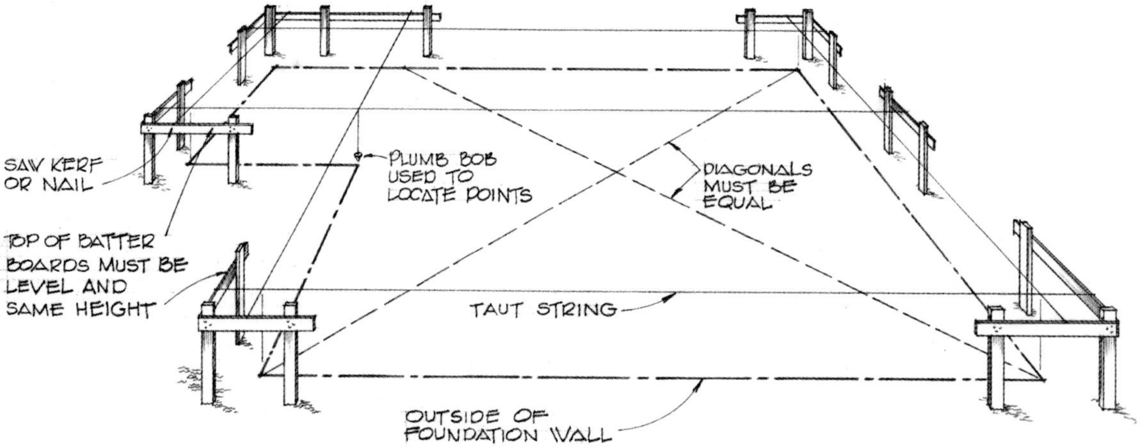

Fig. 7-2 Leveled batter boards are used to layout the foundation of a building.

can be dug the proper depth and concrete poured directly into the trenches to form adequate footings. See Fig. 7-2 for the method of laying out footings.

Frost action below the footing would raise and lower the building during freezing and thawing and soon fracture the foundation as well as disrupt other parts of the building. Naturally, frost lines vary throughout the country; local building codes usually indicate the depth to which footings must be placed below grade. Figure 7-3 shows average frost depths throughout the country compiled by the United States Weather Bureau. The National Building Code prescribes footings to be placed a minimum of 1′–0″ below the frost line. Footings of buildings with basements are deep enough so that frost lines usually need

Fig. 7-3 Average frost depths in inches throughout the United States.

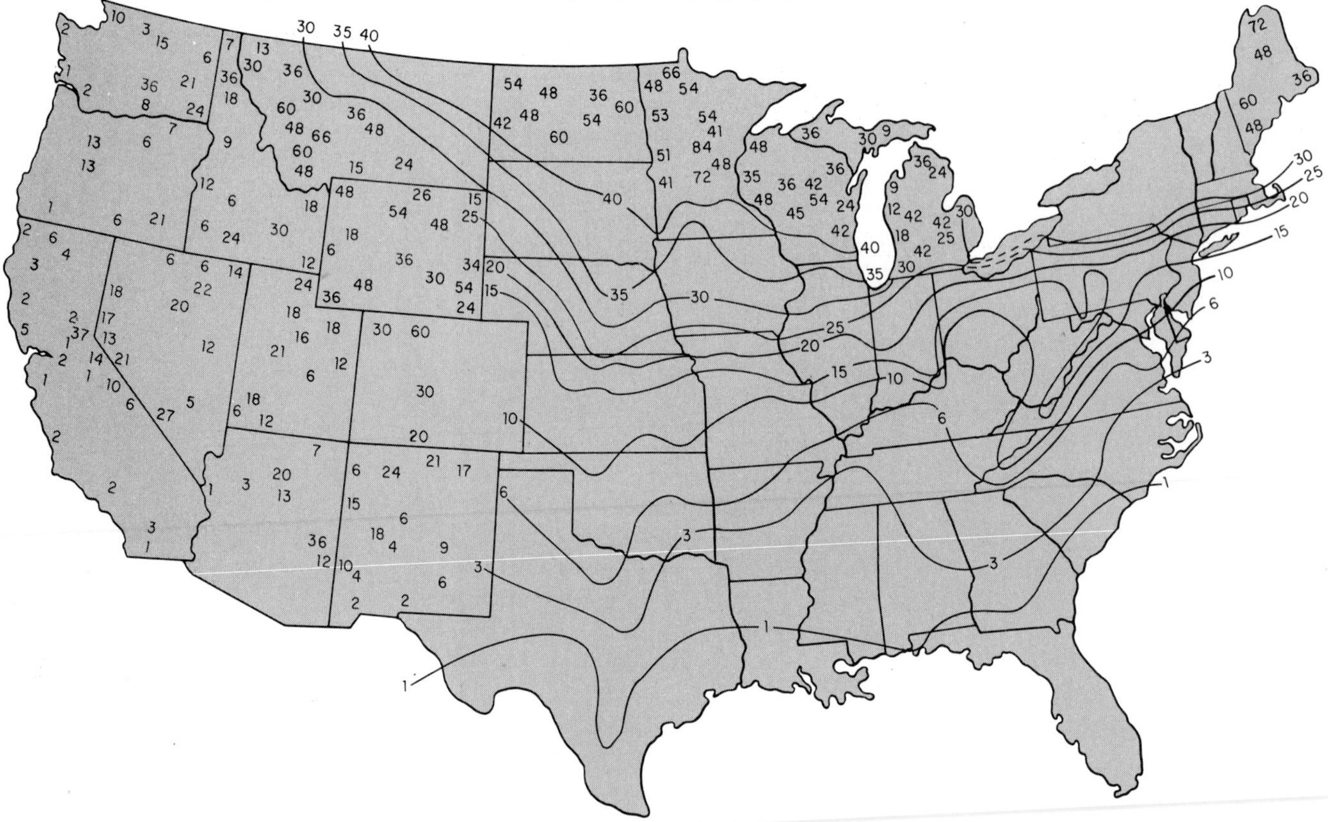

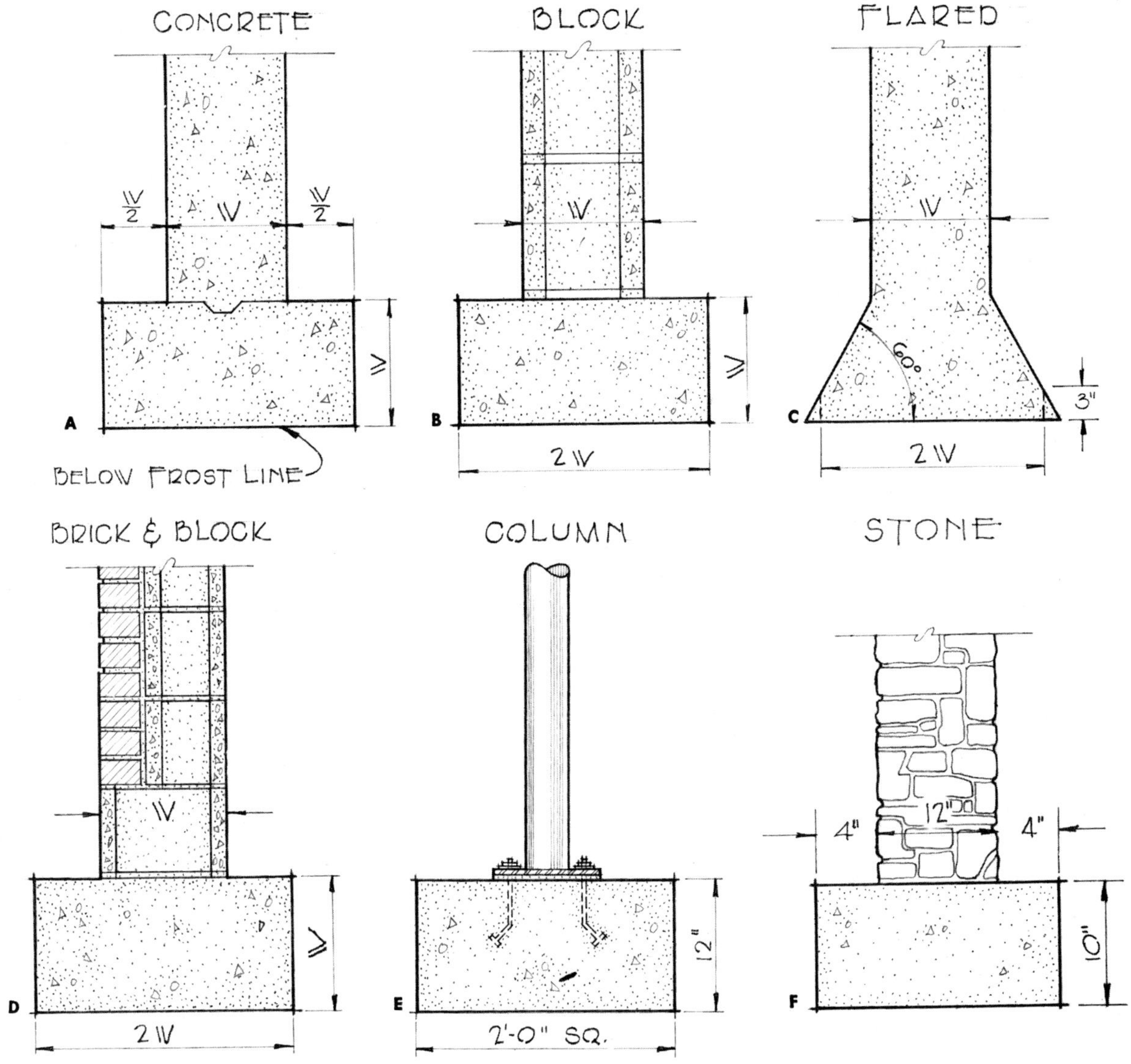

Fig. 7-4 Footings for light construction.

not be considered. In northern areas, the cost of excavating for deep footings often makes the basement more economical than in southern areas where footings are often merely trench footings several feet deep from grade.

Footings should also be placed on undisturbed soil; occasionally, if a building must be put over a fill, the soil should be well tamped and sufficient steel reinforcing should be introduced to the footing, to prevent cracking (Fig. 7-6). Local codes in some areas require steel reinforcing in the footings to counteract specific conditions: (Florida Hurricane Code; California Seismic Code). However, a good rule of thumb is that in firm soil, using light frame construction, the footing can be made twice as wide and the same depth or thickness as the width of the foundation wall (see Fig. 7-4A). Footings should project beyond each side of the wall one-half the wall thickness so that the load is transmitted to the center of the footing.

Stepped Footings are often required on sloping or steep lots where straight horizontal footings would be uneconomical Fig. 7-5). The bottom of the footing is always placed on undisturbed soil and below the frost line, and horizontal runs should be level. The vertical rises of the footing are usually the same thickness as the horizontal portion and are poured at the same time. The vertical distance between steps should not exceed 2′; if concrete block is used for the foundation wall, the vertical

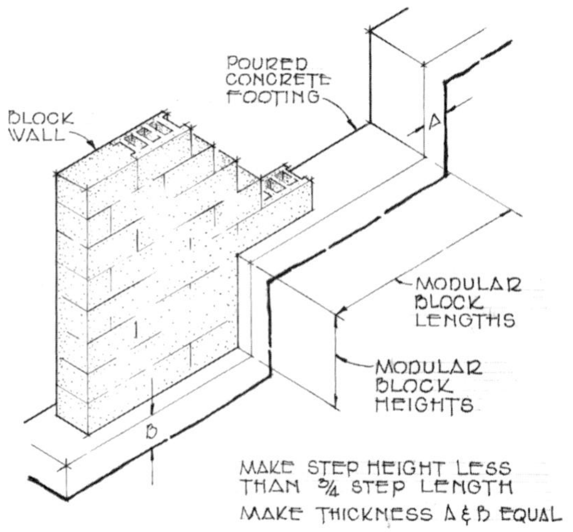

Fig. 7-5 Stepped footings. Check local codes for various restrictions.

height of each step should be compatible with the unit height of the concrete block. Horizontal lengths for the steps are usually not less than 3′.

Column or Post Footings are required to carry concentrated loads within the building. Usually they are square with a tapering pedestal on which the column or post will bear (see Fig. 7-4E). A steel pin is usually inserted into the pedestal if a wooden post is to be used. The footing will vary in size, depending on the load-bearing capacity of the soil and the load it will have to carry. Ordinary column footings for small residences might be 24″ sq by 12″ deep, which would support 16,000 lb if the soil bearing capacity were 4000 lb per sq ft (see Table 7-1).

Footings for chimneys, fireplaces, etc., should be poured at the same time as other footings, and they should be large enough to support the weights they will have to carry. Total weights of different types of masonry construction can be calculated by using Table 7-2.

The soil upon which footings rest must be level and compact. In light soils in which the load-bearing qualities are questionable, it is advisable to introduce steel reinforcing rods at intersecting points between chimney or fireplace footings and wall footings. In soft soils this is advisable also at corners, offsets, and where breaks in direction or size of the footings occur. When footings are subjected to heavier loads, calculations should be made to determine their correct size in order to balance the various footings in relation to their various

Table 7-1 Soil Load-Bearing Qualities

Type of Soil	Safe Load (tons per sq ft)	(lb per sq ft)
Soft clay, loam	1	2000
Dry, firm sand, or clay	2	4000
Compact, coarse sand	3	6000
Coarse gravel	4	8000
Hard pan or hard shale	10	20000
Solid rock	No limit	

Table 7-2 Masonry Weights

Material	Weights (lb per cu ft)
Poured concrete	150
Concrete block	75
Solid brick	120
Clay tile	60

loads. The first consideration is the load-bearing qualities of the soil upon which the footings rest. Table 7-1 indicates typical supporting capacities of different types of soil conditions in tons and pounds per square foot. The soil capacities are only general and cannot be relied on entirely for calculating critical footing sizes. Soils vary considerably even in local areas; also, the moisture content of some soils changes its supporting qualities. Only a soil expert or a local testing laboratory after numerous tests will be able to analyze load-bearing characteristics of a soil for critical footing design. Local practices that have been found successful should be relied upon for this purpose. Careful builders generally have the soil tested before footings are poured. If local codes require steel reinforcing rods, they should be placed near the *top* in wall footings and near the *bottom* in column or isolated footings. Engineers have found that the steel is more effective in case of uneven settlement in the upper part of continuous footings (see Fig. 7-6).

Because residences and frame buildings are comparatively light and seldom require accurate footing design, their footings are generally figured by the above-mentioned rule of thumb. In stable soil the footing for an 8″ foundation wall should be 16″ wide by 8″ deep or thick; the footing for a 12″ foundation wall should be 24″ wide by 12″ deep, etc. However, if the soil is not trustworthy or the building gives indication of being heavier than usual, the following method can be used to calculate the necessary size of the footings. See Tables 7-3, 7-4, and 7-5. Both dead load and live load must be considered in the calculations. *Dead load* refers to the weight of the structure as well as any stationary equipment fastened to it; *live load* refers to varying weights and forces to which parts of the building are subjected: people, furnishings, storage, wind, snow, etc. Both weights are designated in pounds per square foot. Local codes generally require residential floors to be able to carry 40 lb per sq ft live load.

Table 7-3 Typical Weights of Materials Used in Light Construction

Roof	Lb per sq ft
Wood shingles	3
Asphalt shingles	3
Asbestos shingles	4
Copper	2
Built-up roofing, 3 ply & gravel	5.5
Built-up roofing, 5 ply & gravel	6.5
Slate, ¼″ thick	10
Mission tile	13
1″ Wood decking, paper	2.5
2″ × 4″ Rafters, 16″ o.c.	2
2″ × 6″ Rafters, 16″ o.c.	2.5
2″ × 8″ Rafters, 16″ o.c.	3.5
½″ Plywood	1.5
Walls	
4″ Stud partition, plastered both sides	22
Window glass, DSB	5
2″ × 4″ Studs, 1″ sheathing, paper	4.5
Brick veneer, 4″	42
Stone veneer, 4″	50
Wood siding, 1″ thickness	3
½″ Gypsum wallboard	2.5
Floors, Ceilings	
2″ × 10″ wood joists, 16″ o.c.	4.5
2″ × 12″ wood joists, 16″ o.c.	5
Oak flooring, 25/32″ thick	4
Clay tile on 1″ mortar base	23
4″ Concrete slab	48
Gypsum plaster, metal lath	10
Foundation Walls	
8″ Poured concrete, at 150 lb per cu ft	100
8″ Concrete block	55
12″ Concrete block	80
8″ Clay tile, structural	35
8″ Brick, at 120 lb per cu ft	80

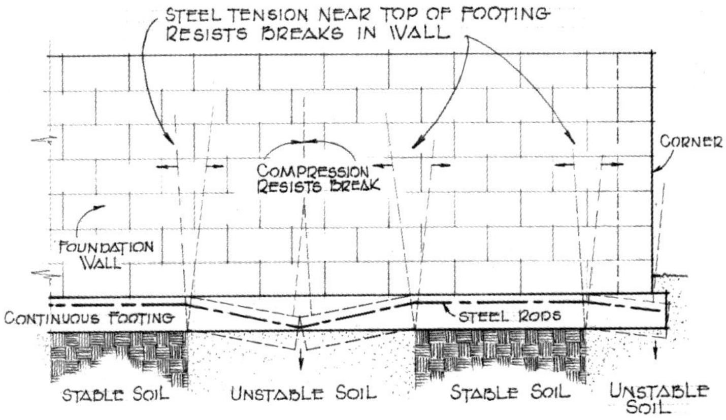

Fig. 7-6 Reinforcing steel becomes most effective if placed in upper part of continuous footings.

Foundation Walls for light construction are generally built of poured concrete or concrete block. In areas where local stone has been found to be economical and dependable, it can be used for foundations. For residential structures, brick or hollow clay tile is used occasionally. Either material has sufficient load-bearing qualities; the choice should be determined by availability, economy, and desired architectural effects.

Poured concrete is considered the most reliable, although it involves considerable labor in preparing forms and also requires time for the concrete to set and harden. The integral, one solid-piece concrete foundation will resist fracturing from settling and differential soil pressures. It lends itself to steel reinforcement at critical points, and dimensions are not restricted by unit sizes as would be the case when using concrete block, brick, etc. Walls thinner than 6″ or 8″ would probably meet the load-bearing requirements for most small structures, yet they have a tendency to fail in shear or to buckle because of earth or water pressures. A good rule of thumb is to limit the height of unreinforced concrete foundation walls to *ten times their thickness;* otherwise vertical reinforcing rods should be used.

Frequently the thickness of the wall is determined by the thickness of the superstructure rather than the load it is to carry. If masonry is used above, the foundation should be as thick as the masonry. If brick or stone veneer frame construction is used, an 8″ thick foundation would be sufficient for 1-story heights. A 2-story building with basement height would require a 10″ thick foundation wall. Brick cavity walls, which are usually 10″ thick, can be supported on

Table 7-4 Calculation for Exterior Wall Footings (Fig. 7-6)

Given: 1-story brick veneer frame, wood shingle roof, plaster interior walls, poured concrete foundation. Load-bearing value of soil 2000 lb per sq ft.

ROOF

	1. Live load, snow, wind (varies locally)	30.0 lb per sq ft	
Dead Load	2. Shingles, wood	3.0	
	3. Wood deck, 1″ thick & paper	2.5	
	4. Rafters, 2″ × 6″, 16″ o.c.	2.5	
	(Length of rafters measures 13′–0″)	38.0 lb per sq ft × 13′	= 494 lb

FIRST-FLOOR CEILING

	1. Live load (attic storage)	20.0	
Dead Load	2. Wood floor, 1″ thick	2.5	
	3. Wood joists, 2″ × 8″, 16″ o.c.	3.5	
	4. Ceiling plaster, metal lath	10.0	
	(Half span of ceiling is 5′–0″)	36.0 lb per sq ft × 5′	= 180 lb

EXTERIOR WALL

	1. Brick veneer	42.0	
Dead Load	2. Sheathing, wood 1″ thick & paper	2.5	
	3. Studs, 2″ × 4″, 16″ o.c.	2.0	
	4. Plaster, metal lath, interior	10.0	
	(Height of wall measures 9′–0″)	56.5 lb per sq ft × 9′	= 509 lb

FLOOR

	1. Live load (usual code requirement)	40.0	
Dead Load	2. Finish oak floor	4.0	
	3. Subfloor, 1″ thick & paper	2.5	
	4. 2″ × 10″ joists, 16″ o.c.	4.5	
	(Half span of floor to center beam is 5′–0″)	51.0 lb per sq ft × 5′	= 225 lb

FOUNDATION

Dead Load	1. Concrete wall, 8″ thick (Height of foundation wall is 9′–0″)	100.0 lb per sq ft × 9′	= 900 lb
	2. Concrete footing, 16″ x 8″	100.0 lb per sq ft × 1.33′	= 133 lb
		Total load on soil per lin ft of wall	= **2471 lb**

$$\textit{Required area of footing} = \frac{\textit{load}}{\textit{soil-bearing cap.}} = \frac{2471}{2000} = 1.23 \textit{ sq ft}$$

Total area of footing required per lin ft of wall = 1.23 sq ft

For convenience use 1.25 : 12″ × 1.25 = *15″ wide footing required.* To be on the safe side, it would be practical to make the footing 16″ wide, which would be the width if calculated by rule of thumb.

Table 7-5 Calculation for Column Footing (Fig. 7-7)

1. Ceiling	180 lb per lin ft
2. Partitions	100
3. First floor	255
Total	535 lb per lin ft

The column supports 10 lin ft of beam

535 × 10 =	5350
Dead load of beam	250
	5600 lb carried by column

$$\frac{\text{Total load}\ 5600}{\text{Soil capacity}\ 2000} = 2.8 \text{ sq ft footing required}$$

$$X = \sqrt{2.8} = 1.7 = 1'\text{–}8''$$

Required column footing size = 1′–8″ × 1′–8″
Make footing 2′–0″ × 2′–0″ × 12″ deep

an 8″ foundation provided the 8″ thickness is corbeled with solid masonry to the thickness of the cavity wall. Long foundation walls, over 25′, should be increased in thickness or designed with integral pilasters at points in the wall where girders or beams rest. The pilasters should be extended one-half the thickness of the foundation wall (see Fig. 7-8).

Moisture conditions in the soil adjacent to the foundation walls may require the walls to be made thicker to ensure a dry basement. Also, exterior waterproofing and proper drainage along the base of the wall may be necessary. When concrete walls are poured separately from the footings, a key is used at their intersection to resist lateral ground pressures (see Fig. 7-9).

Concrete Block foundations, because of their economy and speed of erection, are finding widespread use for foundations of residences as well as other types of buildings. Concrete block

Fig. 7-7 Footing loads.

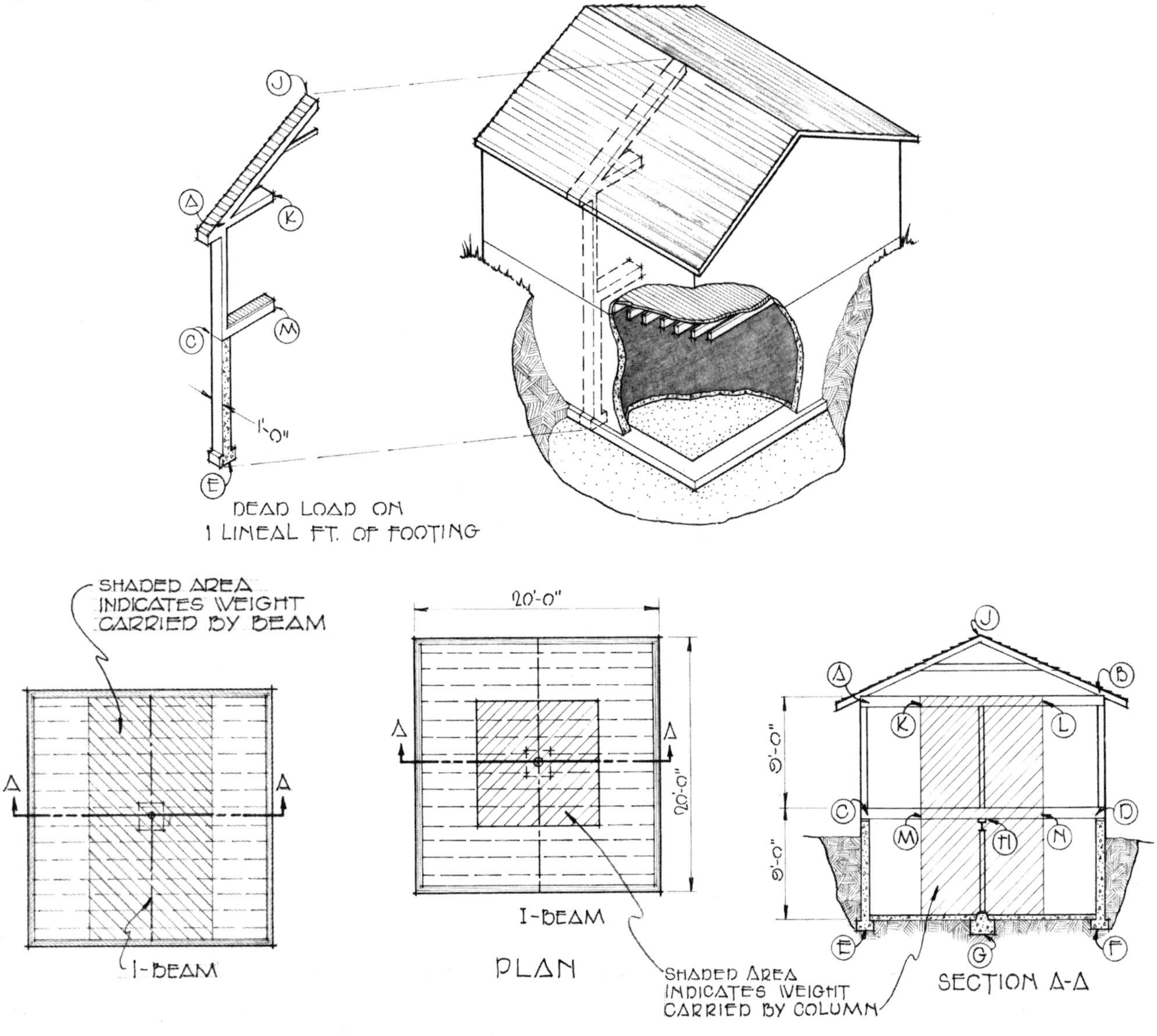

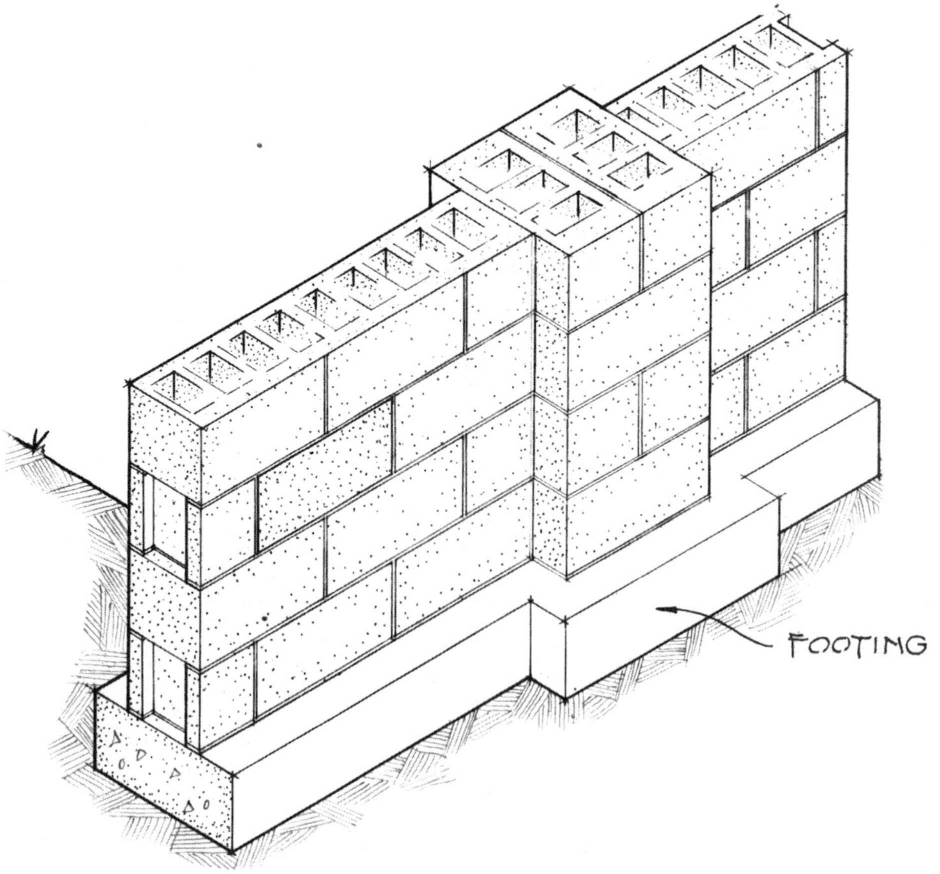

Fig. 7-8 Block wall pilaster.

Fig. 7-9 Dampproofing foundation walls.

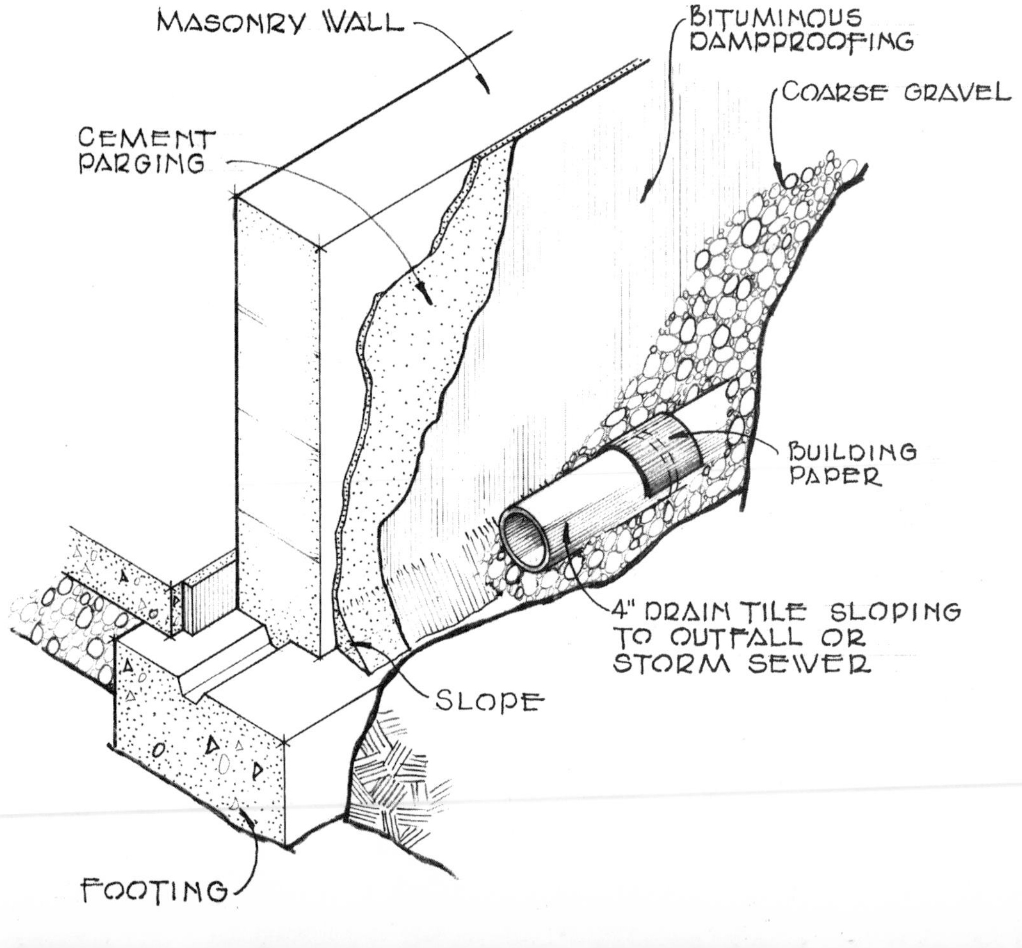

has proven to be satisfactory if correct design has been used and good workmanship has been followed. The majority of foundation walls are made with the nominal 8″ × 8″ × 16″ and/or 8″ × 12″ × 16″ sizes. Their actual sizes are 7⅝″ × 7⅝″ × 15⅝″ and 7⅝″ × 11⅝″ × 15⅝″ (standard sizes vary slightly in different areas). The smaller height and length allow for vertical and horizontal mortar joints to attain modular dimensions. This feature can be a convenience to the designer or draftsman. Common brick can be incorporated into concrete block walls if necessary—three brick courses are equivalent to the 8″ block thickness, three brick wythes are the same as the 12″ block thickness, etc. Block foundation walls should be capped with 4″ high solid cap block. This cap provides a smooth, continuous bearing surface for wood sills and makes the walls more resistive to termite infestation. Corner, joist, jamb, header, and other special units are also made in the standard sizes (see Fig. 7-10). Basement partitions can be built with 4″ or 6″ thick partition block. Very often, concrete block is veneered with face brick to produce economical yet pleasing masonry walls of different thicknesses.

Points on foundation walls of block on which beams or girders rest should have the cores filled with 1:2:4 concrete from the footing to the bearing surface. If heavy loads are anticipated, vertical steel rods should also be introduced to the cores. In long concrete block walls, 8″ × 24″ vertical pilasters should be incorporated to the inside of the wall at a maximum of 10′–0″ intervals, and filled with concrete for rigidity.

The load put on concrete block walls should be limited to 70 lb or 80 lb per sq in., which usually makes the 8″ or 12″ thick blocks adequate for foundations in the majority of light construction buildings. In most situations, the mortar joints are the weakest part of the wall. Codes usually require blocks to be laid in full beds of Portland cement mortar. Fully loaded walls would still have a safety factor of approximately four against failure. Walls supporting wood frame construction should extend at least 8″ above the grade line. Entrance platform slabs, porch slabs, areaways, should be supported or anchored to foundation walls (see Fig. 7-11). In straight walls, blocks should be laid in a lap bond

Fig. 7-10 Typical concrete block units.

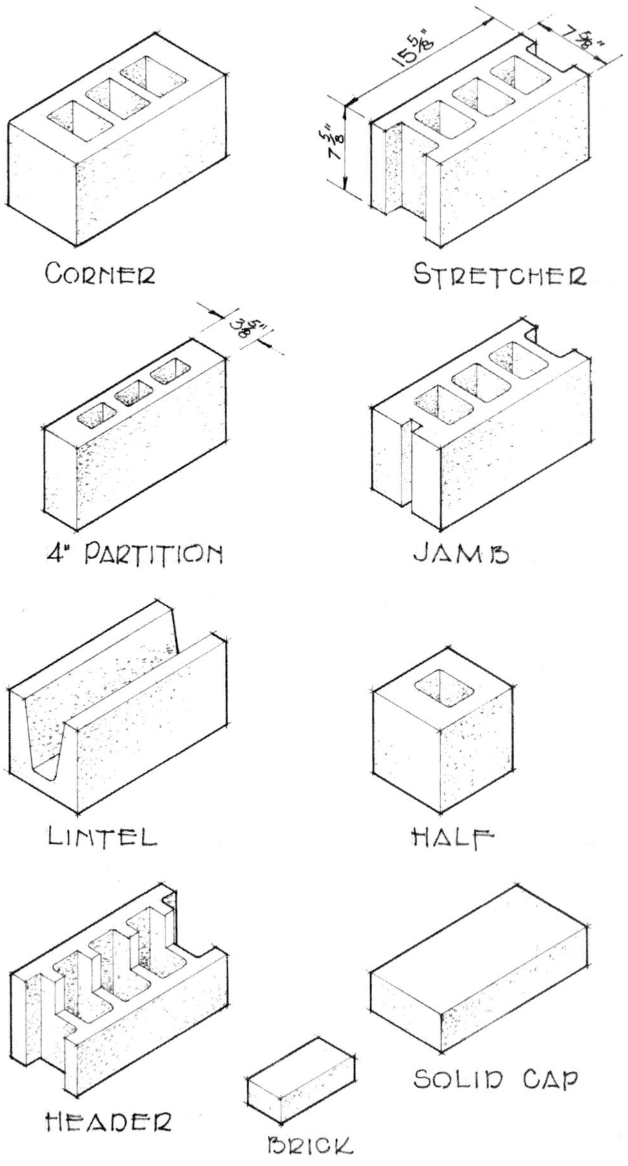

Fig. 7-11 Anchoring exterior slabs to foundation walls.

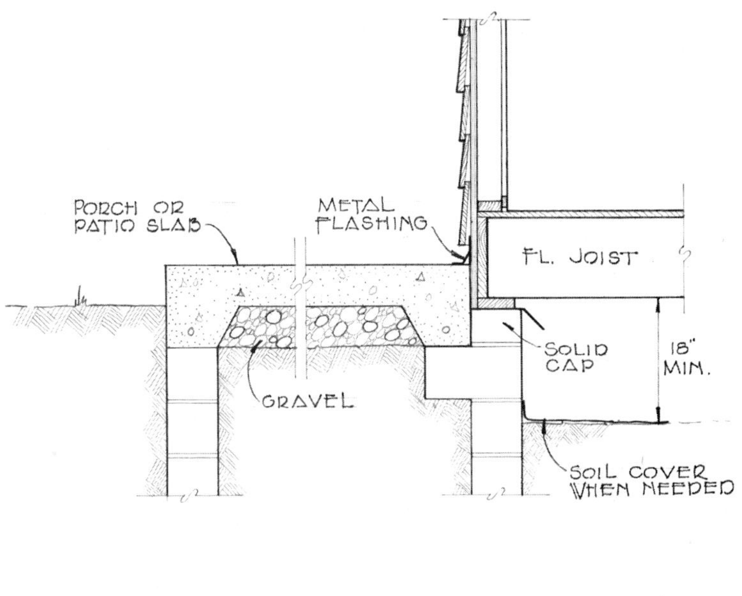

(Fig. 7-8), so that vertical joints in every other course are directly above each other. Intersecting block walls should also be bonded for rigid construction, by interlocking or lapping of alternate courses.

For economy and the sake of good construction, care should be taken to design block walls so that blocks will not have to be cut by the mason. Wall lengths should be in modules of 8″ if the 16″ long block is used. Openings for doors and windows should be placed, if possible, where vertical joints occur; both the width of the opening and the placement of the opening in the wall must be considered. Similarly, heights of block walls should be determined by the heights of the units used. Care taken on the drawing board to provide wall lengths and openings compatible with the block units used will result in sounder walls and neater construction.

Anchor bolts are required by most local codes in foundation walls. They are especially necessary to tie frame constructions such as breezeways, carports, or garages to the foundations. Spaced 6′–0″ apart with at least two bolts in each sill member, anchors will resist winds if they are long enough to extend down into the second course of block. The lower ends of the bolts are secured by embedding a 4″ sq steel washer into the mortar joints and filling the cavities with concrete.

If necessary, the heat loss through 8″ thick concrete block can be reduced 50 percent by putting fill insulation into the cavities of the block.

Fig. 7-12 Lintel block in masonry wall.

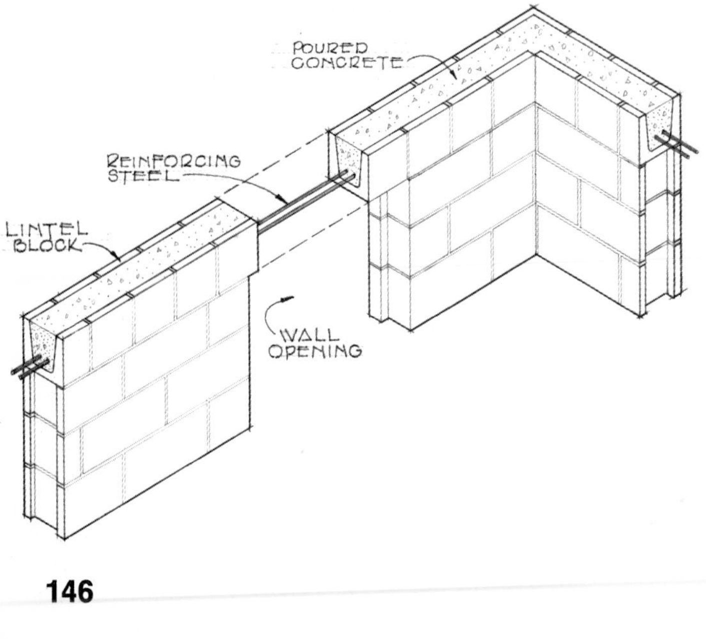

In areas subject to earthquakes, block walls are not practical for foundations. To resist earthquakes, they must be reinforced with vertical rods in cores and there must also be horizontal reinforcement in mortar beds.

Basement concrete block walls should be carefully laid with full, tight mortar joints. If the wall is to be waterproofed, the exterior surface below grade should be parged with a ½″ layer of cement mortar and coated with hot tar or asphalt. In case of extreme moisture conditions, roofing felt is applied over the hot tar and given another coat of hot pitch. Drain tile, set in gravel around the edge of the footings, should also be used to carry off water that may build up around the wall (see Fig. 7-9).

Lintels over wall openings should be reinforced concrete rather than wood. Wood incorporated into block walls for support often shrinks and causes cracks in the block work. Some codes require a reinforced wall header, capping the entire block wall. Precast concrete lintels are available that can be set in mortar above openings by the mason. Because of their weight in handling, split precast lintels are often used over wider openings. Lintel block can also be made into satisfactory lintels. The blocks are set on forms over the opening and filled with concrete and several reinforcing rods (see Fig. 7-12).

Piers are freestanding masonry posts. In basementless houses with wood floors they are spaced 6′–8′ apart to support the girders. Usually they need only be several feet high and 16″ sq in section and capped with 4″ solid cap block. The block should be laid in a lapped bond for strength, and if the piers support heavy loads they should be made larger and filled with concrete.

Stone Foundations using natural stone are not only pleasing to the eye, but are economical as well—especially where the stone can be found locally and has been pronounced suitable for construction work. Stone looks casual, yet gives the impression of solidity; its varied surface textures, uneven contours and sizes present a challenge to the artistry of the mason. Architects realize that stone eliminates the mechanical appearance, so often present when block materials are used. For this reason, stone is popular with architects and they use it frequently, especially in the building of better quality residences.

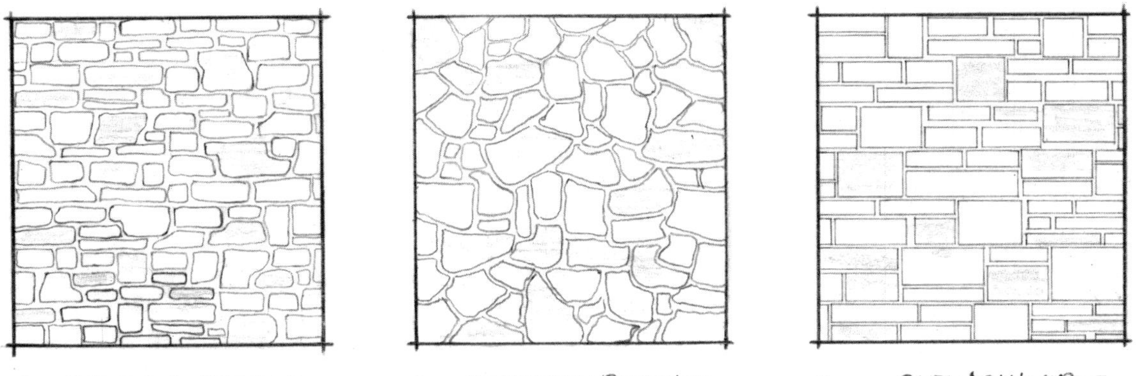

A COURSED RUBBLE B RANDOM RUBBLE C CUT ASHLAR

Fig. 7-13 Stonework textures.

Stonemasonry is generally referred to as either "rubble" or "ashlar." Rubble stonework is made up of individual stones more or less irregular in shape, size, and method of combining. In some masonry the irregularity may be less pronounced to give prominence to the horizontal coursing—hence the expression "coursed rubble." To achieve the effect of horizontal dominance to the courses, the mason must dress the individual stones somewhat, forming horizontal setting beds and continuous uneven horizontal joints (see Fig. 7-13A). "Random rubble" is the term given to the more irregular and rustic-looking stonework, showing no evidence of coursing and very little dressing by the mason. The stones usually are massive in appearance and are combined to avoid the use of chips and fillers (see Fig. 7-13B). Bondstones are stones large enough to extend through the full thickness of the wall; good stonework will show evidence of bondstones at critical places as well as systematically throughout the entire wall. Fieldstones, gathered from river beds or open fields, also produce a rubble-type stonework. They vary in color and size and usually are rounded by nature from water action, weathering, or movement on the earth's surface. Interesting textures on either exterior or interior walls above grade can be achieved with fieldstones, but due to their roundness they are unsuitable for foundation walls, where load-bearing qualities have to be considered.

Pilasters can be incorporated into stone foundations at critical points to serve the same purpose as mentioned for other masonry materials.

"Ashlar stonework" is the term given to masonry making use of custom-dressed and squared stones. The stones are usually processed at the quarry; each stone is cut to specifications to fit an exact place in the building. This type of stonework is costly; for this reason it is used mainly in large commercial or public buildings—seldom in residences. Ashlar stone can also be used as a veneer with other masonry materials as a backing. Ashlar-stone patterns impart the formal look, so prevalent on public buildings.

Any of the granites produce excellent foundations walls; their conchoidal fracture patterns reduce the amount of hammer dressing considerably. The use of granite results in typical random rubble masonry. Hard sandstones, blue shale, and conglomerates also produce suitable rubble walls. Coursed rubble can be conveniently made with the sedimentary type stones, hard sandstones, limestones, etc.

Sedimentary type stone cut into 4″ thick veneering for wood frame construction is generally referred to as "ashlar-stone-veneer." The pieces have rock faces and squared setting surfaces and are combined to form similar horizontal courses.

Residential stone walls should be at least 16″ thick; thinner walls are more difficult for masons to lay. The unit of measurement of stone masonry is called a "perch," usually 25 cu ft of finished wall.

Precast concrete slip sills are usually used in stonemasonry under window and door openings.

Brick and Tile Foundations Brick foundation walls are satisfactory for light frame construction as far as strength and dependability are concerned. However, they require more skilled labor, and care must be used in selecting a hard-burned brick that will withstand below-

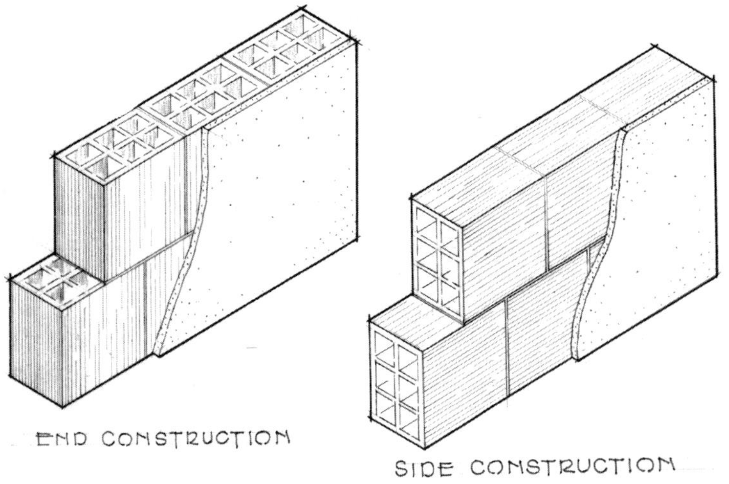

Fig. 7-14 Methods of setting structural clay tile in walls.

grade conditions. Brick must be laid with high-grade Portland cement mortar and mortar joints must be completely filled to prevent water seepage. Poured concrete footings are recommended with either brick or tile foundation walls.

Tile foundations can be laid in either *end construction* or *side construction,* and load-bearing tile; A.S.T.M. designation C34 must be specified. End construction tile is laid with the cells vertical, and side construction tile is laid with the cells horizontal. End construction is considered stronger. Solid masonry units must be inserted into the walls to form load-bearing surfaces for joists and beams to rest on; pilasters can be incorporated into the walls as in other types of walls.

Tile units are generally 12″ long and are referred to in terms of their nominal sizes. Thus, an 88H unit is 8″ × 8″ × 12″ in size. Letter designations refer to the direction of the cells in the unit and to the fitting units as follows:

H—Side Construction (horizontal cell)
V—End Construction (vertical cell)
C—Closure unit, nominal 8″ length
U—Utility unit, nominal 12″ length

For example, a 58VU unit would mean: 5″ nominal wall thickness, 8″ nominal height, end construction (vertical cell), and utility unit, 12″ in length. The tile used for foundation walls is generally 8″ or 12″ thick and is laid with Portland cement mortar (see Fig. 7-14). Load-bearing tile is not as pleasing in appearance as other materials; it can be veneered with brick above grade or stuccoed with a 1″ layer of Portland cement stucco.

Areaways Basements in residences require some method of ventilation and natural lighting. If the basement wall extends only 1′ or 2′ above grade, an areaway is needed so that basement windows that are on or below grade do not let moisture get into the basement (see Fig. 7-15). The areaway walls must be tied to the basement walls, and the same masonry materials are usually used for the areaway as for the foundation. Small areaways can be made of semicircular, corrugated galvanized steel. The bottom of the areaway can have a masonry floor with a drain leading to the storm sewer, or it can be filled with sufficient crushed gravel or stone with drainage tile below to carry the water away from the foundation wall. The areaway walls should extend several inches above grade and at least 4″ below the bottom of the basement window. If the areaway is over 24″ deep, it should be provided with a grill above to prevent children or animals from falling into it.

Fig. 7-15 Areaways for basement windows.

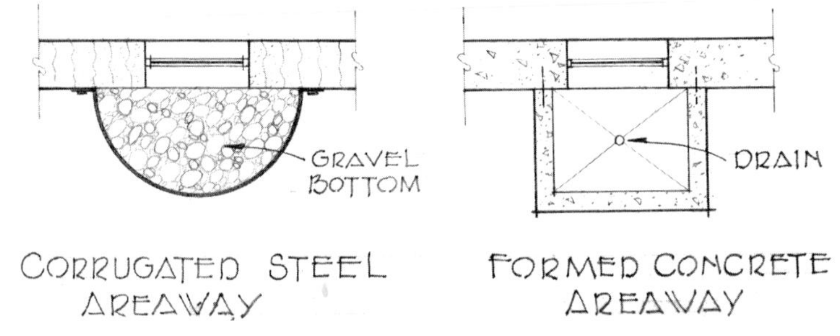

Freestanding Pier Foundations In warmer areas where floors need not be insulated, it is more economical to put 1-story houses on freestanding piers of masonry rather than on continuous foundations around the entire exterior wall (see Fig. 7-16). The piers must be of solid masonry—brick, poured concrete, or concrete filled hollow block. Customarily, piers 18″ or 24″ high above grade are used, never more than three times their least horizontal dimension unless reinforced. Usually 8″ × 16″ or 12″ × 16″ piers spaced not more than 8′ apart are sufficient. Piers should be covered with termite shields where required, and spanned with either wood or metal beams large enough to carry the weight of the exterior walls. The beams act as sills, and the floor is built above the beams, which are well-anchored to the piers.

Brick veneer can be used with freestanding piers by starting the brick veneer on a poured footing below grade. The footings must be poured integrally with the pier footings, and each must be the proper size. Despite masonry piers having been used, this brick-veneer curtain wall gives the exterior the appearance of a continuous foundation. When a brick-veneer curtain wall is used, sufficient ventilation and an access door must be provided as in continuous foundations (see Fig. 7-17).

Grade Beam Foundations One-story frame buildings can be adequately supported on foundations made up of a system of poured concrete piers with suitable footings, and the piers spanned by reinforced concrete beams that have been formed with trenches dug into the ground (see Fig. 7-18). The concrete beams must be designed in accordance with good engineering practice to carry the weight of the building above. Unless the soil below the beam has been removed and replaced with coarse rock or gravel not susceptible to frost action, the bottom of the grade beam must be below the frost line. If structural analysis has not been made, the following minimum conditions (FHA) should be met, based on a 1-story structure with average soil conditions:

1. Piers:
   a. Maximum pier spacing 8′–0″ o.c.
   b. Minimum size of piers, 10″ diam; pier should be reinforced with a No.5 bar for the full length of the pier and extending into the beam.
   c. Depth of pier should extend below the frost line and have a bearing area of at least 2 sq ft for average soils.

2. Grade beam:
   a. Minimum width for frame buildings: 6″; an 8″ beam can be flared if covered by base trim. Masonry or masonry veneer should be 8″ wide.
   b. Minimum effective depth, 14″; if grade beam supports a wood floor, the beam must be deep enough to provide a minimum of 18″ crawl space below the wood floor.
   c. Reinforce the beam with two top bars and two No.4 bottom bars, if frame construction; if masonry or masonry veneer, reinforce with two top bars and two No.5 bottom bars. If grade beam is flared at top, reinforce top with one No.6 bar instead of two No.4 bars.

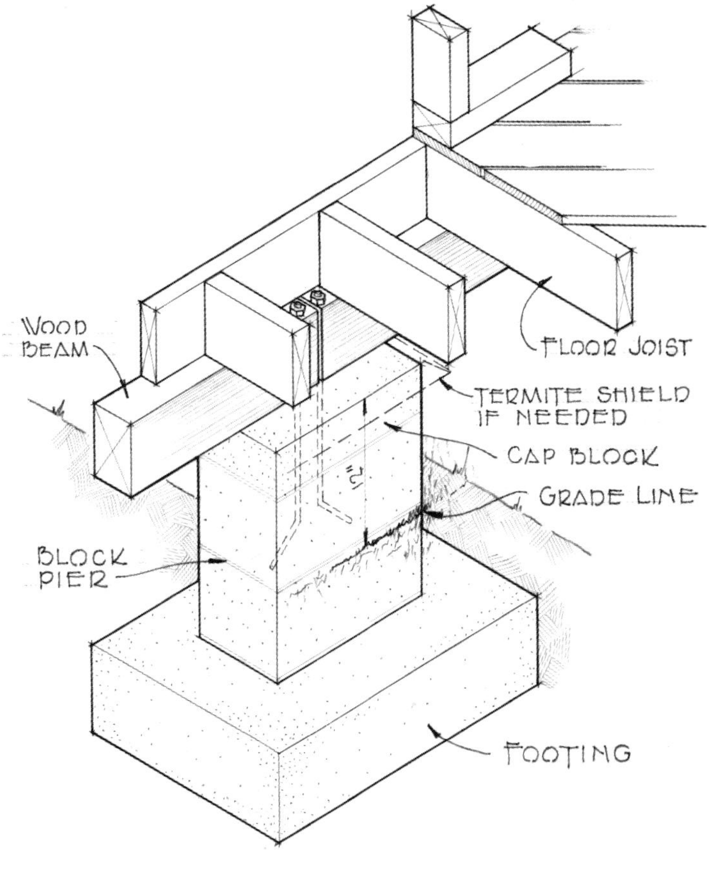

Fig. 7-16 Freestanding masonry pier.

Fig. 7-17 Economical pier construction with brick veneer and crawl space.

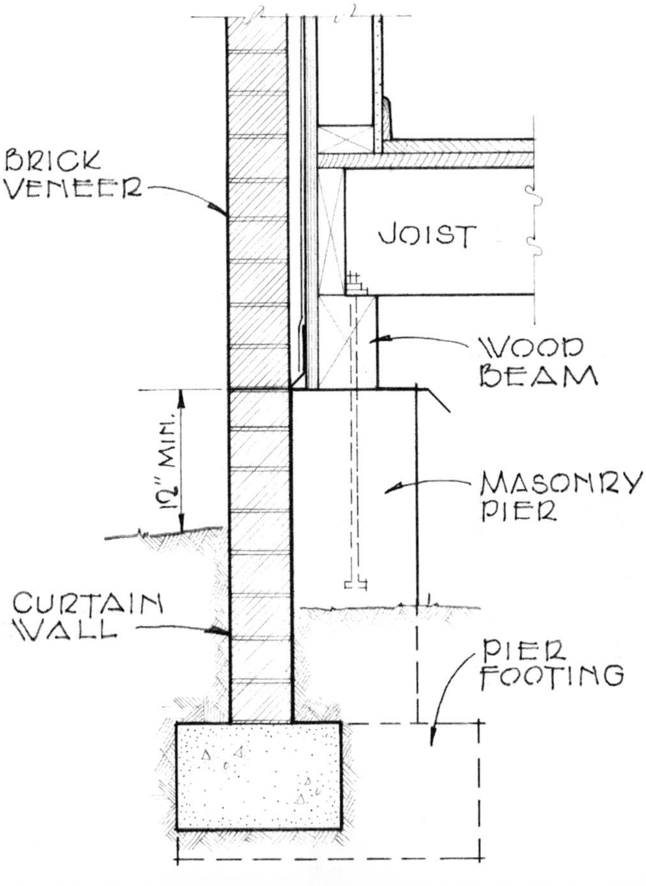

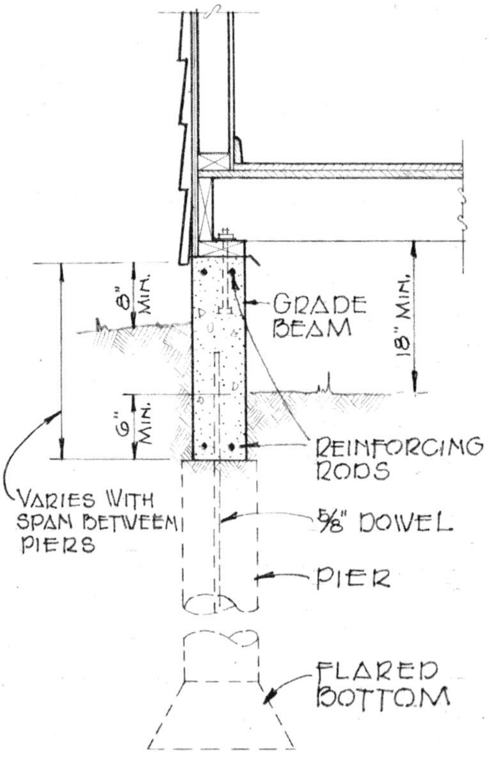

Fig. 7-18 Detail showing the use of grade beam with frame construction.

Concrete Slab-on-ground Construction In recent years basements have been eliminated in many 1-story houses. Formerly, a basement was definitely necessary, for heating plants, fuel storage, and laundry or utility areas. With the advent of liquid and gas fuels, however, the need for bulky fuel and ash storage space has been eliminated. Both heating plants and laundry equipment have become more compact, thus requiring little space in the modern home. Basementless residences have become popular, especially in warmer climates where footings need not be placed so deep in the ground. With the elimination of the basement, one type of floor construction that has been found successful, if properly executed, is the concrete slab-on-ground (see Fig. 7-19).

Precaution should be used in placing a slab on certain lots. Sloping lots would not only require considerable excavation, they also present drainage problems; low lots where moisture often accumulates would also be unfavorable. The ideal area would be a nearly level lot requiring a minimum of excavation and one free of moisture problems. Finish floor should be at least 8″ above grade. Concrete floors have a tendency to feel cold and damp during winter and wet seasons; this can be eliminated by introducing either radiant heating coils or perimeter heating ducts into the slab. Care must be taken to have an absolutely watertight membrane below the slab to prevent moisture from penetrating from the ground, and particularly in northern climates, the periphery of the slab must be well insulated. Concrete slabs can be finished with either of the many types of flooring materials: asphalt, rubber, vinyl, or cork tile in mastic, carpeting over padding, plywood block flooring in mastic; or hardwood strip flooring can be laid on sleepers over a concrete slab.

The following construction requirements should be met in using a concrete slab-on-ground:

1. Finish-floor level should be high enough above natural grade so that the finished grade will provide good drainage away from the building.
2. All debris, topsoil, and organic matter must be removed from below the slab. Loose soil must be tamped. Earth fill should not exceed 12″.
3. All sewer, water, gas, and oil supply lines must be installed before the slab is poured.
4. At least a 4″ layer of coarse gravel or crushed rock must be placed above the soil and tamped well.
5. A watertight vapor barrier must be placed over the crushed stone before the slab is poured, which will prevent the cement fines from working into the voids of the gravel and prevent moisture from seeping up into the slab from the soil.
6. A permanent, waterproof, nonabsorptive type of rigid insulation must be installed around the perimeter of the slab in accordance with the requirements of the climate. In very mild climates insulation may not be required, but an expansion joint should be used.
7. The slab must be reinforced with wire mesh weighing not less than 20 lb per 100 sq ft, or with 6″ × 6″ No.10 wire mesh. The slab must be at least 4″ thick and be troweled to a smooth, hard finish.
8. When ductwork is placed in the slab, it should be of noncorrodible, nonabsorbent material with not less than 2″ of concrete completely surrounding the ductwork. Metal heating coils and reinforcement, if used, must be covered with at least 1″ of concrete.

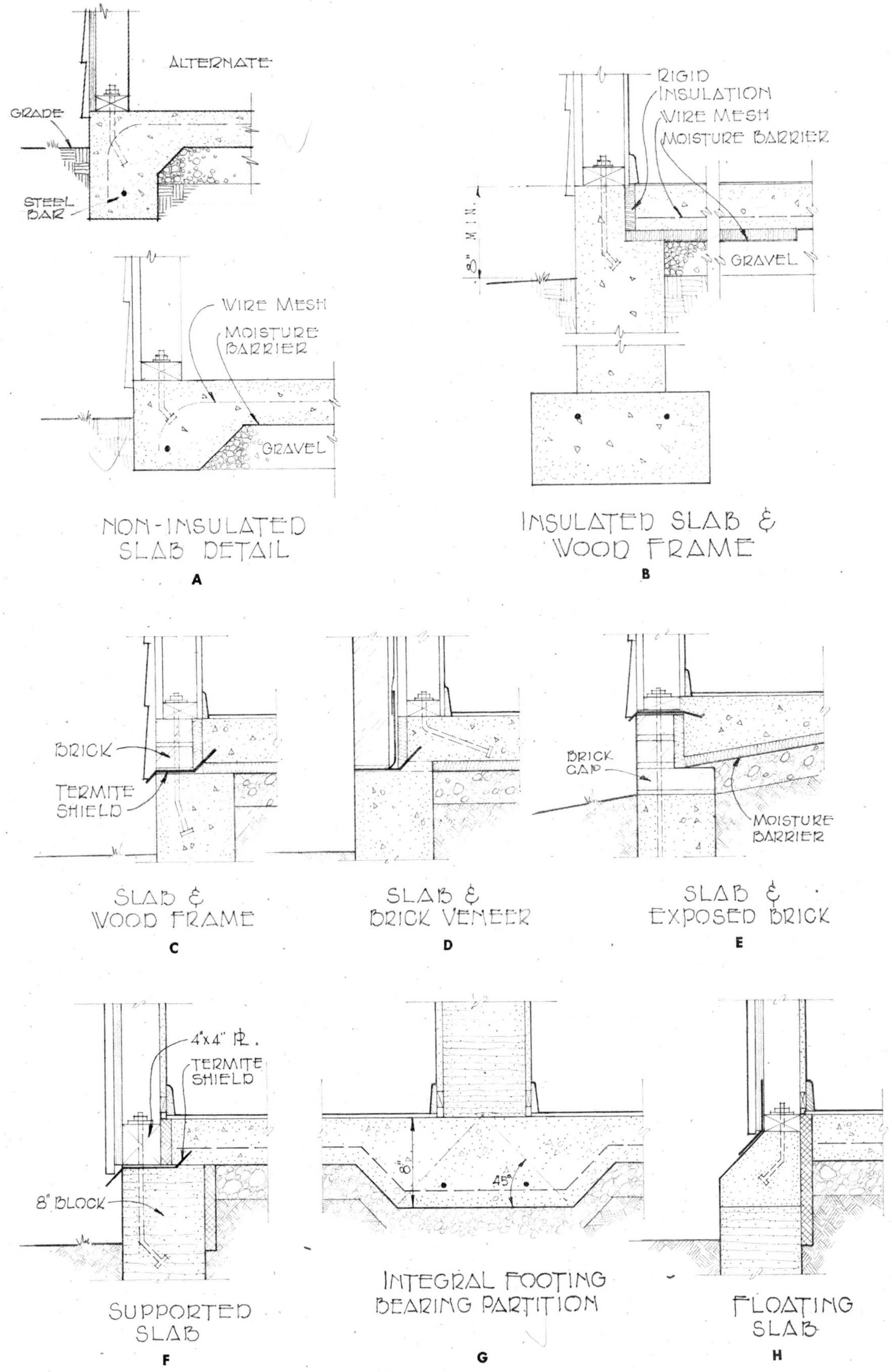

Fig. 7-19 Sill details of slab-on-ground construction.

Slab-on-ground floors permit a lower silhouette in the overall appearance of the house. This lower, more ground-hugging appearance is typical of many of the so-called "ranch-type" houses. In areas where outdoor living spaces adjacent to the house are popular, the slab floor eliminates the need for four or five steps leading from interior floor levels to the surface of the outdoor terrace areas. Consequently, the terrace becomes more usable and more easily accessible from the interior of the house.

Slabs can either be supported by the foundation wall (Fig. 7-19F), or they can be independent of the foundation and supported entirely by the soil below the slab. (Fig. 7-19H.) Either method is satisfactory if the soil below is well-compacted. If settlement should occur below the slab, the "floating" slab construction would be less likely to crack or fracture eventually. If considerable fill is necessary under a slab, it should be done under the supervision of a soil engineer in accordance with good engineering practice. Such a slab should be supported by the foundation wall, as well as by concrete piers or intermediate foundations throughout the center of the slab area. See Fig. 7-20. All load-bearing partitions and masonry nonbearing partitions should be supported on foundations bearing on natural ground independent of the slab, unless the slab is thickened and reinforced to distribute adequately the concentrated load (see Fig. 7-19G).

In northern areas, where insulation from heat loss is of prime importance, several inches of Zonolite or insulating concrete can be used below the regular concrete. Structural clay tiles laid over the entire area provide a satisfactory bed for a concrete slab. The tiles should have a 3″ or 4″ layer of crushed stone or gravel and a waterproof membrane below, and should be laid horizontally with their cells in an alternating pattern to prevent lateral heat flow toward cold exterior walls. Proper rigid insulation should also surround the entire slab (see Fig. 7-19).

Structural Concrete Slabs are designed by a structural analysis of their intended load and contain steel reinforcing to make them strong enough to withstand the load they will bear independent of any central supports below. For example, garages with basements underneath may require structural slab floors.

Integral Slab and Footing Where frost lines are very shallow, slabs and their footings can be poured at one time, thus providing an integral foundation-and-floor, economical for 1-story buildings (see Fig. 7-19A). The footing is merely a flared thickening of the slab around its perimeter. For best results the bottom of the footing should be at least 1′ below the natural grade line and must be supported on solid, unfilled, and well-drained soil. Several No. 4 bars are placed near the bottom of the footing, and the wire mesh of the slab is rolled into the shape of the footing to tie the entire concrete mass together. Gravel fill and a waterproof membrane must be placed below the slab and footing, similar to the other types of slabs. This type of slab is difficult to insulate, but construction time is gained by its use.

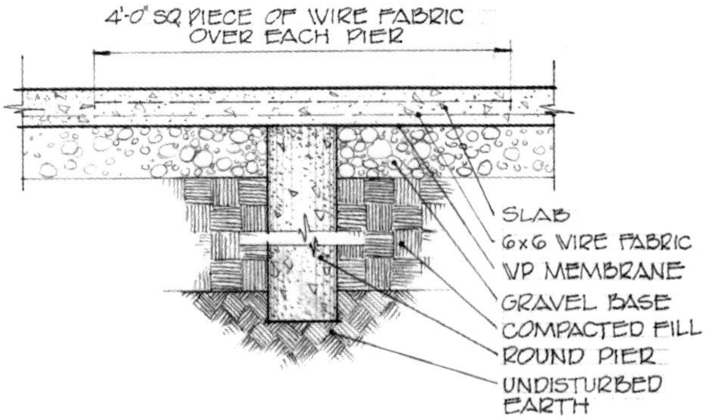

A

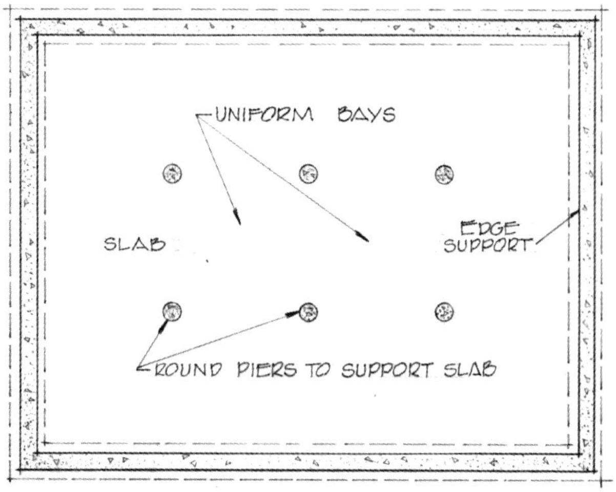

B

Fig. 7-20 Use of piers below slabs on ground.

Termite Protection under Floor Slabs In areas where termite infestation is a problem, certain precautions should be taken for concrete slab-on-ground construction. First, the entire area below the waterproof membrane should be treated with a poisonous chemical. Where insulation or expansion-joint material has been used around the perimeter of the slab, the material should be kept 1″ below the surface of the slab and the space filled with hot tar or asphalt. Insulation containing wood fiber should not be used in termite areas. Circular spaces around all plumbing pipes that pierce the slab should be dug out 1″ deep and also filled with hot pitch. All framing lumber that comes in contact with the slab or is near it should be pressure-treated. All plumbing walls should be provided with an access door for periodic inspection. Openings where anchor bolts are fastened to sill plates must be sealed. Metal flashing should be provided between the wood framing and the slab. If slabs should happen to crack, a plastic waterproof membrane is more reliable than tarred felt membranes.

Insulation for Floor Slabs In most areas of the United States insulation must be installed around residential concrete slabs if the construction is to be satisfactory. Because of the density of concrete, it can be classified as a conductor of heat rather than an insulator—the reverse is true of wood and other cellular types of building materials. Heating engineers maintain that practically all the exterior heat loss from a slab-on-ground takes place along and near the edges of the slab. Very little heat is dissipated into the ground below the slab. See Fig. 7-21. Therefore, careful consideration must be given to the insulation of the slab edges, especially in colder areas. Insulation should be rigid, resistive to dampness, immune to fungus and insect infestation, easy to cut and work, high in crushing strength, and of course resistive to transmission of heat.

Insulating qualities, referred to as *R* factors, are usually given for different insulation materials. The *R* factor for a material would be the temperature difference in degrees Fahrenheit necessary to force 1 Btu per hr through 1 sq ft of the material 1″ thick. Table 7-6 lists the resistance values, or *R* factors, that should be used in determining the minimum amount of insulation recommended for various design temperatures, with and without floor radiant heating. The table indicates also, the minimum depth the insulation should extend below grade.

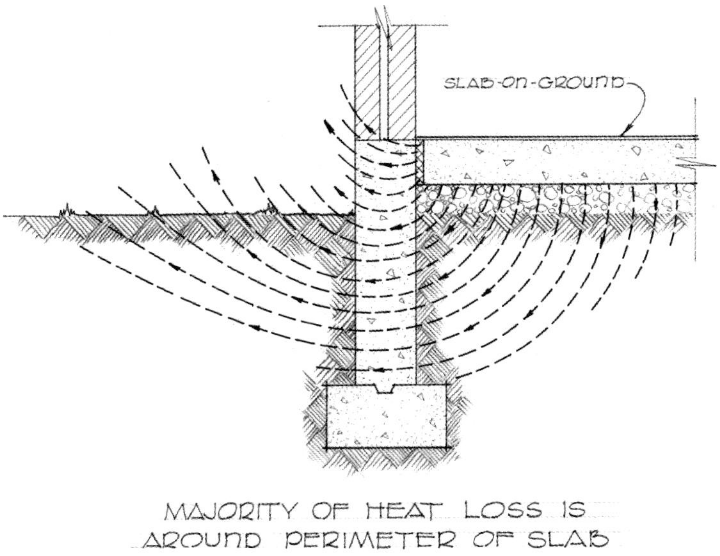

Fig. 7-21 Heat loss of slab on ground.

Table 7-6 Resistance Values for Determining Slab-on-Ground Perimeter Insulations

Heating design temperature (°F)	Depth insulation extends below grade	Resistance (*R*) factor No floor heating	Floor heating
−20	2′–0″	2.00	3.00
−10	1′–6″	1.75	2.62
0	1′–0″	1.50	2.25
+10	1′–0″	1.25	1.87
+20	1′–0″	1.00	1.50

For example, if the table indicates an *R* factor of 2.62 needed, and the insulation selected has an *R* factor of 1.50 per in. of thickness, then the total thickness needed would be calculated as follows:

$$\frac{2.62}{1.50} = 1.74'' \text{ of insulation}$$

For convenience and reliability a 2″ thickness should be used, making the *R* factor: $2 \times 1.50 = 3.00$.

Cellular-glass insulation board, asphalt coated glass-fiber board, synthetic-plastic foam are favorable types of perimeter insulation for concrete slabs.

Steel Reinforcement Poured concrete used in foundations for lintels or structural beams must be reinforced with steel rods to carry the weight imposed upon it. For structural use, concrete in itself possesses good compression resistance qualities but has relatively poor tensile strength. Mild steel and concrete have nearly the same coefficients of expansion and contraction; they are, therefore, compatible in that they will expand and contract practically the same amount during temperature changes, and so do not lose their bond when combined. When a force or weight is exerted downward on the top of a concrete beam, the tensile stresses would react outward on the lower part of the beam and cause it to break. For example, if a heavy weight were put on the center of a horizontal beam, supported on each end, the beam would crack open on its underside. To counteract this, steel, with its high tensile strength, should be placed in the lower part of the beam where the steel becomes the most effective. If the beam has a column or support below it at any point, the steel in the beam should continue over the column but be raised to the upper part of the beam directly over the column (see Fig. 7-22A). The tensile stresses directly above the column are in the upper part of the beam.

Steel wire mesh, used in concrete slabs-on-grade, should be placed in the lower part of the slab for most effectiveness; in a 4″ slab the mesh should be placed 1″ from the bottom of the slab. Steel mesh, also known as "welded wire fabric," is available in 5′ wide rolls, and the 6″ × 6″ mesh

Fig. 7-22 Loading stresses of reinforced concrete beams. Similar stresses exist in wood beams.

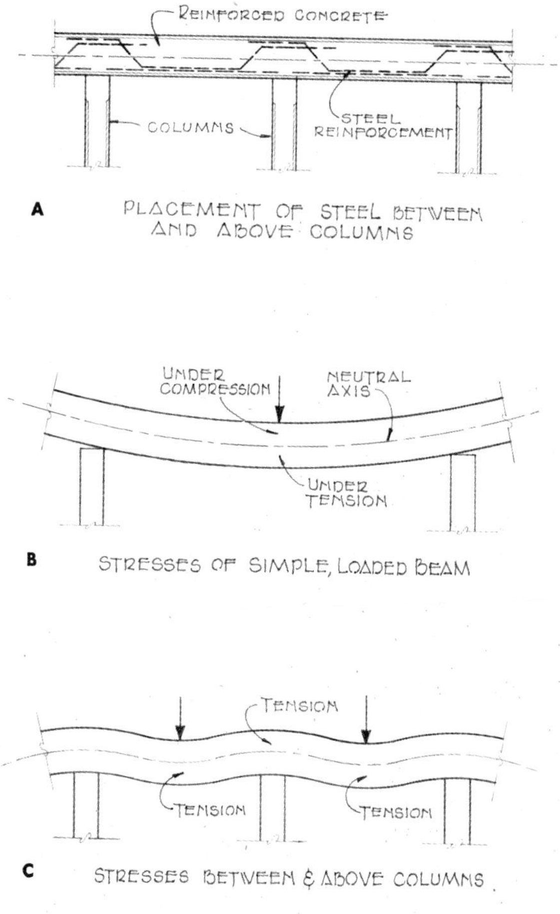

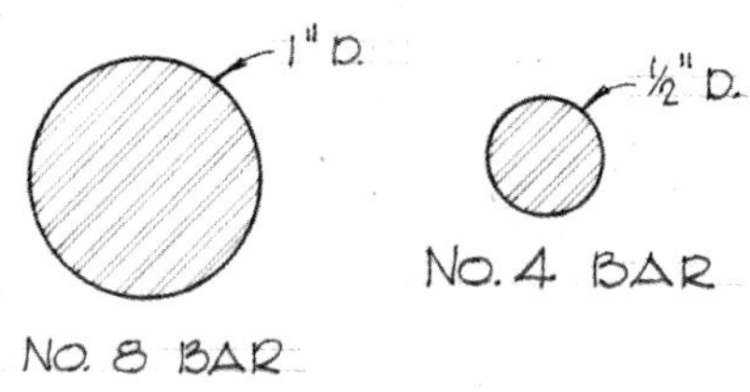

Fig. 7-23 Reinforcing steel is sized according to its diameter.

opening size is usually used in slab reinforcement unless structural slabs are required. Number 10 wire size is sufficient.

In brickwork, steel angles are usually used above openings, unless brick arches or other types of masonry lintels are used. Angle-iron sizes, ¼″ × 4″ × 4″, ¼″ × 4″ × 6″ are often used because they lend themselves to the width of the brick and the mortar joint thickness.

Steel reinforcement rods are available in sizes from No. 2 to No. 11, and they are labeled by their number or by their diameter. See Fig. 7-23. The number labeling is preferable because it indicates how many eighths of an inch the rod is in diameter. A No. 5 rod, for example, would be ⅝″ in diameter, a No. 7 rod ⅞″ in diameter, etc. Deformed rods are rods that have ridges on their surfaces thus providing more mechanical bond between the steel and concrete. Steel reinforcement should be indicated and placed correctly when drawing section details.

7.4 CONVENTIONAL WOOD FRAME CONSTRUCTION

Four out of five houses built in North America employ wood frame construction. A frame structure will give many years of satisfactory service if careful planning has been done on the drawing board and is followed during construction. Correct details and good workmanship are two important factors in realizing durability from a frame building; however, the following methods will further ensure maximum service life from the use of wood:

1. Control the moisture content of the wood;
2. Provide effective termite and insect barriers throughout; and
3. Use naturally durable or chemically treated wood in critical places in the structure.

7.4.1 Platform Frame Construction

Platform frame construction (also referred to as western frame) is identified by its story-level construction—erected by the workmen upon each subfloor or platform (see Fig. 7-24). This method of construction has become popular throughout the country in recent years, mainly for the following reasons:

1. Long studding pieces required in balloon framing are not always available and are usually more costly.
2. The platform built at each level is convenient for carpenters to work on (the construction builds its own interior scaffolding).
3. The construction prevents "flue-action" within the walls in case of fire, thus eliminating the need for fire-stop material in critical places.
4. It lends itself to modern prefabrication methods.

Fig. 7-24 Platform (western) frame construction.

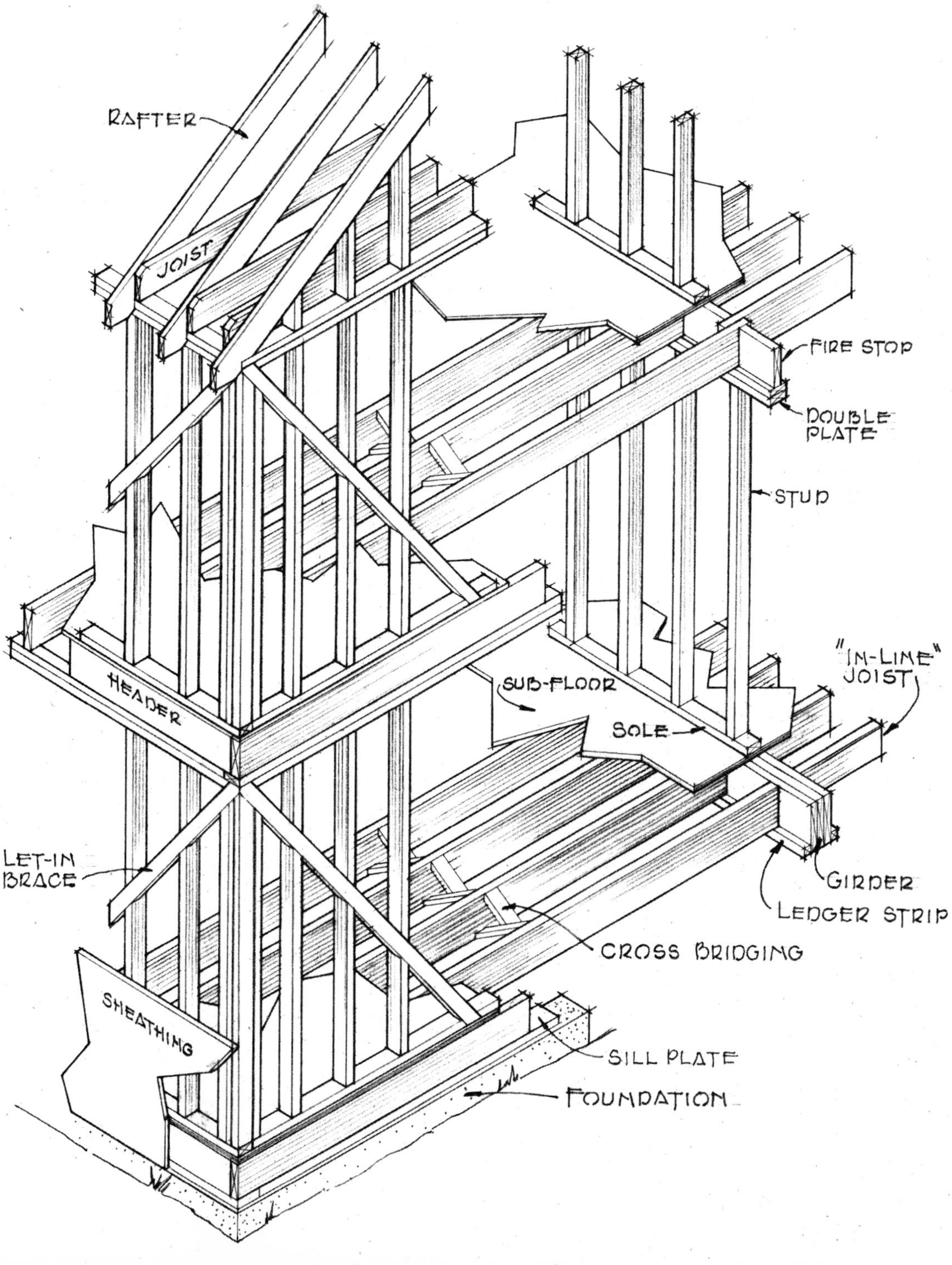

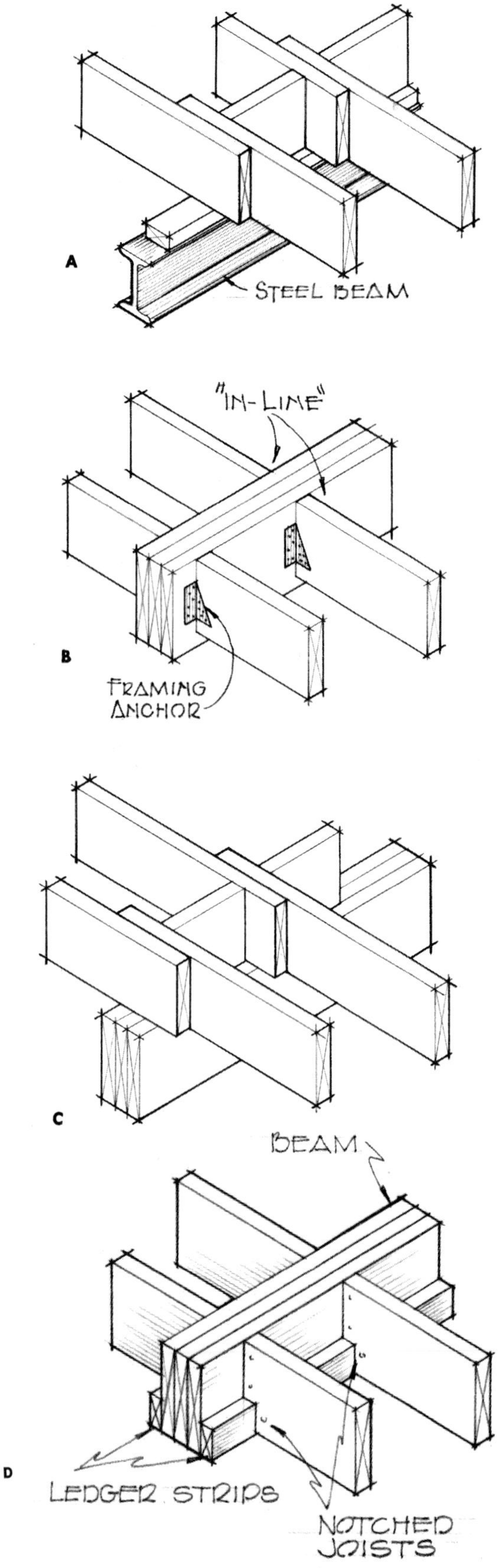

Fig. 7-25 Joist and girder framing.

5. It is quicker to erect—wall sections can be assembled quickly on the horizontal platform and tilted into place.

Beams or Girders Under wood floor framing, unless the joists are long enough to span between exterior walls, some type of heavy beam must be used to support the inner ends of the joists (see Fig. 7-25). If a building is wider than 15′ or 16′, which is generally the case, it is necessary to use additional support under the floor joists to avoid using excessively heavy floor joists. For this, wood or metal beams are used, and they are supported by the exterior foundation walls and piers or columns.

The beams under floors carry concentrated loads, and their sizes should be carefully considered. If steel is selected, I beams are usually used; their sizes for general residential use can be selected from Table 7-7. Steel has the advantage of not being subject to shrinkage. Wood beams can be either solid or built-up of nominal 2″ lumber, usually of the same size lumber used for the floor framing joists. Solid wood beams contain more cross-sectional lumber than built-up beams of similar nominal size. For example, a 6″ × 8″ solid wood beam would have an actual size of 5½″ × 7¼″, whereas a built-up beam of 6″ × 8″ nominal dimension would be actually only 4½″ × 7¼″. However, from a practical standpoint the built-up wood beams have several advantages:

1. Stock-size framing lumber is more readily available;
2. Smaller pieces are easier to handle;

Table 7-7 Maximum Spans for Wood or Light Steel Beams in Residential Construction

Suitable materials		Maximum clear span	
Wood timber (nominal size)	**Light steel beam (B section)**	**1-story dwellings**	**1½- & 2-story dwellings**
4″ × 6″	6B8.5	5′–0″	4′–0″
6″ × 6″	6B8.5	6′–0″	5′–2″
4″ × 8″	8B10	6′–4″	5′–6″
6″ × 8″	8B10	8′–0″	7′–0″
4″ × 10″	10B11.5	8′–0″	7′–0″
6″ × 10″	10B11.5	9′–0″	7′–0″

NOTE: The above spans are based on timber having a minimum fiber stress in bending of 1200 psi.
Unusual joist spans or concentrated loads may require calculations by established engineering practice.

3. They reduce splitting and checking; and
4. They can be nailed to the frame more easily, etc.

It is desirable to locate beams, if possible, under major interior partitions in order to eliminate the need for double joists under the partitions. Bathrooms and kitchens have heavier dead loads, and their weights should be considered in placing the beams. If living space in basements is important, beam sizes are generally made larger to avoid numerous columns throughout the basement. Columns are usually spaced 8′–10′ on center in basements, depending on the beam sizes. Under basementless houses, pilasters are spaced no more than 7′ or 8′ on center. Wood beams should have at least a 4″ bearing on masonry walls or pilasters, with a ½″ air space around the ends of the beams for adequate ventilation, if they are surrounded with masonry. See Fig. 7-26. If splices are necessary in wood built-up beams, they should be staggered and should be placed near the column for sound construction. The top edge of the beams must be the same height as the sill plates if joists are to rest on the beams (see Fig. 7-27). If the joists are to butt into the beams, a ledger strip is nailed to the beam, and either notched or narrower joists are toenailed over the ledger strip to the beams (see Fig. 7-24). Metal angle connectors or steel joist hangers can also be used for butt-fastening joists and beams. Joists butting into beams allow more headroom

Fig. 7-26 Beam pocket in foundation wall.

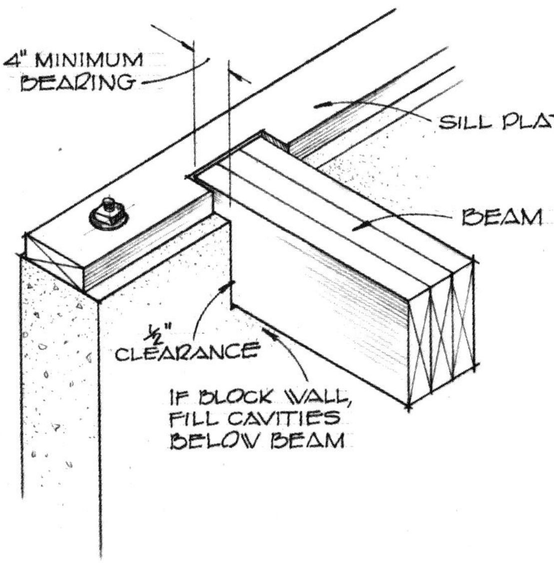

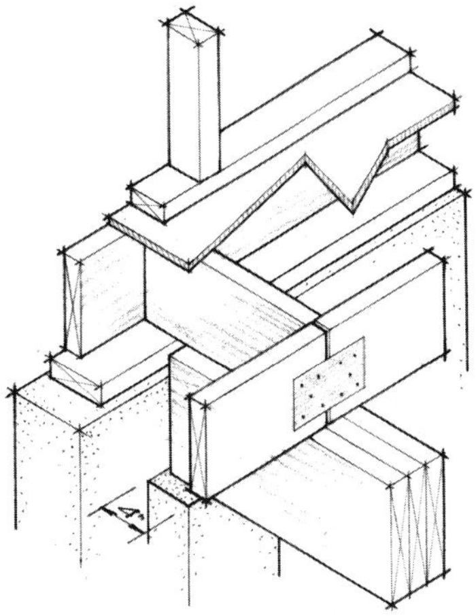

Fig. 7-27 Box sill and girder support construction.

in basements and facilitate installation of ductwork and plumbing under the floor; basement ceilings can without difficulty be finished with unbroken surfaces; and plywood subfloors can be more easily put over "in-line" joists. However, joists resting on the beams is the simpler method of floor framing.

Beams carry half the weight imposed on all the joists that rest on or are attached to the beams (see Fig. 7-7). In 2-story houses, considerable weight is transferred from the upper story to the beams. For convenient selection of beam or girder sizes under wood floor construction, the Federal Housing Administration has published Table 7-7, which designates maximum spans for the usual beam sizes used. The table is for those species of wood with a minimum of 1200 lb fiber stress—such as Douglas fir, southern pine, or western larch. Beams supporting unusually heavy loads would have to be designed according to established engineering practice.

Columns In residential basements, either wood or metal columns can be used under the beams. The columns are usually 6″ × 6″ wooden posts, or preferably, round steel columns, 3″ or 4″ diam, with cap plates welded to both ends (see Fig. 7-28). Steel columns are available in stock lengths, or they can be fabricated in any lengths desired. Other types are adjustable. Select wood column sizes according to loads, unsupported heights, and lumber species (see Table 7-8).

Sills The box type sill (Fig. 7-27) is generally used with platform frame construction. The sill plate, generally measuring 2″ × 6″ or 2″ × 8″, is placed over the foundation wall and

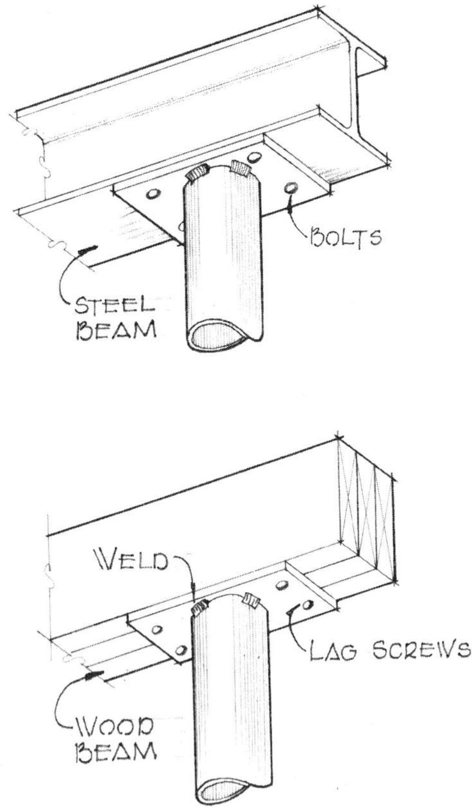

Fig. 7-28 Steel columns supporting girders.

anchored with ½″ anchor bolts, spaced according to local codes—usually 6′ on center. Occasionally, builders use a 4″ × 6″ or 4″ × 8″ treated sill plate in box sill construction. The wood sill must be at least 8″ above finished grade, and a continuous, noncorrosive termite shield should be placed below the sill in termite-infested areas. If exterior wood siding is used on the building, the outside surface of the framing should be placed within the outer edge of the foundation so that the outside surface of the sheathing becomes flush with the outer surface of the foundation wall (see Fig. 7-24). This allows the finish siding to come down over the joint between the sill plate and the masonry wall to make a weathertight joint.

Floor Joists Floor joists are the structural members of the wood floor. Their size, spacing, and direction must be indicated on the floor plan, so they have to be given special consideration by the draftsman. Joists rest on the sill plate, with a minimum of 1½″ bearing surface—preferably 3″ on the plate; this should be worked out on the sill detail. Joists are selected for strength and rigidity. The strength is required to carry both dead and live floor loads; the rigidity is needed to prevent vibration and movement when live load concentrations are shifted over the floor. Joists are usually of 2″ (nominal) dimension thickness; 3″ thick joists could be used, but they are often unavailable. The 6″, 8″, 10″, or 12″ (nominal) depth are used, depending on the load, span, spacing, and species and grade of lumber involved. Generally, joists are spaced 16″ on center; however, 12″ or 24″ spacing can be used when load concentrations vary. Floor framing is simpler if the same depth joists are used throughout the floor, and for greatest rigidity they should run in the direction of the shorter span. Builders can gain additional strength and stiffness in joists by using lumber finished on only two sides—the narrow edges (S2E), although rough lumber will ignite more

Fig. 7-29 Double joists and header blocking.

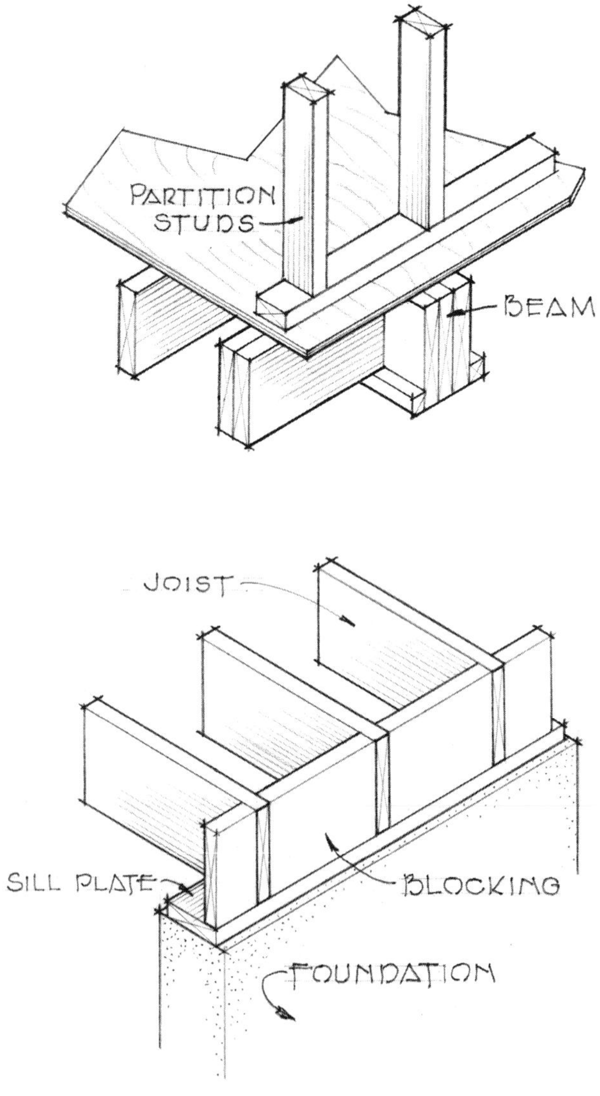

Table 7-8 Loading Capacities of Wood Columns in Wood-Frame Construction

Solid or Glued			Wood Columns	Maximum Loads in Kips (1000 lbs)					
				Heights (Unsupported)					
Nominal Size	Actual Size	Area (sq. in.)	Lumber Species	7′–0″	8′–0″	9′–0″	10′–0″	11′–0″	12′–0″
2″ x 4″	1½″ x 3½″	5.25	Sou. Pine; Douglas Fir	.88	.67	.53	.43	.35	.30
			Redwood	.66	.50	.40	.32	.26	.22
			Hemlock, Eastern	.60	.46	.36	.29	.24	.20
4″ x 4″	3½″ x 3½″	12.25	Sou. Pine; Douglas Fir	11.22	8.59	6.79	5.50	4.54	3.82
			Redwood	8.42	6.44	5.09	4.12	3.41	2.86
			Hemlock, Eastern	7.72	5.91	4.67	3.78	3.12	2.62
4″ x 6″	3½″ x 5½″	19.25	Sou. Pine; Douglas Fir	17.64	13.51	10.67	8.64	7.14	6.00
			Redwood	13.23	10.13	8.00	6.48	5.35	4.50
			Hemlock, Eastern	12.13	9.28	7.33	5.94	4.91	4.12
6″ x 6″	5½″ x 5½″	30.25	Sou. Pine; Douglas Fir	68.47	52.42	41.42	33.55	27.72	23.30
			Redwood	51.35	39.31	31.06	25.16	20.79	17.47
			Hemlock, Eastern	47.07	36.04	28.47	23.06	19.06	16.01
6″ x 8″	5½″ x 7¼″	39.88	Sou. Pine; Douglas Fir	90.26	69.10	54.60	44.22	36.55	30.71
			Redwood	67.69	51.82	40.95	33.17	27.41	23.03
			Hemlock, Eastern	62.05	47.51	37.53	30.40	25.12	21.11
8″ x 8″	7¼″ x 7¼″	52.56	Sou. Pine; Douglas Fir	206.74	158.28	125.05	101.30	83.72	70.34
			Redwood	155.05	118.71	93.79	75.97	62.79	52.76
			Hemlock, Eastern	142.13	108.82	85.98	69.64	57.55	48.36
8″ x 10″	7¼″ x 9¼″	67.06	Sou. Pine; Douglas Fir	263.77	201.95	159.56	129.24	106.81	89.75
			Redwood	197.83	151.46	119.67	96.93	80.11	67.31
			Hemlock, Eastern	181.34	138.84	109.70	88.85	73.43	61.70
10″ x 10″	9¼″ x 9¼″	85.56	Sou. Pine; Douglas Fir	547.82	419.42	331.40	268.43	221.84	186.41
			Redwood	410.86	314.57	248.55	201.32	166.38	139.80
			Hemlock, Eastern	376.63	288.35	227.83	184.54	152.51	128.15
12″ x 12″	11¼″ x 11¼″	126.56	Sou. Pine; Douglas Fir	1198.63	917.70	725.09	587.32	485.39	407.86
			Redwood	898.97	688.27	543.83	440.49	364.04	305.90
			Hemlock, Eastern	824.05	630.91	498.50	403.78	333.70	280.40

quickly in case of fire, and some codes prohibit its use. If joists lap over beams or supports, the lap should be no more than 6″ or 8″ and no less than 4″ for proper nailing together of joists (see Fig. 7-25A). If the lap is excessive, any sag or deflection at the center of the joists will cause the ends of the joists extending over the beams to raise the floor. If joists are supported by a steel beam, a 2″ × 4″ nailing strip should be bolted to the beam and the joists fastened to it.

For economy, the lengths of the joists should be limited to 2′ increments in length. The header joists are end-nailed to each joist with 16-penny nails, and both the headers and the joists are toenailed to the sill plate. If the bearing surface at the ends of the joists is critical, blocks between the joists can be used as a header—the blocks would function very much like block bridging (see Fig. 7-29).

Local codes usually indicate the minimum joist sizes for various conditions. A rule of thumb for joist sizes using either Douglas fir, southern yellow pine, western larch, or hemlock (J & P Grade) would be to make their spans in feet one and one-half times their depth in inches, if the joists are spaced 16″ on center. Thus, a 2″ × 10″ joist of the species indicated would span 15′, if a 40 lb live load is required. Usually, lumber of a higher grade does not increase the allowable span, because rigidity is the controlling factor, which is not contingent on grades. For more accurate joist size selection according to spans required, refer to Appendix D.

Note: As of September 1970, the various national lumber associations have adopted the American Softwood Lumber Standard, PS 20-70, which now unifies dressed lumber sizes as shown:

Nominal Size	Dressed Size (S4S) in inches	
	Surfaced dry	Surfaced green
2 × 4	1½ × 3½	1⁹⁄₁₆ × 3⁹⁄₁₆
2 × 6	1½ × 5½	1⁹⁄₁₆ × 5⅝
2 × 8	1½ × 7¼	1⁹⁄₁₆ × 7½
2 × 10	1½ × 9¼	1⁹⁄₁₆ × 9½
2 × 12	1½ × 11¼	1⁹⁄₁₆ × 11½

Double joists should be used under all partitions running parallel with the joists, or some method of blocking must be employed so that partitions bear on framing rather than on the subfloor between the joists (see Fig. 7-29).

Trimmers and Headers Openings in floor framing for chimneys, stairways, etc. must be surrounded by additional framing members for support. The joists that run parallel to the two sides of the opening are doubled and are called "trimmers." The members that surround the other two sides of the opening are also doubled and are called "headers"; into these headers are framed the shortened joists called "header joists" or "tail joists" (see Fig. 7-30). Headers should not be over 10′–0″ long; if the spans are short and loads around the opening are not heavy, the assembly can be spiked together, otherwise joist hangers or additional support must be used. Framing should not be fastened into chimneys; fire codes require a 2″ space around chimneys between the framed opening, which should be filled with incombustible insulation. If the chimney flues are well surrounded with masonry, corbel masonry may be extended from the chimney on which framing may rest. Tail joists over 6′–0″ long must be connected to headers in the same manner that joists are connected to beams or girders.

Fig. 7-30 Framing around floor and ceiling openings.

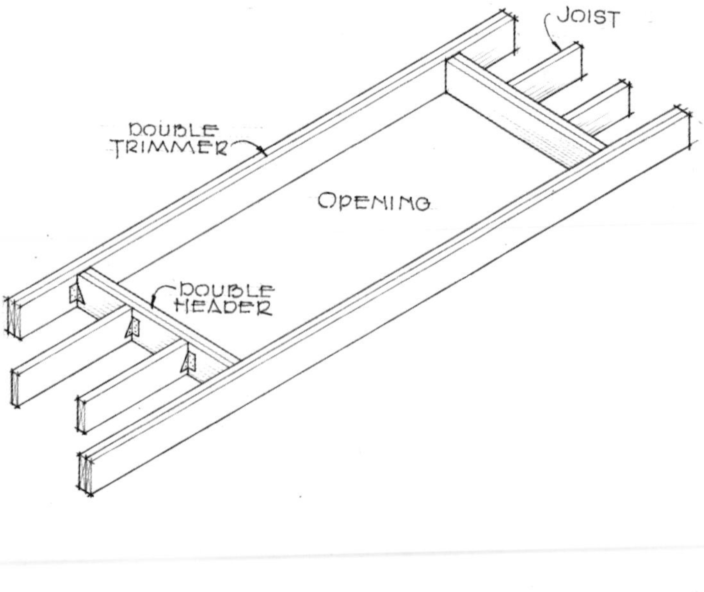

Cutting Openings in Joists The cutting or drilling through of joists that have been set in place should be avoided if possible. However, plumbing or wiring must occasionally pass through floor joists. Small holes, if placed properly, are not too objectional, but larger cuts often result in weakened or dangerous conditions. A horizontal structural member, such as a floor joist, with a load imposed upon it can be considered to be under compression throughout the upper half of its depth; it is under tension throughout its lower half, with a neutral axis in the center of its depth. The farther away the wood fiber is from the center of the depth of the joist, the more important the fiber is to the strength of the member. Therefore, the closer to the center axis a hole is cut, the less destructive it will be. Joists may be notched at top or bottom if the notch does not exceed one-sixth of the depth of the joist, as long as the notch does not occur within the center one-third of the span. Holes with a maximum of 2″ diam can be bored within 2″ of the edges of the joist without causing excessive damage.

Bridging consists of rows of short members between joists to produce a firm, rigid floor. Bridging not only prevents the deep, narrow shape of the floor joists from buckling sideways. but it distributes concentrated live loads to adjoining joists. Rows of bridging should be uninterrupted throughout the floor. Three types of bridging are seen in floor framing: 1″ × 3″ pieces nailed diagonally between the joists; blocks the same depth as the joists nailed in staggered fashion perpendicular to the joists; or light metal bridging pieces nailed diagonally between the joists. Cross-bridging is generally used (see Fig. 7-24); it allows wiring and piping to pass through without cutting. Joists with more than 8′ of span should have one row of bridging, but rows of bridging should be no more than 7′ or 8′ apart in longer spans.

Subfloor Nominal 1″ boards 4″, 6″, or 8″ wide, securely nailed to the joists, have been used for years on subfloors. The boards can be square-edged, tongue-and-groove, or shiplap, and it is preferable to lay them diagonally—45° to the joists. Finish strip-flooring can then be laid in either direction over the subfloor. Joints in the subflooring should fall in the center of the joists and they should be staggered. Square-edge boards laid up too tight often produce squeaky floors; rather, they should be nailed about 1/8″ apart. When subflooring is laid perpendicularly to the joists, the finish floor must be laid perpendicularly to the subfloor.

Because of the speed of erection, fir plywood has become popular for subflooring. Plywood produces a smoother surface for block flooring, tile, carpeting, and other nonstructural flooring materials. Sheets of plywood, usually 1/2″ or 5/8″ thick for subfloors, should be laid with their face-grain across the joists; the end joints of the sheets should be staggered and fall midway between adjoining sheets (see Fig. 7-31). If other than strip wood-flooring is used, the joints around the plywood should have blocking below, or tongue-and-groove edge plywood can be used. Plywood must be securely nailed around its edges as well as throughout central areas where backing occurs.

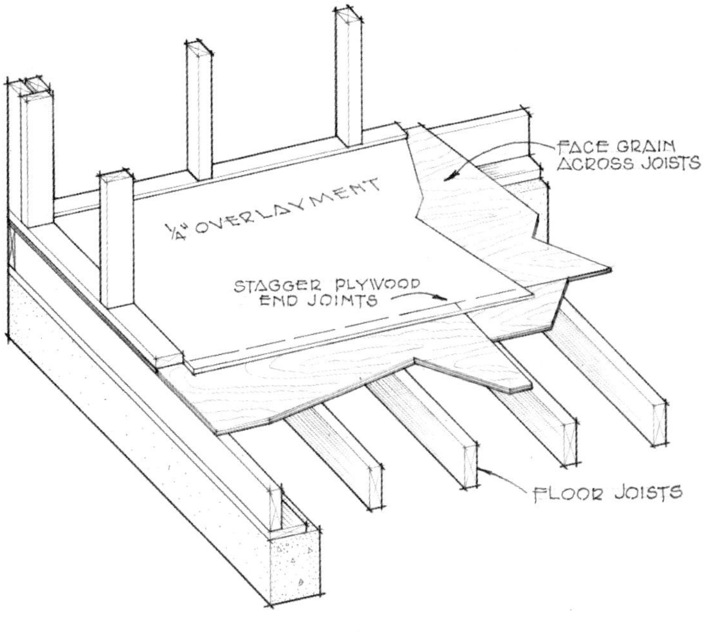

Fig. 7-31 Use of plywood subflooring.

Subfloor under Ceramic Tile In bathrooms and other areas requiring ceramic tile floors, some method must be used to lower the subfloor so that a concrete base for the tile can be provided for. If the joists are adequate for the load, they can be dropped several inches, or the top of the joists can be chamfered and the subfloor dropped 3″ between the joists. If there is no objection to the finished tile floor being an inch or so above the other finished floor surface, the regular subfloor could be left as is. However, in economical construction, ceramic tile can be laid on mastic, which does not require a concrete subfloor, nor does it entail dropping of the wood floor.

Soleplates After the subfloor is in place, 2″ × 4″ plates, called "soles" or "shoe plates," are nailed directly over the subfloor to form the layout for all walls and partitions. Dimensions for this layout must be taken from the floor plan working drawing. It should be noted that unless floor plans show dimensions from the outer edge of the exterior wall framing to the center line of partitions, accurate layout of soleplates by workmen becomes rather difficult. The plates are generally run through door openings, then cut out after the framing and rough openings have been established. Plumbing walls must be built of 2″ × 6″ or 2″ × 8″ studs to enclose soil stacks; partitions between closets can be built of 2″ × 4″ studs set sideways to increase usable space.

Studs usually 2″ × 4″ (16″ on center) are toenailed to the soleplate and are capped with a double 2″ × 4″ cap plate. Double studs, which support proper sized lintels or headers above the openings, should be used around all door and window openings. In 1-story buildings, studs can be spaced 24″ on center, unless limited by the wall covering. If ceiling heights are to be 8′–0″ high, the studs are generally cut 7′–8″ or 7′–9″ in length. Blocking, halfway up the height of the studs, stiffens the wall and prevents the studs from warping. If vertical paneling is to be used as interior wall covering, horizontal blocking must be inserted between the studs in rows every 2′–0″ of vertical height throughout the wall, or else 1″ × 3″ horizontal furring strips will have to be nailed to the studs to back up the vertical paneling.

With platform framing it is convenient for workmen to lay out each wall horizontally on the platform, nail the pieces together without the second cap plate, then lift the wall into place where it can be temporarily braced. All the walls and partitions are set in place and trued carefully. The top piece of the double

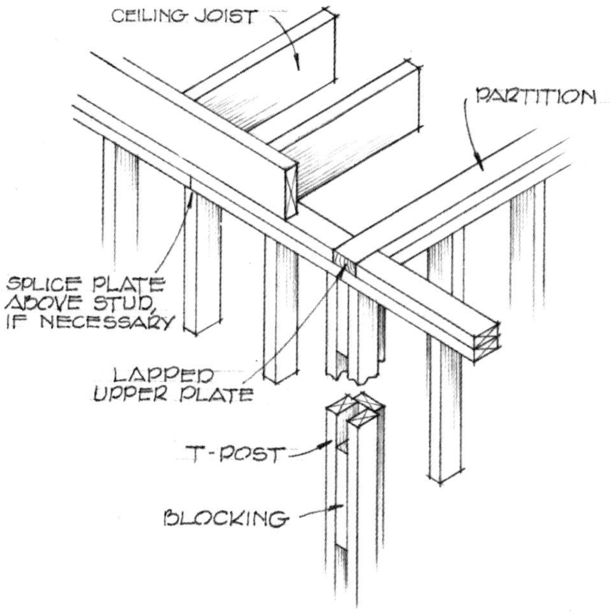

Fig. 7-32 Framing at intersections of walls.

cap plate is then attached so all the walls and partitions are well lap-jointed (see Fig. 7-32). Corner posts, T posts, and posts forming intersections of partitions are built-up of 2″ × 4″'s, well-spiked together in a manner to provide for both inside and outside nailing surfaces at the corners (see Fig. 7-33).

Bracing Sufficient diagonal bracing must be used at the corners as well as in major partitions to counteract wind pressures and to prevent lateral movement of the framing. Let-in, 1″ × 4″ braces placed as close to 45° as possible should be used, and they should be tied into both the top and bottom plates of the wall. If windows or openings are close to the corners, K braces can be used (see Fig. 7-1). Diagonal bracing can be eliminated if wood sheathing is used and nailed diagonally to the studs, or if the frame is sheathed with plywood.

Lintels The horizontal supports above openings, are usually built-up of two pieces of nominal 2″ × 4″, 2″ × 6″, or 2″ × 8″ lumber with the wide dimension vertical. Extra strength and the exact 3½″ stud width can be gained by sandwiching a ⅜″ plywood panel between the two vertical lintel pieces (see Fig. 7-34). Unless unusual loads bear over the opening, two 2″ × 4″s will support openings up to 3′–0″ wide, two 2″ × 6″s up to 4′–0″, two 2″ × 8″s up to 5′–0″; openings exceeding 6′–0″ should be framed with diagonal truss-type framing or steel flitch plates introduced to the lintels. Many southern builders use double 2″ × 12″ lintels above all wall openings; this eliminates the need for cripples or vertical blocking between the lintel and the top plate (see Fig. 7-34). For volume construction, some builders use a double 2″ × 6″ cap plate, set vertically, over all bearing walls, thus eliminating lintels. Such buildings generally have openings no wider than 4′–0″ (see Fig. 7-35).

Second-floor Framing Each story in platform framing is a separate unit; if two stories are planned, the second-floor joists and headers are attached to the top plate of the first floor. The second-story walls are built upon the platform or subfloor of the second floor. Second-story floor joists then become the first-floor ceiling joists. If possible, second-story partitions should fall directly above partitions below; otherwise additional floor joists or blocking is required. Occasionally, second stories are cantilevered out beyond exterior walls below. Joists below cantilevered walls should be perpendicular to the walls and well-anchored (see Fig. 7-36).

Ceiling Joists generally rest on the top wall plate if the roof is put directly above. If an attic floor is required (Fig. 7-37), headers and joists can be built-up to the outside surface of the walls, with the attic floor nailed to the joists, and a 2″ × 4″ soleplate nailed over the floor around its perimeter on which the rafters bear. In ceiling framing, if a gable-type roof is used, it is more desirable to put the ceiling joists parallel to the roof rafters, making the

Fig. 7-33 Stud framing at corners and intersections of walls.

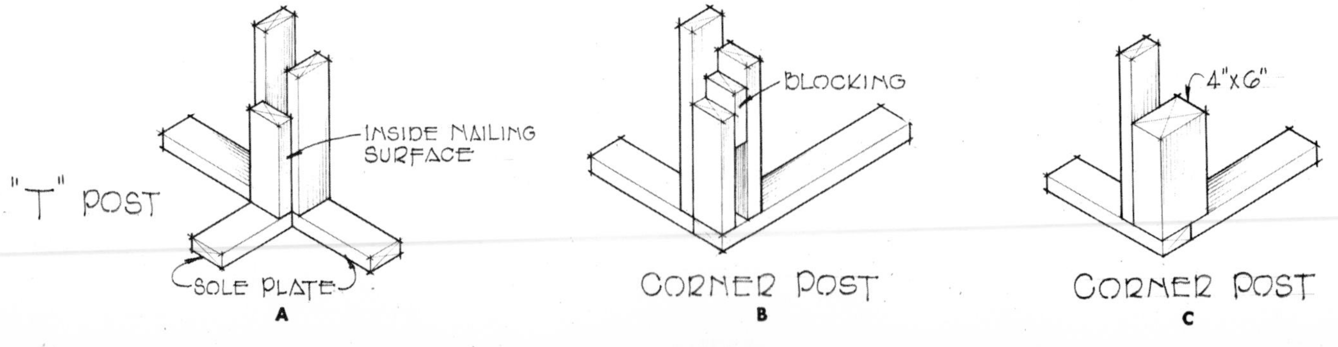

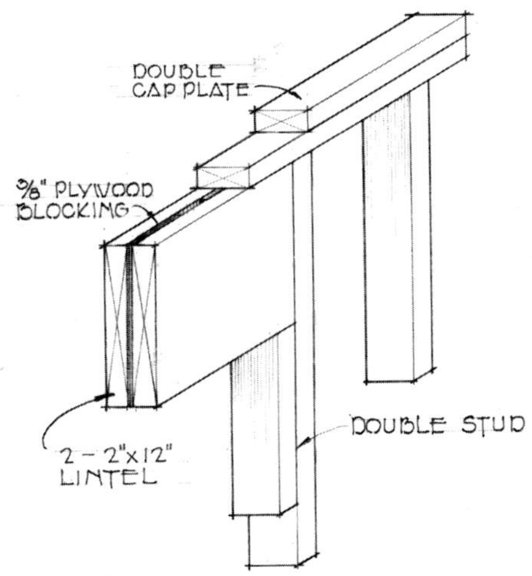

Fig. 7-34 Lintels over typical wall openings.

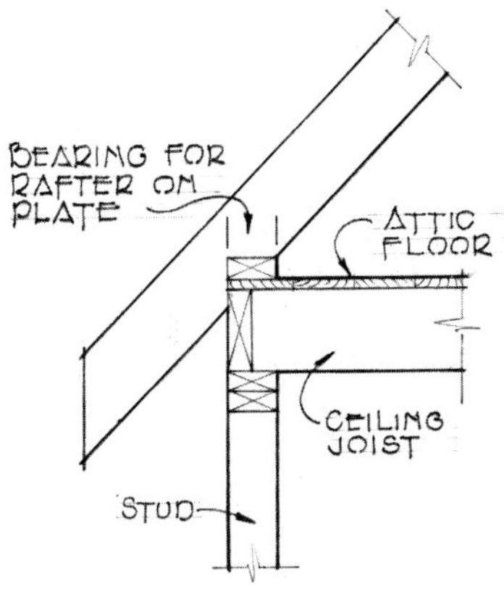

Fig. 7-37 Fastening rafters on attic floor.

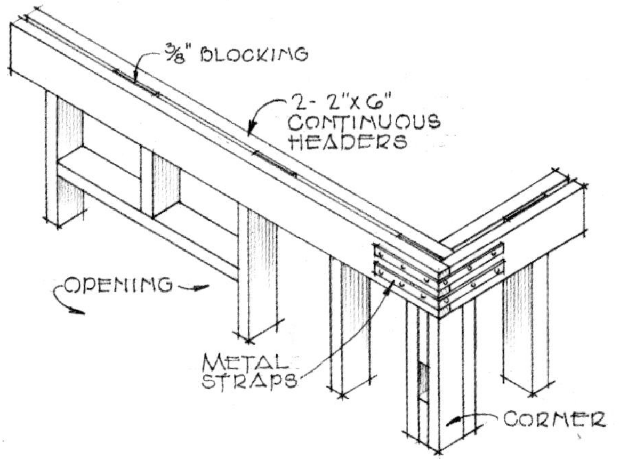

Fig. 7-35 Wall framing with continuous headers instead of double cap plate.

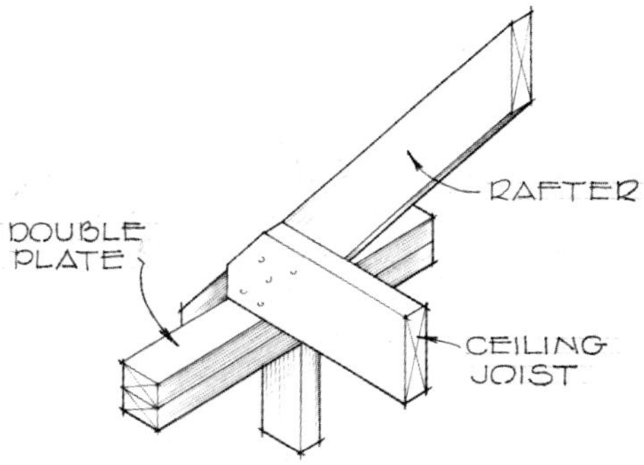

Fig. 7-38 Fastening rafters and ceiling joists.

Fig. 7-36 Framing a second-floor overhang.

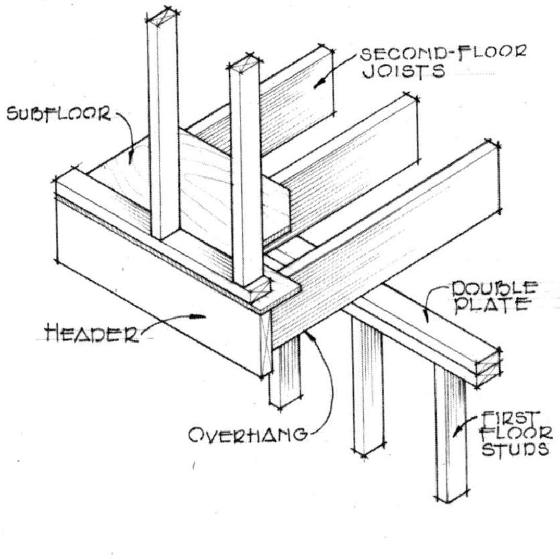

ceiling joists actually bottom chords for the truss shape of the roof rafters. Ceiling joists are nailed to both the top plate and the roof rafters (see Fig. 7-38). A "catwalk" brace for ceiling framing is shown in Fig. 7-39.

When ceiling joists must be placed at right angles to the rafters, short joists are run perpendicularly to the long joists over the plate and nailed to both the plate and the rafters. The inner ends of the short joists are butted and anchored to a double long joist. Metal straps are used to tie the tops of the short joists across at least three of the long joists if no wood flooring is used (see Fig. 7-40).

Gable-roof Rafters (See Fig. 7-41 for roof-framing terminology.) Wind pressures against gable roofs (hip roofs as well) not only exert downward forces on the windward side, but also exert upward pressures on the leeward side, especially if the roof has a considerable overhang. Therefore, rafters must be well-anchored at their lower ends or bearing cuts. The triangular notch cut into the rafters for horizontal bearing is called a "bird's-mouth." It should be

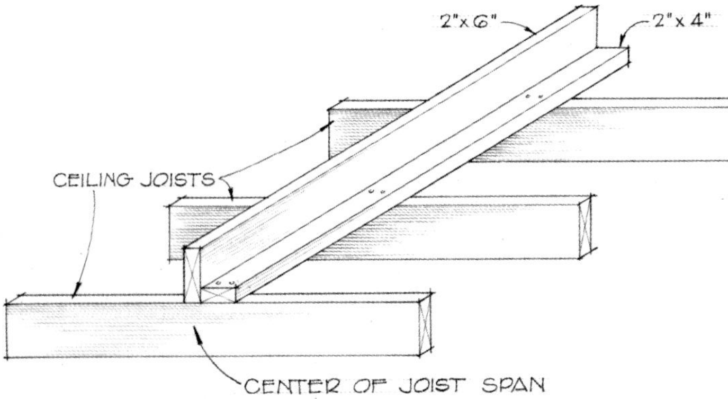

Fig. 7-39 "Catwalk" over ceiling joists.

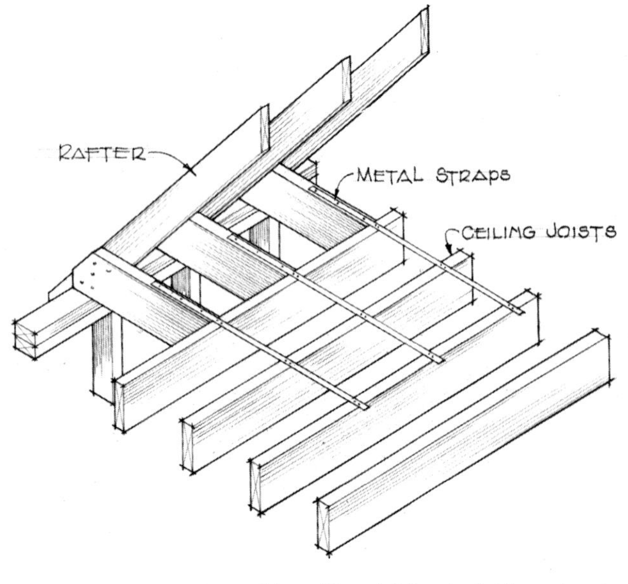

Fig. 7-40 Framing with ceiling joists at right angles to rafters.

Fig. 7-41 Arrangement of opposite rafters and ceiling joists.

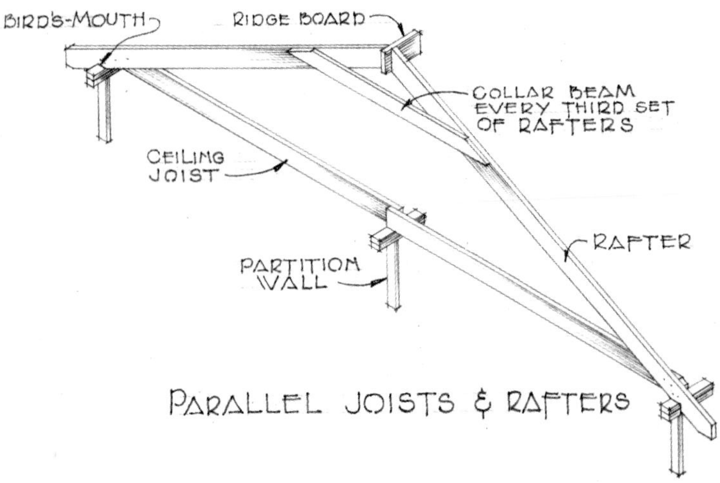

deep enough so that the rafter bears on the full width of the 2″ × 4″ plate. The bird's-mouth is toenailed to the plate, and the rafter is also nailed to the ceiling joist; metal anchors are sometimes employed for more positive anchorage. Rafters are placed directly opposite each other at the ridge so that they brace against each other. Rafter lengths and cuts are carefully laid out on a pattern piece to insure uniformity of all common rafters and to simplify their cutting. The ridgeboard can be either 1″ or 2″ nominal lumber, but it should be 2″ wider than the rafters so that the entire beveled ridge cut will make contact with the ridgeboard.

Valley Rafters Valleys are formed by the intersection of two gable roofs; the rafter directly below the valley is called the "valley rafter" (see Fig. 7-42). Valley rafters carry additional loads and should be doubled, as well as widened to allow full contact with the diagonal cuts of the jack rafters.

Jack Rafters are shorter than common rafters, and run from hip or valley rafters to the plates. If roofs with different ridge heights intersect, the higher roof is framed first and the valley is formed by nailing a plate over the higher roof surface; the jack rafters of the lower roof are then nailed to the plate. Or, the valley rafter can be incorporated into the larger roof framing if attic communication is needed between the gables or hips (see Fig. 7-42).

Hip Rafters like ridgeboards, do not carry any loads and are therefore the same size as the common rafters (Fig. 7-43).

Collar Beams (See Fig. 7-41.) Collar beams are short lengths of 2″ × 4″'s or 1″ × 6″'s, nailed across opposite gable rafters about one-third the distance down from the ridge. They not only stiffen the roof against wind pressures, but they also allow the size of the rafters to be reduced in that they shorten the clear span of the rafters. If the attic is used for occupancy, the collar beams act as ceiling joists as well as rafter ties and must be placed at ceiling height. When the roof pitch is low and the rafter span is long, collar beams are nailed to each pair of rafters; otherwise, to every third pair.

Gable Studs must be framed with the same spacing as studs in the lower walls; they are diagonally cut and notched to fit the underside of the end rafters and butt to the double wall plate (see Fig. 7-44B). It is customary to make provision for a louver, usually screened, near the ridge of the gable end-wall. The net area of

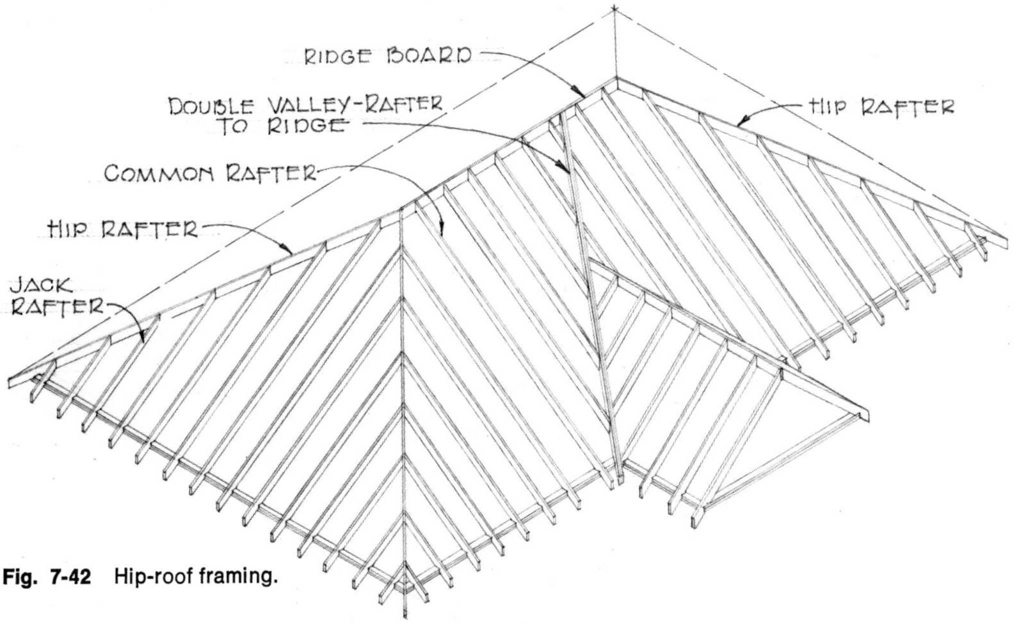

Fig. 7-42 Hip-roof framing.

Fig. 7-43 Roof framing: (A) valley rafter; (B) hip rafter.

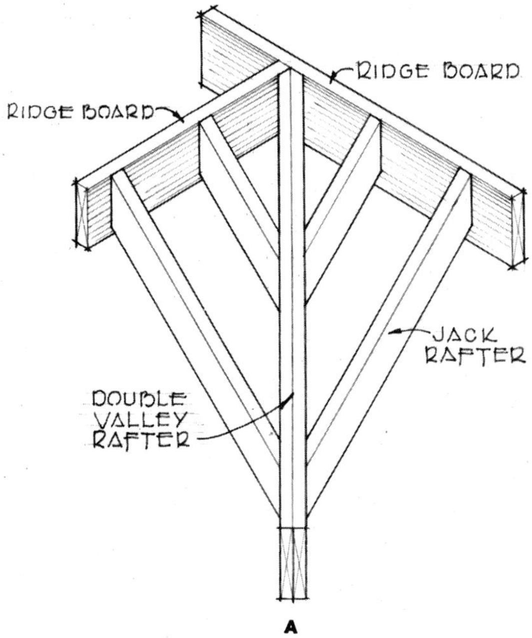

A

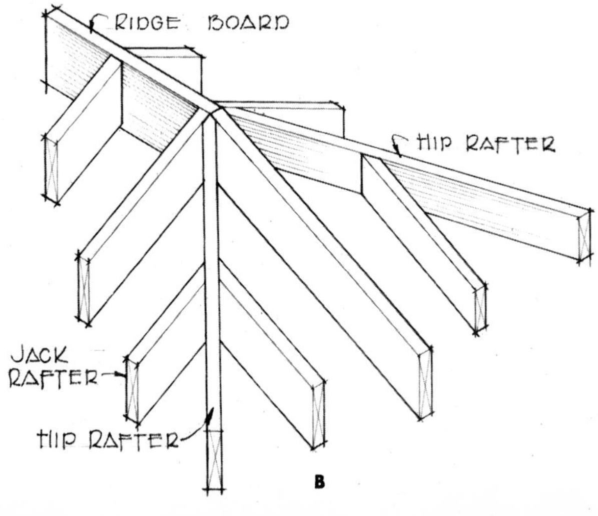

B

the opening should be at least 1/300 of the area of the ceiling below. In most cases prefabricated wood or metal louvers are used; they are inserted into the rough opening after the wall sheathing is applied. If a boxed overhang is required above the gable wall, a ladder-type framing can be cantilevered over the gable wall (see Fig. 7-45). If wood siding is used on the gable wall, and brick veneer is used below, 2″ × 8″ gable studs can be used to bring the gable siding out flush with the brick veneer.

Roof Decking There are several methods of covering the roof framing, depending on the materials used and the type of roof covering. Nominal 1″ matched boards, usually 6″ wide and nailed perpendicularly to the rafters, are often used. They are started at the edge of the roof overhang and laid-up tight to the ridge. Use of shiplap or tongue-and-groove lumber will result in a tighter deck and more solid surface for the roof covering. Splices should be well-staggered and made over the center of the rafters. Long pieces of lumber are desirable for roof decking.

Fir plywood makes a satisfactory roof deck; it goes on fast and makes a rigid roof when properly nailed down. Plywood joints should fall on the rafters, and vertical joints should be midway on succeeding rows. The face-grain of the plywood should be laid perpendicularly to the rafters. See Fig. 7-47. Plywood that is 3/8″ thick can be used as decking when light roof coverings are used; 1/2″ thickness is necessary for the heavier roof coverings. All plywood edges

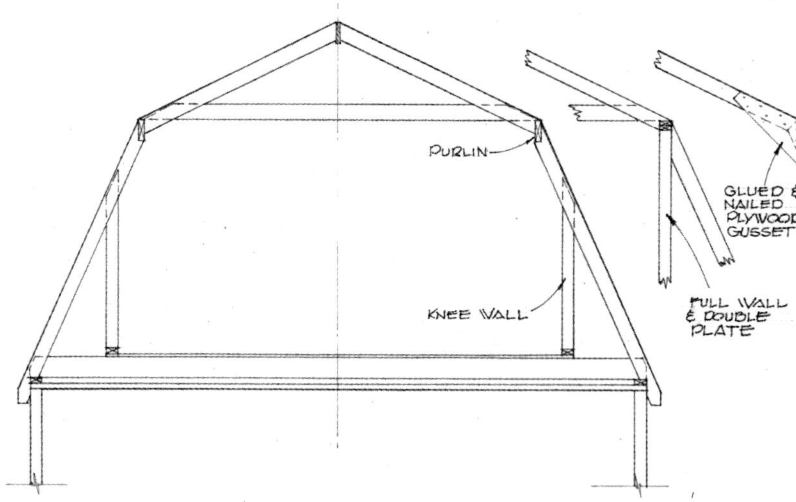

A

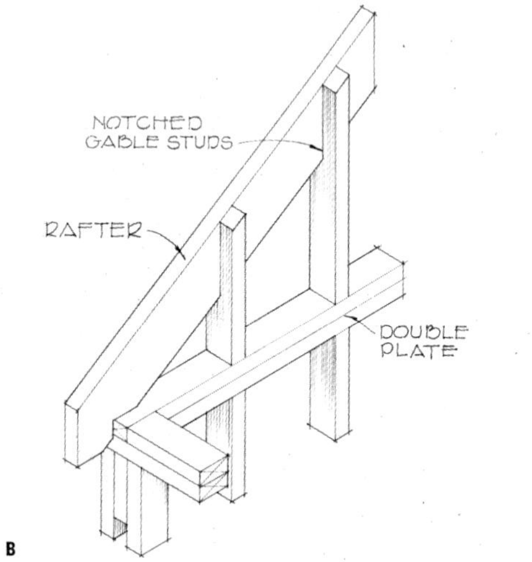

B

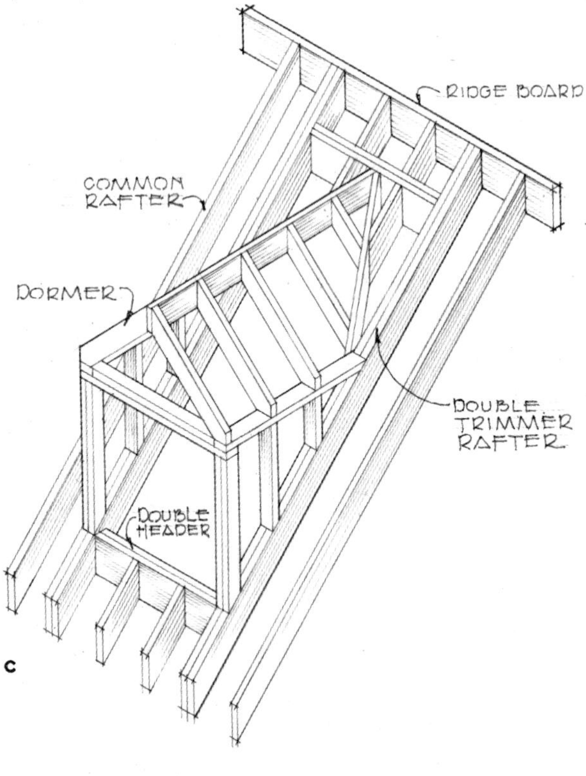

C

Fig. 7-44 (A) Gambrel roof framing; (B) gable studs; (C) dormer framing.

Fig. 7-45 Gable-end roof framing.

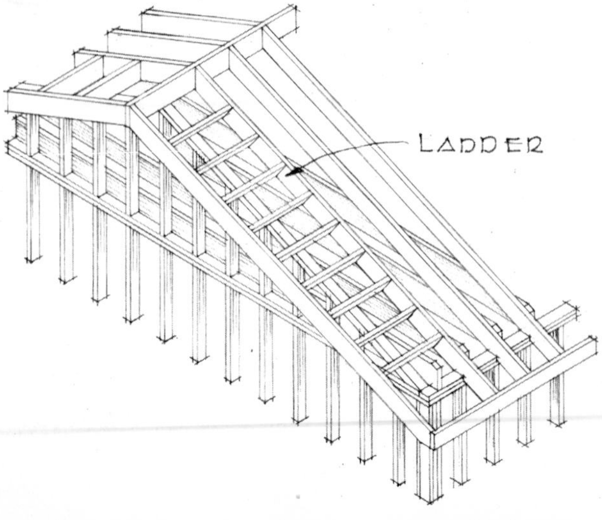

Fig. 7-46 Flat-roof framing at corners.

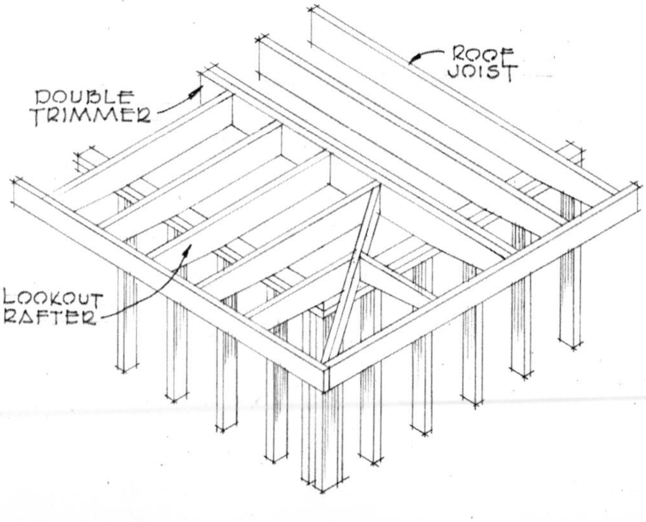

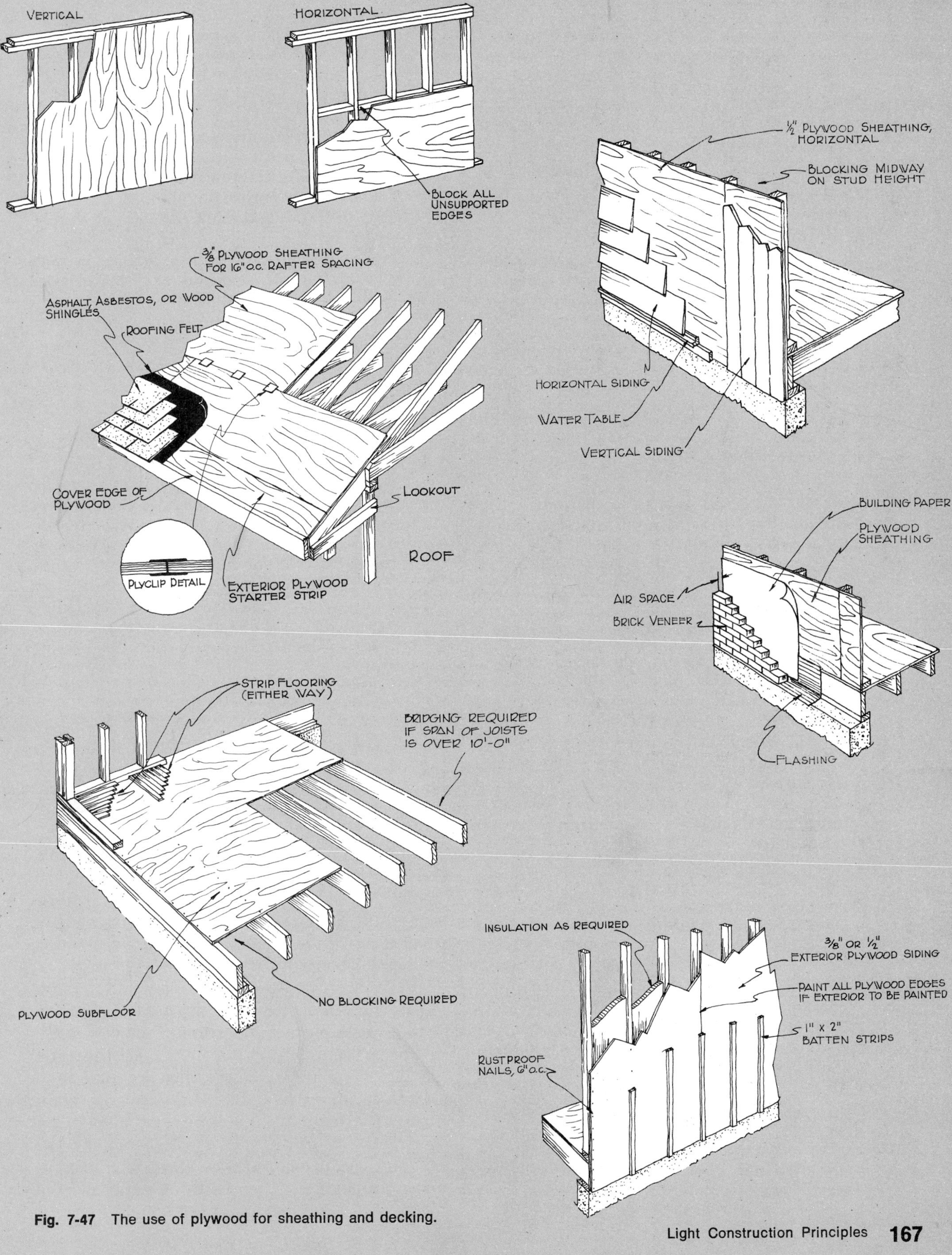

Fig. 7-47 The use of plywood for sheathing and decking.

should be well-covered with molding or trim at the edges of the roof. As soon as the roof deck is completed it is covered with a good grade of roofing paper, preferably 30-lb paper. The paper is edge-lapped and end-lapped with at least a 2″ lap and securely nailed every 6″ with galvanized roofing nails. This covering is very important because it is rainproof and therefore protects the structure while the work is in progress.

If wood shingles are used as the roof covering, then 1″ × 3″ nailing strips can be used instead of solid decking. These strips are spaced the same distance apart as the part of the shingle that is exposed to the weather. The nailing strips provide an air space for ventilation and drying, thereby prolonging the life of the wood shingles. Wood shingle roofs can also have a tight, built-up deck covered with waterproof building paper; the 1″ × 3″ nailing strips are then attached over the paper, to which the wood shingles are nailed.

Wall Sheathing is the outer subwall, which is nailed directly to the studs and framework. Wall sheathing adds both strength and insulation to the building, and forms a base for the exterior siding. The following types of materials are used for wall sheathing:

1. *Wood boards,* 1″ nominal thickness, usually 6″ or 8″ wide—wider lumber will shrink more and leave wider gaps. Wood sheathing can be applied either horizontally or at a 45° angle. The horizontal method is more economical, but requires diagonal let-in bracing at the corners. Diagonal sheathing adds greatly to the rigidity of the wall and eliminates the need for corner bracing. It also provides an excellent tie between the framing and the sill plate. Wood sheathing can be either square-edged, shiplap, or tongue-and-groove. End joints should be staggered and made over studs; two eightpenny nails are used at each stud bearing. Number 2 common lumber is usually specified.
2. *Fiberboard asphalt-coated sheathing* is available in 4′ widths and 8′, 9′, 10′, and 12′ lengths. It can be applied either horizontally or vertically. The latter method usually requires a 9′ long sheet to cover a wall that has 8′–0″ ceilings. Fiberboard sheathing ½″ thick is easy to handle by carpenters, and it goes on quickly compared to wood sheathing. Other types of fiberboard measure 2′ × 8′ and have shiplap or tongue-and-groove edges; they are applied horizontally. Fiberboard must be carefully nailed with galvanized roofing nails.
3. *Plywood* used for sheathing usually comes in 4′ × 8′ sheets and should be a minimum of 5⁄16″ thick over studs spaced 16″ on center (o.c.) and ⅜″ thick over studs spaced 24″ o.c. Sixpenny nails should be used and should be spaced not more than 6″ apart for edge nailing and 12″ apart for intermediate nailing. Plywood is usually applied vertically to permit perimeter nailing without additional blocking. When the 8′ dimension is horizontal, blocking is desirable along the horizontal joints between the studs as a base for the finish-wall nailing. When the finish-wall material requires nailing between the studs (as with wood shingles), the plywood should be at least ⅜″ thick. Wood shingles must be nailed to stripping if 5⁄16″ plywood or other non-nail-holding sheathing is used. Plywood can be applied with power-driven staplers using galvanized wire staples.
4. *Gypsum sheathing,* composed of moisture-resistant gypsum filler faced on both sides with lightweight paper, can be used as a subwall. It is available in 2′ × 4′ and 2′ × 8′ sizes and ½″ thick. Some gypsum sheathing has V-joint edges for easier application and better edge ties; this type is applied horizontally and nailed securely with galvanized roofing nails. Vertical joints are always staggered and made on the center of the studs. If finish siding is used that requires both nailing strips and a smooth base, the nailing strips are fastened directly to the studs, and the gypsum sheathing is nailed over the nailing strips.

7.4.2 Balloon Frame Construction (Fig. 7-48)

The distinguishing feature of ballon construction is that the studs run from the sill to the top plate. These vertical lengths of wall framing minimize the amount of wood shrinkage in the total height of the building. Even though the stud lengths are long, balloon framing is still an important type of construction in that there is less chance of the wood framing reducing in height when used with brick or stone veneer or stucco in 2-story buildings. Generally, in 1-story buildings the platform frame is employed; if ballon frame is used, it can be identified by the studs placed directly on the sill plate, which is called a "solid sill." Wood shrinks considerably more across grain than on end-grain; therefore, the absence of horizontal members, with the exception of the sill and the plate, provides end-grain fiber almost throughout the entire height of the

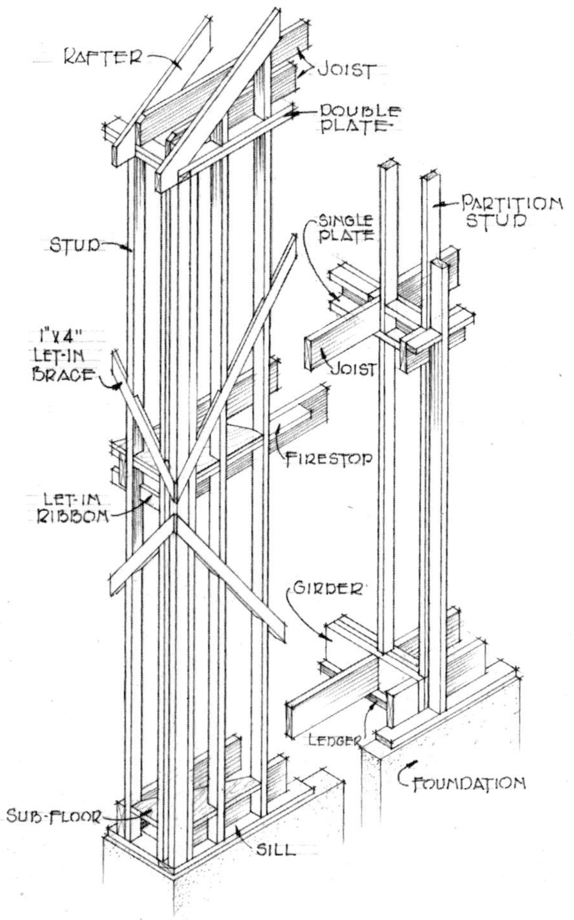

Fig. 7-48 Balloon (eastern) frame construction.

building. Even though balloon frame is not used as often as platform frame, it has features that are noteworthy, and it is sometimes used in combination with platform construction.

Sill The sill plate, as in platform frame, is well-anchored to the foundation with ½″ anchor bolts. If the top of the foundation wall needs trueing, a bed of grout or mortar is placed below the sill; termite shields are also required in applicable areas. The sill is usually a 2″ × 6″ or 2″ × 8″; sometimes a double sill of well-spiked members is used. Both the studs and the first-floor joists rest on the sill plate, forming the solid sill. Usually the sill plate is set the thickness of the sheathing inside the outer edge of the foundation wall.

Floor Joists The size and spacing of the floor joists, as in platform frame, depend on their loads and span (refer to Appendix D). Generally the joists are spaced 16″ on center and are toe-nailed to the sill plate and the beam within the building. Joists can be butted to the beam and anchored, or they can be lapped over the beam. A row of bridging should be used if the joists span more than 10′–0″. There are no headers at the ends of the joists.

Studs The studs are usually spaced 16″ on center, as in other framing, and they run to the top plate. Each stud carries its own load from plate to sill without any lateral distribution by headers or beams. For this reason studs have to be carefully selected, especially in 2-story houses where the studs must be considerably longer. The spacing of the studs must be compatible with the spacing of the floor joists and ceiling joists. This allows the joists in all floors to be nailed directly to the studs. Openings for doors and windows must be surrounded with double studs, and headers or lintels must be carefully selected; openings in first-story walls must have headers over them that are capable of carrying the entire weight of the studs above the openings.

One of the shortcomings of balloon frame is the ease in which a fire in the basement could burn through the sill and enter the cavities between the studs, causing "flue-action" and rapid spread of the conflagration through the entire structure. To eliminate this hazard, codes require 2″ blocking between the joists and studs above the sill plate, and often prescribe that the cavity at the sill be filled with masonry or a noncombustible material.

Ribbon Another typical feature of balloon frame is the method of supporting second-floor joists. Ceiling or second-floor joists rest on a 1″ × 6″ board, let into the studs, called a "ribbon." The joists are also spiked to the studs. The ribbon is necessary only on those walls taking the ends of the joists. Fire-stopping and blocking are also needed at the intersection of second-floor joists and the walls. In addition, horizontal blocking between the studs is also required midway between room heights.

Posts Corner studs and posts at intersections of partitions and walls are built-up, similar to platform frame, so that nailing surfaces will be found on both inside and outside corners. Often balloon framing is used in partitions of 2-story solid-masonry buildings to minimize the vertical shrinkage.

Braces If horizontal board sheathing is used for the subwall, 1″ × 4″ let-in bracing must be used throughtout the framing to resist raking stresses. The use of diagonal wood sheathing or plywood eliminates the need for the bracing.

Diagonal 2″ × 4″ blocking at the corners does not have the strength the let-in braces have, especially if the blocking is not tightly fitted into the stud spacings.

Subfloor Boards, measuring 1″ × 6″, laid diagonally, or plywood is generally used for the subfloor. The subfloor extends to the outer edge of the wall framing and is notched around the studs.

Top Plate and Roof Framing The top plate consists of a double 2″ × 4″, lapped at corners and intersections of partitions, and well-spiked together. If nailing surfaces are necessary for the application of gypsum board or other ceiling coverings, blocking must be inserted between the ceiling joists and spiked to the top plate. Rafters rest on the top plate and are nailed to both the plate and the ceiling joists, similar to platform framing. Metal framing anchors can be used to fasten rafters to the top plate if more rigidity is desired. The roof framing is done similarly to the method indicated in platform framing, and the treatment of the overhang varies with the type of architectural effect required. Some houses have very little overhang at the eaves; others may have as much as a 3′ overhang. Rafters can be left exposed at the eaves, or they can be boxed-in with a horizontal soffit. The treatment of the detail at the junction of the walls and roof plays an important part in the general character of the building (see Fig. 6-49).

7.4.3 Wood Trusses

Lightweight, prefabricated wood trusses, often called trussed rafters, offer many advantages in roof framing of small or average size residences (see Figs. 7-49 and 7-50). Wood trusses can be used with either platform or balloon framing; when spaced 24″ on center, which is usually the case in small buildings, they become compatible with sheet sizes of plywood and other materials. Trusses can be lifted into place and quickly anchored on the job. Complete freedom can be exercised in the placement of partitions within the building; they can be made thinner, and when they are not load-bearing, the foundation can be simplified, which constitutes a saving. The basic shape of the truss is a rigid structural triangle, and with the addition of strut members, the basic shape subdivides into smaller triangles, each reducing the span of the outer members or chords. This reduction of individual member spans allows narrower members and less material is required to carry similar loads as compared to conventional framing.

The fasteners used to join the members of the truss can be nails, bolts, split rings, barb-pointed plates, or plywood gusset plates fastened with nails and glue. Many lumber dealers stock engineered trusses of standard lengths and roof pitches. Volume builders prefabricate their own trusses with simple jigs and production-line efficiency. Fabrication of trusses requires careful workmanship and attention to detail; the joints between members are critical, especially the heel joint which is subjected to more lateral stresses. The heel joint should bear on the wall plate below (see Fig. 7-51). If an overhang is required, the top chords can be extended beyond the heel joint to support the overhang (see Fig. 7-49). Modified trusses are available for complete framing of hip-type roofs. Occasionally, conventional framing is combined with trussed-

Fig. 7-49 An economical wood truss for light construction.

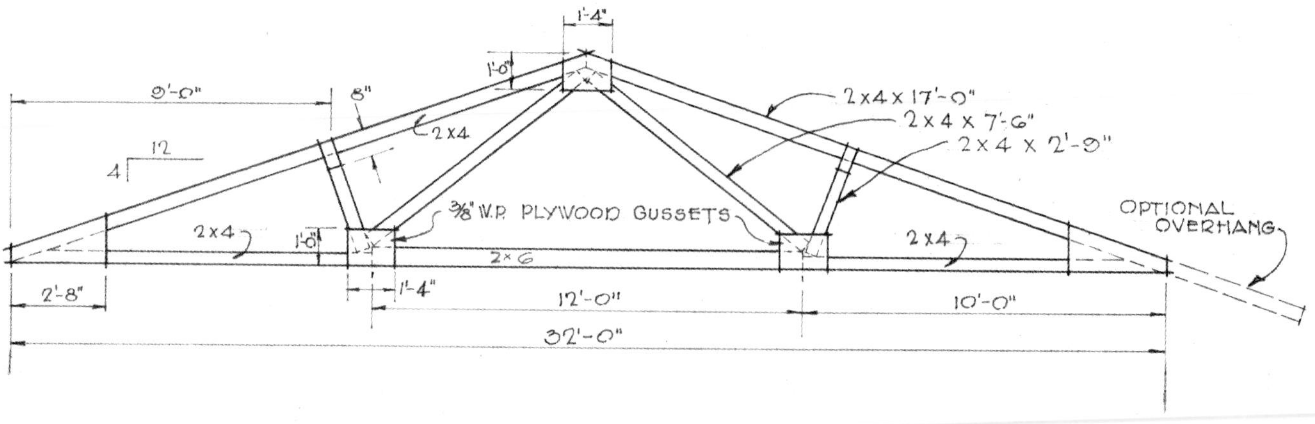

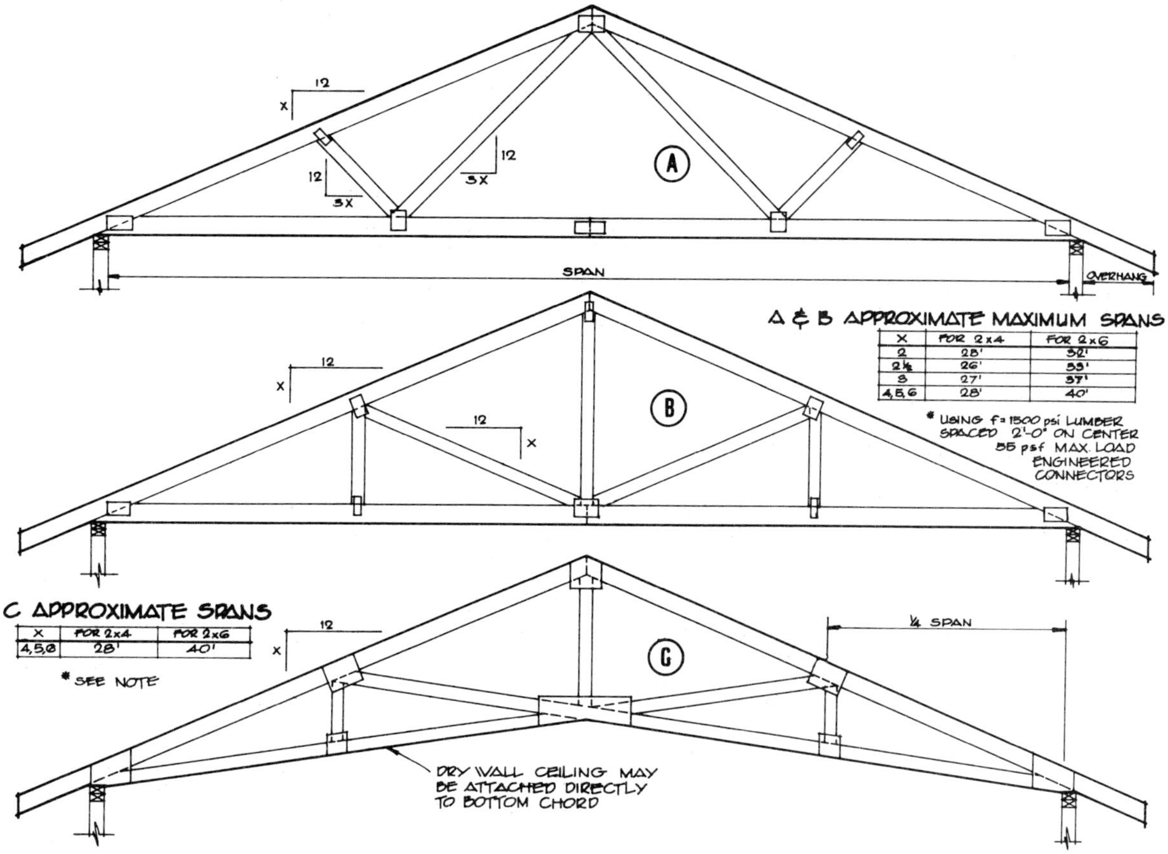

Fig. 7-50 Prefabricated trusses for light construction.

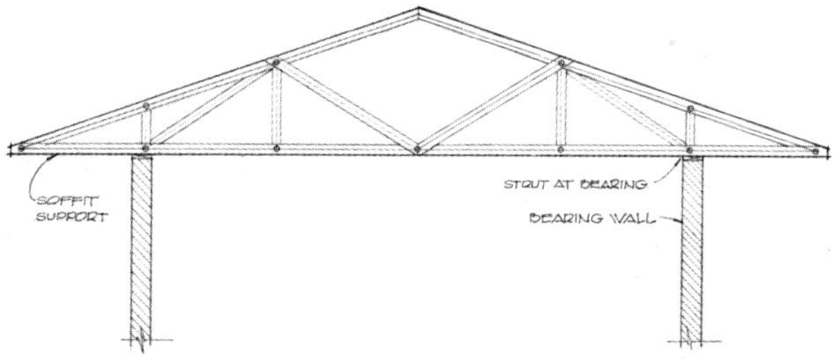

Fig. 7-51 An alternate overhanging truss that transfers load to walls.

rafter framing, the trusses then replace the common rafters of the pitched roof, and conventional framing is used at the intersections of sloping roofs and around the hips of hip roofs.

One of the disadvantages of the trussed rafter is the relatively small amount of usable storage space remaining in the attic. However, if a W-type truss is used, the top of the lower chords between the center webs can be covered with a subfloor and used for storage if a 24″ disappearing stair is introduced between two trusses. The two trusses must be offset several inches from the 24″ spacing to take the stair unit. Also, by necessity, modular limitations with respect to building sizes, shapes, offsets, etc., are encountered in the use of trusses.

Figure 7-49 shows an economical 32′–0″ truss designed by Byron Radcliff of Michigan State College. It is made entirely of 2″ × 4″s with the exception of the center of the bottom chord. The center 10′ section is designed for a 25 lb floor load to permit attic storage. In tests this truss took a 109 lb roof load before breaking, i.e., twice the heaviest snow load for which trusses must be designed anywhere in this country. It requires only 73.1 board ft of lumber.

7.5 PLANK-AND-BEAM FRAME CONSTRUCTION

Plank-and-beam wood framing (see Figs. 7-52 and 7-53), now an established method of residential construction, has been adapted from the older type of mill construction which utilized heavy framing members and thick wood floors and roofs. Plank-and-beam framing is similar to steel skeleton framing in concept; it de-

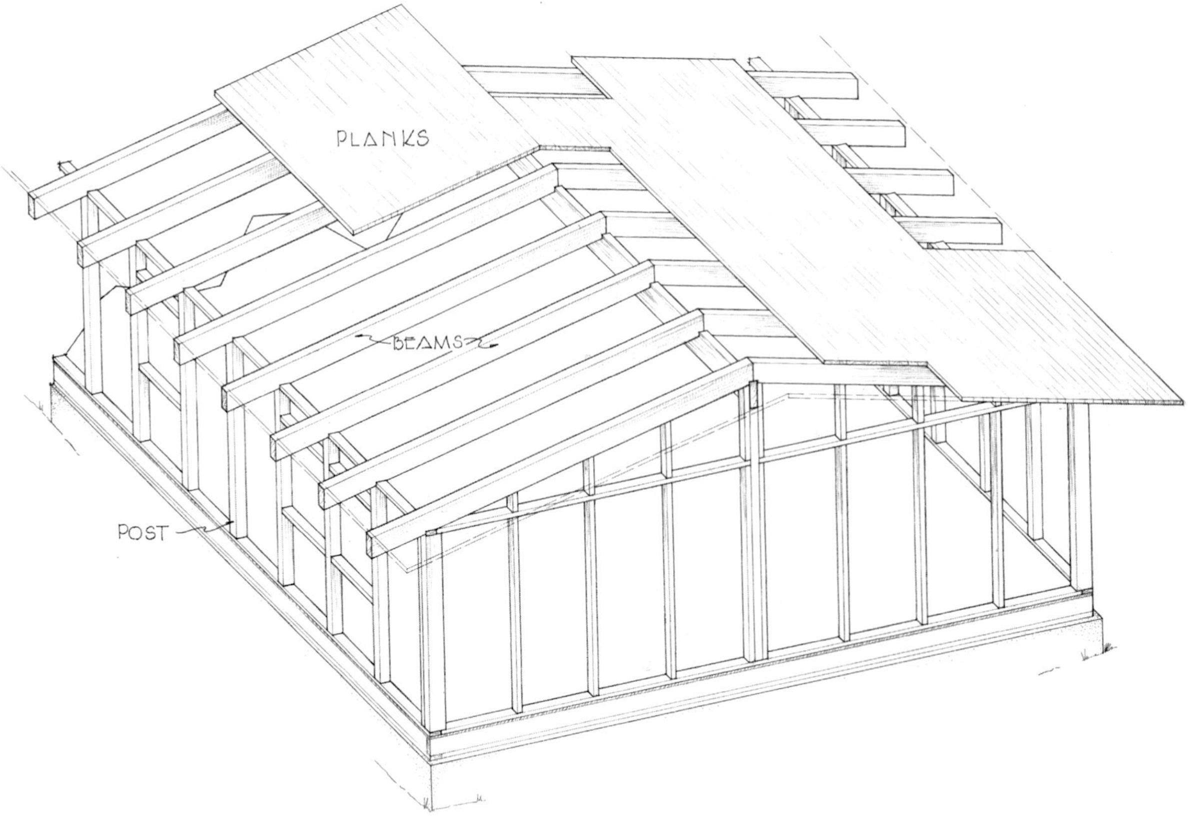

Fig. 7-52 Plank-and-beam construction with transverse beams.

Fig. 7-53 Plank-and-beam construction with longitudinal beams.

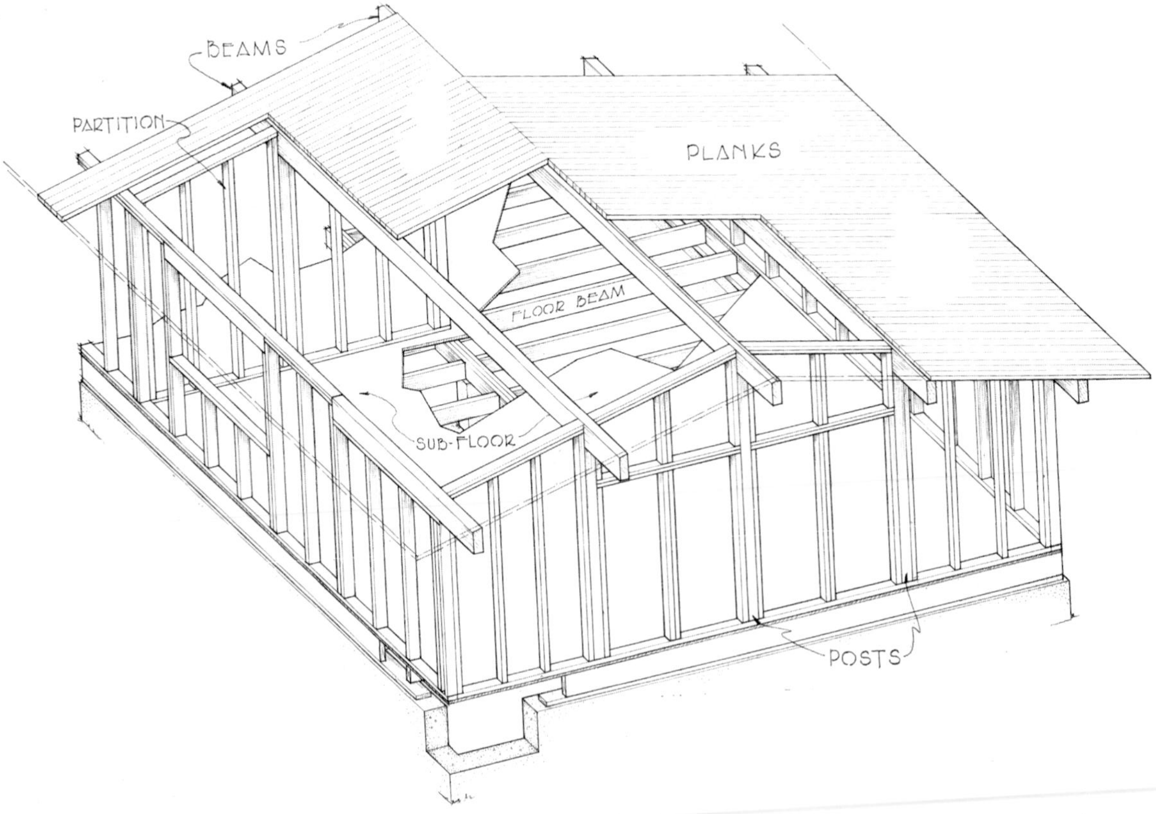

velops structural stability by concentrating loads on a few large members, which in turn transfer their loads directly to the foundation by the use of posts or columns. In structures, these lines of load transfer from the beams should not be interrupted unless special provision has been made for their replacement. Posts needed to support beams in light construction must be at least 4″ × 4″. Where heavy, concentrated loads occur in places other than over main beams or columns, supplementary beams are necessary to carry the loads.

One of the structural advantages of plank-and-beam framing is the simplicity in framing around door and window openings. Because the loads are carried by posts uniformly spaced throughout the walls, large openings can be easily framed without lintels. Large window-walls, which are characteristic of contemporary construction, can be formed by merely inserting fixed glass between the posts. However, a window-wall should have several solid panels in appropriate places to stabilize it against lateral movement. All walls must be braced with diagonal bracing or suitable sheathing.

Plank-and-beam framing requires disciplined planning; savings will be realized by employing modular dimensions to the framing members and wall and roof coverings. (See p. 221 on modular dimensions.) It lends itself to the use of plywood. Stock plywood sizes can be used with a minimum of cutting and waste. Massive, exposed structural members within a house are instrumental in giving it a feeling of stability and rhythmic beauty—attributes that testify to the architect's competence.

With rising relative costs of labor in home building, plank-and-beam framing, which requires the handling of fewer pieces than does conventional framing, offers structural economies to home builders. In a study made by the National Lumber Manufacturers Association, the plank-and-beam method saved 26 per cent on labor and 15 per cent on materials over conventional joist framing. Bridging is eliminated between joists, nails are fewer and larger, inside room heights are increased with no increase in stud or building heights. Masonry piers can be used instead of continuous foundation walls for economy. (The piers must be located under the structural posts.) Eave details and roof overhangs are simpler; usually the 2″ roof decking is cantilevered over the wall and no material is needed for boxing-in the cornice. Conventional framing can be successfully combined with plank-and-beam framing within the same building. Sometimes a plank-and-beam roof is used in only one room of the house, often the living or family area. If so, sufficient column bearing must be provided within the stud walls for the beams of the one roof. If plank-and-beam wall framing supports conventional roof framing, a continuous header should be used at the top of the walls carrying the roof loads, to transfer the load from the closely spaced rafters to the posts. See Fig. 7-54.

There are limitations in plank-and-beam framing, and attention to special details is necessary at these points of construction: partitions must be located over beams, or else supplemental framing must be installed; partitions perpendicular to the beams must rest on a 4″ × 4″ or 4″ × 6″ soleplate to distribute the load across the beam of the floor. Additional beams are needed under bathtubs and other concentrated loads. Because of the absence of concealed air spaces in floors and roofs, wiring and plumbing are more difficult to install. Often built-up cavity beams are used, through which wiring or piping can pass. Flexible wiring cable can

Fig. 7-54 Plank-and-beam interiors.

often be laid in the V joint on the top of 2″ roof decking. Surface-mounted electrical raceways may have to be used for electrical outlets. Plumbing, especially in 2-story houses, may have to be hidden within false beams or furred spaces. Moldings and raceways may have to be employed, and top surfaces of beams may have to be grooved to conceal wiring or piping.

Plank roofs with no dead air space below often require additional insulation and vapor barriers. Insulation is usually applied above the decking, and must be rigid enough to support workmen on the roof. The thickness of the insulation must conform to local climatic conditions. Vapor barriers should be installed between the decking and the insulation. Prefinished insulation board, 2″ to 4″ thick, is available in large sheets to replace decking and insulation combinations. It is light and can be installed rapidly by workmen; no decorating of the underside ceiling is necessary. Prefinished insulation tile or panels can also be applied to the underside of regular wood decking. They can be attached directly to the decking, or furring strips can be used between the underside of the decking and the insulation. When rigid insulation is used above the decking, wood cant strips of the same thickness are fastened around the edges of the roof for application of flashing or gravel stops (see Fig. 7-55). Light-colored coverings for plank roofs also keep the house cooler in summer and warmer in winter.

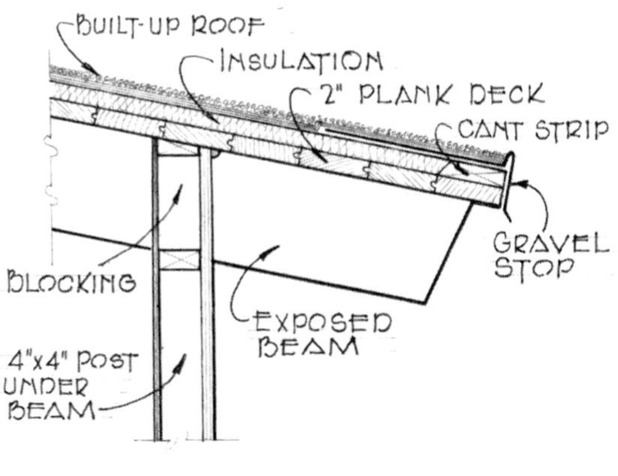

Fig. 7-55 Typical plank-and-beam cornice detail.

Another consideration in plank-and-beam framing is the quality of the exposed structural lumber. Higher grades of framing lumber are required, because large knots, streaks, and resin blemishes are objectional if painted, and are even more unsightly if natural finishes are used. Workmanship in installing the structural pieces is especially important. Finishing nails must be used, metal anchors if used, must be carefully fastened, and no hammer marks should be left on the exposed structural surfaces. Planking should be accurately nailed to the beams, joints should occur above the beams, and the tongue-and-groove planking should be nailed up tightly so that shrinkage between planks will not be objectional. Kiln-dried lumber should be specified, especially for visible ceilings. Blocking, or filler wall, between beams on exterior walls must be carefully fitted and detailed or leaky joints and air infiltration will result when the blocking dries and shrinks. Particular care must be given to connections where beams abut each other and where beams join the posts. These connections must be strong and neatly done. Where gable roofs are used, provision must be made to absorb the horizontal thrust produced by the sloping roof beams (see Fig. 7-56). Partitions and supported ridge beams help relieve this thrust. Metal straps fastened over the ridge beam or metal ridge fasteners are effective in resisting the lateral stresses.

Plank-and-beam roofs can be supported with either transverse beams or longitudinal beams (see Figs. 7-52 and 7-53).

Fig. 7-56 Horizontal thrust of a beam ceiling.

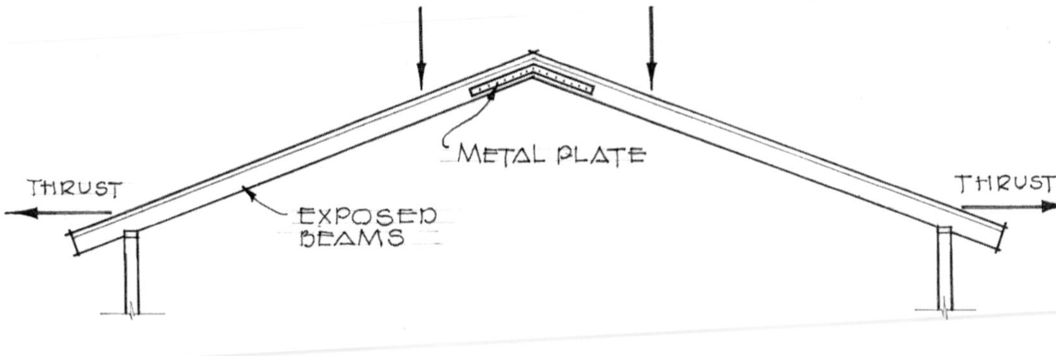

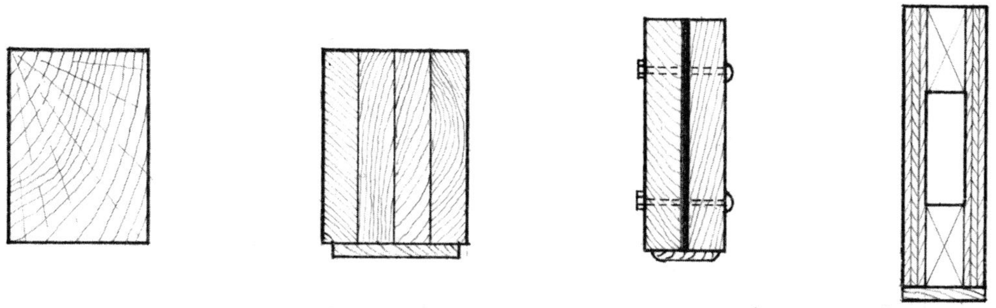

Fig. 7-57 Types of beams used in plank-and-beam construction.

Fig. 7-58 Wood decking used on plank-and-beam ceilings.

Transverse Beams are usually supported at the ridge by a heavy ridge beam and by the long, exterior walls of the building. The planks then span the beams perpendicularly to the slope of the roof, if it is a gable-type as shown. Beams may be solid, glue-laminated, or built-up (see Fig. 7-57) of 2″ lumber, securely fastened together (fasteners are usually concealed). Strength and rigidity of the planks are improved if they are continuous over more than one span. Tests show that a plank that is continuous over two spans is nearly two and one-half times as stiff as a plank extending over only one span, under the same conditions. Planks, usually 6″ or 8″ wide, can be tongue-and-grooved or splined (see Fig. 7-58), and are designed to support moderate loads. If beams are spaced more than 7′ or 8′ apart, noticeable deflection of common species of nominal 2″ planking will result.

Longitudinal Beams running the entire length of the building, can be used instead of transverse beams. In that case, the planking is applied parallel to the slope of the roof—down the slope. For either method, tables are used for the proper selection of beam size, span, and spacing, after the other architectural considerations have been resolved. Exterior beams at corners of gable ends are usually false or short beams, which are cantilevered out from the corner of the long, exterior walls (see Fig. 7-53). Beam sizes can be reduced when interior partitions become supports for the beams.

When either method of plank-and-beam framing is employed, interior partitions are often more difficult to frame than when conventional framing is used. If ceilings are sloping, the top of the partition must meet the underside of the slope and must be made diagonal. Other partitions, running perpendicularly to the slope of the ceiling, will have horizontal cap plates but must be built to different heights. Interior partitions, using 2″ × 4″ studs, can be framed by several methods. first, they can be framed with the studs cut the same length as the exterior walls and a double cap plate put over all the exterior and interior walls, tying them securely together as done in platform framing. Short studs are then attached above the plate to a single top plate that conforms to the slope of the celing and is attached to it. Or, the partitions can be erected after the roof is completed. The various length studs are cut to fit the slope of the ceiling, and each partition with a single 2″ × 4″ cap is fitted into its proper place.

Finish strip-flooring should be nailed at right angles to the plank subfloor, similar to conventional construction. Care must be taken to be sure flooring or roofing nails do not penetrate through the planks when the planks serve as a ceiling. The inside appearance should be considered when spacing beams; moving a beam several inches one way or another near a partition will often be an improvement. Partitions, on the other hand, should be placed in relation to beams so that the beams seem to form a uniform pattern throughout the room. Needless to say, the appearance of exposed beams

Fig. 7-59 A California Redwood home with an interesting roof of planks over laminated beams. *(Courtesy Dandelet.)*

on the exterior of the building is also of importance. Plank-and-beam framing lends itself to "open planning," a characteristic of contemporary houses.

In most areas, structural design of the plank-and-beam framing will be controlled by the local building code to the extent of specifying live load requirements. A live load of 40 lb per sq ft is usually specified for floors. For roofs, some codes specify 20 lb per sq ft, others 30 lb. Beam sizes, spacing, and species necessary for various spans of both roofs and floors can be taken from the plank-and-beam tables found in Appendix E.

Glue-Laminated Structural Members offer many design possibilities in plank-and-beam construction that otherwise would be restricted by the structural limitations of sawed wood members (see Fig. 7-59). Many stock beam shapes are available (see Fig. 7-60) providing variations in conventional building silhouettes. Many church buildings successfully employ either laminated beams or arches for interesting ceilings and roof structures. Special waterproof glues are used for exterior exposures. Usually comparative sectional sizes span one-third more than sawed timbers. Consult manufacturers' catalogues for specific shapes, loads, and spans.

Fig. 7-60 Glue-laminated structural shapes available in wood.

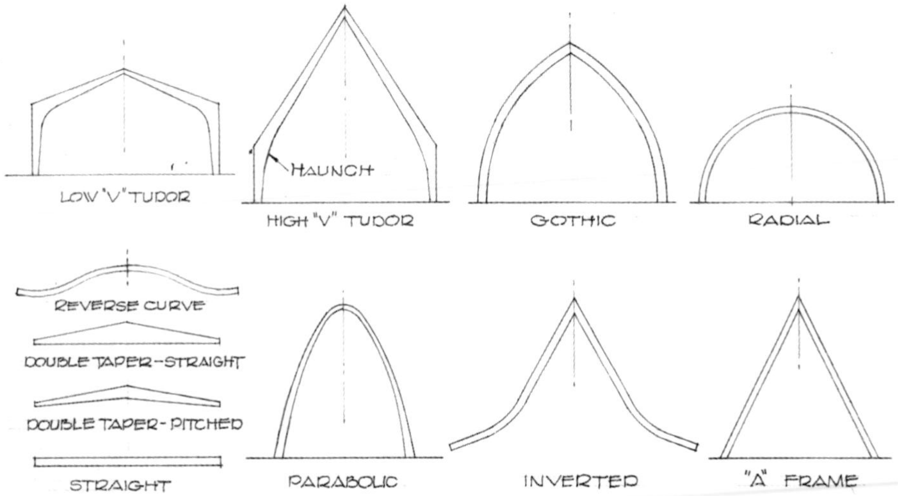

In larger buildings, structural systems such as rigid frames, two-hinged barrel arches, and three-hinged arches, as well as bowstring arches and domes, make use of laminated members. Rigid frames are made of separate leg and arm members carefully joined at the haunch to maintain the desired roof slope. The two-hinged barrel arches must have provision for counteracting outward thrust at their bases with the use of either foundation piers, tie rods, or concrete foundation buttresses. Each support must be engineered to resist the horizontal thrust of the arch. Three-hinged arches such as Tudor and Gothic are popular in contemporary church architecture because of their beauty. Their spans vary typically from 30 to 100 feet. Their base construction is similar to the two-hinged arches. Because of the distance between arches, purlins are commonly placed perpendicularly between arches to carry the roof decking. Arch design data varies with the roof slope and span distance. Metal connectors at critical points insure neat, engineered joining of the laminated members. See Fig. 7-61.

7.6 BRICK AND STONE VENEER CONSTRUCTION

In areas of the country where brick or building stone are economical, veneered frame dwellings are popular. Masonry veneer over wood framing is more economical than solid masonry; the combination wall—masonry over wood, utilizes the good qualities of both materials. The exterior masonry is durable and requires no maintenance; the wood is economical, more flexible, and is a good insulator. Any of the previously mentioned types of wood framing can be used with veneer; the wood frame supports the entire weight of the floors and roof—no loads are put on the masonry veneer. The single wythe of brick or stone is merely an exterior wall covering for the structure (see Fig. 7-62).

Bricks or 4″ or 6″ cut stone can be used for veneering. Hard-burned, moisture-resistant brick should be used. Sandstones and limestones are commonly used for stone veneers. In many southern states, as well as other areas of the country, used brick has become very popular in residential construction. The brick are reclaimed from dismantled commercial buildings or other structures and artistically combined to produce pleasing exteriors and chimneys. Even chipped brick are included to create a casual and weathered appearance. Many brick manufacturers make a simulated old-brick that produces the same effect.

It is common practice to start the veneer at the grade line. Provision must be made on the foundation for the width of the veneer and a 1″ air space between the veneer and the wall sheathing; at least 5″ bearing width is allowed (see Fig. 7-62). Good construction usually starts the veneer lower than the wood sill on the foundation wall. Condensation often develops within the air space, and provision must be made to keep the moisture from penetrating the wood members. The exterior sheathing must be covered with a moisture barrier, such as roofing felt. If asphalt-coated sheathing board is used, the asphalt coating acts as a moisture barrier. At the bottom of the air space, a rustproof base flashing must be inserted under the felt and extended into the lower mortar joint of the veneer. This flashing prevents any moisture from penetrating the wood sill members after gathering at the bottom of the air space. Weep holes can be provided at the bottom course by leaving mortar out of vertical joints about 4′ apart.

Brick or masonry sills under window and door openings must be flashed in the same manner. Water running off from windows and doors onto their sills must be kept from entering the air cavity. Masonry will absorb moisture unless it is waterproofed. Veneer is tied to the wood frame wall with rustproof, corrugated metal ties. The ties are nailed through the sheathing to every other stud and laid into the mortar joints of every sixth course (about every 16″ to 20″ of vertical masonry). Sloping sills of brick, set on edge, are usually used under all openings of brick veneer, and a similar sloping sill must cap brick veneer when it extends only partially up an exterior wall. Combination brick and wood siding exteriors require a bead of caulking where the two materials join together. Stone veneer usually has a cut stone sill under all openings. It also extends out from the face of the veneer, similar to brick, and has a sloping top surface, called a "wash," and a drip underneath to prevent water from running back to the wall. All mortar joints in veneers should be well-tooled to prevent moisture penetration.

Steel angle iron, usually 3″ × 3″ × 1/4″ or 4″ × 4″ × 1/4″ depending on loads, is used for lintels above openings in brick veneer (see

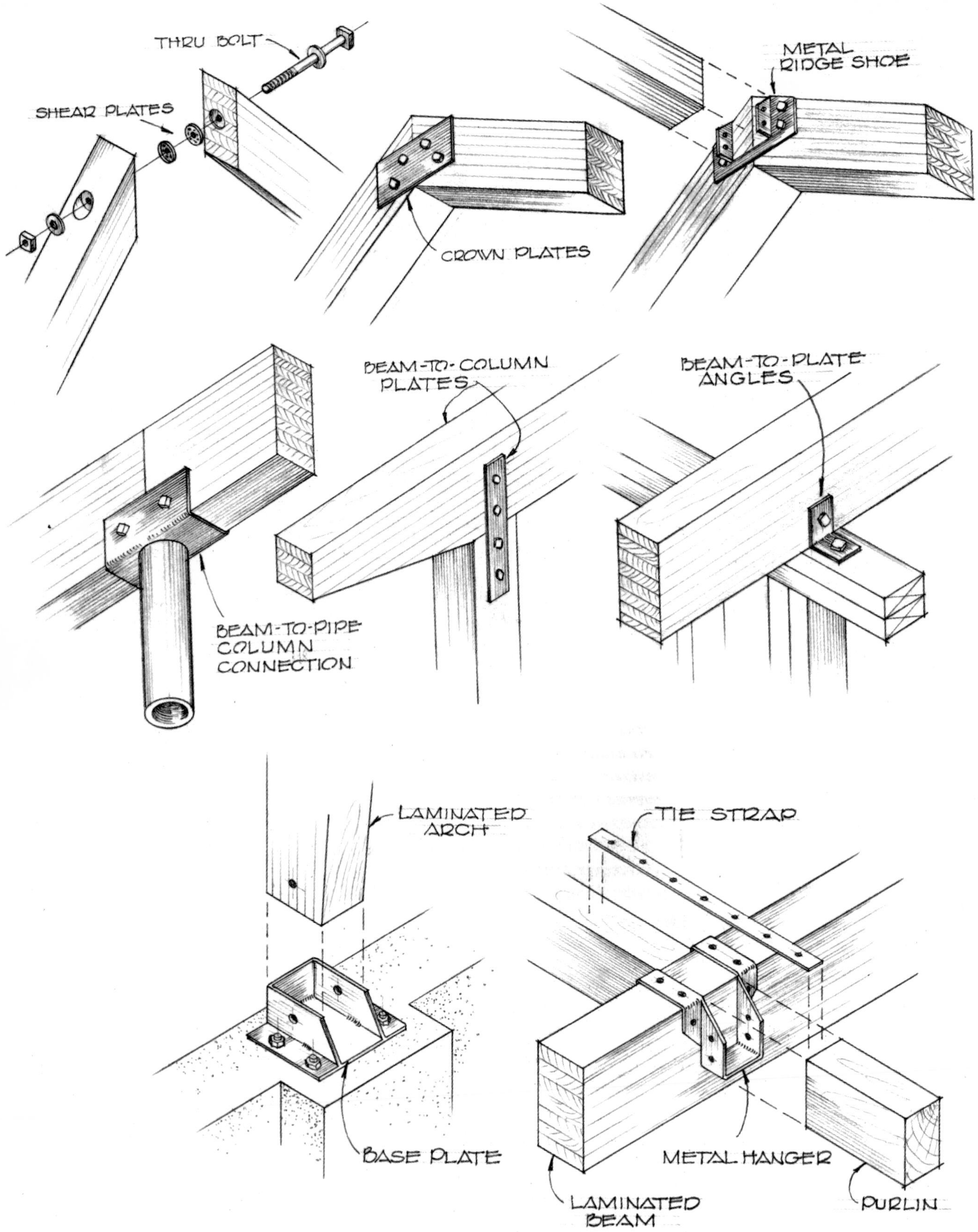

Fig. 7-61 Metal connections for laminated timber members.

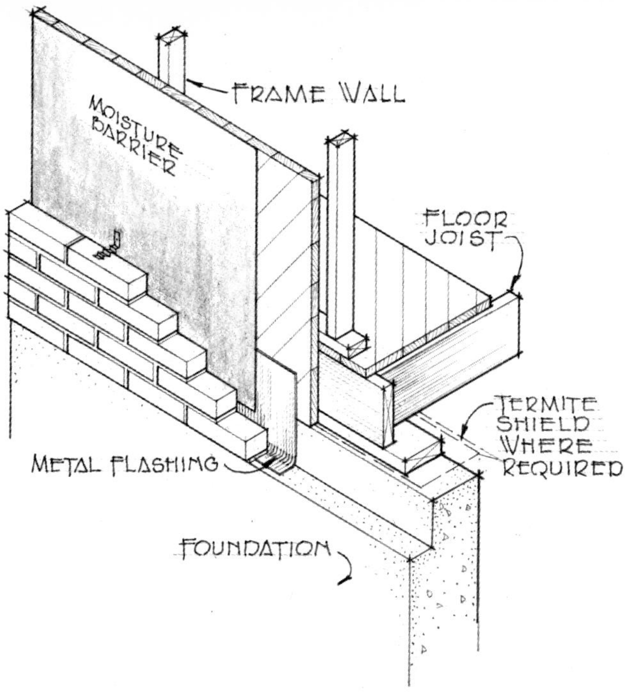

Fig. 7-62 Wood frame construction with brick veneer.

Fig. 7-64 and Table 7-9). Often brick "soldier courses" (Fig. 7-65) are put directly above openings. Some builders eliminate the use of steel lintels above veneer openings in 1-story houses by using a wide trim frieze board and molding above all window and door openings. If a low, boxed-in cornice is used no masonry is necessary above the openings. The wide frieze board continues around the entire house below the cornice, and blocking is used to fur out to the face of the veneer above the windows and doors.

Brick or stone is often used to veneer concrete block and structural clay tile. In low walls, corrugated metal ties can be used to tie the two materials together; in larger walls, more positive bonds are attained with "header courses" of brick set into the masonry backing (see Fig. 7-66).

Table 7-9 Steel Angle Lintels for Light-Frame Brick Veneer Construction

Span	Size
0′–5′	3″ x 3″ x ¼″
5′–9′	3½″ x 3½″ x 5⁄16″
9′–10′	4″ x 4″ x 5⁄16″
10′–11′	4″ x 4″ x ⅜″

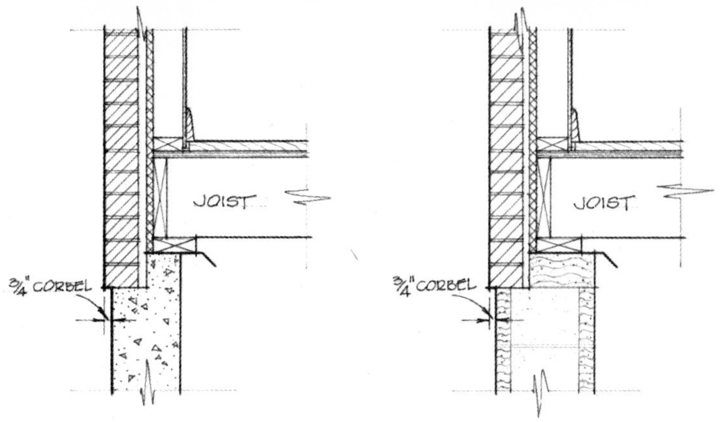

Fig. 7-63 Brick veneer may be corbelled on foundation walls.

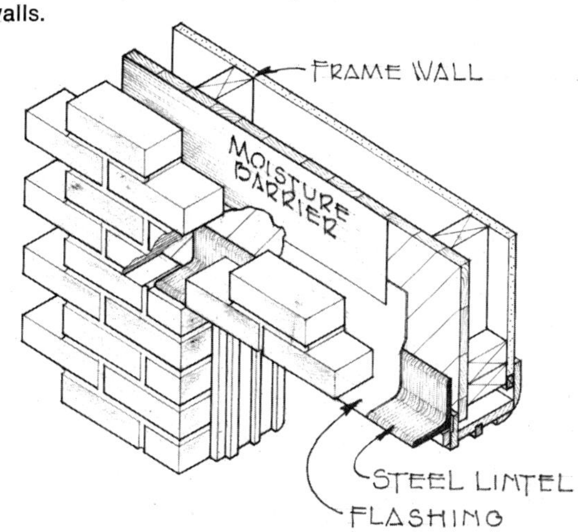

Fig. 7-64 Steel lintel above brick veneer openings.

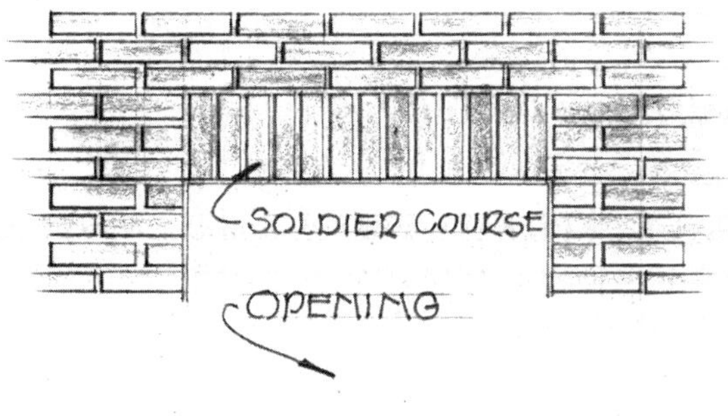

Fig. 7-65 Brick soldier course above opening.

Fig. 7-66 Concrete block and brick veneer wall details.

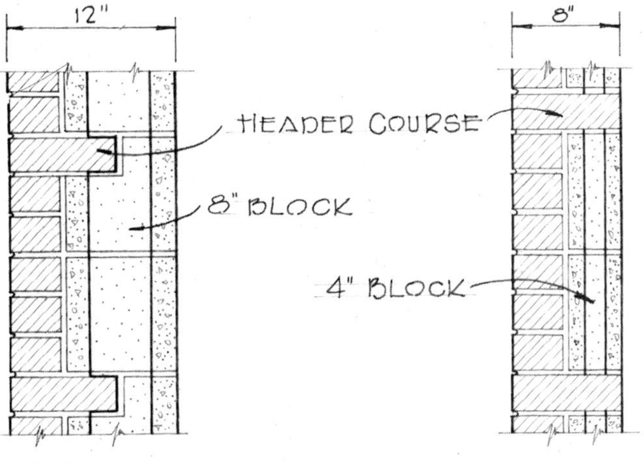

7.7 SOLID MASONRY AND CAVITY WALL CONSTRUCTION

Solid masonry, especially brick and stone, has served man well for centuries as a desirable construction material. Many structures still standing—and still beautiful—are evidence of its pleasing as well as durable characteristics. Both brick and stone are available in many different colors, textures, and sizes to challenge the creativity and artistry of modern designers and builders. Even though many solid masonry buildings have been built of these materials in the past, the present-day trend is to use these materials as exterior veneers only, with either wood frame, concrete block, structural tile, or reinforced concrete as the structural, load-bearing material. Solid stone in residential work is limited mainly to foundations, as mentioned in the previous material on foundations, or small walls; in contemporary residences it is often used to create contrasting walls where the texture and color of the brick or stone is exposed both inside and outside. Many architects feel that the natural beauty of stone provides sufficient textural interest to make any further decoration of the walls unnecessary.

Local codes in some residential areas require solid masonry exterior walls in all structures. Usually 8″ thick brick walls are used in 1-story houses; local codes must be referred to if higher walls are involved. This type of construction, where solid brick walls carry the weight of the floors and roof, is known as "bearing-wall construction." The floors and roof are constructed of wood framing members, similar to conventional framing, except that the floor joists are set into the masonry walls and transfer their loads to them; the rafters rest on wood plates well-anchored to the top of the walls. All the wood structural members of the floors, partitions, and roof are surrounded by the shell-like exterior masonry wall. This shell of incombustible material has the advantage of restricting the spread of fire to surrounding buildings. Floor joists setting in the masonry wall must have a diagonal cut, called a "fire cut," on their ends to prevent the joists from rupturing the wall, should a fire burn through the joists and cause them to drop to the bottom of the building (see Fig. 7-67). The fire cut allows full bearing at the bottom surface of the joist, yet is self-releasing in case of fire.

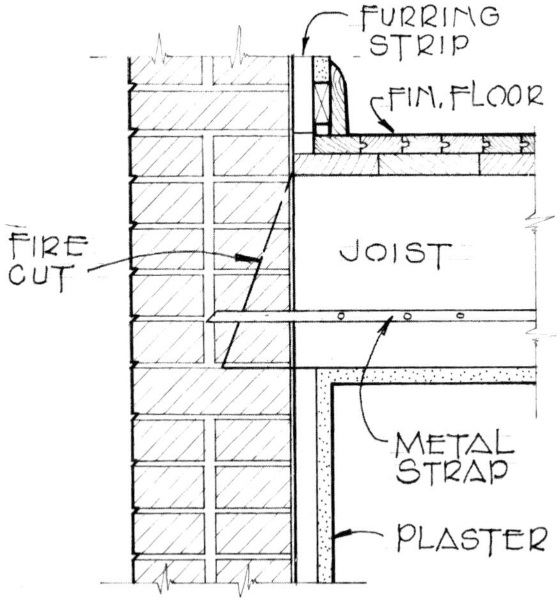

Fig. 7-67 Wood joists in solid-brick wall detail.

Because of the porous and noninsulating nature of sold brick or masonry, some method must be used to prevent moisture penetration and to insulate the exterior walls. The conventional method is to waterproof the inside surface of the masonry with hot asphalt or tar, then fasten 1″ × 2″ furring strips to the inside masonry surface—to which the interior wall covering is applied. Blanket insulation can also be inserted between the furring strips. Another method of furring the masonry wall, to get an air space between the exterior and interior surfaces, is by using furring clay tile. Or a self-furring metal lath can be used, over which ¾″ plaster is applied.

In economical 1-story buildings, a single-wythe brick called Norwegian brick can be used for the masonry load-bearing walls. See Fig. 7-68. Since the Norwegian brick is larger than common brick, a wall can be laid up much faster. It is 5½″ wide, 2$\frac{3}{16}$″ high, and 11½″ long and can be furred with 2″ × 2″ furring strips, fastened to metal clips which are set into the mortar joints throughout the wall. Interior finish materials can be fastened to the furring strips.

Many other hollow brick units are available up to 8″ thick which are suitable for single-unit masonry walls. Interior plaster is often applied directly to the inside surface of these units. Many small commercial buildings are built with this method. For residential construction, however, small brick units are prefer-

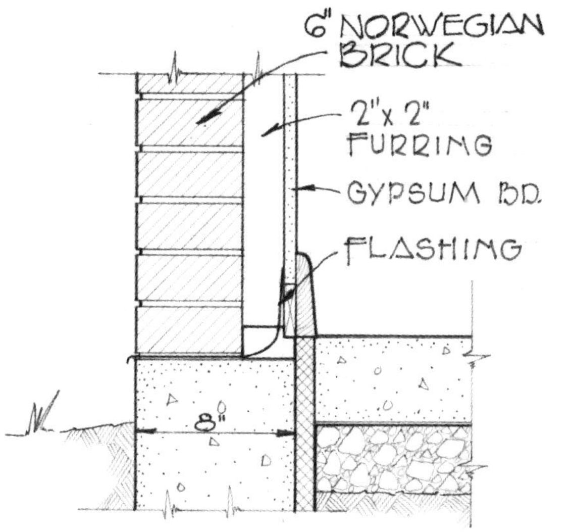

Fig. 7-68 Norwegian brick wall detail for one-story walls.

able because their texture imparts more interest than that of the larger units.

If a brick surface is required for both the outside and inside walls, a *brick cavity* wall can be used (Fig. 7-69). This method of construction was introduced from Europe in the late thirties and has been widely accepted in this country. A 2″ air cavity is used between the wythes of common brick, making the wall usually 10″ thick. Rigid metal ties are placed in the mortar joints spaced 16″ on center horizontally and vertically to tie the two wythes together. No furring is necessary, since the air cavity prevents moisture penetration and insulates the wall. In colder climates, air stops are used at corners to minimize air circulation throughout the cavity. Added insulation can be given by applying rigid insulation to the inside wall of the air cavity; insulation should not touch the outside wythe of brick. Flashing must be used at floor levels, sills, heads of openings, and other critical places. Weep holes must be used in the outer base-course to dissipate moisture accumulating in the lower part of the air cavity. This can be accomplished by omitting the mortar from header joints at intervals of 3′ or 4′. Another method is to insert cotton sash cord, cut 5″ or 6″ long, in the mortar joints every 4′ to produce a wick action and also seal the cavity from insects.

Wood floor joists can rest on the inside wythe of brick; additional metal ties must be used in the course below the joists, and the joists must not project into the cavity. Girders and beams must be supported by solid, 8″ wide pilasters that bond the inner and outer wythes

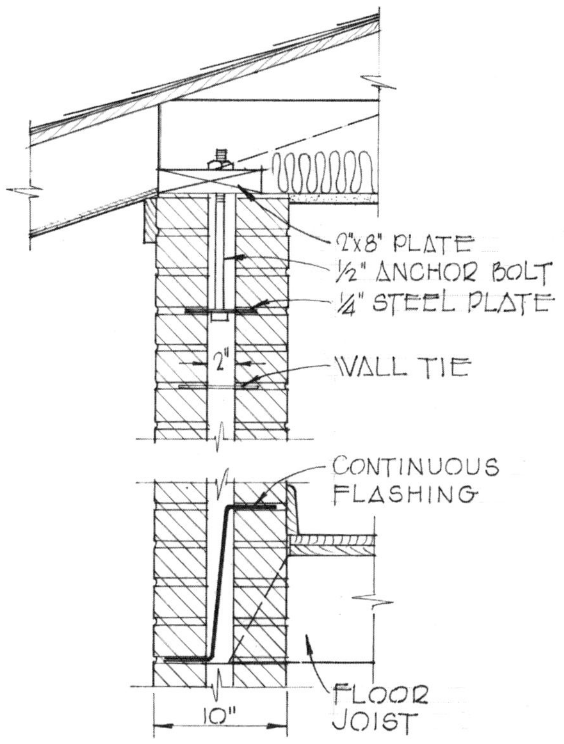

Fig. 7-69 Brick-cavity wall detail.

together. Roof and ceiling construction must be supported by a 2″ thick wood plate that rests on both wythes and is anchored with $\frac{1}{2}''$ anchor bolts 6′–0″ on center. The anchor bolts must extend down into the air cavity about 15″, and a $3'' \times 6'' \times \frac{1}{4}''$ plate is welded to the head of the bolt and anchored in the mortar joints of the brick (see Fig. 7-69). Mortar joints should be well-tooled on both the outer and inner finish surfaces.

Concrete Block has become the most economical building material for small buildings, even for above-ground construction. It is estimated that a block wall costs about 10 per cent less than conventional stud-wall with insulation construction. It is a widely available material that combines structure, insulation, exterior and interior finish surfaces. Many various shapes and sizes of blocks are manufactured; as previously mentioned, the most used sizes are nominal $8'' \times 8'' \times 16''$ and $8'' \times 12'' \times 16''$. (Refer to Fig. 7-10 for other sizes and shapes.) The blocks are made either of dense concrete mixes, which give them good structural qualities, or of lightweight aggregate mixes, which result in blocks that are weaker structurally, but that provide better insulation. Lightweight blocks of foamed concrete are available in some areas; they have the same insulating qualities as stud walls with wood sheathing, siding, and 2″ of insulation.

Improperly cured blocks often result in cracks in concrete block walls. The blocks should be air-cured for at least 28 days, or they should be cured under high-pressure steam, which is the better method for reducing ultimate shrinkage. Steam-cured blocks will shrink from 1/4″ to 3/8″ in a 100′ wall; air-cured blocks will shrink about twice the amount. Cracking can often be eliminated by introducing wire mesh or lightweight block steel reinforcement into every second or third horizontal mortar joint (see Fig. 7-70). Extra reinforcement is required above and below all wall openings. In long concrete block walls, control joints must be used to relieve contraction and other stresses; they are continuous vertical joints through the wall, and are spaced at 20′–0″ intervals.

Concrete block walls are not successful in areas subjected to earthquakes, unless heavy reinforcement is used extensively at each floor and ceiling level. Refer to local seismic codes if blocks must be used.

Fig. 7-70 Horizontal reinforcement in block courses.

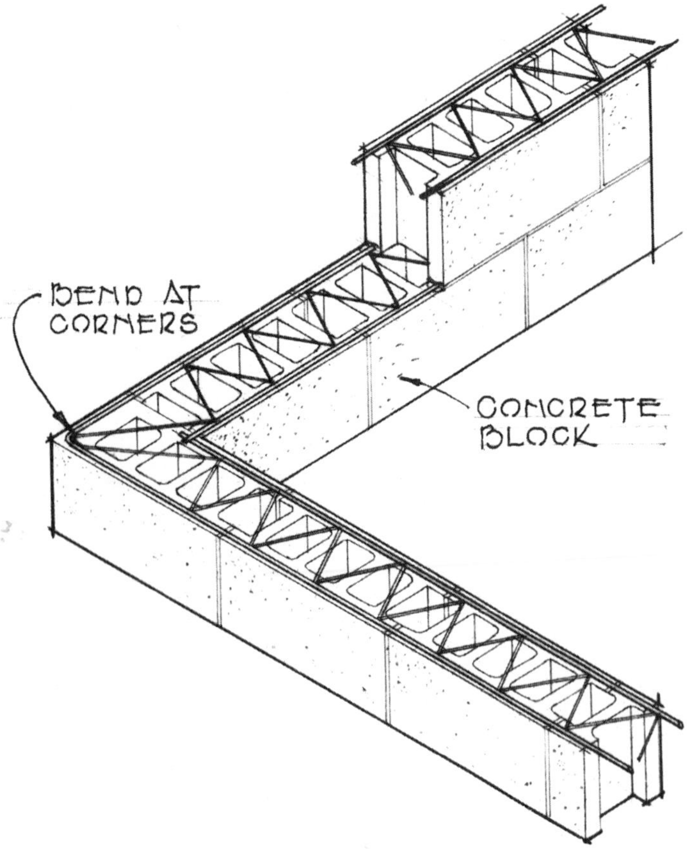

In warm areas such as Florida, Arizona, and parts of Texas, concrete block has become a very popular above-ground construction material, even in fine houses. Blocks can be waterproofed on the exterior with waterproof, cement-base paints, or directly covered with stucco. The inside is usually furred and plastered. Florida hurricane codes require continuous, reinforced concrete "bond beams" above each story-level of block work, which must be tied to the foundation with vertical corner reinforcement (see Fig. 7-12).

Different architectural effects can be achieved by the use of different sized blocks in various combinations; however the half-lapped bond is used in structural walls. A "stacked bond" is occasionally used for novelty effects, but horizontal reinforcement must then be used in the horizontal joints. As mentioned in the material on foundations, i.e., use block modules for lengths, heights, and opening sizes, as well as placement of the openings (see Fig. 7-5). Hollow blocks must be capped with solid cap blocks where framing joists or beams rest on them. Nonload-bearing partitions can be made with 4″ thick hollow blocks.

Steel and Concrete Joists Steel joists are often used in small commercial buildings for the structural support of roofs and light-occupancy floors. Several different types of open-web steel joists are manufactured; details and allowable spans are obtained from manufacturers' catalogues.[1]

Total dead and live loads must be calculated, and preliminary considerations must be studied before open-web steel joists are adopted. After they have been found adaptable in the preliminary planning, a thorough engineering calculation is made of all aspects of their use before the steel joist construction is finally selected for the structure.

Steel joists are available in standard depths of 8″, 10″, 12″, 14″, 16″, 18″, and 20″, each in different weights which can span up to 40′ for roofs. Maximum permissible spacing of the joists for floors is 24″ on center; for roofs 30″ on center. In flat roof construction with 2″ thick tongue-and-grooved decking, a 2″ × 4″ nailing strip is fastened to the top of the joists with metal clips or lag bolts to receive the

[1] Specifications and details can also be obtained from the Steel Joist Institute, 1346 Connecticut Avenue N.W., Washington, D.C. 20036.

decking. Some joists are made with wood nailing strips already attached to both the top and bottom chord. If a ceiling is required below the roof joists, 3/8″ ribbed metal lath can be clipped to the bottom chord and plaster applied over it (see Fig. 7-71). This construction will give the roof a 3/4-hr fire rating according to the National Bureau of Standards Report TRBM-44. Flat-type roof construction with steel joists also employs a 2″ concrete slab poured over paper-backed steel mesh, or a 2″ gypsum slab as the deck. Usually, built-up roofing is applied directly over the slabs, unless rigid insulation is needed. Lightweight, insulating concrete makes a desirable roof. The steel joists rest on the load-bearing masonry walls, or, in wider buildings requiring a steel girder through the center, they would rest on the girder as well as on the walls. Metal bridging is attached to joists between spans. Suspended ceilings of acoustical tile can be supported with hangers and metal channels below the steel joists; the open-web character of the joists allows pipes, ducts, and wiring to be run through the dead air space above the ceiling.

In floor construction with steel joists, the joists are supported in the masonry wall similar to wood framing, as well as on steel girders through the center if the building is wider than the span of one joist. A 2″ or 2½″ poured concrete slab is placed over one of several types of permanent forming material—either paper-backed 6″ × 6″ No. 10 wire mesh, corrugated steel sheets, or 3/8″ expanded metal rib lath. The forming material is left in place. Floor slabs are reinforced with 1/4″ (No. 2) bars, 12″ on center both ways, or with the 6″ × 6″ welded wire mesh; no other reinforcing is generally used.

Precast, reinforced concrete slabs of similar thickness can also be used on floors. Asphalt tile or other floor finishes can be put over the concrete slabs.

Reinforced Concrete Joists are occasionally used in light construction (see Fig. 7-72). In case of a concrete floor with a basement below, or a fireproof flat roof, the use of concrete joists is appropriate. They are manufactured in many areas so that a source can usually be found near any given building site. Depth and reinforcing size are custom-designed according to the loads and spans required. Concrete joists are generally spaced 24″ on center and bear on concrete block walls. The slab can be poured over wood forming placed between the joists; or the permanent forming materials, mentioned above can be used. Another method utilizes filler block, laid tightly between the concrete joists and resting on the joists. A 2″ slab is poured over the filler block to form the floor or roof (see Fig. 7-72). Precast concrete joists are designed for each specific job and delivered to the site ready to be installed.

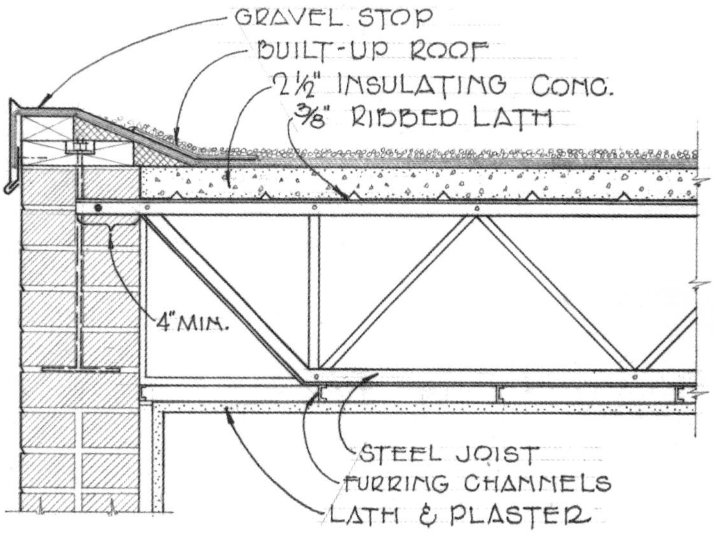

Fig. 7-71 Bearing wall and steel joist detail.

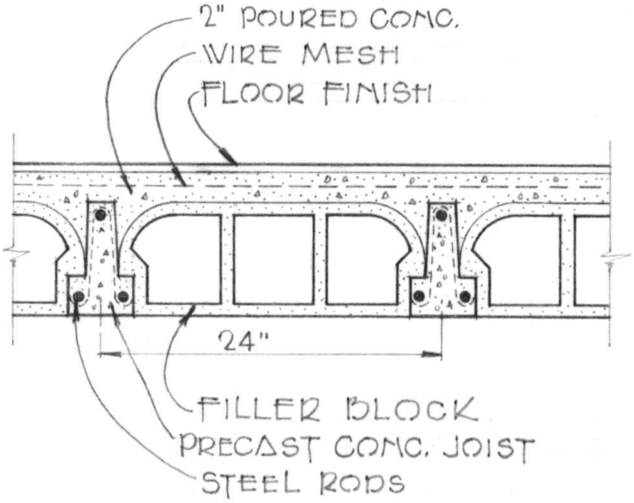

Fig. 7-72 Concrete floor detail (requires no forming).

7.8 ROOF TYPES AND ROOF COVERINGS

The roof is a very important part of any building—large or small, and it should therefore receive careful consideration. One might

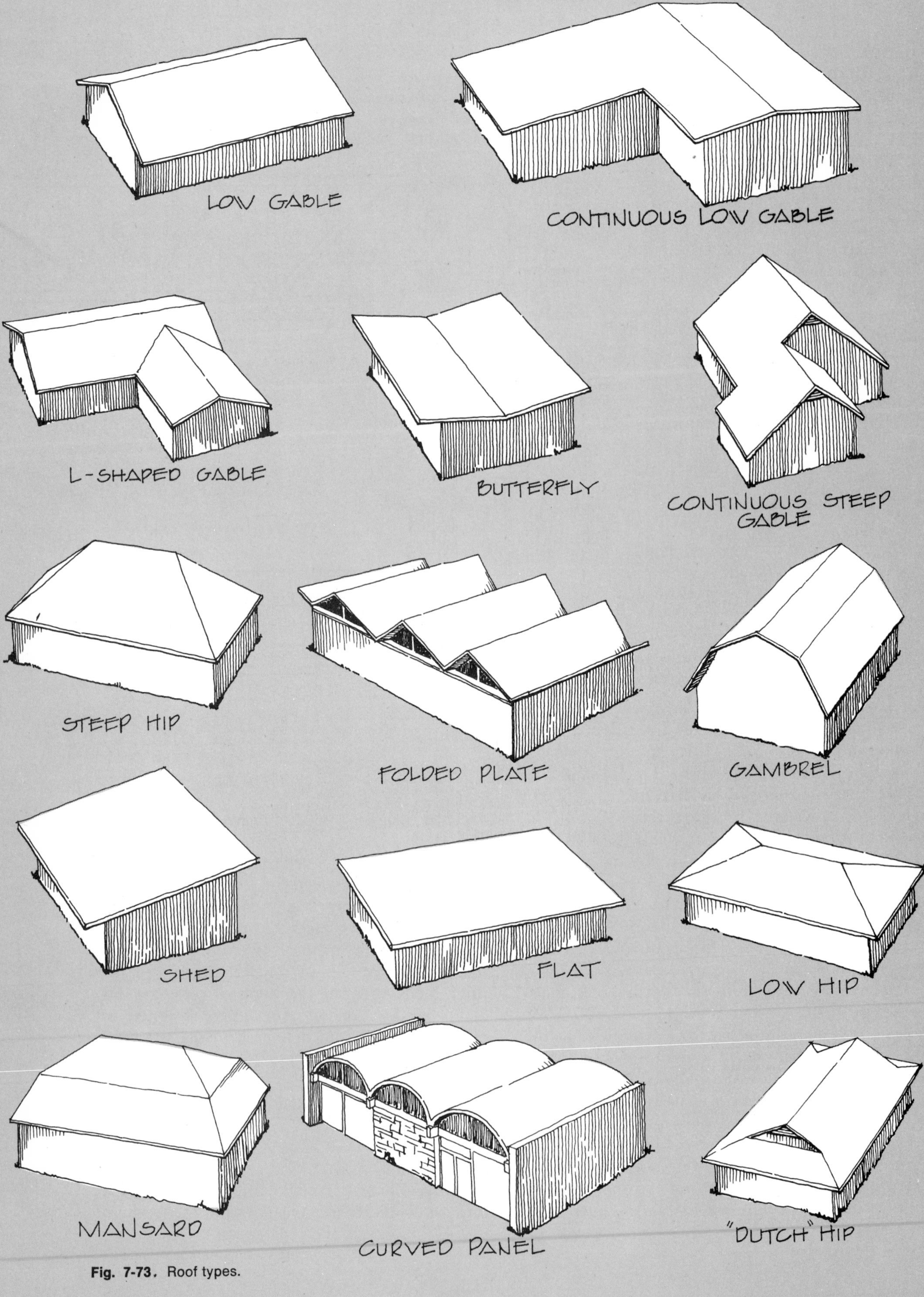

Fig. 7-73. Roof types.

say a house is no better than the roof that covers it. Like an umbrella, it protects the structure from the elements; in some climates it is subjected to intense heat, most everywhere to rain and dampness, and in many areas to driving winds. Not only is the roof extremely functional, but its shape and nature play a vital role in the architectural appearance and styling of a house, which is often designated by its roof type. In commercial buildings however, the roof is often flat and obscured by parapet walls, and therefore less important as far as the building's appearance is concerned.

In years past, the snow load of buildings in northern areas required steep roofs. However, with the improvement of roofing materials and more engineering design in buildings, the design of modern roofs has become less restrictive. Because architects and builders now have available a generous selection of roof coverings for any desired architectural treatment, one finds successful roofs of all types and slopes in almost every area of the country regardless of climatic conditions.

7.8.1 Roof Types

The Flat Roof (see Fig. 7-73) is one of the simplest and most economical roofs as far as material is concerned. The roof joists become the framing members of both the roof and the interior ceiling. Sizes and spans of joists must be adequate to support both the live load of the roof and the dead loads of the roofing and the finished ceiling. The spacing of wood roof joists is generally 16″ on center. Comparatively little air space is provided in a flat roof; therefore, batt-type or blanket insulation with the vapor barrier near the interior side, is recommended between roof joists. All the air cavities between the roof joists must be ventilated. Solid bridging should not be used in flat roofs; the blocking would prevent uniform air circulation.

Overhangs, for reason of weather protection or appearance, vary in width from 1′ to 4′—the usual overhang is 2′ so that 4′–0″ wide plywood panels can be conveniently ripped and used for soffits. Overhangs of the flat roof are simply cantilevered over the exterior wall plates, and the joists are toenailed to the plates, or metal framing anchors can be used. If a boxed-in overhang is used, a header joist is recommended around the periphery of the roof (see Fig. 7-74A). The header joist becomes the backing for the finish fascia board, provides blocking for the soffit material, and tends to straighten the roof line. Overhangs from exterior walls that are parallel to the joists must be framed with look-out joists (sometimes called "tail joists," see Fig. 7-46). Look-out joists are short and butt into a double, long joist. Generally, the distance from the double, long joist to the wall line is the same as the overhang. If wide joists are necessary, because of the span, the joist width is often tapered from the exterior wall to the outside end of the joist. This tapering of the joists prevents the fascia board from appearing too wide and heavy. Occasionally, to avoid wide fascias, narrow outlookers are lap-nailed to the roof joists. Blocking is required on the top wall plate between each roof joist to provide nailing strips for the soffit and crown molding.

Flat roofs have the advantage of ease and flexibility of framing over odd building shapes and offset exterior walls. Other types of roofs often restrict the general shape of the building. Many architects resort to a flat roof when living spaces within the building do not conform to traditional shapes and relationships. Space planning can be almost unrestricted if a flat roof is used. However, the straight, horizontal roof line of a flat roof often appears hard and monoto-

Fig. 7-74 Flat roof with narrow fascia details.

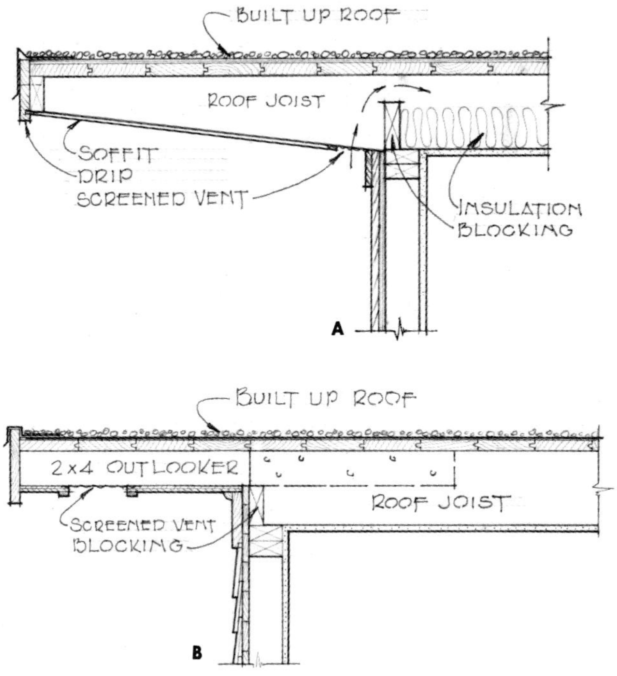

nous; variety and interest can be gained by combining other roof shapes with the flat roof, or by using several roof levels throughout the building. A watertight "built-up" roof covering must be used on a flat roof, and metal gravel stops are put around the edges. The roof can have a slight pitch or it can be perfectly flat. Many flat roofs retain puddles after a rain, but this is not particularly objectional.

The Shed-Type Roof (see Fig. 7-73) is framed very much like a flat roof yet it has a definite slope. As a rule the slopes are made low, unless the shed is used in combination with gable-type roofs. Ceilings can be applied directly to the rafters to provide interest and variety to interior living spaces. The span of a sloping rafter is the horizontal distance between its supports. Shed rafters should be well-anchored to the plates of the exterior wall.

The Gable Roof used for centuries, is the traditional shape of most roofs. It consists of two inclined planes that meet at a ridge over the center of the house and slope down over the sidewalls. The inclined planes form a triangular shape at the ends of the house called a "gable" or "gable end" (see Fig. 7-45). Framing of the gable roof is discussed in the material under platform framing. Many different slopes or "pitches" can be used with the gable roof, depending on the architectural treatment and roofing materials.

Roof pitches must be indicated on drawings, and there are several methods of expressing the slope (refer to Section 9.3).

Details of the framing and architectural treatments of the intersection of the roof and the walls (see Fig. 7-75) are shown in "cornice details," which will be discussed in Chapter 9, under working drawings. Steep gable roofs allow enough headroom for second-story living space, even though the floor area may not be as large as that of the first floor. Light and ventilation can be provided by dormers with windows, which are framed out from the main roof (see Fig. 7-44C). In traditional, colonial-type houses, dormers must be symmetrically spaced on the roof; they should have good proportions so that they will look light and neat. Massive dormers often ruin an otherwise attractively designed colonial-type house.

Low-slope gable roofs are characteristic of the newer, rambling ranch-type house—they

Fig. 7-75 Roof construction at overhang with a boxed-in eave.

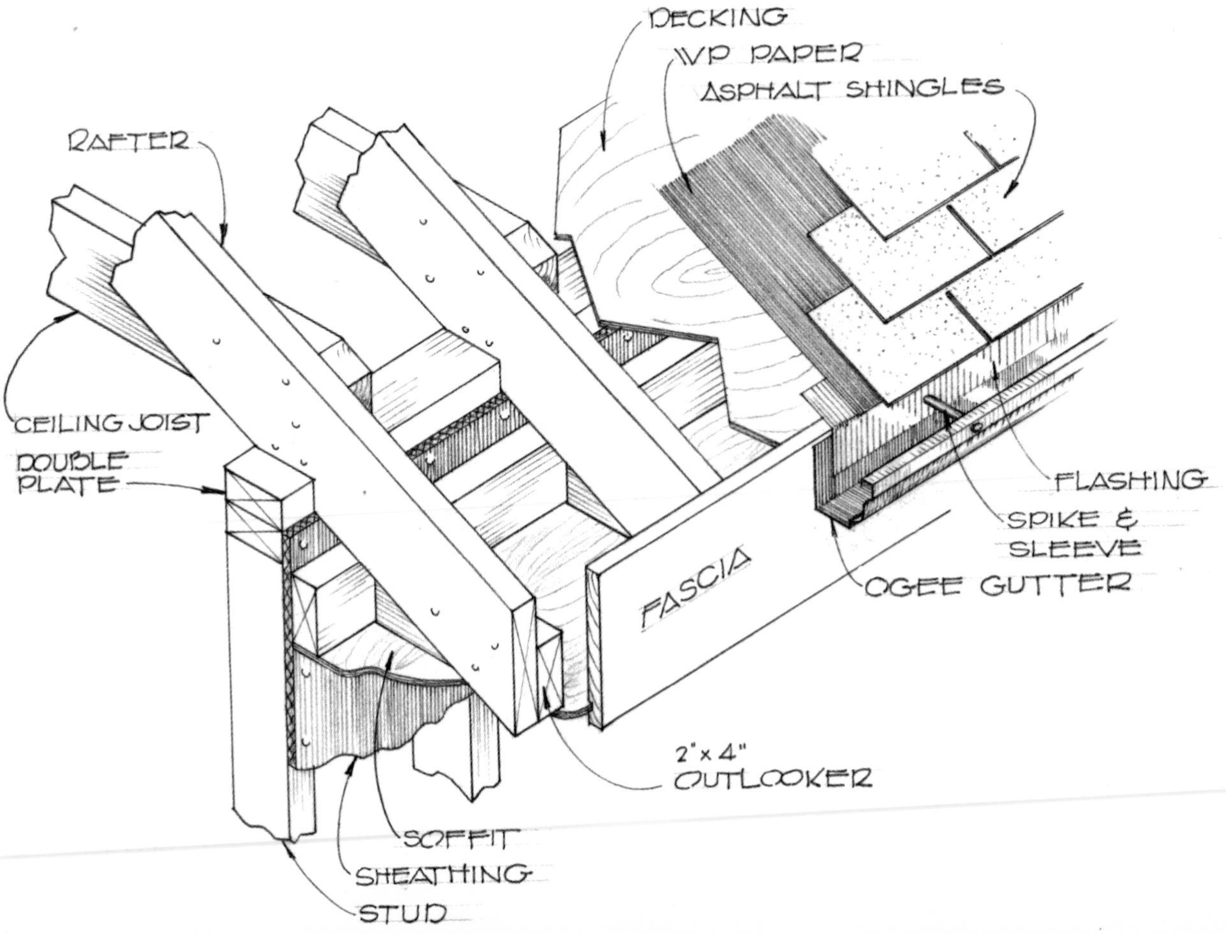

usually have wide overhangs. The space below the roof can be used, if at all, for minor storage.

The Hip Roof is another conventional type roof that is popular in many areas of the country (see Fig. 7-73). The inclined roof planes slope to all outside walls, and the treatment of the cornice and roof overhang is identical around the entire house. It eliminates gable endwalls but requires more roofing material than a gable roof of comparative size. Usually, the plan is rectangular, in which case common rafters are used to frame the center portion of the roof. Hip rafters, which carry very little of the load, are used at the exterior corners of the sloping intersections. Valley rafters, on the other hand, carry considerable loads, and are used at the interior intersections of the roof planes. Short jack rafters join either the hip rafter and the wall plate or the valley rafter and the ridge. More complex framing is required in hip roofs; hip, valley, and jack rafters require compound diagonal cuts at their intersections. For simple hip roofs, a roof layout is not necessary on the working drawings, but more complex roofs with ridges of different heights and other offsets would definitely require a roof layout drawing. Interesting roof lines can be attained by combining a hip roof over part of the structure and gable roofs over other parts.

Trussed rafters are available in some areas for framing standard span and pitch hip roofs. Regular trusses are used in the center section along the ridge, and modified trusses are made to conform to the end slope of the hip.

Like other roofs, hip roofs must be properly ventilated; because the roof covering is continuous over the higher areas of the roof, small metal vents or louvers are often employed on the rear side near the ridge to allow warm air to escape. Air inlets are provided by vents under the eaves.

Steep hip roofs often allow additional living space under the roof, similar to steep gable roofs. To be consistent, dormers on hip roofs usually have hip roofs as well.

The Dutch Hip Roof a variation of the hip roof, is shown in Fig. 7-73. It is framed similarly to the gable roof throughout the center section to the ends of the ridge, where double rafters are used. The end hips are attached to the double rafters and are started below a louver and extend over the corners of the building. The louvers at each end of the ridge allow more positive ventilation under the roof.

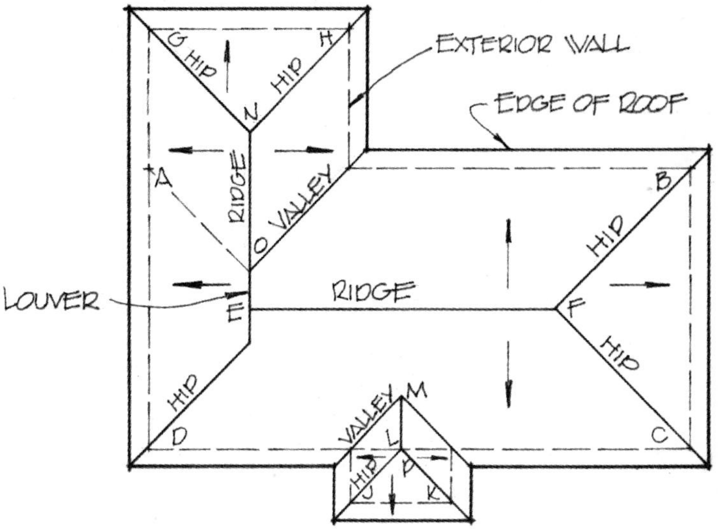

Fig. 7-76 Layout of a hip roof.

Because a hip roof can become more complex to frame than other roofs, the following method is offered *to lay out a working drawing for a hip roof:*

Using Fig. 7-76 as an example, draw the outline of the building including all ells and offsets. Draw the main roof formed by the rectangle ABCD; the 45° hip lines are drawn from the main corners and corners of the ells. The intersections of the 45° hip lines will locate the ridgelines. Draw the 45° valley lines connecting all roof intersections. A Dutch hip is indicated at point E; the ridge end can be indicated at any location along the diagonal hip lines, depending on the size of the louver used on the end elevation of the building. Uniform overhangs can be drawn around the exterior wall lines, and hip lines can be extended to the corners of the overhangs. This layout can be used regardless of the pitch that has been selected—low or steep slope. Hip roofs are more pleasing if the same pitch has been used on all planes of the roof. Rafters are drawn using either 16″ or 24″ o.c. spacing.

The Gambrel Roof is typical of Dutch colonial houses, and it is also found on many farm buildings. Each slope has a break or change of pitch; the lower part is always steeper than the upper (see Fig. 7-44). From a practical standpoint, this roof allows more headroom compared to a gable roof with the same ridge height. More labor is involved in framing a gambrel roof; as a result, it is seldom used in modern construction except on strictly colonial houses.

The Butterfly Roof is similar to an inverted gable roof (see Fig. 7-73). Caution should be exercised in the selection of a butterfly roof; roofers indicate that the intersection of the two inclined planes produces severe strain on the roof covering. Drainage of the valley is difficult, yet this can be accomplished with the use of tapered cant strips under the roofing, which act very much like a saddle that is used to spread water away from a chimney on a sloping roof. A bearing partition should be used below the valley for a stable support for the rafters.

The Barrel-Vault Roof employs precurved plywood panels or regular plywood attached to curved ribs. The panels are custom-designed and made by authorized plywood manufacturers. With relatively thin cross sections, the curved stressed-skin panels permit spanning long distances because of their arching action. Tie rods are usually required to counteract the thrust action when thinner panels are used. Insulation can be incorporated into the panels, and the underside of the panels can be used as the finished ceiling. Supported beams are uniformly spaced below the intersections of the vaults.

The Folded-Plate Roof (see Fig. 7-73) creates a roof line that is truly contemporary in profile. Its form is the result of engineered functional design. Reinforced concrete folded-plate roofs have been in use for years. Corrugated metal, on a small scale, obtains its stiffness similarly because of its folded characteristic. However, it has been largely through the efforts of the Douglas Fir Plywood Association (now the American Plywood Association) that the shape has been adapted to wood construction, mainly because of the high shear strength and rigidity of plywood.

A plywood folded-plate roof differs from conventional pitched roof construction in that the roof sheathing and framing are designed to act together as a large inverted V-shaped beam to span from end to end of the building. A multiple-bay roof is made up of several such "beams" connected together side by side.

The inclined planes of the roof transfer their vertical loads to adjoining ridge and valley intersections, very much as cross-bridging in conventional floor construction transfers a concentrated load to surrounding floor joists. Loads on the inclined planes are carried in shear by the plywood diaphragm action to the ends of the building, and by horizontal thrust action to the sides of the building.

Vertical supports are necessary at the ends of the building under the valleys and along the sides of the building. Either a beam or a bearing wall can be used along the sides. Horizontal thrust that is transferred to the sides of the building must be counteracted by horizontal ties—steel or wood.

The analysis of a multiple-bay folded plate differs slightly in that at the interior valleys additional support is gained by each plane supporting the other; for this reason walls or vertical beams are not required, provided the valley chords are adequately connected. Omission of supports below valleys, of course, increases the shear that must be resisted by the interior sloping planes. Horizontal chord stresses are greater then as well.

The following list points out the advantages and disadvantages of the folded-plate roof as compared to other methods of roof construction.

Advantages:

1. Trusses or other members that span from valley to valley are eliminated, thereby resulting in clear, uncluttered interiors.
2. Inasmuch as the plywood sheathing constitutes part of the "structural unit," long spans are possible with small framing units.
3. A plywood ceiling can also be used as a finish as well as for additional resistance to shear.
4. Assembly can be with nails only; no gluing is required, although it will improve rigidity.
5. Either conventional site construction or prefabrication can be employed. Components of the folded plate can be stressed-skin panels or one or more full-length plates can be prefabricated.
6. Interesting form can be achieved economically for buildings of all sizes—from residences to large industrial structures.

Disadvantages:

1. Drainage requires special attention on multiple-bay structures.
2. A well-designed folded-plate roof necessitates more roofing material. At least a 5 : 12 slope is recommended, since shear in the roof diaphragm diminishes with increase in slope.
3. Folded plates do not readily lend themselves to incorporation of a flat ceiling.

7.8.2 Roof Coverings

There are many roofing materials available for small buildings, and each has its advantages and limitations. Consequently, selection of the proper roofing material is of paramount importance, and in so doing, the following points should be considered:

1. Slope of the roof, if any;
2. Quality or permanence required of the roof;
3. Inherent architectural features of the roofing in relation to the rest of the structure; and
4. Cost of the roofing material.

Built-up Roofing A flat roof or a roof of very little slope must, of necessity, be covered with a completely watertight material. The majority of flat roofs are now covered with built-up roofing (see Fig. 7-77), which, if properly installed, is both economical and durable. On a wood deck, the first heavy layer of felt is nailed to the decking with galvanized roofing nails. Each succeeding layer of felt is mopped with either hot asphalt or hot coal-tar pitch. The top layer is then well-mopped and covered with a thin layer of pea gravel, fine slag, or marble chips. This mineral surface protects the roof to some degree from the elements, and the lighter colors reflect the sun's rays from the building. For every 100 sq ft of roof the use of 400 lb of gravel or 300 lb of slag is recommended.

A 5-ply roof would normally be bonded by roofing contractors for 20 yr; economy 3-ply roofs would be bonded for 10 yr. Over smooth concrete decks fewer plies are required, and the first layer of felt is mopped directly to the slab. Asphalt pitch can be used on steeper slopes than can coal-tar pitch, but the limiting slope for a built-up roof is 2:12, if gravel is expected to stay on the roof. Even on a 2:12 slope gravel will lose its grip during heavy rains. Metal gravel stops, preferably copper, are fastened to the wood deck surrounding the entire roof. Proper use of base-and-cap flashing is shown in Figs. 7-78 and 7-79.

On flat roofs as well as pitched roofs, substantial and rigid roof decks play an important part in the success of the roof covering. Decks should be well-nailed, clean, and dry before coverings are applied.

In roofing terminology, a "square" is an area of 100 sq ft; thus a square of roofing material is the amount necessary to cover 100 sq ft.

When a building has a sloping roof, more consideration must be given to the appearance of the roofing material. Shingles or multiple-unit type roofing materials are designed for sloping roofs; the incline allows water to drain off quickly without readily challenging the watertightness of the roof. The small, individual units of such roofing are also not subjected to stresses or shock from severe temperature changes; each piece can expand and contract individually without producing a noticeable effect, as in a built-up roof. The degree of resistance to water penetration of shingle materials varies directly with the slope of the roof and indirectly with the amount of exposure of each unit to the weather. Usually the steeper slopes will allow more exposure of the units than the flatter slopes because the water drains off quicker. Strong winds tend to drive mois-

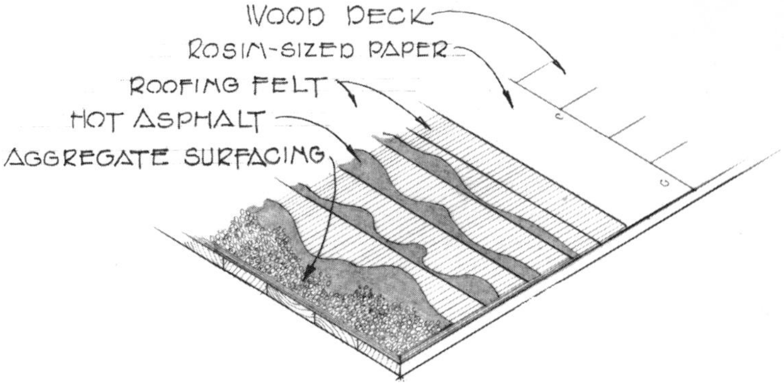

Fig. 7-77 Built-up roofing on wood deck (level to 2″–12″ pitch).

Fig. 7-78 Roof flashing at a parapet wall.

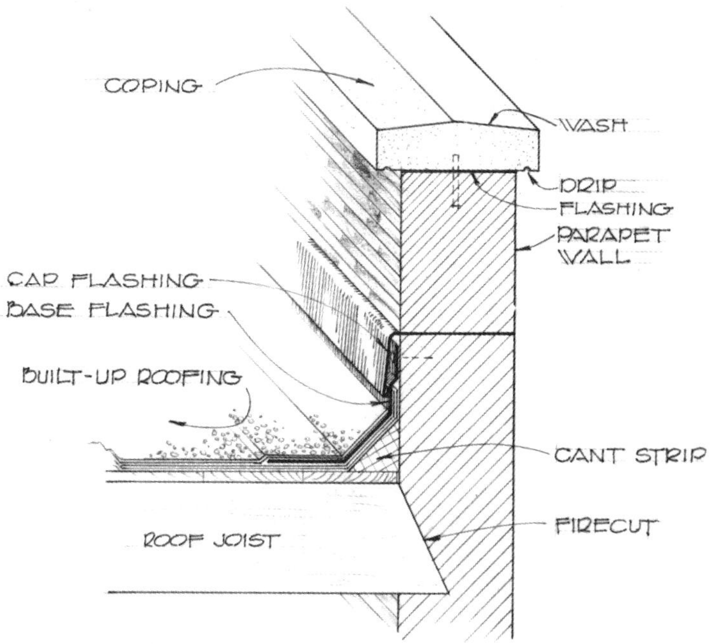

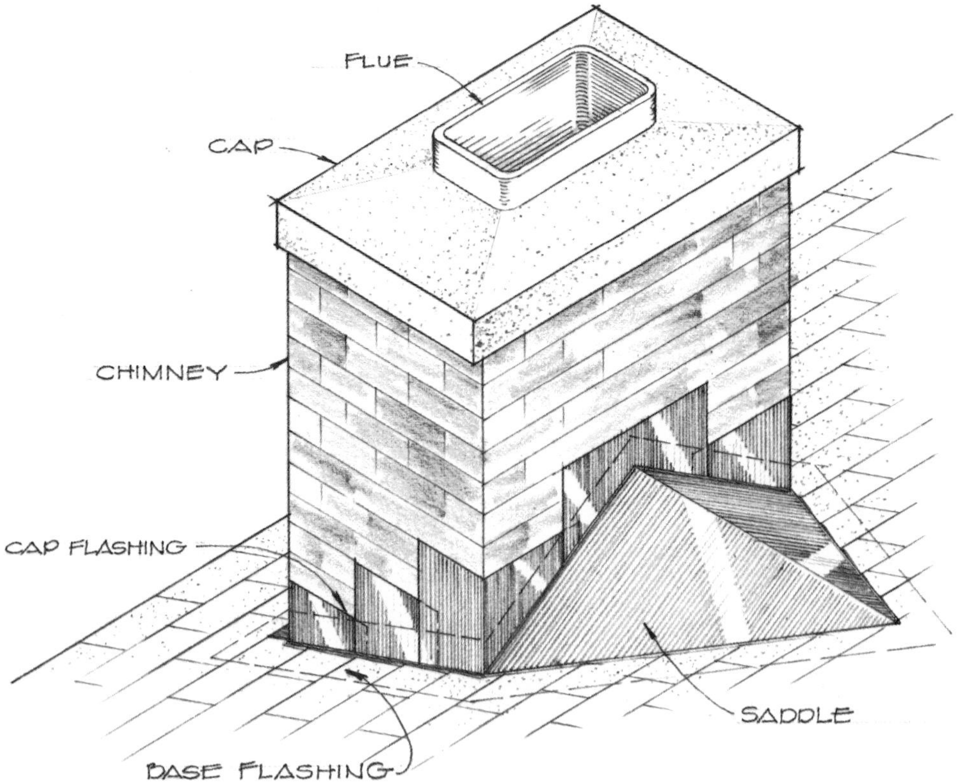

Fig. 7-79 Chimney flashing on a sloping roof.

ture under roof units unless some provision is made for sealing the edges or holding them down. This tendency is especially noticeable on lower slopes. Exposure to the weather is specified in inches; some roofing materials are exposed 4″ between laps; other materials, for example, can be allowed 10″ exposure. However, manufacturers' recommendations should be followed in applying all roofing materials.

Sloping roofs in light construction are generally covered with one of the following roofing materials:

1. Asphalt shingles;
2. Asbestos-cement shingles;
3. Wood shingles;
4. Slate shingles;
5. Clay tile units;
6. Cement tile units; or
7. Metal shingles or panels.

Asphalt Shingles Asphalt-saturated felt, coated with various colored mineral granules, is manufactured into "strip" shingles of different shapes and sizes. The most popular shape is the square-butt strip shingle, 12″ wide and 36″ long, with slotted butts to represent individual shingles at the exposure. Strips with hexagonal exposures are also made. The amount of 4″ or 5″ is the usual exposure to the weather, and weights per square vary according to the quality of the shingles. Quality shingles should weigh at least 235 lb per square. The shingles are attached to the wood deck with 1¼″ galvanized roofing nails—four nails are needed for each strip. Each nail is driven about ½″ above each slot on the square-butt shingles. Two layers of shingles are then fastened with each nail, and the nailhead is just covered with the succeeding course. A double course is fastened at the eave. Occasionally, a starter strip of 55 lb roll roofing or one course of wood shingles is used under the double layer of strip shingles at the eave. Along the gable edge of the roof, a strip of wood bevel siding is often nailed to the deck with the thin edge in, to guide water from the edge as it drains along the incline. Metal edge-flashing can also be used at gable edges. Roof decks should be first covered with 15 lb asphalt felt, lapped 6″ at ends and sides, before asphalt shingles are applied.

Asphalt strip shingles can be used on low-

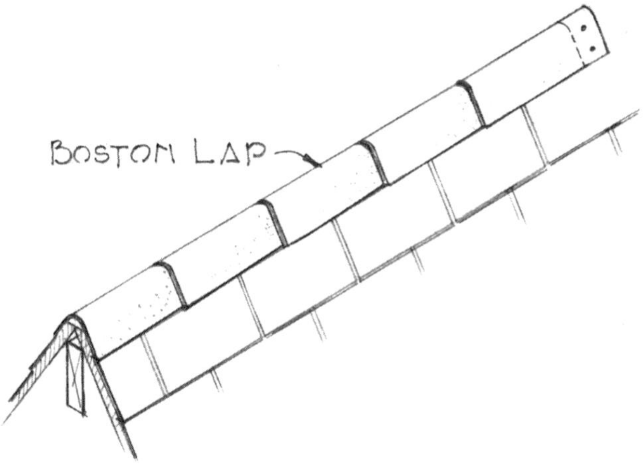

Fig. 7-80 Covering ridge, asphalt shingles.

slope roofs if self-sealing shingles are used. This type has asphalt adhesive under the exposed edges, which seals the edges against driving rains and capillary attraction. Often starter strips near the eaves are full mopped with adhesive, rather than nailed to prevent this moisture penetration.

To cover ridges and hips, strip shingles are cut into smaller pieces and nailed over the ridges in a lapped fashion—called a "Boston lap" (see Fig. 7-80). Intersections of roofs and walls must be flashed with durable metal flashing, preferably copper, and valleys are flashed with similar metal flashing, usually 18″ wide.

Although they burn readily when ignited, asphalt shingles are more resistant to combustion than wood shingles, and many local codes which prohibit wood shingle roofs will allow the use of asphalt shingle materials.

Asbestos-Cement Shingles Shingles made of 15 to 20 percent asbestos fiber and 75 to 85 per cent Portland cement have been found to be very durable and noncombustible, and are successful on many residential roofs. Because of their brittleness, however, care must be taken in applying them to the roof deck as well as walking on them after they are in place. Various manufacturers make asbestos-cement shingles with simulated wood-grain surfaces, yet the hard texture of the material does not mellow beautifully with age as other natural materials seem to do.

Three different shapes of asbestos-cement shingles are used on sloping roofs—"American-method," "Dutch-lap," and "hexagonal" (see Fig. 7-81). When installed, American-method shingles resemble conventional wood shingles. Dutch-lap shingles are larger shingles and are lapped at top and one side, which is economical in both material and labor. Strong shadows are produced from the vertical and horizontal laps. Hexagonal shingles, also known as the "French method," are basically square; by being attached diagonally they create a hexagonal pattern. Because the shingles are rigid, special pieces are made for covering ridges and hips. A cant strip or furring strip is required at the starting eaves, and furring strips are necessary at the ridge and

Fig. 7-81 Asbestos shingle applications.

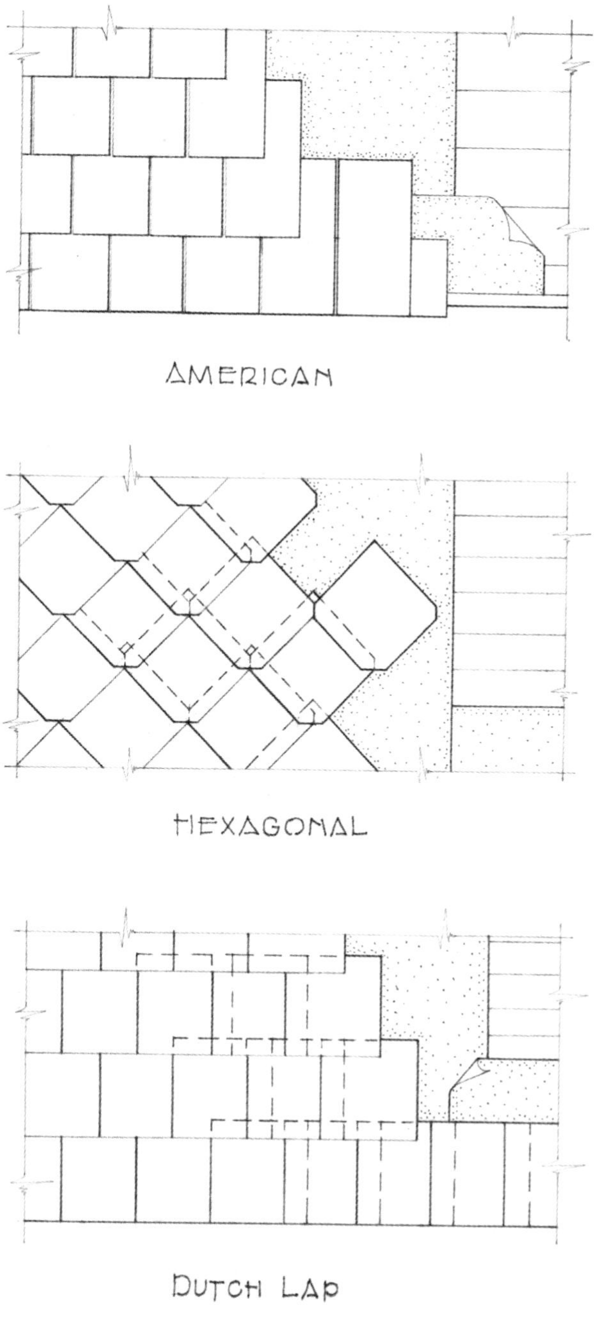

hips to allow ridge and hip shingles to cover adjacent shingles at the correct angle. A roof pitch 5″ to the foot is required for most asbestos-cement shingles; American-method shingles can be used on a 4″ pitch, however. Galvanized iron or copper nails are used to fasten asbestos-cement shingles, a tight roof deck is needed, and 15 lb roofing felt is nailed to the deck before the shingles are applied. Flashing is required at intersections and valleys, as is the case when using asphalt shingles.

Wood Shingles have been used for many years in residential construction. Because of their inherent combustibility, they are prohibited by many local codes, even for small buildings. However, in other than restricted areas, wood shingles are being used in many parts of the country, and they make handsome and durable roofs. Wood weathers to a soft, mellow color after exposure to the elements, and if properly installed can be expected to last 25 yr.

Two types of wood shingles are available: machine-sawed and handsplit. Both kinds are made chiefly of western red cedar, redwood, and cypress—all highly decay-resistant woods. The machine-sawed shingles are made in 16″, 18″, and 24″ lengths and in random widths. They are taper-sawed in shingle mills, and graded No. 1, No. 2, or No. 3 according to the absence of knots and defects. To prevent cupping after exposure, the better grades are cut from the logs so that the annular rings of the log become perpendicular to the flat surfaces of the shingles. Butt ends vary in thickness from ½″ to ¾″.

Handsplit shingles, often called "shakes," are split from the log to reveal a natural, irregular wood-grain surface. Their butts are thicker, ranging from ⅝″ to 1¼″, which produce strong horizontal course lines that give the roof a rustic quality. Thick, natural butt shingles are popular on ranch-type houses. Lengths of handsplit shingles are generally 24″, 32″, 36″, and widths vary from 5″ to 18″. In dry areas, wood shingles are usually put directly on plywood or tight wood decks. In damp areas, installation of nailing strips, spaced the same distance apart as the shingle exposure, provides ventilation directly below the shingles (see Fig. 7-82). Air space below the shingles prolongs the life of the roof.

Fig. 7-82 Wood shingles over sleepers.

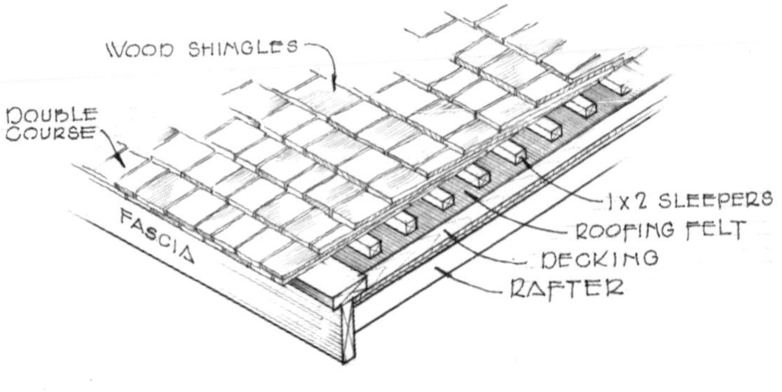

The starting course for wood shingles is doubled at the eave, or better tripled, and projects beyond the edge of the roof board at least 2″ to form a drip. A strip of 30 lb roll roofing felt is first nailed over the overhang, to make the roof watertight over the exterior wall. This precaution will prevent water from penetrating the shingles if ice dams occur on the lower part of the roof in colder areas. A cant strip of bevel siding along the gable edges is also recommended, as mentioned under asphalt shingles.

The standard exposure for wood shingles is 5½″. Longer shingles, however, can be laid with exposures up to 12″, depending on the slope of the roof and method of application. More course-line texture can be obtained by doubling each course, usually with No. 2 grade shingles below. Careful nailing technique must be used to see that joints in preceding and successive courses are staggered or are offset at least 1½″ to allow good drainage and eliminate water penetration into the roof along the edges of the shingles. Shingles are loosely spaced to allow for swelling and shrinking, and zinc-coated or copper threepenny nails should be used; thicker shingles require larger nails. At least two nails must be used for each shingle and three for wider shingles, and care must be taken not to split the shingle when it is nailed. Open valleys are flashed with durable metal flashing; wide shingles are neatly cut to form the valleys. Hips and ridges can be covered by several methods, but the alternating Boston lap is the most popular as it retains the shingle texture to the edge of the ridge.

Many variations can be used in laying shingles. Sometimes every fifth or sixth course is doubled to vary the shadow line throughout the roof, sometimes the shingles are laid at random with no set course, sometimes they are staggered so that alternate shingles project beyond adjoining ones, sometimes the course lines are made wavy to simulate thatch roofs with even the rakes and eaves turned over slightly to emphasize the effect of the thatch. Stained shingles are occasionally used to give definite color to the roof; incidentally, staining prolongs the life of the shingles. Regardless of the treatment and variations that are possible with wood shingles, the basic water-shedding principles of application must be followed.

Slate Roofing Natural slate taken from quarry beds and split into thin sheets has provided builders with one of our more "aristocratic" roofing materials. The marked cleavage of the slate rock imparts a natural, irregular, and pleasing surface to a roof, and the natural color variations of slate from different quarries produce subtle shades ranging from blacks and grays to blues and greens, and even to browns and reds. Some slate changes in color after weathering. A well-laid slate roof is very durable and will outlast the life of the building. Slate is used only on the finest homes and more formal commercial buildings, yet its use has diminished in recent years.

Slate is split, cut into sheets, and punched for nails at the quarry. Common commercial sizes of the sheets, are 12″ × 16″ and 14″ × 20″ and $\frac{3}{16}$″ or $\frac{1}{4}$″ thick. Random sheets vary in size and thickness. Each sheet is attached with at least two copper nails; pieces near ridges and hips are often secured with copper wire and roofing cement. Slate roofs are heavy, and therefore the roof-framing members must be more substantial than those for wood or asphalt shingles or other light roofing materials. Because of the weight of the slate, the sheets hug the roof well against driving wind. Damaged slate sheets are difficult to replace after the roof has been completed; experienced slate roofers are required to properly install a slate roof.

Under most conditions, at least a 6:12 pitch is necessary for slate. Roof boards are nailed up tight, over which a heavy roofing felt is applied and secured with roofing nails. A cant strip is used at the eaves to give the starter course the same slant as successive courses. Usually the starter course is laid along the eave with the long dimension parallel to it, and the doubled course is started flush with the edge. Depending on the slope of the roof, slate should be laid with a 3″ or 4″ head lap. The head lap is the amount a lower edge of a course laps or covers the top edge of the second course underneath it. The amount of slate exposure is found by deducting the lap from the total length of the sheet and dividing the difference by two. For example, the exposure of a 16″ long sheet with a 4″ head lap is $\frac{1}{2}(16 - 4) = 6$. Slate can be laid with different exposures on the same roof, however. As with wood shingles, all joints must be staggered to shed water effectively. After random sizes are sorted, it is preferable for the slater to attach the large, thick slates near the eaves, the medium slates near the center, and leave the smaller, thin pieces for the ridge area. This method produces rather interesting slate textures on a roof.

Hips and ridges are generally finished with the Boston-lap method. Both flashing and roofing cement are used to make the ridges and hips water resistant. Closed valleys, made with trapezoidal pieces of copper flashing placed under each course and lapped at least 3″, are the most popular on slate roofs.

Clay Tile Roofing Many variations of clay roofing tile are manufactured. They are generally very durable, are made from different types of clay, and burnt in kilns as are many other types of terra-cotta building products. Roofs of clay tile are characteristic of Mediterranean and Spanish architecture. The early Jesuits of Mexico first brought tile roof construction to this country when they built the old Spanish missions of California and the Southwest.

Even though there are various patterns or shapes, all clay tile can be divided into two general categories: flat and roll type. The flat tiles vary from simple pieces to pieces with interlocking edges and headers. Roll tiles are available in semicircular shapes, reverse S shapes, and pan and cover types. Each type requires a tightly sheathed roof covered with heavy roofing felt. On low-pitched roofs and on all ridges and hips, the paper should be doubled; cant strips are needed at the eaves, as in slate roofs. Although some flat tile is fastened by hanging it on wooden cleat strips across the roof, the majority is secured with copper nails through prepunched holes. The semicircular roll tile require wooden strips running from the eaves to the ridges between the pans. Tile application requires careful planning inasmuch as tile pieces must fit toegther and very little latitude is allowed in their placing. Allowance must be made for expansion and contraction of the roofing at intersections of walls and pro-

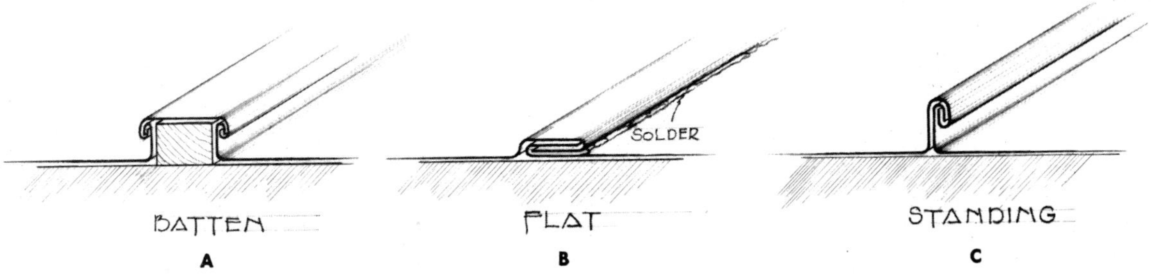

Fig. 7-83 Metal roof seams.

jections. Because clay tile is one of the heavier roofing materials, roof framing must be adequate to support it.

Open valleys are usually used with tile, and copper flashing is placed below. Manufacturers furnish special shapes and pieces for covering hips and ridges, as well as pieces for rake edges and starter strips at the eaves. Often starter pieces at the eaves as well as ridge and eave pieces are set in mastic or cement, both of which are available in colors to match the tile. Ridge rolls often require wood strips along the ridge for fastening the tile. Some tile shapes tend to look bulky on residential roofs; however, if carefully chosen to complement the style of the house, tile will help in creating a picturesque effect.

Cement Tile Roofs This type of roof has become popular in southern Florida for residential construction. Precast concrete panels with wide exposures are attached to the roof (mainly hip roofs) and neatly grouted with mortar. Heavy roofing felt is used below, and white waterproofing cement-base paint is applied as a finish. Cement tile can be used on low pitches, and the roof becomes resistant to sun and heat.

Metal Roofing Occasionally, metal roofing is the most appropriate material to cover residences or light construction buildings. The principal metals used in roofing are copper, terneplate, aluminum, and galvanized iron. Because of the cost of material and labor, metal is generally restricted in use to finer residences and more expensive structures. On moderately priced residences, one often sees metal employed for small dormers, projections over front entrances, and minor roofs, in combination with other roofing material on the major roof. Metal must be applied by experienced roofers, who are aware of the individual properties of the different metals.

Copper is the most durable, as well as one of the more expensive metals for roofing. It is malleable, tenacious, easy to work, and does not require maintenance after installation. It weathers to a gray-green color and looks well in combination with other building materials.

Terneplate is made of sheet iron or steel coated with an alloy of 25 per cent tin and 75 per cent lead. Metal roofers purchase the metal in small sheets that have been shop-coated with an oil-base paint. After application, the top surface must be painted with two coats of paint long in oil. If properly maintained, terneplate will last from 30 to 50 yr. One of the advantages of terneplate is its light weight; also it expands less than copper.

Both copper and terneplate are applied on tight board roof decks covered with rosin-sized paper. On roof pitches from 3″ to 12″, either the standing-seam or batten-seam method is used (see Fig. 7-83). After joining the small sheets into long strips, the standing seam is formed by turning up one edge $1\frac{1}{2}''$, and the adjoining edge $1\frac{1}{4}''$. The edges are bent and locked together without soldering. Cleats are nailed to the roof deck and incorporated into the seam to hold the metal to the deck, but no nails are driven through the sheets.

Batten seams are formed by nailing wood strips, ranging in size from $2'' \times 2''$ to $4'' \times 4''$ to the deck, which run from the eaves to the ridge, and which are parallel to each other. Metal lengths are put between the battens and bent up along the edges of the battens to form pans down the slope of the roof. Cleats of the same metal are nailed to the edges of the battens and are incorporated into lock joints which are formed by the edges of metal caps that rest on the battens, as well as the edges of the metal pans. Batten strips are used on the ridges and hips where necessary. The ends of wood batten strips at the edges of the roof must be covered with metal.

Several types of aluminum roofing are occasionally used on small buildings. Aluminum shingles with baked enamel finishes and several mill-finishes are manufactured. Some are laid beginning at the ridge and continuing down to the eave; others are laid beginning at the eave and proceeding up to the ridge, similar to the method of applying wood or slate shingles. Aluminum sheets are also available for batten-seam type of installation, using aluminum battens and aluminum self-tapping screws.

Corrugated aluminum sheets are employed mainly for temporary buildings. They are fastened directly to the deck with aluminum nails and neoprene washers; the fastening is done through the high portion of the lapped corrugations.

On economy roofs, corrugated galvanized iron sheets can be used. However, galvanized iron has a limited service life as well as an unpleasing appearance. This material should be reserved for temporary or less important structures.

7.9 EXTERIOR FINISH MATERIALS

The exterior finish material plays a very important part in the esthetics of a building, and if maintenance is a factor, the selection of the finish is especially important. Many finish materials are available; some of the more common materials for wood construction are: wood siding, wood shingles, plywood, asbestos shingles, hardboard, aluminum, stucco, and masonry veneer (see Section 7.6 on masonry veneer). Wood siding has been used successfully for years and is typical of American-built houses. Much of it requires periodic repainting; some of the durable wood species, such as redwood, western red cedar, and cypress, can be left natural with merely an application of several coats of water repellent. Kiln-dried lumber is preferred, and select grades with a minimum of knots and defects should be used. Figures 7-84 to 7-86 illustrate some of the more common types of wood siding available.

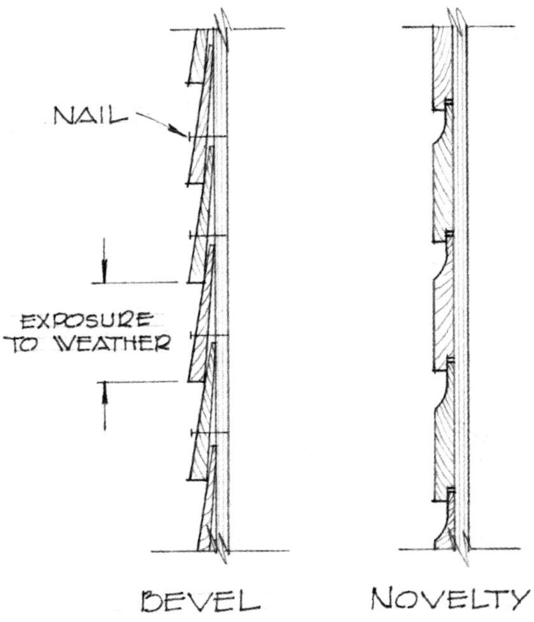

Fig. 7-85 Vertical details of bevel and novelty siding.

Fig. 7-84 Various vertical wood siding as shown through horizontal sections.

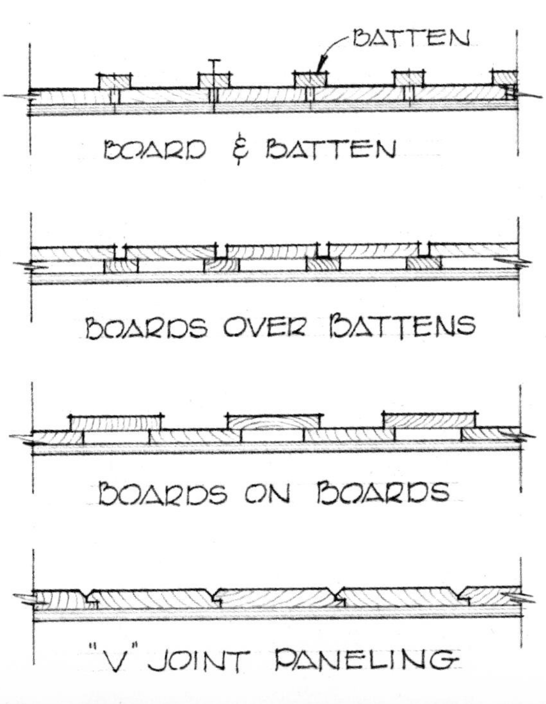

Fig. 7-86 Treatments of outside corners on horizontal wood siding.

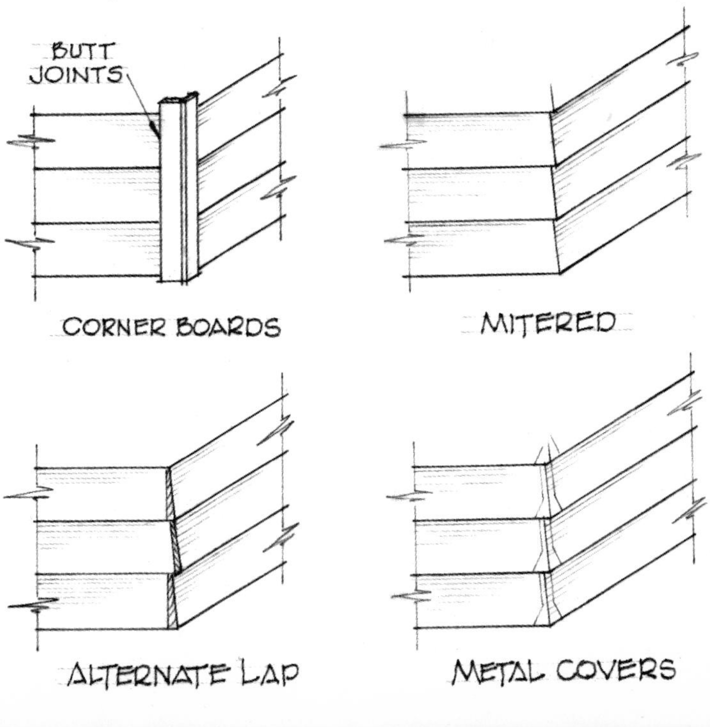

Bevel Siding is widely used in present-day construction. It is cut into widths varying from 4″–12″, and butt thicknesses range from $\frac{7}{16}$″–$\frac{3}{4}$″. The usual amount of lap is from 1″–2″. For example, a bevel siding 6″ wide is usually applied with $4\frac{1}{2}$″ to the weather, a siding 10″ wide is usually applied with 8″ to the weather. Wider sizes have a tendency to cup and warp.

Much of the warping in siding can be prevented by the application of a prime coat of paint to all sides of the siding, including ends, before installation. Rustproof nails should be used—rust stains bleed through the paint film (Fig. 7-85 indicates the correct nailing technique). Notice in the figure that the nails do not pass through the underpiece of the lap—this allows for expansion in the lap without taking the risk of splitting the thin portion of the underpiece, should the nails be put through both pieces of the lap. Widths over $7\frac{1}{2}$″ are generally known as "bungalow siding." Strong horizontal shadow lines are characteristic of bevel siding. Various corner treatments are shown in Fig. 7-86. A starter strip must be nailed to the bottom of the sheathing so that the first course of siding will slope the same amount as succeeding courses. The bottom course is started about 1″ below the top of the foundation wall to weatherproof and hide the wood and masonry joint. Bevel siding exposures are worked out exactly by carpenters, so that horizontal butt lines coincide with sill and head edges of windows and doors, and courses are similar throughout the wall height. Minor variations of exposure on a wall are permissible inasmuch as the are not readily noticeable. Water tables should be used above all windows and doors; a rabbeted trim member is generally used at the top of the wall to cover the thin edge of the top course. Rabbeted bevel siding is also available in various widths and thicknesses.

On economy walls, drop siding, also known as "novelty siding," is acceptable without sheathing. Building felt is tacked directly to the studs and the drop siding is nailed over the felt. Figure 7-85 shows one of the typical profiles of drop siding. Corners can be treated as mentioned under bevel siding, or square-edged corner boards can be nailed directly over the siding.

Board-and-Batten Siding can be used to obtain a rustic texture on exterior frame walls (see Fig. 7-84). Either surfaced or unsurfaced square-edged lumber can be used. The wide boards are nailed vertically with at least an $\frac{1}{8}$″ space between them for expansion. Battens of the same type of lumber, usually only 2″ wide, are nailed over the vertical joints of the wide boards. The 2″ batten strips are also used for trim around doors and windows as well as along the top of the wall. Joints between the wide boards are often caulked before the batten strips are applied. Horizontal blocking must be installed in the stud wall if insulation-board sheathing has been used, so that the boards and battens can be nailed at a minimum of four levels of vertical height throughout a 1-story wall. If nominal 1″ wood sheathing has been used, the boards and battens can be secured by nailing into the sheathing. Care should be exercised in nailing the batten strips; the nails should pass between the wide boards in the joint, or the nails can pass through the batten and one of the wide boards *only* (see Fig. 7-85). This allows expansion of the joint without splitting either the boards or the batten. Only rustproof nails should be specified.

Another interesting effect can be gained by applying the wide boards over the narrow batten strips. This application becomes a reverse board-and-batten method, which produces narrow grooves and a slightly different overall effect. Redwood lumber is frequently applied in this manner.

V-joint, Tongue-and-Groove Paneling can also be used for vertical siding. Adequate wood sheathing or horizontal blocking must also be installed to provide proper nail-anchoring; blind nailing is generally used along the tongue to hide the nails within the joint. Kiln-dried lumber with minimum shrinkage characteristics should be selected, and joints should be nailed up tight so that moisture will not penetrate between the boards. Either random width or uniform width paneling can be used. Bottom cuts at the base of the wall should be beveled to provide a drip. Because of cupping, paneling over 8″ wide should be avoided.

Wood Shingles produce warm and charming exterior finishes that are popular in many areas of the country. The shingles are versatile in that many effects can be obtained by various applications. They can be painted, stained, or left to weather naturally. In warm areas of the Deep South however, unfinished shingles weather unevenly because of projections, overhangs, etc. Handsplit shakes can be used for

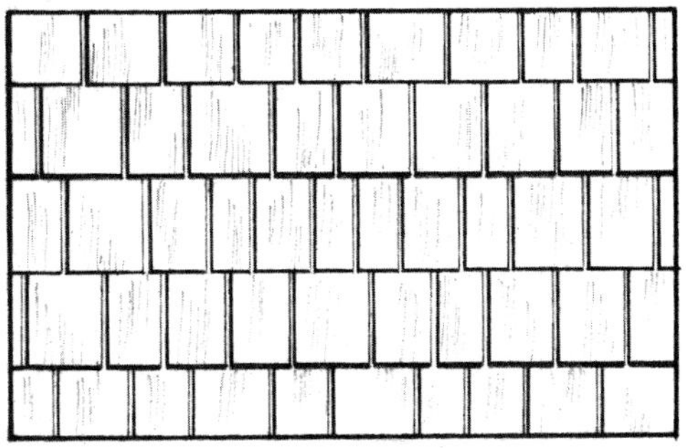

Fig. 7-87 Wood shingle textures.

rustic effects, double courses of regular shingles can be used for strong horizontal shadow lines, or regular shingles can be applied in staggered course lines for unusual effects (see Fig. 7-87). More exposure widths can be allowed on wood shingle walls than is necessary when applying similar shingles to a roof. Table 7-10 can be used in determining the amounts of weather exposure of shingles according to their lengths.

Table 7-10 Maximum Weather Exposure for Wood Shingle Siding

Length of shingle	Single course	Double course
16″	7½″	12″
18″	8½″	14″
24″	10″	16″

Western red cedar is the most popular wood used for commercial shingles, and the application to walls is similar to the methods mentioned under roof coverings (Section 7.8.2). For siding, No. 1 grade is usually specified; No. 2 or No. 3 grade can be used for underlays of double courses. Wood shingles must have substantial wood backing for nailing; if insulation-board sheathing is used on the wall, horizontal nailing strips, usually 1″ × 3″, are nailed over the insulation board. The strips are spaced the same distance apart as the exposure width of the shingles.

Exterior Plywood is now used extensively for siding. Plywood can be applied vertically with 1″ × 2″ batten strips placed vertically either 16″ or 24″ on center to hide the joints of the plywood (see Fig. 7-88). Plywood must be well-painted. Also, texture "one-eleven" ply-

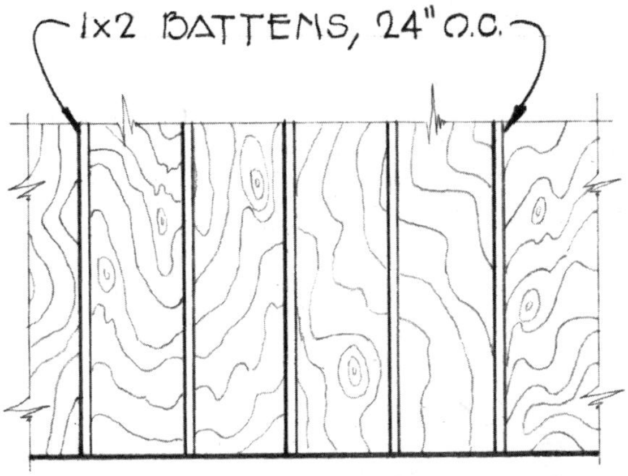

Fig. 7-88 Plywood siding. Battens can be spaced either 24″ or 16″ o.c.

wood, ⅝″ thick, with rabbeted joining edges, can be nailed vertically on stud walls to resemble vertical paneling. Plywood is also available in strips to be applied horizontally similar to shingles.

Asbestos-cement Shingles of several colors and sizes are manufactured for exterior siding, mainly for modestly priced homes and buildings. Asbestos-cement shingles have the disadvantage of being brittle and therefore break easily, in addition, they appear much darker in color when they become wet. Manufacturers' directions should be followed in their application; usually a tight, wood subwall is required, and the vertical joints of the shingles require a 4″ wide asphalt paper flashing-strip backing. The shingles butt against vertical corner boards, which have been flashed with asphalt paper throughout the entire height of the corner.

Sheet Hardboard is comparatively new as an exterior siding material, yet if it is properly applied and painted, it will give satisfactory service. Hardboard is made from natural wood fibers that are subjected to heat and pressure to form sheets of various sizes and thicknesses; it comes in various surface textures—smooth, grooved, and ribbed. Hardboard must have solid backing support, and is durable if kept painted with linseed oil-base paints. Panels can be applied horizontally to resemble wide bevel siding, or larger panels can be applied vertically to resemble board-and-batten siding.

The horizontally applied panels are usually 1′ wide by 16′ long by 3/8″ thick, applied generally with 10 1/2″ or 11″ exposures. Starter strips at the base of the wall and corner treatments are handled similarly to wood bevel siding. Vertical joints should be made over studs, and nailing is done through the lap at each stud location.

For vertical application, 4′ wide panels are used. Lengths are obtainable up to 16′, and recommended thicknesses are 1/4″ and 5/16″. Vertical wood battens spaced 16″ on center can be used to hide vertical joints on smooth hardboard edges; a 1/8″ space must be left between panels, and joints are caulked before batten strips are applied. Grooved and ribbed panels have shiplap edges for concealing the joints. Manufacturers' directions should be followed in applying either type of hardboard exterior panels.

Aluminum Siding is finding acceptance in residential construction and is also used extensively for remodeling exterior walls. Two types of aluminum panels are most popular: those applied horizontally to resemble either narrow or wide bevel siding, and those applied vertically to resemble board-and-batten siding. Both styles are available with baked-on-enamel finishes of various colors, and can be painted if necessary, similar to wood siding. Aluminum siding is light in weight, easy to apply, and resistant to weathering.

The horizontal panels are started at the base of the sheathing with a wood cant strip nailed below the bottom edge of the first course, and each course is nailed to the sheathing along its top edge. Courses are held to the adjacent course with a lock joint. Matching corner pieces, backer strips for end-joints, and trim pieces are furnished by the manufacturers for each type of panel. Horizontal panels are made 12 1/2′ long, with either a bevel exposure 8″ wide or two 4″ bevel exposures.

Vertical aluminum panels are applied by first nailing a starter corner strip vertically along one corner, then locking the first panel into the strip and nailing the panel along the edge opposite the lock joint. This procedure is continued across the wall. Aluminum can be cut with a hacksaw or tinsnips when fitting around openings, etc.; appropriate pieces are furnished by manufacturers to form water tables and trim members. Vertical panels are made in lengths to cover 1-story heights so that joints are eliminated.

Stucco has been used for years as a satisfactory exterior siding material, but present-day use is limited largely to direct application over concrete block and other masonry materials. Some application for stucco over wood frame walls in residential construction is still found, however.

On masonry walls of concrete block, tile, or brick, two coats of Portland-cement stucco are applied like plaster to form a coat 5/8″ thick. This particular stucco should be made of one part Portland cement, three parts sand, and 10 per cent by volume of hydrated lime. Or a prepared Portland-cement stucco may be used and applied according to the manufacturers' directions. The masonry wall is first cleaned with a wire brush and a scratch coat is applied. After the scratch coat is thoroughly dry, the finish coat is applied and given whatever surface texture is desired. A finish may be smooth with a metal trowel finish, sand-finished with a wood float, or stippled by applying various tooling or stroking effects. To render the finish waterproof, cement-base paints are usually applied after the finish coat is completely dry. Colored stucco can be obtained by mixing mineral pigments into the finish coat, or colored cement-base paints may be applied to the final stucco surface.

On wood frame walls, stucco is applied over ribbed metal lath that is backed up with heavy asphalt-treated paper (see Fig. 7-89). Wood or metal furring strips 15″ on center can also be used under galvanized wire fabric, or galvanized furring nails can be used to keep the fabric at least 1/4″ away from the paper and sheathing. Foundations must be adequate to prevent settling and subsequent cracking of the stucco. Stucco-covered 2-story buildings should be constructed with balloon framing to minimize vertical shrinkage. Wherever applicable, termite shields should be provided at the base of all walls to prevent infestation between the stucco and wood frame. Usually a rustproof metal ground strip is placed at the base of the wood

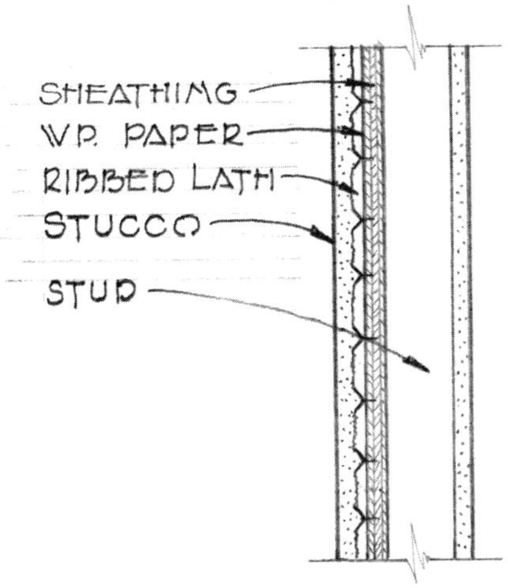

Fig. 7-89 Stucco on wood-frame detail.

wall to close the opening between the stucco and the sheathing. Flashing must be used above all doors and windows, and the tops of stucco walls must be protected by overhangs and trims members. When applied over wood frame walls, a 3-coat stucco job is standard—consisting of a scratch coat, brown coat, and finish coat—to make the stucco $3/4''$ thick.

Stucco is used to produce imitation, "half-timber" type exterior walls used mainly in Normandy style houses. Treated boards representing the timbers are fastened directly to the sheathing, and stucco is applied to the furring lath in the areas between the timbers. In this construction, attention must be given to the prevention of moisture penetration between the timbers and the stucco. Flashing must be used liberally over horizontal timber pieces as well as joints in the timber pieces, which are especially susceptible to the accumulation of moisture.

All of the aforementioned exterior siding materials must be applied over a suitable moisture-resistant building paper that has been fastened to the wall sheathing. This paper is important in preventing moisture penetration under and between siding pieces, and in preventing air infiltration through the exterior walls from wind pressures.

7.10 INTERIOR FINISHES AND TRIM

Gypsum Wallboard commonly called gypsum drywall construction, is now used as the interior finish in the majority of American

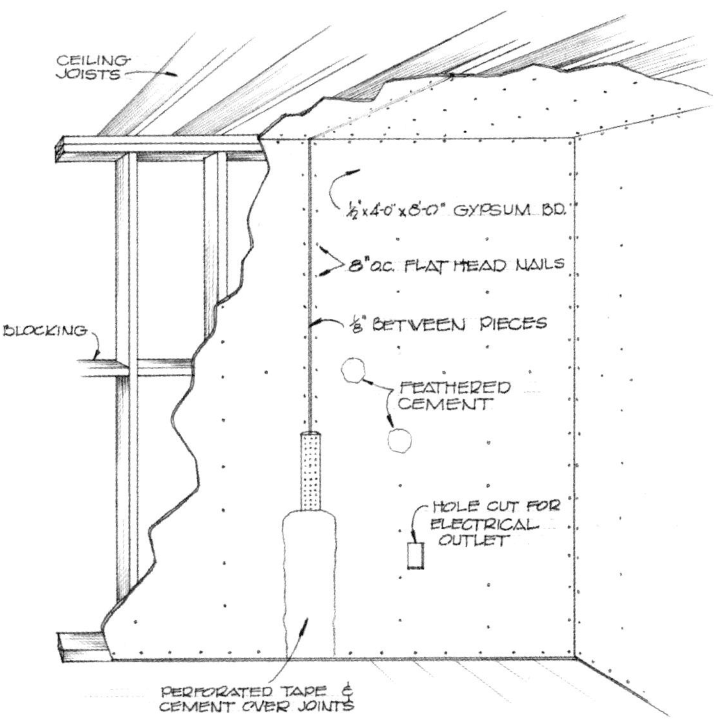

Fig. 7-90 Application of gypsum board applied vertically for interior walls.

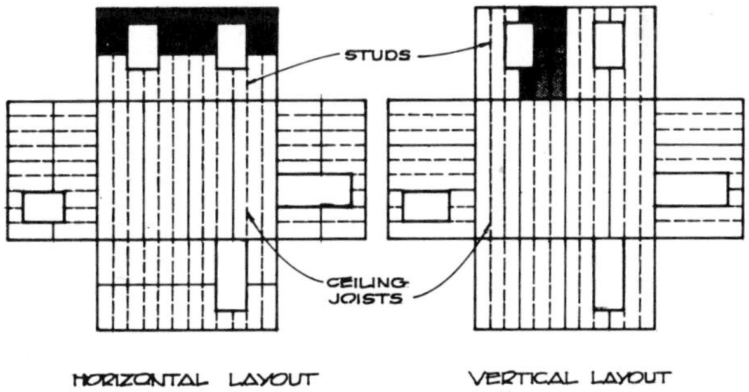

Fig. 7-91 Two methods of gypsum board layout.

homes under construction. The paper-covered gypsum sheets are made in $4' \times 8'$, $4' \times 10'$, and $4' \times 12'$ sizes. Standard thicknesses are $3/8''$, $1/2''$, and $5/8''$. Gypsum is light to handle and has good thermal and fire resistance qualities. The sheets can be easily cut and nailed to framing, joints and nailheads can be smoothly finished with cement and perforated tape, and very little moisture is introduced into the structure from the material, as is the case when plaster is used. See Figs. 7-90 and 7-91.

Plaster is still preferred by many architects for first-class construction. A two-coat job, consisting of $3/8''$ rocklath, a brown coat, and a finish coat results in a $7/8''$ total thickness. Metal lath

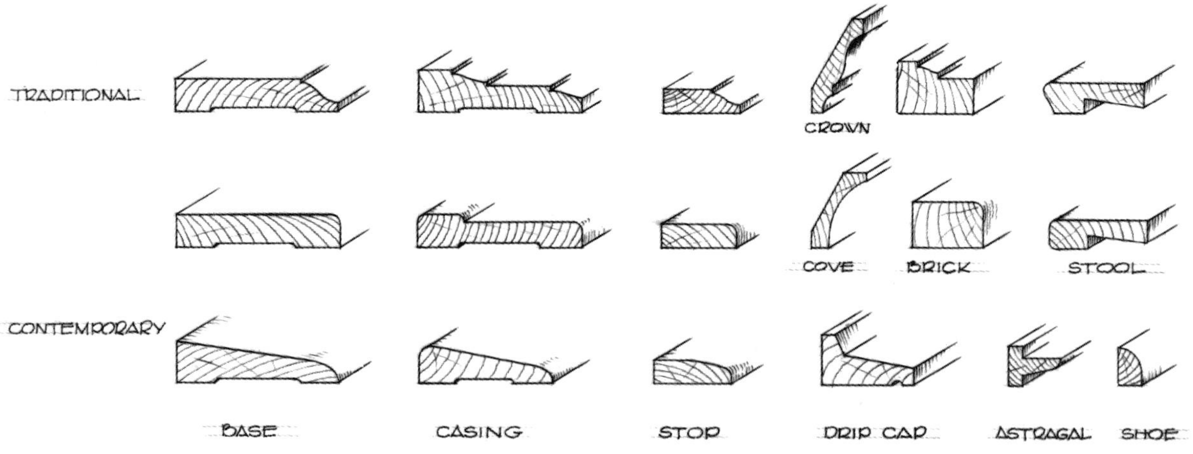

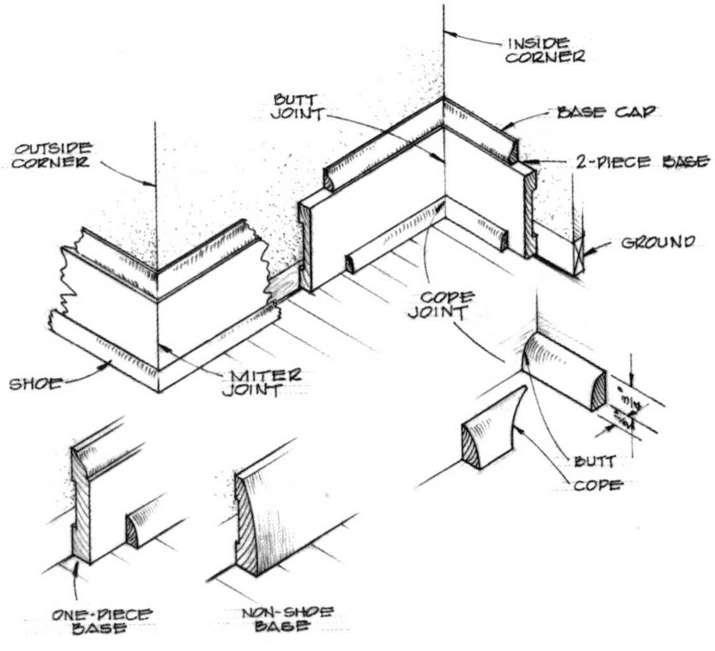

Fig. 7-92 Stock trim and base applications.

strips are fastened in corners and at critical points around openings where cracking tends to occur. If metal lath is used for the entire base instead of the rocklath, a three-coat job—scratch, brown, and finish coat—is required. A water resistant plaster, called Keene's Cement, is usually specified in kitchens and baths.

Prefinished Plywood Sheets in various natural wood finishes are becoming popular in many room interiors. They are blind-nailed directly to studs and never require painting or finishing. Other manufactured sheet materials as well as solid wood paneling are also available for various wall coverings. In order to straighten nailing surfaces when using sheet materials or ceiling acoustical tile, furring strips can be applied perpendicularly to studs or ceiling joists.

Trim is the general term given to molding, base, casing, and various other finish members which must be carefully fitted by trim carpenters to complete the appearance of the structure. See Fig. 7-92. Many stock pieces and patterns are available at lumber dealers. In higher-class construction, custom-made moldings and trim pieces are often shown in detail on the working drawings and therefore must be specially milled. Care must be taken to select consistent patterns to be used throughout a building so that harmony in the trim results. Colonial interiors traditionally require ogee profiles, whereas contemporary styles usually appear best with simpler tapered or teardrop profiles. Casing and finishing nails are used to apply trim members; the nails are driven below the surface of the wood with a nail set so the holes can be filled, and care must be exercised to prevent hammer marks from injuring the surface of the wood.

7.11 INSULATION, VAPOR BARRIERS, AND VENTILATION OF FRAME STRUCTURES

Present-day builders are fully aware that indoor comfort is of primary importance to the individual. Consequently, proper insulation becomes a major consideration in warm climates as well as cold. Many types of insulation are available; the most suitable usually depends upon the details of the construction; the amount depends upon the extent of comfort desired. When care in selection and installation is taken, optimum benefit will be realized. Experience has shown that it is more economical to employ modern insulation materials than to rely on structural materials for insulating requirements.

Heat loss calculations and design of heating and cooling systems are not discussed in this material; however, the general aspects of insulation, such problems as water vapor within buildings and the ventilation of unheated air spaces are of concern to the draftsman if details of construction are to be correctly conceived and drawn.

Basically, all construction materials can be classified more or less as either insulators or conductors, depending on their porosity or density. One must understand that still air is an excellent insulator if confined into small spaces such as the matrix of insulating materials or small cavities within walls. On the other hand, dense materials, such as glass or masonry, are relatively poor insulators. All materials, however, resist the flow of heat to a certain extent, the resistance of the given material being directly proportional to its thickness.

Heat may be transmitted by three different methods—conduction, convection, and radiation. *Conduction* is the transfer of heat by direct molecular contact; metals, for instance, conduct heat more readily than wood, yet all materials conduct heat if a temperature difference exists between their surfaces. It must be remembered that *heat flows from the warm to the cold surfaces*. *Convection* is the transfer of heat by air or other agent in motion. Even though air is a good insulator, when it circulates it loses part of its value as an insulator. Air spaces about ¾″ wide within walls or ceilings are the most restrictive to circulation. In larger spaces the air acts like a conveyor belt, taking heat from warm surfaces and depositing it on cold surfaces. *Radiation* is the transfer of heat through space from a warm surface to a cold surface, very much as light travels through space. Effective resistance to radiation can be provided by shiny surfaces, such as aluminum foil; the more actual surfaces a heat ray has to penetrate, the more effective the reflective insulation becomes. Actual heat transfer through walls and ceilings usually employs all three of the above-mentioned methods of transfer, to various degrees. Of course, some heat is also dissipated from buildings through openings around doors and windows.

To compare the suitability or insulating qualities of different building materials and insulations, a standard of reference must be used. By accurate experimentation, the thermal qualities of individual building materials have been determined; when these materials are incorporated into typical combinations found in walls, floors, roofs, etc., including occasional air spaces, the rate of heat flow or coefficient of transmission, known as the "*U* factor," can be calculated. This factor can be defined as the number of Btu (British thermal units—heat units) that will flow through 1 sq ft of the structure from one air region to another due to a temperature difference of 1°F, in 1 hr.

Easy reference can be made from tables giving the *U* factors with and without insulation, put out by the American Society of Heating and Ventilating Engineers. Tables for *U* factors of typical constructions and various insulation combinations can also be found in the Forest Products Laboratory Report R1740. Comparisons of these *U* factors makes it possible to evaluate different combinations of materials and insulations on a basis of overall heat loss, potential fuel savings, influence on comfort, and cost of installation.

Other than the reflective insulators, commercial insulations are usually made of glass fibers, glass foam, mineral fibers, organic fibers, and foamed plastics. The best materials should be fireproof and vermin-proof, as well as resistant to heat flow. The cellular materials utilize tiny isolated air cells to reduce conduction and convection; the fibrous materials utilize tiny films of air surrounding each fiber. These efficient insulating materials are manufactured into blankets, batts, and sheets in sizes and shapes to fit conveniently into conventional structural spaces. Some have tabs or edges for stapling to wood frame members; others are sized so that they can be tightly wedged into conventional structural cavities. Proper selection depends on initial cost, effectiveness, and the adaptation of the insulation to the construction features. Blankets and batts should be installed between framing members to form isolated air spaces between their faces and the interior wall surfaces. Sheet insulation should be used where rigidity is important, such as on roof decks and perimeters of floor slabs. Fill insulation (loose mineral wool or mineral pellets) is used mainly in ceilings where it can be poured between ceiling joists, or it can be used to fill the cavities of concrete block. Reflective foil insulations are best put into cavities where the reflective surfaces can be adjacent to air spaces. All insulation should be installed according to manufacturers' directions, and care must be taken to cut the material carefully around outlet boxes and other obstructions within the walls. Figure 7-93 illustrates the proper placement of insulation within typical frame buildings.

If the restriction of heat flow were the only consideration in the application of insulation within buildings, it would be a simple matter to provide enough insulation around heated spaces to theoretically reduce fuel bills sufficiently and thereby offset the initial cost of the insulation. However, air usually contains water vapor, and because water vapor acts like a gas to penetrate porous materials and always flows from areas of high temperature to areas of lower temperatures, many types of insulation soon lose their effectiveness if they become saturated with water vapor.

Air is saturated or has a relative humidity of 100 per cent when it contains as much moisture as it will hold. Warm air has the ability to retain more moisture than cold air. If saturated air is lowered in temperature, some of its moisture will be given off as condensation. This point in temperature change at which a specimen of air gives off moisture in the form of condensation is known as its *dew point*. When high temperature differences exist between insulated wall surfaces (between inside and outside air) the dew point often occurs in the insulation itself, where the resistance to heat flow is greater than in the structural members. The condensation which can gather in the insulation from the cooling of the vapor as it passes through a wall, may not only reduce the value of the insulation, but may eventually cause permanent damage to the structural members. This problem generally arises in winter, during the heating season, especially when the humidity within the building is high.

The simplest solution to the problem is to prevent water vapor from getting into the wall structures. This is partially done by providing a vapor barrier near the *inside surface* of the wall. To be effective, the vapor barrier must be as airtight as possible. One of the best and most economical vapor barriers is aluminum foil, which also acts as a reflective insulator. Asphalt and aluminum paints are other effective vapor barriers. The glue layers in plywood act as vapor barriers. Polyethylene film and glossy, asphalt-treated heavy paper are satisfactory barriers; however, ordinary building-paper felt does not offer much resistance to the passage of vapor. Many types of commercial insulation have one

Fig. 7-93 Placement of insulation in wood-frame buildings. Ventilation of attic and crawl spaces is necessary. The fraction indicates the ratio of minimum net vent opening to the ceiling area for proper ventilation of enclosed spaces.

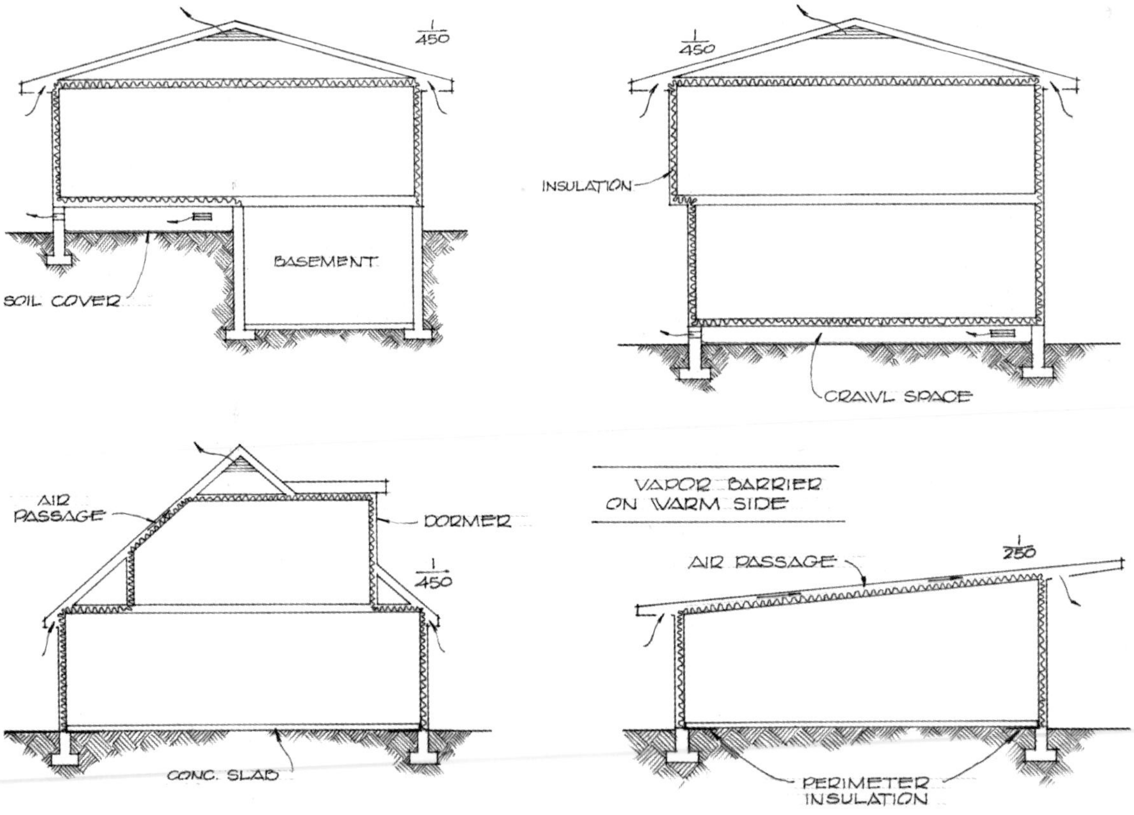

face covered with a vapor barrier—this is the side that should always be placed toward the inside of the building.

Even good vapor barriers do not prevent some moisture from penetrating through minor breaks in the barrier around pipes, electric outlets, joints, etc.; some will even permeate the barrier itself, not necessarily through minor breaks. Water vapor that has possibly found its way into walls can be released to the outside by "cold side venting." This condition requires sheathing paper to be weather-resistant but not vapor-proof. Lightweight roofing felt is satisfactory—it can breathe. Siding materials must not be airtight, yet they must have the ability to shed water and resist driving rains. Many of the newer, water-base exterior paints possess this feature of allowing water vapor from the inside to escape through the paint film.

Another suggestion that will help minimize the vapor problem in homes is the installation of forced-air fans in rooms of excess humidity, such as bathrooms, kitchens, and utility areas. The use of exhaust fans directly to the outside relieves the home of much of the otherwise destructive concentrations of humidity.

Some engineers maintain that no moisture barrier need be used in ceilings below an attic that is adequately vented with louvers. The water vapor can permeate through insulation in the ceiling and be carried out of the building by the air movement in the attic space. For this reason, louvers in vent spaces should never be closed during the winter. If air spaces exist below roofs, and the air spaces are not heated, adequate ventilation must be provided below the roof. Since most roofing materials are resistant to vapor flow, trapped moisture within the spaces would soon cause damage.

In gable roofs, the vents should be a minimum of $1/450$ of the ceiling area. If vents can be provided along the eaves of a gable roof, a more positive circulation will result, and the vents near the ridge on the gable can be made smaller. Hip roofs are more difficult to vent; openings are necessary around the roof in the soffit of the eaves. Small metal outlet vents can also be incorporated into the roofing, near the ridge of the hip, to allow air to circulate and escape. Numerous types of small metal vents are available for hip-roof venting. The area size of vents under hip-roof eaves should be a minimum of $1/900$ of the ceiling area; the outlet vents near the ridge of hip roofs should be at least $1/1600$ of the ceiling area.

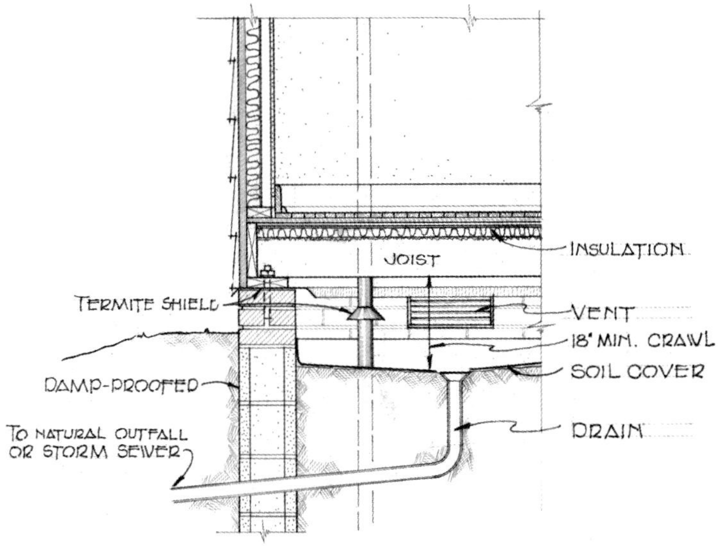

Fig. 7-94 Good crawl-space construction.

Flat roofs should be vented with a continuous vent along the soffit of the overhang (see Fig. 7-73). Spaces between all framing members should have access to outside air if the ceiling material is supported by the roof members. A minimum vent area of $1/250$ of the ceiling area should be provided. All wood-framed roofs with unheated spaces directly below should be adequately vented by either of the above-mentioned methods.

Crawl spaces in basementless houses also require adequate ventilation. At least four foundation-wall vents should be provided, preferably located near the corners. The aggregate net ventilating area should be not less than $1/150$ of the basementless area. Fewer vents can be used if the ground below the floor is completely covered with a vapor barrier.

In colder localities, floors in basementless houses should have insulation applied between the floor joists (see Fig. 7-94). Crawl spaces will be trouble-free if,

1. Insulation is applied below the floors;
2. Sufficient vents are installed in the foundation walls;
3. A vapor barrier is provided over the entire ground area within the foundation walls; and
4. Proper termite shields are installed where applicable.

REVIEW QUESTIONS

1. Why must local frost depths be considered when drawing footings?

2. What is a good rule of thumb for sizing footings in light construction?

3. Describe a stepped footing and indicate its application.

4. What condition may require accurate calculation of footing sizes?

5. List three materials that are commonly used for foundation walls.

6. What is a pier?

7. Indicate the logical application of grade beam foundation construction.

8. What are the advantages of a slab-on-ground floor construction in comparison to crawl space construction?

9. What are the identifying characteristics of platform (western) frame construction?

10. Why are trussed rafters widely used in small home construction?

11. In plank-and-beam framing, how is the load on roof beams transmitted to the foundation?

12. Why should the location of beams in plank-and-beam framing be shown on the working drawings?

13. What part of the construction limits the spacing of beams in plank-and-beam framing?

14. What is a "transverse" beam?

15. List the good points of brick-veneer construction.

16. Explain modular sizing of concrete block walls.

17. What are the important factors in the selection of a roofing material?

18. What is the purpose of a vapor barrier in a wood wall, and why should it be placed facing the interior side?

"All things require skill but an appetite."—George Herbert

8 Drafting Expression

Expression in drafting concerns itself mainly with the manner and technique employed by the draftsman in conveying correct information on working drawings simply and clearly. The preparation of working drawings becomes an important part of architectural service, entailing ideas and skillful graphic communication. Tradesmen, estimators, contractors—all concerned with the construction of a building—must rely on the drawings for much of the technical information needed to execute their work. The drawings, therefore, must be expressive and somewhat tailored to locally accepted conventions, as well as accurately scaled. It helps if the draftsman as he works puts himself in the place of the carpenter or contractor, usually pressed for time, who must search the drawings for each bit of information. The following points on expression draftsmanship will be helpful in communicating your ideas on paper with a minimum of misinterpretation.

8.1 VARY LINE WEIGHTS ACCORDING TO THEIR IMPORTANCE

All lines on a drawing should have significance, or they have no reason for being there. This significance, naturally, varies, and it should be reflected by the weight or width of each line.

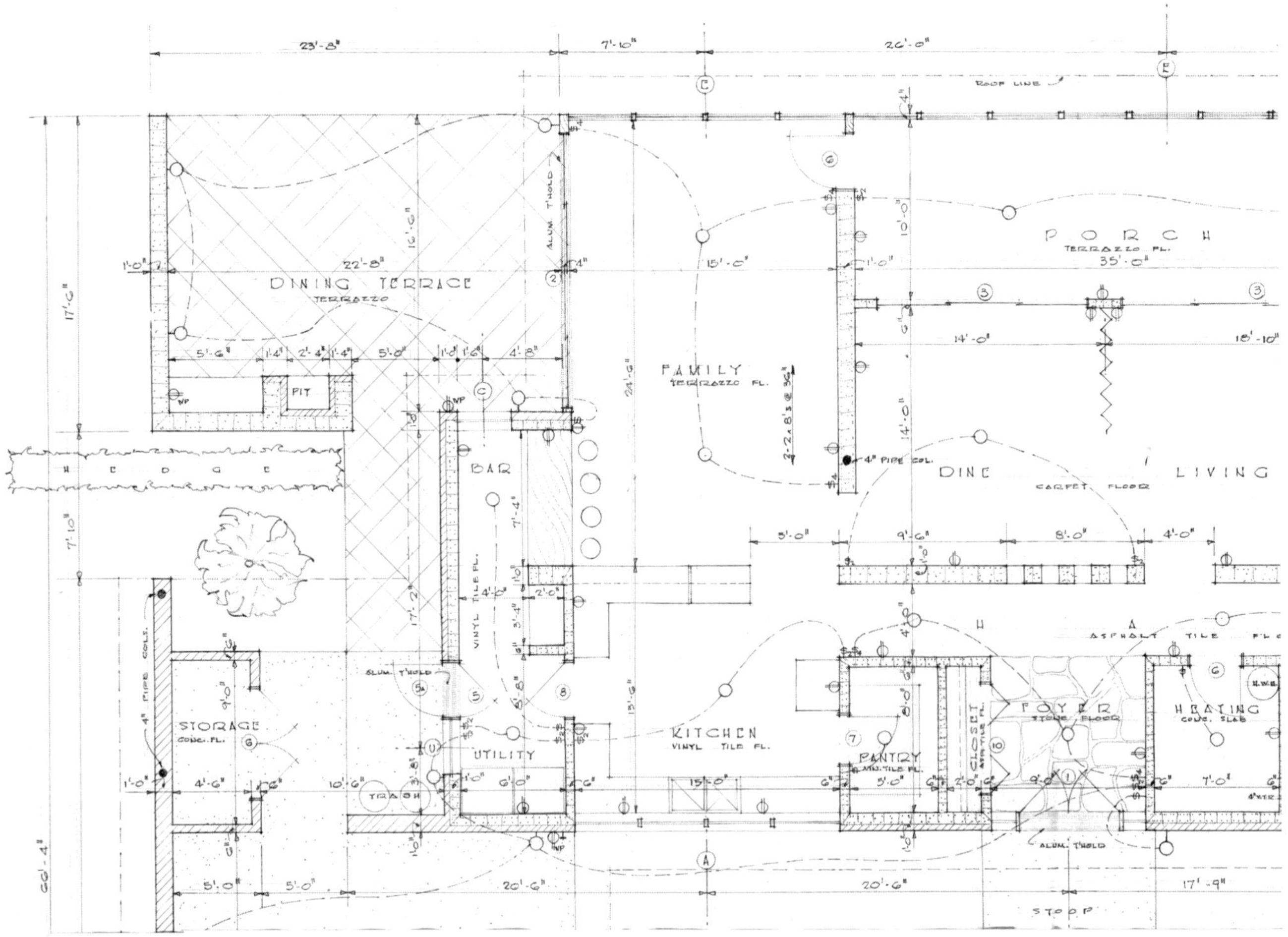

Fig. 8-1 Expressive linework on a working drawing.

If a line has little importance, it should appear light; on the other hand, if a line contributes an important aspect to the drawing, it should appear heavy and prominent. Other lines will have intermediate importance. However, if all the lines on a drawing appear prominent, or if all are made light, the drawing loses much of its expressiveness. We might say, then, that line variations (contrast) contribute definite meaning to drawings (see Fig. 8-1). Students should study various examples of good linework to know where to place the correct emphasis and where to restrain it. For added clarity, heavy lines are effective in more situations than beginners usually realize. For example, a plan or elevation can be improved by a heavy outline, and the silhouette of a section can be made more readable (see Fig. 8-2). Also, grade lines and roof overhang lines on elevation views look more realistic if they are heavy. Features nearer to the observer can add "depth" to the drawing by being outlined with heavy lines. In contrast, center lines, extension lines, and dimension lines require only minor emphasis and should be made fine. Consistent variations in linework are one of the important fundamentals of professional graphic expression. Pencils must be kept sharp, various pressures must be used; it may even be necessary to go over important lines. To gain extreme emphasis, some draftsmen use the drafting fountain pen on a few important lines on a drawing (see Fig. 8-3). The ink can go directly over pencil construction lines with very satisfactory results.

Develop the habit of putting a slight pressure on the beginnings and endings of pencil lines, to make them sharp and distinct, rather than fizzled-out and ragged at their ends. Architectural linework appears more distinctive and pleasing if it extends slightly at corners (Fig. 8-4) rather than ending exactly at the line intersections. This does not mean that lines can extend any haphazard distance from the intersections; they should consistently be about $\frac{1}{16}''$ long.

See the full-size drawing in Fig. 8-5 for actual line weights and lettering sizes.

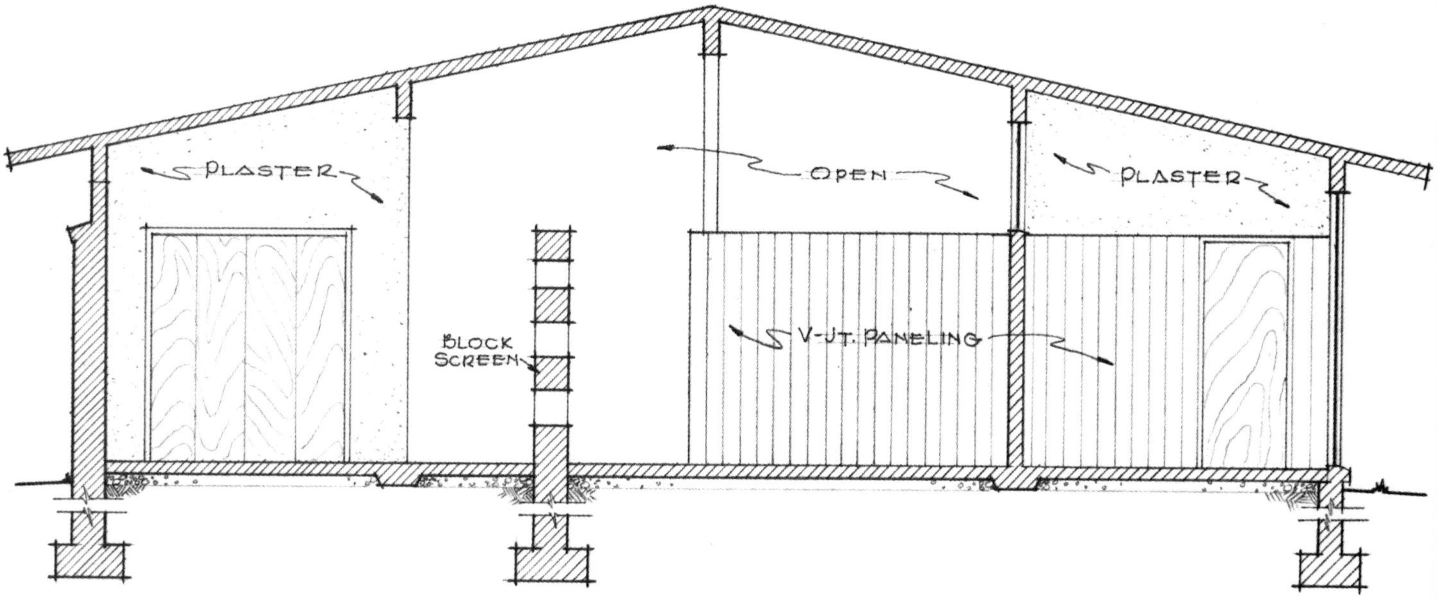

Fig. 8-2 Outline emphasis on section views.

8.2 LEARN TO MAKE CRISP-LOOKING BROKEN LINES

Many types of broken lines are found to be necessary on drawings, and a little care in their execution will pay off in added expression. Broken lines can be "phantom" lines representing hidden surfaces, or they can represent alternate positions of movable features, or they can represent structural pieces, or they can be employed to provide information in other situations. After observing various working drawings, you will notice many uses for dissimilar broken lines (see Fig. 8-6). Like other linework, the dashes in broken lines should be given emphasis at their ends with slight pencil pressure, and the dashes should not be spaced too far apart; that is, they should have more line than openings. Make the dashes uniform in length and spacing. If several features are represented with broken lines, use a different dash length for each representation. Each will then have an obvious meaning. For example, on floor plans, broken lines are used to represent roof outlines, electric outlet and switch connections, etc. When selecting a dash technique for each, the roof outline could have 1″ dashes, the electric outlet and switch connections could have ½″ dashes, etc. Should they cross each other or appear near one another, there will be an obvious difference and no mistake will be made in their identification (Fig. 8-7A). If possible, complete each type of broken line on the drawing before starting other types,

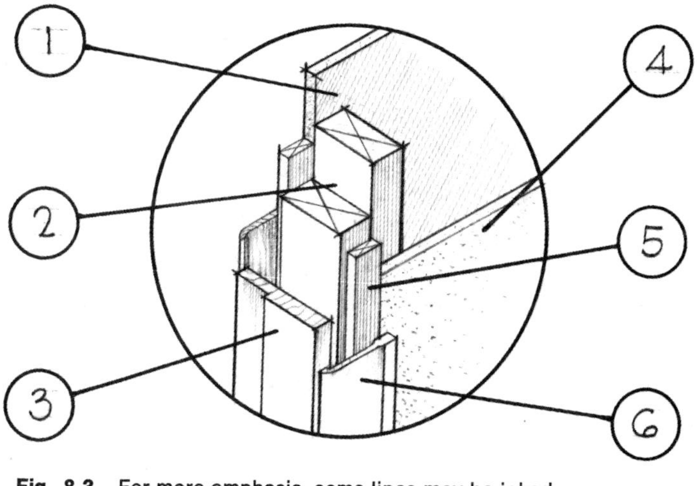

Fig. 8-3 For more emphasis, some lines may be inked.

Fig. 8-4 Intersections of lines on architectural drawings.

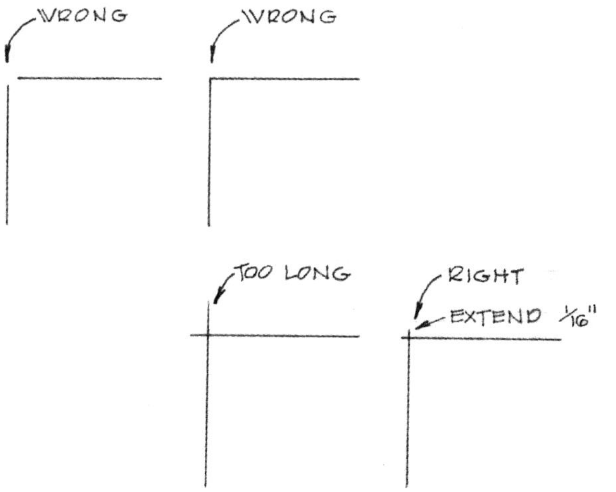

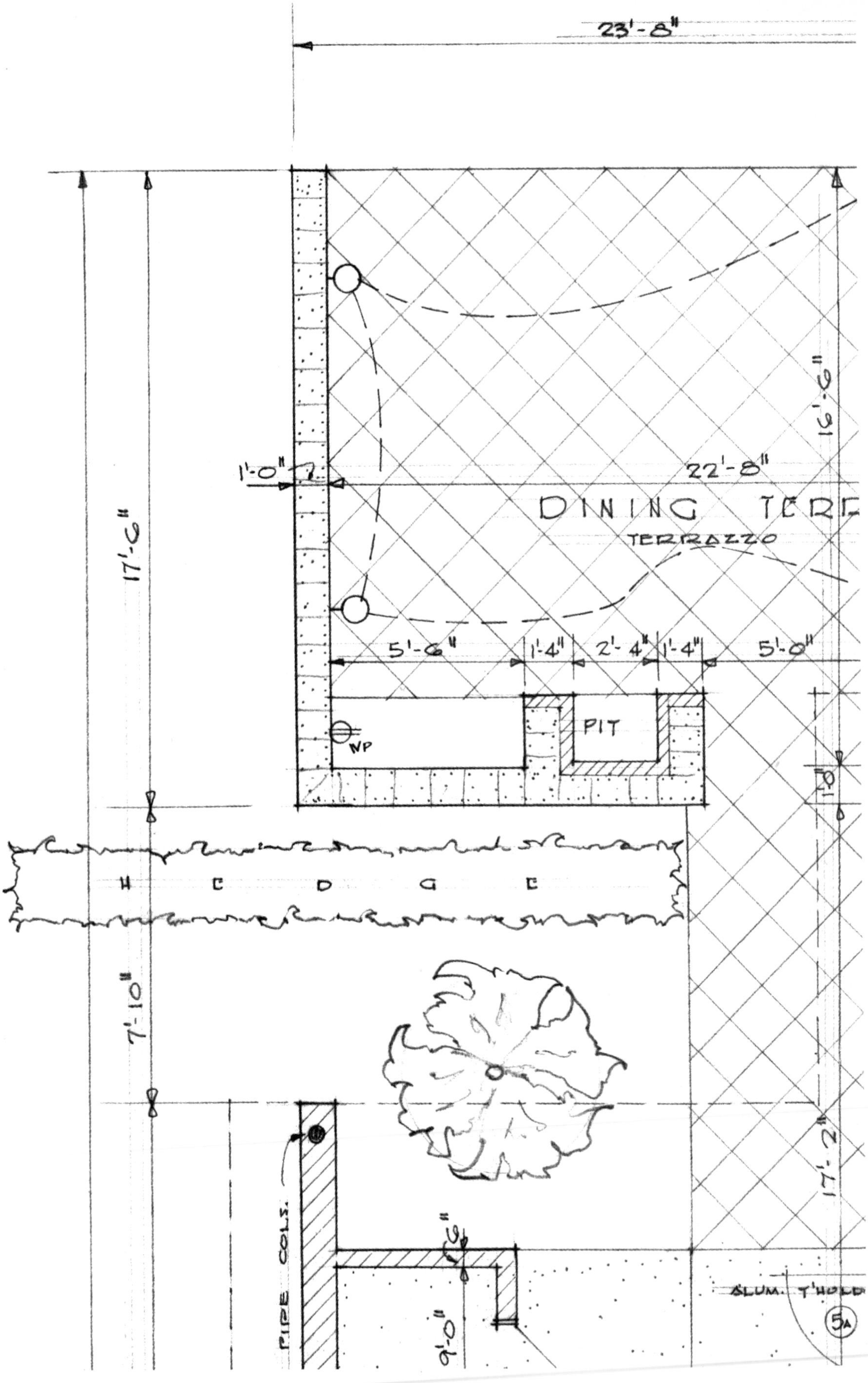

Fig. 8-5 The actual size (partially shown) of the original working drawing in Fig. 8-1. Notice the typical sizes of lettering, symbols, etc. used by the draftsman.

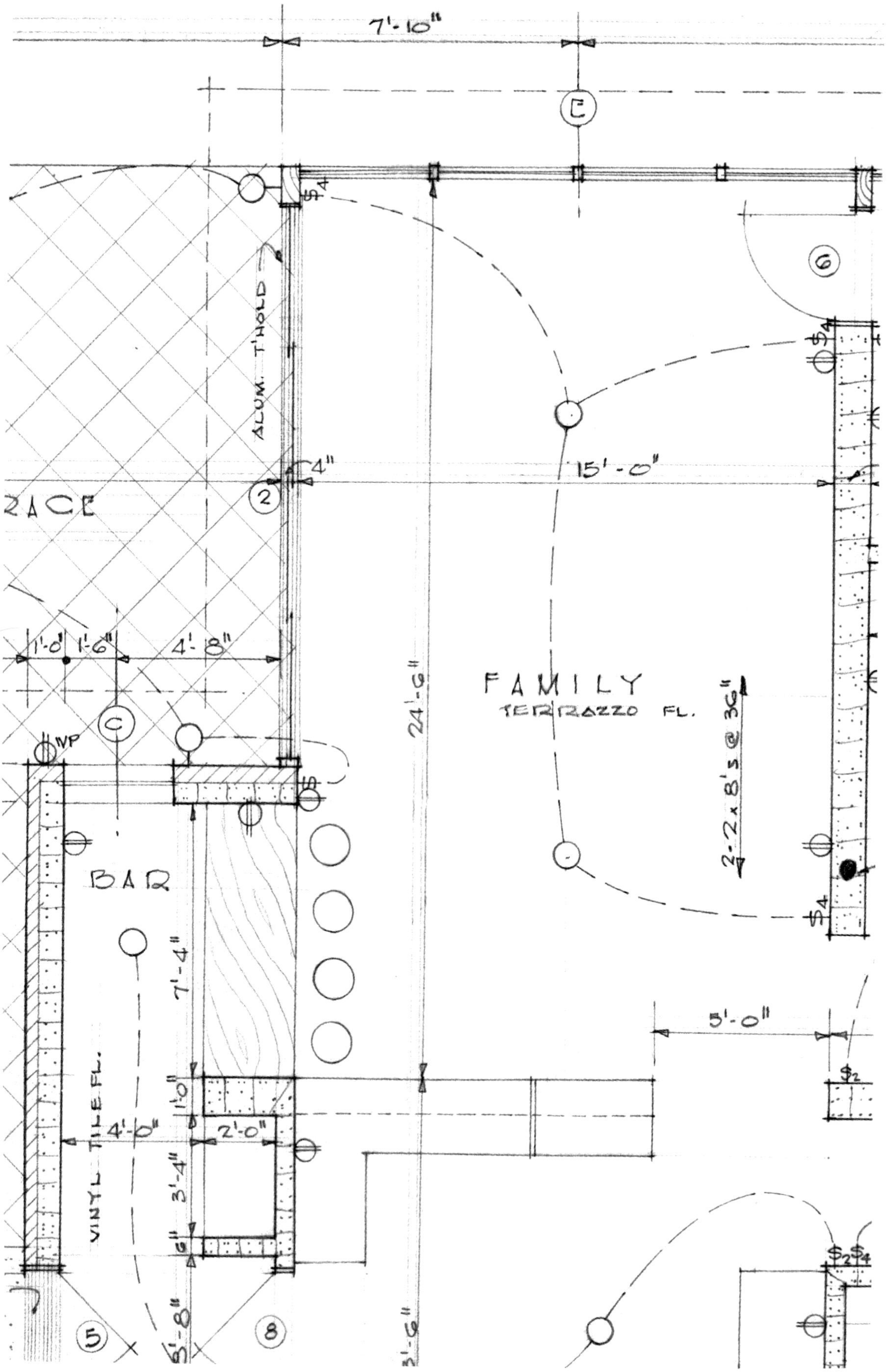
7'-10"
ALUM. T'HOLD
4"
15'-0"
RACE
1'-0" 1'-6" 4'-8"
FAMILY
TERRAZZO FL.
2-2x8's @ 36"
24'-6"
BAR
7'-4"
5'-0"
1'-0"
4'-0"
2'-0"
3'-4"
VINYL TILE FL.
6"
3'-8"
3'-6"

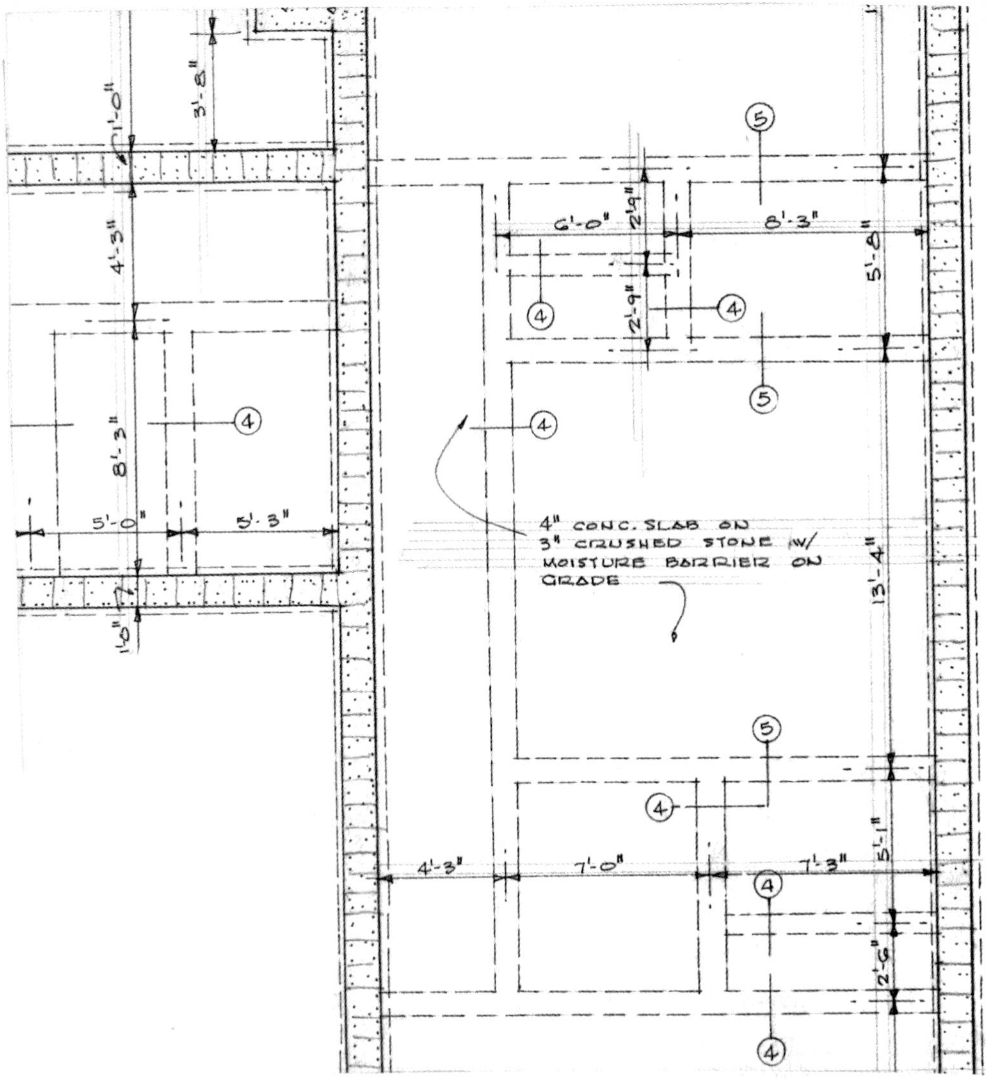

Fig. 8-6 A partial plan showing the use of broken lines.

so that individual techniques will be maintained. When a broken line changes in direction at a corner, make dashes intersect at the actual corner, rather than at an opening with no corner point (see Fig. 8-7B).

8.3 MAKE THE DIMENSIONS EASY TO READ

The usefulness of a working drawing depends to a large extent upon the correctness and manner of placement of its dimensions. If the dimensions are orderly and have been determined with the builder's needs in mind, information is readily obtained from the drawing. Numerous expensive mistakes are often the result of faulty dimensions.

Regardless of the scale of a drawing, numerical dimensions always indicate the actual size of the structure or feature. For example, if the side of a carport is represented by a line 5″ long on a plan drawn to the scale $\frac{1}{4}'' = 1'\text{–}0''$, the numerical dimension shown on the drawing should be 20′–0″, which is the dimension workmen must use to build the wall.

Extension lines are light lines drawn from the extremities of a feature requiring a dimension (see Fig. 8-7C). Extension lines should not touch the feature, but rather they should begin $\frac{1}{32}''$ from the object line and extend about $\frac{1}{8}''$ beyond the arrowhead of the dimension line. If features within a drawing are best dimensioned outside of the view, extension lines pass through the object lines and are unbroken.

Dimension Lines are also light lines and have arrowheads on each end, indicating the exact extremities of the dimension (see Fig. 8-7C).

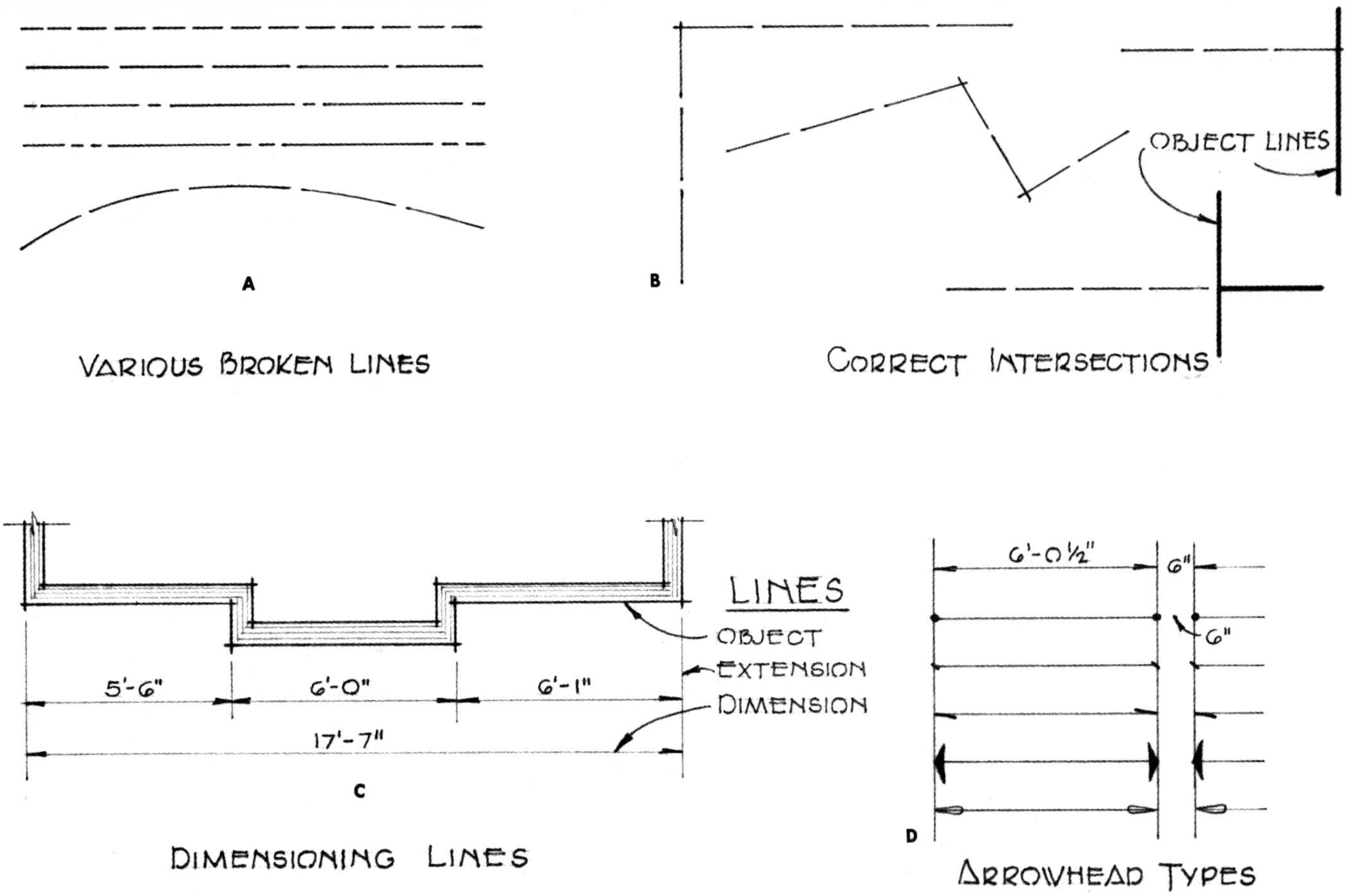

Fig. 8-7 Broken lines, arrowheads, and dimensions.

On architectural and structural drawings, dimension lines are made continuous, and the numerical dimension is placed just above the line, about midway between the arrowheads (see Fig. 8-7C). When placing a numerical dimension above adjacent parallel dimension lines, be careful to place it closer to the line it identifies. On shop or engineering drawings, the dimension line is broken near its center, and the numerical dimension is centered in the opening.

Arrowheads are drawn at the ends of dimension lines. Various types of arrowheads are seen on drawings (Fig. 8-7D), but the student should learn to make conventional arrowheads well before trying other types. Make them neat and uniform, with their points just touching the extension lines. A sharp, narrow arrowhead about 1/8″ long is the most appropriate. Avoid clumsy arrowheads made with dull pencils, giving the drawing a "spotty" appearance.

Dimensions should be neatly lettered, and they should be made to read from the bottom and right side of the drawing—never from the top or left side. Dimensions under 12″ are given in inches, such as 6″, 3 5/8″, 11 1/2″, etc. Over 12″ long they are usually given in feet and inches, such as 3′–4″, 25′–7 1/2″, 12′–0″, etc. However, on detail drawings, some features that are well over 12″ in size are commonly expressed in inches only. For example, joist spacing is usually indicated as 16″ on center, kitchen base cabinets as 36″ high, minimum crawl space as 18″, etc. When lettering dimensions, never place the numbers directly on linework nor allow the numbers to touch lines on the drawing; it often mutilates the figure, and after a print is made of the drawing, the dimension is usually misread.

8.4 PLACE DIMENSIONS FOR OBVIOUS ASSOCIATION WITH THEIR FEATURES

Dimension lines should be placed outside the view or drawing, if possible. On large plans, however, features such as partitions that are well inside the exterior walls must be dimensioned inside the view for obvious association. Dimensions that are too remote from their features are difficult to find, and the excessively long extension lines which are then necessary make the drawing confusing. The placement of dimensions within a drawing should be studied carefully to be sure they do not interfere with other lines on the view. Avoid a dimension line that coincides with an object line at the arrowhead; offset the dimension slightly. Judgment must also be used in placing dimensions around the periphery of a plan or detail. If they are too close, they interfere with the outline of the view, and the numerical dimensions often become crowded; if they are too far away, they give the impression of pertaining to features other than their own.

8.5 LINE UP DIMENSIONS IN SERIES FOR SIMPLICITY

If possible, a series of dimensions should be "lined up" so that they can be quickly drawn with one setting of the ruling edge, even if the view has offset edges (see Fig. 8-8). With arrowheads at each extension line intersection, the continuous dimension-line effect simplifies the appearance of the drawing. The smallest dimensions are placed nearest, and the larger ones are placed farther away from the view. On a floor plan, for example, which often has many features requiring complex dimensions, similar features should be brought to each series for unity. The location of window and door center lines can be dimensioned along one series, closest to the plan; the offsets in the exterior wall and abutting partitions can be dimensioned along another series about ½″ farther out; and the overall length of the building can be shown as a single dimension about the same distance out again. Almost each dimensioning situation requires a different solution. Be sure to check the total of a series, arithmetically, to verify the overall dimension. Occasionally it becomes necessary to cross extension lines, but avoid crossing dimensional lines.

8.6 DO NOT DUPLICATE DIMENSIONS

Basically, dimensions are either *size* dimensions or *location* dimensions. Only those that contribute to the construction of the building or feature should be shown—needless repetition only clutters. Often the method of construction dictates their correct choice. For example, in frame wall construction, the window and door openings are located to their center lines on the plan, whereas in solid-masonry construction, they are dimensioned to their edges (see Fig. 8-9). In frame partitions, the location of doors is often superfluous, inasmuch as their symbol indicates an obvious placement. Correct dimensioning eliminates the need for workmen to make unnecessary addition or subtraction calculations on the job.

8.7 USE LEADERS TO AVOID OVERCROWDING

Leaders are straight or curved lines leading from a numerical dimension or note to the applying feature (see Fig. 8-10A). Usually an

Fig. 8-8 In-line dimensions on a plan view.

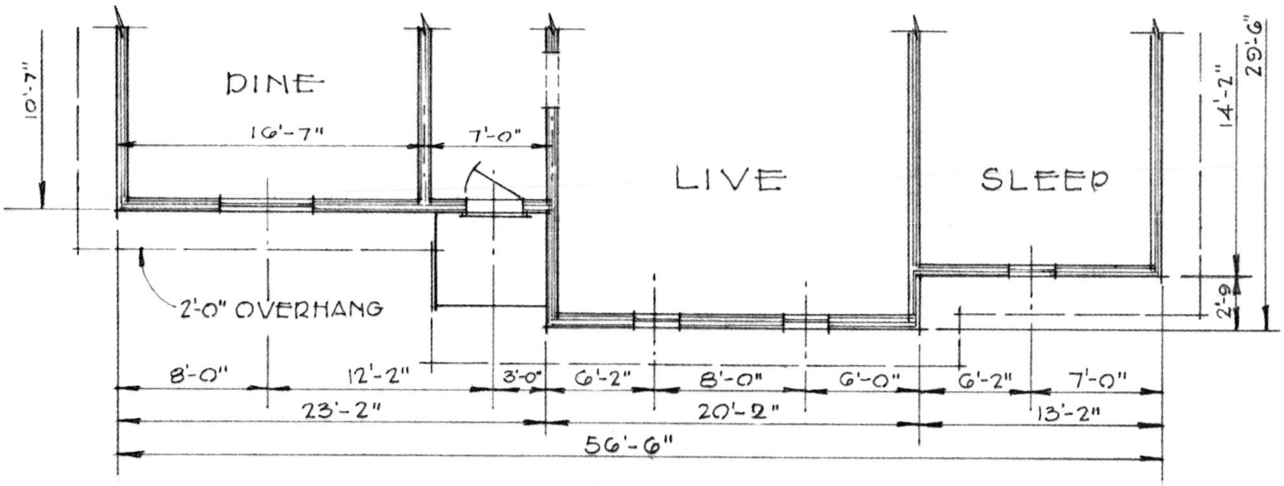

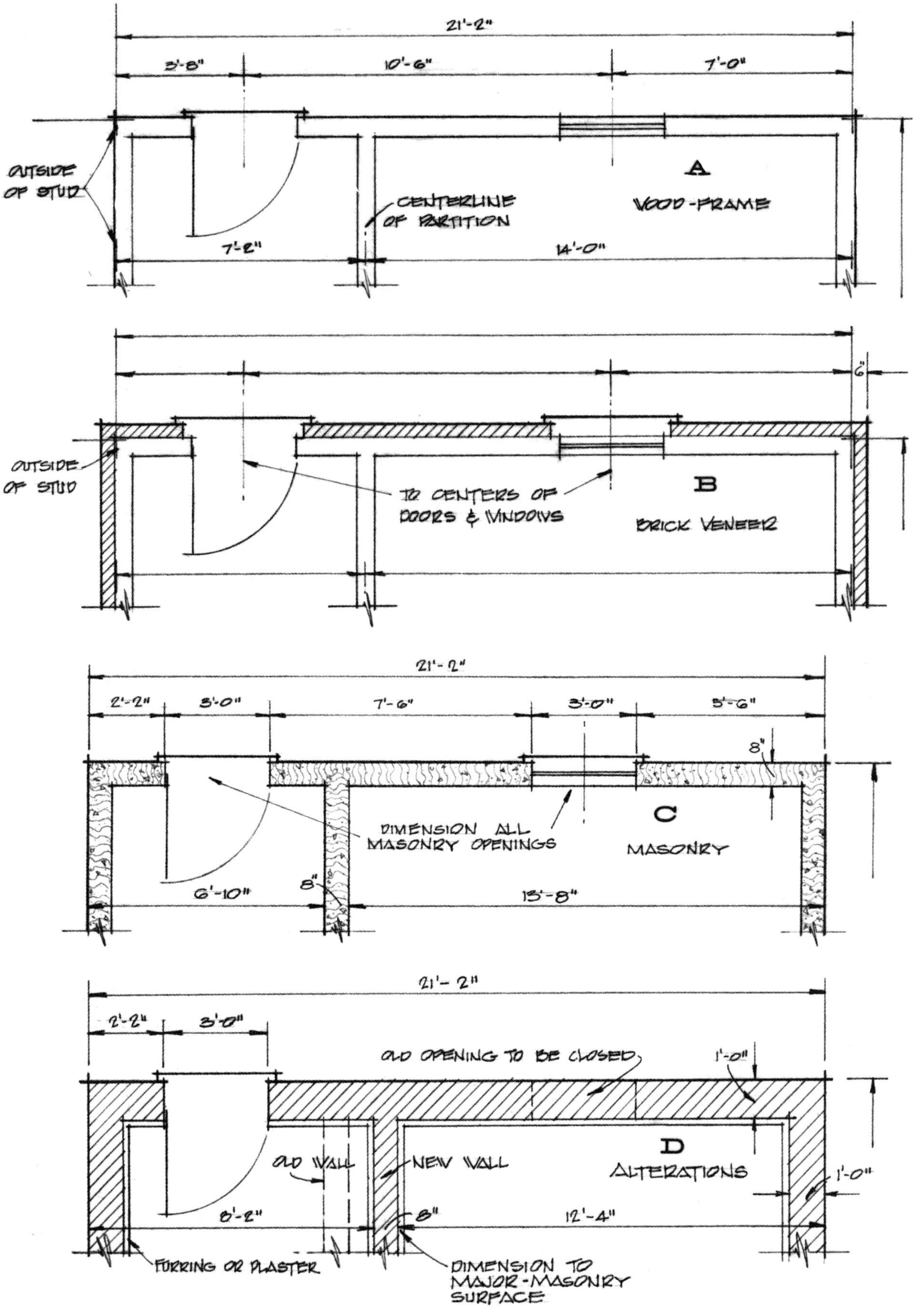

Fig. 8-9 Dimensioning conventions.

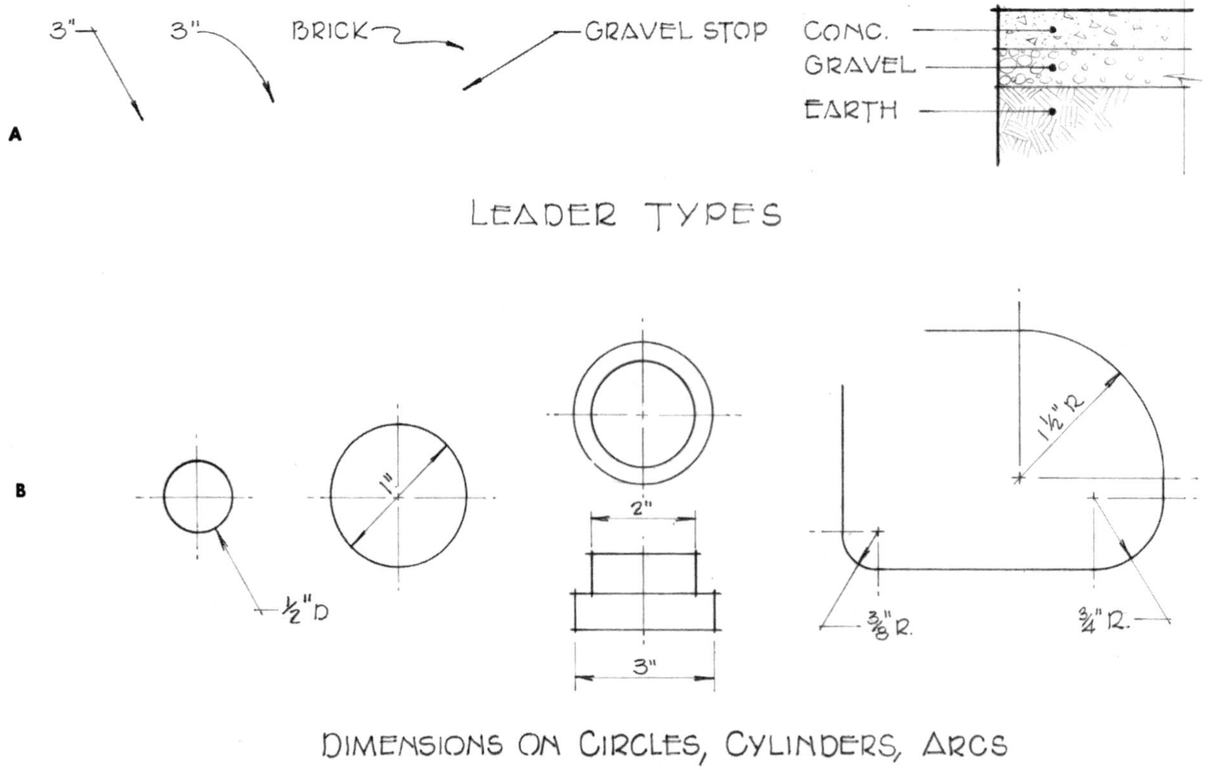

Fig. 8-10 Various types of leaders; dimensions for circles and arcs.

arrowhead or dot is drawn on the feature-end of the leader. Various leader techniques have been devised by draftsmen, but the most effective leaders are those that identify themselves as leaders and do not become confused with object lines or other lines on the drawing. Leaders should appear as connectors only and should not be misinterpreted. This is the purpose for using angular or offset-curve leaders. It is usual practice to add leaders to the drawing after dimension lines have been completed; then satisfactory, uncrowded spaces can be found for the leader-dimension or note, without placing this information too far from the feature. If a series of leaders must identify a number of materials or features, on section views for example, be sure the notes are arranged in a logical sequence so that the leaders do not cross (Fig. 8-10A). For readability, bring the leader to the beginning of a note. Leaders with circles or "balloons" attached are effective for identifying parts of an assembly or similar drawing requiring a sequence of letters or numbers (see Fig. 8-3).

Use angular leaders also to label circular shapes and holes. Place the leader indicating a diameter dimension on the exterior of the circle, with the arrowhead touching the circumference and pointing toward its center. A regular, angular dimension line can be used to label large circles; dimension cylinders on their rectangular view. Draw the leaders indicating the radii of arcs from their radiating points to the arcs, with the arrowhead of the leader on the inner side of the curvature (Fig. 8-10B) and the letter R following the numerical radius.

8.8 USE NOTES SPARINGLY ON A DRAWING

Unless a note clarifies the graphic representation, chances are it can be better included in the written specifications and thereby save the draftsman's time. If a note is needed, however, use small lettering and make it clear and concise. If a note, such as, "See detail A–A" is used, be sure there is a detail A–A to which the reader can refer. Check spelling carefully; even draftsmen need a dictionary occasionally. Extensive notes should be organized in neat blocks away from linework. These lettered areas of unusually long notes (if they definitely must be put on the drawing) should be considered in the sheet layout planning. Allow "breathing space" around a note, regardless of size, so that the reader can understand it.

8.9 ABBREVIATIONS SAVE TIME, BUT THEY ARE OFTEN CONFUSING

Even though the American Standards Association has established abbreviation standards for the construction industry, many variations still exist throughout the country. Some architectural offices insist upon abbreviating every word possible on their drawings, mainly to economize; other offices, knowing the inconsistencies and chances of misinterpretation, will not tolerate the use of abbreviations. The draftsman must use discretion, however, and abbreviate only those words that have commonly identified abbreviations and use them in such a way that they cannot possibly be misconstrued. Capital lettering is usually employed, and as a rule, the period at the end is omitted. If it becomes necessary to use unusual abbreviations throughout a set of drawings, indicate their meanings on a legend. A list of common construction abbreviations is included in the Appendix.

8.10 INDICATE MATERIALS AND FEATURES WITH SYMBOLS

Because most buildings are a complexity of different materials and components, a simplified method of representation is necessary on a drawing—the smaller the scale, the simpler the symbol. Many of the conventional architectural symbols are shown in Fig. 8-11. Study these symbols carefully and commit to memory the important, most-used ones: brick, concrete, stone, earth, wood, concrete block, insulation, glass, gravel, doors, and windows. Notice that most symbols are different on elevations from those in section or on plans. Learn all representations. Like other aspects of architectural drawing, symbols also vary slightly in different areas and in different offices. If nonstandard symbols are used on drawings, a symbol legend can be drawn on one of the sheets. Although simply drawn, all symbols should be indicative of the material they represent; if a symbol is misleading or gives the impression of the wrong material, clarify it with a simple note. Material symbols or "hatching" need not be made with heavy line weights. In fact, their representation in rather large areas will appear more pleasing if the linework "fades out" near the center, thus resembling a highlight on the surface, and it is given more emphasis near the edges (see Fig. 8-12). Make the so-called highlights nongeometric in shape, to eliminate any possibility of their appearing as construction features on the surface. The edges of hatched areas should be distinct. Contrast of adjacent materials is especially important on section views. To aid expression, hatch adjacent pieces on section views in different directions. Otherwise, use the same tone and technique for a material or member reappearing in different places throughout the section. If an overall gray pencil tone is used to indicate a predominant material, usually it is more tidy to apply the shading on the reverse side of the tracing. Wood structural members in section are merely indicated with diagonals (Fig. 8-11); finish lumber is indicated with an end-grain symbol done freehand.

If notes or dimensions must go into hatched areas, leave out enough of the linework so that the number or note can be inserted and can be read without difficulty (see Fig. 8-12).

In drawing wood frame construction, the floor plan of a home can be represented with parallel lines, scaled 6″ apart, which is usually close to the actual thickness of the combined studs, inside material, and outside wall coverings. Parallel lines are often the only symbol needed to represent the wood walls. But by the addition of either straight or wavy lines (resembling wood grain) within the parallel lines, a more prominent outline of the plan is attained (see Fig. 8-13). The tone of the symbol makes the plan more readable. This principle of giving prominence to important features by shading, either freehand or mechanical, is adaptable to many situations in drafting. The symbols for windows and doors on plans drawn at small scales are shown in Fig. 8-9. Several methods are shown for indicating doors. On elevation views, draw windows and doors accurately to reveal their characteristics.

8.11 AVOID UNNECESSARY REPETITION OF SYMBOL HATCHING

When drawing elevation views of a symmetrical nature, the material symbol on one side of the center line often can be omitted if there is no special reason for hatching the entire elevation (see Fig. 8-14). In design drawings, however, completion of the various material tones may be necessary in analyzing the esthetic aspects

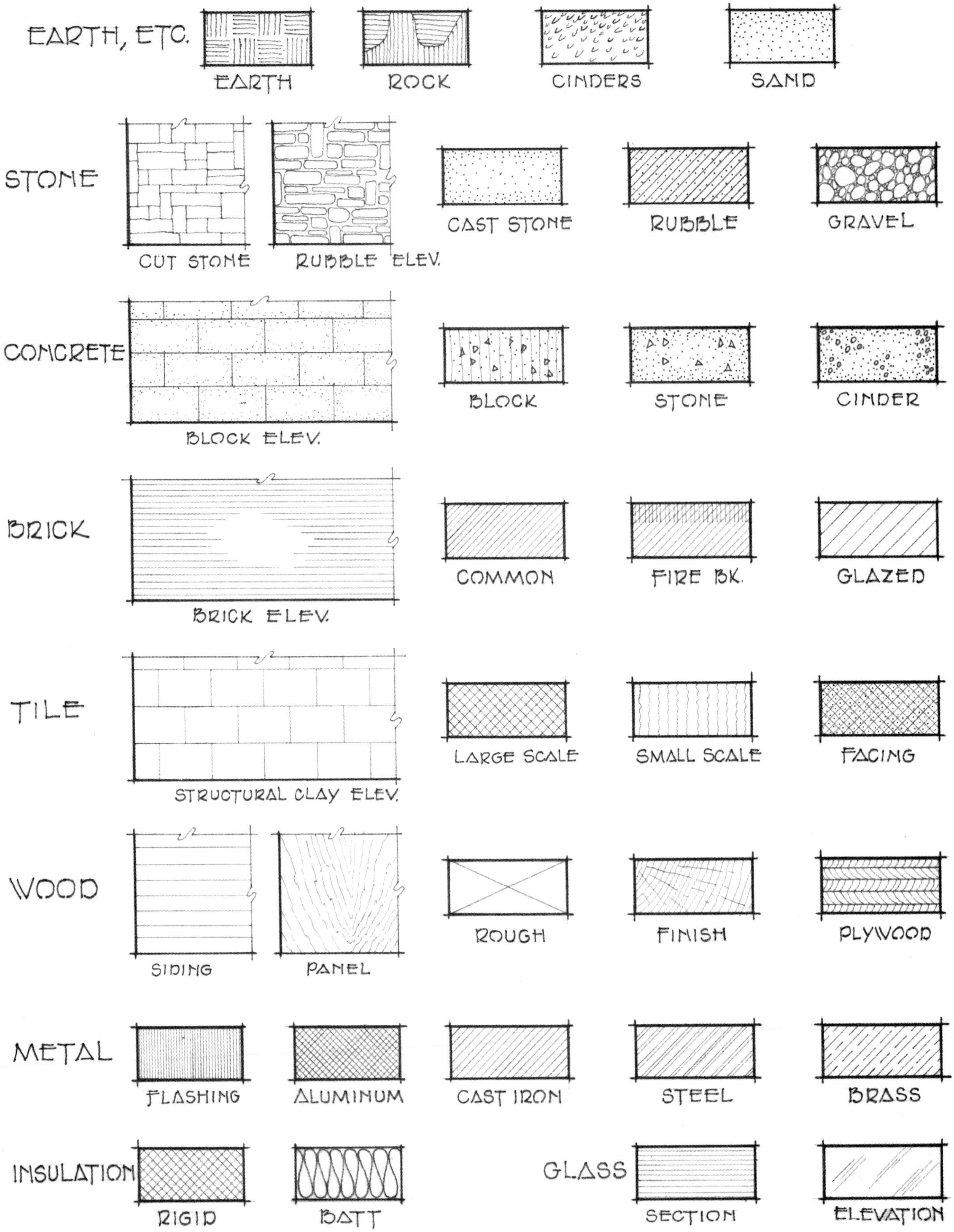

Fig. 8-11 Material symbols used on working drawings.

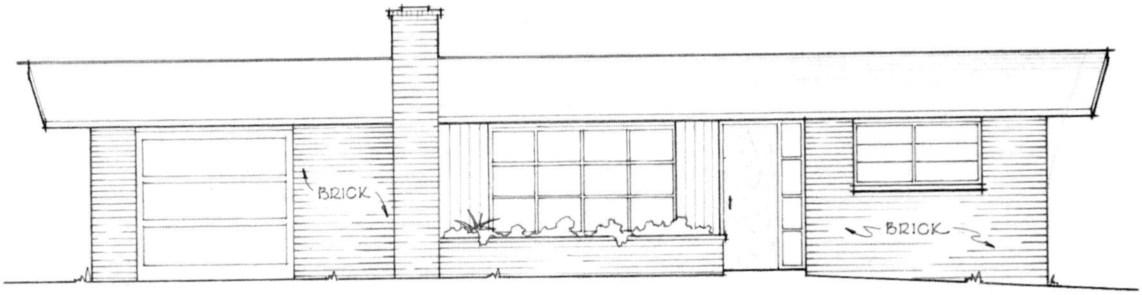

Fig. 8-12 An elevation showing application of material symbols.

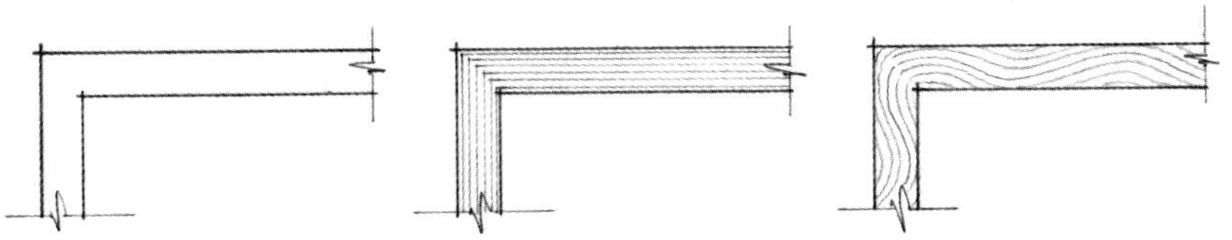

A B C

Fig. 8-13 Representation of wood frame on plan views.

Fig. 8-14 A symmetrical elevation view showing half-symboling.

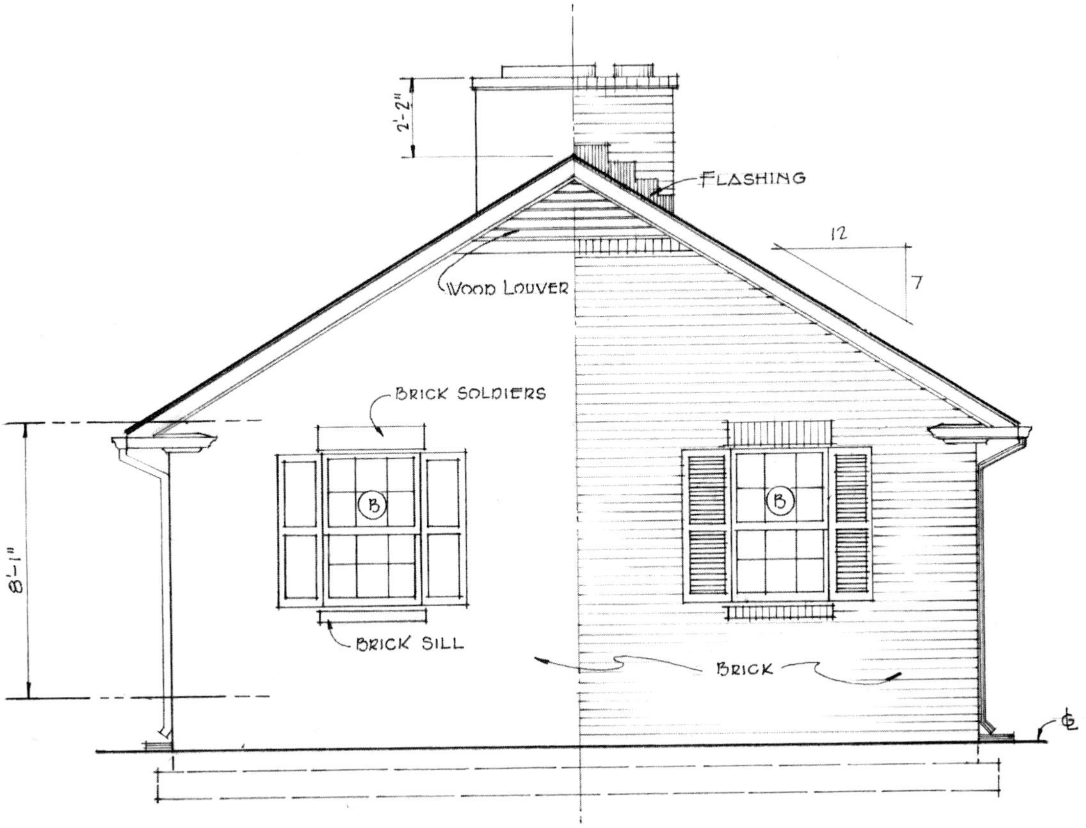

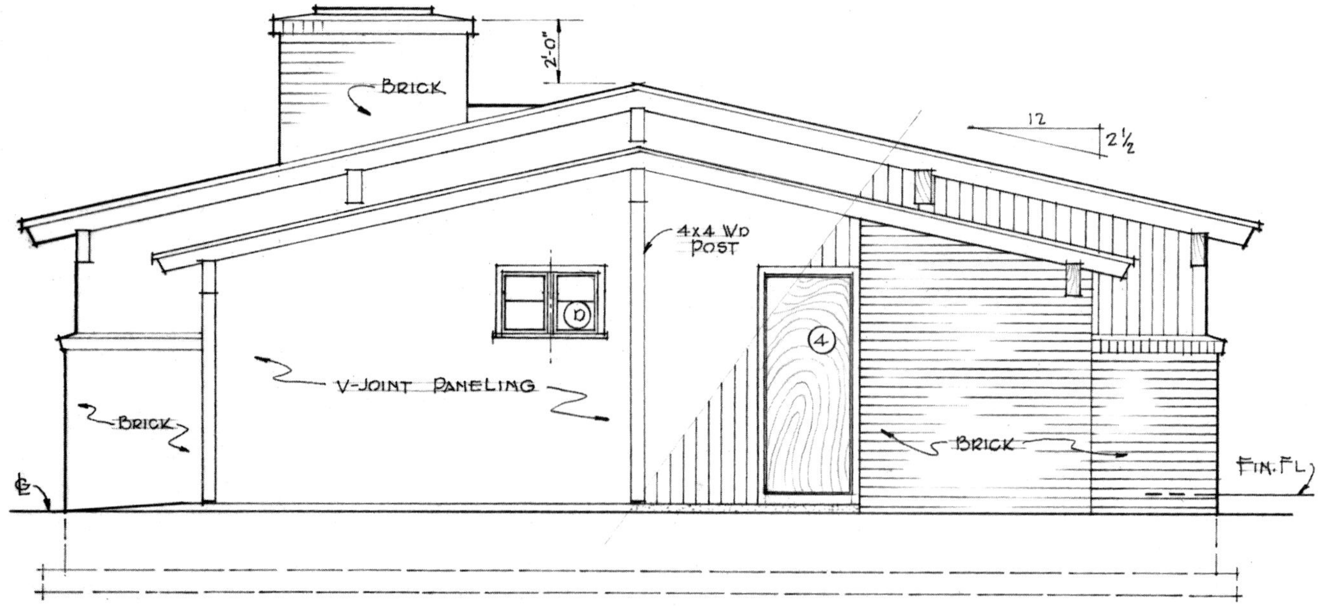

Fig. 8-15 Partial symboling with the use of a diagonal line.

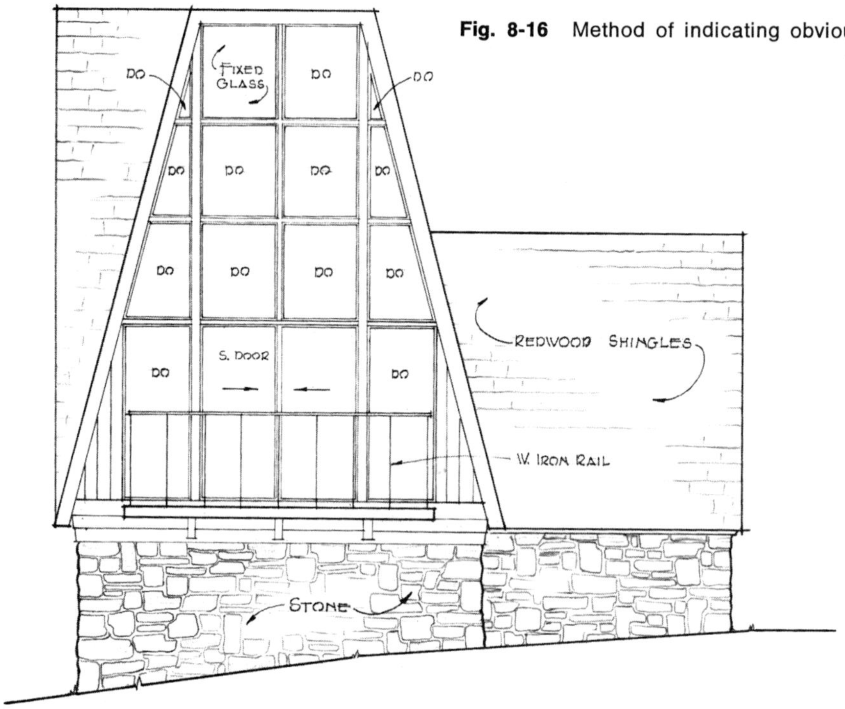

Fig. 8-16 Method of indicating obvious similar features.

Fig. 8-17 A typical window schedule.

WINDOW SCHEDULE

MARK	NO. NEEDED	ROUGH OPNG.	TYPE	MFG. NO.	MULLION	REMARKS
A	2	2'-11" x 4'-6"	DH	BW 2749	NONE	BY BILT-WELL
B	6	3'-10" x 4'-6"	DH	BW 2749	1- 3⅛"	SEE DETAIL
C	4	8'-9" x 4'-6"	DH	BW 2749	2- 3⅛"	DO
D	2	1'-11" x 3'-2"	DH	BW 2749	NONE	DO
E	3	1'-5" x 2'-3⅞"	CAS.	A461	NONE	BY TRUSCON

of the building. Another method of suggesting materials on an elevation without taking the time to hatch the entire drawing is shown in Fig. 8-15. A light diagonal line that does not conflict with other important lines is drawn on the elevation to limit the hatching to a typical area. Sometimes merely a note is sufficient to indicate the material if it does not require careful delineation. When a series of identical features is shown, it is permissible to symbol only one feature completely and add a ditto (DO) note to the remaining ones. (See Fig. 8-16.) Time is saved if laborious hatching is omitted where repetition is not informative.

8.12 USE A DRAFTING TEMPLATE FOR DIFFICULT SYMBOLS

Many symbols such as bathroom fixtures, electrical symbols, kitchen equipment, circles, irregular shapes, etc., can be quickly drawn with appropriate architectural templates (see Fig. 1-1). Refer to Section 1.16 for the correct use of drafting templates.

8.13 USE SCHEDULES TO ORGANIZE EXTENSIVE INFORMATION

A schedule is an organized arrangement of notes or information usually lettered within a ruled enclosure and conveniently placed on the drawing (see Fig. 8-17). Extensive information placed in a schedule, rather than lettered in various places on the drawing, makes the information easily accessible to estimators and builders who appreciate the organized arrangement. Schedules commonly list information pertaining to doors, windows, interior trim, painting, structural detail elements, etc. Door and window schedules are usually placed on the floor plan sheet, where they can be studied in relation to the plan drawing. When drawing a schedule enclosure, make the horizontal ruled lines 1/4″ or 3/16″ apart so that there will be sufficient space between the lines for the lettering (which need be only 1/16″ high) to avoid touching the ruled linework. The title should be slightly larger, and a top-horizontal and a left-vertical column for identifications and headings should be isolated from the remaining spaces with heavy lines. Draw a heavy border line around the entire schedule.

Identify windows with letters (A, B, C, D, etc.), both in the schedule and near the windows on the plan; identify doors with numbers (1, 2, 3, 4, etc.), or vice versa, so that each can be easily distinguished. Rough-opening sizes for windows installed in frame walls is important information, and should be included in the schedule along with window size, type, and material. Often the name of the manufacturer and the item's exact catalogue number are also provided. Instead of a lettered schedule, door information can also be shown by drawing small elevation views of each door type. Sometimes the small elevations are included as part of a lettered schedule. If the doors are similar stock heights, they become simplest to draw if arranged in a horizontal row (see Fig. 8-18). Dimensions and

Fig. 8-18 A method of describing doors on working drawings.

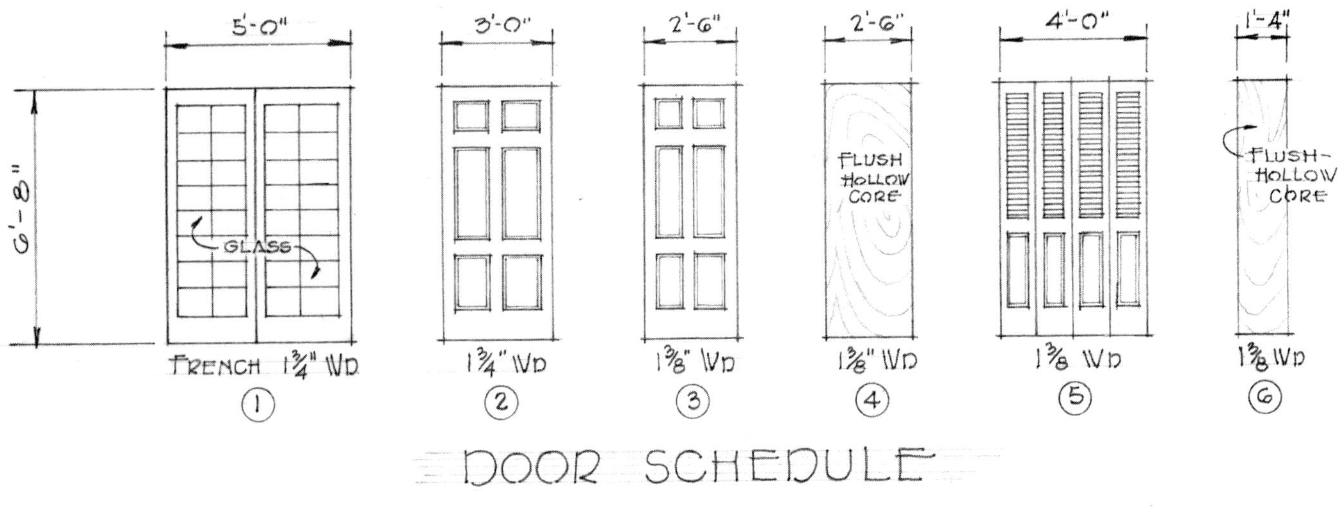

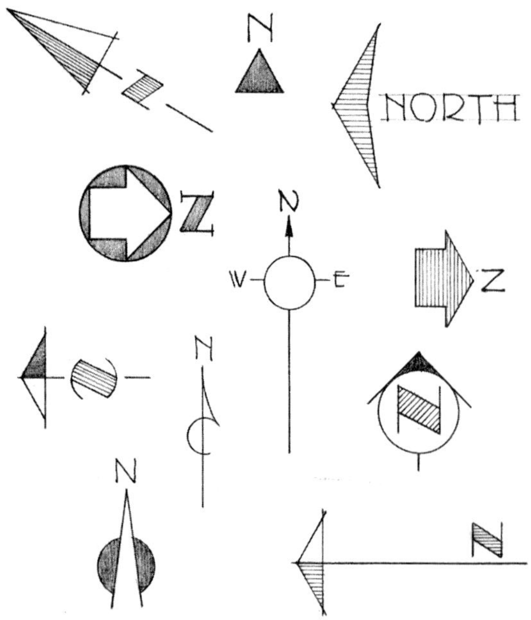

Fig. 8-19 Suggestions for north-point arrows.

material information should both be included in this type of graphic schedule. On noncomplex floor plans using only stock doors, their sizes can be lettered along the door symbol on the plan with a note such as, $1\frac{3}{8}''$ × 2′–6″ × 6′–8″ FLUSH, and no schedule is required.

8.14 AVOID SMUDGED PENCIL LINEWORK

Slight smudging of pencil linework with triangles and instruments cannot be entirely avoided, but care should be taken to refrain from unnecessary rubbing or touching the finished pencil lines. Beginning students, especially, are confronted with the problem of smudged drawings. Listed below are a number of suggestions for keeping a pencil drawing clean while on the drawing board:

1. Use a systematic and organized procedure in the sequence of drawing lines so that instruments will not have to be placed over existing lines any more than necessary, e.g., start from the top of the layout and draw as many major, horizontal lines as possible, proceeding to the bottom of the layout. For vertical lines, start from the left of the layout and draw as many vertical lines as convenient, proceeding toward the right of the drawing (if left-handed, proceed toward the left). In other words, draw lines so that the triangle can be moved away from the lines already completed. This will become a timesaving habit, if conscientiously applied during early training.
2. Sprinkle a conservative amount of material from a dry cleaning pad (small bags available at drafting supply stores) under the instruments. See Fig. 8-20. Or, if this is not handy, use a few erasings from the Artgum eraser. These particles act as tiny rollers under the instruments and prevent direct contact with the paper. When they become soiled, they should be replaced.
3. Protect completed parts of a drawing by covering them with extra sheets of paper. Do this also at the end of the day or work period.
4. Triangles are available with small protrusions on both surfaces of the plastic, which will prevent direct contact with the paper and minimize smudging.
5. Small triangles will reduce smudging if extensive work must be done on small details.
6. Form the habit of raising the T-square blade slightly when moving it up or down on the drawing board. This can be done by merely bearing down on the head as it is moved.
7. Keep the instruments clean by wiping with a damp cloth regularly. Avoid soap and water on wooden parts, but carbon tetrachloride and a clean cloth will do an excellent job of cleaning any of the drafting equipment (note: carbon tetrachloride fumes, if excessively inhaled, can cause permanent injury—avoid them). The fine graphite from pencil leads has the habit of lodging in the surface pores of almost any material. Always wipe the pencil point after sharpening. Do not store the pencil pointer in direct contact with other drafting equipment, either on the drawing board or in portable kits. Keep it in an isolated container.

Fig. 8-20 Using a dry cleaning pad to prevent smudged linework.

Fig. 8-21 Sweeping loose graphite from drawings.

8. Sweep the drawing occasionally with the drafting brush to reduce the amount of loose graphite on the surface. Avoid rubbing the drawing with the hand or any hard objects, as well as with sleeves or cuffs. See Fig. 8-21.
9. Be sure the hands are clean and dry. If necessary, use a little talcum powder on them to reduce perspiration.

8.15 LEARN THE PRINCIPLES OF MODULAR DRAFTING

To meet the rising cost of construction, the building industry has developed a method for simplifying the details of structures so that building components, materials, and equipment can be assembled easily with a minimum of alterations, such as cutting, fitting, and other minor modifications. It is felt that by reducing hand labor for such job-site alterations, the application of this principle effects the only definite economies yet to be realized in present-day construction, and that this fuller utilization of our technical advancements in the building industry can be made without sacrificing any of the architectural qualities of the design. The industry's recommendation is *modular coordination,* which involves these four aspects:

1. Thinking modular during all stages of the design process;
2. Drawing the working drawings so that modular concepts are represented simply, yet with some flexibility;
3. Sizing building products so that they will conform to modular assembly; and
4. Devising construction techniques that will economically utilize coordinated materials with a minimum of modification and waste.

Modular drafting concerns itself with these concepts. Some architectural offices use modular coordination and dimensioning completely on their working drawing; others, because of the occasional difficulty in obtaining a full range of modular products and localized difficulty in obtaining construction personnel who fully understand the system, are reluctant to convert to the modular method. But there is merit in coordination; and, like any advancement in an industry involving large numbers of people in various areas and trades, time is required before the method is universally understood and accepted.

Beginning students should first learn the conventional methods for representing and dimensioning of working drawings. Then, after an intimate acquaintance with construction methods and building products, the benefits of modular methods will become apparent. Well-thought-out conventional drawings often result in modular characteristics, whether it is realized or not. The first step is "thinking modular," both in conceiving the building structurally and esthetically, and continuing this thinking throughout the working drawings. Modular drawings are not necessarily restricted to the use of modular materials only.

With the help of material published by the Modular Building Standards Association,[1] Washington, D.C., the following points are given briefly, to serve as an introduction to the fundamentals of modular drafting.

8.15.1 Use a Modular Grid in Laying Out Preliminary Design Sketches

From the very outset, design-trial sketches must be developed over a modular grid, which has only one restriction—that it be sized in 4″ multiples: 16″, 24″, 4′–0″, 10′–8″, 24′–0″, etc. The selection of the basic grid may be almost any convenient multiple size (see Fig. 8-22). If plywood or other sheet materials are to be a dominant material in the construction, a 4′–0″ × 4′–0″ grid size might be a logical selection. If the spans of structural members seem to sat-

[1] Now defunct. This material, however, is available from other sources.

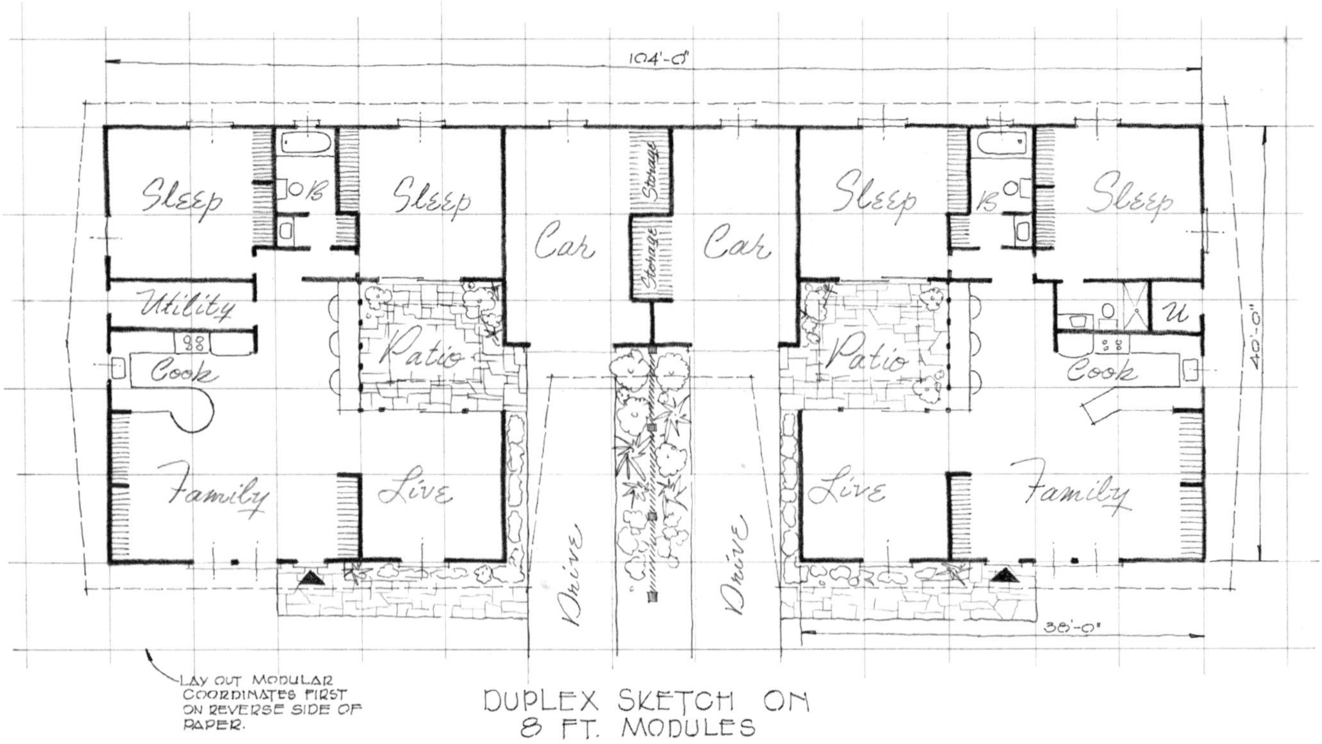

Fig. 8-22 Modular drawings start with preliminary sketches over modular grids.

isfy a 12′–0″ spacing, a grid size of 12′ may be appropriate. If concrete block is to be a major material, a 16″ grid size could be used (it may be a bit small for design sketches, however). The size of the building or repeating spaces within the building should be considered in selecting a design-grid size, just so the selected size of the grid can be divided by four.

Fig. 8-23 The basic module of an architectural volume.

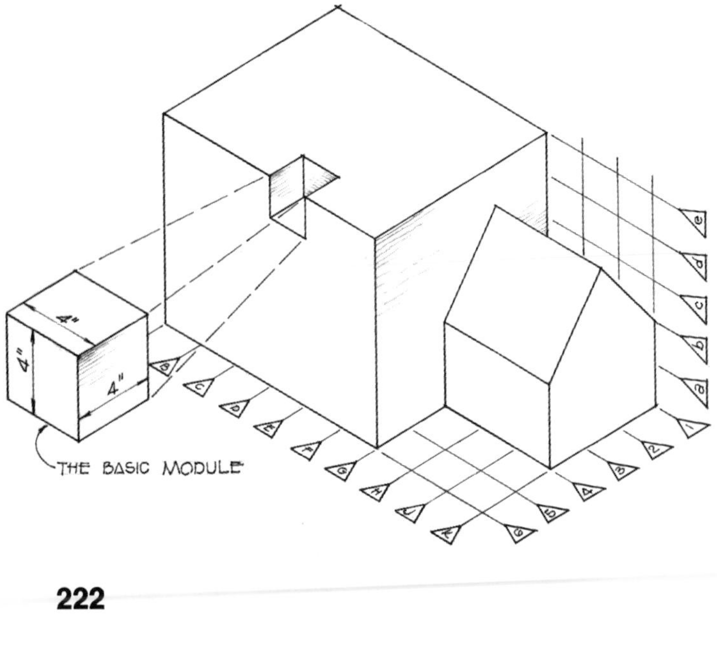

The basic 4″ module was adopted by the American Standards Association, after careful study, as being the most convenient unit from which major materials could be sized and construction features could be dimensioned. The module is 3-dimensional, resembling a 4″ cube (Fig. 8-23), yet it appears in all three principal building planes as a 4″ grid. Some drawings do not show the grids, but because the building was created over a grid, important points will fit, even if the grid lines are imaginary. The basic module is also compatible with sizing of products from countries using the metric system; 4″ is nearly identical with 10 cm.

When the preliminary sketches are converted to large-scale drawings, multiples of the 4″ module become easy to dimension, and all parts of the building can be conveniently related. The design grid can be laid out directly on the sketch paper, or it can be inserted below tracing paper as an underlay. If the structural system and the planning layout can be combined into unified modules, both the working drawings and the construction will be simplified. Grid-disciplined design sketches are the foundation, so to speak, for modular coordination, making possible the benefits of modular drawings.

8.15.2 Develop the Details of the Building on Grid Lines

In developing the details of a building, the 4″ grid lines must be drawn first and become a part of the drawing. The grids can be drawn on the reverse side of the tracing paper, or they can be done in ink so that they cannot be erased if changes must be made. Draw the grids only where each detail will appear; but they must be made to show clearly on the reproduction prints. Because of their small size, 4″ grid lines are not put on a small-scale drawing. Any scale smaller than 3/4″ = 1′–0″ is considered a small-scale drawing. On complex plans and elevations it may be necessary to use reference grid lines to relate the details to their correct placement in the building. Some of the grids in the details may coincide with the reference grids shown on the plans and elevations, others may not; regardless, the continuity of the 4″ module is related with modular dimensions at key points throughout the building.

The accompanying details show where units and surfaces usually best fit within or on grid lines. Each unit of a detail does not necessarily have to fall on grid lines, nor does the modular system restrict the use of only modular materials. However, key points have been worked out in conventional construction to best utilize standard materials in the system. Notice that generally the nominal sizes and surfaces fit the grid lines (see Figs. 8-24 and 8-25). The actual size is usually a fraction of an inch smaller than the nominal size (an exception is the height of a wide-flange beam). For example, the nominal cross-section size of a 2″ × 4″ wooden board actually measures only 1½″ × 3½″; the actual size of the 8″ × 8″ × 16″ concrete block measures 7⅝″ × 7⅝″ × 15⅝″. To eliminate the need for excessive fractions, the grid line conveniently falls within the joint in masonry and just outside the edge of a 2″ × 4″ member, allowing some flexibility. Because 3/8″ is usually the width of a mortar joint between masonry units, 3/16″ is, therefore, a constant dimensional relationship of unit surfaces to the controlling grid. It becomes convenient for grid lines to fall on the center

Fig. 8-24 Actual and nominal sizes of common building materials.

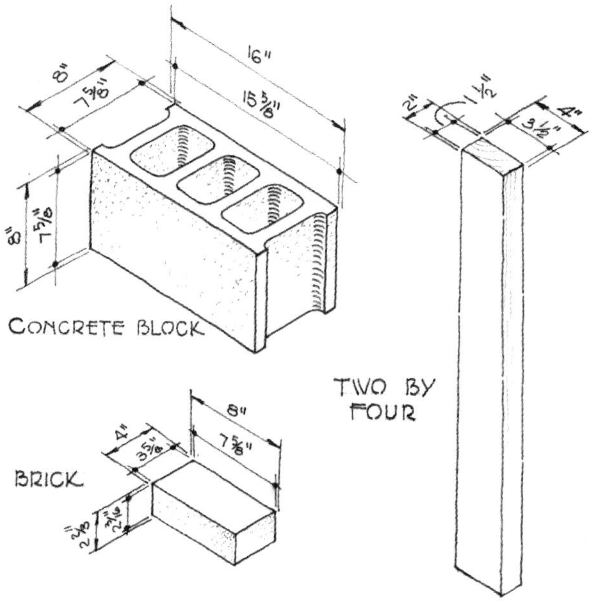

Fig. 8-25 Typical walls and their representation.

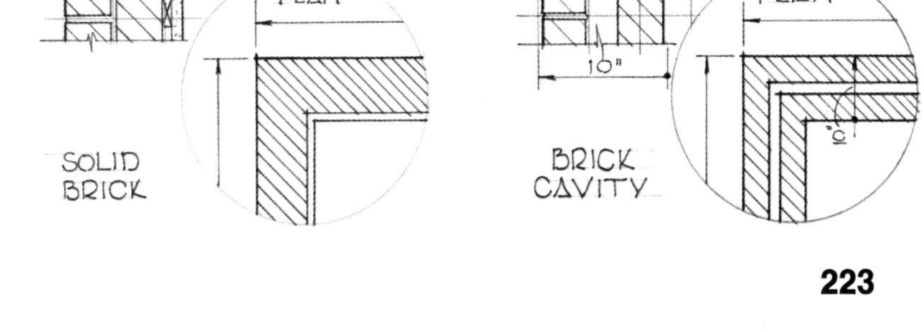

lines of columns, window openings, partitions, etc. When grid lines indicate nominal sizes, it is important that the draftsman as well as the construction contractor is fully aware of this fact. Working drawings can also be based on actual sizes, but a consistent method must be used throughout the drawings. Comparatively few fractions are required in modular drafting, which should make the system of particular interest to draftsmen.

8.15.3 Use an Arrowhead to Indicate a Grid Dimension; a Dot to Indicate a Nongrid Dimension

The dots and arrowheads at the ends of dimension lines have a definite significance on modular drawings. To distinguish between grid and off-the-grid dimensions, an arrowhead is always used to indicate a dimension on a grid line, and a dot to indicate a dimension off the grid lines (see Fig. 8-26). Dimensions that have an arrowhead at each end of the dimension line will be in 4″ multiples. Dimensions that have dots on each end, may or may not be modular, but their extremities do not fall on grid lines. If a dimension has an arrowhead on one end and a dot on the other, it cannot be a 4″ multiple and therefore is not a modular dimension. Even though the grid lines do not actually appear on a modular drawing, the designer or draftsman imagines them to be there, and their presence is always implied by the 4″ multiple dimensions. As we mentioned, reference grids with heavy triangles at their ends, enclosing a consecutive numbering system (see Fig. 8-23), can be used to give additional coordination between details and the plans and elevations. Any point within the total volume of the building can be located with the reference grids.

Fig. 8-26 The use of arrowheads and dots on modular drawings.

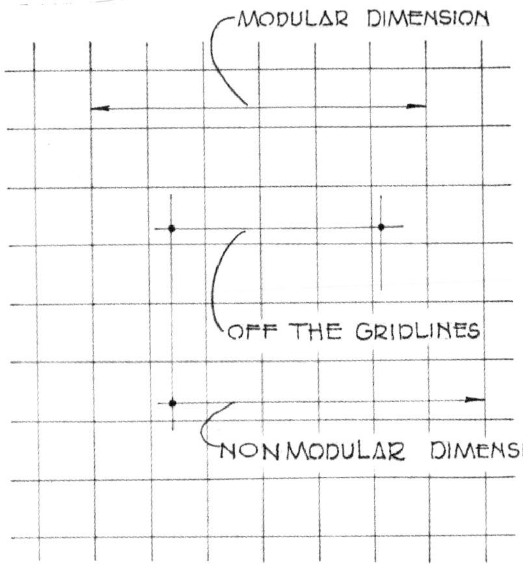

8.15.4 Coordinate Vertical Dimensions with Modular Floor Heights

Usually the nominal finished floor is placed on a grid line; the actual finished floor surface is located $\frac{1}{8}$″ below a grid line (Fig. 8-27). In wood frame construction, however, the top of the subfloor or the surface of a slab-on-ground foundation is placed on a grid line (Fig. 8-28). Three brick heights as well as one 8″ concrete-block height coincide with two grid heights. A difficult point of modular coordination concerns the use of stock doors. If the finished floor coincides with a grid line, then the 6′–8″ or 7′–0″ stock-door heights will not allow enough space for the head jamb to make the rough-opening modular. If special doors and frames are not available to fit the modular heights, consideration must be given to this point in the details. Other important vertical heights are, window-sills, ceiling heights, and table heights.

8.15.5 Use a Note to Indicate the Drawings Are Modular

Because a set of drawings drawn and dimensioned to modular measure appears very much like a set of conventional drawings, a note, stating that the drawings are modular, should be used as a guideline for contractors, bidders, estimators, and workmen. The note, usually placed on the first sheet of the drawings, should be simple and clear; if it is accompanied by several simple drawings illustrating the method of dimensioning employed, as well as by any special representations found on the drawings, all the advantages of modular measure will be readily understood. In order to standardize the modular note, an easily applied translucent appliqué [2] has been devised by the A.I.A. modular

[2] Available from: Standpat Co., 150-42 12th Road, Whitestone, N.Y. 11357.

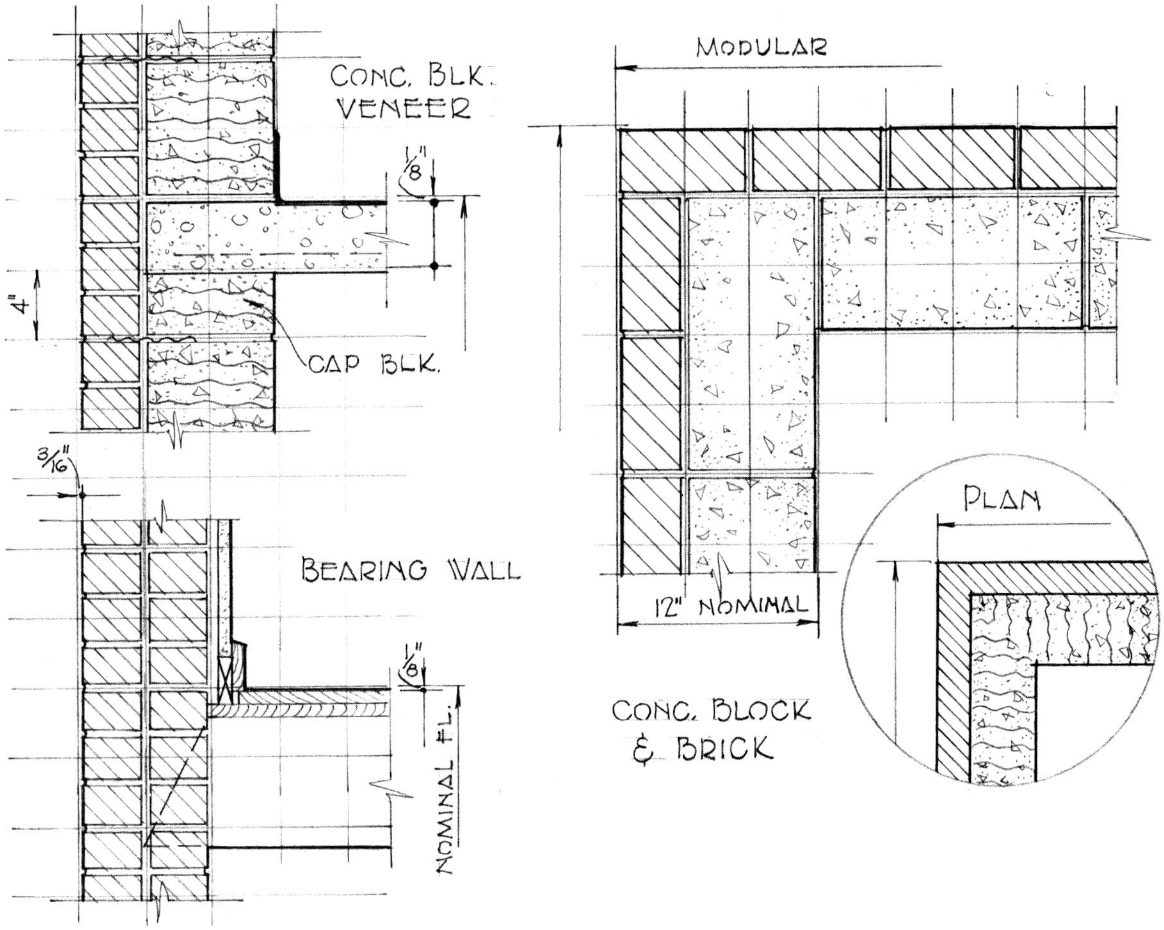

Fig. 8-27 The placement of floor levels within modular grids.

Fig. 8-28 The placement of frame details within modular grids.

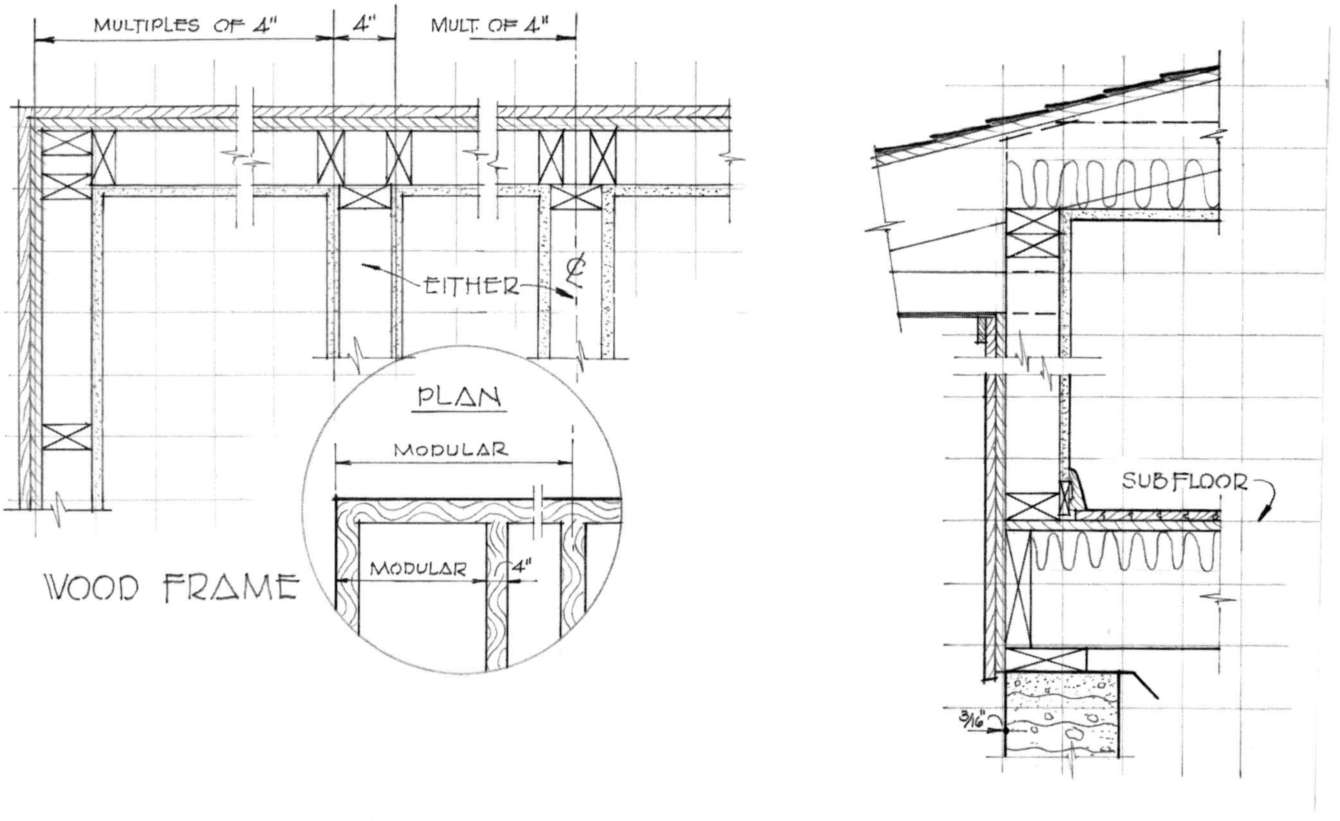

coordinator and is recommended by the Modular Measure Committee of the American Standards Association (see Fig. 8-29). It can be affixed by a pressure-sensitive adhesive to the tracing itself, and will clearly show on all prints. Some architectural offices design their own modular note, and merely letter it, along with any illustrative drawings, directly on the first sheet of their drawings.

Figures 8-30 and 8-31 show a residential floor plan and various details drawn and dimensioned modular.

A type of modular construction for small buildings is shown in Fig. 8-32 (MOD 24, devised jointly by the major U.S. wood products associations). The framing is placed on 24 in. centers so standard 4 ft × 8 ft plywood and sheeting materials can be used with a minimum of waste and

Fig. 8-29 A preprinted applique available for attachment to working drawings to indicate they are modular.

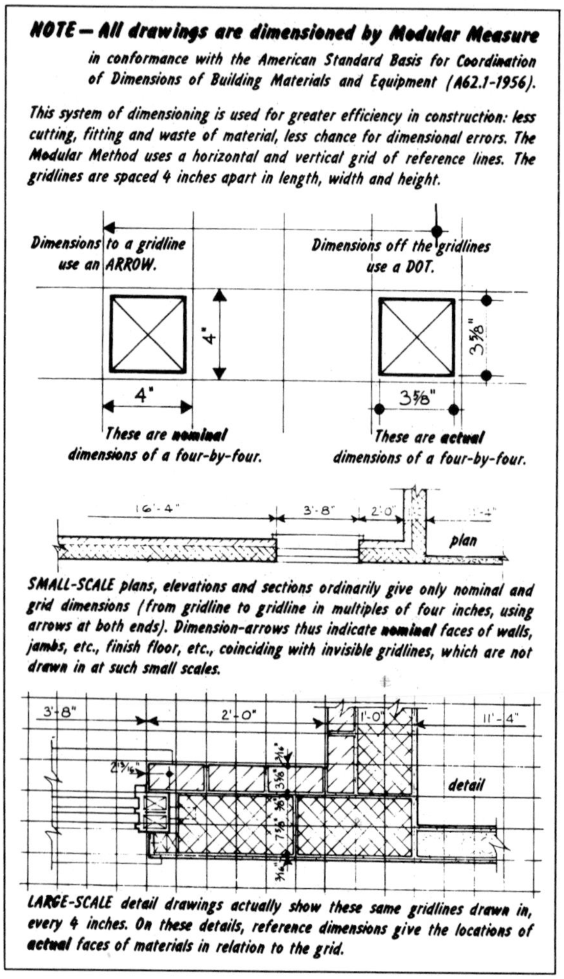

cutting. Many factory-manufactured small homes are now produced using a 4 in. module for sizing.

8.16 METRIC SYSTEM OF MEASUREMENT

It is expected that American industry will eventually convert to the metric system of measurement. In construction, many standards will have to be established before complete conversion will be possible. Lumber, materials, and building components will have to be manufactured in metric measurement before the industry can be expected to adopt the system.

A module of 10 centimeters, almost identical to our present 4 in., would be a logical new module for construction materials (see Fig. 8-33). Otherwise, the *meter* would be a convenient unit for sizing buildings and dimensioning drawings. A suggested method of dimensioning drawings is shown in Fig. 8-34. Until a complete conversion is made, the metric dimension could be placed above the dimension line and the English equivalent placed below.

8.17 REPRODUCTION OF DRAWINGS

The majority of all architectural working drawings are made on either tracing paper, vellum, or film, for the sole purpose of making economical reproductions. Drawings have little value unless they can be satisfactorily reproduced. Sets of the "prints" (often referred to as "blueprints") must be furnished to contract bidders, estimators, subcontractors, workmen, and others who are concerned with the construction of the proposed building; the original drawings are retained by the architectural or engineering office. Several types of reproduction equipment are in use for making prints; each type requires the original tracing to have opaque and distinct linework and lettering in order to produce legible copies. Some architectural offices have their own print-making equipment; others send their tracings to local blueprinting companies, which charge a nominal square-foot fee for the service.

Ozalid Prints are prints produced on paper coated on one side with light-sensitive diazo chemicals. The sensitive paper, with the tracing above it in direct contact, is fed into an Ozalid machine (Fig. 8-35) and exposed to ultraviolet light for a controlled amount of time. The pencil

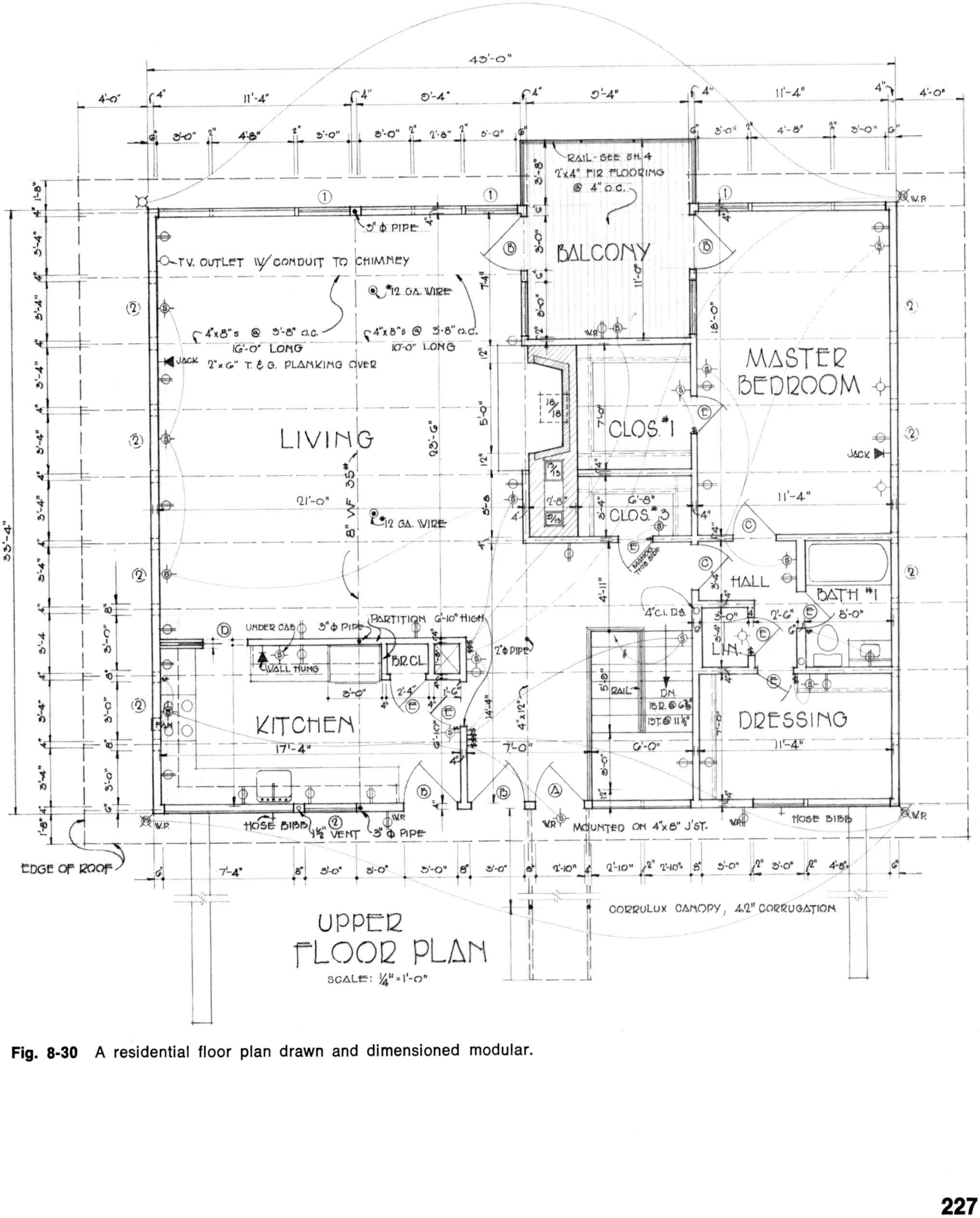

Fig. 8-30 A residential floor plan drawn and dimensioned modular.

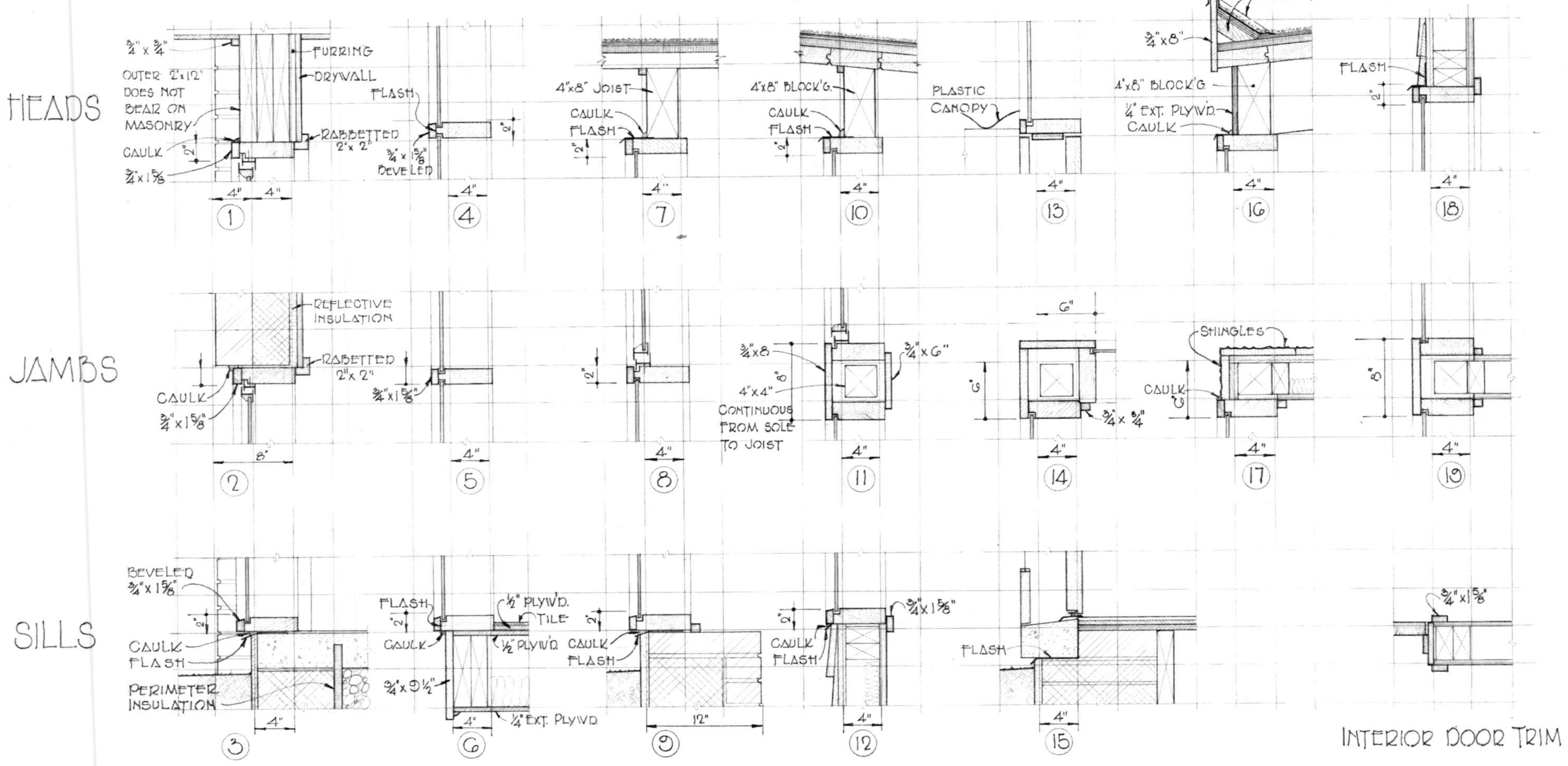

Fig. 8-31 Modular residential details.

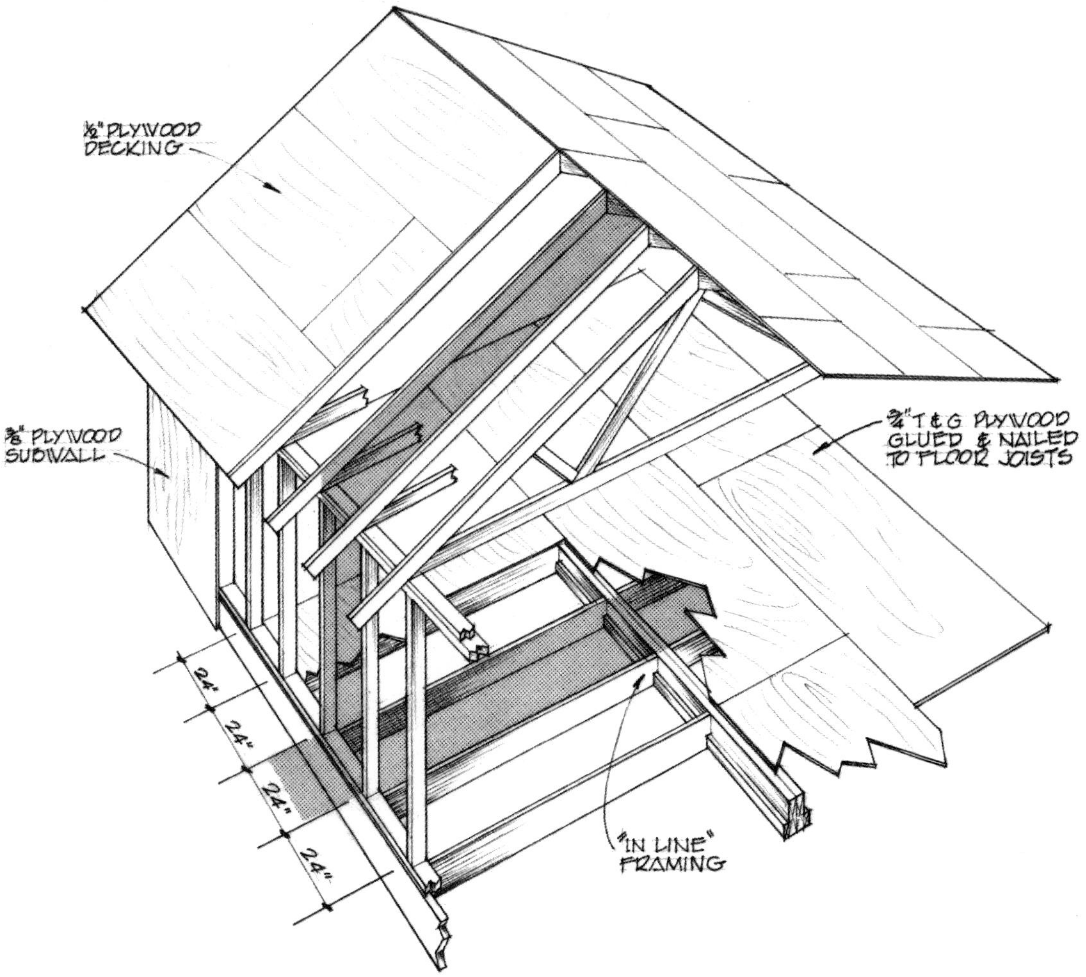

Fig. 8-32 MOD 24, an economical modular framing system for light construction developed jointly by American Plywood Association, Western Wood Products Association, and Southern Forest Products Association.

Fig. 8-33 Suggested modular materials in metric measure.

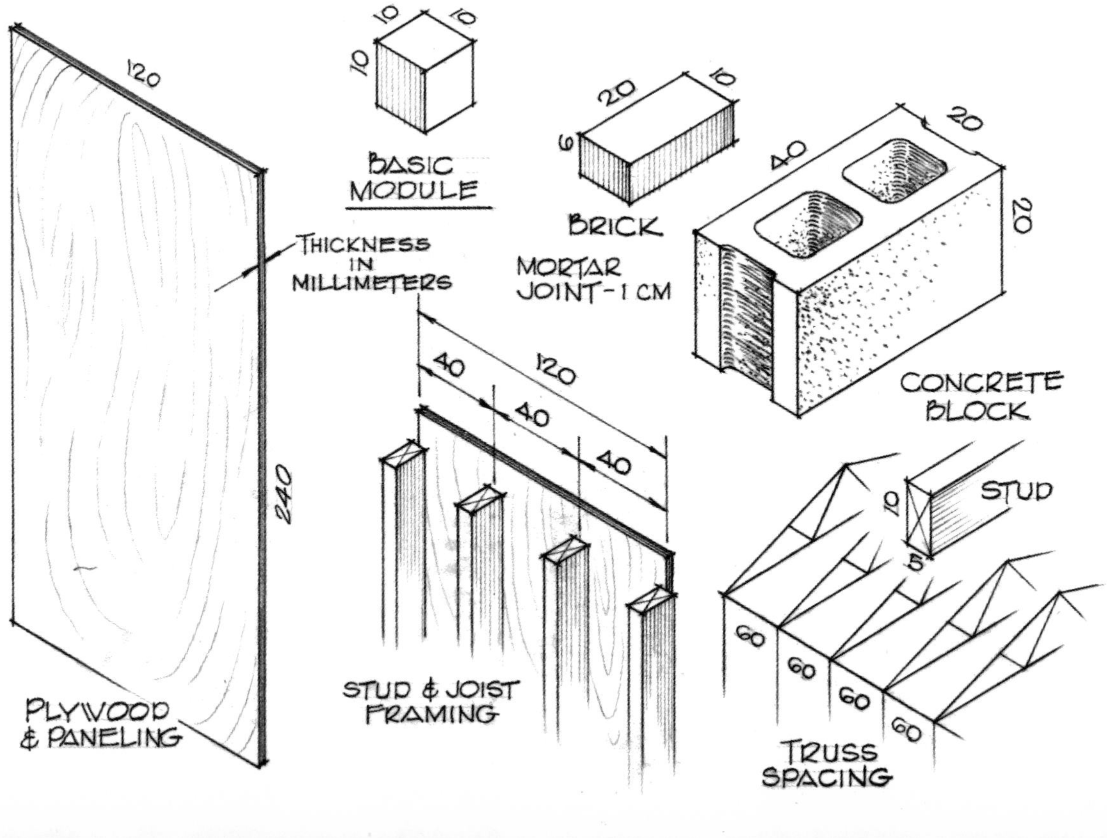

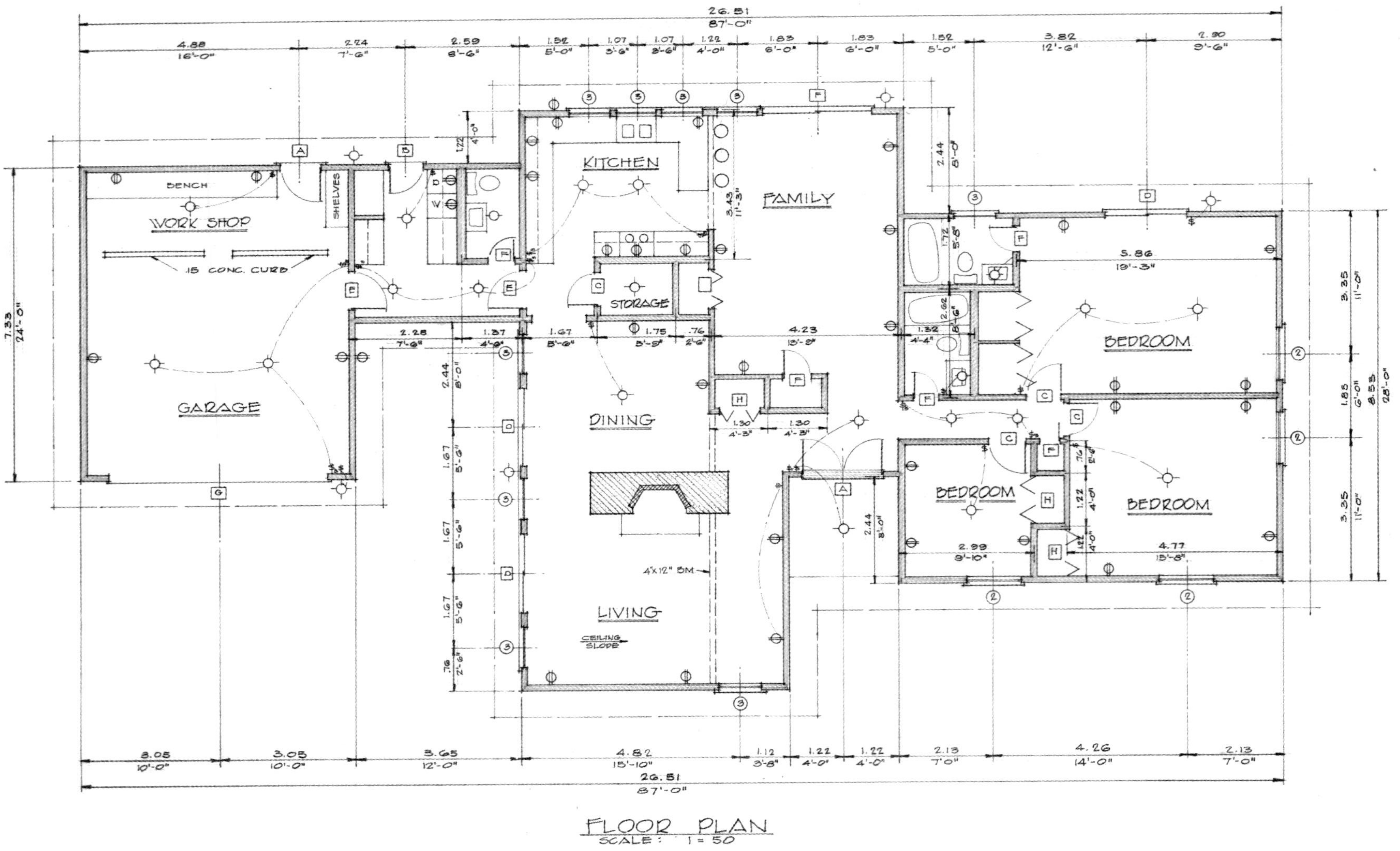

Fig. 8-34 Metric dimensions. Although no standards for metric dimensioning have been yet adopted, one method for converting may be used as shown. The metric dimension is placed above the line and the English units below.

or ink lines of the tracing prevent exposure of the chemical directly below; while the translucent areas are completely exposed. After the exposure, the sensitized paper only is again fed into a dry developer, utilizing ammonia vapors, which turn the background of the print white and the lines either blue, black, or sepia, depending upon which type of paper has been selected. Dry development does not shrink the paper and change the scale of the drawing. The white background of Ozalid prints also allows changes or notes to be added, if necessary, directly on the paper with ordinary pencils.

Blueprints This process has been used extensively for many years as the conventional method of producing prints of all types of technical drawings. The blue nature of the prints has given rise to the common term "blueprints." These prints are made by exposing sensitized paper and tracing paper, in direct contact, in a blueprint machine. They are exposed to ultraviolet light similar to that of the Ozalid machine for a controlled amount of time (the sun could also be used as a light source). The exposure is followed by a fixing bath of potassium bichromate and water, followed by a bath of clear water, which turns the background of the sensitized paper dark blue and the linework white. After the baths, the print must be dried. If a reverse color print is desired, a "Vandyke" paper can be used as an intermediate print. The Vandyke then serves as a negative; it is made from the original tracing and appears dark brown. This negative can be used to make positive, white-background-and-blue-line prints. Both blueprints and Ozalid prints will gradually deteriorate in color if continually left in open sunlight.

Fig. 8-35 A floor model machine for reproducing working drawings.

Photostat Reproductions If it becomes necessary to change the size of a drawing, enlargements or reductions can be made photographically. A large, specially designed camera is used to change the size of drawings made on either tracing paper or regular paper. The direct print has white lines and a black background. This print can be photostated again to produce a positive with black lines and a white background. The process is more expensive than Ozalid or blueprint methods, but the prints are more permanent in nature.

Photocopy Prints A number of manufacturers have photocopy equipment on the market for duplicating drawings. Light-sensitive paper of limited sizes produces prints of high contrast; however, various pencil tones are not clearly defined.

REVIEW QUESTIONS

1. What do we mean by "contrast" in linework?

2. How may broken lines be varied to represent various features on a drawing?

3. What is a typical architectural characteristic of line intersections at corners?

4. From what directions on a drawing are dimensions made to read?

5. Why is a series of dimensions best placed along a continuous line on a floor plan?

6. What is the conventional method of expressing architectural measurement with numbers?

7. Why are the basic structural features of a plan the first dimensions to be given consideration?

8. Why is it preferable to use only those abbreviations that have been standardized and commonly accepted?

9. What is the advantage of using a schedule when considerable information is involved?

10. Describe "modular coordination."

"The better part of every man's education is that which he gives himself."
—Lowell

9

Typical Architectural Details

The word "details" covers the broad category of isolated and enlarged drawings which, together with the plans and elevations, form the complete set of working drawings. Each detail furnishes specific information at key points throughout the construction. Almost every set of drawings requires a different set of details, the choice of which is determined by the architect or draftsman. Only a few standard details may be necessary, however, on drawings of modest structures incorporating conventional construction. In fact, some sets of drawings contain very few details, allowing the builders considerable latitude in the choice of construction, whereas other sets contain details for almost every construction arrangement in the building.

This chapter will be limited to the basic general details found in average residential and light-construction sets of drawings. Other minor details will be discussed in Chapter 10.

9.1 SELECTING THE CORRECT SCALE OF DETAILS

Before starting a detail drawing, take a minute or two to decide upon the most appropriate scale. Suitable scale depends upon the size of members in the detail, the amount of detail that must be shown, as well as the space available in the layout of the sheet; all these factors must be considered. Plan the sheets so that details are placed for their most logical association with other drawings and that all sheets of a set are utilized for economy as well as appearance. Scales for details range from ½″ = 1′–0″ to full size. Small pieces, such as moldings, are usually drawn full size to show clearly profiles and small detail. Larger members or assemblies can be drawn at smaller scales. It is worth noting that the preferable larger scales can be used in minimum spaces if "break symbols" are employed to remove unimportant areas of long members. This method of condensing details to show only the significant points is common practice in architectural drawings since many members are necessarily large, and reducing the scale would only make smaller pieces difficult to show. However, if space permits, the true heights and lengths of important members of a detail are definitely more informative to workmen. Break symbols should be resorted to only when limited space prevents drawing the entire detail.

The choice of scale may also be affected by the units in the detail. For example, if concrete block coursing is used, by selecting the ¾″ = 1′–0″ scale, the 8″ coursing can be easily layed out with the ½″ = 1′–0″ architects' scale.

9.2 DRAWING TYPICAL WALL DETAILS

If the construction of a house is identical throughout all the exterior walls, only one wall section may be necessary; if the construction varies, several sections should be drawn. A typical wall section conveniently incorporates the *footing detail, sill detail,* and *cornice detail*—all properly in line for relative reference (see Figs. 9-1, 9-2, and 9-3).

To draw a wall section, start with the poured footing (usually twice as wide and the same height as the thickness of the foundation wall), and center the foundation wall directly above. If footing depths vary below grade, and even if a basement is required, the foundation wall can be drawn with a break symbol, and only a convenient amount of the wall need be shown.

The construction at the top of the foundation, known as the sill detail, is important, and various arrangements of the framing members at this point determine the height of the finished floor from grade. If the foundation is concrete block, show the courses and insert an anchor bolt through the sill plate into the block wall. Wood members should be kept at least 8″ from grade, and wherever applicable, metal termite shields should be shown between the wood and masonry surfaces. If a wood floor over a crawl space has been decided upon, allow at least 18″ clearance between floor joists and the grade line. This condition usually places the finished floor at least 28″ or 30″ above grade (unless excavation is done within the foundation). Exterior steps to the floor surface, of course, will then be necessary. If a basement is planned, such as in house No. 1 of Fig. 10-3, the foundation must extend far enough above grade to meet local codes and to allow installation of basement windows. If slab-on-ground construction is required, the finish-floor level will usually fall about 8″ above the grade level, requiring one step height for entry. Other variations of the sill detail may result in still other floor heights; usually, it is advantageous to keep the house as low as possible. Draw the grade line after the sill is completed. Be sure the wood joists have at least 3″ bearing surface on the sill plate. In western frame construction, the box sill requires the soleplate and studs to be placed over the subfloor.

In brick-veneer construction, a better sill detail results if the brick starts at, or just below, grade and the wood plate is raised above the bottom of the veneer-and-frame air space (see Fig. 9-2B). This prevents moisture, which usually forms at the bottom of the air space during cold weather, from penetrating the wood framing. Otherwise, the wood members are identical to frame construction. Brick sills (Figs. 9-4F and 9-5) must have flashing below.

In solid-masonry construction, several methods can be used to support wood floor joists. A diagonal "fire cut" can be used at the ends of the floor joists resting within the solid masonry walls (see Fig. 9-4D). Or, the masonry wall can be widened to provide bearing for the floor joists.

The cornice detail shows all the construction at the intersection of the walls and the roof, including the roof overhang. In conventional frame construction, both the notched bird's-mouth of the rafters and the ceiling joists bear on the double wall plate, and the joists usually are shown parallel to the rafters. A bird's-mouth

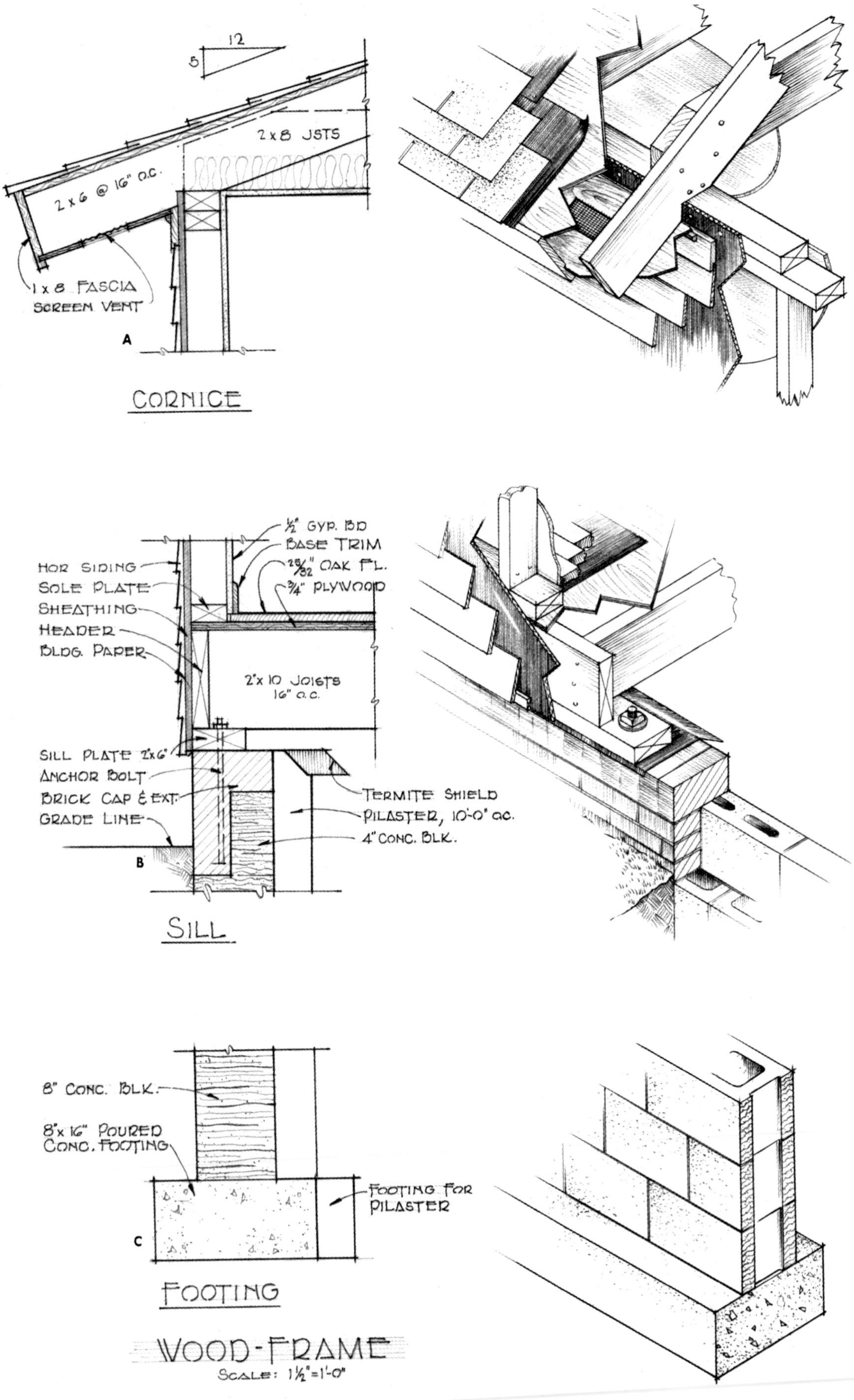

Fig. 9-1 Typical wall details (the isometric views help to visualize the construction).

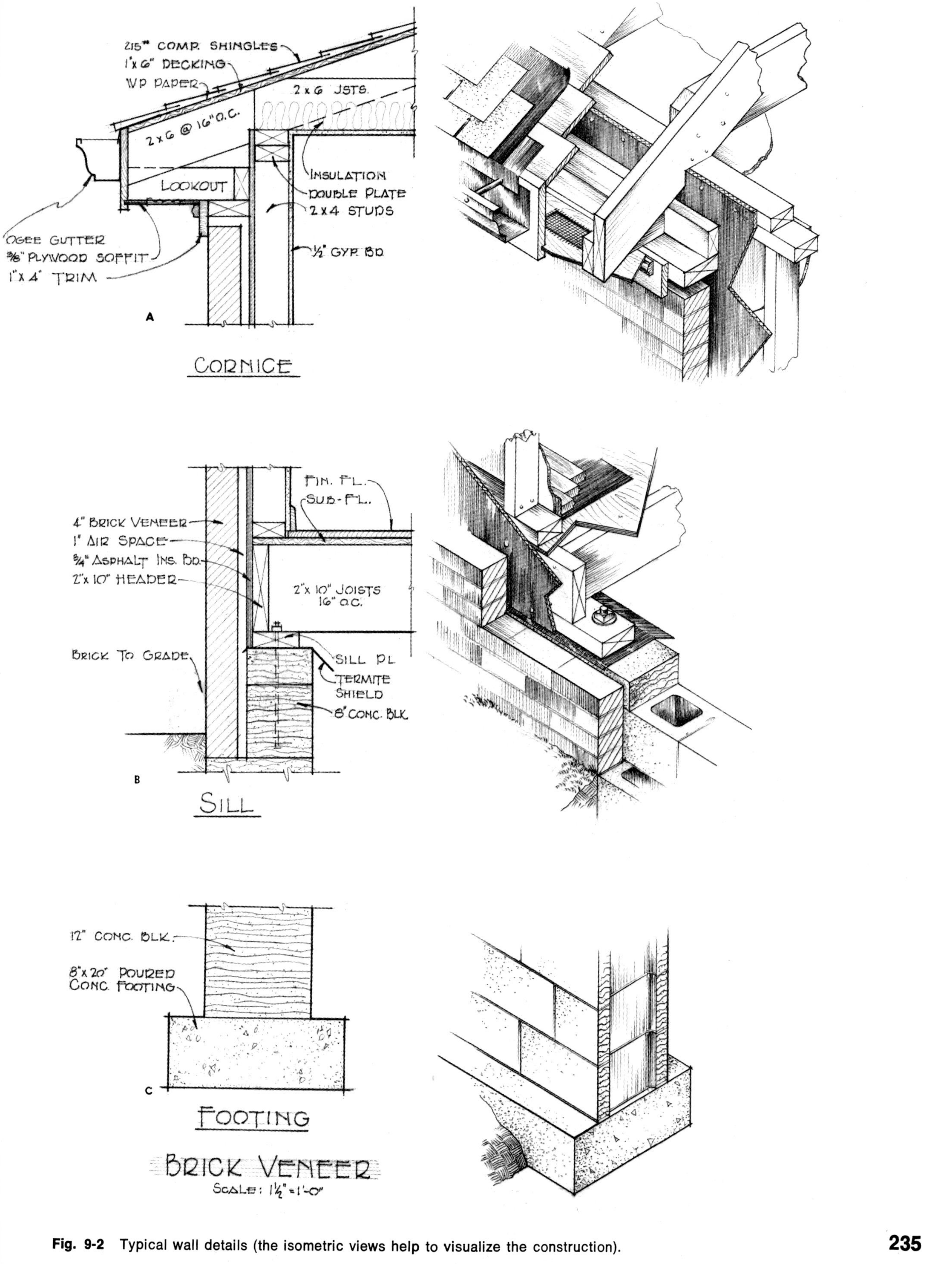

Fig. 9-2 Typical wall details (the isometric views help to visualize the construction).

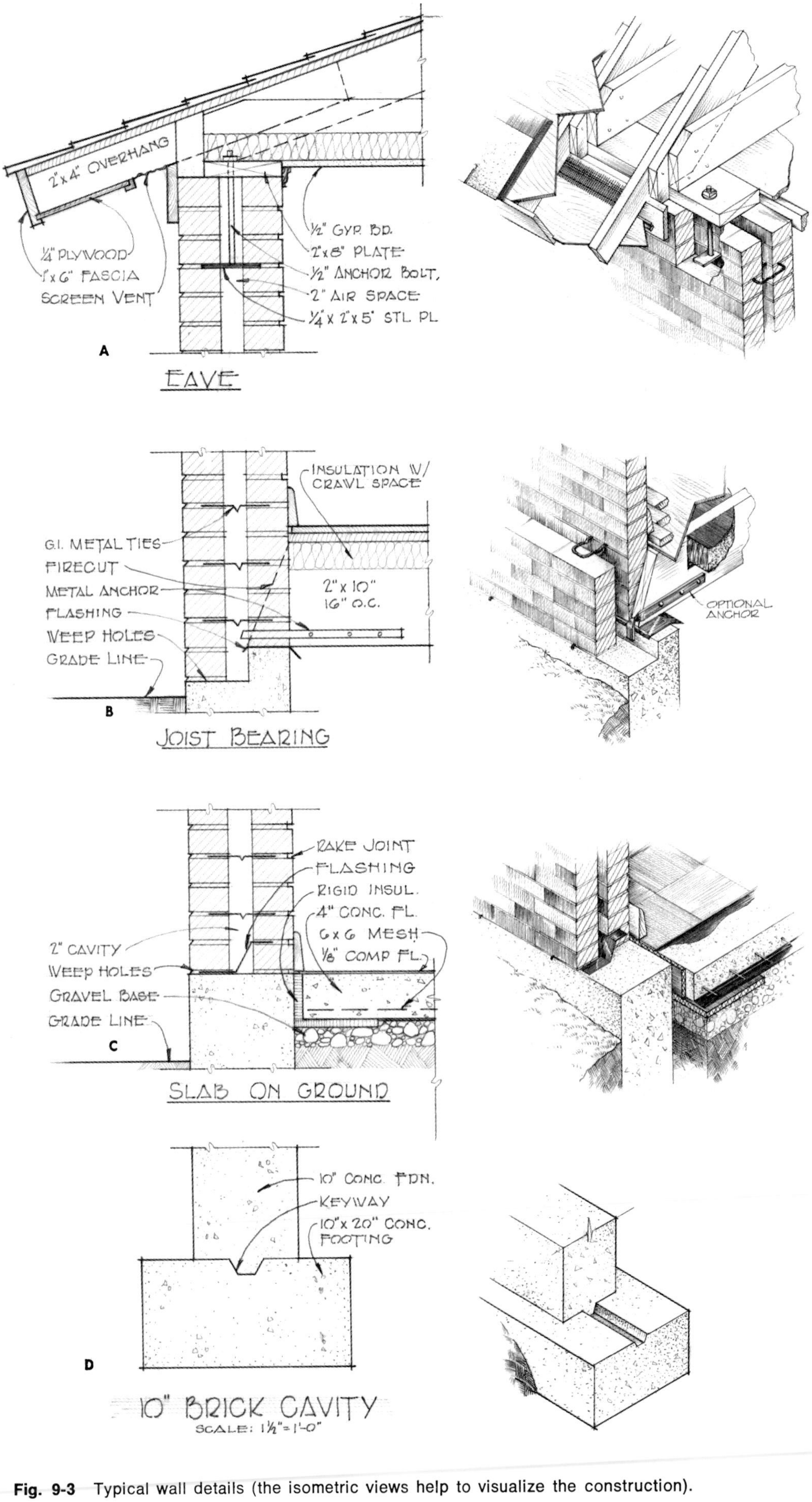

Fig. 9-3 Typical wall details (the isometric views help to visualize the construction).

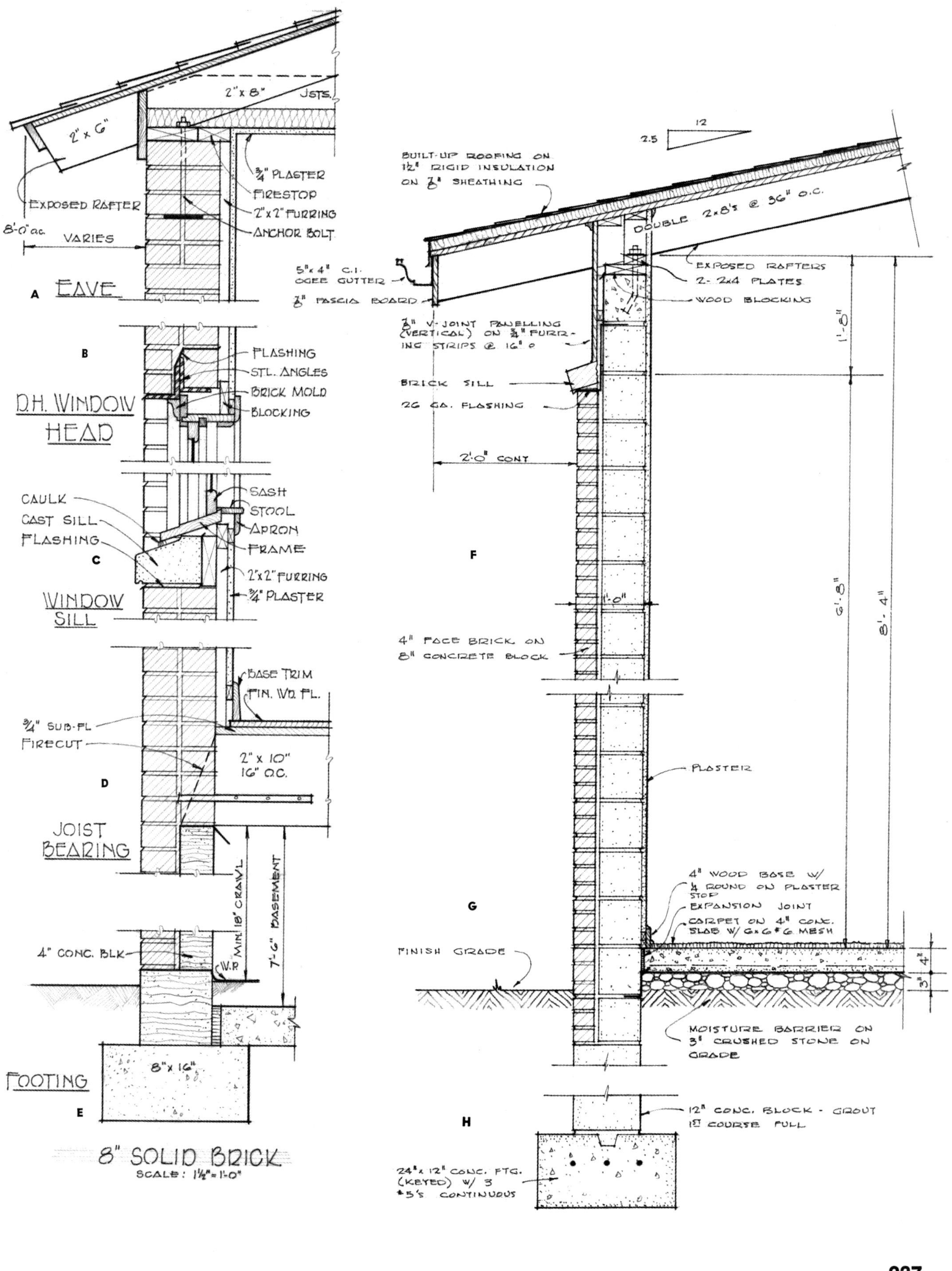

Fig. 9-4 Typical wall details.

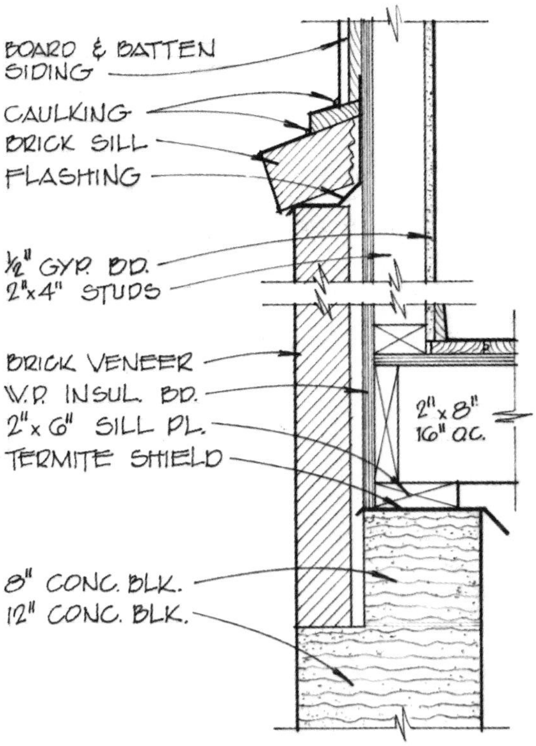

Fig. 9-5 Wood and brick half-wall detail.

cut provides a horizontal bearing surface for the rafters, and because it supports the main weight of the roof, the surface should be a minimum of 3″ wide. **Remember that members in details should be drawn *actual size rather than nominal size.***

Extend the rafters to form the overhang (often at least 2′ on ranch-type homes). The overhang can be given various treatments, depending upon the decisions made on the design sketches. If a wide, boxed-in cornice seems advisable, draw 2″ × 4″ horizontal outlookers from the studs to the rafter ends (Fig. 9-2A). Attach soffit material to the underside of the outlookers, and show a screened vent under the eave when applicable. At the ends of the rafters, draw either a vertical or inclined fascia board, making it wide enough to allow about a 3/4″ drip below the surface of the soffit material. If a sloping soffit is desirable, the soffit material is attached directly to the underside of the rafter overhang; on other treatments, the rafters can be left exposed on the exterior. Cornice details showing exposed rafters, either in conventional or post-and-beam construction, must have blocking and exterior wall covering shown between the rafters. This detail must be carefully conceived to produce an airtight joint between the wall and the underside of the roof decking; exterior trim at this point also requires consideration.

Complete the decking, roofing material, gravel stops, gutter, etc., and include all hatching, notes, and applicable dimensions. Avoid scattering descriptive notes on section views in a disorderly fashion. Plan the notes in a logical sequence with noncrossing leaders touching the identifying part. Line up the notes on a vertical guide line insofar as possible, and make the spacing between notes uniform when they occur in groups. Keep the notes as close to their counterparts as practical for minimum misinterpretation. Outline the section with *bold lines.* See Fig. 9-6 for cutting plane indications. Roof slopes, as discussed below, should be indicated with a roof-slope diagram.

9.3 INDICATING ROOF PITCHES ON DRAWINGS

The slope of a roof largely determines the kind of roofing; this in turn influences preliminary planning when pleasing roof lines have

Fig. 9-6 Methods of indicating cutting planes for sections.

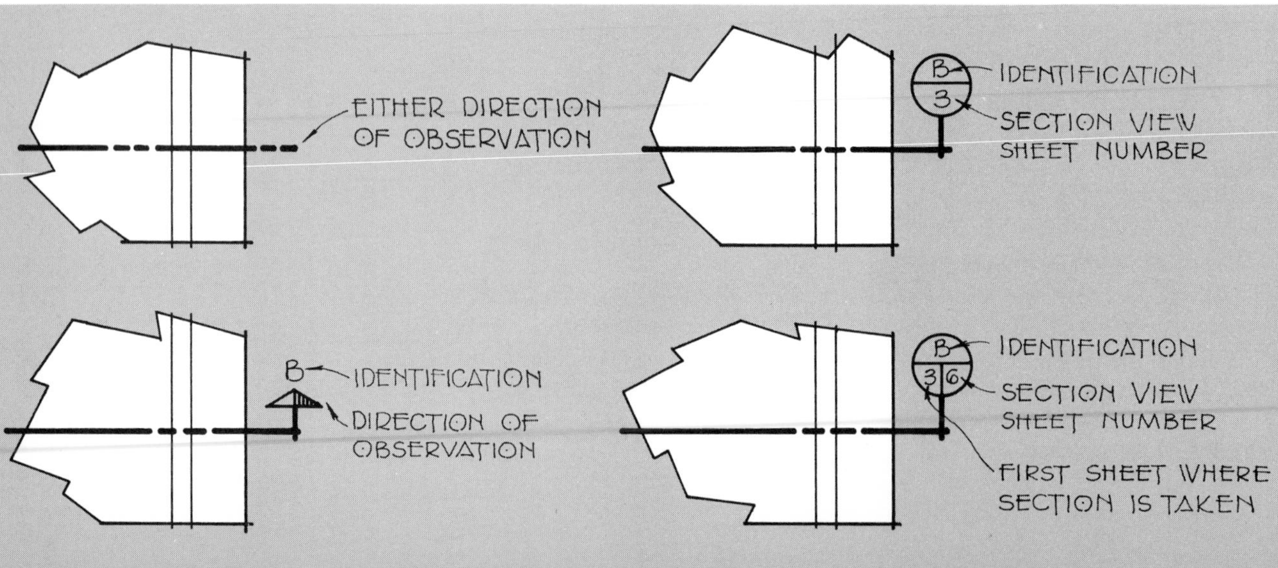

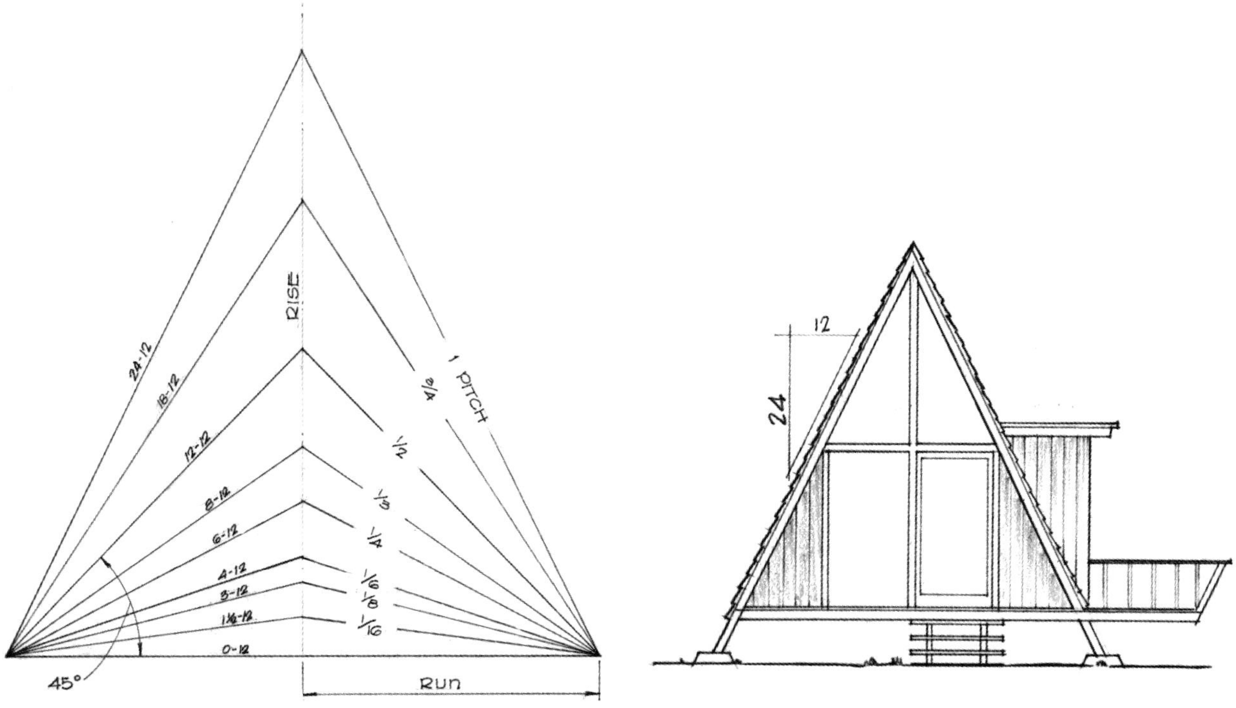

Fig. 9-7 Typical roof slopes.

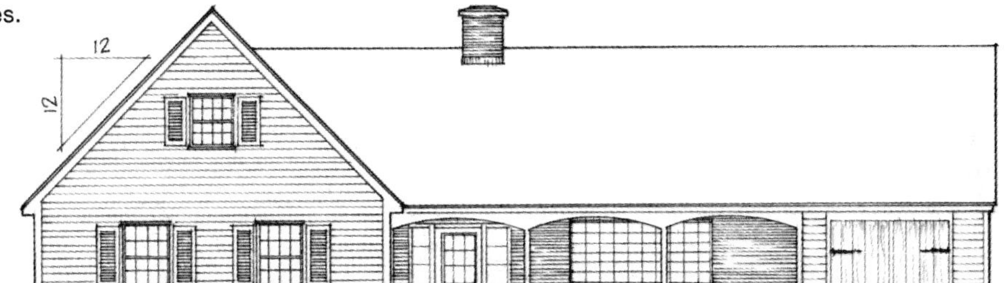

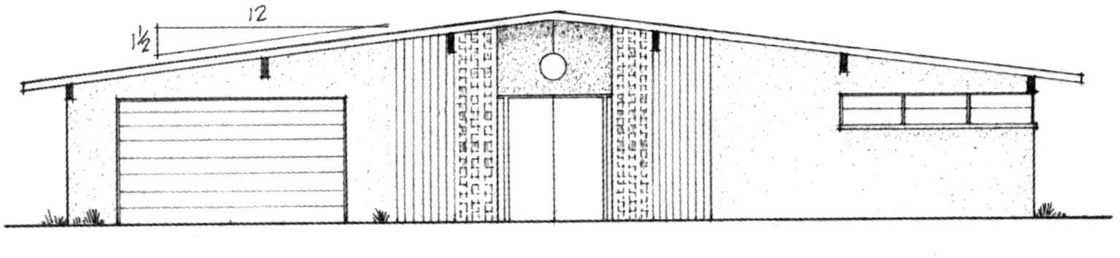

been established. Although any slope can be made workable, it is advisable to modify the roof lines of the sketch slightly if necessary so that the working drawings will have roof slopes that are not too difficult to measure. This affects the appearance very little and makes the construction of the roof somewhat simpler (see Fig. 9-7 for typical roof slopes).

Roof slopes or pitches can be shown by any of three methods on drawings:

1. A slope-ratio diagram;
2. A fractional pitch indication; or
3. An angular dimension.

The slope-ratio triangle is drawn with its hypotenuse parallel to the roof profile; and its opposite sides, representing the rise and run slope ratio, are drawn vertically and horizontally. The horizontal leg of the triangle is usually measured 1″ long for convenience and given a numerical value of 12. The rise value shown on the vertical leg of the triangle can then be easily measured off on the 1″ = 1′–0″ scale. This ratio of the rise of the roof to its run is stated, as for example, 3 : 12, 7 : 12, 1½ : 12, etc., making it consistent with conventional references associated with roofing materials and other construction applications. In Fig. 9-8 the 4 : 12 right triangle symbol

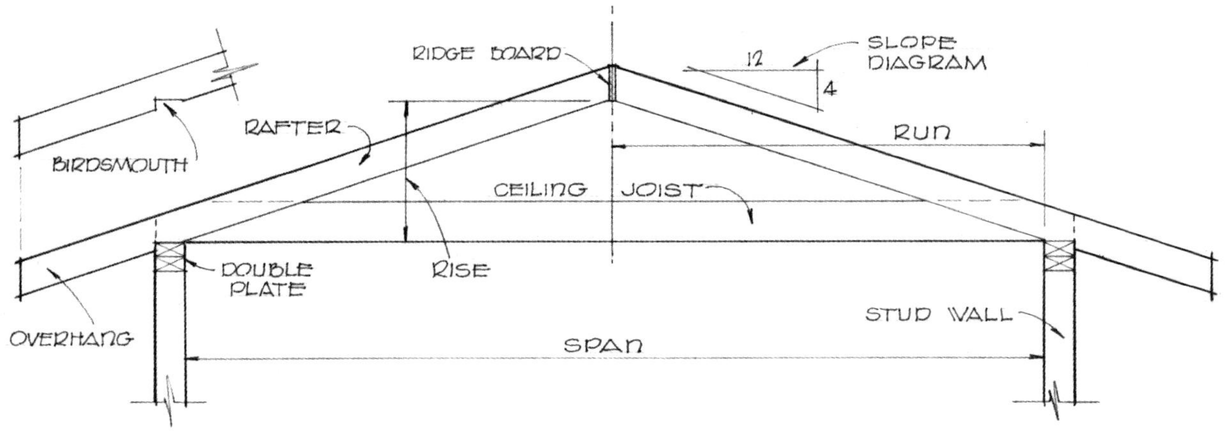

Fig. 9-8 Roof slope and framing terms.

means, briefly, that for every 12″ of horizontal run, the roof rises 4″. Most architects use this method for slope indications.

The fractional pitch of a roof is derived from the standard formula:

$$\text{Pitch} = \frac{\text{Rise}}{\text{Span}},$$

the span being total distance between top-plate supports (twice the run). The pitch of the roof in Fig. 9-8 would be $\frac{4}{24}$ or $\frac{1}{6}$. Fractional pitches are infrequently found on working drawings; yet carpenters have traditionally used fractional pitches for many of their rafter layouts.

Angular slopes are shown with an arc dimension line, revealing the angular dimension in degrees from the horizontal (Fig. 9-7). Its use is limited mainly to minor construction features.

9.4 WINDOWS AND THEIR REPRESENTATION

Windows provide, first of all, the light and ventilation necessary in dwellings; they are the eyes through which the surrounding landscape can be enjoyed, bringing in the outdoors to make the interior more spacious and less confined. Windows, then, must be carefully selected as to size, type, and placement, if they are to provide the desired architectural character to the structure; both practical and esthetic considerations are important in their selection. As a rule, the total window area should be at least 10 per cent of the floor space.

Glassed areas can be either preassembled window units or "fixed glass," which is directly

Fig. 9-9 Major residential window types. (1) Double-hung; (2) casement; (3) horizontal sliding; (4) awning; (5) jalousie; (6) basement; (7) bow or bay; (8) hopper and fixed; and (9) skylight.

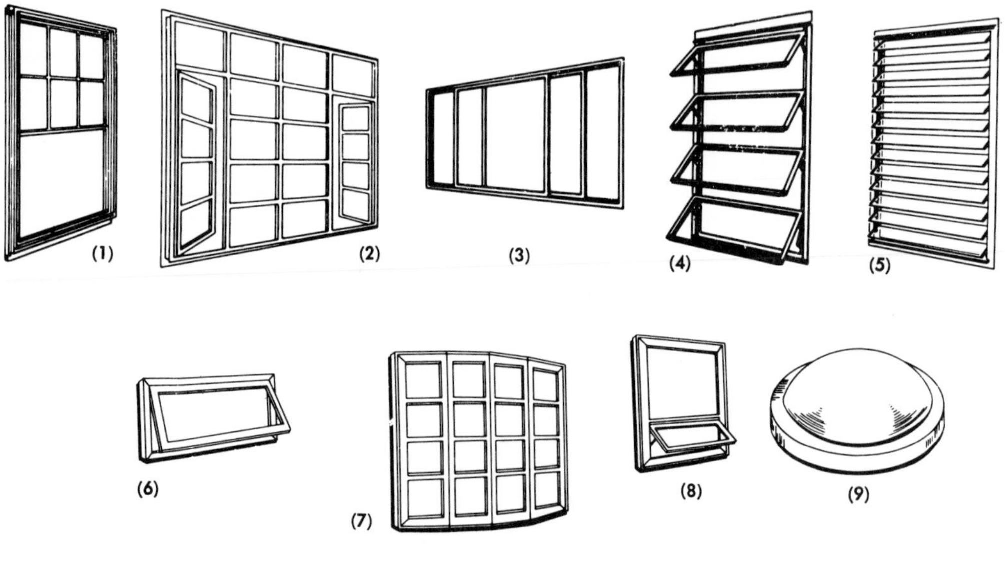

affixed to the framing. The fixed glass allows large window areas to be installed with a minimum of expense, inasmuch as no operating sash, hardware, or screens are necessary. If ventilation is needed, occasional opening sash or panels can be incorporated into window-walls. Today's market offers a wide assortment of preassembled window units; most of them are made of wood, aluminum, or steel. Each material has its merits; their choice should be contingent upon the specific requirements of the design. Units should be selected for appropriateness, durability, and ease of maintenance. Many units are manufactured with insulating (double) glass. This type has the advantage of reducing heat loss (up to 60 per cent over single-glass units); in addition, no damaging condensation can form on the inside pane. Tinted glass is also obtainable. Figure 9-9 shows the major types of window units currently used in residential construction.

Double-Hung or vertical-slide, windows are the most familiar, having two sash that operate vertically. A double-hung window allows a maximum of 50 per cent ventilation and is typically American. The unit, including the two sash, frame, weather stripping, and hardware, is set into the rough opening, plumbed, and nailed to the double studs and header. Inside trim is applied after the interior walls are complete. If units are combined into groups, a structural mullion is shown between the units. The sloping sill member rests on the lower member of the rough opening (see Fig. 9-10).

Casement windows have their sash hinged on the side. Most of them open out, but some are available that open in. Casement sash have the advantage of directing breezes into the room when open, and 100 per cent ventilation is possible. Operating cranks open and close the sash.

Horizontal Sliding windows operate horizontally like sliding doors. Horizontal slide windows, like double-hung windows, allow only 50 per cent ventilation when open. Units are often combined with fixed picture-window sash.

Awning windows open out horizontally, with the hinges of each sash at the top and the cranking hardware operating all the sash in each unit simultaneously. Their major advantage is that they can be left open during rain without adverse effects. Dust collects on the opened windows readily, however.

Jalousie window units have small, horizontal glass panels that operate horizontally, much like awning sash. The individual glass panels do not have frames. The advantages are similar to those of awning windows, except that jalousie windows are seldom as weathertight when closed. Therefore, they should be reserved mainly for glass-enclosed porches or for residences in warmer climates.

Hopper windows have small sash, opening either in or out, which are combined with larger fixed windows. The complete unit is set into the rough opening like other window units.

Skylights are actually roof windows that can be placed over openings in roofs of little or no slope and sealed into the roofing material. Residential skylights are usually "bubble"-shaped plastic units with flanges or sealing rims around the base (see Fig. 9-9). Small skylights are convenient for giving natural light to interior hallways or windowless bathrooms. However, in warm climates the direct glare of the sun through a skylight can be troublesome unless some manner of light control is provided. Caution should be exercised in the use of skylights on roofs.

Clerestory windows are so named because of their placement—usually high in a wall above a lower roof level. They are often a series of small windows; their height affords privacy and permits them to cast dramatic light effects within the room.

Picture Windows so called because usually no muntins interfere with the "framed" view, are fixed-glass units (as a rule rather large), which often become the center unit of several regular windows.

Study the many manufacturers' catalogues for more detailed information of various windows and observe the recommended method of attaching each in different wall openings (see Fig. 9-11). Notice that window sizes and the *rough-opening* sizes are given in the literature. This information is important to the builders. "Rough opening" means the width and height of the framed opening that receives the window unit. In Fig. 9-10 note the method of framing window openings in wood frame construction. As mentioned previously, the units are supported by the wood framing, and the section views reveal the relationship of the unit to the framing, how they are attached, and what trim is necessary for completion. These details

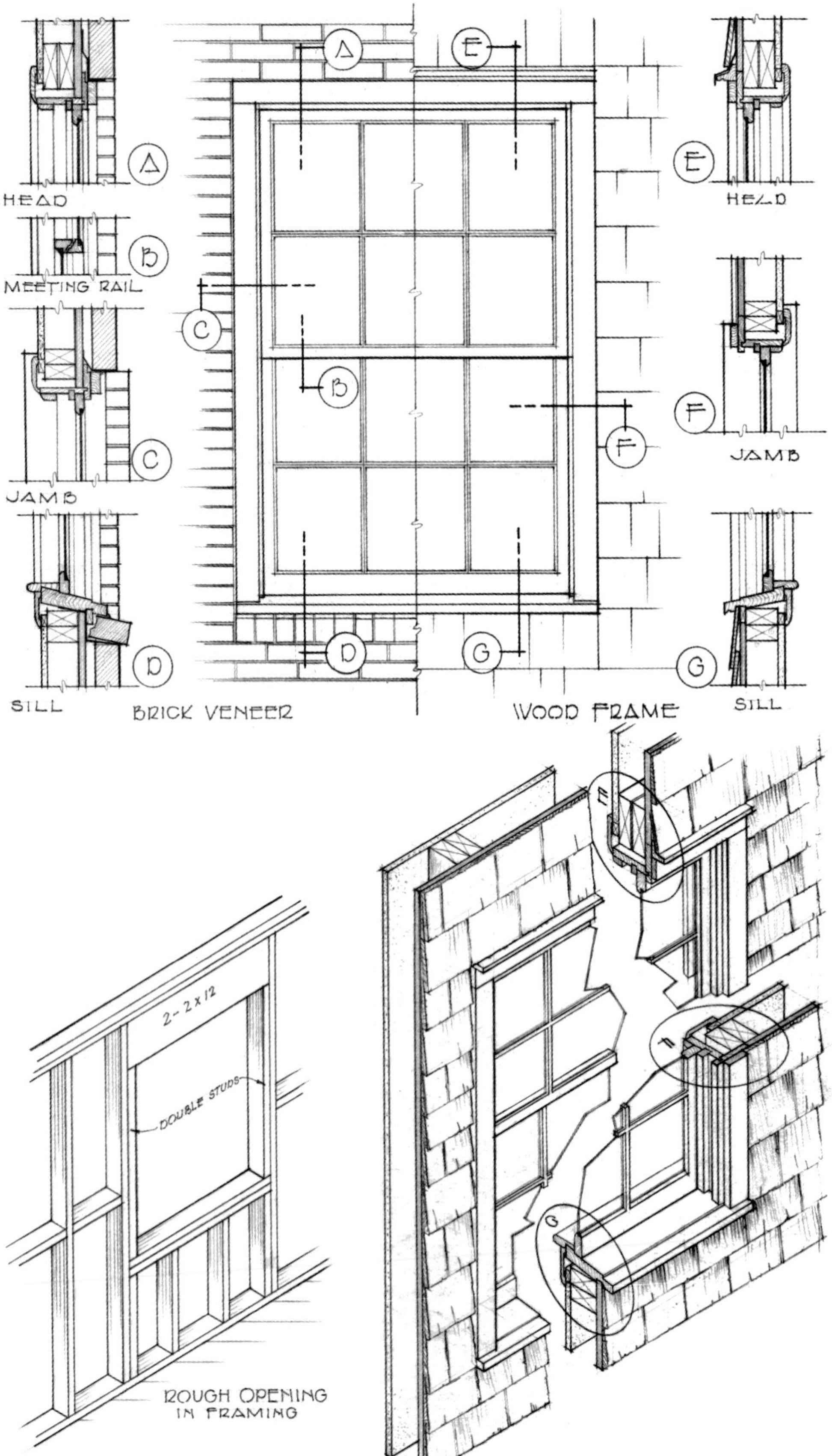

Fig. 9-10 Typical sections of a double-hung window.

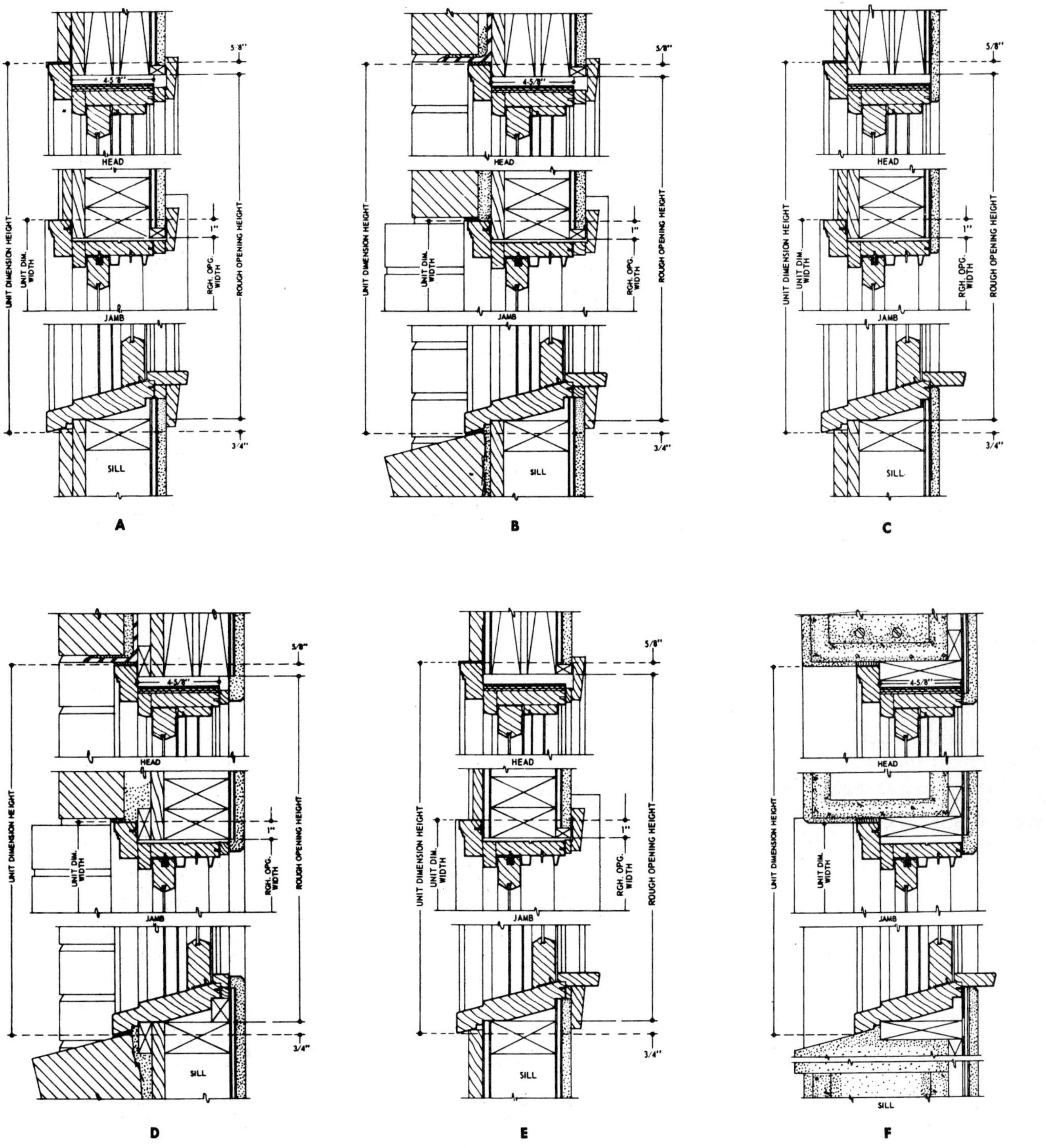

Fig. 9-11 Double-hung window details in various walls.

should be shown on working drawings for proper installation of the windows.

To better understand the **details of a double-hung window**, observe the cutting planes shown on the elevation view of Fig. 9-10. The head, jamb, and sill sections to the left of the elevation clearly explain these important points in the construction. A meeting rail section is also shown merely to familiarize you with the relationship of the two sashes. Note that, for more information, the right side of the elevation appears to be in a brick-veneer wall, and the same sections to the right show typical construction around the double-hung window in brick-veneer construction. The isometric view in Fig. 9-10 describes the pictorial representations of the same head, jamb, and sill sections in wood frame. Study these details carefully. Similar sections of a metal window are shown in Fig. 9-12. Details of windows vary with different manufacturers; therefore, after window selections have been made, details of the windows must be taken from the manufacturers' catalogues.

To draw a window detail, first establish the wood frame members, or the rough openings of masonry, if the window is to go into solid masonry. Use large scales such as 3″ = 1′–0″ or 1½″ = 1′–0″, if small members are present in the section. Then, draw the sheathing and inside wall covering. Next, locate the window frame in relation to the rough-opening surface, and complete the sash, trim, and exterior wall covering. Use the conventional break symbol so that only the necessary amount of detail need be drawn. Be sure that the structural members line up vertically and that the head section is drawn at the top, the jamb in the center, and the sill section at the bottom.

Fig. 9-12 Fixed-glass and metal window detail.

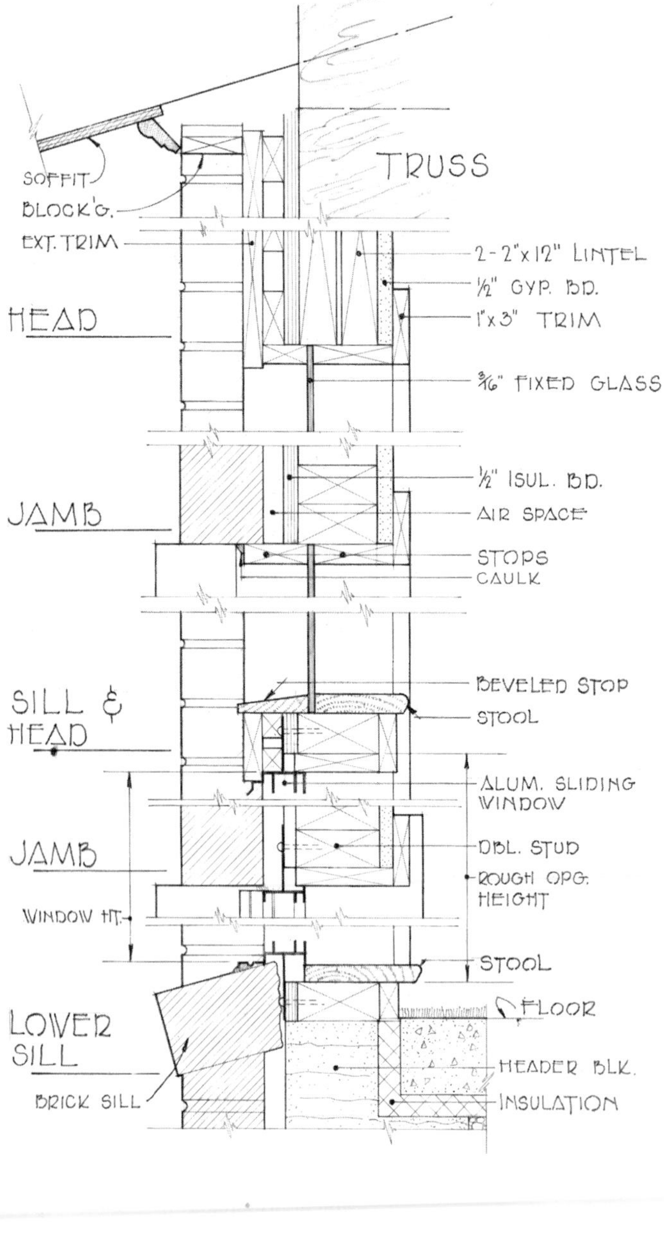

9.5 DOORS AND THEIR REPRESENTATION

Because of their economy and the wide assortment of available sizes, stock doors are universally used in residential and light construction. Two major types are manufactured—flush and panel (see Fig. 9-13).

Flush Doors are built of solid-wood stiles and rails with various wood veneering glued to both sides, producing smooth, easy-to-paint surfaces. This type is popular in contemporary architecture because of its clean-cut appearance and easy-to-maintain features. Various shaped lights can be introduced to flush doors for lighting dark entrances, and decorative moldings can be applied directly to the plywood surfaces for style treatments. Flush doors can be subdivided into two types—*hollow core* and *solid core*. The hollow core have grillage-filled cavities, making them lighter and ideal for interior use. The solid core have their cavities filled with wood blocking, making them heavier and more appropriate for exterior entrances. The heavier construction reduces warping during extreme temperature differences between inside and outside. Many decorative wood-grain veneers are available on flush doors to match natural-wood

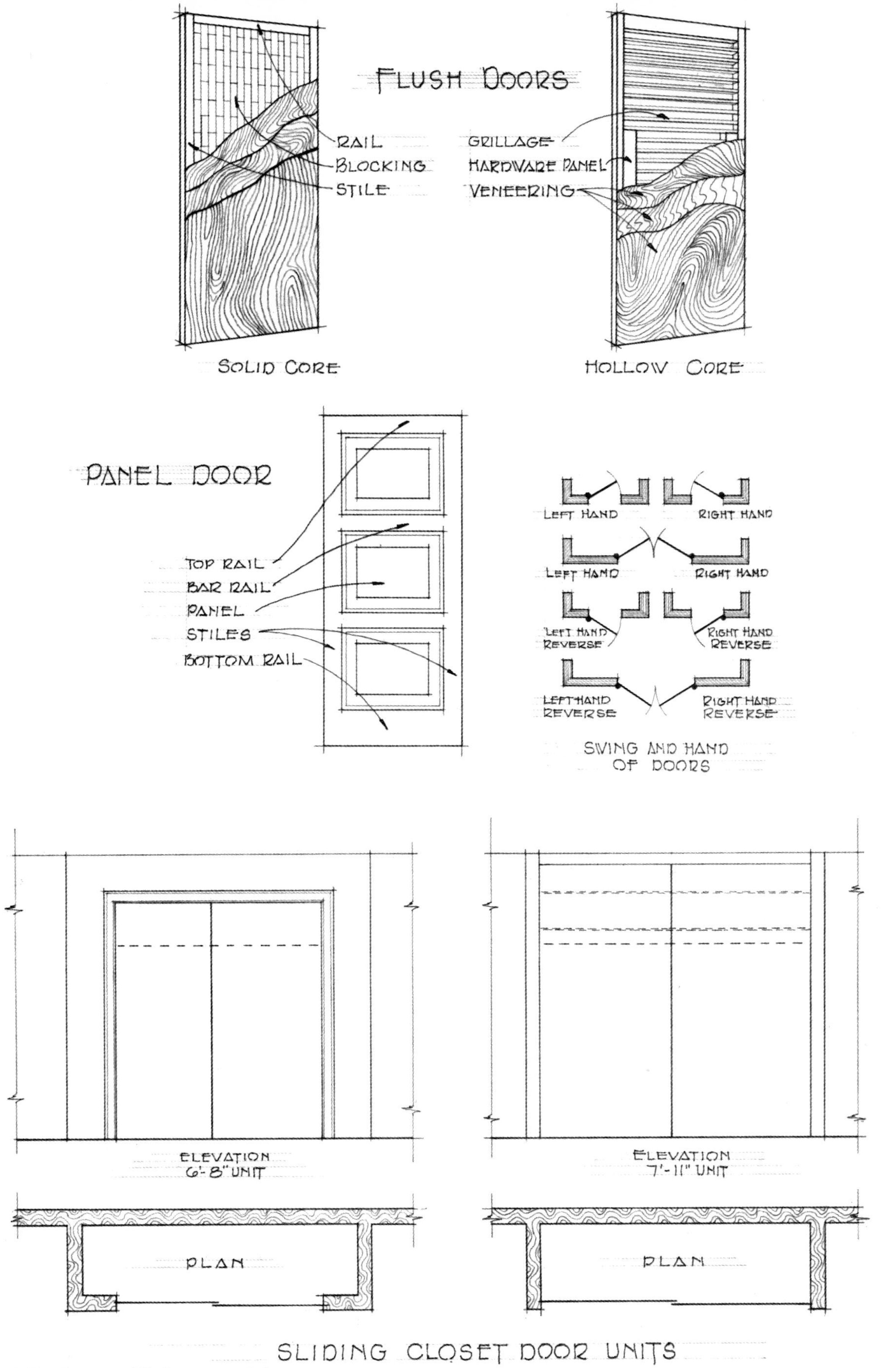

Fig. 9-13 Doors and their representation.

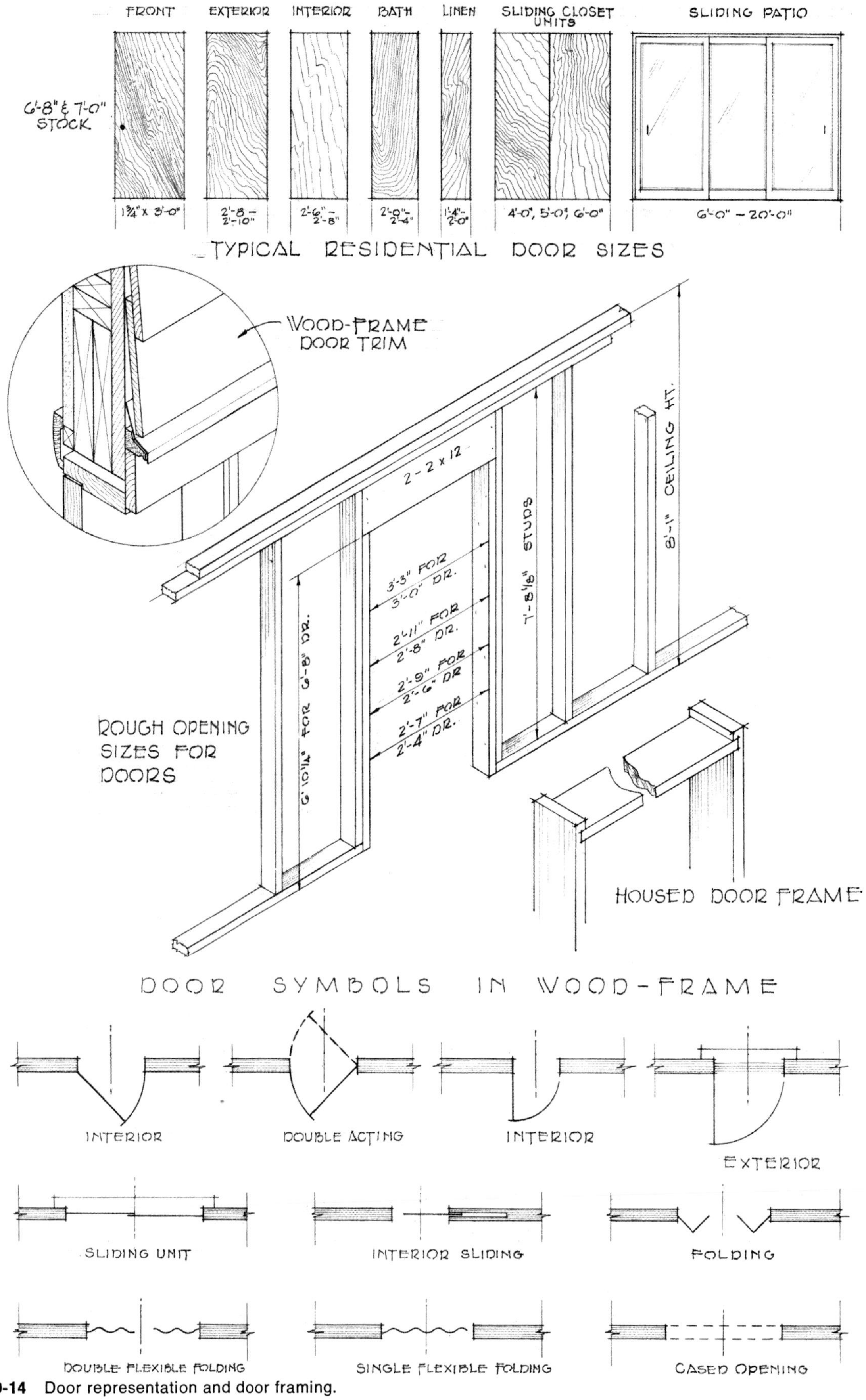

Fig. 9-14 Door representation and door framing.

interior wall coverings. See Fig. 9-14 for typical sizes.

Panel Doors manufactured in a wide variety of styles, are generally made of ponderosa pine or Douglas fir. Various arrangements of the panels and lights are surrounded with stiles and rails, usually of solid wood, to produce handsome and sturdy doors. Panel doors have been used for many years in American homes. Some panel doors are manufactured with glue-and-veneer stiles and rails. They are sometimes preferred for exterior installation. For colonial and traditional homes, panel doors are the most authentic in character. Elaborate panel-door and frame units are available for classic entrances (Fig. 9-15). Variations of the panel door include the following styles:

French Doors having glazed lights separated with muntins throughout, rather than panels. When additional light is needed, or a view is desired between rooms, these doors find application, especially in traditional homes. Often they are used in pairs with an astragal molding between.

Dutch Doors also typical of some colonial styles, are cut in half horizontally, and each half operates on its own set of hinges. The bottom half can act as a gate while the top remains open.

Louver Doors which have horizontal strips placed on the diagonal for vents instead of panels, are attractive in both traditional contemporary settings. They are excellent for closet doors, because of their venting characteristics, but are time-consuming to paint.

Jalousie Doors usually suitable for enclosed porches or exterior doors in warmer climates, have operating glass-panel units inserted within the stiles and rails.

9.5.1 Wood Stock-Door Sizes

Both flush and panel doors are available in $1\frac{3}{8}''$, $1\frac{3}{4}''$, and $2\frac{1}{4}''$ stock thicknesses. Stock heights are 6′–8″ and 7′–0″; narrow doors can be obtained in 6′–6″ heights. Widths are available in 2″ increments, from 1′–6″ to 3′–0″; a few styles are made in 4′–0″ widths. See Fig. 9-14 for the conventional door widths applicable to residential construction.

Fig. 9-15 Details of a traditional entrance.

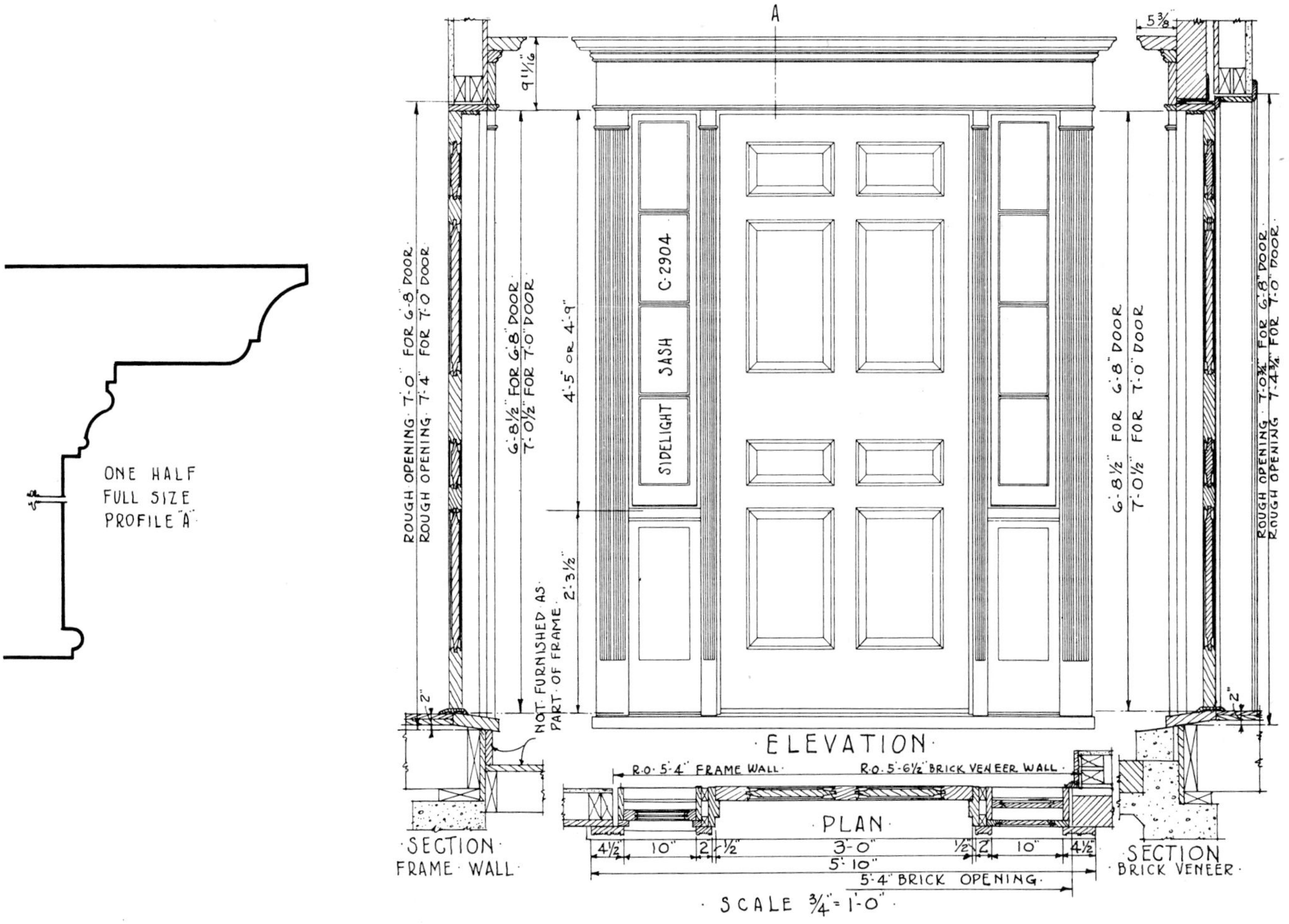

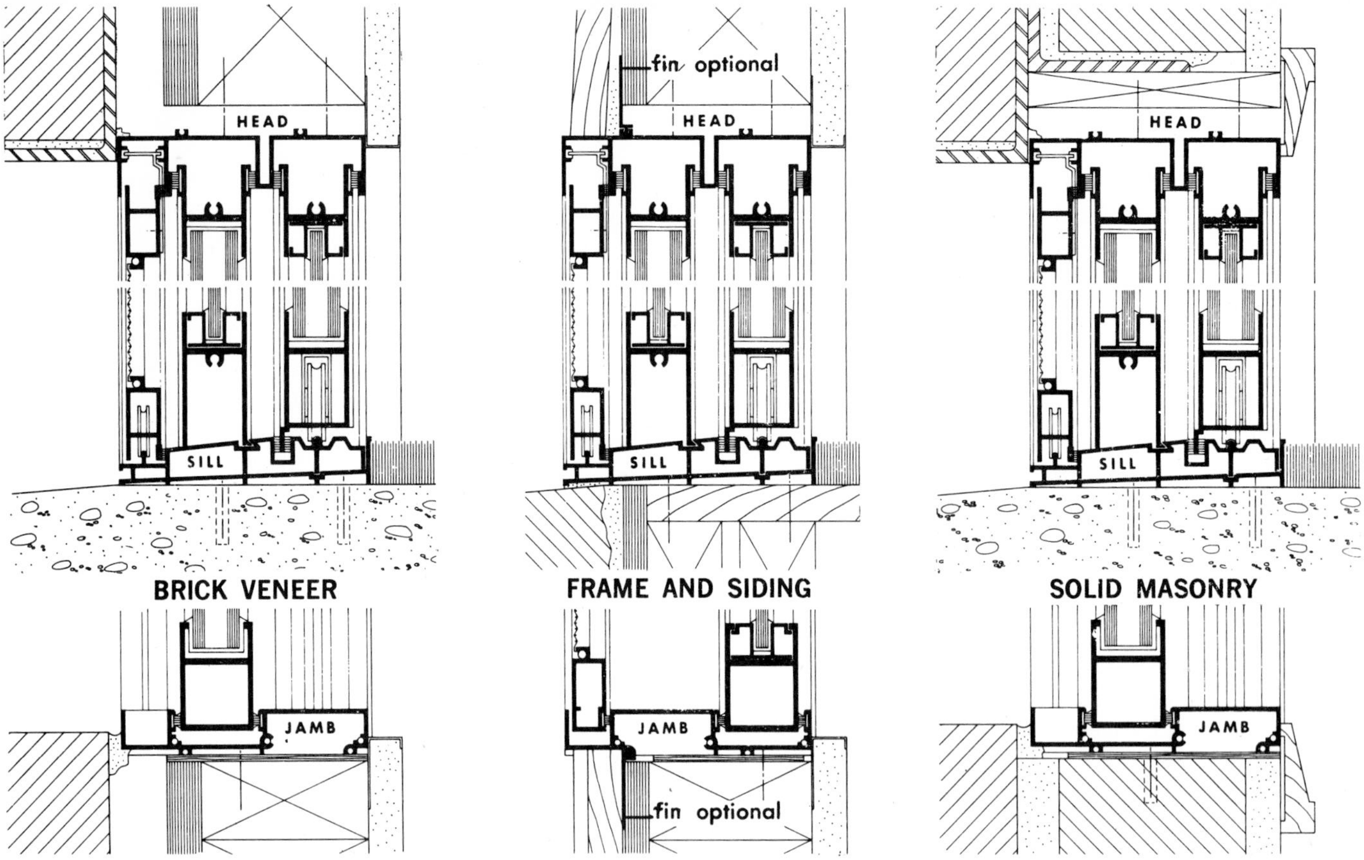

Stock Sizes and Types

Door Types Viewed from exterior	Door Sizes Width	Door Sizes Height	Stock Numbers	Glass Sizes Width only All heights 76¾″	Rough Openings All heights 6′–10½″
XO	5′–11″	6′–10″	G2- 6	33″	5′–11½″
	7′–11″	6′–10″	G2- 8	45″	7′–11½″
	9′–11″	6′–10″	G2-10	57″	9′–11½″
OX	5′–11″	6′–10″	G2- 6	33″	5′–11½″
	7′–11″	6′–10″	G2- 8	45″	7′–11½″
	9′–11″	6′–10″	G2-10	57″	9′–11½″
OXO	8′–10¼″	6′–10″	G3- 9	33″	8′–10¾″
	11′–10¼″	6′–10″	G3-12	45″	11′–10¾″
	14′–10¼″	6′–10″	G3-15	57″	14′–10¾″
OXXO	11′– 8⅞″	6′–10″	G4-12	33″	11′– 9⅜″
	15′– 8⅞″	6′–10″	G4-16	45″	15′– 9⅜″
	19′– 8⅞″	6′–10″	G4-20	57″	19′– 9⅜″

Fig. 9-16 Aluminum sliding glass door details.

9.5.2 Folding or Sliding-Door Units

With the increase in private outdoor living areas, large sliding glass doors have found widespread acceptance. Sliding units are manufactured of aluminum, steel, or wood (see Fig. 9-16). Stock heights are usually 6′–10″, and unit widths, ranging from 6′–0″ to 20′–0″, utilize various sliding and fixed-glass panel arrangements. Like other component sizing indications, door unit widths are given first, such as 8′–0″ × 6′–10″, 12′–0″ × 6′–10″, etc. Exact sizes and specifications should be taken from manufacturers' literature. Because of serious accidents involving large glass doors, many local codes require either tempered glass or protection bars across the doors.

For interior use many types of folding and sliding-door units are appropriate for closet doors and room dividers. Stock sizes conform to the 6′–8″, 7′–0″, and 8′–0″ heights, and custom-built units are available from some manufacturers for special situations. The 8′–0″ high closet-door units (Fig. 9-13) allow an additional amount of accessible storage space in a closet in comparison to lower heights and are highly recommended. Their use reduces the amount of framing around the door as well.

Accordion doors, available in 6′–8″ and 8′–0″ stock heights, and in width ranging from 2′–4″ to 8′–2″, are made of flexible plastic material and require little space at the jambs when open. Distinctive wood folding doors are also made of various wood panels. Sliding closet units come in 3′, 4′, 5′ and 6′ widths.

9.5.3 Fireproof Doors

Flush wood doors filled with heat-resisting materials and treated with fire-resisting chemicals (1 hr fire rating) are available for light construction. Some codes require fireproof doors between the house and attached garages. Many types of metal doors having hollow, grillage-filled, or wood cores are manufactured mainly for commercial and industrial application.

9.5.4 Doorframes

Exterior wood doorframes usually are made and assembled at the mill and delivered to the site, ready for installation into the rough openings. In wood-frame floor construction, the header joist and subflooring below an entrance must be cut out slightly to receive the sloping still member of a doorframe (Fig. 9-15). Frames must be heavy enough to carry the weight of the doors and to take the strain of door closures. Generally, exterior frames are 1¾″ thick, and the sill member is made of hardwood to resist wear. Heavy doors may require thicker jamb members. A planted threshold of either hardwood or metal is necessary to hide the joint between the sill and the finished floor below entrance doors.

Interior doorframes are purchased in sets and usually assembled on the job. Usually 1″ or 1⅛″ thick lumber is satisfactory for interior use. Other dimensions, of course, depend upon the size of the door and the thickness of the walls in which they are installed. To provide simple door installation, planted doorstops are preferred on interior frames.

Metal doorframes, called "door bucks," are being used by some housing developers. They are prefitted and drilled, ready for the installation of the door hardware. Both wood and metal frames are available with prehung doors.

Representations of cased openings are shown in Fig. 9-17. See Fig. 9-18 for various entrance-door frames.

9.5.5 Overhead Garage Doors

Because of their size and weight, garage doors must be operated with counterbalances or springs on overhead tracks. Stock sizes range from 8′–0″ × 7′–0″ to 9′–0″ × 7′–0″ for single garage widths; double garage openings require a 16′–0″ × 7′–0″ door size. Their symbol on plans is merely a line through the opening, accompanied by a dimensional note and the manufacturer's number.

9.5.6 Drawing Door Details

Although accurate details of door sections are seldom shown on working drawings involving conventional construction, the draftsman

Fig. 9-17 Variation in wall-opening symbols on plans.

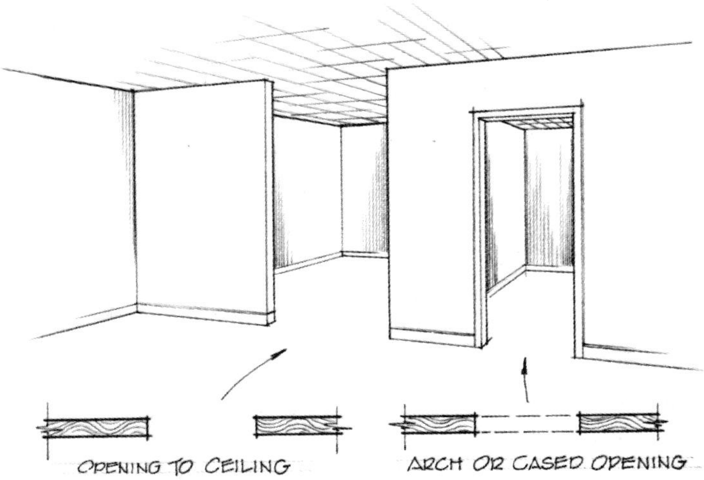

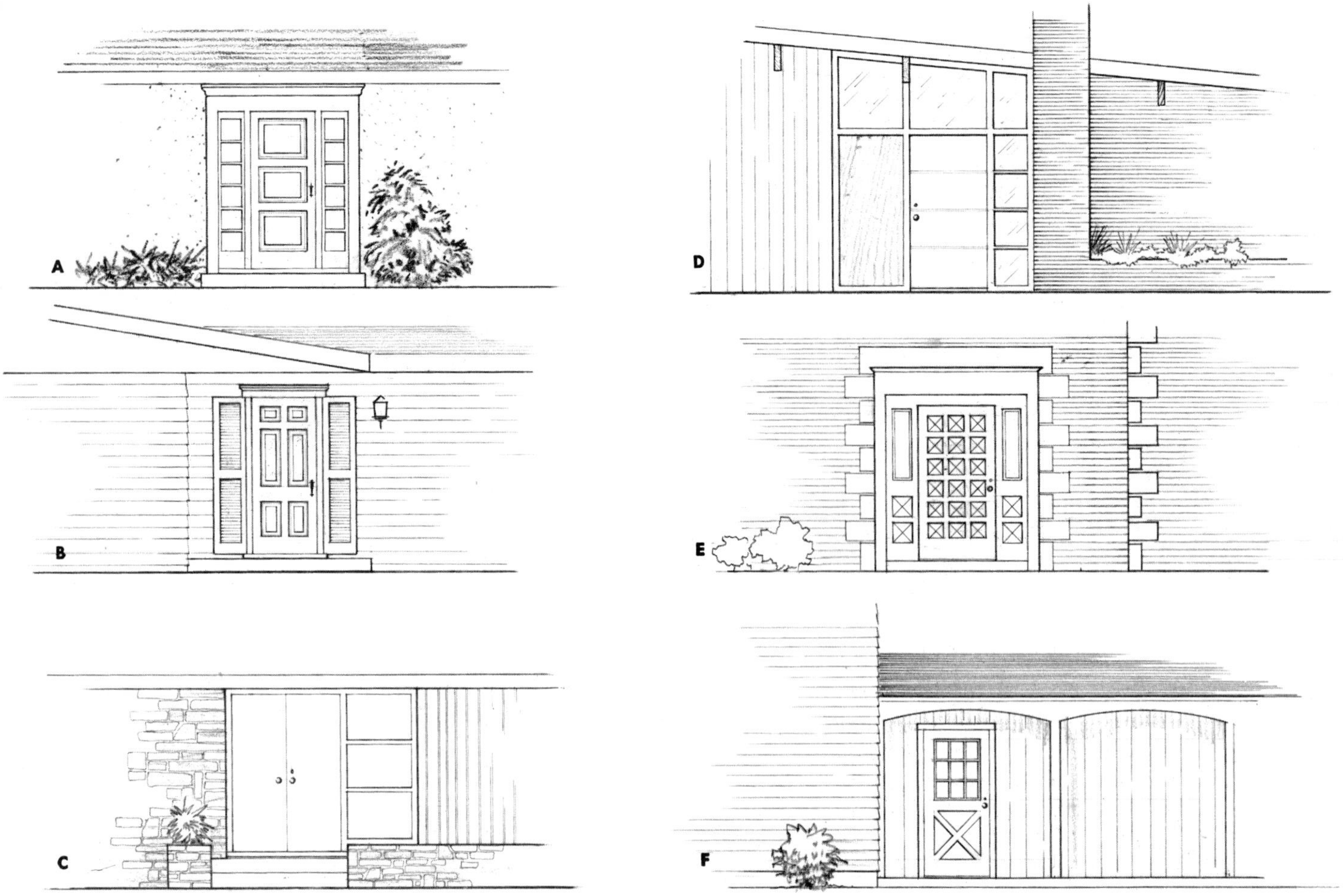

Fig. 9-18 Entrance suggestions.

must choose the size, type, and style to best fit the situation. If doors are incorporated into special framing, or if they are placed in walls of different construction, section views of the jambs and the surrounding construction, as well as the trim, must be drawn. To show the proper installation methods in various types of walls, several door details are included in this material (also refer to Fig. 8-31).

In Fig. 9-15 note that the cutting planes on the door elevation indicate sections similar to window details, described previously. Section A reveals the construction through the head jamb and sill, and the plan section reveals the construction through the side jambs. The sections are placed in a position for convenient projection, as well as for analyzing the relationships of the members. In drawing the sections, start by laying out the frame walls, then the wall coverings, and finally the doorjambs and surrounding trim. In solid-masonry construction, the masonry outlines are drawn first; then the jambs and trim are added. Steel angles or reinforced concrete lintels must be used to support the weight of the masonry above the door opening and must be shown on the head section.

9.6 FIREPLACE DESIGN AND DETAILS

For centuries fireplaces were the only method of heating homes; and even with our modern fuels and central heating systems, the fireplace is still as popular as ever because we have not found a substitute for the sheer fascination of an open fire, which provides warmth and a peaceful gathering place in the home.

Because the old-time "fireplace mason," who knew by experience the necessary dimensional requirements of successful fireplaces, is slowly disappearing, complete working drawings of fire-

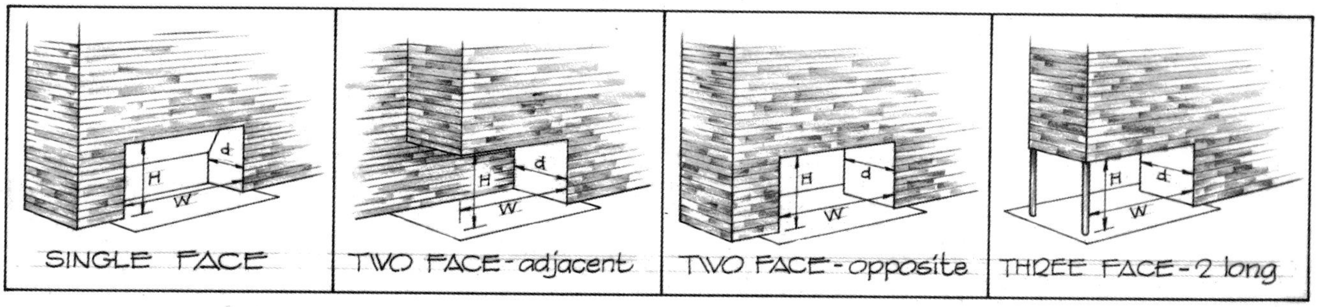

Fireplace Dimensions

Fireplace Type	Opening Height h, in.	Hearth Size w by d, in.	Modular Flue Size, in.
Single Face	29	30 × 16	12 × 12
	29	36 × 16	12 × 12
	29	40 × 16	12 × 16
	32	48 × 18	16 × 16
Two Face— adjacent	26	32 × 16	12 × 16
	29	40 × 16	16 × 16
	29	48 × 20	16 × 16
Two Face— opposite	29	32 × 28	16 × 16
	29	36 × 28	16 × 20
	29	40 × 28	16 × 20
Three Face— 2 long, 1 short	27	36 × 32	20 × 20
	27	36 × 36	20 × 20
	27	44 × 40	20 × 20

Fig. 9-19 Typical fireplace openings and workable dimensions.

places must be included in plans to ensure their correct construction. If an "honest house" is to be built, the fireplace must be honest as well and must be designed to be workable.

Residential fireplaces of various forms and styles are being constructed. Some are merely openings in massive interior masonry walls, with no mantel or other decor other than the texture of the masonry. Some have provision for log storage near the opening; others may have outdoor barbecues incorporated into the chimneys. Many are masonry walls with copper hoods above to concentrate the draft and carry off hot gases and smoke. For general purposes, fireplaces can be divided into the following groups:

1. Single-face fireplaces (conventional).
   a. Wall
   b. Corner
   c. Back-to-back
2. Multiple-face fireplaces (contemporary).
   a. Two adjacent faces (corner)
   b. Two opposite faces (through opening)
   c. Three faces, 2 long, 1 short
   d. Three faces, 1 long, 2 short
   e. Hooded
   f. Freestanding

The successful operation of a fireplace depends upon its construction. Even special fireplaces, which incorporate various shapes and materials, can be made workable if the basic principles of fireplace design are followed, instead of resorting to chance or mere luck. Here are the critical points in single-face fireplace design and construction:

9.6.1 Size of Fireplace Opening

Not only should the fireplace be given a prominent position in a room, away from major travel routes, but the fireplace opening should be in keeping with the room size. Small rooms should have small fireplace openings; large rooms, large ones. The opening should have pleasing proportions; a rectangle is more desirable than a square; the width should exceed the height. A fireplace width of, for instance, 28″–36″ would be adequate for a room of 250 sq ft floor space. In Fig. 9-19, notice some of the more common opening sizes. A raised hearth, usually 16″ above the floor, brings the opening nearer to eye level and often makes the fireplace appear larger. Keep wood trim at least 8″ from the opening and use a steel angle-iron lintel to support the masonry above the opening.

Figure 9-19 shows that fireplace openings have relative proportions of height, width, and depth; however, minor variations may be made to meet the various masonry courses and other restrictions of layout. The size of the opening becomes the starting feature in the design of a fireplace.

9.6.2 Flue Size and Chimney Height

Each fireplace in a building should have an independent flue, unconnected to other vents or flues, and it must start on the center line of the fireplace opening. A chimney can take care of a number of fireplaces, and each flue must continue to the top with as little offset as necessary. Each flue must be large enough in cross-sectional area to create the proper draft through the fireplace opening. Unless the sectional flue area is at least one-tenth of the fireplace opening area (rule of thumb), a troublesome condition may result (see the table that accompanies Fig. 9-20 for exact sizes). Chimney heights under 14′ may even require larger flue sizes, as the height of the chimney, surounding buildings, and prevailing winds affect flue velocities. The higher the chimney, the more draft velocity. For fire protection of the roofing materials, the height of the chimney should be at least 2′ above the highest point of the roof. Flue sizes are important and therefore should be clearly indicated on the drawings; a flue too large is better than one too small. Vitrified-clay flue linings are used to resist high chimney temperatures and to provide smooth flue interiors. Without the lining, cracks tend to develop in the chimney walls. Round linings operate more efficiently, but rectangular types can be more easily fitted into chimney spaces.

9.6.3 Shape of Combustion Chamber

The combustion chamber (Fig. 9-20) is lined with 4″ thick firebrick set in fireclay. It is shaped not only to reflect heat into the room, but to lead hot gases into the throat with increased velocity. If the fireplace is too deep, less heat will be radiated into the room. The sections in Fig. 9-20 indicate the conventional shape of combustion-chamber walls. The back and end walls should be at least 8″ thick. Slight variations are permissible in the layout of the chamber, but long experience has shown that the conventional shapes and proportions are the most satisfactory, as far as operation is concerned.

9.6.4 Design of the Throat

The throat offsets the draft above the chamber, and if a metal damper is used, the door of the damper acts as a valve for checking downdrafts while the fireplace is in operation. The inclusion of a damper is a convenient method of preventing heat loss and outside drafts when the fireplace is not in use. Notice that the door of the damper hinges so that it opens toward the back of the fireplace. The opening of either the damper or the throat should be larger than the area of the flue lining. Also, the damper should be the same length as the width of the fireplace and be placed at least 6″ (preferably 8″) above the top of the fireplace opening. Both steel and cast-iron dampers are available; check manufacturers' catalogues for types and sizes.

9.6.5 Shape of the Smoke Shelf and Smoke Dome

The location of the damper establishes the height of the smoke shelf, which is directly under the flue and which stops downdrafts with its horizontal surface. The smoke dome is the area just above the shelf. Notice that the back wall is built vertically; the only offset on the back is a corbeled brick course that supports the flue lining, where a corbeled brick course is also shown for flue support. Usually the sloping walls are represented with lines drawn 60° from the horizontal.

9.6.6 Support for the Hearth

The hearth is best supported with a reinforced concrete slab, resting on the walls of the fireplace foundation and extending in front at least 18″. (Previously, a brick "trimmer arch" was used to support the forward hearth against the chimney foundation in conventional construction.) Number 3 reinforcing rods are placed near the upper part of the slab, and brick, stone, or other masonry material is applied directly on the slab for a textured hearth covering. If an ash dump is feasible to a basement ash pit or outdoor cleanout door, the reinforced slab is simply formed with ribbed metal lath having a hole cut for the ash dump and any upcoming flues; the concrete is poured over the lath.

In homes with slab floors the fireplace and the hearth are built up from an isolated footing to the floor level. For easy cleaning, the fireplace floor can be made 1″ higher than the outer hearth.

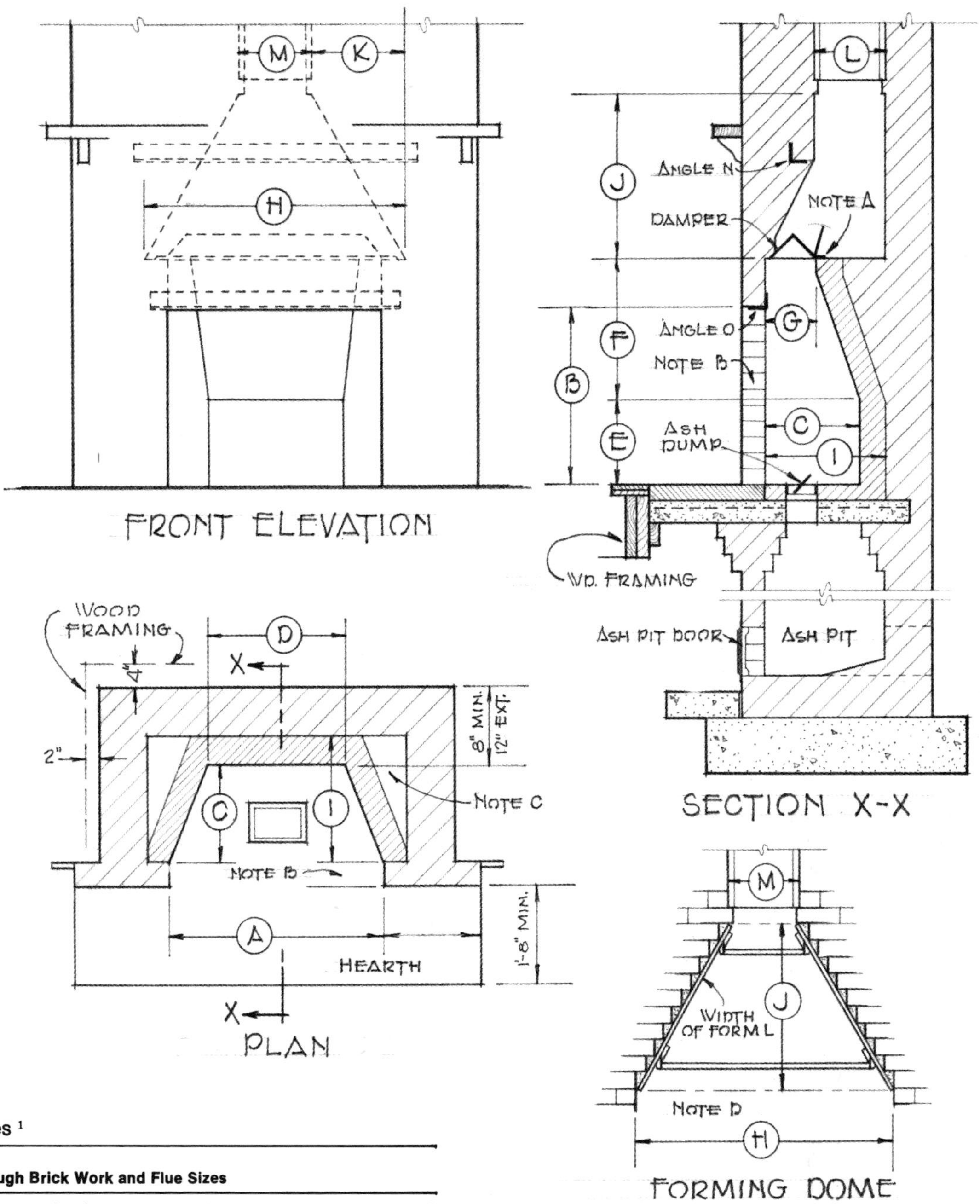

Fireplace Dimensions, Inches [1]

Finished Fireplace Opening							Rough Brick Work and Flue Sizes: New sizes[3]							Old sizes			Steel angles[2]	
A	B	C	D	E	F	G	H	I	J	K	L	M	R[4]	K	L	M	N	O
24	24	16	11	14	18	8¾	32	20	19	10	8	×12	8	11¾	8½	× 8½	A-36	A-36
26	24	16	13	14	18	8¾	34	20	21	11	8	×12	8	12¾	8½	× 8½	A-36	A-36
28	24	16	15	14	18	8¾	36	20	21	12	8	×12	10	11½	8½	×13	A-36	A-36
30	29	16	17	14	23	8¾	38	20	24	13	12	×12	10	12½	8½	×13	A-42	A-36
32	29	16	19	14	23	8¾	40	20	24	14	12	×12	10	13½	8½	×13	A-42	A-42
36	29	16	23	14	23	8¾	44	20	27	16	12	×12	12	15½	13	×13	A-48	A-42
40	29	16	27	14	23	8¾	48	20	29	16	12	×16	12	17½	13	×13	A-48	A-48
42	32	16	29	14	26	8¾	50	20	32	17	16	×16	12	18½	13	×13	B-54	A-48
48	32	18	33	14	26	8¾	56	22	37	20	16	×16	15	21½	13	×13	B-60	B-54
54	37	20	37	16	29	13	68	24	45	26	16	×16	15	25	13	×18	B-72	B-60
60	37	22	42	16	29	13	72	27	45	26	16	×20	15	27	13	×18	B-72	B-66
60	40	22	42	16	31	13	72	27	45	26	16	×20	18	27	18	×18	B-72	B-66
72	40	22	54	16	31	13	84	27	56	32	20	×20	18	33	18	×18	C-84	C-84
84	40	24	64	20	28	13	96	29	61	36	20	×24	20	36	20	×20	C-96	C-96
96	40	24	76	20	28	13	108	29	75	42	20	×24	22	42	24	×24	C-108	C-108

[1] See Fig. 9-20.

[2] Angle sizes: A. 3" x 3" x 3/16"; B. 3½" x 3" x ¼"; C. 5" x 3½" x 5/16".

[3] New flue sizes: Conform to modular dimensional system. Sizes shown are nominal. Actual size is ½" less each dimension.

[4] Round flues.

Note A. The back flange of the damper must be protected from intense heat by being fully supported by the masonry. At the same time, the damper should not be built in solidly at the ends, but given freedom to expand with heat.

Note B. The thickness of the fireplace front will vary with the material used: brick, marble, stone, tile, etc.

Note C. The hollow, triangular spaces behind the splayed sides of the inner brickwork should be filled to afford solid backing. If desired to locate a flue in either space, the outside dimensions of the rough brickwork should be increased.

Note D. A good way to build a smoke chamber is to erect a wooden form consisting of two sloping boards at the sides, held apart by spreaders at the top and bottom. Spreaders are nailed upward into cleats. The form boards should have the same width as the flue lining.

Fig. 9-20 Successful fireplace construction. *(Courtesy Donley Bros. Co.)*

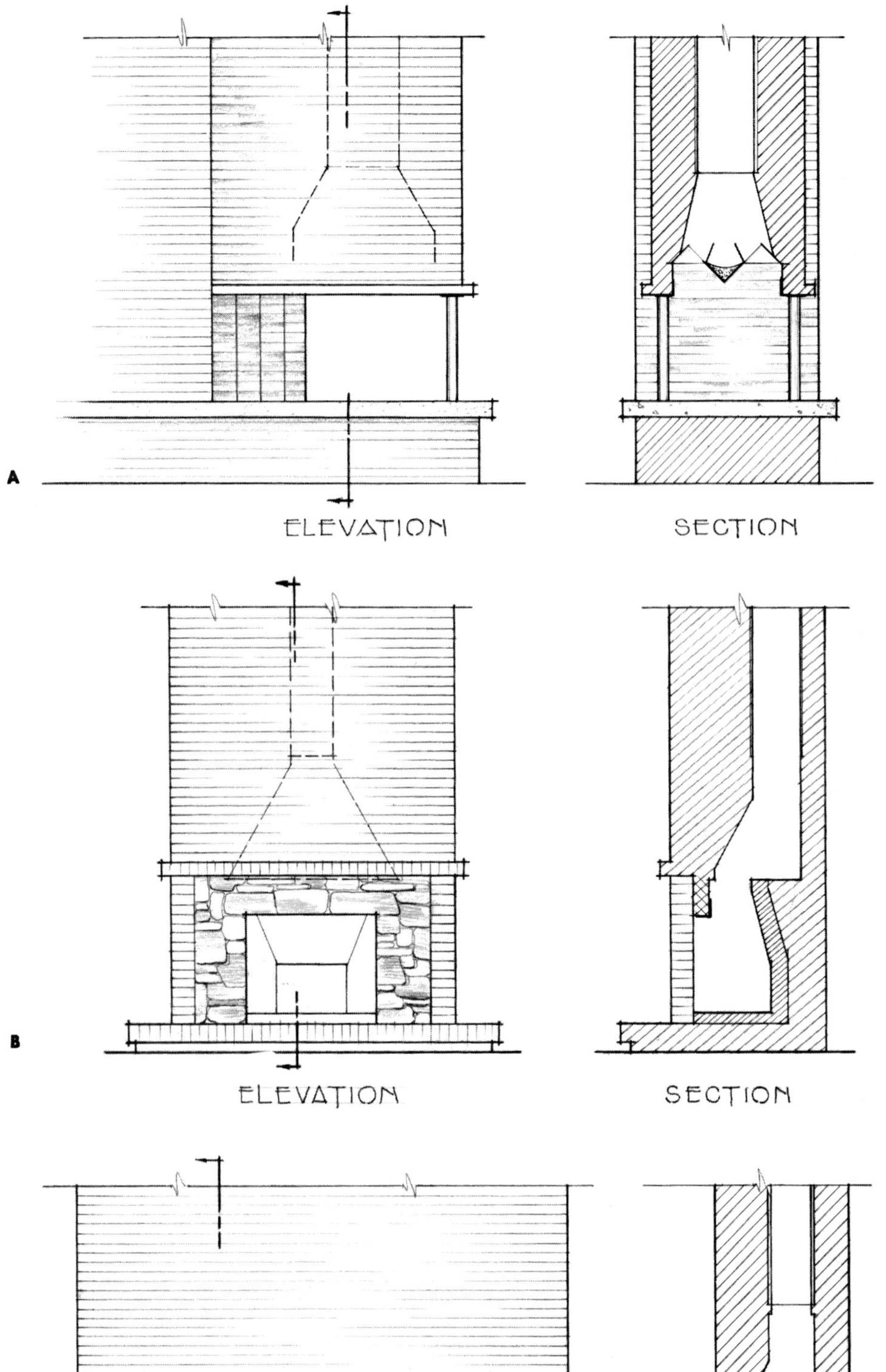

Fig. 9-21 Fireplace suggestions.

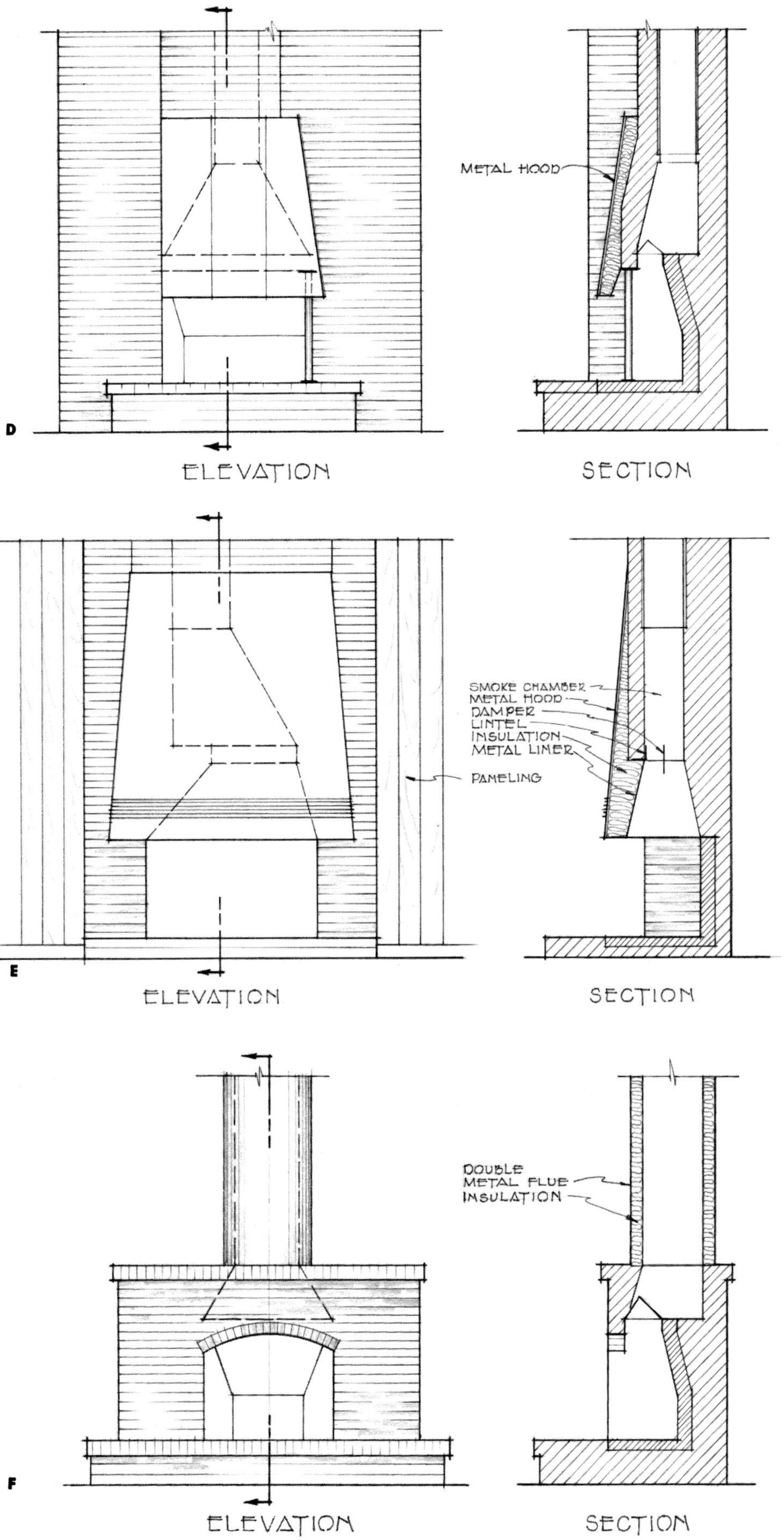

Fig. 9-21 continued

9.6.7 Wood Framing Precautions Around the Fireplace and Chimney

Precautions must be taken when fireplaces or their chimneys pass through wood frame floors, roofs, etc. Fire codes prohibit direct contact between framing members and chimney surfaces (see Fig. 9-20). Usually a 2″ air space is provided between the masonry and wood; this space is filled with incombustible insulating material. Trimmers and headers around wood openings are doubled to give support to the cut joists or rafters, and the sub-flooring or decking is applied closer to the masonry. If the fireplace is wider than the masonry hearth, a cantilever support (Fig. 9-21C) can be used to frame the floor offset support. The hearth slab, which is independent of the wood framing, usually has its outer edge resting on a ledger strip fastened to the headers or floor joists.

9.6.8 Steel Fireplace Boxes

Prefabricated, one-piece, steel fireboxes are available (see *Sweet's Architectural Catalog File*) that combine the combustion chamber, smoke dome, and even a steel lintel for the masonry opening. The firebox is merely set on a masonry hearth, and the brick or stone enclosure is built up around it, thus eliminating any necessity for fireplace design other than the correct flue size. Because they are hollow, the fireboxes can utilize warm-and-cold-air ducts and vents to improve heating efficiency. After the desired openings have been determined, correct catalogue numbers can be established.

9.6.9 Special Fireplaces

Special fireplaces include variations of the multifaced and hooded types, often referred to as "contemporary." Because of their unusually large openings and their complexity of shapes, special fireplaces occasionally cause smoking in the room and poor "draw" through their throats. Generally, if these fireplaces operate poorly, the flue is too small, the damper throat is too narrow, the chimney height is too low, or possibly nearby buildings or trees prevent proper draft through the flues. Also, fireplaces with the sides of the combustion chamber exposed so as to allow roof drafts to pass directly through, such as freestanding or open-back fireplaces, will tend to allow smoke into the room unless room drafts are prevented or glass sides are installed. Special metal smoke-dome-and-damper boxes are available to improve multiface fireplace operation (see *Sweet's File*). Hooded fireplaces require heat-resisting insulation below the metal hoods.

Freestanding, complete fireplace units are sold which require no masonry enclosures nor a masonry chimney. The units, complete with chimney and hearth, can be installed in existing structures.

In drawing special fireplace details, design data can be taken from the fireplace dimensions table and the accompanying drawings (Fig. 9-20); further information can be found in Ramsey and Sleeper's *Architectural Graphic Standards*. But the best source for information about special fireplaces, as well as the equipment needed for regular fireplaces, is from manufacturers' catalogues and literature. See Fig. 9-22 for chimney heights.

Fig. 9-22 Chimney heights.

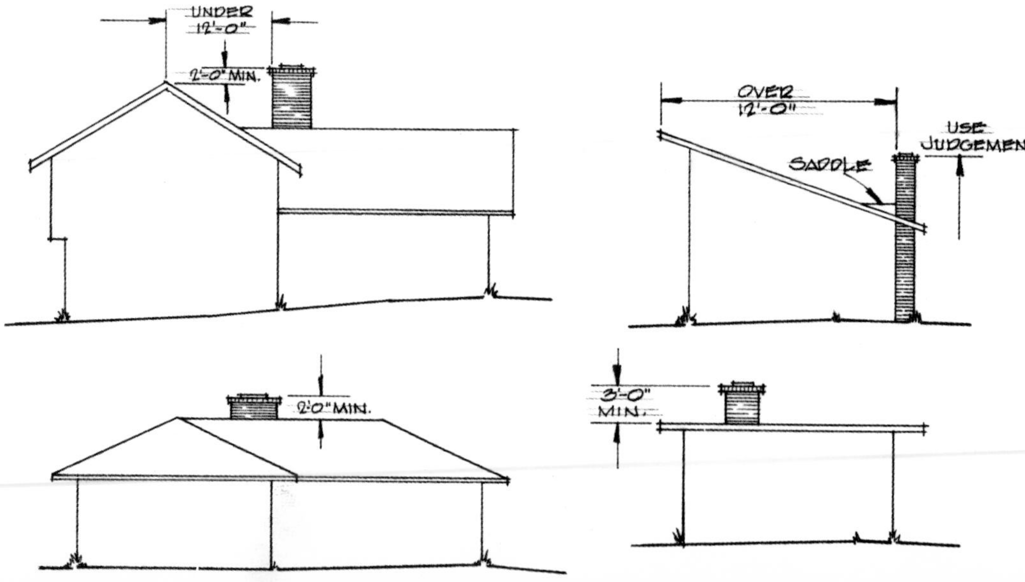

9.7 STAIR DESIGN AND LAYOUT

Let us now consider the problems encountered in stair construction. A flight of stairs is part of the system of hallways communicating the occupied floor levels of a building. In multistory buildings, the stairs, both interior and exterior, must be given careful consideration in the total design. Main stairways in homes, as well as in public buildings, have long been objects of special ornament by architects. Many beautiful staircases are evident in scores of buildings throughout the country. The present trend, however, is toward simplicity and comfort in residential stairs, although dramatic stairways are occasionally found in contemporary public buildings.

Stair Terminology

Stairs have their own terminology in construction work; the following terms are commonly encountered:

BALUSTERS: the thin vertical supports for the handrail of open stairs.

BULLNOSE: the first step on an open stair, which has been extended out forming a semicircle and often receiving the newel post.

CARRIAGE: the rough structural support (usually 2″ × 12″) for treads and for risers of wood stairs, sometimes called string or stringer.

CLOSED STRINGER: the visible member of a stairs which abuts the risers and treads and which is not cut to show the profile of the stairs.

HANDRAIL: the round or decorative member of a railing which is grasped with the hand during ascent or descent.

HEADROOM: the narrowest distance between the surface of a tread and any ceiling or header above.

HOUSED STRINGER: the stringer which has been grooved to receive the risers and treads.

LANDING: the floor at either the top or bottom of a flight of stairs.

NEWEL: the main post of the railing at the bottom of a stair or at changes in direction of the railing.

NOSING: the round projection of the tread beyond the face of the riser.

OPEN STRINGER: stringer which has been cut to fit the profile of the stairs; the riser cut is mitered, the tread cut is square.

PLATFORM: the intermediate landing between various parts of the stair flight.

RAILING: the handrail and baluster forming the protection on open stairs.

RISE: the total floor-to-floor vertical height of a stair.

RISER: the vertical face of the step.

RUN: the total horizontal length of a stairs, including platform.

STAIRWELL: the enclosed chamber into which the stairs are built.

STEP: the combination of one riser and one tread.

STRINGER: the inclined member supporting the risers and treads, sometimes a visible trim member next to the profile of the stairs.

TREAD: the horizontal surface member of each step, usually hardwood.

WINDER: the radiating or wedge-shaped treads at turns of stairs.

9.7.1 Types of Construction

Previously, stair building was a highly specialized craft, especially in home construction; many stairs required considerable hand labor. Today, stairways are often ordered directly from a mill or shops, fabricated according to details furnished by the designer. Usually, first-class construction accepts only shop-made stair units (Fig. 9-23) having expert workmanship, which are delivered to the site and quickly installed by carpenters. Figure 9-24 shows a more economical stair which is built on the job. Usually 2″ × 12″ carriages are cut to the profile of the stairs and the treads are attached. Three carriages are preferred construction if the stair width is 3′–0″ or over. Double trimmers and headers must surround the stairwell framing, and the carriages must have sufficient bearing at both ends.

Other structural methods of stair support have been devised by architects to produce both novel and sturdy stair flights.

Fig. 9-23 Mill-made stair construction.

Fig. 9-24 On-the-job stair construction.

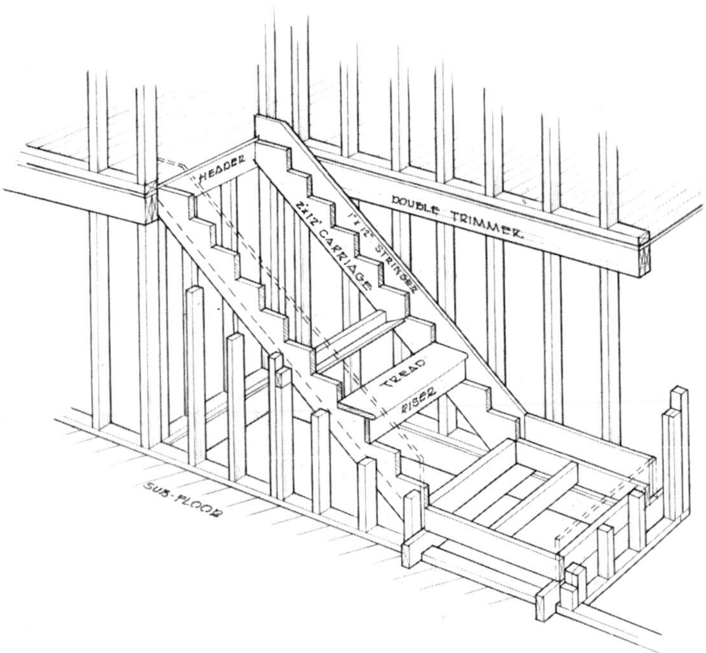

9.7.2 Riser and Tread Proportions

Because considerable effort is expended in ascending and descending stairs, regardless of type, comfort and safety should be the first consideration in their design. In designing a comfortable stair, there must be a definite relationship between the height of the risers and the width of the treads; all stairs should be designed to conform to established proportions. If the combination of riser and tread is too great, the steps become tiring, and a strain develops on the leg muscles and the heart; if the combination is too short, the foot has a tendency to kick the riser at each step in an attempt to shorten the stride, also producing fatigue. Experience has shown that risers between 7″ and 7½″ high with about a 10″ tread result in the most satisfactory combination for principal residential stairs. Minor service stairs may vary somewhat; yet in no case should the riser be more than 8″ high. It will be seen that as the height of the riser is increased, the width of the tread must be decreased for comfort and safety.

9.7.3 Stair Formulae

The following three formulae have been devised for checking riser and tread proportions —exclusive of molding; either will be satisfactory:

Two risers + 1 tread = between 24″ and 25″
Riser × tread = between 70″ and 75″
Riser + tread = between 17″ and 17½″

As an example of formulae application, suppose that a 10″ tread were found suitable on a preliminary stair layout; then after examining either of the stair formulae, it would be seen that a riser height of 7½″ would satisfy either formula. If a 10½″ tread were selected, the riser would have to be 7¼″, etc. Minor variations would still make the stairs workable, but treads are seldom made less than 9″ or more than 12″ wide.

9.7.4 Angle of Stairs

Stair flights should be neither too steep nor too flat in incline. An angle of from 30°–35° from the horizontal is the most comfortable.

Long flights are also tiring; usually a platform about midway in a long flight helps relieve fatigue. There will always be one less tread than there are risers in all stairs.

9.7.5 Plan Layout Variations

Various plan layouts are shown in Fig. 9-25. If space on the plan prohibits the use of a straight run, other layouts are shown for the purpose of flexibility in fitting stairs in restricted spaces, and for lending stairs various character treatments. In limited space, a winder stair (Fig. 9-25E) can be used if necessary; yet it is more hazardous than a platform arrangement. The winder-stair profile should be considered at a line 1′–4″ from the winder corner. Remember that a landing counts as a tread and should be the same width as the rest of the stairs.

Fig. 9-25 Various stair layouts.

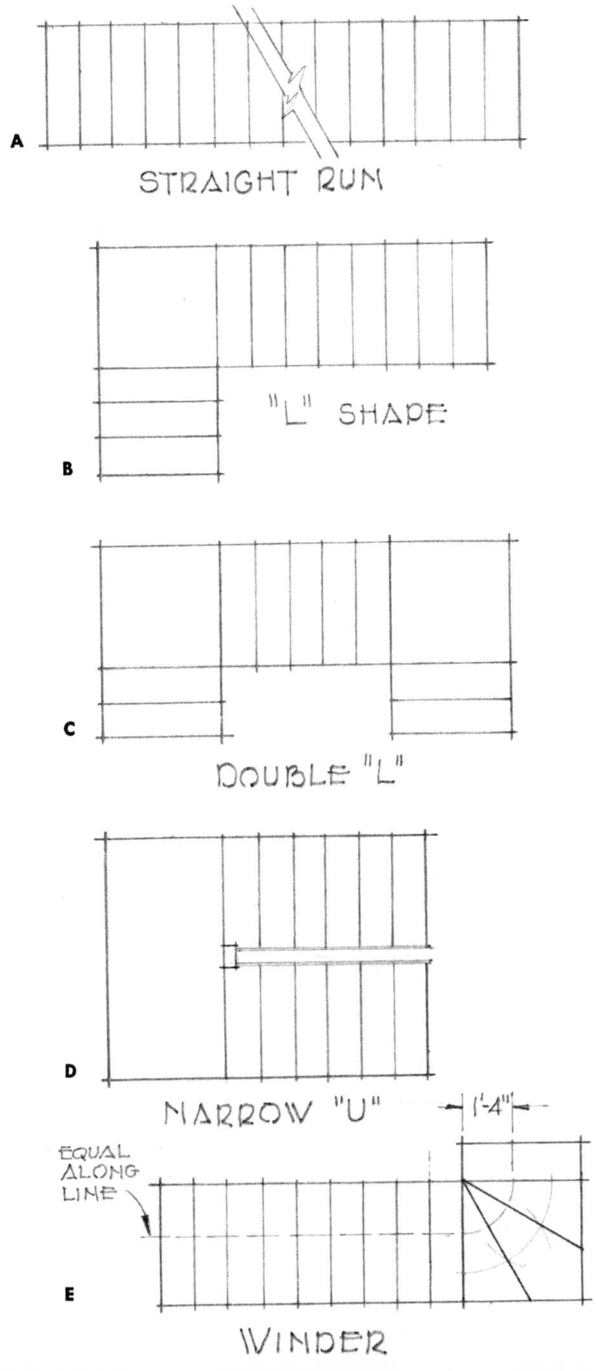

9.7.6 Headroom

Headroom should be between 6′–8″ and 7′–4″ over major stairs; 6′–6″ is usually sufficient over minor flights to the basement or attic: Individual conditions may necessitate slight variations of headroom. Disappearing stairs to attic storage spaces are usually prefabricated units, which can be shown on the plan with a dashed rectangle and a note.

9.7.7 Railings

Whether a stair is open or enclosed between walls, a railing must be installed to be within easy reach in case of stumbling or loss of balance. It is general practice to use a continuous handrail from floor to floor. It can be plain or ornamental—in keeping with the design features of the building—but it should be smooth and sturdy. The most comfortable handrail height is 30″ above the tread surface and 34″ above landings.

9.7.8 Exterior Stairs

Exterior stairs are usually designed with smaller riser heights, and therefore with wider treads than interior stairs. A good proportion is a 6″ riser and a 12″ tread for maximum safety on long flights. Landings should be provided every 16 risers on continuous stairs. If slopes are gradual, ramps (up to 15°) are often preferable to steps for outside use. Usually, masonry with reinforcing and well-anchored footings is the most practical exterior material.

Requirements of all classes of stairs are given in the *Building Exits Code,* published by the National Fire Protection Association. The design of all stairs should meet their specifications.

9.7.9 Drawing Stair Details (Fig. 9-26 and 9-27)

STEP NO. 1. *To draw a stair detail,* first, the finished-floor to finished-floor height must be known, even though carriages rest on rough framing. The number of risers necessary to ascend the height can be found arithmetically by dividing the heights by 7″ or 7½″ (typical risers). If the floor-to-floor dimension is conveniently divisible by either typical riser height, calculation is simplified. But seldom will it come out even, unless ceiling heights have been purposely figured. In Fig. 9-27, the total height or rise needed for the stairs is 107″ (8′–0″ ceiling height, plus 9½″ joist height, plus 1½″ flooring thickness). When we divide 107 by 7, the quotient is 15.28; 107 divided 7½ is 14.26. Since all risers must be the same height, either 14 or 15 risers can be adopted. Either will result in a comfortable stair. If the space is limited, fewer risers result in a shorter run, so that 14 risers is the logical selection. Using 14 risers with 9½″ tread width seems to satisfy either of the stair formulae:

$$\frac{107''}{14} = 7.66'' \text{ riser}$$

$$\text{Rule 1: } 2(7.66) + 9.5 = 24.82$$
$$\text{Rule 2: } 7.66 \times 9.5 = 72.77$$
$$\text{Rule 3: } 7.66 + 9.5 = 17.16$$

Therefore, the stair data for our Fig. 9-27 would be:

Total number of risers	14
Total number of treads	13
Riser height	7.66″
Tread width	9.5″
Total rise	107″
Total run	123.5″

STEP NO. 2. Because odd fractions are difficult to measure on a drawing, the graphic method of stair-profile layout is recommended. Scale the floor-to-floor height and draw the floor lines, between which the stair is to be drawn. Divide the between-floor space into 14 divisions graphically. Divisions on the scale can be used by adopting 14 convenient divisions and adjusting them diagonally across the space and marking to form the tread surfaces (see left side of Fig. 9-26). Draw the 13 vertical-riser surfaces similarly, or measure them if feasible. The top riser meets the second-floor surface. This results in the correct stair profile from floor to floor. Strengthen the profile and erase the construction lines.

STEP NO. 3. Next, locate the ceiling or soffit surface above the stairs, keeping in mind that the headroom for important stairs should be 6′–8″ to 7′–4″ high, if possible; slightly less is permissible if the stairwell above must be made smaller. This headroom line locates the header framing and the sloping ceiling above. In basement stairs, less headroom is satisfactory. To conserve stairwell space, usually two or more flights of stairs are superimposed directly above one another in multistory buildings. Openings for the stairwell can now be dimensioned for the framing, and final adjustments on second-floor walls near the stairs can be made.

STEP NO. 4. If the carriage outline is to be drawn, the thickness of the treads (usually $1\frac{1}{16}$″) is shown below the profile surface, and the thickness of the risers (usually ¾″) shown within the vertical lines. The original profile will remain the surface of the risers and treads. Usually the carriage is cut from 2″ × 10″ or 2″ × 12″ lumber, and at least 3″ of solid material must remain below the depth of the cuts for stability. Nosings commonly extend 1⅛″ beyond the surface of the risers. Basement stairs seldom require covered risers.

STEP NO. 5. For safety, railings are a necessary part of the stairs and should be drawn next. If necessary, details of railings, ornamental newel posts, balusters, and trim can be taken from manufacturers' catalogues. Draw the railing 2′–6″ above surface of the treads. Major stairs should be made from 3′–0″ to 3′–6″ wide.

Complete the stair plan layout by projecting the risers from the elevation detail. Show the riser surfaces and indicate the number of risers; include either an UP or DOWN note and arrow (see Fig. 9-27). About half of the complete stair symbol is shown on each floor plan, and a conventional diagonal break line is drawn near the symbol center. A concrete stair detail is shown in Fig. 9-28.

EXERCISES

1. Draw a typical wall detail of a brick-veneer, 1-story residence, using the scale: 1″ = 1′–0″. Use a crawl space with concrete-block foundation wall. Floor joists: 2″ × 10″; ceiling joists: 2″ × 8″; roof slope 4:12.

2. Draw a typical wall detail of a concrete-block wall with a slab-on-ground floor, using the scale:

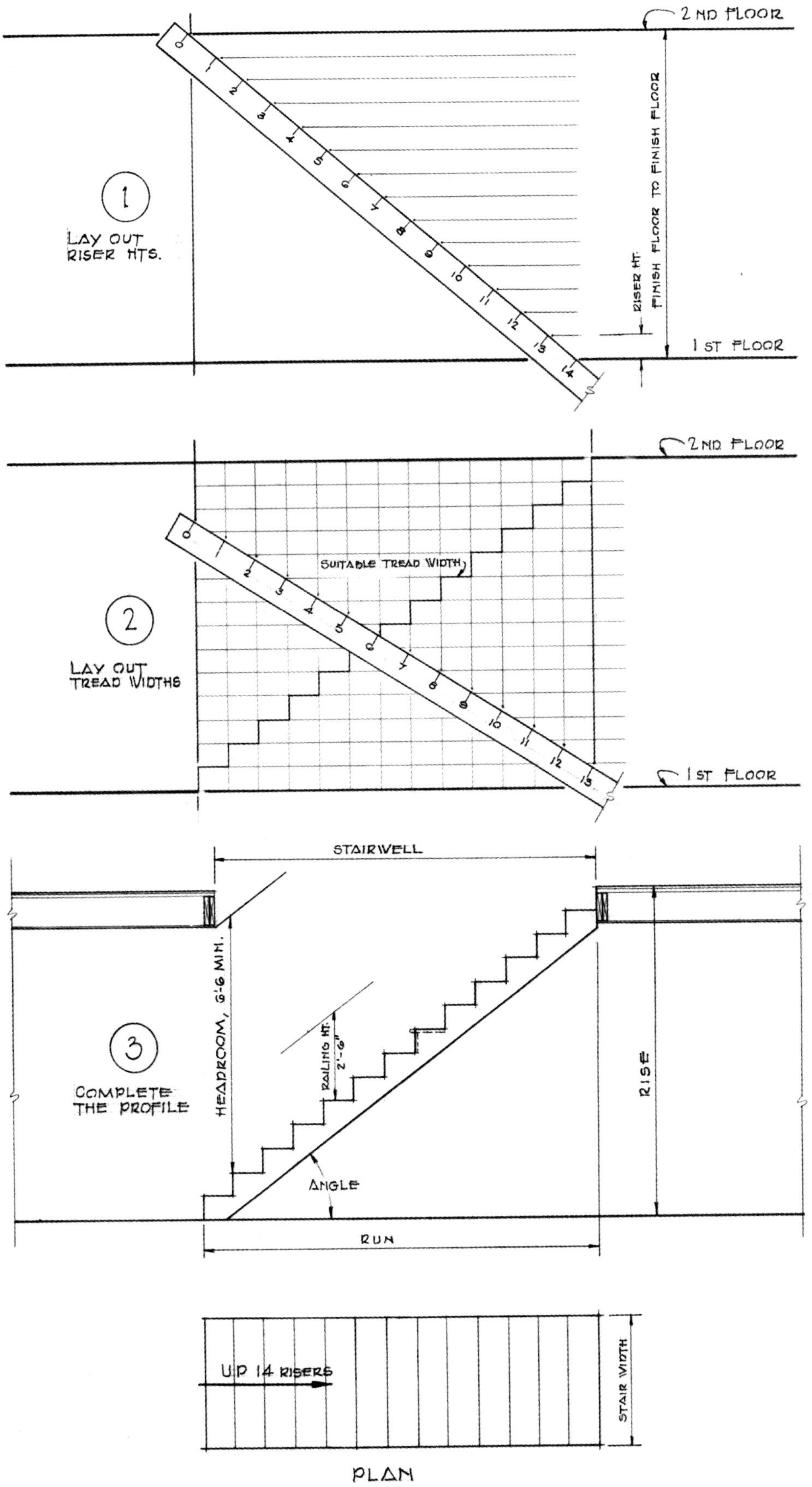

Fig. 9-26 Drawing a stair detail.

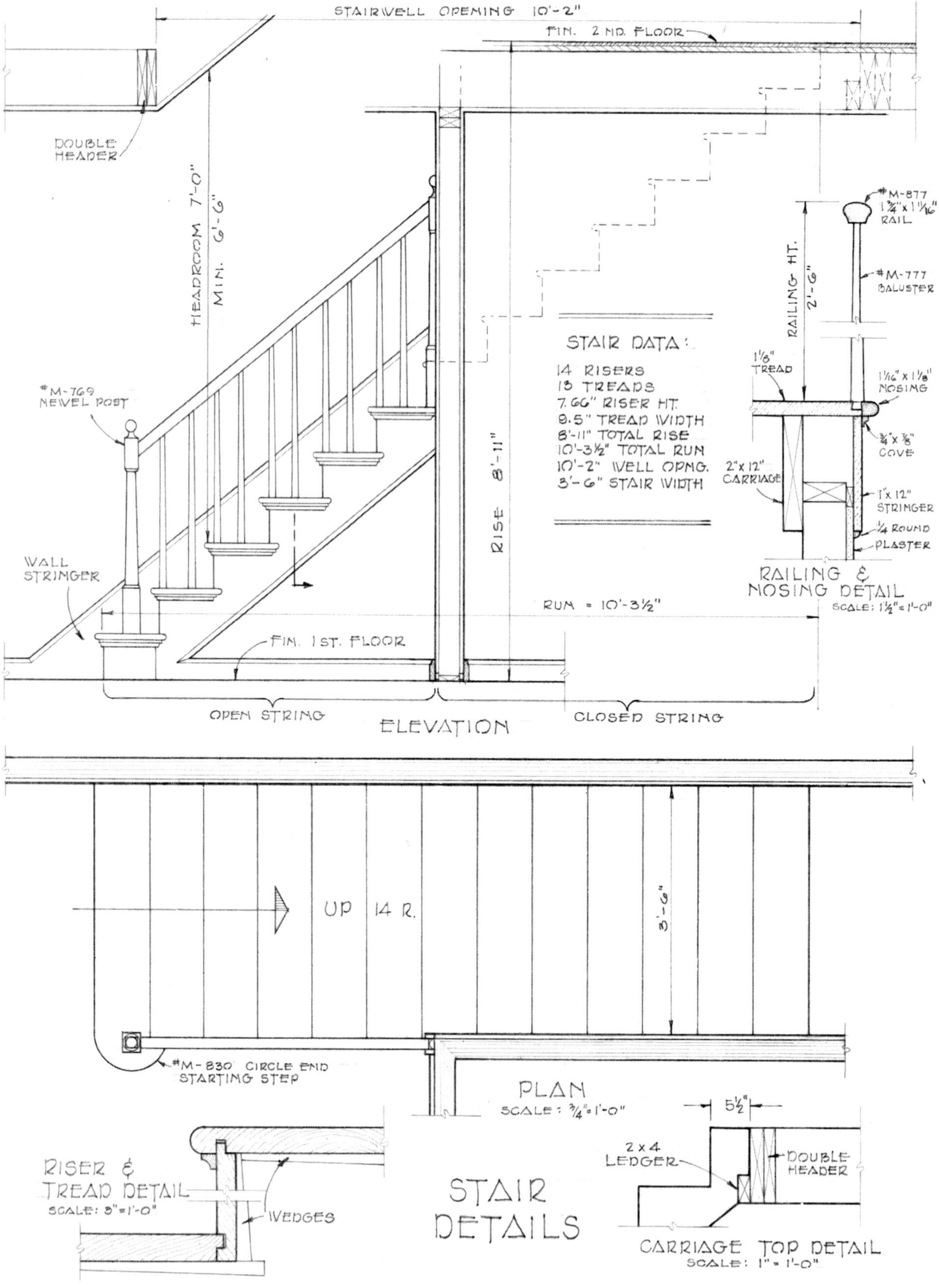

Fig. 9-27 Details of a traditional stairs.

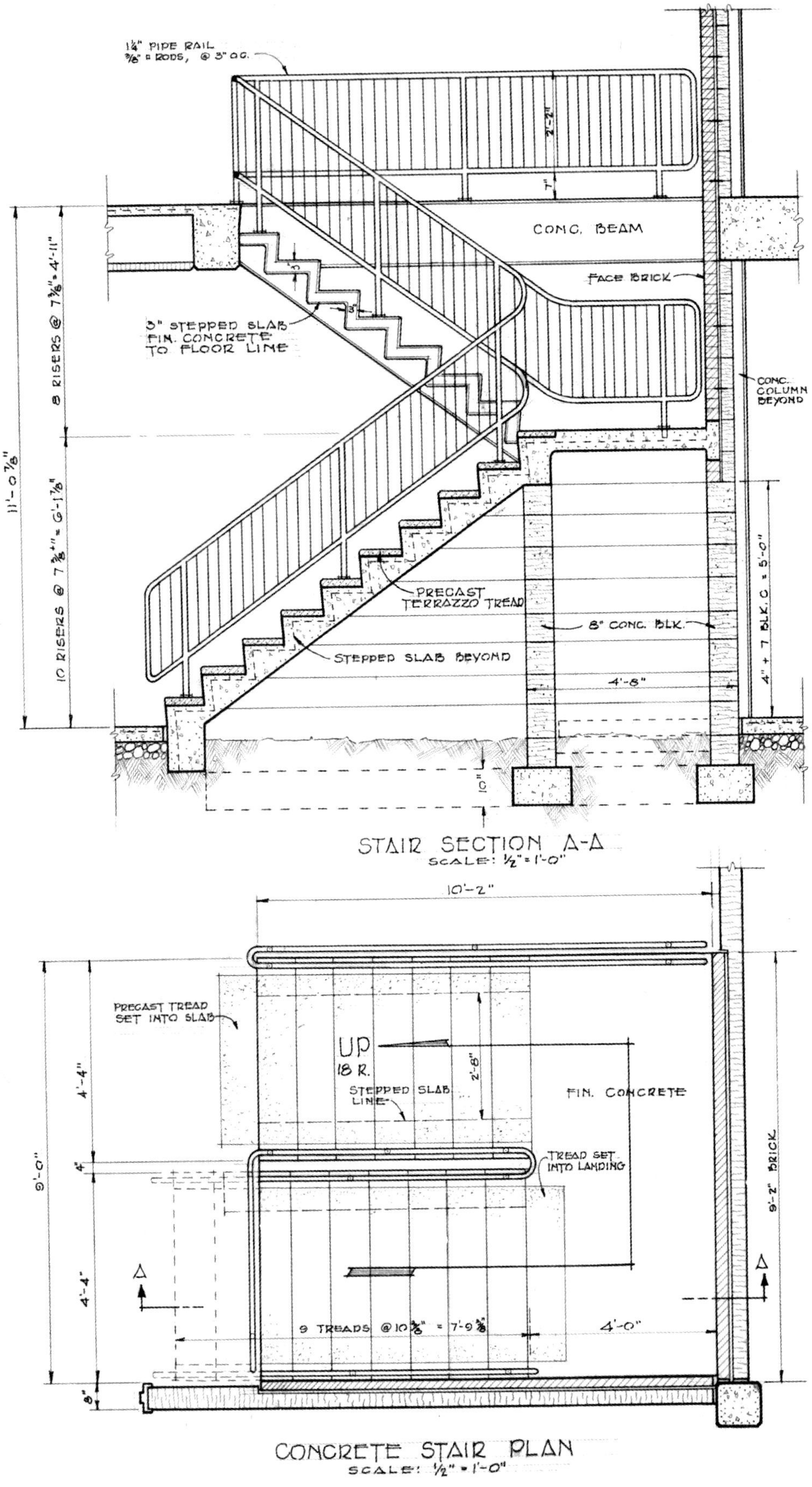

Fig. 9-28 Details of a commercial stairs.

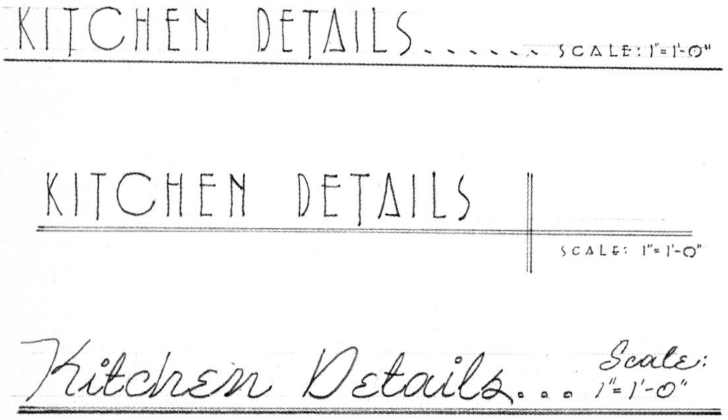

Fig. 9-29 Title layout suggestions for details.

3/4″ = 1′–0″. Show a flat roof with 2″ × 8″ roof joists and box-in the 2′ overhang (see roof overhang details in Chapter 7).

3. Draw a typical wall detail of a frame wall for a house with a basement of 8″ poured concrete walls, using the scale: 1″ = 1′–0″. Use a plank-and-beam roof with 3″ × 8″ beams. Roof slope: 3:12, board-and-batten siding.

4. Draw a section detail of an aluminum awning window, using the scale: 1″ = 1′–0″. Select an actual window from *Sweet's File.*

5. Draw a section and an elevation of a wood hopper window, using the scale: 1½″ = 1′–0″. Use information from a manufacturer's catalogue.

6. Draw the head, jamb, and sill section of a door detail in a solid-brick (8″) wall, using the scale: 3/4″ = 1′–0″. Use 1¼″ wood jambs, suitable trim, and 1¾″ flush door.

7. Draw the elevation, plan, and vertical section details for a contemporary fireplace, using the scale 1″ = 1′–0″. Use stone masonry with a flagstone hearth. Size of fireplace opening: 42″ × 28″.

8. Design and draw the details for a colonial stairs. Single-flight. Finish-floor to finish-floor height: 9′–8″. Select a suitable scale, trim, and railing.

REVIEW QUESTIONS

1. What factors are used to determine the choice of scale when drawing details?

2. What information does a typical wall detail usually show?

3. Why are structural members in detail drawings drawn actual size rather than nominal size?

4. In gable-roof terminology, what is the difference between "span" and "run"?

5. Why must manufacturers' catalogues be consulted when determining rough-opening sizes for windows?

6. Differentiate between a window sash and a window frame.

7. Why are doorjambs usually the only sections needed when drawing door details?

8. What dimensions are first selected in fireplace design, and what should be the basis for their selection?

9. For a workable fireplace, what should be the proportion of the cross-sectional flue area to the fireplace opening area?

10. What two dimensions are the most critical in satisfactory stair design?

"To do easily what is difficult for others is the mark of talent."—Amiel

10

Working Drawings of Small Homes

This chapter is concerned, mainly, with typical working drawings of small, custom-designed homes and the steps necessary for the satisfactory completion of these drawings by the student. To show the conventional representation of various home styles and construction features, two sets of drawings are included. Each set is typical in present architectural practice, and should be studied carefully for its manner of depicting construction information. Occasionally, modifications will be necessary to satisfy local conditions and code requirements.

The *1-story home* (Fig. 10-1) would possibly be ideal for a family with two boys or two girls. The approximately 1100 sq ft of floor space plus basement and carport are efficiently arranged with versatile areas and "open planning" to give the interior a feeling of spaciousness. For economy, the interior walls and ceilings are covered with ½″ gypsum wall board, and the living-dining area boasts a plank-and-beam ceiling for variety. If feasible, the basement can be made into a recreational area. For convenient outdoor eating, the terrace is isolated from the public by a brick extension wall. By detail modification, the house can easily be constructed on a concrete slab, and the stairwell utilized for a central heating unit and utility room.

Fig. 10-1 Pen-and-ink perspective drawing of small one-story home.

The *2-story home* is more traditional in nature, resembling many homes built in New England during colonial times and still popular in many areas. Built over a crawl space with a cantilevered second story, the house has about 3000 sq ft of floor space including the double carport, which makes it suitable for a larger family than the 1-story home. The sleeping area is organized on the second floor for isolation from the downstairs living and eating areas. Because of the overhang, brick veneer is used on the garage-first-floor level, and bevel siding for the walls above.

Instructor assignments—limiting the size of a home, giving the tastes of a tentative client, and indicating the major type of construction and materials, are very much like the actual situations in an architectural office. Usually, the architect first consults with the client about his wishes, design sketches are prepared, and further consultation may be necessary to resolve information about the project. In fact, more sketches may have to be done before all ideas are clearly in mind and working drawings can be started. Student problems should be developed in the same manner—first by sketches, preferably on $\frac{1}{8}''$ coordinate paper, then on tracing paper with instruments. In the architectural office, the sketches of a project, together with any written information are given to an experienced draftsman, or project chief, for their development. Some consultation may be necessary, yet one man usually assumes the responsibility for the completion of a small project. Student drafting assignments provide similar learning situations.

The following plates (Figs. 10-2 through 10-8), showing conventional drafting practice, should serve merely as guides for developing original ideas into complete working drawings. If only manipulative drafting exercise is advisable, the plates can be duplicated directly (they are shown approximately half size). While working on the drawings, the student is urged to continually refer to *Sweet's File,* to Ramsey and Sleeper's *Architectural Graphic Standards,* and other reference sources for additional help.

10.1 START WITH THE FLOOR PLAN

In general, follow these steps in developing the first-floor plan.

STEP NO. 1. *Lay out the major exterior walls with light lines.* Use the $\frac{1}{4}'' = 1'\text{–}0''$ scale and take the dimensions from the sketch. A 3H or 4H pencil works best for preliminary construction lines. Extend the lines beyond their

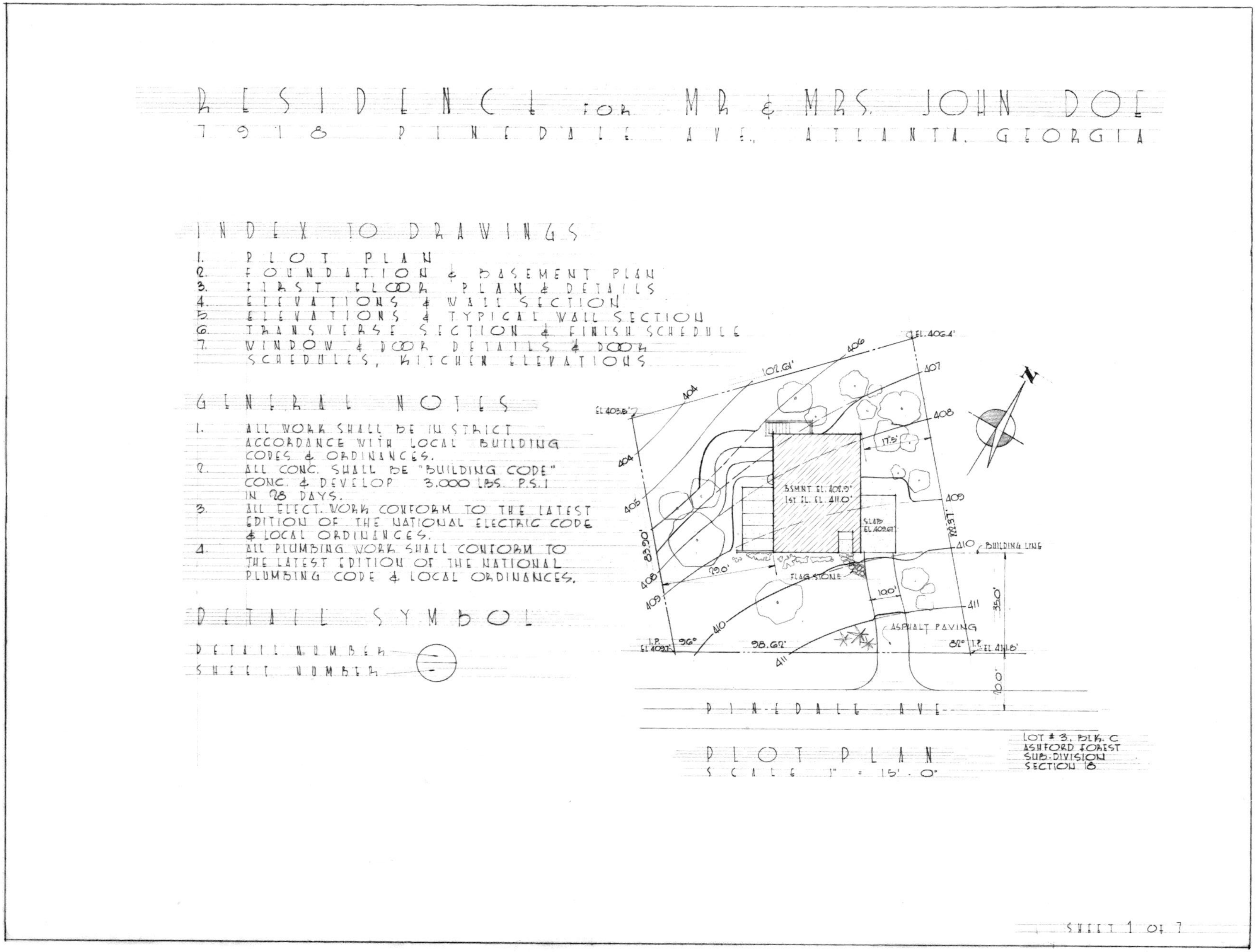

Fig. 10-2 Title page and plot plan of a small one-story home.

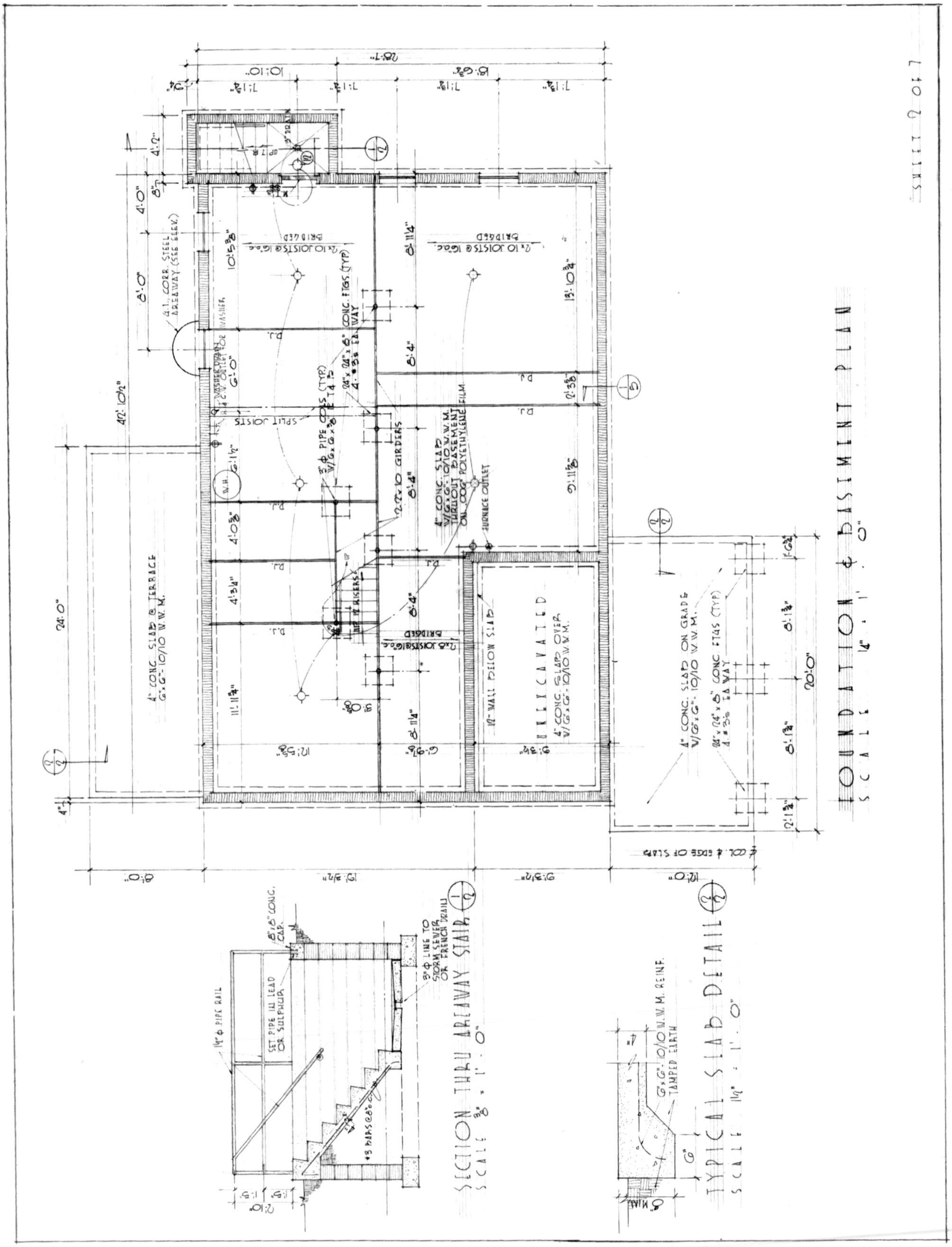

Fig. 10-3 Foundation and basement plan.

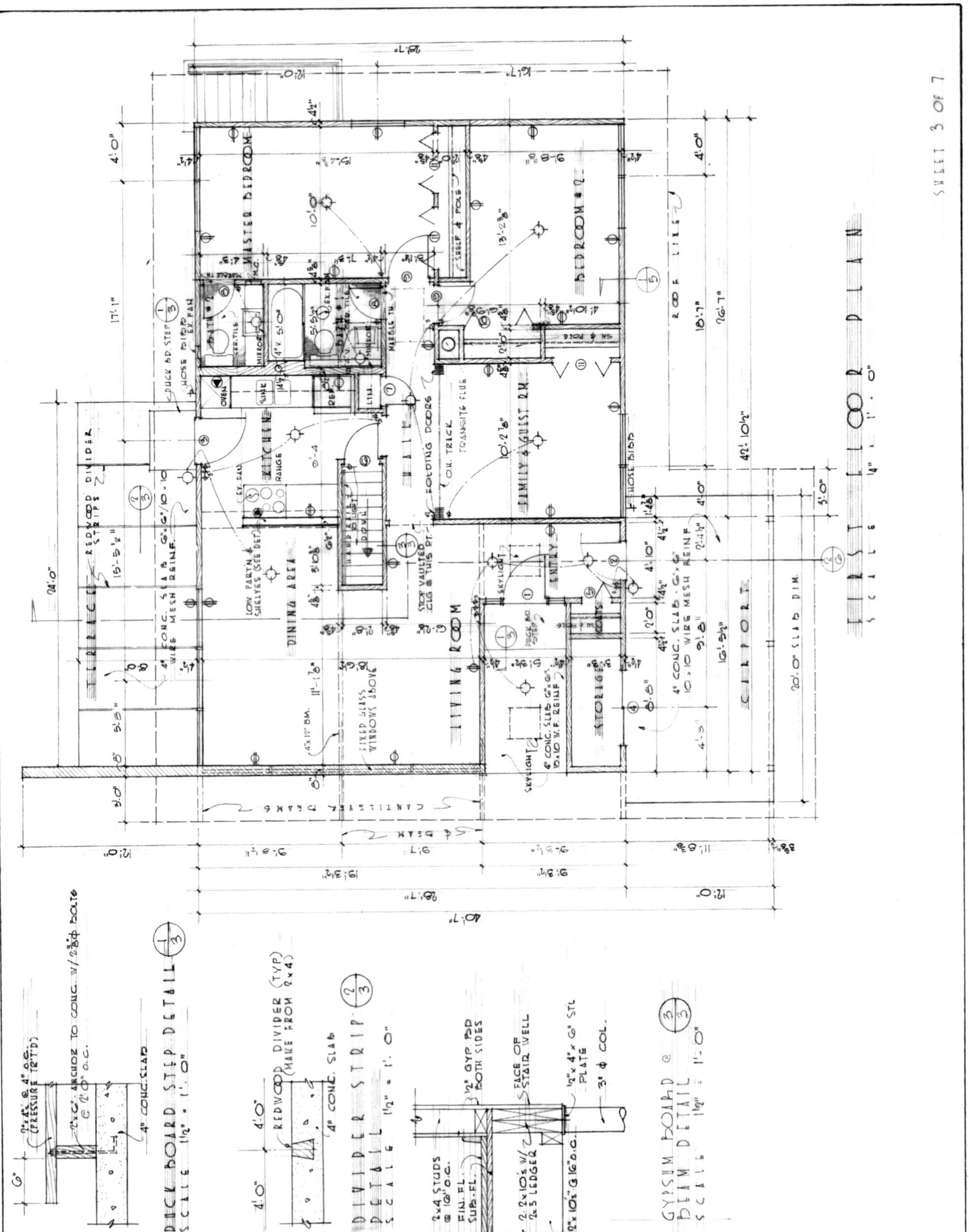

Fig. 10-4 Floor plan and details.

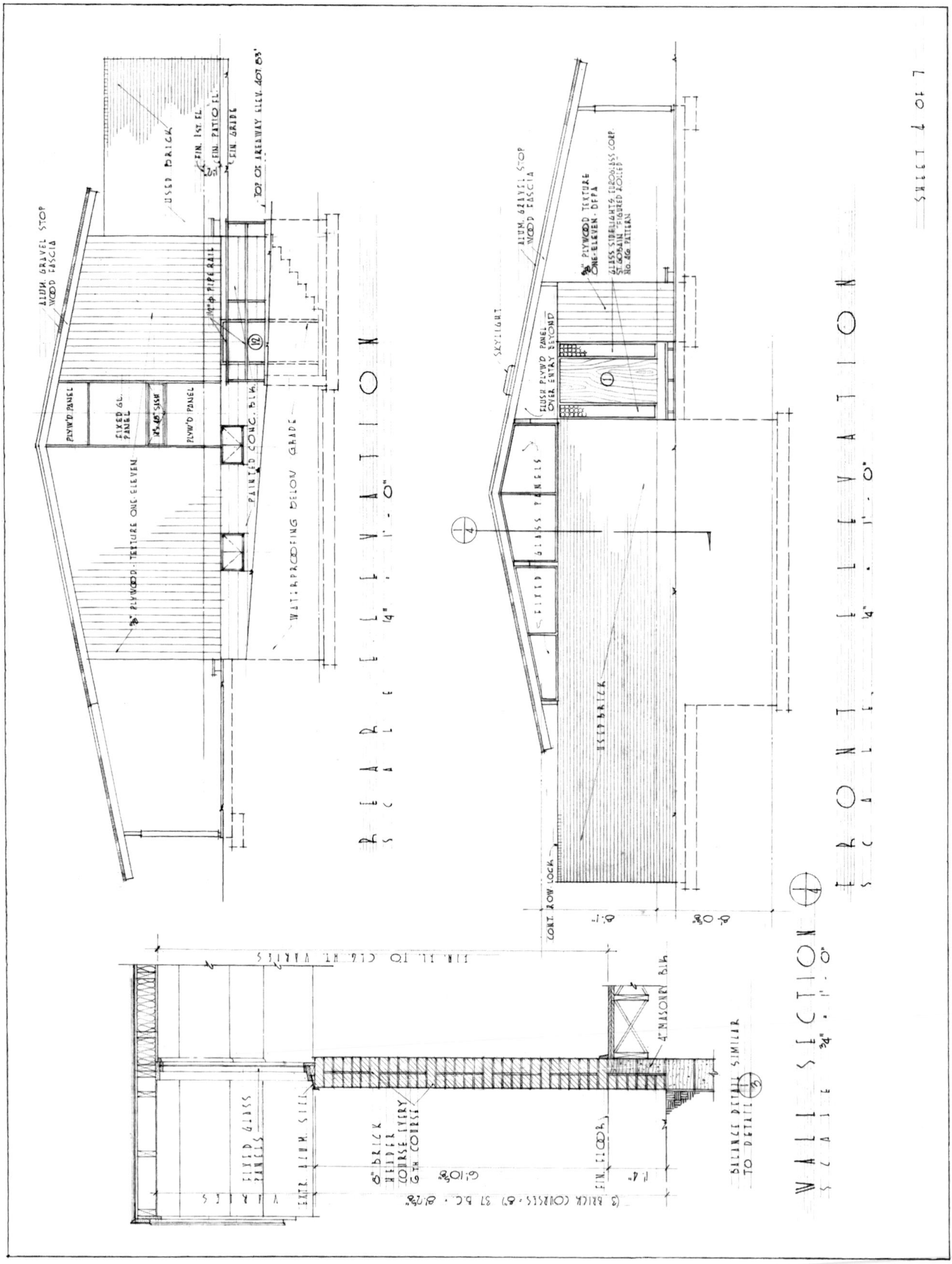

Fig. 10-5 Elevations and wall section.

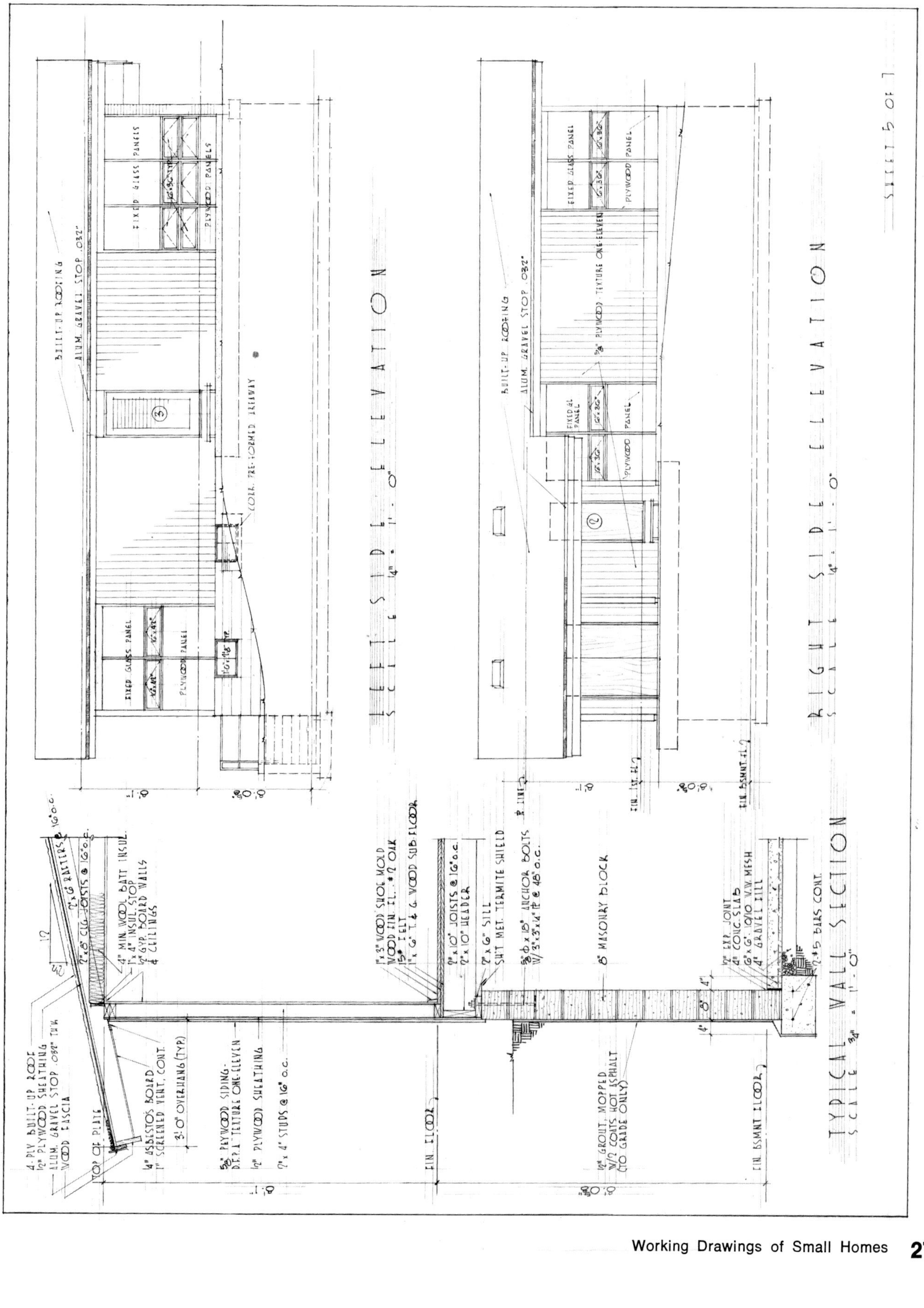

Fig. 10-6 Elevations and typical wall section.

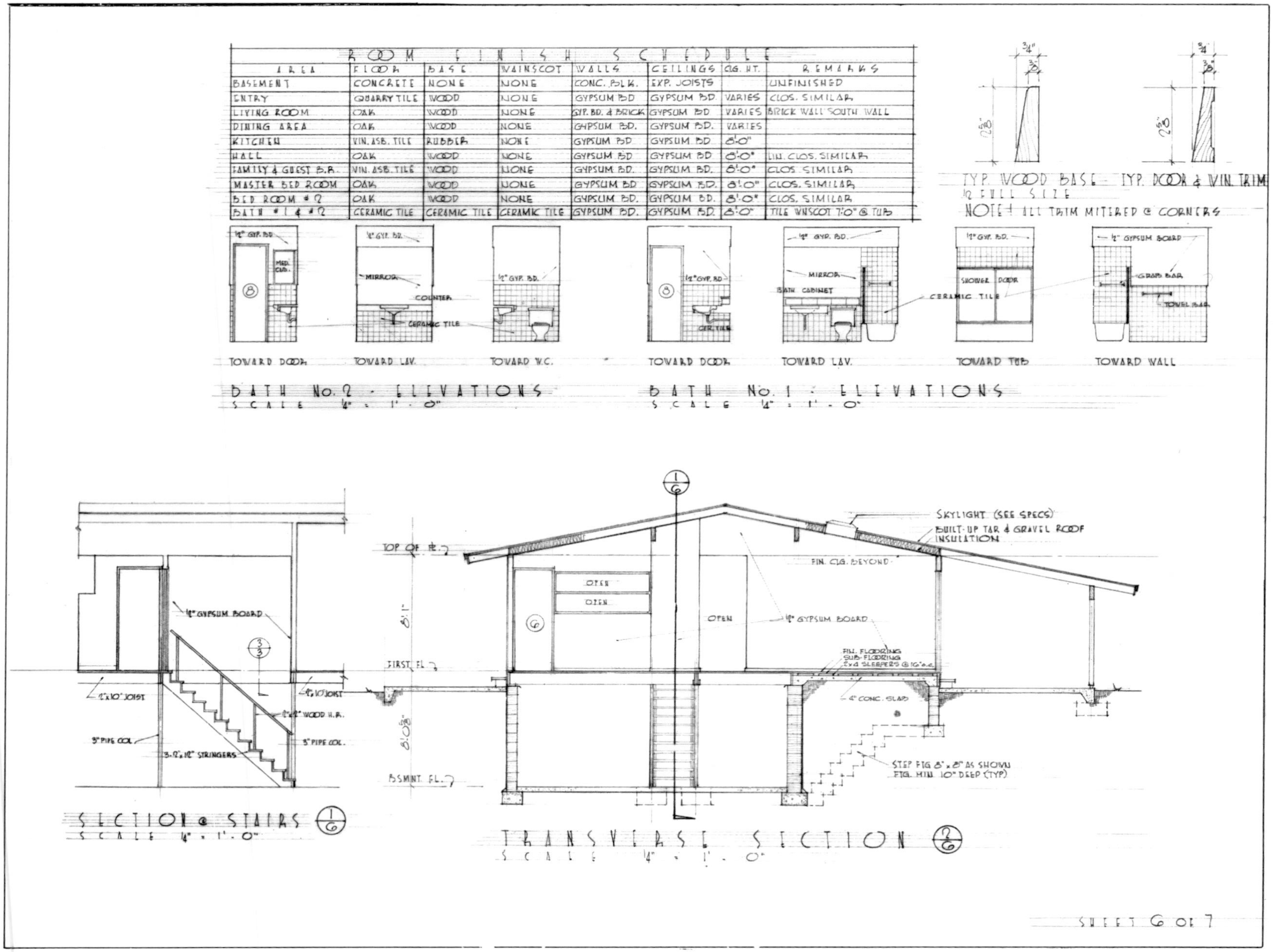

Fig. 10-7 Transverse section and finish schedule.

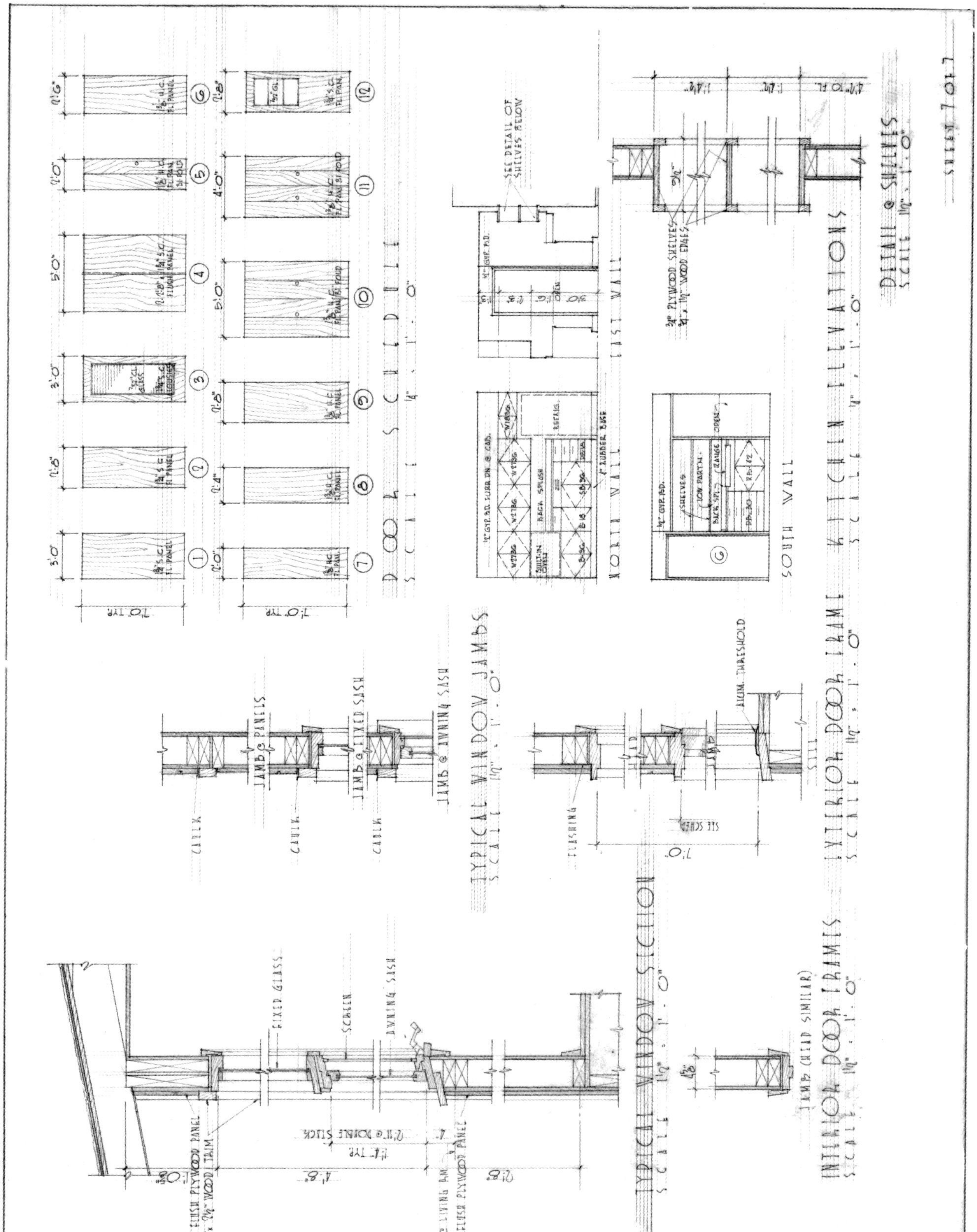

Fig. 10-8 Window and door details, door schedule, and kitchen elevations.

termination points during construction, until definite measurements are established. The following wall thicknesses are satisfactory on small plans, unless special conditions exist:

Wood frame exterior walls	6″
Wood frame partitions	5″
Brick veneer	10″ (4″ brick, 6″ wood)
Concrete block	4″, 8″, 12″ (nominal)
Solid brick	8″, 12″ (plus furring)
Brick cavity	10″ (2″ air space)

Draw the light lines completely through window and door openings at this preliminary stage. Then, lay out all partitions, including if necessary, an 8″ wide wet-wall for the bathroom 4″ vent-stack enclosure. Block-in the areas for stairs, fireplaces, door stoops, etc. Give clothes closets a minimum of 2′ interior width.

STEP NO. 2. *Locate all windows and doors with center lines.* Refer to the elevation sketches, if necessary for window placements, and check manufacturers' catalogues for available sizes (see Figs. 10-4 and 10-11 for various window symbols). Select window types for their practicality and for their harmony with the spirit of the exterior. If elevations are not definite and window changes seem inevitable, draw the window symbols with only light lines and come back later for strengthening after the elevation fenestration is completed. After considering the proper door widths that become necessary in the different rooms (Fig. 9-14), lay out the door symbols. Scale the symbol the same width as the door. Study the traffic flow through doors before indicating their swing. Since interior doors are frequently left open, be sure to provide sufficient clear space for doors when in an open position. Exterior residential doors swing in; interior doors should not swing into hallways. For convenient accessibility, provide either sliding- or folding-door units in closets; louver doors are especially appropriate, since they allow ventilation for the clothes. Two symbols are shown for doors (Fig. 9-14); either is satisfactory. Erase the construction lines within the door symbols before completing the symbols. Indicate doorsills or waterproof thresholds below exterior doors. Cased openings or archways, which drop below ceiling heights, must be shown with broken lines (see Fig. 9-17).

STEP NO. 3. *Draw the layout of the stairs.* If exact ceiling heights have not been established, stair indications on the plan may have to be delayed until stair details (Fig. 9-27) have been completed. However, after stair information is complete, the risers are indicated with lines. An arrow indicating either UP or DOWN and a note showing the number of risers completes the stair symbol. A diagonal break line near the center of the stair-run terminates the amount of stair symbol necessary on each floor. Usually a 10″ tread, requiring about a 7½″ riser, results in a comfortable residential stair.

STEP NO. 4. *If a fireplace is required, draw the outline of the fireplace lightly.* The cutting plane of a fireplace representation passes through the lower part of the opening (see Fig. 9-20). Here again, details may require development on another sheet before the indication on the plan can be accurately drawn. Usually a masonry hearth, 18″ or 20″ wide, is necessary in front of the opening. Size the fireplace opening and the masonry around it according to the proportions of the room in which it will serve. If a metal fireplace lining is used, the size and number should be indicated with a note. Refer to Section 9.6 for fireplace designs, details, and methods of representation.

STEP NO. 5. *Lay out the kitchen cabinets and bath fixtures.* Locate the sink, stove unit, and refrigerator; show the kitchen base cabinets 24″ wide and the wall cabinets 12″ wide. Use broken lines for the wall cabinets inasmuch as they are above the cutting plane of the plan. Carefully locate and draw the symbols for the bathroom fixtures. Sizes and clearances can be taken from Fig. 6-41 or from manufacturers' catalogues. Sizes of bath fixtures should be accurately scaled to indicate correct placement and workability of the arrangement. Bathroom templates save considerable time in this step. Indicate a medicine cabinet if no storage space is provided in built-in lavatory cabinets. Show all other built-in cabinetwork throughout the house in its correct place. All built-in features, which become a permanent part of the construction must be shown on the plan.

STEP NO. 6. *Draw all electrical outlets and switch symbols (see* Fig. 11-30). On ¼″ = 1′–0″ floor plans, use a circle 3⁄16″ in diameter for the majority of the electrical symbols; a circle template will be handy for this. Locate ceiling outlets in the centers of room areas for general lighting. Long, rectangular rooms may require several ceiling outlets in order to distribute light evenly throughout the room. Living areas are best illuminated with table and floor lamps which can be operated from duplex outlets and convenient wall switches. Show a ceiling outlet above the tentative placement of a dining room table. Local lighting should be provided for work centers such as kitchen counters, sewing centers, etc. Place light switches near doors (opposite hinges) where entrance is made into the room. If a room has several entrances, use two 3-way switches (Fig. 11-30) to provide convenient light operation. If necessary, use two 3-way switches and one 4-way switch to operate the lights from three different locations. Place the switches so that the lighting can be turned on before entering a room. Show 3-way switches at the top and bottom of stairways. In addition, outside outlets are needed for entrances, yard floodlights, and terrace requirements. When connecting switch symbols with their outlets, use an irregular curve as a ruling edge and maintain a consistent broken-line technique. Place duplex wall outlets about 8′–0″ apart in living areas, then lamps can be positioned at will throughout the room. Halls should have outlets for vacuum cleaners. It is important to provide a sufficient number of outlets for the many electric appliances now being used in a modern home: refrigerator, food freezer, range, heating units, washer, dryer, motors, and diverse equipment for food preparation, grooming, etc. Some appliances may even require 220 volts, which is easily indicated with a 3-stem symbol. Waterproof outlets are specified for outdoor use. (Refer to Chapter 11 for further information on electrical drawings.)

Step no. 7. *Complete and verify all dimensions.* Several methods of dimensioning the framing can be used on wood frame construction. For example, in one method, applied for the 2-story house, the dimensions are taken from the outside surface of the exterior stud wall to the center lines of the partitions. This method is conventional, and it provides workmen with the necessary dimensions for laying out the soleplates over the subfloors in western frame construction. Even on brick-veneer construction, only the wood framing is dimensioned (refer to Chapter 8 for more details). On the 1-story home, as another method, the outside dimensions start at the surface of the sheathing, which coincides with the surface of the foundation wall on the detail. Continuous dimensions are carried through the house from partition surfaces, and the thickness of each partition is dimensioned. This method gives a better indication of inside room dimensions, and is preferred by some architects. In either method, dimensions are shown to the center lines of windows and doors. Generally, the obvious placement of interior doors in narrow areas, such as hallways, seldom needs dimensions for location. Notice that dimensions are placed on each drawing where they are legible, uncrowded, and related to their features. Make guide lines for all dimension figures no larger than $\frac{1}{8}''$ high. Check cumulative dimensions to be sure they equal the overall dimensions. Dimension solid masonry from wall surfaces, and indicate the thickness of each wall or partition so that masons will have definite surfaces to work from. They need to know the dimensions of door and window masonry openings as well. Avoid duplication of dimensions.

Students should remember that workmen cannot construct frame buildings with the same precision found in, for instance, the machine trades. Finished buildings often show slight variations from dimensions indicated on working drawings. This condition, however, does not give license to careless and inaccurate dimensions on working drawings, but it is a situation that draftsmen should be aware of when dimensioning the drawings.

Step no. 8. *Letter the room titles, notes, and scale of the plan.* Place the room titles near the center of the room, unless dimensions or ceiling electrical symbols interfere and would result in a crowded appearance. Unless a finish schedule is to be used, the finish flooring should be indicated with a small note below the room title. All notes that clarify features on the drawing should be completed; however, avoid excessive notes that can better be included in the specifications. Door sizes must be given either in door schedules or on the door symbols. Scale indications are lettered very small.

Use a note to show the size, direction, and spacing of ceiling or floor joists above (see Fig. 10-10). In conventional framing, ceiling joists must rest on bearing walls. To determine the size and spacing of the joists, based on their longest span, refer to the table on maximum spans for wood joists and rafters in the Appendix.

Ceiling joists on 1-story houses should preferably run parallel with the rafters, to act as lateral ties. On 2-story houses, the ceiling joists become the floor joists of the second floor, and their sizes must be computed as joists capable of supporting 40 lb per sq ft live load. Number 2 common, southern yellow pine or standard and utility grade Douglas fir are widely used in house framing.

STEP NO. 9. *Complete all hatching of materials according to the symbols shown in Fig. 8-11.* If lettering or dimensions fall in the hatching areas, leave enough of the symbol out, to make the lettering readable. Prepare a border and title block similar to Figs. 10-9 through 10-14 or to those shown in Chapter 2.

STEP NO. 10. *Check the plan carefully for discrepancies or omission.* For this the following list will prove helpful.

FIRST-FLOOR PLAN INFORMATION CHECKLIST

_______ 1. All necessary dimensions.
  _____a. Outside walls
  _____b. Interior partitions
  _____c. Window and door center lines
  _____d. Edges and thicknesses of solid masonry
  _____e. Sizes of terraces, walks, and driveways
  _____f. Special construction
  _____g. Arrowheads on all dimension lines

_______ 2. Window symbols, door symbols with swing.
_______ 3. Window and door identification.
_______ 4. Center lines in windows.
_______ 5. Type of passageways through partitions.
_______ 6. Stair symbol and note: UP or DOWN and number of risers.
_______ 7. Steps necessary at exterior doors, different floor levels.
_______ 8. Vent stack in 8″ wet-wall.
_______ 9. Window and door schedules.
_______10. Thresholds under exterior doors or between floors of different flooring materials.
_______11. Symbols for all stationary kitchen, bath, and laundry fixtures.
_______12. Built-in millwork.
_______13. Shelves and rods in clothes closets.
_______14. Fireplace symbol including hearth.
_______15. Broken line indicating roof outline, on 1-story plans.
_______16. All lighting symbols.
  _____a. Ceiling outlets
  _____b. Wall fixture outlets
  _____c. Switches with broken lines to outlets
  _____d. Outside outlets and floodlights
  _____e. Mechanical equipment outlets
  _____f. Sufficient wall outlets
  _____g. Special lighting

_______17. Medicine cabinets in bathroom.
_______18. Ventilating fan in interior baths.
_______19. Note indicating size, spacing, and direction of ceiling framing.
_______20. Dashed lines showing scuttle to attic, if any.
_______21. Any special beams or structural members in overhead construction.
_______22. Any metal or wood columns.
_______23. Symbol for hot-water heater, central heating unit, or fixed mechanical equipment.
_______24. Hose bibbs.
_______25. Note indicating the drainage slope of concrete slabs (usually 1/8″ per ft).
_______26. Cutting-plane lines showing section detail locations.
_______27. Titles for all rooms, hallways, and areas.
_______28. Note indicating finish floor in each room (if no finish schedule is used).
_______29. Correct symbol hatching for materials.
_______30. Floor plan title and scale.

10.2 DEVELOP THE SECOND FLOOR OVER THE FIRST-FLOOR PLAN

If a 2-story house, similar to the one in Fig. 10-15 is to be drawn, the second-floor plan is developed directly over the first-floor drawing. Sometimes architects make a print of the first floor and use it instead of the tracing. Start the second floor by first drawing the outside walls the same size as the walls below, unless a second-floor cantilever arrangement (Fig. 10-14), or a 1½-story house is being drawn. The knee walls under sloping roofs of typical 1½-story houses must be located on end-elevations to determine the proper headroom in the living spaces. Knee walls should be a minimum of 4′–6″ in height. Since light and ventilation are necessary in rooms with sloping walls, dormers must be planned so that the dormer windows will be on vertical planes. The position of the knee wall can be used to locate the position of the vertical dormer face, or smaller dormers can be placed higher on the roof. Additional sketches may be necessary in developing neat-appearing dormers.

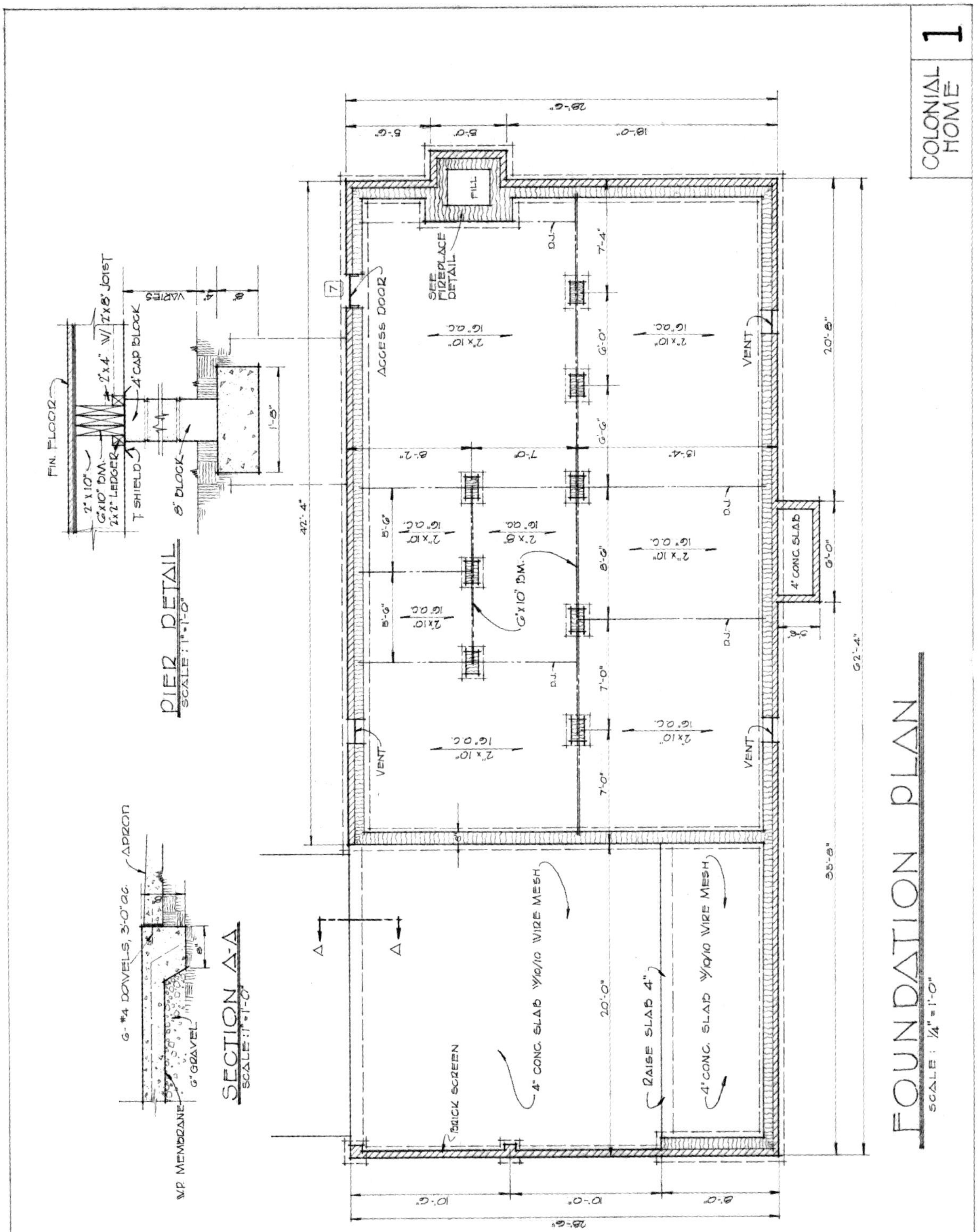

Fig. 10-9 Foundation plan of a two-story home.

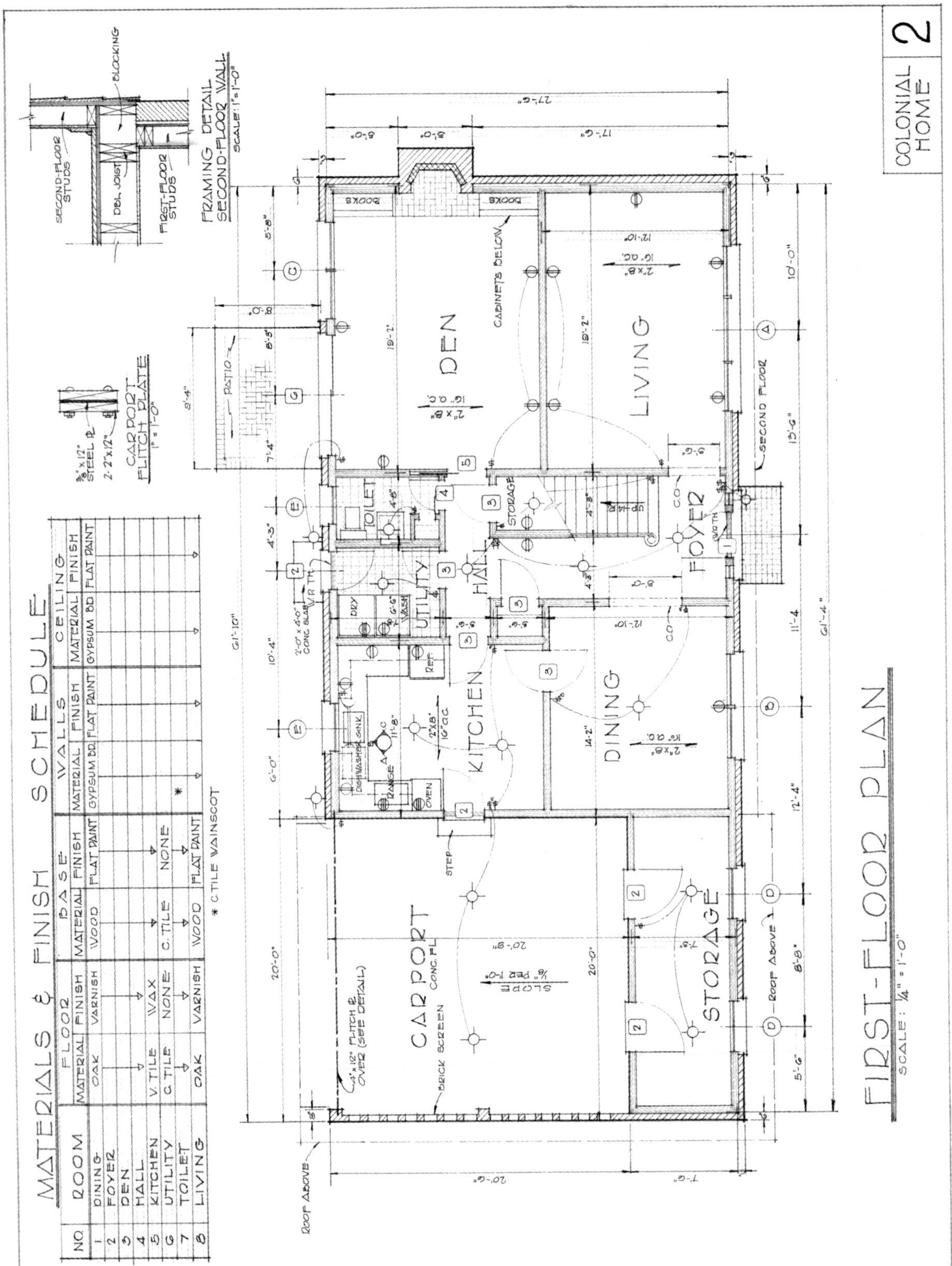

Fig. 10-10 First-floor plan.

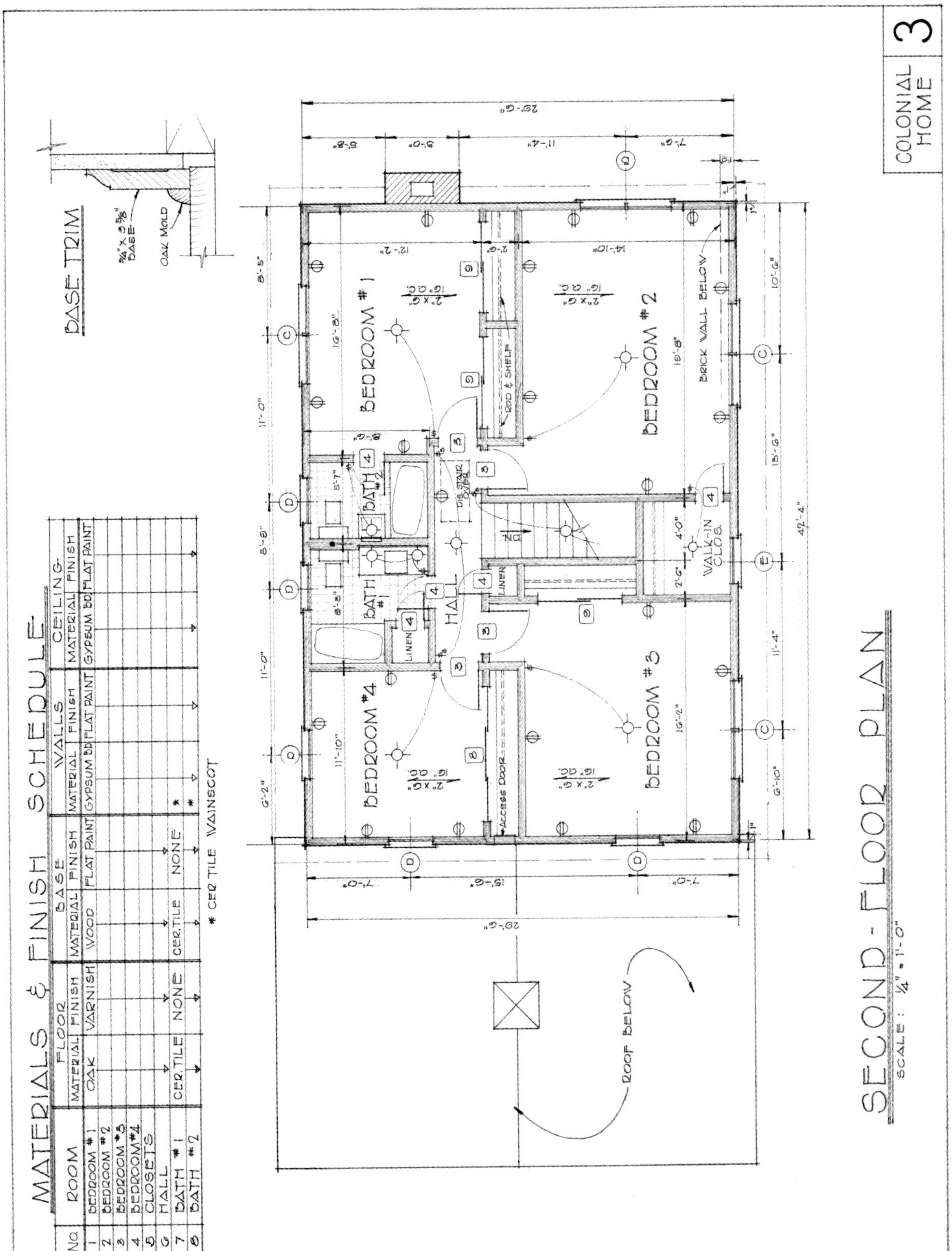

Fig. 10-11 Second-floor plan.

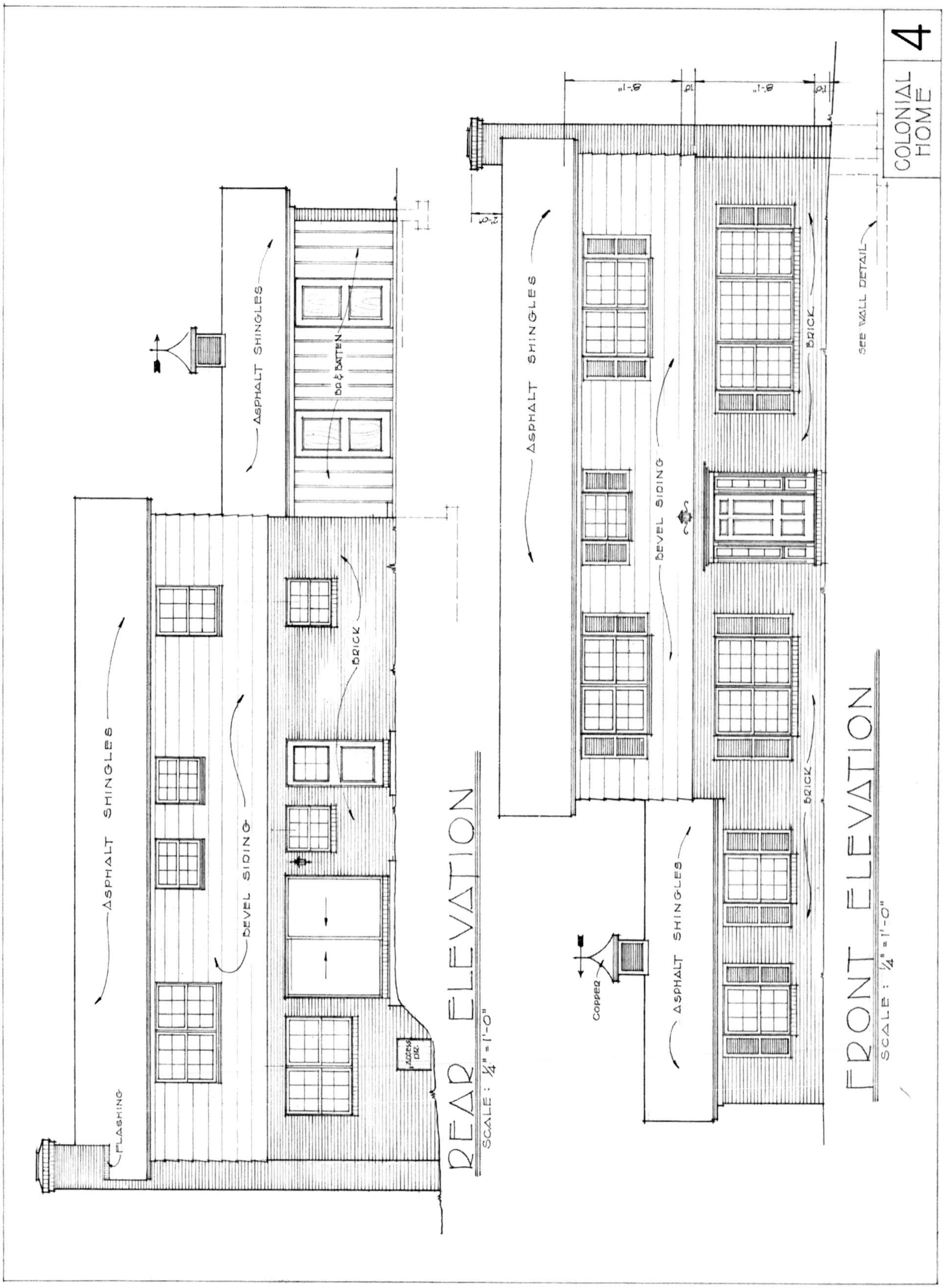

Fig. 10-12 Elevation views.

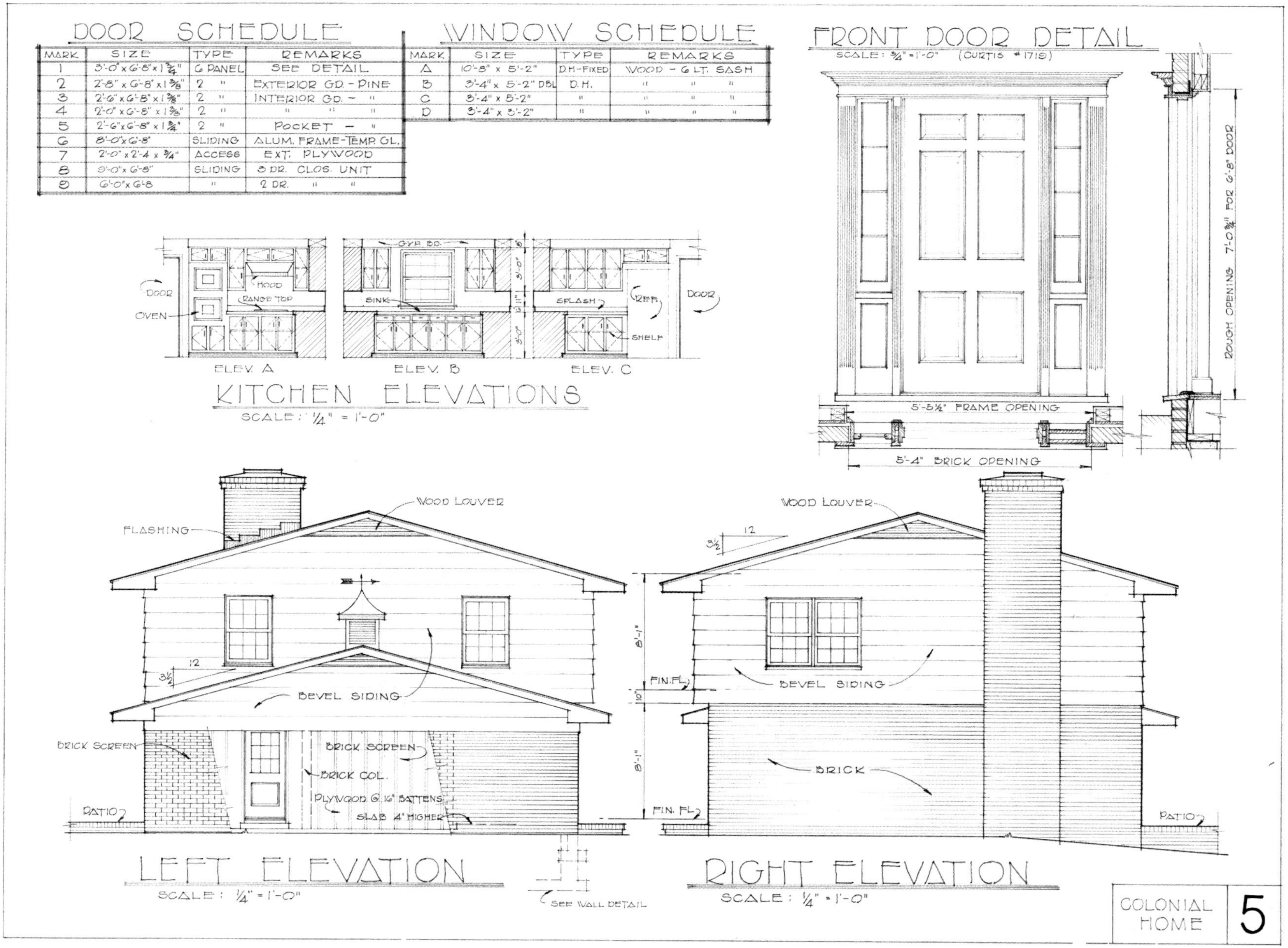

DOOR SCHEDULE

MARK	SIZE	TYPE	REMARKS
1	3'-0" x 6'-8" x 1¾"	6 PANEL	SEE DETAIL
2	2'-8" x 6'-8" x 1⅜"	2 "	EXTERIOR GD. - PINE
3	2'-6" x 6'-8" x 1⅜"	2 "	INTERIOR GD. - "
4	2'-0" x 6'-8" x 1⅜"	2 "	" " "
5	2'-6" x 6'-8" x 1¾"	2 "	POCKET - "
6	8'-0" x 6'-8"	SLIDING	ALUM. FRAME-TEMP. GL.
7	2'-0" x 2'-4 x ¾"	ACCESS	EXT. PLYWOOD
8	9'-0" x 6'-8"	SLIDING	3 DR. CLOS. UNIT
9	6'-0" x 6'-8	"	2 DR. " "

WINDOW SCHEDULE

MARK	SIZE	TYPE	REMARKS
A	10'-8" x 5'-2"	D.H.-FIXED	WOOD - 6 LT. SASH
B	3'-4" x 5'-2" DBL	D.H.	" " "
C	3'-4" x 5'-2"	"	" " "
D	3'-4" x 3'-2"	"	" " "

Fig. 10-13 Elevation views, schedules, and details.

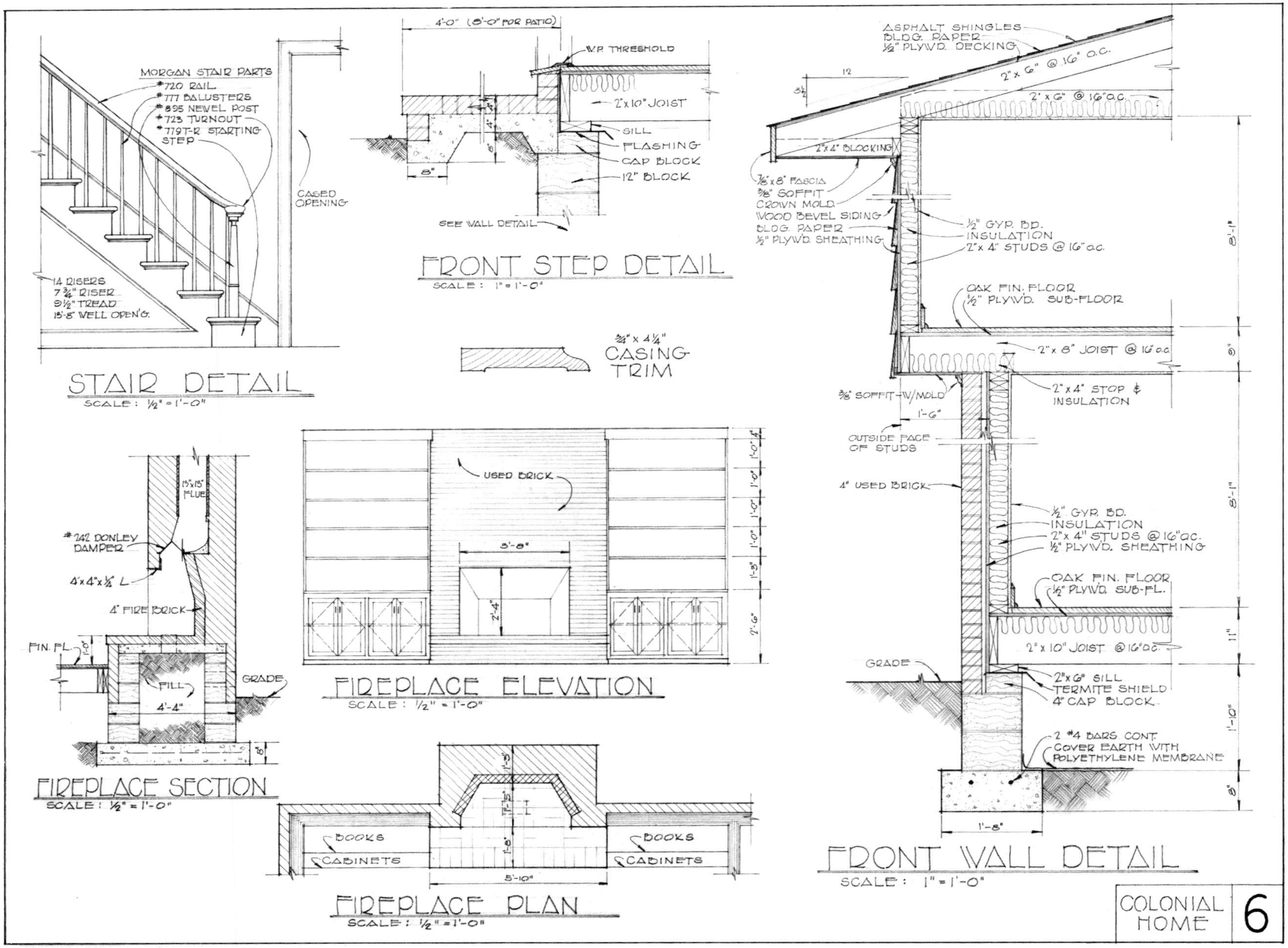

Fig. 10-14 Wall section and details.

Fig. 10-15 Pen-and-ink elevation rendering of a two-story home.

Partition layouts in second floors are somewhat restricted by the bearing walls below. Whenever possible, locate second-floor partitions directly over first-floor walls to avoid the need for additional support. Keep in mind that chimneys, stairs, and plumbing must be relative to the first floor when locating the walls, and that the vent stacks from first-floor plumbing must come up through second-floor partitions. Stairways should begin and end in hallways. Draw the top half of the stair representation from the first-floor half and include the proper note. Locate the center lines of second-floor windows; usually they are located directly above first-floor windows or centered over first-floor wall spaces. Complete the window symbols and identifications. Generally, window and door identifications are incorporated with first-floor schedules. All rooms must communicate with halls. Locate and draw the door symbols with the correct swing. Usually, doors 2′–6″ or 2′–8″ wide are used in bedrooms, and bathroom doors can be 2′–2″ or 2′–4″ wide. Partial, 1-story roofs, which are lower than the second-story roof, should be shown to clearly describe their relationships. Also show scuttles or ceiling exhaust fans with broken lines. Locate and draw all bathroom fixtures and built-in cabinetwork to scale. Show the lighting symbols and dimension partitions, walls, and windows, similar to the first-floor plan. Draw in the hatching symbols for materials, where necessary, and complete all appropriate construction notes.

Because of the similarity between first- and second-floor plan requirements, use the first-floor plan checklist to verify all the necessary second-floor plan information upon completion.

10.3 USE THE FIRST-FLOOR PLAN TO DEVELOP THE FOUNDATION (BASEMENT) PLAN

In modern residential construction basements are not as popular as they once were. Living space above ground is not only more economical, but it is more comfortable. However, a basement is included in the 1-story house to show its correct representation. Foundation plans of houses with crawl spaces would appear similar except that usually masonry piers are employed instead of metal columns for the floor framing supports.

Develop the foundation plan, like the second-floor plan, on tracing paper taped down directly over the first-floor plan. As with other steps in the completion of working drawings, the foundation plan requires information about the total concept of the structure before it can be drawn. Reference must be made to a *typical sill detail* or wall section, in order to relate the framing of the first floor and its position on the foundation wall. This information must be carefully observed if a satisfactory foundation is to be developed for the building. From the typical wall section of the 1-story house, notice that the exterior sheathing surface is flush with the outside surface of the foundation walls, and that the dimensions on the floor plan are given for the sheathing surface. In this case, the outside foundation lines are simply drawn exactly over the floor plan exterior lines. Relationships with other types of sill detail may not be as simple. For example, brick-veneer construction must have a foundation surface about 4″ or 5″ wide beyond the wood framing upon which the brick must bear. Other sill details may require still different relationships between the wood framing and the foundation walls. For this reason, the typical wall construction detail must be worked out (at least on preliminary sketches) before the foundation plan can be started. Study various sill details and observe the relative positions of the wood framing and the foundation wall. Western frame sills are commonly called "box sills."

The general shape of the foundation is drawn first, and since economical 8″ block has been selected for the foundation in this home, the thickness of the wall is scaled 8″ wide. Because the front entrance requires a concrete walk, which is exposed to the weather, this area could not be excavated; yet a block wall, for continuity, surrounds the area. A note is added to indicate the area is not excavated. Represent footing widths with broken lines. A satisfactory footing for 8″ block walls is usually 16″ wide. Even though the footings for the carport and terrace slab are poured integrally, the bearing surface of slabs is also shown with a broken line.

One of the important problems involved in foundation-plan development is the method of supporting the first floor, if wood framing is employed. It becomes obvious that floor joists cannot span the entire width of the plan, even if they are placed parallel to the short dimension. To best utilize the lengths of available joists, and to provide direct support under important points of load-bearing walls above, a 4″ × 10″ wood beam or girder is indicated along the stairwell through the entire length of the basement. This beam is supported by the foundation and equally spaced metal columns. Each column has an independent footing, also shown by broken lines. Columns are also necessary on the opposite side of the stairwell to prevent overloading the header joists at the ends of the stairwell.

As mentioned previously, concrete block piers would be used instead of the metal columns, if a similar wood frame floor were constructed above a crawl space with no basement. Ordinarily, the piers would be 16″ × 16″, hatched like the walls, and shown with independent footings and locating dimensions.

Another important consideration is the support for load-bearing walls above, other than those above the main girder. Outside walls are, of course, directly supported by the foundation walls, but interior walls must depend on floor joists for support. If a partition is perpendicular to the floor joists, no extra support is necessary, since its weight is distributed over a number of joists. But if the partition is parallel to the joists, often no joist falls directly below, and therefore, extra joists must be introduced to carry the load. Notice that double joists are indicated below parallel partitions. The layout of the first-floor plan, then, is a definite help in placing these additional members in the first-floor framing. Extra joists are also necessary below concentrations of bathroom fixtures and other special dead loads.

Place all notes and information pertaining to the first-floor framing on the foundation plan. Notes indicating details of the second-floor framing are included on the first-floor plan. In other words, the framing notes on any plan should pertain to the framing construction *directly overhead*. Use the conventional note for showing the size, spacing, and direction of first-floor joists (see Appendix D for joist sizes).

Windows should be installed in basements to allow light and ventilation. Screened vents and an access door are necessary in crawl spaces. Here again, it may be necessary to refer to elevation sketches or typical sections for more information about the placement of basement windows. Until the elevations are completed, it is usually difficult to determine the level of the grade line, and whether areaways around certain basement windows are necessary. If they are needed, include a section detail on the foundation-plan sheet.

Dimension all masonry (to faces), partitions, columns or piers (to centers), slabs, and special framing; and complete all notes indicating the floor material, windows, doors, and framing sizes. Title the plan and show its scale.

Foundation-Plan Information Checklist

_______ 1. All necessary dimensions.
- _____a. Masonry walls, surfaces, and thicknesses
- _____b. Partitions
- _____c. Columns or pilasters
- _____d. Girders or beams
- _____e. Double joists
- _____f. Outside slabs
- _____g. Arrowheads on all dimension lines

_______ 2. Window symbols, door symbols with swing.
_______ 3. Stair symbol and riser notes.
_______ 4. Footing indications under walls, colums, exterior stoops, piers.
_______ 5. Special floor framing.
_______ 6. Areaways, if necessary.
_______ 7. Lighting symbols.
- _____a. Ceiling outlets
- _____b. Switches with broken lines to outlets
- _____c. Sufficient wall outlets
- _____d. Mechanical equipment outlets

_______ 8. Symbol hatching of materials.
_______ 9. Note indicating unexcavated areas.
_______10. Note indicating floor surfaces.
_______11. Exterior slabs.
_______12. Plumbing fixtures, heating units.
_______13. Foundation-wall vents and access door.
_______14. Fireplace foundation.
_______15. Basement door.
_______16. Foundation-plan title and scale.

10.4 PROJECT ELEVATIONS FROM THE FLOOR PLAN (FIG. 10-16)

Elevations are the "pictures" of the house, revealing not only the height dimensions and exterior materials, but also providing carpenters and workmen a "total view" of the building.

Fig. 10-16 Project elevation views from the plan so correct measurements can be quickly made.

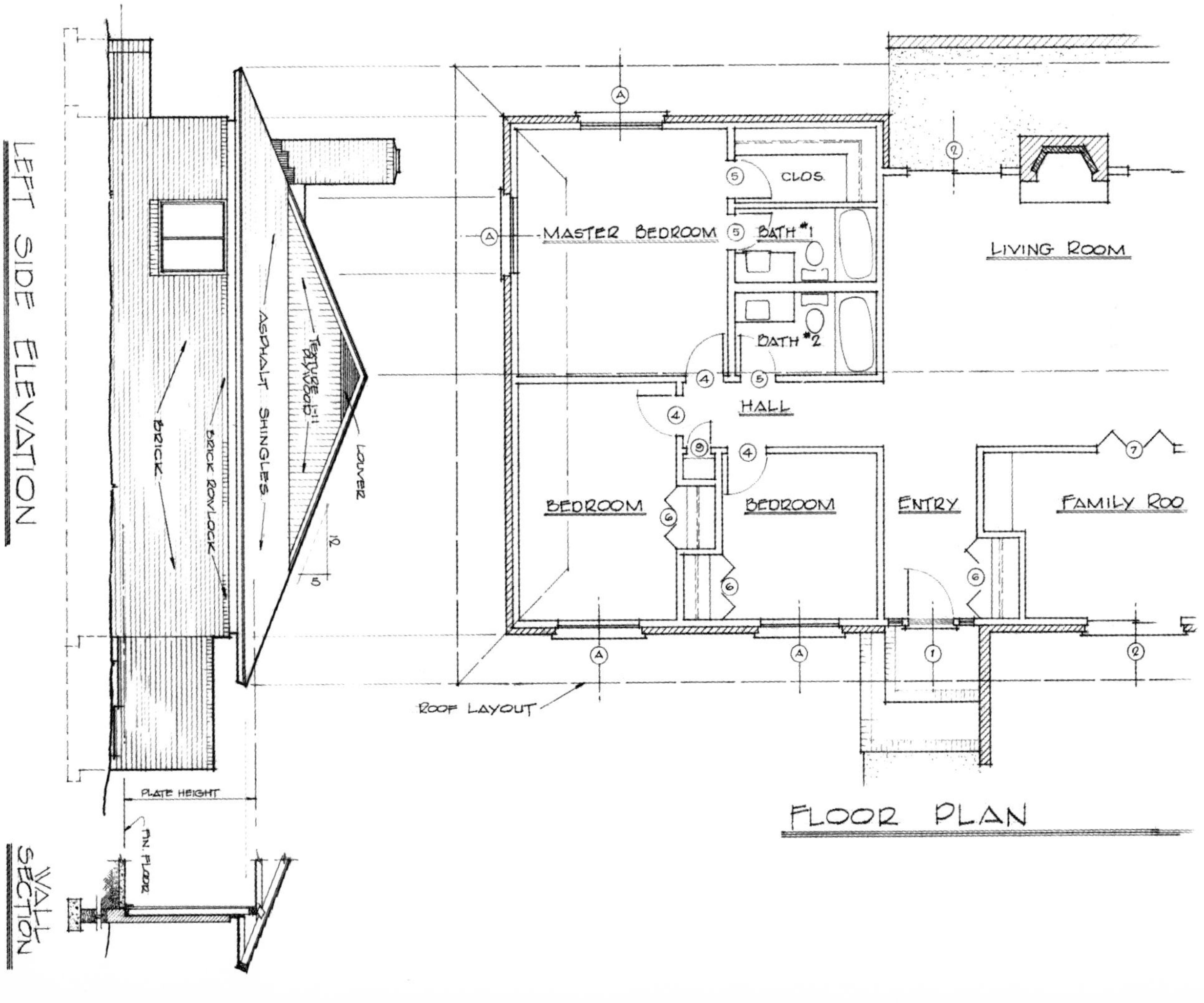

This total representation is more important than generally realized. Specific information about various parts of a building is shown in details, drawn large enough to reveal small members; but unless these details can be related to the total concept of the building, they cannot be understood. The elevations help tie together these bits of information. Also, if minor construction details and dimensions are not shown on working drawings, workmen must continually refer to elevation views for the specified finished appearance. Builders have slightly different methods of arranging members and trim during construction without violating given details. A graphic representation of the correct finished appearance, then, places considerable importance on the elevation views. Drawing these views is not difficult if the proper procedure is followed.

Although we have not discussed wall sections (Figs. 9-1 through 9-4), which are necessary in determining definite elevation-view heights, the student should at this point develop a typical wall section, if he has not already done so for the foundation plan (see Section 9.2). Consideration should also be given to the general roof layout and the amount of roof overhang, especially if offset exterior walls are encountered, which may require a roof plan drawn on another sheet of paper.

Draw the elevations by taking their widths from the plan view and their heights from the developed wall sections. If the house has a gable roof, start with an end-elevation so that the profile of the roof can be established and transferred directly to the other elevations. Tape the plan to the board directly above the intended space for the elevation so that projection can be made with instruments. Or a tick-strip (a narrow strip of paper with the necessary markings) can be used to transfer all outside walls, window and door openings, center lines, and even roof overhangs, to the elevation view. Use the same scale as the plan ($\frac{1}{4}'' = 1'\text{–}0''$), allowing direct transfer. Elevations of larger buildings are usually drawn to the $\frac{1}{8}'' = 1'\text{–}0''$ scale, however.

Inasmuch as an elevation must have a horizontal line from which to spring, the tentative *grade line* is the logical beginning. Draw a light horizontal line (even if the finished grade must be made to slope later) and allow enough space on the paper for the foundation below and the height of the building above. From the sill detail or wall section, lay out the *finish-floor line* lightly —it will become an important reference line later. Various types of construction establish definite dimensions from the grade to the finished floor surface. Ceiling heights are indicated by distances to the top of the double wall plate, which usually are 8′–1″ above the floor line. Draw two plate heights if two stories are required. Remember that both the ceiling framing and roof rafters bear on the top double wall plate.

Take roof pitches and cornice construction from details or sketches and lay out the profile of the roof, after the center line of the ridge is established. On sloping roofs, be sure the roof line allows for the width of the rafters at the bird's-mouth on the top-plate bearing surface (see Figs. 9-1A and 9-2A). If trussed rafters are used, the lower chord of the trusses rests directly on the wall plates. Extend the roof lines beyond the walls to show the proper amount of overhang, draw the fascia board, and complete the exterior treatment of the cornice area. After critical examination, slight changes may be necessary in the roof profile to obtain the desired pleasing appearance.

To establish the heights of windows and doors on the elevation, measure the height of exterior doors (usually 6′–8″ or 7′–0″ stock doors) from the *finish-floor surface,* and extend this height as the head for all windows and doors on the first-floor level. Correct window sizes, taken from manufacturers' literature, are then established from the head height. Features of windows and doors, including trim and brick sills if necessary, are carefully drawn on elevation views. If a number of similar windows are needed, it usually becomes simpler to draw the window accurately on a small piece of paper first, then slip this drawing under each window position and trace it. Second-floor windows are located according to inside requirements and outside appearance; generally upper windows line up with lower windows, and higher windows are reduced in size. Place window identifications (letters or numbers within small circles) directly on the window symbol.

Project chimneys from the plan also, and extend their heights at least 2′ above the ridgeline. Slight changes in position are possible through attic spaces, if chimneys must appear symmetrical after piercing the roof.

Draw the footing and foundation lines below the grade lines with broken lines. Basement heights are usually 7′ or 7′–6″, and footings should extend down below local frost depths. The grade line can be changed, if necessary, to the desired finished level or slope. Strengthen all important elevation lines, especially the outline of the view and the eave line, and show the symbol for the various exterior materials. Portions of the hatching should be left out near the centers of large areas to prevent a mechanical appearance.

Dimensions on elevations need be only those that cannot be shown on details and plans. Dimension the finish-floor and ceiling heights, chimney heights, extended-wall heights, window heights (other than standard door heights), and other features requiring a vertical dimension. To make the elevations informative without appearing too cluttered, simple notes should indicate exterior materials such as flashings, gutters, downspouts, and steps. Indicate the roof pitch with a graphic diagram (see Section 9.3).

Usually four elevations must be drawn for a complete description of the building; project the other elevations from the correct wall of the floor plan and the elevation just completed. It is advantageous to construct subsequent elevations in-line, either vertically or horizontally, so that the layout of major features can be easily projected, even though features appear reversed in opposite elevations. Occasionally, it becomes necessary, even for experienced draftsmen, to make minor changes in the elevations and plans as work progresses. Students surely can expect changes to occur in early exercises, until more facility is attained in handling the many interrelated conditions that exist in developing a complete set of working drawings. But perseverance is rewarding—subsequent drawings will become much easier.

Elevation-Views Information Checklist

_______ 1. All necessary dimensions.
- _____a. Floor-to-ceiling heights
- _____b. Window heights
- _____c. Chimney heights
- _____d. Footing depths
- _____e. Roof overhang
- _____f. Special feature heights or depths

_______ 2. Grade line, floor lines, ceiling lines.
_______ 3. Correct window symbols and identification.
_______ 4. Correct door symbols and identification.
_______ 5. Footing and foundation lines (broken).
_______ 6. Roof-slope indications.
_______ 7. Exterior materials symbols.
_______ 8. Exterior materials notes.
_______ 9. Louvers; attic, crawl space, roof.
_______10. Notes indicating special features.
_______11. Section cutting-plane lines and identifications.
_______12. Exterior steps, stoops, roofed open areas, railings.
_______13. Columns, shutters.
_______14. Necessary dormers.
_______15. Flashing, gutters, downspouts.
_______16. Elevation title and scale.

10.5 SELECT SCALES SUITABLE TO THE DETAILS

To utilize remaining spaces on working drawings, details must be drawn to accommodate the layout. Usually a detail is easier to read if it is drawn to a large scale. When there are many details, one or more additional sheets may be required. Follow the procedure indicated in Chapter 9 when drawing the *wall sections* as well as other major details. For clarity, the typical wall section in the 1-story house has been drawn in its entirety.

10.6 DRAWING TRANSVERSE AND LONGITUDINAL SECTIONS

When buildings have various floor levels or unusual interior construction, such as split-levels, a full section through the entire house is often drawn. Such a section shows features in their relative positions, rather than as isolated details on the drawing, and becomes very informative to workmen on the job. A full section taken through the narrow width of a house is known as a "transverse" section; through the long dimension it is known as a "longitudinal" section. Either can be used, depending upon which plane reveals the necessary information. The cutting plane can be straight across, or it can be offset to conveniently gather in features on several planes, thereby increasing the value of the drawing. Broken lines are also effective in showing, if necessary, important structural members beyond visible surfaces. For convenience, full sections are usually drawn to the same scale as the elevations.

In the drawings for the 1-story house, a transverse section has been included to show, among other things, the construction of the sloping ceiling and roof in the living-dining area and the shape and position of cabinets in the kitchen area. The section also shows the basement and unexcavated foundation clearly, as well as information about the walls and the roof overhang. It gives a good idea about the shape of the total living-dining "volume."

To draw a transverse or longitudinal section, tape the tracing paper directly over the proper elevation view and trace the outline of the house, the floor levels, heights of windows and doors, the foundation, grade line, etc. Considerable time is saved by working directly over the elevation. Interior partitions, stairs, etc., are taken from the plans. Keep in mind the direction and spacing of ceiling and floor framing members, the placement of girders, headers, columns, etc. Limit the notes on the section to important features within the building. Place the cutting-plane indication on the floor plan where offsets, if any, can be seen. Floor and ceiling heights, other vertical dimensions, footing depths, and roof pitch, are easily dimensioned on the full section.

10.7 DRAWING THE KITCHEN DETAILS (INTERIOR ELEVATIONS)

The kitchens in today's homes generally require built-in cabinets for work counters, fixture enclosures, and storage. Builders usually subcontract this millwork and have it installed prebuilt instead of building it on the job.

Kitchen details, showing the size, shape, and general cabinet design, are helpful to the subcontractors, who must not only estimate the cost, but must fabricate and install the units as well. The heights and widths of kitchen cabinets have been standardized according to body measurements, however, often special arrangements and conditions exist in custom-designed kitchens requiring accurately drawn details on the working drawings.

To draw the kitchen details, select a scale that will make the finished elevations neither too large nor too small, usually $\frac{1}{2}'' = 1'\text{–}0''$ is the best scale on residential drawings. Lay out each wall elevation upon which the cabinets are to be installed (keep them in a horizontal row, if space allows) and lightly draw the horizontal heights of the cabinet features—4″ toe space, 36″ base-cabinet height, thickness of the countertop, heights of the wall cabinets, etc. Notice that wall cabinets often only go to a point 14″ below the standard, 8′ ceiling, because of difficulty in reaching any higher. This area above wall cabinets can be furred-out flush with the face of the cabinets, or cabinets can be extended to the ceiling to be used for dead storage. Sometimes a shelf is left above wall cabinets, but it becomes a dust collector. These features must be shown on the details. When the kitchen is U- or L-shaped, the cabinets must return toward the viewer at one or both corners. At this point a "profile" section of the cabinetwork is drawn, and either the cut profile is hatched entirely, or it can be shown as a section with the top, doors, shelves construction, etc., carefully described. After the returning sections are drawn, the remaining cabinet elevation surfaces are carefully laid out to show the doors and drawer faces (they look best if symmetrical and larger drawers are shown at the bottom of the cabinet) with hardware indications simply drawn. Use broken lines to indicate the door swing and the shelves within the cabinets. Show any windows or doors with their trim, which can be seen on the kitchen elevations. If necessary, draw an enlarged plan of the kitchen; otherwise the arrangement of the cabinets shown on the floor plans is satisfactory. Include a symbol on the plan indicating the proper view of each kitchen detail, such as A, B, C, etc. Indicate all installed kitchen equipment, sink, stove unit, range hood, dishwasher, etc., with a note, strengthen important lines, and add appropriate dimensions. Do not forget a "splash" above the countertops, and indicate the countertop covering material.

10.8 DRAWING THE BATHROOM DETAILS (INTERIOR ELEVATIONS)

Here again, details must be drawn of bathroom interiors if ceramic tile or other specially applied surfacing is to be used for the floor and wall covering, so that subcontractors can estimate and satisfactorily complete the work. Many bathrooms have built-in cabinetwork also.

To draw the bathroom details, use a scale similar to the kitchen details (usually ½″ = 1′–0″), and lay out—in a horizontal row if possible—the heights and widths of the walls that are to receive special covering or cabinetwork. Show the height of the wall wainscoting (6′ high around shower areas, and 4′ high on other walls), all mirrors, cabinets, bathroom fixtures, tile fixtures, wall offsets, windows and doors, all at their proper scale and heights. Relate each bathroom elevation to the floor plan layout with a direction indication. Use light horizontal and vertical lines to represent the elevation symbol for ceramic tile, which is scaled 4″ sq. Complete the necessary notes and dimensions, title each view, and show the scale.

10.9 DRAWING FIXED-GLASS DETAILS

With the increased use of glass in many homes, "fixed glass" has become an economical method of providing generous window openings without the expense of prefabricated window units. Some prefabricated units, however, incorporating both fixed glass and opening sash, can be installed into rough openings that have been sized according to the units. Fixed glass installed in framing on the job is not restricted by manufacturers' sizes and can be made satisfactory if well-conceived details are followed. Appearance may require finish lumber for the structural framing around the glass, or finish lumber must surround rough framing when the fixed glass is trimmed out (Fig. 9-12).

In drawing fixed-glass details, sections must be drawn through the sill, jamb, head, and adjoining mullions, showing the following conditions: first, the rough opening must be made substantial enough to eliminate any structural changes in the framing caused by shrinkage or bending of members from overhead wall loads. Proper lintels must be provided above fixed glass to prevent stresses, unless plank-and-beam framing relieves the window opening of this necessity.

Secondly, the surrounds within the rough window opening, which receive the glass, must have rabbets at least ½″ deep to allow a loosely sized piece of glass to be set in a bed of putty and be held firmly, yet allowing slight flexibility. Window stops (usually attached on the interior) must be sized as thick as the rabbets so that their surface coincides with the exterior trim surface in contact with the glass. The trim member forming the exterior sill should be inclined slightly to allow water to drain properly from the sill surface. This principle of water drainage is true of all exposed materials forming ledges on walls. Drips should also be provided on head and sill exteriors to prevent water from running back under the members into the construction. Outside and inside wall edges must be kept in line so that inside casing trim will cover the joint between the surrounds and the interior wall surfacing, and the exterior will work out with exterior surfacing materials. In brick-veneer construction, the glass is placed within the stud wall, yet the trim must be wide enough to cover the air space between the stud wall and the brick. A masonry sill must be shown in masonry wall openings with fixed glass. Inside stools below the fixed glass must extend beyond the inside wall surface and have proper apron trim. Each detail should be labeled and dimensions should be applied to the different trim members. If prefabricated, operating sash for ventilation are incorporated with fixed windows, the glass surface of both should line up on the same vertical plane.

10.10 THE PLOT PLAN ORIENTS THE HOUSE TO THE LOT

The plot plan, showing important natural features, orients the building accurately on the property. Information about lot size, shape, elevation, contours, roads, setback requirements, etc., must be taken from a survey map or legal description of the property and drawn to a convenient scale. Use the civil engineer's scale to lay out and dimension all land measurements in feet and decimal parts of a foot. The dimensions on construction features, however, should be shown in feet and inches. Usually, a scale of 1″ = 20′ or 1″ = 10′ is satisfactory, depending upon the size of the lot; sometimes the scale, $\frac{1}{16}$″ = 1′–0″ is used, but the drawing should be large enough to show features and dimensions clearly.

After the outline of the lot is blocked in, determine the most favorable position of the

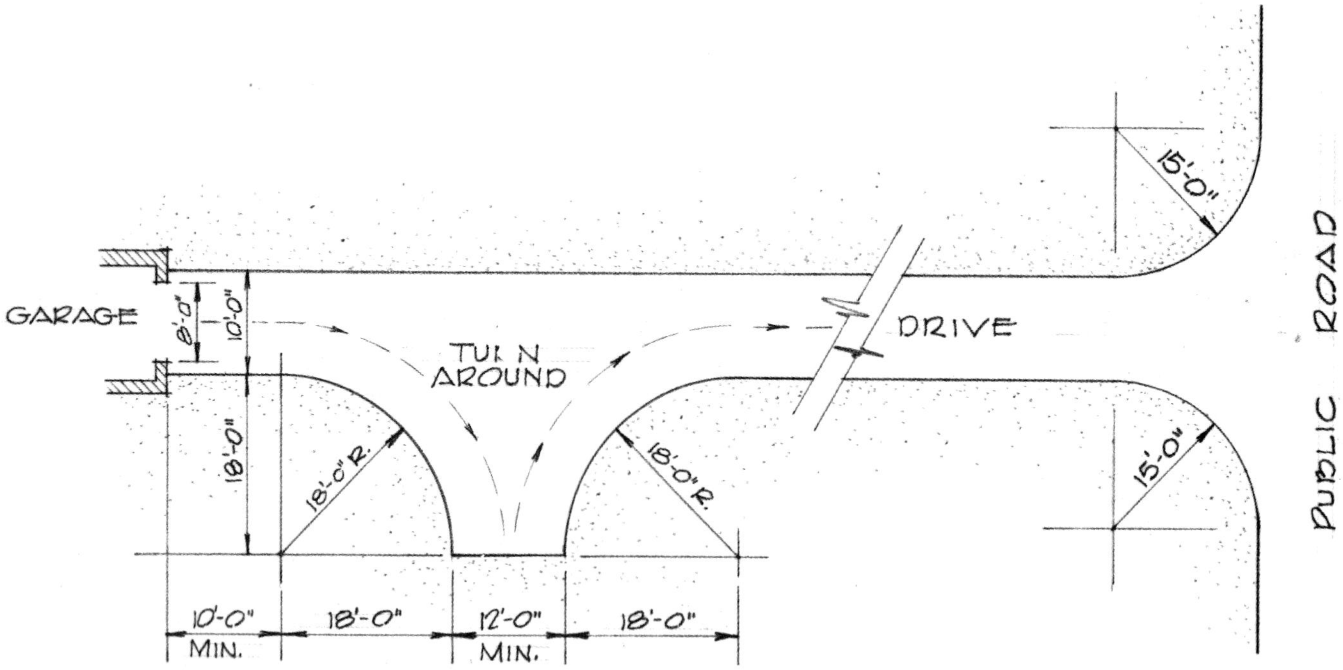

Fig. 10-17 Layout of private drives and turning radii.

house, and draw the outline of the foundation and all the exterior slabs, terraces, walks, drives, etc. (Occasionally a roof plan is drawn instead of the foundation.) If contour lines are available from the survey map, show the original lines broken and the finish contour lines as solid lines. On the plot plan of the 1-story house, the contour lines are shown with 1′ intervals, and upon investigation it will be noticed that the lot slopes toward the left-rear corner. Excavation from the basement has been used to build up the terrace slab to its necessary level, and the finish contour lines indicate this surface change. Hatch the house area to give it prominence, and if necessary, use other hatching variations to show relative contrast on other important indications. Often trees or other natural features are shown on the plot plan to denote their nonremoval during excavation and grading. See Fig. 10-17 for drive layouts.

Use the following checklist, from FHA plot plan information requirements, as a guide for dimensioning and completing the plot plan.

Plot Plan Information Checklist

_______ 1. Scale of the drawing and title.
_______ 2. Dimensions of the plot and north point.
_______ 3. Lot and block number of the plot.
_______ 4. Dimensions of front, rear, and side yards.
_______ 5. Location and dimensions of garage, carport, or other accessory buildings.
_______ 6. Location of walks, driveways, and approaches, with dimensions and materials.
_______ 7. Location of steps, terraces, porches, fences, and retaining walls.
_______ 8. Location and dimensions of easements and established setback requirements, if any.
_______ 9. Elevation level of first floor, floor of garage, carport, or other buildings.
_______ 10. Finish-grade level at each principal corner of the structure.
_______ 11. Finish grade at both sides of abrupt changes of grade such as walls, slopes, etc.
_______ 12. Other elevation levels that may be necessary to show grading and drainage.
_______ 13. Location of a reference bench mark and its elevation, from which contractor can relate all grades.
_______ 14. Existing trees, if any, to be removed or retained and their identification.
_______ 15. Location and identification of utility pipes that will service the structure.
_______ 16. Septic tank and leaching field, if required.
_______ 17. Obstructions such as utility poles, catch basins, hydrants, etc.

REVIEW QUESTIONS

1. When starting a floor plan, why is it necessary to begin with general shapes and light lines?

2. What is meant by a "wet-wall"?

3. On wood frame construction drawings, why is it convenient for workmen to have dimensions shown from the outside of exterior-wall studs to the center lines of partitions?

4. Why are lengthy notes about construction commonly put in the specifications rather than on the working drawings?

5. Why is a floor plan more readable when symbol hatching has been used throughout the walls?

6. Does a joist note, giving size, spacing, and direction, and shown on a floor plan pertain to the framing above or below?

7. Why are piers within a crawl space generally masonry? How is this indicated?

8. What does the term "unexcavated" mean when shown on part of a foundation plan?

9. Of what value is the finish-floor-line indication on an elevation view?

10. What dimensions must necessarily be put on elevation views?

"A comfortable house is a great source of happiness. It ranks immediately after health and good conscience."—Sydney Smith

11

Residential Mechanical and Electrical Systems

Much of the comfort and livability of our present-day structures is provided by the wide variety of mechanical and electrical equipment now available to us. The various methods of conditioning the air within a building, the host of electrical appliances and lighting devices, the accommodations for plumbing facilities, arrangements for use of public utilities—all must be given careful attention by the designer of both homes and commercial buildings. No structure is considered complete without adequate provision for this equipment and the human comfort it affords.

For large jobs, architects commonly employ the services of specialists to design layouts and furnish drawings dealing with mechanical and electrical systems. Engineering firms, who employ draftsmen specializing in this type of work, are equipped to handle the complexity of problems involved. Separate drawings such as a "Heating and Air-Conditioning Plan," "Electrical Plan," "Plumbing Plan," etc., are prepared and combined with the architectural set of working drawings. However, much of the technical information needed on larger installations is not usually required for the majority of residential work; subcontractors can design and install conventional residential equipment with a minimum of information on working drawings. Commonly, this information can be included on the regular floor plan. Of course, when regular floor plans become overcrowded with notes, symbols, and information, it frequently is advisable to draw separate plans for each of these areas of information, especially for the heating system.

Even though subcontractors usually lay out and design conventional residential heating-cooling, plumbing, and electrical systems, the student of architectural drawing, in order to plan for accommodating this equipment, should understand the general characteristics of the currently used systems and the problems involved in making them successful. Their provision in the structure contributes to the workability of the "total concept" and thereby justifies their careful study.

11.1 PLANNING THE HEATING AND COOLING SYSTEM

In homes, the selection of the most appropriate heating system is closely related to other aspects of the building, such as necessity for a utility room, feasibility of a basement, selection of floor construction materials, etc., and probably requires more consideration during early planning than other equipment installations. Type and cost of fuel available in the area are important factors; the client's preference as to the method of heating the house requires attention. Local climate, degree of comfort desired, initial cost of equipment, efficiency, amount of insulation should also be given serious thought. In many areas, year-round air conditioning is now almost a "must," and equipment capable of providing interior comfort in all seasons is a sound investment.

Local and national codes relating to heating and cooling installation must be carefully observed.

11.2 ARCHITECTURAL CONSIDERATIONS FOR HEATING AND COOLING

Comfort and efficiency of heating and cooling equipment begin with incorporating the following construction features into the building during the design stage:

1. Protect the west walls of the house from direct afternoon sun. This can be done by placing the carport or garage on the west side or by using trees, planting, or fences for protection.
2. Use large glass areas on the south side, with sufficient overhangs or sunshades to protect the glass from direct sun during the summer months.
3. Protect the house, if possible, from cold winter winds. This is a matter of orientation and the intelligent use of windbreaks.
4. Use a light-colored roof to reduce heat absorption during summer for more cooling efficiency.
5. Specify sufficient insulation in both the walls and the ceilings. Use 2″ or 3″ in exterior walls, 4″ or 6″ in ceilings for continual year-round comfort.
6. Provide for sufficient ventilation in attics, kitchens, baths, and laundries to eliminate excessive interior moisture.
7. In colder areas, specify insulating (double) glass in all fixed-glass windows and window units. Double panes will not only reduce important heat losses, but will prevent destructive condensation from forming on glass and surrounding wood trim.
8. Locate the heating unit near the chimney or provide as short and direct a smoke pipe as possible.
9. For the most heating efficiency, plan a compact shape of the house perimeter.
10. In 2-story houses, provide coinciding first- and second-floor partitions for heat risers to the second story, chases may even be necessary.
11. Specify weather stripping on all doors and windows.

11.3 CURRENT RESIDENTIAL HEATING SYSTEMS

Employing various fuels and methods of installation, the following basic systems are now generally used for residential central heating:

1. *Forced warm air* which heats the air in a furnace, forces it through ducts with the use of a fan to all the heated areas of the house, returns the cooled air, and filters it.
2. *Hot-water systems,* either 1-pipe or 2-pipe, which heat water in a central boiler and circulate it through piping to the different rooms where various types of convectors, radiators, baseboard, or radiant panels, supply the heat to the air.
3. *Electric radiant systems,* using electricity as an energy source, provide a comfortable radiant-type heat with the use of resistance wiring embedded in either floors or ceilings or mounted in metal baseboards.
4. *Heat pumps,* which use no primary fuel other than electricity to run the motor, operate as a combination heating and cooling system. However, supplementary electric resistance heating

elements may be necessary during extreme temperature drops. The application for heating and cooling purposes is recent; heat pumps have been found adequate primarily in mild climates. A heat-pump unit is basically a refrigeration system using electrical energy to pump the natural heat from either air or water outside the house to produce a useful temperature level within the house. The procedure is reversed during summer cooling.

Although steam heat is occasionally used, its popularity as a method of residential heating is steadily declining.

In warm climates, small wall or floor units are sometimes more satisfactory than central systems. Also, unit heaters can be combined with central systems when isolated areas are difficult to heat with a main system.

11.3.1 Forced Warm-Air Systems

These systems utilize a motor-driven fan to circulate filtered and heated air from the central heating unit, called an exchanger, through a system of ducts to each part of the house. Often provision is made for the introduction of a small amount of fresh outside air to the system. Warm air has become the most popular heating method in the majority of new homes throughout the country, mainly because of its economical initial cost and its compatibility and ease in combining with summer cooling systems. Heat distribution throughout the house is instantaneous—almost as soon as the furnace is turned on. Filters, introduced into the return ductwork, provide clean air throughout the operation. This heating system has an additional advantage: location of the furnaces is not restricted to basements or utility rooms. Furnaces of various types and sizes can conveniently be installed in crawl spaces, attics, small closets, or adjoining garages. In addition, the design features of many modern furnaces make them acceptable for installation in living spaces, such as recreation and play rooms. The furnace can be either the conventional "up-flow" or reverse "counterflow" (see Fig. 11-1), depending upon its placement and necessary duct system. Counterflow furnaces, of course, must be used when ducts are embedded in concrete slab floors or when above-the-floor furnaces must supply the warm air through ducts located in crawl spaces.

Various types of ductwork can be used with warm-air furnaces. Circular sheet-metal ducts are usually the most economical. Fiberglas ducts are often used in attic installations, paper ducts in concrete-slab construction. Many systems utilize a "perimeter" arrangement, both in slabs and crawl spaces, as well as in some basement installations, whereby a continuous duct is placed near the periphery of the building, and a number of "feeder" ducts radiating out from the central plenum supply the perimeter duct with warm air (Figs. 11-2, 11-3, and 11-4). Room registers receive the warm air from the perimeter duct only. Another method utilizes a main trunk duct through the central part of the building, and smaller branch ducts carry the warm air to the different rooms. Rectangular sheet-metal

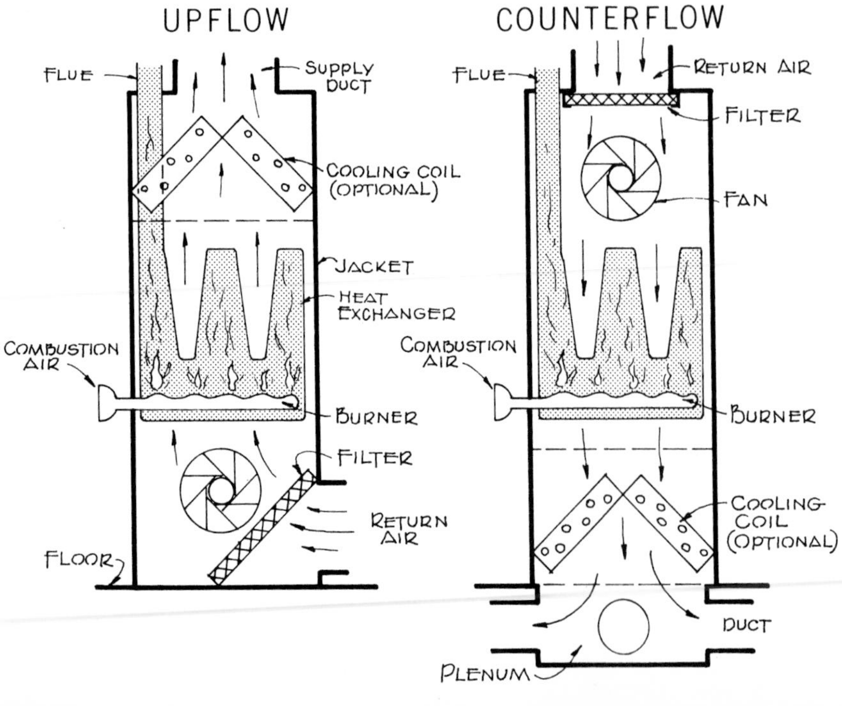

Fig. 11-1 Section diagrams of typical gas-fired furnaces for warm-air heating systems. Similar furnaces are made for other fuels and various furnace shapes are available. Cooling coils are shown for the combination heating-cooling operation. The counterflow furnace is usually used in slab or crawl-space construction.

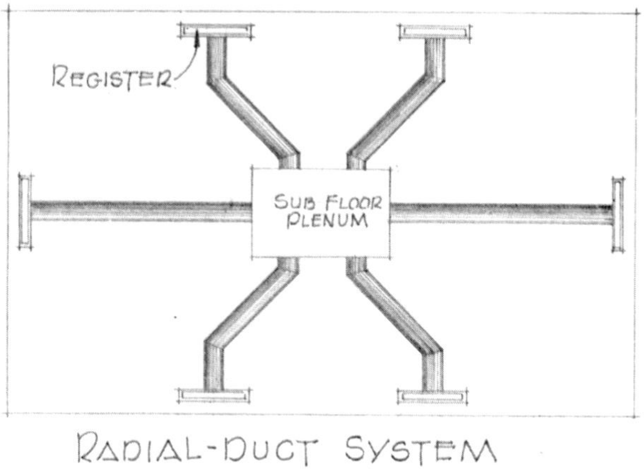

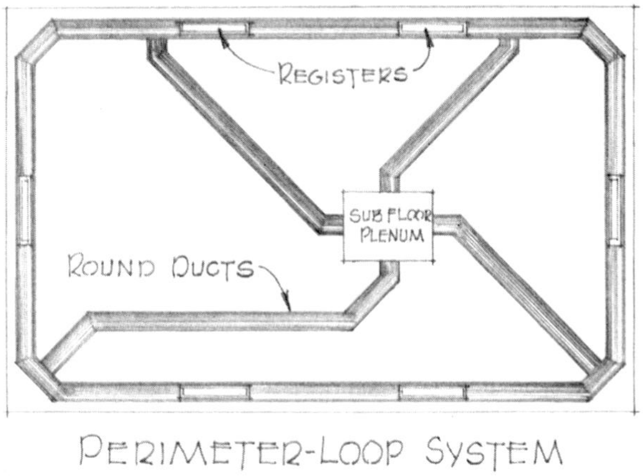

Fig. 11-2 Warm-air duct systems used in slabs and crawl spaces.

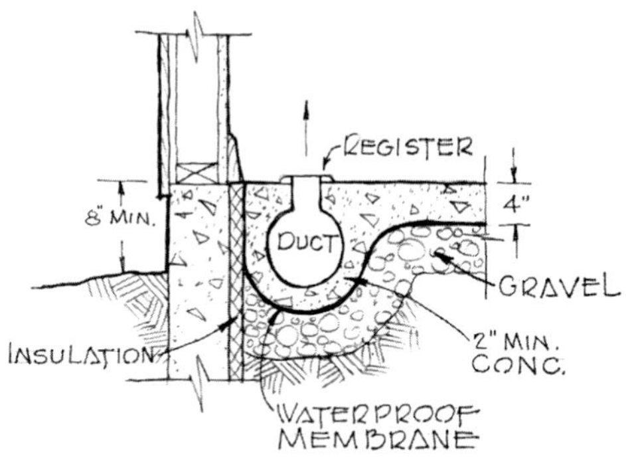

Fig. 11-3 Sketch detail of slab construction and perimeter heat duct.

Fig. 11-4 Typical floor register.

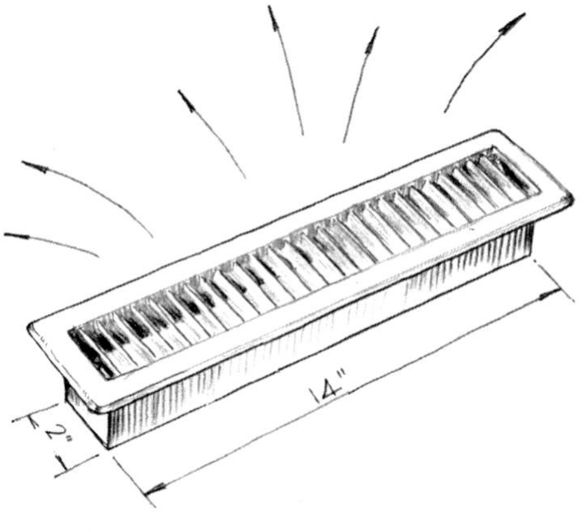

ducts are usually used for this system, and a more compact and neater arrangement for basement installation results. Another system has a large central duct, called an "extended plenum," with small circular ducts to each register (See Fig. 11-5).

Return ducts, usually shorter and larger in cross section, bring the cooled air back to the furnace.

The trend in residential installations is to give more consideration to return air-duct sizing. Many systems now provide for the introduction of fresh air through adjustable outside registers capable of compensating for air not returned from kitchens, baths, and vent fans. This maintains a continual supply of fresh air in the home and, because of infiltration, equalizes return air pressures.

Quite another system of warm-air distribution in 1-story homes is called the "ceiling panel" system. A false or secondary ceiling is constructed 3″ below the regular ceiling, through which the warm air is evenly dispersed with the use of baffles. After giving off the heat by conduction to the lower ceiling, the air is forced back to the furnace through regular ductwork. No heated air enters the rooms themselves, and therefore no drafts are created; yet the heat given off by the ceiling maintains a comfortable temperature level within each room.

We see, then, that various systems of warm-air distribution are available to the home designer and that each system has slightly different characteristics and applications (Figs. 11-5 through 11-9).

The modern warm-air system, comprising the furnace, ductwork, fan, and registers, usually has automatic controls to make it almost self-sufficient in operation. The controls necessary to operate a typical warm-air system are:

1. Room thermostat;
2. Fan thermostat; and
3. High-limit control.

Occasionally, warm-air furnaces are equipped with humidifiers, in which case a "humidistat" is used to control the correct humidity level. However, residential humidifiers are often troublesome and frequently omitted in residential heating systems.

The *room thermostat* automatically turns the burner on when inside temperatures drop below a preestablished setting and turns it off when

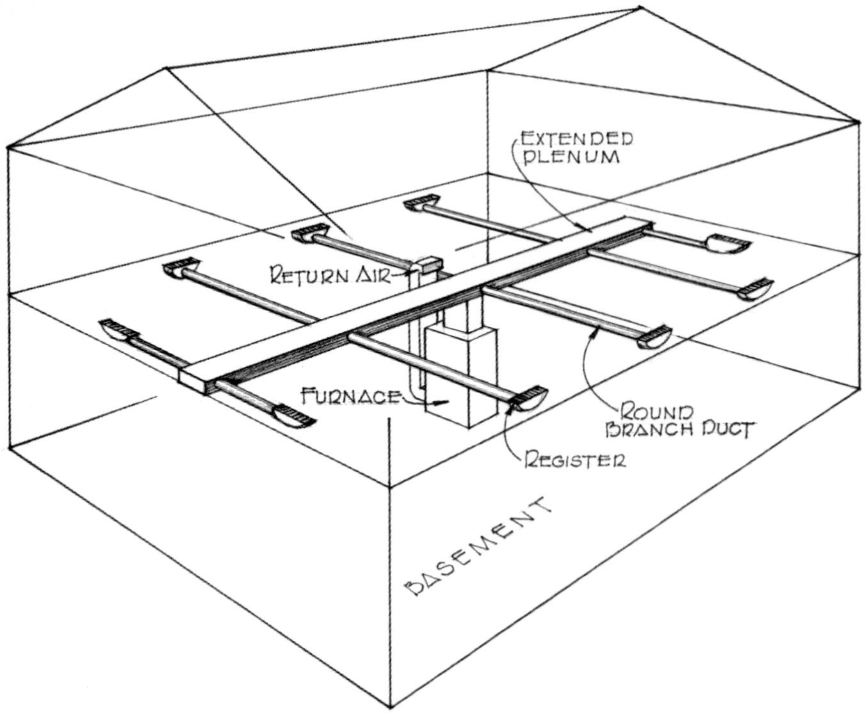

Fig. 11-5 Warm-air distribution system with an extended plenum and round ducts to the room registers. The furnace is located in the basement.

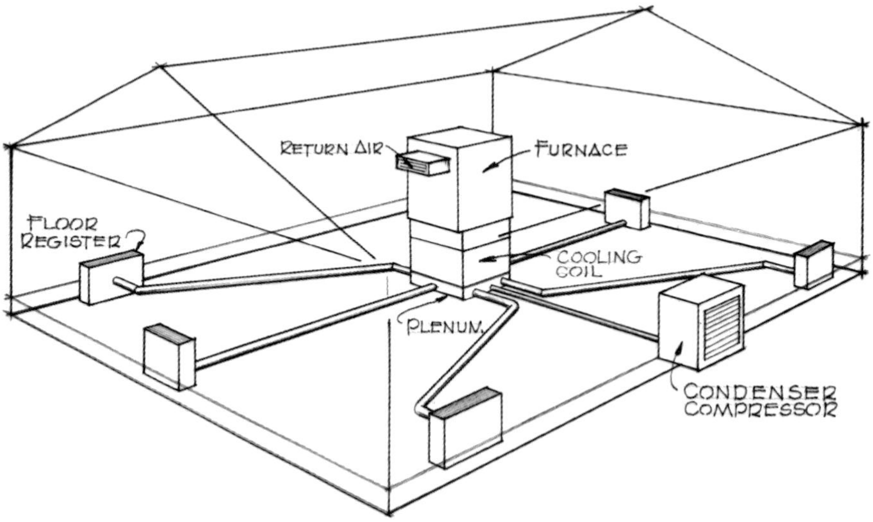

Fig. 11-6 A radial distribution system using round ducts for a slab or for a crawl space. If used for heating only, the cooling coils and compressor-condenser unit are omitted. The counterflow furnace is necessary in this installation.

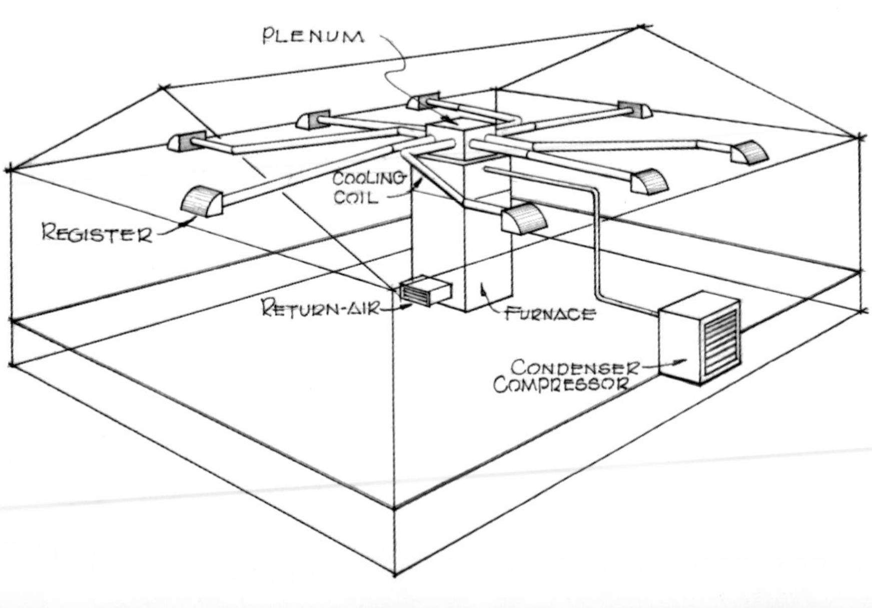

Fig. 11-7 Attic distribution system using round ducts is practical when ceiling registers are used.

Fig. 11-8 Forced-air heating-cooling distribution system using rectangular ducts. The furnace and cooling unit are placed in the basement.

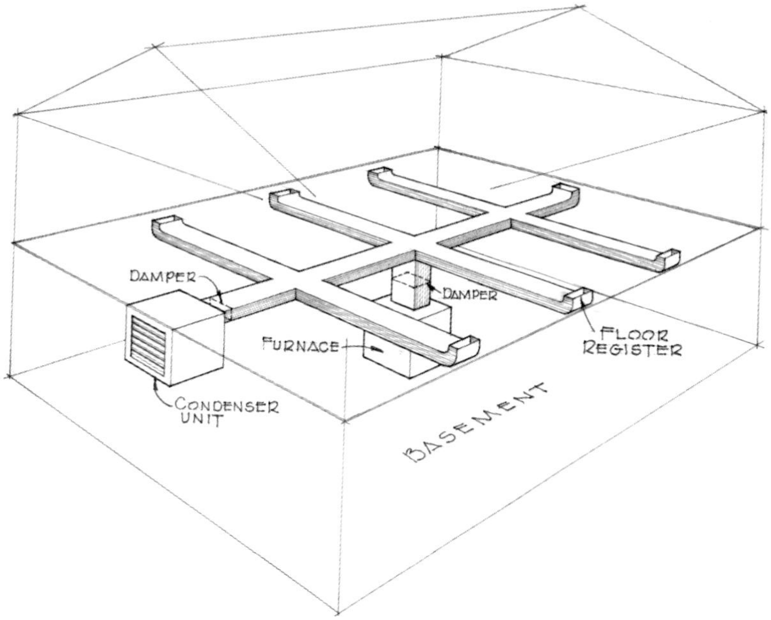

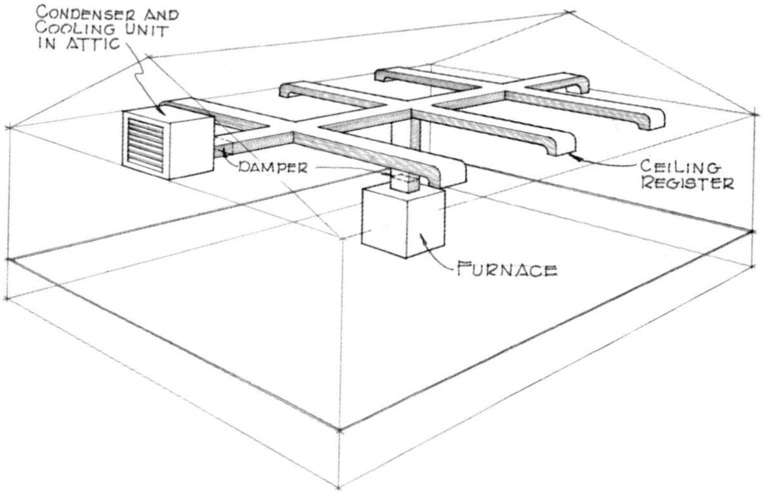

Fig. 11-9 Forced-air heating-cooling distribution system using rectangular ducts to ceiling registers. The furnace is placed on the first floor, and the cooling unit is placed in the attic. Warm-air furnaces can also be placed in the attic, and cooling units are available for placement in crawl spaces.

the desired temperature has been attained. The thermostat should be located 5′ from the floor on an inside wall with free air circulation that will provide uniform temperature levels throughout the house. The *fan thermostat* is located within the furnace unit and turns the fan on when the heated air in the plenum reaches a comfortable temperature for circulation. When the room thermostat turns the burner off, and the air in the plenum drops to a temperature level too low for circulation, the fan is turned off. The *high-limit control,* also located in the furnace unit, is a safety device for the purpose of turning the furnace completely off should a malfunction occur causing the temperature within the plenum to become dangerously high.

11.3.2 Hot-Water Systems (Hydronic Systems)

Heat distribution with the use of water has been in practice for many years and is still considered a very satisfactory method—approximately one-fourth of all new homes built today employ some form of hot-water heating.

The central boiler (Fig. 11-10), utilizing gas, oil, or coal as a fuel, heats water from a cold-water supply to the required temperature (usually 200°F) and pumps it throughout the rooms by means of various piping systems. A simple 1-pipe system, having room converters or radiators connected in series, allows the water to be carried in the main pipe and diverted to the convectors, then returned to the boiler for reheat-

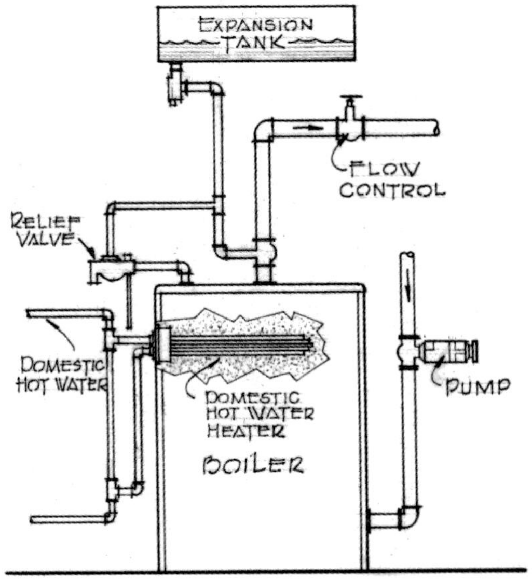

Fig. 11-10 Diagram of a boiler used with hot-water heating systems.

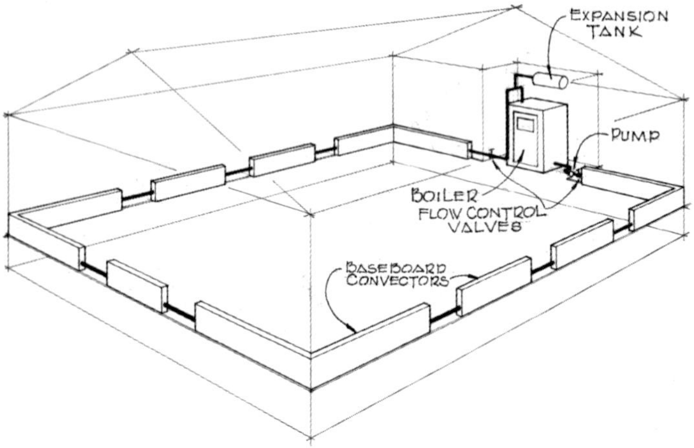

Fig. 11-11 One-pipe hot-water heating system with baseboard convectors in the rooms.

Fig. 11-12 Two-pipe, reverse-return hot-water heating system with baseboard convectors. The boiler is installed in the basement.

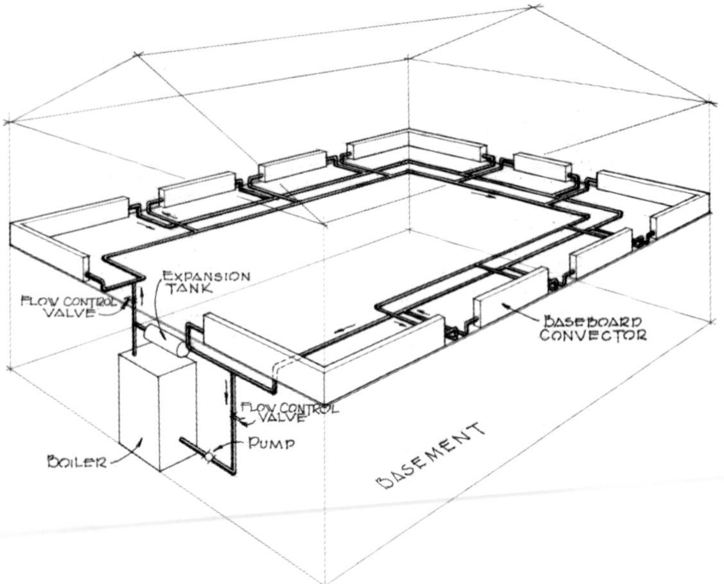

ing. Special fittings allow restricted amounts of water into each convector so that the temperature of the water in the later ones varies only slightly from the convectors closest to the boiler (see Fig. 11-11). A *2-pipe system* works more efficiently; of course, the initial installation cost is higher. One pipe supplies the rooms with hot water, the other, called the "return," carries the cooled water back to the boiler (see Fig. 11-12). The return can be either direct or reverse, meaning the order in which the cooled water returns in relation to the order in which the warm water enters each convector. The reverse-return method is usually preferred.

Another system, referred to as a "radiant system," distributes the hot water through pipes embedded either in concrete floor slabs or plastered ceilings (which, when warm, act as large radiators).

Various types of units can be used to dissipate the heat from the water to the air within each room. The conventional radiator has been used for years, but is a dust collector and uses floor space unless recessed into walls. More popular convectors are enclosed heaters with extended surface coils or finned tubes that give off the heat readily when air circulates through the units. Various sizes are available for wall-hung, recessed, or completely concealed installation.

A popular adaptation of the convector is the baseboard unit. The finned piping is arranged along the base of the outside walls and covered with a metal enclosure to resemble a baseboard. Heat is given off near the floor where it is needed, and various lengths of convectors can be combined with suitable trim to produce unobstructive heaters with pleasing appearances. See Fig. 11-13. Forced-air convectors must be used with residential heating-cooling hydronic systems, and they are adaptable to many commercial applications.

Hot-water furnaces must be located in the basement or in first-floor utility rooms of basementless homes. If coal or oil is used as a fuel consideration must be given to storage space, which should be not too distant from the furnace. Each boiler is equipped with an expansion tank, either closed or open, to compensate for variations of the water volume at different temperature levels and to relieve air pockets from the system.

One of the disadvantages of hot-water systems, if unattended when not in operation, is the possibility of freezing during cold weather.

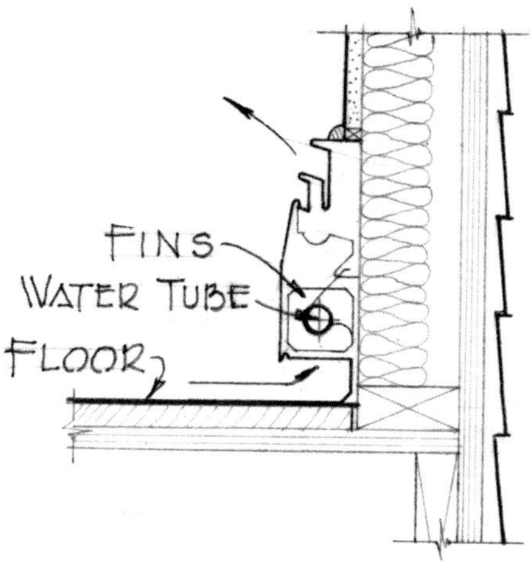

Fig. 11-13 Sectional detail of a hot-water baseboard convector. Fins conduct the heat from the water tube to the air, creating air circulation through the baseboard.

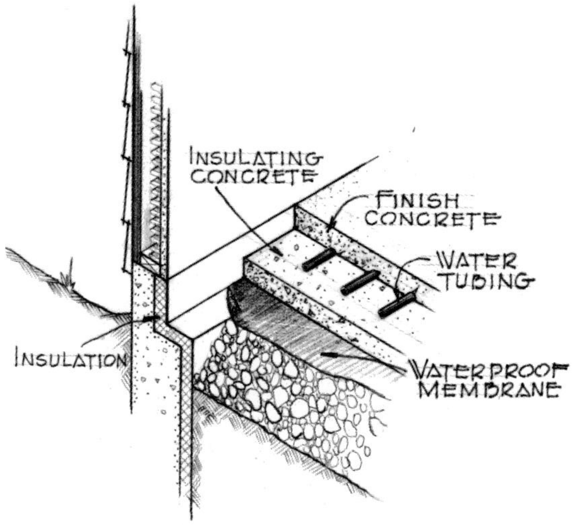

Fig. 11-14 Floor panel hot-water heating embedded in concrete-slab construction.

Radiant-panel hot-water systems employ either iron pipe or copper tubing embedded in floor slabs (Fig. 11-14), or copper tubing in ceiling plaster. Although copper is more expensive than iron, its installation is simpler and cheaper because it can be easily formed to fit panel areas and requires fewer fittings. Usually a serpentine coil system is employed (see Fig. 11-15). Copper, being smaller in diameter and lighter, is practical for ceiling installation; the coils are fastened directly to metal or gypsum lath before the plaster is applied. Heat in floor slabs eliminates the usual coldness of concrete, yet because of its mass, concrete does not respond as quickly to heating as do ceiling panels. Higher surface temperatures (100°F–120°F) are allowable on radiant ceilings than on slab surfaces (80°F–85°F). Radiant surfaces heated to a temperature of 85°F or 86°F will keep the occupants comfortable even with air temperatures slightly less than 60°. Balancing valves, usually located in closets or in other inconspicuous areas, allow complete control of heat within each room. The piping is usually taken off main supply lines to each room and fed back to the boiler by return mains, similar to typical 2-pipe hot-water systems. Standard thermostatic controls cause the pump and boiler burner to maintain comfortable room temperatures. Because of the heat "lag" of slab radiant systems, it becomes necessary in many areas to include an exterior temperature change anticipator (outdoor thermostat), which controls the heat in the system prior to the actual need within the house.

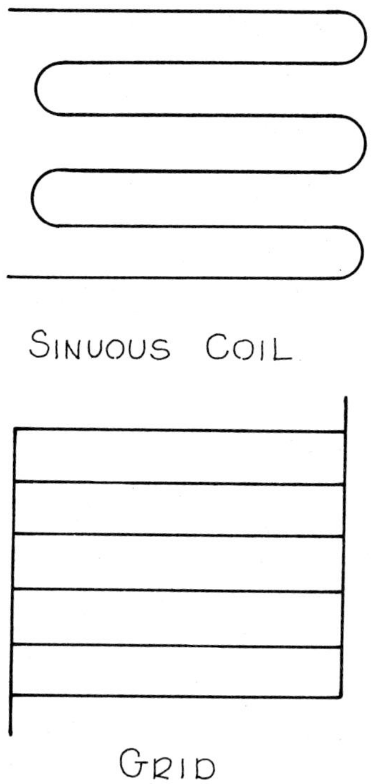

Fig. 11-15 Two methods of installing hot-water pipe in radiant panel systems.

The advantages of radiant-panel heating are that:

1. The heat is "clean," creating little dust and reducing the need for frequent repainting;
2. There are no visible registers or heating units within the rooms; and
3. There are no drafts or noise from blower equipment.

11.3.3 Electric Heating Systems

Basically, electric heating systems convert electrical energy into heat with the use of resistance wiring installed in various ways throughout the structure. Both radiant- and convection-type heat are produced. In areas where electrical energy is economical, this type of fuel produces a very desirable method of heating residences. The heat is clean, easy to distribute and control, and installation of the system is economical. From a standpoint of safety, little damage can be done by fire since elements are designed to operate below 150°. The heat can be placed exactly where it is needed, as for example, bathroom heaters or other auxiliary heaters.

Electrical resistance elements in baseboards, similar in appearance to hot-water baseboard units, can be installed along exterior walls to provide instantaneous and comfortable heat.

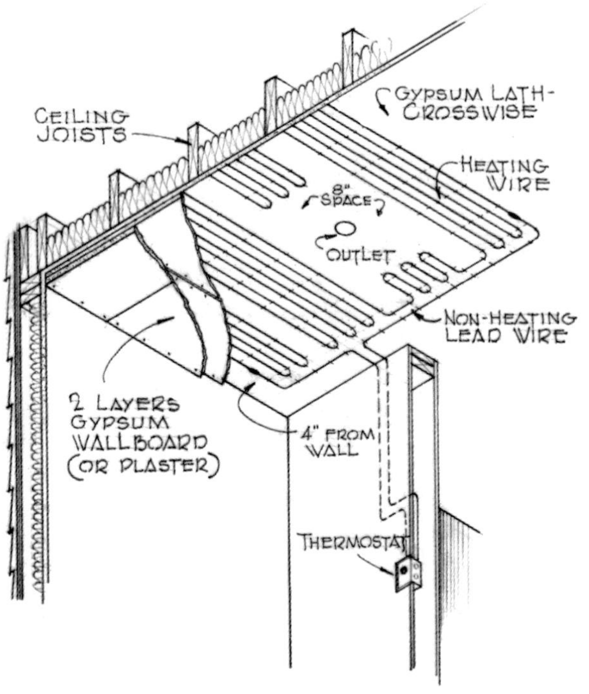

Fig. 11-16 Installation of radiant heating electrical wire in dry-wall ceilings.

Fig. 11-17 Installation of radiant heating electrical wire in concrete floor slabs.

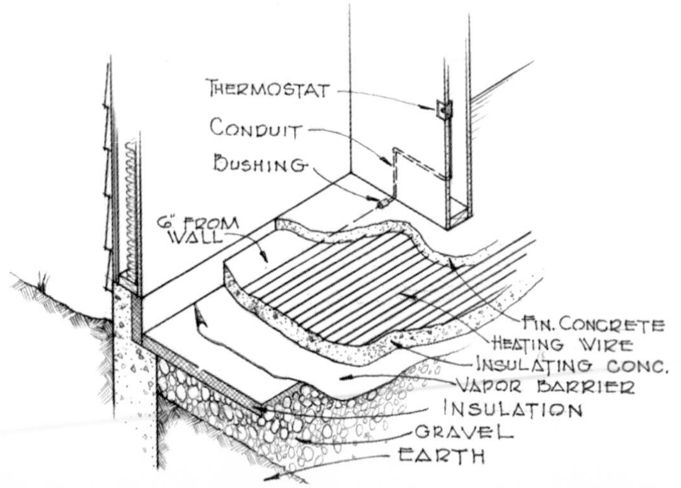

Radiant plaster ceilings are produced by attaching resistance wiring to gypsum lath. The wiring is manufactured in specific lengths to provide exact wattage ratings for a room according to its heat loss. Wattage sizes are based on the conversion ratio: *1 watt = 3.41 Btu*. The wiring is insulated with a protective covering and should not be cut or spliced. After the circuit has been carefully tested, a ½″ brown-and-finish plaster coat is applied. Connector wiring is regular non-heating type. Control thermostats are installed in each room. Care must be taken to keep the embedded wiring at least 6″ from walls and at least 8″ from any ceiling outlet boxes. It is recommended that 6″ of mineral insulation be applied over all radiant ceilings. Resistance wiring can also be installed between two layers of gypsum wall board in dry-wall construction. See Fig. 11-16. Spacing of the wiring on the first layer must allow for the nailing of the second layer, however, and a 3″ wide space below each ceiling joist is left void of the resistance wiring for this purpose. Otherwise, the installation is identical to plastered ceilings.

Resistance wiring can also be embedded in concrete slabs. Usually 3″ of insulating concrete (vermiculite aggregate) is used as a base, the wiring is carefully stapled in place, and 1½″ or 2″ of surfacing concrete is applied over the wiring. See Fig. 11-17. The perimeter of the slab should be well-insulated, and it is advisable to place more wiring near the periphery to compensate for heat loss to the exterior. This method of central heating is not recommended except in mild climates where floor surface temperatures will not have to be made uncomfortably warm. Resistance wiring in slabs is often satisfactory for auxiliary heating and for preventing snow from accumulating on driveways and walks.

One of the architectural advantages of any of the electrical resistance-type heating systems is the fact that no floor space need be reserved for a central heating unit, including chimney or flues. Another point which is often overlooked is that electrical heating installations are subject to minimum wear and therefore require less maintenance.

11.3.4 Heat Pumps

As we mentioned earlier, the heat pump uses no combustion of fuel, such as gas, oil, or coal, as a primary heat source; rather, it operates on the principle that freely available outside air (or

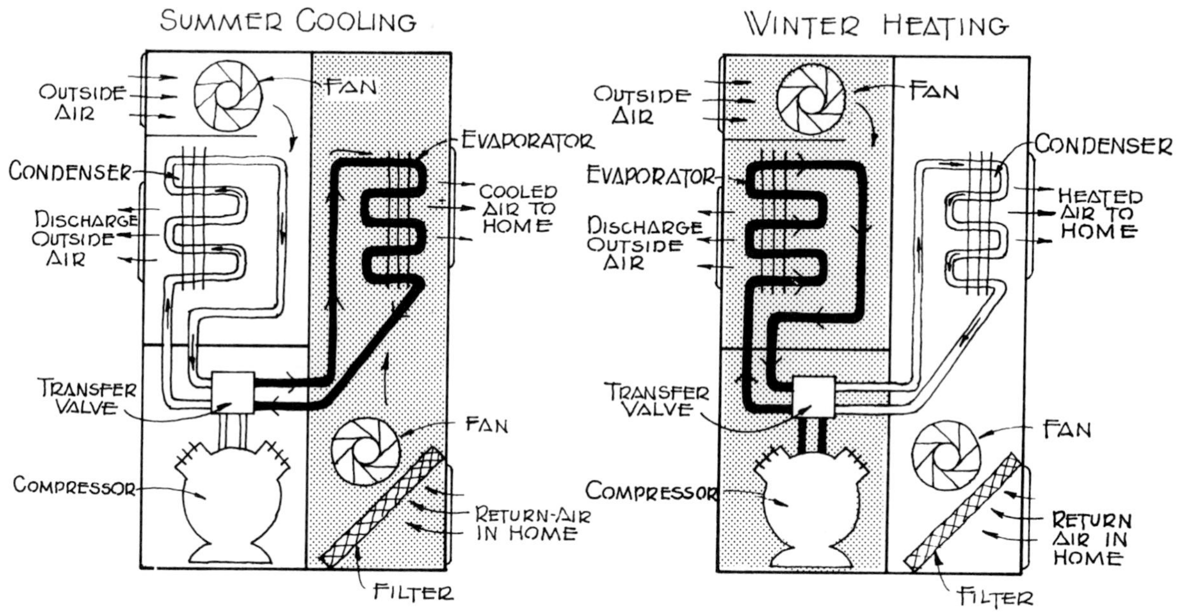

Fig. 11-18 Diagram of the heat-pump operation in summer and winter. The unit acts as a two-directional refrigeration system, taking the heat from the inside air and discharging it outside in summer, and taking the heat from outside air in winter and discharging it inside the house.

an economical water supply) contains useful heat even during colder weather, and that this heat can be controlled and pumped into the house to maintain desirable temperature levels. Like electrical heat, it is clean and free of soot particles. In summer the system operates in reverse, taking the heat from within the house and pumping it to the outside, working on a principle similar to that of the household refrigerator. See Fig. 11-18. Actually, the system is more efficient for cooling than for heating, but since it performs a dual function, the heat pump is commercially feasible for year-round inside comfort.

As a heating method, the system's efficiency drops considerably as the outside air drops in temperature. At a point just above freezing it becomes necessary to supplement the heat supply, usually with resistance-type electric heating elements, in order to maintain a required heat supply. The additional expense for such supplementary electrical equipment may make operation of the pump impractical in many sections of the country, unless electrical rates are low. Experience has shown that the most practical adoption of the heat pump for home heating has been in areas where outside temperatures seldom drop below 30°F.

Several heat source-and-delivery media have been found successful: water-to-water, water-to-air, and air-to-air. When a water-to-water system is used, an economical source of uniform-temperature water must be available for the heat exchanger. Distribution of the conditioned water within the house is handled with conventional piping systems. To date, the air-to-air system has been most highly commercialized for residential use. With this system, the air distribution within the house resembles the forced warm-air heating methods, and consideration must be given to duct sizing and register placement for cooling as well.

In appearance, the heat pump is either a single metal-covered unit, placed outside the house, or it is contained in two cabinets, called a remote unit, with one installed inside—usually in the basement, utility room, or attic near an outside wall—and the other outside. Some manufacturers make a unit that can be hung on an outside wall, but because of noise the condensing unit is more satisfactory if it is not attached to the building in any way.

In operation, the pump draws in outside air (or water), and the refrigerant in the evaporator absorbs the air's natural heat, a compressor pumps the refrigerant to a higher temperature and pressure level, and the condenser gives off the heat to the inside air, creating the heating cycle. The heat pump is considered efficient in operation up to the point where supplemental resistance heat must be introduced. This supplementary heat must be sufficient to supply at least 75 per cent of the total calculated heat-loss requirements (100 per cent is recommended in case of compressor failure). Cooling is done with the fixed-refrigerant circuit by interchanging the air over the evaporator and the condenser. Reversing refrigerant valves makes the changeover possible.

Because frost on the evaporator coils reduces efficiency, automatic hot-gas defrosting cycles or electric defrosters are necessary in air-source systems. Another required control is the inside air-temperature regulating thermostat, similar to other heating and cooling systems, which controls inside temperature, fans, and the heating and cooling changeover. Also, an outdoor temperature-change anticipator is advisable in order to maintain uniform inside comfort during sudden weather changes. An emergency switch should be installed, however, so that outdoor thermostats can be bypassed and the auxiliary heat can be controlled with the indoor thermostat only.

In planning a heat-pump installation, a 220-volt service outlet must be provided. No provision, of course, is necessary for a chimney or smoke vent, but it would be wise to plan for some other type of emergency heat in case of power failure.

11.4 AIR-CONDITIONING METHODS

Summer cooling, commonly called air conditioning, can be done most simply in residences with the use of individual room units, placed in appropriate window openings. Or in new construction, openings the size of window units can be provided in outside walls with electric outlets (usually 220 V) nearby. This method of cooling may be the most economical in regions where summer temperatures are moderate and only one or two rooms in the home may require air conditioning. Basic planning for this type of cooling is not important and is not usually considered on working drawings, other than possibly a note on the floor plan where a unit is to be installed in an opening.

In areas where the cooling season is comparatively long, a central air-conditioning system, usually combined with the heating system equipment, is considered the most satisfactory for year-round inside climate control. As previously pointed out, these central systems, like heating systems, require consideration during initial planning of the structure; usually the type of heating system selected will have a bearing on the most appropriate cooling system. If warm-air heating is selected, cooling equipment utilizing the same circulating fan, ductwork, and registers will minimize the installation cost of the combination arrangement.

A mechanical refrigeration system, as mentioned under heat pumps, requires two basic units connected by closed-circuit refrigerant piping. The one unit, called the evaporator, allows the refrigerant to vaporize under low pressure and absorb heat from the surrounding air or water. This unit must be placed within the house, and is commonly combined within the central furnace jacket of combination systems. The other unit, called the condenser, dissipates the heat absorbed by the evaporator as well as the heat of compression. Higher pressures in the condenser change the vaporized refrigerant into a liquid, requiring the heat taken up in the evaporator to be given off as it circulates through the condenser. The condenser, then, must be placed outside the building where it can give off its heat; or if installed inside, it must be adjacent to an outside wall opening.

Single-package cooling units are manufactured to fit conveniently near louvers in attics, crawl spaces, or basement openings. Yet, dual units are usually incorporated with heating systems requiring the condenser to be located on the exterior of the building. Many types of cooling units are available for combining with warm-air heating systems.

In dry regions, such as the southwestern part of the United States, where outside air contains comparatively little moisture, air-conditioning units utilizing *evaporative cooling* rather than mechanical systems are being used successfully for summer cooling. Dry air can be economically cooled by forcing it through a spray of recirculated water. This system is based on the fact that evaporation is a cooling process. Both individual room units and central systems working on this principle are manufactured.

If the home is to be heated with hot water, an entirely separate cooling unit and ductwork system (split system) may be economically installed in an attic or crawl space to cool the house with air and yet allow the hot-water system to heat the house independently with water. Also, an indirect cooling unit, called a "water chiller," may be combined with a hot-water system to circulate chilled water through the same piping system. During the winter, heated water is piped through the system; during the summer, chilled water for cooling. However, in comparison to cooling with air, chilled water does not have the advantage of removing excess moisture during the cooling process. Water chillers require about the same amount of floor space in basements or utility rooms as the water boilers themselves. If a water-cooled type of condenser is used with the chiller, space must also be planned for a cooling tower near the rear of the building or on a level roof.

Usually the 2-pipe, reverse-return piping system is the most popular with water heating-cooling combinations. One thermostatic control may be used to regulate both the boiler and the water chiller. Circulating chilled water through radiant floor slabs or ceiling panels is not considered practical for cooling, mainly because of condensation problems on cold surfaces.

11.5 RESIDENTIAL VENTILATING FANS

Circulation of fresh air in the home is not the major problem it becomes in public buildings. Usually the home is occupied by comparatively few people, doors are continually being opened and closed, and open windows furnish natural ventilation. And if the need arises, the blower fans in warm-air heating systems may be used during off-season to supply additional ventilation. In public buildings, however, where many people congregate for extended periods, forced-air ventilating systems, usually designed by the same engineer who designs the heating-cooling systems, must be installed to provide a continual supply of fresh air.

Ventilation problems within the home consist mainly of eliminating excess moisture, odors, fumes, etc., from specific areas such as kitchens, bathrooms, and laundry rooms. These areas should be serviced by locally placed exhaust fans, which are available in many models and sizes for almost any situation. Kitchen fans can be installed in ceilings or outside walls, incorporated in range hoods, or included within cabinetwork; if access to the exterior is difficult, forced-air fans with electronic filters can be installed to clean the air without requiring an outside outlet. Bathroom fans for ceiling installation commonly combine the exhaust fan with a light fixture and a supplementary resistance-type heater. Any source of excess moisture should have direct exhaust vents to the outside.

Central ventilating fans are effective as well as economical for cooling purposes when air-conditioning equipment is not installed. In many regions, pulling cool evening air through the house helps to make the interior more comfortable by alleviating the effects of the sun's radiation (the heat retained by the roof and walls) on the structure. These quiet-running fans can be located in central hallway ceilings or other appropriate locations to draw outside air through windows of the lower floors and discharge it through the attic. Fan sizes, based on air-movement capacities, should be selected to provide at least one air change (volume of the house in cubic feet) every 3 min. Some types of fans are made to operate in a horizontal position and others in a vertical position.

The locations of attic fans are usually shown on floor plans by the use of broken lines, drawn to the approximate size; dimensions and type may be inserted with a note or included in the set of specifications. Manufacturers' catalogues must be consulted for detailed information about fans, which, like other types of equipment installed in a building, should be identified with model numbers and relevant size descriptions.

11.6 LOAD CALCULATION AND SIZING OF HEATING EQUIPMENT

To maintain a satisfactory air temperature within the home, the heating plant must be large enough to replace the heat loss of the house during average exterior temperatures; yet it should not be oversized if it is to operate efficiently and provide balanced heating. First, the *design temperature* must be established. Outside design temperature varies with the climate and can be determined for a given locality from tables compiled by The American Society of Heating, Refrigerating, and Air Conditioning Engineers (A.S.H.R.A.E.)—*Heating, Ventilating, Air-Conditioning Guide* and other books on heating design. Usually 75°F is taken as a comfortable inside temperature. If the recommended outside temperature is, say, 5°F for a given area, then the design temperature for the heating system would be 70°F. If an outside design temperature is

20°F, then the design temperature would be 55°F, etc. A correctly designed heating system would be able to furnish enough heat to the interior to maintain the 75°F inside temperature. Only after the rate at which the building loses heat during average extreme temperatures is calculated, can the heating-plant size be determined.

The next step is finding the entire heat loss of the building. This is done by individually computing the heat loss of each room to be heated. The number of square feet of cold partitions, cold ceilings, exposed walls, cold floors, windows and exterior doors is calculated for each room. Then each surface area is multiplied by its *U factor*. Several different factors dealing with heat loss calculation are found in this information and various A.S.H.R.A.E. and N.E.S.C.A. tables available on home heating and cooling. The following definitions of the major ones encountered may clarify their meanings:

U FACTOR: Coefficient of heat transmission through a combination of materials commonly found in walls, floors, ceilings, etc. It is the Btuh flowing from air surface to air surface through 1 sq ft of structure for each degree (F) difference in temperature between the two surfaces.

k FACTOR: Unit conductivity. The rate of heat flow in Btuh through 1 sq ft of a homogeneous material 1" thick per degree (F) difference in temperature between its two surfaces.

R FACTOR: Thermal resistance of materials. It is obtained from the reciprocal of *U* factors and is expressed in degrees (F) per Btuh per sq ft. For example, a ceiling with a *U* factor of 0.20 would have an *R* factor of 1/0.20 = 5.0. The larger the *R* value, the more resistance to heat flow, and therefore the better heat barrier material.

HTM FACTOR: Heat Transfer Multiplier as used in the N.E.S.C.A. *J-Manual* method of heat loss calculation. It is similar to a *U* factor except that *HTM* factors are shown in their tables already multiplied by specific design temperatures and are used with the calculation forms shown in Appendix G. Window and door *HTM* factors also are modified to include infiltration heat losses which simplifies the total calculation.

The larger *U* factors in the tables indicate comparatively poorer insulators. Heat transfer characteristics of the different materials and types of construction, as found in A.S.H.R.A.E. tables have been established under controlled laboratory conditions.

The rate at which a building loses heat depends directly upon the heat-loss characteristics of its structural components and upon the temperature gradient (difference between inside and outside air temperatures). Remember that the areas of doors and windows in outside walls must be subtracted from the gross wall areas, and usually different *U* factors must be used for their calculations. The tables will show that windows and exterior doors have rather high transmission factors.

In heated basements, the masonry walls above grade have a different *U* factor from that of the walls below grade, since the ground absorbs very little heat compared to outside air. Partitions between heated rooms are not considered in heat-loss calculations; one balances the other when uniform inside temperatures are maintained.

To sum up, heat loss by *transmission* will vary in proportion to the area in sq ft (A) of the ceiling and the outside wall areas, to the coefficients of their transmission values (U), and to the difference between the required inside temperature (t_i) and to the outside design temperature (t_o). Thus the formula:

$$H = AU(t_i - t_o)$$

After the heat loss of each different exposed surface of a room is determined, the result will be the heat loss of the room if it were airtight and doors were never opened. But cracks around doors and windows allow heat to escape by what is called *infiltration* and must be considered in an accurate heat-loss calculation.

The amount of heat loss by infiltration varies directly with the wind pressure against the structure and the temperature difference between inside and outside air. In cold, windy climates heat loss is considerable, especially if no weather stripping is used around loose-fitting windows and doors. Naturally, tight construction reduces infiltration. One method of determining heat loss by infiltration is by measuring the length of the cracks around all windows and doors in feet and multiplying the totals by the appropriate infiltration factors, which also can be found in the previously mentioned heating manuals. This method is preferred for accurate calculations, especially in commercial building design.

An approximate, *air change* method is satisfactory for residential heating systems. With this method, the number of air changes within a room per hour has been found by experience to vary from ½ to 2 changes. Under ordinary conditions, then, one air change per hour can be assumed. Therefore, a roomful of air must be reheated every hour to allow for infiltration loss, and the volume of the room in cubic feet is conveniently used. The density of air is taken to be 0.075 lbs per cu ft. The specific heat of air is 0.24 Btu (the heat needed to raise the temperature of one lb of air 1°F). Therefore, 0.075 × 0. 24 = 0.018 gives the Btu of heat necessary to raise one cu ft of air 1°F. The infiltration heat loss can then be stated by the following formula:

$$H = V(.018)(t_i - t_o)$$

in which V = volume of air in room, t_i = inside design temperature, and t_o = outside design temperature.

Totals of infiltration heat losses are combined with the transmission heat losses through walls, ceilings, floors, etc.

In calculating the heat loss of concrete slabs-on-grade, usually only a 10′ wide area around the perimeter of the slab is considered (see the discussion on slab insulation, p. 153). The heat loss to the ground within the interior of the slab is negligible. Transmission factors are available for both heated and unheated slabs.

After heat-loss totals by both transmission and infiltration are determined for each room, the grand total provides the heat loss for the structure. It must be remembered that since *U* factors are given for 1° difference in inside and outside air, room heat-loss calculations must include multiplication by the design temperature. The grand total Btu per hr heat loss is the basis for sizing the heating unit after several points have been taken into account. Usually it is considered good practice to add 20 percent capacity to the unit to compensate for morning pickup when nighttime heating is allowed to drop as low as 55°F. Also, if plenum systems are placed in unheated crawl spaces or attics, the design temperature difference should be 30° greater than when ducts pass only through heated portions of the building. Heat loss in ductwork must also be considered in sizing individual room ducts as well as in sizing the central unit. Heat loss of ducts passing through heated areas is not considered.

At present, the majority of all residential heating-cooling contractors throughout this country and Canada use the N.E.S.C.A. *J Manual* method of load calculation. Their tables and calculation forms have been devised from A.S.H.R.A.E. *U* factors and engineering information. Various shortcuts such as infiltration factors included with door and window factors, and specific design temperatures included with the factors, simplifies either heating- or cooling-load calculation for residential buildings. The form in Appendix G shows the calculation for the heat losses in the one-story house given in Chapter 10. A thorough study of the step-by-step procedures given in the *J Manual* must be made before attempting the calculations. Those students wishing to pursue this area of work would be advised to take one of the short courses offered by N.E.S.C.A. several times each year in various metropolitan and university centers throughout the nation. Write to: *N.E.S.C.A.*, 1501 Wilson Blvd., Arlington, Va., 22209, for further details.

Heating calculations and system design for commercial buildings are traditionally done by registered engineers engaged in this specialized field.

Hot-water boiler sizes must be taken from design tables, distributed by the Institute of Boiler and Radiator Manufacturers (I.B.R.), after total heat-loss calculations have been made. Sizes are usually indicated in Btu per hr output and are determined after the following requirements have been considered:

1. Maximum heat necessary for all the connected radiator or convector units;
2. Heat necessary for domestic hot water, if combined in the boiler;
3. Heat lost in piping (piping factor); and
4. Heat necessary for warming up the radiators or convectors and piping system after starting (pickup factor).

Items No. 3 and 4 are often overlooked, inasmuch as the average boiler possesses enough reserve capacity to overcome the extra load, and in modern residences piping and equipment are usually installed within insulated areas.

Boiler manufacturers' catalogues give boiler dimensions, smoke pipe and flue sizes, according to rated outputs.

Room convectors or radiator sizes and capacities are based upon individual-room heat losses as well as their distance from central boilers.

In hot-water radiant systems, the lineal feet and size of pipe that must be embedded in floors or ceilings is based on emission factors and individual-room heat losses. Tables must be consulted for the emission rates in Btu per hr per ft of piping in order to determine the amount and size of piping necessary to satisfy each room's heat loss. Water design temperatures adopted for the system must also be considered.

11.7 SIZING COOLING EQUIPMENT

In heating, the major problem is the addition of heat and moisture to the interior; in cooling during the summer, on the other hand, the problem becomes just the reverse—the *removal of heat and moisture.*

Many factors—internal and external—affect the cooling load and become part of the cooling calculations. Appliances, such as exhaust fans, for example, which remove heat and moisture from kitchen and baths, aid in reducing the cooling load. However, despite such reductions, the heat gain in the kitchen is rather large, so that it is common practice to compensate for it by adding 1200 Btu to the kitchen heat-gain calculations. Another source of internal heat is that given off by the occupants. For this, 300 Btu is usually allowed for each person living in the home.

The major source of residential heat gain, however, is due to external factors: outside air temperature and the sun shining on glass, roof, and walls. Sun shining on fixed-glass units and windows contributes considerably to cooling loads and should be avoided if possible during early planning, as previously discussed. Also, the radiant heat of the sun, although not considered in heating loads, must be dealt with in air conditioning. Remember that heat has a natural tendency to travel from warm to cold temperatures.

All of these heat sources contribute to the cooling load, and the size of the cooling equipment is based on its capacity (Btu per hr) to remove this heat.

To arrive at the correct cooling load for air systems, design temperatures must be taken from tables similar to those used for heating design. Usually 75°F (50 percent humidity) is used for the desirable inside temperature, and outside design temperature, including factors for daily temperature range, is taken from regional cooling tables. The design temperature difference between inside and outside air will then reveal the temperature reduction necessary for inside comfort.

Finally, the total heat gain within the structure must be calculated. Total exposed areas of walls, warm floors, warm ceilings, windows, and doors are multiplied by the heat-gain factors. Heat gain by air leakage is found by applying the correct factors from tables. Sizes of windows receiving direct sun are multiplied by their factors. To the total heat gain through the structural components (external heat) is added the internal heat produced by people and appliances. Because moisture removal is part of comfort cooling, factors are used also for determining the heat gain from dehumidification (latent heat), which changes the moisture from a vapor to a liquid. Heat gain to ductwork in noncooled areas and other special heat sources are found with the use of factors from tables. All of these sources require attention in arriving at a heat-gain total for each room. To determine the total for sizing the central cooling unit, all the calculated room Btu per hr are added together.

Load calculations, design data, and code requirements for air systems can be taken from *Manual J* and *Manual 9* published by the N.E.S.C.A. Work sheets for job design and installation are also available (see Appendix).

Cooling loads can also be calculated by a method developed by the I.B.R. Although basically similar to the N.E.S.C.A. method, the I.B.R. method bases its tables for determining regional design temperatures on latitude. The I.B.R. has also formulated its own factors for calculating sensible heat gains through walls, roofs, floors, windows, and doors. This method requires that shade lines be determined on walls and glass receiving direct sunlight and that different factors be used for shaded and sunlit portions. In addition, like the N.W.A.H.A.C.A. methods similar calculations must be made for infiltration around doors and windows, internal heat gains, and the latent heat gain (usually taken as one-third of the sensible heat gain).

Cooling units have been rated in tons of refrigeration capacity, 1 ton of refrigeration being the amount of cooling necessary to melt 1 ton of 32°F ice at 32°F in 24 hr. The latent heat of ice is 144 Btu per lb; then 1 ton (2000 lb) of ice absorbs 144 $\times$ 2000 or 288,000 Btu per 24 hr in changing ice to water. The heat gain in buildings is calculated in Btu per hr; therefore, 288,000 ÷ 24 = 12,000 Btu per hr, which is the capacity of 1 ton of refrigeration. *Total heat gains are simply divided by 12,000 to find the tonnage required.* A ton of refrigeration does not necessarily equal 1 hp, although some units are rated in horsepower. Most manufacturers now rate their equipment in Btu per hr, including both input and output.

It must be remembered that if a water chiller is added to an existing hot-water system, new convectors must be installed in the rooms. Combination convectors, having fan, filter, and heating-cooling coils, as well as individual room thermostats, provide a more positive distribution of cooled air. Compared to residential cooling with air, hydronic systems have not become as universally popular.

Duct sizes for air distribution of combination heating-cooling systems are usually based on the total cubic feet of air per minute (CFM) necessary for the cooling. Total CFM circulating through a system is based on unit manufacturers' recommendations, usually from 300 CFM–420 CFM per ton. (Heating ductwork need not be as large.) Tables indicate duct sizes for both main trunk and individual room ducts, based on total and room Btu heat gains. Minor factors such as register distance from the central unit, duct offsets, risers, etc., are also considered. Ducts passing through unheated and uncooled spaces or outside walls must be insulated. Filters are installed in the return-duct side of the system.

11.8 LOCATION OF OUTLETS IN ROOMS

Placement of registers and heat outlets in rooms requires careful consideration if the ultimate in comfort is to be attained from the system, especially in areas of extreme outside temperatures. Generally, it becomes advisable to place outlets in or near outside walls where the greatest amount of heat loss or heat gain occurs. To counteract cold downdrafts below windows, often uncomfortable in winter, low wall or floor outlets that blow the air up along the wall and windows are effective. However, when covered with floor-length window drapes, their maximum efficiency is decreased. Registers can also be placed in partitions near the outside walls to blow the air along the exterior wall and thereby reduce downdrafts. Concrete floor slabs, utilizing the perimeter loop system, should have their registers in the slab. Sheet-metal boots for bringing the ductwork into wall registers placed near the floor may also be used. Generally, in northern regions where heating seasons are comparatively long, registers and heat outlets are located in the floor or low sidewall; in southern areas where cooling seasons are longer, air is dispersed better with high sidewall or ceiling outlets. Aside from these considerations, outlets should be so placed that air distribution is not noticeable to the occupants, no drafts are created, and the conditioned air will not have a tendency to stratify. Registers should be unobstructive and fit into the decorative scheme of the interior, and they should not restrict the placement of furniture. Since many types are available, it is possible to choose registers that fill the requirements of any situation.

Convectors for hot-water systems are mainly the baseboard type or wall units placed low near the floor.

Proper placement of return-air grilles contributes to the dispersion of the conditioned air. In small homes, if centrally located returns are used, air will generally find its way through doorways, halls, and stairwells. Doors normally left closed are usually specified to be undercut ¾″ for an economical method of air return; or a grille may be installed in the door. Returns, however, must be large enough to prevent noise in the ductwork, and their sizes should be based on the volume of air delivered to the supply outlets. Properly sized and placed returns aid considerably in maintaining comfort throughout the building.

It is evident, after studying the problems involved in providing comfort within a building during all seasons of the year, that each installation requires an individual application during planning. Selection of the most satisfactory equipment must necessarily follow a thorough analysis of all the conditions involved. Heat-loss factors of the various building materials and their combinations deserve attention. Initial costs of insulation should be compared in terms of fuel-cost savings over the life-span of the building. Of course, early costs of equipment and insulation generally will vary directly with the degree of comfort required.

11.9 DRAWING THE HEATING AND/OR COOLING PLAN

The "Heating and Air-Conditioning Plan" is basically a floor plan showing walls and structural features of the building with the layout of the central unit, the distribution system, and the room outlets in their correct position (see Figs. 11-19 and 11-20). A plan of each floor involved is usually sufficient to show the important information, supplemented by several small details, if necessary. Information about simple heating or heating-cooling installations could be incorporated into the regular floor plan, but with more complex systems it is usual practice to put the information on a separate plan for easier identification. Use the heating and piping symbols (Fig. 11-25) adopted by the American Standards Association, Inc. (A.S.A.), which have been standardized and universally recognized. Large ductwork is scaled to show its horizontal dimension, and notes are added to indicate their cross-sectional sizes. In residential ductwork it is standard procedure to use only 8″ vertical-duct depths with increased widths for increased air capacities. For example, a smaller duct might be 10″ × 8″ and a larger one may be 16″ × 8″. Notice that the horizontal dimension is given first in the specification. Piping is shown by single lines.

After heat-loss calculations and design information are detemined, start the plan with a freehand sketch of the entire layout. Add all pertinent sizes and information to the sketch. When ready to do the instrument drawing, fasten a clean sheet of tracing paper directly over the regular floor plan and follow these general steps:

1. Trace the structural features (start with basement plan, if applicable) using rather light linework. The linework of the heating or cooling

Fig. 11-19 Basement heating-cooling plan of house No. 1.

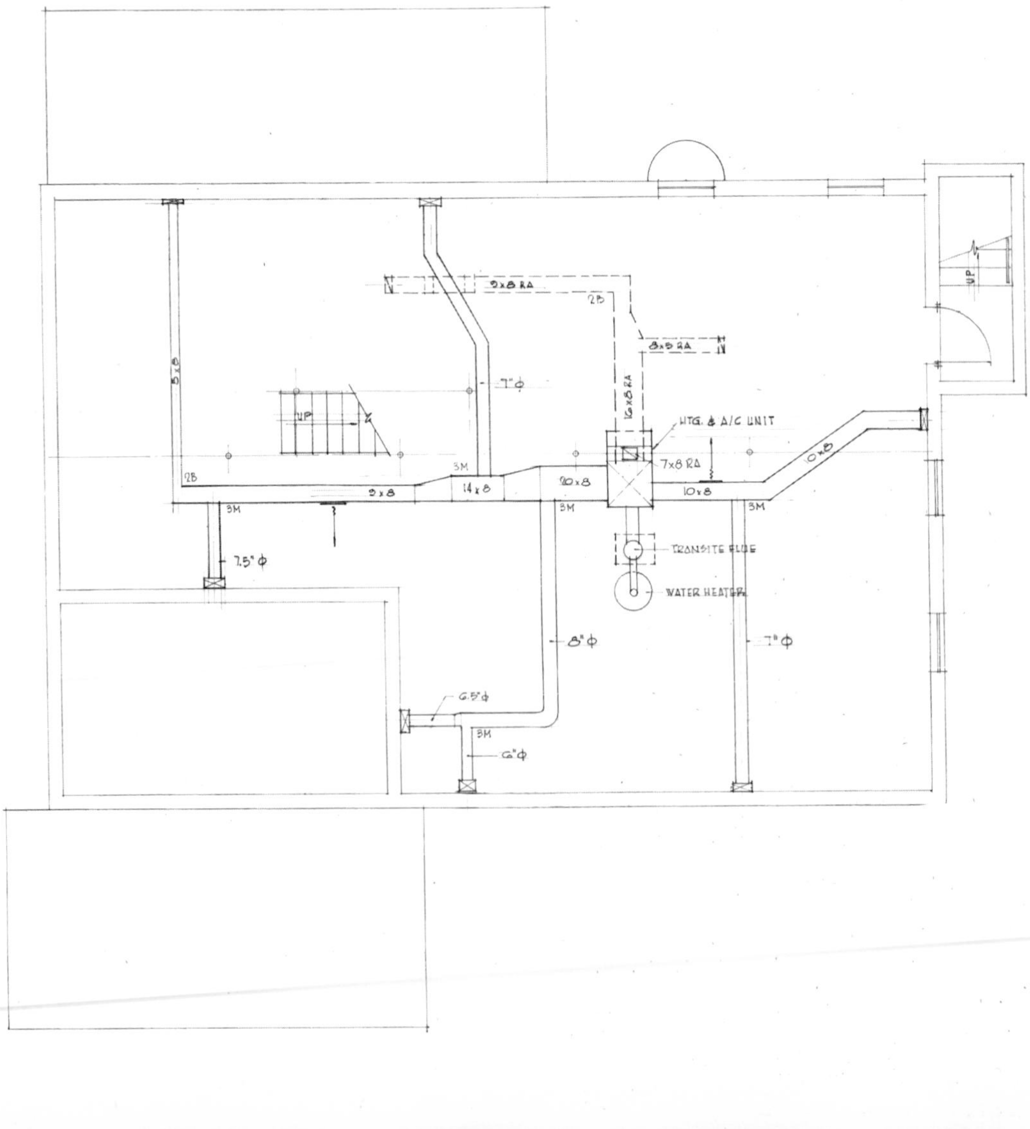

equipment and symbols, drawn later, should dominate the structural features.

2. Scale the floor size of the central unit and locate it where planned; show smoke pipe to chimney or vent. Unit output rating in Btu per hr and manufacturers' catalogue numbers may be added later.
3. Using their correct symbols, locate all room outlets and indicate their sizes and capacities. Locate return outlets with their capacities.
4. If ceiling outlets are indicated, coordinate them with ceiling electrical outlets. Care must be taken near structural girders and plumbing piping.
5. If rectangular ductwork is to be drawn, lay out duct sizes to satisfy room Btu per hr requirements by starting with the outlet farthest from the plenum. In general, one register will handle about 8000 Btu heat loss in heating; for cooling, one register will handle only 4000 Btu heat gain. Indicate each change of ductwork size with a note. Ductwork should be incorporated into the structure as simply and directly as possible. Show standard ductwork fittings with identification numbers.
6. Show circular ductwork with a single line, with a note giving its size.
7. Locate risers for second-story outlets, if necessary. Riser duct sizes are made to pass through stud partitions. Be sure second-floor partitions fall where risers are indicated.
8. In hot-water systems, use a single line for feeder pipes and a broken line for returns. Draw fittings, if necessary, with simple symbols.
9. Complete all notes, schedules, and structural details necessary to accommodate the system.

Fig. 11-20 First-floor heating-cooling plan of house No. 1 showing the layout of the room registers.

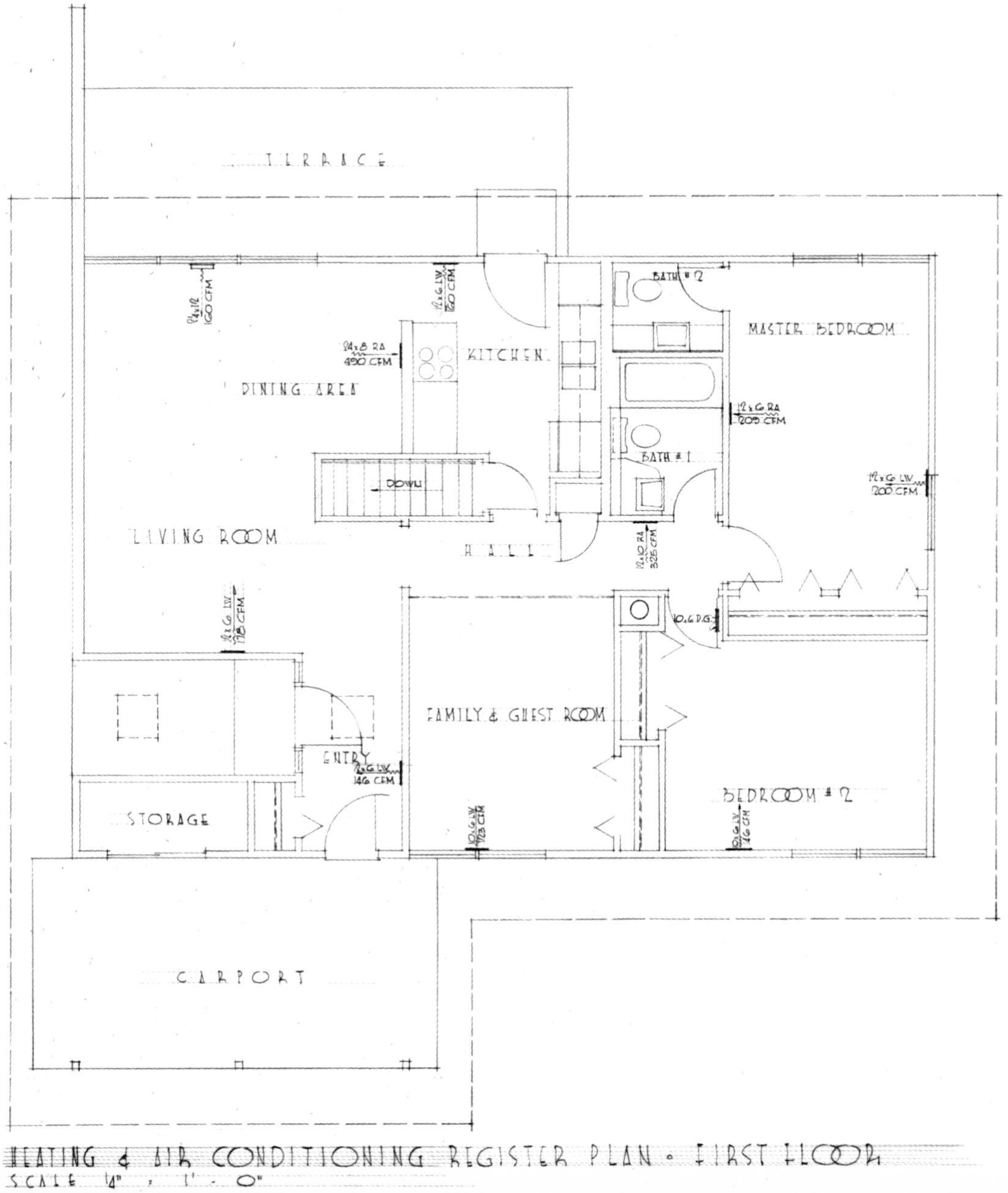

11.10 PLUMBING SYSTEMS AND DRAWINGS

Plumbing drawings are mainly concerned with the piping systems that supply hot and cold water, the pipes that carry waste materials to the sewer or disposal system, and the plumbing fixtures. With the exception of the fixtures, the systems are largely concealed within the structural cavities of the building.

For complex structures, the plumbing system design, like other mechanical or electrical design work, is usually done by competent engineers—frequently specialists. Because these systems are oftentimes complicated, involving the action and control of water and air within pipes, engineers must be well-qualified in the fields of hydraulics and pneumatics.

Small home systems, on the other hand, even though they involve similar basic principles, seldom require the services of plumbing engineers. Usually the responsibility for the design of residential systems falls upon licensed subcontractors who are familiar with local and

The drainage system combines the use of TRAPS, VENTS, WASTE LINES, and SOIL STACKS

VENTS protect the water seals in traps and permit them to operate effectively. By admitting air to the system, vents permit atomspheric pressure on both sides of the trap seal to be maintained, and permit air to enter at the same time as gases escape the drainage system.

TRAPS permit waste and waste water to enter the drainage system and prevent any sewer gases from entering the house. The water seal utilizes a portion of the waste water to act as the barrier.

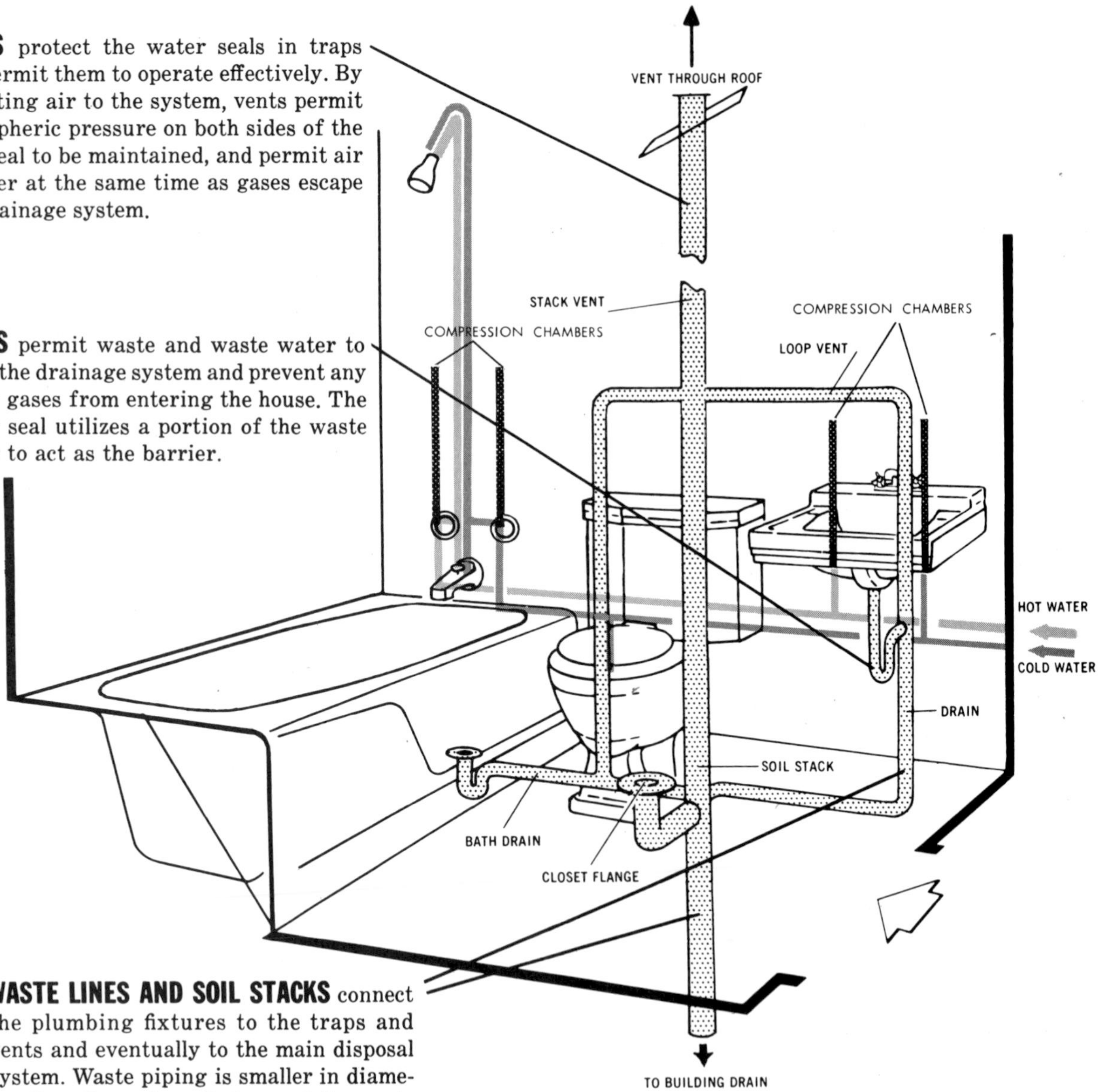

WASTE LINES AND SOIL STACKS connect the plumbing fixtures to the traps and vents and eventually to the main disposal system. Waste piping is smaller in diameter than the main soil pipe, and the waste carried differs in content. Materials carried away by waste piping include such items as grease, hair, lint, food scraps, etc. Because of this function, cleanouts should be located so that the entire system can be opened up if necessary.

Fig. 11-21 The basic parts of a bath plumbing system without reference to code or engineering limitations.

national plumbing codes. Much of residential plumbing is standardized, requiring little more than the location of plumbing fixtures on the working drawings. Simple structures do not always warrant separate plumbing plans, whereas complex commercial buildings may require a number of individual drawings devoted entirely to plumbing information.

Strict compliance with local plumbing codes is mandatory, regardless of the type of building. Plumbing codes, which may vary slightly from area to area, serve to ensure a sanitation standard to protect the health of the community. Students must understand the principles underlying good plumbing practices (Fig. 11-21) and be acquainted with local code restrictions. The most up-to-date requirements can be found in the *National Plumbing Code* published by the American Society of Mechanical Engineers. Many of these recommendations have become part of local plumbing codes throughout the country. Some of the more common terms found in codes are illustrated in Fig. 11-22.

Economy in plumbing costs is the direct result of careful planning when arranging the placement of rooms and fixtures requiring water outlets. Simplification of arrangement and the clustering of plumbing fixtures, usually into one wet-wall, should be the designer's objective in low-cost construction. In multistory construction, definite savings ensue if fixtures are located above each other to benefit from the use of common vents and soil stacks. However, in planning better-class homes, the workability of a good floor plan should not be sacrificed merely because extended plumbing lines constitute an added expense.

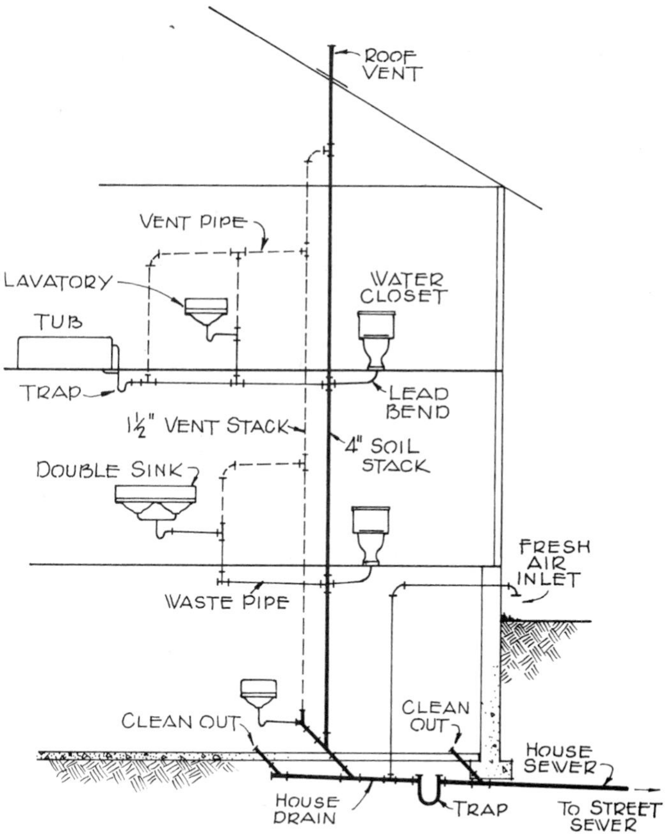

Fig. 11-22 A drainage diagram of a multistory residence.

11.11 BASIC REQUIREMENTS OF THE WATER-SUPPLY SYSTEM

Water-supply piping within the home should be as direct as possible and sized large enough to provide an adequate supply at each outlet. The entrance main pipe must be placed low enough below ground to prevent freezing or mechanical damage. Usually a 1″ or 1¼″ galvanized steel or wrought-iron pipe is sufficient; if copper is used, a ¾″ or 1″ pipe is satisfactory. A shutoff valve near the entry of the line into the house is often a requirement.

One of the important considerations in water supply is the choice of piping material. Three types are commonly used in residences: galvanized steel, galvanized wrought iron, and either hard or soft copper. Galvanized steel is most frequently found in homes, since it is the most economical, and joints are made with standard, tapered pipe thread. Although structurally rigid, steel pipe will eventually become corroded from deposits of water impurities, especially in regions where water has a high mineral content. These deposits can reduce the capacity of the pipe sufficiently to necessitate replacement. This factor must be considered when specifying galvanized steel pipe for plumbing. Wrought-iron pipe, though more expensive than steel, has less tendency to accumulate corrosive deposits. Copper pipe, often called tubing, eliminates the problem of corrosion altogether and is very durable. The diameter of the pipe can be smaller, simple solder joints are easy to make, and minimum water friction is created. Aboveground, in exposed locations, hard-tempered copper produces the most acceptable installation; below ground, the flexible soft-copper tubing is simple to place. Because of its desirable attributes, architects usually specify copper for the better type of construction, and its use is gaining in popularity.

Hot- and cold-water lines are commonly run parallel to each other throughout the structure. However, care is taken to keep the pipes at least 6″ apart, so that the water temperature in either pipe is not affected by the other. Insulating of hot-water lines is recommended, especially if the lines are long. Even cold-water lines in basements may require covering to prevent sweating. When water lines approach each fixture, hot water must be on the left, cold water on the right. Another important point is the provision for "air cushions" in the water lines. These short, sealed-off extensions of the water pipes, attached just above the outlet in the lines, eliminate hammering noises when faucets are quickly turned off. Other types of shock-relief and expansion chambers are available for incorporating into the lines. Much of the noise in plumbing walls can be isolated by having closets or storage rooms adjacent to baths; if this is not feasible, sound-deadening insulation or offset studding may be necessary in the wetwalls.

Table 11-1 Fixture Minimum Pipe Sizes (FHA)

Fixture	Branch hot water	Branch cold water	Soil or waste connections	Vent connections
Watercloset		½″	3″ x 4″	2″
Lavatory	½″	½″	1¼″	1¼″
Bathtub	½″	½″	1½″	1¼″
Sink	½″	½″	1½″	1¼″
Laundry tray	½″	½″	1½″	1¼″
Sink and tray combination	½″	½″	1½″	1¼″
Shower	½″	½″	2″	1¼″

11.12 BASIC REQUIREMENTS OF THE DISCHARGE SYSTEM

Whereas water is supplied into plumbing lines under pressure, drainage lines work on an entirely different principle—gravity. This must be fully understood to ensure their functioning properly. Compared to the water lines, then, the piping for waste discharge must be larger, and branches that carry the wastes horizontally into vertical stacks must be properly sloped (⅛″–½″ per ft) to ensure complete and free drainage. Sewage lines produce offensive and harmful gases that would permeate the entire structure unless *traps* forming offsets in the pipe to retain a water seal are installed near each fixture. Water closets have a built-in trap. Vent stacks through the roof discharge sewer gases to the outside air. These vent stacks and their branch vents have other important functions. They allow a continuous atmospheric pressure to exist within the sewage system, which prevents the siphonage of water from fixture traps and reduces the decay action of bacteria on the sewage while it is in the piping. Sewer gases may possibly emerge through trap seals unless the vents allow the gases to pass readily to the open air. Vent stacks should be installed at least 6″ yet no more than 5 ft from the traps and should extend at least 12″ above the roof. Although minor variations in practice exist, local codes carefully regulate methods of venting fixture traps and drainage lines.

Soil- and vent-pipe sizes vary according to the number of fixtures they serve. In residential systems the main soil stack and house drain are usually 4″ cast-iron soil pipe; waste branches and minor vent stacks generally are 1½″ or 2″ in diameter. The minimum size permitted for a soil stack pipe serving one water closet is 3″; the pipe for stacks handling two water closets must be at least 4″. Vent stacks that run parallel to soil stacks can be half as large as the soil stacks.

The majority of pipe used for sewage lines is asphalt-coated cast-iron pipe, known as "soil pipe." It is manufactured in 10 ft sections with a "bell" on one end to form the female section of the oakum-and-solder joints. Cast-iron pipe is resistant to corrosion, especially in contact with the ground. Other types of drainage pipe are also used, namely, copper, galvanized steel, galvanized wrought iron, brass, or lead. All pipe exposed near fixtures is chrome-plated brass. The sewer pipe running below ground from the house to the public sewer may be cast-iron, vitrified tile, concrete, or fiber pipe; but codes usually require at least 5′ of cast-iron pipe (house sewer) beyond the foundation of the building. Lead pipe connections at fixtures allow slight flexibility in case of shrinkage or movement of wood framing without putting strain on the connected piping. Plumbing fixtures must be solidly supported by the structure. All drainage pipe should be as straight and direct as possible, fittings made to minimize friction, and cleanouts inserted at critical points of the system to allow unclogging if this becomes necessary.

11.13 DOMESTIC WATER HEATERS

To furnish a continual supply of hot water throughout the year, modern homes must be equipped with some type of automatic hot-water heater. The heater and storage-tank combination unit is the most satisfactory, although heaters that supply hot water instantaneously as it is needed are available. Sizes of heaters and their tanks are based upon the number of occupants. Figures show that the average residential occupant uses about 40 gal of hot water per day. This estimate includes consumption for laundry and bath facilities, based on water heated to 140°F. Although tanks holding the minimum of 20 gal are available, a 30 gal tank is more satisfactory for the average family, and one holding 50 gal is necessary for a larger family using automatic laundry equipment. Heaters with slow recovery rates require proportionately larger storage tanks. If a unit has a slow recovery rate, such as an electric water heater, then an 80 gal tank unit would be necessary to furnish hot water at about the same rate as would a 30 gal gas- or oil-fired unit.

In commercial buildings having many hot-water outlets, the consumption per fixture is usually not as great as in residences. However, the demands of the building and the consumption rate during peak hours must be known before the size and type of hot-water heater can be indicated. Because hot-water lines tend to corrode more than cold-water lines, piping from hot-water heaters should be copper. Heaters should be located near their principal outlets, and heaters having adjustable temperature settings are appropriate for such installations.

Indicate hot-water heaters on working drawings with a circle symbol and a W.H. note. Its tank size can also be noted, if necessary.

11.14 PRIVATE DISPOSAL SYSTEMS

In most urban areas, buildings are serviced by public sewage lines that run along street thoroughfares. The house sewer connection is made by merely tapping the public sewer line. But in outlying areas where no public sewage facilities exist, provision must be made for satisfactory disposal of the sewage on the owner's property. The designs of individual disposal systems are closely regulated by local codes, and a number of conditions pertaining to the property must be analyzed before a permit is granted. Conditions affecting the disposal system design are number of occupants of the house, permeability of the soil, groundwater level in the area, size of the property, and the relative location of wells or streams that may be affected by the sewage disposal.

The simplest system (often prohibited by local codes) is a cesspool. This is an underground cylindrical pit with porous walls built of stone or masonry to allow seepage of the discharge into the surrounding ground. The sewage is deposited directly into the pit. If the surrounding soil is permeable enough to carry off the liquid and the underground water table is low enough to prevent contamination, the system may be adequate for retaining a small amount of solid matter. However, experience has shown that cesspools become troublesome when the apertures of the masonry become clogged and the surrounding ground becomes saturated. Secondary cesspools may then be necessary.

Probably the best solution for individual sewage disposal on property having sufficient amount of space is a *septic tank and tile drain field* (see Fig. 11-23). The sewage empties from a cast-iron house sewer into a watertight concrete or steel tank placed below ground. Cast-iron tees or wood baffles at the entrance and discharge end of the tank prevent disruption of the surface scum within the tank and direct the solids to the bottom. Bacteria act on the sewage to break down the solids into a compact sludge, which needs removal only after several years' use. Only after the sewage is about 70 percent purified will the effluent liquid leave the tank and flow through the seepage drains, thus eliminating the possibility of contaminating surrounding water tables. Concrete or clay tile piper (4″–6″ diam), placed in trenches filled with coarse gravel, are set about 1/4″ apart with roofing-paper strips over the joints to allow positive drainage into the soil. The tile lines are placed about 16″ below ground level and sloped from 4″–6″ per 100′, to keep the drainage near the surface and yet maintain a gradual outflow.

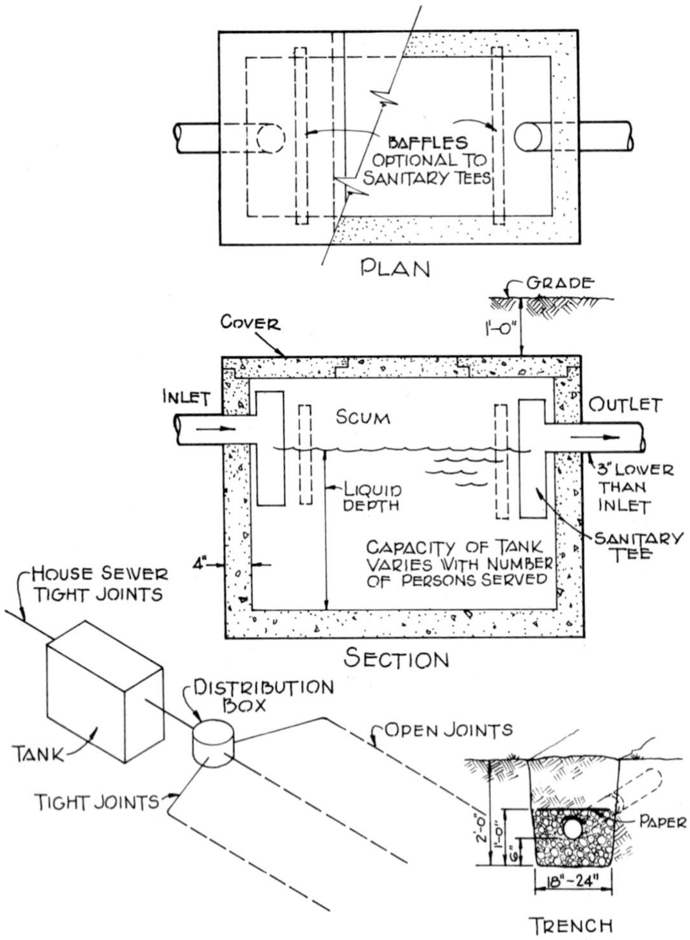

Fig. 11-23 Septic tank details and a disposal field layout used on level ground. Perforated fiber or plastic pipe is commonly used for field lines.

Different arrangements of the tile lines are possible in restricted space and to accommodate various contours; if steep slopes are encountered, line drops to different levels are made with tightly jointed vitrified tile. Lengths of drainage tile lines and sizes of gravel trenches are determined by local codes according to the size of the dwelling and the number of occupants, as well as the absorption rate of the soil. Usually 100′–300′ of tile line is required for the average residence. Tests should be made to determine the rate of water absorption in the disposal area before reliable disposal fields can be designed. Sewage disposal systems should be installed by competent and reliable contractors. Because detergents interfere with the bacterial action in septic tanks, wastes from automatic laundry equipment should be emptied into isolated drainage lines. Also, storm drains should not empty into the septic tank.

Some local codes allow a *seepage pit,* similar in construction to a cesspool, to take the discharge from a septic tank and allow it to release the effluent liquid into the surrounding soil instead of tile lines. Low underground water tables permit the use of a seepage-pit system.

11.15 DRAWING THE PLUMBING PLAN

On drawings of simple, noncomplex buildings, show the plumbing fixtures to scale and locate any other water outlets on the regular floor plan. Usually, this is all the plumbing information that is necessary. Include all exterior hose bibbs and automatic washer outlets from which piping lines can be planned. Use plumbing templates, if available, or simply scale the symbols with instruments. List fixture sizes and manufacturers' catalogue numbers in the specifications, or list them in a plumbing fixture schedule. Public sewer lines and septic tank systems should be located on plot plans.

If the plumbing information is more extensive, draw a separate floor plan showing the walls and main structural features, traced from the regular plan. See Fig. 11-24. In general, follow these steps in completing the plumbing plan:

1. Draw all plumbing fixture symbols to scale (see Fig. 11-25).
2. Locate the cold-water supply line from the street and lay out all cold-water lines to each outlet. Indicate valve, fitting, and pipe sizes.
3. Locate the water-heating equipment and lay out the hot-water lines to all fixtures requiring hot water. Use a hot-water-pipe symbol and label pipe sizes and fittings.
4. Locate the house drain according to public sewer connections or location of the septic tank.
5. With heavy lines, lay out the soil lines after consulting local plumbing codes for pipe sizes and number of fixtures on each line. Show cleanout symbols and vents according to code. Make soil lines as short and direct as possible. Indicate size and description of pipe and fittings.
6. Locate gas-line entrance and show pipeline to outlets. Give the pipe size.
7. Draw a vertical section through the stack and vent lines on drawings of multistory buildings. To show complex piping arrangements, use a single-line isometric layout without standard fitting and fixture symbols.
8. Darken all plumbing information to make it more prominent than the structural outlines.
9. Add appropriate notes and titles.

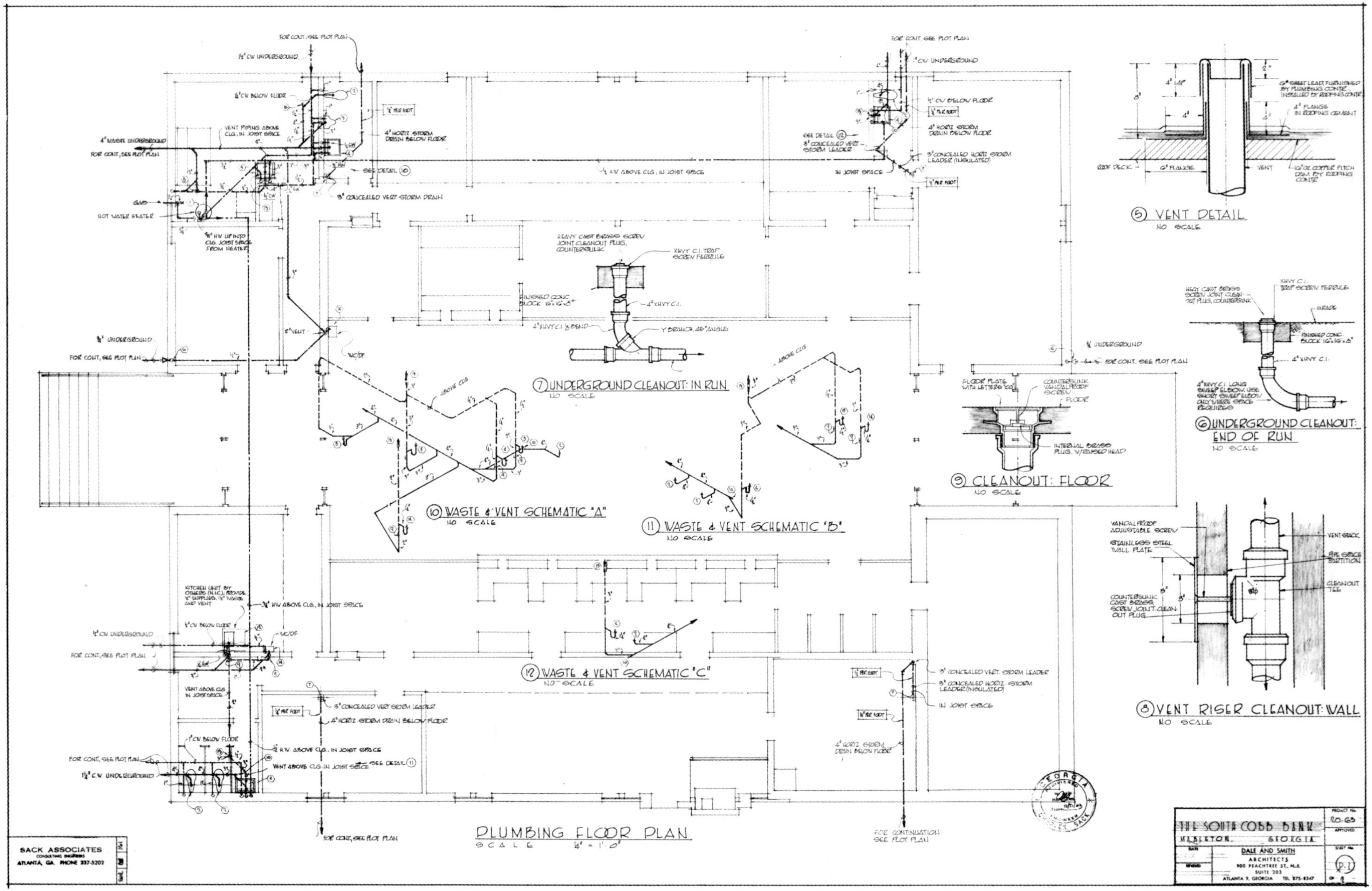

Fig. 11-24 A typical plumbing drawing from the small commercial building (Chapter 14).

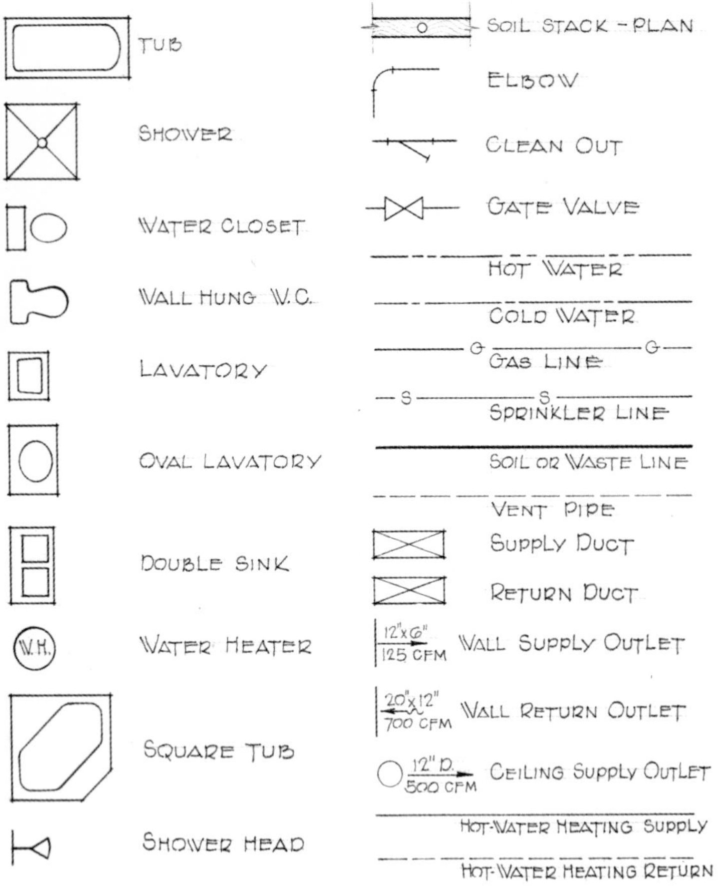

Fig. 11-25 Plumbing and heating symbols.

11.16 HOME ELECTRICAL SYSTEMS

In order to represent electrical systems on the drawing board, the student should have a rudimentary knowledge of the principles of electrical distribution so that he may provide adequate wiring and lighting, not only to meet present demands, but also to anticipate future needs.

In planning an electrical wiring system, safety must be the primary consideration. Electricity passing through a conductor creates heat. Overtaxed wiring is not only inefficient, but dangerous as well. If the conductor is too small to accommodate the amount of current passing through it, the overload results in a breakdown and the melting of the protective insulation of the wiring, thus creating a hazard. Statistics prove that considerable destruction is caused by fire due to outmoded electrical wiring. Minimum requirements for safety standards found in many local codes have been established by the National Electrical Code. Compliance with all applicable codes is the first requisite of the electrical system. A copy of the local electrical code should be studied for requirements of local construction. Also, the pamphlet *Planning Your Home Lighting—HG-No. 138*,[1] 22 pp., will be found helpful.

Like the design of mechanical equipment systems, the design of electrical systems in large buildings requires the services of engineering firms specializing in such work; whereas residential systems of a less complex nature are usually designed and installed by licensed electrical contractors who are familiar with the limitations and requirements of local and national codes. Proper planning for home electrical needs, however, must be done on paper when the total concept is conceived and the major planning is undertaken.

Electrical Terminology

AMPERE: The unit of current used to measure the amount of electricity passing through a conductor per unit of time. (Can be compared to the flow of water in gallons per second.)

CIRCUIT: Two or more wires through which electricity flows from a source to one or more outlets and then returns.

CIRCUIT BREAKER: A switch which breaks the flow of electricity in a circuit automatically, and which performs the same safety function as does a fuse.

CONDUCTORS: Common term for wires that carry the electricity.

FUSE: A safety device containing a conductor that melts when the circuit is overloaded, and thus breaks the circuit.

GROUND: A connection between the electrical system and the earth—it minimizes the damage from lightning and injury from shocks.

HORSEPOWER: A unit of work. One hp = 746 watts. (The term is diminishing in use.)

OUTLET: Any device attached to a circuit that allows electricity to be drawn off for lights or appliances. Receptacles are outlets; so are sockets.

RECEPTACLE: An outlet meant to receive the plugs of electrical cords of portable lighting equipment and appliances.

SERVICE ENTRANCE: The wires and fittings that bring electricity to a building.

[1] Send 35¢ to: Superintendent of Documents, U.S. Government Printing Office, Washington, D.C. 20402.

SERVICE PANEL: The main panel (or distribution box) that receives the electricity and distributes it through various types of branch circuits. It contains a main disconnect switch and fuses or circuit breakers for control of the electrical system in the building.

SHORT CIRCUIT: A condition created by a wrong connection between "hot" conductors or between a "hot" conductor and a neutral wire.

VOLT: The unit used to measure the electrical potential difference.

VOLTAGE DROP: The loss of voltage caused by the resistance in conductors or equipment too small to produce overloading.

WATT: The practical unit of electrical power. (Amperes times volts.) Most appliances are rated in watts to indicate their rate of electrical consumption. Both voltage and amperage are considered.

1 ampere with pressure of 1 volt = 1 watt
1 watt consumed for 1 hour = 1 watt hour
1000 watt hours = 1 kilowatt hour (kwh)

11.16.1 The Service Entrance

Electricity is furnished to the home by a 3-wire service entrance, installed by the local power company. This 3-wire service supplies 240/120-volt single-phase 60-c/s alternating current to the house, now considered standard procedure in most localities. Several methods of firmly anchoring service entrances are shown in Figs. 11-26 and 11-27. If the service is to be attached to a low roof, a masthead (or weatherhead) installation prevents the service wires from being attached too near the ground. The entrance head should be at least 10′ above the ground. A rigid support for the service wires must be furnished by the home owner. Locating the point of attachment should be governed largely by the location of the service panel. Minimum distances between the entrance and the service panel result in wiring economy, less voltage drop, and more electrical efficiency. Generally, the entrance is made near the kitchen or utility area to provide short runs for the important energy outlets.

In some areas, entrance wires are brought to the house below ground. This method conceals the wires and fittings that would otherwise be unsightly. Power meters installed on the exterior of the house are more convenient for both the power company and the home owner.

The size of the entrance wires and conduit is determined by the capacity of the service panel (see Section 11.16.2). A minimum 60-amp service requires No. 6 wires and 1″ conduit; 100-amp service requires No. 2 AWG, type R (or No. 3RHW) wires and $1\frac{1}{4}$″ conduit; 150- or 200-amp service requires No. 1/0 or No. 3/0 (type RHW insulation) and 2″ conduit.

11.16.2 The Service Panel

The service panel (distribution box) is the heart of the electrical system. Encased within a metal box, the equipment contains main disconnect switches, fuses or circuit breakers, and terminals for attaching the distribution circuit wires. Boxes can be either flush or surface mounted. Fuses in the panel are the protective devices in case of overlooking or accidental short circuits, and are sized according to each circuit capacity (replacements must be no larger than the original fuses). In place of fuses, similar protection may be provided by more expensive circuit breakers which automatically break the circuit when overloaded. No replacement is necessary when cut off; a released circuit breaker is merely switched back to its closed position. Show the location of the service panel on the floor plan.

Every electrical system must be grounded to moist earth with the use of a conductor from the ground terminal in the service panel to a metal ground rod or a cold-water pipe.

The size of the service panel size is determined by the estimated load requirements of the building, combined with the anticipated future needs. Lighting and appliance loads can be taken from the Wattage Table and converted into amperes. For example, if a total of 30,000 watts was found to be needed in the home, the minimum service would then be 125 amp (30,000 ÷ 240 = 125).

$$\frac{\text{Watts}}{\text{Volts}} = \text{Amps}$$

A 150-amp service would be the logical selection to take care of future needs. A 20 per cent additional capacity is commonly added for these contingencies.

Although a *60-amp service* is the minimum acceptable by the National Electric Code for houses under 1000 sq ft, a *100-amp service* is

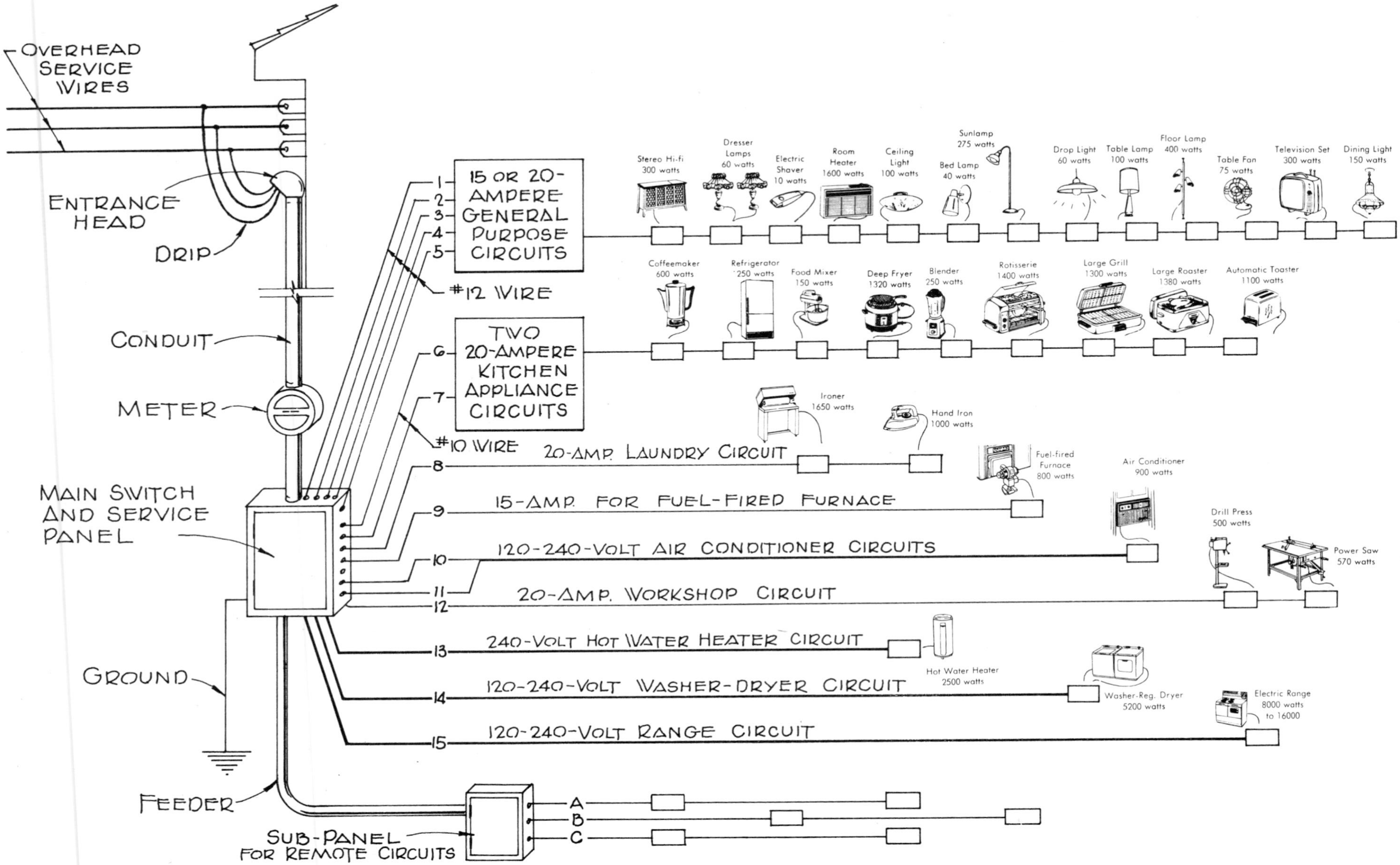

Fig. 11-26 Wiring diagram of a residential electrical system.

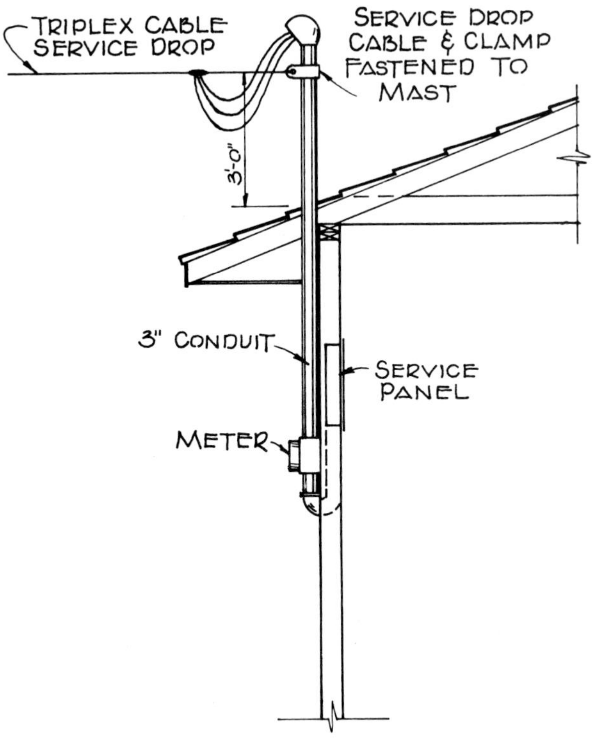

Fig. 11-27 Entrance mast for low roofs.

recommended as the minimum for all new homes up to 3000 sq ft in size. This service will be adequate for lighting and appliances requiring up to about 24,000 watts total load (see Wattage Table). If an electric range, water heater, electric dryer, central air conditioning, along with lighting and the usual small appliances are included, a *150-amp service* will be needed. If electric resistance heating or other unusual loads are to be included with the above loads, a *200-amp service* should be selected. Large homes of 5000 sq ft and over should have at least the 200-amp service. Larger services are also available for commercial installations.

Wattage Table

Home Appliances	Watts
Automatic dryer (regular)	4500
Automatic dryer (high-speed)	8700
Automatic washer	700
Bathroom heater	1500–2500
Dishwasher and waste disposal	1500
Exhaust fan	300
Fuel-fired heating system	800
Hand iron	1000
Home freezer	350
Ironer	1650
Range	8000–13500
Refrigerator	300
Roaster-broiler	1500
Room air conditioner (1 ton)	1500
Television	300

11.16.3 Branch Circuits

Branch circuits have various capacities (15, 20, 30, 40, and 50 amp), depending upon their use. Both 240- and 120-volt circuits are furnished by the service panel. Depending upon local codes, one of the following types of wiring is used in modern construction:

Nonmetallic-Sheathed Cable (Romex) is inexpensive and easy to install. It is flexible and covered with paper and fabric that form the protective covering over the individual insulated copper wires. Both 2- and 3-wire cable is available to be used only in dry locations. For damp locations or underground, a plastic-covered cable is used instead of the fabric-covered kind. Either type is available in sizes from No. 14 to No. 6 wire.

Metal-Armored Cable (BX) is covered with a spiral, flexible-metal sheathing that gives the wiring more protection from physical damage, yet it is unsuitable for damp locations.

Metal Conduit is more expensive and offers still more protection for the wiring. The conduit is installed with the boxes and the outlets during construction; then the wiring is pulled through and connected. All splices must be made in junction boxes.

GENERAL-PURPOSE CIRCUITS (120 volts, 15 or 20 amp) serve the lighting and general-convenience outlets. Good circuitry layout provides several circuits in rooms or wings so that partial lighting will always be available in case of a blown fuse. From a general standpoint, one circuit should be provided per 375 sq ft of floor area in the house. Number 12 wire should be used, which will allow a maximum of 2400 watts in circuits up to 75′ in length; longer circuits require larger wire.

APPLIANCE CIRCUITS (120/240 volts, 3-wire, 20 amp) should be provided in kitchens, dining areas, and laundries to serve appliances requiring heavier loads. Three-wire circuits provide greater capacity with a minimum voltage drop at the outlets. Home workshops should be supplied with a similar circuit. Number 12 wire is used for appliance circuits, and usually two circuits are needed in a residential system.

INDIVIDUAL-EQUIPMENT CIRCUITS are needed to service each of the following permanently installed equipment: electric range, washer-dryer, fuel-fired furnace, dishwasher, electric water heater, central air conditioning, bath heaters, and other similar equipment. The capacity of each circuit must be sufficient for the needs of each piece of equipment.

FEEDER CIRCUITS with subdistribution panel equipment, are sometimes used for remote areas. A 3-wire feeder is run from the main panel to a subpanel and 2-wire branch circuits are extended from the subpanel with a minimum of voltage drop.

A method of wiring that is finding more acceptance is the 240-volt perimeter circuit. The 3-wire circuit is installed completely around the building to allow actually two 120-volt circuits for each wire provided. Receptacles have one 120-volt outlet on each hot wire, yet both hot wires furnish 240 volts in case the voltage is later needed for a room air conditioner or other equipment. Only a simple hookup modification would need to be made.

11.16.4 Low-Voltage Switching

Another variation of the conventional wiring system is the low-voltage switching system. With this system, wall switches control a low-voltage circuit (6–24 volts) through a relay that activates the line voltage at the outlet. Savings can be realized on the low-voltage wiring, since light bell wire can be used. There is no danger of shock at the switch, and any or all of the outlets can be controlled at a central station. Slightly different types of equipment are available for low-voltage systems.

11.16.5 Location of Outlets

For maximum convenience, the probable placement of furniture of each room should be considered before locating outlets. For instance, in a bedroom the outlets would best be on each side of the bed. Since bedrooms and living rooms rely primarily on movable lamps for general lighting, one or two of the outlets should be connected to wall switches. Outlets should generally be placed near the corners of rooms, where they are easily accessible and there is less chance of their being obstructed by furniture. In living areas, no point along a wall should be farther than 6′ from an outlet. Small habitable rooms should have at least three convenience outlets; in larger rooms they should be spaced about 8′ apart along each wall. The conventional height for outlets is 12″ above the floor except in kitchens and dining areas. In kitchens they are placed just above the countertops at 4′ intervals, convenient for work centers; in dining areas they should be located near and just above table surfaces. Baths need an outlet near the lavatory or vanity and one on an opposite wall. Keep all outlets away from tubs or shower stalls, unless they are waterproof. All stationary appliances in kitchens, laundries, and utility rooms require an outlet near their place of installation. Remember to include sufficient outlets in garages, workshops, as well as waterproof outlets near terraces for outdoor living, and one near the front entrance.

11.16.6 Location of Lighting Fixtures

Interior lighting must be adequate for the activities of each area, yet subtle variations in the amount of general light and the careful use of supplementary or accent lighting give the overall lighting a less monotonous quality. Unusual architectural features must be given special consideration. Well-lighted interiors are often decidedly more interesting in the evening than during the daylight. Artificial light must be regarded as a definite part of the total design of the building.

Although fluorescent lighting is more efficient than incandescent, interiors of living areas will usually be more flattering in the warmer light of incandescent lamps. In bedrooms also, such lamps are frequently used with or without the addition of a ceiling fixture. In work areas where abundant lighting is necessary for specific tasks, fluorescent-type light may be found more acceptable. However, glare and harsh light levels should be avoided. For example, a luminous suspended ceiling with uniformly spaced fluorescent tubes above produces a very pleasing method of lighting a kitchen. Fluorescent indirect lighting is also suitable for cove installations. See Fig. 11-28. Work counters in kitchens can often be provided with indirect lighting placed beneath wall cabinets. Other than the general lighting of each room, provision must be made for supplementary-activity lighting with outlets and/or fixtures properly placed. Unusual architectural features can be given added interest by the use of recessed spots or other types of isolated lighting; be sure any special lighting has an outlet symbol indication.

Usually, small rooms have one centrally located ceiling fixture. Larger rooms and long hallways have several fixtures so arranged that uniform lighting is provided throughout. In bathrooms, light should fall on the face of the persons using mirrors and vanities. See Fig. 11-29. In dining rooms, the ceiling fixture should be located directly above the table placement. Closets can be lighted with door-operated or chain-pull outlets, or they may receive sufficient light from adjacent fixtures placed in front of their door openings. All entrances and outdoor living areas should have provision for lighting with outlets operated from inside wall switches.

Students should acquaint themselves with the many types of lighting fixtures now available. Each lighting situation has a variety of workable solutions—only experience can produce the most dramatic results.

11.16.7 Location of Light Switches

Wall switches are generally placed 4′ above the floor and should be located near the latch side of door openings for easy access. Switch placement must conform to the traffic patterns within the house. Switches should be located so that in going from one room to another, lights can be switched on before entering or upon leaving. Rooms with several exits, and stairways, should be provided with a 3-way switch at each exit, so that the lighting can be turned on or off from all exits, or in the case of stairs, from each level. Lighting can be operated from three stations by the use of *two 3-way switches and one 4-way switch* (Fig. 11-30). Usually low-voltage switching is used when it becomes necessary to control the lighting from three or more stations. Low-voltage switches are indicated on the drawing with the same symbols as other switches. Silent mercury switches are recommended in and near bedrooms. In living rooms where variations of light intensity may be useful in creating different moods, dimmer switches can be indicated. Other types of switches are available for providing convenient lighting-outlet control.

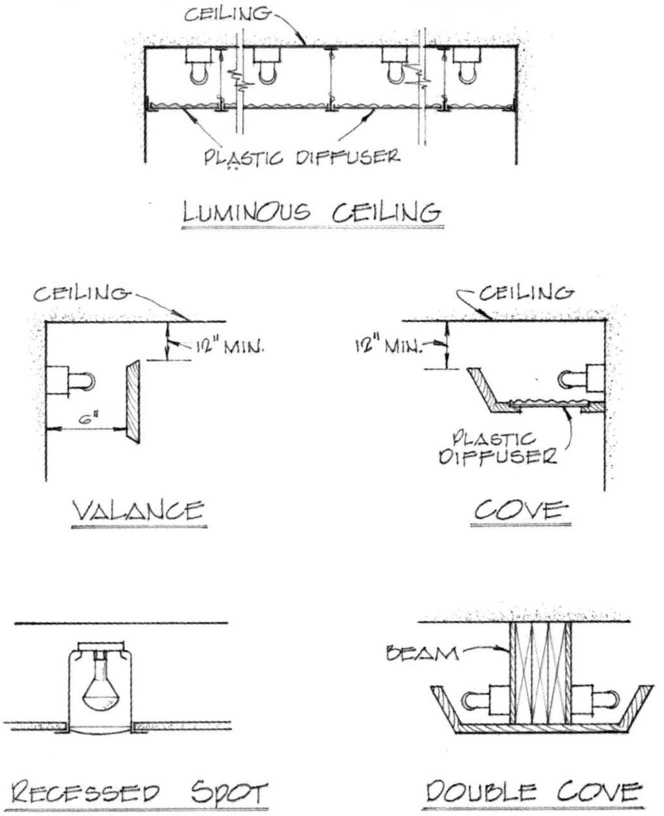

Fig. 11-28 Methods for providing indirect lighting in living areas.

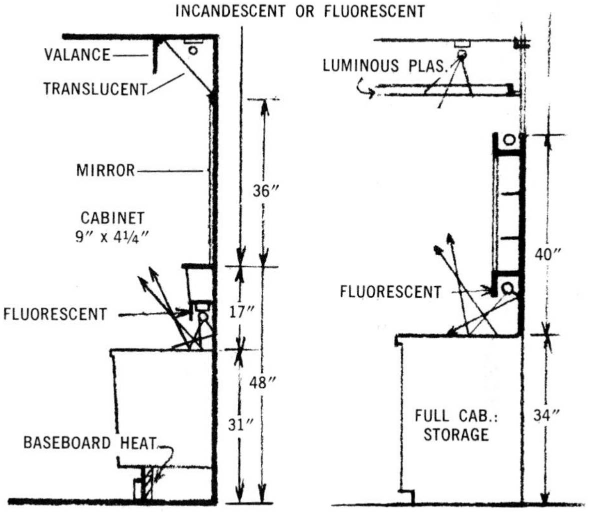

Fig. 11-29 Indirect lighting in bathrooms.

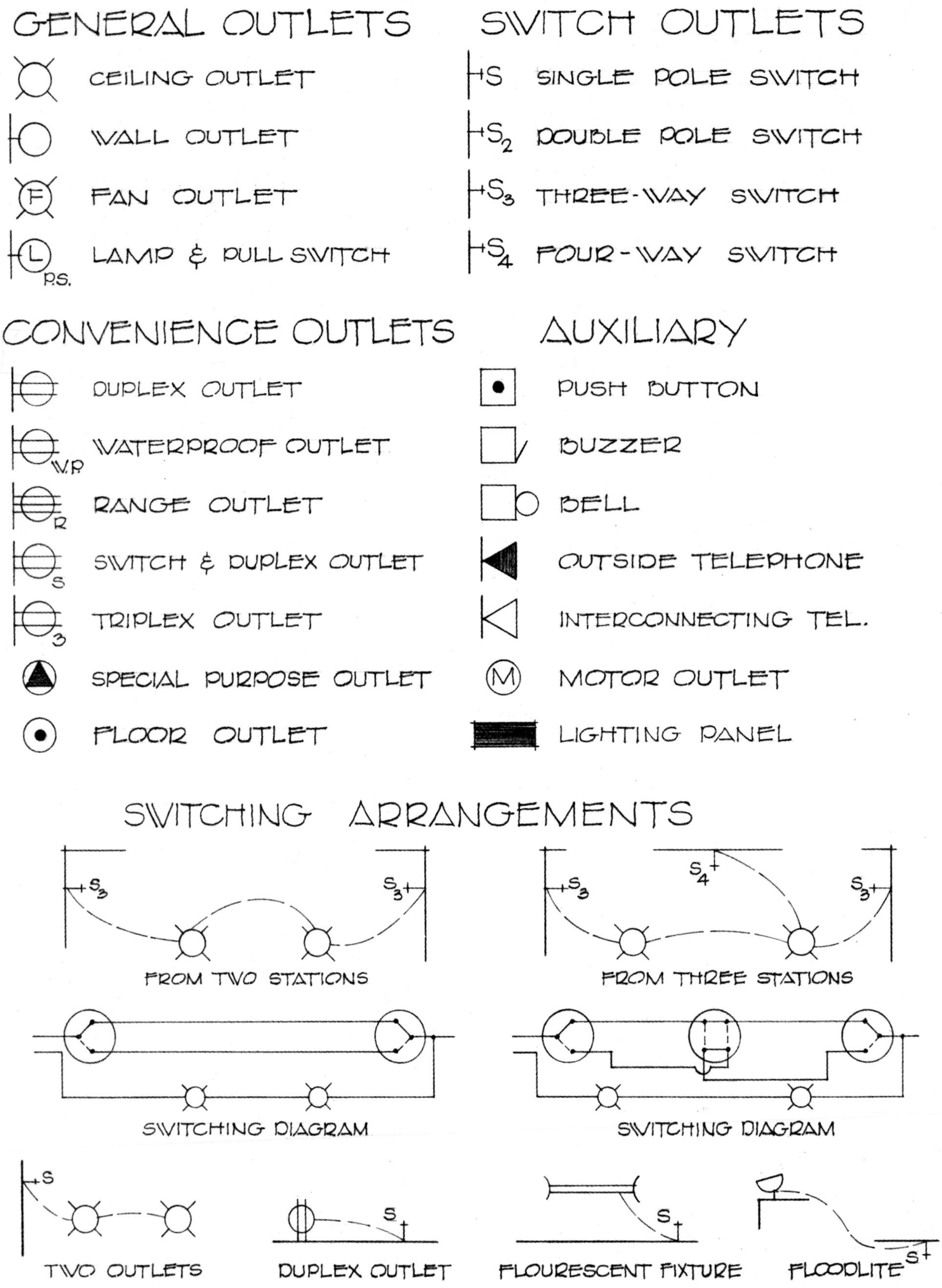

Fig. 11-30 Electrical symbols for working drawings.

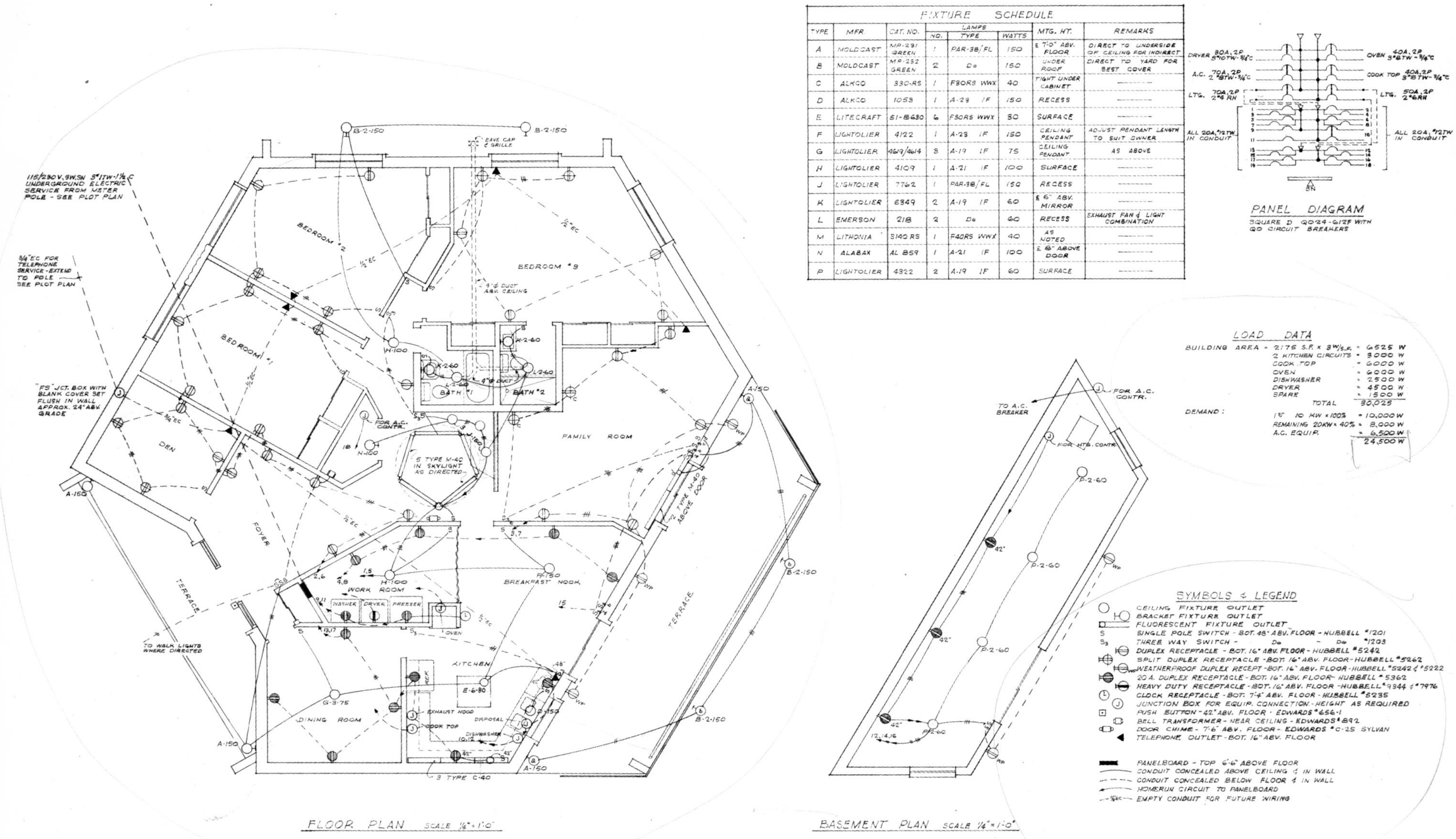

Fig. 11-31 An electrical plan for a residence.

11.16.8 Special Outlets

The following special outlets are usually indicated on the electrical plan with appropriate symbols:

1. *Entrance signals* (bell or chimes) are best located in central locations such as hallways. Low-voltage current is provided by a transformer located near the service panel. Circuits to entrance-door push buttons utilize No. 18 AWG bell wire.
2. Locate *telephone outlets* in convenient locations; wiring is usually done by telephone companies.
3. *Intercom systems* become practical in rambling-type homes; panels and stations are indicated on the plan.
4. *Television-antenna outlets* can be provided in new home construction.
5. *Automatic fire- and/or burglar-alarm systems* are available for home protection. Locate alarm bells in the master bedroom.
6. *Built-in hi-fi* or *stereo systems* can be shown with built-in main and remote speakers located in various living areas.

11.17 DRAWING THE ELECTRICAL PLAN

The electrical information on residential working drawings is usually shown on the regular floor plan, as was mentioned earlier. However, if excessive information requires a separate drawing, as is often needed with complex homes and commercial buildings, use a separate floor plan. See Fig. 11-31. Follow these general steps in drawing the electrical plan:

1. Locate the service panel, show symbol, and indicate its amperage information;
2. Show all convenience-outlet symbols; use 3-wire symbols for all outlets requiring 240 voltage such as range, dryer, air conditioner, etc.;
3. Show all ceiling- and wall-lighting outlets;
4. Show all special outlets such as telephone, door bell, etc.;
5. Show all switches and their outlet connections (use an irregular curve);
6. If necessary, complete an electrical fixture schedule and symbol legend; and
7. Complete titles and necessary notes.

REVIEW QUESTIONS

1. In planning a satisfactory residential heating system, what basic factors must be considered?

2. How can the architecture contribute to the efficiency of the heating and/or cooling system?

3. What is meant by "degree of comfort" in reference to heating-cooling systems?

4. What are the advantages of the forced warm-air heating systems? The hydronic systems? The radiant systems?

5. Would a heat-pump system be efficient for heating a home in your locality?

6. Why are filters placed in the return-duct side of a warm-air heating system?

7. What type of warm-air furnace must be used with heat ducts embedded in a concrete slab-on-ground floor?

8. How is the air that is removed by kitchen and bath exhaust fans usually replaced in a well-designed system?

9. What three controls are necessary in making a warm-air system fully automatic?

10. Why has electricity become popular as a home-heating energy source?

11. Why would the 2-pipe, hot-water system be more satisfactory than the 1-pipe system in home heating?

12. What general type of insulation is the most efficient with radiant heating systems?

13. What two methods of home heating commonly employ baseboard registers?

14. Which type heating system is most easily combined with conventional cooling equipment?

15. If a room has a calculated heat loss of 3200 Btu per hr, what wattage resistance wire would be needed to satisfy the heat?

16. In heat-pump installations, what is the primary source of heat supplied to the rooms?

17. What mechanism reverses the cycles from heating to cooling in the heat pump?

18. What is the purpose of an outside thermostat?

19. What are the disadvantages of water chillers in residential cooling?

20. Are partitions between heated rooms considered when calculating heat losses?

21. Which part of a residential plumbing system operates by gravity? Which part by pressure?

22. How can initial plumbing costs be reduced when designing a home?

23. What is the purpose of a soil trap in plumbing fixtures?

24. What size hot-water heater would be sufficient for a family of three, where the home contains automatic laundry equipment?

25. What factors determine the correct size septic tank and the length of tile drainage lines?

26. What size electrical service panel should be selected for a home of 2000 sq ft?

27. What is a "feeder" circuit?

28. What should be analyzed to determine the location of wall switches?

29. What types of switches are needed to operate an outlet from three locations?

30. Why must lighting be considered in the total concept of a home?

"Thus shadow owes its birth to light."—John Gay

12

Perspective Drawings, Shades and Shadows

It is of great advantage for the architectural draftsman to be able to draw objects as they appear to the casual observer. A realistic representation is still the most effective way of showing a client, who may have a minimal knowledge of graphics, the appearance of a proposed structure. Through the years, architects have used perspectives in presentation drawings and also for preliminary planning sketches. Unquestionably, the value of perspective drawings is due to the fact that architectural designs are shown in the most natural way. Draftsmen with a working knowledge of perspective will be better prepared for presentation work and, equally important, will find themselves with a keener sense of 3-dimensional space visualization. To the beginner, perspective may seem difficult, but after careful study of the principles, even the novice with comparatively little experience will be able to do surprisingly well.

This chapter is not an exhaustive study of the theory of perspective; rather, it is meant to show the beginner the fundamentals and the methods commonly employed in drawing perspectives with the least difficulty and in the most practical way. We will concern ourselves mainly with the "how" rather than the "why" by the use of step-by-step illustrated instructions.

12.1 THEORY AND NOMENCLATURE

Perspective drawing is a pictorial method of representing a building or object, very much as the lens of a camera records an image on film. We can say that a perspective is the projection of an object on a fixed plane from a fixed point. Remember that a view we observe with our eyes is actually two coordinated views from two points, usually not fixed as we move our heads about, producing 3-dimensional realism difficult to obtain on a drawing. The drawing can only show the image as it will appear from one point of view, and of course, that point is fixed. This is a limitation inherent in every perspective drawing. Occasionally, even with the most accurate projection, an entirely unrealistic representation will result. For that reason, slight modifications of points and geometric arrangement in drawing may be necessary before arriving at a satisfactory picture. The student must be willing to make several trials, if need be, for the sake of appearance and true architectural proportions.

The basic theory of perspective drawing assumes that the image is produced upon a transparent vertical plane, called the "picture plane" (Fig. 12-1), very much as the orthographic views (discussed in Chapter 3) are formed on transparent planes—the only difference being that the orthographic have parallel projectors, whereas the perspective views have projectors radiating from a single point, similar to the visual rays of a person's eye (see Fig. 12-1). The outline of these projection points, as they pierce the picture plane, forms the perspective drawing. For comparison, we could produce a perspective on a window glass if we were looking through it at a building across the street and drew the exact outlines as we see them through the glass. On our paper, however, we will plot all the points of the perspective with projection lines from the orthographic plan and elevation view, thereby eliminating any guesswork. A pictorial representation of the planes and points necessary to draw a typical perspective is shown in Fig. 12-2. Later, we will discuss how each is laid out on paper to produce the finished perspective.

Down through the years, many artists and draftsmen have contributed to the system of perspective projection as we know it today. The accompanying woodcut, "Demonstration of Per-

Fig. 12-1 In perspective drawing, the image of an object is produced on a theoretical, transparent plane called the "picture plane" as we look through the plane at the object.

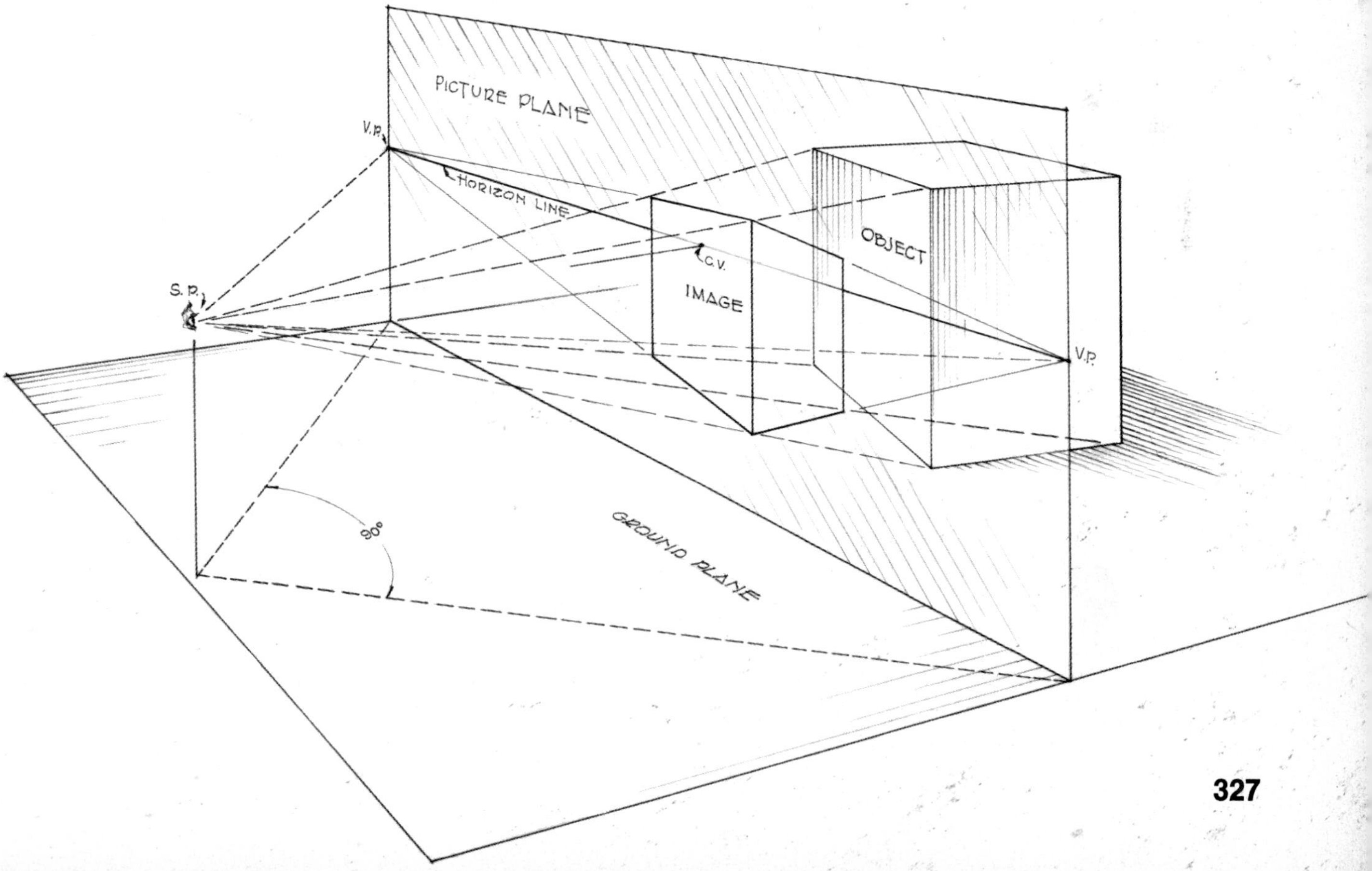

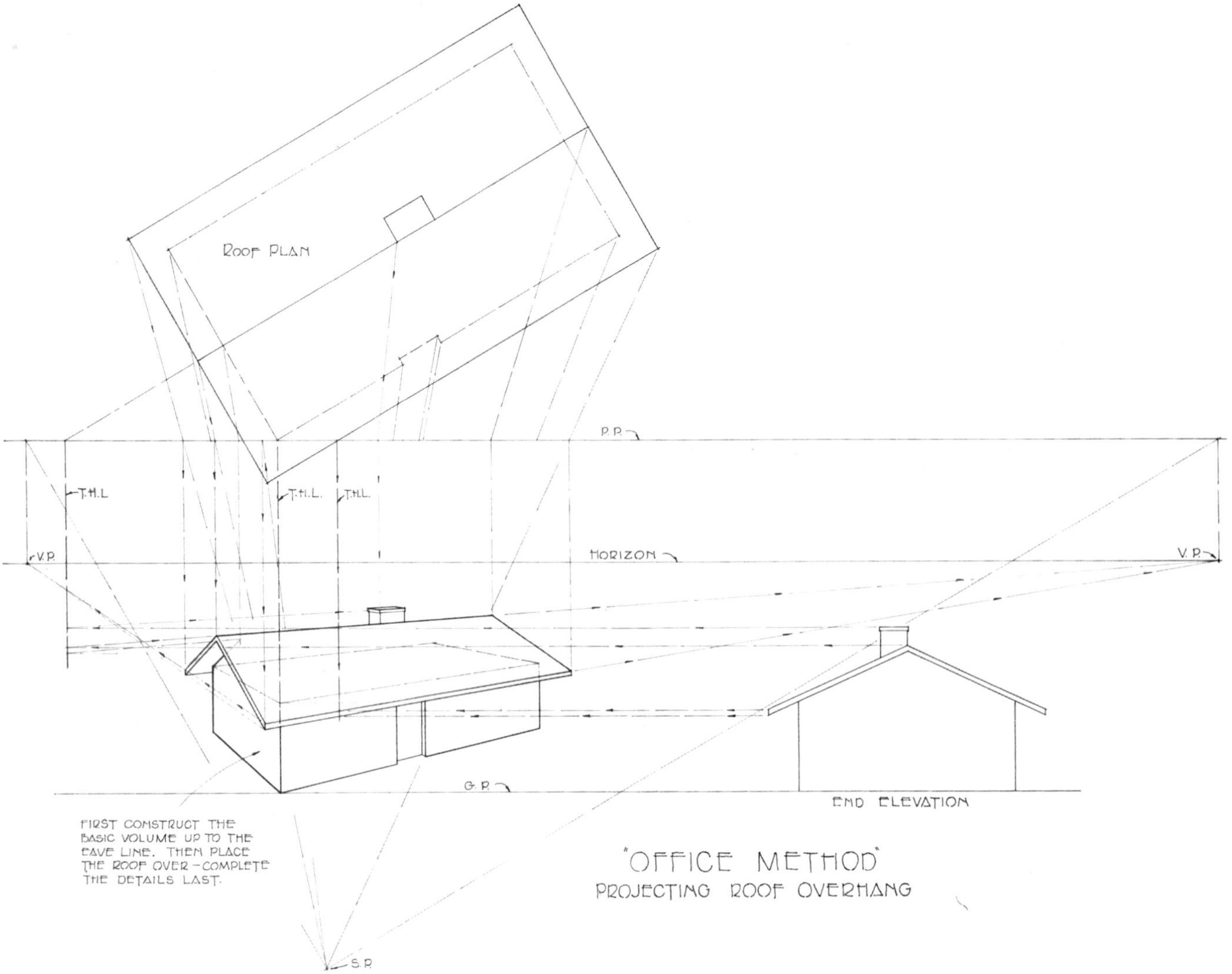

Fig. 12-2 A 2-point perspective done by the office method.

Fig. 12-3 A woodcut by Albrecht Dürer in 1525 verifying the principles of perspective. The string passing through the picture plane locates points to form the image.

spective," by Albrecht Dürer is from the artist's treatise on geometry, written in 1525. It illustrates a rather crude yet effective early attempt to prove the principle of projectors forming a true image as they pierce a vertical plane (Fig. 12-3).

To interpret both the drawings and written material, we must have an acquaintance with perspective terms. It would be wise at this point to study the drawings in this chapter and observe the significance of each of the following terms:

Picture Plane (P.P.) As we mentioned, the picture plane is conveniently thought of as a transparent, vertical plane upon which the perspective is drawn. The lower edge of the plane intersects the ground plane. On the plan-portion view of the layout, it appears as a line parallel to the ground plane and usually is placed between the station point and the object (see Fig. 12-2). All horizontal measurements are established on the picture-plane line and are projected to the perspective. Any part of an object touching the picture plane will have true-height characteristics, and these heights can be projected directly from an elevation of the object or measured directly as long as the feature touches the picture plane. You will notice in the different drawings that the farther back from the picture plane the features fall, the smaller they will appear on the perspective. On the lower, elevation portion of our perspective construction layout, the surface of the paper becomes the picture plane. For convenience, we will label the picture-plane line P.P. on the drawings; the other terms will also be designated by their initial capital letters.

Ground Plane (G.P.) The ground plane must be horizontal and is represented with a line on the elevation portion of our layout. If the object touches the picture plane on the plan, it must also touch the groundline in a similar manner on the perspective (see Fig. 12-2). If the object is placed in back of the picture plane in plan, it will appear above and back of the groundline on the elevation. The groundline is always parallel to the horizon line and represents the intersection of the picture plane and the ground.

Station Point (S.P.) The station point is the origination of the visual rays as the object is observed through the picture plane. It will appear as a point on both the plan and elevation construction. However, it is usually not shown in elevation; yet it would fall on the horizon directly above its plan designation. The placement of the point on the plan view obviously determines the "view" of the building. And this choice of placement would be very much like actually walking around the building to determine the most favorable position for observation. (Generally, it is most expedient to choose the front view showing the entrance.) It also becomes evident that the distance between the station point and the picture plane directly affects the finished size of the perspective (see Fig. 12-7). If they are close together, the perspective will appear small; if they are farther apart, a larger perspective will result. In early attempts, students often make the mistake of placing the station point too near the picture plane. In general, the station point should be placed about twice as far away from the picture plane as the length of the building being drawn. Another method of determining the proper distance for a pleasing perspective is with the use of a 30° triangle. Merely place the triangle so that its sides enclose the extremities of the plan (Fig. 12-4), and the apex will locate a satisfactory station point. Usually, the point is located in the center of vision (see Fig. 12-7B), rather than off to one side. The most desirable placement of station points comes only after experience is gained in dealing with the correct appearances of the many architectural forms and features that are generally encountered.

Horizon Line (H.L.) The horizon line represents the intersection of the sky and the ground, and therefore is only represented on the elevation portion of the drawing. Usually, the horizon line is placed above the ground line; the amount above determines the height of observation, since the horizon plane is always at eye level. If a view from 30′ high were desired, for

Fig. 12-4 A convenient method for locating the station point.

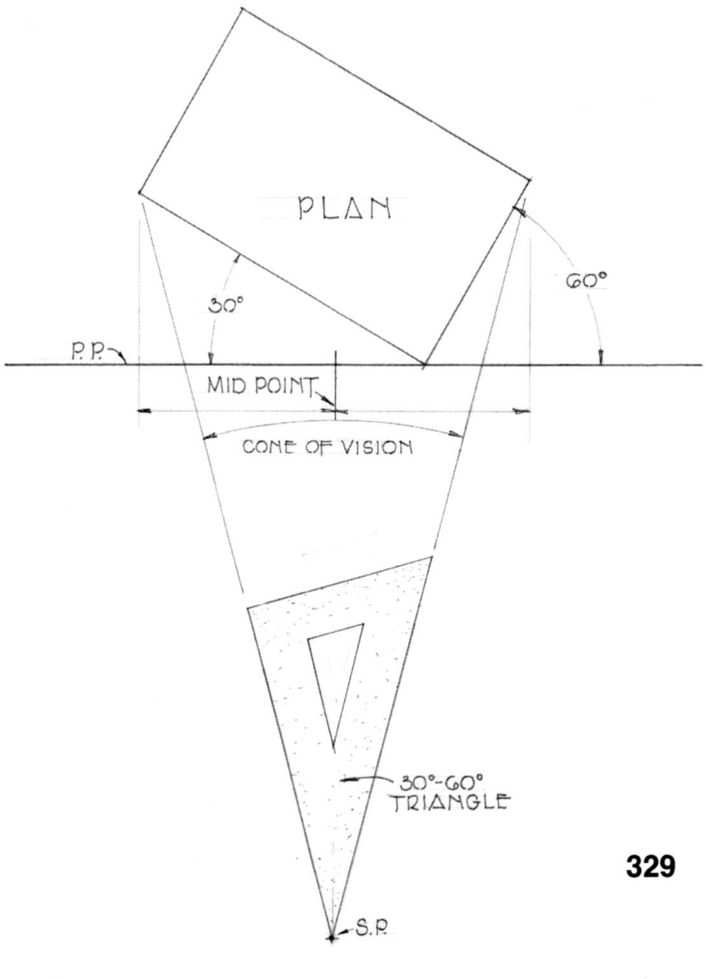

Fig. 12-5 Photograph of a house with major lines extended to locate the vanishing points.

example, the 30′ would be scaled from the groundline to determine the placement of the horizon line.

Vanishing Points (V.P.) Vanishing points always fall on the horizon line. Receding, horizontal lines which are not parallel to the picture plane vanish at these points. See Fig. 12-5. On the plan portion, perpendicular lines parallel to the sides of the building are projected from the station point to locate the vanishing points on the picture plane; to bring the points to the elevation portion of the setup, they are projected down to the horizon line (see Fig. 12-2). This is the method for a 2-point, angular perspective. In a 1-point perspective, the vanishing point is simply placed in the most favorable position on the horizon line. In drawing perspectives, the vanishing points make convenient terminations for the horizontal receding lines, and as long as the proper lines vanish at the correct point, the picture will develop with little trouble. Remember that parallel lines vanish at the same point. Sloping surfaces, which will be discussed later, have vanishing points lying on a vertical trace through the original vanishing points. Unless a 3-point perspective is drawn, all vertical lines are drawn vertically. Very few architectural delineators have found use for the 3-point type of perspective. In reality, the sides of tall buildings would converge vertically as we look up at them. But the distortion does not lend itself to accurate presentation; therefore, we will not concern ourselves with 3-point perspective in this material.

Occasionally, when working on large drawings, the vanishing point falls a considerable distance from the paper. If a large board is not available to overcome this problem, some

Fig. 12-6 Handy method of drawing lines when their vanishing points fall off the drawing board.

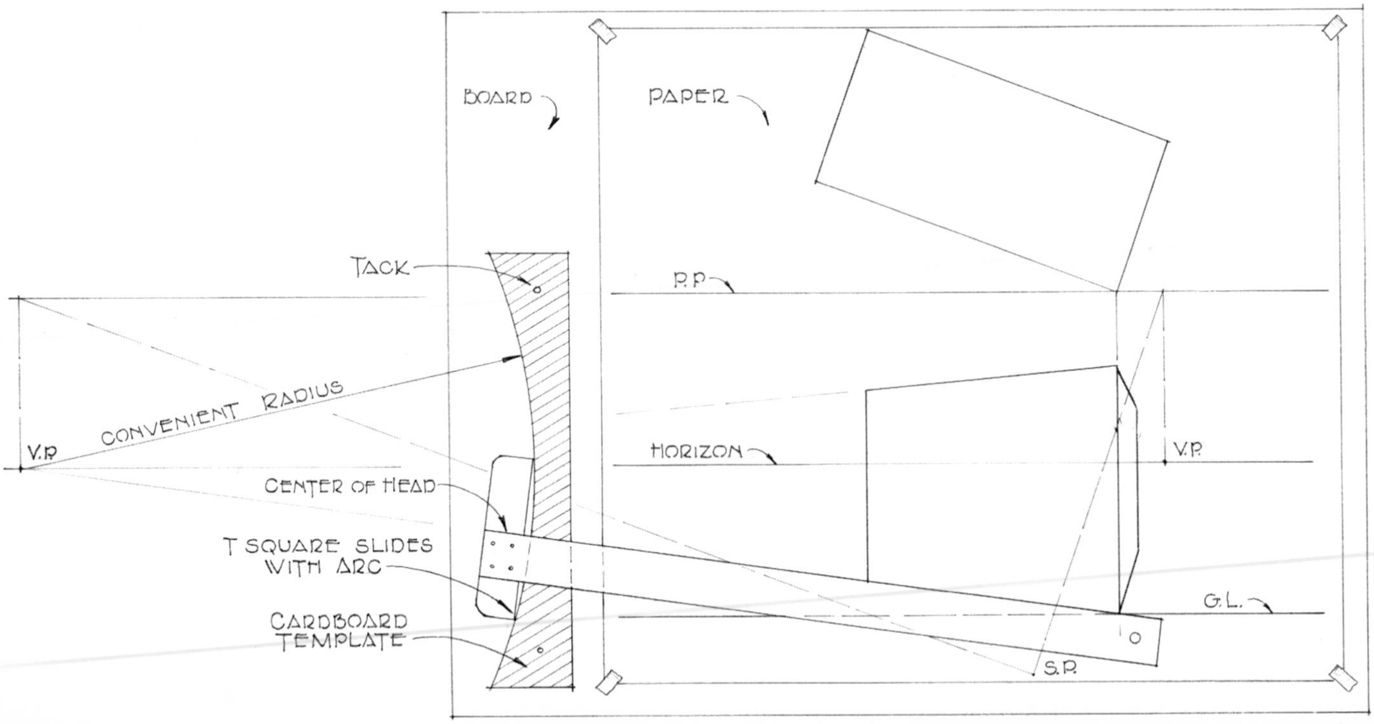

method must be employed to vanish lines at the distant points. Often an adjacent table can be used, and a thumbtack in the vanishing point will aid in aligning an especially long straightedge. Another method is shown in Fig. 12-6 with the use of an offset-head T square and a curved template fastened to the board.

True-Height Line (T.H.L.) If a vertical line of the object touches the picture plane, the line will appear full length on the finished perspective, thus providing a convenient method for projecting true heights: from an elevation view or by measurement directly on the true-height line, if necessary (see Fig. 12-2). If difficulty is encountered in establishing heights for a certain feature of the floor plan with the use of only one true-height line, the problem can be solved by projecting the feature to the picture plane. Wherever the projection intersects the picture plane, a new true-height line can be drawn for measuring the height of that feature only. Remember that height measurements can be made on only those features that touch the picture plane.

12.2 PERSPECTIVE VARIABLES

Briefly, the variables in perspective construction, other than the actual scale change of the orthographic views, are the relationships between the station point, picture plane, and object (see Fig. 12-7). Naturally, there can be an infinite number of relationships, and the draftsman should know the various ways in which these variables can be manipulated for the most desirable pictorial appearance.

The relationship of the object to the picture plane (Fig. 12-7). First of all, a decision must be made as to which sides of the building should appear on the perspective. Ordinarily, the front is shown and given the most emphasis; occasionally an interesting feature in the rear will call for a view from that side. Emphasis is attained by placing the important side at a small angle from the picture plane—the larger the angle, the less the emphasis. Usually, the 30°–60° angles are convenient for laying out the plan in relation to the picture plane, with the 30° angle given to the more important side. A 45° angle produces equal emphasis on the two observable sides of a building, thereby lessening the interesting effect that is achieved when only one side is emphasized.

It is worth remarking that without changing the scale of the orthographic views, the size of the finished perspective can be controlled to a certain extent by merely changing the forward and backward relationship of the plan and picture plane (Fig. 12-7G, H, and I). Usually the front corner of the plan is placed on the picture plane; but by bringing the plan *down,* with more of it (or all of it) in front of the picture plane, a larger perspective will result. Conversely, if a smaller perspective is desired, the plan can be placed in back of the picture plane. This variation obviously controls the size of the perspective slightly, if such becomes necessary.

The distance from the station point to the picture plane After observing the drawings, it will be seen that the closer the station point is to the picture plane, the smaller the perspective becomes. Also, close station points produce images with sharp angles on their forecorners, resulting in distorted and displeasing perspectives. On the other hand, if the station point is placed too far from the picture plane, it will usually fall off the paper and therefore become troublesome. Under ordinary conditions, a station point placed to produce a 30° angle of vision with respect to the extremities of the plan produces quite satisfactory images (see Fig. 12-4). The cone of vision should not be more than 45° in width.

The station point can also be moved to the right or left of the center of vision (Fig. 12-7A, B, and C), but its placement too far either way will produce distortion. Similar effects can be gained by changing the angle of the plan in relation to the picture plane, as previously mentioned. The latter method is advisable since it keeps the station point and the center of vision in a perpendicular relationship to the picture plane, eliminating unnecessary distortion.

The height of the horizon from the ground plane The placement of the horizon line in respect to the groundline determines the eye-level height in observing the building (see Fig. 12-8). The horizon is always at eye level. If it is placed above the height of the roof, a bird's-eye view will result; if it is placed below the foundation of the building, the perspective will give one the impression of looking up at the building from a low position, such as a valley. The normal position of the horizon is 5′–6″ or 6′–0″ above

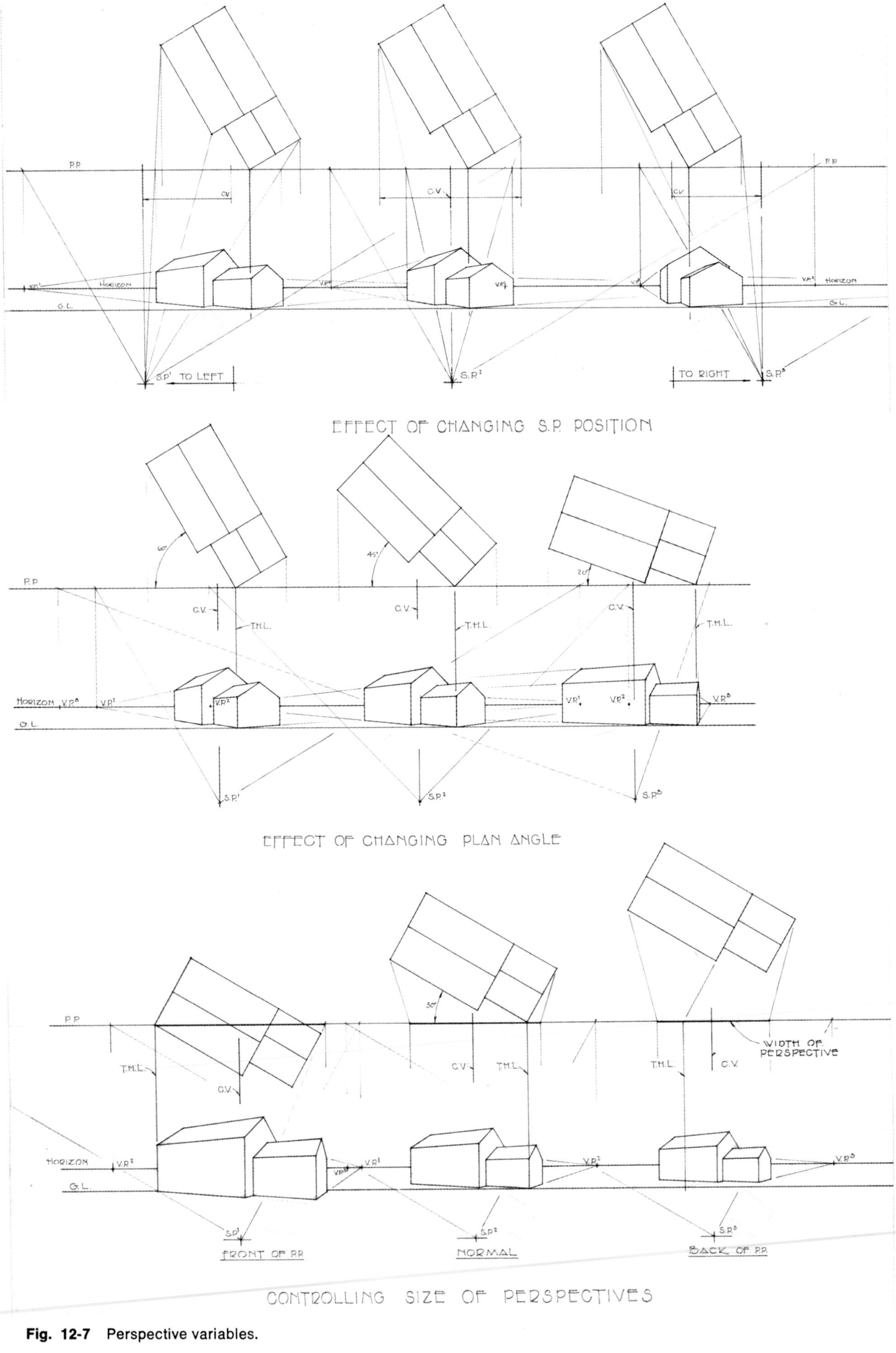

Fig. 12-7 Perspective variables.

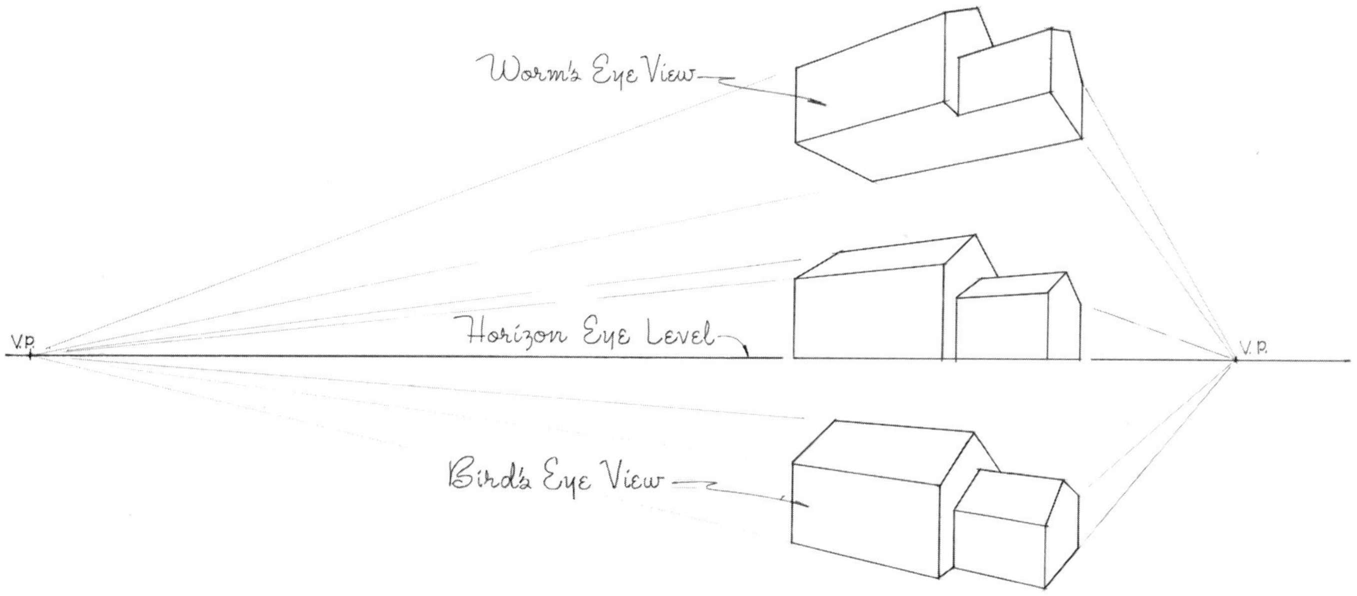

Fig. 12-8 Effect of viewing a building from different heights.

the groundline; this distance represents the eye-level height of the average person standing on level ground. Care should be taken not to place the horizon line at the same height as a dominant horizontal feature on the building, such as a strong roof line. The feature will then coincide with the horizon line and thereby lose much of its interest and importance. Low buildings, such as houses with flat roofs, are usually given more interest if the horizon line is placed 25′ or 30′ high. Although this placement gives prominence to the roof, it nevertheless reduces strong, nearly horizontal roof lines. See Fig. 12-9.

We see that the variables that exist in the setting up of a perspective layout make it possible for the draftsman to adapt a mechanical projection method to a variety of perspective situations. With experience, the modifications can be made to give variety to the perspectives, which will be limited only by a draftsman's reluctance to experiment and improve the quality of his work. Do not forget, however, that interest is important on a drawing, but not at the expense of misrepresenting true architectural conditions.

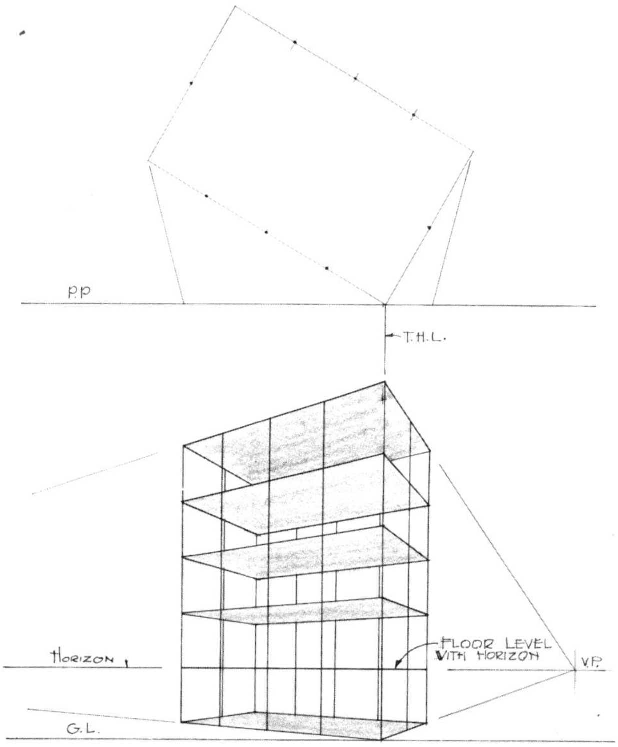

Fig. 12-9 Appearance of floor levels at various heights.

12.3 TYPES OF PERSPECTIVES

All linear perspectives (those defining outlines) used by delineators can be classified as either 2-point or 1-point perspectives (as we stated, 3-point perspective is not effective in architectural presentation). The 2-point angular perspective (Fig. 12-2) is the most popular type for showing the exteriors of buildings. Two sides of the building are seen, and the angular nature of these sides reveals the important information without excessive distortion. Several methods of construction have been developed—namely:

1. The common or office method;
2. The direct projection method; and
3. The perspective-plan method.

The office method is of particular importance to the beginner; it is widely used and most often the simplest method for orientation. Although more complex, the perspective-plan method has more versatility and drawings can be completed quicker once the principles have been mastered. The knowledge of these two methods will be sufficient for any perspective work encountered and will be discussed in what follows.

The 1-point perspective (Fig. 12-18) depicts a building or interior with one side parallel to the picture plane. It will be seen that the horizontal lines of the parallel side are drawn horizontally, producing a true orthographic shape of the side. The receding, parallel sides are formed by lines converging to a single point, the vanishing point, usually placed within the view. Interior views of rooms are often drawn with the 1-point method; it presents an accurate description of the facing wall, combined with observation of both receding sidewalls. Another typical application for 1-point perspective is a street flanked by buildings. Looking directly down the street, the vanishing point falls at the end of the street. The receding building and street lines are then conveniently drawn to the one vanishing point (see Fig. 12-19). Other dramatic applications can be found for the 1-point method, especially when formal architectural arrangements are involved. Many of the principles of 2-point perspective apply equally to the 1-point, only minor variations in setting up the perspective change.

12.4 TO DRAW A TWO-POINT ANGULAR PERSPECTIVE OF AN EXTERIOR (OFFICE METHOD)

Figures 12-10 through 12-12 show the step-by-step sequence usually employed.

Step A

1. Draw the floor plan, or roof plan as shown, on a 30°–60° relationship with the horizontal. Or a separate plan can be taped down in a similar position.
2. Draw the horizontal picture-plane line touching the lower corner of the plan. (Other relationships can be used later, if desired.)
3. Locate the center of vision (C.V.) midway on the horizontal width of the inclined plan.
4. Establish the station point on the center of vision, far enough from the picture plane to produce a 30° cone of vision (refer to Fig. 12-4).
5. From the station point, draw perpendicular projectors, parallel to the sides of the plan, to the picture plane. These points are the vanishing points in plan, and are often called distance points.
6. Draw a horizontal ground-plane line a convenient distance below the picture plane. It will need to be placed only far enough below the picture plane to allow sufficient space for the perspective layout.

Step B

7. Draw the elevation view on the groundline. Place it off to the side of the perspective area; even if projection lines run through the elevation view, no harm will result. This view supplies the heights; therefore it must be drawn to the same scale as the plan. Usually the end elevation is sufficient if the major heights are shown. (If a perspective is being drawn from a separate set of plans, the elevation, like the plan, can merely be taped on the ground plane in a convenient position.)
8. Draw the horizon line as shown. The heights of the elevation view will aid in determining the most effective eye-level height. Usually if a level view is desired, the horizon line is scaled 6′–0″ above the ground-plane line. This distance is optional.
9. Drop vertical projectors from the picture-plane distance points (projectors originating at the station point) to the horizon. These points on the horizon line are the vanishing points of the perspective and should be made prominent to avoid mistaken identity.
10. Draw vertical true-height lines from the corner of the plan touching the picture plane and the extension of the two ridges as they intersect the picture plane. Unless they are "boxed in," ridgelines of gable roofs should be brought to the picture plane, where a true-height line can be established. Usually this is the simplest method of plotting their heights; from the true-height line, the ridge height is vanished to the proper vanishing point.
11. Now we are ready to start the perspective itself. From the intersection of the main true-height line at the corner of the building and the ground plane, construct the bottom of the build-

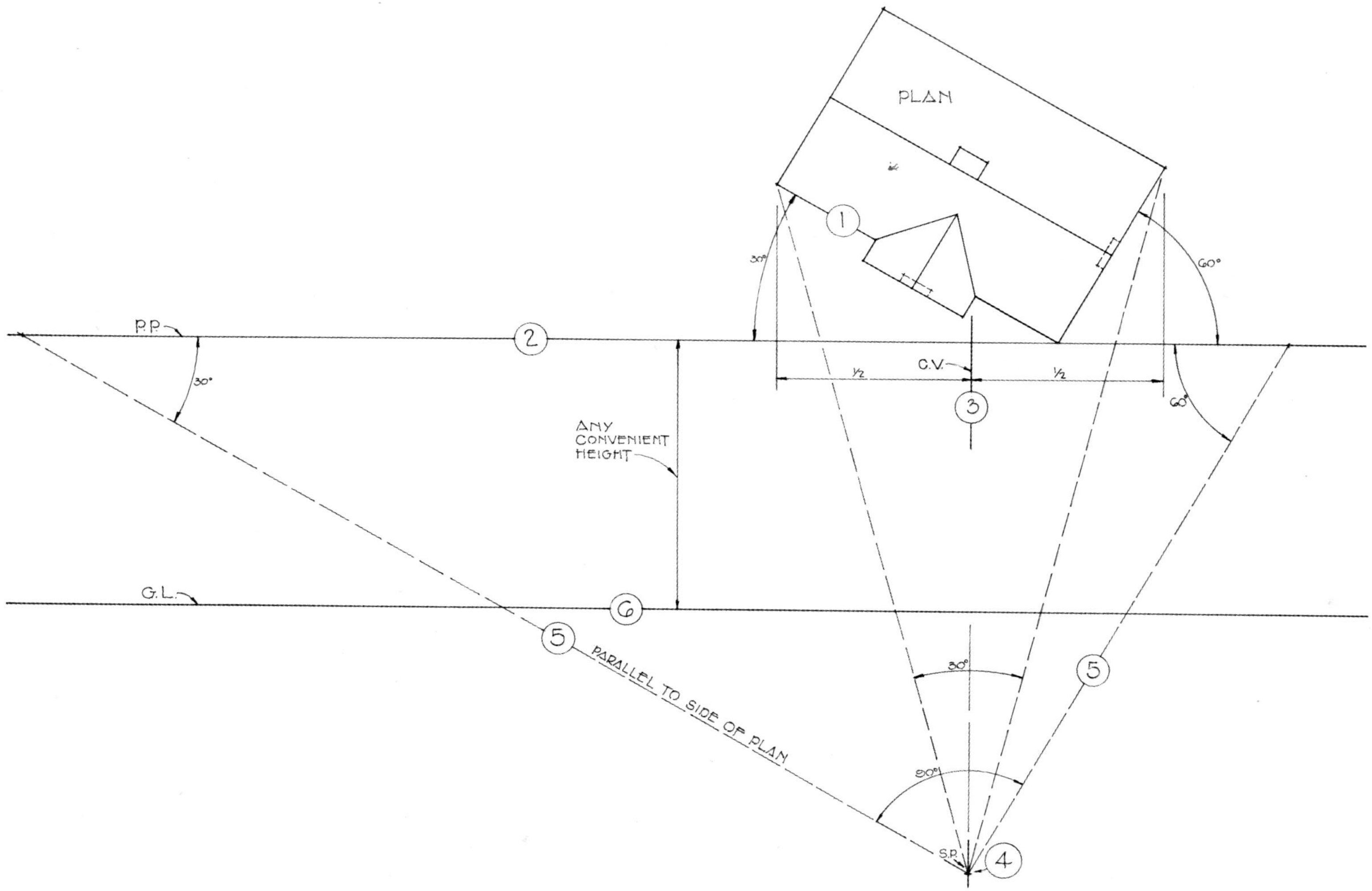

Fig. 12-10 Step A in drawing a perspective by the office method.

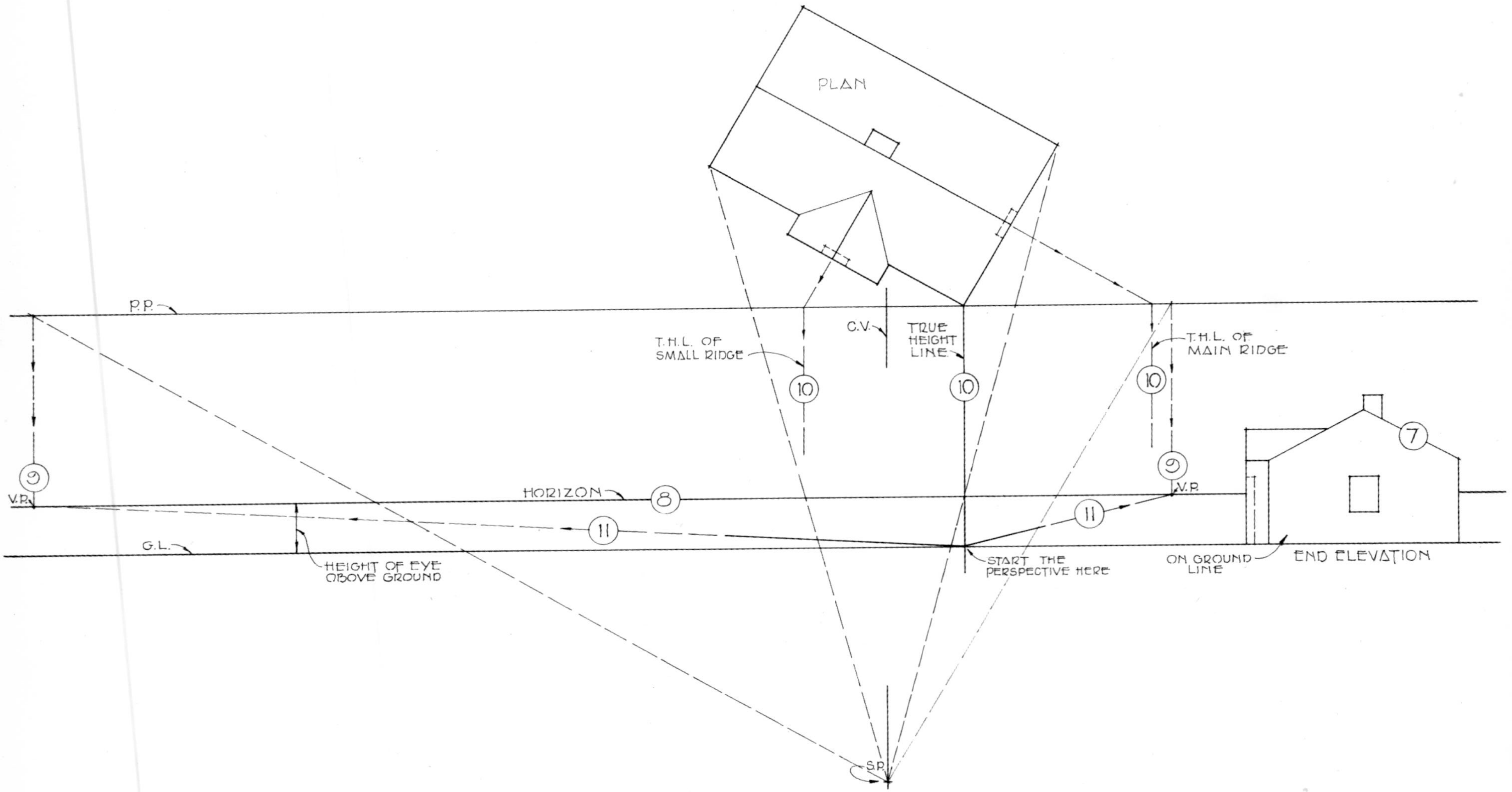

Fig. 12-11 Step B—office method.

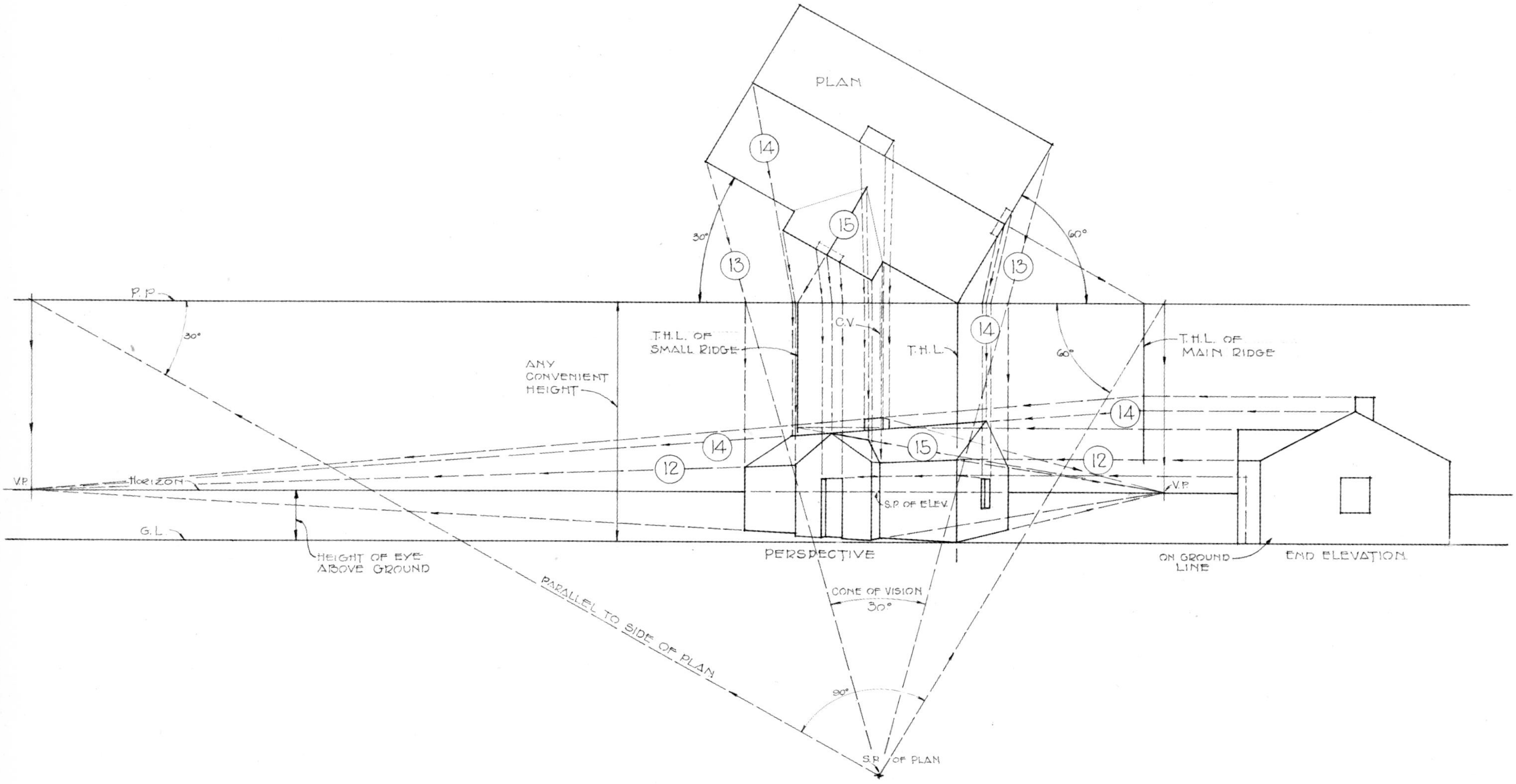

Fig. 12-12 Step C—office method.

ing by projecting the point toward both vanishing points. All perspectives should start at this point.

STEP C

12. Next, continue developing the main blockmass of the building. Take the height of the basic block from the elevation view and project it to the true-height line. This gives us the height of the block on the perspective. Again, project this point on the true-height line to both vanishing points.
13. To find the width of the basic block, we must go to the plan. With a straightedge, project both extreme corners of the plan toward the station point. Where these projectors pierce the picture plane, drop verticals to the perspective. This establishes the basic-block width; the back corner can be located, if desired, by vanishing the outer corners to the correct vanishing points.
14. Next, plot the main ridge so that the roof shape can be completed. Project the height of the ridge from the elevation view to the main ridge true-height line. Vanish this point to the left vanishing point. The ends of the ridge must be taken again from the plan view. Project both ends of the ridge on the plan toward the station point; where the projectors pierce the picture plane, drop verticals to the vanished ridgeline. This defines the main ridge, and the edges of the roof can then be drawn to the corners of the main block.
15. The small ridge of the front gable roof can be established by the same method as above. Because this ridge is perpendicular to the main ridge, the small ridge is vanished to the right vanishing point. The remaining corners and features of the gable extension in front of the main block can be taken from the plan by the method previously mentioned and vanished to the correct vanishing point.
16. Continue plotting the remaining lines and features on the perspective by locating each from the plan as usual and projecting their heights from the elevation view. After heights are brought to the true-height line, they must usually be projected around the walls of the building to bring them to their position. Remember that true heights are first established on the picture plane and then vanished along the walls of the building to where they are needed.

12.5 INTERIOR TWO-POINT ANGULAR PERSPECTIVE (OFFICE METHOD)

Figure 12-13 illustrates the method of drawing an interior view with 2-point perspective. The principles are the same as for exterior views. However, notice that only a partial plan is

Fig. 12-13 Interior 2-point angular perspective (office method).

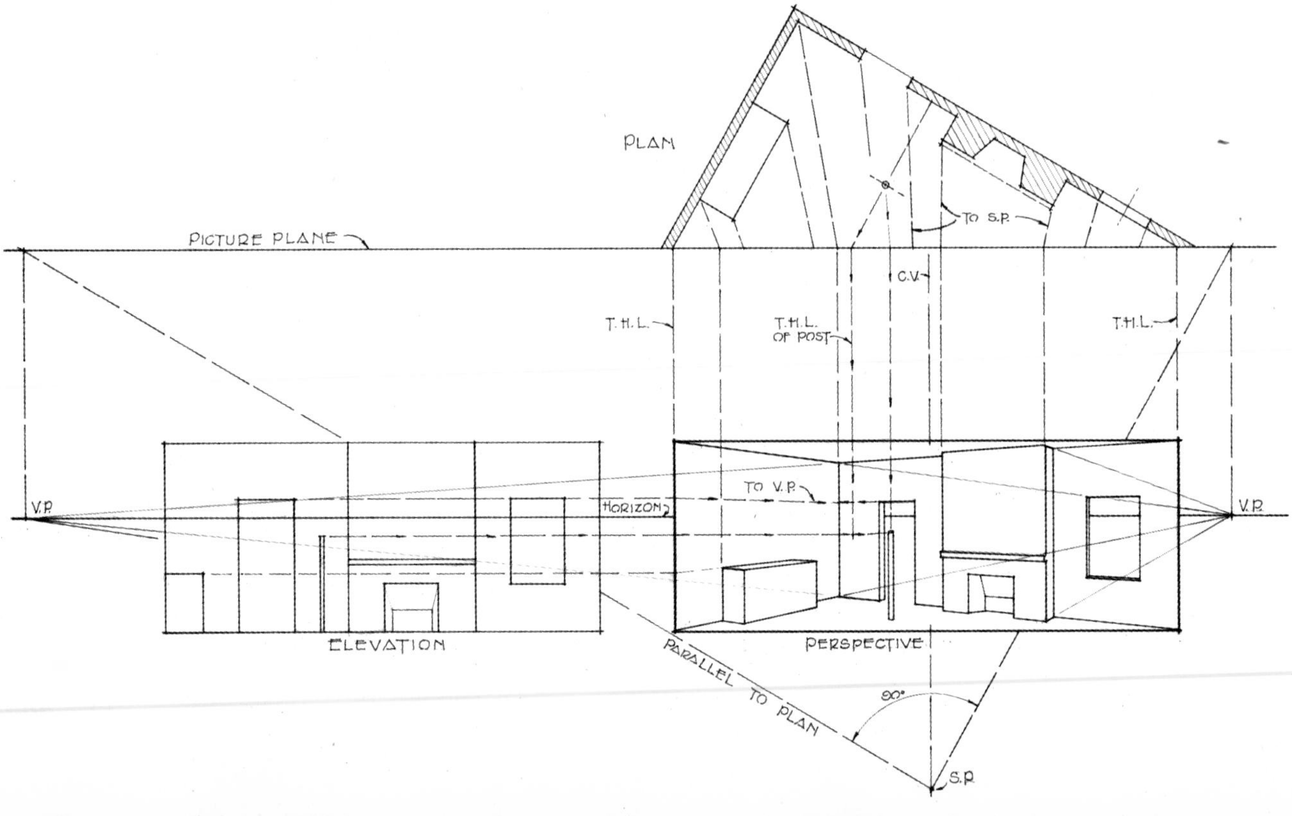

drawn, and the rectangular shape of the interior touching the picture plane is drawn on the perspective. The view forms within this rectangle; later, the rectangle can be removed if a feathered-out drawing is desired.

A pole has been placed in the room merely to indicate the method of plotting any point in space; other points can be located in a similar manner. Heights of features on the walls are projected to the true-height line and carried along the walls to their correct position, which is located from the plan. When setting up the perspective, keep the station point about twice as far from the picture plane as the greatest width of the plan being drawn; this effects a desirable appearance. Coordinates can be laid off on the floor, resembling square tile, if odd locations or shapes are required within the room.

The picture plane can be placed in other positions than shown on the figure; regardless, projectors locating the features must be brought to the picture plane before they are dropped to the perspective.

12.6 THE PERSPECTIVE-PLAN METHOD AND MEASURING LINES

Comparison will show that the perspective-plan method requires less space on the drawing board, has more versatility, and is obviously more sophisticated than the office method. Many professional architectural delineators use the perspective-plan method exclusively. Although several new variations in procedure are encountered, the basic principles of the office method are still applicable.

The plan method requires no orthographic plan from which projections are taken. Rather, the perspective plan is drawn from measurements laid off on a horizontal measuring line. From this plan, vertical projectors establish widths and feature locations on the finished perspective. Heights are measured on a true-height line rather than projected.

It is usual practice to draw a perspective from a set of working drawings. The plot plan serves as a guide for correctly orienting the station point. The plan and elevation views furnish all the measurements for drawing the perspective. Here lies one of the advantages of this method; when transferring the dimensions from the working drawings to the perspective layout, the size of the perspective can be controlled by merely changing the scale of the dimensions during transfer. Also, the method allows trials of various horizon heights without a major amount of reconstruction. With the use of tracing paper over the original perspective plan, experimentation becomes a simple matter.

Figures 12-14, 12-15, and 12-16 illustrate the three major steps necessary in completing a simple perspective by the plan method. The given conditions and dimensions, similar to a typical problem, are shown in Fig. 12-14.

Step A—Locating the preliminary points

1. Start with the horizon line and draw it near the upper part of the paper. For convenience, this line also serves as the picture plane in plan.
2. Establish the station point at the given distance on the center of vision (to scale) and draw the 30°–60° projectors to the picture plane. This locates the left and right vanishing points.
3. Construct the left and right measuring points (M.P.) on the picture plane. To locate the left measuring point, bring the distance between the left vanishing point and the station point to the picture plane with the use of an arc swung from the left vanishing point. From the right vanishing point, scribe the radius (right vanishing point to station point) to the picture plane; this point becomes the right measuring point. These measuring points will be vanishing points for the horizontal measurements we will use in our next step.
4. Draw the ground-plane line 6′–0″ (scaled) below the horizon line. This establishes our eye level.

The orthographic floor plan shown with dotted lines in the figure is unnecessary in an actual layout; it is added merely to give the beginner a visualization of the plan and picture-plane relationship, which, to the more experienced, would be indicated by the points just established on the horizon line.

Step B—Drawing the perspective plan

5. At an arbitrary location below the horizon, draw a horizontal measuring line (H.M.L.). The plan in perspective will develop from this line, making it actually a groundline for the plan only, as well as a line upon which horizontal measurements of the building are laid off. It is helpful to know that projections from the plan to the finished perspective will be more accurate if the measuring line is placed well below the horizon; the exaggerated shape of the resulting plan will not adversely affect the perspective, and also, sufficient space will be gained for the develop-

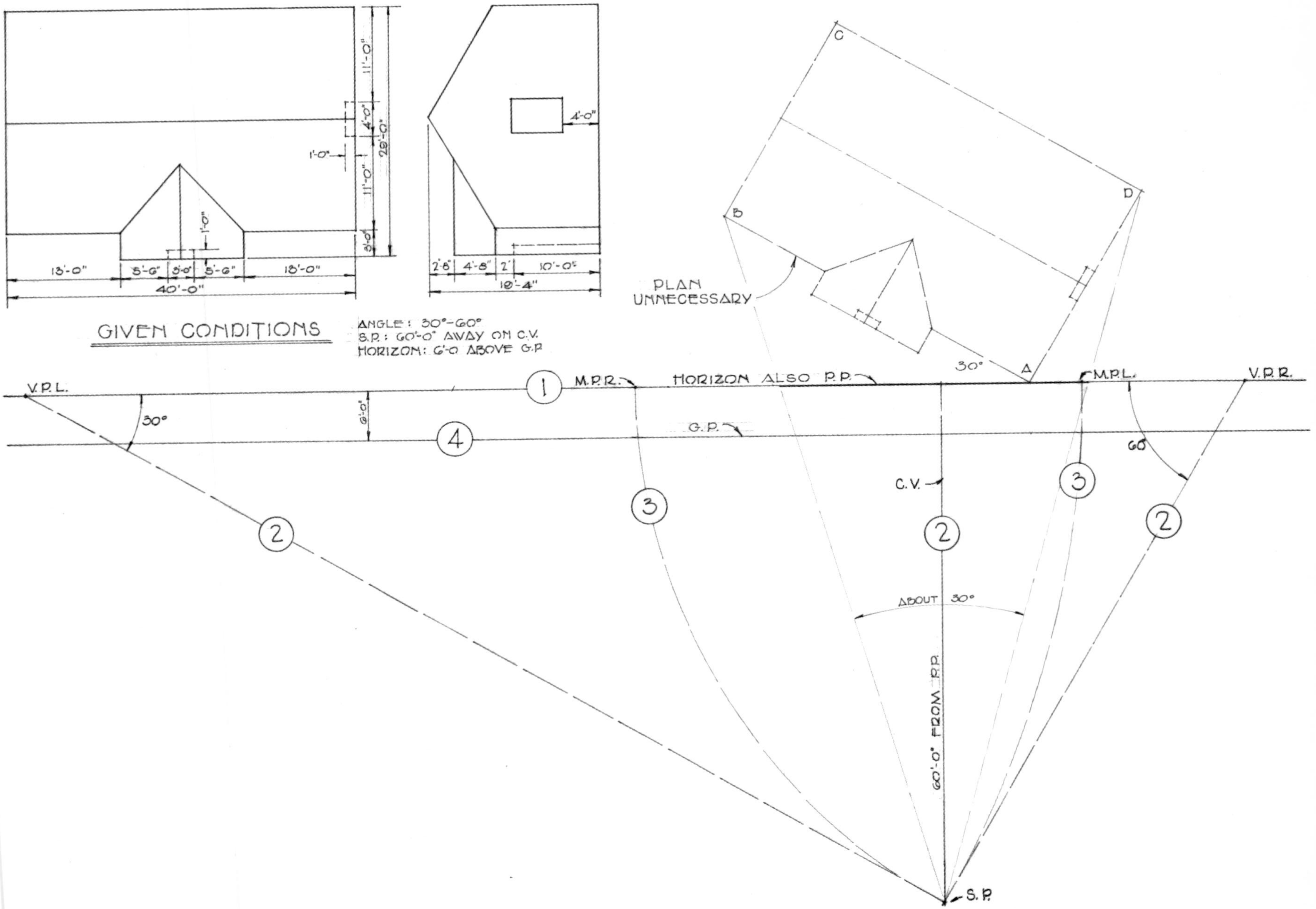

Fig. 12-14 Step A in drawing a perspective by the perspective-plan method.

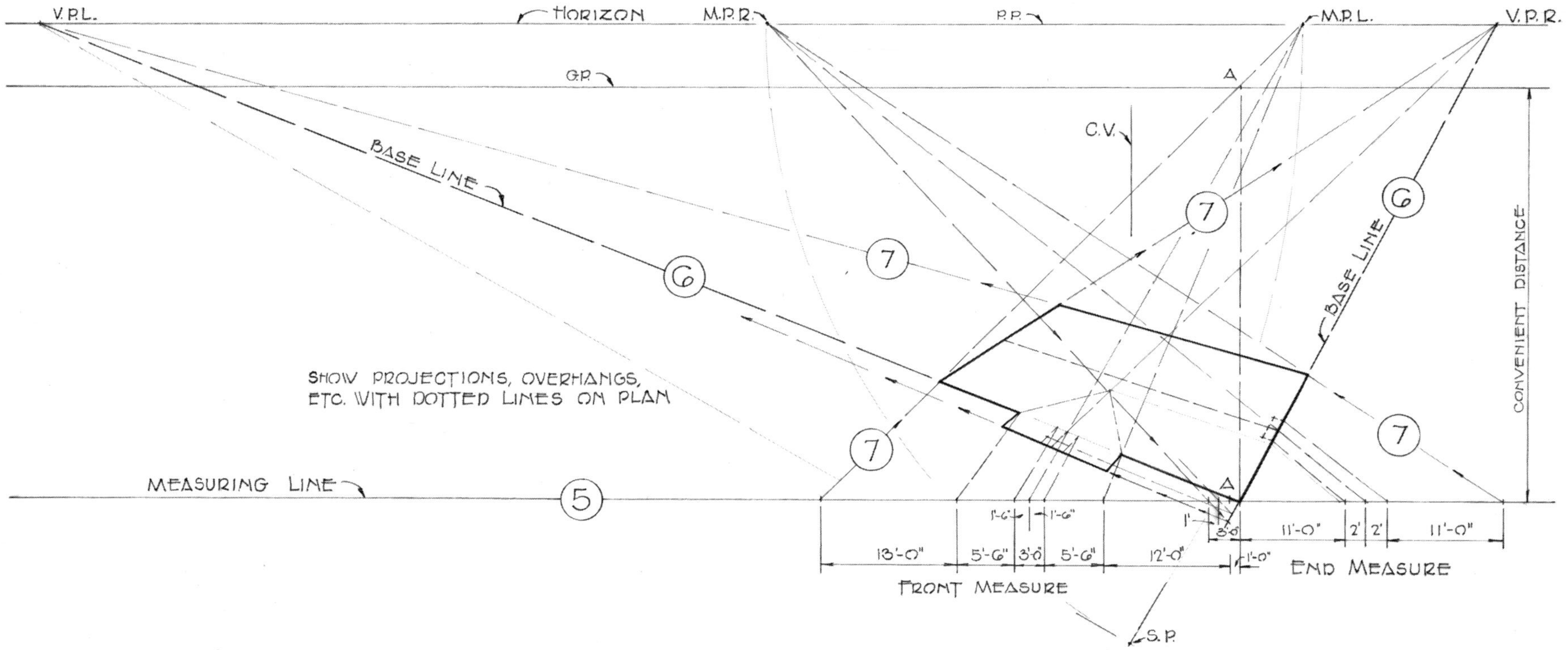

Fig. 12-15 Step B—perspective-plan method.

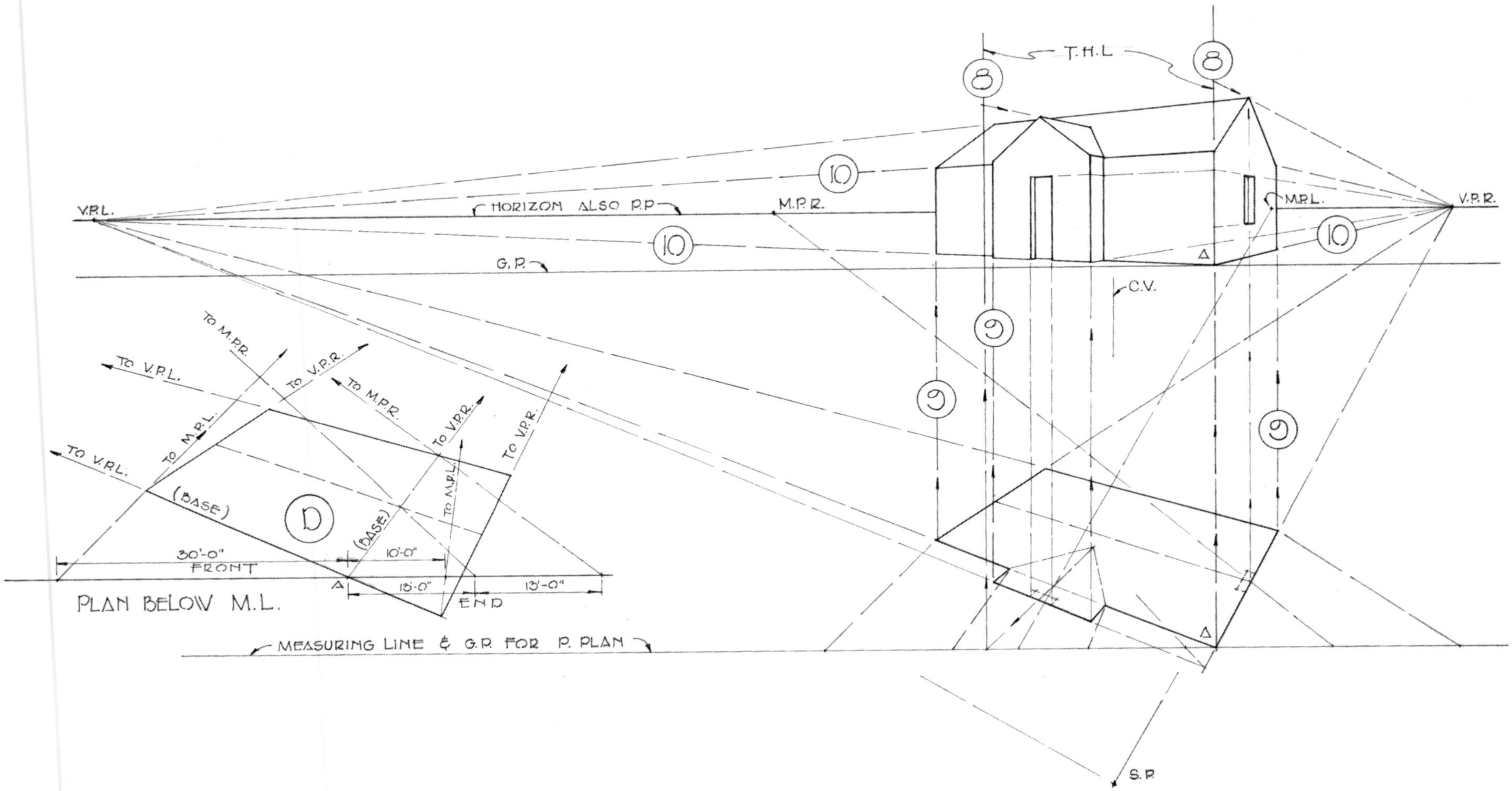

Fig. 12-16 Step C—perspective-plan method.

ment of the picture. Transfer the corner of the building touching the picture plane to the measuring line (point A).

6. From point A, draw lines to both the left and right vanishing points. These lines are the left and right edges of the plan and are referred to as "base lines." Measurements laid off on the measuring line, when projected to the measuring point, will terminate at these base lines. To lay out the dimensions of the plan on the measuring line, start at point A. All the dimensions of the front side of the building (A–B), starting at the forecorner, are stepped off to the left of point A, and those for the right end of the building (A–D) are stepped off to the right of point A. The depth of the small front-entrance projection would necessarily extend in front of point A, and therefore its depth measurement would be laid off *to the left of point A* instead of to the right.

When a part of a plan falls in front of the measuring line (see Fig. 12-16, Part D), the base line must continue through point A below the measuring line; and the measurements also must be laid off in continuity through point A. If the left side is in reference, the measurements of the features extending in front of the measuring line would be laid off *to the right of point A,* and the projection line to the left measuring point would therefore extend below the measuring line to locate the features on the base line. The opposite construction would be needed for similar right-side measurements.

7. To complete the plan, draw lines toward the correct vanishing point from the foreshortened measurements on the base lines.

STEP C—COMPLETING THE FINISHED PERSPECTIVE

8. Lay out a true-height line, projected from point A on the picture plane. Establish the bottom of the line on the ground plane, which has been scaled 6′–0″ below the horizon. This line represents the corner of the building on the picture plane, and all scale heights are measured upon it.
9. Transfer corners and features from the plan to the perspective with vertical projectors.
10. Project heights of the building to the vanishing points as discussed in the office-method construction. Complete the perspective as shown by first blocking in the major forms, then adding the projections, openings, and other minor features after the general shape is found to be satisfactory.

When a number of similar-sloped features are needed on a perspective, and the amount of slope or pitch is given, it may be advisable to locate the vanishing points of the sloping planes (see Fig. 12-17). Slope vanishing points must lie on traces (vertical lines) which pass through the vanishing points located for horizontal surfaces, V.P.L. and V.P.R. Notice that the V.P. for the 30° inclined roof plane, labeled No. 1, is located on the right trace *above* V.P.R. If a V.P. for a horizontal surface is located on the horizon line, then the V.P. for an inclined surface must be located *above* the horizon.

To locate the V.P. for slope No. 1, start at M.P.R. and lay out the given slope (30° in this case) from the horizontal as shown by the shaded area, and extend the line to the right trace. This locates the V.P. of the inclined roof. The V.P. for the declining roof plane on the back part of the house is located from the same M.P.R. and the slope is layed out *below* the horizon and extended to the right trace *below* the V.P.R.

Opposite slope V.P.s are located in a similar manner as shown by the shaded areas Nos. 3 and 4 and their related projection lines.

12.7 ONE-POINT PARALLEL PERSPECTIVE (OFFICE METHOD)

The 1-point perspective has several typical applications, such as interiors, street scenes, and exterior details of entrances or other special features. Sometimes the 1-point method is the only effective way to represent buildings of unusual shape. For example, a U-shaped house being observed toward the U is most faithfully represented with a 1-point perspective. This method is usually easier to draw than the 2-point, angular perspective, and it is the only type that reveals three wall planes. All receding horizontal lines converge at only one vanishing point, and lines parallel to the picture plane in plan are parallel to the horizon in the perspective. Usually, less board space is needed.

Figure 12-18 shows a simple room interior drawn with the 1-point method. Notice that many of the perspective principles previously discussed are applicable. All the variations in respect to the placement of the picture plane, station point, and horizon equally affect the finished 1-point perspective drawing.

To construct a 1-point parallel perspective (Fig. 12-18), start by drawing the plan and elevation views as shown. Establish the picture plane at the lower part of the plan (it may be placed in front, in back, or at an intermediate

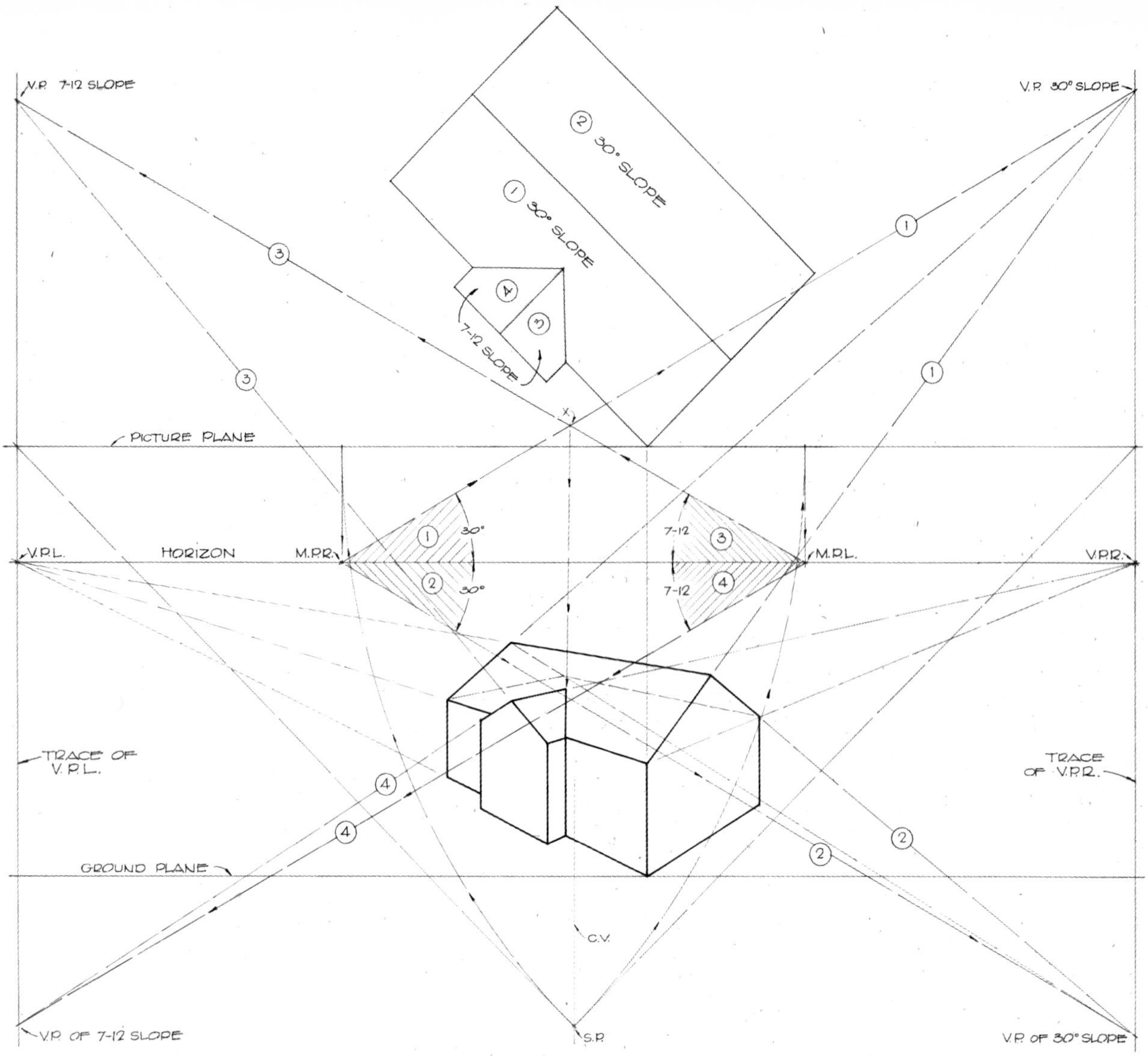

Fig. 12-17 Vanishing points of slopes. Similar numbers indicate relative lines and angles.

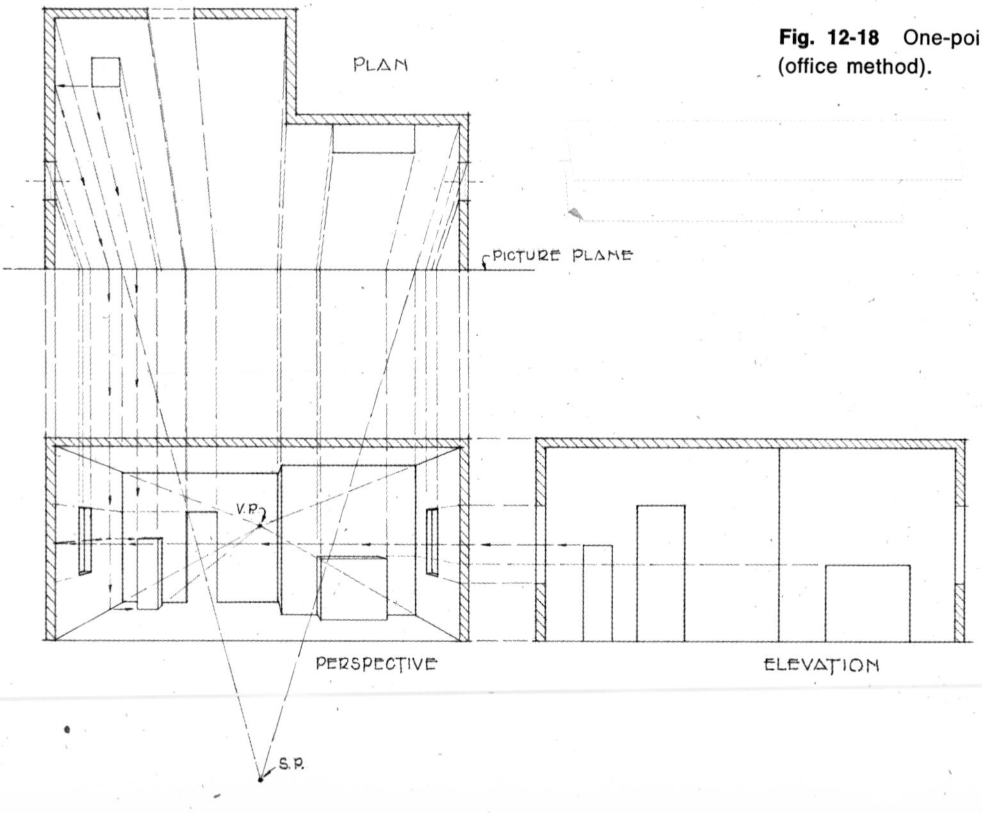

Fig. 12-18 One-point parallel perspective (office method).

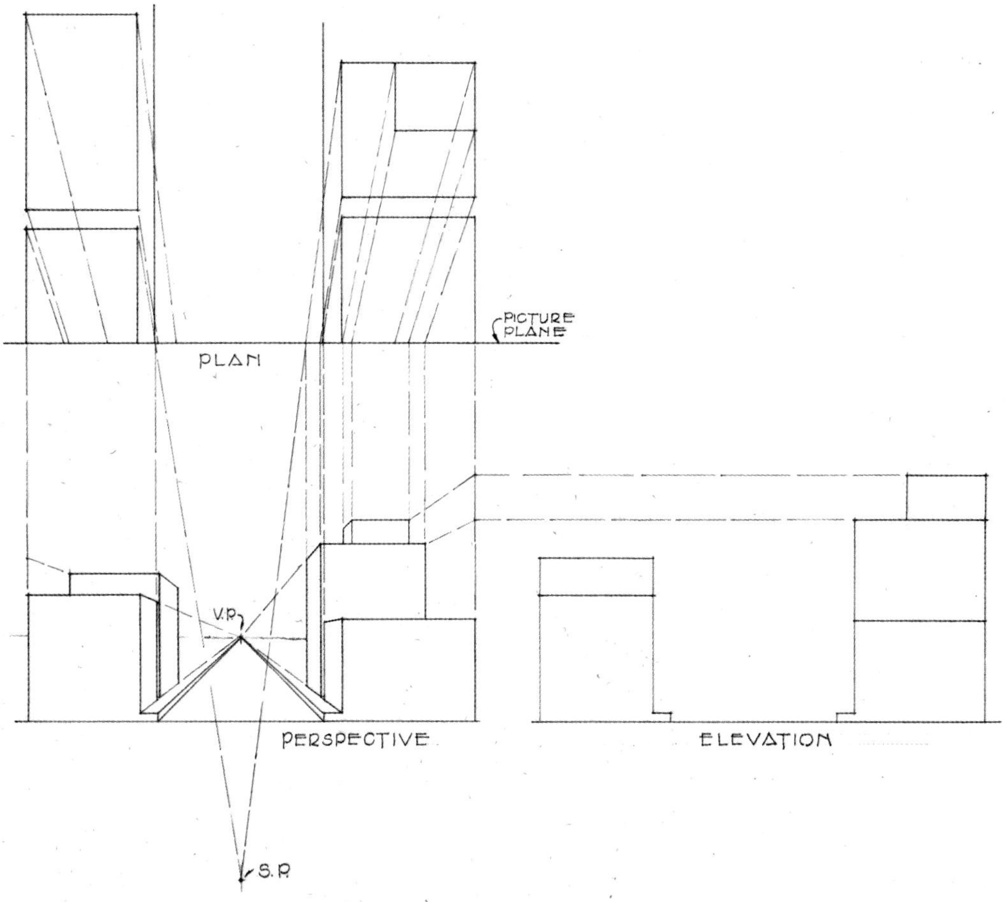

Fig. 12-19 One-point parallel perspective (office method).

area of the plan). On the center of vision below the plan, locate the station point, about the width of the plan away from the picture plane, or a 60° cone of vision in this case will satisfactorily locate the station point. The elevation view can be placed on either side of the area reserved for the perspective drawing. From the plan and elevation views, project the frame of the perspective representing the picture plane in elevation. Locate the one vanishing point within the frame at the desired distance above the groundline (bottom of frame). No horizon line is needed. If other than a room interior is to be drawn, start the perspective by drawing the features touching the picture plane; project their lines from both the plan and elevation views. Project interior wall lines toward the vanishing point. Locate the horizontal spacing of points and vertical lines by projecting the features from the plan toward the station point; at the intersection of the projectors and the picture plane, drop verticals to the perspective in the same manner as described in 2-point perspective (Section 12.4, Step C–13). Project heights from the elevation view to the true-height line. Notice how heights are carried along the walls, floors, or ceilings to where they are needed. Heights for objects away from the walls can be located by first establishing their heights on the nearest wall, then after projecting the objects horizontally to the same wall on the plan view, their heights and locations can be easily brought down to the perspective view. This procedure is indicated by the arrowheads on projectors from the tall box in the room.

The perspective-plan method can also be adapted to 1-point perspective construction, yet the office method is usually less time-consuming.

Figure 12-19 shows the construction of a simple *exterior* perspective using the 1-point method. Notice that the street lines converge at the vanishing point in the center of the drawing, and that the buildings have one wall parallel to the frontal picture plane.

When drawing 1-point perspectives of room

interiors (frequently used by interior designers), the student often finds it difficult to place furniture in its desired position within the floor area. One method that will simplify the location of objects is with the use of grid lines (see Fig. 12-20). Notice that a scaled orthographic plan is first needed with the furniture layed out in its correct position. Convenient grid lines, similar in appearance to large, square floor tile, are lightly drawn on the plan and numbered consecutively if necessary both ways. The same grid lines are then drawn in perspective on the perspective drawing floor area.

Locate all the furniture outlines in perspective from the plan diagram using the correct grids for placement. Next, build up the heights of the furniture with measurements as previously mentioned to have correctly blocked-in forms. To complete the actual appearance of the furniture, add the details last.

Fig. 12-20 Using a floor grid field on a 1-point interior perspective to position furniture correctly.

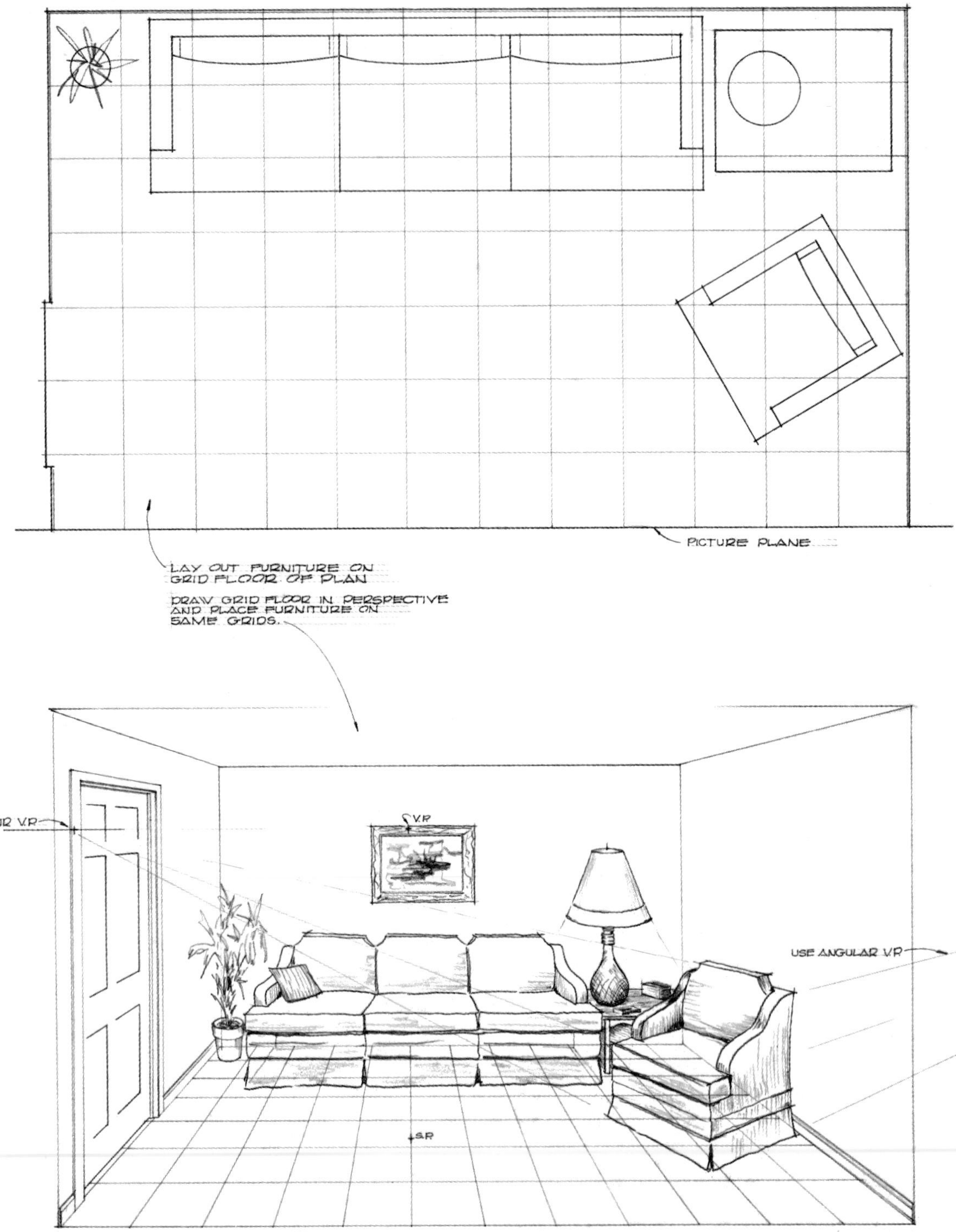

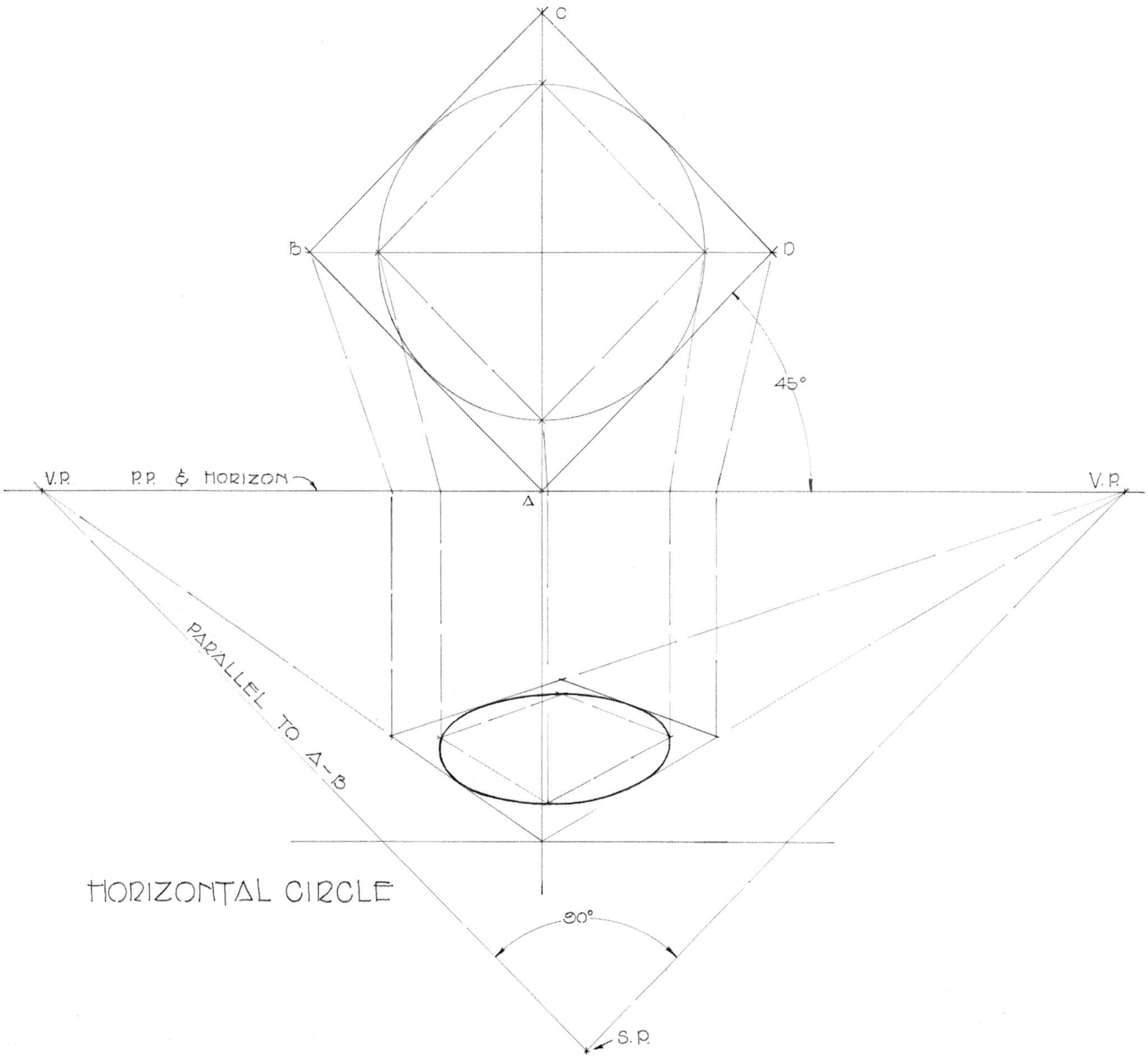

Fig. 12-21 A method of drawing circular shapes in perspective.

12.8 A PROFESSIONAL METHOD OF DRAWING PERSPECTIVES

As we have already seen, setting up the perspective construction for the average building is rather time-consuming for the draftsman. The professional delineator, who is continually concerned with architectural perspective, must adopt a rapid yet versatile system that consistently produces satisfying and faithful drawings. One method having these characteristics combines the perspective-plan and measuring-point principles with a simple way of modifying and controlling the setup during construction. It begins with a pictorial plan of very small scale, drawn by the perspective-plan method, mainly for the purpose of early study before the finish perspective is started. This small, preliminary layout is called a "diagram," and is the secret of good perspectives without unnecessary, large-scale, trial-and-error construction. After a small diagram is perfected as to angle of observance, distance to station point, height of horizon, etc., only the necessary lines and points are enlarged to scale for the final perspective. Several drawings employing this system will convince the student that it is as effective in the classroom as it is in an architectural office. Follow the sequence of the numbers shown in the accompanying drawings and in the written instructions that follow:

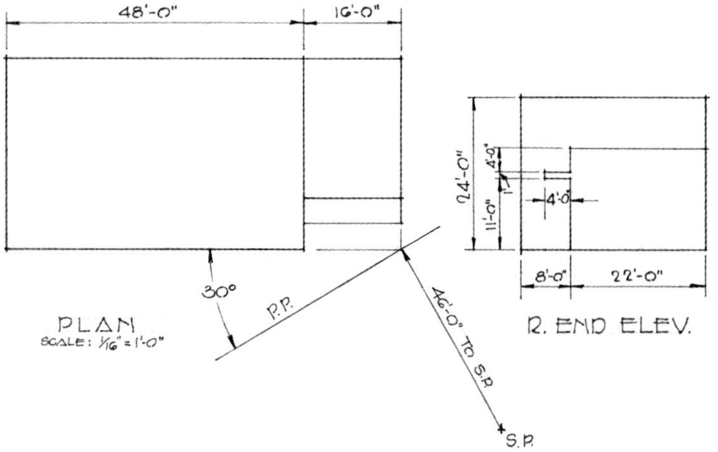

Fig. 12-22 Floor plan and end-elevation for the professional "diagram" perspective.

Fig. 12-23 Preliminary steps for the professional "diagram" perspective.

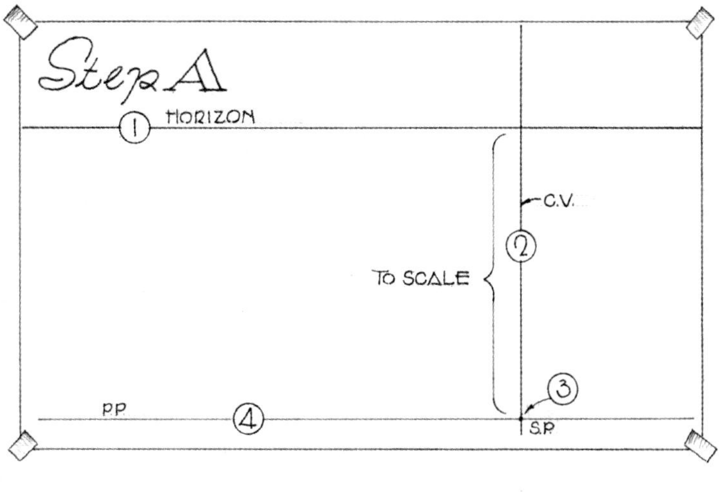

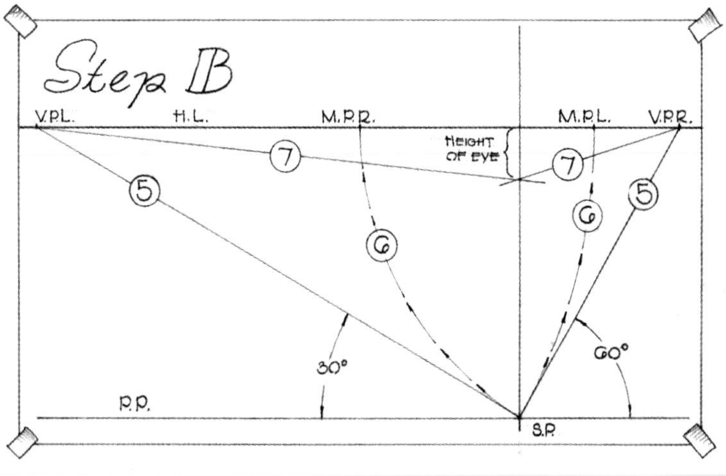

Before beginning to draw, study the plot plan, if available, or proposed site arrangement. Determine which angle of observation will show the important elements of the building. Draw a line on the plot plan indicating the line of sight you have chosen. On this line, establish the station point by laying a 30° triangle on the line so that the angle represents the angle of vision. The apex of the 30° angle, as previously indicated, locates a satisfactory station point when the length across the building forms the length of the side opposite the 30° angle of the triangle. This point will help you visualize the tentative picture and orient you to the problem at hand. Study the elevation views, which will then be visible, and concern yourself only with them; if you are using a set of working drawings, lay the other drawings aside.

Step A (Figs. 12-22 and 12-23)

1. Draw the horizon line as shown.
2. Construct a vertical center-of-vision line. It will also serve as a true-height line later.
3. Establish the station point on the center of vision by scaling the distance you indicated on the plot plan. Use a small scale. The civil engineer's scale can be used for enlargements of scale, if desired; it provides convenient multiples of ten.
4. Through the station point, draw a horizontal line—this will be the picture plane in plan, upon which all horizontal measurements of the building can be made. Occasionally, it may be necessary to construct an auxiliary picture plane for measuring; this will be discussed later.

Step B (Fig. 12-23)

5. Locate the right and left vanishing points on the horizon line, by projecting from the station point as shown (if a 30°–60° angle of observance is satisfactory). Any angle can be used as long as the included angle between the two projectors is 90°. (These projectors can serve as base lines of the perspective plan if the drawing is small and space is not critical.)
6. Next, locate the left and right measuring points on the horizon line. With a compass, swing the distance between the station point and the right vanishing point to the horizon line, using the right vanishing point as a center, to locate the right measuring point. This point will be the vanishing point of all parallel measuring lines laid off to the right station point. Follow the same procedure for bringing the distance be-

tween the station point and the left vanishing point to the horizon line and locate the left measuring point.

7. Establish the desired eye level of the perspective by measuring down (in scale) from the horizon on the center of vision, to locate the corner of the building on grade. From this point, construct lines to both the left and right vanishing points. These lines become the base legs of our basic rectangle in perspective.

STEP C (FIG. 12-24)

In this step it may be advisable to construct a new picture plane in order to keep the drawing lower on the paper when working with larger buildings and scales. On small preliminary diagrams, the picture plane indicated in Step B will usually serve the purpose without being cumbersome. It will be found satisfactory for laying off measurements and constructing the perspective plan. However, if a large building is drawn, requiring a large piece of paper and considerable space on the board, when enlarging the diagram, an auxiliary picture plane will be found more convenient. This new picture plane will replace the original for measurements and is arbitrarily placed between the station point and the ground corner of the perspective. After the vanishing points and measuring points are located on the horizon line, the station point is no longer necessary and can be removed.

8. Draw the auxiliary picture plane, as shown.
9. Draw the new baselines from the intersection of the picture plane and the center of vision to both vanishing points. Use the original vanishing points and extend the lines below the auxiliary picture plane to take care of overhangs and offsets of the plan that occasionally fall outside the basic rectangle.
10. Draw the basic rectangular shape of the plan as shown. Notice that measurements are taken from the working drawings, converted to the working scale, and laid out on the auxiliary picture plane, on both sides from the center of vision. (See Section 12.6, Step B.) Project right-side measurements to the right measuring point and left-side measurements to the left measuring point. When they *intersect the baseline,* vanish them toward the corresponding vanishing point.

STEP D (FIG. 12-24)

11. Lay off measurements and construct all projections, overhangs, and roof lines if necessary. Intersections of sloping roofs will be needed to complete the perspective on gable and hip roofs. To avoid confusion later, when projecting the plan up to eye level, roof intersections, overhangs, exterior stoops, etc., should be drawn as broken lines on the plan.
12. Project all visible corners from the plan up to the perspective. This final step is generally done on a separate tracing paper *overlay*—only the perspective will then be on the clean sheet. All construction is made from points under the overlay. Of course, preliminary diagrams are done on the original sheet for study, when only general shapes are necessary.
13. Take heights from the working drawings and convert to scale. Lay off the heights on the center of vision starting at ground level. The center of vision is on the elevation picture plane and therefore can be used for true-height measurements. If necessary, project heights around the walls of the building to where they are needed, as explained in previous methods. Block in basic shapes first and then make measurements and project details last, to avoid confusion between numerous lines.

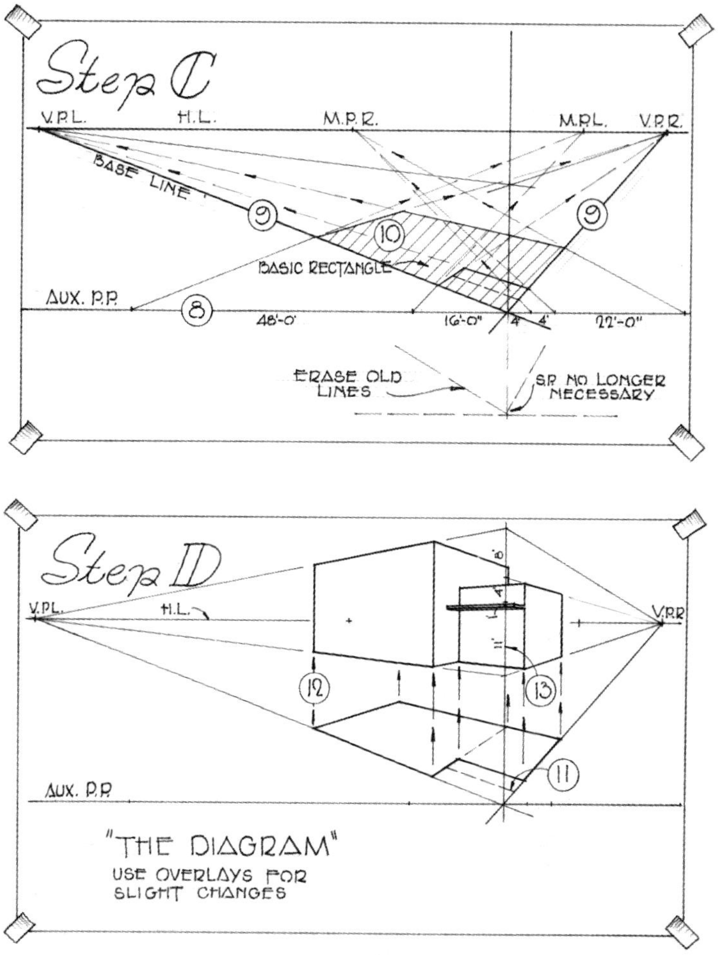

Fig. 12-24 Steps in drawing the diagram.

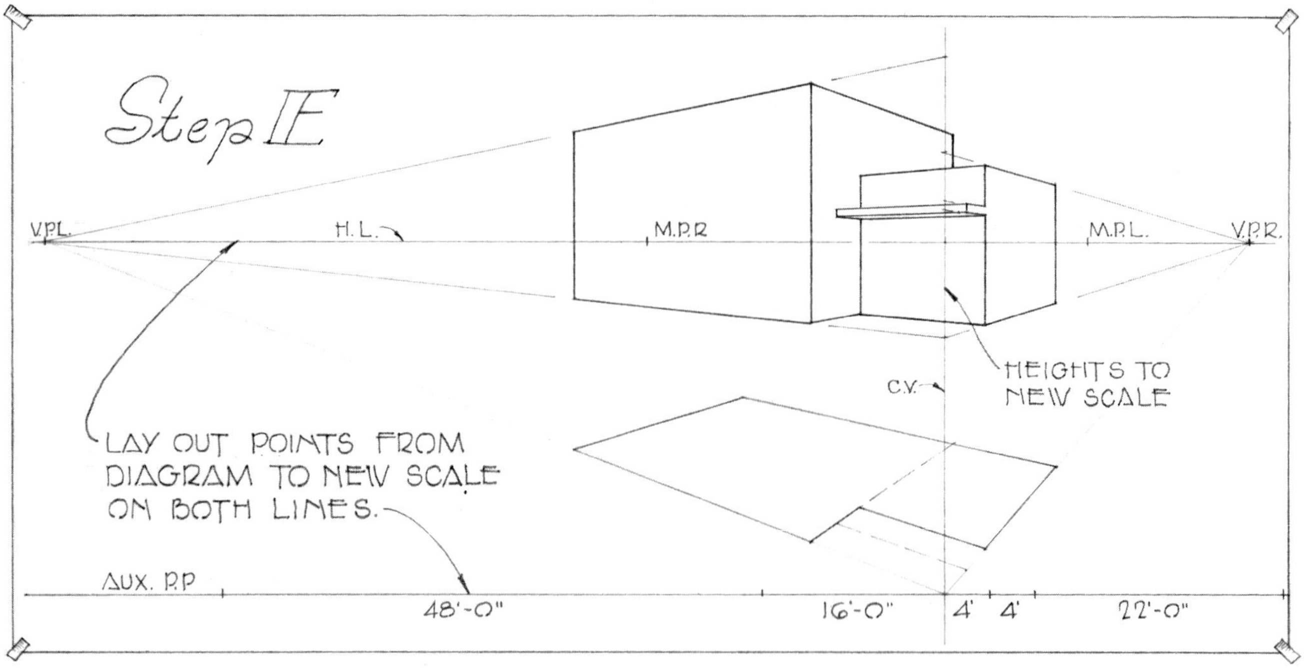

Fig. 12-25 Laying out the perspective at a convenient scale from the diagram.

Step E—enlarging to desired size (fig. 12-25)

After several diagrams are studied and one is found to be satisfactory, a larger perspective can easily be constructed at the desired size. Merely lay out the horizon line and transfer the center of vision and all points from the diagram to a new scale. The size of the finished perspective can be controlled by the scale selected; for example, if the finished perspective is to be four times the size of the diagram, use a scale four times as large as the diagram for the new measurements along the horizon line, center of vision, and auxiliary picture plane.

At larger scales, horizontal measurements for constructing the plan will occasionally fall beyond the paper. To overcome this difficulty, follow the procedure shown in Fig. 12-26. Draw a horizontal line to the edge of the paper from a point on the

Fig. 12-26 A method of making measurements that are too long for the drawing board.

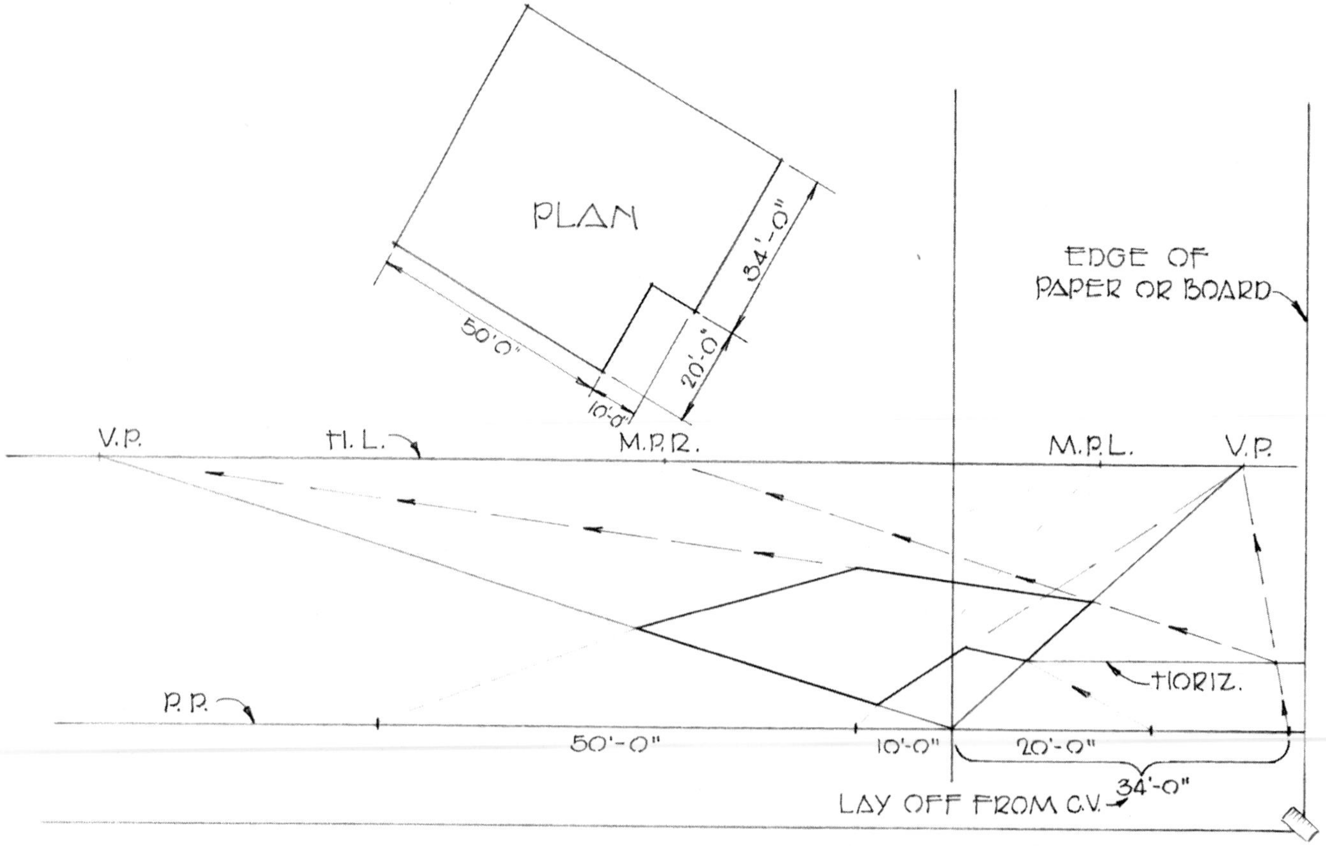

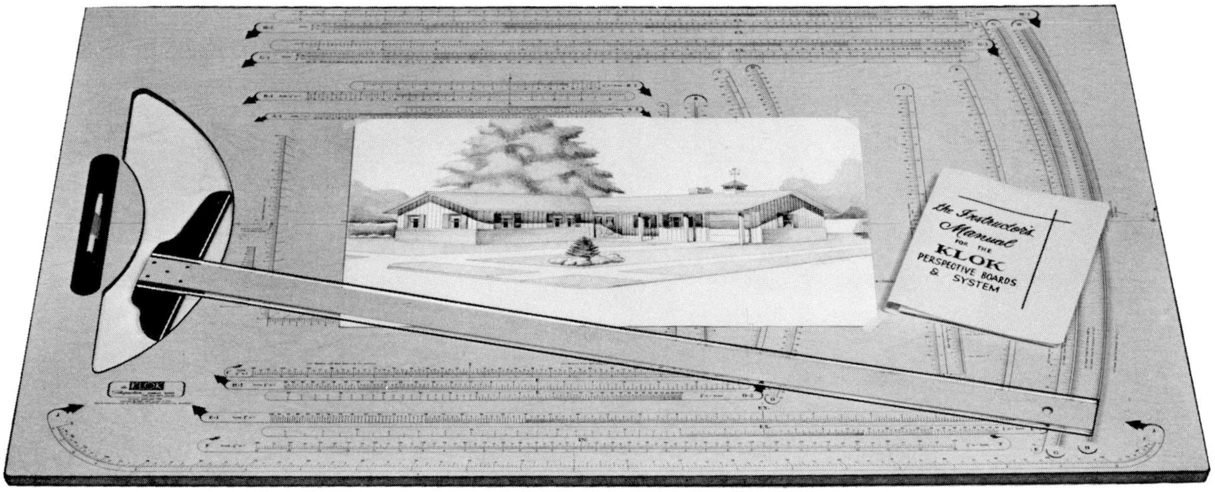

Fig. 12-27 The Klok Perspective Board. A timesaving device for drawing perspective drawings using scales and a modified T square as shown. Manufactured by: Fiberesin Plastics Division, U.S. Gypsum Co., Oconomowoc, Wis. 53066.

base line where the longest measurement has been made. Make the additional measurement from the center of vision, and instead of projecting toward the measuring point, project to the vanishing point on the same side of the center of vision until it intersects the horizontal line. From this point it is treated as previously shown in Step C. The construction merely brings the dimension back in perspective to the point of maximum measurement and lays it off on that plane rather than on the original forward picture plane.

After several drawings have been made, slight variations of the procedure may be found to save time and overcome minor difficulties, should they arise.

12.9 TIMESAVING SUGGESTIONS

The Diagonal Use diagonals of rectangular areas for quickly locating centers and for checking construction of the perspective as it develops.

Similar Perspectives If a number of similar perspectives are to be drawn, use perspective grid charts as an underlay. Various charts are available at drafting supply stores. Or, use a perspective board as shown in Fig. 12-27.

Reflections When showing the reflections of buildings in water or on other shiny surfaces, draw the reflections to the same vanishing point as the building. The water's edge is the dividing line between the reflections and the true images. Locate a reflected point as far below the shiny surface as the point is above (see Fig. 12-28).

12.10 SHADES AND SHADOWS

The geometric forms of light and shade produced by the action of the sun on architectural subjects are of particular interest to the architect and the draftsman. Good architectural forms have the property of producing pleasing shadows regardless of the sun's position. To the observer, shadows are an integral part of an architectural composition, and their representation becomes almost as important as the building itself.

Linear perspective, as we mentioned earlier, produces only the outlines of objects. Realism is attained not by outlines, but by the sensitive selection of values of light and shade as well as texture to represent various surfaces. The effect of light upon surfaces and materials produces the true image; often outlines are almost entirely obscure. The study of shades and shadows is a further step in creating graphic realism. First the student must understand the action of light, then he must define it geometrically as it creates various patterns. These areas or patterns are then given the correct value or tone, in keeping with composition, contrast, and visual interest, to produce the desired pictorial effect.

On actual renderings, shadows can be overdone; if they are too mechanical and hard, much of their 3-dimensional expression is lost. The uniformity of the shades and shadows on the illustrations in this material is for the introduction of principles only and should not be

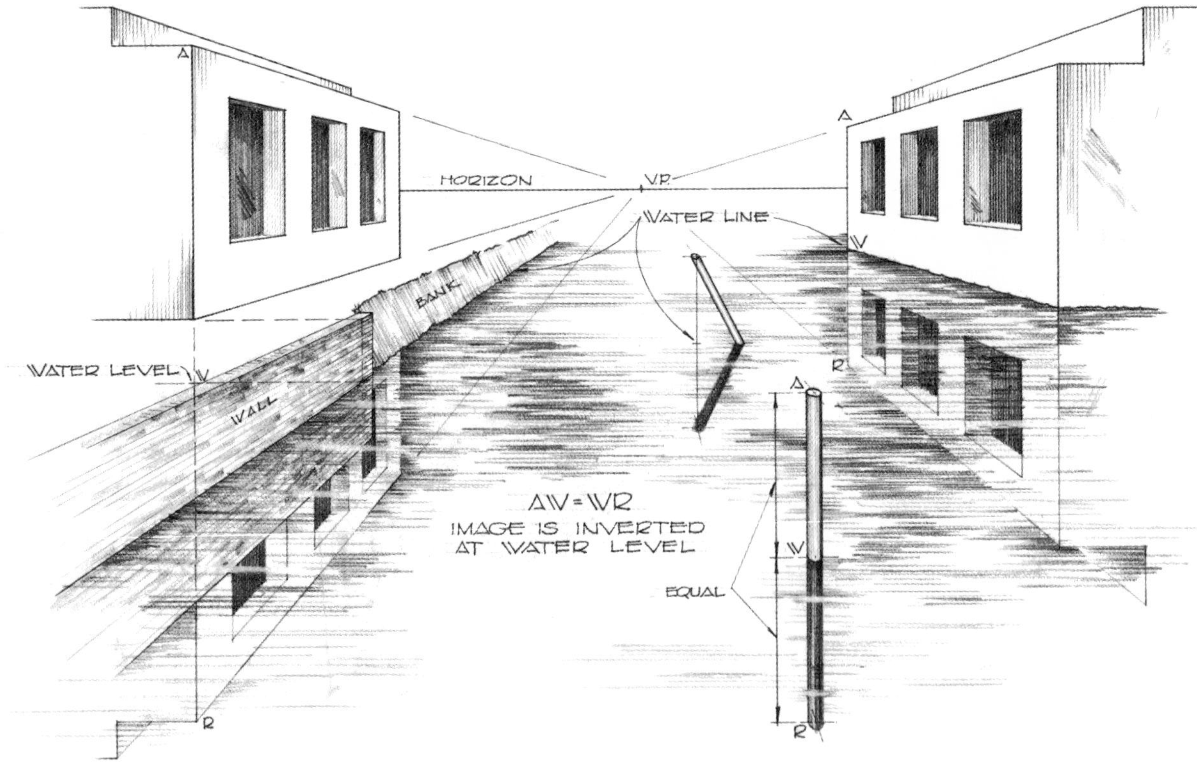

Fig. 12-28 Reflections on water or other shiny surfaces can be quickly projected with the use of points as shown.

taken as the correct representation of shadow values. Other finished perspectives (see Fig. 12-29) should be observed for displaying this quality. It will be seen that shades and shadows of finished work seldom have uniform tones throughout; in fact, the interplay of reflected light usually produces a graduation of tone. Shadows on architectural subjects are generally most prominent close to the observer, near the center of interest, and those farther away from the center of interest become more neutral and indefinite as they recede. Contrast and intensity of shadows near the observer, then, should be given the most consideration by the draftsman.

The Light Source Usually, on elevation-view shadowing, the light source is considered to be coming from the upper left. The conventional method illustrating a light-ray direc-

Fig. 12-29 A perspective rendering showing the use of shadows to reveal important architectural features.

tion is by showing it passing through a cube diagonally, from upper left to lower right (see Fig. 12-30). Notice that it appears as a 45° line on both elevations and plan and can be easily drawn with the triangle. Another advantage of using the conventional 45° light source is that it conveniently reveals depth-dimensional characteristics. Shadows will fall to the right and below the object. The shadow of a point will be the same distance below as it is to the right of the original point. Therefore, the shadow clearly indicates the depth of recessed features. By its convenience for transferring distances from the horizontal to the vertical, and vice versa, the 45° triangle actually serves as a handy tool for measuring when plotting shadows. However, if a different shadow effect is desired, the 30°–60° triangle can also be used. In casting shadows, light rays are assumed to be parallel.

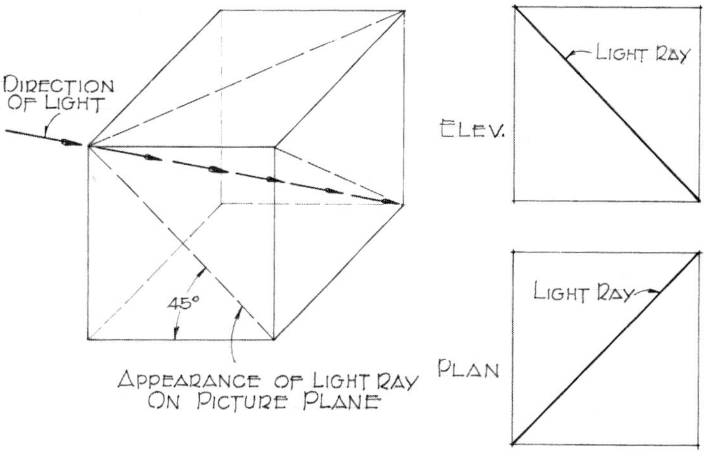

Fig. 12-30 Conventional light source on orthograpnic views.

Orthographic Shadows As an introduction to the characteristics of shades and shadows, it would seem logical to begin with shadows produced on orthographic views. One might ask, "Why learn to put shadows on orthographic views, which are commonly used only for working drawings?" It is true that orthographic views are mainly for working drawings, and that they show depth information by association with related orthographic views. Yet many architectural offices have found that front elevations of buildings (as well as other elevations), if skillfully applied with texture indications and shadows, make very adequate and often very attractive presentation drawings (see Figs. 12-31 and 12-32). Such drawings are used to show clients the tentative appearance of a building. The greatest advantage of shadowed elevations over perspectives is the tremendous saving in preparation time, and time and cost are usually important.

At the very outset, we can say that the casting of shadows is affected by three conditions:

1. The direction of the light source;
2. The shape of the object; and
3. The manner and shape of the surface upon which the shadow falls.

Fig. 12-31 An elevation rendering showing the use of shadows.

Fig. 12-32 An elevation-view rendering of a small commercial building showing the use of shadows.

In analyzing the action of light, the student is encouraged to observe the shadows of buildings and different objects about him in everyday life—even those of models in an artificial light source; the importance of astute observation of actual shadows cannot be overemphasized. After observing actual shadows and studying the accompanying shadow drawings, a number of *consistencies* become obvious. A few general ones are listed below and should be remembered:

1. Only an object in light casts a shadow.
2. A shadow is revealed only when it falls on a lighted surface.
3. The shadow of a point must lie on the light ray through that point.
4. On parallel surfaces, a shadow is parallel to the line that casts it.
5. The shadow of a plane figure will be identical to the outline of the figure if the shadow falls on a plane parallel to the outline of the figure.
6. The shadow of a line perpendicular to the picture plane will be inclined if it falls on a surface parallel to the picture plane.

In plotting orthographic shadows, usually two views are necessary for the projection (see Figs. 12-33 through 12-38). Sometimes it may be a plan and an elevation, other times it may be two elevations. The important view is the one having the surface that receives the majority of shadows appear as a line. Plot each point or corner casting a shadow and complete the one shadow profile before going to the next. Check the resulting shadow to be sure each point is accounted for. If the result does not appear logical to the eye, the construction is usually faulty.

Fig. 12-33 Plotting shadows of simple forms in orthographic views.

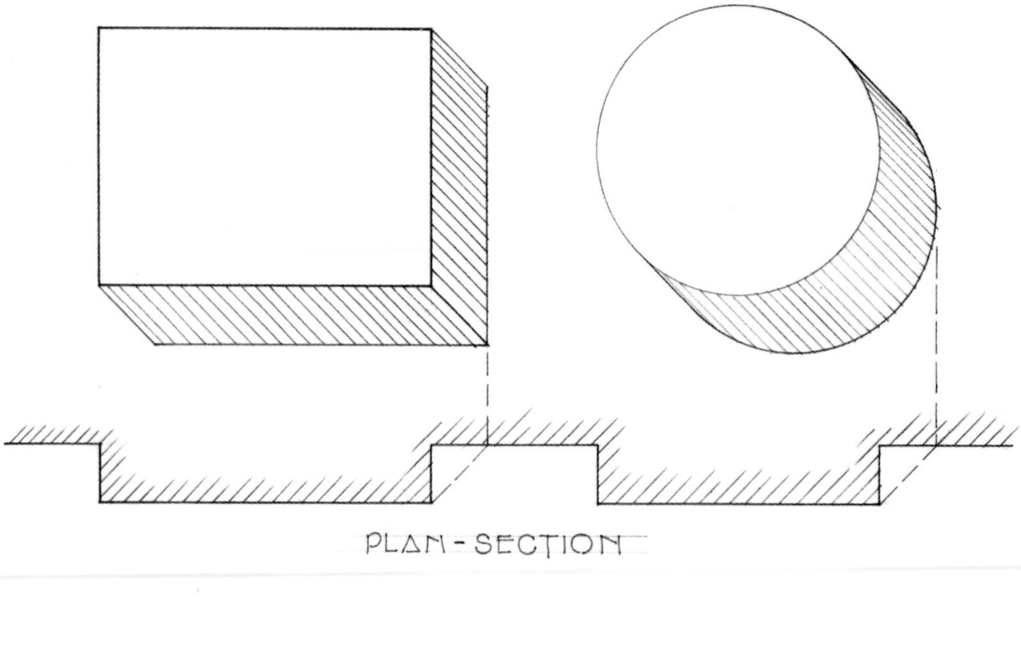

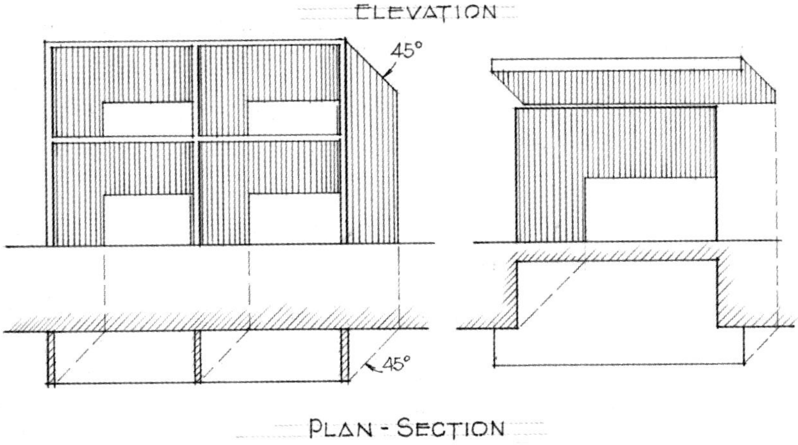

Fig. 12-34 Plotting shadows to show relief in orthographic views.

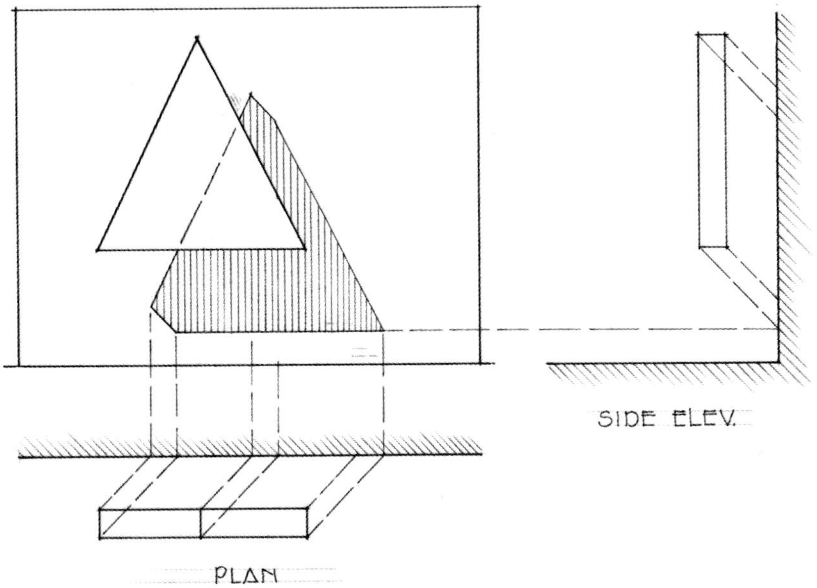

Fig. 12-35 Plotting shadows on removed surfaces in orthographic views.

Fig. 12-36 Plotting shadows on architectural features in orthographic views.

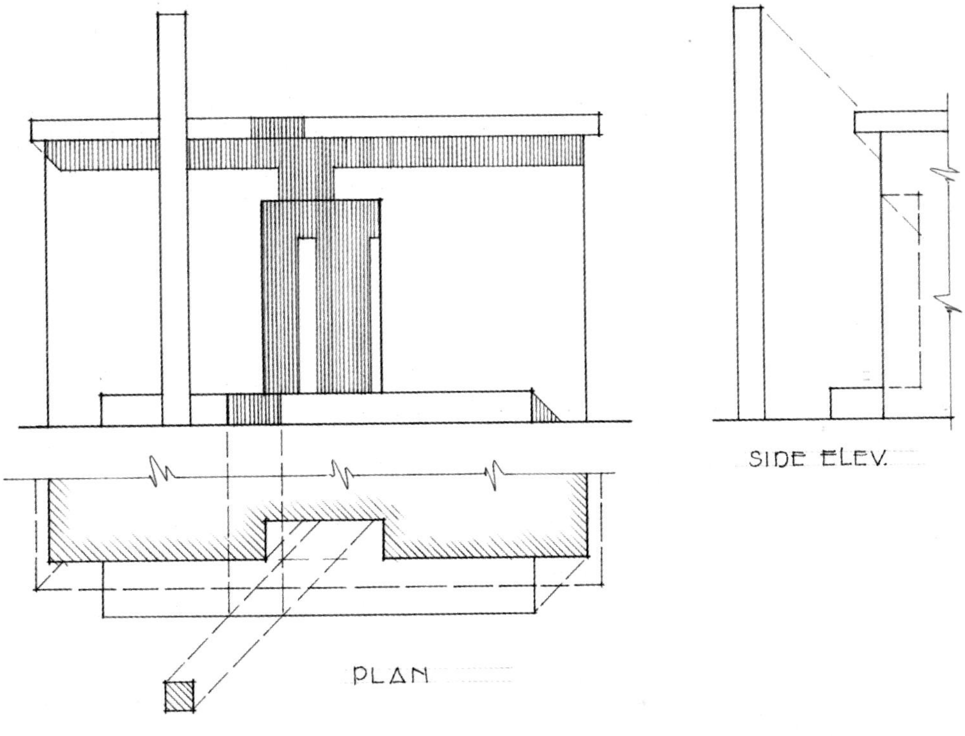

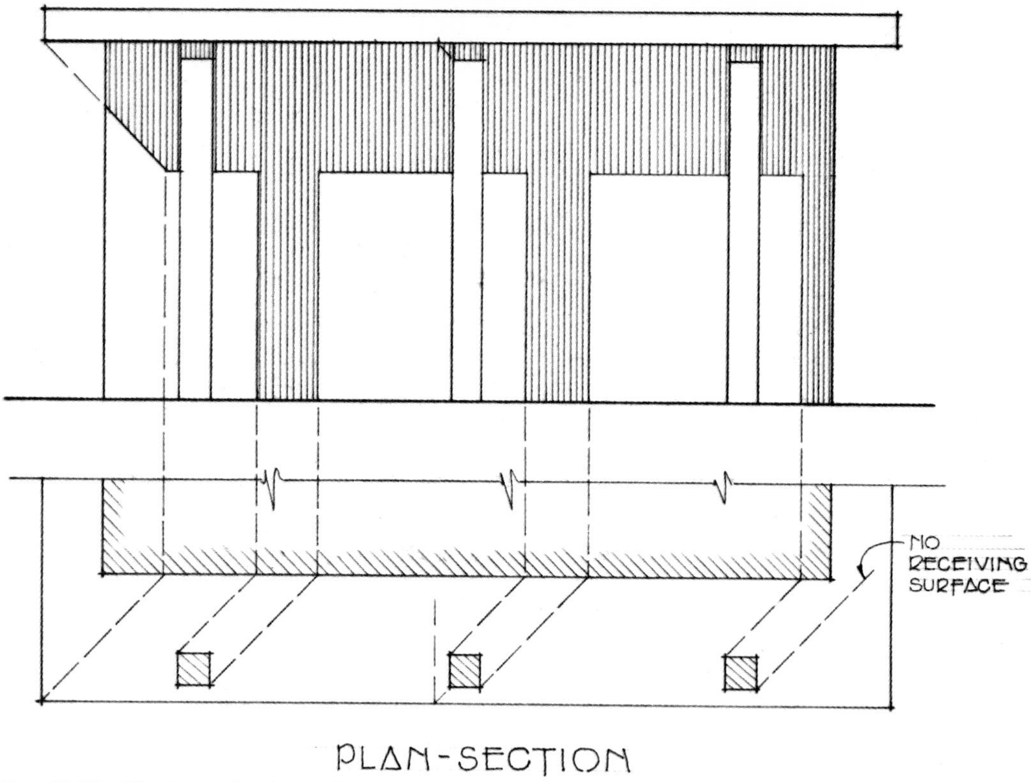

Fig. 12-37 Shadows of columns in an orthographic view.

Fig. 12-38 Plotting shadows falling upon inclined planes in an orthographic view.

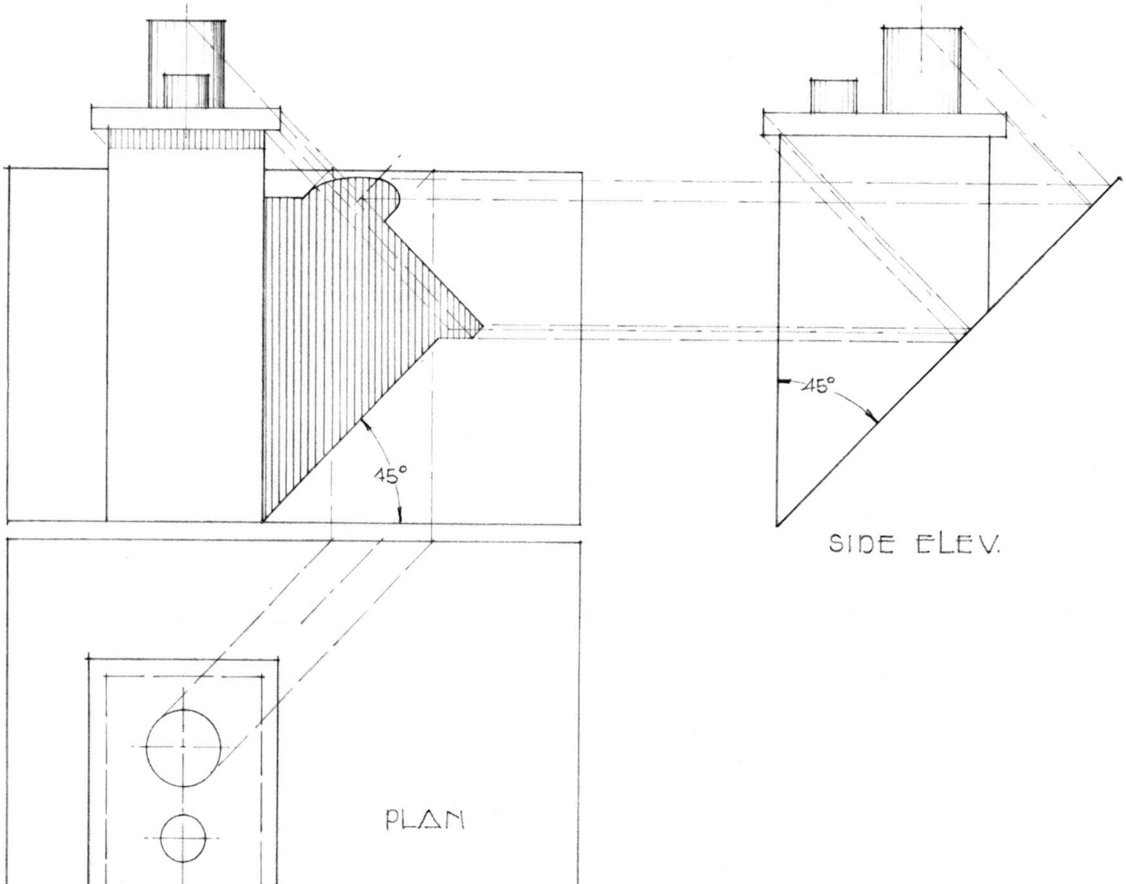

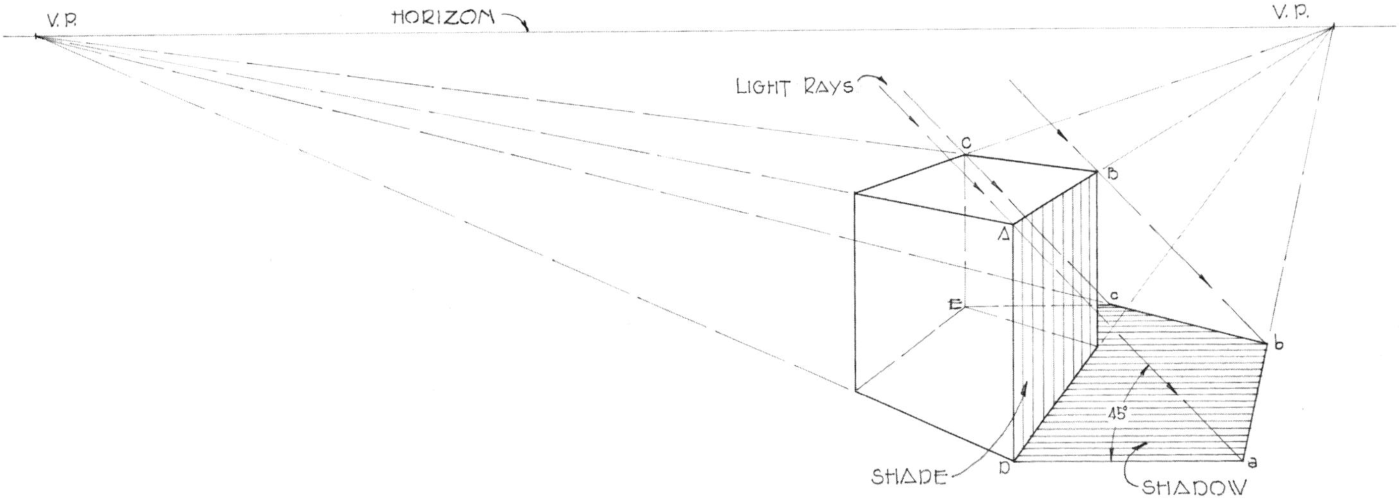

Fig. 12-39 Perspective shadows falling upon a horizontal plane.

Perspective Shades and Shadows Similar principles to those we found in orthographic shadow casting are encountered in plotting shadows of pictorial subjects. On perspective drawings, often entire surfaces are on the opposite side from the light source and therefore receive no light. These surfaces must be shown in darker tones; yet they are not shadows. We refer to the darker surfaces of the object not receiving light as "shades" (see Fig. 12-39). Determining the outlines of both shades and shadows (as well as occasional highlights) plays an important part in giving realism to perspective drawings.

Notice that the same vanishing points are used for both the shadows and the horizontal lines of the perspective itself (Fig. 12-39). If the light source is parallel to the picture plane, the shadows of horizontal lines will vanish at the same point as the object lines themselves. Also, the shadows of vertical lines will appear as horizontal shadows if they fall on a horizontal surface. Plotting shadows with a light source parallel to the picture plane, of course, limits shadow casting to either the right or left of the object, never in an oblique manner. In angular perspective, then, one exposed wall will be in light and one will be in shade. Various shadow characteristics can be obtained by using different angles of the light source. A high angle produces a narrow shadow on a horizontal plane such as the ground, whereas a low angle of light produces a wide shadow. Usually 45°, 60° or 30° angles are most convenient because of the construction with drafting triangles. See Fig. 12-40. For the student, casting shadows on 2-point,

Fig. 12-40 On perspective drawings, a light source parallel to the picture plane is convenient for casting shadows.

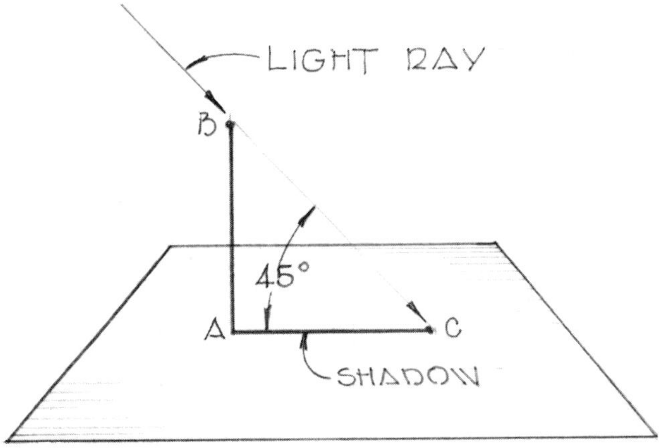

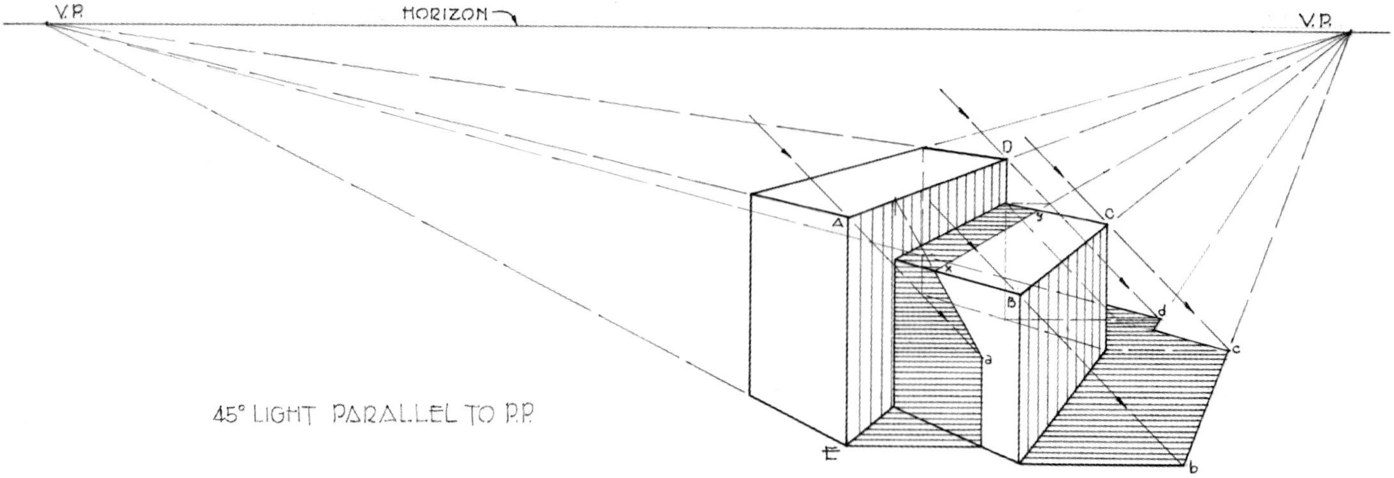

Fig. 12-41 Perspective shadows falling upon a vertical plane.

angular perspectives with the *light source parallel to the picture plane* will produce adequate realism for most situations. For that reason, we will concern ourselves mainly with this method of shadow construction.

Actually, light striking an object such as a building that is drawn in an angular position, produces rather interesting and revealing shadows when the light source is parallel to the picture plane. The shadows from overhangs, offsets, and other features can be made to contribute effective composition elements to the finished drawing.

In Fig. 12-39, a 45° light source produces the shade and shadow of a perspective cube as shown. Point A casts its shadow at point a, point B casts its shadow at b, and point C casts its shadow at c. The shadow of line A–D is drawn horizontal, inasmuch as the shadow falls on a horizontal plane. Line A–B creates the shadow line a–b, which must vanish at the same right vanishing point as line A–B. Line b–c is the shadow of B–C and therefore must vanish at the same left vanishing point. By plotting points, and then the lines connecting these points, the entire shadow outline is completed. Notice that the shadow of the hidden corner C–E is plotted on the figure merely to show the horizontal relationship of E to c. From Fig. 12-39 we see that:

1. The shadow cast by a vertical line on a horizontal plane is horizontal; and
2. On parallel surfaces, a shadow is parallel to the line that cast it, and therefore vanishes at the same vanishing point.

Figure 12-41 shows the shadow of a vertical line being interrupted by a vertical wall plane. The shadow of point A cannot be established until the horizontal shadow line from point E is projected to the receiving wall. The remaining diagonal line above point a is a part of the shadow of line A–D, and is completed after the horizontal shadow of line A–D is projected on the top of the small block (line x–y). Line a–x–y is the shadow of A–D falling on perpendicular surfaces. From Fig. 12-41 we see that:

1. The shadow of a vertical line is vertical if it falls on a vertical surface; and
2. The shadow of a horizontal line is inclined if it falls on a vertical surface.

We see in Fig. 12-42 the effects of a horizontal shadow cast upon various level of a simple stairs. The shadow is located on each level, vanished to the right vanishing point, and the shadows on the vertical risers merely connect the shadows falling upon the treads. Notice the convenient points used to establish the width of each horizontal shadow.

Shadows falling upon inclined surfaces (Fig. 12-43) present interesting projection problems. The shadow of the chimney is found by projecting the ridge at point A to point B on the forepart of the chimney. Point B is projected horizontally back to the ridge at point C. The line C–D will then be the shadow line of corner D–E; the 45° projection from corner E to e describes its length. To find the shadow of point F, we can consider a theoretical horizontal plane extending back from the ridge height. The shadow of F will fall at f on the imaginary plane; by projecting f to the ridge we have the shadow of line E–F on the inclined roof. A similar procedure is needed to plot the shadow of the flagpole after it reaches the incline of the roof.

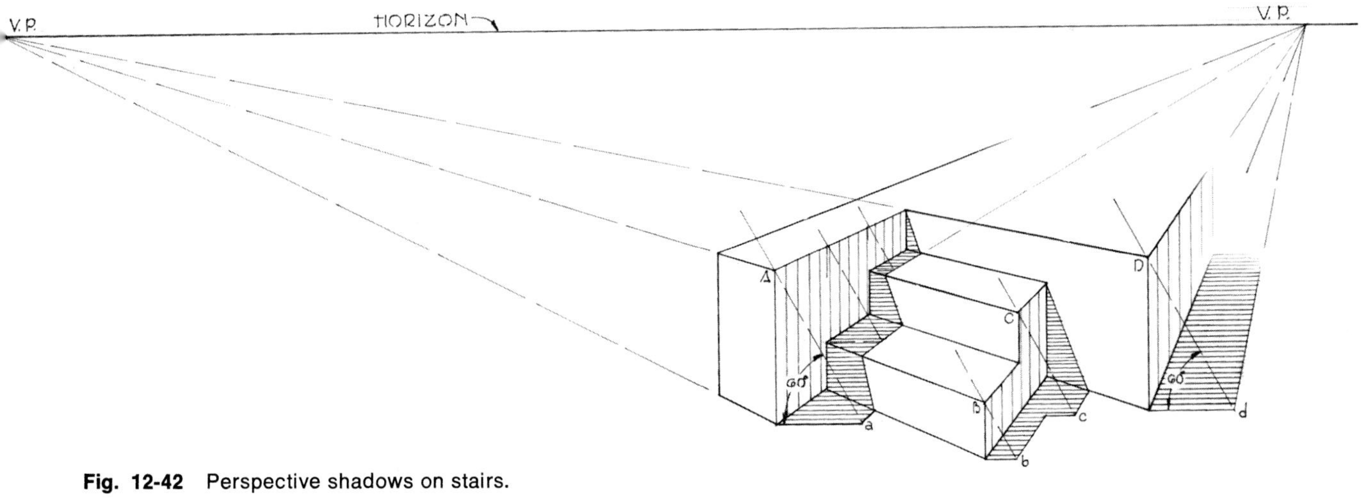

Fig. 12-42 Perspective shadows on stairs.

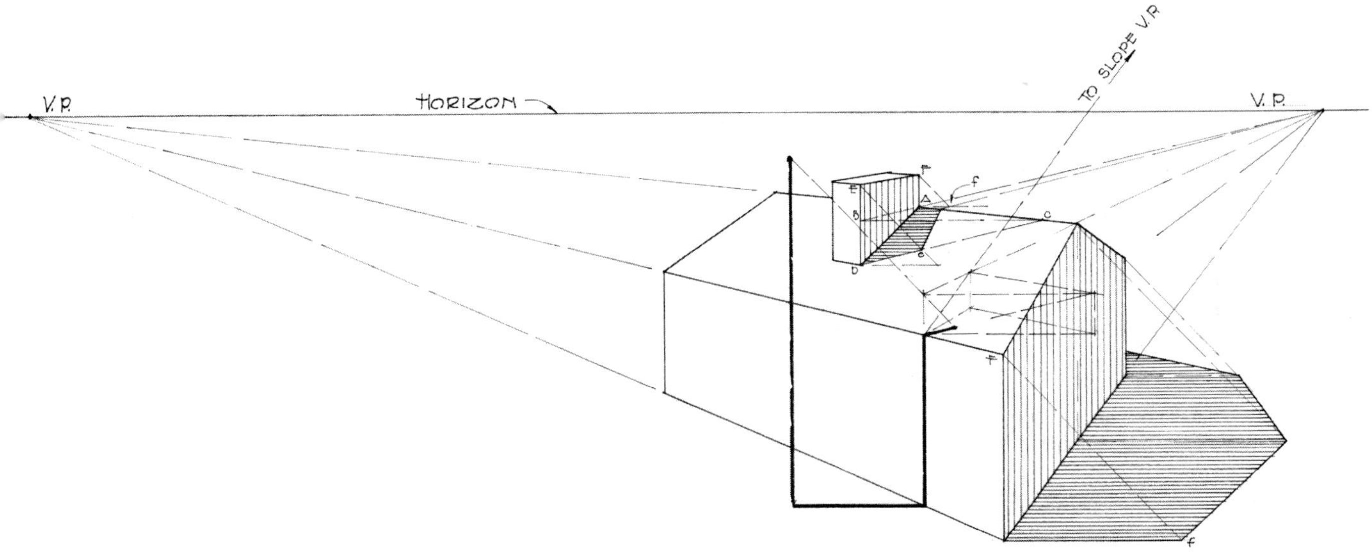

Fig. 12-43 Perspective shadows falling upon inclined surfaces.

Notice that a line extending up the incline from the shadow at the eave produces a similar condition as the chimney provided. The shadow of the flagpole top is brought down to the vertical plane of the wall (just above the eave on a vertical line); from that point a theoretical horizontal plane is assumed that will intersect the roof, and a horizontal plane is assumed at the eave level. The diagonal connecting both planes will be the shadow of a vertical, such as the flagpole, as it falls upon the inclined roof. This is plotted in the same manner as the shadow of vertical line D–E of the chimney. From Fig. 12-43, it can be deduced then that the shadows of vertical lines are inclined if they fall upon inclined surfaces. From Fig. 12-44 it will be seen that shadows from surfaces parallel to an incline will be parallel to the inclines.

Perspective shadows with the light source *oblique* to the picture plane can be projected if an actual exterior light condition is desired. See Fig. 12-45. Notice that two shadow-vanishing-points are needed. They can be located at random or by actual bearing and altitude angles of the light source. The light bearing V.P. is on the horizon and the altitude V.P. is on a trace through L.H.V.P.

Shadows from a single source such as a light fixture in an interior can be plotted as shown in Fig. 12-46.

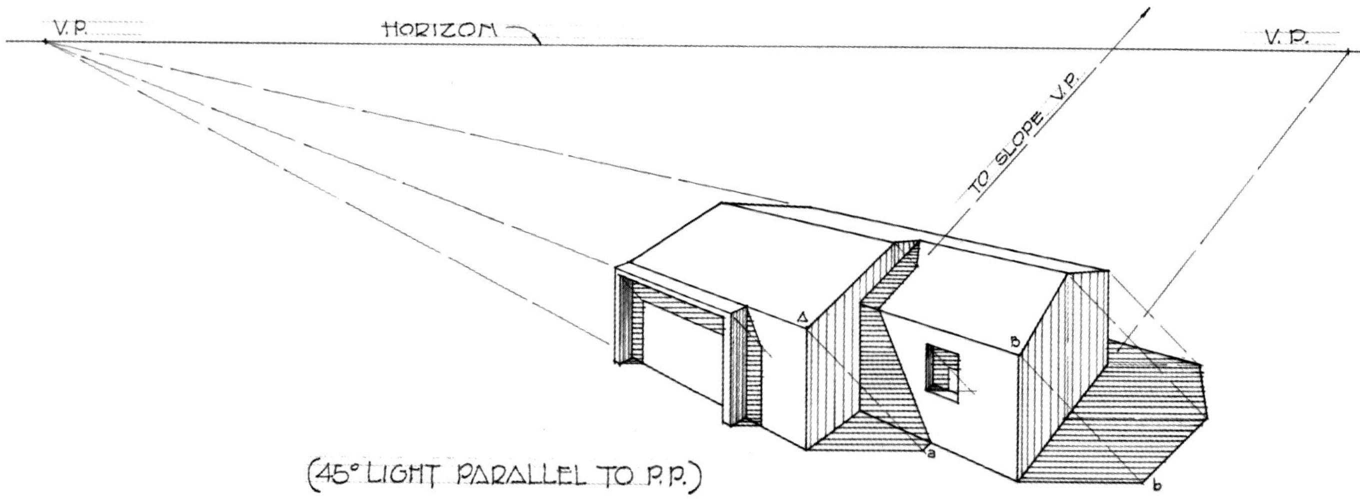

Fig. 12-44 Various shadows showing the characteristics of buildings.

Fig. 12-45 Perspective shadows with the light oblique to the picture plane. Notice that two shadow vanishing points are needed. They can be located at random or by bearing and altitude angles of the light source. The light bearing V.P. is on the horizon and the altitude V.P. is on a trace through L.H.V.P.

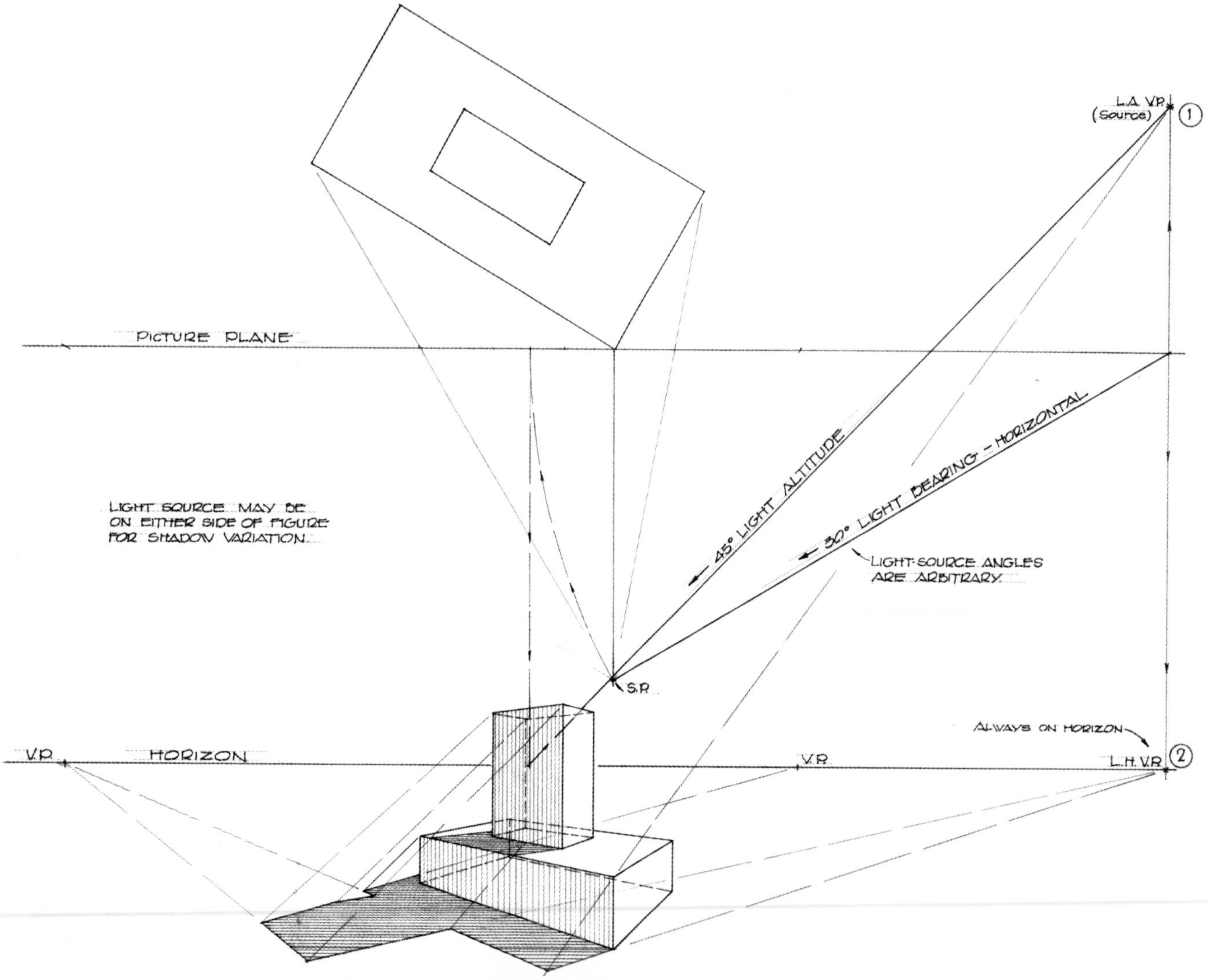

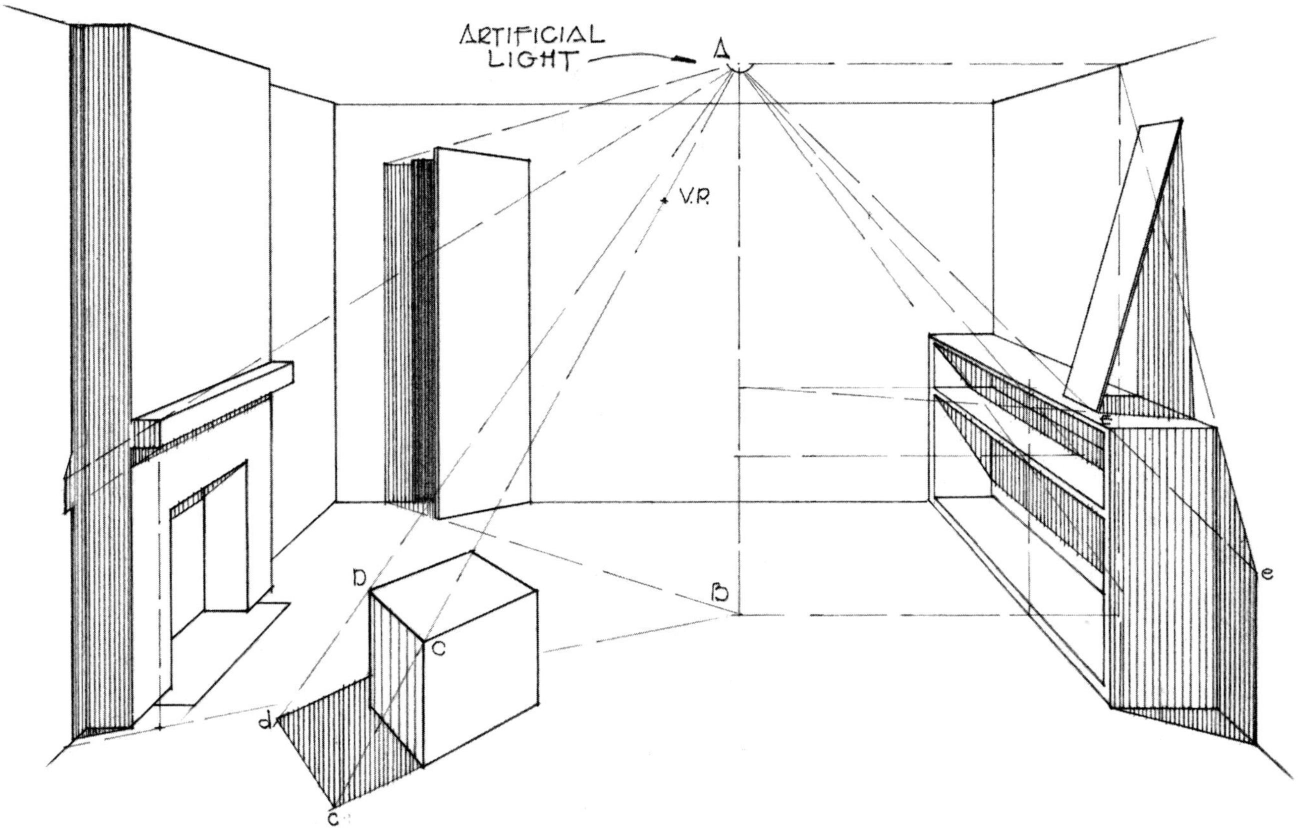

Fig. 12-46 Plotting shadows from a single light source on an interior perspective.

EXERCISES

1. Using the office method, draw an angular perspective of Figs. 12-47A, B, and C.

2. Using the office method, draw an angular perspective of the interior views of Figs. 12-48A and B.

3. Using the perspective-plan method, draw an angular perspective of Fig. 12-49; Figs. 12-50A, B, C, and D; and Fig. 12-51.

4. Using the 1-point perspective method, draw a parallel perspective of Fig. 12-52 and Fig. 12-48A.

5. Construct the shadows on the orthographic views of Figs. 12-47B and C; Fig. 12-52; and Fig. 12-53.

6. Draw the angular perspective of Figs. 12-47A, B, and C; Figs. 12-50A, B, C, and D; and Fig. 12-54; and complete their shades and shadows as indicated. Use a light source parallel to the picture plane. Make the shadows a darker tone than the shades.

REVIEW QUESTIONS

1. What is meant by linear perspective?

2. How does the projection of a perspective view to the picture plane differ from the projection of an orthographic view?

3. What is the point called that approximates the eye when a person draws an object in perspective?

4. What effect is produced on a perspective when the horizon line is raised in relation to the groundline?

5. What effect is produced on a perspective when the object is placed farther away from the picture plane?

6. Why must true heights of an object be established only on the picture plane?

7. If an object is placed in an oblique position in relation to the picture plane, why are two vanishing points necessary?

8. What are the advantages of using the perspective-plan method for drawing a perspective?

9. In a 1-point parallel perspective view of an interior, is the single vanishing point used to draw a piece of furniture that is in a diagonal position?

10. Why is the action of light on architectural subjects important to the designer?

11. Why is it convenient to use a 45° light-source direction?

12. Explain the difference between a "shade" and a "shadow."

13. What purpose do orthographic shadows serve?

14. When the light source is parallel to the picture plane, is the shadow of a vertical corner drawn vertically when it falls upon a wall?

Fig. 12-47 Geometric forms to be drawn in perspective. Enlarge the plan and elevation to suit your paper.

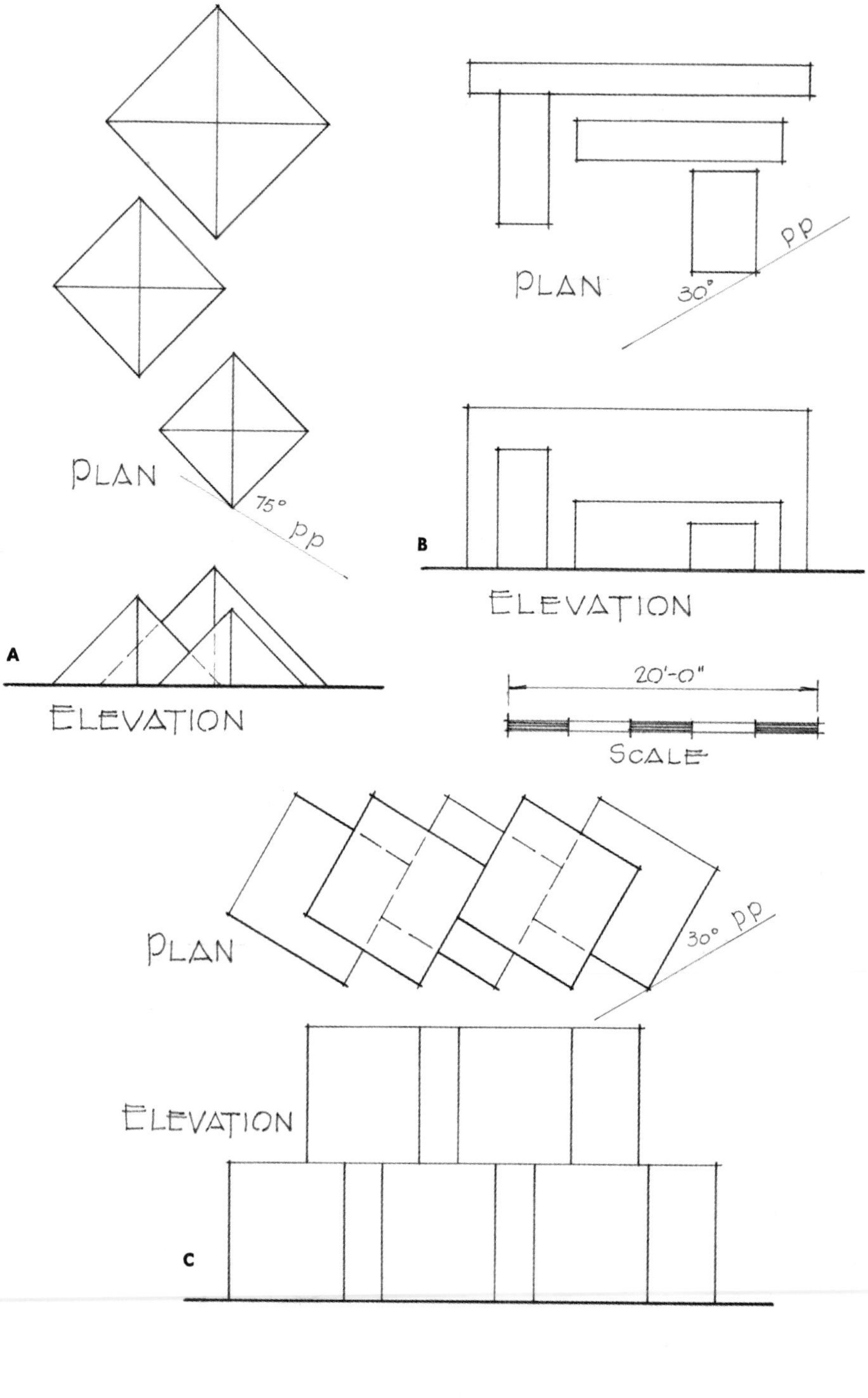

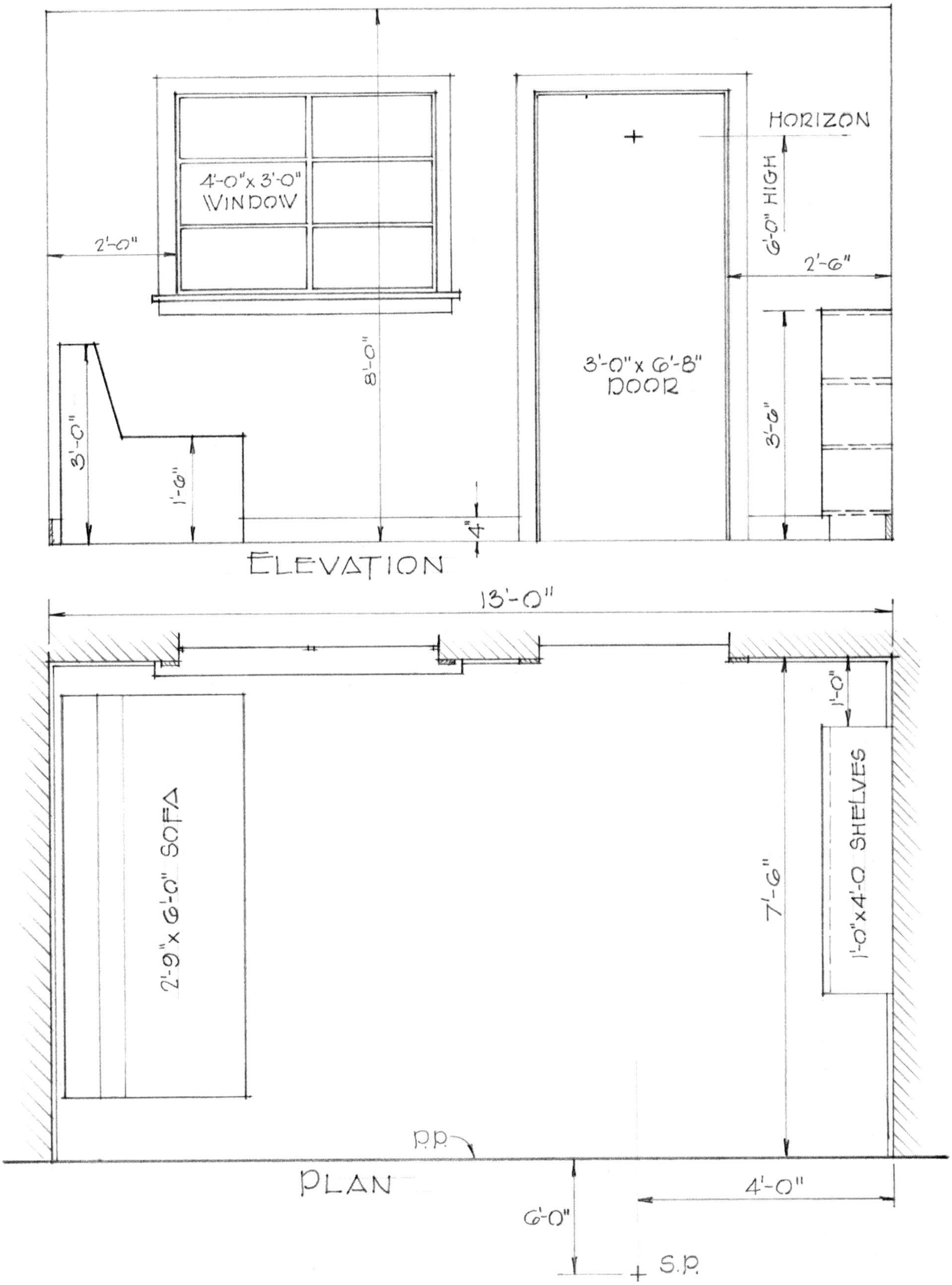

Fig. 12-48A Problem for 1-point interior perspective.

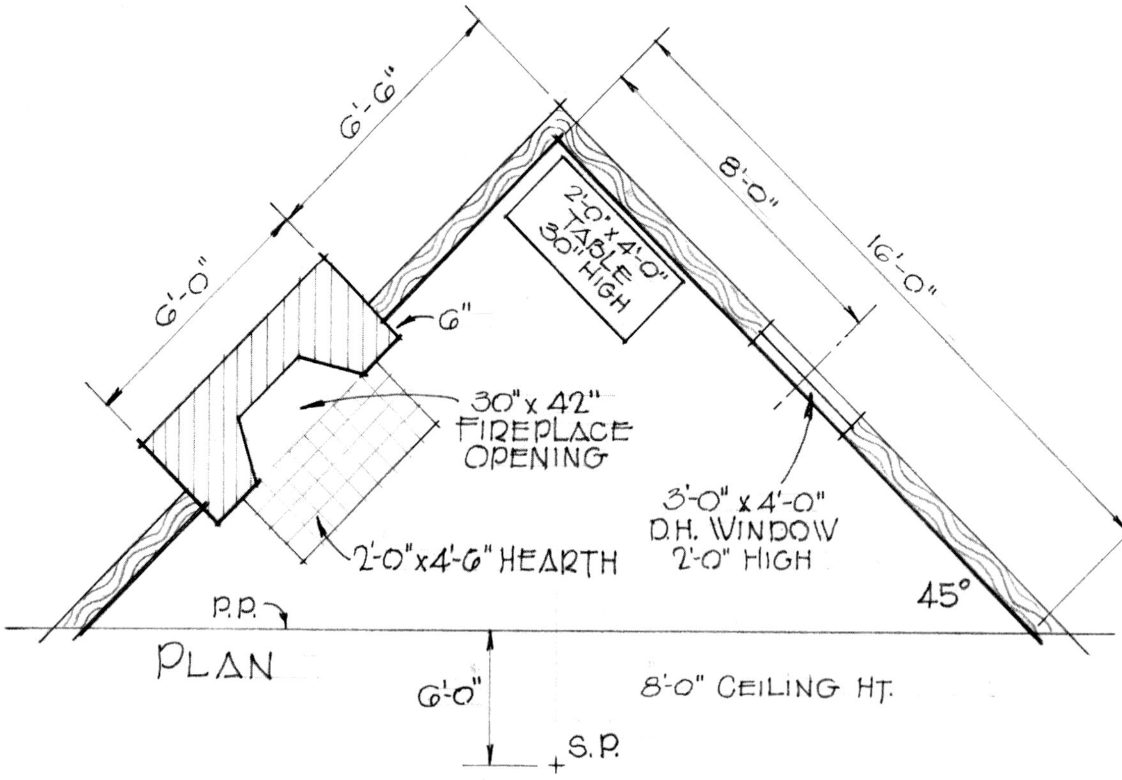

Fig. 12-48B Problem for 2-point interior perspective.

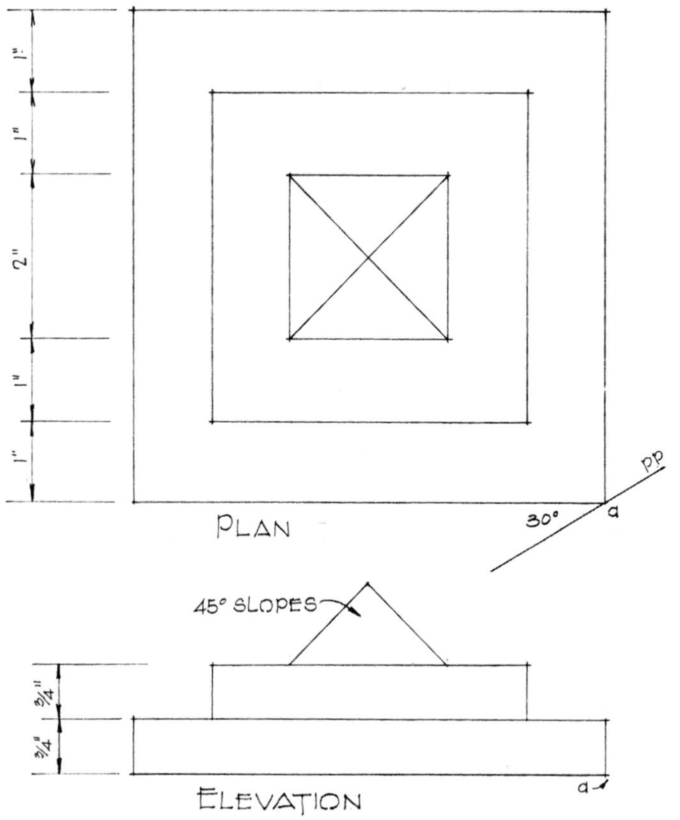

Fig. 12-49 Problem for drawing a perspective using the perspective-plan method. Place the station point 6″ below picture plane and 3″ to the right of point *a*. Place groundline (1) 3″ below the picture plane and groundline (2) 11″ below the picture plane.

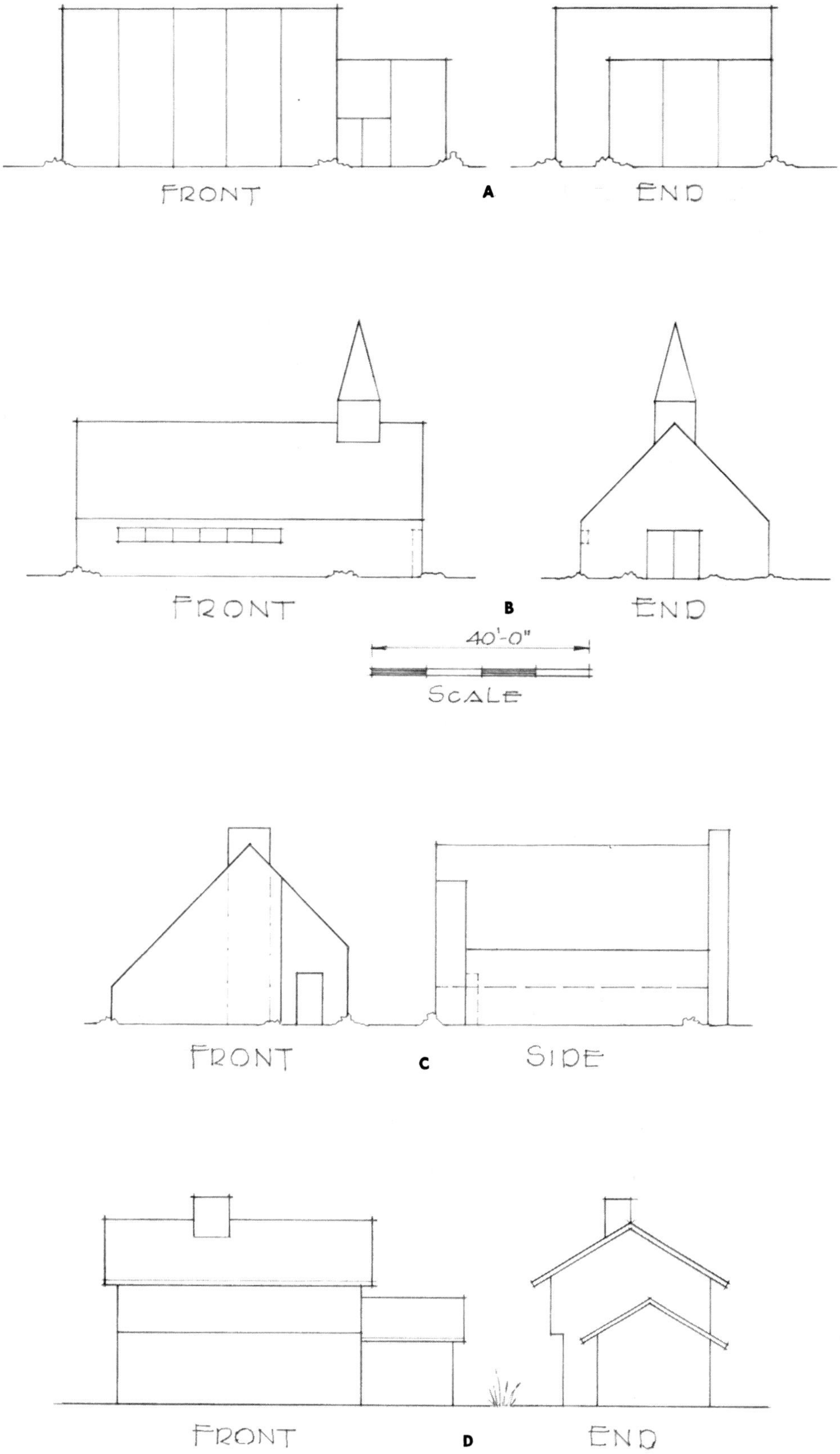

Fig. 12-50 Architectural forms to be drawn in perspective. Draw the enlarged plan and elevation from the given elevation views.

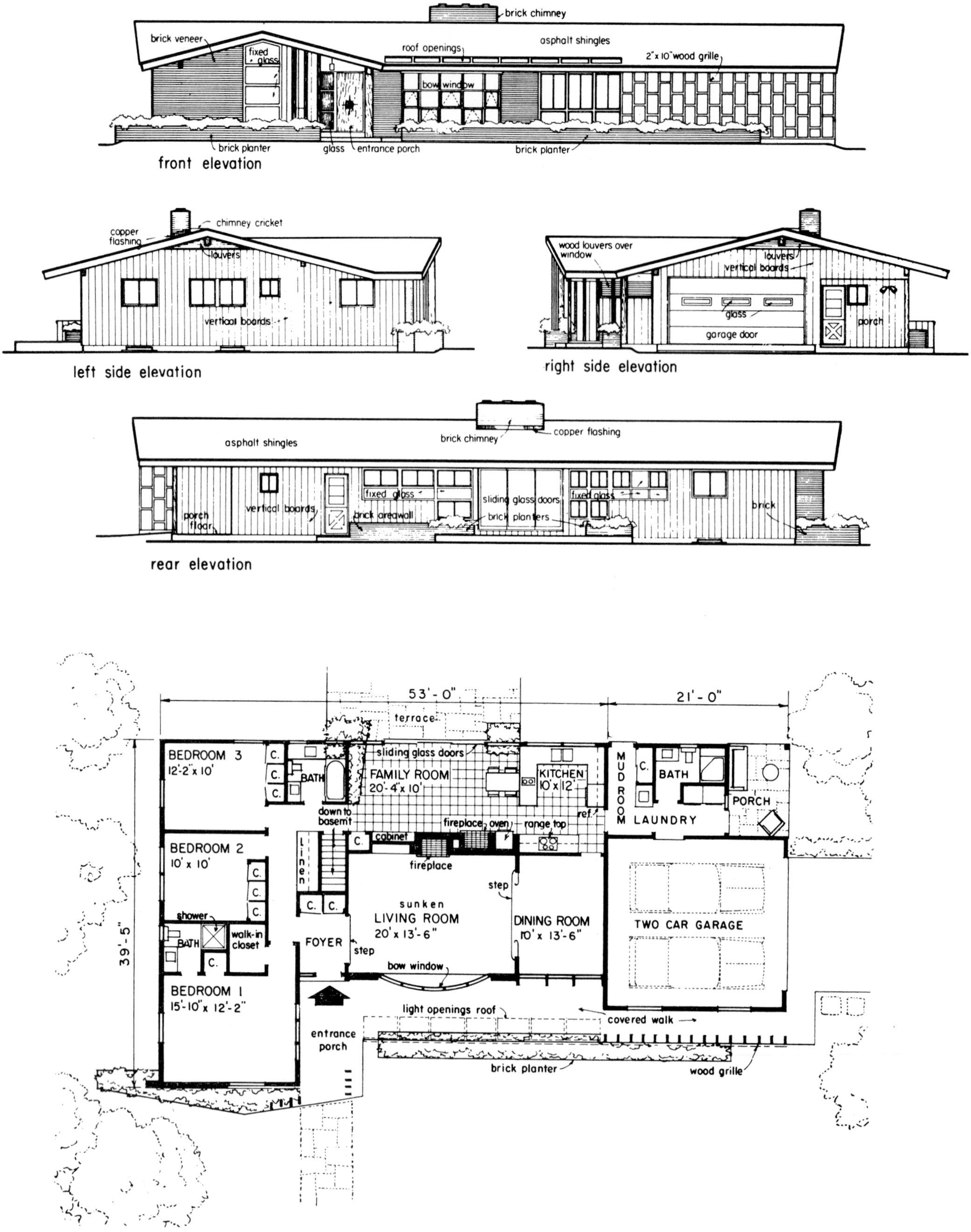

Fig. 12-51 Scale a floor plan and elevation of this house and draw the perspective.

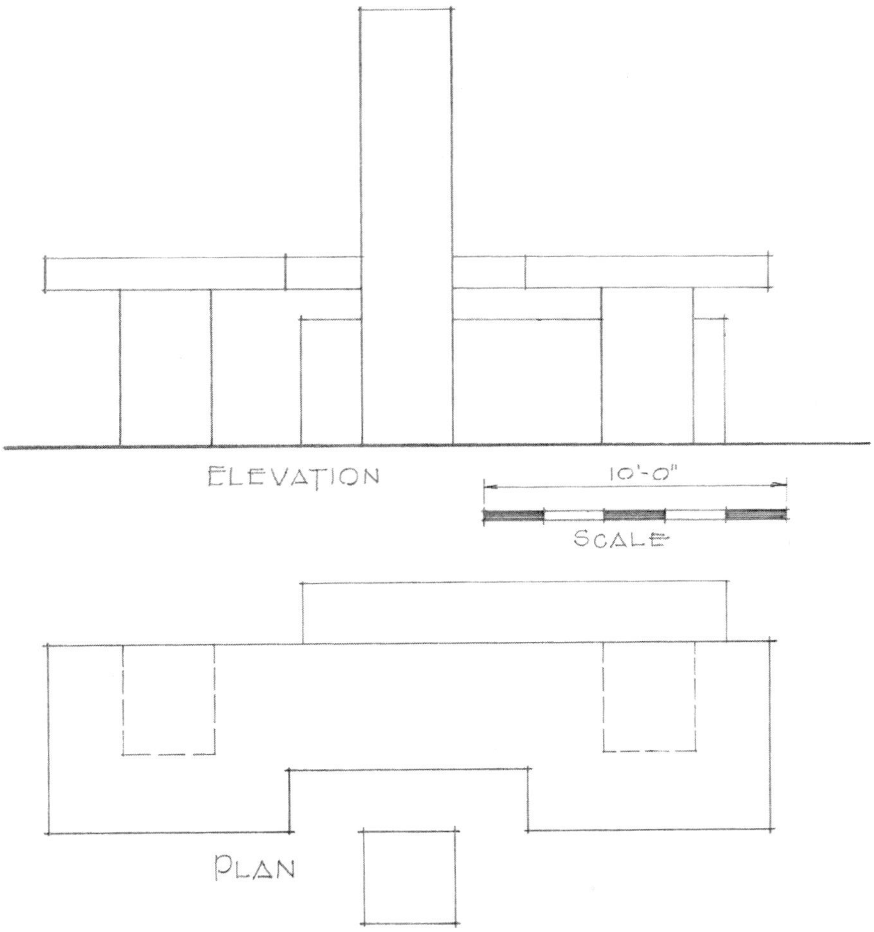

Fig. 12-52 A problem for plotting orthographic shadows, or for drawing a perspective.

Fig. 12-53 A problem for plotting orthographic shadows, or for drawing a perspective.

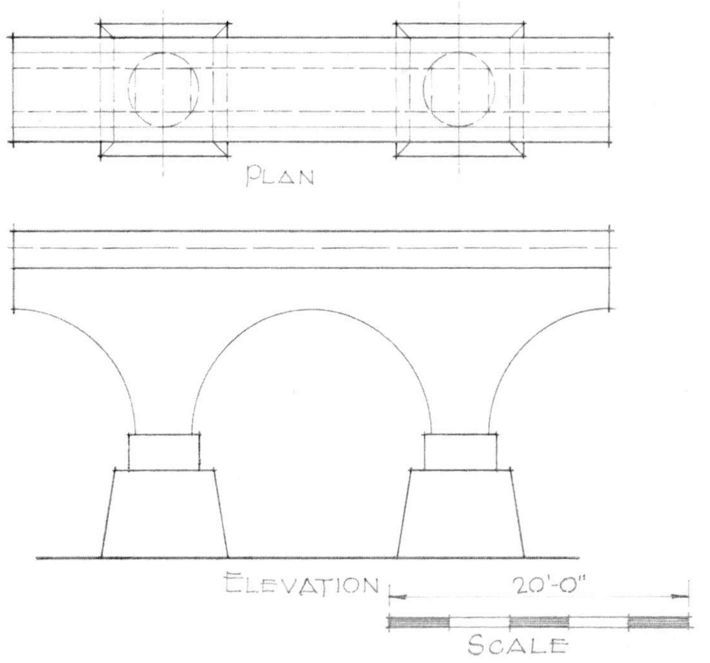

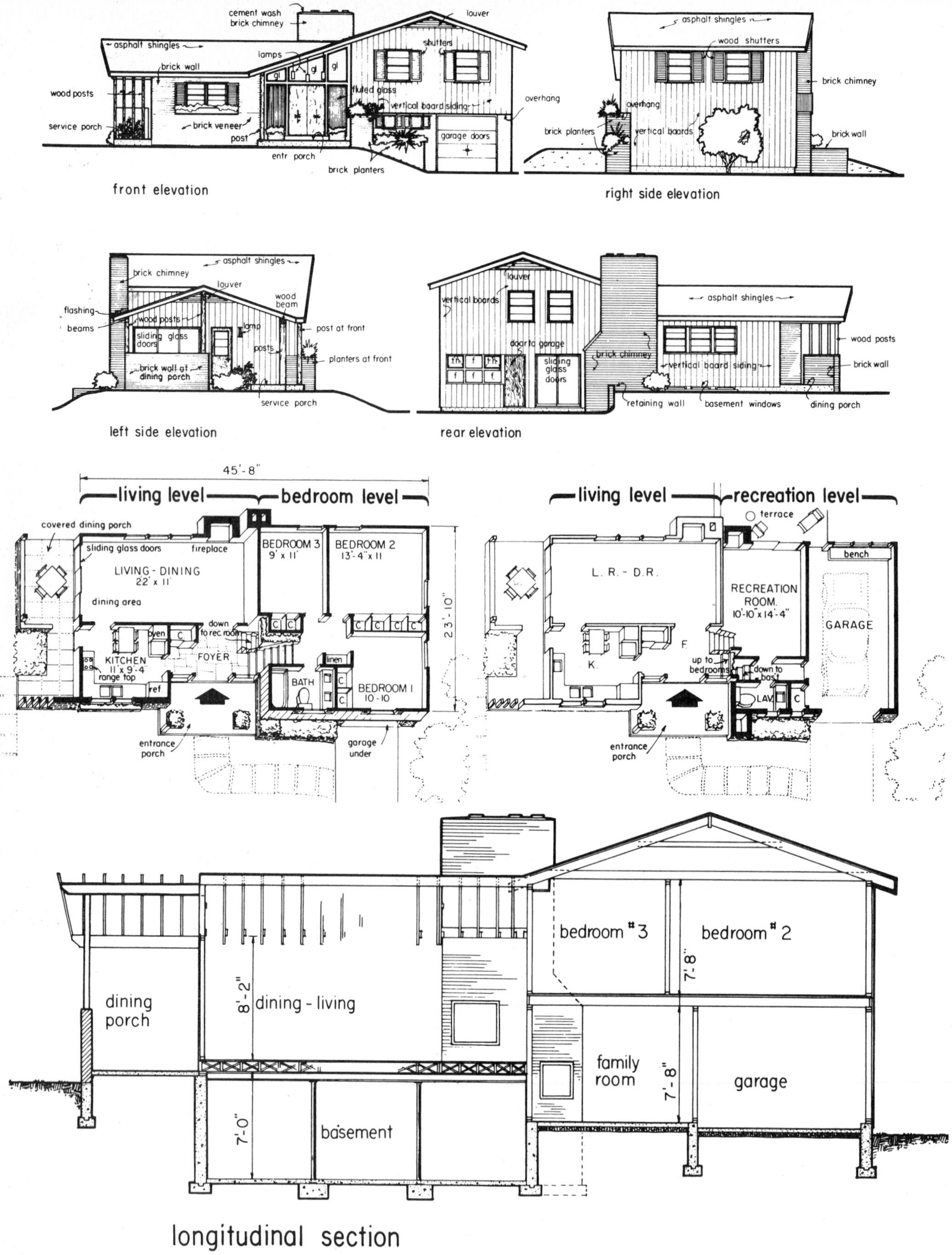

Fig. 12-54 Scale a floor plan and elevation of this split-level house and draw the perspective.

"Good painting is like good cooking: it can be tasted, but not explained."
—Valaminck

13

Presentation Drawings and Renderings

Before working drawings can be started it is generally necessary to prepare a presentation drawing of the tentative structure. This is done for several reasons. First, it combines the efforts of preliminary planning into a tangible proposal for a client's approval, making the presentation an actual "selling" instrument. Secondly, if offers a means for careful study of the structure's appearance, by all concerned, upon which improvements or changes for final development can be based.

The presentation is the designer's graphic concept of a building, in its natural setting, made to represent the structure honestly, realistically, artistically, and in a manner easily understand by the layman. A great deal of unnecessary technical information is avoided to make the general concept more pronounced. Rendered perspective or elevation views showing the realism of light and shade, landscaping, and textures, are usually the most effective elements of successful presentation drawings. However, considerable latitude in the selection of views is possible, depending upon the nature of the proposal and the time allowed for its completion. Student projects usually include a perspective, a floor plan, several elevations, and a plot plan. The duplication of similar information on the various selected views should be avoided so an attractive yet uncluttered graphic proposal results.

13.1 TYPES OF PRESENTATION DRAWINGS

Many presentations consist of a perspective only. In fact, an architectural office will often give presentation work of expensive buildings to professional delineators, specialists in this type of work, for elaborate perspective renderings—frequently in color. Many of such presentations have sufficient artistic merit to be used for promotional work, in brochures, and even in national publications.

If time is limited, effective presentations can be made with only a floor plan and a rendered elevation. Others may include a transverse section view or an interior perspective, if such features seem worthy of special consideration. Often residential presentations include a plot plan to show the proposed orientation of the home and grounds. In other situations a well-executed freehand sketch may be adequate in showing a client sufficient information about a structure. We see, then, that on a presentation drawing, the draftsman can give his creative abilities free rein in depicting the most interesting qualities of a building.

Successful presentations are done in almost all of the different art media; the most frequently used are: pencil, pen and ink, colored pencil, water color, tempera, pastel, and charcoal pencil (see Figs. 13-1 through 13-8). Usually the mastery of one medium or another is the deciding factor in making the choice. After experimentation the draftsman will find that

Fig. 13-1 Pencil presentation of a small chapel.

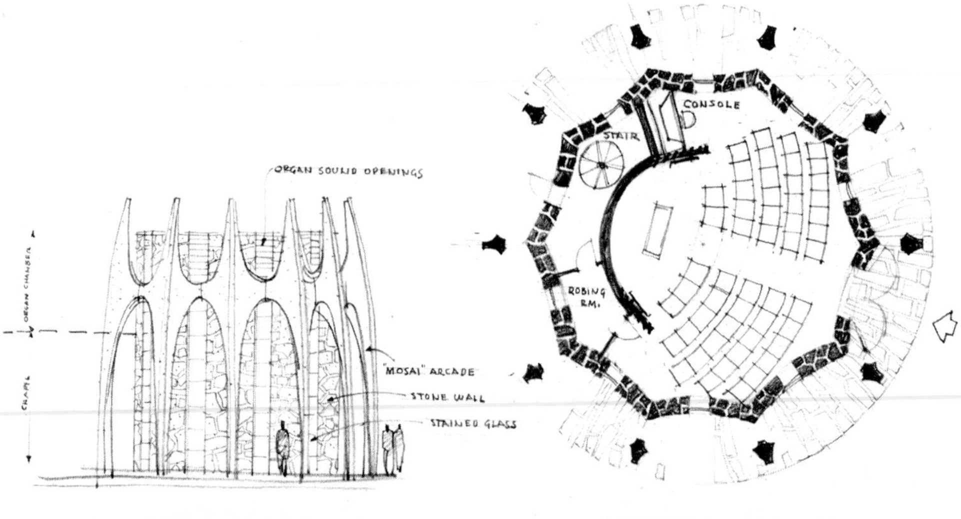

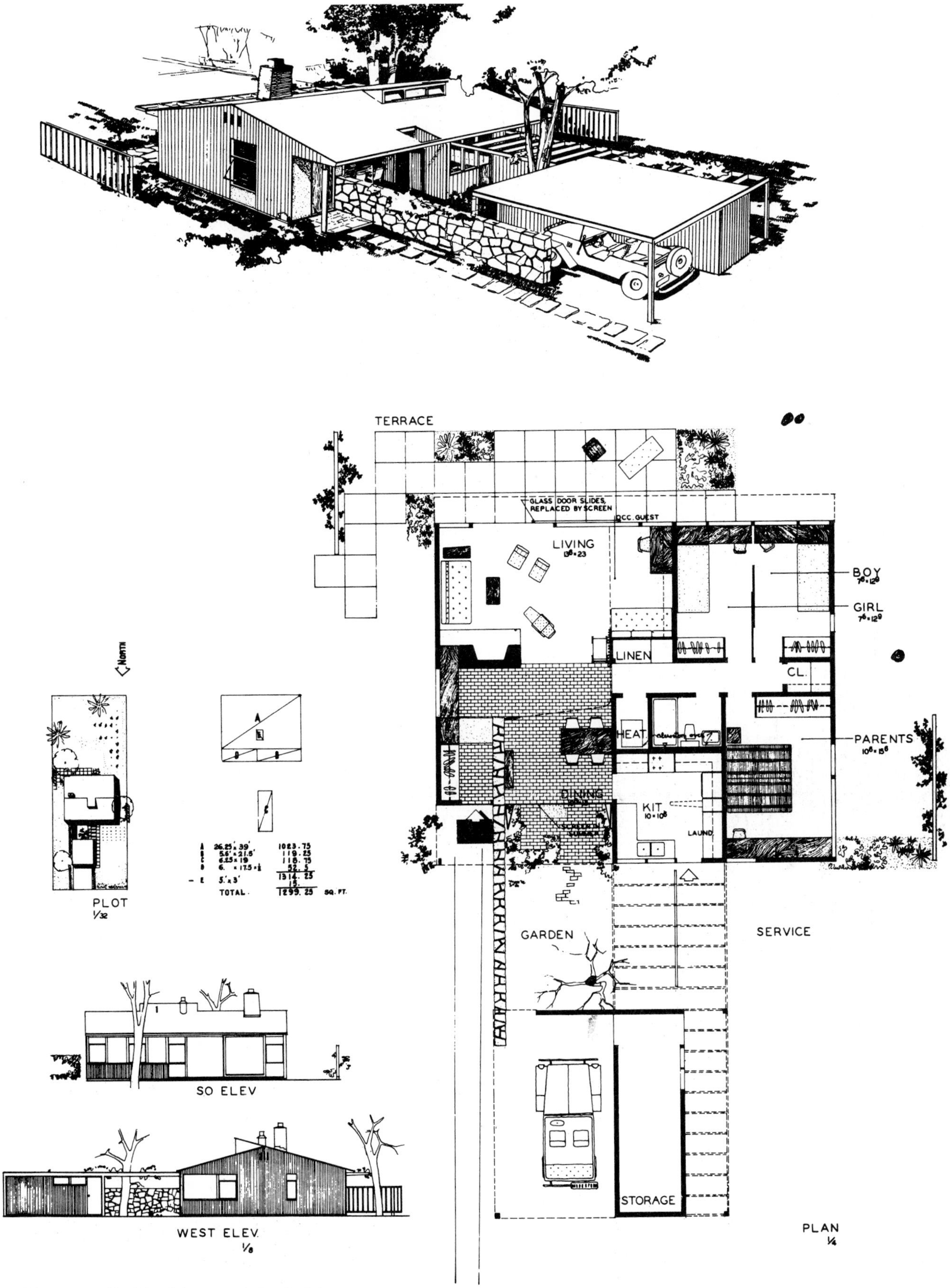

Fig. 13-2 Residential presentation in ink.

each medium has advantages as well as limitations. Pencil and pen and ink, for example, capable of executing sharp, fine lines can be used to reveal small details and various textures. But they are time-consuming when covering large areas. The pencil is comparatively easy to control, yet it should be selected as the medium for rather small drawings—as should pen and ink. The combining of pencil or ink linework with transparent watercolor wash for large areas overcomes this limitation and is often an intelligent choice of media for many architectural subjects. Although color commands attention and excites the viewer, it requires considerable skill in handling, especially in representing finer detail.

The beginning student woud be wise in developing his ability in pencil work first, before attempting other media. After some degree of skill is acquired in representing values, textures, light and shade, trees and shrubbery; and after command of composition and balance is attained, facility in other media becomes only a matter of mechanics.

13.2 PRESENTATION PAPER OR BOARD

Pencil drawings may be done on a good grade of tracing paper, for convenient reproduction, or they may be done on illustration or Bristol board stock for more rigid display drawings. As we mentioned earlier, tracing paper, because of its transparency, aids trial and error composition with little wasted effort. Elements can be taken from previous sketches, rearranged to suit the composition with the final tracing as an overlay, and even improved upon when one does the finish work. Also, weak points of the composition, when viewed from the reverse side, can be quickly observed.

If necessary, drawings on tracing paper can be mounted on thick illustration board with the use of ordinary white library paste. Thin

Fig. 13-3 A student presentation in ink and tempera.

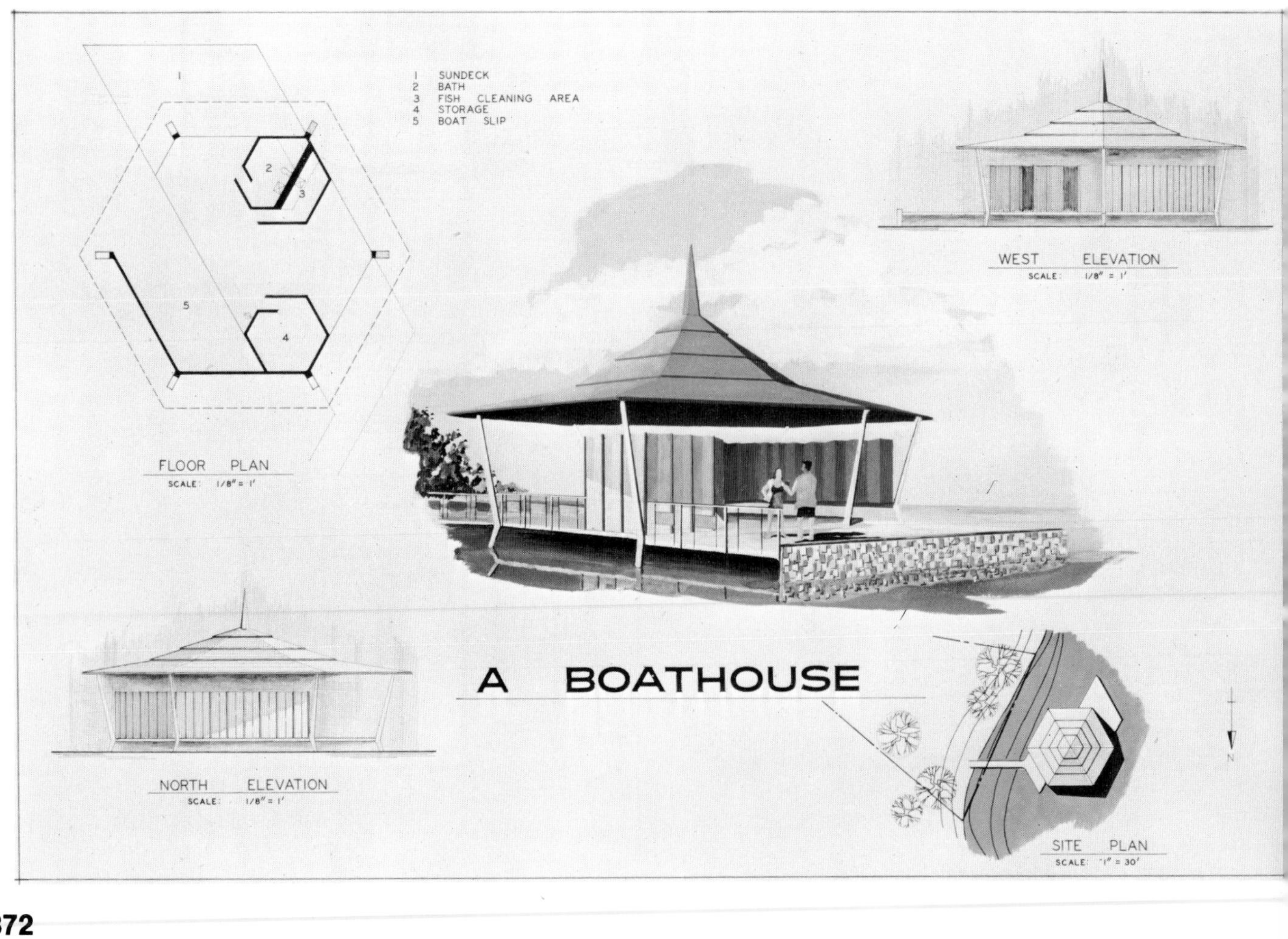

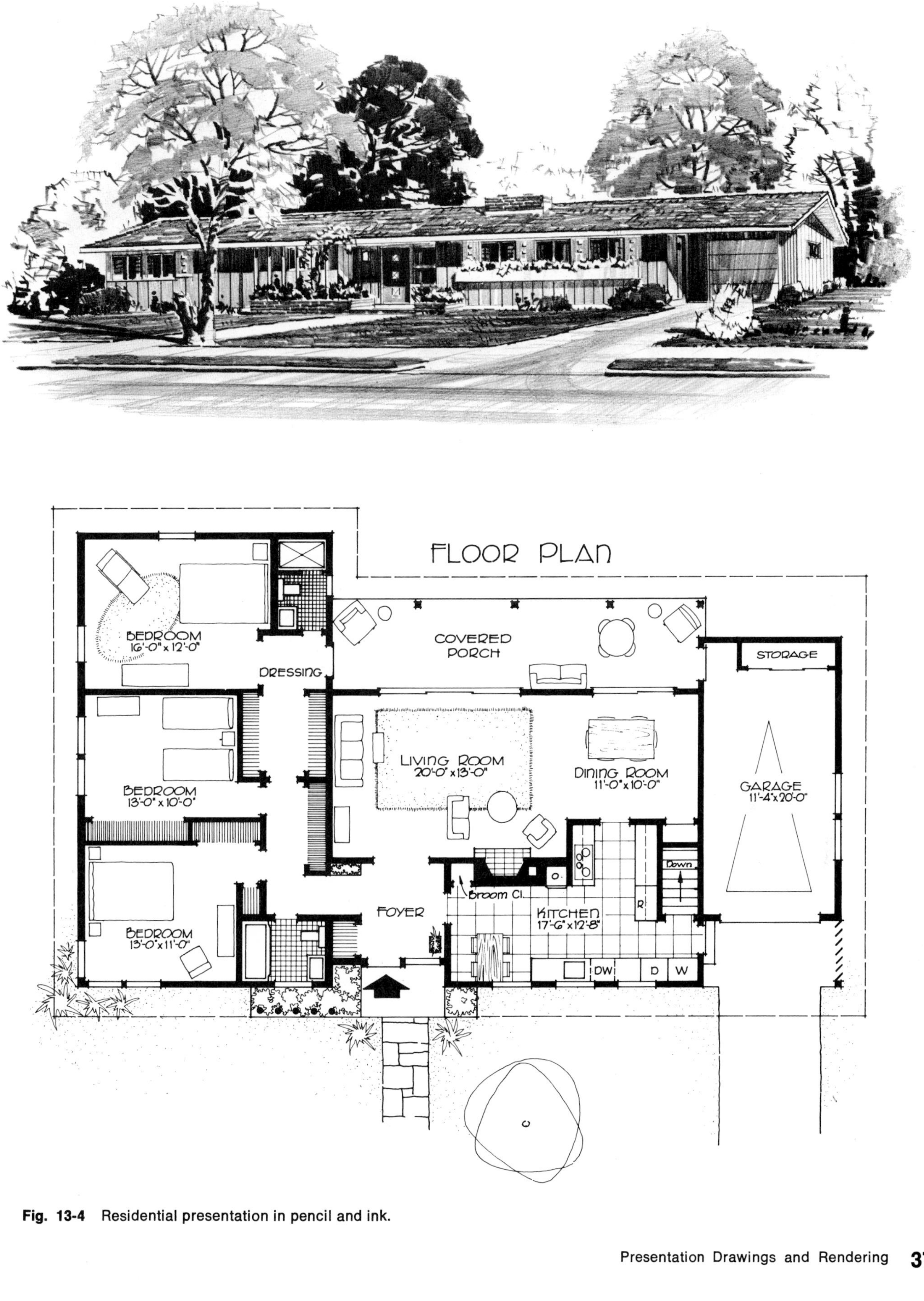

Fig. 13-4 Residential presentation in pencil and ink.

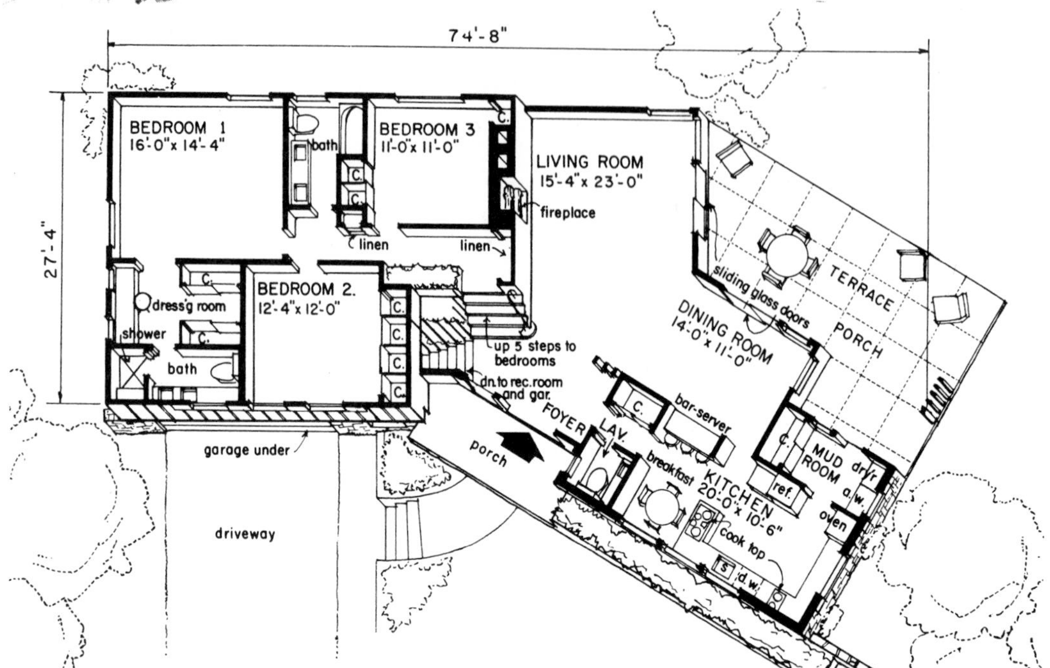

living and bedroom levels

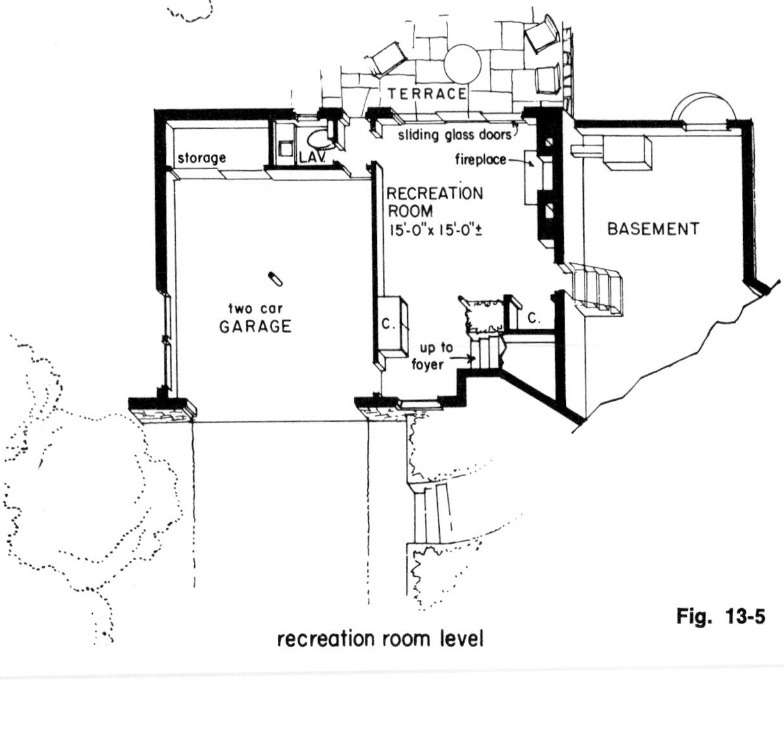

recreation room level

Fig. 13-5 Residential presentation in pencil and ink.

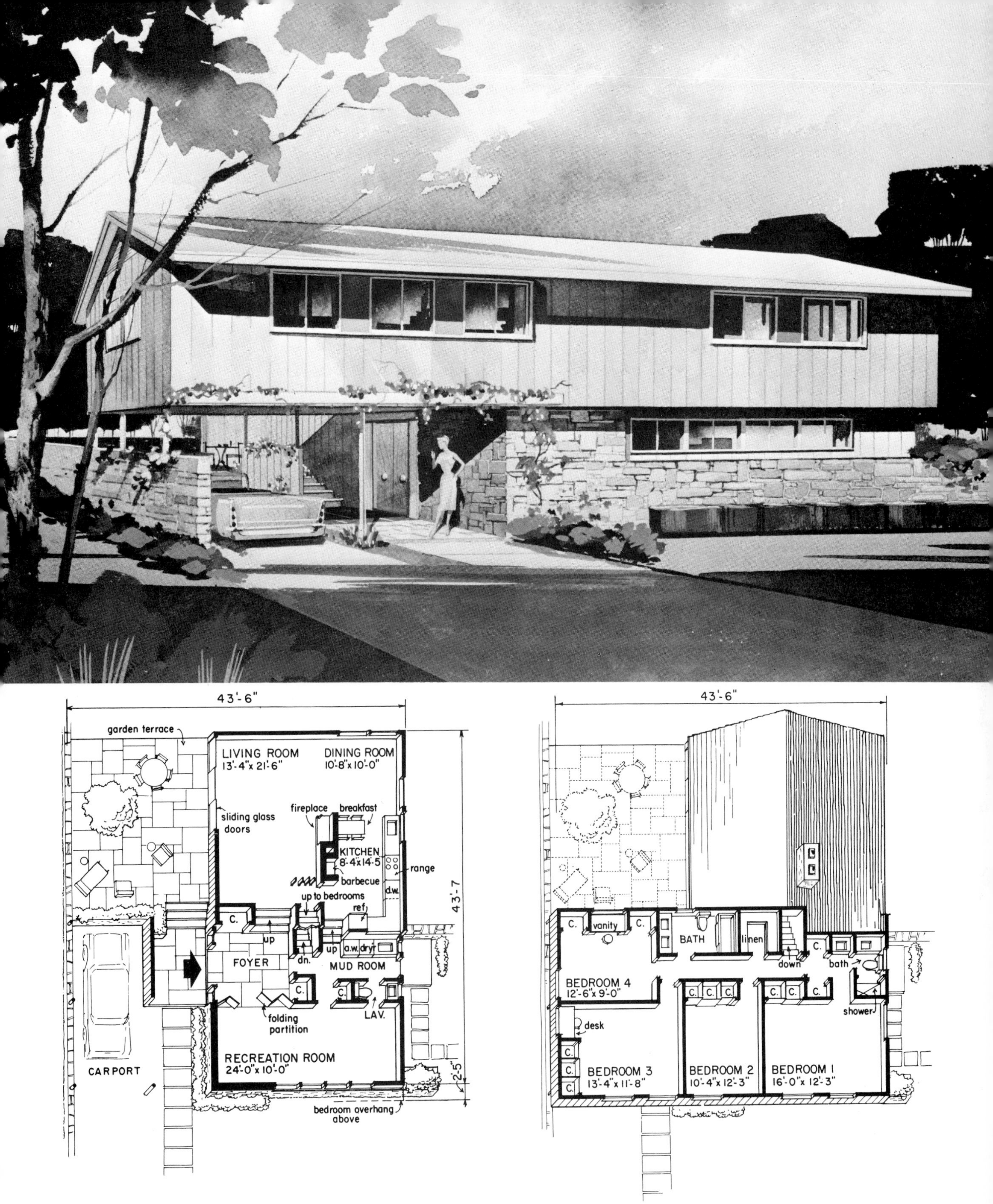

Fig. 13-6 Residential presentation in watercolor and ink.

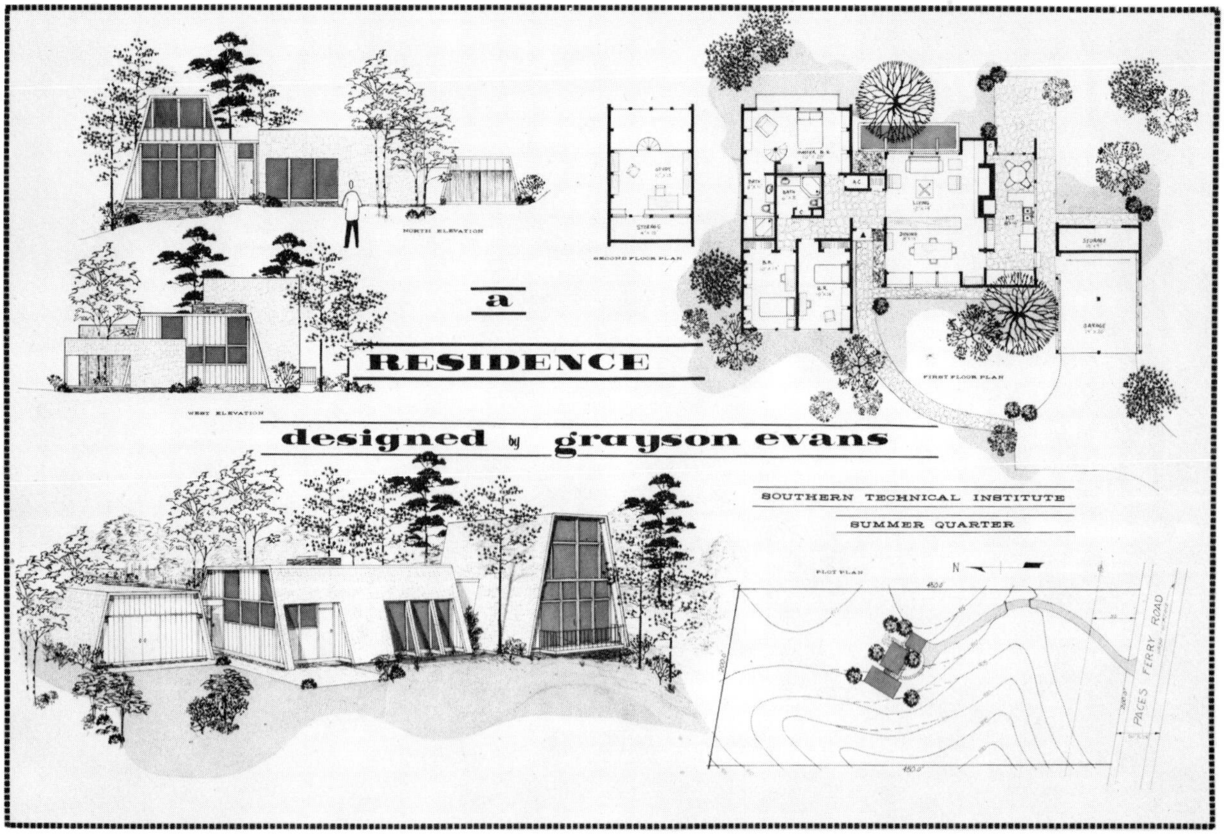

Fig. 13-7 Student presentation made with ink and pressure-sensitive tape, lettering, tonework, and landscaping applied.

Fig. 13-8 Student residential presentation made with ink and watercolor.

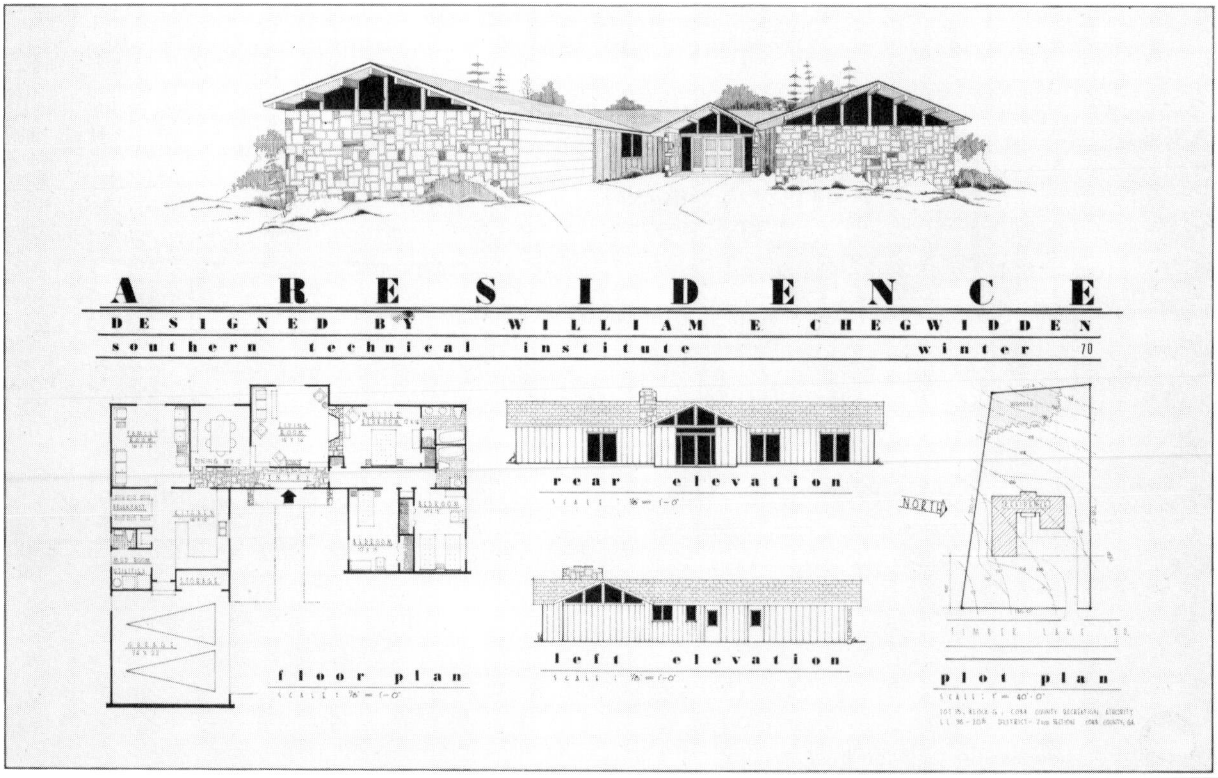

the paste to a creamy consistency with water and apply evenly to the back of the tracing and the face of the mounting board. Smooth out wrinkles with a large plastic triangle. To prevent the board from warping, apply a sheet of similar tracing paper to the back of the board, using the same procedure as mentioned above. Keep the board flat with weights until dry. Or a finished tracing may be merely taped to a suitable mounting board and surrounded with a neat frame cut from mat board stock (see Fig. 5-44).

When preparing a presentation on heavy illustration or Bristol board, first draw each drawing on tracing paper. This is especially important when a number of views or drawings must be arranged into a pleasing composition. Cut out all views so that they are individual units. Next, arrange the views on the board for balance and interest. Do not hesitate to try two or three completely different arrangements before you are satisfied that you have the best possible one. To transfer drawings from tracing paper to the board, scrub each drawing on its reverse side with a soft pencil to act as a carbon, making sure there is sufficient graphite in back of each line. Then tape each view in place and go over the linework with a 2H pencil to transfer the drawings to the board. The illustration board is then ready for final rendering.

Fig. 13-9 Avoid uniform foliage shape around the building.

13.3 COMPOSITION

Composition is the art of arranging lines, values, spaces, masses, and other elements into a thing of beauty. Whether rendering a single perspective or a presentation drawing having a number of views, the principles of composition are equally important. Often a well-designed building will appear rather mediocre if the presentation is poorly planned. Thorough study of professional work will indicate the careful attention given to composition, which to the layman is not readily apparent. To a fortunate few, pleasing composition comes easily and may require little more than a chance to experiment. To others, it means acquiring a thorough knowledge of composition by repeated applications in an effort to improve. Even if beginning work seems disappointing, composition can be mastered and the following suggestions may be of help.

Begin with pleasing forms Study the basic geometric shapes involved in the layout. Be sure the simple forms, both in themselves and in the surrounding spaces, are harmonious and attractive. There must be variety. Avoid mechanical and uniform patterns, unless minor repetition is necessary for emphasis. Avoid strong lines near and parallel to the edges of the paper; an outline of distant trees should not parallel a strong roof line (see Fig. 13-9). Avoid two or three strong elements in a straight line.

Provide optical balance in the composition (Fig. 13-10) Each element is affected by a feeling of gravitational pull and therefore has optical weight. Larger elements have more weight than smaller, darker elements more weight than lighter, and intense colors more effect than pale colors. These graphic weights must balance, and they must be placed to prevent the composition from appearing bottom-heavy. Make the building the dominating element, or one view the dominating view; the other elements should be subordinate to it. Provide a center of interest, usually an entrance on a perspective, which acts as an optical fulcrum from which the various other elements are balanced. Avoid a static bal-

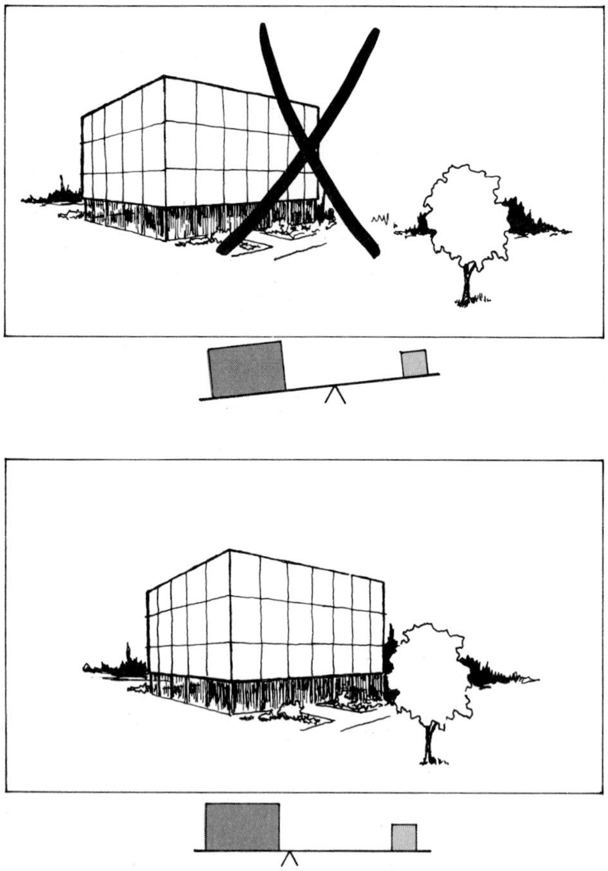

Fig. 13-10 Keep the composition balanced.

Fig. 13-11 Use contrast for emphasis.

ance, yet combine features and spaces to appear restful and to retain attention without carrying the eye off the paper. Avoid placing the building or other prominent element in the dead center of the paper.

Use contrast for producing emphasis Contrast in a composition is achieved by adjoining entirely different elements. They may be contrasting in value, size, shape, texture, or a combination of either. An important architectural feature, for example, shown in a very light tone can be given emphasis by surrounding it with a dark background of tree forms or a dark shadow nearby. Conversely, a light background can be made to emphasize a dark feature. Usually the building is shown bathed in warm sunlight, and subordinating areas, whether shadows, foliage, sky, or similar elements, are shown in various darker tones to lend emphasis as well as relief to the building. See Fig. 13-11. Also, occasional strong contrasts create interest. *Remember that carefully drawn shadows help explain the surfaces upon which they fall.* In planning contrasts and values, of course, one of the very first decisions that must be made is the direction of light. This is very important. Even though you have certain liberties in this choice, adopt the most advantageous direction from the standpoint of revealing the major architectural features as well as producing the most interesting shadow patterns.

In general, features in the foreground can be made darkest, features in mid-distance intermediate, and distant features the lightest. Other value arrangements may also be found satisfactory. Usually a dark shadow falling across the foreground in front of a building is effective in creating a feeling of depth. Make sure the structure appears firmly attached to the ground and has space around, behind, and in front of it. Temper hard architectural lines with planting. Planting is also helpful in emphasizing an important entrance, by leading the eye to it with a hedgerow or a similar strong contrast along a walkway. The strong outline created by extreme contrasts, however, must be interesting.

When using color, one may achieve emphasis by making important features bright and subordinate elements subdued or grayed. On line drawings, emphasis, of course, is produced by line weights. Heavy lines become more important than thin, light lines. Give the center of interest the strongest lines and the various subordinate features weaker lines, often actually fading out near the edge of the composition. Variety holds the attention of the viewer.

Hold the composition together Avoid strong isolated elements which tend to fall away from the layout. To tie elements together, indicate trees, shrubs, or grass, but do not place a large tree in the foreground which will detract or hide important information about the building. This problem can be eliminated, if need be, by making the tree in the foreground appear almost transparent, or several branches with foliage might be made to look as though they were part of a tree behind the viewer. Tree forms and planting indications must also be typical of the area where the building is to be built; palm trees around a New England residence would be ludicrous. Avoid strong indications of clouds or sky, birds, or smoke coming from a chimney; they are rarely needed on an architectural presentation.

Do not overburden the composition with too much detail Pick out essentials and leave some of the detail to the imagination. Carefully detail important features of the structure for interest and avoid details on subordinating elements. To create rhythm, however, some elements must reoccur throughout the composition. Too much of any one surface or texture representation will be found monotonous. On pencil drawings, you will find the eraser an important tool in composing. Erasing areas of superfluous detail can often add considerable interest to the finished drawing.

Keep all elements of the composition in proportion To maintain reality, do not overscale a tree or other feature. Occasionally, a simple human figure or group of figures, if drawn the correct size, contributes an easily associated relative scale. The size of the building is then easily compared to the size of the figure. Sometimes a related object such as a vehicle can be shown to suggest the activity for which the building is designed. Keep these suggestions simple (see Figs. 13-2 and 13-6) and in the correct scale; avoid laborious, diligent studies. Also, consider the building itself in proportion to the size of the paper; the effect will not be pleasing if the building appears to be lost in the space or is so big as to appear overpowering. Beginning students often make the mistake of placing important elements of a composition too close to the outside edges of the paper or board. The finished drawing must give the impression of being tailor-made for the sheet upon which it is placed.

Learn to represent the basic architectural textures Correct indications of the materials used in construction should be evident to the observer, especially in the foreground. In the distance, the various materials usually will appear only as values. The viewer should be able to distinguish between stone, brick, concrete masonry, wood, glass, roofing materials, etc. Notice that some appear rough and others smooth, some dark and others light. In bright sunlight, even a rough texture is occasionally lost and therefore left completely white.

Study the silhouettes and character of trees and shrubs Get to know their forms, their trunk and branch structures, their foliage textures, and the manner in which they appear in groups. Notice the action of light and shade on the different types of foliage and on the bark, giving individuality to the representation of each species. Many draftsmen simplify and stylize their representations of trees and planting; this is advisable for the student so long as he retains the basic natural characteristics of the subject. Study the planting on professional renderings and the way they relate to the total development. Sketch trees and outdoor scenes from nature to learn firsthand this necessary element of architectural presentation. Effective tree indications can be shown with only trunk and branch structures (as they would appear in winter) as long as their skeleton character is faithfully maintained.

13.4 RENDERING IN PENCIL

For pencil rendering it is recommended to have available two each of the H, HB, 2B, 4B, and 6B drawing pencils. Sharpen one of each grade to a cone point (Fig. 5-1A) for outlines and fine detail work. Remove about $\frac{3}{8}''$ of the wood on the other set and sharpen or wear down to a chisel point (Fig. 5-1B and C) for laying in various tones—often referred to as "pencil painting." In beginning work, the pencil will be more expressive if both sharp and broad points are employed. Later, your individual style—developed after much experimentation and practice—dictates the use of either fine line or broad stroke linework.

Hold the pencil in a natural position, similar to writing, with the hand resting comfortably on the paper. (Always place a small sheet of paper under the hand to eliminate smudging the finished drawing.) Work in a restful, uncramped position. If you are working on thin paper, be sure you have several sheets of underlay paper underneath; this makes the drawing paper more responsive to pencil stroking. One of the secrets of velvety pencil tones is continual *extreme pressure* on the pencil—even on light tones. It makes the strokes more definite and minimizes grainy pencil work. Use harder pencils for lighter tones and softer ones for darker tones. If a tone seems to be too dark when pressure is applied, pick up a harder pencil—but always maintain firm pressure on the pencils if you want to develop interesting textures. Give each stroke identity, especially at its beginning and ending. Notice that occasional white areas left out between strokes contribute sparkle and variety. Artists develop individuality by going about a drawing in their own way; hence, a student must feel free to develop a drawing in his own way, as long as the results are satisfactory. Each person's work will differ, much like his handwriting. The student will find it interesting and also very helpful to observe how professionals treat various features. In addition, it will be good experience—and many accomplished artists have profited by it—to reproduce some of the drawings of the old masters found in art museums.

Fig. 13-12 A pencil presentation and photograph of the finished building.

One point the student must remember is that he must exaggerate features such as contrast between light and dark areas in his composition occasionally, rather than try to make the rendering resemble a photograph (see Fig. 13-12). Plan a well-balanced tone arrangement (with values ranging from extreme darks to white, as shown in Fig. 13-14) before you start rendering. Have the main outlines carefully laid out with light lines, even major shadows, so you will avoid mistakes and not lose control of your drawing. Fine detail such as window muntins can be omitted in the preliminary layout. Landscaping and tree studies are first done on tracing paper overlays. When their composition and general effect are satisfactory, they are transferred to the final drawing with light lines. While most of the strokes representing natural foliage and tone work are done freehand, strong roof lines and other architectural edges may be completed with the help of the straightedge.

Practice Strokes With a grade B pencil sharpened to a conical point, practice the fine line strokes shown in Fig. 13-13A, B, E, F, and G. Try all of these several times to develop discipline in pencil control. The exercises are mainly for showing outline information and suggestions of surfaces and textures. Keep the pencil uniformly dressed throughout the exercises. With a softer pencil (2B or 3B) sharpened to a chisel point, and, using its flat surface, practice the broad stroke exercise shown in Fig. 13-13 C, D, and N. These strokes become useful for pencil washes and various background tones throughout a drawing. Notice that definite pressure is required at the ends and beginnings of strokes. Try graduated tone exercises which will be continually useful in areas varying from a dark to a light value. Try the strokes in the full range of

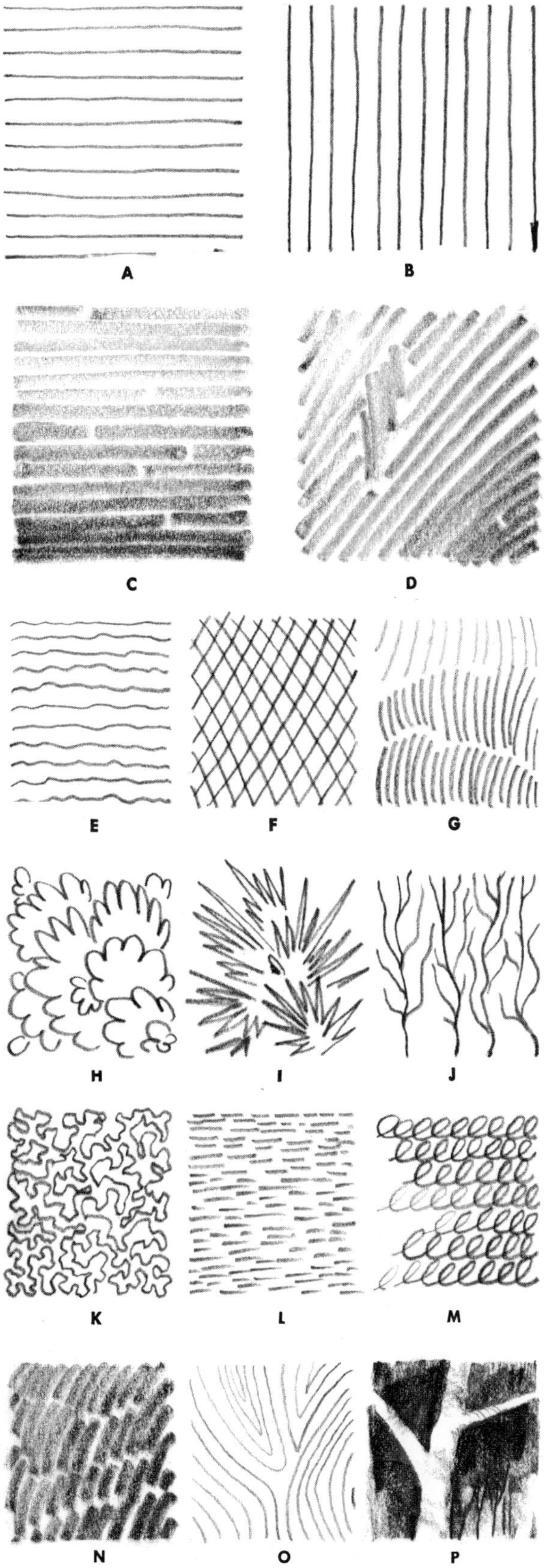

Fig. 13-13 Practice strokes in pencil.

values, from darks to light. Experiment with other methods of your own for creating other tones, since there are unlimited ways of representing them with a pencil. Before applying pencil tones to a final rendering, evaluate their suitability first on practice paper.

For filling large areas, a broad sketching pencil, resembling a carpenter's pencil and available at art supply stores, can be useful, and a graphite stick may also be found appropriate for showing sharp edges and gradual, uniform tones. The wide pencil will save time in laying in larger backgrounds and in representing many other features. Observe the manner in which E. A. Moulthrop has so ably given a charming and casual quality to typical architectural subjects with the use of a broad sketching pencil (Figs. 13-14 and 13-15). These drawings were originally done on tracing paper.

Pencil Textures DRAW BRICKWORK DIFFERENTLY AT DIFFERENT SCALES. The need for rendering brick walls arises frequently in architectural subjects. For this, pencil is especially suitable because it is a medium that lends itself well to soft, tonal variations. Care must be taken to plan the general tone of all the brick surfaces in respect to light and shade in the composition. In full sun, for instance, the tone value of brick will usually be very light, shown with generous areas of white, devoid of detail. In shade, the values become darker tones with more of the brick detail in evidence. Corners, where contrast is intense, must be carefully done to reveal the rough nature of the brick coursing joints. When drawing brick, first establish basic background values with the broad stroke; put in shade and shadow areas where they seem necessary. Change the direction of some of the strokes to avoid monotony. Usually, shadow lines are suggested and allowances made for reflected light during this step. The representation of the actual brick is then applied over the tonework.

For drawing brick at a small scale, use a series of parallel wavy lines, broken occasionally, to produce a convincing texture (see Fig. 13-16A). It is important that the lines are in perspective and that their width and spacing are scaled properly. Remember that the height of one brick course with a mortar joint is only about 2½″. Although the linework is broken at irregular intervals, vertical joints of the brick are ignored. Do not try to indicate each brick; even the use of occasional diagonal strokes, similar in value to

Fig. 13-14 Rendering done with the broad sketching pencil.

Fig. 13-15 Rendering showing various textures in pencil.

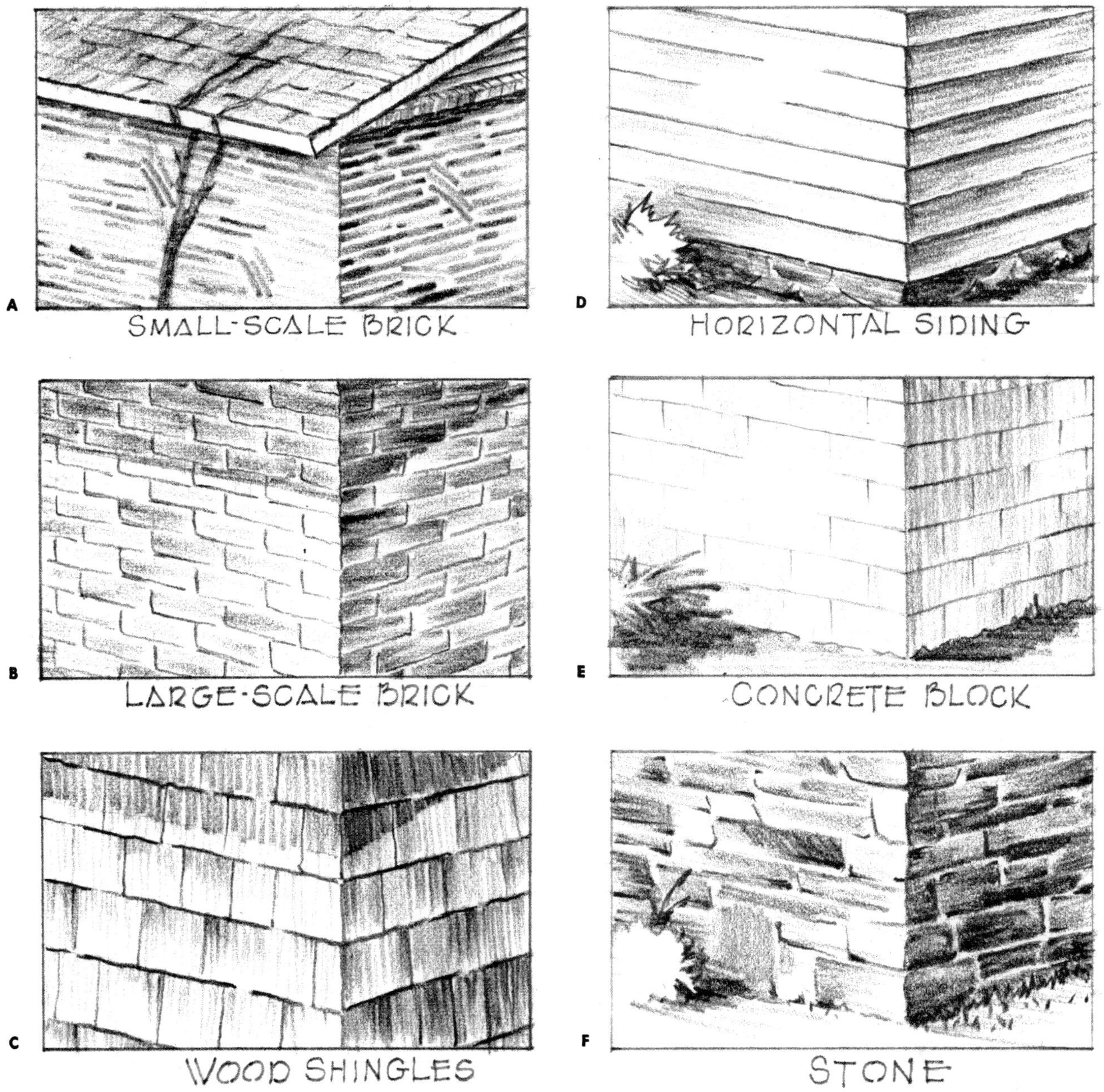

Fig. 13-16 Architectural textures in pencil.

surrounding linework, will help relieve the tedious regularity of coursing. As suggested previously, let a bit of pure white show in a few areas. Be sure that shadows expressing the relief of corners, offsets, and reveals at window and door openings, are carefully handled. Brick walls can often be a dark value at corners opposite the light, and as they recede, they can be made gradually lighter, to where extremely dark tree backgrounds provide sharp contrasts.

Brick surfaces near the viewer must be larger in scale and must therefore be given more individual brick detail (see Fig. 13-16B). For best results, use a pencil dressed to the proper brick width and show (with various short strokes) the brick and mortar joints between. Go over occasional strokes to bring out variations in color. Make bold sharp-ending strokes. Fine line shadows along the lower edge and side of the individual brick, here and there, help emphasize the texture. Give brick in shadow a very dark value. Do not forget the shadows below brick windowsills. Shadows from nearby foliage falling upon a wall will help create interest; they are drawn with vertical strokes briskly applied over the finished brick.

Stonework can appear smooth or rough. Much of the artistry of stonework is provided by the arrangement of the various unit sizes and the mortar joint pattern throughout the wall. The appearance of stone varies greatly, depending upon coursing, unit sizes, and roughness. Cut stone usually has uniform coursing and a rather smooth texture, whereas rubble stonework may have various unit sizes, and shadows indicate that the stones are rough and irregular. The rendering should capture the intended texture. The bold treatment of the stonework contributes to the rustic appearance of a building.

Begin stonework by lightly indicating the unit pattern throughout the wall, regardless of the desired texture. As a rule, patterns showing a dominance of horizontal courses are the most pleasing (see Fig. 13-16F). Place larger stones at corners for stability, and vary the sizes and shapes of the smaller ones in between to avoid regularity. Next, shade each stone with parallel broad strokes, making sure that the stones vary in value for interest and that the strokes change in direction occasionally. Leave generous amounts of white areas, especially if you plan dark features in back of the stone. Possibly, the suggestion of shadows, drawn in fine lines emanating from the lower edge of a few stones, may be all that need be shown in these areas. Let the mortar joints remain light and not very wide. As in brickwork, treat stone corners carefully, particularly where strong light and shade contrasts appear, and where stone is bordered by sky. Emphasize stone textures near the center of interest where they should be darkest.

Use a dotted technique to represent stucco (Fig. 13-26I); a similar method can be used for concrete block, by merely adding a few fine lines to suggest coursing.

Wood siding is drawn with parallel lines. The general tone of wood siding must be considered with respect to composition and light and shade—also to color, if painted. If it is painted white, only the shaded areas may require a background value. If, on the other hand, the wood is to be stained, more of the values will appear darker. However, use white highlights even on the darker wood surfaces to prevent monotony. Apply background values with the broad stroke mainly in the direction of the wood grain.

Show clapboard siding with fine horizontal lines (occasionally a few heavy lines may be needed), which represent the shadow below each board (see Fig. 13-16D). Spacing of the linework depends upon the width of the boards to the weather. Vary the weight of the lines, but in areas of a wall where light intensity is the strongest, omit them altogether. Be sure the lines are in perspective. Care must be taken to represent the sawtooth profile at corners or where the clapboards abut vertical wood trim. Show wood louvers in a similar way—with parallel lines and a sawtooth shade at the shadow side of the louver strips.

Represent board-and-batten siding by carefully drawing the edges of each vertical batten strip with light lines. Give the boards between the strips a light gray value and leave the strips white, except in shade. Accent the shadow side of the batten strips with a fine dark line. In shade, darken the boards rather than the battens (see Fig. 13-17). Shadows falling across the wall must give evidence of the batten offsets.

Wood shingle siding is rendered by first drawing the horizontal coursing with freehand wavy lines to indicate the shadow at the butts. Break the lines frequently and vary their darkness to give the wall a weathered, rustic effect. Draw staggered vertical joints between shingles only here and there with the fine point. Then apply broad strokes in slightly varying tones vertically throughout (to simulate the wood grain); the tone value of these strokes should create a pleasing overall value composition. Indicate shadows with dark, bold strokes.

Roofing shingles must be given an identification value in the composition; usually it will vary throughout the roof surface. Coursing is drawn with wavy, horizontal lines, and very few vertical strokes are shown. Background tones are drawn down the slope of the roof to indicate a slight weathered effect. In some roofing materials the shingle coursing is not pronounced; the drawing must make this clear. Built-up roofing may be indicated with a dot technique in shadow and at important corners only.

Glass is usually dark. In general, glass appears dark unless there are drapes, blinds, or shades directly in back of it to receive the sunlight. Highlights on glass appear white. To indicate the dark areas, make definite broad strokes with a 3B or 4B pencil. The upper part of the shaded area is made the darkest. For highlighting, leave white openings that slope in the direction of the light—these will suggest the smoothness of the glass. Reflections of foliage or of surrounding features will add interest (see Fig. 13-17). In direct sunlight or on planes facing the viewer, windows are especially dark and more reflective on their shaded sides or on planes slant-

Fig. 13-17 Pencil rendering showing reflections in glass.

ing away from the viewer. Leave muntins and mullions white if they are in direct sunlight. Large glassed areas may require suggestions of furniture within, since an expanse of glass admits a considerable amount of light to the interior.

The surface of glass is generally recessed several inches or more from the surface of the wall. This means that reveals and surrounding trim must be carefully drawn. When drawing window units such as double-hung or casement (or even entire glass walls), show drapery or curtains along the inside edges where they would ordinarily be seen. Indicate the folds of drapery with vertical light and dark areas, and show shadows from muntin bars as wavy lines across the drapery (see Fig. 13-17). Curtains or other window treatment should look realistic. Remember that muntins and division bars, though white in sunlight, appear darker on the shadow side.

TREES PROVIDE A NATURAL SETTING. Trees, drawn in correct proportion to a building, establish the relative scale in the viewer's mind and add a note of softness and charm to the rendering. Often they are drawn in natural groupings as background, or a few may be shown in the foreground to achieve good composition. Earlier in this chapter we stressed the importance of direct observation from nature. This is particularly helpful in familiarizing the student with the individual characteristics of different tree species, and before long, he will be able to draw trees from memory. Their silhouette, their trunk and branch structure, their bark texture, their appearance at the base of the trunk, and their foliage clusters and leaf forms—all play a part in giving tree species identity.

Before drawing a tree, study its silhouette (Fig. 13-18) so that you get to know the character and form of the trunk and the angle of the branches in relation to it. Then lightly lay out the trunk and branch structure, which becomes the skeleton of the tree. Give the structure personality but do not overly distort it—this only detracts from the building; reserve slight distortions for needed interest in an otherwise weak composition. Notice that branches radiate in all directions—in front and back of the trunk, as well as the sides—and become consistently smaller toward the top. The pine tree, however, has a slightly different trunk system. The thickness of the trunk remains similar for most of its height and only near the top does it gradually diminish, where small branches radiate almost horizontally with needle clusters of various sizes. No two trees, even of the same species, are exactly alike; the drawing should show slight variations, yet the identifying characteristics should be present.

Fig. 13-18 Shapes of various species of trees.

After the basic structure is established, draw the clusters of foliage lightly (see Fig. 13-19B) with some darker areas to indicate shade; strive to make the general pattern a pleasing one. In the foreground, of course, more detail must be shown on tree representations. Render the foliage with the broad stroke using a 4B pencil, starting with the darkest values. Have various tones throughout the foliage, using a fanlike series of continuous pencil strokes. Some foliage may be better represented by slightly different stroking, but accent the bottom edges of foliage clusters. Leave branches or parts of the trunk white where dark foliage falls in back of them. Remember as you work that highlights on leaf clusters appear white, similar to the highlight of a sphere; whereas shade appears dark below clusters. Treat the trunk as a cylindrical form to give it volume. Then draw coarse bark, if the species requires it, with most of the bold dashes near the edges of the trunk to give it a rough, uneven appearance. In direct sunlight leave some of the trunk entirely white. Soften any harsh vertical lines at the base of the tree by indicating grass or shadows. Undulating tree shadows falling on grass provide a convenient way of showing rise and fall of the terrain.

Show shrubbery near the building. Evergreen shrubs used for foundation planting and as accents help to tie building and ground together and eliminate hard vertical architectural lines, especially at corners. Pleasing groups of various indigenous species contribute a landscaped appearance and help to emphasize the center of interest, usually the front door. Shrubs can be shown in their natural forms, or trimmed

Fig. 13-19 Steps in drawing a tree.

into continuous geometric forms, such as a hedge along a walkway (see Fig. 13-20).

In rendering shrubbery, outline the groupings first before applying the broad stroke patterns shown in Fig. 13-13. Again, leave white areas. On some, show indications of the branch structure, and be sure that the darkest values are near the ground where shadows appear. Shrubs in front of a building should be rendered before drawing the linework on the building. This eliminates needless erasing of wall textures and lines.

Tie elements together with grass indications. Grass may be represented with broad horizontal lines, drawn with a T square if necessary, and accented along edges of drives and walks. Make the indications lighter in sun, of course, than in shade. Grass can be suggested by drawing it only where shadows fall along the ground, leaving lighted areas entirely white; too much grass might de-emphasize the center of interest. Short, vertical strokes made with the fine point can then be shown along borders and edges. Some delineators use a series of looping strokes drawn horizontally and close together to represent grass (see Fig. 13-13M); others use rows of short vertical strokes, varying in value, throughout the shaded areas. Be sure the edge of grass indications, extending to the edge of the rendering, forms an interesting outline. See Fig. 13-21.

Clouds and sky are usually not indicated on pencil renderings. If they seem necessary for the composition, make clouds rather subdued and remember that sky appears lightest near the horizon and gradually darker above.

As we previously mentioned, trees and shrubbery on a rendering should be merely suggestive rather than too complex—subordinate to the architecture. For that reason many renderings

Fig. 13-20 Shrubbery suggestions.

Fig. 13-21 Representing grass in foreground.

are shown with stylized indications (see Fig. 12-32). In this technique, trees and planting are simplified, often showing only outlines or branch structures, others only flat tones of foliage masses. The treatment is effective if the natural forms and tree characteristics have been retained. Nature must be the source for ideas in arriving at authentic stylized treatments. Even the representation of people can be simplified (Fig. 13-22).

Fig. 13-22 Indications of people must be drawn to the correct scale.

Use a value scale to plan values and contrast. Nearly everything we see is made up of an almost unlimited number of shadings of colors or grays ranging from black to white. The variation of lightness or darkness of color or grays is known as *value*. To the beginner most subjects appear to be muted in values that are difficult to distinguish. Early trials by students often result in dull gray renderings that are composed of nearly identical values. But this dullness must be avoided at all costs.

Contrast is defined as the striking difference in adjacent elements of a composition, whether by the use of color, value, texture, outline, or treatment. We know that the appearance of contrast is relative (Fig. 13-23). A black value next to a gray value will not appear as dark as a black value adjacent to a white area. Likewise, a relatively loud sound in a quiet bedroom may be very disturbing, whereas the same sound in a busy street may go unnoticed.

Before starting a drawing, develop a value scale that ranges from black to white similar to the one shown in Fig. 13-24. A value scale to the artist is similar to a score to the musician. Each produces a sense of order to the creation—the musician with sound value, the artist with color

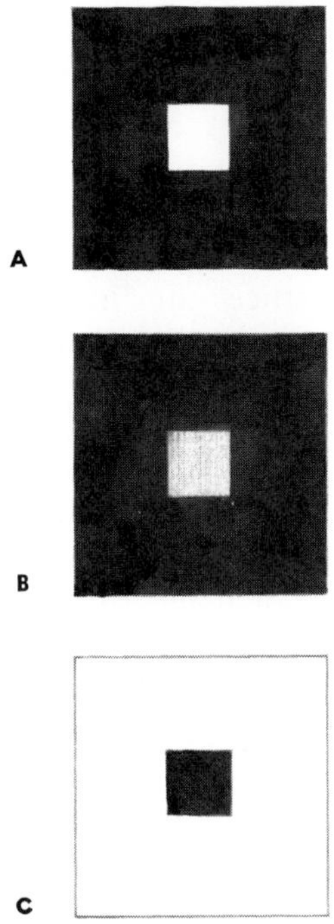

Fig. 13-23 Contrast of values.

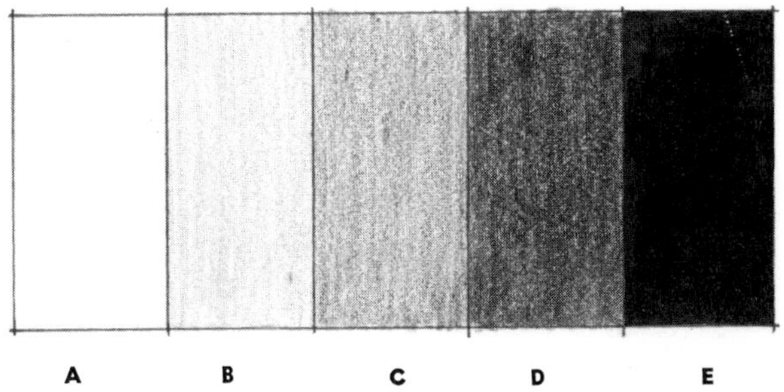

Fig. 13-24 Use a value scale to help you plan the light and dark areas.

value. White and black with three or four intermediate grays between are satisfactory for the range of most drawings. Plan your drawings with the use of the value scale so that important features are accented with extreme contrasts; whites against blacks or blacks against whites, and make less important features or outlines with lesser amounts of contrast. Plan a definite arrangement of the values. This is necessary even if reality is exaggerated to some degree. But if you want sparkle and interest in your pencil drawings, have light and dark values provide contrast where the dominance counts most. The size of the white or black areas also plays a part in developing brightness. Position the values in the composition so they have variety yet balance (Fig. 13-25). Use dramatic profiles where the

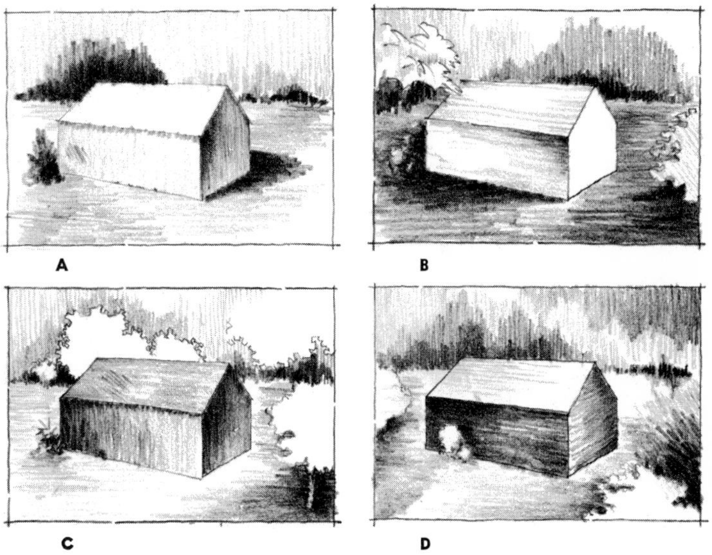

Fig. 13-25 Planning value layouts.

highest contrast occurs. This *shape accent* should be reserved for the dominating features only, since too many accents tend to cancel out each other. The pattern or repeating quality which holds the whole together is known as *matrix*.

13.5 RENDERING IN INK

Materials

1. Black waterproof India ink—the standard brands; can be diluted with water for gray washes or gray ink linework;
2. Technical fountain pen, points No. 0, No. 2—for lettering and other uniform linework;
3. Ruling pen—for various width ruled lines;
4. Hunt's No. 102 Crow Quill pen—a fine, flexible point for delicate linework;
5. Hunt's No. 99 pen—a nibbed point for general work;
6. Speedball No. B–6—a round nib pen for bold linework;
7. Small pointed watercolor brush; and
8. Small bottle of white tempera color.

Select a strong paper or board that will take ink well. A smooth surface is preferable, because a rough surface tends to interfere with fine pen stroking. Good grades of tracing paper and illustration board are satisfactory; plate-finish Bristol board, if available, will be found very desirable.

Pen and ink drawing requires more care in planning than pencil. Pencil can be erased or darkened by repeated strokes until a desired

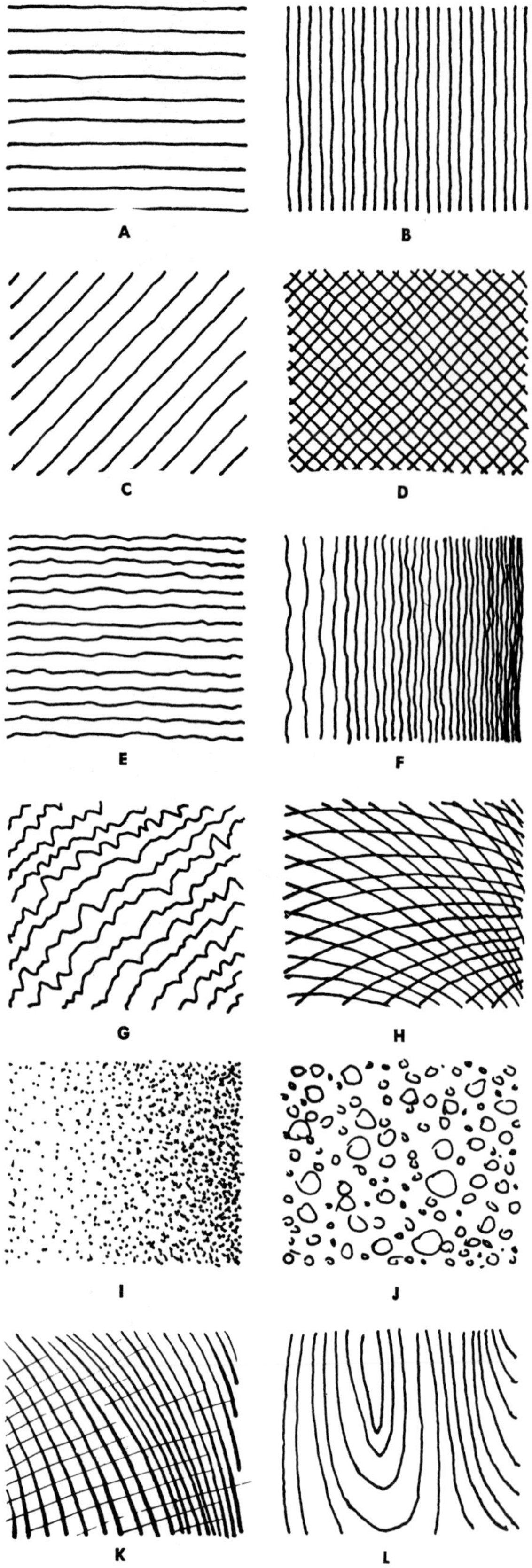

Fig. 13-26 Practice strokes in pen and ink.

value is attained; but ink work is difficult to remove or modify once it is put on paper. Successful pen renderings also require a careful balanced composition of white, black, and intermediate values. Various line or dot techniques must be found to represent the intermediate values since the ink remains black unless, of course, it is diluted. Elements of the composition must therefore be reduced to their simplest expression to give the rendering a crisp yet delicate appearance. Photographic realism should not be the objective with pen and ink.

Before you begin, a word of advice: do not make the mistake of using the same width pen point throughout your entire drawing. Unless you are experienced in pen and ink technique, this is likely to make the drawing look monotonous and uninteresting. Use two or three points of different widths to give the lines character. If you want to soften the appearance of the ink rendering, do all the linework freehand; it is usually more appealing. To obtain a quality of perspective depth, draw tree and planting indications in the far background with a fine pen, the mid-distance trees with an intermediate point, and the foreground features with a broader pen.

Begin by practicing the various pen strokes shown in Fig. 13-26. Acquaint yourself with the capabilities of each pen; try each tone shown in the exercise. Experiment with the tone representations before you use them on your finish rendering. By all means, have the outlines and edges of all values laid out lightly in pencil (as well as other major linework), using care not to groove the paper, before you do any inking. Pencil lines can be easily erased when the ink is thoroughly dry. If you are not pressed for time, make a *value study* of the composition. After the perspective is completed in pencil, place a sheet of tracing paper over it and quickly establish the general value patterns rather roughly, using a soft pencil or charcoal. Avoid details on the study; instead, strive for pleasing value patterns that can be created by contrasts of light and shade and from the landscaping composition. When finished, this becomes your guide for choosing line technique, values, and landscaping on the final ink drawing. See Figs. 13-27 and 13-28.

To avoid smearing ink lines, start at the top of the drawing and work down. Remember that ink work cannot be rushed. To save time in

A

B

Fig. 13-27 (A) Partially completed pen and ink rendering of the small home discussed in Chapter 10; (B) completed pen and ink rendering of small home.

Fig. 13-28 A student ink drawing.

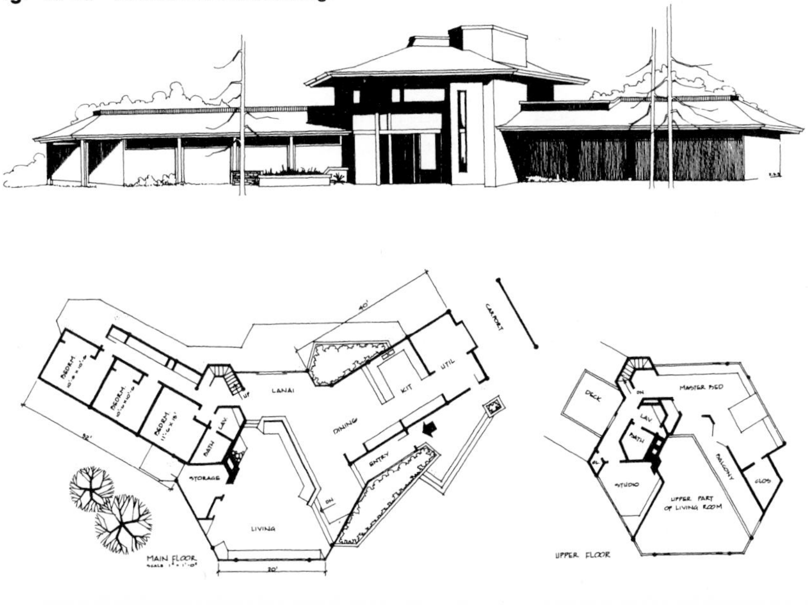

filling large black areas, outline them with the pen and fill in the remainder with a small watercolor brush. Be sure there are sufficient areas left white to give the impression of strong light, as we mentioned earlier. If a minor mistake should occur in the linework, white tempera applied with a brush will cover it. Check the value study from time to time to see that the total desired effect is developing. The same basic principles of composition that were discussed in connection with pencil rendering apply equally to work done in ink.

13.6 RENDERING WITH COLOR

After you have made a number of pencil and pen and ink renderings, you may have the urge to try working in color. There is something exciting about color work. It is dramatic and commands attention, and there is no question about its compelling qualities on architectural presentations if the color has been carefully handled. If, on the other hand, the coloring appears hard, unharmonious, and detracting, it would have been better if the presentation had been done in black and white. Color is a completely different graphic dimension requiring mental application not required in other work. The study of color is rather extensive, entailing scientific and psychological aspects, and there are many good books covering the subject. Here, we can only discuss the major points, primarily to introduce the beginning student to the basic principles of color and to clear up any misconceptions he may have.

Let us start our study with an examination of the color wheel (inside the front cover) showing the interrelationship of basic colors. The color wheel, as you will notice, places colors in an organized position around the circle, relative to each other, for convenient reference by the student or color artist, and the wheel is the result of extensive study about color characteristics. It is handy for selecting actual color combinations or as an aid in mixing pigments to arrive at a desired color on the palette. Many of the rules governing the effective use of color are based on the relationship of the colors on the wheel. It does not solve all the problems concerning color, yet it can guide the bewildered novice in his early work; later these color characteristics will come automatically.

Color Term Definitions

PRIMARY COLORS: Red, yellow, and blue, from which, theoretically, all other colors can be made.

SECONDARY COLORS: Orange, green, and purple, made by mixing adjacent primary colors on the color wheel.

TERTIARY COLORS: Colors located between primary and secondary colors on the color wheel and made by mixing adjacent colors.

HUE: The term used to designate the name of a color. Red, blue-green, orange, blue, etc., are different hues.

VALUE: The lightness or darkness of the same hue, such as light red or dark red.

CHROMA: The intensity or purity of a color, namely the degree to which it has been diluted or neutralized.

SHADE: A darkened value of a color.

TINT: A lightened value of a color, usually by the addition of white.

COMPLEMENTS: Colors located opposite each other on the color wheel and considered harmonious. Complements mixed together will produce a gray if the result ends midway between the two colors. A color can be darkened by adding a slight amount of its complement. Complements of equal chroma and value are usually not pleasing, but by varying their values or chromas in a subtle manner—for example a dark green and a light red—a more pleasing color combination results.

MONOCHROMATIC: A color scheme using values of only one color. For instance sepia produces a very artistic monochromatic color scheme.

ANALOGOUS: A color scheme employing two or three adjacent colors on the color wheel; usually more interest is created if one of the colors predominates the scheme. For example, yellow, yellow-green, and green, with the yellow predominating.

WARM COLORS: Reds, oranges, and yellows, which seem to advance toward the viewer.

COLD COLORS: Blues, greens, or violets, which appear cool and seem to recede when seen from the same distance as warm colors. Gray can be either cold or warm.

Pure pigments, made from plants or minerals, reflect particular colored waves, while absorbing others. Pigments do this in varying degrees, so that experimentation in mixing various colors is necessary—arriving at the desired colors is a matter of trial and error. When mixing colors it will become apparent that certain pigments have a greater affinity for one color than for another.

Colors on renderings, as we mentioned, should be kept soft and subdued, often grayed. Greens for foliage, for instance, should be yellowish green hues, rather than hard, high-intensity greens. If you will look about at the surrounding landscape you will notice that nature's colors are restful to the eye. Few abrupt, hard colors exist unless put there by man. Even the coloring on buildings should utilize soft, natural colorings of building materials to complement the landscape. Try to have three basic harmonious colors in your composition: one in the foreground, one in the mid-distance, and one in the background. In general, these three distinct planes can be treated in a monochromatic color scheme, by using various values of one color for light-and-shade effects. Stay with simple, uncomplicated color combinations; usually a few colors will be sufficient and more appropriate and also easier to handle than many colors. The choice of colors, of course, is a personal thing, and you will find with experience that impressions created by color are affected by many things—light, adjacent colors, paper, patterns of the drawing, etc. Make it a habit to "see" the colors around you, learn to identify them, and you have taken the first step in trying to master this troublesome technique.

Colored Pencils One of the simplest methods of coloring a rendering is with colored pencils. Although many colors are available, they lack subtlety because a direct application is required. Some pencils, however, have water-soluble colors; the lines made by this type can be blended in with a wet brush to create a watercolor effect.

A rather effective color pencil rendering can be done on a dark black-line Ozalid print of an elevation view. The pencil tracing is run through the machine so that the background of the print becomes gray rather than white, giving it an intermediate tone throughout the paper. Light pencil colors are used to bring out the architecture and to contrast the gray background. Major colored areas are filled in with close, parallel lines made with instruments, and the foliage indications are added in an abstract manner. An elevation rendering, for example, can be done very quickly in this manner (see Fig. 13-29).

Watercolor Down through the years, watercolor has been an important medium in architectural presentation. One distinguishes between two general types of watercolor work—transparent and opaque. As the name of the former implies, *transparent* type watercolor pigments are used. Thin washes are spread over special paper stretched carefully on the drawing board, or over commercially prepared watercolor board. In some cases the washes may have to be superimposed over each other to arrive at desired values and effects. *Opaque* watercolors, either tempera or casein, are slightly different in that they have the capacity of covering different colors beneath. They are applied in a creamy consistency rather than as a thin wash. Although the techniques of transparent and opaque watercolors are basically different, beautiful work can result by using both media, separately or in combination.

Because tempera does not necessarily have to be diluted, and because of its opaqueness, it is the ideal medium for the student's early work. Tempera can be put on regular inexpensive illustration board; and even though the paint is water-soluble, it can easily be applied in successive layers, making it ideal for the beginner. He will gain self-confidence when he sees that mistakes can be covered without much trouble or carefully sponged off with a damp sponge. However, tempera colors possess strong, vivid qualities that require toning down, done by mixing with white, gray, or with

Fig. 13-29 Rendering of a front elevation with colored pencils.

their complements. In mixing, as well as in method of application, tempera paints handle much like artist's oil colors.

Purchase the materials shown in the material list at your art or drafting supply store. You will find that the more expensive brands are more enjoyable to work with. Brushes must be cleaned in water before the tempera dries; never allow brushes to rest on their bristles, since they would soon lose their shape and become worthless.

Materials for Tempera Rendering

COLORS (in tubes)	BRUSHES
Chinese White Alizarin Crimson Cadmium Red—Medium Cadmium Yellow—Pale Yellow Ochre Prussian Blue Ultramarine Blue Viridian Ivory Black Burnt Sienna Burnt Umber	1 No. 4 red sable, pointed watercolor brush 1 No. 1 and 1 No. 4 red sable "Brights" flat-end brush 1 No. 5 flat bristle color brush 1 Regular painter's nylon bristle brush—1″

GENERAL
Muffin tin Pint jar (for water) Old dinner plate (for a palette) Baby sponge

Painting a Color Wheel To acquaint yourself with the tempera pigments, make your first color exercise the duplication of a color wheel. It will not only be a helpful exercise but it will also become a serviceable reference when doing other color work. Lay out the wheel on illustration board using a 6″ outer and a 4″ inner diameter. Divide it into twelve equal 30° segments as shown. Allow a small amount of white space between each segment so that the colors do not run together. Paint the primary colors first, making sure that you have enough remaining pigment to mix the other colors. Use cadmium yellow—pale for the yellow, alizarin crimson with a bit of cadmium red for the red, and Prussian blue mixed with a little ultramarine blue for the blue. In mixing the secondary colors, see if you can get them from the primaries; otherwise you may have to draw on the other tube pigments. Viridian requires a touch of yellow for the proper green. Then mix and paint in the tertiary colors to complete the color wheel. Label all the colors correctly.

Further experience will be gained by mixing various pigments and noting the results. See what happens when white is mixed with other colors. Try mixing a slight amount of black with the various colors as well. Try mixing complements. Be sure you feed small amounts of a strong color into a weaker color when mixing; otherwise you may end up with more color than you need. All this experimentation will be helpful before attempting an actual rendering. Other exercises should include architectural textures such as stone, brick, wood, etc., and the painting of trees, shrubs, and foliage. Study professional tempera renderings for ways of handling these features.

Helpful Hints Some artists cover the entire rendering with a thin sepia or pale yellow transparent wash before applying the tempera.

Do not overstroke the paint, let some of the brush work give character to the forms.

Blending can be done with a finger while the paint is wet. Blends can also be accomplished with a *drybrush* technique.

Avoid using too much white for light value tints. The overuse of white pigment results in a "chalky" painting, often appearing cold and lifeless.

Values in color rendering are just as important as they are in black and white renderings. Here too, careful value studies are necessary in planning color renderings. See Fig. 13-30.

To create harmonious color combinations, the renderer does not have to stay with the colors found in nature—green grass, blue sky, etc. Slight modifications of natural colors, as long as they are plausible and not extreme, create interest and a note of abstraction.

If the tempera painting is to occupy only a small rectangular area of a larger presentation, surround the area with masking tape before starting to paint so it will stay within bounds.

Start the painting with flat tones in the major areas; then add the texture indications and the detail strokes in a systematic manner over the backgrounds.

When painting the landscaping, apply indications in the distance first, usually with flat tones along the horizon, then add the mid-distance foliage, and finally the trees and shrubs in the foreground. Paint any figures last.

Fig. 13-30 Rendering in tempera.

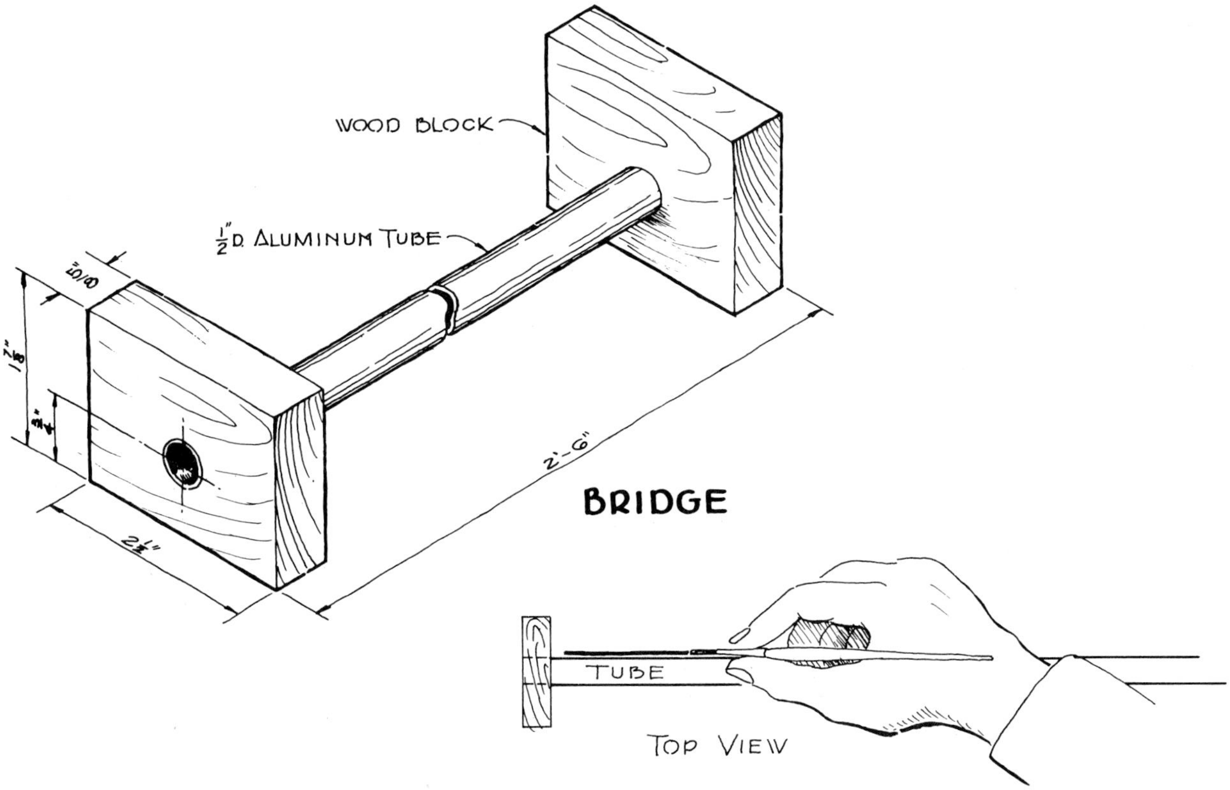

Fig. 13·31 Convenient handrest for tempera painting.

If necessary, tempera can be reduced to a thin wash and brushed over underlying colors to soften their appearance and yet retain their identity.

Paint mullions over the general glass areas with a pointed brush or a ruling pen; or use a small (No. 1) flat-end brush if the mullions have more width. The flat brush is easier to control.

For painting straight lines on a building, use a "bridge" such as shown in Fig. 13-31, which can be made from an aluminum tube or wooden dowel (about 30″ long) with blocks of wood at each end. Have about $\frac{1}{2}$″ clearance between the tube and the working surface. When using the bridge, rest several fingers and the thumb comfortably along the tube, with the brush held between the thumb and forefinger as you move the brush uniformly along the surface. For more versatility, make the clearance at the top of the blocks $\frac{7}{8}$″ so that it can be turned over and used with larger brushes.

A more economical bridge can be made with an ordinary brass-edged ruler having art gum erasers (cubes) glued to each end (Fig. 13-32).

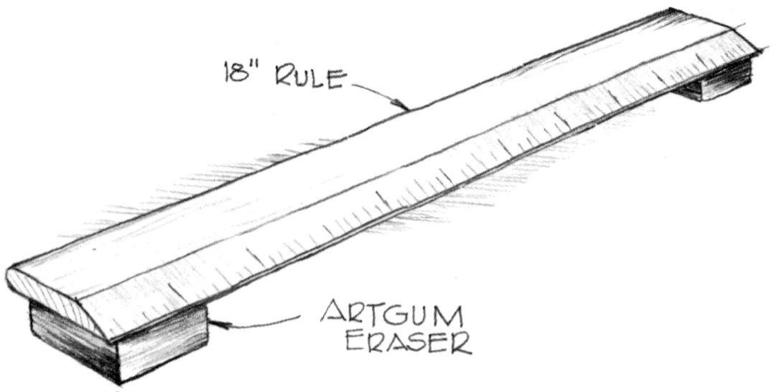

Fig. 13-32 An inexpensive bridge can be made by gluing artgum erasers to a brass-edge rule.

EXERCISES

1. On $8\frac{1}{2}$″ × 11″ white drawing paper, lay out six equal rectangles with $\frac{1}{2}$″ space between as shown in Fig. 13-16. Using a soft pencil, render the following material textures in the rectangles: brick, rubble stone, coursed ashlar stone, concrete block, board-and-batten wood siding, and wood shingle siding.

2. Draw a realistic deciduous tree; a coniferous tree; a group of evergreen shrubs—all in pencil.

3. Using the scale $\frac{1}{4}$″ = 1′–0″, draw the elevation view shown in Fig. 13-6 and render it in pencil; add appropriate landscaping.

4. On $8\frac{1}{2}$″ × 11″ white drawing paper, duplicate the ink textures shown in Fig. 13-26.

5. Using the scale $\frac{1}{4}$″ = 1′–0″, make a pencil presentation drawing of a lakeside cabin. Use 20″ × 30″ illustration board and include a plot plan, floor plan, and perspective view.

6. Make an ink presentation drawing of an original home design, using the scale $\frac{1}{8}$″ = 1′–0″. Use 20″ × 30″ illustration board and include a plot plan, floor plan, two elevations, and a perspective view.

7. Make an ink presentation drawing of a small commercial building; include a floor plan and a perspective view, using the scale $\frac{1}{8}$″ = 1′–0″.

8. With colored pencils, render the front elevation of a residence drawn to the scale $\frac{1}{4}$″ = 1′–0″. Use either 20″ × 30″ illustration board or a black-line Ozalid print of the elevation view.

9. On 20″ × 30″ illustration board, render a small commercial building in tempera color. Show only the perspective view that has been drawn in pencil from the floor plan.

10. Make an ink and tempera presentation drawing of a contemporary golf shelter. Draw a plot plan, floor plan, and elevation view in ink; render a perspective in tempera color. Use 20″ × 30″ gray illustration board and draw the views other than the colored perspective with black ink and white tempera to give variety to the linework.

REVIEW QUESTIONS

1. What are the advantages—for client and architect—of preparing a presentation drawing of an architectural proposal?

2. For what reason are perspective views generally effective in presentation work?

3. What is meant by "optical balance"?

4. Why are plumbing fixtures and furniture usually shown on presentation plan views?

5. What media are appropriate for rendering small drawings?

6. On perspective renderings, why should the details nearest the observer be made more prominent than those in the distance?

7. What methods can the renderer employ to produce emphasis?

8. What do landscaping indications contribute to a perspective? Indications of people?

9. What is meant by a "value study"?

10. How are analogous colors related to each other on the color wheel?

"Money is a good slave but a bad master."—Horace

14

Drawing a Small Commercial Building

The planning of commercial buildings requires considerable research on the part of the designer or student. Each type of building presents problems that are unique—problems that must be resolved if the project is to be successful. One might say that success or failure of a commercial venture is frequently contingent on the qualities of the building itself. Because of the individual nature of each project, only general comments can be made about planning. For more specific information and to acquire a good background in this area of architecture, students must resort to personal observation, library references, and architectural magazines. Of course, in actual practice the designer would have to work closely with a client, who most likely would furnish definite requirements for a project. The designer nevertheless must thoroughly understand the activities for which the building is intended before he can do a creditable job of planning the project and completing the set of drawings. The following general factors are often encountered in planning a small commercial building:

1. Code restrictions and zoning regulations;
2. Efficient use of land and construction economy;
3. Floor space requirements for various activities;
4. Public traffic flow;
5. Accommodation for: manufacturing, shipping-

receiving, secretarial work, sales, administration, storage spaces, special equipment, and building maintenance;
6. Layout of parking facilities;
7. Layout of counters, display cases, and show windows;
8. Provision for public and employee rest rooms;
9. Provision for communication between spaces (halls, stairs, elevators, etc.);
10. Provision for noise control;
11. Provision for air conditioning;
12. Selection of materials for permanency; and
13. Selection of colors for harmony.

Many small commercial buildings for offices and trade are constructed with load-bearing masonry walls, slab-on-grade floors, and steel bar joists for the roof structure (See Fig. 14-1). The joists rest on a reinforced bond beam formed with lintel block as the top course of the exterior walls. A fiberboard accoustical ceiling (Fig. 14-2) is merely hung from the joists at the desired height with the use of wires and channel sections as shown on the detail. In this economical construction, the concrete block sub-walls are frequently left exposed and painted with masonry paints to form the interior wall surfaces. With various modifications interior partitions are commonly 4″-thick concrete block painted as well. Codes usually do not allow wood-frame stud partitions in commercial areas. Vinyl or asbestos tile set in mastic provide satisfactory finish floors over the slab unless subjected to unusual wearing conditions.

Front entrances and display windows are frequently constructed of stock aluminum tubing cut to size and fabricated according to dimensions shown on the drawings. Doors, plate glass, and insulated panels of prefinished materials can be combined into the aluminum frames to form functional and attractive front wall units (see Fig. 14-3). Notice that manufacturers' stock numbers are shown on the drawings to indicate the correct frame profiles, and complete unit dimensions are given to provide a basis for fabrication. (Check *Sweet's Architectural File* for the various stock frame materials available for store fronts.)

Often landscape architects are employed to devise interesting settings for commercial buildings which soften the architecture and provide a natural relationship to the land. An example of a typical landscape plan is shown in Fig. 14-4.

The following drawings (Figs. 14-5 through 14-12) are the major ones from a complete set for a small suburban bank building; only some of the detail drawings have been omitted. They are reproductions of the actual architectural tracings originally drawn in pencil on 22″ × 34″ tracing paper and reduced to page size. This completed project represents a typical economical solution to the needs of a client who desired an efficient yet pleasant-appearing structure. The drafting technique is an example of professional work. On similar original projects, students will find that many of the features found on these drawings will be adaptable to theirs.

Like most architectural projects, this bank building required numerous preliminary sketches before problems were resolved and before final working drawings could be started. All the needs and activities of a small bank had to be considered in refining the sketches. Private offices, bookkeeping areas, vaults, boardroom, storage spaces, rest rooms, teller cages, mechanical equipment had to be allotted their proportional amount of floor space after the general size of the building had been determined. Naturally, customer traffic flow had to be considered and sufficient space provided for it. Notice that even an outside teller's cage was required.

The logical structural solution seemed to be a 1-story steel frame building with steel joists used to support the poured gypsum and built-up roof. Structural unity was maintained around the modular column spacings, 15′–0″ on center. Where possible, the steel-tube columns were placed within masonry walls; and where convenient on exterior walls, they were placed between fixed glass to form mullions requiring no additional trim. Brick and concrete-block cavity walls were selected for the major exterior walls for durability, insulation, and appearance. Because of the column unity, the exterior brick walls were divided into uniform panels by the vertical fixed-glass windows. Tinted glass was specified to furnish soft, natural light and reduce glare. The vertical windows, brick panels, and copper fascia and battens give the building its specific character, and all minor details were devised to complement these design features. A raised central ceiling allowed narrow clerestory windows to flood the public lobby with natural light without restricting the placement of offices and minor rooms completely around this large customer area. The two main entrances provided unobstructed traffic flow from front to back.

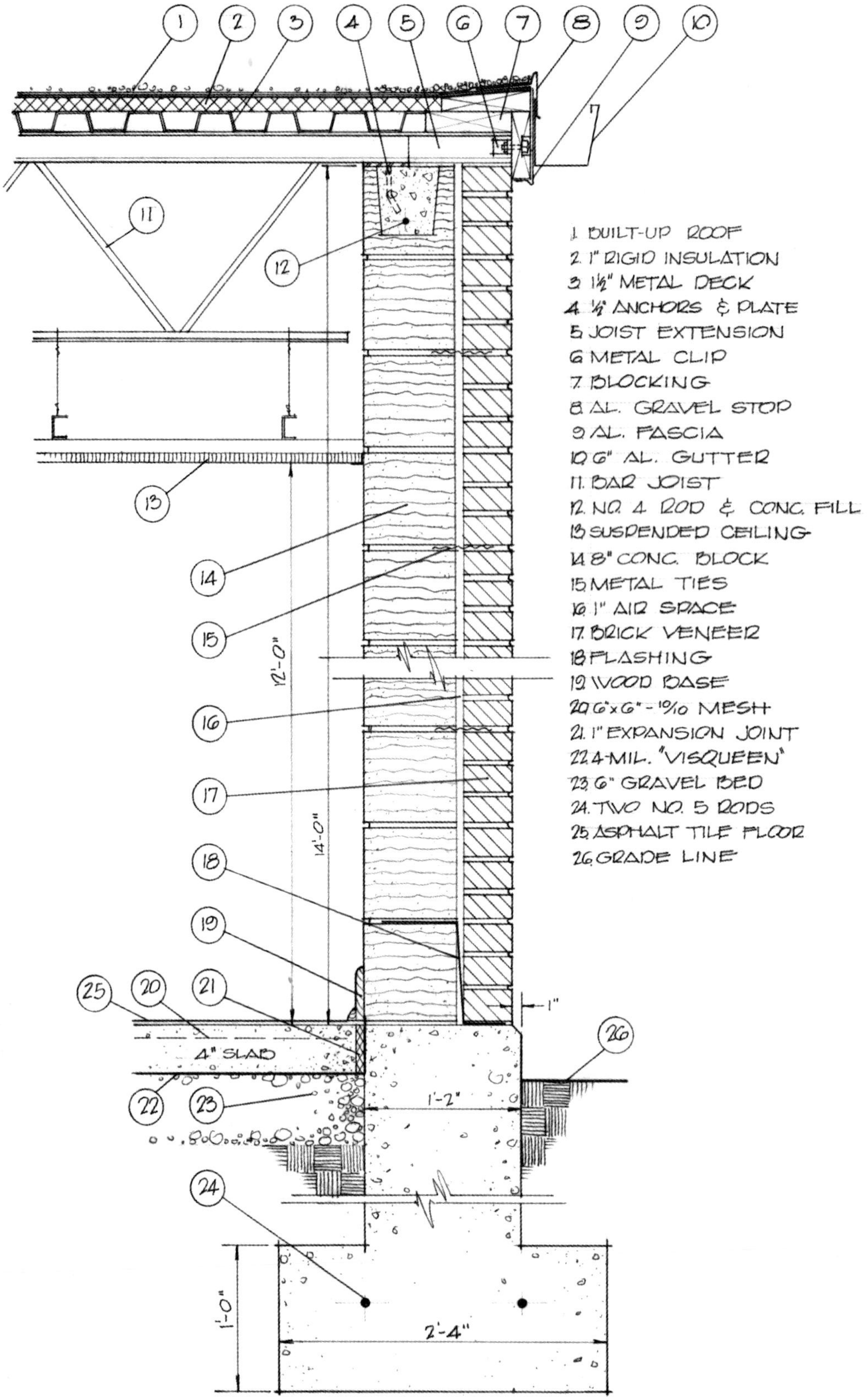

Fig. 14-1 Typical wall section for a small commercial building.

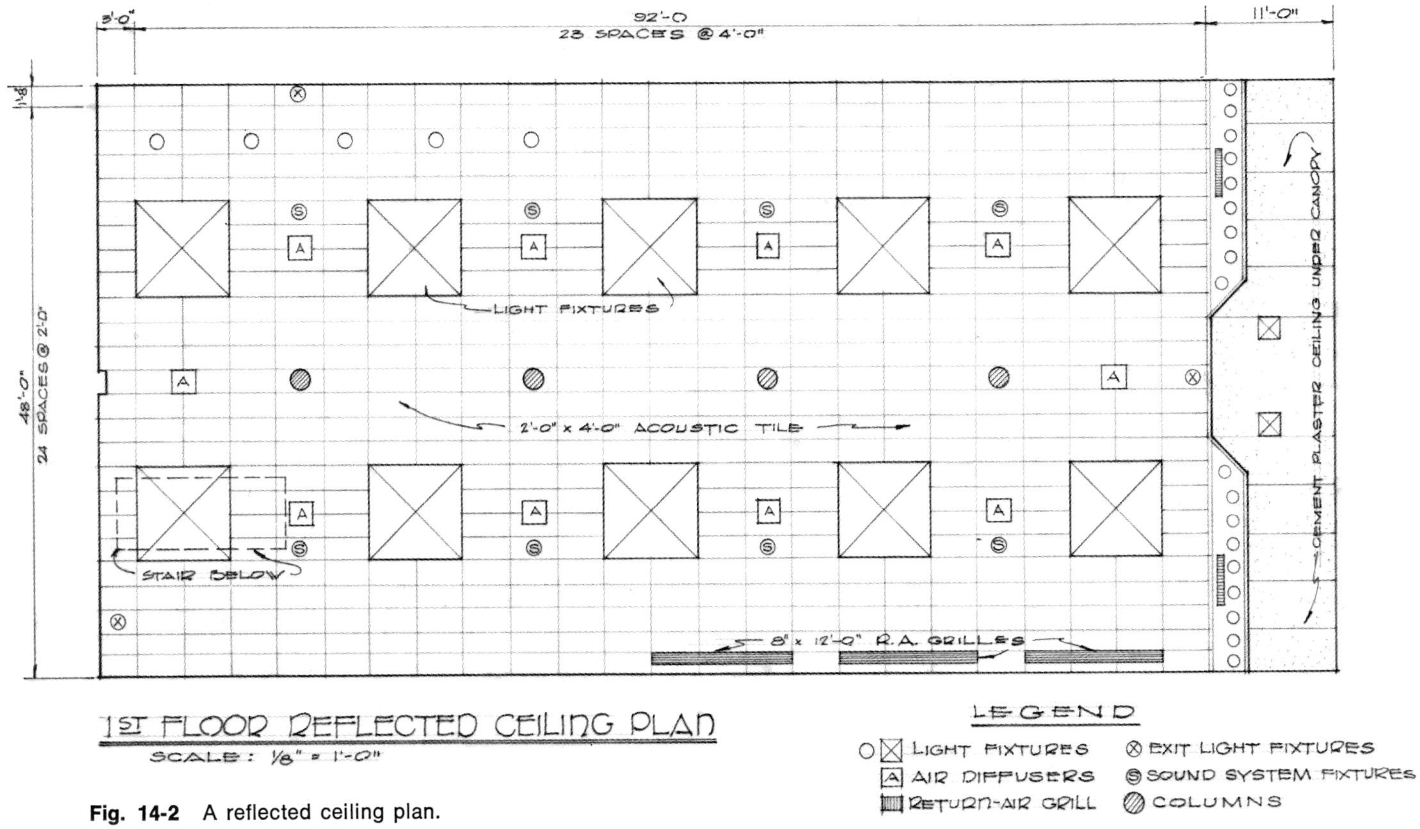

Fig. 14-2 A reflected ceiling plan.

Fig. 14-3 Entrance details for a small commercial building.

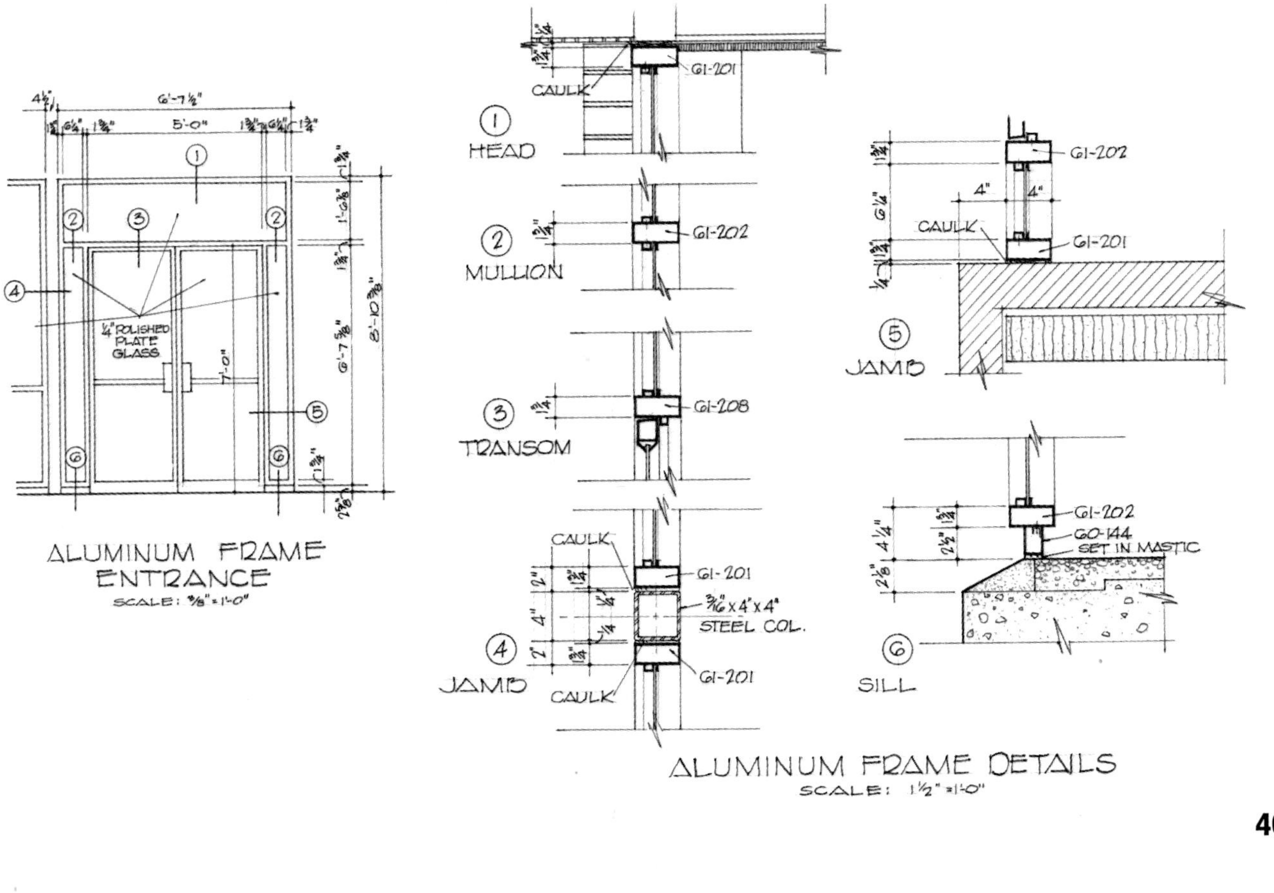

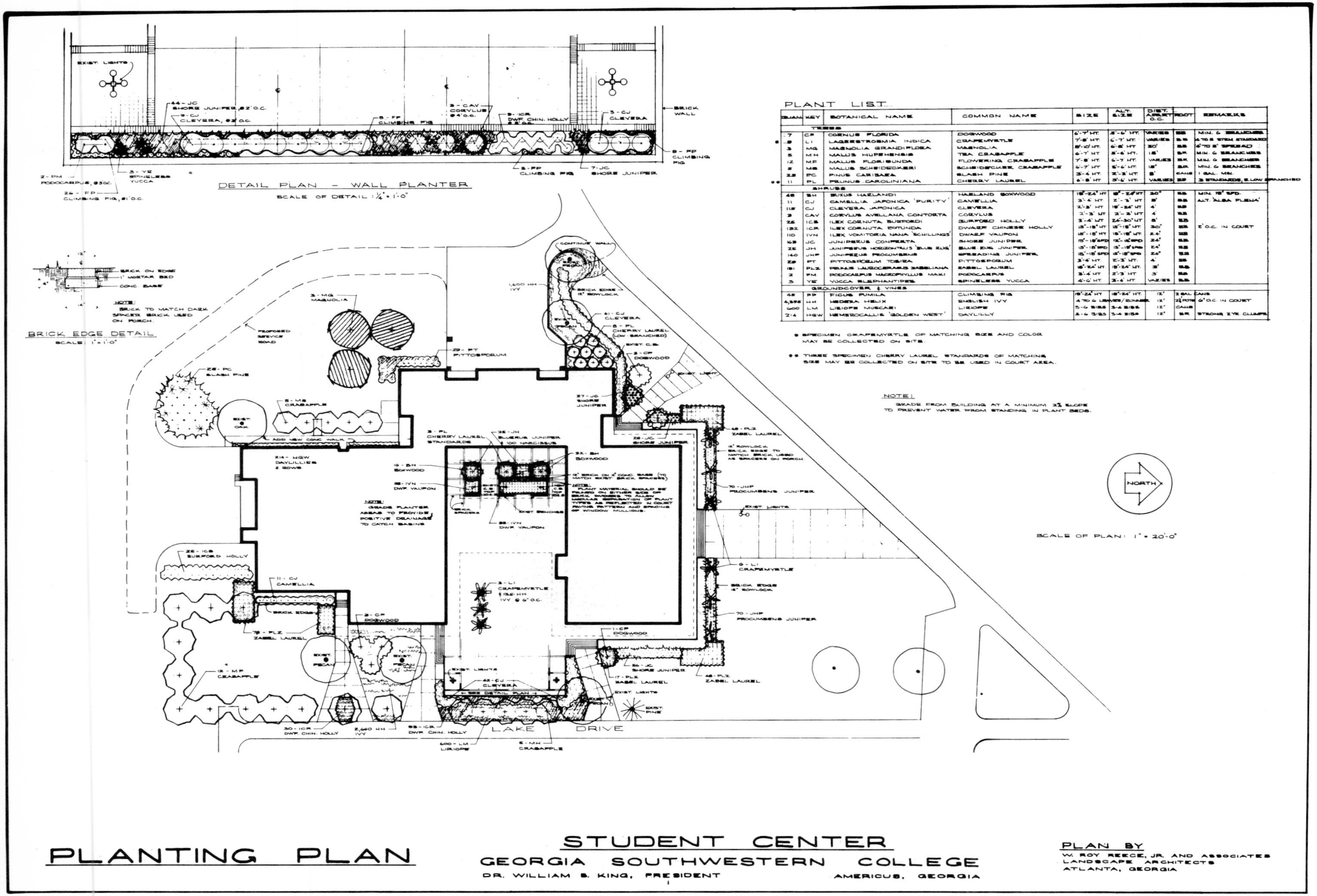

Fig. 14-4 A landscaping plan.

To simplify the floor system, a slab-on-grade was used. Terrazzo surfacing on the public lobby floor satisfied the demand for resistance to hard wear. The floor was kept low to minimize the number of steps needed near the rear entrance. To give the elevations a stable appearance and to provide a foundation planter arrangement, a stone curb-wall was placed 16″ beyond the actual foundation.

On the inside, several vaults were needed. Reinforced-concrete walls and ceiling, 1′ thick, provided complete protection for the safe deposit boxes and cash reserves, whereas the record vault, requiring mainly fire protection, was more economically surrounded with brick masonry. Floor space was reserved for the mechanical equipment—heating and cooling. Notice that it was necessary to fur down the ceiling in portions of the plan to accommodate the ductwork (see Heating-Cooling Plan, Fig. 14-12). To reduce heating and cooling loads, double entrance doors were selected. All plumbing was kept near one end of the plan, for additional economy.

Most of the interior concrete block walls were left exposed and were painted; however, for variety, wood paneling was specified in the president's office and the large boardroom. Interior walls were arranged in such a way that construction was simple and neat. When laying out the tellers' cages and other built-in cabinet work, sizes of standard bank furniture had to be taken into consideration. The acoustical tile ceiling had to be suspended from the steel joists with a metal channel system, similar to systems currently popular in many commercial buildings.

14.1 PLANNING THE DRAWING LAYOUT

Because of the size of the bank building, it became convenient to draw the plans and elevation to the $\frac{1}{4}'' = 1'\text{–}0''$ scale; larger buildings, naturally, may necessitate the use of the $\frac{1}{8}'' = 1'\text{–}0''$ scale, provided the corresponding size tracing paper is used. Each plan view became suitable for placing on a single sheet; and two elevations or complete sections made the layout of elevation sheets a simple procedure. The detail sheets required more careful planning. To show the many small members clearly, the cornice details were drawn to large scales and were therefore organized on a separate sheet. Various window and door details, requiring less space, were combined on another sheet.

14.2 DRAWING THE PLAN

The first step in drawing a plan of this type with modular-spaced columns is the layout of the center lines or grid lines of the columns. Although the grid lines are not needed in the public lobby area, they are drawn completely through the entire plan for reference and then erased later. Sometimes reference grid lines are drawn on the reverse side of the tracing paper to simplify erasing. After the exact widths of the masonry wall are determined, the outline of the plan is blocked in, and all partition walls are lightly drawn without regard for window and door openings. Then, after reference is made to modular masonry-length tables, the door and window openings are located according to the scheme of the exterior and the traffic flow of the interior. Only construction lines are used up to this point. The walls are then darkened and refined; window and door symbols are drawn; and minor wall outlines are completed. Manufacturers' literature is consulted before drawing the aluminum entrance doors. Plumbing fixtures are drawn with the use of a template. In the public lobby area, the tellers' cages and other built-in cabinet work are located and drawn the correct size. The terrazzo divider strips are completed, and other minor details are added throughout the plan. Exterior platforms and steps are drawn with the help of information from the plot plan contour levels and preliminary stair layouts. Then door identification is shown; room titles are lettered; and all general call outs are added. Next, dimensions are inserted—in positions where they do not interfere with linework. Notice that, along with important exterior dimensions placed around the periphery of the plan, a continuous line of dimensions is shown through the interior in each direction to locate all partitions accurately and show their thicknesses.

In some cases it is advisable to begin a project with a typical wall section rather than the plan. Needless to say, much of the wall information must be known before the plan can be drawn.

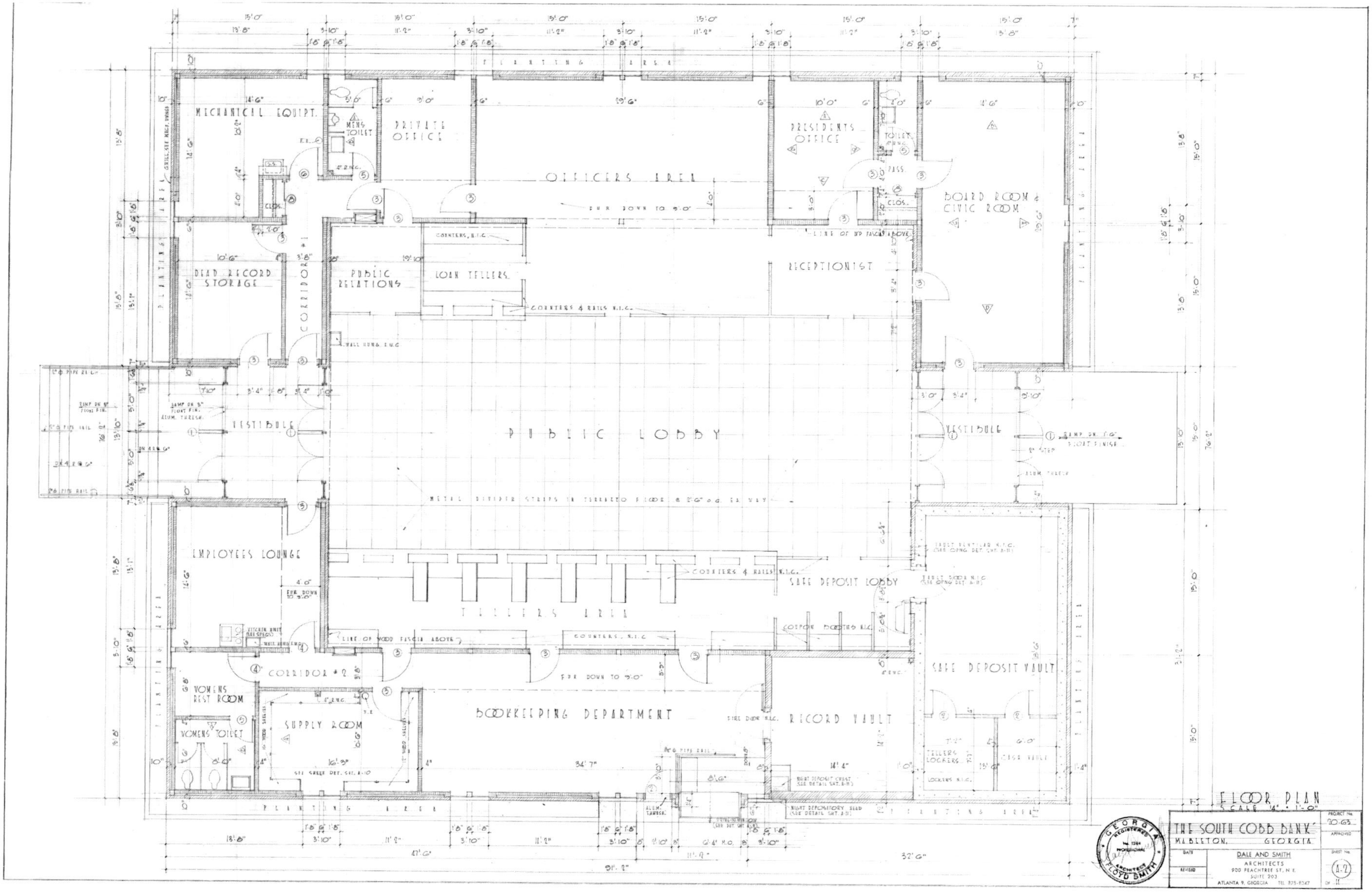

Fig. 14-5 Floor plan of small bank building.

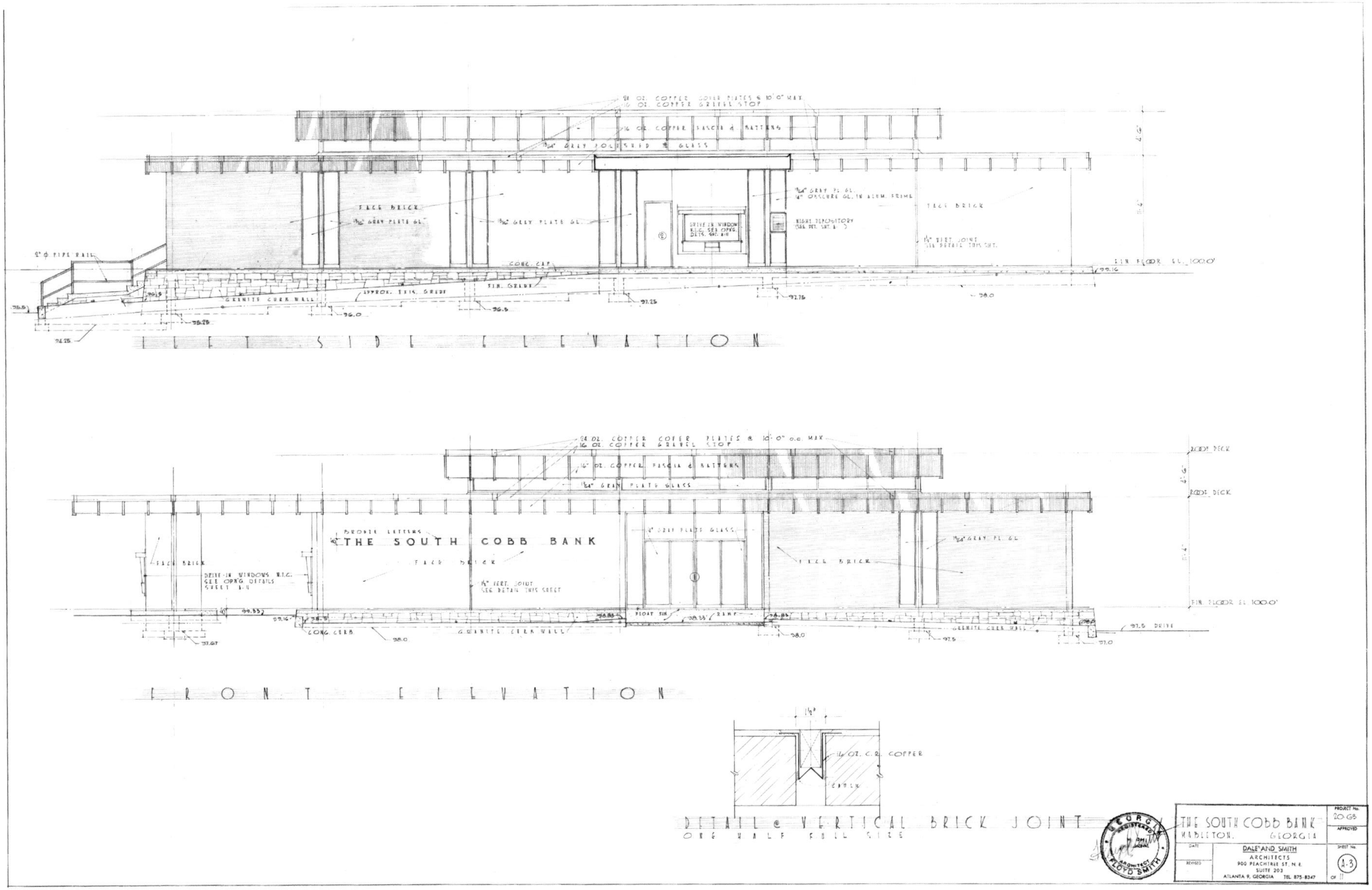

Fig. 14-6 Elevations of small bank building.

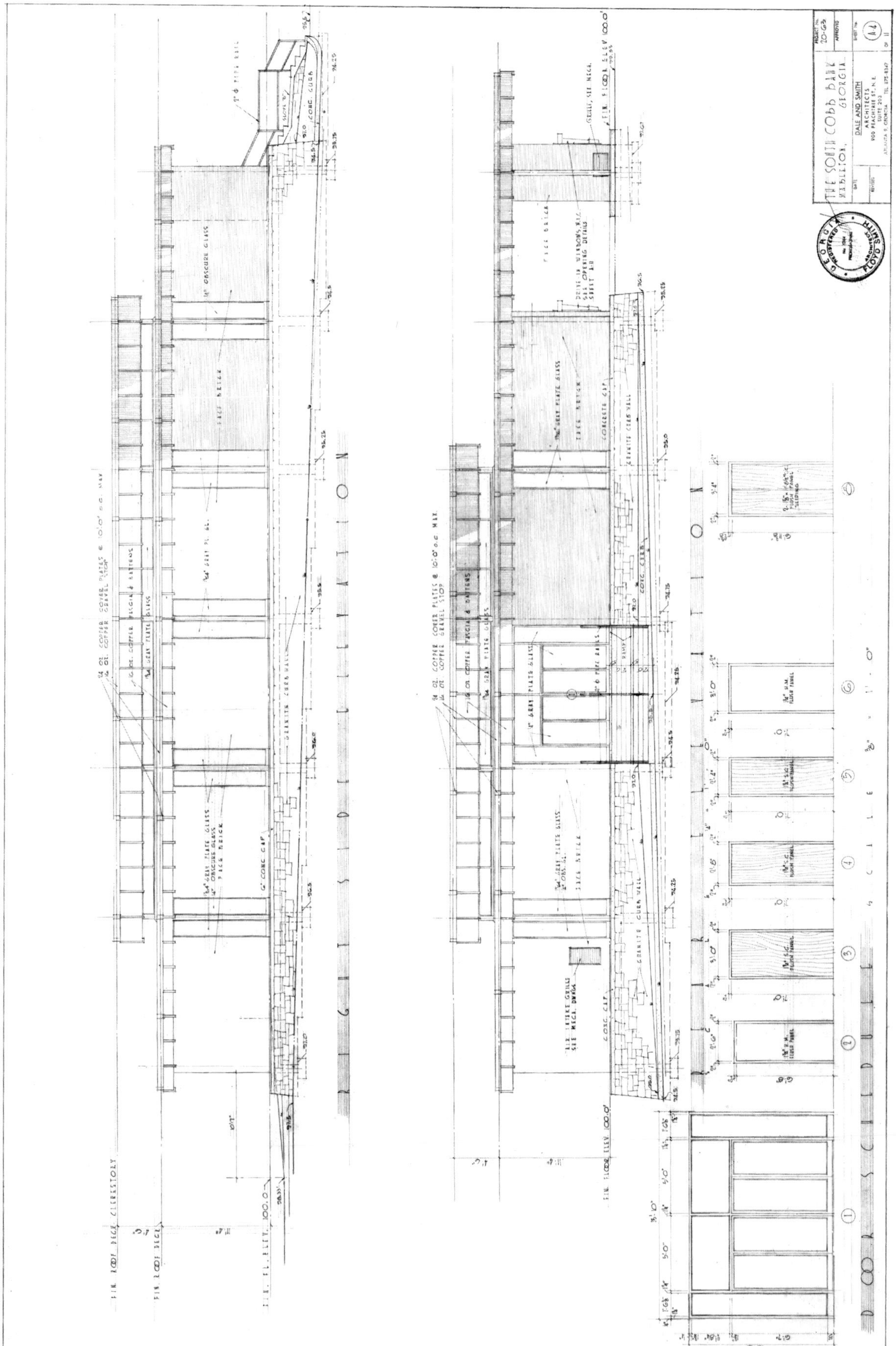

Fig. 14-7 Elevations and door schedule of small bank building.

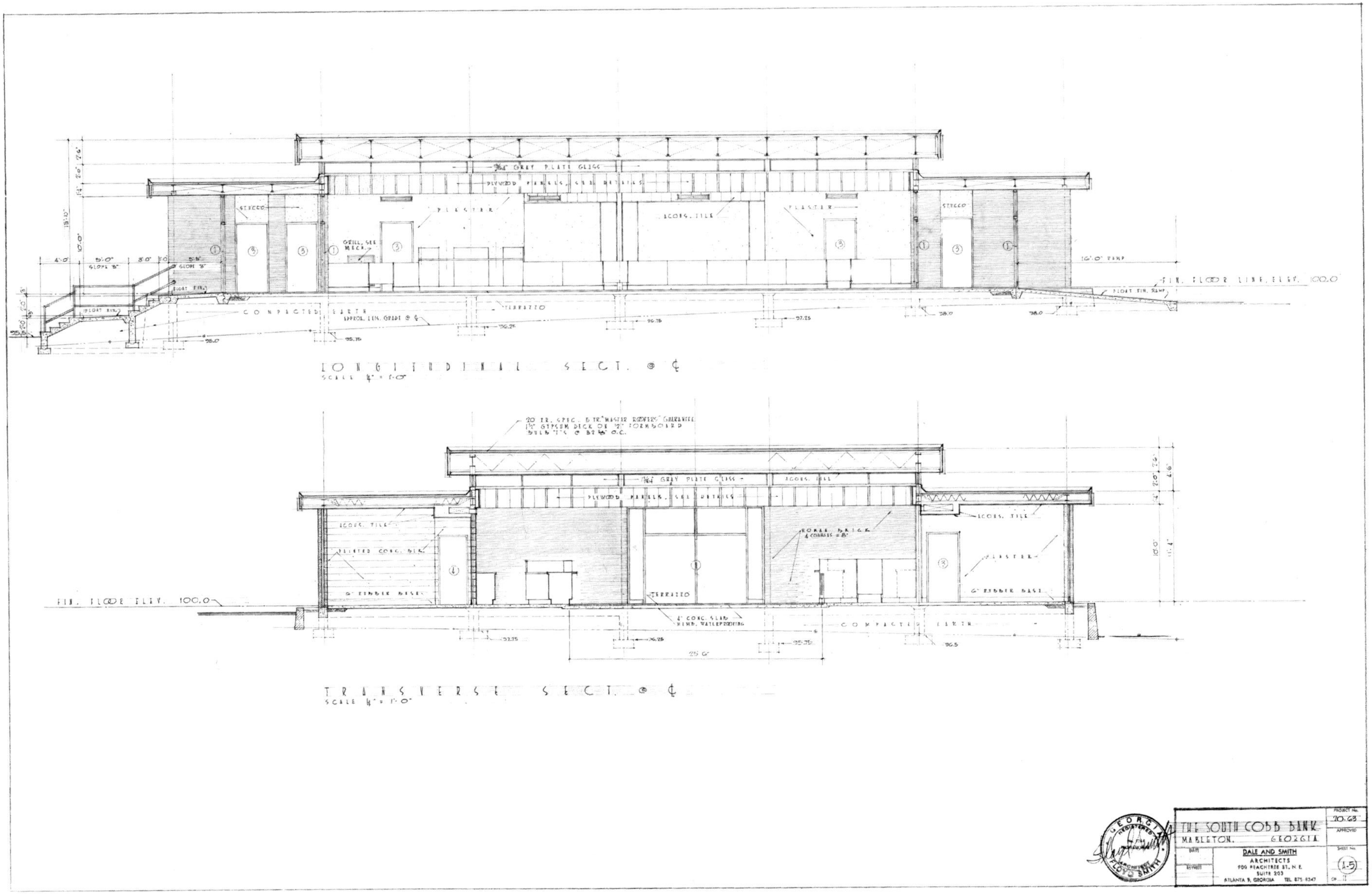

Fig. 14-8 Longitudinal and transverse sections of small bank building.

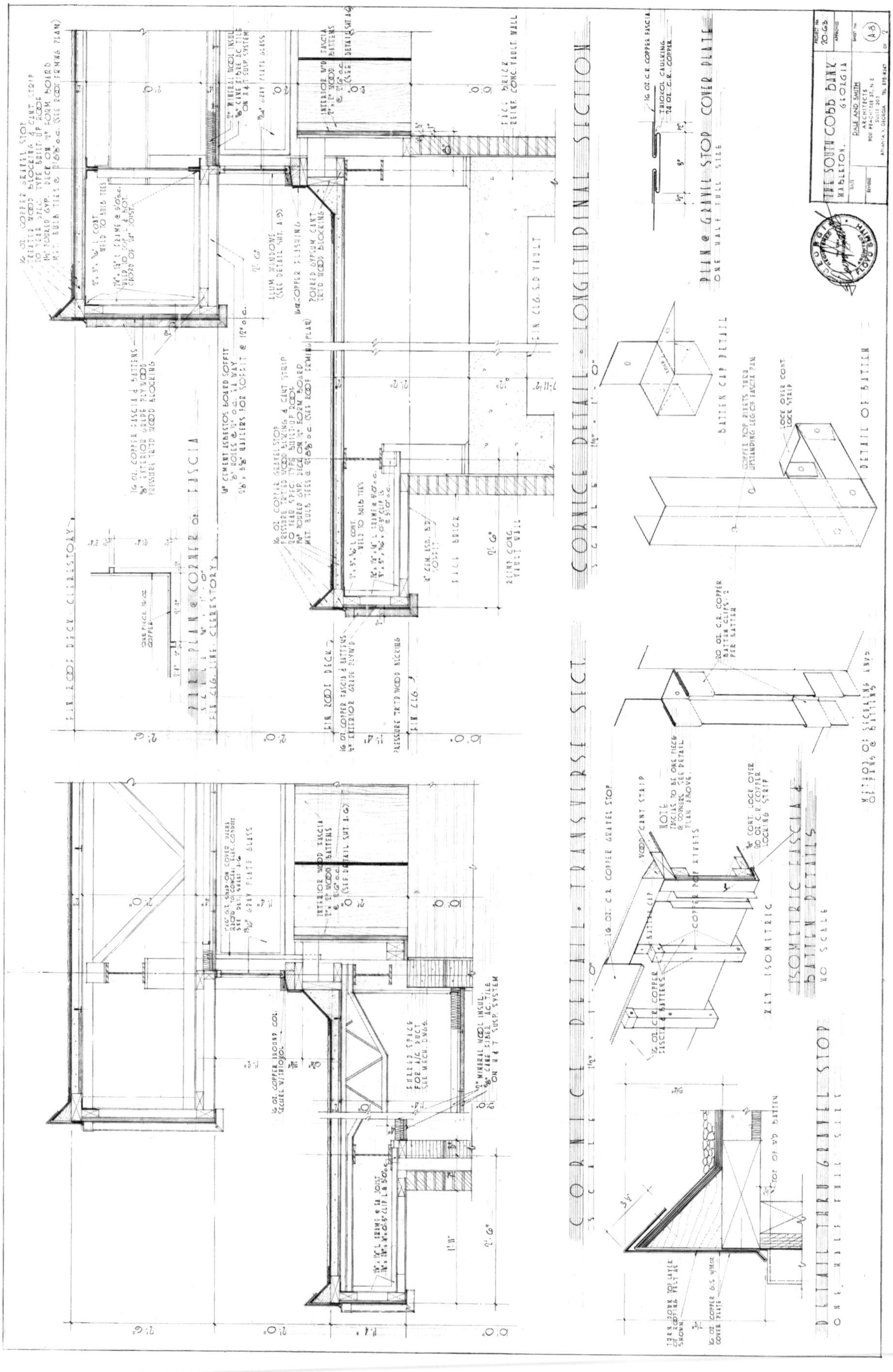

Fig. 14-9 Cornice details of small bank building.

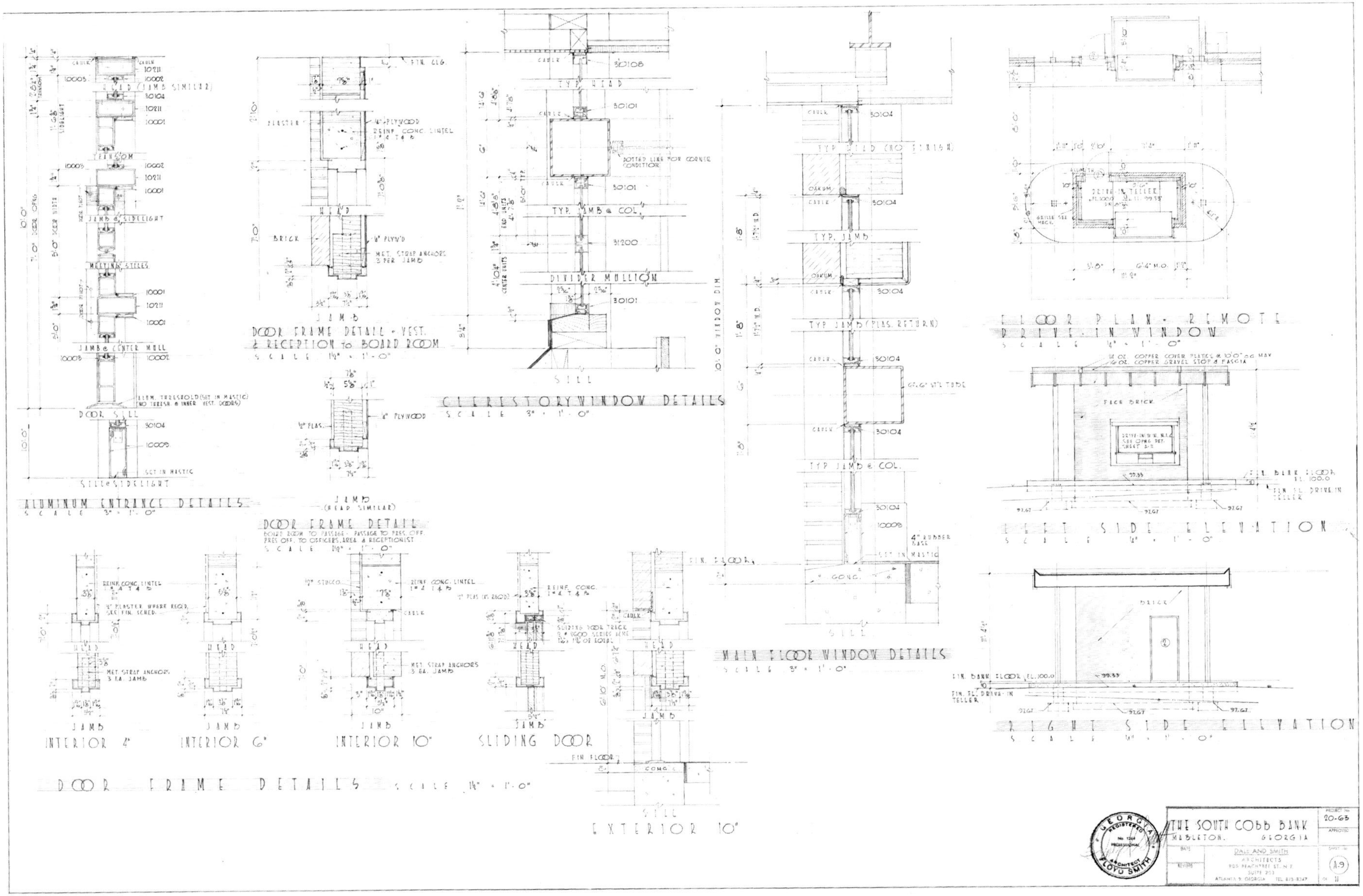

Fig. 14-10 Details of small bank building.

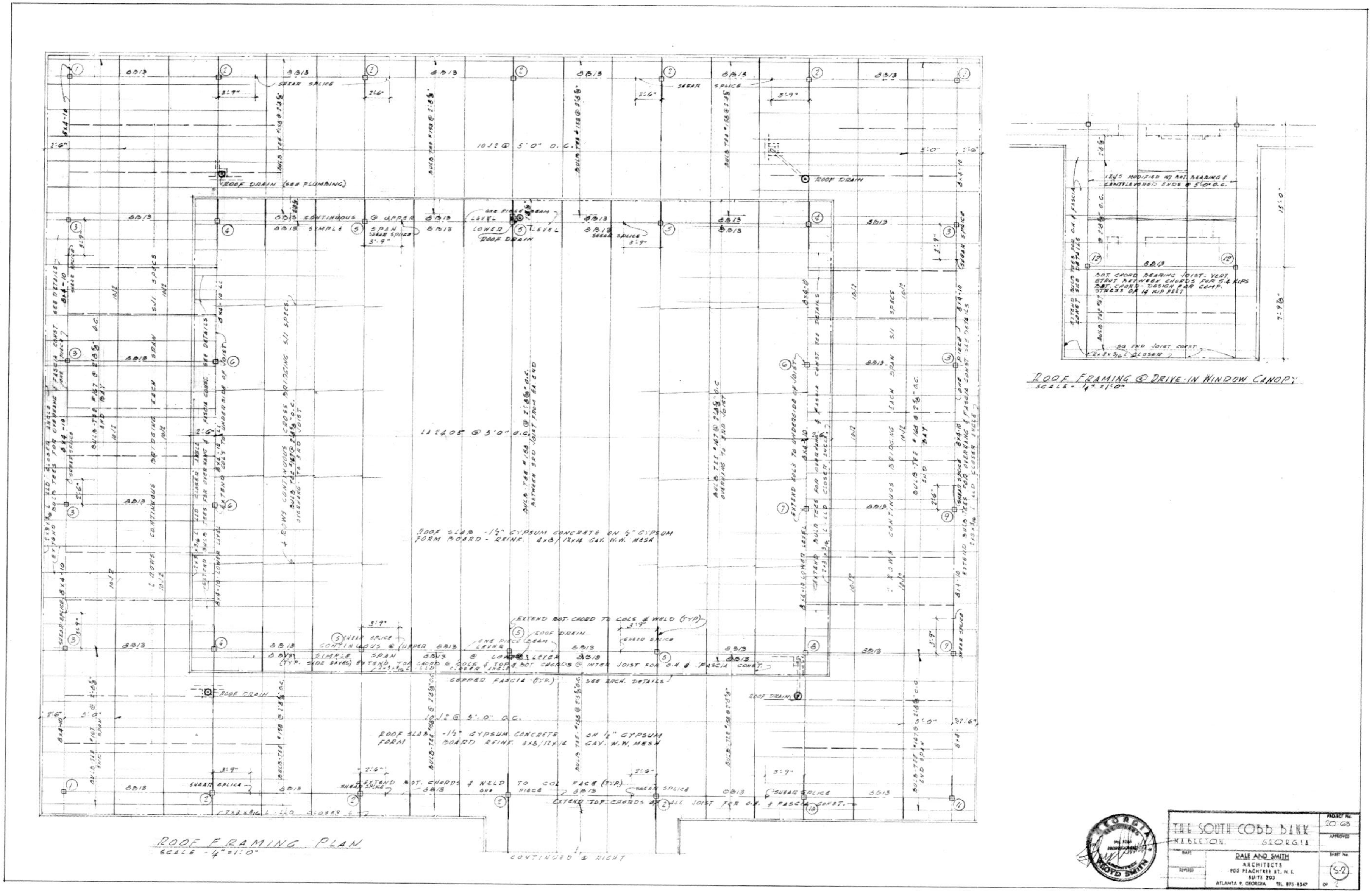

Fig. 14-11 Roof-framing plan of small bank building.

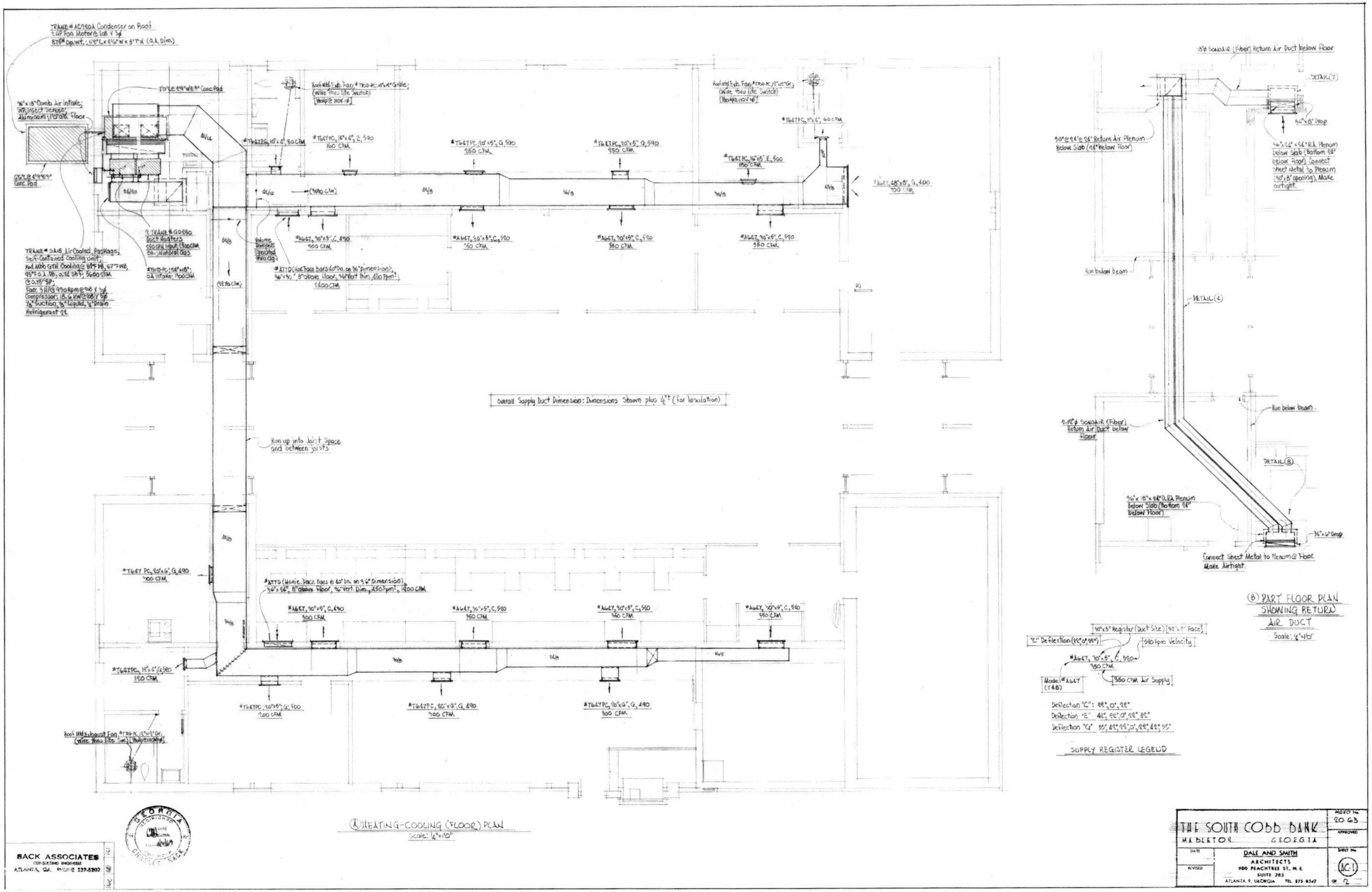

Fig. 14-12 Heating-cooling plan of small bank building.

14.3 DRAWING THE ELEVATIONS

Before starting the elevations, sizes of the steel joists, both in the public lobby ceiling and the lower surrounding ceiling, had to be calculated from handbooks (see Chapter 7); and with this information a typical wall section was drawn. Because of the long span and the depth subsequently required for the lobby joists, the upper fascia had to be made wider than the fascias around the outer walls. In starting the elevations, the finish-floor level is drawn, then, after establishing the desired ceiling heights, the major horizontal lines are drawn from information taken from the preliminary section view. Lengths of the elevation view features, however, are projected directly from the plan, as in residential drawings. Windows, offsets, doors, planter walls, and other features are drawn from preliminary sketches with the help of manufacturers' literature. Sizes of fixed-glass units are determined by their most pleasing proportions, which were developed on the sketches. It is necessary to space the battens on the copper fascia by accurate measurement. Vertical center lines of the modular columns can be left on the elevations to show their relative spacing. The clerestory windows under the upper roof are sized and drawn to complement the batten treatment of the fascias. Where indicated, the trim members are completed, and the finish-floor and roof level are added. To complete the drawing, the grade line, footings, stair railings, material symbols, notes, and titles are added as shown. For convenience in construction, the column-footing surfaces are labeled for their correct elevation below grade. To save time, portions of the symbols may be omitted. The highlights on the copper fascia produce realism of smooth metal.

14.4 DRAWING THE FULL SECTIONS

The longitudinal and transverse sections are drawn after all detail information has been completed on both the plan and elevations. These section views reveal all visible interior information on the center-line cutting planes completely through the building. To conserve time, the longitudinal section is blocked in on the sheet placed directly over the left-side elevation drawing, and the transverse section over the front elevation drawing. In both cases, the floor plan is oriented and attached to the board above the section view so that interior features can be easily projected. The 5′ spacing of the ceiling joists is clearly evident on the longitudinal section, whereas the side view of the joists is visible on the transverse section. Dimensions of the bank's furniture had to be verified for those views, and in completing the sections, it occasionally became necessary to duplicate information found on elevation views.

14.5 DRAWING THE DETAILS

Although the drawing of details is a time-consuming part of the architectural routine, the draftsman is required to draw all those necessary for each project. Details should be made consistent with each other as well as with the general concept of the building. Major details have to be accurately drawn before portions of the plan or elevations can be completed; inaccuracies may result in costly building errors.

As stated previously, in drawing details, reference must continually be made to *Sweet's File* or manufacturers' catalogues for actual sizes and other information about pertinent materials. Measurements of masonry coursing must conform to the heights and widths of the individual units. Steel members are accurately scaled, and all wood members are drawn actual rather than nominal size. The relationship of members in details and especially the joining of different materials must be well thought out before the detail is drawn.

A detail may be typical in that it represents similar construction throughout the building, or it may be the construction of an individual feature; in either case their titles should correctly describe their application. Take for example the raised cant-strip arrangement in the gravel-stop detail. This wood strip around the edge of the built-up roof not only retains the gravel or slag on the roof, but it raises the edge of the roofing felt so that the copper gravel stop can be placed on top of the felt, thereby permitting it to "breathe" with expansion and contraction. If the copper and felt were sealed together, changes in temperature might eventually rupture the felt. Because of the cant strip, however, roof drains were needed on both roof levels (see Roof Framing Plan, Fig. 14-11). Isometric drawings clearly show the fabrication of the copper battens and their application to the fascia.

Various masonry wall thicknesses throughout the building make it necessary to draw a number of doorframe details. In dimensioning detail drawings, important sizes are shown, and care must be taken to include dimensions that relate the detail to major dimensions shown on the plan or elevation. Titles and scale are shown on each detail drawing. Efficient organization of small details on a large sheet comes with drafting experience—neatness is the result of careful planning.

14.6 STRUCTURAL DRAWINGS

The roof-framing plan (Fig. 14-11) has been included mainly to show its relation to the architectural drawings and to show the conventional method of representing structural drawings. Usually these drawings, which become part of the complete set, are done by structural engineers. A plan of this type is drawn over the modular layout of the steel columns. All the steel joists in the roof framing are indicated with single lines, as well as I-beam members. Beam splices are accurately located. Placement of continuous bridging is indicated between joists. All information needed for the fabrication of the structural steel must be shown on the drawing, including welded joints of beams and columns. Often member schedules, describing and locating each piece of steel, accompany the structural drawing. In this case for instance, a column schedule was shown on another sheet to list the various column lengths.

For further information on structural drawing we suggest the book by Milo S. Ketchum, listed in the Bibliography.

EXERCISES

Exercises in planning and drawing commercial buildings are best undertaken under the supervision of your instructor, who can check them occasionally and offer helpful criticism during their development. Start all exercises with sketches.

1. Wayside rest station. Design and prepare the working drawings for a masonry rest station to be located on a level, 1-acre lot along a federal highway. Provide for the following facilities:
   a. Parking for 10 cars
   b. Parking for 5 semitrailer trucks
   c. Rest rooms for men and women
   d. Trash receptacles
   e. Water fountain
   f. Two picnic tables and benches

   Draw the plan, elevations, plot plan, and necessary details.
2. Suburban hardware store. Design and make the working drawings for a small hardware store on a commercial lot 80′ wide and 125′ deep. Use brick bearing-wall construction with a concrete slab-on-ground floor and a steel joist roof structure. Provide for the following facilities:
   a. Floor area of 5000 sq ft
   b. Display window across entire front
   c. Storage space in rear with unloading doors
   d. Private office of 150 sq ft
   e. Rest rooms
   f. Checkout counter and merchandise counters and racks
3. Small chapel. Design and draw the working drawings for a small chapel, intended for people of all faiths in a resort area. Use massive stone walls and a wood-plank ceiling supported by laminated wood beams. The lot is 200′ from the sea. Provide for the following facilities:
   a. The nave to seat 300 people
   b. Private office of 175 sq ft
   c. Choir loft to seat 20 people
   d. Rest rooms for men and women
   e. Provision for mechanical equipment and janitorial care
   f. Parking space for 150 cars
4. Fraternity house. Design and draw the working drawings for a college fraternity house to accommodate 60 students. The lot is 175′ wide by 300′ deep, and it slopes to the rear, allowing for a daylight basement recreational area to be placed on the lower level. Use as many floor levels as necessary and use fireproof construction throughout. Provide the following facilities:
   a. Double-occupancy rooms (200 sq ft)
   b. Common toilets and showers on each floor
   c. General storage on each floor
   d. Small study desk, book shelves, and closet space for each student
   e. Mechanical equipment room
   f. Apartment for the housemother
   g. Kitchen and dining area for the students
   h. Recreational area
   i. Parking for 60 cars
   j. Telephone on each floor

5. SIX-STORY OFFICE BUILDING. Prepare the presentation drawings for a metropolitan office building with six floor levels. Use reinforced concrete structural frame with cast-concrete-panel curtain walls. The floors and roof are to be poured concrete. The basic width to be 72′–0″ and the length 96′–0″. The first floor-to-floor height to be 12′–0″, remaining floor-to-floor heights to be 10′–8″. Put concrete columns on 24′–0″ centers; use a center core for one elevator, two separate stairwells, toilets, and janitorial space on each floor. Reserve space for air-conditioning equipment. Reserve the first floor level for a lobby and three small business concessions. On the remaining floor levels, provide office suites of various sizes with convenient hall arrangements within the interior of the building.

Draw the following views, using the scale, 1/8″ = 1′–0″.

a. Two floor plans, first floor and typical office floors
b. Two elevations
c. Site plan (convenient scale)
d. Perspective

REVIEW QUESTIONS

1. Why must codes dealing with public buildings be carefully regulated?

2. List three general structural systems commonly used in commercial buildings?

3. Why did it become necessary to make the upper fascia on the suburban bank building wider than the lower fascia?

4. Why are enclosed vestibules often used in public entrances?

5. When laying out plan views of buildings with multiple floor levels, why is it important for the draftsman to reserve suitable space for vertical plumbing and mechanical chases?

6. What detail is commonly drawn before starting the plans and elevations?

7. What factors must be considered in deciding upon the spacing of modular columns in the planning of a commercial building?

8. In dimensioning, how are features in detail views made to relate to major features on plan and elevation views?

9. Why must masonry coursing sizes be accurately drawn on details?

10. What types of professional services are usually engaged by architectural firms to complete their sets of working drawings for commercial buildings?

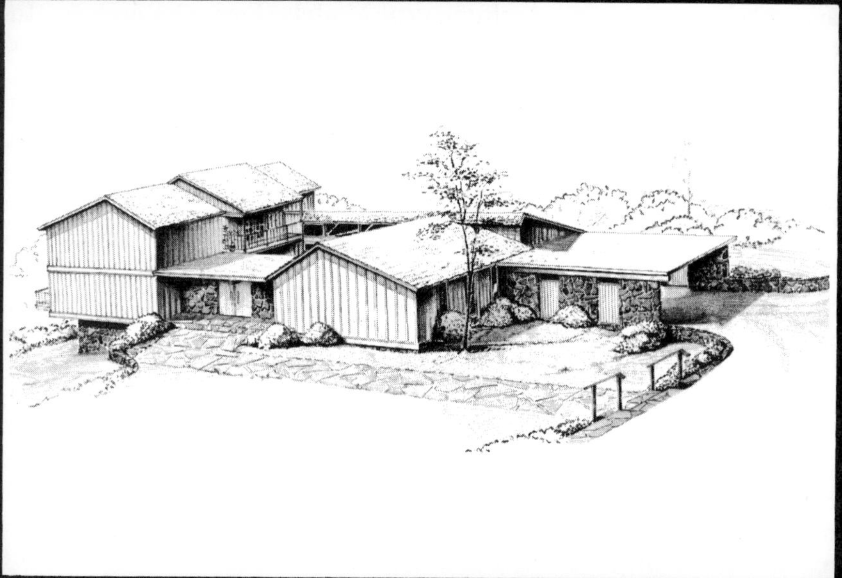

"This modest charm of not too much, part seen, imagined part."—Wordsworth

15

Building Models

There are some who may contend that model building does not belong in a book on drawing —that the construction of a model house, for instance, like the building of model airplanes, is mainly for those who enjoy tinkering with miniature things. (Model building is one of the more pleasant aspects of architecture and it has become an important creative expression for professionals as well as students.) Many architects rely on 3-dimensional models for final evaluations of their designs and sometimes reserve work space in their offices exclusively for this interesting phase of their activity. When the scope of a project justifies it, some offices engage the services of professional model builders to construct impressive and realistic models. If promotional methods have to be relied upon to raise funds for a specific building project, executive boards or organization planning groups will find a model most advantageous. Lending institutions also will usually approve loans more readily when shown an impressive model of the projected structure.

Landscape architects find that models are the most expedient method for site planning and landscaping. City planners, plant layout experts, and safety engineers, all make invaluable use of models.

To the layman a model is usually the most telling means of visualizing all aspects of a building, including proportion and relationship of features, appearance of tentative materials, and its other 3-dimensional qualities. Often the designer himself catches a features on the model that may have been overlooked on the working drawings. The model, then, is visual proof that the spatial concepts of a design are workable and pleasing. Generally, the draftsman is called upon to construct a model after preliminary plans are drawn, or occasionally after the final working drawings have been completed.

For the student, models are unquestionable learning instruments. In teaching architectural drawing, the author has found model building to be one of the most convincing methods of helping students to determine, for example, the correct choice of details to be included in their final drawings or to discover why the choice of a roof slope was not becoming to the building. No other means, except perhaps working on an actual construction job, offers the student such an effective way of relating all the views of a drawing into a total building concept. Besides, the model has the advantage of small scale, which can be related to the drawing because of its similarity in size, and it allows the project to be viewed in its entirety.

15.1 TYPES OF MODELS

Depending upon their purpose, several types of models can be constructed.

Architectural Models (Figs. 15-1 and 2) Intended primarily to show the exterior appearance of the design only, this type of model is usually constructed of heavy illustration board, thin balsa-wood panels, or if need be, of hardboard, $\frac{1}{8}''$ thick, with surface textures applied directly to the board and scaled $\frac{1}{4}'' = 1'\text{–}0''$ ($\frac{1}{8}'' = 1'\text{–}0''$ for larger buildings). It is constructed directly from the drawings; and the elevations, roofs, walks, drives, landings, etc., are cut out with a sharp model-builder's knife and attached to the base. Contours are usually built up with layers of economical chip board; their edges are left to appear very much like contour lines on a plot plan (see Fig. 15-1). All exterior surfaces are neatly painted to represent the given materials; contours are made to look like grass or ground cover. Trees and shrubs of the same scale are carefully glued in place. In addition, many commercially printed papers are available that simulate various material textures. On smaller-scale city-planning models, neatly painted solid wooden blocks may be used to show building masses.

Structural Models (Figs. 15-3 and 15-4) For school projects or models requiring a visual analysis of their structural systems, larger-scale models (usually $\frac{1}{2}'' = 1'\text{–}0''$ or $\frac{3}{4}'' = 1'\text{–}0''$) are built to correspond exactly to the construction of the actual building. Framing members of either balsa or soft pine are cut to scale and assembled to represent the building's actual framing system. When assembling, of course, quick-drying model-builder's cement is used in-

Fig. 15-1 Architectural model showing a building complex and built-up contour levels.

Fig. 15-2 Student architectural model of a residence. Roof is detachable to reveal interior room layout.

Fig. 15-3 Student structural model of a residence.

Fig. 15-4 Student structural model of a residence showing conventional construction.

Fig. 15-5 Student architectural model of a boat house showing the use of glass to represent water.

stead of nails or other fasteners. Considerable amounts of the exterior surfacings, especially rear elevations, are omitted to allow full view of the structure as well as of the interior room arrangements. The termination of the wall and the roof are made to show the layers of materials within the actual construction. Usually front elevations are completed in detail to reveal the important esthetic qualities of the design. Models of residences often include major interior cabinet work, plumbing fixtures, and even appliances or furniture. Leaving some areas open by omitting part of the roofing allows complete observation of these features. This type of model is the most rewarding for the student, since it requires solutions to structural problems that are not always evident on the drawings and that nevertheless must be considered when the final drawings are done.

The qualities necessary for a successful model builder are patience, care in attention to detail, and the ability to track down simple, everyday items that will faithfully represent building materials at the small scale. See Fig. 15-5. Some items, such as sponges for shrubbery and small plastic figures and autos, are inexpensive; others, such as sandpaper, pins, bird gravel, and pieces of burlap or felt material, are common household items.

15.2 MODEL-BUILDING TOOLS

The following list indicates the basic equipment needed for model building:

1. Model-builder's knife (Stanley, Exacto);
2. Sharpening stone;
3. T square, triangles, architect's scale;
4. Metal straightedge;
5. Tweezers;
6. Small hammer;
7. Handsaw;
8. Several small paint brushes;
9. Shears;
10. Sandpaper and masking tape; and
11. A sturdy table.

Although a minimum number of tools is generally required, supplementing these with other small hand tools facilitates working with diverse materials. If available, more elaborate tools can save time and produce more professional work. In constructing structural models, a miter box can be useful. Power shop tools can be very helpful, especially a power table saw for cutting structural lumber to scale, as we will discuss later; a power sander is also quite useful.

15.3 CONSTRUCTING ARCHITECTURAL MODELS

Working drawings, either preliminary or final, are necessary to construct a model, regardless of type. Dimensions must be taken from the drawings or prints of the drawings, and reference must be continually made to them throughout the model construction.

Start with a substantial base, either $\frac{1}{2}''$ or $\frac{3}{4}''$ plywood, upon which the model is to be attached. Use $\frac{1}{4}''$ thick plywood or hardboard, if the model will be rather small and size the base to allow for sufficient landscaping without making it unwieldy. Cut the walls from heavy illustration board or balsa-wood sheets of a thickness proportionate to the scaled-wall thickness. Work from the elevation views of your drawing and cut window and door openings to scale; allow for corner joints, either lapped or mitered. Avoid exposing end-grain of wood any more than necessary. If raised contours are to be applied to the base, allow for the height of the grade line above the base when cutting the wall pieces. It is best to glue the walls directly to the wood base, using triangles to keep them plumb. Occasionally, gluing small wooden blocks to the inside may be necessary to insure a sturdy attachment to the base. If a detachable roof is planned, cut out partitions of a similar material and glue in place after exterior walls are finished and after the floor level has been constructed. The floor panel may have to be supported with blocking below. All work to be done on the interior should be completed before the roof is constructed.

Before gluing the exterior wall panels in place, apply the basic material texture to them. This is easier when the panels can be laid flat on the table.

Natural-Wood finishes can be represented with balsa, placed with the wood grain in the proper direction, stained with a suitable color, and wiped with a cloth. Avoid getting glue on a wood surface that is to be stained; the stain will not penetrate evenly. Batten strips, for example, should be glued in place *after* the board surfaces have been stained. Uniform grooves to represent paneling are easily scored in the soft balsa with a stylus or empty ball-point pen.

Brickwork is simulated by painting the walls with a subtle variation of the basic brick color, usually earth colors, and occasional mortar joints drawn with white linework. Use white ink in a ruling pen.

Stonework can be represented in a similar manner. Paint subtle variations of the basic stone color—grays or dark ochres—with light-color mortar joints applied according to the desired stonework patterns, or actual small stones can be used (Fig. 15-6). Be sure to keep the textures in the same scale as the model.

Stucco is shown by mixing sand and paint and applying this mixture as a final coat.

For the most part, use the subdued, opaque paints for model finishing. Tempera or casein colors are handy for color mixing, and rubber-base wall paints are suitable for covering large areas. Avoid enamels and glossy paints, which are unsatisfactory because of light reflections. Because of its quick-drying qualities, lacquer is frequently used by professional model builders when spray painting is applicable.

After the walls have been fastened in place, the next step is the roof. Select a rigid material for roof panels to prevent warping. Work from a roof plan if necessary to insure neat-fitting pieces; on complex roofs, such as hip roofs with offsets, it will be found simplest to project exact shapes carefully from roof drawings and lay them out on the material with drawing instruments before cutting. Use a sharp knife for clean, straight edges. Sloping roofs usually need several wood bracing members below, particularly on detachable roofs, if they are to remain rigid. Chimneys piercing the roof may be cut from wood blocks and merely glued to the roof.

To represent built-up type roofing, apply coarse sandpaper to the roof with contact cement applied to both surfaces. Asphalt-type shingles may be represented with strips of construction paper, cut to appear as strip shingles, and painted the desired color if necessary.

Next, work on the construction of grade levels or lot contours. If the model requires no contouring and is to be shown on a perfectly flat lot, the base can be painted dark green and covered with flock (tinted fibers that adhere to the wet paint, giving the surface a velvety appearance), or it can be covered with model-builder's simulated grass (sawdust dyed green). Use a thick, oil-base paint to hold the grass material securely. If suitable, apply a stippled surface of texture paint and finish it with green color.

Raised contours, if needed, are cut from heavy chip board and glued over each other to the correct heights. This stepped surface looks best if merely painted a dull green; walks, drives, etc., are cut from separate pieces, painted, and glued over the contoured surface. The easiest way to make steep lot surfaces is to build them over wire screen or hardware cloth that has been blocked up to the correct height from below and covered with a layer of molding plaster or papier-mâché. After it has cured, paint and apply grass material as mentioned above. (See Fig. 15-7.)

Exterior details such as window and door trim, cornice moldings, etc., are applied after the contour levels are fixed. Cut the trim members from thin balsa sheets, using the metal straightedge and sharp knife. Small dowels, toothpicks, and model-builder's pieces may also

Fig. 15-6 Student architectural model made with molding plaster.

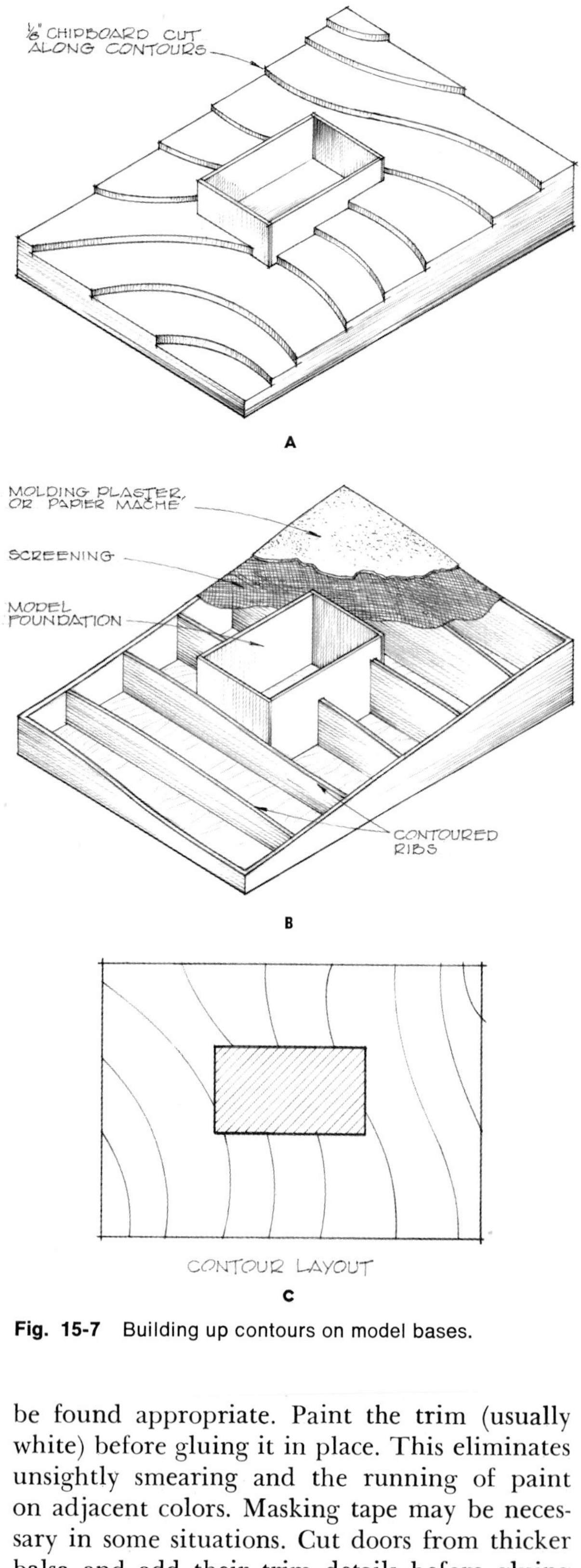

Fig. 15-7 Building up contours on model bases.

be found appropriate. Paint the trim (usually white) before gluing it in place. This eliminates unsightly smearing and the running of paint on adjacent colors. Masking tape may be necessary in some situations. Cut doors from thicker balsa and add their trim details before gluing them in position; they can be left partially open rather than closed. Thin plastic may be fastened to the interior of window openings to represent glass, although windows are nearly as effective without it if the window trim has been carefully applied. On large glassed areas, muntin strips are usually glued directly to the plastic.

Complete the landscaping as the last step. Show fences, walls, terraces, swimming pools, and other outdoor features which will enhance the model. Water surfaces look realistic if represented with ripple window glass embedded in the surfacing material. Paint the area under the glass a light blue. For foundation planting, tear pieces of spong (natural or synthetic) into various shrubbery shapes, dye them several shades of green, and glue them in natural-appearing groups near the model corners and entrances. Green lichen is also available at model-supply stores for this purpose and is similarly secured with glue. To simulate trees, take actual twigs or small branches having the proper scale and formation and glue pieces of the sponge or lichen throughout the small branches to shape the trees' foliage. Then drill a hole in the base and insert the tree trunk with glue.

Dress the edge of the base panel with suitable stock molding or trim; miter the molding neatly at the corners to give it a finished appearance. Incidental objects such as autos, people, furniture, bath fixtures, if necessary to further elaborate the model, may be found generally at hobby shops or dime stores. Be sure they are the right scale. These items can also be carved from white or colored soap. However, avoid superfluous items, which only clutter the model and detract from the architecture instead of supplementing it.

Many architectural offices use a material called *chip board* for the majority of their models. The material is a gray, economical paper board, about $3/32''$ thick, available at most drafting supply stores. All cuts are neatly made with a sharp knife, and pieces are glued together and held in place with straight pins or rubber bands until the glue has set. The board has good stability, takes tempera or latex paint well, and does not seem to be greatly affected by humidity changes. Clean-cut appearing models can be quickly made with this versatile model material. (See Fig. 15-8.)

Another material that should be investigated by the model builder is basswood. The wood possesses a fine, uniform grain and can be cut, glued, finished, and painted similar to other model materials. Textured basswood sheets representing many of the traditional architectural

Fig. 15-8 Student architectural model made with chip board.

surfaces are available from many model-supply stores and hobby centers. Polystyrene sheets, available from similar sources, are also finding application to model building. This clear, colorless plastic material can be scribed, tooled, sawed, scored, and textured, and bonds quickly with the model cements mentioned in the next section. Other preformed plastic features such as windows, doors, people, and autos are available in several scales from dealers, but generally those that are custom-made give the model a more professional appearance.

15.4 CONSTRUCTING STRUCTURAL MODELS

To build a model as a true miniature of the tentative building requires a working knowledge of the various framing systems. (Chapter 7). Because of the many small pieces involved in a structural model, scales must necessarily be larger (½″ = 1′–0″ or ¾″ = 1′–0″) than architectural models, which are meant to show mainly exterior appearances. Small buildings such as residences, then, become the most practical projects when using these larger scales.

Structural models provide varied learning situations for students and lend themselves to classroom projects where groups can work together to solve the problems involved. The situations and problems encountered parallel actual construction jobs and offer interesting and informative experience to drawing students. A foreman, similar to an actual job superintendent, should be designated in the model crew to plan individual tasks of the construction and keep the model moving along smoothly. Considerable time and work are involved. If a student's original design is used, the model definitely creates added enthusiasm.

Framing lumber for structural models is best cut from ponderosa or sugar pine stock on a power table saw. Equip the saw with a *hollow-ground blade* to produce neat cuts and smooth surfaces requiring no sanding. When cutting the lumber, it is most convenient to scale it down to its *nominal size* rather than actual size. For example, 2″ lumber would be scaled exactly 2″ thick. Use convenient lengths (about 3′) of the stock and cut the narrow dimension first. Although balsa wood is available for structural pieces, pine gives the model more stability.

Use model cement (Testor's, duPont Duco) for most of your gluing work. A very satisfactory cement for joining clear plastic pieces and other materials is No. 527 Bond Cement.[1] When small pieces can be quickly assembled, use the *extra-fast-drying* type of cement to save time in setting. For stronger wood joints use white wood glue with pressure, if possible; on thin paper use contact cement to prevent wrinkling.

Base for the Model First build a sturdy base for the model, making it large enough to

[1] Manufactured by Bond Adhesives Company, Box 406, Jersey City, N. J. 07303.

accommodate the floor plan and leave sufficient space around it to show exterior features and landscaping. Remember that if the base is built too large the model will become difficult to display and move about. Usually 1/4″ plywood with 1″ × 2″ framework (set vertically) is satisfactory if securely nailed (see Fig. 15-9). Use diagonal bracing to insure rigidity throughout the plywood.

Foundation Walls Lay out the outline of the foundation on the base and proceed with the foundation walls. If a basement or lot contours are planned, consideration must be given to floor-level heights, and the base surface as a reference level should be indicated on the typical wall section detail of the working drawings. Heights then can be quickly scaled from this reference point. If the house is to have a concrete-slab floor, represent the slab with 1/4″ plywood, and according to the drawings, fasten it directly to the base or block it up to the required height. Slabs may also be cast of molding plaster or spackling compound. Basements must have full-height foundation walls of the proper thickness with raised lot contours to be finished as a later step. Construct crawl space foundations according to the foundation plan and show walls and piers correctly placed. Build the foundation of wood, scaled the correct thickness; and be sure it is built the same height above grade as indicated on the drawings. The foundation is a major step of the model construction and is important in getting it started correctly.

If termite shields are indicated on the working drawings, use strips of aluminum or copper foil and attach them on foundation walls and piers as shown.

Wood Framing Next, construct the wood framing (if applicable) according to the typical wall detail; follow good framing practice. Start with the sill plate and glue all members together in the same manner and sequence that carpenters would use on the full-size construction. If a wood floor is indicated, insert all wood built-up girders or steel beams to support the floor framing. Steel beams can be made from three strips of thin wood, glued together and painted orange to resemble structural steel. Space the floor joists, insert them in the direction shown on the drawings, and cover with the subflooring. To expose portions of the floor framing, cut circular free-form holes in the subflooring near the center of several rooms; then the flooring layers—subfloors, building paper, and finish floor—can be exposed by cutting similar holes just a little larger for each succeeding layer. Similar openings in ceilings and roofs are then planned directly above these floor openings so that the structure will be exposed completely through the model.

After the walls and partitions are laid out on the subfloor according to the plan, construct each wall section with the use of a jig on the table top. In gluing the studs and plates together to form the wall sections, remember to place the studs 16″ on center (if conventional framing), insert the proper posts at corners (corner posts) and intersections of walls (T posts), provide double studs and lintels around window and door openings, cut the studs about 7′–9″ long for 8′ ceilings, build the sections with the sill and only *one* top plate (the other 2″ × 4″ plate should be attached after the wall sections are set in place), and allow enough plate length

Fig. 15-9 Details for constructing a satisfactory model base.

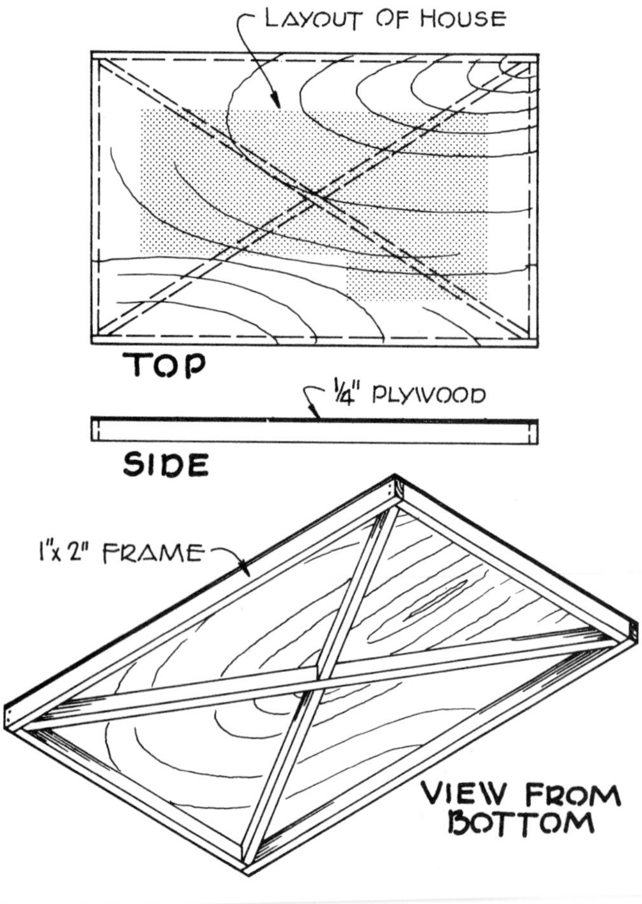

for corner joints (see Framing Details in Chapter 7). Be sure there will be nailing surfaces on both inside and outside wall corners. Glue the wall sections to the subfloor, using your triangles or tri-square to keep them plumb. Now the second top plate is applied over the walls (see Fig. 15-10B), overlapping the other top plate at corners and at intersections to produce a rigid wall framework. Do not forget diagonal braces at outside corners.

Complete all work to be done within room interiors before applying ceiling joists. Show suggestions of major floor finishes such as oak strip, parquet, tile, carpeting, ceramic, flagstone, etc. Usually only portions of the various finishes need to be shown. Areas of the interior walls may be indicated with illustration board or wood paneling; however, avoid covering too much framing. Letter the room titles on small strips of white board and glue to the floor; place them so that they read from the front of the building.

While the interior is accessible, insert all permanent fixtures and built-in cabinet work. Bathroom fixtures may be carved from soap, as we mentioned earlier, and glued in place. Scaled fixtures of various types are available at hobby shops. Make cabinets from wood blocks. Cabinet doors may be made from thin balsa and glued to the blocks. Paint or stain the cabinets before installing.

Next, attach ceiling joists to the wall framing according to the drawing. On gable roofs, joists are usually parallel to the rafter direction and fastened to them above the plate. Cut common rafters from a pattern drawn out on paper, if need be. Hip and valley rafters may require projection layouts as well. Place the sloping rafters in pairs opposite each other and glue to the plate adjacent to the ceiling joists. This forms a strong framing arrangement. If feasible, temporarily fasten the ridgeboard in place before attaching the rafters. Keep the edges of the overhangs straight. If truss rafters are employed, set up a triangular jig on the table and build the identical trusses before setting them in place on the model.

In plank-and-beam framing, sand and stain ceiling beams *before* gluing them in place. Use cripples above top plates to bring partitions up to sloping plank-and-beam ceilings; or, diagonal-top partitions may be built with full-height studs after the ceiling slopes have been established. Use double studs or 4″ × 4″'s within the walls to support the ceiling beams. See Fig. 15-11A. Treat the rafter or beam overhang as shown on the drawings, using thin balsa for soffit material if a boxed cornice is called for. After the framing is complete, reinforce major corners and roof joints with common pins, shortened if necessary, to prevent observers from accidentally damaging the structure.

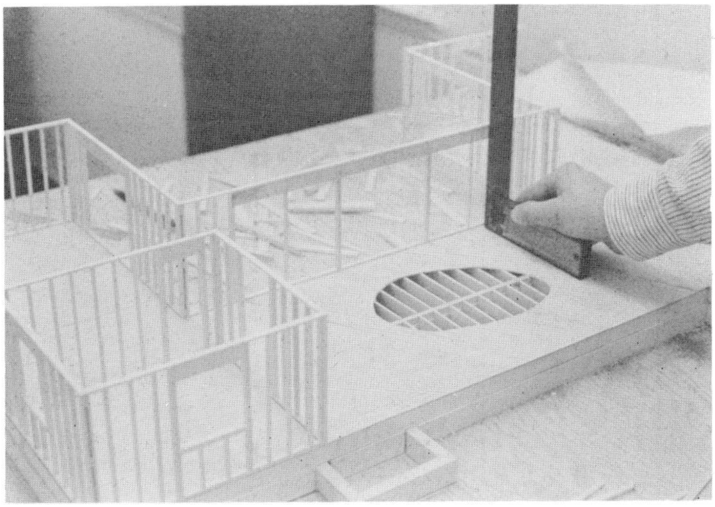

A

B

Fig. 15-10 (A) Checking the plumb of wall framing; (B) applying the double plate on structural models.

Exterior Walls Apply exterior wall materials next; include subwall, building paper, and insulation, if applicable. Avoid covering walls around the entire building; usually the back walls can be left exposed so that the interior and structure are easily visible. Complete the front in detail, on the other hand, to provide a basis for analyzing the design qualities.

Make brick veneer of balsa sheets that have

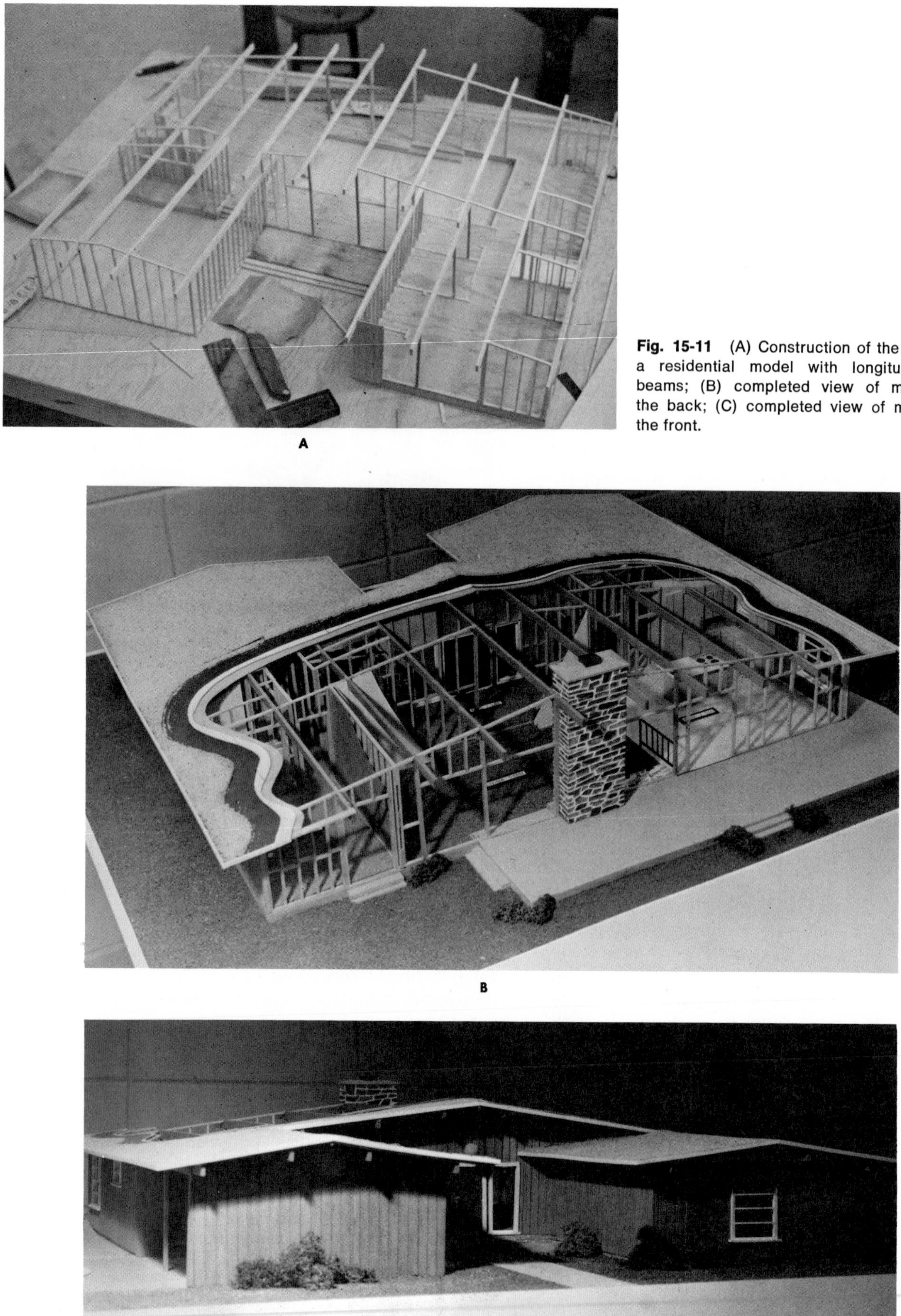

A

B

C

Fig. 15-11 (A) Construction of the framing in a residential model with longitudinal roof beams; (B) completed view of model from the back; (C) completed view of model from the front.

been sized to fit the framing, cut for door and window openings, and mitered at outside corners. Show brick sills extending out from the brick surface under windows with balsa strips glued in place. Before fastening the veneer in place, complete the brick texture by scoring the balsa with horizontal grooves to represent the brick coursing; do this with a blunt-tipped instrument such as a stylus. Of course, provision must be made for the erection of the brick panels on the foundation. To paint the brick, first coat the entire surface with white color (tempera works fine), making sure the grooves are filled. Then apply the basic brick color with a drybrush technique, covering mainly the brick surfaces and leaving the mortar grooves white. Use subtle color variations to give the brick a realistic appearance. If you want to represent used brick, tone down the basic brick color by applying over it a wider variety of colors, primarily earthy reddish-brown shades. This is best done in the drybrush technique also. Keep all the panels of similar value and check their development by viewing them at a little distance, rather than up close.

Stone textures are done in a similar manner; or relief is gained by cutting individual stones from thin balsa (1/32″ thick) and gluing them to the panels. Paint the panels white before applying the stones. Be sure the stone pattern is pleasing and the pieces are glued in place with their wood grain in the same direction—usually horizontal. The stones are then painted in slight variations of gray or earth colors.

It may be worth mentioning that very attractive masonry walls and textures can be produced with molding plaster or spackling compound, available at builder's supply stores. First build a wooden mold or form for each masonry wall or unit required, then mix sufficient plaster and water in a container and carefully pour into one form at a time and screed. Add the plaster to the water when mixing; to prevent air bubbles, avoid vigorous mixing. You must work rather hurriedly, as the plaster sets quickly and cannot be left or worked too long. Avoid spilling the plaster, since it is difficult to remove from clothes and floor. After the plaster is sufficiently hard, remove it from the form without breaking. Repair any imperfections and carve stone, brick, or other masonry textures on the surface with a suitable tool. The plaster carves easily if not entirely cured. When dry, coat with white shellac to seal the surface and paint the masonry units the desired colors, leaving the mortar joints white. Chimneys can be cast as a unit by this method, as well as replicas of many precast panels now in use in construction.

For even more textural stonework realism, small pea gravel or other aggregate can be placed in the bottom of forms to produce the face of the masonry panels, and a thick mixture of the molding plaster is poured over it. When these aggregate panels or units are cured and cleaned, they look very authentic and are extremely effective. Take precautions to construct the forms in the correct size and to scale. Join the panels at intersections with a thin mixture of the plaster as an adhesive, or use white wood glue.

Make the various types of wood siding from balsa wood. Whether painted or stained surfaces are required, balsa can be easily cut and finished to resemble many wood exterior finishes. Glue the siding to the exterior walls after the subwall materials have been applied. Before attaching siding to the walls, carefully cut the openings for doors and windows, groove if necessary, and paint or stain. As mentioned previously, be sure the wood grain runs in the same direction as it would on the actual building and that stain is applied before glue is used. To simulate horizontal clapboard siding, apply thin strips of balsa in a lapped fashion, allowing the correct amount of exposure to the weather. Paint after all the siding is in place. Make wood shingle siding from small balsa pieces, which are cut and glued in place individually.

Build landings, steps, planters, etc., from wood blocks, and veneer with thin balsa if necessary for uniform masonry textures; paint off-white to represent concrete. Chimneys rising up through wood framing must be independent of the framing and may be made from cast molding plaster or constructed of soft wood and veneered with thin balsa to obtain horizontal wood grain completely around the unit. Show flue extensions and a sloping wash at the top. If needed, fireplace openings can be carved out with a chisel or a knife, and the cavity painted a dull black. When completed, fasten the chimney to the base before framing the roof structure around it.

Roofing Because of the comparatively small nature of models, their roofs are a predominant feature and therefore necessitate a great deal of care in finishing. Select a stable material such as balsa for the roof decking, rather than paper board, which has a tendency to warp when the roofing materials are glued on. At this point you should plan which parts of the roof surfaces are to be left exposed for viewing the framing members and the interior structure of the model. See Fig. 15-12. For this purpose leave off most of the sloping surfaces in the rear. On gable or hip roofs, cover a considerable amount of the front slopes so that the front view gives the impression of completion. Roofing over important roof edges and ridges is necessary. On flat roofs, leave a large portion of the central area without covering, since it does not detract from the appearance of the elevations. Use black construction paper to represent roofing felt, usually cut to expose the multiple layers of a built-up roof. Fasten coarse sandpaper as the final aggregate surface to this type of roof or use sand or bird gravel glued to the felt. Various abrasive sheets can be fashioned into strip asphalt shingles and glued to the roof, placing them so that they overlap. For realistic wood shingles, take actual cedar shingles and cut the miniatures from the thin ends. Copper foil (gasket stock) will be found attractive and easy to shape for metal roofs and flashing applications. Many similar materials can be found to simulate other types of roofing; some will require painting. Half the enjoyment of building models is the challenge offered in finding simple, inexpensive materials that will represent building textures at the correct scale.

Details Minor details should be one of the last operations in the construction of the model, even though it often becomes tempting to add a few during the construction to see how they will appear. By details we mean the small features such as doors, windows, cornice trim, shutters, etc., which give the model its finished touch. When trim pieces are to be different in color from adjacent surfaces, paint the trim before attaching. Avoid using aluminum paint on models; it generally appears tacky. If an aluminum window is specified, paint the pieces white. Positioning small pieces may require the use of a pair of tweezers. Cut window members, surrounds, sills, muntins, etc., from thin balsa, making sure that the type and scale of the window are accurately reproduced. Some of the muntin bars of a double-hung window, for instance, must be made very thin.

For exterior doors, cut each one from balsa after the trim around their openings has been affixed and give them their correct detail according to the door schedule. To represenet various treatments you may score a balsa door with a stylus to show panels, glue stile and rail strips on the door, or glue small panels on the door. Flush doors are smooth except possibly for suggestions of the latch hardware. Take time to detail the front entrance carefully. Form wrought-iron work from soft wire, solder the joints, and spray a dull black. Other minor details may be added if they contribute additional character to the model.

Landscaping Landscaping on structural models is done in a similar manner as was suggested for smaller architectural models, the important thing is maintaining scale. See Fig. 15-7.

If necessary, build up the lot contours with wire screen and blocking, covering the surface grade with molding plaster, spackling compound, or papier-mâché. Papier-mâché may be made from shredded newspapers soaked in water until they become a fibrous mass. Drain and mix the fibers with wallpaper paste and sawdust to make a sticky, plastic material for covering the screen. Large areas of papier-mâché require considerable time in drying and may split when dry unless shrinkage joints are provided.

Paint the grass surfaces green and cover with model-builder's grass material (green sawdust), or use green flocking over the paint. When painting drives, walks, etc., use masking tape to maintain neat edges between the adjacent colors. Drives and walks may be edged with small balsa strips to make them definitive and give them a clean-cut appearance.

For the trees and shrubs use green sponges or lichen, properly shaped and sized. For trees, merely cement the forms to the twigs or branches; to attach the trees follow the same procedure as for architectural models. Fasten the shrubbery in interesting groups near corners of the model and in other areas where the architectural lines need to be softened. Also, use plantings to emphasize the front door, or place them as natural screens for privacy.

If edge-grain shows around the periphery of the base, select a suitable molding or stock casing for covering the edge. Nail the trim about $\frac{1}{8}''$ above the surface of the grade line to prevent the grass material from dropping off. Miter the corners of the trim and either paint or stain with a suitable finish.

A

B

Fig. 15-12 (A) Residential structural model; (B) an enlarged view of the framing.

REVIEW QUESTIONS

1. What part does the model of a building play in architectural service?

2. What characteristics of an architectural proposal does a model most effectively show?

3. Why is balsa wood a favorite material for many model builders?

4. How are lot contours usually represented on architectural models?

5. Why is the scale so important when selecting model-building materials?

6. Why must the model builder use particular care in the direction in which wood grain is placed on exterior textures?

7. Why is soft pine recommended for structural lumber rather than balsa wood?

8. What is the disadvantage of using glossy enamels on model surfaces?

9. Names various materials convenient for representing roofing textures.

10. Why can landscaping problems be more easily solved on a model than on a landscaping plan?

"Nothing is achieved before it is thoroughly attempted."—Sir Phillip Sidney

16

Writing Specifications

In the light of what has been said about graphic description, it will be seen that working drawings, however well-drawn, cannot be entirely adequate in completely revealing all aspects of a construction project. Many things cannot be shown graphically. For example, how would one show on a drawing the quality of workmanship required on a kitchen cabinet, except by an extensive hand-lettered note? Or who is to be responsible for securing a building permit? It becomes standard procedure, then, to supplement working drawings with written specifications.

16.1 PURPOSE OF SPECIFICATIONS

These detailed instructions, commonly called "specs," become an important part of architectural service and require considerable time in writing. They become, along with the drawings, a legal document forming part of the contract, a basis for bidding, and written instructions for the construction, defining and limiting the materials and fabrication according to the intent of the architect or designer. Generally, complete detail specifications are necessary to ensure positive control of the construction and to eliminate possible misinterpretations. For small projects, however, such as project houses, for example, abbreviated (streamlined) specifications, outlining only the major features of the work to be done, may suffice.

In small architectural offices, draftsmen who have had experience with materials and construction frequently compile the entire set of specifications; in larger offices, however, specification writers are engaged for this specialized work only.

16.2 RELATIONSHIP OF SPECIFICATIONS AND DRAWINGS

Information in the specifications should be compatible with information found on the working drawings. Should there be a discrepancy, the specifications usually take precedence over the drawings. A statement to that effect is generally contained in the specifications "General Conditions," to avoid a conflict.

Draftsmen and specification writers soon learn from experience which information is best put on the drawings and which is best reserved for the written specifications. In general, the drawings should show the placement, arrangement, dimensions of features, and basic types of materials, whereas the specifications should state the supplementary, defining information about the materials and the exact methods of fabrication. For example, the drawings might indicate "brick" as a material on an elevation, and the specifications would then state the exact requirements of the brick, whether it is common or face, the color, the grade, the cost, or other information. It is customary to show window, door, and finish schedules on the working drawings. However, further information about windows and doors, as well as interior finish, is usually contained in the specifications.

16.3 SPECIFICATION MATERIAL SOURCES

To make up a completely new set of specifications for each job would be unnecessarily time-consuming. Instead, specification writers rely on various sources for reference material and standard specifications from which they can compile a set for each new job. Specifications that have repeatedly proved satisfactory in the past are heavily relied upon. Some may have to be modified to fit the conditions of a given job; many can be used word for word. Listed below are the major sources from which specification material is available:

1. City and national codes and ordinances;
2. Testing societies (A.S.T.M.; A.S.A.);
3. Government agencies (FHA; NHA; U.S. Government Printing Office);
4. Manufacturers' catalogues (*Sweet's File*);
5. Manufacturers' associations (N.L.M.A.);
6. Model specifications;
7. Individual file of previously written specifications;
8. Books on specifications;
9. Federal specifications (General Services Administration); and
10. Construction Specifications Institute (*Construction Specifier Magazine*).

The specification writer must not only be familiar with construction methods, new materials, and building techniques, but he must be able to accumulate reference material and organize it for easy access when it is needed.

16.4 SPECIFICATION ARRANGEMENT

A set of specifications, commonly divided into "sections," must have a logical arrangement of information so that each trade or type of work completed by one contractor will be conveniently placed in one section. It is also customary to list the sections in the same sequence as the disposition of the work on the job. For example, the carpentry section is listed before the section on roofing, since carpentry work precedes the installation of roofing. However, because all projects vary slightly, and contractors must use workmen in the most efficient manner, specifications naturally cannot always have this similar sequence.

On *small jobs* such as residences the following arrangement of sections is commonly used:

1. General Conditions;
2. Excavation;
3. Concrete and Masonry;
4. Waterproofing;
5. Miscellaneous Metal;
6. Rough Carpentry;
7. Finish Carpentry and Millwork;
8. Roofing and Sheet Metal;
9. Weather Stripping, Insulation, Caulking, and Glazing;
10. Plastering or Dry-wall Construction;
11. Ceramic Tile;
12. Flooring;
13. Painting and Decorating;
14. Plumbing;
15. Mechanical Equipment;
16. Electrical; and
17. Landscaping.

The general conditions section (usually the first section) is reserved for information relating to the work of all the trade sections. Items such as relationship of all parties to the contract, legal rights, responsibilities, insurance, terms of payment, guarantees, completion of work, and similar items are included in this important section. With specifications of small jobs, it is usual practice to include the *A.I.A. Short Form of Agreement Between Owner and Contractor* as a part of the general conditions. With larger jobs, the more complete *Standard A.I.A. General Conditions Form* is used[1] Occasionally the section "Special Conditions" accompanies standardized general conditions when revisions or supplements to specific articles must be made.

When using the above arrangement of sections for small jobs, a *block form* of page format (see Fig. 16-1) can be used to save typing time, yet provide a simple method of listing the information in each section. Notice that the lines in each paragraph are single-spaced, with double-spacing between paragraphs. Paragraph indentation is not necessary. Other page formats using indentations and standard outline numbering systems may be used for more complex specifications, as long as the style is consistent throughout the entire set.

1 These standard forms and other construction contract document forms are available from the American Institute of Architects, 1735 New York Avenue, N. W., Washington, D. C. 20006.

16.5 GENERAL POINTS FOR PREPARING SPECIFICATIONS

The following points should be kept in mind when writing specifications:

1. Use simple, direct language and accepted terminology, rather than abstract legal terminology;
2. Use brief sentences requiring only simple punctuation;
3. Specify standard items and alternates where possible, in the interest of economy, without sacrificing quality;
4. Avoid repetition; use cross-references if they apply and seem logical;
5. Avoid specifications that are impossible for the contractor to carry out; be fair in designating responsibility;
6. Avoid including specifications that are not to be part of the construction;
7. Clarify all terms that may be subject to more than one interpretation;
8. Be consistent in the use of terms, abbreviations, format, arrangement of material;
9. Specify numbers, names, and descriptions of

Fig. 16-1 Sample page format for small job specifications.

SECTION 6 — 6-1

CARPENTRY & MILLWORK

FRAMING LUMBER: All framing lumber including joists, studs, rafters, headers, trimmers, plates, sills, shall be K. D. No. 2 Dimension S4S Southern Yellow Pine, or No. 2 J & P Douglas Fir, or No. 2 Dimension Western Larch.

SUBFLOORING,WALL AND ROOF DECKING: Board lumber shall be No. 2 S4S Southern Yellow Pine. Plywood shall be 1/2" Douglas Fir, Utility Grade.

MOISTURE CONTENT: All lumber shall be kiln dried with a moisture content not to exceed 15%.

JOISTS: Shall be the sizes and placed in the direction shown on the plans. Spacing of joists shall be 16" o.c. except under bathroom floors which shall be spaced 12" o. c. Joists shall be doubled under each partition running parallel to the joist run. Floor framing shall be kept 2" from chimney masonry and all floor openings shall be surrounded with double headers and trimmers. All joists shall have at least 2" bearing surfaces at both ends.

BRIDGING shall be 1" x 3" material cut on bevel and double nailed at each end. Bottom ends shall be nailed up tight after subflooring is installed. Joists 8'-0" in span and over shall have one continuous row; joists 12'-0" and over shall have two rows.

STUDS: Studding shown on the drawings marked 7" shall be 2" x 6" set 16" o. c.; marked 3" shall be 2" x 4" set the 2" way 24" o. c.; all other studding shall be 2" x 4" set the 4" way 16" o. c., doubled around all openings and built-up solid on all corners.

WALL OPENINGS: Over all window and door openings supporting usual loads the following size headers shall be used:

Two 2" x 4"s on edge, maximum span 3'-6"
Two 2" x 6"s on edge, maximum span 4'-6"
Two 2" x 8"s on edge, maximum span 6'-0"
Two 2" x 10"s on edge, maximum span 7'-6"
Two 2" x 12"s on edge, maximum span 10'-0"

PLATES: Bottom sole plates shall be single 2" x 4" and top bearing plates for rafters and ceiling joists shall be two 2" x 4".

RAFTERS shall be spiked to the wall plates and tied to the ceiling joists where possible. Opposing rafters shall be directly opposite each other at the ridge and shall bear on a 1" x 8" ridge board.

HIPS & VALLEYS: All hip rafters shall be 2" x 8". All valley rafters shall be 2" x 8" placed at each valley with one valley rafter extending from the wall plate to the ridge where applicable.

materials from the *latest editions* of manufacturers' catalogues;

10. Capitalize the following: major parties to the contract, such as Contractor, Owner, Designer, Architect; the contract documents, such as Specifications, Working Drawings, Contract, Special Conditions; specific rooms within the building, such as Kitchen, Living Room, Office; grade of materials, such as No. 1 J & P Douglas Fir, Heart Redwood, Grade A White Oak; and of course all proper names;
11. Differentiate between "shall" and "will"—"The Contractor shall . . . ," "The Owner or Architect will . . .";
12. Avoid the term "a workmanlike job" or similar vague phrases; rather, describe the quality of workmanship or exact requirements to be expected;
13. Use accepted standards when specifying quality of materials or workmanship required, such as "Lightweight concrete block shall meet requirements of A.S.T.M. C–90–52";
14. Number all pages and include a table of contents; and
15. Keep in mind that bidders and subcontractors of different trades will have to use the specifications to look up information in their respective areas and that the information dealing with their work should be stated in the logical section and not "hidden" throughout the various sections.

16.6 METHODS OF WRITING SPECIFICATIONS AND REPRODUCTION

As we mentioned, it is common procedure to start writing specifications with a previously completed set—possibly from a similar project. In doing so, merely cross out material not applicable and add new material, either from other sources or self-written, where necessary. Or, the "cut-and-paste" method may be employed: Cut out specification paragraphs from different sources and fasten in their proper order to clean sheets of paper with paste or cellophane tape. Make corrections or additions in longhand, if necessary, and carefully check for accuracy and organization. Then type the set in its final form from this makeup. Compile the index after the final typing is done so that page numbers will be correct.

Inasmuch as a number of sets of specifications are needed for each job, it is customary to have them reproduced by an economical method. Contractors, subcontractors, owners, lending institutions, and city permit offices usually require copies; the architectural office or designer also retains a copy for future reference. Usually the set is reproduced by spirit duplication (Ditto) or by mimeograph. If the size of the project warrants it, the specifications may be duplicated by offset lithography or by letterpress. Occasionally only the title cover is printed by letterpress for appearance. The sets are then bound into neat booklets. Some offices type small sets on tracing paper ($8\frac{1}{2}'' \times 11''$), reproduce them in the same machine as the working drawings, and bind them with the drawings.

16.7 THE C.S.I. FORMAT

The Construction Specifications Institute[2] has for a number of years engaged in a program of standardizing specification format. The Institute has found, after questioning its members, that a universal need exists for more uniformity in format arrangement and that a consistent national format would prove beneficial not only to the writers of specifications, but to the contractors and material suppliers as well. After evaluating the various comments, the Institute has compiled a format that provides the advantages of standardization, yet has sufficient flexibility to allow writers throughout the country enough latitude in expression to accommodate local codes and trade-practice variations. Only the arrangement in the format is restrictive, so that a set of specifications, like the alphabet, or numbering system, will be universally useful because of its consistency. The benefits of the format will be realized mainly from its widespread usage. Although nearly every set of specifications varies in content because of variations in circumstance, it has been found that arrangement of content can be identical.

The C.S.I. format is based upon the "Division-Section" concept. The word *section* denotes the "trade section" or "technical section" and defines a basic unit of work or necessary material, whereas the broader term *division* arranges the similar sections into logical trade-work groups, usually according to the similarity of the

[2] Dupont Circle Building, Washington, D. C. 20036.

work involved. The system provides for convenient major divisions, forming the permanent backbone of the format; and the sections, forming the flexible units of information, are the meat of the specifications. The divisions are given numbers (1, 2, 3, 4, 5, etc.); and the sections within each division are given numbers and letters (1A, 1B, 1C, 1D, or 9A, 9B, 9C, 9D, etc.).

The format is adaptable to small jobs as well as large. When divisions are not applicable to information needed on the particular job, the division number and title are shown nevertheless, and the note "None on this job" is placed below it.

The C.S.I. format is shown on the following pages in the interest of standardization in specification arrangement and in recognition of its merit (by permission of the Construction Specifications Institute). Also, the following complete set of specifications for house No. 1 (Chapter 10) is an example of the C.S.I. format as used in residential specification writing:

The C.S.I. Format

BIDDING REQUIREMENTS

CONTRACT FORMS

GENERAL CONDITIONS
(And Supplementary General Conditions)

SPECIFICATIONS

Division 1: General Requirements
Includes most requirements that apply to the job as a whole, or to several of the technical sections, especially those requirements normally referred to as Special Conditions.
General Conditions and supplementary General Conditions are not included within the divisions of the Specifications.

Division 2: Site Work
Includes most subjects dealing with site preparation and development.
Exceptions: site utilities in Divisions 15 and 16.

Division 3: Concrete
Includes most items traditionally associated with concrete work.
Exceptions: paving, piling, waterproofing, terrazzo.

Division 4: Masonry
Includes most materials traditionally installed by masons.
Exceptions: paving interior flooring.

Division 5: Metals: Structural and Miscellaneous
Includes most structural metals and those metals not falling under the specific provisions of other divisions.
Exceptions: reinforcing steel, curtain wall, roofing, piling, doors, and windows.

Division 6: Carpentry
Includes most work traditionally performed by carpenters.
Exceptions: wood fences, concrete formwork, doors, windows, finish hardware

Division 7: Moisture Protection
Includes most items normally associated with preventing the passage of water or water vapor.
Exceptions: paint, water stops and joints installed in concrete or masonry, and gaskets and sealants for curtain walls.

Division 8: Doors, Windows, and Glass
Includes metal and wood doors, windows, and frames; metal and glass curtain walls; transparent and translucent glazing.
Exceptions: glass block, and glass mosaics.

Division 9: Finishes
Includes interior finishes that are not traditionally the work of the carpentery trade.

Division 10: Specialties
Includes finish hardware and most other factory assembled, prefinished assemblies.

Division 11: Equipment
Includes most items of specialized equipment.

Division 12: Furnishings
Includes most items that are placed within the finished building.

Division 13: Special Construction
Includes on-site contruction that consists of items which normally would fall under several other divisions but which require the control that can be attained only by including all parts in a single section.

Division 14: Conveying Systems
Includes those systems that utilize power to transport people or materials.

Division 15: Mechanical
Includes most items that have been traditionally associated with the mechanical trades.

Division 16: Electrical
Includes most items that have been traditionally associated with the electrical trades.

S P E C I F I C A T I O N S

FOR THE

CONSTRUCTION

OF A

RESIDENCE

FOR

MR. & MRS. JOHN DOE

1918 Pinedale Ave.

Atlanta, Ga.

ARCHITECTS

DATE

JOB NO.

INDEX

NOTE: This index is for the convenience of the Contractor only. Its accuracy and completeness are not guaranteed and not to be considered part of these specifications.

BID FORM

Place ____________________

Date ____________________

TO: Mr. John Doe
Atlanta, Georgia

FROM: ____________________

____

Dear Sir:

Having carefully examined the plans and specifications entitled "A Residence for Mr. and Mrs. John Doe", Atlanta, Georgia, dated, __________, prepared by the office of ______________________________, Architect, and having visited the site to become familiar with all conditions affecting the cost of the work, the undersigned hereby proposes to furnish all labor, materials, equipment, and incidentals, and perform all work in a manner called for in the said documents for the sum of ________________ dollars, ($____________).

If awarded the contract, the undersigned agrees to furnish within 14 days, all Bonds and Insurance required; agrees to commence actual physical work within 10 days from date of notification to proceed, and that all work will be completed within 120 days.

The undersigned further agrees to execute the agreement entitled A.I.A., The Short Form of Agreement Between Owner and Contractor #A107, Sept., 1963 Ed., within 30 days after notification in writing.

Respectfully submitted,

____
(Individual or Firm Name)

By ____________________

Title ____________________

____
(Legal Address)

(This must be an Individual or Firm licensed to do business in the State of Georgia)

INSTRUCTION TO BIDDERS

1. SCOPE: This proposal is for the construction of a residence for Mr. & Mrs. John Doe, Atlanta, Georgia.

   The Construction shall consist of a one-story residence with basement as detailed on the plans and described in the following specifications.

2. BIDS: Bids shall be made in duplicate on the form provided hereto and shall be dated. All blanks must be filled in. Base bid amount shall be stated both in writing and in figures. Signature must be in long hand by a principal duly authorized to make contracts.

   The owner reserves the right to reject any and all bids and to waiver informalities. Unbalanced bids will be subject to rejection.

   Sealed bids will be received by Mr. & Mrs. John Doe, Atlanta, Georgia, up until 4:00 P.M., E.S.T., __________ __________.

3. CONTRACT: The form of the Contract will be THE SHORT FORM OF AGREEMENT BETWEEN OWNER AND CONTRACTOR of the American Institute of Architects, AIA Doc. #A107, Sept., 1963 Ed.

4. BID GUARANTY: Bidder shall furnish with his proposal a Bid Bond equal to at least 5% of his base bid, in a specifically stated amount. The Bond shall be made payable to the owner. Bid Bond shall guarantee that Contractor will not withdraw his bid for a period of 30 calendar days from the date of the receipt of the bid; it shall further guarantee that Contractor will, if notified within a 30-day period, enter into a contract with the Owner to perform the work as agreed to and set forth in the Contract. If the successful Bidder defaults in executing the Contract, or in furnishing the Owner's Protective Bond, his bond will become the property of the Owner.

5. VISITING BUILDING SITE: The bidder, before submitting a bid on this proposal, is assumed to have visited the building site for the purpose of observing first hand any conditions relevant to the completion of the work. No consideration will be given any claim based on lack of knowledge of existing conditions, except where contract documents make definite provision for adjustment of cost or extension of time due to existing conditions not readily forseeable.

6. PERFORMANCE AND PAYMENT BOND: Contract, if awarded, will be a stipulated sum basis. Both a Performance and Payment Bond will be required in an amount equal to 100% of contract price.

GENERAL CONDITIONS

1. STANDARD A.I.A. FORMS: The General Conditions of A.I.A. Short Form for Small-Construction Contracts, Doc. #A107, Sept., 1963 Ed., is hereby made a part of this specification to the same extent as if bound herein. The modifications and General Conditions herein included, shall be a part of the Contract and shall apply to all Contractors and Sub-Contractors. Copies of the General Conditions may be examined or obtained at the Architect's office, located at ____________ ______________________.

2. ARCHITECT'S SUPERVISION: The Architect will not have continuous supervisory responsibility for this job, but will be called in on occasion by Owner when needed. When Architect is not functioning as such, the word "Owner" shall be substituted in the A.I.A. General Conditions for "Architect".

3. DETAIL DRAWINGS AND SPECIFICATIONS CONFLICTS: Should a conflict occur in or between drawings and specifications, the order of precedence shall be as follows:

   (a) General Conditions
   (b) The Detail Specifications
   (c) Large Scale Drawings
   (d) Small Scale Drawings

4. EXAMINATION OF SITE: The Contractor shall visit the site of the building, examine for himself as to the nature and bearing power of the soil. He shall furnish all labor and materials necessary to prepare the site for execution of this contract.

5. GRADES, LINES, LEVELS, AND SURVEYS: The Owner will establish the lot lines and restrictions. The building shall be located on the lot as shown on the Plot Plan. The finished floor shall be established as near the same relation to grade as shown on the plans.

6. MATERIALS: Article 3 of the A.I.A. General Conditions is amended by the addition of the following paragraph:

   When reference is made in the specifications to trade names or to the names of Manufacturers, such references are made solely to designate and identify quality of material or equipment, and not to restrict competitive bidding. In case Contractor wishes to use materials or equipment of trade names which differ from those mentioned in the specifications, prior written approval of Architect and Owner must be obtained. The Architect and Owner will approve such material or equipment changes upon written request, if they are considered suitable and equal to those specified. Whenever "approved", "satisfactory", "as directed", or similar phrases are used in these specifications, they shall be understood to mean that material or construction methods referred to shall be approved by, satisfactory to, or as directed by the Architect or Owner.

7. PROTECTION: Article 6 of the A.I.A. Short Form General Conditions shall be amended by the addition of the following paragraph:

   The Contractor shall, at all times, provide protection against weather, rain, wind, storms, frost or heat so as to maintain all work, materials, apparatus, and fixtures free from injury or damage. At the end of the day's work, all new work likely to be damaged shall be covered. If low temperatures make it impossible to continue work, the Contractor shall cease work and shall so notify the Owner. Any work damaged by failure to provide protection as above required shall be removed and replaced with new work at the Contractor's expense.

8. MANUFACTURER'S DIRECTIONS: All manufactured articles, material and equipment shall be applied, installed, connected, erected, used, cleaned and conditioned as directed by the manufacturers, unless herein specified to the contrary.

9. WORKMANSHIP: Compliance with the drawings and specifications with regard to materials and methods of assembly will, not in itself, assure acceptance of the construction. Of equal importance is good workmanship, the lack of which will be sufficient cause to refuse acceptance of the construction.

10. WORK AND MATERIALS NOT COVERED IN SPECIFICATIONS: Any item of work necessary to the proper completion of construction under this contract which is not specifically covered in the drawings and specifications shall be performed in a manner deemed good practice of the trade involved.

    Materials and equipment not specifically covered by the drawings and specifications shall be of a standard equal to good practice commensurate with the class of dwelling being constructed.

******

DIVISION 1: GENERAL REQUIREMENTS

(Special Conditions)

A. LOCATION OF WORK: Work included in this contract is to be located at the Owner's property at Atlanta, Georgia.

B. OWNER: The Owner referred to in these Specifications is Mr. John Doe, Atlanta, Georgia.

C. SCOPE OF WORK: Contractor shall furnish and install all material and equipment shown, listed, or described on the drawings or in these Specifications, subject to qualifications, conditions, or exceptions as noted. Contractor also, shall furnish all labor, scaffolding, and tools necessary to complete the work.

D. MEASUREMENTS & DIMENSIONS: Before ordering material or commencing work which is dependent for proper size and installation upon coordination with building conditions, Contractor shall verify all dimensions by taking measurements at building site and shall be responsible for their correctness. Any discrepancies between drawings and/or specifications and existing conditions shall be referred to the Architect for adjustment before any work affected thereby is begun.

E. LAYING OUT WORK: All work of every character and description shall be laid out on premises, or otherwise, by Contractor, who will be held responsible for any errors and for its correctness.

F. SPECIFICATIONS DIVISIONS: The separation of specifications into divisions is not intended to control Contractor in dividing work among sub-contractors, but is for the purpose of uniform coordination of the work of the different trades. It shall be the General Contractor's entire responsibility for proper coordination and completion of all work described in these specifications, whether performed by the General Contractor or by sub-contractors.

G. SUB-CONTRACTORS: All sub-contractors shall be approved by Owner.

H. FOREMAN: Contractor shall have at the building site, from start to finish of construction, a responsible foreman. In addition, Contractor shall give his personal supervision to the work. Foreman shall be on duty during all working hours. Any instructions or notices given to him shall have same importance as if given to the Contractor in person.

J. TEMPORARY PROVISIONS: Contractor shall be responsible for providing and maintaining the following temporary provisions:

   1. Temporary toilet, which shall be located as directed and maintained in sanitary condition, for the use of workmen.

   2. Temporary water supply, including lines, valves, hose, and similar equipment for construction purposes.

   3. Temporary light and power, including wiring, lamps, and connections as required for the completion of the work.

   4. Temporary heat, as needed during cold and wet weather for the purpose of protecting and drying construction and materials.

K. CONTRACTOR'S INSURANCE: Contractor will maintain such insurance as will protect him from claims under Workman's Compensation Acts and other employee benefits from claims for damages because of bodily injury, including death, and for claims for damages to property which may arise out of and during operations under this Contract, whether such operations be by himself or by any sub-contractor or anyone directly or indirectly employed by either of them. The Contractor shall file with the Owner certificate for property damage insurance in the limits of $50,000 for each accident and $100,000 for the aggregate of operations.

L. FIRE INSURANCE: Owner shall effect and maintain "Builders' Risk--Completed Value Form" insurance as specified in Article 15 of Short Form General Conditions.

M. PROTECTION OF TREES: Near construction operations, Contractor shall provide adequate wood frames around valuable trees, as directed, to protect them from damage.

N. PROTECTION OF FOUNDATION WALLS: Immediately after backfilling has been completed, Contractor shall rough grade a strip 4 feet wide surrounding the building and cover with building paper or polyethylene film for the purpose of protecting the lower wall against mud and dirt stains. This protective covering shall be maintained until finish grading and planting operations are started.

******

DIVISION 2: SITE WORK

A. GENERAL:

   1. Secure permits, and pay fees required for work in this division.

   2. Protect and maintain conduits, drains, pipes, sewers, wires which are to remain on property, or which are to remain until new permanent installations are complete.

   3. Take precautions necessary to protect adjoining property, from excessive drainage, debris, and assume full responsibility for damages resulting from negligence of these items. No trespassing will be allowed on adjoining property.

   4. Provide and place any additional earth needed to bring existing grades to new grades indicated on plans, and dispose of any excess earth on property where indicated.

   5. Excavation and backfill necessary for sewers, water and gas piping, plumbing, heating, and electrical work are included in other divisions.

   6. Visit site; examine existing conditions and conditions surrounding site; determine requirements under which work will be performed.

B. CLEARING OF SITE: Completely remove all trees, shrubs, stumps, sod, and all other organic debris from areas to be covered by the building, walks, terraces, and driveway. All such debris shall be disposed of at the Contractor's expense.

   Box and protect all trees and shrubs which have been designated to remain; maintain boxing until finished grading is completed. Remove interfering branches and roots of remaining trees without injuring trunks. Cutting and trimming shall be done as directed by Owner.

C. TOPSOIL: Strip topsoil to its entire depth from areas to be covered by building, walks, terraces, driveway, and areas to be graded; pile topsoil neatly away from construction on property until finish grading is completed. Stripped topsoil shall be free from clay, large stones, and debris. Use topsoil exclusively for the finished grade.

D. EXCAVATION: Excavate to elevations and dimensions indicated, plus sufficient space to permit erection of forms and inspection of foundations. Excavation for footings may be cut to accurate sizes to form trenches, and side forms omitted, if care is taken to dig cleancut trenches, and concrete is poured without cave-ins.

Footings and foundations shall not be placed on earth fill. Any excess cut under footings and foundations shall be filled with concrete only. All foundation elevations shall have depth conforming to local building codes and practices, and in all instances shall extend to solid, undisturbed earth. Bottoms of footings shall be approximately level, and clean and clear of loose materials and water.

Excavation, required and included herein, consists of earth and materials of whatever nature encountered, with the exception of rock, which shall be paid extra for at a unit cost agreed upon before execution of the rock excavation.

E. BACKFILL: Before backfilling, remove all forms, debris, and other loose material from fill areas. Backfill promptly after footings, foundations. and other related work has been completed and approved. All trench backfill shall be firmly compacted. At no time shall power equipment used for backfilling be allowed to touch foundation walls or completed masonry work. Any damage to masonry will be the responsibility of the Contractor.

All necessary fill under concrete slabs shall be deposited in thin layers, slushed, tamped, and compacted. Slabs shall not be poured until all settlement has occurred and earth has been inspected and approved by the Architect. Fill immediately beneath basement slab and entrance slab shall be crushed stone or gravel 4" deep.

F. GRADING: Provide such cutting, grading, and filling as necessary to transform existing grades to finish grades as indicated on the drawings. Slope finish grades to drain away from the house on all sides.

G. PLACING TOPSOIL: As soon as practicable, after rough grading has been completed and approved, spread topsoil previously stripped and retained, over all graded areas. Prepare topsoil to receive grass by removing stone, debris, and unsuitable material. Hand rake to remove water pockets and irregularities completely around building.

H. CLEANUP: During construction and cleanup, do not dump debris on any part of the property or on any unauthorized place. Clean graded areas of all rocks, roots, and debris; remove same from premises. Debris may not be buried on property.

J. SODDING: Sodding of graded areas is not included in this contract.

******

DIVISION 3: CONCRETE

A. GENERAL: This division is intended to cover all concrete work and related items necessary to complete work shown on drawings and herein specified. Contractor shall furnish all materials, labor, and equipment required to complete footings, basement slab, entrance slab, carport slab, terrace slab, drive and turn-around area, sidewalk, and all related items.

B. MATERIALS: Materials to be incorporated in the concrete work shall comply with the following requirements:

1. Cement: Shall be a domestic Portland Cement, standard brand, Type 1, conforming to ASTM C-150.

2. Concrete: Shall be "Ready-Mixed" by Supplier approved by the Architect, and shall be 2500 lb. "Building Code Design Concrete", No. 57 aggregate, 5" slump range. (1:2:4) Mix.

3. Reinforcing Steel: Shall be intermediate grade conforming to ASTM A15.

4. Expansion Joint Material: Shall be asphalt mastic strips (Preformed) composed of cane fibre of cellular nature, or other suitable and approved fibre impregnated with a durable asphaltic compound. Install where exterior and interior slabs abut masonry. Thickness throughout to be 1/2".

5. Vapor Barrier: Shall be Sisalkcraft Moistop, or equal. Vapor barrier shall be used over gravel fill under basement, entrance, and carport slabs. Film shall be purchased in 8'-0" or wider rolls.

6. Gravel Fill: Shall be clean, washed gravel 3/4" to 1 1/2" in size, or crushed stone of same size, and shall be placed under all slabs where indicated on plans, at least 4" deep.

7. Anchor Bolts: Shall be furnished and set in all exterior walls in accordance with size and spacing indicated on drawings. Unless otherwise noted, they shall be 5/8" dia. x 18" long with a 3" x 3" x ¼" plate which shall be embedded under the second course of block below the sill and placed 48" o.c.

C. PLACING VAPOR BARRIER: Prior to placing vapor barrier, sub-grade shall be smooth and rolled to prevent protrusions which may cause damage to barrier, and soil below treated with termite poisoning (See Article K, this division). Vapor barrier shall be lapped not less than 6", with top lap placed in same direction concrete is to be spread. Use under all slabs resting on gravel fill. Run continuous as much as possible. Workmen shall avoid walking on film before slabs are poured.

D. PLACING REINFORCEMENT: Basement slab, entrance slab, carport and terrace slab shall be reinforced with 6" x 6", 10/10 welded wire mesh, unless otherwise specified. Reinforcement shall be at least 1" up into bottom of 4" slabs. Mesh shall be lapped at least 12"

at all joints, and run continuous where possible. Reinforcement bars in footings shall be two #5 rods, placed 2" down from top of footings.

E. CONCRETE MIXES: Concrete for job to be mixed, designed, handled, protected, and cured in accordance with provisions of the "Specifications for Ready-Mixed Structural Concrete", adopted by the Concrete Advisory Board of Greater Atlanta on September 17, 1958, revised 1960.

F. PLACING CONCRETE: Before pouring foundation footings, see that bottoms of excavations are of undisturbed earth, free from frost, properly leveled, and tamped. Before pouring concrete basement slab, be sure that termite poisoning has been applied, reinforcing is as specified, and column footings have been properly located and poured.

Concrete will not be poured without prior approval of Architect.

Concrete shall be mixed and placed only when temperature is over 40°F.; concrete shall have a temperature of between 60°F. and 90°F. when placed. Maintain concrete temperature of at least 50°F. for 72 hours after placing, when regular Portland Cement is used, and 24 hours when early-strength concrete is used. Method of heating materials and protecting concrete shall be approved by Architect.

Concrete shall be delivered to the point of pouring directly from troughs of trucks or by carts, and shall not be dumped into carts or forms with a fall of more than six (6) feet.

Tamp freshly poured concrete into place with steel rammer and slicing tools until concrete is thoroughly compact and without voids. Screed slabs to true planes, lines, and grades indicated on drawings.

G. CONCRETE FINISH: Concrete slabs shall be finished as follows:

1. Basement slab--smooth metal trowel finish

2. Carport slab--broom finish

3. Driveway and turn-around--broom finish

4. Entrance slab--broom finish on exterior portion and metal trowel finish on interior storage and entrance area.

Floating and troweling: When slabs have hardened sufficiently they shall be floated to a compact and smooth surface, with no coarse aggregate visible. Broom finish slabs shall be floated with a wood float, and after proper hardening shall be finished with neat, even cane-broom striations. Metal trowel slabs may be finished by hand metal-troweling or machine troweling. After leveling and compacting, the surface shall be thoroughly troweled by either hand steel trowel or by a motor driven rotary trowel. The final troweling shall be for the purpose of burnishing and shall be performed sufficiently late so that a sheen will show on the surface. Hand troweling or machine troweling operations shall leave a smooth, hard, impervious

even surface, with no trowel marks.

Edges of exposed slabs shall be finished with a rounded edging tool, leaving the exposed corners slightly rounded and cleancut, free from burrs and obstructions.

H. SLAB PROTECTION: Protect concrete from injury by freezing, the elements, or defacement during construction and curing. Cover concrete with 2" of sawdust or wood shavings and keep moist for 7 days.

J. REMOVAL OF FORMS: Care shall be taken in removal of forms not to damage surfaces of concrete. Floor slab forms shall not be removed in less than seven (7) days.

K. TERMITE TREATMENT: After placing gravel fill under basement and entrance slabs, and prior to placing vapor barrier, apply the following dosages of 0.5% Dieldrin in oil solution or water emulsion:

1. Foundation walls: Apply each side at rate of 1 gallon per 2½ lineal feet per foot of depth.

2. Floor slabs and carport slab: Apply uniformly at the rate of 1 gallon per seven (7) square feet.

3. Concrete block foundation wall voids: Apply at the rate of one gallon per five (5) lineal feet.

Treatment shall be made when weather permits and soil is dry. Protect treated areas from human or animal contact until covered by soil or concrete.

******

DIVISION 4: MASONRY

A. GENERAL: This section includes the furnishing by Contractor of all materials, labor, and equipment necessary to complete concrete block and brick walls as shown on drawings, and specified herein.

1. Work related to other items: Build in door frame, basement windows, sheet metal work, termite shields, metal reinforcement, ties, anchors, bolts, structural members, and built-in items required by other trades.

2. Protection: Contractor shall protect his work while under construction by placing roofing felt and boards over walls at night and during rainy weather. No masonry shall be laid in weather below 50°F. without approval of Architect.

3. Cutting and Patching: Consult other trades in advance, make provisions for installing their work to avoid cutting or patching. Do necessary cutting and patching of masonry to accommodate work of others.

4. Masonry reinforcement: Dur-O-Wall or equal masonry reinforce-

ment shall be placed in block and brick work as specified.

B. MATERIALS: Masonry materials shall comply with the following requirements:

1. Concrete block: Lightweight, manufactured from expanded shale aggregate produced by the rotary kiln method in accord with Autoclave Building Products Association Standards and meet requirements of ASTM C-90-52, Grade A.

2. Used brick: Shall be of suitable quality to resist spalling and deterioration. Type and color to be selected by Owner. Contractor shall make allowance of fifty dollars ($50.00) per thousand for used brick in bid.

3. Mortar mix: For laying brick and concrete block--1 part cement, 1 part lime putty, and 6 parts sand. (1 part approved masonry cement and 3 parts sand) For exterior masonry use admix, 1 lb admix per 1 bag of cementuous material. Mortar ingredients shall comply with the following requirements:

   a. Aggregates: ASTM C-144-52T
   b. Water: Clean, fresh, free from acid, alkali, sewage or organic material
   c. Portland cement: ASTM C150-55, Type 1
   d. Masonry cement: ASTM C-91-55T, Type 11
   e. Hydrated lime: ASTM C-207-49T, Type S
   f. Admix: Horn's "Hydratite Plus", Master Builder's "Omicron", or Truscon "Mortite."

4. Horizontal reinforcement: Furnish for all concrete block and brick walls. Dur-O-Wall or equal shall conform to requirements of ASTM Standard A82-34, and shall be placed in first and second bed joints (8" c to c) above and below openings and in every second bed joint (16" c to c) throughout remainder of walls. Reinforcement in first bed joint immediately above and below openings shall be continuous. In second bed joint it shall extend two feet beyond each side of opening. At splices, it shall be lapped sufficiently (6" minimum) to insure continuity. Corners shall be cut and bent to conform to surface of bed. Reinforcement shall not pass through control joints.

C. WORKMANSHIP:

1. General: Brick and block shall be stacked at site and protected from damage and mud stain. Work to be done by skilled masons experienced in the various types of masonry work. Work which fails to conform to best standards of practice, and to drawings and specifications, will be replaced. Work out coursing and check with a story pole. Make corners square and joints uniform in width. Units to be fully bedded in full, except as noted, mortar joints. No tamping or moving of units will be allowed after mortar has begun to set, resulting in a broken bond. Keep tops of walls dry and protect from frost.

2. Cutting: Cut all concrete block, where required, with a power

driven masonry saw. Used brick shall be broken to conform to the character of the units, and no unit shall be smaller than a half stretcher.

3. Laying used brick: Each brick shall be shoved into place, with beds full, solid, and uniform. Fill head joints completely with mortar. During hot, dry weather, dampen brick to reduce absorbancy; in cold, wet seasons, lay brick dry. Lay out work to avoid cutting.

   Use a running bond, with stretchers overlapping each other one-half brick. Joints to be approximately 3/8",to give coursing 2-2/3" vertically and 8-1/2" horizontally. Strike off joints flush, and when partially set, rake all exposed joints 3/8" deep and tool firmly to produce a smooth surface. Exterior brick wall extending from house shall have a rowlock course cap, throughout entire length.

4. Laying concrete block: Concrete footings to receive block shall be laid dry. Butter all joints in such a manner to result in full mortar joints, both horizontally and vertically. Dur-O-Wall reinforcement shall be completely enclosed in mortar.

   Use a running bond, with stretchers overlapping each other one-half block. Joints to be 3/8". Tool all joints with round steel tool to obtain a smooth concave joint. Tool shall be 24" long with ends turned up to give a uniform straight joint.

D. CLEANING:

1. Used brick: Remove excessive chunks of mortar with knife or chisel. Do not clean with acid solution.

2. Concrete block: Point-up all voids and open joints with cement mortar. Scrape entire surface with a piece of flat concrete block, removing all excess mortar and dirty spots. Do not clean with acid solution.

E. WATERPROOFING CONCRETE BLOCK: (Refer to Article E, Division 7)

******

DIVISION 5: METALS: STRUCTURAL & MISCELLANEOUS

A. STRUCTURAL METAL: (None on this job)

B. MISCELLANEOUS METALS:

1. General: Contractor shall furnish and install items of miscellaneous metal work specified herein and/or shown on drawings.

2. Railing for basement entrance: Railing shall be black iron pipe, 1/2" diameter, with welded joints as shown on drawings. Finish railing by grinding all welds smooth. Pipe shall be well anchored into concrete block retaining wall, with metal pipe sleeves at least 8" below surface of block. Pipe shall

be welded into sleeves.

3. Steel basement columns: Columns shall be 3" diameter with 3/8" x 4" x 6" welded cap and base plates. (six required)

4. Galvanized areaway: Metal areaway shall be of 20 gauge galvanized iron, with horizontal corrugations, size as shown on drawings, and shall be well anchored to foundation wall with galvanized anchor bolts and nuts. Furnish 6" crushed gravel below areaway to a level 3" below bottom of basement window.

5. Aluminum thresholds: Thresholds shall be installed in all exterior entrances, and shall be exterior weather seal type. Anchor securely in bed of caulking compound.

6. Termite shields: Termite shields shall be 24-gauge galvanized sheet metal in 8 ft lengths. Break metal to form a 2" flange at a 45-degree angle. Solder all joints and apply mastic under holes for anchor bolts to form a tight barrier between masonry and wood.

******

DIVISION 6: CARPENTRY & MILLWORK

A. GENERAL: This division is intended to cover carpentry, millwork, and related items necessary to complete work shown on drawings and/or herein specified and is a part of this contract. Contractor shall furnish all materials, labor, and equipment necessary to complete the work, including rough hardware, installation of finish hardware, and miscellaneous specialty items.

B. PROTECTION OF MATERIALS: Deliver lumber and carpentry materials in a dry condition and store lumber to insure proper ventilation and drainage. Protect lumber from elements with tarpaulin. Protect millwork from injury and dampness during and after delivery. Do not store or install millwork in building until concrete, masonry, or related work is thoroughly dry.

C. LUMBER GRADING REQUIREMENTS:

1. Moisture content: Framing lumber not to exceed 19% and finish lumber and millwork not to exceed 12%.

2. Grade & Trade Mark: Graded in accordance with latest grading rules of manufacturer's association under which rules lumber is produced and bear the grade and trade mark of the association.

3. Quality: Lumber must be sound, thoroughly seasoned, well manufactured, and free from warp which cannot be corrected by bridging or nailing. Woodwork exposed to view on exterior or interior of building shall be dressed (S4S).

D. GRADES AND SPECIES OF LUMBER:

1. All rough framing lumber except studs and wall plates: To be No. 2 Common kiln dried SL Sou. Yellow Pine. Treat lumber in contact with masonry or concrete by the Celcure process impregnated by pressure in accord with Standard C2 of the American Wood Preservers' Association.

2. Studs, sole, and double wall plate: To be Coastal Region, Douglas Fir (Utility grade).

3. Bridging, blocking, furring, grounds, etc.: To be No. 1 Common Sou. Yellow Pine.

4. Sub-flooring: To be No. 1 Common Sou. Yellow Pine, 1" x 6" T & G, laid diagonally.

5. Wall sheathing and roof decking: To be 1/2" x 4' x 8' DFPA plywood, CD interior grade. Lower 24" of roof decking to be covered with exterior grade DFPA plywood of same thickness. Roof sheathing shall be applied with surface grain at right angles to rafters. End joints shall be supported on bearings and staggered, with alternate courses in line. Plywood shall be fastened with 8d nails spaced 6" at edge supports and 12" at intermediate supports.

6. Exterior soffit: Shall be 1/4" asbestos board, fastened with flat-head galvanized nails. Carport ceiling shall be the same material.

7. Exterior siding: To be 5/8" x 4' x 9' DFPA exterior plywood, "texture one-eleven", blind nailed where possible with 8d galvanized finishing nails.

8. Fascia board: To be 5/4" x 6", B or better SYP, kiln dried.

9. Exterior trim: To be B or better SYP, kiln dried, of sizes shown.

10. Interior woodwork, painted: Shall be B or better SYP, kiln dried or "D select" Ponderosa Pine. All interior woodwork to be machine sanded at mill and hand sanded on job.

11. Exterior plywood panels: Those exposed to weather such as, panels above and below fixed glass and front entrance, shall be genuine Douglas Fir plywood, exterior grade, and shall carry the EXT-DFPA trade mark as evidence of waterproof glue-line. Thickness shall be as indicated on drawings, and grades shall be "Plyshield", AC face grade.

12. Shelving: Construct shelving as shown and detailed on drawings from 3/4" fir plywood, DFPA grade AB int. with solid Douglas Fir edges set-in. Shelving shall be supported on wood cleats or as otherwise detailed.

13. Laminated plastic cabinet and vanity tops: To be 1/16" thick,

standard grade, high-pressure laminated plastic surfacing material, conforming to NEMA standards, color and pattern to be selected by Owner.

a. Bond laminated plastic with phenol resorcinol water-proof adhesive to exterior grade plywood countertops and splash, as detailed, in accordance with manufacturer's standards. Form integral splash with glue and screws to plywood top.

b. Seal plywood edges at sink cutout with mastic approved for purpose by manufacturer.

c. Countertop edges: Shall be self-edged, laminated plastic of same material, as indicated on drawings.

E. WORKMANSHIP: Carefully lay out, cut, fit, and erect all framing, sheathing, bridging, blocking, and other items of carpentry in such a manner as to minimize shrinkage and insure stability. Do all cutting and carpentry work required for installation of work of other trades. Brace, plumb, and level all members and secure with sufficient nails, spikes, and bolts to insure rigidity.

F. JOISTS: Shall be 2 x 10's spaced 16" o.c., except where otherwise indicated. All joists shall be doubled under partitions and around stairwell as shown.

G. CROSS BRIDGING: Joists over 8'-0" in span shall be bridged with one row of 1" x 3" cross bridging, cut on bevel and nailed up tight after sub-flooring has been applied.

H. LIVING AREA BEAMS: Shall be 4" x 12" No. 1, J & P, Douglas Fir.

J. WALL AND PARTITION FRAMING: Shall be 2" x 4" studs spaced 16" o.c., with single sole plate and double cap plate. Studs shall be doubled at the sides of all wall openings.

K. CEILING JOISTS AND RAFTERS: Ceiling joists shall be 2" x 8" spaced 16" o.c. Rafters to be 2" x 6" spaced 16" o.c., with 3'-0" overhang, unless otherwise noted. Rafters shall have 1" x 4" collar beams on every third set. Gypsum board ceiling to be attached directly to rafters in Living-Dining and Front Entrance area.

L. DRYWALL CONSTRUCTION: Provide and install 1/2" thick gypsum wallboard, meeting Federal Specifications SS-51a and ASTM Specifications C36, on all ceilings and walls as indicated on drawings. Wallboard shall be erected and joints taped in strict conformity to specifications of manufacturer. Use metal corner beads on all exterior gypsum board corners. Metal bead trim shall be U. S. Gypsum No. 200-A Metal Trim. Nails shall be GWB-54 1 5/8" long annular ring, meeting the requirements of ASTM C380.

Apply gypsum wallboard first to the ceilings and then to the sidewalls; plan wallboard lengths to minimize end joints. Do not force boards up tight when nailing. Space nails not more than 7" apart on ceiling panels and not more than 8" apart on walls. Dimple the nail heads slightly below the surface of the wallboard with the

final hammer blow, taking care not to break the paper face.

Finish joints, nail dimples, corners and edges using the three-coat cement and tape system. Allow 24 hours for drying between applications of cement. Sand each coat after it is dry to a smooth, even surface.

Gypsum wallboard installation shall be done by an experienced drywall applicator, normally engaged in this trade.

M. INTERIOR TRIM AND MILLWORK: Carefully erect interior woodwork, with closely fitted joints and free from hammer marks. Miter exterior angles, butt and cope interior angles, and 45° miter all running joints of moldings.

All exposed millwork shall be machine sanded to a smooth finish, with all joints tight and formed to conceal shrinkage. Set all finish work straight, plumb, and level in true alignment; rigidly secure in place. In general, set all work in place by concealed methods. Where nails are unavoidable, countersink. Accurately set and brace frames to hold their positions and shapes. Complete all work free from warp, open joints and other defects.

N. CLOSET HANGING RODS: Furnish and install where indicated on drawings; rods shall be 1" diameter iron pipe, and supported at least 4'-0" o.c.

O. WOOD FLOORING: All sub-floors to be broom clean and covered with building paper before finish floors are laid.

Wood flooring, where scheduled, to be 25/32" x 2-1/4" T & G end matched Select Oak. All flooring to be laid evenly, driven tight, and blind nailed every 16" without tool marks. All nails must be countersunk and filled with a paste filler where necessary to face nail. These floors are to finish level with other floors. Flooring shall be sanded and left in a perfectly smooth and first class condition to receive finish.

P. INSULATION: Complete all thermal insulation as shown on the drawings or herein specified or both, as follows:

1. Materials: On all ceilings shall be mineral wool batts, 4" thick with reflective foil vapor barrier on room side. Barrier shall have flanges for attaching to wood supports.

All exterior walls shall be mineral wool batts, 2" thick with reflective foil vapor barrier on room side.

2. Installation:

a. Vertical surfaces between studs: Start first batt at bottom of wall on plate and snugly fit each succeeding one. Cut batts to fit irregular spaces, leaving flange on inside for nailing. In removing wool to fit around pipes, etc., do not cut vapor barrier unless necessary. Where necessary to cut vapor barrier, make a minimum cut and fit neatly around all pipes, conduits, and boxes.

b. Horizontal surfaces between ceiling joists: Install insulation before attaching finish ceiling. Fit each batt snugly and securely between joists. Install so foil vapor barrier does not touch gypsum wallboard surface. Cut vapor barrier only where absolutely necessary. Construct wood blocking above exterior walls to contain batts near ends of joists. Care shall be taken to ensure proper circulation of air from soffit vents through attic area. Above Living-Dining area, openings shall be made in ridgeboard to allow circulation between rafters.

c. Insulation which is torn, displaced, water soaked, or otherwise damaged to be removed and replaced with new acceptable material.

Q. CLEAN-UP: Upon completion of work, all surplus and waste materials resulting from the work in this division shall be removed from the premises, and the entire structure and involved portions of the site shall be left in a neat, clean and acceptable condition.

******

DIVISION 7: MOISTURE PROTECTION

A. GENERAL: The Contractor shall furnish all labor and materials to complete the following items shown on the drawing, or herein specified, or both, as follows:

1. Four-ply built-up roof with marble chips over.

2. Sheet metal flashing and gravel stops as related to roof.

3. Skylights as shown on roof (two required).

4. Caulking required around openings, joints, and abutments of different materials.

5. Waterproofing of basement walls below grade.

B. Built-up Roof Materials:

1. Roofing shall be Johns-Manville asphalt saturated rag felt, #15 (perforated), applied in accordance with the manufacturer's specifications (15 year guarantee). Work shall be done by a roofing contractor approved by the manufacturer. (Spec. No. 902)

2. Pitch shall be Johns-Manville asphalt roofing pitch, grade specified for sloping roof. Not less than 95 lbs. of pitch shall be used for each 100 sq. ft. of completed roof.

3. Marble chips shall be of white marble, graded from 1/8" to 1/2" in size, and shall be durable and dry, free from sand, dirt, or other foreign substance.

C. APPLICATION OF BUILT-UP ROOFING:

1. Over wood decking, lay one thickness of J-M Red Rosin sized sheathing paper, lapping the sheets not less than one inch and nail with large-head galvanized roofing nails. Nails shall not penetrate through the decking.

2. Apply two layers of No. 15 Asphalt-saturated Rag Felt (perforated) lapping each felt 19" over the preceding one. Nail sufficiently to hold in place.

3. Apply two layers of No. 15 Asphalt-saturated Rag Felt (perforated) lapping each felt 19" over the preceding one. Mop the full width under each felt with J-M Standard 190 Asphalt using 25 lbs per square. Nail at 24" centers adjacent to the back edge.

4. Over the entire surface pour from dippers a uniform flood coat of J-M Standard 190 Asphalt using 70 lbs per square. While still hot, embed not less than 400 lbs of marble chips, evenly distributed, per square.

D. SHEET METAL FLASHING & GRAVEL STOPS:

1. Flashing shall be 24-gauge, best commercial grade, galvanized copper-bearing steel, and shall be used for all pipes or vents penetrating the roof.

2. Gravel stops shall be formed of .032" thick aluminum of 8 ft lengths. One edge shall extend onto roof not less than 4". Bend the gravel stops to form a 1" high stop and a 45° drip over facia. Stops shall be securely nailed to deck with aluminum nails, and length shall be lock jointed. Provide for expansion on long runs.

3. Where dissimilar metals come in contact, apply a heavy coat of asphaltic paint to both adjoining surfaces.

E. CAULKING: Joints and faces to be caulked shall be clean, free from dust and dirt, and dry. Joints more than 1/2" deep shall be packed with cakum to 1/4" of surface before applying caulking. Caulk joints before final coat of paint is applied to adjacent work. Caulk exterior facings of all window and door frames using Thiokol base compound. Caulking shall be done with a gun and applied by an experienced mechanic. After caulking compound has been applied, glaze and smooth surface by brushing surface with a fine hair brush dipped in mineral spirits. Paint caulking bead to match surrounding material.

Bed metal thresholds in caulking compound.

F. WATERPROOFING BASEMENT WALLS BELOW GRADE: All Concrete block walls below grade shall be pargeted with a 1/2" thick layer of Portland Cement grout, well forced into pores of block. After completely cured, mop two coats of hot Asphaltic Pitch over entire area. Cant the grout over the edge of footings as shown.

G. PLASTIC SKYLIGHTS: Skylights shall be "Acrylite" skydomes, Model SI-2424 with W-36 plastic and aluminum rims, as manufactured by American Cyanamid Co., or equal.

******

DIVISION 8: DOORS, WINDOWS, AND GLASS

A. GENERAL: The Contractor shall provide all materials and labor to complete the following items shown on the drawings or scheduled, or herein specified, or both, as follows:

1. Wood doors and wood door frames
2. Hanging and fitting of doors
3. Folding door in Family Room
4. All window units
5. Glazing of fixed-glass windows
6. Mirrors in bathrooms

B. WOOD DOORS:

1. All doors shall be flush type, sizes and thicknesses as shown and scheduled, except Kitchen entrance door, which shall be D.F. solid stiles and rails with aluminum jalousie insert.

2. Flush doors shall be "Weldwood" as manufactured by U.S. Plywood Corp., or "Roddiscraft" as manufactured by Roddis Plywood Corp. Exterior flush doors shall be solid core; interior doors shall be hollow core.

C. WOOD DOOR FRAMES: Frames shall be dadoed together at head with joints set in white lead. All frames shall be accurately set, plumb, level and true, with space in back of all butts solidly shimmed. Exterior frames shall have integral stops.

D. HANGING AND FITTING OF DOORS: Each door shall be accurately cut, trimmed and fitted to its frame. Allow clearance for paint as well as possible swelling, and for weatherstripping on exterior doors. All doors shall operate freely without binding and all hardware shall be adjusted properly. No nails for temporary pulls.

E. FOLDING DOOR IN FAMILY ROOM: Folding door shall be Pella wood folding door with joining end-post and jamb attaching panels as manufactured by Rolscreen Co. Finish to be Ash with scratch-resistant lacquer. Height to be standard 6'-8" and width of complete double section to be 10'-6". Attach track on jamb trim so door operates freely.

F. ALUMINUM THRESHOLDS: (See Division 10B)

G. WOOD WINDOWS: Window units shall be Anderson "Flexivent" out-swinging awning type, sizes as shown on elevations. Aluminum screens with hardware to be furnished with units.

H. FIXED-GLASS WINDOWS: Fixed-glass as shown on drawings shall be 3/16" sheet glass, Double-Strength, as manufactured by Pittsburg Plate Glass Co. or Libby-Owens-Ford Co. Panes shall be cut 1/4" smaller than openings and pressed into non-hardening glazing compound around entire opening. Exterior wood stops to be installed by glazer according to window detail. Rebates receiving glass shall be primed with one coat of lead-base paint before glass is installed. Glazing compound shall conform to Fed. Spec. TT-C-598.

J. CLEANING AND REPLACING GLASS: Prior to final inspection, broken or damaged glass shall be replaced with glass of like kind and quality without cost to the Owner. Upon completion of work, remove labels, stains, excess compound, and leave glass in a clean, polished condition.

K. BATHROOM MIRRORS: Mirrors shall be 1/4" silvered plate glass with copper backing, of first quality, in sizes shown on bath details. Mirrors shall be neatly installed directly on wall with mastic and metal clips and carefully fitted to abutting cabinetwork, tile, fixtures, and walls at edges.

******

DIVISION 9: FINISHES

9A. CERAMIC & QUARRY TILE

a. GENERAL: Furnish all labor and materials necessary to install ceramic tile in both bathrooms and the quarry tile floor in the front Entry, as shown on the drawings and specified herein. No tile will be required on walls or floors in back of or under built-in cabinets unless otherwise detailed on drawings.

b. SAMPLES: Submit samples of all ceramic and quarry tile in this division for Owner's approval as to color and texture prior to installation. Samples shall be of sufficient size to indicate true color and texture.

c. CERAMIC TILE: All ceramic tile shall be standard grade of a quality as manufactured by American Olean Tile Co., or equal, and shall meet requirements of Simplified Practice Recommendation R-61 issued by U.S. Dept. of Commerce.

1. Wall Tile shall be matte glazed 4¼" x 4¼" in size. Setting shall be by conventional mortar method with all cove, bullnose, and trim pieces furnished to neatly finish to the dry wall construction.

2. Floor Tile shall be unglazed mosiac with smooth edges in 1" x 1" sizes of a similar color to wall tile.

3. Accessories shall be vitreous china in colors to match the wall tile. Bath No. 1 shall be furnished with the following accessories: paper holder, soap holder, toothbrush & tumbler holder, soap holder & grab rail in tub enclosure, and two towel bars; bath No. 2 shall include: paper holder, soap holder, toothbrush and tumbler holder, and two towel bars. Verify mounting locations with Owner.

d. LAYING CERAMIC TILE: Wall tile shall be set first. Scratch coat shall be brought to the proper surface or plane to receive the tile setting bed. All tile over wood framing shall be backed with 15-lb. asphalt impregnated felt and flat-ribbed metal lath.

Lay out tile on floors and lengthwise on walls so that no tile less than half size occurs. For heights, maintain full courses to produce nearest obtainable heights shown on drawings without cutting tile. Heights of wainscoting shall be 4'-0" and 6'-0" in tub enclosure, unless otherwise shown. Align joints in wall tile and trim vertically and horizontally with no staggered joints.

Use white cement for grouting wall tile and natural grey cement for grouting floor tile. Do not permit traffic on floor tile for at least 24 hours after laying. Leave finish tile work clean and free from cracked, chipped, or broken tile. Tile work shall conform to applicable requirements of the latest edition of "Basic Specifications of Tile Work", as issued by Tile Manufacturers Association, Inc.

e. MARBLE THRESHOLDS: Marble thresholds shall be installed the same width as bathroom door openings. Thresholds shall be Georgia Marble, or approved equal, 7/8" thick and 2" wide.

f. QUARRY TILE: Quarry tile for Entry floor shall be 6" x 6" x ½" standard dark red, as manufactured by Murray Tile Co., Louisport, Kentucky, or approved equal. Tile shall conform to the requirements of Simplified Practice Recommendation R-61 issued by the U.S. Dept. of Commerce. Set tile on approved cement mortar bed with ¼" aligned joints in both directions. Mortar bed on concrete slab shall bring tile surface to same plane as the finish floor in adjoining area. Run tile in closet floor. Setting bed shall consist of 1 part Portland Cement, 1/10 part hydrated lime, and 5 to 6 parts of dry sand. Pointing mortar shall consist of 1 part Portland Cement, 1/5 part hydrated lime, 2 parts dry sand, and applied depth of joint. Place setting bed on slab, screed, and compact.

9B. RESILIENT FLOORING

a. GENERAL: Contractor shall furnish materials and install the vinyl asbestos tile floor in the Kitchen, as shown in the Finish Schedule. Tile will not be required under built-in kitchen cabinets.

b. MATERIALS:

1. Vinyl Asbestos Tile shall be 1/8" thick, 9" x 9", as manu-

factured by Armstrong Cork Co., Robbins, or equal. Color and style to be selected by Owner.

2. Adhesive shall be the type recommended by the tile manufacturer.

3. Rubber Base shall be 4" cove type, to be installed around walls and base of kitchen cabinets.

c. PREPARATORY WORK: No tile shall be installed on floors that are not clean, dry, level, and in suitable surface condition to insure first-class installation. Areas not level or in suitable condition shall be treated with underlayment in strict accordance with manufacturer's recommendations before the installation of the tile.

d. INSTALLATION: Cut and fit the tile neatly to walls, cabinets, and fixtures. Install edging strips where edge of tile is terminated at other floors. Tile and base shall be installed by experienced workmen in strict accordance to manufacturer's printed specifications.

e. CLEANING AND WAXING: At completion of entire work, just before acceptance of building, tile floor shall be thoroughly cleaned and given a wax treatment specially prepared for this type of flooring, then burnished with a floor finishing machine. Upon completion, leave floor in first-class condition.

9C. PAINTING

a. GENERAL: Furnish labor, materials, tools, ladders, scaffolding, and other equipment necessary to properly execute a complete job of exterior and interior painting.

Painting Contractor shall not apply any paint or finish to surfaces not in proper condition for finishing. The Contractor shall notify the Architect of any surface which is not in satisfactory condition. Painting or finishing of any surface will be considered acceptance of that surface by the Painting Contractor. Aluminum gravel stop and flashing not to be painted.

b. MATERIALS: Paint, stains, sealers, fillers, linseed oil, shellac, lacquers, turpentine, and other painting materials shall be of the highest quality, as manufactured by Devoe & Reynolds Co., Inc., Sherwin-Williams Co., Martin-Senour Co., or similar reputable manufacturer.

All materials shall be delivered to site in manufacturer's labeled containers. Labels shall give manufacturer's name, type of paint, color, and instructions for reducing. Application and thinning of paint shall be done in strict accordance with manufacturer's directions.

c. COLOR SELECTION: Colors shall be selected by Owner and Architect. Architect will furnish Contractor with color cards and Finish Schedule indicating where various colors shall be used.

If color mixing is required, Contractor shall prepare samples at job to indicate intended mixtures.

d. PROTECTION OF OTHER WORK: Painting Contractor shall furnish drop cloths and lay cloths in areas where painting is being done to protect floors and other adjoining work from damage during painting. In cases where coverings cannot be used, Contractor shall notify Foreman and request work to be protected in a satisfactory manner. Paint droppings shall be removed, and any damaged surfaces shall be restored to a condition satisfactory to the Architect.

e. PREPARATION OF SURFACES: Contractor shall properly prepare all surfaces before painting by cleaning, filling, removing rust, sealing knots, etc., to insure smooth and uniform surfaces without blemishes and to insure maximum durability of the finish.

1. General: Before painting, remove hardware, accessories, plates, lighting fixtures, and similar items, or provide careful protection for such items. Upon completion of each living space, replace the above items. If necessary, remove doors for painting top and bottom edges; do not remove hinges. Only skilled mechanics shall be used for removing and replacing the above items.

2. Wood: Sandpaper to a smooth, even surface and then dust off. After sealing or priming or stain coat has been applied, thoroughly fill nail and other holes, and cracks with plastic wood or putty; for natural-finish work, putty shall be colored to match wood. Cover knots with shellac.

3. Steel & Iron: Remove grease, rust scale, and dirt. Touch-up any chipped or corroded places on items which have been shop coated. If steel or iron have a heavy coating of scale, it shall be removed by wire brushing or sand blasting as necessary to produce a satisfactory surface for the prime coat.

4. Galvanized Metal: Thoroughly clean with gasoline and coat with vinegar or a solution consisting of 4 oz. copper sulfate in 1 gal. water. Permit coating to remain on surface for at least 12 hrs. and dust off with stiff brush.

f. WORKMANSHIP:

1. Flow the finishes on smoothly, with the proper thickness, without runs, skips, sags, or defects. Paint neatly around glass and other termination edges. Work only during favorable weather and lighting conditions to produce first class work. No painting to be done unless surfaces are thoroughly dry and sufficient time has been allowed between coats. Only skilled mechanics to be employed.

2. Tint all undercoats and/or intermediate coats of colored paint or enamel a shade slightly lighter than succeeding

coat. Wood finishes to be lightly sanded between coats.

3. If stains, discolors, or undercoats show through final coat, work shall be covered by additional coats until finish is of uniform color satisfactory to Architect.

4. Back-prime all exterior trim before installing.

5. Painting Contractor shall protect his work at all times. Upon completion of work, he shall remove from premises all accumulated materials and rubbish caused by the painting operation. Leave work in a clean, orderly, and acceptable condition.

g. SCHEDULE OF PAINTING: Type of finish material and number of coats required on various surfaces shall be as follows:

1. Exterior Wood Trim and Plywood Siding
   One (1) coat of approved oil-base undercoat
   Two (2) coats of approved oil-base house paint
   (Use this finish on all exterior plywood panels, ceilings, soffits, and any other exterior painted wood)

2. Exterior Ferrous Metal
   One (1) coat of approved red lead primer (If surface is shop coated, omit this coat except for abraded or damaged spots)
   Two (2) coats of approved oil-base outside trim paint

3. Exterior Wood Doors
   Two (2) coats of Monsanto colortone Cedar Rez (Apply first coat as soon as possible after doors are installed, allow 24 hours drying between coats)
   One (1) coat dull exterior-grade Spar Varnish

4. Interior Wood Trim & Doors (not including folding door)
   One (1) coat of approved enamel undercoat & sealer
   Two (2) coats of Egg-Shell enamel, tinted proper color

5. Interior Bathrooms, Kitchen, and Utility Area
   One (1) coat of approved enamel undercoat & sealer
   Two (2) coats of approved Egg-Shell enamel, tinted proper color (Use this finish on walls, ceilings, cabinets, and wood trim)

6. Interior Gypsum Walls and Ceilings
   One (1) coat approved pigmented primer & sealer
   Two (2) coats of approved Alkyd flat enamel
   (Use this finish on all walls and ceilings except those specified for Egg-Shell enamel finish)

7. Interior Exposed Beams in Living-Dining Area
   Two (2) coats of Monsanto colortone Cedar Rez
   One (1) coat of dull interior-grade Spar Varnish

8. Interior Birch Kitchen Cabinets
   One (1) coat of waterproof lacquer sealer
   Two (2) coats of clear waterproof lacquer (Semi-gloss)

9. Interior Oak Wood Floors
   One (1) coat of paste wood filler, rubbed smooth
   Two (2) coats of approved floor sealer, clear

******

DIVISION 10: SPECIALTIES

10A. KITCHEN APPLIANCES

a. GENERAL: Owner will purchase and Appliance Dealer will connect the following kitchen appliances. The Contractor shall provide proper spaces for and do any cutting necessary to accommodate the appliances purchased. Appliance Dealer will provide Contractor with diagrams showing dimensions and clearances necessary.

1. Refrigerator: Install where shown on drawings.

2. Range Top: Install where shown on drawings.

3. Oven: Install as shown in accordance with Manufacturer's recommendations.

10B. FINISH HARDWARE

a. GENERAL: Contractor shall furnish and deliver to building all items of finish hardware and be responsible for their storage. The Contractor shall provide in his bid the sum of five hundred ($500.00) dollars for the purchase of the finish hardware not including the cost of installation. Should the cost of finish hardware exceed the allowance, the net excess will be added to the Contract sum; if the hardware cost is less than the allowance, the difference shall be deducted from the Contract sum. The Owner will select the finish hardware.

b. MATERIALS:

1. Exterior hinged doors shall have Dull Brass, keyed lock sets and 1½ pair Dull Brass butts 4½" x 4½".

2. Interior hinged doors shall have Dull Brass lock sets and one pair paint-primed butts 3½" x 3½". (Bathrooms shall have polished chrome lock sets)

3. Kitchen cabinets and bath vanities shall have polished chrome door pulls and hardware.

4. All hinged doors swinging into adjacent walls shall have

Dull Brass door stops attached to doors.

5. Exterior hinged doors to have anodized aluminum thresholds size 4" x ½" x 1/8" x width of opening.

6. Exterior hinged doors to have brass weatherstripping.

7. Closet folding doors to have concealed unit track and hardware, as manufactured by Knope & Vogt Manufacturing Co., Grand Rapids, Mich., or equal.

8. Tub enclosure to be #701 Economy Line, two panel sliding enclosure, using #701 rail, 5'-0" x 58½" high, satin anodized as manufactured by American Shower Door Co., Los Angeles. Glazing to be 1/8" Acrylic Plastic.

******

DIVISION 11: EQUIPMENT

(None on this job)

******

DIVISION 12: FURNISHINGS

(None on this job)

******

DIVISION 13: SPECIAL CONSTRUCTION

(None on this job)

******

DIVISION 14: CONVEYING SYSTEMS

(None on this job)

******

DIVISION 15: MECHANICAL

A. PLUMBING

a. GENERAL: Contractor shall furnish and install all plumbing and related items shown on the drawings or herein specified, or both, as follows:

1. Complete sanitary drainage system, including fixtures,

roughing connections, piping, hangers, stacks, soil wastes, cleanouts, vents, fittings, fresh-air vents, traps, and running house sewer to and connecting with sanitary sewer in street.

2. Complete cold-water service system from source of supply in street (including all valves, piping, and connections) to connection of hot water storage tank, connections of all fixtures, and all hose bibbs.

3. Complete domestic hot water system, including hot water heater and piping from the hot water tank to all fixtures except water closets and hose bibbs.

4. Complete piping from street main to all natural gas outlets.

b. ORDINANCES AND PERMITS: All workmanship and materials covered by these specifications, all details of the piping, and all manner of installation, shall conform to all municipal, county and state laws, ordinances and regulations affecting this type of work. The Contractor shall obtain all permits necessary for the installation of the work and shall pay all expenses in connection therewith. He shall obtain and deliver to the Owner, without charge, all certificates of inspections from authorities having jurisdiction.

c. MATERIALS:

1. Cast Iron Pipe and Fittings shall be asphalt coated, heavy bell-and-spigot type.

2. Lead Pipe for water closet bends, fixture and vent connections shall be seamless drawn pipe weighing at least 2 lbs. per inch diameter and per foot length.

3. Copper Pipe shall be type "K" for underground service and type "L" hard drawn for above ground service, conforming to ASTM Standards B-88. Fittings shall be sweat-soldered type of cast bronze or wrought copper.

d. PIPE INSTALLATION:

1. Joints in cast iron piping shall be made by caulking with treated oakum and sealed with not less than twelve ounces of bar lead for each inch of pipe diameter.

2. Joints between lead pipe and cast iron pipe shall be made by solder wiping and approved brass ferrule to lead pipe and then caulked into hub of cast iron pipe.

3. Joints in copper pipe shall be made by first cleaning tube-end and fitting-socket thoroughly with steel wool, then evenly applying heat to the joint and using 50-50 solder for sealing.

4. Horizontal drain and waste pipe inside the building shall

be carried with a minimum fall of 1/4" per foot. All changes in horizontal direction of soil and other drainage pipes shall be made with long radius fittings or with Y branches and 1/8 or 1/16 bends.

5. All water lines shall be properly graded for drainage. Hot water pipes shall be kept at least 6" away from cold water pipes.

e. HANGERS & SUPPORTS:

1. Cast iron soil, waste, and vent piping shall be supported near or at each hub, not including the fittings, at intervals not to exceed 5 feet.

2. All copper tube lines shall be supported by means of copper tube hangers, of size and type adequate to support the lines, and these shall be properly supported from the building construction. Pipe 3/4" and smaller shall have hangers placed at intervals not to exceed 7 feet and shall be provided with a hanger at each change of horizontal direction. Hangers supporting tubing 1" and larger shall be placed at intervals not to exceed 9 feet with a hanger at each change of horizontal direction. It is important that no galvanized hangers be permitted with copper tubing lines.

f. CUTTING AND REPAIRING: Cutting and repairing of walls, floors, ceilings, etc., necessary for the installation of this work, shall be performed by the Contractor.

g. TESTS:

1. Drainage lines shall be filled with water to the highest point before soil and waste pipe are covered. Any leaks shall be stopped and tests repeated until no leaks remain in the system.

2. Water lines shall be subjected to a hydrostatic pressure 50 lb per sq inch.

h. PIPE INSULATION: All hot water piping shall be insulated with at least 1" of approved pipe insulation. Insulation shall be applied to the piping in a neat manner after system has been tested and approved.

i. EXCAVATION & BACKFILL: All excavation and subsequent backfill required for this work shall be done by this Contractor. Cast iron pipe underground shall be firmly bedded on solid ground and bell holes shall be provided in all trenches. Backfill shall be well tamped and placed in layers not over 6" thick.

j. GUARANTEE: This Contractor shall furnish the Owner with a written guarantee covering workmanship and materials for a period of one (1) year after acceptance by the Owner. All materials and equipment shall be covered by this guarantee,

and the manufacturers' guarantee shall not relieve this Contractor of responsibility for equipment furnished under this specification.

k. PLUMBING FIXTURES:

1. American Standard plumbing fixtures have been used as a guide. Kohler or Crane fixtures in similar design as approved by the Architect will be accepted. Colors will be selected by the Owner.

2. Bath Tub: "Master Pembroke" recess tub 5'-0" long, 1'-4" high; R 1020 bath and shower combination; R 1700 pop-up drain; quality trim. Shower head to be Victor ball-joint R-1311.

3. Water Closets: "Master One-Piece", 29" x 14"; F 200-1 OP 200 closed front seat, white.

4. Lavatories: "Dresslyn" 18" x 20"; R 2101-8 combination supply and pop-up drain fitting; aerator; R2604, 3/8" supply pipes with stops to wall; R 7000 "P" trap; quality trim.

5. Kitchen Sink: "Harvest", double 14" x 15½" bowls; model SA 410; stainless steel sink with conventional rim.

6. Domestic Hot Water Heater: American Standard Arcoglas standard hot water heater; forty (40) gallon; Model G-40AG for natural gas installation. Water heater to carry a 10 year factory warranty.

B. AIR CONDITIONING (Heating and Cooling)

a. GENERAL: Contractor shall furnish and install the complete winter-and-summer air conditioning system as shown on the drawings and specified herein.

b. CODES, PERMITS, AND ORDINANCES: Installation shall conform to all local codes and ordinances and regulations of Board of Fire Underwriters. All electrical equipment shall be U.L. approved as installed. Obtain all permits necessary, paying all fees in connection therewith. At completion, have work inspected by proper authorities and furnish the Architect or Owner an inspection certificate showing approval of installation.

c. PROTECTION OF EQUIPMENT: Pipe openings shall be closed with caps or plugs during installation. Equipment shall be tightly covered and protected against dirt, water, chemical, or mechanical injury. Chipped or scraped paint shall be retouched to match. At completion of all work, the equipment shall be thoroughly cleaned and left in a condition satisfactory to the Architect.

d. SPACE CONDITIONS: All apparatus shall fit into available

spaces in the building and must be introduced into the building at such times and in such manner as not to cause damage to the structure. Where deviations from the Plans are required in order to conform to the space limitations, such changes shall be made at no additional cost to the Owner, and shall be subject to the approval of the Architect. All equipment normally requiring service shall be made easily accessible.

e. CUTTING AND PATCHING: All cutting and patching necessary for the installation of the system shall be performed by trades whose work will require cutting. It is, however, the Contractor's responsibility to lay out work in advance and coordinate with other trades to insure that cutting will be minimized.

f. DESIGN DATA:

1. The capacity of the cooling equipment is based on a design condition of 95° F DB, 76° F WB entering the evaporator, and 75° F inside temperature.

2. The capacity of the heating equipment is based on a design condition of 10° F outside temperature, 75° F inside temperature, and 170° bonnet temperature.

g. GAS FIRED FURNACE: Provide gas fired furnace (upflow) complete with gas burner, diaphragm gas valve, 100% pilot safety, fan and limit control, ten year warranty heat exchanger, squirrel cage blower and motor, and draft diverter, in insulated cabinet.

Furnace shall have an AGA input rating of 110,000 BTUH and an output rating of 88,000 BTUH, and shall be AGA approved for 1125 cfm air against the resistance of 0.25" SP. Furnace shall be Lennox, Model G8-110, or equal. Motor shall be wound for 115 volts, single phase, 60-cycle current.

h. AIR CONDITIONING UNITS: Air cooled condensing unit shall be complete with hermetic or access-hermetic motor for 230-volt, single phase, 60-cycle current; finned condenser coil, condenser fan and motor, high-low pressure cutout, filter-dryer, and overload protection, encased in acoustically and thermally insulated cabinet with baked enamel finish. Condenser shall be Lennox No. HS6-311V, or equal.

Finned evaporator coils shall be complete with expansion valve or capillary tube, enclosed in factory-built insulated enclosure designed to match furnace. Evaporator shall be Lennox No. CI-41V, or equal. Manufacturer of air conditioning units shall be the same as the furnace unit.

j. DUCTWORK AND FLUES:

1. Metal ducts shall be galvanized steel of gauges and construction as recommended by the latest issue of ASHRAE Guide, and shall be securely hung from building construc-

tion with galvanized straps at a maximum of 5 ft. on centers.

2. Fitting numbers shown on ductwork layout conform to NWAHACA Manual 9, 7th Edition.

3. Inside of ducts visible through grills or registers shall be painted flat black.

4. Flexible connection shall be provided between the unit and supply duct and shall be of fireproof material such as "Ventglas."

5. Flues through roof shall be Transite or metalbestos with 24-gauge metal cap and flashing. Vents from furnace and hot water heater to flues shall be 24-gauge steel.

k. GRILLES AND REGISTERS: Provide grilles and registers as sized and shown on drawings.

1. Floor diffusers: A & A Register Co., Cleveland, Ohio, No. P-28 Oak finish.

2. Low wall registers: A & A Register Co., Cleveland, Ohio, No. M-32 with beige baked enamel finish and damper control.

3. Return air grilles: A & A Register Co., Cleveland, Ohio No. A-05, steel, unfinished.

l. INSULATION OF AIR DUCTS: All supply and return air ducts shall be insulated with one (1) inch of flexible foil-faced glass fiber insulation. Foil to be placed on the exterior to insure a positive vapor barrier. Insulation shall be securely and neatly taped around ducts and at all joints.

m. CONTROLS: Provide a complete system of automatic controls as recommended by equipment manufacturer. Heating and cooling control shall be Minneapolis-Honeywell T861A clock thermostat and Q426A sub base with "Heat-Off-Cool" and "Fan on-Auto" switch. Thermostat shall be located in central Hall.

n. TESTING AND ADJUSTING:

1. The Architect shall be notified in advance when system is ready for testing. Testing and adjusting shall be done by a qualified representative of the installing Contractor.

2. Contractor shall make all required adjustments in the system so the required temperatures will be maintained throughout the rooms.

3. Before final acceptance of the work, the Contractor shall furnish the Owner with all operating instructions and service manuals of the equipment.

o. GUARANTEE: This Contractor shall warrant all equipment and materials to be in perfect condition when installed and

guarantee to replace entirely at his own expense any portion of the equipment or materials which shows defects or faulty workmanship for a period of one (1) year beginning with the acceptance of the system.

p. EXHAUST FANS: Bath and Kitchen exhaust fans specified under Electrical.

******

DIVISION 16: ELECTRICAL

A. GENERAL: The Contractor shall furnish all materials and labor to complete the lighting and appliance electrical system according to the drawings and herein specified.

B. CODE REQUIREMENTS: All wiring to be done in strict accordance with the National Electric Code and all applicable city and county codes, and Contractor shall furnish Owner with an inspection certificate from inspectors having jurisdiction. All equipment shall bear the U.L. label of approval.

C. SERVICE: The service supplied to the structure shall be 3 wire, 115/230 volts, 60-cycle, single-phase. The service is to be brought to the structure by the Power Company. The Contractor shall install the meter on the exterior as required by the Power Company.

D. SERVICE PANEL: The main service panel shall have 150 amp capacity with automatic circuit breakers. Panel shall include main circuit breaker having a grounded neutral and arranged for service specified and having a rating of 200 amp.

E. WIRING: The system of wiring throughout shall be with approved Romex cable. Service entrance and feeder to panel shall be thick-wall galvanized conduit. Romex cable shall have grounding conductor.

F. WORKMANSHIP: All interior wiring shall run concealed. All work shall be carefully done by capable, experienced electricians.

G. SPECIAL OUTLETS: The Contractor shall furnish and install receptacles, and switches if required, for the following special outlets:

1. Exhaust fan in each Bath and Kitchen

2. Electric range top in Kitchen

3. Oven in Kitchen

4. Air conditioning unit in basement

5. Electric dryer in basement

H. BOXES: Switch and receptacle boxes of galvanized steel shall be

installed in framework with metal mounting brackets. Outlet boxes shall be 4" octagonal or round galvanized steel and mounted in a similar manner.

J. RECEPTACLES AND SWITCHES: Receptacles and switches shall be installed as shown on drawings and wired to provide switch control as indicated. Receptacles shall be duplex type of Ivory Bakelite. Wall receptacles shall be placed 18" above the floor; cabinet receptacles 3'-6" above floor and above cabinets. Switches shall be placed 48" above floor, and shall be flush Mercury-Type silent switches of Ivory Bakelite and similar cover plates.

K. TELEPHONE OUTLETS: Furnish and install telephone wiring with one outlet in Living-Hall and one outlet in Master Bedroom. Outlets to be 12" above floor.

L. EXHAUST FANS: Furnish and install exhaust fan in Kitchen and each Bath as indicated on drawings. Fans shall have at least 300 cfm free delivery. Motor shall operate on 115 volts. Fans shall be complete with trim and exit flues.

M. SIGNAL CHIMES: Furnish and install in central hall a set of chimes with a circuit connected to approved transformer and light circuit. Provide outside push button at each door. Chimes shall be Edwards No. C-32 flush mounted, push button Edwards No. 643, or approved equal.

N. LIGHTING FIXTURES: Install lighting fixtures according to locations shown on drawings and allow the sum of three hundred dollars ($300.00) in the proposal for their purchase. Adjustment to Contract sum shall be made upon selection of fixtures by Owner. Contractor shall submit breakdown to Owner on this item.

O. ACCEPTANCE OF WORK: All portions of the electrical system shall be in operating condition satisfactory to the Owner before the work will be accepted.

******

16.8 COMPUTER SPECIFICATIONS

Today's specification writer has the computer to aid him. In larger architectural and engineering offices where complex building projects often require lengthy sets of specifications, the computer can be called upon to do much of the work and do it more accurately.

To utilize the computer, a library of master specs is assembled from various sources. These masters are carefully worded descriptions of the major construction operations that usually repeat themselves in conventional projects and the materials that are commonly used with them. Each new spec that has any possibility of being reused again is also included in the master set until a very comprehensive library is assembled. These master specs are continually punched into cards, loaded on magnetic tape, or fed into memory disks so they can be filed for easy access and be in usable form for the computer.

When the specifications for a new project are ready for compiling, the applicable cards, tape, or disks are taken from the master library, deletions are made or necessary paragraphs are added to customize the stored information for the new project. This final assembly is then fed into the computer. The printout from the computer in typed form is carefully organized and reflects the added or deleted information. If necessary, the printout can be typed on mimeograph stencils or offset masters so reproductions can be easily made. Much of the time usually needed for checking and hand typing is saved, and a more accurate set of specs results.

Several organizations now offer a complete computer specification-writing service using the CSI format. The service is available to architectural and engineering offices desiring to farm out this phase of their work.

REVIEW QUESTIONS

1. What qualifications are required of a construction specification writer?

2. Why has it become standard practice to include window, door, and finish schedules on the drawings rather than in the specifications?

3. List five sources for specification reference material.

4. Why are construction material manufacturers' associations interested in furnishing material to specification writers?

5. Who requires a copy of the specifications? How are these copies usually made?

6. How is the information in the general conditions related to the other technical sections?

7. How do dimensions given in the specifications differ from the dimensions required on the working drawings?

8. Why must requirements in specifications be made fair and just to all parties of the contract?

". . . Blessed is the man who has some congenial work, some occupation in which he can put his heart, and which affords a complete outlet to all the forces that are in him."—John Burroughs

17 Careers in Construction

Many fascinating and rewarding careers are open to young people interested in architectural drawing and construction. High school students learning the material in this book will be glad to know that their efforts can lead to a wide variety of vocations in architecture, construction technology, or related types of engineering. Even without further formal study, your interests can provide a valuable background in acquiring the skills needed for many of the trades commonly associated with construction—carpentry, masonry, plumbing, heating, and air conditioning, as well as literally hundreds of other trade skills necessary in tomorrow's work force.

The construction industry, one of America's largest industries, employs nearly five million people in various capacities. Thousands of workers, tradesmen, craftsmen, designers, technologists, technicians, supervisors, contractors, engineers, and architects are gainfully employed in this important industry. They build our homes, apartments, factories, offices, stores, schools, and the highways and bridges upon which we travel. They plan the buildings, provide the working drawings and specifications, and furnish the know-how to erect the often complex structures.

Some are employed as professional-technical people such as the architects, engineers, technologists, or draftsmen. Others work as managers,

Fig. 17-1 Architects and engineers spend much of their time planning both esthetic and structural features.

foremen, inspectors, contractors, and officials within the many construction companies both large and small. Many people of the aforementioned categories are employed by federal, state, and local governments to carry out vast numbers of important public projects. Even a host of secretaries, clerical workers, typists, and accountants, making up about five percent of the total work force, are needed in the industry. Unskilled and semiskilled workers such as laborers, apprentices, helpers, truck drivers, machine operators, and kindred workers in large numbers are employed.

The future of construction points to a healthy trend, even considering the economy-related variations with which major industries must contend. Construction, naturally, thrives in a flourishing economy. But even if depressed periods come and go, young students must plan their futures on general trends of an occupation over a long period of time. As the population increases, the employment trend can be expected to surge rapidly. Because of the tendency of our modern population to shift from rural to urban centers, new and better buildings will continue to occupy our attention. As the wealth of a country increases, architecture, both domestic and commercial, reflects this increase. Many of our larger cities will continue in a state of urban renewal, often with the help of federally-appropriated funds. Speculative building will continue, and better highway systems will be necessary. Even with more sophisticated building technology, and with a rising skill-level of future workers, the industry will need increased numbers of personnel in the years ahead. In a growing economy, a large percentage of the yearly profits of both individuals and corporations is invested in better housing, new factories, and income-producing properties, which represent sound real estate securities of a healthy nation.

17.1 ARCHITECTS

Probably the most important occupation within the construction industry is that of the architect. Architecture, like engineering, is a profession open to the exceptional student.

The architect is responsible for creating the original design of a building and must answer to society for the integrity of his creation. He must be an artist, businessman, draftsman, psychologist, and an expert on construction and building materials. He must coordinate the work of structural engineers and other technical specialists who contribute to the planning of buildings. He must deal with clients, contractors, material suppliers, and lending institutions in his everyday activities. He must know building codes, zoning laws, fire regulations, and local safety ordinances. But he derives a supreme satisfaction in seeing his building completed, in serving the community well, and in enhancing the local landscape. Both men and women are successfully occupied in this challenging career.

Fig. 17-2 The work area in a typical architect's office.

Aside from the impact that a new building will have on the community, the architect must must be concerned with future considerations such as the preservation of the environment and the economics of the building as an investment. If the building he designs is not profitable for the owner, the project will almost never reach construction stage.

Nearly half of our registered architects are self-employed, usually conducting their profession in or near metropolitan centers. Many architects work together in planning departments of major corporations or in private firms where they can contribute specialized backgrounds. Some are employed by federal or state governments; others teach in colleges or technical institutes.

Becoming an architect requires a rigorous college training. Accredited architectural schools offer a bachelor's degree requiring five years of study. Some schools require even longer periods. The programs are strong in drawing and design, science, English, and mathematics. After graduation three years of practical experience are commonly needed to become eligible for the state licensing examination. The purpose of the examination, offered and required by the various states, is the protection of the general public. Upon passing the state-board test, the graduate is then licensed to practice architecture within the state. Graduate schooling is not usually required for the practice of architecture, although it is often essential for research or teaching positions.

Fig. 17-3 Many technically trained people are needed in the construction of buildings.

High school students contemplating architectural school should take courses in mathematics, science, social sciences, English, and art, as well as architectural drawing courses. Even summer work on construction projects will be helpful. Those young people with the foregoing interests and a desire to study architecture can look forward to an interesting and challenging life's work in their years ahead.

More information on this professional career can be obtained from:

The American Institute of Architects
1785 Massachusetts Avenue
Washington, D.C. 20036

17.2 ENGINEERS

Except for teaching, engineering is the largest profession in number—over 300,000 are occupied in the construction industry alone. Several of the engineering disciplines contribute important expertise to building design, mainly commercial buildings. Civil engineering, representing the specialists in steel and concrete structures, highway and bridge construction, and site planning and surveying, is that category of the profession generally associated with construction. Mechanical and electrical engineers design the climate, lighting, and power systems so necessary within the buildings. All contribute to give us our modern, engineered architecture.

Engineers throughout the years have been the ones mainly responsible for the material advancement that mankind now possesses. Because of their contributions, we now enjoy comfortable homes, rapid transportation, far-reaching roads and bridges, world-wide communication systems, television, and many of the work-saving devices available to almost everyone. We have been able to walk on the moon and even probe deeper into outer space to learn more about the universe. In our hospitals we now have engineered equipment which has extended our life span. Existence for the average person has not only become longer and easier, but it has become more enlightened due to the contributions by various engineers in our vast world of technology.

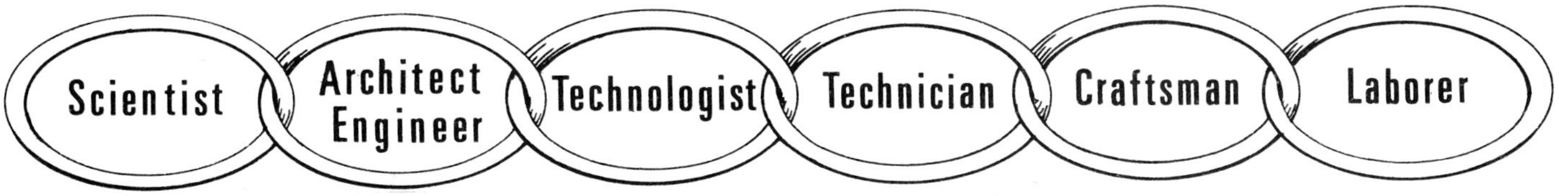

Fig. 17-4 Construction occupational spectrum.

There are those, however, who maintain that the development of technology and engineering, like a devouring monster, will eventually deplete our resources, contaminate our air and water, and finally leave our cities as almost uninhabitable places. No doubt, this is a real and pressing problem, even more critical for young people in the future. But engineering discipline teaches one thing well—that of *problem solving*. Engineers have always been faced with problems in the past, yet their solutions have been amazingly successful. Furthermore, we must not lose faith in man's future.

Engineering is known as a profession because the engineer is held accountable to society for his contributions, and he is pledged to uphold the dignity of his calling in keeping with high standards of conduct. The rewards are consistent with the stringent training. Graduate engineers have consistently been among the highest paid of the professions. The training has also been found favorable for attaining high-paying managerial positions in large corporations.

Armed with the ever-increasing wealth of knowledge now available to them, future engineers will, from all indications, solve the serious problems now facing the industrial nations of the world. The challenge is a real one for the capable young person with superior ability. Like architecture, engineering is a profession requiring rigid college training, especially in mathematics and the sciences. Although a few individuals without degrees have been able to become engineers after years of experience and some college-level training, a bachelor's degree in engineering is the generally accepted educational requirement for entering engineering positions.

The passing of state board tests, similar to those required of architects, is prerequisite to a graduate's registration for practice. In recent years, specialized graduate degrees have been required for many industrial positions, and the trend is increasing. Good engineering schools are located in nearly every state in the nation. The training is devoted to developing a substantial command of mathematics and the sciences. Experience in creative thinking and problem solving is also included. The engineer must be conscious of the needs and the aspirations of his fellowman if the physical principles learned are to be beneficially applied. This, of course, requires that he also learn to communicate both orally and by written word. Since the sphere of scientific and technical knowledge is expanding tremendously, the engineer's education is continual in order to keep abreast of the field. Many engineers after several years of practical experience obtain graduate degrees in business administration to enhance their opportunities for top management positions in major companies.

Inasmuch as engineering careers require a strong mathematics background, high school students contemplating this field should take as many math and geometry courses as possible. Also, several units of science and English are required for entrance into engineering colleges. Economics, social science, mechanical drawing, and sketching are other courses that will be found useful in preparing for college training.

17.3 ENGINEERING TECHNOLOGISTS AND TECHNICIANS

The terms *technologist* and *technician* are rapidly growing categories of specialized technical occupations lying between the engineer and the craftsman in the job spectrum. See Fig. 17-4. At least two years of college-level training are necessary for the technician category, whereas a four-year bachelor's degree is needed for the technologist. The four-year curricula include more courses in the humanities than the two-year programs. Two-year graduates receive the Associate Degree, while those in the four-year earn the Bachelor's Degree in Engineering Technology.

Most graduates in these categories are trained in technical institutes. Some technology programs are offered in separate divisions of engineering schools, and technician programs may be offered in some junior colleges or vocational-technical schools found throughout most states.

A technician is expected to become a specialist in whatever field he or she selects, and therefore some degree of skill is required in training. This does not, however, compare with the manual skill needed in preparing the craftsman or mechanic, who is usually expected to serve as an apprentice until usable skills are developed. Both mathematical and scientific principles are important in training, yet more emphasis is placed on their application and specialization than in engineering study. Technologists and technicians usually work directly with architects or engineers in a wide variety of capacities. Many jobs within the construction industry fall within these groups. Duties such as draftsmen, estimators, foremen, designers, specification writers, and inspectors, to name a few, are representative of the job titles.

Trained draftsmen, for example, take the architect's or engineer's rough sketch and general design ideas and devise construction details and the final working drawings. Skill in drafting opens many technical positions, but the individual most in demand is the one who has acquired specialized training to supplement his drafting skill. Besides the many employed by architects and engineers, scores are needed by the manufacturers of the sundry components that go into buildings. Many are employed to install, service, and sell the components and materials used in construction. Steel shop drawings, installation diagrams, catalogues, and illustrations of various types must be done, as well as the working drawings. Draftsmen are indispensable in landscape architecture, city planning, land development, home-plan services, land surveying, heating and air-conditioning, and kitchen cabinet manufacturing. Even the teaching of drafting and related courses in the hundreds of technical schools throughout the country requires a background in graphic principles.

Both oral and written communication are also necessary in technical training. Team projects often involve individuals in group efforts for which explicit exchange of ideas is important. Because specification writing becomes a major part of architectural service, technologists and technicians must be able to write clearly and express themselves well. They are often called upon to handle people from supervisory or foreman positions aside from their technical capacities. Frequently, it is desirable to understand the fundamentals of computer programming to aid in data analysis and problem solving.

Civil technology programs are similar to the architectural, yet they place more emphasis on structural and surveying courses. Either type qualifies graduates for immediate employment. Some schools offer cooperative programs in which students spend alternate periods or quarters in paid employment with architects or construction companies to supplement their training. One quarter is spent in school and the next is spent on the job.

Working conditions and pay scales are very favorable for technical people as openings continue to grow and their importance continues to be recognized. Technologists can expect slightly higher starting salaries than technicians.

Who are potential successes in this category of work? If you are contemplating this field, look over the following list of characteristics. Those who are most likely to enjoy technical jobs in construction are those who:

1. Like drawing and have a flair for graphic expression;
2. See significance in blueprints, layouts, diagrams, and flow charts;
3. Like to analyze devices to find out how they work; like to build things such as models;
4. Are handy around the house, like to use tools, and enjoy adjusting or fixing objects that are not working right;
5. Are attracted to construction sites and like the sights and sounds of a building rising in place;
6. Are sensitive to their surroundings; and
7. Thrive on hard work and don't mind putting in long hours to complete a task in the proper way.

In preparation for technical institute careers, high school students should take courses in mathematics, science, English, social sciences, and drafting courses.

17.4 CONSTRUCTION TRADESMEN

Attaining a job as a tradesman requires high school courses such as industrial arts and/or vocational courses closely associated with the trade in which you are interested. By all means complete your high school study. After graduation it would be wise to take further specialized courses at local trade and vocational schools if such are available. Bona fide correspondence

Fig. 17-5 Thousands of skilled carpenters find employment in construction.

schools offer many of these courses that can be studied during spare time, but it is usually more satisfactory to study under a competent instructor who has had considerable trade experience. Employment is frequently secured after comparatively short periods of training. Good-paying jobs are available if you apply yourself and if you don't mind serving periods of apprenticeship while learning. Employment is generally on an hourly basis with building contractors or subcontractors.

17.5 SUMMARY

Students should discuss their interests with teachers and counselors while in school. Helpful literature and college catalogues are commonly available from those trained in counseling. If you are unacquainted with potential schools, ask the librarian in your public library for a list of them and their addresses. Most libraries have many school catalogues available. Write to several prospective institutions offering construction or architectural programs and ask for information; they will be only too happy to send it to you. Visit nearby technical schools and talk to admission personnel and department heads. Talk to friends and relatives who may be graduates of similar institutions about their impressions and suggestions. Acquaintances can often be instrumental in finding jobs when schooling is completed. Statistics reveal that, in general, the more education you attain beyond high school, the more monetary rewards await you in years to come.

It must be emphasized that career planning starts with an in-depth analysis of one's own capacities—physical, mental, and emotional, and often the amount of time and cost that can be devoted to training. All must be weighed carefully. Various scholarships are available to capable young people who otherwise could not afford to spend years in college. This help, however, must be pursued through counselors or college registrars. Training programs that are selected should be ones that are approved by recognized evaluating associations. In engineering and technology, approval by the Engineers' Counsel for Professional Development (E.C.P.D.) indicates a highest-standard curriculum.

Study the manpower projections, work environment, health restrictions, skills needed, educational requirements, job mobility, and pay scales in an occupation before you try to

Fig. 17-6 Specialists in various tradework contribute to the completion of a building.

match-up your own characteristics and interests with that required for a potential life's work. Establish a personal goal and a desired life style. If necessary, secure a part-time job as a non-skilled worker on a construction project near your home. This may be an effective way to explore first-hand the various areas of work in this industry. According to the Engineering Manpower Commission, engineers and technical people who graduated in recent years enjoy greatly improved job prospects.

Many publications offered by the *U.S. Office of Education,* Washington, D.C., are helpful in choosing a career and furthering your education. A useful publication by the U.S. Department of Labor, *Occupational Outlook Handbook,* the latest edition, will be especially enlightening.

REVIEW QUESTIONS

1. Why is proficiency in written expression so important in technical training?

2. List some of the occupations which require close coordination by a practicing architect.

3. Is drafting considered a profession?

4. Which level of government is responsible for the licensing of architects and engineers?

5. What analysis becomes the first step in planning a career?

6. Why is the counselor an important person to know while in school?

7. Where can a student seek information about available scholarships to help him further his education?

8. What is meant by *life style* in reference to planning a career?

9. Why is a high degree of integrity expected and required in the engineering profession?

10. Should the amount of pay be the most compelling factor in job selection? Why?

11. What economic factors directly affect the construction industry?

12. How would you rate artistry and good taste in importance when evaluating an architect?

13. What formal degree is now required for the *technologist* job title?

14. What federal government department publishes yearly manpower and occupational trends information?

Fig. 17-7 A typical job application form (reduced from page size) used by many employers.

APPLICATION FOR EMPLOYMENT

Print name (last name first) ______

Present address ______

______

How long in residence? ______

Any previous address ______

How long in residence? ______

Age ____ Birth date ____ Place of birth ______

S. S. number ______ Telephone ______

Height ____ Weight ____ Color eyes ______

Marital status ______ No. of dependents ______

Present state of health: Excellent ___ Good ___ Fair ___ Poor ___

Do you have any disabilities? ____ If so, list them ______

______

List major diseases you have had ______

EDUCATION: Circle last year completed: 6 7 8 9 10 11 12

College: 1 2 3 4

High school attended: ______

WORK EXPERIENCE: List last 3 employers, starting with last:

Month and year	Name and address of employer	Salary	Position	Reason for leaving
From To				
From To				
From To				

REFERENCES: List 3 persons, excluding relatives and former employers, who have known you at least 1 year:

Name	Address	Occupation	Years known

"No one thing pleases all: one man gathers thorns and another roses."—Petronius

Appendices

APPENDIX A: SELECTED BIBLIOGRAPHY

Basic Drawing and Lettering

Earle, James H., *Engineering Design Graphics.* Reading, Mass.: Addison-Wesley Publishing Company, 1969.

French, Thomas E., and Charles J. Vierch, *Engineering Drawing and Graphic Technology* (11th ed.). New York: McGraw-Hill Book Company, 1972.

Giachineo, Joseph W., and Henry J. Beukema, *Engineering-Technical Drafting and Graphics.* Chicago: American Technical Society, 1961.

Gieseke, Frederick E., et al., *Technical Drawing* (6th ed.). New York: The Macmillan Company, 1974.

Hammond, Robert H., et al., *Engineering Graphics for Design, Analysis, and Communication* (2nd ed.). New York: The Ronald Press Company, 1971.

Hoelscher, Randolph P., and Clifford H. Springer, *Basic Drawing for Engineering Technology.* New York: John Wiley & Sons, Inc., 1964.

Luzadder, Warren J., *Fundamentals of Engineering Drawing* (6th ed.). Englewood Cliffs, N.J.: Prentice-Hall, Inc., 1971.

Building Construction

Anderson, LeRoy O., *How to Build a Wood-Frame House*. New York: Dover Publications, 1973.

Callendar, J. H., *Time Saver Standards for Architectural Design Data* (5th ed.). New York: McGraw-Hill Book Company, 1974.

Hornbostel, Caleb C., *Materials for Architecture*. New York: Reinhold Publishing Corp., 1961.

Hornbostel, Caleb C., and William J. Hornung, *Materials and Methods for Contemporary Construction*. Engelwood Cliffs, N.J.: Prentice-Hall, Inc., 1974.

Hornung, William J., *Blueprint Reading*. Englewood Cliffs, N.J.: Prentice-Hall, Inc., 1961.

Ketchum, Milo S., *Handbook of Standard Structural Details for Buildings*. Englewood Cliffs, N.J.: Prentice-Hall, Inc., 1956.

Merritt, Frederick S. (ed.), *Building Construction Handbook* (2nd ed.). New York: McGraw-Hill Book Company, 1965.

Muller, Edward J., *Reading Architectural Working Drawings*. Englewood Cliffs, N.J.: Prentice-Hall, Inc., 1971.

National Forest Products Association, *Manual for House Framing* (Wood Construction Data, No. 1). Washington, D.C., 1970.

———, *Plank-and-Beam Framing for Residential Buildings* (Wood Construction Data, No. 4). Washington, D.C., 1970.

Parker, Harry, et al., *Materials and Methods of Architectural Construction* (3rd ed.). John Wiley & Sons, Inc., 1958.

Principles of Clay Masonry Construction. Washington, D.C.: Structural Clay Products Institute.

Ramsey, Charles G., and Harold R. Sleeper, *Architectural Graphic Standards* (6th ed.). New York: John Wiley & Sons, Inc., 1970.

Reiner, Laurence E., *Methods and Materials of Construction*. Englewood Cliffs, N.J.: Prentice-Hall, Inc., 1970.

Schmidt, Lewis O., *Construction Lending Guide* (American Savings and Loan Institute). New York: McGraw-Hill Book Company, Inc., 1966.

Small Homes Council—Building Research Council, *Circular Series*. Urbana, Ill.: University of Illinois Bulletin. Various circulars on small home planning and construction. Published several times each year.

Smith, Ronald C., *Principles and Practices of Heavy Construction*. Englewod Cliffs, N.J.: Prentice-Hall, Inc., 1967.

———, *Principles and Practices of Light Construction* (2nd ed.). Englewood Cliffs, N.J.: Prentice-Hall, Inc., 1970.

Steel Construction Manual. New York: American Institute of Steel Construction (7th ed.), 1973.

Wass, Alonzo, and Gordon A. Sanders, *Building Construction: Roof Framing*. Englewood Cliffs, N.J.: Prentice-Hall, Inc., 1960.

Residential Planning

Faulkner, Ray N., and Sarah Faulkner, *Inside Today's Home* (3rd ed.). New York: Holt, Rinehart & Winston, Inc., 1968.

Kennedy, R. W., *House and the Art of Its Design*. New York: Reinhold Publishing Corp., 1959.

Record Houses 1974, by Architectural Record editors. New York: McGraw-Hill Book Company. Published annually.

Townsend, Gilbert, and James R. Dalzell, *How to Plan a House* (3rd ed.). Chicago: American Technical Society, 1958.

Architectural Drawing

Goodban, William T., and Jack J. Hayslett, *Architectural Drawing and Planning* (2nd ed.). New York: McGraw-Hill Book Company, 1972.

Hepler, Donald E., and Paul I. Wallach, *Architecture Drafting and Design* (2nd ed.). New York: Webster Division, McGraw-Hill Book Company, 1971.

Hooper, Lee, *Introduction to Construction Drafting*. Englewood Cliffs, N.J.: Prentice-Hall, Inc., 1971.

Kicklighter, Clois E., *Architecture, Residential Drawing and Design*. South Holland, Ill.: The Goodheart-Wilcox Company, Inc., 1973.

Patten, Lawton M., and Milton L. Rogness, *Architectural Drawing* (3rd ed.). Dubuque, Iowa: William C. Brown Company, 1968.

Stegman, G. K., and H. J. Stegman, *Architectural Drafting, Functional Planning and Creative Design*. Chicago: American Technical Society, 1966.

Stern, Ben J., *Opportunities in a Drafting Career.* New York: Universal Publishing and Distributing Corp. (235 East 45th Street), 1967.

Weidhaas, Ernest R., *Architectural Drafting and Design* (2nd ed.). Boston, Mass.: Allyn and Bacon, Inc., 1972.

Building Equipment

Burkhardt, Charles H., *Residential and Commercial Air Conditioning.* New York: McGraw-Hill Book Company, 1959.

Kinzey, Bertram Y., and Howard M. Sharp, *Environmental Technologies in Architecture,* Englewood Cliffs, N.J.: Prentice-Hall, Inc., 1963.

Laub, Julian M., *Air Conditioning & Heating Practice.* New York: Holt, Rinehart & Winston, Inc., 1963.

McGuinness, William J., and Benjamin Stein, *Mechanical and Electrical Equipment for Buildings,* et al. (5th ed.). New York: John Wiley & Sons, Inc., 1970.

National Environmental Systems Contractors Association, *Load Calculation for Residential Winter and Summer Air Conditioning* (3rd ed.) (Design and Installation Manual J). Arlington, Va., 1967.

Sweet's Architectural Catalogue File. New York: F. W. Dodge Corporation. Published each year.

Threlkeld, James L., *Thermal Environmental Engineering* (2nd ed.). Englewood Cliffs, N.J.: Prentice-Hall, Inc., 1970.

Perspective, Sketching, and Rendering

Atkin, William W., et al., *Pencil Techniques in Modern Design.* New York: Van Nostrand Reinhold Company, 1953.

Guptill, Arthur L., *Pencil Drawing Step by Step* (2nd ed.). New York: Van Nostrand Reinhold Company, 1959.

———, *Drawing With Pen and Ink* (rev. ed.). New York: Van Nostrand Reinhold Company, 1961.

Halse, Albert O., *Architectural Rendering; The Technique of Contemporary Presentation* (2nd ed.). New York: McGraw-Hill Book Company, 1972.

Hogarth, Paul, *Creative Pencil Drawing.* New York: Watson-Guptill Publications, Inc., 1964.

Kautzky, Theodore, *Pencil Broadsides* (2nd ed.). New York: Van Nostrand Reinhold Company, 1960.

———, *Painting Trees and Landscapes in Watercolor.* New York: Van Nostrand Reinhold Company, 1952.

Martin, C. Leslie, *Design Graphics* (2nd ed.). New York: The Macmillan Company, 1968.

Taubes, Frederic, *Pen and Ink Drawing* (2nd ed.). New York: Pitman Publishing Corporation, 1962.

Watson, Ernest W., *How to Use Creative Perspective.* New York: Van Nostrand Reinhold Company, 1955.

———, *Gallery of Pencil Techniques.* New York: Van Nostrand Reinhold Company, 1958.

———, *Perspective for Sketchers.* New York: Van Nostrand Reinhold Company, 1964.

Model Making

Hohauser, Sanford, *Architectural and Interior Models.* New York: Van Nostrand Reinhold Company, 1970.

Taylor, John, *Model Building for Architects and Engineers.* New York: McGraw-Hill Book Company, 1971.

Specifications

Abbett, Robert W., *Engineering Contracts and Specifications* (4th ed.). New York: John Wiley & Sons, Inc., 1963.

Edwards, H. Griffith, *Specifications* (2nd ed.). Princeton, N.J.: D. Van Nostrand Co., Inc., 1961.

Lewis, Jack R., *Construction Specifications.* Englewood Cliffs, N.J.: Prentice-Hall, Inc., 1975.

U. S. Federal Housing Administration, *Minimum Property Standards for One and Two Living Units* (FHA No. 300). Washington, D.C.: U. S. Government Printing Office, 1965.

Watson, Donald A., *Specifications Writing for Architects and Engineers.* New York: McGraw-Hill Book Company, 1964.

Periodicals

Architectural Record. McGraw-Hill, Inc., 1221 Avenue of the Americas, New York 10020.

Better Homes and Gardens. Merideth Corporation, 1716 Locust Street, Merideth Building, Des Moines, Iowa 50336.

House and Garden. Conde Nast Publications, 420 Lexington Avenue, New York 10017.

House and Home. McGraw-Hill, Inc., 1221 Avenue of the Americas, New York 10020.

House Beautiful. 717 Fifth Avenue, New York 10022.

Interiors. Whitney Publications, 130 East 59th Street, New York 10022.

Landscape Architecture. American Society of Landscape Architecture, 1500 Bardstown Road, Louisville, Kentucky 40205.

Progressive Architecture. Reinhold Publications, 600 Summer Street, Stamford, Connecticut 06904.

APPENDIX B: GLOSSARY OF CONSTRUCTION TERMS

Also see: Electrical Terms, p. 316
Stair Terms, p. 257
Typical Residential Terms, p. 137

A

ABUT: Joining the end of a construction member.

ACRE: A unit of land measurement having 43,560 sq. ft.

ADHESIVE: A natural or synthetic material, usually in liquid form, used to fasten or adhere materials together.

ADOBE CONSTRUCTION: Construction using sun-dried units of adobe soil for walls; usually found in the southwestern United States.

AIR-DRIED LUMBER: Lumber that has been dried by unheated air to a moisture content of approximately 15 per cent.

ANCHORS: Devices, usually metal, used in building construction to secure one material to another.

APRON: Inside window trim placed under the stool and against the wall.

ARCADE: An open passageway usually surrounded by a series of arches.

ARCH: A curved structure designed to support itself and the weight above.

AREAWAY: Recessed area below grade around the foundation to allow light and ventilation into basement window.

ARRIS: The sharp edge formed by two surfaces; usually on moldings.

ASBESTOS BOARD: A fire-resistant sheet made from asbestos fiber and Portland cement.

ASH PIT: An enclosed opening below a fireplace to collect ashes.

ASPHALT SHINGLES: Composition roof shingles made from asphalt impregnated felt covered with mineral granules.

ASTM: American Society for Testing Materials.

ASTRAGAL: T-profiled molding usually used between meeting doors or casement windows.

ATRIUM: An open court within a building.

ATTIC: The space between the roof and the ceiling in a gable house.

AWNING WINDOW: An outswinging window hinged at the top of the sash.

AXIS: A line around which something rotates or is symmetrically arranged.

B

BACKFILL: Earth used to fill in areas around foundation walls.

BALCONY: A deck projecting from the wall of a building above ground level.

BALUSTERS: Small, vertical supports for the railing of a stairs.

BALUSTRADE: A series of balusters supporting the railing of a stairs or balcony.

BANNISTER: A handrail with supporting posts on a stairway.

BARGEBOARD: The finish board covering the projecting portion of a gable roof.

BASEBOARD: The finish trim board covering the interior wall where the wall and floor meet.

BATT: A type of insulation designed to be installed between framing members.

BATTEN: The narrow strips of wood nailed vertically over the joints of boards to form board-and-batten siding.

BATTER BOARDS: Horizontal boards at exact elevations nailed to posts just outside the corners of a proposed building. Strings are stretched across the boards to locate the outline of the foundation for workmen.

BAYS: Uniform compartments within a structure, usually within a series of beams, columns, etc.

BAY WINDOWS: A group of windows projecting from the wall of a building. The center is parallel to the wall, and the sides are angular. A bow window is circular.

BEARING PLATE: A metal plate that provides support for a structural member.

BEARING WALL: A wall that supports a weight above in additional to its own weight.

BENCH MARK: A mark on some permanent object fixed to the ground from which land measurements and elevations are taken.

BLIND NAILING: Method of nailing to conceal nails.

BOARD MEASURE: The system of lumber measurement. A unit is 1 board ft which is 1′ sq by approximately 1″ thick.

BOND: The arrangement of masonry units in a wall.

BRICK VENEER: A facing of brick on the outer side of wood frame or masonry.

BRIDGING: Thin wood or metal pieces fastened diagonally at midspan between floor joists to act as both tension and compression members for the purposes of stiffening and spreading concentrated loads.

BUCK: Frame for a door, usually made of metal.

BUILT-UP ROOF: A roofing composed of layers of felt impregnated with pitch, coal tar, or asphalt. The top is finished with crushed stone or minerals. It is used on flat or low-pitched roofs.

BULLNOSE: Rounded edge units.

BUTT: Type of joint having the pieces edge to edge or end to end. Also a type of door hinge allowing edge of door to butt into the jamb.

C

CALL OUT: A note on a drawing with a leader to the feature.

CANT STRIP: An angular board used to eliminate a sharp, right angle, usually on roof decks.

CAP: Covering for a wall or post.

CARPORT: A garage not fully enclosed.

CASEMENT WINDOW: Window with one or two sash that hinge on their sides. They may open either in or out.

CASING: Trim around a window or door opening.

CAULKING: A soft, waterproof material used to fill open joints or cracks.

CHAMFER: The beveled edge formed by removing the sharp corner of a material.

CHASE: A vertical space within a building for ducts, pipes, or wires.

CHORD: The lower horizontal member of a truss.

CLEAT: A small board fastened to another member to serve as a brace or support.

COLLAR BEAM: A horizontal member tying opposing rafters below the ridge in roof framing.

CONDUIT, ELECTRICAL: A metal pipe in which wiring is installed.

COPING: A cap or top course of masonry on a wall to prevent moisture penetration.

CORBEL: A projection of masonry from the face of a wall, or a bracket used for support of weight above.

CORE: The inner layer of plywood. It may be veneer, solid lumber, or fiberboard.

CORNER BOARD: Vertical board forming the corner of a building.

CORNER BRACE: Diagonal brace at the corner of a wood-frame wall to stiffen and prevent racking.

CORNICE: The molded projection of the roof overhang at the top of a wall.

CORNICE RETURN: The short portion of a molded cornice that returns on the gable end of a house.

COUNTER FLASHING: Flashing used under cap flashing.

COVE: A concave molding usually used on horizontal inside corners.

CRAWL SPACE: The shallow space below the floor of a house built above the ground. Generally it is surrounded with the foundation wall.

CRICKET: A device used at roof intersections to divert rain water.

CRIPPLE: A structural member that is cut less than full length, such as a studding piece above a window or door opening.

CROWN MOLDING: A molding used above eye level, usually the cornice molding under the roof overhang.

Cul-de-sac: A court or street with no outlet which provides a turn around for vehicles.

Cupola: A small, decorative structure placed on a roof, usually a garage roof, and can be used as a ventilator.

Curtain wall: An exterior wall that provides no structural support.

D

Dado joint: A recessed joint on the face of a board to receive the end of a perpendicular board.

Damper: A movable plate which regulates the draft through a flue or duct.

Dead load: The weight of the structure itself and the permanent components fastened to it.

Dimension lumber: Framing lumber which is 2″ thick and from 4″–12″ wide.

Dome: A roof in the shape of a hemisphere used on a structure.

Doorjamb: Two vertical pieces held together by a head jamb forming the inside lining of a door opening.

Doorstop: The strips on the doorjambs against which the door closes.

Dormer: A projection on a sloping roof framing a vertical window or vent.

Double glazing: Two pieces of glass with air between to provide insulation.

Double hung: A type of window having two sash which can be operated vertically.

Downspout: A pipe for carrying rainwater from the roof to the ground or sewer connection.

Dressed size: The actual finish size of lumber after surfacing.

Drip: A projecting construction member or groove below the member to throw off rainwater.

Dry-wall construction: Interior wall covering with sheets of gypsum rather than traditional plaster.

Ducts: Sheet metal conductors for air distribution throughout a building.

Duplex outlet: Electrical wall outlet having two plug receptacles.

E

Easement: A right or privilege to a piece of property held by someone other than the owner. Usually the right to run utility lines, underground pipe, or passageways on property.

Eaves: The lower portion of the roof that overhangs the wall.

Efflorescence: The forming of white stains on masonry walls from moisture within the walls.

Ell: An extension or wing of a building at right angles to the main section.

Escutcheon: The decorative metal plate used around the key-hole on doors or around a pipe extending through the wall.

Excavation: A cavity or pit produced by digging the earth in preparation for construction.

Expansion joint: A flexible joint used to prevent cracking or breaking because of expansion and contraction due to temperature changes.

F

Facade: The face or front elevation of a building.

Face brick: Brick of better quality used on the face of a wall.

Fascia: The outside horizontal member on the edge of a roof or overhang.

Fill: Sand, gravel, or loose earth used to bring a subgrade up to a desired level around a building.

Firecut: An angular cut at the end of a floor joist resting on a masonry wall.

Fire-stop: A tight closure of a concealed space with incombustible material to prevent the spreading of fire.

Fire wall: A fire resistant masonry wall between sections of a building for the purpose of containing a fire.

Flagstone: Thin, flat stones used for floors, steps, walks, etc.

Flashing: Sheet metal or other material used in roof or wall construction to prevent water from seeping into the building.

Flitch beam: A built-up beam formed by a metal plate sandwiched between two wood members and bolted together for additional strength.

Floor joist: Structural member of a floor.

Flue: The passage in a chimney through which smoke, gases, and fumes escape to the outer air.

Footing: Poured concrete base upon which the foundation wall rests.

Frieze: The flat board of cornice trim which is fastened to the wall.

Frostline: The deepest level of frost penetration in soil. This depth varies in different climates. Footings must be placed below the frostline to prevent rupturing the foundation.

Furring strips: Thin strips of wood fastened to walls or ceilings for leveling and for receiving the finish surface material.

G

Gable: The triangular end of a gable-roofed house.

Gambrel roof: A roof with two pitches, the lower slope steeper than the upper.

Girder: Heavy structural member supporting lighter structural members of a floor or roof.

Glazing: Placing of glass in windows and doors.

Gradient: The inclination of a road, piping, or the ground, expressed in percent.

Gravel stop: A strip of metal with a vertical lip used to retain the gravel around the edge of a built-up roof.

Grounds: Wood strips fastened to walls before plastering to serve as screeds and nailing base for trim.

Gusset: A plywood or metal plate used to strengthen the joints of a truss.

Gutter: A metal or wood trough for carrying water from a roof.

H

Hanger: A metal strap used to support piping or the ends of joists.

Header: In framing, the joists placed at the ends of a floor opening and attached to the trimmers. In masonry work, the small end of a masonry unit.

Hearth: The incombustible floor in front of and within the fireplace.

Heartwood: The central portion of wood within the tree, which is stronger and more decay-resistant than the surrounding sapwood.

Hip rafter: The diagonal rafter that extends from the plate to the ridge to form the hip.

Hip roof: A roof that rises by equally inclined planes from all four sides of a building.

Hose bibb: A water faucet made for the threaded attachment of a hose.

House drain: Horizontal sewer piping within a building which carries the waste from the soil stacks.

House sewer: The watertight soil pipe extending from the exterior of the foundation wall to the public sewer.

Humidifier: A device, generally attached to the furnace, which supplies or maintains correct humidity levels in a building.

I

Incandescent lamp: A lamp within which a filament gives off light when sufficiently heated by an electric current.

Insulating concrete: Concrete with vermiculite added to produce lightweight, insulating concrete for subfloors and roofs.

Interior trim: General term for all the finish molding, casing, baseboard, etc., applied within the building by finish carpenters.

J

Jack rafter: A rafter shorter than a common rafter; especially used in hip-roof framing.

Jalousie: A type of window having a number of small, unframed yet movable pieces of glass.

Jamb: The vertical members of a finished door opening.

Joinery: A general woodworking term used for all better-class wood-joint construction.

Joist: A horizontal structural member supported by bearing walls, beams, or girders in floor or ceiling framing.

Joist hanger: A metal strap to carry the ends of floor joists.

K

Kiln-dried lumber: Lumber that has been properly dried and cured to produce a higher grade of lumber than that which has been air dried.

King post: The center upright strut in a truss.

Kip: A unit of 1000 pound load.

Knee wall: A low wall resulting from 1½-story construction.

Knocked down: Unassembled; refers to construction units requiring assembly after being delivered to the job.

L

Lally column: A steel column used in light construction.

Laminated beam: A beam made of superimposed layers of similar materials by uniting them with glue and pressure.

Landing: A platform between flights of stairs or at the termination of stairs.

Lap joint: A joint produced by lapping two similar pieces of material.

Lath: Metal, wood, or gypsum base for plastering.

Lattice: Framework of crossed or interlaced wood or metal strips.

Leader: A vertical pipe or downspout that carries rainwater from the gutter to the ground or storm sewer.

Ledger strip: A strip of lumber fastened to the lower part of a beam or girder on which notched joists are attached.

Light: A single pane of glass in a window or door.

Lineal foot: A 1′ measurement along a straight line.

Lintel: A horizontal support member across the head of a door or window opening.

Load-bearing wall: A wall designed to support the weight imposed upon it from above.

Lookout. A short wooden framing member used to support an overhanging portion of a roof. It extends from the wall to the underside surfacing of the overhang.

Lot line: The line forming the legal boundary of a piece of property.

Louver: An opening or slatted grill allowing ventilation while providing protection from rain.

Luminaire: An electric lighting fixture used within a room.

M

Mansard roof: A hip-type roof having two slopes on each of the four sides.

Mantle: The shelf above a fireplace opening.

Masonry: A general term for construction of brick, stone, concrete block, or similar materials.

Mastic: A flexible adhesive for adhering building materials.

Matte finish: A finish free from gloss or highlights.

Metal wall ties: Corrugated metal strips used to tie masonry veneer to wood walls.

Miter joint: A joint made with ends or edges of two pieces of lumber cut at a 45° angle and fitted together.

Millwork: A general term that includes all dressed lumber which has been molded, shaped, or preassembled at the mill.

Modular construction: Construction in which the size of all components has been based upon a standardized unit of measure.

Moisture barrier: A sheet material that retards moisture penetration into walls, floors, ceilings, etc.

Monolithic: Term used for concrete construction poured and cast in one piece without joints.

Mortar: A mixture of cement, sand, lime, and water used to bond masonry units.

Mortice: A hole, slot, or recess cut into a piece of wood to receive a projecting part (tenon) made to fit.

Mosaic: Small colored tile, glass, stone, or similar material arranged to produce a decorative surface.

Mullion: The structural member between a series of windows.

Muntin: A small bar separating the glass lights in a window.

N

Newel post: The main post supporting a handrail at the bottom or top of a stairs.

Nominal size: The size of lumber before dressing, rather than its actual size.

Nonbearing wall: A wall supporting no load other than its own weight.

Nonferrous metal: Metal containing no iron, such as copper, brass, or aluminum.

Nosing: The rounded edge of a stair tread.

O

On center: A method of indicating the spacing

between framing members by stating the measurement from the center of one member to the center of the succeeding one.

OUTLET: Any type of electrical box allowing current to be drawn from the electrical system for lighting or appliances.

OVERHANG: The projecting area of a roof or upper story beyond the wall of the lower part.

P

PALLET: A rugged wood skid used to stack and mechanically handle units of masonry.

PANEL: A flat, rectangular surface framed with a thicker material.

PARAPET: A low wall or railing; usually around the edge of a roof.

PARTITION: A wall that divides areas within a building.

PARGE COAT: A thin coat of cement plaster applied to a masonry wall for refinement of the surface or for dampproofing.

PARQUET FLOORING: Flooring, usually of wood, laid in an alternating or inlaid pattern to form various designs.

PARTING STOP: Thin strips set into the vertical jambs of a double-hung window to separate the sash.

PARTY WALL: A wall between two adjoining buildings in which both owners share, such as a common wall between row houses.

PENNEY: A term used to indicate the size of nails, abbreviated "d". Originally, it specified the price per hundred nails (i.e., 6 penney nails cost 6¢ per hundred nails).

PERGOLA: An open, structural framework over an outdoor area usually covered with climbing shrubs or vines to form an arbor.

PERIPHERY: The entire outside edge of an object.

PIER: A masonry pillar usually below a building to support the floor framing.

PILASTER: A rectangular pier attached to a wall for the purpose of strengthening the wall. Also a decorative column attached to a wall.

PITCH: The slope of a roof usually expressed as a ratio.

PLAT: A graphic description of a surveyed piece of land, indicating the boundaries, location, and dimensions. The plat, recorded in the appropriate county official's office, also contains information as to easements, restrictions, and lot numbers, if any.

PLATE: The top horizontal member of a row of studs in a frame wall.

PLUMB: Said of an object when it is in true vertical position as determined by a plumb bob or vertical level.

POCHÉ: The darkening in of areas on a drawing to aid in readability.

POST AND BEAM CONSTRUCTION: A type of building frame in which roof and floor beams rest directly over wall posts.

PRECAST: Concrete units that are cast and finished at the plant rather than at the site of construction.

PRIME COAT: The first coat of paint that serves as a filler and sealer in preparation for finish coats.

PURLINS: Horizontal roof members laid over trusses to support rafters.

Q

QUARRY TILE: Unglazed, machine-made tile used for floors.

QUARTER ROUND: Small molding presenting the profile of a quarter circle.

QUARTER-SAWED OAK: Oak lumber, usually flooring, which has been sawed so that the medullary rays showing on end-grain are nearly perpendicular to the face of the lumber.

QUOINS: Large squared stones set in the corners of a masonry building for appearance's sake.

R

RABBET (or rebate): A groove cut along the edge or end of a board to receive another board producing a rabbet joint.

RADIANT HEATING: A method of heating with the use of radiating heat rays.

RAFTER: A roof structural member running from the wall plate to the ridge. There are jack, hip, valley, and common rafters. The structural members of a flat roof are usually called roof joists.

RAKE JOINT: A mortar joint that has been recessed by tooling before it sets up.

RAKE MOLDING: Gable molding attached on the incline of the gable. The molding must be a different profile to match similar molding along the remaining horizontal portions of the roof.

Random rubble: Stonework having irregular shaped units and coursing.

Register: Opening in air duct, usually covered with a grill.

Reinforced concrete: Concrete containing steel bars or wire mesh to increase its structural qualities.

Retaining wall: A heavy wall that supports an earth embankment.

Reveal: The side of an opening for a window or door, between the frame and the outer surface of a wall.

Ribbon: A wood strip set into studs to support floor joists in balloon framing.

Ridge: The top edge of a roof where two slopes meet.

Ridgeboard: The highest horizontal member in a gable roof; it is supported by the upper ends of the rafters.

Riprap: Irregular stones thrown together loosely to form a wall or soil cover.

Rise: The vertical height of a roof or stairs.

Rocklath: Paper covered gypsum sheets used as a plaster base.

Rough hardware: All the concealed fasteners in a building such as nails, bolts, hangers, etc.

Rough opening: An unfinished opening in the framing into which doors, windows, and other units are placed.

Rubble: Irregular broken stone.

Run: The horizontal distance of a flight of stairs, or the horizontal distance from the outer wall to the ridge of a roof.

S

Saddle: A small gable roof placed in back of a chimney on a sloping roof to shed water and debris.

Sash: An individual frame into which glass is set.

Scab: A short piece of lumber fastened to a butt joint for strength.

Schedule: A list of similar items and information about them, such as a window schedule.

Scribing: Marking and fitting a piece of lumber to an irregular surface such as masonry.

Scuttle: A small opening in a ceiling to provide access to an attic or roof.

Section: A unit of land measurement usually one mile square. A section contains approximately 640 acres, and there are 36 sections to a township. (Also a drawing showing the cut-open view of an object.)

Septic tank: A concrete or steel underground tank used to reduce sewage by bacterial action.

Shake: A handsplit wood shingle.

Sheathing: The rough boarding or covering over the framing of a house.

Shim: A thin piece of material used to true up or fill a space between two members.

Shoe mold: The small molding covering the joint between the flooring and the baseboard on the inside of a room.

Shoring: Planks or posts used to support walls or ceilings during construction.

Siding: The outside finish covering on a frame wall.

Sill: The horizontal exterior member below a window or door opening. The wood member placed directly on to the foundation wall in wood frame construction.

Skylight: A window in a flat roof.

Sleepers: Wood strips placed over or in a concrete slab to receive a finish wood floor.

Smoke chamber: The enlarged portion of a chimney flue directly above the fireplace.

Soffit: The underside of an overhang such as an overhang or stairs.

Soil stack: The vertical pipe in a plumbing system that carries the sewage.

Soleplate: The horizontal member of a frame wall resting on the rough floor, to which the studs are nailed.

Span: The horizontal distance between supports for joists, beams, or trusses.

Specifications: The written instructions that accompany a set of working drawings.

Square: A unit of measure—100 sq ft. Commonly used in reference to the amount of roofing material to cover 100 sq ft.

Stile: The vertical member on the door or panel.

Stirrup: A metal U-shaped strap used to support the end of a framing member.

Stool: Horizontal interior member of trim below a window.

Stretcher course: A row of masonry in wall with the long side of the units exposed to the exterior.

Stringer: The inclined structural member supporting the treads and risers of a stairs; sometimes it is visible next to the profile of the stairs.

Stucco: A cement plaster finish applied to exterior walls.

Studs: The vertical framing members of a wall.

Subflooring: Any material nailed directly to floor joists. The finish floor is attached over the subflooring.

T

Tail joist: A relatively shorter joist that joins against a header or trimmer in floor framing.

Tensile strength: The greatest longitudinal stress a structural member can bear without adverse effects (breaking or cracking).

Terrazzo flooring: Wear-resistant flooring made of marble chips or small stones embedded in cement that has been polished smooth.

Thermal conductor: A substance capable of transmitting heat.

Termite shield: Sheet metal placed over masonry to prevent the passage of termites into wood.

Terra cotta: Baked clay and sand formed into masonry units.

Thermostat: An automatic device for controlling interior temperatures.

Threshold: The beveled metal, stone, or wood member directly under a door.

Title: Legal evidence to the ownership of property.

Toe nail: Nailing at an angle to the wood fiber.

Tongue: The narrower extension on the edge of a board that is received by the groove of an adjacent board.

T-post: A post built up of studs and blocking to form the intersection of the framing of perpendicular walls.

Transom: A hinged window over a door.

Trap: A U-shaped pipe below plumbing fixtures to create a water seal and prevent sewer odors and gases from being released into the habitable areas.

Tread: The horizontal surface member of a stairs upon which the foot is placed.

Trim: A general term given to the moldings and finish members on a building. Its installation is called finish carpentry.

Trimmer: The longer floor framing member around a rectangular opening into which a header is joined.

Truss: Structural members arranged and fastened in triangular units to form a rigid framework for support of loads over a long span.

V

Valley rafter: The diagonal rafter at the intersection of two intersecting sloping roofs.

Vapor barrier: A watertight material used to prevent the passage of moisture or water vapor into and through walls.

Veneered construction: Type of wall construction in which frame or masonry walls are faced with other exterior surfacing materials.

Vent stack: A vertical soil pipe connected to the drainage system to allow ventilation and pressure equalization.

Vestibule: A small entrance room.

W

Wainscot: The surfacing on the lower part of an interior wall when finished differently from the remainder of the wall.

Wallboard: Large sheets of gypsum or fiberboard that are usually nailed to framing to form interior walls.

Wall tie: A small metal strip or steel wire used to bind tiers of masonry in cavity-wall construction, or to bind brick veneer to the wood-frame wall in veneer construction.

Water table: A horizontal member extending from the surface of an exterior wall so as to throw off rainwater from the wall.

Weather stripping: A strip of fabric or metal fastened around the edges of windows and doors to prevent air infiltration.

Weep hole: Small holes in masonry cavity walls to release water accumulation to the exterior.

Winder: The radiating or wedge-shaped treads at the turns of some stairs.

Wythe: Pertaining to a single-width masonry wall.

APPENDIX C: ABBREVIATIONS USED IN ARCHITECTURAL DRAWING

Alternate	ALT
Aluminum	AL
American Institute of Architects	A.I.A.
American Institute of Electrical Engineers	A.I.E.E.
American Institute of Steel Construction	A.I.S.C.
American Society of Heating, Refrigerating, and Air-Conditioning Engineers	A.S.H.R.A.E.
American Society for Testing Materials	A.S.T.M.
American Standards Association, Inc.	A.S.A.
American Wire Gauge	AWG
Apartment	APT
Avenue	AVE
Bathroom	B
Bedroom	BR
Board	BD
Board measure	BM
British thermal unit	BTU
Building	BLDG
Building line	BL
Cast iron	CI
Ceiling	CLG
Center to center	C to C
Center line	CL or ℄
Cleanout	CO
Closet	CLO
Column	COL
Combination	COMB
Composition	COMP
Concrete	CONC
Construction Specifications Institute	C.S.I.
Cubic feet of air per minute	CFM
Cubic foot	CU FT
Cubic inch	CU IN
Cubic yard	CU YD
Diameter	DIA(M)
Dimension	DIM
Dining room	DR
Ditto	DO or ″
Divided or division	DIV
Door	DR
Double-hung window	DHW
Double-strength grade A glass	DSA
Double-strength grade B glass	DSB
Downspout	DS
Dozen	DOZ
Drawing	DWG
Dressed and matched (4 sides)	D4S
East	E
Enclosure	ENCL
Entrance	ENT
Exterior	EXT
Federal Housing Authority	FHA
Feet per minute	FPM
Finish	FIN
Flashing	FLG
Floor	FL
Footing	FTG
Foundation	FDN
Gallon	GAL
Galvanized iron	GI
Gauge	GA
Glass	GL

Head	HD
Heat- and moisture-resistant rubber insulation	RHW
Height	HGT
Hexagonal	HEX
Horsepower	HP
Hose bibb	HB
Hundred	C
I beam	I
Institute of Boiler and Radiator Manufacturers	I.B.R.
Insulate or Insulation	INS
Interior	INT
Joist and plank (lumber designation)	J & P
Kiln dried	KD
Kitchen	K
Laundry	LAU
Lavatory	LAV
Light (pane of glass)	LT
Linen closet	L CL
Living room	LR
Medicine cabinet	MC
Minimum	MIN
Modular	MOD
Molding	MLD
National Environmental Systems Contractors Association	NESCA
National Housing Authority	NHA
National Lumber Manufacturer's Association	N.L.M.A.
North	N
Number	NO. or #
On center	OC
Plaster	PLAS or PL
Plate	PL or ⅊
Plywood	PWD
Quart(s)	QT
Refrigerator	REFR
Riser	R
Room	RM
Rubber	R
Second	SEC
Single-strength grade B glass	SSB
South	S
Specifications	SPEC
Standard	STD
Telephone	TEL
Temperature	TEMP
Terra-cotta	TC
Thousand	M
Threshold	THR
Tongue and groove	T & G
Tread	T or TR
Unfinished	UNFIN
Ventilation	VENT
Water closet	WC
Water heater	WH
Waterproof or waterproofing	WP
Wide flange (steel)	WF or W
Wood	WD

APPENDIX D: JOIST AND RAFTER SIZES

Joist and Rafter Spans

SPANS BASED ON AMERICAN SOFTWOOD LUMBER STANDARDS (PS 20-70) SIZES

SELECTED SPECIES AND GRADES		SOUTHERN YELLOW PINE No. 1 Kiln Dried $F_b = 1900$ $E = 1{,}900{,}000$	SOUTHERN YELLOW PINE No. 2 $F_b = 1200$ $E = 1{,}400{,}000$	DOUGLAS FIR-LARCH No. 2 $F_b = 1450$ $E = 1{,}700{,}000$	EASTERN SPRUCE Structural $F_b = 1300$ $E = 1{,}300{,}000$	SOUTHERN YELLOW PINE No. 1 Kiln Dried $F_b = 1900$ $E = 1{,}900{,}000$	SOUTHERN YELLOW PINE No. 2 $F_b = 1200$ $E = 1{,}400{,}000$	DOUGLAS FIR-LARCH No. 2 $F_b = 1450$ $E = 1{,}700{,}000$	EASTERN SPRUCE Structural $F_b = 1300$ $E = 1{,}300{,}000$
Nominal Size	**Spc'g. " o.c.**	**FLOOR JOISTS — 30# Live Load**				**40# Live Load**			
2" x 6"	12	12–6	11–3	12–0	11–0	11–4	10–3	10–11	10–1
	16	11–4	10–10	10–11	10–0	10–4	9–4	9–11	9–2
	24	9–11	8–8	9–7	8–9	9–0	7–9	8–8	7–11
2" x 8"	12	16–6	14–11	15–10	14–6	15–0	13–6	14–5	13–2
	16	15–0	13–6	14–5	13–2	13–7	12–3	13–1	12–0
	24	13–1	11–6	12–7	11–6	11–11	10–3	11–3	10–6
2" x 10"	12	21–0	19–0	20–3	18–6	19–1	17–3	18–5	16–10
	16	19–1	17–3	18–5	16–10	17–4	15–8	16–9	15–3
	24	16–8	14–7	16–1	14–8	15–2	13–1	14–6	13–4
2" x 12"	12	25–7	23–1	24–8	22–6	23–3	21–0	22–5	20–6
	16	23–3	21–0	22–5	20–6	21–1	19–1	20–4	18–7
	24	20–3	17–9	19–7	17–11	18–5	15–11	17–6	16–3
		CEILING JOISTS — No Attic Storage—Drywall Ceiling				**Limited Attic Storage—Plaster Ceiling**			
2" x 4"	12	13–2	11–10	12–8	11–7	9–1	8–3	8–9	8–0
	16	11–11	10–9	11–6	10–6	8–3	7–6	8–0	7–3
	24	10–5	9–5	9–11	9–2	7–3	6–6	7–0	6–4
2" x 6"	12	20–8	18–8	19–11	18–2	14–4	12–11	13–9	12–7
	16	18–9	16–11	18–1	16–6	13–0	11–9	12–6	11–5
	24	16–4	14–2	15–7	14–5	11–4	10–0	10–11	10–0
2" x 8"	12	27–2	24–7	26–2	24–0	18–10	17–0	18–2	16–7
	16	24–8	22–4	23–10	21–9	17–2	15–6	16–6	15–1
	24	21–7	18–8	20–6	19–0	15–0	13–2	14–5	13–2
2" x 10"	12	34–8	31–4	32–9	30–7	24–1	21–9	23–2	21–2
	16	31–6	28–6	29–9	27–9	21–10	19–9	21–1	19–3
	24	27–6	23–1	26–0	24–3	19–1	16–10	18–5	16–10
		LOW SLOPE ROOF RAFTERS (3" in 12" or less) — 20# Live Load—No Finished Ceiling				**40# Live Load—No Finished Ceiling**			
2" x 6"	12	16–5	14–2	15–4	14–4	13–0	11–0	11–11	11–5
	16	14–8	12–4	13–3	12–10	11–9	9–6	10–3	9–11
	24	12–8	10–0	10–10	10–5	9–9	7–9	8–5	8–1
2" x 8"	12	21–7	18–9	20–3	19–4	17–2	14–6	15–8	15–1
	16	19–6	16–3	17–6	16–10	15–6	12–7	13–7	13–1
	24	16–8	13–3	14–4	13–9	12–11	10–3	11–1	10–8
2" x 10"	12	27–6	23–11	25–10	24–6	21–10	18–6	20–0	19–3
	16	24–8	20–8	22–4	21–6	20–0	16–0	17–4	16–8
	24	21–3	16–11	18–3	17–7	16–6	13–1	14–2	13–7
2" x 12"	12	33–5	29–1	31–4	30–0	26–6	22–6	24–4	23–5
	16	30–0	25–2	27–2	26–2	24–4	19–6	21–1	20–3
	24	25–10	20–6	22–2	21–5	20–0	15–11	17–2	16–7
		HIGH SLOPE ROOF RAFTERS (over 3" in 12") — 20# Live Load—Light Roofing				**40# Live Load—Heavy Roofing**			
2" x 4"	12	11–6	10–3	11–0	9–11	8–5	7–4	7–8	6–11
	16	10–5	9–1	9–6	8–7	7–3	6–4	6–8	6–0
	24	8–6	7–4	7–9	7–0	5–11	5–2	5–5	4–11
2" x 6"	12	18–1	15–0	16–2	15–7	13–2	10–6	11–4	10–11
	16	16–4	13–0	14–0	13–6	11–5	9–1	9–10	9–5
	24	13–4	10–7	11–5	11–0	9–4	7–5	8–0	7–9
2" x 8"	12	23–8	19–9	21–4	20–6	17–5	13–10	14–11	14–5
	16	21–6	17–1	18–5	17–9	15–1	12–0	12–11	12–6
	24	17–7	13–11	15–1	14–6	12–4	9–9	10–7	10–2
2" x 10"	12	30–3	25–2	27–2	26–2	22–2	17–8	19–1	18–4
	16	27–5	21–10	23–7	22–8	19–3	15–3	16–6	15–11
	24	22–5	17–10	19–3	18–6	15–8	12–6	13–6	13–0

APPENDIX E: DESIGN DATA FOR PLANK-AND-BEAM FRAMING [1]

Design Data for Planks

Design data for plank floors and roofs are included in **Table 1.** Computations for bending are based on the live load indicated, plus 10 pounds per square foot of dead load. Computations for deflection are based on the live load only. The table shows four general arrangements of planks as follows:

Type A—Extending over a single span.
Type B—Continuous over two equal spans.
Type C—Continuous over three equal spans.
Type D—A combination of Types A and B.

On the basis of a section of planking 12 inches wide the following formulas were used in making the computations:

For Type A: $M = \frac{wL^2}{8}$ and $D = \frac{5wL^4\ (12)^3}{384EI}$

For Type B: $M = \frac{wL^2}{8}$ and $D = \frac{wL^4\ (12)^3}{185EI}$

For Type C: $M = \frac{wL^2}{10}$ and $D = \frac{4wL^4\ (12)^3}{581EI}$

For Type D:

$$M = \frac{wL^2}{8} \text{ and } D = \frac{1}{2}\left(\frac{5wL^4\ (12)^3}{384EI} + \frac{wL^4\ (12)^3}{185EI}\right)$$

To use **Table 1**, first determine the plank arrangement (Types A, B, C or D), the span, the live load to be supported and the deflection limitation. Then select from the table the corresponding required values for fiber stress in bending (f) and modulus of elasticity (E). The plank to be used should be of a grade and species which meets these minimum values. The maximum span for a specific grade and species of plank may be determined by reversing these steps.

For those who prefer to use random length planks (instead of arrangements Type A, B, C or D), similar technical information concerning it is included in *Random Length Wood Decking,* a publication of the National Forest Products Association.

Design Data for Beams

Design data for beams are included in **Tables 2 through 10.** Computations for bending are based on the live load indicated plus 10 pounds per square foot of dead load. Computations for deflection are based on the live load only. All beams in the table were designed to extend over a single span and the following formulas were used:

For Type A: $M = \frac{wL^2}{8}$ and $D = \frac{5wL^4\ (12)^3}{384EI}$

To use the tables first determine the span, the live load to be supported and the deflection limitation. Then select from the tables the proper size of beam with the corresponding required values for fiber stress in bending (f) and modulus of elasticity (E). The beam used should be of a grade and species which meets these minimum values. The maximum span for a beam of specific size, grade and species can be determined by reversing these steps.

Notations

In the preceding formulas and in the tables the symbols have the following meanings:

w = load in pounds per linear foot.
L = span in feet.
M = induced bending moment in pound-feet.
f = fiber stress in bending in pounds per square inch.
E = modulus of elasticity in pounds per square inch.
I = moment of inertia in inches to the fourth power.
D = deflection in inches.

Lumber Sizes

Tabular data provided herein are based on net dimensions (S4S) as listed in American Softwood Lumber Standard, VPS 20-70.

1 From *Plank-and-Beam Framing for Residential Buildings* (Manual #4). By and with permission from the National Forest Products Association.

Table E-1 Nominal Two-Inch Plank

Required values for fiber stress in bending (f) and modulus of elasticity (E) to support safely a live load of **20, 30,** or **40,** pounds per square foot within a deflection limitation of $l/240$, $l/300$, or $l/360$. For instructions on use of table see Design Data for Planks on page 465.

PLANK SPAN IN FEET	LIVE LOAD psf	DEFLECTION LIMITATION	TYPE A		TYPE B		TYPE C		TYPE D	
			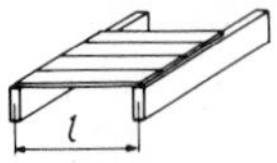		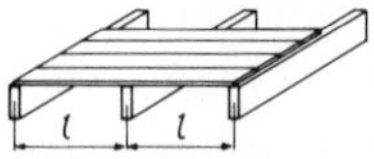		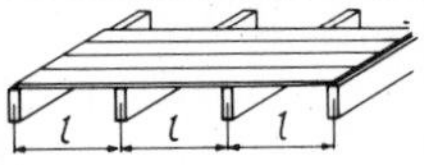		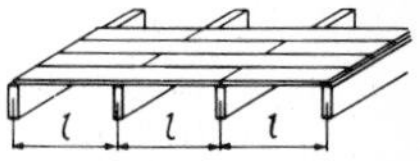	
			f psi	E psi	f psi	E psi	f psi	E psi	f psi	E psi
6′	20	$\frac{l}{240}$	360	576000	360	239000	288	305000	360	408000
		$\frac{l}{300}$	360	720000	360	299000	288	381000	360	509000
		$\frac{l}{360}$	360	864000	360	359000	288	457000	360	611000
	30	$\frac{l}{240}$	480	864000	480	359000	384	457000	480	611000
		$\frac{l}{300}$	480	1080000	480	448000	384	571000	480	764000
		$\frac{l}{360}$	480	1296000	480	538000	384	685000	480	917000
	40	$\frac{l}{240}$	600	1152000	600	478000	480	609000	600	815000
		$\frac{l}{300}$	600	1440000	600	598000	480	762000	600	1019000
		$\frac{l}{360}$	600	1728000	600	717000	480	914000	600	1223000
7′	20	$\frac{l}{240}$	490	915000	490	380000	392	484000	490	647000
		$\frac{l}{300}$	490	1143000	490	475000	392	605000	490	809000
		$\frac{l}{360}$	490	1372000	490	570000	392	726000	490	971000
	30	$\frac{l}{240}$	653	1372000	653	570000	522	726000	653	971000
		$\frac{l}{300}$	653	1715000	653	712000	522	907000	653	1213000
		$\frac{l}{360}$	653	2058000	653	854000	522	1088000	653	1456000
	40	$\frac{l}{240}$	817	1829000	817	759000	653	968000	817	1294000
		$\frac{l}{300}$	817	2287000	817	949000	653	1209000	817	1618000
		$\frac{l}{360}$	817	2744000	817	1139000	653	1451000	817	1941000
8′	20	$\frac{l}{240}$	640	1365000	640	567000	512	722000	640	966000
		$\frac{l}{300}$	640	1707000	640	708000	512	903000	640	1208000
		$\frac{l}{360}$	640	2048000	640	850000	512	1083000	640	1449000
	30	$\frac{l}{240}$	853	2048000	853	850000	682	1083000	853	1449000
		$\frac{l}{300}$	853	2560000	853	1063000	682	1354000	853	1811000
		$\frac{l}{360}$	853	3072000	853	1275000	682	1625000	853	2174000
	40	$\frac{l}{240}$	1067	2731000	1067	1134000	853	1444000	1067	1932000
		$\frac{l}{300}$	1067	3413000	1067	1417000	853	1805000	1067	2415000
		$\frac{l}{360}$	1067	4096000	1067	1700000	853	2166000	1067	2898000

Table E-2 Floor and Roof Beams

Required values for fiber stress in bending (f) and modulus of elasticity (E) for the sizes shown to support safely a live load of **20** pounds per square foot within a deflection limitation of *l*/240. For instructions on use of table see Design Data for Beams on page 465.

SPAN OF BEAM	NOMINAL SIZE OF BEAM	MINIMUM "f" & "E" IN psi FOR BEAMS SPACED:					
		6′-0″		7′-0″		8′-0″	
		f	E	f	E	f	E
10′	2-3x6	1070	780000	1250	910000	1430	1040000
	1-3x8	1235	680000	1440	794000	1645	906000
	2-2x8	1030	570000	1200	665000	1370	760000
	1-4x8	880	485000	1030	566000	1175	646000
	3-2x8	685	380000	800	443000	915	506000
	2-3x8	615	340000	720	397000	820	453000
	2-2x10	630	273000	735	219000	840	364000
11′	2-3x6	1295	1037000	1510	1210000	1730	1382000
	1-3x8	1490	905000	1740	1056000	1990	1206000
	2-2x8	1245	754000	1450	880000	1660	1005000
	1-4x8	1065	647000	1245	755000	1420	862000
	3-2x8	830	503000	970	587000	1105	670000
	2-3x8	745	453000	870	529000	995	604000
	2-2x10	765	363000	890	424000	1020	484000
12′	2-3x6	1545	1346000	1800	1571000	2060	1794000
	1-3x8	1775	1175000	2070	1371000	2370	1566000
	2-2x8	1480	980000	1725	1144000	1970	1306000
	1-4x8	1270	840000	1480	980000	1690	1120000
	3-2x8	985	653000	1150	762000	1315	870000
	2-3x8	890	588000	1035	686000	1185	784000
	1-6x8	755	483000	880	564000	1005	644000
	2-2x10	910	472000	1060	551000	1210	629000
	1-3x10	1090	566000	1275	660000	1455	754000
13′	2-3x6	1815	1711000	2110	1997000	2415	2281000
	1-3x8	2085	1494000	2430	1743000	2780	1991000
	2-2x8	1740	1245000	2025	1453000	2315	1660000
	1-4x8	1490	1067000	1735	1245000	1985	1422000
	3-2x8	1160	830000	1350	969000	1545	1106000
	2-3x8	1045	747000	1215	872000	1390	996000
	1-6x8	885	614000	1040	716000	1185	818000
	2-2x10	1070	600000	1245	700000	1420	800000
	1-3x10	1280	719000	1495	839000	1710	958000
14′	2-2x8	2015	1555000	2350	1815000	2685	2073000
	3-2x8	1340	1037000	1570	1210000	1790	1382000
	2-3x8	1210	933000	1410	1089000	1610	1244000
	1-6x8	1025	766000	1200	894000	1370	1021000
	1-3x10	1485	899000	1730	1049000	1980	1198000
	2-2x10	1235	749000	1445	874000	1650	998000
	1-4x10	1060	642000	1240	749000	1415	856000
	3-2x10	825	499000	965	582000	1100	665000
	2-3x10	740	449000	865	524000	990	598000
15′	3-2x8	1540	1275000	1800	1488000	2055	1699000
	2-3x8	1390	1148000	1620	1340000	1850	1530000
	1-6x8	1180	943000	1375	1100000	1570	1257000
	1-3x10	1705	1105000	1990	1289000	2270	1473000
	2-2x10	1420	921000	1660	1075000	1895	1228000
	1-4x10	1220	789000	1420	921000	1625	1052000
	3-2x10	950	614000	1105	717000	1265	818000
	2-3x10	850	553000	995	645000	1135	737000
	1-6x10	735	464000	855	541000	980	618000
	4-2x10	710	461000	830	538000	945	614000
	2-2x12	960	512000	1120	597000	1280	682000
16′	3-2x8	1755	1548000	2045	1806000	2340	2063000
	2-3x8	1580	1393000	1840	1626000	2105	1857000
	2-2x10	1615	1118000	1890	1305000	2155	1490000
	1-4x10	1385	958000	1615	1118000	1845	1277000
	3-2x10	1075	745000	1260	869000	1435	993000
	2-3x10	970	671000	1130	783000	1290	894000
	1-6x10	835	563000	975	657000	1130	750000
	4-2x10	810	559000	945	652000	1080	745000
	1-8x10	615	413000	715	482000	815	550000
	1-3x12	1310	746000	1530	871000	1750	994000
	2-2x12	1090	621000	1275	725000	1455	828000
17′	2-2x10	1825	1341000	2125	1565000	2430	1787000
	1-4x10	1565	1149000	1825	1341000	2085	1532000
	3-2x10	1215	894000	1420	1043000	1620	1192000
17′	2-3x10	1095	804000	1280	938000	1460	1072000
	1-6x10	945	675000	1100	788000	1260	900000
	4-2x10	910	670000	1065	782000	1215	894000
	1-8x10	690	495000	805	578000	910	660000
	1-3x12	1480	894000	1725	1043000	1975	1192000
	2-2x12	1235	745000	1440	869000	1645	993000
	1-4x12	1060	639000	1230	746000	1410	852000
	3-2x12	820	497000	960	580000	1095	663000
18′	2-2x10	2045	1592000	2385	1858000	2725	2123000
	1-4x10	1755	1364000	2045	1592000	2340	1819000
	3-2x10	1365	1061000	1590	1238000	1815	1415000
	2-3x10	1270	955000	1480	1114000	1695	1273000
	1-6x10	1060	801000	1235	935000	1415	1068000
	4-2x10	1020	796000	1195	929000	1365	1062000
	1-8x10	780	588000	910	686000	1040	784000
	1-3x12	1660	1062000	1935	1239000	2210	1416000
	2-2x12	1380	885000	1615	1033000	1845	1180000
	1-4x12	1185	758000	1385	885000	1580	1011000
	3-2x12	920	590000	1075	688000	1230	786000
	2-3x12	830	531000	970	620000	1105	708000
19′	3-2x10	1520	1248000	1775	1456000	2025	1664000
	2-3x10	1365	1123000	1595	1310000	1825	1497000
	1-6x10	1170	943000	1365	1100000	1560	1257000
	4-2x10	1140	936000	1330	1092000	1520	1248000
	2-4x10	975	802000	1140	936000	1300	1070000
	1-8x10	860	691000	1005	806000	1145	921000
	1-3x12	1850	1249000	2155	1457000	2465	1665000
	2-2x12	1540	1041000	1800	1215000	2055	1388000
	1-4x12	1320	892000	1540	1041000	1760	1190000
	3-2x12	1025	694000	1200	810000	1370	926000
	2-3x12	925	624000	1080	728000	1230	832000
	1-6x12	805	531000	940	620000	1070	708000
20′	3-2x10	1685	1456000	1965	1699000	2245	1942000
	2-3x10	1515	1310000	1770	1529000	2020	1747000
	1-6x10	1300	1099000	1515	1282000	1735	1465000
	4-2x10	1260	1092000	1475	1274000	1685	1456000
	2-4x10	1080	936000	1265	1092000	1445	1248000
	1-8x10	960	806000	1120	941000	1280	1075000
	2-2x12	1705	1214000	1990	1417000	2275	1619000
	1-4x12	1465	1040000	1710	1214000	1950	1387000
	3-2x12	1140	809000	1330	944000	1520	1079000
	2-3x12	1025	728000	1195	850000	1365	971000
	1-6x12	970	620000	1130	723000	1295	826000
	2-4x12	730	520000	855	607000	975	694000
21′	3-2x10	1855	1685000	2165	1966000	2475	2247000
	2-3x10	1670	1516000	1950	1827000	2225	2088000
	1-6x10	1430	1273000	1670	1485000	1905	1697000
	4-2x10	1390	1264000	1625	1475000	1855	1686000
	2-4x10	1195	1083000	1390	1264000	1590	1444000
	1-8x10	1050	933000	1225	1089000	1400	1244000
	2-2x12	1880	1405000	2195	1640000	2510	1874000
	1-4x12	1615	1204000	1880	1405000	2150	1606000
	3-2x12	1255	937000	1465	1093000	1670	1249000
	2-3x12	1130	843000	1320	984000	1505	1124000
	1-6x12	970	717000	1130	837000	1295	956000
	2-4x12	805	602000	940	702000	1075	802000
22′	1-6x10	1580	1463000	1845	1707000	2105	1951000
	4-2x10	1525	1453000	1780	1696000	2035	1938000
	2-4x10	1310	1245000	1530	1453000	1745	1660000
	1-8x10	1160	1073000	1355	1252000	1545	1431000
	1-4x12	1770	1384000	2065	1615000	2360	1846000
	3-2x12	1375	1077000	1605	1257000	1835	1436000
	2-3x12	1240	969000	1445	1130000	1655	1291000
	1-6x12	1080	825000	1260	963000	1440	1100000
	2-4x12	885	692000	1035	807000	1180	922000
	4-2x12	1035	808000	1205	943000	1375	1078000
	5-2x12	825	646000	965	754000	1105	862000
	3-3x12	825	639000	965	746000	1105	852000

Table E-3 Floor and Roof Beams

Required values for fiber stress in bending (f) and modulus of elasticity (E) for the sizes shown to support safely a live load of **20** pounds per square foot within a deflection limitation of *l*/300. For instructions on use of table see Design Data for Beams on page 465.

SPAN OF BEAM	NOMINAL SIZE OF BEAM	MINIMUM "f" & "E" IN psi FOR BEAMS SPACED: 6′-0″ f	6′-0″ E	7′-0″ f	7′-0″ E	8′-0″ f	8′-0″ E
10′	2-3x6	1070	975000	1250	1138000	1430	1300000
	1-3x8	1235	850000	1440	992000	1645	1133000
	2-2x8	1030	712000	1200	831000	1370	949000
	1-4x8	880	606000	1030	707000	1175	808000
	3-2x8	685	475000	800	554000	915	633000
	2-3x8	615	425000	720	496000	820	566000
	2-2x10	630	341000	735	398000	840	455000
11′	2-3x6	1295	1296000	1510	1512000	1730	1727000
	1-3x8	1490	1131000	1740	1320000	1990	1508000
	2-2x8	1245	942000	1450	1099000	1660	1256000
	1-4x8	1065	809000	1245	944000	1420	1078000
	3-2x8	830	629000	970	734000	1105	838000
	2-3x8	745	566000	870	660000	995	754000
	2-2x10	765	454000	890	530000	1020	605000
12′	2-3x6	1545	1682000	1800	1963000	2060	2242000
	1-3x8	1775	1469000	2070	1714000	2370	1958000
	2-2x8	1480	1225000	1725	1429000	1970	1633000
	1-4x8	1270	1050000	1480	1225000	1690	1400000
	3-2x8	985	816000	1150	952000	1315	1088000
	2-3x8	890	735000	1035	858000	1185	980000
	1-6x8	755	604000	880	705000	1005	805000
	2-2x10	910	590000	1060	688000	1210	786000
13′	1-3x8	2085	1867000	2430	2179000	2780	2439000
	2-2x8	1740	1556000	2025	1816000	2315	2074000
	1-4x8	1490	1334000	1735	1557000	1985	1778000
	3-2x8	1160	1037000	1350	1210000	1545	1382000
	2-3x8	1045	934000	1215	1090000	1390	1245000
	1-6x8	885	767000	1040	895000	1185	1022000
	2-2x10	1070	750000	1245	875000	1420	1000000
	1-3x10	1280	899000	1495	1049000	1710	1198000
	1-4x10	915	642000	1070	749000	1220	856000
14′	3-2x8	1340	1296000	1570	1512000	1790	1727000
	2-3x8	1210	1166000	1410	1361000	1610	1554000
	1-6x8	1025	957000	1200	1117000	1370	1276000
	1-3x10	1485	1124000	1730	1312000	1980	1498000
	2-2x10	1235	936000	1445	1092000	1650	1248000
	1-4x10	1060	802000	1240	936000	1415	1069000
	3-2x10	825	624000	965	728000	1100	832000
	2-3x10	740	561000	865	655000	990	748000
	1-6x10	640	471000	745	550000	850	628000
	4-2x10	620	468000	720	546000	825	624000
	2-2x12	835	520000	975	607000	1115	693000
15′	3-2x8	1540	1594000	1800	1860000	2055	2125000
	2-3x8	1390	1435000	1620	1675000	1850	1913000
	1-6x8	1180	1179000	1375	1376000	1570	1572000
	1-3x10	1705	1381000	1990	1612000	2270	1841000
	2-2x10	1420	1151000	1660	1343000	1895	1534000
	1-4x10	1220	986000	1420	1151000	1625	1314000
	3-2x10	950	767000	1105	895000	1265	1022000
	2-3x10	850	691000	995	806000	1135	921000
	1-6x10	735	580000	855	677000	980	773000
	4-2x10	710	576000	830	672000	945	768000
	2-2x12	960	640000	1120	747000	1280	853000
	1-4x12	825	549000	960	641000	1100	732000
16′	2-3x8	1580	1741000	1840	2032000	2105	2321000
	2-2x10	1615	1397000	1890	1630000	2155	1862000
	1-4x10	1385	1197000	1615	1397000	1845	1596000
	3-2x10	1075	931000	1260	1086000	1435	1241000
	2-3x10	970	839000	1130	979000	1290	1118000
	1-6x10	835	704000	975	821000	1130	938000
	4-2x10	810	699000	945	816000	1080	932000
	1-8x10	615	516000	715	602000	815	688000
	1-3x12	1310	932000	1530	1087000	1750	1242000
	2-2x12	1090	776000	1275	905000	1455	1034000
	1-4x12	935	666000	1090	777000	1250	888000
	3-2x12	730	518000	850	604000	970	690000
17′	2-2x10	1825	1676000	2130	1956000	2435	2234000
	1-4x10	1565	1437000	1825	1677000	2085	1915000
	3-2x10	1215	1117000	1420	1303000	1625	1489000
	2-3x10	1095	1005000	1280	1173000	1460	1340000
	1-6x10	945	844000	1100	985000	1260	1125000
	4-2x10	910	837000	1065	977000	1215	1116000
	1-8x10	690	619000	805	722000	910	825000
	1-3x12	1480	1117000	1725	1303000	1975	1489000
	2-2x12	1235	931000	1440	1086000	1645	1241000
	1-4x12	1060	799000	1230	932000	1410	1065000
	3-2x12	820	621000	960	725000	1095	828000
	2-3x12	740	559000	865	652000	990	745000
18′	1-4x10	1755	1705000	2045	1990000	2340	2273000
	3-2x10	1365	1326000	1590	1547000	1815	1767000
	2-3x10	1270	1194000	1480	1393000	1695	1592000
	1-6x10	1060	1001000	1235	1168000	1415	1334000
	4-2x10	1020	995000	1195	1161000	1365	1326000
	1-8x10	780	735000	910	858000	1040	980000
	1-3x12	1660	1327000	1935	1549000	2210	1769000
	2-2x12	1380	1106000	1615	1291000	1845	1474000
	1-4x12	1185	947000	1385	1105000	1580	1262000
	3-2x12	920	737000	1075	860000	1230	982000
	2-3x12	830	664000	970	775000	1105	885000
	1-6x12	720	565000	840	659000	960	753000
19′	3-2x10	1520	1560000	1775	1820000	2025	2079000
	2-3x10	1365	1404000	1595	1638000	1825	1871000
	1-6x10	1170	1179000	1365	1376000	1560	1572000
	4-2x10	1140	1170000	1330	1365000	1520	1560000
	2-4x10	975	1002000	1140	1169000	1300	1336000
	1-8x10	860	864000	1005	1008000	1145	1152000
	1-3x12	1850	1561000	2155	1822000	2465	2081000
	2-2x12	1540	1301000	1800	1518000	2055	1734000
	1-4x12	1320	1115000	1540	1301000	1760	1486000
	3-2x12	1025	867000	1200	1012000	1370	1156000
	2-3x12	925	780000	1080	910000	1230	1040000
	1-6x12	805	664000	940	775000	1070	885000
20′	3-2x10	1685	1820000	1965	2124000	2245	2426000
	2-3x10	1515	1637000	1770	1910000	2020	2182000
	1-6x10	1300	1374000	1515	1603000	1735	1831000
	4-2x10	1260	1365000	1475	1593000	1685	1819000
	2-4x10	1080	1170000	1265	1365000	1445	1560000
	1-8x10	960	1007000	1120	1175000	1280	1342000
	2-2x12	1705	1517000	1990	1770000	2275	2022000
	1-4x12	1465	1300000	1710	1517000	1950	1733000
	3-2x12	1140	1011000	1330	1180000	1520	1348000
	2-3x12	1025	910000	1195	1062000	1365	1213000
	1-6x12	970	775000	1130	904000	1295	1003000
	4-2x12	855	759000	995	886000	1135	1012000
21′	2-3x10	1670	1895000	1950	2211000	2225	2526000
	1-6x10	1430	1591000	1670	1857000	1905	2121000
	4-2x10	1390	1580000	1625	1844000	1855	2106000
	2-4x10	1195	1354000	1390	1580000	1590	1805000
	1-8x10	1050	1166000	1225	1361000	1400	1554000
	2-2x12	1880	1756000	2195	2049000	2510	2341000
	1-4x12	1615	1505000	1880	1756000	2150	2006000
	3-2x12	1255	1171000	1465	1366000	1670	1561000
	2-3x12	1130	1054000	1320	1230000	1505	1405000
	1-6x12	970	896000	1130	1046000	1295	1194000
	4-2x12	940	878000	1100	1025000	1255	1170000
	2-4x12	805	752000	940	877000	1075	1002000
22′	4-2x10	1525	1816000	1780	2119000	2035	2421000
	2-4x10	1310	1556000	1530	1816000	1745	2074000
	1-8x10	1160	1341000	1355	1565000	1545	1787000
	1-4x12	1770	1730000	2065	2019000	2360	2306000
	3-2x12	1375	1346000	1605	1571000	1835	1794000
	2-3x12	1240	1211000	1445	1413000	1655	1614000
	1-6x12	1080	1031000	1260	1203000	1440	1374000
	4-2x12	1030	1010000	1205	1179000	1375	1346000
	2-4x12	885	865000	1035	1009000	1180	1153000
	5-2x12	825	807000	965	942000	1105	1076000
	3-3x12	825	799000	965	932000	1105	1065000

Table E-4 Floor and Roof Beams

Required values for fiber stress in bending (f) and modulus of elasticity (E) for the sizes shown to support safely a live load of **20** pounds per square foot within a deflection limitation of *l*/360. For instructions on use of table see Design Data for Beams on page 465.

SPAN OF BEAM	NOMINAL SIZE OF BEAM	MINIMUM "f" & "E" IN psi FOR BEAMS SPACED:					
		6′-0″		7′-0″		8′-0″	
		f	E	f	E	f	E
10′	2-3x6	1070	1170000	1250	1365000	1430	1560000
	1-3x8	1235	1020000	1440	1192000	1645	1359000
	2-2x8	1030	855000	1200	997000	1370	1140000
	1-4x8	880	727000	1030	847000	1175	969000
	3-2x8	685	570000	800	667000	915	759000
	2-3x8	615	510000	720	600000	820	679000
	1-6x8	525	419000	615	489000	700	558000
11′	2-3x6	1295	1555000	1510	1815000	1730	2073000
	1-3x8	1490	1357000	1740	1584000	1990	1809000
	2-2x8	1245	1131000	1450	1320000	1660	1507000
	1-4x8	1065	970000	1245	1132000	1420	1293000
	3-2x8	830	754000	970	880000	1105	1005000
	2-3x8	745	679000	870	793000	995	906000
	1-6x8	635	558000	740	651000	845	744000
12′	1-3x8	1775	1762000	2070	2056000	2370	2349000
	2-2x8	1480	1470000	1725	1716000	1970	1959000
	1-4x8	1270	1260000	1480	1470000	1690	1680000
	3-2x8	985	979000	1150	1143000	1315	1305000
	2-3x8	890	882000	1035	1029000	1185	1176000
	1-6x8	775	724000	880	846000	1005	966000
	2-2x10	910	708000	1060	826000	1210	943000
	1-3x10	1090	849000	1275	991000	1455	1132000
13′	2-2x8	1740	1867000	2025	2179000	2315	2490000
	1-4x8	1490	1600000	1735	1867000	1985	2133000
	3-2x8	1160	1245000	1350	1453000	1545	1659000
	2-3x8	1045	1120000	1215	1308000	1390	1494000
	1-6x8	885	921000	1040	1074000	1185	1227000
	2-2x10	1070	900000	1245	1050000	1420	1200000
	1-3x10	1280	1078000	1495	1258000	1710	1437000
	1-4x10	915	771000	1070	900000	1220	1028000
14′	3-2x8	1340	1555000	1570	1815000	1790	2073000
	2-3x8	1210	1399000	1410	1633000	1610	1866000
	1-6x8	1025	1149000	1200	1341000	1370	1531000
	1-3x10	1485	1348000	1730	1573000	1980	1797000
	2-2x10	1235	1123000	1445	1311000	1650	1497000
	1-4x10	1060	963000	1240	1123000	1415	1284000
	3-2x10	825	748000	965	873000	1100	997000
	2-3x10	740	673000	865	786000	990	897000
	1-6x10	640	565000	745	660000	850	753000
	4-2x10	620	561000	720	655000	825	749000
	2-2x12	835	624000	975	728000	1115	832000
15′	3-2x8	1540	1912000	1800	2232000	2055	2548000
	2-3x8	1390	1722000	1620	2010000	1850	2295000
	1-6x8	1180	1414000	1375	1650000	1570	1885000
	1-3x10	1705	1657000	1990	1933000	2270	2209000
	2-2x10	1420	1381000	1660	1612000	1895	1842000
	1-4x10	1220	1183000	1420	1381000	1625	1578000
	3-2x10	950	921000	1105	1075000	1265	1227000
	2-3x10	850	829000	995	967000	1135	1105000
	1-6x10	735	696000	855	811000	980	927000
	4-2x10	710	691000	830	807000	945	921000
	2-2x12	960	768000	1120	895000	1280	1023000
	1-4x12	825	659000	960	769000	1100	878000
16′	2-2x10	1615	1677000	1890	1957000	2155	2235000
	1-4x10	1385	1437000	1615	1677000	1845	1915000
	3-2x10	1075	1117000	1260	1303000	1435	1489000
	2-3x10	970	1006000	1130	1174000	1290	1341000
	1-6x10	835	844000	975	985000	1130	1125000
	4-2x10	810	838000	945	978000	1080	1117000
	1-8x10	615	619000	715	723000	815	825000
	1-3x12	1310	1119000	1530	1306000	1750	1491000
	2-2x12	1090	931000	1275	1087000	1455	1242000
	1-4x12	935	799000	1090	932000	1250	1066000
	3-2x12	730	622000	850	725000	970	828000
	2-3x12	655	559000	765	652000	875	745000
17′	2-2x10	1825	2011000	2125	2347000	2430	2680000
	1-4x10	1565	1723000	1825	2011000	2085	2298000
	3-2x10	1215	1341000	1420	1564000	1620	1788000
	2-3x10	1095	1206000	1280	1407000	1460	1608000
	1-6x10	945	1012000	1100	1182000	1260	1350000
	4-2x10	910	1005000	1065	1173000	1215	1341000
	1-8x10	690	742000	805	867000	910	990000
	1-3x12	1480	1341000	1725	1564000	1975	1788000
	2-2x12	1235	1117000	1440	1303000	1645	1489000
	1-4x12	1060	958000	1230	1119000	1410	1278000
	3-2x12	820	745000	960	870000	1095	994000
	2-3x12	740	671000	865	782000	990	894000
18′	3-2x10	1365	1591000	1590	1857000	1815	2122000
	2-3x10	1270	1492000	1480	1671000	1695	1909000
	1-6x10	1060	1201000	1235	1402000	1415	1602000
	4-2x10	1020	1194000	1195	1393000	1365	1593000
	1-8x10	780	882000	910	1029000	1040	1176000
	1-3x12	1660	1593000	1935	1858000	2210	2124000
	2-2x12	1380	1327000	1615	1549000	1845	1770000
	1-4x12	1185	1137000	1385	1327000	1580	1516000
	3-2x12	920	885000	1075	1032000	1230	1179000
	2-3x12	830	796000	970	930000	1105	1062000
	1-6x12	720	678000	840	790000	960	904000
	4-2x12	690	663000	805	774000	920	884000
19′	3-2x10	1520	1872000	1775	2184000	2025	2496000
	2-3x10	1365	1684000	1595	1965000	1825	2245000
	1-6x10	1170	1414000	1365	1650000	1560	1885000
	4-2x10	1140	1404000	1330	1638000	1520	1872000
	2-4x10	975	1203000	1140	1404000	1300	1605000
	1-8x10	860	1036000	1005	1209000	1145	1381000
	2-2x12	1540	1561000	1800	1822000	2055	2082000
	1-4x12	1320	1338000	1540	1561000	1760	1785000
	3-2x12	1025	1041000	1200	1215000	1370	2055000
	2-3x12	925	936000	1080	1092000	1230	1248000
	1-6x12	805	796000	940	930000	1070	1062000
	4-2x12	770	780000	900	910000	1025	1040000
20′	2-3x10	1515	1965000	1770	2293000	2020	2620000
	1-6x10	1300	1648000	1515	1923000	1735	2197000
	4-2x10	1260	1638000	1475	1911000	1685	2184000
	2-4x10	1080	1404000	1265	1638000	1445	1872000
	1-8x10	960	1209000	1120	1411000	1280	1612000
	2-2x12	1705	1821000	1990	2125000	2275	2428000
	1-4x12	1465	1560000	1710	1821000	1950	2080000
	3-2x12	1140	1213000	1330	1416000	1520	1618000
	2-3x12	1025	1092000	1195	1275000	1365	1456000
	1-6x12	970	930000	1130	1085000	1295	1239000
	4-2x12	855	911000	995	1063000	1135	1214000
	2-4x12	730	780000	850	910000	975	1040000
21′	4-2x10	1390	1896000	1625	2212000	1855	2529000
	2-4x10	1195	1624000	1390	1896000	1590	2166000
	1-8x10	1050	1399000	1225	1633000	1400	1866000
	1-4x12	1615	1806000	1880	2107000	2150	2409000
	3-2x12	1255	1405000	1465	1639000	1670	1873000
	2-3x12	1130	1264000	1320	1476000	1505	1686000
	1-6x12	970	1075000	1130	1255000	1295	1434000
	4-2x12	940	1054000	1100	1230000	1255	1404000
	2-4x12	805	903000	940	1053000	1075	1203000
	3-3x12	750	834000	875	973000	1000	1112000
	1-8x12	720	789000	840	921000	960	1052000
	1-10x12	570	623000	665	727000	760	830000
22′	2-4x10	1310	1867000	1530	2179000	1745	2490000
	1-8x10	1160	1609000	1355	1878000	1545	2146000
	3-2x12	1375	1615000	1605	1885000	1835	2154000
	2-3x12	1240	1453000	1445	1695000	1655	1936000
	1-6x12	1080	1237000	1260	1444000	1440	1650000
	4-2x12	1035	1212000	1205	1414000	1375	1617000
	2-4x12	885	1038000	1035	1210000	1180	1383000
	5-2x12	825	969000	965	1131000	1105	1293000
	3-3x12	825	958000	965	1119000	1105	1278000
	1-8x12	790	907000	920	1058000	1055	1209000
	1-10x12	625	716000	730	835000	835	954000

Table E-5 Floor and Roof Beams

Required values for fiber stress in bending (f) and modulus of elasticity (E) for the sizes shown to support safely a live load of **30** pounds per square foot within a deflection limitation of *l*/240. For instructions on use of table see Design Data for Beams on page 465.

SPAN OF BEAM	NOMINAL SIZE OF BEAM	MINIMUM "f" & "E" IN psi FOR BEAMS SPACED:					
		6′ - 0″		7′ - 0″		8′ - 0″	
		f	E	f	E	f	E
10′	2-3x6	1430	1170000	1670	1365000	1905	1560000
	1-3x8	1645	1020000	1920	1190000	2195	1360000
	1-4x8	1175	727000	1370	848000	1565	969000
	3-2x8	915	570000	1070	665000	1220	760000
	2-3x8	820	510000	955	595000	1095	680000
	2-4x8	590	364000	690	425000	785	485000
	2-2x10	840	409000	980	477000	1120	545000
11′	2-3x6	1725	1555000	2015	1815000	2300	2073000
	1-3x8	1990	1357000	2320	1584000	2655	1809000
	1-4x8	1420	970000	1660	1132000	1895	1293000
	3-2x8	1105	754000	1290	880000	1475	1005000
	2-3x8	995	679000	1160	792000	1325	905000
	2-4x8	710	485000	830	566000	945	646000
	2-2x10	1020	544000	1190	635000	1360	725000
12′	1-4x8	1690	1260000	1970	1470000	2255	1679000
	3-2x8	1315	979000	1535	1142000	1755	1305000
	2-3x8	1185	882000	1385	1029000	1580	1176000
	2-4x8	845	630000	985	735000	1125	840000
	1-6x8	1005	724000	1175	845000	1340	965000
	2-2x10	1210	708000	1410	826000	1615	944000
	3-2x10	810	472000	945	551000	1080	629000
	2-3x10	725	424000	845	495000	965	565000
13′	1-4x8	1985	1600000	2315	1867000	2645	2133000
	3-2x8	1545	1245000	1805	1453000	2060	1659000
	2-3x8	1390	1120000	1620	1307000	1855	1493000
	2-4x8	990	801000	1155	935000	1320	1068000
	1-6x8	1180	921000	1375	1075000	1575	1228000
	2-x10	1425	900000	1665	1050000	1900	1200000
	3-2x10	950	600000	1110	700000	1265	800000
	2-3x10	855	540000	1000	630000	1140	720000
	1-4x10	1220	923000	1425	1079000	1625	1230000
14′	3-2x8	1790	1555000	2090	1815000	2385	2073000
	2-3x8	1610	1400000	1880	1634000	2145	1866000
	2-4x8	1150	1000000	1340	1167000	1535	1333000
	1-6x8	1370	1149000	1600	1341000	1825	1532000
	2-2x10	1650	1123000	1925	1310000	2200	1497000
	3-2x10	1100	748000	1285	873000	1465	997000
	2-3x10	990	673000	1155	785000	1320	897000
	1-4x10	1415	963000	1650	1124000	1885	1283000
	1-6x10	915	943000	1070	1100000	1220	1257000
	2-4x10	705	481000	825	561000	940	641000
15′	2-4x8	1320	1230000	1540	1435000	1760	1640000
	1-6x8	1570	1414000	1830	1650000	2095	1885000
	2-2x10	1895	1381000	2210	1612000	2525	1841000
	3-2x10	1260	921000	1470	1075000	1680	1228000
	2-3x10	1135	829000	1325	967000	1515	1105000
	1-4x10	1620	1183000	1890	1380000	2160	1577000
	1-6x10	980	696000	1145	812000	1305	928000
	2-4x10	810	592000	945	691000	1080	789000
	4-2x10	945	691000	1105	806000	1260	921000
	1-8x10	720	510000	840	595000	960	680000
	2-2x12	1280	768000	1495	896000	1705	1024000
	1-4x12	1095	658000	1280	768000	1460	877000
16′	2-2x10	2155	1677000	2515	1957000	2875	2235000
	3-2x10	1435	1117000	1675	1303000	1915	1489000
	2-3x10	1290	1006000	1505	1174000	1720	1341000
	1-4x10	1845	1437000	2155	1677000	2460	1915000
	1-6x10	1115	844000	1300	985000	1485	1125000
	2-4x10	925	719000	1080	839000	1235	958000
	4-2x10	1075	838000	1255	978000	1435	1117000
	1-8x10	815	619000	950	722000	1085	825000
	2-2x12	1455	931000	1700	1086000	1940	1241000
	1-4x12	1250	799000	1460	932000	1665	1065000
	3-2x12	970	621000	1130	725000	1295	828000
	2-3x12	875	559000	1020	652000	1165	745000
17′	3-2x10	1620	1341000	1890	1565000	2160	1787000
	2-3x10	1460	1206000	1705	1407000	1945	1607000
	1-4x10	2085	1723000	2435	2011000	2780	2297000
	1-6x10	1255	1012000	1465	1181000	1675	1349000
	2-4x10	1040	862000	1215	1006000	1385	1149000
	4-2x10	1215	1005000	1420	1173000	1620	1340000
	1-8x10	920	742000	1075	866000	1225	989000
	2-2x12	1645	1117000	1920	1303000	2195	1489000
	1-4x12	1410	958000	1645	1118000	1880	1277000
	3-2x12	1095	745000	1280	869000	1460	993000
	2-3x12	985	671000	1150	783000	1313	894000
	4-2x12	820	559000	955	652000	1095	869000
18′	2-3x10	1695	1432000	1980	1671000	2260	1909000
	1-6x10	1415	1201000	1650	1401000	1885	1601000
	2-4x10	1170	1023000	1365	1194000	1560	1364000
	4-2x10	1360	1194000	1590	1393000	1815	1592000
	1-8x10	1040	882000	1215	1029000	1385	1176000
	2-2x12	1840	1327000	2150	1549000	2455	1769000
	1-4x12	1580	1137000	1845	1327000	2105	1516000
	3-2x12	1230	885000	1435	1033000	1640	1180000
	2-3x12	1105	796000	1290	929000	1475	1061000
	4-2x12	920	663000	1075	774000	1225	884000
	2-4x12	790	569000	920	664000	1055	758000
	5-2x12	735	531000	860	620000	980	708000
19′	2-4x10	1300	1203000	1515	1404000	1735	1604000
	4-2x10	1520	1404000	1775	1638000	2025	1871000
	1-8x10	1145	1036000	1335	1209000	1525	1381000
	1-4x12	1760	1338000	2055	1561000	2345	1783000
	3-2x12	1370	1041000	1600	1215000	1825	1388000
	2-3x12	1230	936000	1435	1092000	1640	1248000
	4-2x12	1025	780000	1195	910000	1365	1040000
	2-4x12	880	669000	1025	781000	1175	892000
	5-2x12	820	624000	955	728000	1095	832000
	1-6x12	1070	796000	1250	929000	1425	1061000
	3-3x12	820	617000	955	720000	1095	822000
	1-8x12	785	584000	915	681000	1045	778000
20′	4-2x12	1680	1638000	1960	1911000	2240	2183000
	1-8x10	1280	1209000	1495	1411000	1705	1611000
	3-2x12	1520	1213000	1775	1415000	2025	1617000
	2-3x12	1365	1092000	1595	1274000	1820	1456000
	4-2x12	1025	910000	1195	1062000	1365	1213000
	2-4x12	975	780000	1140	910000	1300	1040000
	5-2x12	910	728000	1060	849000	1215	970000
	1-6x12	1295	930000	1510	1084000	1725	1239000
	3-3x12	910	720000	1060	840000	1215	960000
	1-8x12	870	682000	1015	795000	1160	909000
	1-10x12	690	538000	805	628000	920	717000
	4-3x12	680	546000	795	637000	905	728000
21′	1-8x10	1400	1399000	1635	1633000	1865	1865000
	3-2x12	1670	1405000	1950	1640000	2225	1873000
	2-3x12	1505	1264000	1755	1475000	2005	1685000
	4-2x12	1255	1054000	1465	1230000	1675	1405000
	2-4x12	1075	903000	1255	1054000	1435	1204000
	5-2x12	1005	843000	1175	984000	1340	1124000
	1-6x12	1295	1075000	1510	1255000	1725	1434000
	3-3x12	1005	833000	1175	972000	1340	1110000
	1-8x12	960	789000	1120	921000	1280	1052000
	1-10x12	760	623000	885	727000	1015	830000
	4-3x12	750	632000	875	737000	1000	842000
	2-3x14	1085	774000	1265	903000	1445	1032000
22′	2-3x12	1655	1453000	1930	1696000	2205	1940000
	4-2x12	1375	1212000	1605	1414000	1835	1615000
	2-4x12	1180	1038000	1380	1211000	1575	1384000
	5-2x12	1100	969000	1285	1131000	1465	1292000
	1-6x12	1440	1237000	1680	1443000	1920	1649000
	3-3x12	1100	958000	1285	1118000	1465	1277000
	1-8x12	1055	907000	1230	1058000	1405	1209000
	1-10x12	830	716000	970	835000	1105	954000
	4-3x12	825	727000	965	848000	1100	969000
	2-3x14	1190	890000	1390	1039000	1585	1186000
	1-6x14	1045	765000	1220	893000	1395	1020000
	3-3x14	795	589000	930	687000	1060	785000
	2-4x14	820	601000	955	701000	1095	801000

Table E-6 Floor and Roof Beams

Required values for fiber stress in bending (f) and modulus of elasticity (E) for the sizes shown to support safely a live load of **30** pounds per square foot within a deflection limitation of *l*/300. For instructions on use of table see Design Data for Beams on page 465.

SPAN OF BEAM	NOMINAL SIZE OF BEAM	MINIMUM "f" & "E" IN psi FOR BEAMS SPACED:					
		6'-0"		7'-0"		8'-0"	
		f	E	f	E	f	E
10'	2-3x6	1430	1462000	1670	1706000	1905	1948000
	1-3x8	1645	1275000	1920	1488000	2195	1699000
	1-4x8	1175	909000	1370	1061000	1565	1212000
	3-2x8	915	712000	1070	831000	1220	949000
	2-3x8	820	637000	955	743000	1095	849000
	2-4x8	590	455000	690	531000	785	606000
	2-2x10	840	511000	980	596000	1120	681000
11'	1-3x8	1990	1696000	2320	1979000	2655	2261000
	1-4x8	1420	1212000	1660	1414000	1895	1615000
	3-2x8	1105	942000	1290	1099000	1475	1255000
	2-3x8	995	849000	1160	991000	1325	1132000
	2-4x8	710	606000	830	707000	945	808000
	2-2x10	1020	680000	1190	793000	1360	906000
	1-3x10	1220	817000	1425	953000	1625	1089000
12'	1-4x8	1690	1575000	1970	1838000	2255	2099000
	3-2x8	1315	1224000	1535	1428000	1755	1631000
	2-3x8	1185	1102000	1385	1286000	1580	1469000
	2-4x8	845	787000	985	918000	1125	1049000
	1-6x8	1005	905000	1175	1056000	1340	1206000
	2-2x10	1210	885000	1410	1033000	1615	1180000
	3-2x10	810	590000	945	688000	1080	786000
	2-3x10	725	530000	845	618000	965	706000
13'	1-4x8	1985	2000000	2315	2334000	2645	2666000
	3-2x8	1545	1556000	1805	1816000	2060	2074000
	2-3x8	1390	1400000	1620	1634000	1855	1866000
	2-4x8	990	1001000	1155	1168000	1320	1334000
	1-6x8	1180	1151000	1375	1343000	1575	1534000
	2-2x10	1425	1125000	1665	1313000	1900	1500000
	3-2x10	950	750000	1110	875000	1265	1000000
	2-3x10	855	675000	1000	788000	1140	900000
	1-4x10	1220	1154000	1425	1347000	1625	1538000
14'	3-2x8	1790	1944000	2090	2268000	2385	2591000
	2-3x8	1610	1750000	1880	2042000	2145	2333000
	2-4x8	1150	1250000	1340	1459000	1535	1666000
	1-6x8	1370	1436000	1600	1676000	1825	1914000
	2-2x10	1650	1404000	1925	1638000	2200	1871000
	3-2x10	1100	935000	1285	1091000	1465	1246000
	2-3x10	990	841000	1155	981000	1320	1121000
	1-4x10	1415	1204000	1650	1405000	1885	1605000
	1-6x10	915	1179000	1070	1376000	1220	1572000
	2-4x10	705	601000	825	701000	940	801000
15'	2-4x8	1320	1537000	1540	1794000	1760	2049000
	1-6x8	1570	1767000	1830	2062000	2095	2355000
	2-2x10	1895	1726000	2210	2014000	2525	2301000
	3-2x10	1260	1151000	1470	1343000	1680	1534000
	2-3x10	1135	1036000	1325	1209000	1515	1381000
	1-4x10	1620	1479000	1890	1726000	2160	1971000
	1-6x10	980	870000	1145	1015000	1305	1160000
	2-4x10	810	740000	945	863000	1080	986000
	4-2x10	945	864000	1105	1008000	1260	1152000
	1-8x10	720	637000	840	743000	960	849000
	2-2x12	1280	960000	1495	1120000	1705	1280000
	1-4x12	1095	822000	1280	959000	1460	1096000
16'	2-2x10	2155	2096000	2515	2446000	2875	2794000
	3-2x10	1435	1396000	1675	1629000	1915	1861000
	2-3x10	1290	1257000	1505	1467000	1720	1675000
	1-4x10	1845	1796000	2155	2096000	2460	2394000
	1-6x10	1115	1055000	1300	1231000	1485	1406000
	2-4x10	925	899000	1080	1049000	1235	1198000
	4-2x10	1075	1047000	1255	1222000	1435	1395000
	1-8x10	815	774000	950	903000	1085	1032000
	2-2x12	1455	1164000	1700	1358000	1940	1552000
	1-4x12	1250	999000	1460	1166000	1665	1332000
	3-2x12	970	776000	1130	905000	1295	1034000
	2-3x12	875	699000	1020	816000	1165	932000
17'	3-2x10	1620	1676000	1890	1956000	2160	2234000
	2-3x10	1460	1507000	1705	1759000	1945	2009000
	1-6x10	1255	1265000	1465	1476000	1675	1686000
	2-4x10	1040	1077000	1215	1257000	1385	1435000
	4-2x10	1215	1256000	1420	1466000	1620	1674000
	1-8x10	920	927000	1075	1082000	1225	1236000
	2-2x12	1645	1396000	1920	1629000	2195	1861000
	1-4x12	1410	1197000	1645	1397000	1880	1596000
	3-2x12	1095	931000	1280	1086000	1460	1241000
	2-3x12	985	839000	1150	979000	1315	1118000
	4-2x12	820	699000	955	816000	1095	932000
	2-4x12	705	599000	820	699000	940	799000
18'	2-3x10	1695	1790000	1980	2089000	2260	2386000
	1-6x10	1415	1501000	1650	1752000	1885	2000000
	2-4x10	1170	1279000	1365	1492000	1560	1705000
	4-2x10	1360	1492000	1590	1741000	1815	1989000
	1-8x10	1040	1102000	1215	1286000	1385	1469000
	2-2x12	1840	1659000	2150	1936000	2455	2211000
	1-4x12	1580	1421000	1845	1658000	2105	1894000
	3-2x12	1230	1106000	1435	1291000	1640	1474000
	2-3x12	1105	995000	1290	1161000	1475	1326000
	4-2x12	920	829000	1075	967000	1225	1105000
	2-4x12	790	711000	920	830000	1055	948000
	5-2x12	735	664000	860	775000	980	885000
19'	1-6x10	1570	1767000	1830	2062000	2095	2355000
	2-4x10	1300	1504000	1515	1755000	1735	2005000
	4-2x10	1520	1755000	1775	2048000	2025	2339000
	1-8x10	1145	1295000	1335	1511000	1525	1726000
	1-4x12	1760	1672000	2055	1951000	2345	2229000
	3-2x12	1370	1301000	1600	1518000	1825	1734000
	2-3x12	1230	1170000	1435	1365000	1640	1560000
	4-2x12	1025	975000	1195	1138000	1365	1300000
	2-4x12	880	836000	1025	976000	1175	1114000
	5-2x12	820	780000	955	910000	1095	1040000
	1-6x12	1070	995000	1250	1161000	1425	1326000
	3-3x12	820	771000	955	900000	1095	1028000
20'	1-8x10	1280	1511000	1495	1763000	1705	2014000
	3-2x12	1520	1516000	1775	1769000	2025	2021000
	2-3x12	1365	1365000	1595	1593000	1820	1819000
	4-2x12	1025	1137000	1195	1327000	1365	1516000
	2-4x12	975	975000	1140	1138000	1300	1300000
	5-2x12	910	910000	1060	1062000	1215	1213000
	1-6x12	1295	1162000	1510	1356000	1725	1549000
	3-3x12	910	900000	1060	1050000	1215	1200000
	1-8x12	870	852000	1015	994000	1160	1136000
	1-10x12	690	672000	805	784000	920	896000
	4-3x12	680	682000	795	796000	905	909000
	2-3x14	985	836000	1150	976000	1315	1114000
21'	3-2x12	1670	1756000	1950	2049000	2225	2341000
	2-3x12	1505	1580000	1755	1844000	2005	2106000
	4-2x12	1255	1317000	1465	1537000	1675	1755000
	2-4x12	1075	1129000	1255	1317000	1435	1505000
	5-2x12	1005	1054000	1175	1230000	1340	1405000
	1-6x12	1295	1344000	1510	1568000	1725	1791000
	3-3x12	1005	1041000	1175	1215000	1340	1388000
	1-8x12	960	986000	1120	1151000	1280	1314000
	1-10x12	760	779000	885	909000	1015	1038000
	4-3x12	750	790000	875	922000	1000	1053000
	2-3x14	1085	967000	1265	1128000	1445	1289000
	1-6x14	950	832000	1110	971000	1265	1109000
22'	4-2x12	1375	1515000	1605	1768000	1835	2019000
	2-4x12	1180	1297000	1380	1513000	1575	1729000
	5-2x12	1100	1211000	1285	1413000	1465	1614000
	1-6x12	1440	1546000	1680	1804000	1920	2061000
	3-3x12	1100	1197000	1285	1397000	1465	1596000
	1-8x12	1055	1134000	1230	1323000	1405	1511000
	1-10x12	830	895000	970	1044000	1105	1193000
	4-3x12	825	909000	965	1061000	1100	1212000
	2-3x14	1190	1112000	1390	1298000	1585	1482000
	1-6x14	1045	956000	1220	1116000	1395	1274000
	3-3x14	795	736000	930	859000	1060	981000
	2-4x14	820	751000	955	1114000	1095	1001000

Table E-7 Floor and Roof Beams

Required values for fiber stress in bending (f) and modulus of elasticity (E) for the sizes shown to support safely a live load of **30** pounds per square foot within a deflection limitation of *l*/360. For instructions on use of table see Design Data for Beams on page 465.

SPAN OF BEAM	NOMINAL SIZE OF BEAM	MINIMUM "f" & "E" IN psi FOR BEAMS SPACED:					
		6′ - 0″		7′ - 0″		8′ - 0″	
		f	E	f	E	f	E
10′	2-3x6	1430	1754000	1670	2047000	1905	2338000
	1-3x8	1645	1530000	1920	1785000	2195	2039000
	1-4x8	1175	1091000	1370	1273000	1565	1454000
	3-2x8	915	854000	1070	997000	1220	1138000
	2-3x8	820	764000	955	891000	1095	1018000
	2-4x8	590	546000	690	637000	785	728000
	2-2x10	840	613000	980	715000	1120	817000
11′	1-3x8	1990	2035000	2320	2375000	2655	2713000
	1-4x8	1420	1454000	1660	1697000	1895	1938000
	3-2x8	1105	1130000	1290	1319000	1475	1506000
	2-3x8	995	1019000	1160	1189000	1325	1358000
	2-4x8	710	727000	830	848000	945	969000
	2-2x10	1020	816000	1190	952000	1360	1088000
	1-3x10	1220	980000	1425	1144000	1625	1306000
12′	1-4x8	1690	1890000	1970	2206000	2255	2519000
	3-2x8	1315	1469000	1535	1714000	1755	1958000
	2-3x8	1185	1322000	1385	1543000	1580	1762000
	2-4x8	845	944000	985	1102000	1125	1258000
	1-6x8	1005	1086000	1175	1267000	1340	1448000
	2-2x10	1210	1062000	1410	1239000	1615	1416000
	3-2x10	810	708000	945	826000	1080	944000
	2-3x10	725	636000	845	742000	965	848000
	1-4x10	1040	909000	1215	1061000	1385	1212000
13′	3-2x8	1545	1867000	1805	2179000	2060	2489000
	2-3x8	1390	1680000	1620	1960000	1855	2239000
	2-4x8	990	1201000	1155	1401000	1320	1600000
	1-6x8	1180	1381000	1375	1612000	1575	1841000
	2-2x10	1425	1350000	1665	1575000	1900	1799000
	3-2x10	950	900000	1110	1050000	1265	1200000
	2-3x10	855	810000	1000	945000	1140	1080000
	1-4x10	1220	1385000	1425	1616000	1625	1846000
	1-6x10	735	679000	855	792000	980	905000
14′	2-4x8	1150	1500000	1340	1750000	1535	1999000
	1-6x8	1370	1723000	1600	2011000	1825	2297000
	2-2x10	1650	1684000	1925	1965000	2200	2245000
	3-2x10	1100	1122000	1285	1309000	1465	1496000
	2-3x10	990	1009000	1155	1177000	1320	1345000
	1-4x10	1415	1445000	1650	1686000	1885	1926000
	1-6x10	915	1415000	1070	1651000	1220	1886000
	2-4x10	705	721000	825	841000	940	961000
	4-2x10	825	842000	960	983000	1100	1122000
	1-8x10	625	622000	730	726000	835	829000
15′	2-2x10	1895	2071000	2210	2417000	2525	2760000
	3-2x10	1260	1381000	1470	1612000	1680	1841000
	2-3x10	1135	1243000	1325	1450000	1515	1657000
	1-4x10	1620	1775000	1890	2071000	2160	2366000
	1-6x10	980	1044000	1145	1218000	1305	1392000
	2-4x10	810	888000	945	1036000	1080	1184000
	4-2x10	945	1037000	1105	1210000	1260	1382000
	1-8x10	720	764000	840	891000	960	1018000
	2-2x12	1280	1152000	1495	1344000	1705	1536000
	1-4x12	1095	986000	1280	1151000	1460	1314000
	3-2x12	855	768000	1000	896000	1140	1024000
	2-3x12	770	691000	900	806000	1025	921000
16′	3-2x10	1435	1675000	1675	1955000	1915	2233000
	2-3x10	1290	1508000	1505	1760000	1720	2010000
	1-6x10	[illegible]	1266000	1300	1477000	1485	1687000
	2-4x10	925	1079000	1080	1259000	1235	1438000
	4-2x10	1075	1256000	1255	1466000	1435	1674000
	1-8x10	815	929000	950	1084000	1085	1238000
	2-2x12	1455	1397000	1700	1630000	1940	1862000
	1-4x12	1250	1199000	1460	1399000	1665	1598000
	3-2x12	970	931000	1130	1086000	1295	1241000
	2-3x12	875	839000	1020	979000	1165	1118000
	4-2x12	730	699000	850	816000	975	932000
	2-4x12	625	599000	730	699000	835	798000
17′	2-3x10	1460	1808000	1705	2110000	1945	2410000
	1-6x10	1255	1518000	1465	1771000	1675	2023000
	2-4x10	1040	1292000	1215	1508000	1385	1722000
	4-2x10	1215	1507000	1420	1758000	1620	2009000
	1-8x10	920	1112000	1075	1298000	1225	1482000
	2-2x12	1645	1675000	1920	1955000	2195	2233000
	1-4x12	1410	1436000	1645	1676000	1880	1914000
	3-2x12	1095	1117000	1280	1303000	1460	1498000
	2-3x12	985	1007000	1150	1175000	1315	1342000
	4-2x12	820	839000	955	979000	1095	1118000
	2-4x12	705	719000	820	839000	940	958000
	5-2x12	655	671000	765	783000	875	894000
18′	2-4x10	1170	1535000	1365	1791000	1560	2046000
	4-2x10	1360	1790000	1590	2089000	1815	2386000
	1-8x10	1040	1322000	1215	1543000	1385	1762000
	2-2x12	1840	1991000	2150	2323000	2455	2654000
	1-4x12	1580	1705000	1845	1990000	2105	2273000
	3-2x12	1230	1327000	1435	1549000	1640	1769000
	2-3x12	1105	1194000	1290	1393000	1475	1591000
	4-2x12	920	995000	1075	1161000	1225	1326000
	2-4x12	790	853000	920	995000	1055	1137000
	5-2x12	735	797000	860	930000	980	1062000
	1-6x12	960	1016000	1120	1186000	1280	1354000
	3-3x12	740	787000	865	918000	985	1049000
19′	2-4x10	1300	1805000	1515	2106000	1735	2406000
	1-8x10	1145	1554000	1335	1813000	1525	2071000
	3-2x12	1370	1561000	1600	1822000	1825	2081000
	2-3x12	1230	1404000	1435	1638000	1640	1871000
	4-2x12	1025	1170000	1195	1365000	1365	1560000
	2-4x12	880	1003000	1025	1170000	1175	1337000
	5-2x12	820	936000	955	1092000	1095	1248000
	1-6x12	1070	1194000	1250	1393000	1425	1592000
	3-3x12	820	925000	955	1079000	1095	1233000
	1-8x12	785	877000	915	1023000	1045	1169000
	1-10x12	620	692000	725	807000	825	922000
	4-3x12	615	702000	715	819000	820	936000
20′	3-2x12	1520	1819000	1775	2123000	2025	2425000
	2-3x12	1365	1638000	1595	1911000	1820	2183000
	4-2x12	1025	1364000	1195	1592000	1365	1818000
	2-4x12	975	1170000	1140	1365000	1300	1560000
	5-2x12	910	1092000	1060	1274000	1215	1456000
	1-6x12	1295	1394000	1510	1627000	1725	1858000
	3-3x12	910	1080000	1060	1260000	1215	1440000
	1-8x12	870	1022000	1015	1193000	1160	1362000
	1-10x12	690	806000	805	941000	920	1074000
	4-3x12	680	818000	795	955000	905	1090000
	2-3x14	985	1003000	1150	1170000	1315	1337000
	1-6x14	860	862000	1005	1006000	1145	1149000
21′	2-3x12	1505	1896000	1755	2213000	2005	2527000
	4-2x12	1255	1580000	1465	1844000	1675	2106000
	2-4x12	1075	1355000	1255	1581000	1435	1806000
	5-2x12	1005	1265000	1175	1476000	1340	1686000
	1-6x12	1295	1613000	1510	1882000	1725	2150000
	3-3x12	1005	1249000	1175	1457000	1340	1665000
	1-8x12	960	1183000	1120	1380000	1280	1577000
	1-10x12	760	935000	885	1091000	1015	1246000
	4-3x12	750	948000	875	1106000	1000	1264000
	2-3x14	1085	1160000	1265	1354000	1445	1546000
	1-6x14	950	998000	1110	1165000	1265	1330000
	3-3x14	725	769000	845	897000	965	1025000
22′	4-2x12	1375	1818000	1605	2122000	1835	2423000
	2-4x12	1180	1556000	1380	1816000	1575	2074000
	5-2x12	1100	1453000	1285	1696000	1465	1937000
	3-3x12	1100	1436000	1285	1676000	1465	1914000
	1-8x12	1055	1361000	1230	1588000	1405	1814000
	1-10x12	830	1074000	970	1253000	1105	1432000
	4-3x12	825	1091000	965	1273000	1100	1454000
	2-3x14	1190	1334000	1390	1557000	1585	1778000
	1-6x14	1045	1147000	1220	1338000	1395	1529000
	3-3x14	795	883000	930	1030000	1060	1177000
	2-4x14	820	901000	955	1051000	1095	1201000
	4-3x14	595	667000	695	778000	795	889000

Table E-8 Floor and Roof Beams

Required values for fiber stress in bending (f) and modulus of elasticity (E) for the sizes shown to support safely a live load of **40** pounds per square foot within a deflection limitation of *l*/240. For instructions on use of table see Design Data for Beams on page 465.

SPAN OF BEAM	NOMINAL SIZE OF BEAM	MINIMUM "f" & "E" IN psi FOR BEAMS SPACED: 6'-0" f		7'-0" f		8'-0" f	
		f	E	f	E	f	E
10'	2-3x6	1785	1560000	2085	1820000	2380	2079000
	1-3x8	2055	1360000	2400	1587000	2740	1813000
	2-2x8	1710	1134000	1995	1323000	2280	1512000
	1-4x8	1470	969000	1715	1131000	1960	1291000
	1-6x8	875	558000	1020	651000	1165	744000
	2-2x10	1050	545000	1225	636000	1400	726000
	1-3x10	1260	655000	1470	764000	1680	873000
11'	2-2x8	2070	1509000	2415	1761000	2760	2011000
	1-4x8	1775	1293000	2070	1509000	2365	1723000
	1-6x8	1055	743000	1230	867000	1405	990000
	2-2x10	1275	725000	1490	846000	1700	966000
	1-3x10	1525	872000	1780	1017000	2030	1162000
	1-4x10	1090	623000	1270	727000	1455	830000
	3-2x10	850	484000	990	565000	1135	645000
12'	1-4x8	2110	1680000	2460	1960000	2810	2239000
	1-6x8	1255	965000	1465	1126000	1670	1286000
	3-2x8	1645	1305000	1920	1523000	2190	1739000
	2-2x10	1510	944000	1760	1101000	2010	1258000
	1-3x10	1820	1132000	2125	1321000	2425	1509000
	1-4x10	1300	808000	1515	943000	1735	1077000
	3-2x10	1010	629000	1180	734000	1345	838000
	2-3x10	905	565000	1055	659000	1205	753000
13'	1-6x8	1475	1228000	1720	1433000	1965	1637000
	2-3x8	1735	1493000	2025	1742000	2315	1990000
	2-4x8	1235	1068000	1440	1246000	1645	1423000
	2-2x10	1780	1200000	2075	1400000	2370	1600000
	3-2x10	1185	800000	1380	934000	1580	1066000
	1-3x10	2130	1439000	2485	1679000	2840	1918000
	2-3x10	1070	720000	1250	840000	1425	960000
	1-4x10	1525	1230000	1780	1435000	2035	1640000
	2-4x10	760	514000	890	600000	1015	685000
14'	2-4x8	1435	1333000	1675	1555000	1915	1777000
	3-2x10	1375	997000	1605	1163000	1830	1329000
	2-3x10	1235	897000	1440	1047000	1645	1196000
	1-4x10	1770	1284000	2065	1498000	2360	1711000
	2-4x10	880	641000	1025	748000	1175	854000
	3-3x10	825	599000	960	699000	1100	798000
	1-6x10	1145	1257000	1335	1467000	1525	1675000
	1-8x10	780	553000	910	645000	1040	737000
	4-2x10	1030	749000	1200	874000	1375	998000
	2-2x12	1395	832000	1630	971000	1860	1109000
15'	3-2x10	1575	1228000	1840	1433000	2100	1637000
	2-3x10	1420	1105000	1655	1289000	1890	1473000
	2-4x10	1010	789000	1175	921000	1345	1052000
	3-3x10	945	737000	1100	860000	1260	982000
	1-6x10	1225	928000	1430	1083000	1635	1237000
	1-8x10	900	680000	1050	793000	1200	906000
	4-2x10	1180	921000	1375	1075000	1575	1228000
	2-2x12	1600	1024000	1865	1195000	2130	1365000
	3-2x12	1065	683000	1240	797000	1420	910000
	1-3x12	1920	1229000	2240	1434000	2560	1638000
	4-2x12	800	512000	935	597000	1065	682000
	2-3x12	960	614000	1120	716000	1280	818000
16'	3-2x10	1795	1489000	2095	1738000	2395	1985000
	2-3x10	1610	1341000	1880	1565000	2145	1787000
	2-4x10	1155	959000	1350	1119000	1540	1278000
	3-3x10	1075	894000	1255	1043000	1435	1192000
	1-6x10	1395	1125000	1625	1313000	1860	1500000
	1-8x10	1020	825000	1190	962000	1360	1100000
	4-2x10	1345	1117000	1570	1303000	1790	1489000
	2-2x12	1820	1241000	2120	1448000	2425	1654000
	3-2x12	1210	828000	1410	966000	1610	1104000
	4-2x12	910	621000	1060	724000	1215	828000
	5-2x12	730	497000	850	580000	975	662000
	2-3x12	1095	745000	1280	869000	1460	993000
17'	2-3x10	1825	1608000	2130	1876000	2430	2143000
	2-4x10	1300	1149000	1520	1341000	1735	1532000
	3-3x10	1215	1073000	1420	1252000	1620	1430000
	1-8x10	1150	989000	1340	1154000	1535	1318000
	3-2x12	1370	993000	1600	1159000	1825	1323000
	4-2x12	1025	745000	1195	869000	1365	993000
	5-2x12	820	596000	955	695000	1095	794000
	2-3x12	1230	895000	1435	1044000	1640	1193000
	3-3x12	820	590000	955	688000	1095	786000
	2-4x12	880	639000	1025	746000	1175	852000
	1-6x12	1070	761000	1250	888000	1425	1014000
	1-8x12	785	558000	915	651000	1045	744000
18'	2-3x10	2120	1909000	2475	2228000	2825	2545000
	2-4x10	1460	1364000	1705	1592000	1945	1818000
	3-3x10	1365	1273000	1595	1485000	1820	1697000
	1-8x10	1300	1176000	1515	1372000	1730	1568000
	3-2x12	1540	1180000	1800	1377000	2050	1573000
	4-2x12	1150	884000	1340	1032000	1530	1178000
	5-2x12	920	708000	1075	826000	1225	944000
	2-3x12	1380	1061000	1610	1238000	1840	1414000
	3-3x12	920	700000	1075	817000	1225	933000
	2-4x12	990	759000	1155	886000	1320	1012000
	1-6x12	1200	903000	1400	1054000	1600	1204000
	1-8x12	880	663000	1025	774000	1175	884000
19'	1-8x10	1430	1381000	1670	1612000	1905	1841000
	3-2x12	1710	1388000	1995	1620000	2280	1850000
	4-2x12	1280	1040000	1495	1214000	1705	1386000
	5-2x12	1025	832000	1195	971000	1365	1109000
	2-3x12	1540	1248000	1795	1456000	2050	1663000
	3-3x12	1025	823000	1195	960000	1365	1097000
	2-4x12	1100	892000	1280	1041000	1465	1189000
	1-6x12	1335	1061000	1560	1238000	1780	1414000
	1-8x12	980	779000	1145	909000	1305	1038000
	3-4x12	735	595000	860	694000	980	793000
	4-3x12	770	624000	900	728000	1025	832000
	2-6x12	670	1063000	780	1240000	895	1417000
20'	3-2x12	1900	1617000	2220	1887000	2530	2155000
	4-2x12	1280	1213000	1495	1415000	1705	1617000
	5-2x12	1135	971000	1325	1133000	1515	1294000
	3-3x12	1135	960000	1325	1120000	1515	1279000
	2-4x12	1220	1040000	1425	1214000	1625	1386000
	1-6x12	1620	1240000	1890	1447000	2160	1653000
	1-8x12	1085	909000	1265	1061000	1445	1212000
	3-4x12	810	693000	945	809000	1080	924000
	4-3x12	850	728000	990	849000	1135	970000
	2-6x12	740	620000	865	723000	985	826000
	1-10x12	860	717000	1005	837000	1145	956000
	2-3x14	1230	891000	1435	1040000	1640	1188000
21'	3-2x12	2090	1873000	2440	2186000	2785	2497000
	4-2x12	1570	1405000	1830	1640000	2095	1873000
	5-2x12	1255	1124000	1465	1312000	1675	1498000
	3-3x12	1255	1111000	1465	1296000	1675	1481000
	2-4x12	1345	1204000	1570	1405000	1795	1605000
	1-8x12	1200	1052000	1400	1228000	1600	1402000
	3-4x12	895	803000	1045	937000	1195	1070000
	4-3x12	935	843000	1090	984000	1245	1124000
	2-6x12	820	717000	955	837000	1095	956000
	1-10x12	950	831000	1110	970000	1265	1108000
	2-3x14	1355	1032000	1580	1204000	1805	1375000
	1-6x14	1190	887000	1390	1035000	1585	1182000
22'	4-2x12	1720	1616000	2005	1886000	2295	2154000
	5-2x12	1375	1292000	1605	1508000	1830	1722000
	3-3x12	1375	1277000	1605	1490000	1830	1702000
	3-4x12	985	923000	1150	1077000	1315	1230000
	4-3x12	1030	969000	1200	1131000	1375	1292000
	2-6x12	900	825000	1050	963000	1200	1100000
	1-10x12	1035	955000	1205	1114000	1380	1273000
	2-3x14	1485	1187000	1730	1385000	1980	1582000
	1-6x14	1305	1020000	1525	1190000	1740	1360000
	2-4x14	1025	801000	1195	935000	1365	1068000
	3-3x14	995	785000	1160	916000	1325	1046000
	3-4x14	680	534000	795	623000	905	712000

Table E-9 Floor and Roof Beams

Required values for fiber stress in bending (f) and modulus of elasticity (E) for the sizes shown to support safely a live load of **40** pounds per square foot within a deflection limitation of *l*/300. For instructions on use of table see Design Data for Beams on page 465.

SPAN OF BEAM	NOMINAL SIZE OF BEAM	MINIMUM "f" & "E" IN psi FOR BEAMS SPACED: 6'-0"		7'-0"		8'-0"	
		f	E	f	E	f	E
10'	1-3x8	2055	1700000	2400	1984000	2740	2266000
	2-2x8	1710	1417000	1995	1654000	2280	1889000
	1-4x8	1470	1211000	1715	1413000	1960	1614000
	1-6x8	875	697000	1020	813000	1165	929000
	2-2x10	1050	681000	1225	795000	1400	908000
	1-3x10	1260	819000	1470	956000	1680	1092000
	1-4x10	900	585000	1050	683000	1200	780000
11'	2-2x8	2070	1886000	2415	2201000	2760	2514000
	1-4x8	1775	1616000	2070	1886000	2365	2154000
	1-6x8	1055	929000	1230	1084000	1405	1238000
	2-2x10	1275	906000	1490	1057000	1700	1208000
	1-3x10	1525	1090000	1780	1272000	2030	1453000
	1-4x10	1090	779000	1270	909000	1455	1038000
	3-2x10	850	605000	990	706000	1135	806000
12'	1-6x8	1255	1206000	1465	1407000	1670	1607000
	3-2x8	1645	1631000	1920	1903000	2190	2174000
	2-2x10	1510	1180000	1760	1377000	2010	1573000
	1-3x10	1820	1415000	2125	1651000	2425	1886000
	1-4x10	1300	1010000	1515	1179000	1735	1346000
	3-2x10	1010	786000	1180	917000	1345	1048000
	2-3x10	905	706000	1055	824000	1205	941000
	1-6x10	785	594000	915	693000	1045	792000
	2-4x10	650	505000	760	589000	865	673000
13'	1-6x8	1475	1535000	1720	1791000	1965	2046000
	2-3x8	1735	1866000	2025	2178000	2315	2487000
	2-4x8	1235	1335000	1440	1558000	1645	1779000
	3-2x10	1185	1000000	1380	1167000	1580	1333000
	2-2x10	1780	1500000	2075	1750000	2370	2000000
	1-3x10	2130	1799000	2485	2099000	2840	2398000
	2-3x10	1070	900000	1250	1050000	1425	1200000
	1-4x10	1525	1537000	1780	1794000	2035	2049000
	2-4x10	760	642000	890	749000	1015	856000
14'	2-4x8	1435	1666000	1675	1944000	1915	2221000
	3-2x10	1375	1246000	1605	1454000	1830	1661000
	2-3x10	1235	1121000	1440	1308000	1645	1494000
	1-4x10	1770	1605000	2065	1873000	2360	2139000
	2-4x10	880	801000	1025	935000	1175	1068000
	3-3x10	825	749000	960	874000	1100	998000
	1-6x10	1145	1571000	1335	1833000	1525	2094000
	1-8x10	780	691000	910	806000	1040	921000
	4-2x10	1030	936000	1200	1092000	1375	1248000
	2-2x12	1395	1040000	1630	1214000	1860	1386000
15'	3-2x10	1575	1535000	1840	1791000	2100	2046000
	2-3x10	1420	1381000	1655	1612000	1890	1841000
	2-4x10	1010	986000	1175	1151000	1345	1314000
	3-3x10	945	921000	1100	1075000	1260	1228000
	1-6x10	1225	1160000	1430	1354000	1635	1546000
	1-8x10	900	850000	1050	992000	1200	1133000
	4-2x10	1180	1151000	1375	1343000	1575	1534000
	2-2x12	1600	1280000	1865	1494000	2130	1706000
	3-2x12	1065	854000	1240	997000	1420	1138000
	1-3x12	1920	1536000	2240	1792000	2560	2047000
	4-2x12	800	640000	935	747000	1065	853000
	2-3x12	960	767000	1120	895000	1280	1022000
16'	3-2x10	1795	1861000	2095	2172000	2395	2481000
	2-3x10	1610	1676000	1880	1956000	2145	2234000
	2-4x10	1155	1199000	1350	1399000	1540	1598000
	3-3x10	1075	1117000	1255	1303000	1435	1489000
	1-6x10	1395	1406000	1625	1641000	1860	1874000
	1-8x10	1020	1031000	1190	1203000	1360	1374000
	4-2x10	1345	1396000	1570	1629000	1790	1861000
	2-2x12	1820	1551000	2120	1810000	2425	2067000
	3-2x12	1210	1035000	1410	1208000	1610	1380000
	4-2x12	910	776000	1060	905000	1215	1034000
	5-2x12	730	621000	850	725000	975	828000
	2-3x12	1095	931000	1280	1086000	1460	1241000
17'	2-3x10	1825	2010000	2310	2345000	2430	2679000
	2-4x10	1300	1436000	1520	1676000	1735	1914000
	3-3x10	1215	1341000	1420	1565000	1620	1787000
	1-8x10	1150	1236000	1340	1442000	1535	1647000
	3-2x12	1370	1241000	1600	1448000	1825	1654000
	4-2x12	1025	931000	1195	1086000	1365	1241000
	5-2x12	820	745000	955	869000	1095	993000
	2-3x12	1230	1119000	1435	1306000	1640	1492000
	3-3x12	820	737000	955	860000	1095	982000
	2-4x12	880	799000	1025	932000	1175	1065000
	1-6x12	1070	951000	1250	1110000	1425	1268000
	1-8x12	785	697000	915	813000	1045	929000
18'	2-4x10	1460	1705000	1705	1990000	1945	2273000
	3-3x10	1365	1591000	1595	1857000	1820	2121000
	1-8x10	1300	1470000	1515	1715000	1730	1959000
	3-2x12	1540	1475000	1800	1721000	2050	1966000
	4-2x12	1150	1105000	1340	1289000	1530	1473000
	5-2x12	920	885000	1075	1033000	1225	1180000
	2-3x12	1380	1326000	1610	1547000	1840	1767000
	3-3x12	920	875000	1075	1021000	1225	1166000
	2-4x12	990	949000	1155	1107000	1320	1265000
	1-6x12	1200	1129000	1400	1317000	1600	1505000
	1-8x12	880	829000	1025	967000	1175	1105000
	3-4x12	660	632000	770	737000	880	842000
19'	3-3x10	1520	1872000	1775	2184000	2025	2495000
	3-2x12	1710	1735000	1995	2025000	2280	2313000
	4-2x12	1280	1300000	1495	1517000	1705	1733000
	5-2x12	1025	1040000	1195	1214000	1365	1386000
	2-3x12	1540	1560000	1795	1820000	2050	2079000
	3-3x12	1025	1029000	1195	1201000	1365	1372000
	2-4x12	1100	1115000	1280	1301000	1465	1486000
	1-6x12	1335	1326000	1560	1547000	1780	1767000
	1-8x12	980	973000	1145	1135000	1305	1297000
	3-4x12	735	744000	860	868000	980	992000
	4-3x12	770	780000	900	910000	1025	1040000
	2-6x12	670	1329000	780	1551000	895	1771000
20'	3-2x12	1900	2021000	2220	2358000	2530	2694000
	4-2x12	1280	1516000	1495	1769000	1705	2021000
	5-2x12	1135	1214000	1325	1417000	1515	1618000
	3-3x12	1135	1200000	1325	1400000	1515	1600000
	2-4x12	1220	1300000	1425	1517000	1625	1733000
	1-6x12	1620	1550000	1890	1809000	2160	2066000
	1-8x12	1085	1136000	1265	1326000	1445	1514000
	3-4x12	810	866000	945	1011000	1080	1154000
	4-3x12	850	910000	990	1062000	1135	1213000
	2-6x12	740	775000	865	904000	985	1033000
	1-10x12	860	896000	1005	1046000	1145	1194000
	2-3x14	1230	1114000	1435	1300000	1640	1485000
21'	4-2x12	1570	1756000	1830	2049000	2095	2341000
	5-2x12	1255	1405000	1465	1640000	1675	1873000
	3-3x12	1255	1389000	1465	1621000	1675	1851000
	2-4x12	1345	1505000	1570	1756000	1795	2006000
	1-8x12	1200	1315000	1400	1535000	1600	1753000
	3-4x12	895	1004000	1045	1172000	1195	1338000
	4-3x12	935	1054000	1090	1230000	1245	1405000
	2-6x12	820	896000	955	1046000	1095	1194000
	1-10x12	950	1039000	1110	1212000	1265	1385000
	2-3x14	1355	1290000	1580	1505000	1805	1719000
	1-6x14	1190	1109000	1390	1294000	1585	1478000
	2-4x14	930	871000	1085	1016000	1240	1161000
22'	4-2x12	1720	2020000	2005	2357000	2295	2693000
	5-2x12	1375	1615000	1605	1885000	1830	2153000
	3-3x12	1375	1596000	1605	1862000	1830	2127000
	3-4x12	985	1154000	1150	1347000	1315	1538000
	4-3x12	1030	1211000	1200	1413000	1375	1614000
	2-6x12	900	1031000	1050	1203000	1200	1374000
	1-10x12	1035	1194000	1205	1393000	1380	1592000
	2-3x14	1485	1484000	1730	1732000	1980	1978000
	1-6x14	1305	1275000	1525	1488000	1740	1700000
	2-4x14	1025	1001000	1195	1168000	1365	1334000
	3-3x14	995	981000	1160	1145000	1325	1308000
	3-4x14	680	667000	795	778000	905	889000

Table E-10 Floor and Roof Beams

Required values for fiber stress in bending (f) and modulus of elasticity (E) for the sizes shown to support safely a live load of **40** pounds per square foot within a deflection limitation of *l*/360. For instructions on use of table see Design Data for Beams on page 465.

SPAN OF BEAM	NOMINAL SIZE OF BEAM	MINIMUM "f" & "E" IN psi FOR BEAMS SPACED: 6'-0"		7'-0"		8'-0"	
		f	E	f	E	f	E
10'	1-3x8	2055	2040000	2400	2381000	2740	2719000
	2-2x8	1710	1701000	1995	1985000	2280	2267000
	1-4x8	1470	1453000	1715	1696000	1960	1937000
	1-6x8	875	837000	1020	977000	1165	1116000
	2-2x10	1050	817000	1225	953000	1400	1089000
	1-3x10	1260	982000	1470	1146000	1680	1309000
	1-4x10	900	702000	1050	819000	1200	936000
11'	1-4x8	1775	1939000	2070	2263000	2365	2585000
	1-6x8	1055	1114000	1230	1300000	1405	1485000
	2-2x10	1275	1087000	1490	1268000	1700	1449000
	1-3x10	1525	1308000	1780	1526000	2030	1743000
	1-4x10	1090	934000	1270	1090000	1455	1245000
	3-2x10	850	726000	990	847000	1135	968000
	2-3x10	765	654000	890	763000	1020	872000
12'	1-6x8	1255	1447000	1465	1689000	1670	1929000
	3-2x8	1645	1957000	1920	2284000	2190	2609000
	2-2x10	1510	1416000	1760	1652000	2010	1887000
	1-3x10	1820	1698000	2125	1981000	2425	2263000
	1-4x10	1300	1212000	1515	1414000	1735	1615000
	2-3x10	905	847000	1055	988000	1205	1129000
	3-2x10	1010	943000	1180	1100000	1345	1257000
	1-6x10	785	713000	915	832000	1045	950000
	2-4x10	650	606000	760	707000	865	808000
13'	2-4x8	1235	1602000	1440	1869000	1645	2135000
	2-2x10	1780	1800000	2075	2100000	2370	2400000
	3-2x10	1185	1200000	1380	1400000	1580	1600000
	2-3x10	1070	1080000	1250	1260000	1425	1440000
	1-4x10	1525	1845000	1780	2153000	2035	2459000
	2-4x10	760	771000	890	900000	1015	1028000
	3-3x10	710	719000	830	839000	945	958000
	1-6x10	920	906000	1075	1057000	1225	1208000
	4-2x10	890	899000	1040	1049000	1185	1198000
14'	2-4x8	1435	1999000	1675	2333000	1915	2665000
	3-2x10	1375	1495000	1605	1745000	1830	1993000
	2-3x10	1235	1345000	1440	1570000	1645	1793000
	2-4x10	880	961000	1025	1121000	1175	1281000
	3-3x10	825	898000	960	1048000	1100	1197000
	1-6x10	1145	1885000	1335	2200000	1525	2513000
	1-8x10	780	829000	910	967000	1040	1105000
	4-2x10	1030	1123000	1200	1310000	1375	1497000
	2-2x12	1395	1248000	1630	1456000	1860	1663000
	3-2x12	930	832000	1085	971000	1240	1109000
15'	3-2x10	1575	1842000	1840	2150000	2100	2455000
	2-3x10	1420	1657000	1655	1934000	1890	2209000
	2-4x10	1010	1183000	1175	1380000	1345	1577000
	3-3x10	945	1105000	1100	1289000	1260	1473000
	1-6x10	1225	1392000	1430	1624000	1635	1855000
	1-8x10	900	1020000	1050	1190000	1200	1360000
	4-2x10	1180	1381000	1375	1612000	1575	1841000
	2-2x12	1600	1536000	1865	1792000	2130	2047000
	3-2x12	1065	1024000	1240	1195000	1420	1365000
	1-3x12	1920	1843000	2240	2151000	2560	2457000
	4-2x12	800	768000	935	896000	1065	1024000
	2-3x12	960	921000	1120	1075000	1280	1228000
16'	2-3x10	1610	2011000	1880	2347000	2145	2681000
	2-4x10	1155	1438000	1350	1678000	1540	1917000
	3-3x10	1075	1341000	1255	1565000	1435	1787000
	1-6x10	1395	1687000	1625	1969000	1860	2249000
	1-8x10	1020	1237000	1190	1443000	1360	1649000
	4-2x10	1345	1675000	1570	1955000	1790	2233000
	2-2x12	1820	1861000	2120	2172000	2425	2481000
	3-2x12	1210	1242000	1410	1449000	1610	1655000
	4-2x12	910	931000	1060	1086000	1215	1241000
	5-2x12	730	745000	850	869000	975	993000
	2-3x12	1095	1117000	1280	1303000	1460	1489000
	3-3x12	730	737000	850	860000	975	982000
17'	2-4x10	1300	1723000	1520	2011000	1735	2297000
	3-3x10	1215	1609000	1420	1878000	1620	2145000
	1-8x10	1150	1483000	1340	1731000	1535	1977000
	3-2x12	1370	1489000	1600	1738000	1825	1985000
	4-2x12	1025	1117000	1195	1303000	1365	1489000
	5-2x12	820	894000	955	1043000	1095	1192000
	2-3x12	1230	1342000	1435	1566000	1640	1789000
	3-3x12	820	885000	955	1033000	1095	1180000
	2-4x12	880	958000	1025	1118000	1175	1277000
	1-6x12	1070	1141000	1250	1331000	1425	1521000
	1-8x12	785	837000	915	977000	1045	1116000
	3-4x12	585	639000	680	746000	780	852000
18'	3-3x10	1365	1909000	1595	2228000	1820	2545000
	1-8x10	1300	1764000	1515	2058000	1730	2351000
	3-2x12	1540	1770000	1800	2065000	2050	2359000
	4-2x12	1150	1326000	1340	1547000	1530	1767000
	5-2x12	920	1062000	1075	1239000	1225	1416000
	2-3x12	1380	1591000	1610	1857000	1840	2121000
	3-3x12	920	1050000	1075	1225000	1225	1400000
	2-4x12	990	1138000	1155	1328000	1320	1517000
	1-6x12	1200	1354000	1400	1580000	1600	1805000
	1-8x12	880	994000	1025	1160000	1175	1325000
	3-4x12	660	758000	770	884000	880	1010000
	4-3x12	690	796000	805	929000	920	1061000
19'	4-2x12	1280	1560000	1495	1820000	1705	2079000
	5-2x12	1025	1248000	1195	1456000	1365	1663000
	2-3x12	1540	1872000	1795	2185000	2050	2495000
	3-3x12	1025	1234000	1195	1440000	1365	1645000
	2-4x12	1100	1338000	1280	1561000	1465	1783000
	1-6x12	1335	1591000	1560	1857000	1780	2121000
	1-8x12	980	1168000	1145	1363000	1305	1557000
	3-4x12	735	892000	860	1041000	980	1189000
	4-3x12	770	936000	900	1092000	1025	1248000
	2-6x12	670	1594000	780	186000	895	2125000
	1-10x12	775	923000	905	1077000	1035	1230000
	2-3x14	1110	1146000	1295	1337000	1480	1528000
20'	4-2x12	1280	1819000	1495	2123000	1705	2425000
	5-2x12	1135	1456000	1325	1699000	1515	1941000
	3-3x12	1135	1440000	1325	1680000	1515	1919000
	2-4x12	1220	1560000	1425	1820000	1625	2079000
	1-8x12	1085	1363000	1265	1591000	1445	1817000
	3-4x12	810	1039000	945	1212000	1080	1385000
	4-3x12	850	1092000	990	1274000	1135	1456000
	2-6x12	740	930000	865	1085000	985	1240000
	1-10x12	860	1075000	1005	1254000	1145	1433000
	2-3x14	1230	1336000	1435	1559000	1640	1781000
	1-6x14	1075	1149000	1255	1341000	1430	1532000
	2-4x14	845	903000	985	1054000	1125	1204000
21'	5-2x12	1255	1686000	1465	1967000	1675	2247000
	3-3x12	1255	1666000	1465	1944000	1675	2221000
	2-4x12	1345	1806000	1570	2107000	1795	2407000
	1-8x12	1200	1578000	1400	1841000	1600	2103000
	3-4x12	895	1204000	1045	1405000	1195	1605000
	4-3x12	935	1264000	1090	1475000	1245	1685000
	2-6x12	820	1075000	955	1254000	1095	1433000
	1-10x12	950	1246000	1110	1454000	1265	1661000
	2-3x14	1355	1548000	1580	1806000	1805	2063000
	1-6x14	1190	1330000	1390	1552000	1585	1773000
	2-4x14	930	1045000	1085	1219000	1240	1393000
	3-3x14	905	1032000	1055	1204000	1205	1375000
22'	5-2x12	1375	1938000	1605	2262000	1830	2583000
	3-3x12	1375	1915000	1605	2235000	1830	2553000
	3-4x12	985	1384000	1150	1615000	1315	1845000
	4-3x12	1030	1453000	1200	1695000	1375	1937000
	2-6x12	900	1237000	1050	1443000	1200	1649000
	1-10x12	1035	1432000	1205	1671000	1380	1909000
	2-3x14	1485	1780000	1730	2077000	1980	2373000
	1-6x14	1305	1530000	1525	1785000	1740	2039000
	2-4x14	1025	1201000	1195	1401000	1365	1600000
	3-3x14	995	1177000	1160	1373000	1325	1569000
	3-4x14	680	801000	795	935000	905	1068000
	1-8x14	955	1122000	1115	1309000	1275	1495000

Table E-11 Lumber Design Values

Species and commercial grade	Size classification	Allowable unit stresses in pounds per square inch: Extreme fiber in bending "F_b" Single-member uses	Extreme fiber in bending "F_b" Repetitive-member uses	Tension parallel to grain "F_t"	Horizontal shear "F_v"	Compression perpendicular to grain "F_{CI}"	Compression parallel to grain "F_C"	Modulus of elasticity "E"	Grading rules agency
EASTERN HEMLOCK—TAMARACK (Surfaced dry or surfaced green. Used at 19% max. m.c.)									
Select Structural	2″ to 4″	1550	1750	1050	85	365	1200	1,300,000	
No. 1	thick	1300	1500	875	85	365	1050	1,300,000	Hardwood
No. 2	6″ and	1050	1200	700	85	365	900	1,100,000	and Pine
No. 3	wider	625	725	400	85	365	575	1,000,000	Manufacturers
Appearance		1300	1500	875	85	365	1300	1,300,000	Association
CALIFORNIA REDWOOD (Surfaced dry or surfaced green. Used at 19% max. m.c.)									
Select Structural		1750	2000	1150	100	425	1550	1,400,000	
Select Structural, Open grain		1400	1600	925	100	270	1150	1,100,000	
No. 1	2″ to 4″	1500	1700	975	100	425	1400	1,400,000	
No. 1, Open grain	thick	1150	1350	775	100	270	1050	1,100,000	Redwood
No. 2	6″ and	1200	1400	800	80	425	1200	1,250,000	Inspection
No. 2, Open grain	wider	950	1100	625	80	270	875	1,000,000	Service
No. 3		700	800	475	80	425	725	1,100,000	
No. 3, Open grain		550	650	375	80	270	525	900,000	
SOUTHERN PINE (Surfaced dry. Used at 19% max. m.c.)									
Select Structural		1800	2050	1200	90	405	1400	1,800,000	
Dense Select Structural		2100	2400	1400	90	475	1650	1,900,000	
No. 1		1500	1750	1000	90	405	1250	1,800,000	Southern
No. 1 Dense	2″ to 4″	1800	2050	1200	90	475	1450	1,900,000	Pine
No. 2	thick	1050	1200	700	75	345	900	1,400,000	Inspection
No. 2 Medium grain	6″ and	1250	1450	825	90	405	1050	1,600,000	Bureau
No. 2 Dense	wider	1450	1650	975	90	475	1250	1,700,000	
No. 3		725	825	475	75	345	650	1,400,000	
No. 3 Dense		850	975	575	90	475	750	1,500,000	

Table E-12 Lumber Design Values, Western Woods

STRUCTURAL JOISTS and PLANKS and APPEARANCE—2″ to 4″ Thick, 6″ and Wider
Recommended Design Values in Pounds Per Square Inch[1]

Grades Described in Sections 62.00 and 50.00 WWPA 1970 Grading Rules

Species or Group	Grade	Extreme Fiber Stress in Bending "Fb"		Tension Parallel to Grain "Ft"	Horizontal Shear "Fv"	Compression		Modulus of Elasticity "E"
		Single	Repetitive			Perpendicular "Fc ⊥"	Parallel to Grain "Fc"	
DOUGLAS FIR-LARCH	Select Structural	1800	2050	1200	95	385	1400	1,800,000
	No. 1 /Appearance	1500	1750	1000	95	385	1250/1500	1,800,000
	No. 2	1250	1450	825	95	385	1050	1,700,000
	No. 3	725	850	475	95	385	675	1,500,000
DOUGLAS FIR SOUTH	Select Structural	1700	1950	1150	90	335	1250	1,400,000
	No. 1/Appearance	1450	1650	975	90	335	1150/1350	1,400,000
	No. 2	1200	1350	775	90	335	950	1,300,000
	No. 3	700	800	450	90	335	600	1,100,000
HEM-FIR	Select Structural	1400	1650	950	75	245	1150	1,500,000
	No. 1/Appearance	1200	1400	800	75	245	1000/1200	1,500,000
	No. 2	1000	1150	650	75	245	850	1,400,000
	No. 3	575	675	375	75	245	550	1,200,000
MOUNTAIN HEMLOCK	Select Structural	1500	1700	1000	95	370	1100	1,300,000
	No. 1/Appearance	1250	1450	850	95	370	1000/1200	1,300,000
	No. 2	1050	1200	675	95	370	825	1,100,000
	No. 3	625	700	400	95	370	525	1,000,000
MOUNTAIN HEMLOCK-HEM-FIR	Select Structural	1400	1650	950	75	245	1100	1,300,000
	No. 1/Appearance	1200	1400	800	75	245	1000/1200	1,300,000
	No. 2	1000	1150	650	75	245	825	1,100,000
	No. 3	575	675	375	75	245	525	1,000,000
SUBALPINE FIR (White Woods) (Western Woods)	Select Structural	1050	1200	700	60	195	800	900,000
	No. 1/Appearance	900	1050	600	60	195	700/850	900,000
	No. 2	750	850	475	60	195	600	900,000
	No. 3	425	500	275	60	195	375	800,000
ENGELMANN SPRUCE (Engelmann Spruce-Lodgepole Pine)	Select Structural	1150	1350	775	70	195	800	1,200,000
	No. 1/Appearance	975	1150	650	70	195	725/875	1,200,000
	No. 2	800	925	525	70	195	600	1,100,000
	No. 3	475	550	300	70	195	375	1,000,000
LODGEPOLE PINE	Select Structural	1300	1500	875	70	250	1000	1,300,000
	No. 1/Appearance	1100	1300	750	70	250	900/1050	1,300,000
	No. 2	925	1050	600	70	250	750	1,200,000
	No. 3	525	625	350	70	250	475	1,000,000
PONDEROSA PINE-SUGAR PINE (Ponderosa Pine-Lodgepole Pine)	Select Structural	1200	1400	825	70	250	950	1,200,000
	No. 1/Appearance	1050	1200	700	70	250	850/1000	1,200,000
	No. 2	850	975	550	70	250	700	1,100,000
	No. 3	500	575	325	70	250	450	1,000,000
IDAHO WHITE PINE	Select Structural	1250	1450	825	65	240	1000	1,400,000
	No. 1/Appearance	1050	1200	700	65	240	925/1100	1,400,000
	No. 2	875	1000	575	65	240	775	1,300,000
	No. 3	500	575	325	65	240	475	1,100,000
WESTERN CEDARS	Select Structural	1250	1450	850	75	295	1100	1,100,000
	No. 1/Appearance	1050	1250	725	75	295	975/1150	1,100,000
	No. 2	875	1000	575	75	295	825	1,000,000
	No. 3	525	600	325	75	295	525	900,000

These design values apply to lumber when used at a maximum moisture content of 19% such as in most covered structures. For other conditions of use, see Section 140.00 of WWPA 1970 Grading Rules.

Table E-13 Properties of Sections (S4S)

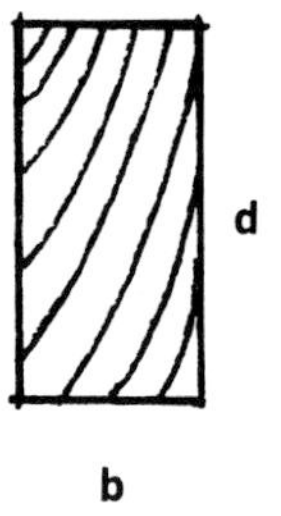

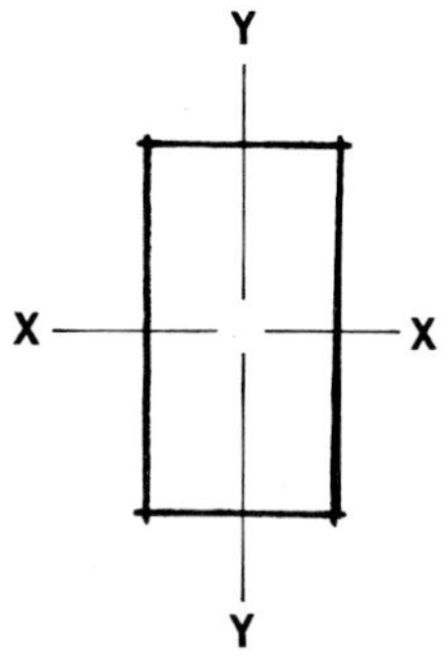

Nominal Size Inches b d	Actual Size Inches b d	Area In.^{2}	AXIS XX S In.^{3}	AXIS XX I In.^{4}	AXIS YY S In.^{3}	AXIS YY I In.^{4}	Board Measure per Lineal Foot	Weight per Lineal Foot Lbs.
2 x 2	1-1/2 x 1-1/2	2.25	.56	.42	.56	.42	.33	.63
3	2-1/2	3.75	1.56	1.95	.94	.70	.50	1.05
4	3-1/2	5.25	3.06	5.36	1.31	.99	.67	1.46
6	5-1/2	8.25	7.56	20.80	2.06	1.55	1.00	2.29
8	7-1/4	10.88	13.14	47.63	2.72	2.06	1.33	2.98
10	9-1/4	13.88	21.39	98.93	3.57	2.62	1.67	3.87
12	11-1/4	16.88	31.64	177.98	4.23	3.18	2.00	4.68
14	13-1/4	19.88	43.89	290.77	4.97	3.75	2.33	5.50
3 x 3	2-1/2 x 2-1/2	6.25	2.61	3.25	2.6	3.24	.75	1.73
4	3-1/2	8.75	5.10	8.93	3.64	4.56	1.00	2.43
6	5-1/2	13.75	12.60	34.66	5.73	7.16	1.50	3.82
8	7-1/4	18.13	21.90	79.39	7.56	9.53	2.00	5.03
10	9-1/4	23.13	35.65	164.88	9.63	12.16	2.50	6.44
12	11-1/4	28.13	52.73	296.63	11.75	14.79	3.00	7.83
14	13-1/4	33.13	73.15	484.63	14.91	17.34	3.50	9.18
4 x 4	3-1/2 x 3-1/2	12.25	7.15	12.50	7.14	12.52	1.33	3.39
6	5-1/2	19.25	17.65	48.53	11.23	19.64	2.00	5.34
8	7-1/4	25.38	30.66	111.15	14.82	26.15	2.67	7.05
10	9-1/4	32.38	49.91	230.84	18.97	33.23	3.33	8.98
12	11-1/4	39.38	73.82	415.28	23.03	40.30	4.00	10.91
14	13-1/2	46.38	106.31	717.61	27.07	47.59	4.67	12.90
6 x 6*	5-1/2 x 5-1/2	30.25	27.73	76.25	27.73	76.25	3	8.40
8	7-1/2	41.25	51.56	193.35	37.81	103.98	4	11.46
10	9-1/2	52.25	82.73	392.96	47.89	131.71	5	14.51
12	11-1/2	63.25	121.23	697.07	57.98	159.44	6	17.57
14	13-1/2	74.25	167.06	1127.67	68.06	187.17	7	20.62
8 x 8*	7-1/2 x 7-1/2	56.25	70.31	263.67	70.31	263.67	5.33	15.62
10	9-1/2	71.25	112.81	535.86	89.06	333.98	6.67	19.79
12	11-1/2	86.25	165.31	950.55	107.81	404.30	8	23.96
14	13-1/2	101.25	227.81	1537.73	126.56	474.61	9.33	28.12
10 x 10*	9-1/2 x 9-1/2	90.25	142.89	678.75	142.89	678.75	8.33	25.07
12	11-1/2	109.25	209.39	1204.03	172.98	821.65	10	30.35
14	13-1/2	128.25	288.56	1947.80	203.06	964.25	11.67	35.62
12 x 12*	11-1/2 x 11-1/2	132.25	253.48	1457.51	253.48	1457.51	12	36.74
14	13-1/2	155.25	349.31	2357.86	297.56	1710.98	14	43.12
14 x 14*	13-1/2 x 13-1/2	182.25	410.06	2767.92	410.06	2767.92	16.33	50.62

**Note: Properties are based on minimum dressed green size which is ½ inch off nominal in both b and d dimensions.*

APPENDIX F: MODULAR VERTICAL BRICK COURSING [1]

Module	Course	Dim.	Module	Course	Dim.
	1C	2⅝″		37C	8′–2⅝″
	2C	5⅜″		38C	8′–5⅜″
1M	3C	8″	13M	39C	8′–8″
	4C	10⅝″		40C	8′–10⅝″
	5C	1′–1⅜″		41C	9′–1⅜″
2M	6C	1′–4″	14M	42C	9′–4″
	7C	1′–6⅝″		43C	9′–6⅝″
	8C	1′–9⅜″		44C	9′–9⅜″
3M	9C	2′–0″	15M	45C	10′–0″
	10C	2′–2⅝″		46C	10′–2⅝″
	11C	2′–5⅜″		47C	10′–5⅜″
4M	12C	2′–8″	16M	48C	10′–8″
	13C	2′–10⅝″		49C	10′–10⅜″
	14C	3′–1⅜″		50C	11′–1⅜″
5M	15C	3′–4″	17M	51C	11–′4″
	16C	3′–6⅝″		52C	11′–6⅝″
	17C	3′–9⅜″		53C	11′–9⅜″
6M	18C	4′–0″	18M	54C	12′–0″
	19C	4′–2⅝″		55C	12′–2⅝″
	20C	4′–5⅜″		56C	12′–5⅜″
7M	21C	4′–8″	19M	57C	12′–8″
	22C	4′–10⅝″		58C	12′–10⅝″
	23C	5′–1⅜″		59C	13′–1⅜″
8M	24C	5′–4″	20M	60C	13′–4″
	25C	5′–6⅝″		61C	13′–6⅝″
	26C	5′–9⅜″		62C	13′–9⅜″
9M	27C	6′–0″	21M	63C	14′–0″
	28C	6′–2⅝″		64C	14′–2⅝″
	29C	6′–5⅜″		65C	14′–5⅜″
10M	30C	6′–8″	22M	66C	14′–8″
	31C	6′–10⅝″		67C	14′–10⅝″
	32C	7′–1⅜″		68C	15′–1⅜″
11M	33C	7′–4″	23M	69C	15′–4″
	34C	7′–6⅝″		70C	15′–6⅝″
	35C	7′–9⅜″		71C	15′–9⅜″
12M	36C	8′–0″	24M	72C	16′–0″

[1] The module corresponds to 8″ concrete block course heights.

WORKSHEET FOR MANUAL J

LOAD CALCULATIONS FOR RESIDENTIAL AIR CONDITIONING

For: Name MR. & MRS. JOHN DOE
Address 1918 PINEDALE AVE.
City and State or Province ATLANTA, GA.
By: Contractor
Address
City

Winter Design Conditions

Outside 10° F Inside 75° F Temperature Difference 65° Degrees

(Insert data below only after all heat loss calculations have been completed)

Total Heat Loss (Btuh) 66,535 (From Line No. 15) Model No. LENOX G-8-110
Serial No. Manufactured by LENOX
Rating Data: Input 110,000 Btuh Output at Bonnet 88,000 Btuh
Description of Controls

Summer Design Conditions

Outside 95° F Outside Wet Bulb 76° F Inside 75° F
North Latitude 35 Degrees Daily Range MEDIUM

(Insert data below only after all heat gain calculations have been completed)

Total Heat Gain (Btuh) 33,280 (From Line No. 21 or 22, if used)
Equipment Capacity Multiplier .89 Model No. COND. HSG-311V; EV. C1-41-V
Serial No. Manufactured by LENOX
Rating Data: Cooling Capacity 30,000 Btuh Air Volume 1,125 Cfm
Description of Controls

Winter Construction Data (See Table 2)

Walls and Partitions 7a & 8a

Windows and Doors 20a & 27a

Ceilings 11c

Floors 15a

Summer Construction Data (See Table 14)

Direction House Faces SE
Windows and Doors 6a

Walls and Partitions 7a & 8a

Ceilings 11c

Floors —

FILE

FORM J—1 WORKSHEET—HEAT LOSS AND HEAT GAIN CALCULATIONS

DO NOT WRITE IN SHADED BLOCKS

Line	Type of Exposure		Const. No.	HTM Htg	HTM Clg	Entire House Area or Crack	Entire House Btuh Htg	Entire House Btuh Clg	1 Living & Area or Crack	Living & Btuh Htg	Living & Btuh Clg	2 Dining Rm. Area or Crack	Dining Rm. Btuh Htg	Dining Rm. Btuh Clg
1	Name of Room								LIVING &			DINING RM.		
2	Running Ft Exposed Wall								19 x 16					
3	Ceiling Ht, Ft								8					
4	Room Compass Directions								S.E. & S.W					
5	Gross	a	8a						152					
	Exposed	b	7a						196					
	Walls and	c												
	Partitions	d												
6	Windows	a	1a						76	5,550				
	and	b	6a											
	Doors	c	1c											
	(Heating)	d												
7	Windows	S.W.			48				76		3,650			
	and	N.E.			40									
	Doors													
	(Cooling)	S.E.			78									
			6a											
8	Net	a	8a		7.9				152	4,720	1,200			
	Exposed	b	7a		6.0				120	2,040	720			
	Walls and	c	8h											
	Partitions	d												
9	Ceilings	a	11c		5.1				304	3,040	1,550			
	SKY LIGHT	b	—											
10	Floors	a	15a											
		b												
11	Infiltration	a	27b						48	3,120				
	and	b	20b											
	Ventilation	c												
	(Heating)	d												
12	Infiltration or	a	20		1.5				368		552			
	Ventilation (Cooling)	b												
13	Sub Total Btuh Loss									18,470				
14	Duct Btuh Loss									—				
15	Total Btuh Loss						66,535			18,470				
16	People				@300				4		1,200			
17	Appliances				1200									
18	Sensible Btuh Gain (Structure)										7,672			
19	Duct Btuh Gain										—			
20	Sum of Lines 18 and 19 (Cooling)										7,672			
21	Total Btuh Gain (Line 20 x 1.3)				1.3						8,872			
22	Btuh for Air Quantities							33,280			4,435			4,435

Line	Type of Exposure		3 Kitchen Area or Crack	Kitchen Btuh Htg	Kitchen Btuh Clg	4 Family-Guest Area or Crack	Family-Guest Btuh Htg	Family-Guest Btuh Clg	5 B.R. #2 Area or Crack	B.R. #2 Btuh Htg	B.R. #2 Btuh Clg
1	Name of Room		KITCHEN			FAMILY-GUEST			B.R. #2		
2	Running Ft Exposed Wall		10								
3	Ceiling Ht, Ft		8			8			8		
4	Room Compass Directions		S.W			N.E.			N.E. & N.W.		
5	Gross	a	80			101			192		
	Exposed	b									
	Walls and	c									
	Partitions	d									
6	Windows	a				32	2,300		35	2,550	
	and	b									
	Doors	c	21	800							
	(Heating)	d									
7	Windows	S.W.									
	and	N.E.				32		1,260	35		1,400
	Doors				1,640						
	(Cooling)	S.E.									
8	Net	a									
	Exposed	b	59	1,000	350	69	1,170	414	157	2,670	945
	Walls and	c									
	Partitions	d									
9	Ceilings	a	130	650	260	186	930	410	181	905	398
	SKY LIGHT	b									
10	Floors	a									
		b									
11	Infiltration	a				16	1,040		16	1,040	
	and	b									
	Ventilation	c									
	(Heating)	d									
12	Infiltration or	a	80		120	88		132	140		210
	Ventilation (Cooling)	b									
13	Sub Total Btuh Loss			2,450			5,440			7,165	
14	Duct Btuh Loss										
15	Total Btuh Loss			2,450			5,440				
16	People				2,370	2		600			
17	Appliances				1,200						
18	Sensible Btuh Gain (Structure)				3,570			2,816			2,953
19	Duct Btuh Gain				—						
20	Sum of Lines 18 and 19 (Cooling)				3,570			2,816			2,953
21	Total Btuh Gain (Line 20 x 1.3)				4,650			3,670			3,840
22	Btuh for Air Quantities										

Line	Type of Exposure		6 Master B.R Area or Crack	Master B.R Btuh Htg	Master B.R Btuh Clg	7 Entrance Hall Area or Crack	Entrance Hall Btuh Htg	Entrance Hall Btuh Clg	8 Basement Area or Crack	Basement Btuh Htg	Basement Btuh Clg
1	Name of Room		MASTER B.R			ENTRANCE HALL			BASEMENT		
2	Running Ft Exposed Wall					10					
3	Ceiling Ht, Ft		8			8			8		
4	Room Compass Directions		S.W. & N.W.			S.E. & N.E.					
5	Gross	a	232								
	Exposed	b									
	Walls and	c									
	Partitions	d									
6	Windows	a	56	4,080		14	1,020		25.	1,830	
	and	b				42	1,390				
	Doors	c									
	(Heating)	d									
7	Windows	S.W.	56		2,690				12.5		580
	and	N.E.							125		480
	Doors					14		1,090			
	(Cooling)	S.E.				42		534	21		250
8	Net	a							74	2,200	585
	Exposed	b	176	3,000	1,060	80	1,360	480			
	Walls and	c							916	3,660	
	Partitions	d									
9	Ceilings	a	198	990	435	46	460	235			
	SKY LIGHT	b				4	260	356			
10	Floors	a							1,088	4,350	
		b									
11	Infiltration	a	28	1,820					40	2,600	
	and	b				40	2,600		20	1,300	
	Ventilation	c									
	(Heating)	d									
12	Infiltration or	a	232		348	20		300	94		745
	Ventilation (Cooling)	b									
13	Sub Total Btuh Loss			9,890			7,090			16,030	
14	Duct Btuh Loss										
15	Total Btuh Loss										
16	People										
17	Appliances										
18	Sensible Btuh Gain (Structure)				4,533			2,995			2,040
19	Duct Btuh Gain										
20	Sum of Lines 18 and 19 (Cooling)				4,533						
21	Total Btuh Gain (Line 20 x 1.3)				5,900			3,900			2,450
22	Btuh for Air Quantities										

Modernized Metric Syste

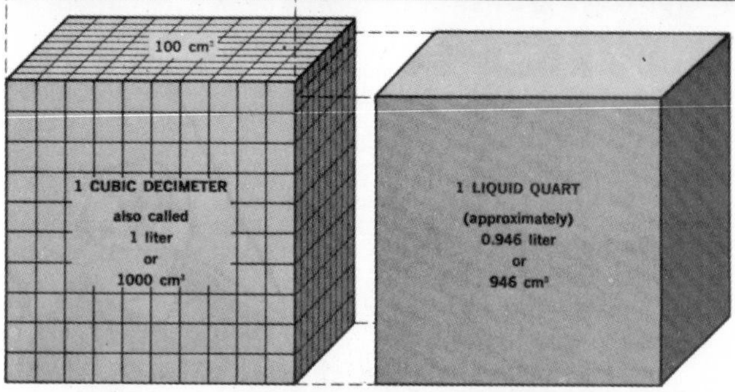

THE International System of Units—officially abbreviated SI—is a modernized version of the metric system. It was established by international agreement to provide a logical and interconnected framework for all measurements in science, industry, and commerce. SI is built upon a foundation of base units and their definitions, which appear on this chart. All other SI units are

The Six Base Units

Length METER–m

The meter is defined as 1 650 763.73 wavelengths in vacuum of the orange-red line of the spectrum of krypton-86.

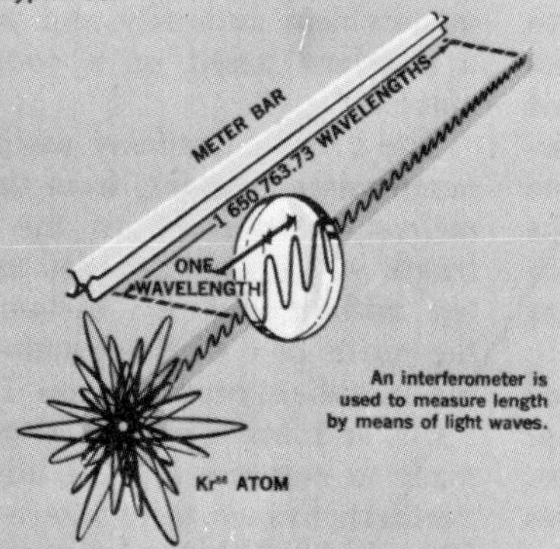

The SI unit of area is the square meter (m^2). Land is often measured by the hectare (10 000 square meters, or approximately 2.5 acres).

The SI unit of volume is the cubic meter (m^3). Fluid volume is often measured by the liter (0.001 cubic meter).

National Bureau of Standards Special Publication 304 A

For sale by the Superintendent of Documents, U.S. Government Printing Office, Washington, D.C. 20402 - Price 20 cents

References:

NBS Spec. Publ. 330, International System of Units (in press)
NBS Misc. Publ. 247, Weights and Measures Standards of the United States, A Brief History, 40 cents
NBS Misc. Publ. 286, Units of Weight and Measure, Definitions and Tables of Equivalents, $2.25

Time SECOND–s

The second is defined as the duration of 9 192 631 770 cycles of the radiation associated with a specified transition of the cesium atom. It is realized by tuning an oscillator to the resonance frequency of the cesium atoms as they pass through a system of magnets and a resonant cavity into a detector.

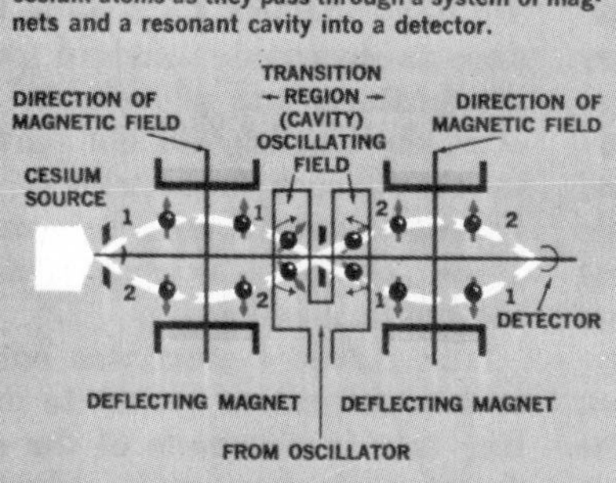

A schematic of an atomic beam spectrometer. The trajectories are drawn for those atoms whose magnetic moments are "flipped" in the transition region.

The number of periods or cycles per second is called frequency. The SI unit for frequency is the hertz (Hz). One hertz equals one cycle per second.

Standard frequencies and correct time are broadcast from NBS stations WWV, WWVB, WWVH, and WWVL, and stations of the U.S. Navy.

Many shortwave receivers pick up WWV on frequencies of 2.5, 5, 10, 15, 20, and 25 megahertz. The standard radio broadcast band extends from 535 to 1605 kilohertz.

Dividing distance by time gives speed. The SI unit for speed is the meter per second (m/s).

Rate of change in speed is called acceleration. The SI unit for acceleration is the meter per second per second (m/s^2).

Mass KILOGRAM–kg

The standard for the unit of mass, the kilogram, is a cylinder of platinum-iridium alloy kept by the Inter national Bureau of Weights and Measures at Paris A duplicate in the custody of the National Bureau o Standards serves as the mass standard for the Unitec States. This is the only base unit still defined by ar artifact.

Closely allied to the concept of mass is that o force. The SI unit of force is the newton (N). A force of 1 newton, when applied for 1 second, will give to a 1 kilogram mass a speed of 1 meter per seconc (an acceleration of 1 meter per second per second).

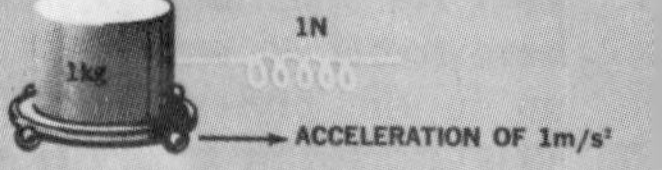

$$1\text{N} = \frac{1\text{kg} \cdot 1\text{m}}{1\text{s}^2}$$

One newton equals approximately two tenths of a pound of force.

The weight of an object is the force exerted on it by gravity. Gravity gives a mass a downward acceleration of about $9.8 m/s^2$.

The SI unit for work and energy of any kind is the joule (J).

$$1\text{J} = 1\text{N} \cdot 1\text{m}$$

The SI unit for power of any kind is the watt (W).

$$1\text{W} = \frac{1\text{J}}{1\text{s}}$$

The International System of Units (SI) and its relationship to U.S. customary units

U.S. DEPARTMENT OF COMMERCE
National Bureau of Standards

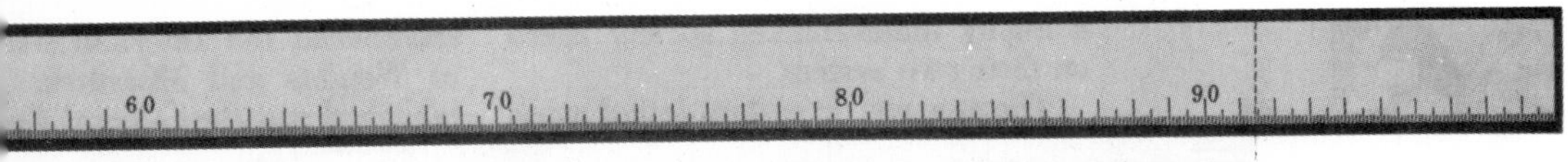

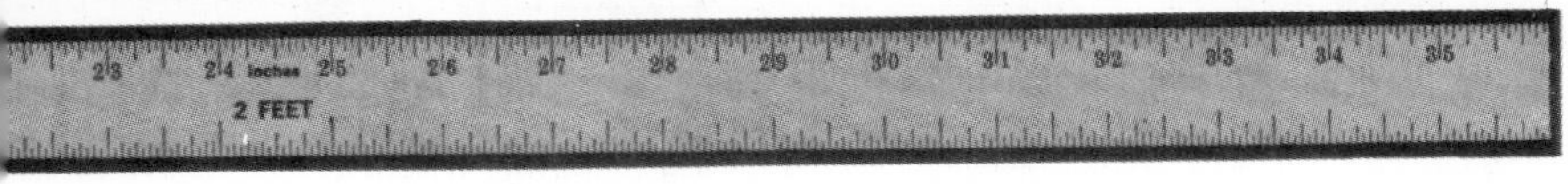

lerived from these base units. Multiples and submultiples ıre expressed in a decimal system. Use of metric weights ınd measures was legalized in the United States in 1866, ınd our customary units of weights and measures are de-ined in terms of the meter and the kilogram. The egal units for electricity and illumination in the United States are SI units.

The comparative dimensions of the meter and the yard, the liter and the quart, and the kilogram and the pound are shown.

1 pound = 0.453 592 37 kg

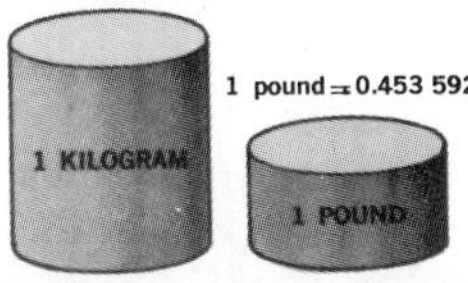

ɔf Measurement definitions, symbols, and some SI units derived from them

Temperature KELVIN–K

The thermodynamic or Kelvin scale of temperature used in SI has its origin or zero point at absolute zero and has a fixed point at the triple point of water defined as 273.16 kelvins. The Celsius scale is derived from the Kelvin scale. The triple point is defined as 0.01 °C on the Celsius scale, which is approximately 32.02 °F on the Fahrenheit scale. The relationship of the Kelvin, Celsius, and Fahrenheit temperature scales is shown below.

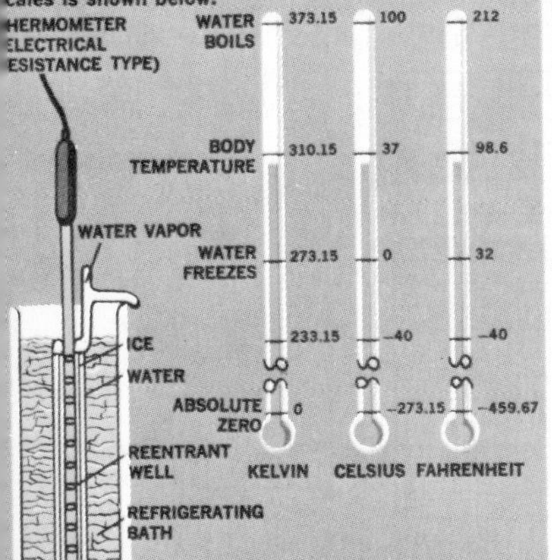

Temp F+40=1.8(Temp C+40)
Temp F=1.8(Temp C)+32
Temp C=(Temp F−32)/1.8
Temp K=Temp C+273.15

TRIPLE POINT CELL

The triple point cell, an evacuated glass cylinder filled with pure water, is used to define a known fixed temperature. When the cell is cooled until a mantle of ice forms around the reentrant well, the temperature at the interface of solid, liquid, and vapor is 0.01 °C. Thermometers to be calibrated are placed in the reentrant well.

Electric Current AMPERE–A

The ampere is defined as the magnitude of the current that, when flowing through each of two long parallel wires separated by one meter in free space, results in a force between the two wires (due to their magnetic fields) of 2×10^{-7} newton for each meter of length.

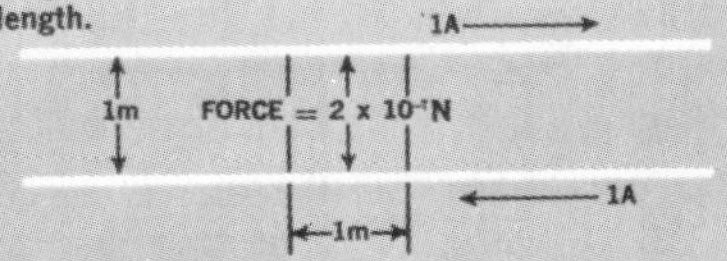

The SI unit of voltage is the volt (V).

$$1\text{V} = \frac{1\text{W}}{1\text{A}}$$

The SI unit of electrical resistance is the ohm (Ω).

$$1\Omega = \frac{1\text{V}}{1\text{A}}$$

Luminous Intensity CANDELA–cd

The candela is defined as the luminous intensity of 1/600 000 of a square meter of a radiating cavity at the temperature of freezing platinum (2042 K).

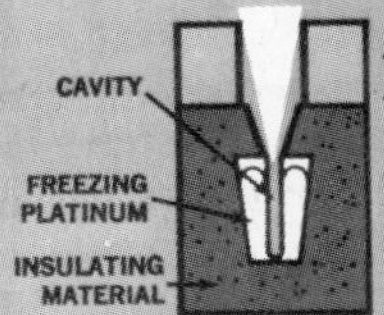

The SI unit of light flux is the lumen (lm). A source having an intensity of 1 candela in all directions radiates a light flux of 4π lumens.

A 100-watt light bulb emits about 1700 lumens

COMMON EQUIVALENTS AND CONVERSIONS

Approximate Common Equivalents		Conversions Accurate to Parts Per Million	
1 inch	= 25 millimeters	inches x 25.4*	= millimeters
1 foot	= 0.3 meter	feet x 0.3048*	= meters
1 yard	= 0.9 meter	yards x 0.9144*	= meters
1 mile	= 1.6 kilometers	miles x 1.609 34	= kilometers
1 square inch	= 6.5 sq centimeters	square inches x 6.4516*	= sq centimeters
1 square foot	= 0.09 square meter	square feet x 0.092 903 0	= square meters
1 square yard	= 0.8 square meter	square yards x 0.836 127	= square meters
1 acre	= 0.4 hectare †	acres x 0.404 686	= hectares
1 cubic inch	= 16 cu centimeters	cubic inches x 16.3871	= cu centimeters
1 cubic foot	= 0.03 cubic meter	cubic feet x 0.028 316 8	= cubic meters
1 cubic yard	= 0.8 cubic meter	cubic yards x 0.764 555	= cubic meters
1 quart (lq)	= 1 liter †	quarts (lq) x 0.946 353	= liters
1 gallon	= 0.004 cubic meter	gallons x 0.003 785 41	= cubic meters
1 ounce (avdp)	= 28 grams	ounces (avdp) x 28.3495	= grams
1 pound (avdp)	= 0.45 kilogram	pounds (avdp) x 0.453 592	= kilograms
1 horsepower	= 0.75 kilowatt	horsepower x 0.745 700	= kilowatts
1 millimeter	= 0.04 inch	millimeters x 0.039 370 1	= inches
1 meter	= 3.3 feet	meters x 3.280 84	= feet
1 meter	= 1.1 yards	meters x 1.093 61	= yards
1 kilometer	= 0.6 mile	kilometers x 0.621 371	= miles
1 sq centimeter	= 0.16 square inch	sq centimeters x 0.155 000	= square inches
1 square meter	= 11 square feet	square meters x 10.7639	= square feet
1 square meter	= 1.2 square yards	square meters x 1.195 99	= square yards
1 hectare †	= 2.5 acres	hectares x 2.471 05	= acres
1 cu centimeter	= 0.06 cubic inch	cu centimeters x 0.061 023 7	= cubic inches
1 cubic meter	= 35 cubic feet	cubic meters x 35.3147	= cubic feet
1 cubic meter	= 1.3 cubic yards	cubic meters x 1.307 95	= cubic yards
1 liter †	= 1 quart (lq)	liters x 1.056 69	= quarts (lq)
1 cubic meter	= 250 gallons	cubic meters x 264.172	= gallons
1 gram	= 0.035 ounces (avdp)	grams x 0.035 274 0	= ounces (avdp)
1 kilogram	= 2.2 pounds (avdp)	kilograms x 2.204 62	= pounds (avdp)
1 kilowatt	= 1.3 horsepower	kilowatts x 1.341 02	= horsepower

† common term not used in SI

* exact

THESE PREFIXES MAY BE APPLIED TO ALL SI UNITS

Multiples and Submultiples	Prefixes	Symbols
1 000 000 000 000 = 10^{12}	tera (tĕr′ȧ)	T
1 000 000 000 = 10^{9}	giga (jĭ′gȧ)	G
1 000 000 = 10^{6}	mega (mĕg′ȧ)	M *
1000 = 10^{3}	kilo (kĭl′ō)	k *
100 = 10^{2}	hecto (hĕk′tō)	h
10 = 10	deka (dĕk′ȧ)	da
0.1 = 10^{-1}	deci (dĕs′ĭ)	d
0.01 = 10^{-2}	centi (sĕn′tĭ)	c *
0.001 = 10^{-3}	milli (mĭl′ĭ)	m *
0.000 001 = 10^{-6}	micro (mī′krō)	μ *
0.000 000 001 = 10^{-9}	nano (năn′ō)	n
0.000 000 000 001 = 10^{-12}	pico (pē′kō)	p
0.000 000 000 000 001 = 10^{-15}	femto (fĕm′tō)	f
0.000 000 000 000 000 001 = 10^{-18}	atto (ăt′tō)	a

*Most commonly used

APPENDIX I: SET OF RESIDENTIAL WORKING DRAWINGS

SHEET No.	DATE: MAR. 7, '76	FOUNDATION, BASEMENT, FIRST & SECOND FLOOR FRAMING PLANS		
1	PROJ. No 7402	RESIDENCE FOR	CHARLES H. STORMES • DESIGNER	
	DRAWN BY: CHS	MR. JEFF STUPAR	3310 SHALLOWFORD ROAD	
of 7	REVISED:	TURTLE COVE, LAKE JACKSON, GEORGIA	ATLANTA, GEORGIA 30341	

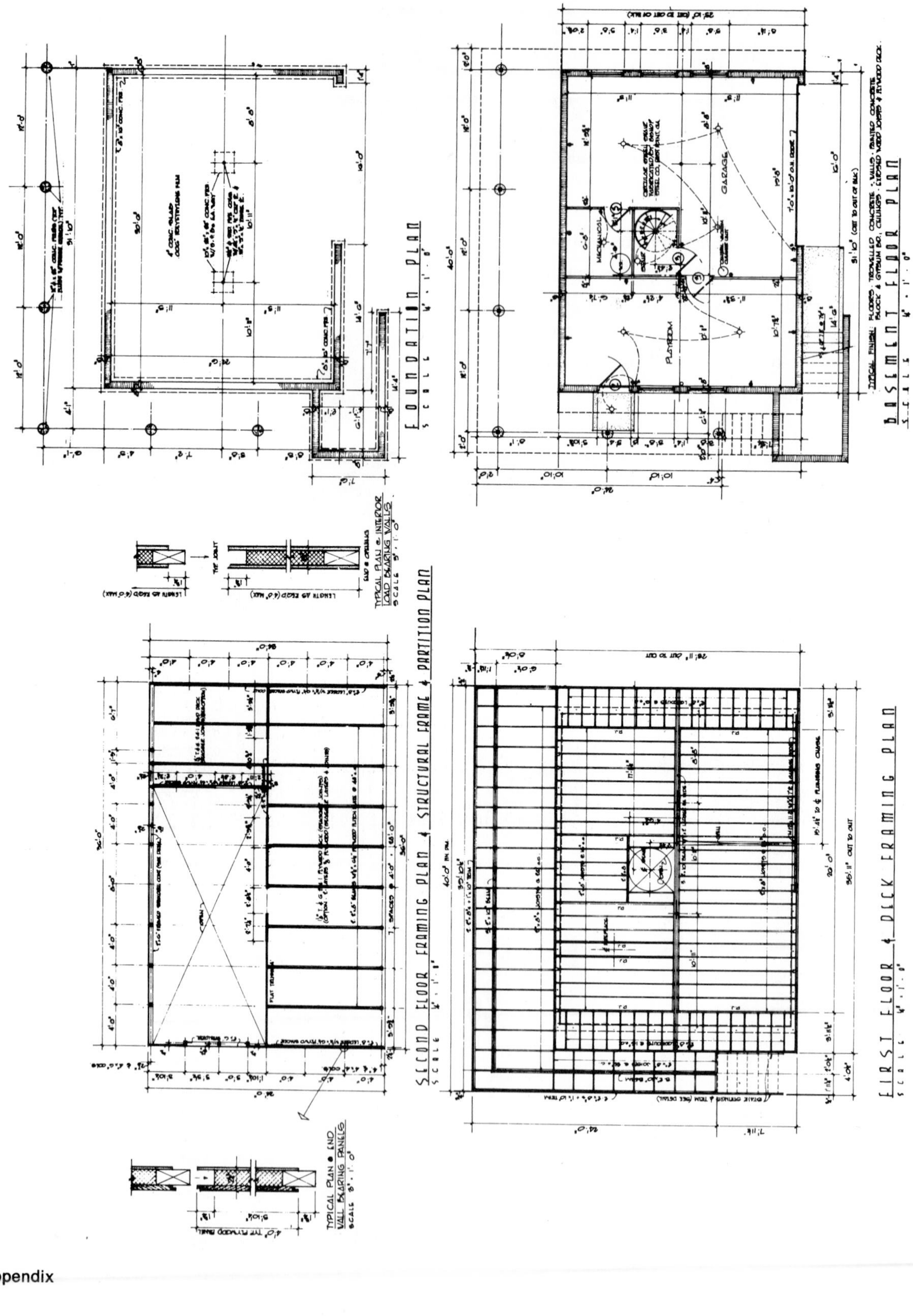

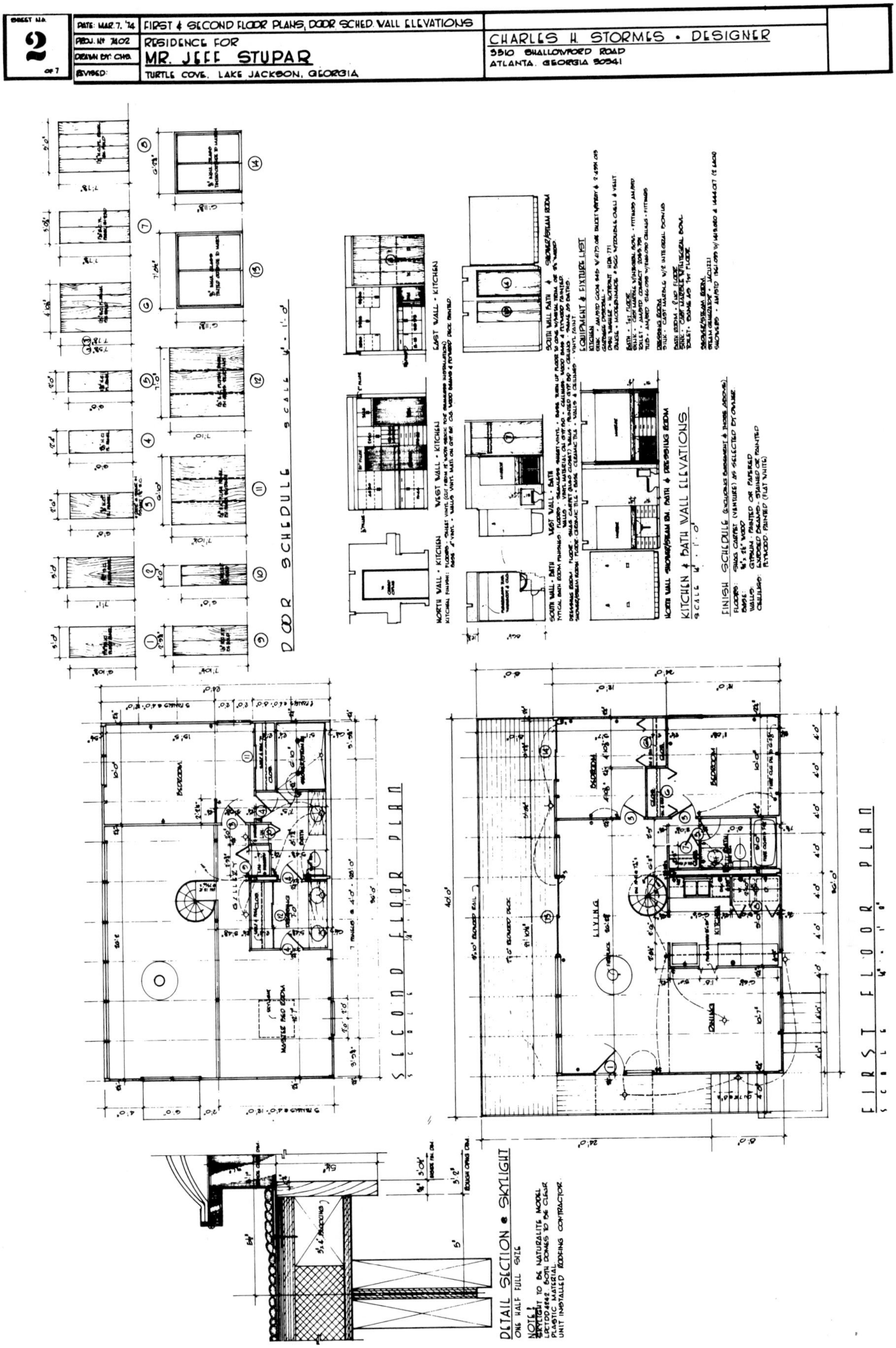
SHEET NO. 2 OF 7
DATE: MAR. 7, '74
PROJ. Nº 7402
DRAWN BY: CHS
REVISED:
FIRST & SECOND FLOOR PLANS, DOOR SCHED. WALL ELEVATIONS
RESIDENCE FOR
MR. JEFF STUPAR
TURTLE COVE, LAKE JACKSON, GEORGIA
CHARLES H. STORMES • DESIGNER
5510 SHALLOWFORD ROAD
ATLANTA, GEORGIA 30341

SHEET NO				
3 OF 7	DATE: MAR. 7, '74	ELEVATIONS		
	PROJ. NO 7402	RESIDENCE FOR	CHARLES H. STORMES • DESIGNER	
	DRAWN BY: CHS	MR. JEFF STUPAR	3510 SHALLOWFORD ROAD	
	REVISED:	TURTLE COVE. LAKE JACKSON, GEORGIA	ATLANTA, GEORGIA 30341	

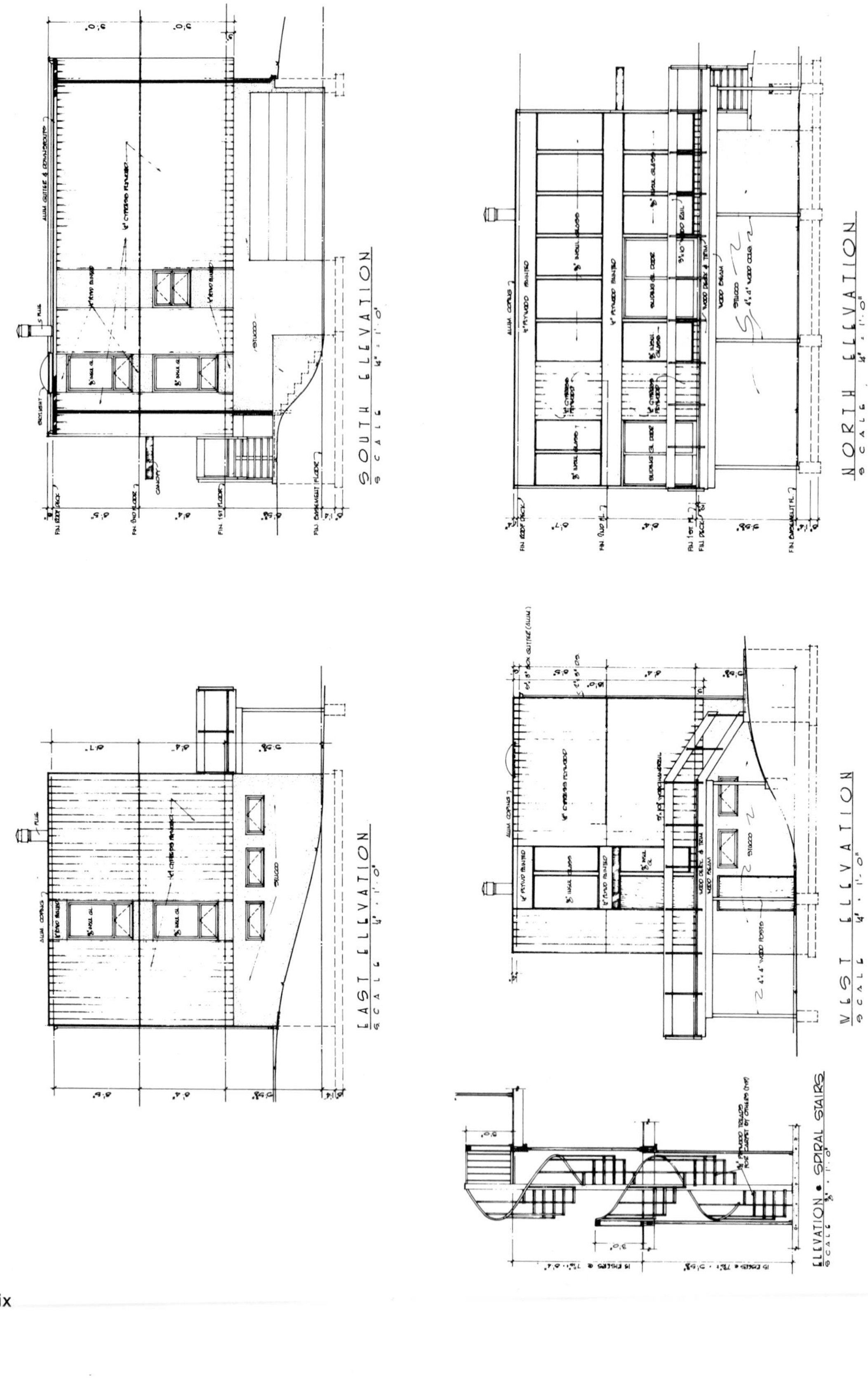

SHEET NO. 4 OF 7	DATE: MAR. 7, '74	WALL SECTIONS & DETAILS	CHARLES H. STORMES • DESIGNER
	PROJ. Nº 7402	RESIDENCE FOR	3510 SHALLOWFORD ROAD
	DRAWN BY: CHS	MR. JEFF STUPAR	ATLANTA, GEORGIA 30341
	REVISED:	TURTLE COVE, LAKE JACKSON, GEORGIA	

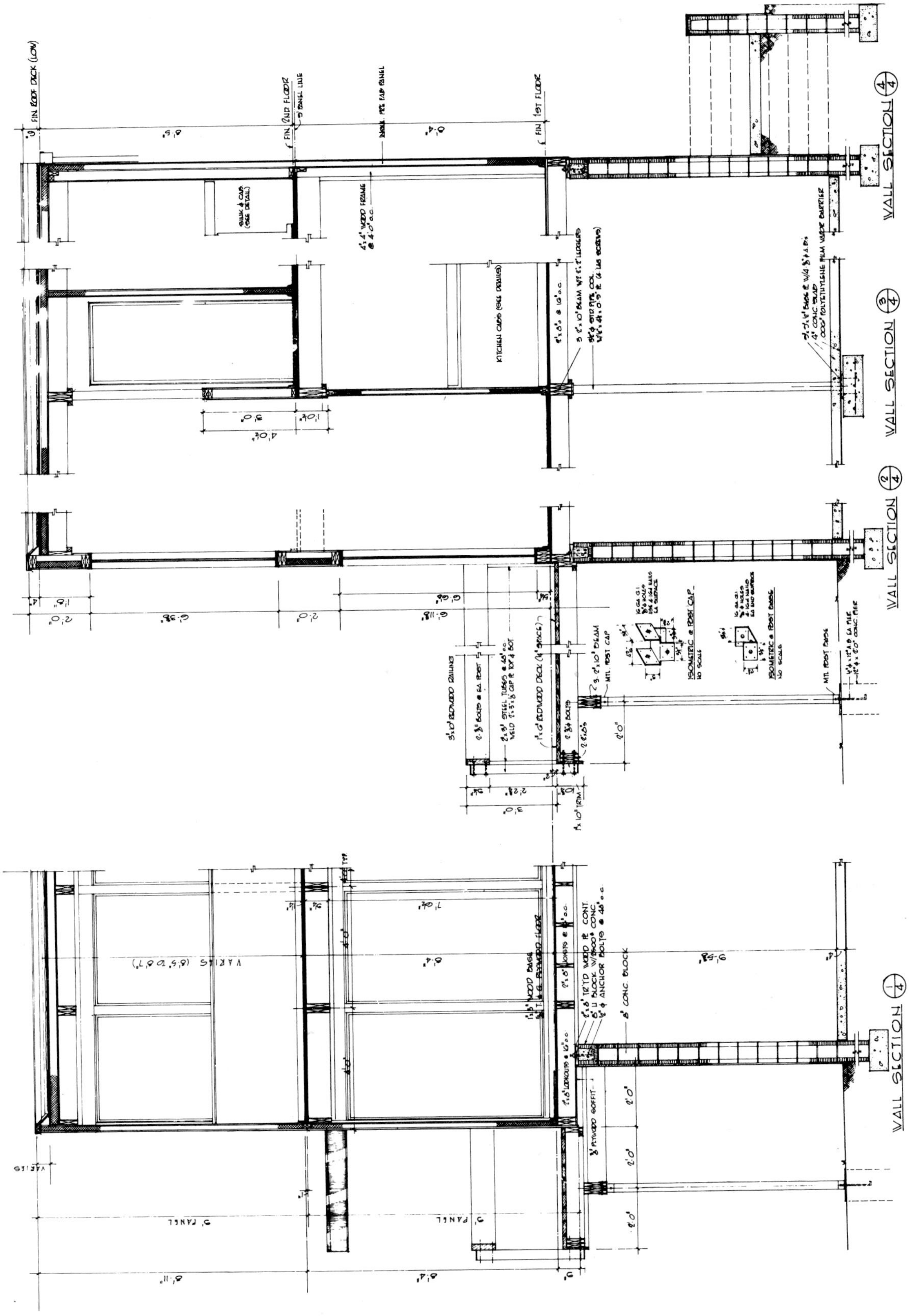

Sheet No.			
5 of 7	DATE: MAR. 7, '74	ROOF FRAMING PLAN & CONSTRUCTION DETAILS	
	PROJ. No 7402	RESIDENCE FOR	CHARLES H. STORMES • DESIGNER
	DRAWN BY: CHS	MR. JEFF STUPAR	3510 SHALLOWFORD ROAD
	REVISED:	TURTLE COVE, LAKE JACKSON, GEORGIA	ATLANTA, GEORGIA 30341

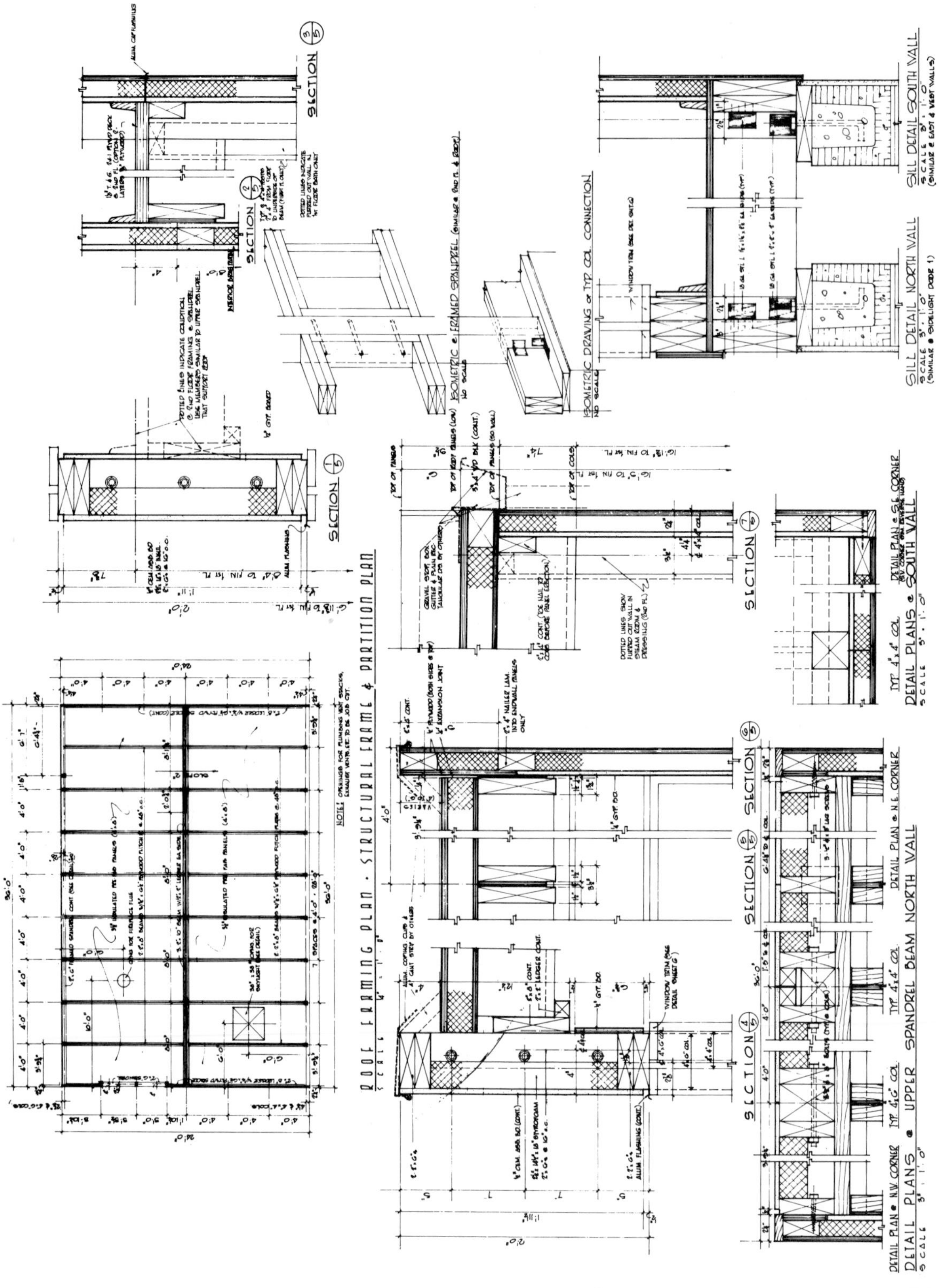

SHEET No. 6 of 7	DATE: MAR. 7, '74	CONSTRUCTION DETAILS
	PROJ. No 7402	RESIDENCE FOR
	DRAWN BY: CHS	MR. JEFF STUPAR
	REVISED:	TURTLE COVE, LAKE JACKSON, GEORGIA

CHARLES H. STORMES • DESIGNER
3510 SHALLOWFORD ROAD
ATLANTA, GEORGIA 30341

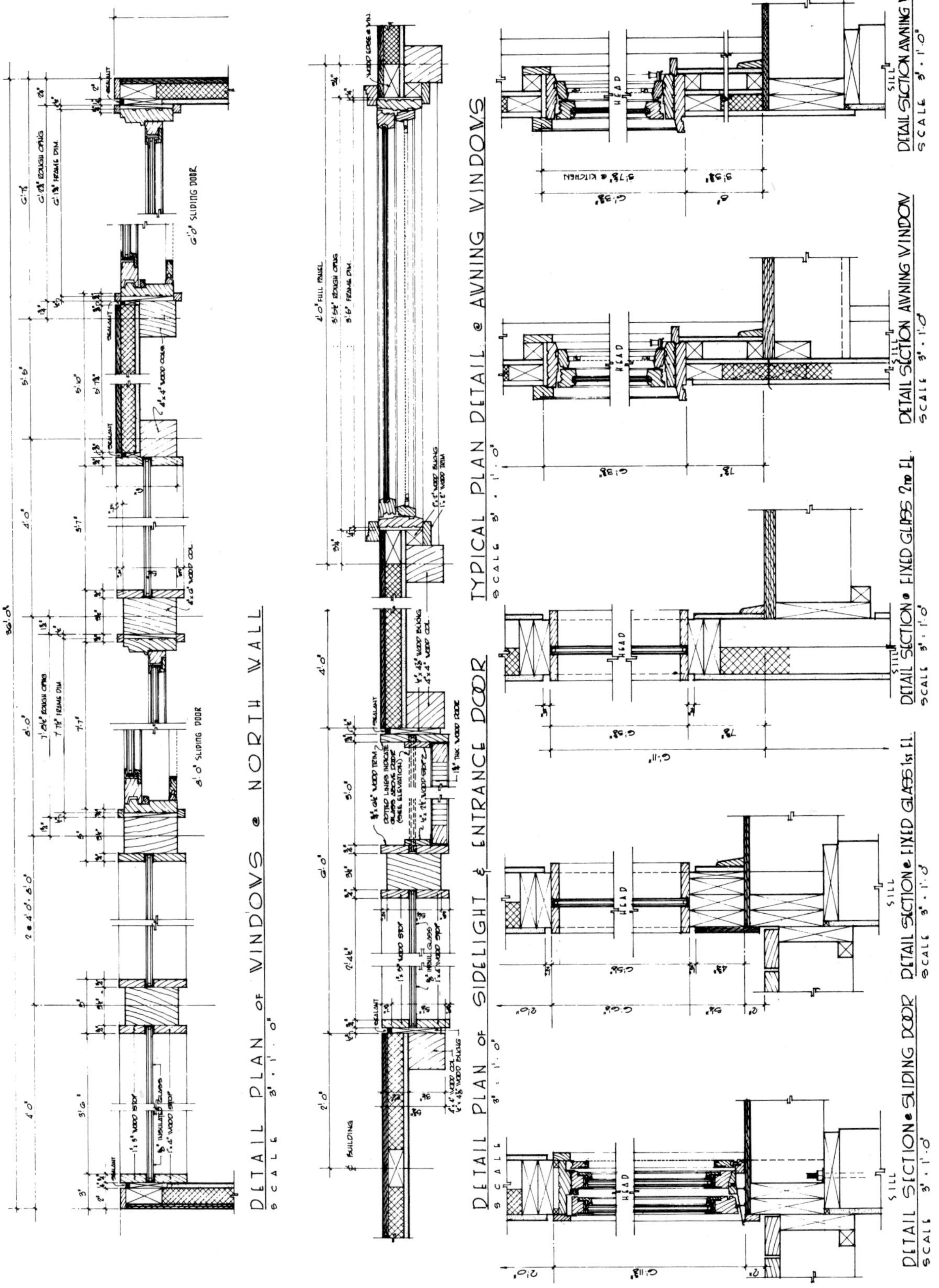

SHEET No. 7 of 7

DATE: MAR. 7, '74
PROJ. No 7402
DRAWN BY: CHS
REVISED:

DOOR FRAME DETAILS & SHOWER/STEAM ROOM SECTIONS

RESIDENCE FOR
MR. JEFF STUPAR
TURTLE COVE, LAKE JACKSON, GEORGIA

CHARLES H. STORMES • DESIGNER
3510 SHALLOWFORD ROAD
ATLANTA, GEORGIA 30341

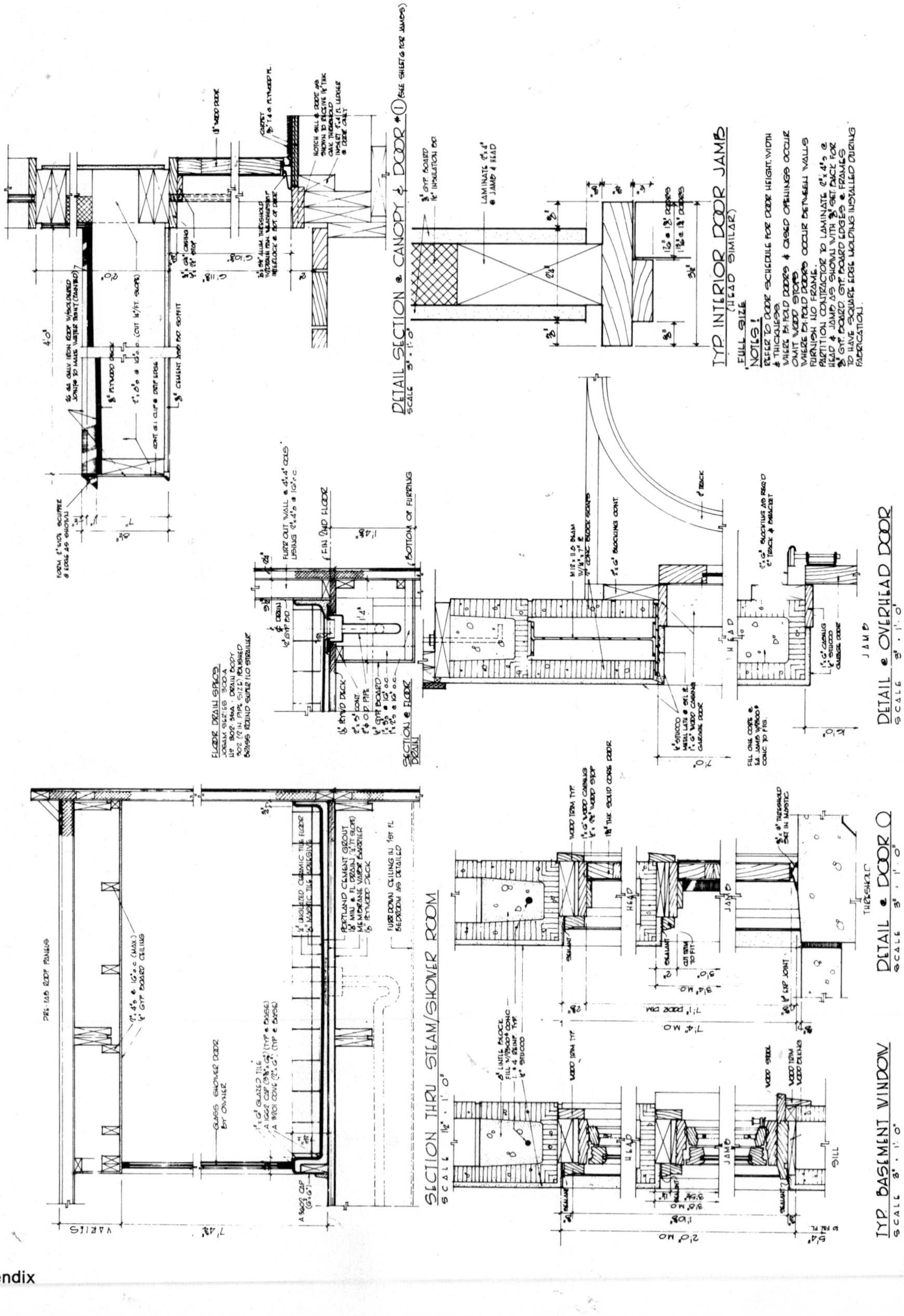

"It is the peculiarity of knowledge that those who really thirst for it always get it."—Richard Jefferies

Index

C

D

R

S

T

U

V

W

Z